An Exposition Upon the Epistle of Jude

An

Exposition

upon

The Epistle of Jude

delivered in Christ Church, London

By the Rev. William Jenkyn

A.D. 1652, Lecturer on Christ-Church

A.D. 1653, Rector of Blackfriars

revised and corrected
by the Rev. James Sherman

Solid Ground Christian Books
Birmingham, Alabama USA
Fall 2006

Solid Ground Christian Books
715 Oak Grove Road
Homewood AL 35209
205-443-0311
sgcb@charter.net
http://solid-ground-books.com

An Exposition upon the Epistle of Jude

William Jenkyn (1612-1685)

Originally published in London in 1653
Reprinted by James Nichol in Edinburgh, Scotland in 1863
Reprinted by James & Klock in Minneapolis, MN in 1976

Solid Ground Puritan Classics

First SGCB edition November 2006

Cover image is of Newgate Prison where Jenkyn died as a martyr.

Cover produced by BORGO DESIGN

ISBN: 1-59925-092-6

Table of Contents

Biographical Sketch by Dr. Joel Beeke	i
Memoir of the Author by Rev. James Sherman	iii
Dedication of the Original of Part I	vi
Dedication of the Original of Part II	viii
Outline of the Contents of the Epistle of Jude	xi
Exposition of Jude 1	1
Exposition of Jude 2	26
Exposition of Jude 3	52
Exposition of Jude 4	73
Exposition of Jude 5	106
Exposition of Jude 6	125
Exposition of Jude 7	153
Exposition of Jude 8	171
Exposition of Jude 9	189
Exposition of Jude 10	210
Exposition of Jude 11	217
Exposition of Jude 12	245
Exposition of Jude 13	279
Exposition of Jude 14	295
Exposition of Jude 15	307
Exposition of Jude 16	311
Exposition of Jude 17	325
Exposition of Jude 18	327
Exposition of Jude 19	332
Exposition of Jude 20	338
Exposition of Jude 21	344
Exposition of Jude 22	349
Exposition of Jude 23	352
Exposition of Jude 24	357
Exposition of Jude 25	359
General Index	361

Biographical Sketch

William Jenkyn was born in 1612 into a staunchly Puritan family in Sudbury, where his father, William Jenkyn, was vicar. His father was disinherited for his Puritan convictions, and his mother was the daughter of Richard Rogers, the godly preacher of Wethersfield in Essex, and the granddaughter of John Rogers, the Protestant martyr under the reign of Mary Tudor.

At the age of fifteen, William, Jr. went to St. John's, Cambridge to study under Anthony Burgess. After earning a bachelor's degree in 1628, he moved with Burgess in 1634 to Emmanuel College, earning a master's degree there in 1635. In 1639, he became lecturer at St. Nicholas Acons in London, then minister of St. Leonard's, Colchester. In 1643, he was appointed vicar of Christchurch, Newgate Street.

Jenkyn was one of the most zealous Presbyterians in London. His congregation soon became a center of Presbyterian zeal. His parish elected five elders, including William Greenhill, a godly publisher, and John Vicars, a Puritan activist.

Jenkyn was also one of the London ministers, who, along with Christopher Love and Thomas Watson, were imprisoned in 1651 for their attempts to assist in restoring the exiled Charles II to the throne via the power of the Scots army. Parliament used the plot's failure to silence the London Presbyterian ministers that supported it. While Love was executed, Jenkyn escaped with his life because he signed a submissive recantation. After he was restored to his ministry at Christchurch, Jenkyn preached for a few years about the names given to Christ in the Scriptures.

Under the Cromwellian protectorate, Jenkyn's reputation was publicly restored. In 1654, he replaced William Gouge as minister at St. Anne Blackfriars. His first task was to preach Gouge's funeral sermon. Jenkyn returned to Christchurch a few years later, and was officially reinstituted there in 1658. About that time, he preached his renowned series of sermons on Jude.

Jenkyn's Exposition of the Epistle of Jude remains unsurpassed today. It powerfully exhibits Jenkyn's piety and learning. Spurgeon says of it: "Earnest and popular, but very full, and profoundly learned. A treasure-house of good things." Thomas Manton said that the "elaborate commentary of [his] revered, Mr. William Jenkyn" was done so well, that for some time he regarded the publication of his own work on Jude as unnecessary.

Though Jenkyn probably welcomed the restoration of Charles II, he soon lost the favor of the new regime, and was ejected from the pulpit in 1662 as a Nonconformist. He settled in a home he owned in Hertfordshire, where he held conventicles, preaching privately to his neighbors and in the vicinity until he was restored to public ministry in 1672. He then returned to London, where his friends built a chapel for him in Jewin Street. He preached to a large congregation there and also served as lecturer at Pinner's Hall. However, in 1682, the rights of nonconformist preachers were revoked, and Jenkyn was deprived of his ministry. He continued to meet with congregants in private houses to proclaim the truths of the gospel.

In September 1684, officers stormed the house where Jenkyn was preaching. All the other ministers escaped, including John Flavel and Edward Reynolds. However, Jenkyn did not escape because he was busy helping a lady out of the house. At age seventy-one, Jenkyn was imprisoned at Newgate under severe restrictions. He was forbidden to pray with any visitors, even his own daughter, and was not allowed to leave prison even to baptize his own grandchild. He lamented, "A man might be as effectively murdered in Newgate as at Tyburn."

Jenkyn's health rapidly deteriorated in prison. The royal court showed no mercy. "Jenkyn shall be a prisoner as long as he lives," was the response to the petition sent to the court for his release.

Four months after his imprisonment, Charles playfully asked his musicians to play Jenkyn's Farewell one evening at Whitehall Palace. "Please, your majesty," said a nobleman in waiting, "Jenkyn has got his liberty." Surprised, the king responded, "Aye, and who gave it to him?" The man replied, "A greater than your Majesty, the King of kings—Jenkyn is dead." The date was January 19, 1685.

More than 150 coaches accompanied Jenkyn's body to the nonconformist cemetery at Bunhill Fields. There, Jenkyn's daughter Elizabeth gave out mourning rings with the inscription: "William Jenkyn, murdered in Newgate." The Latin inscription on Jenkyn's grave is translated:

Sacred to the remains of WILLIAM JENKYN, Minister of the Gospel, who during the heavy storms of the Church was imprisoned in Newgate. Died a martyr there in 72nd year of his age and 52nd of his Ministry, 1684.

Jenkyn's wife, Elizabeth Lovekin, preceded him in death by ten years. Together, they had ten children.

Joel R. Beeke
Puritan Reformed Theological Seminary
Grand Rapids, MI

MEMOIR OF THE AUTHOR.

The Rev. William Jenkyn, M. A., author of the following Exposition, and descended from a wealthy family at Folkstone, was born at Sudbury, in the year 1612. His father dying while he was very young, his wealthy grandfather took him under his charge till he was nine years of age, when his mother, fearing the absence of a religious education, brought him home, and with his father-in-law carefully trained him in godliness. At fourteen he was sent to Cambridge, and placed under the tuition of the Rev. Anthony Burgess, where his eminent piety, progress in learning, and sprightly genius gained him many admirers. Some time after taking his degree of M. A. he was chosen lecturer of St. Nicholas Acons, London; and from thence he became the minister of Hythe, near Colchester. Here he married; but the dampness of the situation, and the solicitations of his friends, induced him to return to London. In the year 1641 he was chosen vicar of Christ Church, Newgate Street, and some months after lecturer of St. Ann's, Blackfriars, which offices he continued to fill with great diligence and acceptance till the destruction of the monarchy, when upon refusing to observe the public thanksgivings appointed by parliament, he was sequestered from his benefices, suspended from his ministry, and banished twenty miles from London.

"About six months after his retirement to Billericay," says Bishop Kennet, "he returned to London, and was sent to the Tower, from 'Love's plot.'" It appears from the same authority, and Oldmixon, that he was prevailed upon, by the advice of friends, to petition (the Rump) parliament for his release. "Dr. Arthur, minister of Clapham, drew up the petition for him, and with great difficulty he, Dr. Lazarus Seaman, and others, prevailed on him to sign it." It is entitled, "The humble and penitent Petition of William Jenkyn, presented to parliament in the year 1651 : Most humbly showeth,

"That your petitioner is unfeignedly sorrowful for his late miscarriages, whether testified against him, or acknowledged by him, and for the great unsuitableness of them to his calling and condition," &c.

On which parliament resolved, "That Mr. William Jenkyn be pardoned both for life and estate, for and in respect of treasons and crimes whereof he is accused," &c.

Mr. Feak, who had embraced the strange notion of the fifth monarchy, having been presented to the living of Christ Church by the government, Jenkyn would not eject him, though upon his discharge from sequestration he had a right to do so. His parishioners, however, anxious to enjoy his ministry, established a lecture for him at seven o'clock on Lord's-day mornings, and remunerated him for his disinterestedness by raising a large subscription on his behalf. He continued this lecture, and that of Blackfriars, from which he had not been ejected, till the death of Dr. Gouge, when he was chosen rector of that parish.

The government after a short time removed Mr. Feak from the living of Christ Church, to which the governors of Bartholomew's Hospital, from their high estimation of his character, immediately presented Mr. Jenkyn. Here he exercised his ministry on the sabbath morning and afternoon to a crowded auditory with eminent success among his parishioners, but especially to occasional hearers, who came from all parts to hear him. He seemed to have adopted the apostle's motto with a lively assurance of its importance, " I am determined not to know any thing among you, save Jesus Christ, and him crucified;" for during several years he preached from the names given to Christ in the Scripture. He had a peculiar manner of gaining a powerful hold of the conscience, and not allowing the sinner to escape by any ancient or modern subterfuge; so that if his hearers were not converted, they were convicted and self-condemned—an eminent and greatly to be desired ministerial talent. Baxter styles him " that elegant and sententious preacher."

Upon the restoration of Charles II. his loyalty was suspected, and he was ordered to appear before the council, respecting which we find the following minute: " Tuesday, Jan. 2, 1661-2. Council Chamber in Whitehall. Mr. W. Jenkyn, the minister of Christ Church Hospital, being sent for this day, made his appearance at the board, and was reproved for not praying for the king," &c.

When the Act of Uniformity and the Oxford Act passed, not being able to subscribe to the required oaths, he retired to his own house at Langley, in Hertfordshire, where he preached in private to his neighbours. When the indulgence was granted in 1671, he returned to London, and his friends erected him a chapel in Jewin Street, where he soon raised a numerous congregation. He was also chosen lecturer at Pinner's Hall. Upon the revocation of the indulgence he was specially favoured by the authorities, who permitted him to continue his services on the Lord's day without interruption until Bartholomew's Day, 1682. After this he preached in private, as opportunity and secrecy permitted, till Sept. 2, 1684, on which day he, and Mr. (afterwards Bishop) Reynolds, Mr. John Flavel, and Mr. Keeling had met a numerous body of their friends, in a place which they thought sufficiently secluded from danger, for the purpose of prayer and communion, when a company of soldiers rushed into the congregation while in the act of worship. All the ministers made their escape except Mr. Jenkyn, who (says Mr. Flavel) might have escaped as well as the rest, had it not been for a piece of vanity in a lady, whom Mr. Jenkyn out of too great politeness had allowed to pass before him, and her long train hindered his going down-stairs. Knowing that it would be acceptable at court, the officers who apprehended him, and the magistrates, Sir James Edwards and Sir James Smith, before whom he was brought, treated him rudely and severely. They rejected his offer of £40, which the law empowered them to take, and committed him to Newgate, though they were assured by medical authority that at his advanced age of seventy-one the confinement of Newgate would cost him his life. He presented a petition to the king, by pleading for whose restoration to the throne he had suffered imprisonment before, entreating him to grant his release. The petition was accompanied by certificates from his physicians, that his life was in imminent danger from his close imprisonment; yet all the answer which could be obtained from the ungrateful monarch was, " Jenkyn shall be a prisoner as long as he lives." Chambers says, " The inveteracy of Charles II. against him seems unaccountable. He had been a great sufferer for loyalty to Charles I., and was one of those who not only resisted the decrees of parliament, but was even implicated in ' Love's plot,' the object of which was the restoration of the king."

The restrictions to which he was subjected in Newgate were exceedingly severe. The keepers were prohibited from allowing him to pray with any visitors—even his own daughter; nor was he permitted to leave the prison to baptize his grandchild, though a considerable sum, and security for his return, were offered for that liberty. Soon after his confinement his health began to decline, but his soul was filled with unspeakable joy and comfort. To one of his friends he remarked, "What a vast difference is there between this and my first imprisonment! Then I was full of doubts and fears, of grief and anguish; and well I might, for going out of God's way and my own calling to meddle with things that did not belong to me. But now, being found in the way of my duty, in my Master's business, though I suffer even to bonds, yet I am comforted beyond measure. The Lord sheds abroad his love in my heart; I feel it; I have the assurance of it." Then, turning to some who were weeping by him, he said, "Why weep ye for me? Christ lives: he is my Friend; a Friend born for adversity; a Friend that never dies. Weep not for me, but weep for yourselves and your children."

After four months' confinement and suffering, he died in Newgate, Jan. 19, 1685, in the seventy-second year of his age, and fifty-second of his ministry. The news of his death soon reached the court. A nobleman in waiting had the courage to say to the king, "May it please your majesty, Jenkyn has got his liberty." Upon which he asked with surprise, "Aye, who gave it to him?" The nobleman replied, "A greater than your majesty, the King of kings!" with which the king seemed struck, and remained silent.

On Jan. 24th he was buried at "Tyndall's burial-place," since called Bunhill Fields, by his friends with great honour, "his corpse being attended, says L'Estrange, by at least one hundred and fifty coaches."

Jenkyn has been accused, and not without cause, of being a changeable man—not in his theology, but in his politics. Some passages in his history are difficult to reconcile with stedfastness of purpose and stern integrity; but unless we had all the circumstances before us, it would be equally wrong at this distance of time to justify or condemn. Political partisans write of him in derision if he was opposed to their views, and in eulogy if his sentiments accorded with their own. It is, however, quite certain, from friends and foes, that he was an eminent minister of Christ—that crowds attended his sermons—that his parishioners were devotedly attached to his person and labours—that other parishes beside his own were anxious to obtain his services—that he preferred to suffer rather than to act contrary to his conscience—that he died in the triumphs and enjoyments of the gospel, and was buried with remarkable honour, not less than six hundred mourners following his body to the grave!

The following Exposition is the most considerable of his works, and exhibits his piety, diligence, and learning. It was delivered at Christ Church, Newgate Street, in the ordinary course of his ministry, and met with great acceptance; two editions having been published during the life of the author, both of which have been carefully collated for the present publication. The editor believes that, from the great pains taken to render the work perfect, few errors have escaped detection. He now commits it to the favour of God, who, judging from the testimonies received from many ministers, has crowned the Expositions previously published with a large share of his blessing. May the desire of the author for his work be eminently realized by this edition, "that the souls of its readers may reap the benefit of the whole, and that it may advance the spiritual progress of the church;" and in every work which we undertake and accomplish for God, may we review it with the same feelings and sentiments as this Exposition was concluded by its author: "For myself, all good that I can do, or in this or any other service have done, I humbly desire may be returned only to the honour and praise of my most dear and blessed Lord and Saviour Jesus Christ, whose grace was the principle of all that is rightly done in it, whose Spirit was my guide in doing it, whose word was my rule, whose glory was my end, whose merit can alone procure acceptance for me and all my services, and the everlasting enjoyment of whose presence is my soul's desire and longing. Amen."

DEDICATION

TO PART I. OF THE ORIGINAL EDITION.

TO THE RIGHT WORSHIPFUL AND OTHER

MY BELOVED AND CHRISTIAN FRIENDS,

INHABITANTS IN THE PARISH OF CHRIST-CHURCH, LONDON.

THE souls of men may as certainly be destroyed by poisoning as by starving. If Satan cannot prevent some kind of tasting and receiving the grace of the gospel, he often poisonously perverts it, by making men turn it into lasciviousness, and even by freedom from sin allow themselves in sinning freely. The seducers crept into the church in Jude's time, and under pretence of Christian liberty introduced unchristian libertinism. No cheaper stuff than grace would serve their turn wherewith to clothe lasciviousness, and no other patron than the Lord Christ himself to protect their impieties. Whether they were the disciples of Simon Magus, or Nicolaitanes, or Gnostics, (as Epiphanius thinks,) I do not inquire; sure I am, they were of the synagogue of Satan; he was both their father and master, whom they resembled, and whose works they did. In this Epistle the apostle Jude not only with holy zeal opposes them himself, but sounds a trumpet to rouse up the Christians, (upon whose quarters these seducers had fallen, to surprise their treasure, the doctrine of faith,) earnestly to contend for the preservation of so precious a depositum, once, and once for all, delivered to their keeping. The arguments used by the apostle are cogent, his directions prudent, and it is probable that his pains were in some degree successful. I know no spiritually skilful observer but perceives too great a resemblance between their faces and those of our times. Sins in our days are not only committed under the enjoyment, but, in pretence, by the encouragement of grace; men who now dare not sin, are by some derided as ignorant of their Christian liberty; and evident it is that many live as if, being delivered from the fear of their enemies, they were delivered from the fear and service of their Deliverer; and as if the blood of the Passover were not intended by God to be sprinkled upon the door-posts to save them, but upon the threshold of the door for them to trample upon. Beloved friends, if God hath appointed that you should resemble these Christians to whom Jude wrote in the danger of your times, it is your duty to embrace the directions delivered to these Christians for your defence from those dangers. A gracious heart considers not how bitter, but how true; not how smart, but how seasonable, any truth is. My aim in publishing these Lectures is to advance holiness, and, as far as I could do it, by following the mind of the apostle, to oppose those sins, which if people hate not most, are like to hurt them most; and to advance those duties with which, if people be not most in love, yet in which they are most defective, and thereby most endangered. And now again, I beseech you, that I may testify my unfeigned affection as well by my epistle as my book—labour to keep close to God in a loose age; spend not your time in complaining of the licentiousness of the times, in the mean while setting up a toleration in your own hearts and lives. That private Christian who does not labour to oppose profaneness with a river of tears, would never, if he could, bear it down with a stream of power. Lay the foundation of mortification deep. Reserve no lust from the stroke of Jesus Christ. Take heed of pleasing yourselves in a bare formal profession. Labour to be rooted in Christ. He who is but a visible Christian, may in a short time cease to be so much as visible; he who speaks of Christ but notionally, may in time be won to speak against him. Love not the world. Beware of scandals; take them not where they are, make them not where they are not. The common sin of our times, is to blacken religion, and then to fear and hate it. Despise not the providences of God in the world; they are signs of God's mind, though not of his love. Delight in the public ordinances, and highly esteem faithful ministers; they and religion are commonly blasted together. Shun seducers. Sit down under a minister as well as under a preacher. He who will hear every one, may at length be brought to hear none; and he who will hear him preach who ought not, may soon be left to learn that which he ought not. Preserve a tender conscience; every step you take fear a snare; read your own hearts in the wickedness of others. Be not slight in closet services; and oft think of God in your shops, for there you think you have least leisure, but sure you have most need to do so. Let your speech be alway with grace, and a word or two of Christ in every company, if possible; and yet not out of form, but feeling.

These Lectures here presented might sooner have seen the light, had I not lately met with such hinderances (sufficiently known) as I once expected would have stopped them altogether. The main of this employment hath lain upon me since that time, which, considering my many other employments, hath not been long, though otherwise long enough to have performed this work much more exactly. I here present you, though not with half of the Epistle, yet with more than the one half of that which upon the whole I preached. I have not knowingly left out any passages delivered in the pulpit. The other part I promise in a similar volume to this, so soon as God gives strength and more leisure, if this find acceptance with the church of God. And now (brethren) I commend you to God, and to the word of his grace, which is able to build you up, and to give you an inheritance among all them which are sanctified; resting

Your servant in the work of Christ,

WILLIAM JENKYN.

DEDICATION

TO PART II. OF THE ORIGINAL EDITION.

TO MY DEAR FLOCK AND MUCH HONOURED FRIENDS,

THE CHURCH OF GOD,

IN THE PRECINCT OF BLACKFRIARS, LONDON

Christian and respected Friends,

It cannot seem strange that I, who have lately given myself to the service of your souls, should now dedicate my book to you for that purpose. Nor can any wonder, since you have lately imitated your predecessors in the loving and unanimous call of your now unworthy pastor, that he should endeavour to follow the steps of those excellent servants of Christ your former ministers, who, in their times, both by preaching and printing, bestowed their labours upon you for your spiritual benefit.

I have frequently heard that Blackfriars is one of those places in London commonly accounted and called privileged, in respect of sundry civil immunities bestowed upon it. But what are all those political, in comparison of the spiritual, privileges which God has afforded to you of this place? in respect of which I much question whether any congregation in London, (I think I may take a far larger compass,) has been equal to you in the privilege of enjoying so long a continuance of an able, orthodox, and soul-saving ministry. Those two excellent and eminently faithful servants of Christ, Mr. Egerton, and Doctor Gouge, lately deceased, spent, as I am informed, about seventy years in their ministerial labours among the people of Blackfriars.

The gospel in your congregation has continued, I think, beyond the remembrance of the oldest (the Lord grant that it may outlive the youngest) now living among you. God has, as it were, made his sun to stand still upon your Gibeon, and his moon upon your Ajalon, to give you light to overcome your spiritual enemies. How many learned and pithy expositions, savoury discourses, and excellent tractates have had their conception in your parish, and their birth in your pulpit! You have enjoyed the monthly administration of the Lord's supper, as your late reverend pastor informed me, these five and forty years, without any interruption. I mention not these things to occasion your glorying in men, or any outward privileges, but only to put you upon self-reflection and holy examination how you have thriven in holiness under all these enjoyments. Church privileges, I grant, are excellent mercies in their kind: without the ordinances, places are commonly as void of civility as

Christianity; they are but *magna latrocinia*, dens of robbers, and places of prey, dark places of the earth filled with violence. Church privileges, so far as they are visibly owned, make men visible saints in opposition to the world; yea, and in their due and holy use real and true saints in opposition to hypocrites. But notwithstanding all these, the means of grace, without grace by those means, leave those who enjoy them in the same condition, in respect of any saving benefit, with those who want them. The ark at Shiloh, Jer. vii. 12, the sacrifices devoured by Ariel, Isa. xxix. 1, 2, circumcision in the flesh, Rom. ii. 25, 28, 29; Jer. ix. 25, 26, the temple of the Lord, Hag. ii. 9, the rock and manna, the Lord's supper at Corinth, 1 Cor. xi. 20, were privileges which did not savingly profit the enjoyers, who were not holy by their holy things, but their holy things rather were made unholy by them. Nay, bare outward privileges increase condemnation. The valley of vision has the heaviest burden. The Israelites, who had not monthly, but daily sacraments, eating and drinking them every meal, were most severely destroyed. These were but as Uriah's letters, which they carried to their own destruction. The higher Chorazin and Bethsaida's elevation was, the greater was their downfal. Justice will pluck the unreformed from the altar of privileges. Sermons do but heat hell, and sacraments are but oil and pitch to make its flame scald and consume the more painfully. The barren oak was not so near cursing as the barren fig-tree; nor are weeds on the dunghill so near plucking up as those in the garden: by none is the name of God so much dishonoured, mercy so much abused, hypocrisy so odiously veiled, the power of godliness so bitterly hated, as by many who have most enjoyed church privileges. Put not off your souls therefore, dear Christians, with outward privileges, without inward grace by those privileges. What is it more to have a name to live, and to be spiritually dead, to have titular sanctity and real impiety, than for a starving man to be praised for a plentiful housekeeper? When God had bestowed upon Abram a new name, and changed it to Abraham, he gave him also a new blessing. The unprofitable under the means of grace are therefore worse than those who want those means, because they are not better. The more a ship is laden with gold, the deeper she sinks; the more you are laden with golden privileges, the deeper, if you miscarry, will be your destruction. Though the minister's industry without success acquits him, yet it condemns his people. He may be sincere, yet unsuccessful; but then the people in the mean time, if unprofitable, show themselves hypocritical. You never commend your ministers but by getting the saving impressions of what they preach upon your hearts. Christ reproved the young man for calling him "Good master," because, saith Calvin, he had never received any saving good from Christ. The sheep only praise the care of the careful shepherd by their wool, milk, fruitfulness, and fatness. Let it never be said that God gives the food of life to you, as a rich man gives a nurse good diet for the benefit of his child, only for the thriving of strangers. Be not as Indians, who go naked and beggarly in the midst of all their heaps of gold. Let not sermons be as jewels only to hang in your ears, but let them be locked up in the cabinets of your hearts. Consider, ordinances are never yours till you get the savour of them upon your spirits. Meat upon the table may be taken away, but not when by eating it is turned into a man's substance. Books may be stolen out of a scholar's study, but a thousand thieves can never take away the learning which he has gotten into his head by studying those books. The grace of privileges is only safe. You shall be stripped of these when you come to die, but the grace of them will stick by you for ever. Christ may say to those at the last day, "Depart," who have eaten and drunk with him, and cast out devils; but never will he say so to those who, having eaten and drunk with him, have also eat and drunk himself, who have cast lust out of their souls, and gotten a broken heart for sin, or obtained the least dram of sanctifying grace. Oh how much is a drop of inward holiness better than a sea of outward privileges!

This book with which I here present you, is the second part of my Exposition upon the Divine and excellent Epistle of Jude. The apostle's scope in writing this Epistle was to stir up these Christians to oppose those who would have seduced them to libertinism, and to contend for the faith against those who turned the grace of God into wantonness; who allowed themselves to live, or rather, like beasts, to wallow in all filthiness, under pretence of advancing free grace; and who laboured to make the saints, by being Christians, to become heathens, as the apostles had made them of heathens to become Christians. The endeavour of Satan was to drive people from one extreme to another; and since he could not, by keeping some under Judaism, cause them to deny that Christ had purchased for them any liberty at all, he most earnestly laboured, by driving them to atheism and looseness, to make them believe that now they had liberty to be as bad as they would; and that the worse they were, the better they were; and the lower they were in sin, the higher in Christian perfection. And hence it was that these later Epistles, one of the last of which was this of Jude, are principally spent in opposing a feigned, workless, lifeless faith, and in administering antidotes against those doctrines of profaneness and libertinism, wherewith the times grew the more infested, as the doctrine of grace grew the more to be cried up and advanced.

It is now a complete year since I began to put pen to paper for preparing this second part for the press. And it might long since have been finished, had not many other employments hindered. It has cost me, I confess, some studious hours; but the kind acceptance which the first part found from the church of God encouraged me to look beyond the difficulty of the work, and made me unwilling to leave this Commentary longer unfinished. I shall conclude with my earnest and humble supplication to the Father of lights, that this endeavour, among others, may advance the spiritual progress of the church, and principally of you, my dear and beloved friends, so in grace here that you may be fitted for glory hereafter. So prays, sirs,

Your affectionate and faithful servant,

for the good of your souls,

WILLIAM JENKYN.

Blackfriars, Feb. 22, 1653.

THE EPISTLE CONSISTS OF THREE PARTS.

  I. The TITLE, ver. 1, 2.
 II. The SUBJECT MATTER, to ver. 24.
III. The CONCLUSION, to the end.

I. The TITLE, containing,

1. **The author** of the Epistle, set forth three ways.
   1. By his name; Jude, ver. 1.
   2. By his office; a servant of Jesus Christ.
   3. By his alliance; the brother of James.

2. The persons to whom he wrote, described by a threefold privilege.
   1. Sanctification; wherein,
      1. The sort of the privilege; sanctified, ver. 1.
      2. The Author thereof; God the Father.
   2. Preservation; where,
      1. The nature of the privilege; preserved, ver. 1.
      2. The means whereby; in Christ Jesus.
   3. Vocation,
      The ground of both the former; called, ver. 1.

3. The prayer, or salutation; wherein three particulars.
   1. The blessings requested;
      - Mercy, ver. 2.
      - Peace.
      - Love.
   2. The measure wherein } he desires they may be bestowed; { be multiplied, ver. 2
   3. The person on whom } { on you.

II. The SUBJECT MATTER of the Epistle, containing an earnest exhortation, wherein are four parts.

1. Reasons of sending the exhortation.
   1. His love to those Christians; Beloved, ver. 3.
   2. The furthering their welfare, showed,
      1. In his obligation to endeavour it; I gave all diligence, ver. 3.
      2. The work whereby he endeavoured it; to write.
      3. The weight of the subject about which he wrote.
   3. The needfulness of the exhortation; it was needful for me to write, ver. 3.

2. The sum of the exhortation.
   1. What the apostle did, he exhorted them, ver. 3.
   2. What the Christians were to do; where,
      1. The thing to be defended; the faith,
         1. Delivered, ver. 3.
         2. To the saints.
         3. Once.
      2. The manner of defending it; earnestly to contend, ver. 3.

1. The dangerous society of seducers, set forth by,
   1. Their entrance, illustrated four ways.
      1. From their nature; they were men, ver. 4.
      2. Their number, indefinite; certain men.
      3. Their subtlety in entrance; crept in unawares.
      4. The vindicating of God's honour in this their entrance, by their punishment, described by,
         - Its severity; this condemnation, ver. 4.
         - Its certainty; they were of old ordained to it.
   2. Their impiety, being entered; expressed,
      1. Generally; ungodly men, ver. 4.
      2. Particularly in their opposing of
         - Grace; where,
            1. Their enjoyment; the grace of our God, ver. 4.
            2. Misimproving it; turning it into lasciviousness
         - God; where,
            1. Whom they opposed; the only Lord God, and our Lord Jesus Christ, ver. 4.
            2. How; denying him.

3. The arguments to urge the Christian to embrace the exhortation; which are two.

1. Examples of God's wrath upon others for sin, viz. upon,
   1. The Israelites, ver. 5, wherein,
      1. A preface, containing,
         1. Jude's duty; I will put you in remembrance, ver. 5.
         2. The Christians' commendation; though ye once knew this.
      2. The example itself, where,
         1. A deliverance, wherein,
            1. The deliverer; the Lord saved, ver. 5.
            2. The delivered; the people.
            3. From what they were delivered; out of the land of Egypt.
         2. A destruction, where,
            1. When it was; afterward destroyed them, ver. 5.
            2. Why it was; that believed not.
   2. The fallen angels, ver. 6, wherein,
      1. Their defection; where consider,
         1. Who made it; the angels, ver. 6.
         2. From what it was made;
            1. Their first estate, ver. 6
            2. Their own habitation.
         3. Wherein it stood, viz.
            1. In not keeping their first estate, ver. 6.
            2. In leaving their own habitation.
      2. Their punishment,
         1. In person;
            1. In everlasting chains.
            2. Under darkness.
         2. At the bar.
            1. To what they shall come; the judgment, ver. 6.
            2. When; the great day.
   3. Sodom and Gomorrha; where consider,
      1. The places punished, viz. Sodom and Gomorrha, ver. 7. The cities about them.
      2. The deserving cause of their punishment, their sin, in,
         1. The sorts thereof; fornication, yea, even uncleanness with strange flesh, ver. 7.
         2. The degree,
            1. Of some; in like manner, ver. 7.
            2. Of all, Gave themselves over, ver. 7. Went after.
      3. The severity of their judgment, set out,
         1. Generally; vengeance, ver. 7.
         2. Particularly;
            1. By what they were punished; fire, ver. 7.
            2. How long; eternal fire.
      4. The end of their punishment; for an example, ver. 7.

2. The imitation of those sins by the seducers; wherein,
   1. The fountain of their wickedness, Security. Delusion. Dreamers, ver. 8.
   2. The faults themselves,
      1. Specified;
         1. Defiling the flesh, ver. 8.
         2. Opposing of lawful authority;
            Despising dominion, ver. 8.
            Speaking evil of dignities.
      2. Aggravated,
         1. From their sinning, notwithstanding punishment on them; likewise also, ver. 8.
         2. From the contrary example of the archangel, in contending with the devil; which example is here,
            1. Propounded, where,
               1. The combatants;
                  1. Michael, ver. 9.
                  2. And the devil.
               2. The strife,
                  1. General; they contended, ver. 9.
                  2. Particular; disputed about the body of Moses, ver. 9.
               3. The carriage of Michael,
                  1. Inward; he durst not bring a railing accusation, ver. 9.
                  2. Outward; he said, The Lord rebuke thee.
            2. Applied to these seducers, by showing their contrary deportment,
               1. Of reviling, notwithstanding ignorance; speak evil of what they know not, ver. 10.
               2. Of corrupting themselves by their knowledge; but what they know, &c.

2. Their ruin; where he propounds,

- **A denunciation of destruction for that imitation; which denunciation is,**
  1. **Propounded; woe to them, ver. 11.**
  2. **Expounded by a mixed description of their sin and misery; and this,**
     1. From the three suitable examples of
        - Cain, Balaam, Core,
        - In whose way they going, in respect of
          - Cruelty,
          - Seduction,
          - For gain,
          - Sedition,
        - should with them perish miserably, ver. 11.
     2. From five elegant comparisons:
        1. Spots in feasts, where,
           1. What they are called; spots, ver. 12.
           2. Where they conversed; in feasts of charity.
           3. What they did there; wherein,
              1. Their employment;
                 - Feed themselves, ver. 12.
                 - Feast.
              2. The manner of their doing it; without fear, ver. 12.
        2. Clouds without water, carried about, &c, where,
           1. To what creatures they are compared; clouds, ver. 12.
           2. To what clouds:
              - Empty; without water, ver. 12.
              - Unstable; carried about of the winds.
        3. Corrupt trees, whose
           - Fruit at best was withering; whose fruit withereth, ver. 12.
           - Fruit therefore was no fruit; without fruit.
           - Want of fruit was joined with a total want of life; twice dead.
           - Want of life was followed with the loss of their place; plucked up by the roots.
        4. Raging waves of the sea, foaming, &c, where,
           1. What they are; raging waves of the sea, ver. 13.
           2. What they get, shame; foaming out their own shame.
        5. Wandering stars, to whom is reserved, &c, where,
           1. Their title; wandering stars, ver. 13.
           2. Their estate to which they are reserved; the blackness of darkness for ever.
  3. **From the ancient and infallible prophecy of Enoch, which is declared; wherein,**
     1. The preface, containing,
        1. His name; Enoch, ver. 14.
        2. Descent; seventh from Adam.
        3. Employment; prophesied of these.
        1. An incitement to attend to the description of the judgment; Behold, ver. 14.
     2. The prophecy itself of the judgment, wherein,
        2. The description itself, where,
           1. The coming of the Judge to judgment, where,
              1. His title; the Lord, ver. 14.
              2. His approach; cometh.
              3. His attendants, where,
                 1. Their quality; holy, or saints, ver. 14.
                 2. Their quantity; ten thousand.
                 3. Relation; his.
              4. Action; coming with their Lord.
           2. The manner of judgment,
              1. By conviction; to convince, ver. 15.
              2. By execution; to execute.
           3. All the parties judged; all the ungodly, ver. 15.
           4. The causes of the judgment:
              1. Works. Ungodly committed for their manner.
              2. Words. Ungodly for their nature, ver. 15.
                 1. What they were; hard speeches, ver. 15.
                 2. By whom spoken; ungodly sinners.
                 3. Against whom; him.

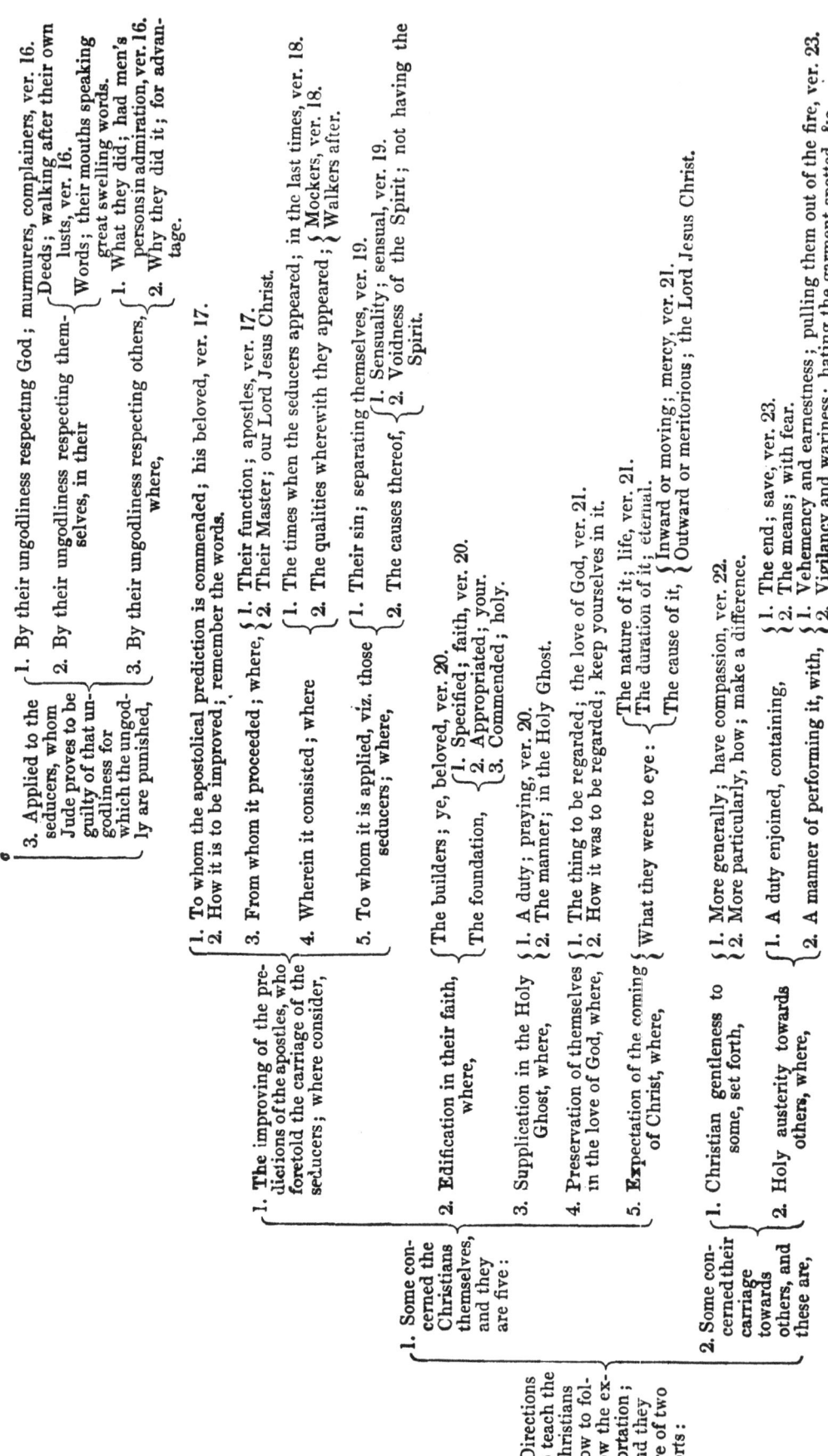

III. THE CONCLUSION of the Epistle, containing a suitable Doxology, or praising of God: wherein consider,

1. The person to whom the praise is given, and that is Christ, who is set forth three ways:
   1. By his power,
      1. To keep them from falling, ver. 24.
      2. To present them faultless in heaven, where their happiness is,
         1. Generally propounded; to present you before the presence of his glory, ver. 24.
         2. Particularly exemplified;
            1. Privatively, by removing all deformity; faultless, ver. 24.
            2. Positively, by fulness of comfort; with exceeding joy.
   2. By his wisdom, where,
      1. Its subject; God, ver. 25.
      2. Its excellency; only wise.
   3. By his goodness; our Saviour, ver. 25.

2. The praise given to that person;
   Glory, ver. 25.
   Majesty.
   Dominion.
   Power.

3. The manner how this praise is given, denoted in the word Amen;
   Assent, ver. 25.
   Desire.
   Trust.

(1) Jude, the servant of Jesus Christ, and brother of James, to them that are sanctified by God the Father, and preserved in Jesus Christ, [and] called: (2) Mercy unto you, and peace, and love, be multiplied.

(3) ¶ Beloved, when I gave all diligence to write unto you of the common salvation, it was needful for me to write unto you, and exhort [you] that ye should earnestly contend for the faith which was once delivered unto the saints. (4) For there are certain men crept in unawares, who were before of old ordained to this condemnation, ungodly men, turning the grace of our God into lasciviousness, and denying the only Lord God, and our Lord Jesus Christ.

(5) ¶ I will therefore put you in remembrance, though ye once knew this, how that the Lord, having saved the people out of the land of Egypt, afterward destroyed them that believed not. (6) And the angels which kept not their first estate, but left their own habitation, he hath reserved in everlasting chains under darkness unto the judgment of the great day. (7) Even as Sodom and Gomorrha, and the cities about them in like manner, giving themselves over to fornication, and going after strange flesh, are set forth for an example, suffering the vengeance of eternal fire. (8) Likewise also these [filthy] dreamers defile the flesh, despise dominion, and speak evil of dignities. (9) Yet Michael the archangel, when contending with the devil he disputed about the body of Moses, durst not bring against him a railing accusation, but said, The Lord rebuke thee. (10) But these speak evil of those things which they know not: but what they know naturally, as brute beasts, in those things they corrupt themselves. (11) Woe unto them! for they have gone in the way of Cain, and ran greedily after the error of Balaam for reward, and perished in the gainsaying of Core.

(12) ¶ These are spots in your feasts of charity, when they feast with you, feeding themselves without fear: clouds [they are] without water, carried about of winds; trees whose fruit withereth, without fruit, twice dead, plucked up by the roots; (13) Raging waves of the sea, foaming out their own shame; wandering stars, to whom is reserved the blackness of darkness for ever. (14) And Enoch also, the seventh from Adam, prophesied of these, saying, Behold, the Lord cometh with ten thousands of his saints, (15) To execute judgment upon all, and to convince all that are ungodly among them of all their ungodly deeds which they have ungodly committed, and of all their hard [speeches] which ungodly sinners have spoken against him.

(16) ¶ These are murmurers, complainers, walking after their own lusts; and their mouth speaketh great swelling [words], having men's persons in admiration because of advantage. (17) But, beloved, remember ye the words which were spoken before of the apostles of our Lord Jesus Christ; (18) How that they told you there should be mockers in the last time, who should walk after their own ungodly lusts. (19) These be they who separate themselves, sensual, having not the Spirit.

(20) ¶ But ye, beloved, building up yourselves on your most holy faith, praying in the Holy Ghost, (21) Keep yourselves in the love of God, looking for the mercy of our Lord Jesus Christ unto eternal life. (22) And of some have compassion, making a difference: (23) And others save with fear, pulling [them] out of the fire; hating even the garment spotted by the flesh.

(24) ¶ Now unto him that is able to keep you from falling, and to present [you] faultless before the presence of his glory with exceeding joy, (25) To the only wise God our Saviour, [be] glory and majesty, dominion and power, both now and ever. Amen.

AN EXPOSITION

UPON

THE EPISTLE OF JUDE.

I BEGIN with the first part of the Epistle, the title of, or entrance into it, contained in the first two verses, which are these:

Ver. 1, 2. *Jude, the servant of Jesus Christ, and brother of James, to them that are sanctified by God the Father, and preserved in Jesus Christ, and called: mercy unto you, and peace, and love, be multiplied.*

This title contains three principal parts:
I. The person who wrote the Epistle.
II. The persons to whom he wrote it.
III. The prayer: wherein the person writing salutes the persons to whom he wrote.

I. The person who wrote this Epistle is described these three ways.
1. From his name, Jude.
2. From his office, A servant of Jesus Christ.
3. From his alliance, The brother of James.

1. The description of the penman of this Epistle from his name, Jude. In the consideration whereof I shall proceed by way of exposition, and of observation.

(1.) The name of the author of the Epistle considered by way of exposition; wherein two things are to be opened: The signification of the name Judas, or Jude; and, The subject of that name, or who the person was to whom it is here applied.

[1.] For the signification of the name Jude. It is found fully expressed Gen. xxix. 35. The occasion of first imposing it, was Leah's apprehension of God's goodness to her, in giving her a fourth son, whom therefore she called Judah, signifying יהודה praise, confession, or celebration. She made his name a monument of her thankfulness to God for him, as also of her son's duty to live to the praise of so good a God: a fruitful wife to Jacob in children, and a fruitful daughter to God in thankfulness. The learned Rivet well observes, that in imposing this name she was directed by the Spirit of God; this Judah being that son of Jacob, of whom Christ, according to the flesh, was to come, for whom God is principally to be praised, he being the choicest gift that ever God bestowed, turning every other gift into a mercy. Only those who have him, and bear him, can praise God; to others God comparatively gives nothing, and they return nothing. God shows superlatively how rich he is, in giving his Son; so God "loved the world, that he gave his only begotten Son," John iii. 16.

[In qua nominis impositione, non dubito quin eam direxerit Spiritus sanctus, cum Judah fuerit is qui inter Jacobi filios, pater futuri Messiæ constitutus erat. Riv. in loc.]

[2.] The subject of this name is to be considered, to which it is here applied. It is applied in Scripture to a threefold subject.
1. To a tribe. Frequent mention is made of the tribe of Judah, 1 Kings xii. 20; Psal. lxxvi. 1.
2. To a country or region, 2 Chron. xx. 3; Jer. xvii. 25.
3. And properly, to persons: and so in Scripture we read of six several persons that had this name.
  1. Judah the patriarch, Gen. xxix. 35.
  2. Judah in whose house Saul lodged at his first conversion, Acts ix. 11.
  3. Judas surnamed Barsabas, Acts xv. 22.
  4. Judas of Galilee, a seditious person, Acts v. 37.
  5. Judas Iscariot the traitor, Matt. x. 4; John xiv. 22.
  6. Judas the apostle, the author of this Epistle. Concerning whom the Scripture intimates, besides his apostolical office and relation to James,
    1. His parentage: his father being Alphæus, spoken of Matt. x. 3; Mark iii. 18; and his mother held to be that Mary spoken of Matt. xxvii. 56; because Alphæus and Mary are said to be the parents of James, to which James, in Luke vi. 16; Acts i. 13, and here in this Epistle, this Judas is said to be brother.
    2. The Scripture expresses a manifest distinction between him and Judas Iscariot, John xiv. 22, calling him Judas, not Iscariot; taking especial care that he might not be taken for him, their hearts and persons being as different as their names were agreeable; for one was *sectator*, the other *insectator Domini*; the one following Christ as a disciple, the other as a blood-hound; one confessed him, the other betrayed him; the one carried himself according to his name, the other was a mere living contradiction to

[In sacra dodecada fuerunt duo qui nomen Judæ gessere; unus fuit sectator, alter insectator. Aug. Tr. 76. in Joh. Unus nomini suo convenienter se gessit (Judas enim Confessorem significat,) alter per antiphrasin nomen istud a se geri ipsis operibus demonstravit. Gerh. Har. in loc.]

B

his name. When the evangelist saith, Judas, not Iscariot, he intended a difference betwixt him and this holy Jude.

3. The Scripture expresses a humble question propounded by him to Christ: "Lord, how is it that thou wilt manifest thyself to us, and not unto the world?" John xiv. 22. Concerning which question, although I meet with different opinions, yet I see not why, with Musculus, we may not conceive that Jude propounded it from a humble and modest consideration of himself and the apostles, in partaking of the gracious manifestation of Christ to them, there being a passing by of others more famous and better accomplished than were the disciples. A question which, thus understood, shows, 1. The freeness of him that gives; so, 2. The humility of them that receive grace; who, instead of insulting over others that have less than themselves, admire the goodness of him that gives more to them than to others; nay, 3. The tender-heartedness and pity of the godly towards the souls of those wicked ones, who are commonly cruel and unkind to their bodies.

4. The Scripture expresses concerning this apostle, that he was πολυώνυμος, had sundry names; for he that in Luke vi. 16 is called "Judas the brother of James," is in Matt. x. 3 called Lebbæus and Thaddæus; the reason whereof I meet with sundry opinions among writers. 1. Some conceive that he had this diversity of names from a usual custom among the Jews, that if any name had in it three or more of the letters of Jehovah, יהוה it should not be used in ordinary speech, but that some other name like it should be substituted for it. Now Judah יהודה containing in it all the four letters in the name Jehovah, (having besides the letter ד) this apostle had other names by which he was ordinarily called; but this reason seems, whatever is the superstition of the later Jews, not to have taken place in our Jude, or in any other of whom we read: the patriarch Judah, the son of Jacob, had no other name than Judah bestowed upon him by his mother or friends, nor did the custom appear upon Judas Iscariot. 2. Others conceive that these names were conferred upon him, to distinguish him from Judas (of the same name) the traitor, grown detestable for his execrable fact and heinous treason; for which cause our apostle may in the title of this Epistle style himself also "the brother of James;" the name of Judas being so odious in the church, that, as a learned man observes, though a good name in itself, Christians have in all ages abstained from imposing it, and that very rarely is it to be found mentioned in any history. And there seems to be an exact care in the evangelist, that when this holy apostle was named, John xiv. 22, he might not be taken for the traitor, speaking thus, "Judas, not Iscariot." Nor was it any change of his name that answered the purpose; for it was no less wisely than piously heeded, that those other names, Thaddæus and Lebbæus, should be suitable to the person upon whom they were bestowed; Thaddæus signifying in the Syriac the same thing, תודה praise or confession, with Judah in Hebrew; the imposers of this name intimating the constancy of this holy man in confessing Christ, what name soever he had. Nor can it be thought, but that the other name, Lebbæus, was applied fitly and suitably to him, as being derived either from the Hebrew word Labi, לביא which signifies a lion, (the emblem of another Judah, Gen. xlix. 9, of which tribe this Jude was,) to show his holy resolution and courage for God, in opposing sin and the enemies of the truth, even as with a lion-like heart; or from the Hebrew word Leb, which signifieth a heart: thereby denoting (say some) that he was a man of much wisdom and understanding in his place and conduct; for he who was of greatest discretion and prudence, was formerly accustomed to be called *Corculum*, from *cor*, a heart; and a wise, understanding man is usually termed *homo cordatus*, a man with a heart: or denoting (say others) that he was *cordis cultor*, a man that laboured much about his heart, studying diligently its purity and sanctifying. This for the expository part of the first thing considerable in the description of the penman of this Epistle, viz. his name.

(2.) From the sameness or commonness of the name Judas to a holy apostle, and a perfidious traitor, together with that seditious Galilean, I observe,

1. That names commend us not to God, nor conduce any thing to our true happiness. Many who have holy and blessed names come much short of them, as Adonijah, Judas, &c. Absalom signifies, the father's peace; but he that was so called, proved his father's trouble. On the other side, many have unpromising and infamous names, who are excellent persons, and have lost nothing thereby. It is not a holy name, but a holy nature, that makes a holy man. No outward titles or privileges profit the enjoyer; "neither circumcision, nor uncircumcision, but a new creature." A peasant may have the name of a prince; a traitor, the name of a holy apostle. It is all one with God to call thee holy, and to make thee so. Oh, beg of him inward renovation, more than outward estimation; otherwise, a great name for holiness will prove but a great plague hereafter. Hell is a wicked Judas's own place. A good name with an unchanged nature, is but white feathers upon a black skin. A great privilege unsanctified is a great punishment.

Obs. 2. That wicked men make the best names and things odious by their unholy carriage. Judas the traitor makes the name Judas by many to be despised. Eli's sons made the people to abhor the Lord's offering, 1 Sam. ii. 17. God tells the people, that they had profaned his holy name, while the heathen said, "These are the people of the Lord," Ezek. xxxvi. 20. Scandalous Christians have brought an odium upon Christianity. It is the duty therefore of those who are conversant about holy things to be holy; to tremble lest any should think the worse of ordinances, of the ministry, or of sanctity, for them. The blood of seeming saints will not wash away the scandal they have brought upon true sanctity, nor make amends for the evil report which they have brought upon the Canaan of godliness; and yet we should take heed of thinking the worse of holiness, or of any way of God, for the wickedness of any person whatever. Eli's sons sinned in making the people abhor the Lord's offering; and yet the text saith the people sinned too in abhorring it, 1 Sam. ii. 24.

Obs. 3. That our baptismal names ought to be such as may prove remembrancers of duty. Leah and Alphæus, in imposing names on their children, made use of such as might induce parents and children another day to seek holiness. God called Abram Abraham, to strengthen his faith: Hannah gave the name of Samuel to her son, because he was a son of prayer. It is good to impose such names as express our baptismal promise. A good name is a thread tied about the finger, to make us mindful of the errand we came into the world to do for our Master.

Obs. 4. That ministers, especially, ought so to behave themselves, as that they may not be ashamed of their names. That their name prefixed may be a crown, a credit to their writings; that whensoever their names are spoken of, the hearer may bless them: that their names may be as a sweet perfume to their actions. Many Christians' names are so odious, that what they say or do is blemished, because it comes from them: it had been good if it had been another's. He is a dead man among the living that has a hateful name. It is a great mercy when our names outlive us; it is a great punishment when we outlive our names. They that honour God shall have the spirit of glory rest upon them. He that is a Jude, a confessor of Christ, shall never want that honour.

Obs. 5. That we should not do that to which we are ashamed or afraid to own or put our names. I deny not but in some cases it may be lawful to change our names, or forbear to mention them, either by tongue or pen; but then we should not be driven to such straits by the badness of our actions, as the most are, so as to be ashamed to own them; but by the consideration of God's glory, or the church's good, or our own necessary preservation in time of persecution, which may be the more advanced by concealing our names. Thus Bucer, in times of trouble for the gospel, called Aretius, Felinus. Calvin's Institutions were printed under the name of Alcuinus. But these did not conceal themselves for sin, but for safety; nor yet so much for safety as for God's glory.

I pass from the name, and proceed to describe,

2. The author of this Epistle, in his office, A servant of Jesus Christ.

Of this, by way of explication, and of observation.

For explication. Here two points are to be opened. In what respect Jude was the servant of Christ? and why he here so styles himself?

[1.] In what respect Jude was the servant of Christ? He was so in three respects.

1. In respect of creation and sustention, as are all creatures. All are thy servants, from the highest angel to the lowest worm, Psal. cxix. 91. "All things were created by him, and for him, and by him all things consist," Col. i. 16, 17. The world is but his family, altogether at his finding: should he shut his hand, the house would be famished: if he withdraw his maintenance, the world would fall.

2. In respect of redemption from the power of sin and Satan, Heb. ii. 15; from their condemning and destroying power, Rom. viii. 1; from their corrupting and defiling power. And that this was a redemption calculated to make us servants to the Redeemer, Rom. vi. 18; Eph. vi. 6, appears, in that it was not only by conquest, and vindication from our enemies, Luke i. 74; as the conqueror might have destroyed us as well as taken us, or destroyed them, in which respect, according to all usage and equity, we ought to be for ever his servants; but a redemption also by purchase, the Lord Jesus having paid no less price than his own precious blood, 1 Pet. i. 18, 19. From which consideration the apostle strongly argues, that we are not our own, but serve for the glorifying of another, 1 Cor. vi. 20.

3. This apostle was the servant of Christ, more peculiarly, by way of special office and function. Christ himself, Moses, David, Cyrus, Zerubbabel, &c., were called God's servants; so are the prophets in the Old, the apostles and ministers in the New Testament called servants. Although it is granted that the apostles were servants in a different way from other ministers, both with respect to the manner of their calling, which was by immediate mission and appointment from God, and also to the extent of their power, which was not confined to one place, but granted to them for planting and governing churches in any part of the world. In which respect, some think, they are called the salt of the earth.

On account of this function, and office of apostleship, Jude principally calls himself a servant of Christ: though not barely and solely on account of God's calling him to it, but in respect also of his own diligence and faithfulness in endeavouring to discharge his office to which he was called: as Peter exhorts, 1 Pet. iv. 10; and, as Paul speaks, Christ keeps no servants only to wear a livery, 1 Cor. ix. 16. As he is not a titular Lord, so neither are his servants titular servants. All their expressions of service reach not the emphasis either of their desires or duty.

[2.] The thing to be opened secondly, is the cause why the apostle here styleth himself the servant of Christ.

Some think, to show his humility and modesty. He who might have used the title either of apostle, or brother of the Lord, rather contents himself with this note of duty and service common to every Christian.

Others, better, for the confirming and comforting himself in his work; because his Lord whom he served, and had set him on work, would stand by him, both in protecting his person and prospering his work.

Others, and those upon clearest grounds, conceive that the apostle here embraces this title of servant on account of others, that his doctrine might with more respect and readiness be received by those to whom he wrote; seeing that he was called to his work, and, that by such a Master, whose service added not more dignity to him, than it required duty from them.

This for explication: the observations follow.

Obs. 1. They who undertake any public employment for Christ, must receive a call from him to be his servants, if with comfort to themselves, or benefit to others, they will go about his work. It is a great shame, if all who are prophets are not the Lord's people; but it is a gross error to think that all the Lord's people are ministerially prophets. Their being the Lord's people makes them fit to hear, but not fit to preach; fit sheep, not fit shepherds. Suppose that, which constant experience contradicts, they have the fitness of gifts, have they therefore a sufficient call to preach by way of office, and ministry? Is it enough, to be a king's servant, or a nobleman's steward, for a person to have abilities to discharge those places? is there not required commission or call also? and are not ministers called servants and stewards? At this time I doubt it would hardly be accounted true doctrine, that every one who has military gifts, courage and policy, may be a commander of a regiment, or captain of a troop, and that he might gather his followers without commission. Is it enough for a man to be a prince's ambassador, because he has sufficient gifts, for wit, and good expression, &c.? must not the king also give him the authority to be an ambassador? Is every one who can run a messenger? must he not be sent likewise? Besides, whosoever has a commission to preach has a commission to baptize, as is plain from Matt. xxviii. 19. Preaching and baptizing reaching alike the ministry of all ages. But has every gifted man such a commission? Further, does not our Saviour, Matt. x. 41, clearly distinguish between a righteous man and a prophet? if they had been all one, why would he have done so? and if gifts make a minister, is it not as true that gifts make a magistrate? and then every one who had understanding and other good governing parts were a lord mayor. Nay, then why might not women preach, (as lately they have done,) many of whom have better gifts than some men? And how could that agree with the apostolical prohibition for women to speak in the church?

Besides, all who are called to preach are bound to increase their gifts, by giving attendance to reading, to doctrine, and by giving themselves wholly to these things, which cannot be done, unless earthly occupations are laid aside: but gifted men are not bound to this; so they have not this call which they pretend. To conclude, every one that hath this ministerial call, has that pastoral care lying upon him, mentioned Heb. xiii. 17, To watch over souls as those that must give an account with joy, and not with grief: but this can in no wise be said of every one who is a gifted man; and therefore gifted persons, as such, must forsake their pretended claim to a ministerial call. Nor can it be evinced, because the apostle says, All may prophesy, 1 Cor. xiv. 31, therefore every gifted person may preach. For, besides that the gift of prophecy was extraordinarily bestowed in that age of the church, not procured by study and industry, but immediately conferred by the Spirit upon some, as were also miracles, the gift of healing, and diversities of tongues, all which are now ceased, it is most plain, that the word *all* in that place is not to be taken in its full latitude, as if all the men, or every believer in the church of Corinth, might stand up and prophesy, for that is expressly contrary to 1 Cor. xii. 29, where by an interrogation the apostle vehemently denies that all are prophets; but it is to be taken restrictively, to those that were in office, and set by God in the church for that purpose, as the apostle speaks, "God hath set some in his church, first apostles, secondarily prophets," &c. 1 Cor. xii. 28. Other cavils are weaker than deserve to be mentioned; as, to argue from that place, that because women are forbid to speak in the church, therefore any man may speak, 1 Cor. xiv. 34. What greater strength is in this argument than to reason thus: Because no woman may be a justice of peace, therefore every man may? Because no woman may speak publicly, therefore some men must, (namely, such as are in office,) had been a much better consequence. Nor is there more strength in that allegation of Moses's wish, that all the Lord's people were prophets, to prove that all might prophesy; for in his desiring that all might be prophets, he includes a required condition, that they might be called by God to that employment.

Obs. 2. Alliance in faith, spiritual relation to Christ, is much dearer and nearer than alliance in flesh. Jude might have called himself a near kinsman to Christ, or Christ's brother, as indeed he was, and was so accounted, Matt. xiii. 55, as much as James, who is called the Lord's brother, Gal. i. 19; but that which includes a spiritual relation is to him much sweeter: to be a servant of Christ is more desirable than to be a brother of Christ. What had it profited to have been his kinsman, unless his servant? Many who were his kinsmen according to the flesh, wanted the honour of this spiritual affinity; but such of them who had this honour bestowed upon them, had all their other glory swallowed up in this, as Christ expressed himself, He is my brother, and sister, and mother. Blessed be God, that this great privilege is not denied to us even now; though we cannot see him, yet love him we may; though we have not his bodily presence, yet we are not denied the spiritual; though he be not ours in house, in arms, in affinity, yet in heart, in faith, in love, in service he is.

Obs. 3. There is a peculiar excellency and worth in the title of servant, with which our apostle, and others before him, were so frequently delighted. It might furnish them and us with a fivefold consideration full of sweet delight. (1.) That he much honours us. To serve Christ is to reign. It is more honour to serve Christ than to serve emperors; nay, than to have emperors serve us; for, indeed, all things do so. (2.) That he will assist us in our works: if he gives employment, he will give endowments too; if an errand, a tongue; if work, a hand; if a burden, a back: "I can do all things through Christ which strengtheneth me," saith Paul. And herein he goes beyond all other masters, who can toil and task their servants sufficiently, but cannot strengthen them. (3.) That he will preserve us. He will keep us in all our ways; and surely then he will so in all his own work. Safety evermore accompanies duty. His mercy is over all his works, but peculiarly over all his workers. Men are never in danger but when they leave working. Jonah was well enough till he attempted to run away from his Master. When our enemies do us the greatest hurt, they remove us above hurt. A servant of Christ may be sick, persecuted, scorned, imprisoned, but never unsafe; he may lose his head, but not one hair of his head perish. (4.) That he will provide for us. He can live without servants, but these cannot live without a Master. Verily his family-servants shall be fed. The servants of Christ shall want no good thing: if they are without some things, there is nothing they can want; they shall have better, and enough of better. Can he that has a mine of gold want pebbles? Can it be that a servant of Christ should want provision, when God can make his very work meat and drink to him? nay, when God can make his wants meat and drink? How can he want, or be truly without any thing, whose friend has and is all? No good thing shall they want, nothing that may fit them for and further them in duty. It is true they may be without clogs, snares, hinderances; but those things are not good which hinder the chief good. If God gave them, he would feed his servants with husks, nay, with poison. (5.) That he will reward them. The Lord gives grace and glory: great is their reward in heaven; nay, great is their reward on earth. There is a reward in the very work; but God will bestow a further recompence hereafter. We should not serve him *for*, but he will not be served *without* wages, even such as will weigh down all our work, all our woes.

Oh the folly of them that either prefer that cruel and dishonourable service of sin, before the sweet and glorious service of Christ; or that, being servants to Christ, improve it not for their comfort in all their distresses!

Obs. 4. We owe to God the duty and demeanour of servants.

(1.) To serve him solely, not serving sin or Satan at all, nor man in opposition to Christ; not serving ourselves or the times, Matt. vi. 24. Who keep servants to serve others, enemies? Christ and sin are contrary masters; contrary in work, and therefore it is an impossibility to serve both; contrary in wages, and therefore it is an infinite folly to serve sin.

(2.) Christ must be served obediently, submissively, [1.] In bearing when he corrects. A beaten servant must not strike again, nor word it with his master: we must accept of the punishment of our iniquities. It is chaff that flies in the face of him that fanneth. [2.] We must be submissive servants, in being content with our allowance, in forbearing to enjoy what we would, as well as bearing what we would not: the proper work of a servant is to wait. Stay thy Master's pleasure for any comfort. All his servants will have what they want, and therefore should be content with what they have. The standing wages are set, the vails are uncertain. [3.] Submissive in not doing what we please, not going beyond our rule, our order. Ministers are his servants, and therefore must not make laws in his house, either for themselves or others, but keep laws; not of themselves lay down what they publish, but publish what he has laid down. Ministers are not owners of the house, but stewards in the house. Laws are committed to us, and must not be framed by us. No servant must do what is right in his own eyes. [4.] Submissive in doing whatever the Master please. Not picking out this work, or rejecting that: nothing must come amiss to a servant. We must not examine what the service is which is commanded, but who the Master is that commands. We must not prefer one thing before another; or refuse a service that most crosses our inclinations, or opposes our ease and interest. A servant must come at every call, and say, Lord, I hear every command, Acts x. 33. [5.] We must serve Christ obediently in doing what is commanded, because it is commanded: this is to serve for conscience' sake. If the eye be not to the command, the servant acts not with obedience, though the thing be done which is commanded; nay, it is possible a work, for the matter, agreeable to the command, may yet be an act of disobedience, in respect of the intention of the performer. Oh how sweet is it to eye a precept in every performance! to pray, hear, preach, give, because Christ bids me! Many do these works for the wages; this is not to be obedient: they sell their services, not submit in service.

(3.) Christ must be served heartily. We must not be ὀφθαλμόδȣλοι, eye-servants, we must "do the will of God from the heart," Eph. vi. 6; Col. iii. 23. Paul speaks of serving God in the spirit, Rom. i. 9. There are many complimental servants of Christ in the world, who place their service in saying, Thy servant, thy servant, Lord; lip servants, but not life, heart servants; such as the apostle speaks of, Gal. vi. 12, that εὐπροσωπῆσαι, make a show only, but the heart of a service is wanting. The heart makes the service *sacrificium medullatum*, the marrow of a performance. Bodily service is but like the fire in the bush, that appeared to burn, but did not; or like the glow-worm in the night, that shines, but heats not: these only act service, but are no servants; servants only in profession. To those who would not profess Christ seriously, Christ will hereafter profess seriously, "I never knew you: depart from me, ye that work iniquity," Matt. vii. 23.

(4.) Christ must be served cheerfully, Psal. xl. 8. He, as he was his Father's servant, delighted to do his will; it was his meat and his drink, John iv. 34. God loveth a cheerful servant in every piece of service, 2 Cor. ix. 7. This makes the service pleasing to Master and servant too; acceptable to the former, easy to the latter. Nothing is hard to a willing mind; willingness is the oil to the wheel. A servant cheerful at his work is as free as his master: if his master make him not free, he makes himself free. The preaching of the gospel must be performed willingly, 1 Cor. ix. 17. Love to souls should make us cheerful in that service; not mourning at our own pains, but at people's unprofitableness; not that we do so much, but that they get no more.

<small>Si non possint a Dominis liberi fieri, suam servitutem ipsi quodammodo liberam faciunt. Aug. de C. D. l. 19. c. 15.</small>

(5.) Christ must be served diligently. These two, "fervent in spirit," and "serving the Lord," are most properly joined together, Rom. xii. 11. Hence it is most necessary, that whatever we do, should be done with all the might, Eccl. ix. 10. Abraham's servant was diligent when he went to procure a wife for Isaac: he would not eat bread till he had done his errand; when it was done, he staid not upon compliments, Gen. xxiv. 33. They whose service is in soul marriage, should spend no time needlessly. It is a pity that Satan's emissaries should be more diligent than Christ's servants; impostors, than pastors. How diligent a servant was Paul, that passed over so many countries with so much speed! "I laboured more than they all," was spoken as commendably as truly; not *plus profui*, I was more successful, but *plus laboravi*, I took more pains: diligence may be a companion and comfort, where success is a stranger.

(6.) Christ must be served perpetually. There must be no end of working, till of living. The dead are they who rest from their labours. Life and labour are of equal continuance. We can never begin too soon, nor continue too long, in the service of Christ: none ever repented of either, many of the contrary to both. Faithfulness to the death hath the only promise of the crown of life. Better never to have begun, than to apostatize. It is an unanswerable dilemma, If the service of Christ were bad, why did you enter into it? if good, why did you depart from it?

Obs. 5. That they who expect to persuade others to serve Christ, must be servants themselves. Jude, a servant of Christ, hopefully exhorts others to continue in his service, and to contend for his faith. The best way to move others, is to be moved ourselves: words that come from the heart, are most likely to reach to the heart. It is not sufficient for ministers to discourse of his service, but to embrace it. A blurred finger is unfit to wipe away a blot. It is woeful when the function and the conversation oppose each other. If the service of Christ be bad, why exhort we others to submit to it? if good, why accept we not of it ourselves? A titular service shall never receive a real reward. "Depart from me, ye that work iniquity," shall be the doom of some that cast out devils, and prophesy in the name of Christ.

Thus much for the second particular in the description of the author of this Epistle, viz. his office, "A servant of Jesus Christ." Now follows the last particular considerable in his description,

3. His kindred and alliance, "The brother of James."

Of which, by way of explication and observation. For explication, two things are to be opened: Who this James was; and, Why this apostle here calls himself his brother.

(1.) Who this James was.

The Scripture speaks of two of that name: the one, James the son of Zebedee, the brother of John the evangelist, mentioned under these relations, Matt. x. 3; iv. 21; called by Christ; leaving father and ship; slain by Herod, Acts xii. 2; named by Christ, with his brother, Boanerges, Mark iii. 17, the sons of thunder. The other, this James here mentioned; concerning whom much is said in Scripture, and in ecclesiastical history; but in both he is spoken of very honourably.

[1.] In Scripture. First, His kindred and alliance are often mentioned. His father is said to be Alphæus, Matt. x. 3; Mark iii. 18; Luke vi. 15; Acts i. 13. His mother was Mary, spoken of Matt. xxvii. 56; Mark xvi. 1; Luke xxiv. 10; Mark xv. 40. His brethren are said to be Simon, Joses, and Judas, Matt. xiii. 55; Mark vi. 3; two whereof were apostles, viz. Simon and Judas, Matt. x. 3, 4; Luke vi. 15, 16; Acts i. 13; and the other, viz. Joses, or Joseph, was competitor with Matthias (as is generally supposed) for the apostleship, in the room of Judas Iscariot, Acts i. 23. Particularly, this James is said to be the brother of the Lord, Gal. i. 19, though, together with him, his brethren, Joses, Judas, and Simon, are also called Christ's brethren, Matt. xiii. 55; Mark vi. 3. Not as if Mary, the mother of Christ, had afterward borne children unto Joseph, as the erroneous Helvidius (whom Hierom confutes at large) laboured to maintain. Nor as if James and the rest were called the brethren of Christ as being the sons of Joseph, Christ's reputed father, by another wife; for the Scripture tells us frequently they were the sons of Alphæus; and it is the received opinion, that Joseph was never the husband of any but the blessed Virgin, though haply some have the more earnestly asserted it from their high esteem of virginity. But some suppose this James and his brethren are called the brother and brethren of Christ, because they were the cousins-german of Christ by the mother's side, or Christ's mother's sister's children: and Hierom thinks their mother is that Mary, called the sister to the Virgin, and the wife of Cleophas, John xix. 25; her first husband Alphæus either being dead, or else one and the same husband being adorned with two names, Alphæus and Cleophas; which might well be, because, among the Hebrews, those names that agree in the same radical letters, lose not their notion and signification by the addition of other letters to them, a rule applicable to these two names, Alphæus and Cleophas. And Gerhard also thinks, that this Mary, the sister of the Virgin, and the wife of Cleophas, was the mother of James, &c.; because, as in John xix. 25, Mary the wife of Cleophas and sister of the Virgin, is joined with Mary Magdalene standing by the cross; so, in the other evangelists, Mary the mother of James, upon the very same occasion, is joined with Mary Magdalene, Matt. xxvii. 56; Mark xv. 40. Some conceive this Mary the wife of Cleophas was mother of James, but was not own sister to the Virgin Mary, because, say they, it is not the custom for the same parents to put the same names on several children; but that she is called sister to the Virgin Mary because her husband Cleophas, or Alphæus, was the brother of Joseph, the husband of the Virgin Mary, brothers' wives being frequently called sisters. The most probable opinion is, that Joseph and Alphæus were of near relation, perhaps natural brethren, and therefore Joseph, being the reputed father of Christ, the children of his brother Alphæus, among whom this James was one, are called the brethren of Christ; it being usual in Scripture to call those persons brethren who are near of kin. As we see Abraham and Lot are called brethren, Gen. xiii. 8, although Lot was his nephew, Gen. xiv. 12. So Jacob calls his uncle Laban brother, Gen. xxix. 12, 15. See Gen. xxxi. 36, 37, 46.

Thus the Scripture speaks of James in respect of his kindred or alliance.

Secondly, The Scripture speaks worthily of him on account of his office; not only because he was an apostle, but also of great honour and respect among the apostles, and in the church, he being, Acts xv., a principal member, some say president, in the council of Jerusalem, where he gave his advice in a great controversy, which was highly esteemed and followed: and on account of his high esteem in the church, and usefulness, he, Cephas, and John, are called pillars, Gal. ii. 9; for although all the apostles were equal in degree of office, yet there were some of them endowed with more eminent gifts, and had greater esteem than the rest; and therefore we read of Paul's comparing himself with the chiefest of the apostles, 2 Cor. xi. 5; xii. 11, of which James was one. And whereas he is called "James the less," Mark xv. 40, it is conceived it was not to distinguish him from the other James the son of Zebedee, as if the Scripture hereby would denote our James less in respect of age, calling to apostleship, or of stature, much less of esteem: but he may be called "the less" in comparison of his father, who, as a learned man thinks, was called James also, as well as Alphæus; which opinion of his he probably confirms in his Exposition upon this place.

[2.] Ecclesiastical history speaks of him also as a most worthy person, both for the admirable and rare holiness of his life, and his constancy in professing Christ at his death.

1. For his life: Hierom, in allusion to his name, James, or Jacob, calls him the supplanter of sin and vice of those times wherein he lived, preached, and wrote. And as many write most highly in commendation of him, so particularly Eusebius, in his second book, chap. i. and xxii. For his holiness he was called the Just, one that was much in fasting and prayer for the pardon of that sinful people the Jews: with his frequent and long praying his knees were hard. The Jews were generally much convinced of his holiness; insomuch, as the enemies of Christ hoped, if they could procure him to deny Christ, that most of those who professed, would abandon the faith of Christ.

2. For his death: The scribes and Pharisees earnestly besought him to disclaim Christ openly; and to that end they set him upon the temple, that in the sight and audience of the people he might declare that Jesus was not Christ. But to admiration he professed his own faith in Christ, telling the multitudes that Christ was in heaven "at the right hand of God," and that in the clouds he should come again to judge the world; with which profession his enemies, being enraged, cast him down from the temple, and afterwards murdered him, he before his death praying that God would pardon their sin unto them. The same author, and also Josephus, lib. xx. Antiq. cap. 8, testifies that those who were of the wiser sort thought that this detestable fact was that which shortly after drew down the judgment of God, to the utter destruction of that bloody city Jerusalem, that had, among others, butchered so holy a man. Thus far Eusebius.

Though I do not relate this as canonical, yet neither do I look upon it as fabulous, it being by many famous and godly writers testified. And this for the first particular to be explained, Who this James was.

(2.) Why Jude styles himself the brother of this James.

Of which I find two reasons given, both probable.

1. That he might difference himself from others of that name, especially Judas Iscariot; of which also the Scripture seems to take especial care. Hence he is spoken of with the addition of "not Iscariot," John xiv. 22, this traitor's name having grown detestable; on account of which it is generally con-

ceived that he had the names of Thaddæus and Lebbæus put upon him, Mark iii. 18; Matt. x. 3 (as was before noted): and thus he wisely preserves himself and Epistle from undue prejudice, and by the clearness of his person prevents dislike of his performance.

2. He expressed this near relation between himself and James, because this apostle James being better known than himself, of high estimation and reputation in the church, commonly known by the title of the Lord's brother, respected by Peter, Acts xii. 17, famous for his sanctity of life, accounted a pillar in the church, Gal. ii. 9, president of the council of Jerusalem, Jude might hereby win attention and credit to himself and his Epistle from those to whom he wrote. And this is the reason that Œcumenius writes to this effect: The fame of James for his virtue would put the greater authority upon Jude's doctrine; especially when it should be seen that Jude was as near him in his practices and conversation, as in blood and kindred. Besides, by the naming of James with so much respect, it could not be imagined but that he consented with him in that wholesome doctrine for which James was famous in the church; and yet though our apostle provides for the acceptation of his doctrine, neither he nor his brother James ambitiously advance their own reputation; both of them, though the Lord's brethren, contenting themselves with that humble, though indeed truly honourable, title of the servant of Jesus Christ.

Jacobi celebris ob virtutem apud omnes fama effectura erat, ut hujus apostoli doctrina apud auditores majorem haberet authoritatem, libentiusque admitteretur; præsertim si is, qui genere et sanguine cognatus esset, non alienus a cognati moribus, sed sub uno Domino Christo degens, idem servitutis jugum cum fratre, &c.

I come to the observations flowing from his using this title of the brother of James.

Obs. 1. How needful is it for a minister to be of an untainted reputation! Jude provides for it, both by making it known how far he was from Iscariot, and how near to James. A bishop must be of good report, saith Paul, 1 Tim. iii. 7. It is necessary for his own salvation that he should be good; and for the salvation of others, that he should be accounted so. How great was Paul's care that the gospel should not be blamed! 2 Cor. vi. 3. Sometimes the people are induced to love the word by the worth of the minister; though we should love the minister for the word. A cracked bell is not good to call men together, nor is a minister of cracked reputation fit to persuade others to holiness. To have all speak well of us, is not more impossible than suspicious. When Antisthenes the Athenian heard that some unworthy men highly commended him, he said, I fear I have done some evil that I know not of. And another would frequently say, Would we know a man, we should observe the life of him that praiseth him. Rarely will one praise him that takes contrary courses to himself. But this should be the care of the best, to keep himself from being spoken of reproachfully and truly at the same time by the worst. Nor is it less the sin of people to blemish the name of him that deserves well, than it is the sin of any one to deserve ill. The apostle is tender of receiving an accusation against an elder: certainly, he who is so much against receiving, would be much more against thieving.

Obs. 2. It is lawful to use human helps for the advantage of truth. This help, the title of "the brother of James," was warrantably prefixed. Paul, where the fruit of his ministry was hazarded by omitting titles, mentions them at large; as to the Corinthians and Galatians, 1 Cor. ix. 1; Gal. i. 1; and where concealment of his titles might do as well, or better, he omits them, as in both the Epistles to the Thessalonians: the like is requisite for us. In these things ministers should consider what tends most to the benefit of souls. I have known ministers of great learning and worth, who have been despicable among idiots, because birth, or university degrees, or alliance, have not commended them; perhaps they had not a James to their brother. The heathen's testimonies are not refused by the apostle to advantage truth, 1 Cor. xv. 33; Tit. i. 12; Acts xvii. 28. If naming a father in a sermon tends more to ostentation than edification, it may better be forborne, otherwise be lawfully used. Human authority was an introduction to Austin's faith; afterward, as the Samaritans, he believed upon firmer grounds. Certainly, we never so well improve our human advantages, as when Christ is advanced by them. How sweet to observe ministers set Christ upon their names, titles, parts, reading!

Obs. 3. The beauty of consent and agreement between the ministers of Christ, either in doctrine or affection. Both these the prefixing of James's name argued between him and Jude. Readily and rashly to dissent from other faithful and approved ministers of Christ is not like our apostle's carriage. Indeed, we must not admire men too much, though of greatest learning and piety; not so affect unity, as to forsake verity; or so follow men, as to forget God. The best men in the world are but rules regulated, not regulating: we must only so far set our watch according to theirs, as they set theirs according to the Sun. Satan endures no mediocrity: all ministers he represents as dwarfs or giants, none of a middle stature; either they must be worshipped, or stoned. Avoid we both extremes; neither proudly dissenting from, nor imprudently assenting to them, either in practice or opinion. Their gifts must neither be adored nor obscured; their falls and slips neither aggravated nor imitated: we must avoid both sequaciousness to follow them in any thing, and singularity to dislike them in every thing. The middle way of a holy, Scripture consent, joining in what we may, and meekly forbearing in what we may not, is a gracious temper. Ministers must not so study to have multitudes of followers, as to scorn to have any companions; to vilify others for the advancement of themselves; to build up their own reputation upon the ruin of another's. Consent as much as may be, is no more than should be. If ministers labour after a holy peace with all men, much more with one another: there is not more beauty than strength in their union. How pleasant is it to read Peter mentioning his agreement with his beloved brother Paul, 2 Pet. iii. 15; that Paul who had withstood him to the face! Gal. ii. 11. There is no repugnancy in Scripture; why should there be betwixt them that handle it? If the penmen of the Scripture are at peace in writing, ministers must not be at war in preaching: they must not seek more their praise for wit, than the profit of souls. When children fall out in interpreting their father's will, the orphans' patrimony becomes the lawyer's booty. Heretics are the gainers by the divisions of them who should explain the word of Christ. The dissension of ministers is the issue of pride. If there must be strife, let it be in this, who shall be foremost in giving honour; if emulation, in this, who should win most souls to Christ, not admirers to themselves. It is good to use our own parts, and not to contemn others. The apostles in the infancy of their calling were not without pride; Christ laboured to allay it both by precept and example.

Obs. 4. Grace and holiness are not only ornaments to the person himself who is endowed with them, but even to those who are related to him. The holiness of the child is an ornament to the father, that of the father to the child, the grace of the husband to the wife; the holiness of one brother beautifies another. It is true, every one must live by his own faith: it is a folly to boast of the holiness of our parents, and neglect it ourselves: if thy father be holy for himself and thee too, he shall go to heaven for himself and thee too. The grace of thy friends doth not beget grace in thee, but beautify it. The saints have oil of grace little enough for their own lamps; and where holiness is abhorred by the child, that of the parent is but an addition to the child's shame and punishment, in being so unlike him spiritually, whom he resembles naturally. It was but a poor privilege for the Jews to have Abraham for their natural, and the devil for their spiritual father: but when a child, a brother, a wife, love and labour for that grace which those of near relation have attained, it is their honour and ornament, that they who are near them are nearer to God. Indeed, it is often seen that they who have most spiritual loveliness have least love from us. The godly want not beauty, but carnal friends want eyes. A blind man is unmeet to judge of colours: how possible is it to entertain angels, and not to know it! The love of grace in another requires more than nature in oneself. Blood is thicker (we say) than water; and truly the blood of Christ beautifying any of our friends and children, should make us prefer them before those, between whom and us there is only a watery relation of nature. But how great a blemish often doth the gracelessness, the unholiness of a parent, a husband, a brother, bring upon those who are nearly related to them! It is a frequent question that was propounded by Saul to Abner, Whose son is this stripling? 1 Sam. xvii. 56. How disgraceful is such an answer as this; The son of drunkard, a murderer, an oppressor, a traitor, a whoremaster! Love to our friends, our posterity, &c., as well as to ourselves, should make us love grace.

Thus much for the third and last particular in the description of the author of this Epistle, "The brother of James;" and so for the first part of the title of the Epistle, the description of the penman of it. Hence follows,

II. A description of those persons to whom he wrote; which persons are described from a threefold privilege:

They are sanctified by God the Father, preserved in Jesus Christ, and called.

1. The first branch of this description is, They are sanctified by God the Father; wherein I consider two particulars: The sort or kind of the privilege bestowed upon them, viz. sanctification, "To them that are sanctified." The author thereof, or by whom it was bestowed, "By God the Father."

(1.) Of the kind of privilege, sanctification. Of which I shall speak by way of explication, and observation.

[1.] Of the privilege, sanctification, by way of exposition. ἡγιασμένοις, " To them that are sanctified." Beza speaks of two copies that read it ἠγαπημένοις· and from thence the Vulgate renders it *Dilectis*, To them that are beloved of God the Father; which manner of speech, as Beza well remarks, is unusual in Scripture, which speaks of us being for and in Christ beloved of the Father. And Estius, though a papist, acknowledges that the former reading, sanctified, is not only more pure, but more suitable to the scope and drift of the apostle, who by calling them sanctified, would deter them from, and make them take heed of, those unholy and impure seducers against whom he was now about to write.

The word here used by the apostle admits of and signifies in Scripture several kinds of sanctification: as,

1. Sanctification by way of destination or separation. To this purpose the Greeks use the word ἀφορίζω, i. e. when things are separated to a holy use: so the Lord sanctified the sabbath day, by separating it from other days, and appointing it for the duties of his own service. Thus also the tabernacle, Exod. xxix. 44, the temple, 1 Kings ix. 3; 2 Chron. vii. 16; the first-born, were sanctified. God commands Moses to sanctify all the first-born, Exod. xiii. 2; which he explains, ver. 12, "Thou shalt set apart unto the Lord all that openeth the matrix."

2. There is a sanctification by way of celebration, acknowledging, manifestation, declaration of the goodness of a thing: thus the creature sanctifies the name of the Creator, "They shall sanctify my name, and sanctify the Holy One of Jacob," Isa. xxix. 23.

3. Sanctification by way of fruition, comfortable use, and blessed enjoyment of the gifts of God: so, "The unbelieving husband is sanctified by the wife," 1 Cor. vii. 14; and, Every creature of God is sanctified, 1 Tim. iv. 5.

4. Sanctification by way of application; to apply a thing to such a holy use as God appointed: so we sanctify the sabbath, Exod. xx. 8, i. e. employ it to the holy use for which God ordained it.

5. By exhibition, introduction, or bestowing actual holiness; by putting holiness really and properly into one. This the Creator only can do to his creature: this God doth by his Spirit, which is called the Holy Ghost, and the Spirit of sanctification, 2 Thess. ii. 13. And thus man particularly is sanctified or made holy three ways:

(1.) Of not holy negatively: and so Christ as he was man was sanctified; for there was a time whenas Christ had not this holiness in his human nature, when his human nature was not.

(2.) Of not holy privately: and so man that had lost totally his holiness, is made holy by regeneration or effectual vocation.

(3.) Of less holy: and so God's children are sanctified, by being enabled to the exercise of an actual mortifying of sin, and living in holiness, with proceeding in both.

The sanctification here spoken of presupposes the second, afterward in the word "called" more particularly to be handled; and intends the third, namely, the actual exercise of the abolition of our natural corruption, and the renovation of God's image in us, begun in grace here, and perfected in glory hereafter.

So that this sanctification stands in an actual putting off of corrupt qualities; a putting on the new and sanctified. A burial; a resurrection. A mortification of the old; a vivification of the new man. One thing is destroyed and pulled down; another set up. A taking away of what is redundant; an addition of what is wanting. The killing power of the cross; the quickening power of the resurrection of Christ, Eph. iv. 22—24; Col. iii. 9, 10; Gal. ii. 20; v. 24; Rom. vi. 5, 8; Gal. vi. 14; Col. iii. 5; Eph. ii. 1.

1. Mortification of the old man is the first part of sanctification, whereby the strength, power, and tyranny of sin is weakened, and more and more abolished: like John Baptist, it decreases; like old folks in a house, who are going out of the world, and crowded out, as it were, by the younger, the heirs. The living of the old man is only as a clog and eyesore to the new.

This work of mortification stands principally in these three acts, or degrees of acting: An act of discerning; detesting; destroying sin, the soul's enemy. Knowing causeth hatred; and hatred puts us upon seeking the destruction of an enemy.

(1.) An act of discerning. Sin may hurt us when we know it not; but we do not hate it unless we know it. Sin always had deformity, but we had not always eyes to see it. It was Leah that lay by Jacob all night, but he discerned her not till the morning. Sin is now discovered as it is, not as it is coloured over by Satan. Sin is uncomely only to a renewed understanding. Nature never sets up a light to discover its own deformities. Of others it is often said, They know not what they do: in understanding they are children, nay, brutes; they see with Satan's spectacles. But a renewed mind discerns between things that differ, looks upon the old bosom favourite as a traitor: there are new apprehensions of the old man. The apostle not without an emphasis speaks of those things whereof we are now ashamed; *now*; not formerly: nay, heretofore sin was gloried in; but now the soul sees it is not only unsafe, and its own death, but unsuitable, and was the death of Christ. It was striking at me, saith a gracious heart, but Christ stepped between me and the blow. Herein stands sin's great deformity, as that of drunkenness in a man's wounds.

(2.) Detestation. The eye increases loathing. It cannot meet this ugly guest in any corner of the house, but the heart rises against it: this hatred of evil, Psal. xcvii. 10, is more than of hell; it is a killing look that the soul casts upon every corruption. He that hateth his brother is a man-slayer; he that hateth his lust is a sin-slayer: not he that hateth the sins or practices of his brother, but the person of his brother; so, not he that hateth the effects and fruits of sin, but the nature of sin; not he that hateth sin for hell, but as hell. Every evil, by how much the nearer it is, by so much the more it is hated. An evil, as it is so to our estate, names, children, wife, life, soul, as impendent, adjacent, incumbent, inherent, admits of several degrees of hatred: sin is an inward, a soul foe. Love turned into hatred becomes most bitter: brethren's divisions are hardest to reconcile: the soul's old love is turned into new hatred; the very ground sin treads upon is hated. There is a kind of hatred of oneself for sin; every act that sin hath a hand in is hated, our very duties for sin's intermixing with them; and we are angry with ourselves that we can hate it no more.

(3.) This hatred puts forth itself in labouring the destruction of sin. Love cannot be hid, neither can this hatred. The soul seeks the death of sin by these ways and helps.

[1.] By lamentation to the Lord, when we feel its strength with the apostle, "O wretched man that I am!" was there ever a soul so sin-pestered! Ah, woe is me, Lord, that I am compelled to be chained to this block! Never did a slave in Egypt or Turkey so sigh under bondage, as a mortifying soul does under corruption. The sorrows of others are outward, shallow, in the eye, the look; but these are in the bottom of the soul, deep sorrows. It is true, a man may give a louder cry at the drawing of a tooth, than ever he did pining under the deepest consumption; but yet the consumption, which is the harbinger of death, afflicts him much more; and though outward worldly grief, as for the death of a child, &c., may be more intense and expressive, yet grief for sin is more deep, close, sticking, oppressive to the soul, than all other sorrows: the soul of a saint, like a sword, may be melted, when the outward man, the scabbard, is whole.

[2.] The soul of a sin-subduer fights against sin with the cross of Christ, and makes the death of Christ the death of sin; (1.) By depending on his death as the meritorious cause of sin's subduing, of sanctification and cleansing, Eph. v. 25, 26. Christ's purifying us being upon the condition of his suffering, and so it urges God thus, Lord, hath not Christ laid down the price of the purchase? 1 Cor. vi. 20; why then is Satan in possession? Is Satan bought out? Lord, let him be cast out. (2.) By taking a pattern from the death of Christ for the killing of sin, we being planted into the similitude of his death, Rom. vi. 5, sin itself hanging upon the cross, as it were, when Christ died. Oh (saith a gracious heart) that my corruptions may drink vinegar, that they may be pierced, and nailed, and never come down alive, but though they die lingeringly, yet certainly! Oh that I might see their hands, feet, side, and every limb of the body of death bored, the head bowing, and the whole laid in the grave; the darkness, error, and vanity of the understanding, the sinful quietness and unquietness of my conscience, the rebellion of my will, the disorder of my affections! (3.) And especially the soul makes use of the death of Christ as a motive or inducement to put it upon sin-killing. Ah, my sin is the knife (saith the soul) that is coloured with my Redeemer's blood. Ah, it pointed every thorn on his head, and nail in his hands and feet. Lord, art thou a friend to Christ, and shall sin that killed him live? Thus a sin-mortifying heart brings sin near to a dead Christ, whom faith beholds bleeding afresh upon the approach of sin; and therefore it lays the death of Christ to the charge of sin. The cross of Christ is sin's terror, the soul's armour. The blood of Christ is *old sures-be* (as holy Bradford was wont to say) to kill sin. As he died for sin, so must we to it; as his flesh was dead, so must ours be. "Our old man is crucified with him," Rom. vi. 6. It is not a pope's hallowing a cross that can do it, but the power of Christ by a promise, which blesses this cross to mortification. Mr. D. Rogers Pr. Cat.

[3.] The soul labours to kill sin by fruitful enjoyment of ordinances. It never goes to pray, but it desires sin may have some wound, and points by prayer (like the sick child) to the place where it is most pained. How doth it bemoan itself with Ephraim, and pour forth the blood of sin at the eyes! It thus also improves baptism; it looks upon it as a seal to God's promise, that sin shall die; we being buried with Christ in baptism, that the Egyptians shall be drowned in the sea. It never hears a sermon, but (as Joab dealt with Uriah) it labours to set its strongest corruption in the forefront of the battle, that when Christ shoots his arrows, and draws his sword in the preaching of the word, sin may be hit. An unsanctified person is angry with such preaching, and cannot endure that the wind of a sermon should blow upon a lust.

[4.] By a right improving all administrations of providence. If God send any affliction, the sanctified soul concludes that some corruption must go to the lions. If there arise any storms, presently it inquires for Jonah, and labours to cast him overboard. If God snatches away comforts, (as Joseph fled from his mistress,) presently a sin-mortifying heart saith, Lord, thou art righteous, my unclean heart was prone to be in love with them more than with Christ, my true Husband. If God at any time hedge up her way with thorns, she reflects upon her own gadding after her impure lovers. If her two eyes, profits, pleasures, be put out and removed, a sin-mortifier will desire to pull down the house upon the Philistines, and to bear every chastisement cheerfully, even death itself, that sin may but die too.

[5.] By consideration of the sweetness of spiritual life. Life is sweet; and therefore what cost are men at to be rid of diseases, to drive an enemy out of the country! The soul thinks how happy it should be, could it walk with God, and be upright, and enjoy Christ, be rid of a tyrant, and be governed by the laws of a Liege, the Lord Jesus. How heavy is Satan's yoke to him who sees the beauty and tastes the liberty of holy obedience! A sick man confined to bed, how happy does he think them who can walk abroad about their employments! Oh, saith a gracious heart, how sweetly does such a Christian pray! how strictly does he live! how close is he in duty! how fruitful in conversing! But I, alas! how feeble, how dead, how unable! I am held under by a tyrant; oh that I could be his death!

[6.] By recollecting its former folly in loving sin: thinking thus; Formerly I loved that which now I see would have murdered me: what a deal of pains, care, cost, time, laid I out to satisfy my lusts! oh that I could recall these follies as I recollect them! but since I cannot make them never to have been, I will labour to hinder them for time to come. Oh that my hatred might be greater than ever my love was to them! A soul that has been mad upon sin, afterward is as vehement against it. This is the apostle's argument, "As you have yielded your members servants to uncleanness, so now to righteousness," Rom. vi. 19; and, "The time past of our lives may suffice us to have wrought the will of the Gentiles," 1 Pet. iv. 3.

[7.] By withdrawing those things which have been as fuel and fodder to corruption. Fire is put out as well by taking away wood, as casting on of water. A sin-mortifying heart forbears the using of that which it has heretofore abused; it knows that often Satan lies in ambush behind lawful enjoyments. He that has taken physic in wine, afterward is ready to loathe that very sort of wine in which his loathed medicine was given him: he that has been sin-sick, dreads those temptations in which Satan was wont to wrap sin up; he considers, that he who always goeth as far as he may, sometime goes further than he should. He feeds not without fear, Jude, ver. 12, but trembles in every enjoyment, lest it may be an inlet to sin, and his own corruption get advantage by it; he fears a snare under his very trencher, and poison (for his soul) in every cup of wine, especially if he has been formerly bitten thereby. Whereas a carnal heart ingulfs itself in occasions of sin, if in themselves lawful, sees no enemy, and therefore sets no watch: he "makes provision for the flesh," Rom. xiii. 14, he cuts not off the food which relieves his enemy; whereas a sin-mortifier, as an enemy that besieges a city, hinders all the supplies and support of lusts, that so he may make himself more yieldable to holiness.

[8.] By reinforcing the fight after a foil; by gaining ground after a stumble, by doubling his guard after unwariness, strengthening the battle after a blow; praying more earnestly, contending more strenuously, laying on more strongly after sin hath been too hard: thus Paul was the more earnest with God against sin; he besought the Lord thrice after the messenger of Satan had buffeted him, 2 Cor. xii. 8.

[9.] By a holy vexation with the constant company and troublesome presence of sin. Thus was holy Paul put upon opposing of sin: he complains, sin was always present with him, even when he would do good, Rom. vii. 21. And sin is called encompassing, easily besetting, εὐπερίστατος, Heb. xii. 1. It dwells in us; it is a leprosy not ceasing till the wall is pulled down, the house of our mortality dissolved; it is as near as the skin upon the back, bowels in the body; it goeth along with a saint in every duty, sabbath, ordinances, like Pharaoh's frogs into the king's chambers, pestering a saint at every turn: the apprehension hereof puts the soul upon endeavouring sin's ruin. The nearer an enemy is, the more hateful he is; the closer the conflict is, the quicker are the strokes, the fiercer the fight.

To conclude, A holy insulting and rejoicing in God follows, if at any time he has given the soul victory, and any heads of these uncircumcised; it blesses God, as Paul, "I thank God through Jesus Christ our Lord," Rom. vii. 25; going about duty more cheerfully, and yet humbly. A man may read the good news of a victory in a saint's countenance. Does he not say to Christ, when some lust hath been smitten, (as Cushi to David,) I would that all the enemies of my Lord were as that one young man? Lord, when will there be a perfect riddance of these vermin? Oh how sweet will heaven be, when I shall trample upon every Goliath, and see every Egyptian dead upon the shore! when I shall have neither tear in my eye, nor lust in my soul!

Having stated the first thing in the nature of sanctification, viz. mortification, we proceed to the

2. Vivification, whereby we live a new and spiritual life. The scriptures proving it are abundant: "I live (saith Paul); yet not I, but Christ liveth in me," Gal. ii. 20. "If ye be risen with Christ, seek those things that are above," Col. iii. 1. The life of Jesus is "made manifest in our mortal flesh," 2 Cor. iv. 11. As the death of Christ is the death of corruption, so the same power of God by which he raised Christ from the dead, frames us to the life of Christ's holiness, Eph. i. 19, 20. Christ, by the power of his Deity, whereby he raised himself, having communicated spiritual life to all his members, (as life is communicated from the head to the other members,) enables them to manifest it accordingly. "As Christ was raised up from death by the glory of the Father, even so we also walk in newness of life," Rom. vi. 4. "Reckon ye yourselves alive unto God through Jesus Christ," ver. 11. "We are his workmanship, created in Christ Jesus to good works, which God hath before ordained that we should walk in them," Eph. ii. 10. "He that abideth in me, and I in him, the same bringeth forth much fruit," John xv. 5.

These brief considerations may show in what respects a sanctified person lives a new life, a life of holiness.

(1.) A sanctified person lives a holy life, in moving and acting from a principle of holy life. All vital actions are from an inward principle: a body without a soul lives not, moves not naturally; nor without an internal principle of spiritual life received from Christ does any one live spiritually. The body of every living creature has a heart, which is the forge of spirits and the fountain of heat. True holiness proceeds from an implanted seed, 1 John iii. 9, the fear of God in the heart, Jer. xxxii. 40, the law put into the inward man, Jer. xxxi. 33. Sanctity, unless Christ be in us, is but a fable. "Christ liveth in me," saith the apostle, Gal. ii. 20; and so he speaks of living to God by Christ, Rom. vi. 11. Christ must abide in us, John xv. 5; he is formed, Gal. iv. 19, and dwelleth in us, Col. i. 27. The actions of a sanctified person are from a vital principle, the spirit within: the holiness of another is but from without, begins at his fingers' ends; he is drawn by outward inducements; his motions are not the motions of a living creature, but like those of a clock, or some image, which move not from within, but from weights without: when his weights are down, his work is done. A person spiritually enlightened, hath *Duceris ut nervis alienis mobile lignum. Hor. Ser. l. 2.* not only *Spiritum adstantem*, but *assistentem:* should he have all the encouragements of honour or profit from without, he could never do any thing cheerfully, but would ever be complaining, unless he enjoyed the supplies of the Spirit, viz. inward quickenings and enlivenings of heart in duty by the Spirit of Christ.

(2.) A sanctified person lives a holy life, as in

acting from, so according to, a principle of holy life. Now his actings are according to his principle of holiness,

[1.] In respect of their kind: they are of the same sort or nature with the principle of holiness. Water in the stream is of the same nature with that in the fountain. He that is sanctified lives like himself, his regenerated self. A spiritual life produces spiritual living: the seed of God puts forth itself in the fruits of godliness; if he be a fig-tree, he bears no thistles. The working of a saint follows his being. The understanding acts in a sound, efficacious, operative, influential knowing both of God and ourselves, Eph. i. 17, 18; Col. iii. 10. The conscience acts in a holy tenderness and remorsefulness for sin, 2 Chron. xxxiv. 27, and in a pious peaceableness and quietness, giving witness of a person's reconciliation to (Rom. v. 1) and walking with God sincerely. This is our rejoicing, the testimony of a good conscience, 2 Cor. i. 12. The memory retaining heavenly things as a treasury, repository, or spiritual storehouse of the word, an ark for the two tables, Psal. cxix. 11; Heb. ix. 4. The will acts by a pliable yielding to God in all things, both to do what God enjoins, and to undergo what God inflicts; in both it is flexible, Psal. xxxix. 9; it desires to please God in all things, though it finds not always to perform, Rom. vii. 18. The affections act in a holy regularity and order, being streams not dried up, but diverted. Love is " out of a pure heart," 1 Tim. i. 5, a spark flying upwards, set upon God principally, and that for himself, Psal. xviii. 1, 2; set upon man for God, either because we see God in him, or desire we may. Hatred is now of those things that God hates, and that hate God, Psal. cxxxix. 21, 22. Joy is now spiritual in the Lord, in communion with him, in serving of him, though in tribulation. Sorrow is now for our sins and those of others, and the sufferings of the church, not for such poor things as worldly trifles; the pearls of tears not being cast upon the dunghill. Our desires are now set upon the presence and pleasing of God, pardon of sin, a soft heart, fruitfulness under the means, the prosperity of Zion, the appearance of Christ. Our zeal is not now hot for ourselves, and cold for God; like fire well ordered, burns for the service, not the consuming of the house. Hope is now lively and well-grounded, not false and carnal. This spiritual acting outwardly reaches the body, making it a weapon of righteousness: fire within will break out. The whole body is the soul's instrument, in all its members being obedient to effect good actions, according to the dictate of renewed reason, and the command of the sanctified will. The eye is (as it were) a watchman, the tongue a spokesman, the ear a disciple, the arm a champion, the leg a lackey, all at the disposal of God. If the wares of holiness be in the shop, those of the same kind will be on the stall. The life of a saint is a visible sermon of sanctification: he who hath his heart ordered aright, hath his conversation ordered aright, Psal. l. 23; the hand of the clock goes according to the wheels. Out of the good treasury of the heart he brings forth good things. The body will be the interpreter of a gracious heart: the law is written in the heart, and commented upon in the life: a clean stomach sends forth a sweet breath. The matter of our actions will be warranted by the word, Psal. cxix. 35; the manner humble, cheerful, resolute, sincere, Micah vi. 8. In a word, glorious ends are propounded, and our workings, if God require, shall cross our own interest, ease, profit, Acts iv. 19. To have a good heart and a wicked life is a walking contradiction, Matt. vii. 16—20. A sanctified person is not as Ephraim, a cake not turned, only baked on one side.

[2.] The actings of a sanctified person are conformable to his principle of sanctification, as that principle is extensive to and puts upon all the ways of holiness, and as it is a seed of all the fruits of sanctification. A sanctified person embraces every holy duty; he fructifies in every good work, Col. i. 10, has respect to every precept, esteems every precept concerning all things to be right, Psal. cxix. 6, 128. There is a concatenation of all graces; they are linked together in a divine league: he has not any grace who wholly wants any. The instructions of the law are copulative; he that would seem to make conscience of keeping all the commandments of God save one, observes none at all out of any obedience to God, who has alike commanded all, James ii. 10. A sanctified person prefers not one command before another, 1 Tim. v. 21; his foot, being sound, can endure to walk in a stony as well as a sandy path; he will do, not many things, but all, even to the parting with Herodias, and the putting down the calves as well as Baal; he is not double diligent in some matters, and negligent in others: he is neither maimed, to want any limb; nor a monster, one part excessively outstripping another. Non est justa causatio cur præteruntur aliqua, ubi facienda sunt omnia. Salv. de Pro. l. 3.

[3.] The actings of a sanctified person are conformable to the principle of spiritual life, as it is the same, a permanent, abiding principle; not sometimes in us, and at other times quite gone from us, but at all times remaining in us. A sanctified person is holy in a continued course, he walks with God; he applies himself to keep the commandments continually, Psal. cxix. 112. He is not holy upon extraordinary occasions; his duties are not like a miser's feast, all at one time, nothing at another. He is not holy by fits and pangs, upon a rainy day reading only, good in thunder and lightning, or in a storm at sea; moved passionately with an affectionate sermon, trembling for the present, and presently after following bribery, Acts xxiv. 25, 26. At the first coming on to profession seething hot, after awhile lukewarm, at length key-cold; slashing with Peter at the first, and shortly after flying, and denying. His infirmities and falls are but for a fit, but his holiness is constant; his goodness is not like the " morning cloud, and early dew," Hos. vi. 4; not like the redness of blushing, but the ruddiness of complexion; his religion is not operative in company, silent in secret: he is not like water, that conforms itself to the shape of every thing into which it is poured; or like a picture that looks every way; his religion leaves him not at the church doors, he retains his purity wherever he lives. He has a principle like a fountain in him, that supplies him in the time of drought; not like a splash of water, licked up with an hour's heat of the sun: the music allures him not, the furnace affrights him not from God.

[3.] As the actings of a sanctified person are from, and according to, a renewed principle of life, so are they for it; and that both in respect of preservation of life in himself, and also for the propagation of it to others.

1. A sanctified person acts for his sanctified principle of spiritual life, in respect of preserving it in himself; which he expresseth, (1.) In shunning whatever may prejudice and impair it, much more than a man avoids that which would shorten a natural life, as sword, poison, diseases, &c.; that which parts between God and the soul being more hurtful, than that which parts betwixt soul and body. What shifts have some made to scramble from death, throwing estates into the sea, leaving them and sweetest relations, running through rivers, fire, &c.! And have

not holy men suffered more to keep from sin, which tends to spiritual death? have they not left goods, lands, children? have they not run through fire, water, nay, into them, even embracing death temporal rather than death spiritual? A man would give all the world rather than lose one natural life; but a Christian would give a thousand lives rather than lose the life spiritual. Lord, (saith he,) I desire but to live, to keep Christ, who is my life, Psal. lxiii. 3; Col. iii. 4. (2.) In prizing that food which upholds life. He loves what nourishes him,—delights in the law of God,—hungers after the "sincere milk of the word," 1 Pet. ii. 2,—accounts it sweeter than the "honey and the honey-comb," Psal. xix. 10,—has a most ardent affection to uncorrupted truths,—estimates a famine of the word the sorest,—esteems the bread of life the staff of life. When he was dead, he had no hunger, the word was as food in a dead man's mouth, found no savour or entertainment: now, though God give him never so much of other supplies, yet it is a famine with him, if he have not bread; like an infant king, that prefers the breast before his crown. Though he be rich in grace, yet he is poor in spirit; he desires grace, having the grace to desire. He never says, I have enough; truth of grace ever puts him upon growth. (3.) A sanctified person labours to preserve his inward principle of life, in using the means that may recover him when his life is endangered by sickness, desiring earnestly that God would heal him, Jer. xvii. 14; Psal. xli. 4; embracing the sharpest administrations, the bitterest reproofs, taking down the most loathed pill, bearing the heaviest affliction, being willing to be cut, sawed, seared, so as to be saved. His great request is, that he may be whole, walk holily, that the pain and impotency of his disease, the filthiness and hurtfulness thereof, were both removed.

2. A sanctified person acts for his principle of spiritual life, in labouring to communicate it to others, as well as to preserve it in himself. The life of a spiritually-quickened soul is generative of itself. All living creatures have a seminary for propagating their kind: the spirit of life is fruitful, endeavouring to communicate itself from one to another. You never heard of a soul that loved to make a monopoly of Christ. Grace may be imparted, not impaired. Samson, when he had found honey, gave his father and mother some with him. The woman of Samaria, being called, calls others to Christ, John iv. 29. How diffusive of Christ was blessed Paul! like the wall which reflects upon the passenger when the sun shines upon it. How suitable was that wish of his to a sanctified soul; "I would to God that thou, and all that hear me this day, were almost, and altogether such as I am, except these bonds!" Acts xxvi. 29. Every Christian labours to raise up seed to his elder Brother. The great design of the soul is to set up Christ more in itself and others, to leaven others with grace; and this gaining of souls is a Christian's greatest covetousness.

So much for the explication of the sort or kind of their first privilege, sanctification. The observations follow in the second place.

Obs. 1. Grace whereby we are changed, much excels grace whereby we are only curbed. The sanctification wherewith the faithful were said to be adorned, was such as cured sin, as well as covered it; not a sanctification that did *abscondere*, but *abscindere*; not only repress, but abolish corruption. The former, restraining grace, is a fruit only of general mercy over all God's works, Psal. cxlv. 9; common to good and bad, binding the hand, leaving the heart free; withholding only from some one or few sins; tying us now, and loosing us by and by; intended for the good of human society, doing no saving good to the receiver: in a word, only inhibiting the exercise of corruption for a time, without any real diminution of it; as the lions that spared Daniel were lions still, and had their ravenous disposition still, as appeared by their devouring others, although God stopped their mouths for that time. But this sanctifying grace with which the faithful are here adorned, as it springs from God's special love in Christ, so it is proper to the elect, works upon every part in some measure, body, soul, and spirit, abhors every sin, holds out to the end, and is intended for the salvation of the receiver. It not only inhibits the exercise of corruption, but mortifies, subdues, diminishes it, and works a real change; of a lion making a lamb; altering the natural disposition of the soul, and making a new man in every part and faculty.

Obs. 2. This sanctification changes not the substance and faculties of soul and body, but only the corruption, and disorder, and sinfulness thereof. It rectifies, but destroys not; like the fire in which the three children were, it consumes the bonds, not the garments; it does not slay Isaac, but only the ram; it breaks not the string, but tunes it. The fall of man took not away his essence, but only his holiness; so the raising of man destroys not his being, but his unholy ill-being. Grace beautifies, not debases nature; it repairs, not ruins it. It makes one a man indeed; it tempers and moderates affections, not abolishes them; it does not extinguish the fire, only allay it that it may not burn the house. It does not overthrow, but order thy love, hatred, sorrow, joy, both for measure and object. Thou mayst be merry now thou art sanctified, but not mad-merry; thy rejoicing will now be in the Lord, elevated, not annihilated. They are mistaken that think sanctification unmans a man, that he must now always be sad, and sour, and solitary; that, as they said of Mary, a Christian looking toward heaven is always gone out to weep: no, there is nothing destroyed by sanctification but that which would destroy us; we may eat still, but not be gluttons; drink, but not be drunken; use recreation, but not be voluptuous; trade, but not deceive; in a word, be men, but holy men.

Obs. 3. The people of God even in this life are saints. Perfectly indeed hereafter, but inchoatively here. A child has the nature, though not the stature of a man. A Christian has here as truly grace, though not so fully as in heaven. Grace is glory in the bud; this life is the infantage of glory; "Ye are sanctified," 1 Cor. vi. 11. They who look upon sanctity as an accomplishment only for heaven, are never like to get thither. It is common to hear a reproved sinner give this answer, I am no saint. Were this an accusation, and not an excuse for his unholiness, it might be admitted; but he is no saint, nor desires to be one; holiness and holy ones are his scorn. Such in this condition shall never see God: heaven must be in us, before we be in heaven. "Depart from me" will be the doom of them that work iniquity; dogs shall be without, Rev. xxii. 15. Ye who here cannot be merry without scoffing at purity, hereafter shall mourn for your want of purity; ye who account purity and sanctification inconsistent with nobleness, breeding, and generosity, will see that these were nothing without purity. That which is the beauty of heaven, the glory of angels, is it an ignominy upon earth, the shame of worms? You are not too good for holiness, but holiness for you. I confess, it is a great sin and shame, and should be a sorrow, that there are so many counterfeit, unsanctified saints, who have made sanctity so hateful; but yet for thee by these to be scandalized at sanctity, is thy woe as well as theirs. Let the pope's calendar only saint the dead, the Scripture requires sanctity in the living.

Obs. 4. Holiness cannot lie hid. Holy life is holily active: if a living man hold his breath long, it is death to him. Saul was no sooner converted than he prays, he breathes. A regenerated person speaks to God as soon as he is born. If God be dishonoured, he speaks for God; he cannot learn the wisdom of our times, to dissemble his religion, to be still when God is struck at; he must show whose image and superscription he bears: wicked men proclaim their sin as Sodom, and he proclaims his grace; and yet not that he may be seen, but that he may be serviceable. The Spirit of God is compared to fire, wind, a river; it will bear away any opposition, rather than be kept in. The world thinks a saint is mad of suffering when he appears for God; they are mistaken, he is not desirous of it, but fearless of it when God requires: he is neither profuse when he should spare, nor penurious when he should spend himself for God.

Obs. 5. How great the change that is wrought upon a person when God comes with sanctifying grace! There is no difference in the world greater, than between a man and his former self. The world, and men of it, need not take it ill that a saint differs so much from them, he differs as much from himself: a sanctified person is utterly opposite to all he was and did before; the stream is turned: he sees now, he was blind before; he loves that which formerly he loathed, he loathes that which formerly he loved; he unlives his former life; he picks it out, as it were, stitch by stitch. The wicked are said to think the course of sanctified persons strange, 1 Pet. iv. 4; ξενίζονται, the word is, they are like men in a strange country, that see strange sights, which before they were altogether unacquainted with. Oh the power of grace! a lion is now a lamb, a goat is now a sheep, a raven is now a dove, and, which is more, a sinner is now a saint: he that before rushed into sin, now trembles at it; he that before persecuted holiness, now preaches it. They in the gospel hardly knew the man that had sight restored to him, but said he was like the blind man, John ix. 9. Did the alone recovery of sight make such a difference in him from what he was formerly? what a difference is wrought then by grace, which makes not only a new eye, but a new tongue, ear, hand, heart, life!

Obs. 6. The holiness of a sanctified person is not purely negative. It stands not altogether in labouring not to sin. It is not enough for the tree that escapes the axe not to bring forth bad fruit, unless it also bring forth good; nor is it sufficient for the sanctified soul to put off filthy, unless it put on beautiful, garments. The old man must be put off, and the new put on. We are not content with half happiness, why should we be with half holiness? The holiness of the most is not to be as bad as the worst; few labour to be as good as the best. Men love to be complete in every thing but that which deserves exactness. We must not cut off the garment of holiness at the midst. Our eternal happiness will not only consist in being out of hell, but in being in the fruition of heaven: we must not mete to God one measure, and expect from him another.

Obs. 7. Sanctification admits no coalition between the new and the old man. This latter is abolished as the former is introduced. The new man is not put upon the old, as sometimes new garments are put upon old, but in the room of it, Col. iii. 9, 10; Eph. iv. 22, 24. In sanctification there is no sewing of a new piece to an old garment, which always makes the rent the wider. It is one thing for sin to be, another thing to be allowed; one thing for sin to be in us, another thing for us to be in sin. Sin is a saint's burden; a thorn in his eye, not a crown on his head; it is his daily task to weaken and impair it: if he cannot fully conquer, yet he faithfully contends. Sin and holiness are like a pair of balances, when the one goes up, the other must needs go down. Christ knows no partners in government, he will not drink of a fountain where Satan puts his feet; his church is a garden enclosed, open only to heaven, shut on every side. The faithful have a broken, not a divided heart. *Nescit de turbato fonte amicus bibere.* Bern.

Obs. 8. As a sanctified person allows no mixtures with grace, so he puts no limits to grace. He desires that the grace he has should be perfect as well as pure; and as he loves that no part of him should be defiled, so, that none should be destitute; he is sanctified throughout; he "perfects holiness in the fear of God," 2 Cor. vii. 1. A saint's complaints of his wants and deficiencies rather proves him covetous than poor; his strong appetite rather speaks him healthful than empty; his desires of clothing, rather growing than naked: he desires that the dominions of Christ may be as large as ever were those of sin, even extending to the whole man. He is not like an upstart gallant, who, unable to furnish himself with new attire for every part, is new and adorned in some parts, and uncomely in all the rest; he labours for furniture for every room, to see a whole Christ formed, to have graces for every faculty. There is no grace he sees in another, but he wishes he had it too: he never thinks he has lived enough, or done enough for God; he never thinks his work done while he is on this side heaven. Who ever was the man that so thoroughly mortified sin, as to leave no life in it? who ever had such a degree of spiritual life, as not to want a further increase? Thy sword must never be thrown away while so many enemies remain. The means of preserving a holy life must never cease, till grace be consummated in glory. He that has holiness enough, never had any. Sanctified persons are always adding to grace, and taking away from sin. Sanctification is a progressive work. The least saint has grace enough to be thankful, the greatest not enough to be idle. To neglect the helps of sanctification never was a Scripture sign of sanctity; to live above ordinances is to live below a saint. Abstinence from spiritual food is so far from proving a strong Christian, that it proves but a sick Christian at the best. He who gives over, never truly began; he who goes not forward, goes backward. Till the flame be out, we must never cease crying for water; till sin be quite extinguished, we must ply the blood of Christ. How short do the best come of their duty, of what God doth and they should desire!

Obs. 9. Outside, superstitious mortification is but a shadow of the true. Penance, fasts, starvings of the body, abstinence from marriage, are not blessed to kill sin; they have no blood in them; sin and Satan fear no such holy water. It is the death of Christ that must be the death of sin; the mortifying or macerating of the carcass, is but the carcass of the duty; there is more labour required to let the blood out of our corruptions, than out of our bodies. A child of God takes more pains with his heart in a day, than a papist with his skin in a year; the one indeed whips himself, but the other denies himself; the one scratcheth his skin, the other pulls out his right eye; the one afflicts the flesh, the other the soul; the one something without himself, the other his very self.

Obs. 10. The Lord estimates his people by the better part, their bent and strain, not their defects. They are here called sanctified; but, alas, how imperfect is their sanctification! Yet their Father looks upon them as they would be, not as they are or do: Not I, (saith the apostle, Rom. vii. 20,) "but sin that dwelleth in me." Corn full of weeds we call corn. Christ loves what he sees of himself in the midst of much more he sees of us; he casts not away the honey because of the honey-comb; he spies a grain of grace in a heap of corruption; he considers what we aim to be now, and what we are to be hereafter, more than what we are now. The owner of an orchard that knows the goodness of every tree in it, although a tree which is of a good kind hath fruit upon it which for the present is green, and as hard as a stick, yet he will say, This is an excellent apple, &c., considering its kind, and what it will be when ripe.

Obs. 11. How causelessly the world complains of those who are truly sanctified! The contentions of a saint are most with himself; the destructions he makes are bloodless; if he thirsts after any blood, it is that of a lust; the tyrants he brings to punishment are those in the soul. Were all his enemies in the world overthrown, and those in the heart spared, those Mordecais still in the gate, what would all avail him? Men have little reason to blame sanctity for distracting the times; there is more reason to blame the want of it. If a good man carry himself turbulently, it is because he is no better, not because he is good. He is, or should be, at peace with every thing but sin: if he shuns any company, it is not for hatred of the person, but the plague-sore; if he reproves, he wounds not destructively, but medicinally: his greatest heats are pious, God is in his flame; his very anger is patient, his indignation humble; he participates of the dove, as well as of the fiery tongues, as the Spirit that fills him had both shapes. Doth he reprove sharply and openly? he prays for thee secretly. A saint, when he acts like himself, is always doing good, diffusive of holiness, a benefactor to the age in which he lives, a conduit-pipe of blessings to a whole kingdom. If his endeavouring to make thee holy make thee hate him, he will be hated still.

<small>Duplici sub specie Divinus Spiritus se mundo ostendit, Columbina et ignea, quia omnes, quos implet, et columbæ simplicitate mansuetos, et igne zeli ardentes exhibet. Greg. 2. p. past. cap. 11. Moses causam populi apud Deum precibus, causam Dei apud populum gladiis allegavit. Greg. Charitas pie solet sævire, patienter novit irasci, humiliter indignari. Bern. Ep. 2. ad Fulc. Molestus ast medicus furenti phrenetico, et pater indisciplinato filio; ille ligando, iste cædendo, sed ambo diligendo. Aug. Ep. 1. ad Bon.</small>

(2.) The author by whom sanctification is bestowed, "God the Father."

I shall briefly explain two particulars. How they are said to be sanctified by God; and, How by God the Father.

[1.] How they are said to be sanctified by God. 1. Not *transferendo essentiam*, by transferring his essence unto them; but *operando gratiam*, by way of operation and working holiness in them, Eph. ii. 10; Acts v. 31; 1 Thess. v. 23; Heb. xii. 10; not by bestowing his Deity upon them, but by setting up the Divine nature in them, 2 Pet. i. 4, <small>Θεία φύσις.</small> as fire warms by its virtue and operation.

2. God was the author of their sanctification, not *excludendo media*, as if he made not use of the ministry of the gospel for accomplishing it. The word cannot sanctify without him; and ordinarily he will not sanctify without it: he sanctifies by the word, John xvii. 17, enlivening and actuating it, making it his power to salvation, bestowing upon it an enlightening power, to discover our misery and deformity by reason of unholiness, as also to discover the beauty of holiness, and the happiness laid up for holy ones; bestowing also upon it an inclining power, to bow us to embrace and obey his holy will, the pattern of all holiness.

3. From God we have our sanctification, not by traduction from our parents. Grace is not of an equal extent to nature; grace is not native, but donative; not by generation, but by generation; it is from the Father of spirits, not fathers of our flesh. Who can bring a clean thing out of filthiness? The new birth is "not of blood, nor the will of the flesh, nor of man," John i. 13. The purest seed-corn brings forth the stalk, the husk, and chaff; and the holiest men have a posterity with a nature covered over with corruption.

4. God sanctifies so that the first infusion of the habit of grace is without the active concurrence of any abilities of our corrupted nature to the acquiring of grace in the heart. The plantation of grace in us is purely supernatural. God's manner of working is altogether Divine, beyond the power and without the help of any thing in man, only he being a rational creature is a subject capable of grace, and thereby in the work of sanctification has a passive concurrence; for of ourselves we are not sufficient to think a good thought, but our sufficiency is of God. He worketh in us both to will and to do. We are dead in trespasses and sins, &c. New-begotten, new-created, &c. Grace is an habitual quality, merely infused by Divine virtue, not issuing out of any inward force of human abilities, howsoever strained up to the highest pitch of their natural perfection. All civility, sweetness of nature, ingenuity of education, learning, good company, restraint by laws, and all moral virtues, with their joint force, cannot quicken our souls to the least true motion of a spiritual life.

5. God sanctifies so that in the practice of sanctification man actually concurs with God. For, being sanctified, and inwardly enabled in his faculties by spiritual life put into them, he moves himself in his actions of grace, although even in these actions he cannot work alone, he being only a fellow worker with the Spirit of God, not in equality, but in subordination to him. Nevertheless, though these actions are performed by the special assistance of the Spirit, yet because man is the next agent, they are properly said to be man's actions.

[2.] God the Father sanctifies. And yet, Eph. v. 26; 1 Cor. i. 30, Christ is said to sanctify, and to be sanctification. And most frequently the Holy Ghost is said to sanctify; grace being called "the fruits of the Spirit," Gal. v. 22; the whole work of sanctification styled by the name of Spirit, Eph. v. 9; and the Scripture expressly speaks us sanctified by the Spirit, Gal. v. 17; and the Holy Ghost is called the Spirit of sanctification. Yet when the Scripture says we are "sanctified by God the Father," it does not contradict itself.

For the explication whereof I shall briefly set down this distinction, and these conclusions.

All the attributes of God are either, 1. Essential, which are the very Divine essence, and pertaining to the very nature of God, as to be a Spirit, omniscient, eternal, true, good, powerful, merciful, &c. Or, 2. Relative; and that, either, 1. Inwardly, to the persons within themselves; as for the Father to beget, the Son to be begotten, the Holy Ghost to proceed from Father and Son. Or, 2. Outwardly; and that either, 1. To the creatures, as to create, sustain, &c.; or, 2. To the church, as to redeem and sanctify, &c.

Conclusion 1. The attributes which appertain to the nature or essence of God, are common to the Three Persons, as to be a Spirit, omniscient, eternal, &c.

Concl. 2. The attributes or properties which inwardly belong to the Persons among themselves, are peculiar and proper to each of them, both in respect of order of being and working. The Father has his being from himself alone, the Son has his being from the Father alone, the Holy Ghost has his being from them both. The Father alone begets, the Son is alone begotten, the Holy Ghost proceeds from the Father and the Son.

Concl. 3. All works external, and in reference to the creatures, as to create, to govern, to redeem, to sanctify, &c., are, in respect of the things wrought, equally common to the three Persons of the Trinity; who, as they are all one in nature and will, so must they be in operation, all of them working one and the same thing together, John v. 17, 19. Most true is that of Christ, Whatsoever things the Father doth, these also doth the Son: the like may be said of the Holy Ghost: so that we are sanctified by Father, Son, and Holy Ghost; there being the same power and will of all three: and in works external, and in respect of the creature, when only one Person or two are named, the whole Trinity is to be understood.

Concl. 4. Though the works of three Persons toward the creature, world, or church, in respect of the thing wrought, are common to all the three; yet in respect of the manner of working, there is distinction of Persons that work; for the Father works through the Son, by the Holy Ghost. The Father works from none, the Son from the Father, the Holy Ghost from both, John v. 19; viii. 28; xvi. 13, there being the same order of working in the Trinity that there is of existing. The Father works by the Son and the Holy Ghost, sending them, and not sent by them; the Son works by the Holy Ghost, sending him from the Father into the hearts of believers, and is not sent by him, but by the Father; the Holy Ghost works, and is sent from the Father and the Son, not from himself. The works therefore of the Trinity are considerable, either absolutely, or in regard of the works wrought, and so they are the works of the whole Trinity in common; or relatively, when we consider in what order the Persons work, which Person works immediately, which by another. And so the Persons are distinguished in their works.

This considered, Jude in ascribing sanctification to God the Father, is easily reconciled to those that ascribe it to God the Holy Ghost, and the Son; these last-named Persons being by Jude included in the working of sanctification, and only the order of working of the blessed Trinity noted. The Father sanctifying through the Son, by the Holy Ghost; the Father sanctifying by sending the Son to merit, and giving his Spirit to work; the Son, by meriting; the Holy Ghost, by working our sanctification, and immediately sanctifying us; in which respect he has the title of Holy, and sanctification most commonly is expressed as his work.

This for the explication of the second particular in the first privilege of the faithful to whom Jude wrote, viz. The author of their sanctification, "God the Father."

Obs. 1. Even our holiness administers matter of humility. Our very graces should humble us as well as our sins; as these latter because they are ours, so the former because they are none of ours. Sanctity is adventitious to nature. Heretofore holiness was natural, and sin was accidental; now sin is natural, and holiness accidental. When God made any of us his garden, he took us out of Satan's waste; we are not born saints: the best, before sanctification, are bad, and by nature not differing from the worst. The members that God accepts to be weapons of righteousness, were before blunted in Satan's service: when God sanctifieth us, he melts idols, and makes of them vessels for his own use. Before any becomes as an Israelite's wife, he is as a captive, unpared, unwashed, unshaven. Sanctification is a great blessing; but was this web woven out of thine own bowels? The best thou didst bring to thine own sanctification, was a passive reception of it, which the very worst of heathens partake of in common with thee, having a human nature, a rational soul; and was there not with that a corrupt principle of opposition to God, and all the workings of God? was not God long striving with a cross-grained heart? How many denials had God before he won thee to himself! how far was the iron gate of thy heart from opening of its own accord! and if he had not wrought like a God, omnipotently, and with the same power wherewith Christ was raised, had thy resistance been ever subdued? Eph. i. 19, 20. And when the being of grace was bestowed, from whence had thy grace at any time its acting? Didst thou ever write one letter without God's guiding thy hand? didst thou ever shed one penitential tear till God unstopped thy eyes, smote thy rock, and melted thy heart? didst thou hunger after Christ, till God who gave the food gave the stomach also? Was ever temptation resisted, grace quickened, corruption mortified, holy resolution strengthened, power, either to do or will, received from any but from God? Doth not every grace, the whole frame of sanctification, depend upon God, as the stream on the fountain, the beam on the sun? When he withdraws his influence, how dead is thy heart in every holy performance! only when he speaks the word effectually, bidding thee go, thou goest; and do this or that, thou dost it.

Obs. 2. The reason why all graces of a sanctified person are for God, they are from him. God's bounty is their fountain, and God's glory must be their centre. He planted the vineyard, and therefore he must drink the wine. We are his workmanship, and therefore we must be his workmen. All our pleasant fruits must be laid up and out for our Well-beloved. All things, but particularly our graces, are from him and for him: we can never give him more or other than his own, when we give all we can. The streams will rise as high as the fountain-head; and so should our graces ascend as high in duty as he who gave them. Where should God have service, if a sanctified person denies it?

Obs. 3. Is God the author of sanctification? then mark its excellency and worth. It is a rare work certainly that has such a Workman; a beauteous structure that has such a Builder. What is a man to be desired for, but his sanctification? If we see a beauty on that body which has a soul, how much more on that soul which has the reflection of God himself upon it! Every saint is a wooden casket filled with pearls. "The King's daughter is all glorious within." Love Jesus Christ in his work-day clothes, admire him in his saints; though they be black, yet they are comely. Did the people of God but contemplate one another's graces, could there be that reproaching, scorn, and contempt cast upon one another that there is? Certainly, their ignorance of their true excellency makes them enemies; they strike one another in the dark.

Obs. 4. Great must be the love that God bears to sanctification. It is a work of his own framing, a gift of his own bestowing. God saw that the work of the first creation was very good; much more that of the second. Wonder no more that the faithful are called his garden, his jewels, his treasure, his temple, his portion. God has two heavens, and the sanctified soul is the lesser. How does he accept of saints even in their imperfections, delight in their performances, pity them in their troubles, take care of them in dangers! He that has given his Son for them, promised heaven to them, and sent his Spirit into them, what can he deny them? Jesus Christ never admired any thing but grace when he was upon the earth: the buildings of the temple he contemned, in comparison of the faith of a poor trembling woman. Certainly, the people of God should not slight those graces in themselves that God so values, as they do when they acknowledge not the holiness that God has bestowed upon them. Shall they make orts of those delicates that Jesus Christ accounts an excellent banquet?

Obs. 5. The love of God is expressive, really and effectually in us, and upon us, even in sanctifying us. Creatures, when they love, will not put off one another with bare words, of bidding be clothed, fed, &c., much less does God. If there be love in his heart, there will be bounty in his hand. Thou sayest that God is merciful, and loves thee; why, what did he ever do for thee, or work in thee? has he changed thy nature, mortified thy lusts, beautified thy heart with holiness? Where God loves, he affords love-tokens; and such are only his soul-enriching graces. No man knows love or hatred by what he sees before him, but by what he finds in him. If our heart moves toward God, certainly his goes out toward us: the shadow upon the dial moves according to the motion of the sun in the heaven.

Obs. 6. We are to repair in our wants of sanctification to God for supply. He is the God of grace; "The Lord will give grace and glory." He has the key of the womb, the grave, the heavens, but chiefly of the heart. He that sitteth in heaven can only teach and touch the heart. How feeble a thing and unable is man, whether thyself or the minister, to do this! He has the winds in his own keeping; and till he send them out of his treasury, how necessarily must thy soul lay wind-bound! Whither shouldst thou go but to him? And how canst thou go but by him? The means of grace are to be used in obedience to him, not in dependence upon them. A golden key cannot open without him, and a wooden can open with him. Man may, with the prophet's servant, lay the staff upon the forehead, but God must give life. How many fat and rich ordinances have been devoured, the soul after all remaining as lean as before, for want of seeking God aright for a blessing!

<small>Parum prodest Lectio, quam non illuminat Oratio.</small>

Obs. 7. How careful we should be to maintain that which God has set up in us, and how fearful lest it should be pulled down by Satan! Christ destroys the works of the devil, and Satan labours to oppose the work of Christ. Every plant indeed that God hath not planted is to be plucked up; but the plants that God's own hand hath planted are to be nourished. What God hath joined together none should separate; grace and the soul are of God's joining together. Who laments not the destruction of man's workmanship, the overthrow and demolishing of beautiful buildings, the rooting up of corn-fields and pleasant gardens by swine? But what are these to the destructions made by sin in the hearts and lives of people? Who can give way to sin, but it must be with a sinful patience? "Keep thy heart with all diligence," Prov. iv. 23: the best endowment is to be most carefully preserved. Who loves not to keep his body healthful? and yet who regards the keeping of his soul holy? The whole Trinity of Persons adorn the heart with holiness; each of them is to have a corner in it, nay, the whole. Let not Satan have wells which he never digged, inhabit houses which he never built. If the Philistines tread not on the threshold on which Dagon fell, let not Satan lodge in the heart that God sanctifies.

This for the first branch considerable in the description of the parties to whom the apostle wrote, " Sanctified by God the Father." Then follows,

2. " Preserved in Jesus Christ."

Wherein I consider two particulars: A privilege or enjoyment received, viz. preservation; " Preserved," &c. The means or way of enjoying it; and that was, " In Jesus Christ." Of both these briefly.

(1.) The privilege bestowed is preservation, " To them that are preserved," &c. In the handling whereof I shall briefly give, The explication of it, and, The observations from it.

For the explication. The word used by the apostle is τετηρημένοις· properly signifies, solicitously to be kept, as a thing lest it be lost, or taken away by others. 1 John v. 18, it is spoken of a regenerate person's keeping himself from being touched by the wicked one: τηρεῖ ἑαυτὸν, keepeth himself as with watch and ward; guardeth himself so accurately, as he that watcheth a prisoner for fear of his escape. So Acts iv. 3, it is said, the apostles were put by the priests εἰς τήρησιν, in hold. So Acts v. 18, they put them ἐν τηρήσει, in prison. And of these preserved ones it is said, They " are kept by the power of God," φρουρούμενοι, kept as a town is kept with a garrison from the enemies; *præsidio circumvallati,* encircled with military strength: so <small>Conservati, ne decepti a seductoribus, pereant. Estius in loc.</small> are these saints preserved by Christ, lest being deceived by seducers, they should perish.

This preservation of the godly is threefold. 1. Temporal, and of the body. 2. Spiritual, chiefly of the soul. 3. Eternal, of both in heaven.

1. The first, though it be not here intended, as indeed it is frequently denied to the faithful, yet it is often in Scripture bestowed upon them, and that several ways: sometimes when their enemies want means to effect their desires upon them, though they have poison, yet no power, no arms or instruments of force, 2 Sam. viii. 2; or when the enemies of the church have outward strength and forces, but are diverted another way, by reason of enemies coming against them from another place, 1 Sam. xxiii. 27; or when the enemies spend their hatred and forces upon one another, Judg. vii. 22; or when their forces are by the providence of God timely discovered, so that the people of God taking refuge in some place of security, strength, or distance, the enemy cannot at all come at them, 2 Sam. xvii. 16; or when there is such a curb of restraint put upon the spirits of enemies, as, though they find them, and have them in their hand, yet they shall not be able to put forth their inward poison against them; thus even the natural force of fire, seas, beasts shall be bridled up, when God will, from hurting his people, Dan. iii. 26; or when the enemies of the church are discomfited, either by their own preposterous fear or oversight, 2 Kings vii. 6, or the instrumentalness of the senseless creatures against them, Judg. v. 20, or the puissance of the church's forces, not only spiritual, but even visible and worldly; or when the faithful being taken, are delivered out of their hand, Gen. xiv. 12, 16; or when God makes an enemy of his church to be his own destroyer, to twist and use his own halter, 2 Sam. xvii. 23; or when God inclines the hearts and dispositions of the haters of his people to pity, tender, and favour them, though they are far from love to their grace; or when God works a really sanctifying change upon their hearts, making them to wash the stripes, and lick the wounds whole, which they have made, Acts xvi. 33; or when God takes his people out of this life from the evil to come, housing his flock against a storm, taking down his ornaments when he purposes to destroy the house; and this he ordinarily does by a natural death, though he can translate his people, and take body and soul immediately into heaven, as in the case of Elijah.

2. But principally, the care of God is in this life expressed toward his people in spiritual preservation.

This spiritual preservation of believers in this life is, (1.) From punishment. The curse of the law, the wrath of God, Gal. iii. 13. Not from the law of God as giving precepts, but as being a covenant exacting perfect obedience, and condemning for an imperfect performance, Rom. vi. 14; 1 Tim. i. 9; —from the terror of the law, forcing for fear of punishment, as bond-slaves by the whip, Rom. viii. 15, the people of God being made a voluntary people, and worshipping God without servile fear, Psal. cx. 3. The faithful also are preserved from the guilt and condemning power of sin, Eph. i. 7, "God not imputing their trespasses," 2 Cor. v. 19; preserved from the curse of all external punishments, as they are the effects of vengeance. Sin may be, and may not be, in the godly; it is in them by habitation, not by dominion: so punishments are on them, and are not on them; on them as sensible pains, on them as castigations to better them, on them as consequents of sin, and God's expression of his dislike of sin; not on them as curses, not on them to satisfy wrath. The wrath of God lies not upon them, when the hand of God lies upon them: every affliction is *medicina*, not *laniena;* sent to kill sin, not the man: the edge, the soul, the sting, the malignity of every trouble, is removed, so that it has little more than the notion of a misery. God's people are not delivered from evils as oppressive to nature, but as satisfactory to justice: whatever they suffer, though it be death itself, they may say, Christ hath laboured, and we enter into his labours, John iv. 38; he has borne the heaviest end; death lost its sting in his side. There is honey in the carcass of this lion; this serpent is but a gentle rod being in his hand. (2.) This spiritual preservation of believers is from sin, and in the state of holiness; their grace being preserved, and the image of God never totally obliterated in them: God preserving the jewel oft when not the casket; a man's self, his soul, though not his carcass; and from that which is the greatest enemy and evil, sin, so oft in Scripture called "the evil," John xvii. 15, and that which makes the very devil himself both to be and to be called the evil one, Matt. v. 37, he both having most and dispersing most of that evil; the world to be called an evil world, 1 John v. 19; Gal. i. 4; and men, evil men, Luke vi. 45. And so this privilege of preservation from sin, and in the state of holiness, aptly follows sanctification; the elect being not only made holy, but kept holy. Hence we read of "him that is able to keep us from falling," Jude 24; of Christ praying that his disciples, though not taken out of the world, yet should be kept from the evil, John xvii. 15, the world kept out of them, though not they out of the world; of the faithful, their being "kept by the power of God through faith unto salvation," 1 Pet. i. 5; of the evil one's not touching him that is born of God, 1 John v. 18; and of his not sinning; of God's delivering Paul "from every evil work," 2 Tim. iv. 18; of preserving blameless to the coming of Christ; of finishing the good work begun unto the day of Christ, Phil. i. 6. All which places intend this spiritual preservation mentioned by Jude, which is that gift of God whereby the elect, being united to Christ by his Spirit and faith, continue in him, and can never totally and finally fall from holiness.

Sundry ways God preserves from sin, and in holiness. 1. Sometimes by keeping his people from the very outward temptation to sin, if he sees it would be too hard for them; often dealing with his servants, as the people did with David, who would not let him go down to battle, lest the light of Israel should have been put out, 2 Sam. xxi. 17; as Gideon dealt with his soldiers, suffering not the fearful to go to fight, Judg. vii. 3; as we preserve a lighted candle in a windy night, by putting it into a lantern. 2. Sometimes by making them conquerors even for the present over the temptation: he strengthens them so with his Spirit, as that they break the strongest cords, with Samson, bearing away the very gates of the city, and overthrowing whole troops of temptations. Thus was Joseph preserved, Gen. xxxix., as Chrysostom expresses it, in a fiery furnace, even when it was heated seven times hotter than ordinary; the power of God being put forth therein, more than in preserving the three children. Thus were the blessed martyrs preserved from sin. We read in that holy martyrology, Heb. xi. 35, they "were tortured, not accepting deliverance." How many have overcome fire with fire; the fiery flame with love to Christ hotter than fire! their holy resolution rising the higher the more opposition they had, as a flood that meets with an obstacle; or as a ball, the harder it is thrown against the ground, the higher it rebounds. 3. Always God so preserves his saints from sinning, that they sin not finally, they sin not away all their holiness; their faith fails not, Luke xxii. 32; there is something in them that sins not, the seed of God, a grain of mustard-seed, a principle of holiness, which, as it opposes, so it will overcome their distempers; as a fountain works out its muddiness when dirt is thrown into it; as life in a man, his diseases. Gratia nec totaliter intermittitur, nec finaliter amittitur. A saint is not delivered fully from the being of sin, but from the total prevalency of it, from finally apostacy; so that his soul still continues in the state of grace, and has the life of holiness, for the essence, though not always in the same degrees: he may *aliquo modo recedere, non penitus excidere*. Grace may be abated, not altogether abolished: he may *peccare*, not *perire;* sin, but not to death; intermit the actings of grace, not lose the habit. Faith may be shaken in, not out of the soul; the fruit may fall off, but the sap not totally dry up. It is true, grace in itself considered, as a creature, might totally fail; our permanency is not *respectu rei*, but *Dei;* not from our being holy, but from our being kept holy. We are kept by the power of God; and if so, it will be to salvation. Actus omittitur, habitus non amittitur; actio pervertitur, fides non subvertitur; concutitur, non excutitur; defluit fructus, latet succus: jus ad regnum amittunt demeritorie, non effective. Pr. l. Effectus justificationis suspenditur, at status justificationis non dissolvitur. Suffr. Br. p. 187. Notwithstanding the power of sin in us, and the power of Satan without us, the frowns and the smiles of the world, the music and the furnace, the wind and the sun, the tide of nature and the wind of example, holiness, though in the least degree, shall never be lost to be of no degree. Satan doth *soli perseverantiæ insidiari*, he only aims to take away grace; he would never care to take away gold, or names, or comforts, &c., if it were not to make us sin. He that offers to give these things to make us sin, would not snatch them from us but for that end. God was not delighted that Job should be tormented, but that his grace should be tried; nor Satan so much that Job should be tormented, as that his grace should be destroyed. But though he winnow never so violently, he shall never winnow out all our grace, Luke xxii. 31. All the power of hell shall never prevail against the God of heaven.

The immutable, eternal decree of God is the foundation of perseverance. Now the counsel of God shall stand, Isa. xlvi. 10. The elect cannot be deceived, Matt. xxiv. 24. The impossibility of seduction is grounded upon the stability of election: the foundation of God abideth sure, 2 Tim. ii. 19; it can never be moved out of its place. The purpose of

God according to election must stand, Rom. ix. 11. Of all that God hath given Christ by election he will lose nothing, John vi. 39.

Quod datur ex efficaci intentione infallibiliter servandi illam personam cui donatur, illud ex decreto dilectionis dimanare manifestum est. Suffr. Br. p. 197.

And that preservation flows from the decree of election, is most manifest, because it is given with a previous intention of infallibly bringing him to salvation, to whom it is given; for what is election, but to ordain infallibly to obtain salvation?

And this immutable purpose the all-powerful and faithful God backs with infallible promises. "The mountains shall depart, but the covenant of his peace shall not," Isa. liv. 10. "I will put my fear into their hearts, that they shall not depart from me," Jer. xxxii. 40. "My sheep shall never perish, neither shall any man pluck them out of my hand," John x. 28. "I will betroth thee unto me for ever," Hos. ii. 19. "Christ shall confirm you to the end," 1 Cor. i. 8. Nay, this stableness of his counsel he shows by an oath also; which was, "That we being delivered," &c., "might worship him without fear, in holiness and righteousness, all the days of our life," Luke i. 74, 75.

This purpose, and these promises, God even in this life backs with such performances as prove perseverance infallibly to follow; he bestows upon his people an inward continuing principle of holiness, the seed of God remaining in God's people, which makes them that they cannot sin, 1 John iii. 9. "A well of water springing up unto everlasting life," John iv. 14. An anointing abiding in them, 1 John ii. 27. The Spirit abiding for ever, John xiv. 16. The fear of God in their hearts not suffering to depart from God, Jer. xxxii. 40. "Gifts without repentance," Rom. xi. 29.

Upon these performances of God believers have been assured, and are commanded to labour for the assurance of their salvation; a privilege not to be attained, if assurance of perseverance were impossible; for without perseverance there is no salvation, 1 John v. 13; Heb. iii. 6; 2 Pet. i. 10.

3. The third and fullest preservation is eternal, which shall be perfectly from every enemy that may hurt in a way of sin and misery, truly called *fœlix securitas, et secura fœlicitas*, happy safety, and safe happiness; when the people of God shall neither offend, nor be offended; when there shall be neither a sin in the soul, nor a sinner in their society; when Satan shall no more solicit; when the faithful shall not only be exempted from foils, but even from fighting; when instead of swords, they shall only have palms in their hands. O blessed condition! to have rest on every side, fulness of grace, perfection of peace, to be freed from all fears, to be lodged in the bosom and locked up in the embraces of God to eternity, to be in our haven, our centre, our Father's house. O my soul! it is a heaven to hope it; what then is it to have it!

And this for the explication of the nature of this preservation, the second kind of privilege bestowed upon the faithful.

Obs. 1. Sanctified persons have many enemies. It is true, none are safe but such, and yet none so much solicited as such. What need this τήρησις, this careful preservation, this garrison of God's power, if there were none feared to give and take the possession of thy soul from God? Is there not a false party within? The best governed city has some traitors, and so has the best governed heart: nay, is not the better party in the soul by far the lesser? and how oft do the disaffected conspire to let in the enemy without! which they had long ago done, and destroyed the good party too, for grace left to itself falls, had it not been for God's power.

Perfectiones sibi relictæ, sunt pondera ad ruinam. Gers.

The great design of Satan is to surprise sanctity. The thief gotten into the house, presently inquires where the jewels and money are laid up. The devil had rather catch one fish than a hundred frogs; he is sure already (he thinks) of his own. Besides, they do not much credit his cause; but could he bring over to himself one sanctified person, he would boast in such an addition to his kingdom. It is the tree that bears fruit which is plucked and cudgelled; under other trees which have only leaves, men sit and walk indeed, but they pluck them not: and of all trees which bear fruit, those which bear the best are pulled and beaten most. It is the richly laden ship that is most endangered by the pirates; the soul enriched with holiness for which Satan lies most in wait. There are as many miracles wrought, as a saint is preserved minutes. Let us neither be secure nor discouraged. Not secure; we live in the midst of enemies. He that will be always safe, must never be secure: we cannot trust God too much, nor our own hearts too little; the former is our keeper, the latter is our traitor. No Christian is his own keeper: we can neither stand nor rise alone; all we can do alone is to fall. Not discouraged: thy many robbers show thou hast something worth taking from thee: thy enemies, though they endanger thy holiness, yet grant it; in opposing thee, they speak thee none of theirs; nay, they engage Jesus Christ to oppose them, who will lose none of his; to pity thee, who will not suffer thee to be tempted above thy power. Let the world fall, yet a Christian falls not, as long as Christ stands.

Cadit mundus, sed non cadit Christianus, quia non cadit Christus. Aug.

Obs. 2. God keeps most graciously when he keeps us from sin: then he keeps us as his own people. He keeps from sickness or poverty by way of a general providence, but from sin by way of peculiar preservation: whatever other preservation he bestows without this, it is but a reservation to eternal ruin. Christ, that loves all his members most tenderly, never desired of his Father to keep them free from outward troubles: he prays not that he should take his disciples "out of the world, but keep them from the evil," John xvii. 15; not that they should be exempted from sufferings, but preserved from sin, the evil: that they might never side with the times against God; that they might never apostatize, or forsake the truth. Every one seeks safety, but who desires this true safety, this soul safety? Worldly policy would that a man sleep in a whole skin, but true wisdom puts a man upon preserving a whole conscience: a whole skin countervails not for a wounded conscience. And yet this is the study of the times, every one labours to save one, to fall upon his feet, to keep from being plundered, &c.; but who study to be kept from offending God? If thou couldst as easily keep thyself from God's wrath as from man's, by all thy projects, thy policy would be a good pattern: gain in the chest, and loss in the conscience, is but a bad exchange. He that will save his life when he should lose it, shall lose it when he would save it. Fear not troubles, because He sleeps not that preserves thee; but fear sin, because He sleeps not that observes thee. Account it a greater mercy, in all the sinful agitations of these times, that God has kept thee from being an actor, than a misery that God hath made thee a sufferer.

Obs. 3. The people of God are never unsafe, Psal. xxxvii; xci. If the Lord be the watchman, what though it be an estate, a life, nay, a soul that is the city, we should not fear the loss of it. The meanest of the people of God stir not out without their life-guard; if they wanted, there is not a creature in heaven or earth but would take their part; they are the hidden, the secret, the preserved ones. Security is not so great a sin as distrust, our Friend being much more able to help than our foes to hurt. What one said sinfully, every child of God may say holily, "I shall never be moved," Psal. xxx. 6. We must commit ourselves "to God in well-doing," 1 Pet. iv. 19; ii. 23. Christ, though he committed himself not to man, knowing what was in man, yet himself living and dying he committed to his Father: we do quite contrary. Find out the danger in which God cannot keep, or the time when God did not keep, or the saint, for to him I speak, that God hath not kept, and then distrust him. Say not, If worse times yet come, what shall I do to be kept? Will not he that provided a city of refuge for those that killed men, find out a city of refuge for thee, when men labour to kill thee for God? Hath God so many chambers, so many "mansions in his house," John xiv. 2, so many hiding-places upon the earth, (his, with the fulness of it,) in the earth, in heaven, and shall his children be shut out? Thy work is not to be solicitous how to be kept, but how to be fit to be kept. Labour to be always in well-doing; then who will harm thee? Keep faith and a good conscience; keep no sin allowedly in thy soul; do thy part, and let God alone with his. But this is our busy sinfulness, we will needs be doing God's work, and neglect our own.

Agnoscit se justæ dedisse stultæ securitatis pœnam; est etiam filiis Dei pia securitas. Calv. in loc.

Obs. 4. A strong engagement lies upon God's people to endeavour the preservation of God's honour. It is true, in this case, protection draws allegiance. If he be a wall of fire to us, to our souls and bodies, let not us be a rotten hedge when we should defend his name, servants, ordinances; if he be a tower, let not us be a tottering wall. Let us labour to say, Lord, he that toucheth thine honour, toucheth the apple of mine eye. If we expect that God should keep us in our, we must maintain his cause in its, danger.

Obs. 5. The gainsayers of perseverance are deceived. Their doctrine most clearly, as hath been proved, opposes Scripture, and most incurably wounds a Christian's comfort. What joy can we have that our names are written in the book of life, if again they may be blotted out? The life of our mortal life is the hope of an immortal; but how unsteady a foundation of hope is the stedfastness of our wills! nay, thus faith's foundation is overturned, which is this, "He that believes shall be saved:" but this opinion says, Some that believe shall not be saved; for it maintains, that some who truly believe do not persevere; and those which do not persevere shall not be saved: it makes the decree of God to depend upon man's most uncertain will. Arminians say that believers shall persevere, if they be not wanting to themselves, if they always will persevere. But what is this, but to say, Believers shall persevere if they persevere? for always to will to persevere, and to persevere, are all one. It is a prodigious error, to hold that God works nothing in us for perseverance, the effectual use of which depends not upon man's free-will. God gives, saith an Arminian, to persevere if we will; but God gives, say we, to will to persevere. And how can we pray to God for perseverance, the condition whereof depends upon man's will, and not upon God's working? Christ promises, John xiv. 16, to pray the Father to give his disciples his Spirit, which shall abide with them for ever: now the cause of the abiding of the Spirit for ever with them, is not their will to have the Spirit abide in them; but the abiding of the Spirit was the cause of their willingness. I conclude, according to this Arminian error of falling from grace, it is possible that there may not be one elect person; for if one finally fall away, why may not another? And by the same reason, why not all? and then where is the church, and to what end is the death of Christ?

Nobis qui vere Christo insiti sumus, talis data est gratia, ut non solum possimus si velimus, sed etiam ut velimus in Christo perseverare. Aug. de Cor. et gra. c. 11 et 12. Non solum ut sine isto dono

perseverantes esse non possint, verum etiam ut per hoc donum non nisi perseverantes sint.

Obs. 6. He that will approve himself a true, must show himself a stedfast Christian. All the sanctified are preserved. Instability is an argument of insincerity. He was never a true friend that ever ceases to be a friend. What has levity to do with eternity? an inconstant Christian with an eternal reward? Not he that comes in first, in this race of Christianity, is crowned; but he that holds out to the last. All that which is done of any thing, is held as nothing, as long as any thing remains to be done. "If any one draw back, my soul shall have no pleasure in him," Heb. x. 38. A thatched roof suits not a precious foundation; nor a wicked conclusion, beautiful beginnings of Christianity. Within a while all possibilities of falling will be removed; one stile or two more, and thou art haply at thy Father's house: the longer thou continuest, the sweeter will be the ways of God. It is harder often to begin than once to persevere. Take heed of falling from thy stedfastness. God preserves us, but we ourselves must not be negligent. Get a sound experience of the truth thou professest; tasting the sweetness, as well as hearing of its sweetness. Follow not religion, as some hounds do the game, only for company. Love the truth for single, not sinister respects: let Christ be sweet for himself. Tremble at the very beginnings of sin; look upon no sin as light; keep a tender conscience; as our apparel, so our consciences, when spotted, become neglected. Apostacy has modest beginnings. The thickest ice, that bears a cart, begins with a tender film, not able to bear a pebble: the least enemy must not be neglected. Presume not on thy own strength. He that carries grace in a proud heart, carries dust in the wind. A proud man is *arbor decorticata*, a tree whose bark is off: humility keeps in the sap of grace. Shun the occasions of sin; it is easier to pass by the snare than to get out. Lastly, pray to be preserved: from God is it that we stand: we are reeds tied to a pillar. The wicked go out of the way, and they call not upon God, Psal. xiv. 3, 4.

Οὐδεὶς ἐραστὴς ὅστις οὐκ ἀεὶ φιλεῖ. Arist. Roh. l. 2. c. 21.

This for the handling of the first particular in the second privilege; viz. the kind of it, preservation.

The second follows; viz. The ground of this their preservation: "In Jesus Christ."

For explication. The faithful may be said to be preserved in Christ two ways.

1. *Merito passionis*, by the merit of his suffering; and thus he saves from the wrath and curse of God: "There is no condemnation to them that are in Christ Jesus," Rom. viii. 1. He saveth "from the wrath to come," 1 Thess. i. 10. "The chastisement of our peace was upon him, and by his stripes we are healed," Isa. liii. 5. He was as the brazen serpent in healing the beholders. All miseries, as curses, have left their stings in his side. He was the true Passover, for whom all the judgments of God pass over us: his cross is the tree cast into the waters of Marah, to take away their bitterness; his ignominy is our glory; his poverty our patrimony.

2. We are preserved in Christ, *efficacia operationis*, by his effectual working in us, and bestowing upon us such supplies of grace, as that we never fully and

finally depart from God; and this is effected two ways: On Christ's part, He sending his Spirit to work in us. On our parts, Faith is enabled by his Spirit to receive continued supplies of strength from him.

(1.) His Spirit of grace, called "the Spirit of Christ," Rom. viii. 9, is bestowed upon us, Gal. iv. 6, he interceding with his Father for that end: "I will pray the Father," (saith he,) "and he shall give you another Comforter," John xiv. 16. "If I depart, I will send him unto you." And this presence of the Spirit working and continuing grace, is the fruit of those prayers for the preservation of his people. "I have prayed for thee, that thy faith fail not," saith Christ to Peter, Luke xxii. 32; and, "I pray that thou wouldst keep them from the evil," John xvii. 15. And the apostle, Rom. viii. 34, 35, from the intercession of Christ, infers the certainty of perseverance: "Who also maketh intercession for us. Who shall separate us from the love of Christ?" &c. Now this Spirit, sent by Christ into the hearts of his people, preserves them, both by working and strengthening their union with Christ. In the former, conveying a life, and bestowing a permanent principle of holiness upon them; putting into them a seed that shall never die, 1 John iii. 9, infusing a habit of holiness never to be lost. In the latter, affording daily supplies, Phil. i. 19, and strengthening them with might, Eph. iii. 16; Phil. iv. 13, to resist all temptations, to bear all burdens, to go through all conflicts, to thrive by all ordinances, to rest upon all the promises, to act their graces with vigour, to mourn for sin committed, to call and cry for grace which is wanting; the Spirit directing in doubts, quickening in deadness, comforting in sorrows, and interceding in prayer, Rom. viii.

(2.) On our part we are preserved in Christ by his operation, when faith is enabled by the Spirit to adhere and cleave unto him, to unite and fasten us unto him, making Christ to dwell in our hearts, incorporating us into him as the branches are in the tree, or as the root is fastened in the soil, the member in the body, or the house upon the foundation; this grace joining and making us adhere to Christ so strongly, that having fastened upon him, there is no plucking the soul from him, John xv. 4, 6; Eph. iii. 17.

And thus, as Christ lays hold upon us, and takes us by the hand with his Spirit; so we lay hold upon him, and take him by the hand with our faith, whereby the union is complete and reciprocal, our Beloved ours, and we his. And from this uniting and closing work of faith, by the Spirit, flows the preservation of a Christian, as the weak branches of a vine are upheld by fastening about the prop, and the house by abiding on the foundation, or a weak, slender reed by being tied to a pillar. But yet faith rests not here, but improves this union, and by virtue of it draws continual supplies of grace and strength from Christ, as the root from the soil, or the branches from the root, or the pipe from the fountain. Hence it is that we live by faith, Gal. ii. 20, because our faith is the instrument that draws virtue from Christ to relieve and sustain us in all our wants, faith and Christ being well met: Christ is very full, and loves to be giving; faith very empty, a covetous grace, and loves to be receiving of his fulness, John i. 16. It suffices not faith to be in the fountain, unless it drink of the fountain; to be in Christ, unless it receive from Christ; to unite us as members to the Head, unless it supplies us as members from the Head; from the Head all the body by joints and bands hath nourishment ministered, Col. ii. 19. The Spirit on the part of Christ, and faith on ours, are those ἁφαί, those joints and instruments of connexion betwixt Christ and us, whereby a Christian is not only knit to Christ his Head, and a kind of spiritual continuity between Christ and him is caused; but has nourishment ministered, ἐπιχορηγεῖται, is furnished or supplied with all suitable furniture plentifully, necessary to preservation of grace, "all things that pertain to life and godliness," 2 Pet. i. 3; justifying grace to preserve us from the guilt of sin, Rom. viii. 10, supplies of sanctifying grace to preserve us from the filth of sin in us, 2 Cor. v. 15, and the force of temptation without us; in both respects faith drawing preservation from Christ, in whom life is, 1 John v. 11, nay, "who is our life," Col. iii. 4. And faith makes use of the ordinances, but as conduit-pipes or watercourses, to convey from Christ those supplies of grace it wants, esteeming prayer, the word, and sacraments, without Christ, but as a vial without a cordial, a plaster without salve, a pipe without water.

Habemus sapientiam, justitiam, sanctitatem Christi, non quatenus speculamur Christum quatenus longe a nobis existentem, sed quatenus incorporamur Christo, quatenus habemus Christum in nobis manentem. De fonte hujus spiritualis plenitudinis accipere non possumus, nisi in illo simus; et hoc discriminis est inter fontem naturalem et spiritualem. Dau. in Col. p. 248.

This for the explication of the person in whom they were preserved, "In Jesus Christ."

Obs. 1. Every one out of Christ lies open to all danger. His temporal preservation is at best but by common providence; but it is cursed as well as common: he is reserved to the day of wrath, not preserved to that everlasting kingdom of which Paul speaks, 2 Tim. iv. 18. Kept he is, but as a prisoner, whose provisions only strengthen him to go to execution: he has no guard from wrath, because no shelter from sin. Sinner, thy security is not from want of danger, but discerning; and didst thou know it, thou wouldst no more rest one hour without labouring for Christ, than a man would securely go to bed when his house is on fire about his ears. Is it not a curse for thy soul to be Satan's for egress and regress? for God to let thee lie as a common without a hedge, to wander as a lamb in a large place, without a shepherd, without a fold, a prey to every beast of prey? Thou wilt not let God be a hedge to keep thee from straying, and he will not be a hedge to preserve thee from devouring. How dreadful is it to be at the cruel courtesy of every devil, every temptation! Thou labourest to keep thy treasure safe; nay, thou hast a hole to hide thy swine in; but thy poor soul has not where to hide its head. What is it to have the protection of a state for thy goods and body, to have the benefit of the law; and to be without the protection of God in Christ, and to want the benefit of every promise in the Bible? Was it dangerous to be shut out of the ark, when the water swelled; to be shut out of a city of refuge, when the avenger of blood pursued; to want blood upon the door-posts, when the angel was destroying? and is it not dangerous to be without a Jesus to deliver thee from the wrath to come? You that will not be preserved from Satan as a seducer in your life, shall not be preserved from him as a destroyer at your death: Christ will then be a shelter worth having; get into him while you live. The drowned world called to Noah too late for admission, when the waters were come to the top of the mountains. The heavens are black, the times gloomy, the storms swift and sweeping; oh let not thy approaches to thy shelter be delayed. Run to thy tower, not the paper tower of thine own merits. Lock up thyself in the wounds of Christ; nothing else can profit in the day of wrath; the storm will go through every other refuge.

Obs. 2. Hypocrites will not be stedfast. One out of Christ cannot be preserved, or be persevering: they who are not built on the rock, cannot stand in the fury of floods. Union to Christ is the cause of permanency. The hope of the hypocrite is as the spider's web; nor is his holiness more permanent. It is not a union by profession, but by real implantation, that makes thee persevere. A stake thrust into the ground may easily be plucked up; it is the rooted tree that will stand. A painted profession will never hold out; fire and water never be endured by it: if the heart be not set aright, the spirit will not be stedfast with God, Psal. lxxviii. 8. There are many end in apostacy; the reason is, they never begun in sincerity. How few real saints are there in suffering times! An unsound body discovers itself in a cold season; a rotten apple in a windy day. Never think to stand long, if thou standest loose from Christ. Loose things that lie close upon the land, will be parted in the water; so will Christ and a hypocrite in sufferings. He that hath no strength from Christ, will prove too weak to bear burdens. He that believes not, will never be established. A poor, humble, dependent soul will stand when he fears he shall fall; a proud hypocrite will fall when he thinks he stands.

Obs. 3. In all dangers it is our wisdom to have recourse to Christ, and improve our interest in him. It is not enough to have, unless we use Christ, and fly to this tower in which we have a propriety, that we may obtain preservation. It is the grand design of Satan, to encourage a presuming sinner to make use of Christ, and to discourage a humble believer from approaching toward him; to suffer the multitudes boldly to throng about Christ, but to dismay a poor trembling woman to touch the hem of his garment: he imboldens thieves to possess what is another's, but disheartens owners from using what is theirs: because he cannot destroy a believer's grace, he labours to disturb a believer's peace. But if fear of wrath assault the conscience, there is preservation from that in Christ: there is room enough in his wounds to hold, and readiness enough in his heart to receive, all that fly unto him. Christ is a shadow against the heats of justice, a city of refuge against the pursuits of wrath, an ark against the flood of vengeance, a passover in nearness of destructions. "He is able to save to the uttermost them that come unto God by him;" and if any come unto him, he will in no wise cast him out. In the solicitations of sin, improve the death of Christ; beg of him to lend thee the quenching power of his blood, when lust is kindling. In the feebleness of thy graces, the deadness of thy heart, the faintness of thy faith, the gasping of thy gifts, the decays of thy fervour, beseech him not to take away his Spirit, but to strengthen thee in the inward man with supplies of spiritual life, and influences of his grace, Psal. li. In sufferings from the world, go to him for strength that has overcome the world, to make thee find thy enemies conquered, and thyself more than a conqueror, John xvi. 33; that his comforts may be real, and the sufferings from the world but appearing.

Obs. 4. How fearful should we be of that which weakens our union to Christ! Nothing but sin endangers the soul's preservation, because nothing but that endangers Christ's departure, and so puts it out of Christ's protection. Sin obstructs supplies of strength from Christ, and so stops the spouts of mercy: sin cuts off the locks, and makes believers a prey to Philistines. Christ and preservation, sin and unsafeness, are undivided couples. The faithful enjoying Christ, are quiet and confident in the midst of all their troubles; but letting in sin, they are fearful and unsafe in the midst of all their pleasures. A child at play complains not of the dust in which it rolls and tumbles, but if the least dust get into the eye, it immediately begins to cry. The people of God, while troubles are upon them, are safe; but when they are within them, when sin sends away Christ, then begins their woe. Sin can never quite bereave a saint of his jewel, his grace; but it may steal away the key of the cabinet, his assurance: he may not know where to find his grace when he stands most in need of it. Grieve not that Holy Spirit which unites Christ to the soul, and supplies the soul with Christ. Grieve not that Spirit in thy joys, which only can rejoice thee in thy griefs. The Spirit of Christ is a tender thing. When Joseph manifested himself to his brethren, the Egyptians were made to go forth; and when the Spirit discovers the love of Christ to us, there must not be a lust allowed in us.

Obs. 5. See the great happiness by the Second, above what was enjoyed from the first Adam. We were holy in the first, but are preserved only in the Second Adam; in the former holiness was perfect only, in the latter it is permanent; in Adam we had a power to stand if we would, in Christ we have grace that makes us will. Adam had life, but lost it, and imparts death; Christ hath life, keeps it, and communicates it. Oh the goodness of God, that he should take occasion by man's hurting himself to do him good; and after his falling, not only to raise him, but to keep him up, to keep him, as the apostle saith, from falling! A mercy, which as it requires thankfulness, so it opposes high-mindedness. Job on the dunghill was more safe than Adam in that place which was the beauty of the earth. Though the faithful may be cast into miseries, yet they perish not with the miserable. But though we stand longer than Adam stood, yet by ourselves we stand not at all: we live in a continued dependence upon Christ; if he withdraw his manutenency, the higher we are in grace, the lower we shall be in sin. We bear not the root, but the root bears us; let us not be high-minded, but fear, Rom. xi. 18, 20. Whoever is preserved in Christ, must not arrogate his preservation to himself: Christ must have the glory both of our setting out and holding out. *Felicior Job in sterquilinio, quam Adamus in Paradiso. Subjiciuntur miseriis, non rejiciuntur cum miseris.*

This for the second privilege from which the faithful to whom Jude writes are described, viz. Their preservation in Christ. Then follows,

3. Their vocation. Last in the order of the apostle's writing, though indeed first in the order of God's working; the apostle hereby expressing the ground of their sanctification, and their perseverance therein, viz. Their true and effectual vocation from sin to God at the first; "Called."

By way of explication. The word here used signifies sundry sorts of callings.

(1.) Not to speak of calling personal, 1 Cor. vii. 24; Rom. i. 1; Gal. i. 1, or to a function and office, whether economical, military, magistratical, or ecclesiastical, Acts i. 26, immediate or mediate, as not being here intended.

(2.) Nor of that general calling of all persons in the world by the works of creation, and the light of nature; by which God speaks to heathens, Rom. ii. 15; i. 19, 20; Psal. xix. 1; Acts xvii. 27; xiv. 17.

(3.) But of that spiritual calling afforded only unto some, which is, to seek happiness and blessedness in Christ.

This is twofold: 1. Only external and ineffectual. 2. Internal also, and effectual.

[1.] Only external, and by the ministry of the gospel, bestowed sometimes upon cities, kingdoms, commonwealths, Psal. cxlvii. 19, 29; Acts xvii. 30; a calling according to means, common to the elect and reprobates. "Many are called, but few are chosen," Matt. xx. 16. It is often inefficacious, as to the saving good of the hearer. Christ would have gathered

Jerusalem's children, and they would not, Matt. xxiii. 37. The word preached profited not, because it was not mixed with faith, Heb. iv. 2. God by this external calling showing what is man's duty, and what was once his ability to perform; the impairing of which latter is no exemption from the former; and hereby rendering men inexcusable, they knowing what they should do, and not doing what they know, John xv. 22, 24. And also by this merely outward calling men are held in external order, abstain from sundry great and heinous sins, are profitable instruments in a commonwealth, observe civil justice, &c., which God oft rewards with temporal blessings.

[2.] The other sort of this spiritual vocation is internal and effectual; this bringing us into the invisible church, as the other into the visible; this uniting us to Christ the Head, the other tying us to the members; this bringing to illumination of faith, the other to illumination of knowledge only; this making us members, the other professors of Christ; this curing and changing, the other only curbing us; this being a calling according to purpose, and flowing from election, the other a calling according to means only. The general way leading to the knowledge of God by the creatures and natural light, or the mere external revelation of the will of God in the Scriptures, sufficing not, without the effectual operation of the Spirit upon the heart; in respect whereof, (as the learned Rivet well observes,) the psalmist throughout the 19th Psalm sets down a threefold school by which God teacheth us, and calls us. 1. That which is common to all men, by the contemplation of the creatures. 2. That which is proper to the church, standing in God's committing his oracles unto it. 3. That which is internal, and of special grace, efficacious, and to be referred to the unction of the Spirit, which teaches and calls after a saving manner. And this is the calling here intended, being that powerful work of God, calling persons to be what they are not, of sinners to become saints, of enemies to become sons; whereby grace is not only offered, but conferred; a work of God's Spirit, whereby the elect are not only morally invited, but efficaciously incited, to come to Christ.

Totus Psalmus in tres partes distribui potest; Prima agit de prima schola, quæ est universalis, seu omnium hominum communis. Secunda, de schola particulari, propria ecclesiæ, penes quam Deus oracula sua deposuit. Tertia, de schola specialis gratiæ, interna, efficaci, quæ ad unctionem Spiritus refertur, quæ docet vero et salutari modo. Riv. arg. Psal. xix.

For the explanation of which, I shall briefly touch upon six considerations, which sweetly agree in three pairs or couples, with the ordinary calls or invitations which are between man and man.

1. The state from which we are called; with,
2. The state to which we are called.
3. The Caller, or who it is that calleth; with,
4. The persons called.
5. The voice wherewith he calleth; with,
6. The answer to the voice of the Caller.

1. The state from which we are called. It is a sinful and damnable state of nature; expressed in Scripture under terms of greatest terror: We are called out of darkness, 1 Pet. ii. 9; turned from darkness, Acts xxvi. 18; translated from the power of darkness, Col. i. 13. Man before his calling is dark in his understanding, Eph. iv. 18; v. 8; as a blind man is said to be dark, he knows no truth savingly, sees no commanding beauty in any of the ways of God, accounts them foolishness, 1 Cor. ii. 14; being blind, he loves darkness, John iii. 19, and his works are the works of darkness, Eph. v. 11; he falls every step, sins in every action; every comfort he uses is a stumblingblock, he is afraid of the stirring of every leaf, stirs not a foot in holiness, as the Egyptians, who in darkness sat still, never enjoying the light of God's countenance, always full of grief and trouble, of which darkness is the emblem, and ready to fall into utter darkness. An uncalled person is under the power of darkness, Col. i. 13, born in the kingdom and under the dominion of Satan, walking "according to the prince of the power of the air," Eph. ii. 2, led captive by him at his will. In a word, we are called from a state, not of darkness only, and blindness, but slavery, rebellion, poverty, pain, ignominy, banishment, nakedness, filthiness, deformity, sickness, the company of lions and leopards, death, perdition, and every thing that is miserable. All the woes of the world, were they a thousand times greater, are but a faint representation of the misery of wicked men; they are miserable within, without, here, hereafter, in life, in death, after death; liable to the loss of the glorious and soul-ravishing presence of God to all eternity, and to be tortured with a fire, to which ours is but painted.

2. The state to which we are called. It is a state of all blessedness; the good of grace here, and the good of glory hereafter. "Called into his marvellous light," 1 Pet. ii. 9, the light of saving knowledge of the will of God; such a light as is influential, like the light of the sun, not that of a torch; a commanding light, to believe and love what we know; this being a knowledge of things as they are, a seeing divine beauty in every word and will of God; accounting the things of God foolishness no more: a light that discovers the deeds of darkness, and makes them loathsome; that makes the called walk as children of the light, and of the day; which discovers heaven in every grace, and hell in every lust, Isa. xlii. 7; Acts xxvi. 18; 2 Cor. iv. 6; John viii. 12; Luke xvi. 8. This calling is also to the light of joy, "sown for the righteous," Psal. xcvii. 11, and only stowed upon them; this oil of joy being only put into a vial clean, and without cracks; joy beyond the joy of harvest; joy, more than that of corn and wine, spoil, treasures, nay life, Psal. iv. 7; this light coming from the Sun, the face of God, without which all the candles of the world could never make a day for a gracious heart: in a word, a light that leadeth to eternal light, the inheritance with the saints in light, Col. i. 12. In which respect the faithful are not only said to be called with a holy, 2 Tim. i. 9, but partakers of a heavenly, calling, Heb. iii. 1; and it is the apostle's prayer, that they may know the hope of their calling, Eph. i. 18; they being called to a kingdom, 1 Thess. ii. 12, to the obtaining the glory of Christ, 2 Thess. ii. 14; deservedly therefore termed a high calling, Phil. iii. 14. But why attempt I to give you an inventory of the benefits by vocation, when eternity shall be little enough to contemplate them? Who can think what it is to be called to sanctification, to have of every grace, the least dram or drop of any one whereof is infinitely more worth than an ocean, a world of wealth and treasures? to be called to the privileges as well as the graces of a Christian, justification of our persons, freedom from the wrath of God, and all those millions of mountains of sins that before lay upon us? to be called out of a dungeon of woe, as Joseph out of prison, to be favourites of the King of glory? to be called to the adoption of sons, liberty of children, comfortable enjoyment of all blessings, admission with boldness to the throne of grace, exemption from the least drop of curse in the greatest deluge of crosses? in a word, to be called to the full fruition of God in heaven; from not only corruption by and with sin, the world, and the devil, but even from their very company; not only from curses, but even crosses too; to have the perfection of all happiness in our God, in whom all delights are concentred, and in comparison

whereof the world's ocean of pleasure is not a drop; and to see and have all this to eternity, without either intermission or amission? Psal. xvi. 11. This, and ten thousand times more, is not a shadow of that substantial happiness laid up in the consideration of this *terminus ad quem*, this term to which a Christian is called.

This for the states of vocation, the first pair of parallels between man's calling man, and God's calling man.

2. The next pair is, The Caller, and The called.

(1.) The Caller is God. He "hath called us with an holy calling," 2 Tim. i. 9. He that calleth us is holy, 1 Pet. i. 15. "Faithful is he that hath called," 1 Thess. v. 24. "He hath called out of darkness," 1 Pet. ii. 9. "The God of all grace hath called us," 1 Pet. v. 10. Our calling depends, 1. Upon his purpose, it being therefore said to be according to purpose, Rom. viii. 28; 2 Tim. i. 9, he purposing the means with the end. 2. Our calling depends upon his power, 2 Pet. i. 3. He must draw, otherwise we never follow: he only calls things that are not, as if they were: he only can call so loud, that the deaf, the dead should hear, John v. 28; Eph. ii. 1: he only who creates can call; and the work of creation is in effectual vocation: he who created the light, can only make us see, 2 Cor. iv. 6: he who made, can only remake. 3. The happy estate of our calling is only from his bounty; exemption from death, Satan, the world, condemnation; the bestowing of grace, Eph. ii. 8, fellowship with Christ, 1 Cor. i. 9, and the kingdom of glory, 1 Pet. v. 10. Eternal life is the gift of God.

(2.) The called in this doctrine of vocation fall under a double consideration. 1. In respect of themselves; and so they are sinners with others. Paul tells us, that we are called not according to works, 2 Tim. i. 9: we are not called because of our good works; but because we are called, therefore are our works good. When Abraham was called, he worshipped other gods, Josh. xxiv. 2. Paul was called when he breathed out threatenings and slaughter against the church, Acts ix. 1; Gal. i. 13. Rich Zaccheus, when an extortioner, nothing better by nature than the rich glutton in hell. God calls those to his kingdom, that are, with Saul, seeking of asses, and running after worldly trifles. Such were some of you, (saith Paul,) fornicators, idolaters, &c.; but ye are washed, ye are sanctified, &c., 1 Cor. vi. 9—11. Elijah and Elisha walked together before the fiery chariot separated them, then one was taken up into heaven, and the other left upon the earth: so, till effectual vocation makes the difference, there is no difference betwixt persons, but they all run to the same excess of riot. 2. Persons effectually called considered in respect of God, are they, and only they, who are elected; this eternal decree and purpose of God being the foundation of election: Whom he hath predestinated, them he also called, Rom. viii. 30. And, "As many as were ordained to eternal life believed," Acts xiii. 48; and, "God hath called us with an holy calling, not according to works, but according to his own purpose and grace, which was given us in Christ Jesus before the world began," 2 Tim. i. 9. This purpose of God made the difference betwixt Esau and Jacob, Moses and Balaam, David and Saul, Jude and Judas.

Prædestinavit nos Deus antequam essemus, vocavit cum aversi essemus, justificavit cum peccatores essemus, glorificavit cum mortales essemus. Nemo dicat ideo, Me vocavit, quæ colui Deum: Quomodo coluisses, si vocatus non fuisses? Aug. ser. 16. de verb. Ap.

3. The third couple or pair of parallels betwixt man's calling man, and God's calling man, is, The voice of the Caller, and The answer of the called.

(1.) The voice the Lord uses is the ministry of his word; it being the ordinary means appointed by God, as the Spirit accompanies it, for this purpose; in the preaching whereof, the law of God first convinces of the sinful distance we are from God, manifests our misery by reason of sin, and so tames a wild sinner, Rom. vii., that now he will stand still while God speaks to him, although of late he was like the wild ass, snuffing up the wind, Jer. ii. 24. The terrible convictions and consternations of the law are not to commend us to God, but God to us; not deserving grace, but preparing for it; though that preparation be also from God. Nor are they alike in every one: God comes to some as on Mount Sinai, in thunder and lightning; to others, more still and sweetly; yet to all in a way of conviction of sin, and loss in themselves, if they remain in this condition of distance from God, John xvi. 8. To old sinners, who have long lived in sin, God makes conversion more painful, as they say the pains of child-bearing are to women who are more aged than common; and they who have been famous for pleasure in sin, are commonly made famous by their greater apprehensions of wrath for sins. Men of deep insight and perspicuity, see sin more in its colours, than those of duller capacity. Those whom God intends most to comfort afterwards, he often deals most sharply with at first; as the ball which rises highest is thrown against the ground hardest; or as landlords that take a great fine of those from whom they are to receive but little rent. However, the terrifyings of the law are not intended to kill, but to prepare for curing him whom God is calling, 2 Thess. ii. 14; the wounds made by the law but making way for the oil of the gospel, the blood of Jesus Christ. This gospel, inviting the poor soul to Jesus Christ, is, as it is actuated and used by the Spirit, the power of God, Rom. i. 16, an efficacious organ, a spiritual channel for conveying grace into the soul; it is the seed cast into the womb of the soul, and blessed by the forming power of the Spirit, for begetting grace in it, imprinting the image of Christ, and bestowing the Divine nature upon it, we being his workmanship by this efficacious instrument, the gospel, John i. 13; iii. 6; 1 Pet. i. 23; 2 Pet. i. 4.

(2.) The answering to the call stands in its effectualness and prevalency in making the called obedient to the Caller's voice, when the heart is so prevailed with, that it is made what it is invited to be, enabled to do what it is exhorted to, Rom. iv. 17; when the law is written in the heart, Rom. vi. 17, which is cast into divine doctrine, as into a mould, and comes forth bearing the stamp and figure of it; when, beholding the glory of the Lord in the glass of the gospel, we "are changed into the same image from glory to glory," 2 Cor. iii. 18; when the heart echos to that voice, "Seek my face," thus, "Thy face, Lord, will I seek," Psal. xxvii. 8; when the gospel comes "not only in word, but in power, and the Holy Ghost, and much assurance," 1 Thess. i. 5; when the ear is bored, Psal. xl. 6, the heart opened, Acts xvi. 14, the heart of stone, the uncircumcised heart, taken away, and the heart of flesh, the circumcised heart, is bestowed, Ezek. xi. 19. In a word, God speaks to the dead heart, which is made to hear his voice, and live, John v. 28; being now inclined to embrace that will of God, to which it was refractory, against which it rebelled formerly; being now made soft, pliable, receptive, yielding, bowed, and obedient.

This for the explication of the third privilege belonging to the faithful, viz. calling.

Obs. 1. They are mistaken, who teach, That the reason of God's calling some rather than others by his gospel, is in regard of

Joh. Arnold. cont. Til. p. 397.

the greater worthiness of some to partake of it than of others. We are all in a state of greatest distance from the Caller, and opposition to his call. What worth above others was in the Corinthians, when the gospel came first to them? The apostle tells them, "Such were some of you;" namely, "fornicators, idolaters, adulterers, effeminate, abusers of themselves with mankind, thieves, covetous, drunkards," &c. 1 Cor. vi. 9—11. Commonly, it is the darkest time of ignorance and profaneness in places immediately before the dawning of the gospel, God washing us when we are in our blood, most polluted, persuading to reconciliation in greatest enmity, calling in most open distance: our calling is not "according to works, but according to purpose," 2 Tim. i. 9: so resolved by Christ, Even so, Father, because it seemed good to thee, Rom. ix. 18; Matt. xi. 26. Else why God calls one rather than another, do not judge, if thou wouldst not err. Before calling, we were not only without strength, and full of impotency, but enemies, and full of antipathy, Rom. v. 6, 10: we are not holy, or willing to be so, and therefore called; but called, and therefore holy. Men find a thing lovely, and love it; God loves a thing, and thereby makes it lovely.

Ex duobus, ætate jam grandibus, impiis, cur iste ita vocetur, ut vocantem sequatur: Ille autem non ita vocetur, ut vocantem sequatur, nolito judicare, si non vis errare. Inscrutabilia sunt judicia Dei; cujus vult misereretur. Aug. de Bon. Pers. cap. 8.

Obs. 2. With as gross an error are they deluded, who make this calling of God to stand in moral persuasions; in the persuading power of threatenings, exhortations, promises of the word, whereby men (say they) are moved or drawn in a most suitable way to their own nature. That God uses the persuasion of precepts and promises, &c. in his word, it is granted; but that in effectual vocation he uses no more, we deny. Illumination of the understanding barely by the word, is but natural and common, natural reason being thereby only perfected, not spiritualized, and with its clearest light apprehending spiritual objects but naturally. And all the motions of the will towards any objects which are so apprehended, are but common and carnal motions. Upon a natural man's understanding of threatenings or promises, when his will puts forth its motions in fear, love, hope, joy, hatred toward good or evil, all these motions are proportionable to the light of the understanding which bred them; and therefore, as they were caused by apprehensions of good or evil to oneself, so they amount to no more than natural propensions to self-preservation. But spiritual illumination, whereby we see a ravishing beauty and excellency in holiness, and apprehend Christ the chiefest of ten thousand, valuing every way of God above all the pleasures of sin, is joined with a spiritual motion of the will towards every way of God in a holy resolution, vehemency, constancy. How can a bare representation of God's will, an objective representation by way of proposal of threatenings, promises, &c., create or work any real effect upon the heart? Why then are not those who know most, most obedient? why are not those who have the best gifts in knowing how to represent truths, most successful in their ministry? why are not Satan's seducements to evil always more effectual than the word's persuasion to holiness, he both re-representing sinful objects, and our natural corruption in understanding and will being on his side? How can the bare proposal of an object make a dead, a deaf man regard? How frequently have moral entreaties been rejected, when used by the best of men! What is all the outward shining of light to

Remonst. Col. Hag. p. 260.

Interna et ineffabili potestate operantur in cordibus hominum, non solum veræ revelationes, sed bonæ voluntates. Aug. cont. P. l. 1. c. 24.

a blind man? Deut. xxix. 3, 4; John xii. 37; Neh. ix. 29; John vi. 36, 37; Isa. liii. 1. How is bare moral persuasion that strength which raised up Christ from the dead? Eph. i. 19. Or what is it in comparison of that new creation, resurrection, renovation, new birth, afforded in effectual vocation? Moral suasion only moves objectively, and in the strength of the proposal of a good. Now as a man is, so will any thing that is propounded seem to him: so long therefore as a man is natural, and not born again, supernatural blessings propounded to him cannot so affect the will, that he should embrace and receive them; but the will must be wrought upon by a powerful operation, overcome and changed, before an offered good can be effectually embraced. All the verbal entreaties in the world to a man spiritually dead, are but as the rubbing of and putting hot waters into the mouth of one that is naturally dead. We are taught, therefore, to whom to seek for saving benefit in our enjoyment of the word. The word is only God's by way of ordination, and his only by way of benediction; though he hath not taken away his word from us, yet if he take away himself from his word, it will not profit. Whither should we go but to him; and how, but by him? Draw us, Lord, and we shall follow thee.

Istam aliquando gratiam fateatur, qua futuræ gloriæ magnitudo non solum promittitur, verum etiam creditur; nec solum revelatur sapientia, sed et amatur; nec suadetur solum quod bonum est, sed et persuadetur. Aug.

Obs. 3. As much overseen as the former, are they who labour to maintain, that notwithstanding all the power put forth in our effectual vocation, there is a liberty in the will to oppose the work of conversion, even to the frustration and defeature of it; or, that putting all the operations of grace that need to be put into the balance, a man's free-will must turn the scales, and determine the case, whether a man shall be converted or no, accept of grace or refuse it. But according to this heterodox position, it will follow, that not God by his grace, but man by his free-will, is the principal cause of his conversion. For if God by putting forth all his strength in man's conversion, does no more than afford to the will a middle kind of state of indifference, he concurs to the act of conversion, or to the change of the will from that indifference, not principally, or predominantly, but only by way of concomitancy, contingently and conditionally; namely, if the will please by its natural power to move from its indifference: so that the will receives from God the less, which is, to be put into a middle state of indifference to convert, or not convert; and that which is the greater, and which determines the act, the will performs of itself. And in conversion more must be attributed to man's will than God's work; for none is therefore holy because he may be so if he will, but because he is truly willing to be so; only the former this opinion attributes unto God, and the latter to free-will. And how can the patrons of this error ever truly pray to God for the grace of his Spirit? What should they pray for? sufficient grace to convert if they will? No; that is universal, and received by the worst. Or shall they pray for the good use of that grace? Neither; for the good use of grace they hold to come from the will, which must by no means be determined by God, but be indifferent, whether to convert or not: and if God only gives a power to will to convert, but it is alone from the will to will to convert, it follows, that God's grace affords no more help to John who is converted, than to Judas who is not; and so it will inevitably follow, that John made himself to

Corvin. contr. Bogerm. p. 263.

Joh. Goodwin Yo. Eld. p. 66.

Si nobis libera quædam voluntas ex Deo est quæ adhuc potest esse bona vel mala, bona vero voluntas ex nobis sit; melius est id quod a nobis, quam quod ab illo. Aug. de pecc. mer. et rem. l. 2. c. 18.

differ from Judas by some act of his own, which he received not from grace, contrary to that of the apostle, "Who made thee to differ?" 1 Cor. iv. 7. For John and Judas are not really made to differ by grace, neither of them receiving any other grace but to convert if they will, and they are not made to differ by what they equally receive; therefore they differ in that John would make use of grace afforded, and Judas would not: whence it follows, that John might thus glory before God; Lord, I give thee thanks that thou didst afford me the help of thy grace, which was a power for me to will to convert; but the same help thou didst afford to Judas, only I added that which supernaturally thou didst not give me, namely, to will to convert, and to will to use thy help: and when I received no more from thee than Judas did, yet I have effected that which Judas did not, I being converted, and he not; and therefore I am no more indebted to thee, than that Judas who is not converted. But how would such a speech as this grate upon Christian ears! And therefore it must be yielded, that John received from God not only a power to be willing to convert, but also the will itself: and this very thing, "to will," is ascribed to God by the apostle, Phil. ii. 13, "It is God that worketh in you to will." It is not devotion to attribute to God almost all in our conversion, but deceit to keep back even the least. Now God hath promised to give us even the will itself to believe. "I will cause you to walk in my commands," Ezek. xxxvi. 27. And if God work in us this only, to be able to will to convert, but man himself the will to convert, the greatness of that mystery of predestination mentioned by the apostle comes to nothing: and that profound question, why God calls many to salvation, to whom he gives not effectual grace whereby they may will to be converted, this question, I say, may easily be answered; for, according to the Arminians, who say, God gives a power only to convert, and the person called has it from himself actually to convert; it may be answered, Those who being called, God foresaw to be willing to convert, he elected to life; and those whom he foresaw not willing to convert, these he passed by: and hereby that speech of the apostle will be altogether superfluous, Who art thou, O man, that reasonest against God? Rom. ix. 20; and that admiration of the apostle, "O the depth," &c. Rom. xi. 33. Nor need an Arminian fear so much, by granting this irresistible, indeclinable, invincible work upon the heart of one that is converted, that the will would be ravished, and forced to consent contrary to its bent, whether it would or no; for when God by his efficacious grace works in the will to will, this efficacious grace puts into the will a nonresistance, and taketh away actual resistance: so that it is as impossible that these two should coexist and meet together in the will, to be wrought upon with efficacious grace, and to resist, as for the will in the same moment to resist, and not to resist; to will to resist, and to will not to resist. So that it is a contradiction to say, When efficacious grace determines invincibly and indeclinably man's will, it compels the will, in working upon it whether it will or no; for that which grace works in it is this, to will; the will being never against the working, when under the working of efficacious grace; the sweetness of grace inspired by the Holy Ghost making the soul more to be delighted with what is commanded, than with what would hinder it; which (as Augustine calls it) is a delight victorious and conquering.

And the truth is, this efficacious determination of the will by grace, is a most happy adjutory to the will's liberty, taking away nothing but only the pravity and rebellion of it; the Holy Ghost tempering its working to the disposition of the will, that it may act with such liberty as becomes its own nature, and by grace never be destroyed, but perfected; the Spirit of God not taking away the natural liberty of the will which is by creation, but only the pravity thereof, which comes into it by man's corruption; grace not slaying, but sanctifying, and not abolishing, but elevating it to move to a supernatural good.

Obs. 4. How are we bound to bless God for his gospel, which is his voice to call us from sin and misery! Admire his goodness, that when he only calls the most with his works, he should also call us with his word. What could God do more for a nation? What are kingdoms without the gospel, but dens of thieves, dungeons of darkness, but as the world without a sun? The heathen have not the knowledge of his law, Psal. cxlvii. 19, 20. He made his gospel dawn when we were in our darkest and deepest idolatry: he called Britain from the worshipping of Apollo and Diana, dumb idols, to serve the living God. What was there in us worth calling to us, when we lay weltering in such abominations? When men call either to God or man, it is to get good; but God's call was to give good: he called us not because we were good, but to make us so. Let us not receive the grace of God in vain. In a land of light, tremble to live in the works of darkness. We, having the light of the gospel, should do our work better than those who only have the dim light of nature. O England, be not weary of it. Take heed of shutting your eyes against the light, or putting out the light because it shines in your eyes. Be not weary of God. Forget not your ornaments and attire. Run not away when God calls. Think it not a disgrace to attend the hearing of that which it is your greatest honour to obey. Let not your stomach decay because your food is so plentiful. Rejoice in the light not for a season only, John v. 35. Let not the proverb take place here, Every thing is pretty while it is young: the longer you enjoy, the more rejoice in the word. Let new food find new stomachs; or rather, the same food continually new brought. Take heed lest wantonness under procure a want of the word. While you are on this side Canaan, love to feed on manna. What a shame is it, that God should call louder to us than ever he did to any, and yet that we should hear worse than ever any did!

Obs. 5. The dignity and duty of the ministers of the gospel. (1.) The dignity; in that God calls by them: they are his mouth, as the gospel is his voice. God beseeches by them to be reconciled: they are his ambassadors, his stewards, his fellow workers, they are fathers, saviours; their work is for the good of souls; not for the estate, with lawyers, nor for the body, with physicians: it is the heavenly inheritance which they teach you to procure, the blood of Christ which they direct you to receive. You are led by them to Christ. Augustine speaks to God thus concerning Ambrose, who was an instrument of his conversion: I was led by thee to him unawares, that by him I might through knowledge be led to thee.

(2.) Their duty. Ministers should labour to uphold the dignity of their calling: the way to do so, is more to desire to be profitable than pompous. Ministers are to call, and cry: if they be silent, who should speak? If people's lusts hate a faithful minister, yet their consciences (even then) honour him, as is clear in Herod. Ministers must call aloud; they must tell people of their sin, thunder out the judgments of God against sleepy sinners: they who must not be dumb dogs, must neither bite the children in the house, nor spare the thieves. If any sin in a minister be unpardonable, it is silence. They must call often, giving line upon line, not being weary of calling, waiting with patience when a sinner may repent: importunity at length may prevail. They are *animarum proci*, wooers of souls to Christ: one denial must not discourage them. All the day long they must stretch out their hands; they must never be speechless till they die. They must call in the language of God, 1 Pet. iv. 11; they must speak as the words of God, 2 Cor. ii. 17, with demonstration of the Spirit. There must not be a sinful curiosity in handling the word: better the grammarian should reprehend, than the people not understand. Ministers must not so call as to cause astonishment, but understanding in people: pithy plainness is the beauty of preaching. What good doth a golden key that opens not? "The kingdom of God is not in word, but power." And as preaching must not be curious, so neither over-slight, consisting of raw, sudden, indigested meditations. The word must not be torn, but divided; not tossed, but handled; the text not named only, but followed: there must be a diligent kind of negligence in handling the word. They must not forbid and unbid in their lives, whom they call in their doctrine. They who are callers, must live like called ones themselves, not neglecting that to which they persuade others. The health of a minister's honour can never be maintained in the air of a corrupt life. If we would have none to despise us, we must be examples.

Obs. 6. The called of God should live suitably to their calling. They must walk worthy of it. If men be called to an office, they must wait upon it accordingly, Rom. xii. 7. A base deportment becomes not those in high place. Joseph called to stand before Pharaoh, throws away his prison garments: Saul called to a kingdom, had another heart. The virtues of him that calleth must be shown, 2 Thess. i. 11; 1 Pet. ii. 9. (1.) Humility and self-debasing, considering so great a God regarded so poor a worm. Remember, as it was a dunghill from whence God took thee, so thy unwillingness was great to leave it; and how long God was making thee willing to do good to thyself; how thou hadst nothing to set up with; that thy portion was nothing but pride and poverty. (2.) Pity to those who are uncalled. The elect of God must put on bowels: they that have obtained mercy, must pray that others may do so. Look upon others' sins with more trouble than thine own sorrows: pity those that cannot pity themselves; weep over their dying souls; thy soul hath been in the state of theirs. Call after others, if God has called thee, and pray that God would make them hear, Luke xxii. 32. Embrace the company of the worst, to make them good, not as a companion, but a physician. (3.) Contempt of the world. Acknowledge thy dignity; be above those trifles which thou, as a child, didst magnify. A Christian is called (2 Thess. ii. 14) to a "kingdom," Col. i. 13; 1 Thess. ii. 12; he has a "high calling," Phil. iii. 14: all that the world can give him he should lay at his feet. His heart must be where his treasure is, and his treasure only where Christ is. Only he can look upon the world as small, who has looked upon Christ as great. How unsuitable is it to see a king raking in the dunghill, or making hay with his sceptre! (4.) A preferring that voice before all others which called thee: "It is the voice of my Beloved," Cant. ii. 8. "My sheep hear my voice," John x. 3, 16. Let not the voice of a stranger withdraw thee; be not tossed up and down "with every wind of doctrine," Eph. iv. 14; be not a follower of men: walk by rule, not example. Whensoever the world or thy own heart calls thee, rather fear them than follow them. Follow others as they Christ. Love that voice of Christ that calls thee from thy sweetest sin: value one promise of his above the sweetest music. Let every Scripture threat be more dreadful than a thunder-clap. (5.) Delight in calling upon him that called thee. Prayer is the called soul's echo back again to God: as soon as Paul was called, he prayed, Acts ix. 11. God saw nothing in thee, and yet he called after thee: how much is there in God for which thou shouldst call after him! Desire him to draw thee nearer to himself, to call thee to him closer, to keep thee, as he has called thee to him, 1 Thess. ii. 12; 2 Thess. ii. 14. (6.) Be thankful for thy vocation, that God should call thee when there was nothing but woe and unwillingness, and should pass by others better accomplished. Let his free grace have all the glory. Who shall speak of God, if thou art silent? Let heart, and tongue, and life advance him.

Hitherto of the two first parts of the title: viz. I. The person who wrote this Epistle; and, II. The persons to whom he wrote it. Now follows,

III. The prayer; wherein the person writing salutes the persons to whom he wrote, contained in these words:

Ver. 2. *Mercy unto you, and peace, and love, be multiplied.*

In which prayer we consider,

1. The blessings which the apostle requests may be bestowed; which are three, "Mercy, peace, love."
2. The measure in which the apostle desireth they may be bestowed, "Be multiplied."
3. The persons upon whom he prays that these blessings may be in this measure bestowed, "Unto you."

1. We will consider the blessings which the apostle requests: the first of them is "mercy." Concerning which,

For the expository part. Mercy is referred either to man or God.

(1.) To man: and so mercy is, according to some, a grief of heart arising from the apprehension of another's misery; according to Scripture, such a holy compassion of heart for the misery of another, as inclines us to relieve him in his misery. It is a compassion of sympathy, because it makes the merciful heart a partaker of the misery of him who is distressed; and therefore, say some, called *misericordia*, because it translates the misery of another into the heart of the merciful. And for this cause it is called the "bowels of compassion," Col. iii. 12; 1 John iii. 17; Phil. i. 8; ii. 1. So likewise by the LXX., Prov. xii. 10. And to have compassion is usually set out in Scripture by a verb that signifies to have the bowels moved, Mark vi. 34; Matt. xiv. 14; xv. 32; Mark i. 41; Luke vii. 13, &c., because mercy expresses itself in the bowels especially; he that is affected vehemently

Misericordia est dolor et ægritudo animi, ex miseria alterius injuria laborantis conceptus. Cic. in Tus. 4.
Misericordia est alienæ miseriæ in nostro corde compassio, qua utique, si possimus, subvenire compellimur. Aug. de C. D. l. 9. c. 5.
Ex eo appellata est misericordia quod miserum cor faciat condolescentis alieno malo.

with another's sufferings, having his very bowels moved and rolled in him, Hos. xi. 8, and is affected as if the bowels of him that is in misery were in his body. Nor is this Scripture compassion a foolish pity, whereby a man unlawfully tenders him that is in deserved misery, as Ahab pitied Benhadad, and Saul Agag, against God's command; but such a compassion as God approves, a fruit of the Spirit, commanded and commended in the word. In this grace of mercy is also comprehended a forwardness to succour the miserable; the bowels of the merciful not being shut up, 1 John iii. 17. This grace the Scripture honours with many precepts and promises, Matt. v. 7; Luke vi. 36; x. 37; 1 Pet. iii. 8; Col. iii. 12. A merciful man is God's almoner, his conduit-pipe to convey his blessings, his resemblance, like unto his heavenly Father, who is the Father of mercy.

Ἔστω ἔλεος λύπη ἐπιφαινομένῳ κακῷ φθαρτικῷ καὶ λυπηρῷ τοῦ ἀναξίου τυγχάνειν. Arist.
Nemo parricidæ supplicio misericordia commovetur. Cic. Tusc. 4.

(2.) To God; and so it is referred in this place by Jude. In which consideration of mercy as referred to God, there are three things to be explained.

How mercy can be attributed to God.

What sorts of mercy are attributed to God.

What are the properties of the sorts of mercy attributed to God.

[1.] How mercy can be attributed to God. Not as it is an affection of grief for the misery of another; but, 1. As it signifies a promptitude and forwardness of the will to succour the miserable. Not as it is *miseria cordis*, or as to be merciful is taken passively, for one to be a fellow sufferer; but as it is *miseria cordi*, as learned Zanchy distinguishes, and as to be merciful is taken actively, for one so to be mindful of the miseries of others, that he desires and is willing from the heart to help them. Suffering with the distressed in their miseries is not essential to mercy, but only accidental, in regard of our nature, which is so subject to passions, that without a fellow feeling we cannot look upon the miseries of those whom we love; and this is not in God: but a propension and inclination of will to relieve the miserable, which is the essential part of mercy, is most properly and abundantly in God, although sympathy or fellow feeling is often attributed to God improperly, and by way of resemblance to human affections, for relieving our capacities, and strengthening our faith. And in respect of this propenseness and willingness in God to help the distressed, are we to understand those scriptures where God calls himself "merciful," and " of great mercy," Zech. ii. 8; Acts ix. 4; Exod. xxxiv. 6, 7; Psal. c. 5; cxlv. 9; that is, of a most forward nature to help us in our distresses. 2. Mercy is attributed to God, as it signifies God's actual helping and relieving us in our distresses; as he bestows those blessings upon us, spiritual or bodily, which proceed from his mercy alone: and thus are those places of Scripture to be understood, where God is said to have or show mercy; as, " He hath mercy on whom he will," Rom. ix. 18. " I found mercy, because I did it ignorantly," 1 Tim. i. 13. In which places mercy is put for calling to Christ, and all graces which follow it. These works or effects of mercy being various and innumerable; so Psal. cxxxvi.; Rom. xi. 31; 2 Tim. i. 18; it comes to pass, that (though mercy be single and one in God) the

Zanc. de Nat. Dei, 1. 4. c. 4, q. 1. Misericordem hominem appellare solemus, non passive, qui miserum habet cor (talis enim potius est miser, quam misericors); sed active, hoc est, illum qui misero homini ex corde cupit succurrere. Si licuit Augustino, dicere quod sit cordis miseria, ex alterius miseria concepta: cur non liceat nobis dicere, misericordiam dici, quia nobis sit cordi alterius miseria? Misericordia duo importat; unum tanquam essentiale, aliud tanquam acciuentale: Primum est promptitudo voluntatis ad subveniendum miseris; alterum est passio tristitiæ, quæ oritur in appetitu ex cognitione miseriæ alterius; quantum ad primum summe est in Deo, non quantum ad secundum. Rich. d. 46. a. 2. qu. 1. lib. 4.

Scripture speaks of it in the plural number; as Gen. xxxii. 10; 2 Cor. i. 3; Rom. xii. 1.

[2.] For the sorts or kinds of God's mercy. It is either, 1. A general mercy, extended to all creatures in common, as there is no creature in any misery which in some respect he does not succour: he gives food to the hungry; warmth by wool, and sundry sorts of skins, to the naked; medicine by many kinds of herbs; the sun, the clouds, the winds, the rain, to refresh the earth severally: and thus he is merciful to the elect and reprobate, just and unjust, nay, men and beasts, Psal. cxlvii. 9; Matt. vi. 26, &c.; Psal. cxlv. 15. Or, 2. A special mercy bestowed upon the elect alone, different from the former both in regard of God's will to help, and also in regard of the effects of that will. It is the will of God, John vi. 39, that the elect should be delivered from their sins, his wrath, Satan's power, the sting of death, and that they should obtain eternal life in Christ. The will and pleasure of God is to do them good, they are his "Hephzi-bah," Isa. lxii. 4; but he hath no pleasure in or special love to others, Mal. i. 10. The effects likewise of his will to help are different toward the elect from those he expresses upon the reprobate; he calling effectually, justifying, redeeming, glorifying the elect, Rom. ix. 15, 18; 1 Tim. i. 13. "The Lord pitieth them that fear him," Psal. ciii. 13. " He that trusteth in the Lord, mercy shall compass him about," Psal. xxxii. 10. The Lord is "plenteous in mercy to them that call upon him," Psal. lxxxvi. 5. Of others he saith, " I will deal in fury; mine eye shall not spare, neither will I have pity," Ezek. viii. 18. The elect are vessels of mercy, the other of wrath. To the former he is merciful in bestowing upon them an eternal, to the latter in affording a temporal, life. These two differing as much as the mercy with which a man regards his beast does from that wherewith he tenders his son: the beast is fed to be slain, or to be fit for labour; the son to be preserved, and out of a paternal care for his good. To the wicked God affords a drop, to the godly a draught of mercy; to the wicked, the crumbs under the table, to the godly, Christ with all his benefits, that bread of life which endureth to eternal life.

This special mercy of God here prayed for by the apostle, is distinguished according to those several miseries of his people in which he succours them. Take a taste of the kinds of it.

God is merciful, 1. With a preventing mercy, when he makes us holy of unholy ones: he loved us first. He waited to show mercy, Isa. xxx. 18; he doing good to us when we knew him not; pitying us when we were in our blood, Ezek. xvi. 22; regarding us when we neither regarded him nor ourselves; keeping us from falling into the sins to which of ourselves we were prone. So that, as in respect of good, we are what we are from God's mere mercy; so, in respect of evil, we are not what we are not from the same mercy.

2. He is merciful to his with a forgiving mercy; fully freeing them from wrath: their sins are as if they had never been, "blotted out as a cloud," Isa. xliv. 22, thrown "into the bottom of the sea," Micah vii. 19, though sought for, yet not to be found, Jer. l. 20. In a sea of affliction there is not a drop of wrath. The faithful are looked upon as sons, not as malefactors; their sufferings are not to satisfy God, but to sanctify them, Heb. xii. 6, 7, 12.

Deus vindictæ gladium miserationis oleo exacuit.

3. He is merciful with accepting mercy; taking in good part the desires of the soul when it finds not to perform; accepting a sigh instead of a service; a cup of cold water, a mite, a broken reed, smoking flax, a groan, instead of a duty; the stammerings of

his child above the eloquence of a beggar; a broken heart as the box of spikenard.

4. He is merciful with reaccepting mercy; looking upon a returning prodigal as a son; pitying as a father, not punishing as a judge; multiplying to pardon, receiving backsliders again, Hos. xiv. 4; Isa. lv. 7.

5. He is merciful with providing mercy, Psal. xxiii.; supplying all our wants, 2 Pet. i. 3; suffering no good thing to be wanting to us, Psal. lxxxiv. 11; always giving what we need, if not what we would; either assuaging or answering our desires; bestowing temporal blessings in subordination, not opposition, to eternal blessedness; giving us, if not riches with godliness, contentment with our poverty.

6. He is merciful with directing mercy in our doubts; guiding us by his counsels, Psal. lxxiii. 24; showing us the way wherein we are to walk, Gal. vi. 16; being eyes to us in our blindness, light in our darkness, a teacher in our ignorance, a pillar and a cloud in every wilderness; giving his word for a rule, his Spirit for a guide.

7. He is merciful with sustaining mercy; upholding us in all our distresses, Psal. xciv. 18, making every affliction fordable, and carrying us through, visiting us in prison, feeding us through our grate, knowing our souls in adversity, leading us gently, proportioning our burdens to our back, casting a tree into every Marah, shining through every shower, sending supplies in every siege, making his grace sufficient for us in all our buffetings, 2 Cor. xii. 9, keeping us from being swallowed up of sin, and our grace from being totally obliterated, Luke xxii. 32.

8. He is merciful with quickening, enlivening mercy to any holy duty; so that we can do all things, Phil. iv. 13; making us a willing people, oiling the wheels of our souls, putting into us delight in his law, so that we account it sweeter than our appointed food, and run the ways of his commandments; he giving us work, wages, and hands, Psal. cxix.

9. He is merciful with a restoring, recovering mercy; and that not only from sin and miseries, but even by them. (1.) From them; bringing out of every distress, bodily and spiritual; causing every cloud to blow over; making the longest night to end in a morning; raising us after the foulest fall, and out of the deepest grave; making faith to work out of the greatest eclipse: he chides not for ever, Psal. ciii. 9, but repents him of the evil, Joel ii. 13; through his mercy he suffers us not to be consumed, Lam. iii. 22; in wrath he remembers mercy, Hab. iii. 2. (2.) By sin and miseries; making our afflictions, nay, our very sins, to work for our good, Rom. viii. 28; and all the smutchings with both to make us brighter, more humble, watchful; and our fiery trials to burn in sunder only our bonds.

10. He is merciful with crowning mercy, when he brings us into heaven; there he perfectly frees us not only from the contagion by, but even the company of, every sin; nay, the fear of ever being annoyed again thereby; delivering us from impure hearts and imperfect graces, from foils, from fighting, from all our causes of complaint: then giving for every combat we have had, a crown; for every tear, a pearl; for every light affliction, a mass of glory; for a drop of gall, a sea of joy; for appearing troubles, real blessedness: this is the mercy of that day, crowning mercy, 2 Tim. i. 18.

[3.] For the properties of God's mercy. It is full; it is free.

1. It is a full and unmeasurable mercy: the unmeasurableness whereof is set forth, (1.) More generally, when God is said to be plenteous in mercy, Psal. lxxxvi. 5. abundant, 1 Pet. i. 3, rich in mercy, Eph. ii. 4, his mercy great, above the heavens, Psal. cviii. 4, his mercies unsearchable, high as the heaven is from the earth, Psal. ciii. 11; multitudes of tender mercies, Psal. li. 1. (2.) More particularly, the unmeasurableness of his mercy is set forth, 1. In that there is no creature in heaven or earth but tastes of it. "His mercies are over all his works," Psal. cxlv. 9; the very dumb creatures speak him merciful. The whole earth is full of his goodness, Psal. xxxiii. 5: he preserves man and beast; nay, his enemies, Matt. v. 45. 2. In that resemblances to set forth his mercy are taken from the most tender-hearted creatures. He draws with the cords of a man, Hos. xi. 4. He pities as a father; nay, more than the most tender-hearted mother doth her sucking child, Isa. xlix. 15. He gathers people as a hen doth her chickens. He has bowels of mercy, and such as sound, Jer. xxxi. 20; and therefore his mercy pleases him; he delights to show mercy, he forgets not his mercy. 3. He is the fountain of the mercy and mercifulness in all the creatures in the world toward one another: the mercies of all parents to their children, of every mother to her little ones, of every Christian, of every tender-hearted person, of every beast and fowl to their young ones, are but drops that come from the sea of God's mercy; he is the Father of mercies, 2 Cor. i. 3. 4. He can deliver from every misery. Bread takes away hunger, drink thirst, clothes nakedness, knowledge ignorance, but no creature can take away every misery: whereas God is the God of all comfort, 2 Cor. i. 3; he supplies all our wants, Psal. xxiii. 1; Phil. iv. 19; Psal. xxxiv. 10, comforts in every trouble, he has a plaster for every sore, is a Physician for every disease, inward and outward; and so merciful is he, that in the very not removing of miseries he is merciful. Were it not for trouble, how should corruption be killed, holiness increased, 1 Cor. xi. 32; Heb. xii. 10, heaven be sweet, eternal crowns and triumphs be enjoyed? 4. He is merciful to his enemies; full of patience and forbearance, expecting their return many years together; giving them rain and fruitful seasons, filling their hearts with gladness, Acts xiv. 17; Matt. v. 45, notwithstanding they sin and fight against him with all his goodness; yea, so merciful is he, that in their greatest enmity to him he has often done them the greatest good, changing their hearts, and making them his friends, Rom. v. 10. 6. He bestows mercy with greatest frequency and reiteration: he has many, manifold mercies, mercies for thousands more than can be expressed. Innumerable are the sins of one man; how innumerable then are the sins of the whole world! how numberless then are those mercies of forbearance expressed every time sin is committed, there being so many millions of sinners, every one committing so many millions of sin! Innumerable are the morsels of food, drops of water, the motions, deliverances, provisions received by one man; what then are those received by a whole world! and every such expression is a mercy, Psal. li. 1; xl. 5. 7. The mercy of God is eternal, and therefore immeasurable: he keepeth mercy for ever, 1 Kings viii. 23: he will not take away his mercy from his servants; it shall follow them all the days of their life, Psal. xxiii. 6: his mercy shall be built up for ever, Psal. lxxxix. 2; it endureth for ever, Psal. cxxxvi.; it is "from everlasting to everlasting," Psal. ciii. 17. He may hide his face for a moment, though that is but according to our thinking, but with everlasting mercies will he gather us. The hills may be removed, and the mountains may depart, but God's covenant of peace shall not be removed, Isa. liv. 7, 10. God never repented himself of bestowing his best mercies.

8. God's mercy is so immeasurable, that to help us out of our miseries he that was God sustained them himself. It had been mercy to have helped us by speaking comfortably to us; more, to have helped us by the bounty of his hand; but to help us out of misery by bearing our miseries, by coming to man, by becoming man, by suffering so much pain, hunger, ignominy, griefs, wounds, nay, death for man! oh, immeasurable mercy! O my soul, acknowledge thine insufficiency either to conceive or requite it.

2. The mercy of God is not only full, but free, without desert on our parts. We deserve no healing from his mercy, unless by being sore and sick; no riches from mercy, unless by our poverty; no deliverance from mercy, unless by being captives; no pardon from mercy, unless by being guilty; no preservation from mercy, unless by being in danger; no mercy, unless by being miserable. God is not tied to one man more than another, Eph. i. 5, 6; he hath mercy on whom he will, Rom. ix. 18: he hath mercy on the beggar, as well as the king; on the barbarian, as well as the Grecian; the bond, as well as the free; the Jew, as well as the Gentile. Election is the election of grace, 2 Tim. i. 9; vocation is according to grace; faith is said to be given, Eph. ii. 8; justification is freely by God's grace, Rom. iii. 24; every good motion is of God's working, Phil. ii. 13; life eternal is God's gift, Rom. vi. 23; the putting away of every sin is for his own sake, Isa. xliii. 25. God is merciful because he will be so; his arguments of mercy are drawn from his own pleasure. What can our works deserve, that are not ours, but his working, 1 Cor. iv. 7; Rom. xi. 36; that are all due to him, if a thousand times more and better, Luke xvii. 10; that are all maimed and imperfect, that are all vitious and polluted, that are all unequal to the recompence? Rom. xi. 35; viii. 18.

This for the explication of the first benefit which the apostle requesteth for these Christians, "mercy." The observations follow.

Obs. 1. How unbeseeming a sin is pride in any that live upon mercy! Mercy, our highest happiness, calls loudest for a lowly heart. He that lives upon the alms of mercy must put on humility, the cloth of an almsman. Renounce thyself and thine own worthiness both in thy receiving and expecting blessings. (1.) In receiving them. If thou hast spiritual blessings, mercy found thee a bundle of miseries, a sinner by birth, a sinner in life, deserving to be a sufferer for both, Eph. ii. 1, 3; without grace, nay, against it; by thy birth, a poor outcast, in thy blood, as naked of grace as of clothes, Ezek. xvi. 22. The apostle therefore speaks of putting on the graces of the Spirit, Col. iii. 12: the spots upon these clothes are only thine; the garment itself was another's before it was thine. Thou art beholden to mercy for any endowment of mind or body; wisdom, estate, riches, honours, &c., Job i. 21; 1 Chron. xxii. 16; Gen. xxiv. 35; xxxiii. 5, 11. It is hard to be high in place, and low in our own esteem. Sacrifice not to thine own yarn or net; let mercy have the praise of all thou art and hast. Pride is the moth of mercy; nay, the wind that dries up the streams both of God's bounty and thy gratitude. That which by mercy was thine, by thy pride may become another's. He is truly great in his riches, that thinks not himself great by riches. The greater our receipts, the less room for pride, the greater cause of thankfulness. (2.) In expecting blessings, only have an eye to mercy. In desires of pardon for sin, acceptance of services, obtaining of heaven, renounce thine own worthiness, either in what thou art or dost.

Magnus dives est, et major divitiis suis, qui non ideo magnum se putat quia dives est. Aug.

How purely unprofitable to God is thy greatest goodness! it is nothing to him: he is neither the better for thy goodness, nor the worse for thy wickedness. Is it any benefit to the fountain, that thou drinkest of it; or to the light, that thou seest? How full of mixtures of sin are thy holiest services! in the sense whereof holy Augustine prayed, Regard, O Lord, in me not my work, but thine own. If thou regardest mine, thou damnest me; if thine own, thou crownest me: whatever good I have is from thee, and it is rather thine than mine. How full of pride is thy humility, thy faith of distrustfulness, thy zeal of lukewarmness, of self-seeking thy performances! What darkness is in thy light, how unrighteous thy righteousness! If God should contend with us we cannot answer for one of a thousand, Job ix. 2, 3. He that boasts of the perfection of holiness, wants its very beginning, Phil. iii. 13. That which appears beautiful in thine eyes, is foul in God's. The wisest counsel is, to cover over thyself and wind up thy soul in Christ's death, to set that between God and thy soul; to acknowledge his mercy thy only merit. Death is a stipend; life is a donative, a free gift, not a due debt. God crowns with mercy; but a swoln head is not fit to have that crown put upon it. Who can say, he hath cleansed his heart? We want a thousand times more grace than we have: though sin be cast down in regard of its regency, yet it is not cast out in regard of its inherency. Thy rectitude compared to thy rule is crookedness. It is not thy purity, but thy pardon, that must save thee. If there shall be judgment without mercy to those that showed no mercy, James ii. 13, then must it be with mercy even to those also which show mercy. It is mercy that must stand Onesiphorus in stead at that day, 2 Tim. i. 16. The crown of righteousness Paul speaks of, 2 Tim. iv. 8, is a crown of mercy too; the bestowing it is of justice, but the promising it was of mercy.

Ideo Deus meus, quia bonorum meorum non indiget: Omne bonum nostrum aut ipse est, aut ab ipso. Aug. de Doc. Ch. l. 5. c. 31.

Qui de perfectione se erigit, habere se bene vivendi nec initium indicat. Gr. Mo. l. 9. c. 1.
In sola Christi morte te totum contege; huic morti te involve; et si Deus te voluerit judicare, dic, Domine, mortem Domini mei objicio inter me et te. Ans. de art. Mor.
Meritum meum miseratio Domini. Bern. Serm. 61. in Cant.
Prece post justitiam indiget, ut quæ, succumbere discussa poterat, ex sola judicis pietate convalescat. Gr. Mor. l. 9. cap. 14.
Etsi ad opus virtutis excrevero, ad vitam non ex meritis, sed ex venia convalesco. Id. ib.
Sordet in districtione judicis, quod in æstimatione fulget operantis. Gr. Mor. l. 5. c. 7.

Obs. 2. The duty of contentment in our greatest wants, or smallest receipts. If one not engaged to us deny us a courtesy, we have no cause of discontentment: when God gives, it is free mercy; when he withholds, he uses his liberty. Thy supplies are without desert, and thy wants must be without discontent. Wonder not at the blessings thou dost not enjoy; wonder more at those thou dost. Thy condition is begging, and thy part is not choice. Repine not if thou canst not reach thy richest neighbour, who hast nothing to say against God, should the poorest overtake thee. Murmur not for what is lost, but be thankful for what is left. We must not control God in the disposing of his alms, as if he did not distribute with equality. We should bring our hearts to his hand: where he stays his bounty, there must we stint our desires.

Cum aspexeris quot te antecedant, cogita quot sequantur. Sen. Ep. 15.

Obs. 3. The impiety and folly of those that abuse mercy, that spurn against God's bowels. Sins against mercy are double-dyed. This is the provocation, to see God's works of love and care forty years, and yet to sin, Heb. iii. 8; this is to sin against the remedy: other sinners *may*, these who thus sin *must* die. These sin at a higher rate than others. These in sin cast not off God only, but even the very man; nay, are shamed by the beasts, Isa. i. 3. If to requite good for evil is our duty in reference to man, surely, to requite evil for good, and that to God, must needs be impiety. This sin renders inexcusable. God appeals to the very consciences of mercy-despisers, and offers themselves to judge of the righteousness of his proceedings in punishment, Isa. v. 3, 4; nay, the recollecting of abused mercy will be the most scalding ingredient in that fiery lake, when the flaming sufferer remembers, He that is now mocking at my calamity, once wept over my unkind soul; he who is now harder than flint and marble against me, was once a tender-hearted God toward me; he who now thunders in wrath against me, formerly sounded in his bowels for me: the way of mercy was once open and plain, but now the bridge of mercy is drawn, my possibilities are ended. I am now in a gulf of woe, that heretofore was unprofitably a gulf of mercy. How many kingdoms, nay worlds, would I now give for but one drop of that love, the sweet and swelling streams whereof I heretofore but paddled in! O Christian, sin not against mercy; if that be thine enemy, what shall justice be? when love itself shall be inexorable, who shall plead for thee? Let mercy make thee blush, that justice may not make thee bleed. Trifle not away the day of grace. The wine of mercy is to refresh the sorrowful with hope, not to intoxicate the sinner into presumption. If mercy cannot thaw thee, it will burn thee. O let the longsuffering of God be salvation, 2 Pet. iii. 15.

Obs. 4. Great is the heinousness of sin, that can provoke a God of much mercy, to express much severity. That drop of gall must needs be bitter, which can imbitter a sea of honey. How offensive is sin, that can provoke God, to whose ocean of pity the sea is but a drop! Ephraim (saith the prophet) provoked God to anger most bitterly, or, with bitternesses, Hos. xii. 14. God afflicts not willingly: he gives honey naturally, but stings not till provoked. Every sufferer coins his own calamities. There is no arrow of judgment which falls down upon us, but was first, in sinning, shot upwards by us; no shower of miseries that rains down, but was caused by the ascent of the vapours of sin; no print of calamity upon the earth, but sin was the stamp that made it. What a folly is it, in our sufferings to be impatient against God, and to be patient towards sin; to be angry with the medicine, and in love with the disease! Let us justify God in all our sufferings, and condemn ourselves. God commands, that if a man were found dead, the city that by measure was found to be nearest to the place where he was found, should offer up a sacrifice, Deut. xxi. 1—9. In all our deaths and woes, would we measure impartially, we should find sin nearest; let us sacrifice it.

Obs. 5. It should be our care to obtain the best and choicest of mercies. God hath mercies of all sorts: wicked men are easily put off with the meanest; their inquiry is, "Who will show us any good?" But, O Christian, let nothing please thee but the light of God's countenance: so receive from God, as that thou thyself mayst be received to God. Desire not gifts, but mercies from God; not pebbles, but pearls. Labour for that which God always gives in love. There may be angry smiles in God's face, and wrathful gifts in his hand; the best worldly gift may be given in anger. Luther, having a rich present sent him, professed with a holy boldness to God, that such things should not serve his turn. A favourite of the King of heaven rather desires his favour than his preferment. We are accustomed to say, when we are buying for the body, that the best is best cheap: and is the worst good enough for the soul? The body is a bold beggar, and thou givest it much; the soul is a modest beggar, asking but little, and thou givest it less. O desire from God that thy portion may not be in this life, Psal. xvii. 14; that what thou hast in the world, may be a pledge of better hereafter; that these things may not bewitch thee from, but admonish thee what is in Christ. The ground of Paul's thanksgiving was, that God had blessed the Ephesians with spiritual blessings in Christ, Eph. i. 3.

Obs. 6. How little should any that have this God of mercy for theirs be dismayed with any misery! Blessed are those tears which so merciful a hand wipes off; happy twigs, that are guided by so indulgent a Father! All his severest ways are mercy and truth to those in covenant, Psal. xxv. 10; if he smiles, it is in mercy; if he smites, it is in mercy: he wounds not to kill thee, but sin in thee. The wounds of mercy are better than the embraces of anger. If sickness, poverty, dishonour be in mercy, why dost thou shrink at them? Wrath in prosperity is dreadful, but mercy makes adversity comfortable. It is the anger of God which is the misery of every misery. Peter, at the first, was not willing that Christ should wash his feet; but when he saw Christ's merciful intent therein, feet, and hands, and head are all offered to be washed. A child of God, when he sees the steps of a Father, should be willing to bear the stripes of a child. God will not consume us, but only try us: he afflicts not for his pleasure, but for our profit, Heb. xii. 10. God visits with rods, yet not with wrath; he takes not away his loving-kindness, Psal. lxxxix. 33. Mercy makes the sufferings of God's people but notions. It would do one good to be in troubles, and enjoy God in them; to be sick, and lie in his bosom. God gives a thousand mercies to his people in every trouble, and for every trouble. He burdens us, but it is according to our strength: the strokes of his flail are proportioned to the hardness of the grain, Isa. xxviii. 27; and merciful shall be the end of all our miseries: there is no wilderness but shall end in Canaan; no water but shall be turned into wine; no lion's carcass but shall be a hive of honey, and produce a swarm of mercies. The time we spend in labouring that miseries may not come, would be spent more profitably in labouring to have them mixed with mercy, nay, turned into mercies when they come. What a life-recalling cordial is the apprehension of this mercy of God to a fainting soul under the pressure of sin! Mercy having provided a satisfaction, and accepted it; nay, which is more, it beseeches the sinner to believe and apply it. That fountain of mercy which is in God, having now found a conveyance for itself to the soul, even Jesus Christ, through whom such overflowing streams are communicated to us, as are able to drown the mountains of our sins, even as easily as the ocean can swallow up a pebble. O fainting soul, trust in this mercy. If the Lord takes pleasure in those that hope in his mercy, Psal. xxxiii. 18; cxlvii. 11, should not we take pleasure to hope in it? Mercy is the only thing in the world more large than sin, Exod. xxxiv. 7. It is easy to presume, but hard to lay hold upon mercy, Psal. lxxvii. 7. O beg, that since there is an infinite fulness in the gift, and a freeness in the Giver, there may be a forwardness in the receiver.

Obs. 7. It is our duty and dignity to imitate God in showing mercy; a grace frequently commanded and encouraged in the Scripture. Mercy we want, and mercy we must impart, 1 Pet. iii. 8; Matt. v. 45; Luke vi. 36. As long as our fellow members are pained, we must never be at ease, Col. iii. 12; Rom. xii. 15. When we suffer not from the enemies of Christ by persecution, we must suffer from the friends of Christ *Plus est aliquando compati, quam dare: nam qui exteriora largitur, rem extra se positam tribuit; qui compassionem, aliquid sui-ipsius dat. Gr. Mor. 20.*

by compassion. When two strings of an instrument are tuned one to the other, if the one be struck upon and stirred, the other will move and tremble also. The people of God should be so harmonious, that if one suffer and be struck, the other should be moved and sympathize. Holy men have ever been tender-hearted, grace not drying up, but diverting the streams of our affections, Jer. ix. 1; Luke xix. 41; 2 Cor. xi. 29. Christ was mercy covered over with flesh and blood; his words, his works, life, death, miracles, were all expressions of mercy, in teaching, feeding, healing, saving men: if there were any severity in his miracles, it was not toward man, but the swine and the barren fig-tree. Insensibleness of others' miseries is neither suitable to our condition as men, nor as Christians: according to the former, we are the same with others; according to the latter, grace hath made the difference. Mercy must begin at the heart, but must proceed further, even to the hand: they whose hands are shut, have their bowels shut also. We are not treasurers, but stewards of God's gifts.

Sic mens per compassionem doleat, ut larga manus affectum doloris ostendat. Greg.

Thou hast so much only as thou givest. The way to get that which we cannot part with, is by mercy to part with that which we cannot keep. Our good reacheth not to Christ's person, it must to his members. Jonathan is gone, but he hath left many poor lame Mephibosheths behind him. We must love Christ in his working-day clothes. We cannot carry these loads of riches to heaven; it is best to take bills of exchange from the poor saints, whereby we may receive there what we could not carry thither. Especially should our mercy extend itself to the souls of others: as soul miseries, so soul mercies, are the greatest. They who are spiritually miserable cannot pity themselves; though their words speak not to us, yet their woes do. We weep over a body from which the soul is departed; and can we look with tearless eyes upon a soul from which God is departed? If another be not afflicted for sin, grieve for him; if he be, grieve with him. If thou hast obtained mercy, thou dost not well (as said the lepers) to hold thy peace: mercy must never cease till its objects do; in heaven both shall, Luke xiv. 14; Gal. vi. 9.

Thus much for the first blessing which the apostle prays may be bestowed upon these Christians to whom he wrote, viz. "mercy."

The second follows, viz. "peace;" which we shall first explain, and then present you with some practical observations.

Peace is a word very comprehensive, and is ordinarily used to denote all kind of happiness, welfare, and prosperity. And, 1. I shall distribute it into several kinds. 2. Show the excellency of that here intended.

1. There is *pax temporis*, or external, among men.
2. *Pax pectoris*, or internal, in the heart.
3. *Pax æternitatis*, or eternal, in heaven. Or more distinctly thus:

1. There is a peace between man and man.
2. Between man and other creatures.
3. Between man and, or rather in man with, himself.
4. Between God and man.

1. Peace between man and man; and that is public or private.

(1.) Public; and that either political of the commonwealth, when the politic state is in tranquillity, and free from foreign and civil wars: There shall be peace in my days, 2 Kings xx. 19. "In the peace thereof ye shall have peace," Jer. xxix. 7. This is either lawful, and so a singular mercy; or unlawful, as when one people is at peace with another against the express will of God, as the Israelites with the Canaanites and Amalekites; or when they join in any sinful attempt, as did the Moabites and Ammonites against the Israelites. Or ecclesiastical, and of the church, when its public tranquillity and quiet state is not troubled within by schisms and heresies; or without, by persecuting and bloody tyrants. "Pray for the peace of Jerusalem," Psal. cxxii. 6. "The churches had rest," Acts ix. 31; and Acts iv. 32; 1 Cor. xiv. 33.

(2.) Private; and that either between the good and the good, or between the bad and the bad, or between the good and the bad. 1. Between the good and the good: "Love as brethren," 1 Pet. iii. 8; and, "Let brotherly love continue," Heb. xiii. 1; and, "The love ye have to all saints," Col. i. 4. 2. Between the bad and the bad. "Is it peace, Jehu?" 2 Kings ix. 22. And that either lawfully, for their own preservation; or wickedly, against the people of God; or to strengthen one another in some sinful attempt, and to that end, joining hand in hand. 3. Between the good and the bad; which is either lawful, as Abraham's with Abimelech; and commanded, Render to no man evil for evil; but, if it be possible, have peace with all men, Rom. xii. 17, 18. So Psal. cxx. 7, "I am for peace." And sometimes caused by a work from God upon the hearts of wicked men, as in the case of Daniel, chap. i. 9, and in Esau's love to Jacob; according to that of Solomon, "The Lord will make his enemies at peace with him," &c., Prov. xvi. 7. Or unlawful, when against the mind of God the godly make leagues with them, or agree in any way of sin.

2. There is a peace between man (the faithful I mean) and other creatures. The good angels are at peace with, and are ministering spirits to them, Heb. i. 14. As Job v. 23, "Thou shalt be in league with the stones of the field, and the beasts of the earth shall be at peace with thee;" and Hos. ii. 18, "I will make a covenant for them with the beasts of the field, and with the fowls of heaven, and with the creeping things of the earth." The meaning is, There shall be such a work of God upon the beasts and fowls, &c., for the good of the church, as if God had bound them to do them good by way of covenant; so that although the beasts, the fowls, the stones, &c. may annoy them, nay, kill them, the true safety of the church shall not be hindered by them; yea, all things shall work together for their good: neither nakedness, nor sword, nor death, nor any of these things shall separate them from the love of God in Christ; and if God sees it for their good, all the creatures in the world shall be so far from hurting the godly, that they shall all agree to advance their temporal good and welfare. There is mention, Jer. xxxiii. 20, of God's "covenant of the day, and of the night;" that is, the establishment of God's decree upon the day and the night, whereby they come to be in such and such a way from the creation to the end of the world.

Hujus fœderis vigore, mala hujus vitæ sic lædunt pios, ut non noceant, non perdant, sed prosint. Ubi notandum est, vocabulum fœderis accipi μεταληπτικῶς, et per similitudinem effectus. Riv. in Hos. ii. 18.

3. There is a peace in man with himself; and that is either false, or sound. False peace is, when sinners, thinking themselves free from the fear of dangers, falsely promise safety to themselves: "When they shall say, Peace and safety," &c., 1 Thess. v. 3. Sound peace in man with himself is twofold: (1.) Of assurance, when sanctified conscience ceaseth to accuse and condemn us, speaking comfortably in us and for us before God, 1 John iii. 21. This sweet quietness and tranquillity of conscience is the immediate fruit of our atonement with God; "that peace of God which passeth all understanding." Phil.

iv. 7, and in which the apostle places the kingdom of God, Rom. xiv. 17; the peace that Hezekiah was not destitute of, when he said, "Remember now, O Lord, I beseech thee, how I have walked before thee in truth," &c., Isa. xxxviii. 3. This peace sweetens every condition, is as music within, when the rain and storms fall upon the house; a friend, as Ruth to Naomi, that will go along with us in every distress: though we change our place, our garments, our conditions, our companies, yet our enemies cannot take this from us; it is "a continual feast," Prov. xv. 15. This peace preserves our hearts and minds (Phil. iv. 7) in all afflictions, and puts into us a holy security and neglectiveness of all dangers, Psal. iv. 8. (2.) Of subordination, when the will, affections, and inclinations of a man submit themselves to the mind savingly enlightened by and subjugated to God; which, although it be not perfect, by reason of that repugnant law in our members, yet it is true and progressive, the imperfection of it occasionally being an incentive to godliness, making us more fervent in prayer, humble, broken-hearted, and receptive of that peace we long for.

4. There is a peace with God, both in this life and in the next.

(1.) In this life; and so it is twofold. 1. A peace of reconciliation; and, 2. Of contentment. 1. Of reconciliation, whereby God and Christ is at one with man. "The chastisement of our peace was upon Christ:" the wrath deserved by us for our sins Christ sustained, and satisfied Divine justice fully; so that now God, not requiring satisfaction twice for the same offences, is at peace with us, Isa. liii. 5; John i. 29. This, the foundation of all the former and following kinds of good peace, is purchased by Christ the Prince of peace, Isa. ix. 6, and our peace, Eph. ii. 14; and proclaimed in the preaching of the gospel, the glad tidings of peace, Rom. x. 15, by the ministers of it, the ambassadors of peace, 2 Cor. v. 20; and accepted by faith, whereby we therefore enjoy and have peace with God, Rom. v. 1. 2. Of contentment, or holy submission, by which a man is peaceable, and not murmuring or impatient against God, but quietly accepting whatsoever is his will; the way indeed to live a truly quiet life, and (as one says well) ever to have our will; the waves of unquietness being ever raised by the wind of pride and unsubmissiveness, Phil. iv. 11.

(2.) Peace with God in the next life, or peace eternal, is the perfect rest which the saints shall enjoy in heaven; called "life and peace," Rom. viii. 6, and the "rest that remaineth for the people of God;" their resting from their labours, both inward and outward; not only from hurt, but from danger by, nay, from the presence of any thing that ever did molest them.

The apostle in this salutation, by peace, intends principally, peace with ourselves; that "peace of God which passeth all understanding," so often commended; which includes peace with men, commanded, and peace with the other creatures, promised to accompany it, and peace with God, presupposed as its cause and original.

2. This sanctified tranquillity and quietness of conscience (a singular blessing, often requested by the apostles for the faithful to whom they wrote) is of rare excellency, Rom. i. 7; 1 Cor. i. 3; Col. i. 2; 2 Pet. i. 2.

(1.) For its author and original. It is from God, he being called the God of peace, 1 Thess. v. 23; 2 Cor. xiii. 11, and it the peace of God, Col. iii. 15; Phil. iv. 7. He is the author of external peace in church and commonwealth; the peace of Jerusalem must be begged of him; he maketh wars to cease, and all stirs to be hushed; he maketh peace between us and the creatures, making a covenant for us with them: he is the author of eternal peace; for eternal life is the gift of God. But after a special manner is he the God of internal peace, the peace of conscience, at which St. Jude aims: for, 1. He sent his Son, [1.] To merit it for us, when we lay in the horror of an accusing conscience; who is therefore called in himself, the Prince of peace, Isa. ix. 6; and in respect of us, our peace, Eph. ii. 14: and the peace we speak of is said to be his peace, John xiv. 27, he making peace by slaying hatred on the cross, Eph. ii. 16, by his perfect obedience abolishing whatsoever God might hate in us. [2.] He sent his Son to preach and publish this peace, and to invite men to it, and that, first, in his own person. "The Spirit of the Lord is upon me, to preach glad tidings," &c., Isa. lxi. 1; Luke iv. 18. Secondly, in his ministers. "Christ came and preached peace to you who were afar off," Eph. ii. 17; he thus preaching it to the world's end. As he sent his Son to merit and preach this peace; so, 2. He sent his Spirit to apply and seal this peace in the hearts of the elect; it being called a fruit of the Spirit, Gal. v. 22; this Spirit enabling us to cry for this peace, Gal. iv. 6, and working faith in our hearts, whereby we have peace with God, Rom. v. 1, and boldness and access to the throne of grace, Eph. iii. 12, creating the fruit of the lips to be peace, Isa. lvii. 19. Nothing that the world either is or has, nay, neither men nor angels, can give peace; they may wish and publish it, God only gives it. Some say there is a disease which only the king can heal; I am sure a broken heart, a wounded conscience, can be healed only by the Prince of peace.

(2.) The excellency of this peace appears in the subject of it; and that both in respect of the parties that have it, and of the part of each of those parties in which it resides.

1. The parties that enjoy it are only the faithful. [1.] It is only promised to them, the true children of the church: "Great shall be the peace of thy children," Isa. liv. 13. "The Lord will bless his people with peace," Psal. xxix. 11. "The meek shall delight themselves in the abundance of peace," Psal. xxxvii. 11. "He will speak peace to his people," Psal. lxxxv. 8. "Lord; thou wilt ordain peace for us," Isa. xxvi. 12. "The end of that," the upright, "man is peace," Psal. xxxvii. 37. "He shall enter into peace," Isa. lvii. 2. God will reveal unto such abundance of peace, Jer. xxxiii. 6.

[2.] It is only reported of the faithful, that they have peace; they are the sons of peace, Luke x. 6. The justified only have peace with God, Rom. v. 1. "There is no peace to the wicked," Isa. lvii. 21. "The way of peace they know not," Isa. lix. 3. "Great peace have they which love the law," Psal. cxix. 165.

[3.] Peace is only wished and requested for the faithful. For others, either only as they were with an eye of charity looked upon as faithful; or as in those requests the terms upon which they should obtain this peace are also included; namely, the disturbing of their own unsound peace, the accepting of him that deserves the true peace, and the walking in the ways of holiness. But peace from God is never desired for men to continue in a state of war against God, Rom. i. 7; 1 Cor. i. 3; Gal. i. 3; Phil. i. 2; Col. i. 2, &c.; Gal. vi. 16; 2 Thess. i. 2.

[4.] The faithful only have taken the right course to obtain peace. They alone are freed from God's wrath, Rom. v. 9, 10, more dreadful than the roaring of a lion, or the wrath of all the kings of the world, it destroying the body and soul in hell: they only have pardon of sin, Rom. v. 1. The other, like guilty malefactors, are in an hourly expectation of the worst of deaths, through the fear of which they die before they die, Heb. ii. 15; Job xv. 20, 21. The faithful only have Christ, who is our peace, and the Prince of peace; the Spirit of God, of which peace is a fruit and effect, Gal. v. 22: they alone rejoice in hope, Eph. ii. 12; Rom. xii. 12, and live in expectation of a crown incorruptible, an everlasting kingdom; others live a hopeless, heartless life.

2. The part of these parties in which this peace resides, is the heart and conscience. The peace of God rules in the heart, Col. iii. 15. "Your heart shall rejoice," John xvi. 22; and, "Thou hast put gladness into my heart," Psal. iv. 7; and, "The peace of God shall preserve your heart," Phil. iv. 7; in which respect, (1.) It is a sustaining, strengthening, reviving peace. So long as the heart is kept safe, a man falls not, faints not; when the heart is relieved with a cordial, a fainting man revives: now the peace of God keeps up the heart; it brings aid and relief to it in all dangers, when sin and Satan, temptation and persecution, lay siege to it; it brings strong consolation, Heb. vi. 18. It is a banner over us in war, a cordial, an antidote against all poison; it makes Paul and Silas sing in prison, Acts xvi. 25, Paul ready to die for the name of the Lord Jesus, Acts xxi. 13, the faithful to be comforted in all tribulation, 2 Cor. i. 3, 4, and consolation to abound as sufferings abound, Rom. v. 3, 5; Heb. x. 34; it makes the faithful in a cold winter of persecution to be warmest within, causing a martyr to go as merrily to a stake, as another to a feast. (2.) The seat of this peace, the heart, Prov. xiv. 10, denotes, as our sustentation by it, so the soundness, truth, and reality of it: it is not *in cortice*, but *in corde*; in the heart, not in the habit; in the conscience, not in the looks; it is in the breast, not in the brow; not suffering a man to be like some prisons, beautiful without, but full of horror, blackness, chains, and dungeons within. It is a peace not residing in the hall of the senses, but in the closet of the heart. A saint's peace is a silent calmness, an unseen quietness; meat, of which those without know not; like the windows of Solomon's temple, narrow without, broad within; the worst, the unbeautiful, the black side of his cloud is seen, when the bright is hidden.

φρουρήσει τὰς καρδίας ὑμῶν. Phil. iv. 7.

(3.) The seat of this peace, the heart, implies its seriousness, weightiness, greatness, that the ground of it is not slight and toyish, but some great matter; not lightly pleasing the fancy, and superficially bedewing the senses, but like a ground-shower, soaking even to the heart-root. The peace of a saint is not like the mirth of a child, caused more by a doll or a toy, than by a conveyance of a thousand pounds a year; or like our laughter which is more at a jest, than at the finding of a bag of gold of ten thousand pounds. No, his peace is not idle, frothy, and ludicrous merriment, but deep, and affecting the heart with apprehensiveness of an interest in the great things of eternity; a "peace that passeth understanding." Light, either griefs or contentments, are easily expressed; not so those which are deep and weighty: these are joys unspeakable, glorious, and superabundant, 1 Pet. i. 8; 2 Cor. vii. 4. (4.) The seat denotes the safety of this peace. The heart is too deep for a man to reach: a saint's peace is laid up in a cabinet that man cannot open; men may break into his house, but not into his heart: "Your joy," saith Christ, "no man taketh from you," John xvi. 22. The power of adversaries is but skin-deep. There is a threefold impotency of man in reference to a Christian's peace: 1. Man cannot give this peace. 2. He cannot hinder it from entering. 3. He cannot remove it, or hinder it from abiding. It continues like a fountain in the hottest summer, and is warmest in the coldest winter of affliction; like a candle which is not overwhelmed, or quenched in the dismal darkness of the night, but is made thereby to give the clearer light. David in greatest straits comforted himself in God. The faithful glory in tribulation, James i. 2; 2 Cor. vii. 4; Rom. v. 3; they are commanded to rejoice evermore, Phil. iv. 4; 1 Thess. v. 16; as the sufferings of Christ abound in them, so their consolations abound by Christ. The faithful have oft drawn matter of joy from their sufferings; they "yield the peaceable fruit of righteousness," Heb. xii. 11. A sick man may rejoice at the coming of the surgeon, though he knows he will put him to pain. I know (saith the apostle) that this shall turn to my salvation, Phil. i. 19. The light affliction that lasteth but for a moment, procureth "a far more exceeding and eternal weight of glory," 2 Cor. iv. 17. If we suffer for Christ, we shall also reign with him, 2 Tim. ii. 12. None can separate us from Christ, Rom. vii. 38, 39, and therefore not from peace: the Spirit of peace by us may for a time be sinned away, but he cannot by enemies be persecuted away. The sun may as easily be blown out with bellows, as true peace be driven away by sufferings. (5.) The seat of this peace, the heart, imports the spiritualness and sublimity of it. It is not sensual, earthly, and drossy; the heart is no more relieved with worldly comforts, than are the stomach, bags, and barns filled with grace and holiness. What is it to the soul, that thou hast goods laid up for many years? The rarest delicacies of the earth are not such food as the soul loves; spiritual blessings of communion with God, enjoying Christ, a view of our names as written in heaven, alone pacify the heart. This peace is upheld by the promises of God, not of men; by Scripture, not politic props. The Father of spirits is only the physician of spirits. Thus the jewel of peace is rare, obtained but by a few, the faithful; and regarded, laid up in the casket of the heart; there is the subject of it.

Illud verum et solum est gaudium, quod non de terra, sed de Cœlo est; quod non de creatura, sed de Creatore accipitur. Bern. Ep. 114.

3. The excellency of this peace appears in its effects. (1.) It most disturbs sin, when it quiets the soul most. A pacified conscience is pure: the soul at the same time tastes and fears the goodness of God, Hos. iii. 5: the sun of mercy thaws the heart into tears for sin. Peace with God increases fear of transgression, as it diminishes fear of damnation, making us who formerly feared because we sinned, now to fear lest we should sin. If mercy be apprehended, sin will be hated: spiritual joy causes godly grief. As God is wont to speak peace to the soul that truly mourns for sin; so the soul desires most to mourn for sin, when God speaks peace to it. The pardoned traitor, if he have any ingenuousness, most grieves for offending a gracious prince. Godly peace at the same time banishes slavish horror, and causes filial fear. Besides, the more quietness we apprehend in enjoying God, the more are we displeased with that trouble-heart sin.

(2.) Another effect of this peace is activeness and stirring in holy performances. When the faithful are most quiet, they should be least idle: when David had rest from his enemies, he then was careful how to build God a house: when the soul sees it is redeemed from the hands of his enemies, it is most engaged to serve the Redeemer in holiness and righteousness, Luke i. 74, 75. This peace is as oil

Tu illum judicas gaudere qui ridet? animus debet esse alacer. Res severa est verum gaudium, cæteræ hilaritates leves sunt; frontem remittunt, pectus non implent. Sen. Ep. 23. Ego neminem posse scire arbitror, quid sit, nisi acceperit. Bern. in Cant. Melius impressum quam expressum innotescit. In his non capit intelligentia nisi quantum attingit experientia. Id. ibid.

to the wheels, to make a Christian run the ways of God's commandments. The warmth of the spring draws out the sap of trees into a sprouting greenness, and the peace of God refreshes the soul into a flourishing obedience. Jonathan having tasted honey, his eyes were enlightened; and the soul which has tasted the sweetness of inward peace, is holily enlarged. Some who profess they enjoy an ocean of peace, express not a drop of obedience: suppose their profession true, they defraud God; but it being false, they delude themselves. The joy of God's people is a joy in harvest; as it is large, so it is laborious: they are joyful in the house of prayer, Isa. lvi. 7.

(3.) This inward peace from God inclines the heart to peaceableness toward man. A quiet conscience never produced an unquiet conversation: the nearer lines come to the centre, the nearer they are one to another; the peaceable approaches of God to us, will not consist with a proud distance between us and others, 1 Pet. iii. 8, 9. This peace of God makes those who have offered wrong to others, willing to make satisfaction; and those who have suffered wrong from others, ready to afford remission. *Pax ista reddit offendentes ad satisfaciendum humiles, et offensos ad remittendum faciles. Dau. in Col. iii. 15.* The equity of the former stands thus: If the great God speaks peace to man when offended by him, should not poor man speak peace to man when offending of him? The equity of the latter thus: If God be pacified toward man upon his free grace, should not man be pacified toward man, it being a commanded duty? and if God by his peace have sealed to man an acquittance from a debt of ten thousand talents, should not man by his peace acquit man from the debt of a hundred pence? Matt. xviii. 21—35. In a word, this peace from God makes us peaceable toward all; it keeps us from envying the rich, from oppressing the poor; it renders us obedient to superiors, gentle to equals, humble to inferiors; it preserves from sedition in the commonwealth, from schism in the church; it cools, it calms, it rules in heart and life.

(4.) Peace from God makes us commiserate those who are under his wrath. A pacified soul loves to impart its comforts, and is most ready to give a receipt of what eased it; it labours to comfort those that are in trouble, by the comfort wherewith it is comforted, 2 Cor. i. 4. The favourites of the King of heaven envy not his bestowing favour also upon others; they pity both those who please themselves with an unsound peace, and also those who are pained with the true wounds of conscience.

(5.) This peace from God makes us contented and quiet in every affliction. Since the Lord hath spoken peace in the first, we shall take it well, whatsoever he speaks in the next place: whatever God does peaceably, the soul bears it patiently. The great question of a godly heart, when any trouble comes, is that of the elders of Bethlehem to Samuel, "Comest thou peaceably?" and if it answers, "Peaceably," is entertained with welcome. Lord, thou hast pardoned my sin, saith a pacified soul, and now do what thou pleasest with me. Men destitute of this peace are like the leaves of a tree, or a sea, calm for the present, moved and tossed with every wind of trouble; their peace is nothing else but unpunished wickedness.

And this for the explication of the second blessing which the apostle requests for these Christians, viz. "peace."

The observations to be drawn from it follow.

Obs. 1. They who are strangers to God in Christ, are strangers to true peace. True peace comes from enjoying the true God. A quiet conscience, and an angry God, are inconsistent; a truth deducible as from the preceding exposition of peace, so even from the apostle's very order in requesting peace. First he prays for mercy, then for peace. If the Lord do not help us, how shall we be helped to this blessing? "out of the barn-floor, or the wine-press?" 2 Kings vi. 27. The garments that we wear must receive heat from the body, before they can return any warmth again to it; and there must be matter of peace within, ere any peace can accrue from any thing without. If God be against us, who can be for us? if he disquiet us, what can quiet us? if he remain unpacified, the conscience will do so, notwithstanding all other by-endeavours. A wicked man's peace is not peace, but at the best only a truce with God. The forbearance of God to strike is like a man's, who thereby fetcheth his blow with the greater force and advantage; or like the intervals of a quartan, the distemper whereof remaining, the fits are indeed for two days intermitted, but return with the greater violence. A wicked man's conscience is not pacified, but benumbed; and the wrath of God not a dead, but a sleeping lion. A sinner's peace is unsound and seeming, in the face, not in the heart; a superficial sprinkling, not a ground-shower: he having in laughter his heart sad, may truly in it say with Sarah, I laughed not; he being in his rejoicing, as well as in his mourning, a hypocrite. Ask not the countenance, but the conscience of a sinner, whether he rejoices. The guilt of his sin is an unseen sore, a hidden scourge. His peace relieves him not; it is no preservative to his heart in persecution or distress; it leaves him, like Absalom's mule, when he hangs in any woe, and stands most in need thereof. His peace stands only in the avoiding of troubles, not in the sweet enjoying of God in his troubles; it is as uncertain as a dream, or as the crackling of thorns under a pot, Job xx. 5, 7; Eccl. vii. 6. His days of mourning will shortly come. Deluded he is with a groundless conceit of vain hopes; he is like a child in a siege, not apprehensive of his danger, but busy at sport, while the parents are at the breach, and the city ready to be sacked: he is secure, but not safe. *Vides convivium, lætitiam: interroga conscientiam. Amb. Off. l. 1. cap. 12. Evasisse putas quos diri conscia facti mens habet attonitos et surdo verbere cædit, occultum quatiente intus torture flagellum.*

Obs. 2. It is a mistake to think there is no peace to be found in the good ways of God. True peace is a fruit of God's Spirit, Gal. v. 22, and a branch of Christ's kingdom, Rom. xiv. 17. Godliness does not quell, but qualify mirth, not consume, but correct it; it deprives not of the use of nor comfort in any lawful delights, being procured by Christ, and bestowed by God as fruits of love. As for sinful and inordinate delights, which have no more pleasure in them than is found in the scratching of some unsound part when it itches, a saint being now healed of his disease, it is no pain for him to part with them. *Isaacum, i. e. gaudium jugulandum tibi formidas? securus esto; non Isaac, sed Aries mactabitur; non peribit tibi lætitia, sed contumacia, cujus utique cornua vepribus hærent, et sine punctionibus anxietatis esse non potest. Bern.* If holy men want peace, it is because they, or others, or both, are not more holy; nor are they sad because they are now holy, but because they were no sooner so. Their greedy desire of more holiness, often hinders them from taking notice of what already they have. They judge not aright of their present state; they have a pardon signed and sealed, but haply they cannot read it, because some sin has blotted it, or Satan casts some mist before their eyes. *Vid. Gataker's Just Man's Joy.* If the holiest will sport with, they must expect to smart for sin; Satan, who was their tempter, will soon prove their torturer. And in mercy doth God correct a wandering child home, when in wrath he suffereth a vagabond to take his course; and the tears of the godly for sinning are full of peace, they are a shower mixed with a sunshine; and more delight is there in godly grief than in sinful pleasures, in mourning with Christ than in sporting with Satan. Or it may be, sorrowing saints are but newly entered into the ways of God. Millstones, though they are hewed fit either to other, yet they grind not well till they have wrought some time together. Apparel, though made fit, is not so easy at the first putting on, as when it hath been worn a while. Christ's yoke seems heavy at first putting it on us, but it becomes easy and delightful when we have borne it a while, Matt. xi. 30. Nor is the peace of a saint to be estimated by its not appearing; his peace is inward, and often makes but little show in the face. The wealthy merchant cries not his rich wares, worth many thousands, about the street, when the poor, who carry toys, proclaim them in every corner of the city. The godly have their souls fraught with inward joys, though their looks outwardly show them not, while the hypocrite boldly voiceth up his supposed happiness: as the glory, so the joy of a saint is most within. In a word, this life is the time of obscurity to a saint's happiness; it is in some sort a winter with him, while it is a summer with the wicked: now the lofty oak in winter seems dead, while the dunghill grass is fresh and green; but when summer comes, the oak is flourishing, and the grass is withered, or made hay of, Job xvi. 22. The happiness of the people of God is hidden in their root, in this winter of affliction and desertion: they are now the sons of God, but it doth not yet appear what they shall be, 1 John iii. 2: their life is hid with Christ; but when Christ, who is their life, shall appear, then shall they appear also with him in glory, Col. iii. 3, 4. But then at the approach of this Sun shall that *fœnea fœlicitas*, as Augustine calls it, that grass-like happiness of wicked men, consume and wither.

Grave dum tollis, suave dum tuleris. Greg. in Ezek. l. 2. c. 7.

Gramen hieme virescit, æstate arescit: arbor (arescente gramine) virescit. Aug in Psal. 36.

Obs. 3. How careful should the people of God be to preserve their peace! Shall a blessing so excellent in its original, nature, use, and so earnestly desired by this and all the other apostles for the faithful, be by them neglected? O forfeit not, disturb not this happy peace.

(1.) Preserve in thee a fear of God. As sin gets in, peace goes out: nor is it the being, but the allowing of it in us that makes the soul unquiet. No sin shall destroy peace in us, but that which finds peace from us. The tares of dissension between God and us are only sown by the enemy sin. This was the instrument which broke the bones, and wounded the conscience, of David and Peter; this is the mint of a saint's misery, the source of his sorrows. Every sin has a bitter farewell: sin is nothing else but sorrow in the seed. Whenever thou art tempted, before thou consentest, take up and weigh thy sin in thy meditations, as a porter doth his burden before he agrees to carry it, and ask thy soul whether thou art able to go through with thy burden. (2.) Delight in the ordinances. These are the food of peace: "They shall be joyful in my house of prayer," Isa. lvi. 7. Prayer is fitly called the leech of cares; it is a breathing out the heats of inward grief, and a breathing in the cooling delights of God's Spirit. The gospel has glad tidings in its very name. A promise spread with the blood of Christ is the only plaster for a wounded conscience. The directions of the word are the ways of peace: Great peace have they that love the law, and "walk according to that rule," Gal. vi. 16. (3.) Be sincere and upright in thy services. "The end of the upright man is peace," Psal. xxxvii. 37. Sincerity and walking before God with an upright heart, darted a beam of peace into Hezekiah's shower of tears, Isa. xxxviii. 3. God puts not the oil of peace into a cracked vial. Heart peace is a companion only of heart purity. (4.) Love not the world; for it is enmity with God. The sunshine of earthly enjoyments puts out the fire of spiritual peace: the thorns of worldly cares make the peace of many a saint to go but with a scratched face. They who have suffered with joy the spoiling, have suffered sorrow for the loving of their goods: when men sweat in outward employments, their peace is coldest inwardly.

Obs. 4. Holiness makes no man unpeaceable and turbulent. The more God quiets us, the less shall we sinfully discontent men. The world condemns the godly as authors of dissension; but the true reason why they are accounted unpeaceable by the world, is, because they will not lose their peace with God: to find trouble in the world is their portion, but to cause trouble in the world is not their property. They are wont indeed to disquiet men's lusts; but are wicked men and sin so near, that the one cannot be distinguished from the other? The will of a saint is for peace, but it is necessity that makes him contend. Peace rules in his heart, Col. iii. 15; it doth βραβεύειν, it sits as the judge or umpire was wont to do in the public games of wrestling or running, who ruled and ordered the runners or wrestlers, deciding their controversies, and giving rewards to the conquerors: so this peace of God, when the troublesome affections of anger, hatred, and revenge arise in our hearts, appeases strifes, ends controversies, and renders us peaceable. As for wicked men, who seem sometimes to be very peaceable among themselves in sin, they must know that agreement against God is not peace, but conspiracy, and such a rotten peace makes way for a real war, both with others and within themselves.

Apostolus innuit hoc esse hujus virtutis officium ut agat brabeutem sive agonothetam inter cæteros affectus ; nam βραβεύειν id significat. Cum igitur insurgunt in cordibus nostris turbidi affectus iræ, odii, vindictæ, hæc pax Dei debet suum officium facere ; id est, instar agonothetæ, lites dirimere, tumultuantes affectus compescere, et omnia ad pacem deducere. Davenant in Col.

Obs. 5. It is most suitable to a minister's function to further and pray for the peace of others. As they are Christians, they are called to peace, Col. iii. 15; and as ministers, they are called to be ambassadors of peace, 2 Cor. v. 20. The bodily peace of others should be prayed for by them, James v. 14. Brotherly peace should they promote among their people. An unpeaceable people among themselves, will be an unprofitable people under him, James iii. 16. Ministers should endeavour the civil peace, put people "in mind to be subject to principalities and powers," Tit. iii. 1, and to take heed of treason and rebellion. To revile them for this is to be angry with the fifth commandment. But especially should ministers labour to bring people into peace with God, and to pray them to "be reconciled to God," 2 Cor. v. 20; and by ministerial directions to help them to attain peace of conscience within themselves. Confident I am, that while men's lusts speak ministers contentious, their consciences speak them peaceable.

The third and last blessing desired by this apostle for these Christians is "love."

For the expository part, I shall, 1. Specify the several kinds of love, principally that at which the apostle seems most to aim. 2. Set down the excellent properties of this kind of love which make it so desirable.

Ἀγάπη dicitur vel ab ἄγαν παρεῖν, vel ab ἄγειν κατὰ πᾶν, i. e. seipsum toto animo in rem dilectam, vel ab ἄγειν et παύεσθαι, quod est, valde in re amata acquiescere. Ita ἀγάπη significat vehementem affectum, ardentemque amorem, quo quis alicui sese intime adjungit, et in eo totus quiescit ; unde et pater Cœlestis de Filio suo, Hic est (inquit) filius meus ἀγάπητος, et mox, quasi etymologiam subdens, in quo mihi complaceo. Zanc. de Na. Dei. l.

4. c. 3. Amicitia est quasi habitus. Amor autem et dilectio significant actum vel passionem. Charitas autem utroque modo accipi potest; differenter tamen significatur actus per ista tria : nam amor est aliquid communius inter ea ; omnis enim amor dilectio est vel charitas, sed non e converso. Addit dilectio super amorem, electionem præcedentem; unde dilectio est in sola voluntate rationalis creaturæ, charitas autem ultra amorem addit perfectionem amoris in quantum illud quod amatur, carum, i. e. magni pretii æstimatur. Tho. 1. 2. qu. 16. Art. 3.

Amor aliarum rerum est, charitas inter solos homines, dilectio ad Deum spectat: diligimus Deum; charos habemus parentes, liberos, &c., amamus omnes. Aret. in Probl.

Not to stay upon the consideration of the word ἀγάπη, love, or of its agreement with those other expressions ordinarily used to set forth the same thing; as charity, friendship, &c. This love, in the general, being that inclination or tendency of any thing to the good beloved, or that principle whereby one joins himself to and rests in an object, is of sundry sorts.

Not to speak of those which are either far from, or contrary to, the scope of the apostle; as of natural love, which is that quality in any thing following its form, by which it tends to and rests in what is agreeable to it. Nor of animal love, whereby the sensitive appetite in men or beasts tends to its good, and rests in it; nor of love merely rational, or intellectual, whereby the will freely embraces any object presented to it by the understanding; nor of angelical love; nor of that love which God has towards himself, as the chief good.

There are three sorts of love, any of which may be desired from God as a blessing; namely, a love of, 1. God to man. 2. Man to God. 3. Man to man, himself, or others.

Since the apostle had desired that these Christians might receive mercy from God, and that every particular believer might have peace in himself, I conceive that he seems now in the last place to pray, that they might again both return love to God, and render it also to one another.

1. There is a love of God to man, though without passion, sympathy, or any imperfection or weakness; these being attributed to him only to relieve the weakness either of our faith or apprehensions. And this love is,

(1.) Considered as a love of desire; as love desires to be carried to the union of the thing beloved. This desire of union with man God shows many ways; as, 1. By being near unto, nay, present with him, by his universal care and providence; he being "not far from every one of us: for in him we live," &c., Acts xvii. 27, 28. 2. By assuming the nature of man into a personal conjunction with himself in the Mediator, Christ. 3. By conversing with man by signs of his presence, extraordinary visions, dreams, oracles, inspiration; and ordinarily by his holy ordinances, wherewith his people, as it were, abide with him in his house. 4. By sending his Holy Spirit to dwell in man, and bestowing upon man the Divine nature. 5. By taking man into an eternal habitation in heaven, where he shall be ever in his glorious presence, Psal. xvi. 11.

(2.) There is a love of God to man, considered as a love of benevolence, or of good-will, or of willingness to do good to the thing beloved: what else was his eternal purpose to have mercy upon his people, and of saving them, but, as it is expressed concerning Jacob, this loving them? Rom. ix. 13. And to whom can a will of doing good so properly agree, as to Him whose will is goodness itself?

(3.) There is a love of God to man, considered as a love of beneficence, bounty, or actual doing good to the thing beloved. Thus he bestows the effects of his love, both for this life, and for that which is to come. And the beneficence of God is called love; "Behold what manner of love the Father hath bestowed upon us, that we should be called the sons of God," 1 John iii. 1. And John iii. 16, "God so loved the world, that he gave," &c. By this love of beneficence he bestows the good things of nature, grace, and glory. God does good to every creature, hating, though the iniquity of any one, yet the nature of none; for the being of every creature is good, Gen. i. 31, and God has adorned it with many excellent qualities. According to these loves of benevolence and beneficence, God loves not his creatures equally, but some more than others; inasmuch as he wills to bestow, and also actually bestows, greater blessings upon some than upon others. He makes and preserves all creatures, but his love is more especially afforded to mankind; he styles himself from his love to man, Tit. iii. 4, and not from his love to angels, or any other creature. He is called φιλάνθρωπος, a lover of man, but never φιλάγγελος, or φιλόκτιστος, a friend of angels or creatures without man. His love is yet more peculiarly extended to man in creating him after his own image, Gen. i. 27, and in giving him lordship over the creatures, Psal. viii. 5; in giving his Son to take upon him man's nature, Heb. ii. 16, and exalt it above heavens (Matt. xxviii. 18) and angels, to die for sinning, dying man; offering him to man in the dispensation of the gospel with wooing and beseechings. And yet of men he loves some more especially and peculiarly than others; namely, those whom he loves with an electing, calling, redeeming, justifying, glorifying love. God loves all creatures, and among them the rational, and among them the members of his Son, and much more the Son himself.

Omnia diligit Deus quæ fecit, et inter ea, magis creaturas rationales; et de illis, eas amplius quæ sunt membra unigeniti, et multo magis ipsum unigenitum. Aug. 1. 9. in Joh.

(4.) There is a love of God to man, considered as a love of complacency, and delight in the thing beloved. He is pleased through his Son with his servants; and he is much delighted with his own image wheresoever he finds it. He is pleased with the persons and performances of his people : " He hath made us accepted in the Beloved." "The Lord taketh pleasure in them that fear him," Psal. cxlvii. 11. They reflecting his excellencies, and showing forth his virtues; he rejoicing over them with joy, and resting in his love, Zeph. iii. 17: accounting a believer amiable; his soul, a lesser heaven ; his prayers, melody; his sighs, incense; his stammerings, eloquence; his desires, performances.

2. There is a love of man to God; which is, when the soul is moved, drawn, and called out to desire the participation of his presence; yielding up and conforming itself to his will, and quietly resting in the enjoyment of him. This love is considerable in its several kinds.

(1.) It is *amor concupiscentiæ*, a love of desire to enjoy him for ours as the source of all our happiness. The soul loves God, under the apprehension of the greatest good, and therefore puts forth itself in strongest desires toward him. This love is as strong as death, and can take no denial. It is the wing and weight of the soul, that carries all the desires into an intimate unity with the thing beloved, stirs up a zeal to remove all obstacles, works an egress of the spirits, and as it were a haste of the soul to entertain and meet it; according to those expressions of the saints in Scripture : "The desire of our soul is to thy name," Isa. xxvi. 8. "With my whole heart have I sought thee," Psal. cxix. 10. "My soul fainteth for thy salvation," ver. 81. "My soul breaketh for the longing it hath to thy judgments at all times," ver. 20. "My soul thirsteth for God," Psal. xlii. 2. "I am sick of love," &c., Cant. ii. 5. Oh the vehement panting, breathing, and going forth of the

Amor concupiscentiæ non requiescit in quacunque extrinseca aut superficiali adeptione amati, sed quærit habere quasi ad intima illius perveniens. Aq. 1. 2æ. q. 2ß. ar. 2.

soul of one toward God who is in love with him! He contemns the most serious worldly employments when he is taken up with this, and whoever discourses with him of earthly concerns speaks as with one not at home; all the world not satisfying him without the kisses of the lips of his Beloved, his desires being a thousand times more for one smile of his face than for all the wealth under the sun. No difficulty so great, no danger so imminent, nay, no death so certain, which this love carries not through to obtain the thing beloved; this love being a falling mountain, that breaks down all that stands betwixt it and the place of its rest. In a word, no means will be left unused which are appointed by God to obtain our Beloved; inquiries of or from others how to find him; letters of love, sighs, tears, sobs, groans unutterable, are sent to win him; desires to hear again from him in his promise of grace are expressed. The soul is never near enough till it be in the arms, the bosom of God in heaven. It saith not, as Peter of his tabernacles, Lord, let there be one for me, and another for thee; but let us both be together in one. It is ever night with one who loves Christ till the sun of his presence arise. He is like a certain kind of stone, of which some report, that if it be thrown into the water whole, it swims; if broken, it sinks: he never droops in any trouble, unless he apprehends a breaking between him and Christ. He is like the marigold, that opens with the shining, and shuts with the setting of the sun. His heart is locked up in sorrow when God hides his face, and he cannot find another key fit to open it again among all the keys in the house. What is all the world to him without the presence of God, but as a sieve plucked out of the water? His comforts are only full when God is in them. What are companions to him in whom he sees nothing of God, but objects either irksome or pitied? What are ordinances, unless with Christ, but as candles that have no light put to them? Nay, what would the joys of heaven itself be, if it were not for the presence of God, but as a funeral feast or banquet, where is much provision, but no cheer?

2. There is *amor complacentiæ*, a love of complacency and delight, when the soul having arked itself in God's embraces, now with infinite sweetness and security reposes itself in them, saying then as David, "Thou hast put gladness into my heart more than when their corn and wine increased. I will lay me down in peace, and sleep," Psal. iv. 7, 8; and with Peter, "Lord, it is good to be here;" and with the spouse, I charge you, stir not up, nor awake my Beloved. And when Christ meets it sweetly in prayer, sacraments, or a sermon, breathing thus, "Oh that, Lord, this meeting might never end! dear Jesus, why comest thou so seldom, and stayest no longer?" All the night long do thou lodge between my breasts. "A day in thy house is better than a thousand elsewhere," Psal. lxxxiv. 10. "My soul is satisfied as with marrow and fatness." "He brought me into the banquetting-house, and his banner over me was love. Thy left hand is under me, thy right hand embraceth me," Cant. ii. 4, 6. How contented could the soul be in such an income of Christ, were not his pleasure otherwise, that it had no avocation to take it off; no earthly employment, no family, feeding of body, or relations, to call it away from those secret enjoyments of such a Beloved! Oh, thinks the soul, what a blessed place will heaven be, where I shall never be severed one moment from the embracements of Christ to eternity!

3. There is *amor amicitiæ*, a love to be set upon God, for the goodness and excellency which are in himself. To love God for the creatures is not to enjoy, but to use God. To love him for another end than himself, is to turn the ultimate end into a means. Love to God, grounded upon human inducements, is but spurious. When the inducement, suppose it to be profit, or preferment, is removed, that love will discover its falseness. And by the very reason for which men contend for the outward appearance and profession of love to God, viz. because they love their pleasures and profits, which without such a profession they cannot peaceable enjoy; by that very reason, I say, they will be beaten off even from their outside appearing profession, when those profits and pleasures which they love so much are in hazard. It is a dead love to God that cannot stand unless it be shored up. True love will stand alone, without politic props. To shroud our own private ends under the name of love to God, is not *amicitia*, but *mercatura*; not to love, but to make merchandise of him. The love that cannot be warm any longer than it is rubbed with the warm clothes of preferment, is but the carcass of love. Then has this love a soul, when God himself is the object of it, when it is not of what he has, but of what he is; when he is beloved though we beg with him, or though all his rings and ornaments are plucked off; nay, when he plucks off ours: in a word, all his ways, ordinances, people, will have our love drawn out to them, for that of God which is imparted to them. The word will be received in its purity and power, most loved, when least adulterated; when it discovers most of God to us, and most of sin in us; when the dearest corruption is struck at, the closest duty urged, the secret corners of the soul searched; when the spiritual sword is laid on with severest blows. The persons also in whom most shines the beauty of God's likeness, we shall most be taken with; and those will have our love shine upon them, who can reflect nothing back again but holiness.

4. There is *amor benevolentiæ*, a love set upon God, endeavouring to bring to him, so far as creatures can to an infinite Creator, to whom their good extendeth not, Psal. xvi. 2, all service and honour. This love returns to God not only a heart, but a tongue of praises, and a hand of obedience. All its pleasant fruits are laid up for its Beloved; all it is and has is accounted too little. Lord, saith the soul, that I could love thee more, and serve thee better! how impure is my heart! how poor and imperfect are my performances! what I have is neither enough, nor good enough, for thee; but had I something better than myself, and oh that I myself were a thousand times better for thy sake! it should be bestowed upon thee. A soul in love with God is boundless in duty; the smallness of his obedience is the greatness of his trouble. When another man observes his zeal and vehemency, his tears, and sobs, and wrestling in prayer, and sees him so strict and exact in living, he thinks it a great matter, and is ready, as the disciples, who looked upon the beautiful buildings of the temple, to admire him; but the party himself that loves Christ thinks all this as nothing, in comparison of what Christ deserves: he looks upon his services as Christ foretold of the temple, as if there were not one stone left upon another. This love causes a universal, cheerful, constant obedience to the commands of Christ, John xiv. 23: in it all our services are steeped, and with it made easy to us; and coming from faith, are acceptable to God. Nor will love think it too much to suffer much for Christ; nay, it accounts it little to endure all things, 1 Cor. xiii. 7, for him who hath borne our burdens, and shed better blood for us than any we have to shed for him.

Faith works by love. Love is the instrument in the hand of faith. A hand alone can lay hold and receive; and so the proper work of faith is to lay hold upon Christ: but a hand without an instrument cannot cut any thing; no more can faith practise any moral duties without love. Faith in justification is alone, but in the life of man it works by love.

From this love to God flows another sort, in respect of the object, of love, namely, 3. Love to man; whereby our neighbour is loved as ourselves.

This comprehends a love of ourselves, and of others.

(1.) Of ourselves. It is made the rule of loving others, Matt. xxii. 39. None is so near us, after God, as ourselves. Frequent are the commands of Scripture to regard ourselves. "Take heed to yourselves," Acts xx. 28. "Take heed to thyself," 1 Tim. iv. 16. "Work out your own salvation," Phil. ii. 12. Let every one examine himself, 1 Cor. xi. 28. And ver. 31, "If we would judge ourselves," &c. "Examine yourselves, whether ye be in the faith; prove yourselves," 2 Cor. xiii. 5. Every one is bound to wish to himself that good, which to wish is truest love; namely, the everlasting enjoyment of God. None can love God, but at the same time he loves himself; for he that loves God, desires to enjoy him; but whosoever desires to enjoy such a good, must needs love himself. And this enjoyment of God a man more desires for himself than for another; and if it could be communicated to no more than one, a man should desire it rather for himself than any one: for there are more causes concur why a man should thus love himself than any other; for another man may miss of true blessedness without either my fault or misery, but I myself cannot. And though this direct precept is not expressed in terms, Thou shalt love thyself; yet where we are commanded to love God, we are at the same time enjoined to love ourselves; for to love God is to desire to enjoy him for ours, who is the chief good; and this is the chiefest love. And some remark that the written law of God was given for help and relief of the law of nature, which was much defaced and darkened in every one by sin; but the law of nature was not impaired, as it moved and put men upon loving and caring for themselves; and therefore an express command of loving ourselves was not needful. And whereas the love of ourselves is noted in the Scripture as a great sin, 2 Tim. iii. 2; there is a threefold love of ourselves.

Precepto non est opus ut se quisque et corpus suum diligat; quoniam id quod sumus et id quod infra nos est, inconcussa naturæ lege diligimus, quæ in bestiis etiam promulgata est, restabat ut et de illo quod supra nos est, et de illo quod juxta nos est, præcepta sumeremus. Aug. de Doct. Chr. l. 1. c. 25, 26.

[1.] *Naturalis;* whereby every creature by nature's instinct desires its own preservation; and this is not discommended.

[2.] *Spiritualis;* or *amor charitatis;* a true charitative love, whereby a man desires to obtain divine and spiritual good; and this damps not, but inflames the love of God: none can desire a divine good too much. This is commended and commanded.

[3.] *Inordinatus;* love which only respects good things that please the sense. Such a love which so makes us love ourselves, as to contemn God, and to neglect spiritual good things: this inordinate love of ourselves is reproved by the apostle. We should not so love our bodies as to neglect God, but we must so love God as to neglect, nay, to hate our bodies; and this hatred of our bodies is true love to ourselves, because it is most profitable for us. A man may be willing to have a limb cut, nay, cut off, and yet this man may love himself; nay, because he loves himself, and desires the preservation of the rest, he therefore yields to lose one limb. To love ourselves, is not *curare cutim,* but *animam,* to regard our souls, not our skins; and to regard the soul, is to love God, and loathe sin. He that sinneth, hateth his own soul, Prov. viii. 36. He that loves a garment, hates the moth that eats it. Neither can he love his neighbour well, who does not so love himself; as he cannot write a straight line, who writes by a wrong rule. It were better that some man should say to one, I love you as well as my swine, than as well as my soul.

Jav. 2. 105.

(2.) Love to man comprehends a love to all others, who are meant by the word neighbour; "Thou shalt love thy neighbour." Now he is our neighbour, and to be beloved with a love both of benevolence and beneficence, who is not only our friend, as the Pharisees thought, Matt. v. 43, but every one who stands in need of our help, Luke x. 37. He is a neighbour who may want our relief, and whose relief we may want. A neighbour is to be esteemed not by the nearness of blood, but by the society of reason.

Proximus est, vel cui a nobis præbendum est, vel a quo nobis præbendum est officium misericordiæ. Aug. l. 11. c. 30. de Doct. Chr. Proximus non sanguinis propinquitate, sed rationis societate penitus adunus est. Aug. E. 52.

[1.] Even those who are most remote in respect of place, are to be beloved, and are comprehended within this neighbourhood. They of Macedonia and Achaia made "a contribution for the poor saints at Jerusalem," Rom. xv. 26. Gaius is commended for his love to strangers, 3 John 5. A good man, having ability, is as diffusive as a common treasury, or a fountain. A great fire will warm those that sit far from it, and love that is fervent will extend to them that are most remote.

Quod præstamus nostris per affectum, præstamus aliis per humanitatem. Lactant.

[2.] Our enemies. It is the command and example of Christ to love our enemies: "Bless them that curse you, do good to them that hate you," Matt. v. 44; 1 Pet. ii. 23; Luke vi. 27; Psal. xxxv. 13, 14; Rom. xii. 13, 15. Every one can love his friend, but it is only a Christian that can love his enemy. Love, like fire in cold weather, must be made the hotter by the sharpness of cold unkindness. Our Saviour and Stephen prayed for their enemies. David's imprecations are rather prophecies than curses. His and Paul's were both against men as they were known to be enemies to God, and incurable sinners. In our enemy we may find something to be beloved; a participation of that nature which may possibly partake of holiness and eternal blessedness. Theodosius being moved to execute one who had reviled him, answered, "That if his enemy were dead, he had rather restore him to life, if it were in his power, than being alive, to put him to death." It is not manhood, but childishness, to be quieted with striking the thing that hurt us. Though enemies are not worthy to be loved by us, yet malice is unworthy to be lodged in us. It is true, the precept of loving enemies is contrary to unsanctified nature. It was once said by a good man, Either this precept is a fable, or we are no Christians: but God alone knows how to punish our enemies without passion and inequality. It is our duty to weary persecutors with patience. A Christian must not, like the flint, seem to be cool, but be fiery when struck. He that takes up fire to throw, (though against his enemy,) hurts himself most. To be kind to the kind, argues civility; to be unkind to the unkind, argues corruption; to be unkind to the kind, argues devilishness; to be kind to the unkind, argues Christianity. He has nothing supernatural in charity, that comes not to this, To be ready to requite evil with good; publicans doing good for good, and heathens abstaining from returning evil for evil. When the godly in Scripture have rejoiced in the destruction of their

Amicos diligere omnium est, inimicos solorum Christianorum. Tert. ad Scap.

enemies, it was not out of delight in the punishment of their enemies, whom they loved not; but in the justice of God, whom they loved: *non de malo inimici, sed de bono Judice;* not that their enemies suffered such evil, but that they had so good and upright a Judge. We must not so much as use the magistrate to revenge us on our adversary; for this were to make God's ordinances an instrument of our malice. Violent things have the more force upon those that resist them. A sword may be spoiled with the force of lightning, the scabbard not being hurt at all. To give place to wrath, Rom. xii. 19, is counsel both wise and holy. "Anger rests in the bosom of fools," Eccl. vii. 9. Love to an enemy is a token of a truly noble mind. When David spared Saul, having power to kill him, Saul told him, he knew that he should be king, 1 Sam. xxiv. 20. It is a sign of a weak stomach not to be able to concoct light meats, and of a weak mind not to digest injuries, Prov. xvi. 32. Wicked men account revenge to be valour. These are not like Adam in his innocency, that gave names to things according to their natures. It is an unhappy victory to overcome a man, and to be overcome by a lust. The wisdom of the world and the word are contrary. Is it not a thrice noble conquest to overcome our own and our enemies' passions, and Satan's temptations, three enemies at one blow, and all this without shedding blood? Nay, not only not to hurt an enemy, but to help him, to feed him, give him drink in his hunger and thirst; nay, to feed him cheerfully, tenderly; such being the feeding commanded by Paul, Rom. xii. 20, 21, who bids us ψωμίζειν, feed our enemies, as birds feed their young; or as sick folks and young children are fed, with much tending and tenderness, their meat being minced and cut; or as a man feeds his friend, carving him the best. And the Hebrew word, rendered, Give him drink, signifieth most properly, *propina,* Drink to him as a token of true love.

Infelix victoria, ubi superans virum, succumbis vitio. Bern.

Ψωμίζω proprie significat cibum concisum et intinctum frustulatim veluti in os indere, ut puerulis et ægrotis solemus. Non significat simpliciter pascere, sed indulgenter pascere, ut in conviviis fieri solet, quum quis alteri ministrat de iis quæ ipsi apponuntur. Significat et abundanter pascere; frustulatim distribuere. Pisc. Tollet. Eras. Bez. Steph. שָׁקָה (ex הִשְׁקָה propina illi: Quod verbum in conviviis locum habet. Salaz. in Prov. xxv. 1.

[3.] The wicked are not excluded the line of love and neighbourhood. It is true that holy men are chiefly the objects of our love. With these we have communion both of nature and grace also. "Let us do good unto all, especially to the household of faith," Gal. vi. 10. The love of complacency must be set upon the good. The love of benevolence must not be denied to the bad. As those objects are best seen which are most in the light, because light is that by which every object is seen; so those men are most to be beloved which are nearest to God, because he makes every object to be beloved. Yet wicked men also are to be beloved, because being men they may be good; as are good men, because being saints they are good. If a man be degenerate into a beast, and wandering from God, bring him to his Master again. As the nature of man must not make his vices loved, so neither must the vices of man make his nature hated. St. Augustine thinks that Stephen's prayer was a great means of Paul's conversion. The denouncing of curses against wicked men by ministers must not be poisonful, but medicinal.

Non hoc ago ut sim homine conviciando superior, sed errorum convincendo salubrior. Aug. con. lit. Pet. l. 3. c. 1.

[4.] The faithful call for the chiefest room in our love, and are eminently to be looked upon as neighbours. With our heavenly Father he is not in the communion of sons, who is not in the charity of brethren. The bond of grace is the strongest: creation has made us friends, but redemption has made us brethren. The frequent inculcating of the command of love of the brethren, the brotherhood, the household of faith, of brotherly love, and of being kindly affectionate with brotherly love, &c., 1 Pet. i. 22; ii. 17; iii. 8; John xiii. 34; 2 Pet. i. 7; Col. iii. 14; Rom xii. 10; 1 Thess. iv. 9; Heb. xiii. 1, insinuates the necessity and common disesteem of this duty. In pursuance of this duty, contentions, strifes, and controversies among brethren are forbidden. It is a fault for brother to go to law with brother, 1 Cor. vi. 6, 7. Let there be no strife between us, said Abraham to Lot, for we are brethren, Gen. xiii. 8. "Why do ye wrong one another?" said Moses, since ye are brethren, Acts vii. 26. The sowing of discord among brethren, is one of the abominations which God's soul hateth, Prov. vi. 1. In this respect likewise the Scripture opposes inward hatred and rancour among brethren, Gen. xxxvii. 4. How dear did this sin cost Joseph's brethren! "He that hateth his brother is in darkness," 1 John ii. 11. "He is a murderer," 1 John iii. 15. As also anger, which is a short hatred, as hatred is a long anger. This causeless anger puts us "in danger of the judgment," Matt. v. 22. Anger is not allowed by Christianity. Most opposite also to brotherly love is the contempt and despising of any brother. "Despise you the church of God?" said Paul, 1 Cor. xi. 22. The poorest brother concurs to make up the perfection of Christ. When the mother of Darius had saluted Hephestion, who was Alexander's favourite, instead of Alexander the Great, she blushed and was troubled; but Alexander said to her, It is well enough done, for he is also Alexander. The meanest saint is to be beloved for what of Christ is in him; he is an old casket full of pearls. But above all, how destructive to brotherly love is oppression, defrauding, and grinding our brethren! "Let no man," saith Paul, "defraud his brother in any matter," 1 Thess. iv. 6. Even the Jew, who might take usury of a heathen, might not take it of his brother. If lilies rend and tear lilies, what may thorns do? Nor must a Christian content himself in not hurting a Christian: his care must be to benefit him, to do him good; and that for his soul. All thy spiritual gifts of knowledge, utterance, &c., must profit thy brother, 1 Cor. xii.; xiv. 26. Comfort him in his troubles of mind, direct him in his doubts, reprehend him gently for his faults. Not to rebuke him, is to hate him, Lev. xix. 17. To be angry with the sin of our brother, is not to be angry with our brother. To love the soul, is the soul of love; so to love thy brother, as to labour to have him live in heaven with thee. For his name; not casting aspersions on him, but wiping them off; not receiving, much less raising accusations against him, but laying hold upon the thief that pillaged his name, as knowing that the receiver in this case is as bad as he. For his body; visiting and sympathizing with him in his sickness; helping him, to thy utmost ability, to find the jewel of health. For outward necessaries; pitying him in his low estate; casting the dung of thy wealth on the barren soil of his poverty; making his back thy wardrobe, his stomach thy barn, his hand thy treasury. For body and soul; praying for him, calling upon God as "our Father," not thine alone. In the primitive times, saith one, there was so much love, that it was *ad stuporem Gentilium,* to the wonder of Gentiles; but now so little, that it may be to the shame of Christians. That which was the motto of a heathen, *Dic aliquid ut duo simus,* Say something that we may be two, must not belong to Christians. It is best that dissension should never be born among brethren; and next,

Non erit tibi concordia cum Christiano, si sit discordia cum Christiano.

Apud summum patrem, qui non fuerit in charitate fratrum, non habebitur in numero filiorum. Leo. Ser. 11. de quadr.

Tert. Apol. c. 39.

that it should die presently after its birth. When any leak springs in the ship of Christian society, we should stop it with speed. The nearer the union is, the more dangerous is the breach. Bodies that are but glued together, may (if severed) be set together as beautifully as ever; but members rent and torn cannot be healed without a scar. What a shame is it that the bond of grace and religion should not more firmly unite us, than sinful leagues do wicked men! A true Christian, like the true mother, to whom Solomon gave the child, may be known by affection. As the spleen grows, the body decays; and as hatred increases, holiness abates, 1 John iii. 14; v. 1; iv. 7, 8, &c.

In sum, this love to the faithful must put forth itself both in distributing to them the good they want, and in delighting in them, and rejoicing with them, for the good they have. Both these, how profitable, how honourable, how amiable are they! Most honourable it is for the meanest Christian to be a priest to the high God, to offer a daily sacrifice with which God is well pleased, Heb. xiii. 16; to resemble God in doing, rather than in receiving good; to be the hand of God to disperse his bounty, to have God for his debtor, to lend to the Lord of heaven and earth. What likewise is more profitable than that our distribution to saints, like an ambassador, by lying lieger abroad, should secure all at home? that this most gainful employment should return us pearls for pebbles, jewels for trifles, crowns for crumbs; after a short seed-time, a thousandfold, measure heaped, shaken, thrust together, and running over? What, lastly, so amiable, as for members of the same body, children of the same Father, and who lay in the same womb, suck at the same breasts, sit at the same table, and expect for ever to lodge in the same bosom, to be at union with and helpful to one another? And on this side heaven where should our complacency centre itself, but upon the truly excellent, Psal. xvi. 3, noble, illustrious ones, who are every one kings, and more magnificent than ever were worldly monarchs? For their alliance, having the Lord of heaven and earth for their Father; the King of kings for their elder Brother; a queen, the church, the spouse of Christ, for their mother, Psal. xlv.; having for their treasures those "exceeding precious promises," 2 Pet. i. 4, "more to be desired than gold, yea, than fine gold," Psal. xix. 10; in comparison of which a mountain of gold is but a heap of dung. For their guard, having the attendance of angels, Psal. xxxiv. 7; nay, the wisdom, care, and strength of God. For their food, having bread that endures to eternal life, John vi. 27, drink better than wine, and a continual feast. For their apparel, having the robes of Christ's righteousness here, which makes them as beautiful as angels, all fair, and without spot, Cant. iv. 7; and attire to be put on hereafter, Rev. vii. 9, which will shine more gloriously than a hundred suns made into one. For their habitation, a palace of glory, "a building of God, a house not made with hands, eternal in the heavens," 2 Cor. v. 1.

Having thus first explained this love here desired by the apostle in its several sorts, I come now,

II. To touch briefly upon those rare and excellent properties of this grace of love, both as it is set upon God, and upon man.

1. The properties of this grace of love to God.

(1.) This grace of love set upon God, is true, cordial, and sincere; not in word or outward profession, but in truth, and in the inward man; not complimentary, but real; the inward purpose of the heart having an emphasis of love that hypocrisy and expressions cannot reach.

Eph. vi. 24. ἐν ἀφθαρσίᾳ.

And the truth is, our loving God is not so properly said to be sincere, as to be our very sincerity. Then, and then alone, a duty is done in sincerity, when it is done in love; and herein stands hypocrisy, when, though there is much doing, yet there is no loving. The love of a hypocrite to Christ, like the shining of the glow-worm, is without any inward heat, and stands only in a glistering profession; or like some spices, which are cold in the stomach, though hot in the mouth; or like the fire in Moses' bush, it burns not while it blazes: it proceeds from human inducements of education, countenance, or commands of superiors, interest;—an apprehension of the love of Christ barely to mankind; or from this, that Christ is out of sight, and troubles not his lusts; or from some accidental, circumstantial ornaments which attend the ministry and truth, as wit, learning, expression, elocution, or credit of visible conformity to them; not from an inward apprehension of the proportionableness, suitableness, and fitness of Christ to all his desires and capacities, as being the fairest of ten thousand, Cant. v. 10, or from any real interest and propriety in Christ, which are the grounds of love, when true and sincere, Luke vii. 47; 1 John iv. 16, 19.

(2.) This love to God is superlative; it surpasses all other love: the soul in which it abides, seeing infinitely more loveliness in one God, than in all the combined, assembled excellencies of all worldly objects, loves him infinitely more than them all. It often not only steps over them, but kicks them away; not only laying them down as sacrifices, but hating them as snares, when they would draw from Christ. When Christ and the world meet (as it were) upon so narrow a bridge, that both cannot pass by, Christ shall go on, and the world shall go back. Christ in a Christian shall have no rivals; as Christ bestows himself wholly upon a Christian, wholly upon every one, as every line hath the whole indivisible point, so a Christian gives himself wholly to Christ; he shares not his heart betwixt him and the world; all within him he sets on work to love Christ, keeping nothing back from him, for whom all is too little. The greatest worth that it sees in any thing but Christ is this, that it may be left for Christ; ever rejoicing that it has any thing to which it may prefer him. To a soul in which is this love, Christ is as oil put into a vial with water, in which, though both be never so much shaken together, the oil will ever be uppermost; or as one rising sun, which drowns the light of a numberless number of stars. It loves the world as always about to leave and loathe it; not as that for which it lives, but as that without which it cannot live. The world has not the top and strength of its affection; it loves nothing much but Him whom it cannot love too much. It lodges not the world in its best room, and admits not such a stranger into the closet of the heart, but only into the hall of the senses.

(3.) It is a jealous or zealous love; suspicious lest any thing should, and burning in a holy heat of indignation against any thing that does, disturb the soul's Beloved. Love is a solicitous grace, and makes the soul account itself never sufficiently trimmed for Christ's embraces, never to think that any thing done is well enough done. All the soul is and can is esteemed too little for him, who is its *optimus maximus*, its best and greatest. The more brightly shining the beams of love to Christ are, the more motes and imperfections the soul ever sees in its services. Its fear only is, lest by sin, and unsuitable carriage, it stirs up and awakes the Beloved, Cant. iii. 5. It cannot put up a disgrace, expressed by the greatest, against Christ. It zealously contends for his word, ways, worship, worshippers, kingdom, Gal. iv. 16, 18;

Acts xv. 2; xvii. 16; xviii. 25; xix. 8; Jude 3. All its anger is against those intercurrent impediments that would stop it in advancing Christ; it labours to bear down those hinderances of God's glory with a flood of tears, if it cannot with a stream of power. The meekest soul in love with God knows how to be holily impatient; and, like Moses, though when with God to pray for men, yet when with men to contend for God. Every sin by how much the nearer to it, by so much is it more detested by it. Of all sins therefore its own have the deepest share of hatred; for what it cannot remove, it mourns heartily, crying out of the body of death, the sin that doth so easily beset it, Rom. vii. 24; Heb. xii. 1, as of the constant company of a noisome carcass; endeavouring that every sin may be more bitter to remember, than it was ever sweet to commit; looking upon the want of sorrow after sin, as a greater argument of want of love than was the sin itself.

(4.) It is a chaste, a loyal love; not set upon what God has, so much as upon what God is; not upon his, but him; not upon his rings, but his person; not upon his clothes, but his comeliness; upon a Christ, though not adventitiously adorned: his gifts are loved for him, not he for them; he is sweet without any thing, though nothing is so without him. Love desires no wages, it is wages enough to itself, it pays itself in seeing and serving the beloved. A nurse does much for the child, and so does the mother; but the former for the love of wages, the latter for the wages of love. Love carries meat in the mouth: the very doing of God's will is meat and drink to one who loves him. A heart in love with Christ is willing, with Mephibosheth, that others should take all, so it may behold the King. Worldly comforts shall not *fallere*, but *monere;* only they shall be used to admonish how much worth is in Christ, not to bewitch the soul from Christ; as spectacles by which the soul may read him the better, or as steps by which it may be raised up to him the nearer: and no further shall they be delighted in, than as they are pledges of, or furtherances unto, the enjoyment of him. Should God give all to one who loves him, and not give himself, he would say, with Absalom, What doth all avail me, so long as I see not the King's face? 2 Sam. xiv. 32. Communion with God is the heaven of him who loves God. It is heaven upon earth for God to be with him, and the heaven of heaven for him to be with God.

<small>Si ista terrena diligitis, ut subjecta diligite, ut munera amici, ut beneficia domini, ut arrham Sponsi. Aug. Med.</small>

(5.) It is an active, stirring, expressive love. The fire of love cannot be held in, it will break out at lips, hands, feet, by speaking, working, walking, John xiv. 23; Psal. cxix. 111, 140, 159. Love saith, as Elijah to Obadiah, "As the Lord liveth, I will show myself," 1 Kings xviii. 15: the strength of love will have a vent. "The love of Christ constraineth," 2 Cor. v. 14, and, as the word συνέχει, used by the apostle, signifies, hems in, shuts up, pinfolds the heart, that it cannot wind out from service, and cannot choose but do for Christ. Love is a mighty stream, bearing all before it. It cares not for shame or loss; it carries away these, as did Samson the other, gates upon its shoulders, Judg. xvi. 3. "It is strong as death," Cant. viii. 6. A man in love with God, is as a man who is carried away in a crowd, who cannot keep himself back, but is hurried without his own labour with the throng. Love with ease despatches great employments: the commands of God are not grievous to it. Love is the wing, that weight and holy proclivity of the soul, which, if it finds not, makes a way; nay, it is so speedy and present an affection, that it endures no delays. It accounts not the least time little in which God is withdrawn. It follows hard after God, and puts not off its pursuits of duty or comfort till to-morrow, or to a more convenient time.

<small>ἀγάπη, from ἀγαν ποιεῖν, say some.</small>

(6.) It is an expensive, bountiful, costly love. It will not offer that which cost it nothing; even the meanest gift (as, alas, how much below Christ is all we are or do!) comes from a kingly heart. Love contends after excellency and perfection in attending upon that object which it loves under the apprehension of the greatest good. How willingly did those converts lay down all their goods at the apostles' feet! Acts iv. 35; and those afterwards burn their books of curious arts, though of great value! Acts xix. 19. How great was David's expense for the temple, 1 Chron. xxii. 14—16, and his desire that his purchase which he bought of Araunah should be (being for his God) costly! 2 Sam. xxiv. 24. How bountiful was that formerly sinful woman in her expression of love to Christ! How freely were her tears, hairs, kisses, ointment employed! The greatness of the debt forgiven her made her love much, and the greatness of her love made her spend much, Luke vii. 45, 46. What, save love, made Zaccheus part with half of his goods to the poor, and a fourfold restitution to the wronged by false accusation? Luke xix. 8. Love will make Peter willing to feed the sheep of Christ, John xxi. 15—17, and Paul not to account his life dear to him to finish his ministry, Acts xx. 24. Joseph loved Benjamin most, and gave him a mess five times so much as any of the rest, Gen. xliii. 34. He that loves God most will lay out most for God. More than once we read in the Scripture of the labour of love, 1 Thess. i. 3; Heb. vi. 10. Love rests in its labour, and then rests most when it labours most. Nothing labours more, or thinks it labours less, than love. I have heard of one that was asked for what sort of men he laboured most; he answered, for his friends. He was again asked, for whom then he laboured least; he answered, for his friends. Both answers were true; for love made him think he did least for those for whom indeed he did most.

(7.) It is a submissive, stooping, patient love, bearing from, and forbearing for, the beloved any thing. It puts us upon things below us, to please him whom we love; it make us undertake that which another may esteem weakness and indecency. David's love to God's presence transported him to leaping and dancing, thereby (though Michal esteemed it baseness) to honour God. Parents, out of love to their children, play, and lisp, and stammer: Christ himself emptied and humbled himself (Phil. ii. 8) for our sakes. Love flies not, like chaff, in the face of him that fans. The soul that loves is reconciled to God, though it sees not that God is reconciled to it. It has a child-like ingenuity to have and stay with a father that scourges it, not a servile unsubmissiveness, to threaten, presently after stripes, departure. It *iratum colere numen*, follows a frowning father. It lives contented with God's allowance. It will patiently be without what he thinks either fit to remove, or not fit to bestow; and all this not upon force, but upon choice. It loses its own will in God's, and had rather will as doth God, than understand as doth an angel. It takes with joy the spoiling of its goods. It ever thinks it hath enough left, so long as God takes not away himself. It bears the indignation of the Lord, and accepts the punishment of its iniquity, and is willing to receive evil as well as good, because from the hand of a God whom it loves. For his sake it is willing to be killed all the day long, Psal. xliv. 22; Rom. viii.

<small>Omnia quæ horribilia audis, servire, mori, expiata et sancta sunt amori. Nier. de art. vol</small>

36; nor can the waters of death extinguish the taper of love.

(8.) It is a conforming love. The will of God is the compass by which it steers. It fashions not itself according to the world. It walks not by example, but by rule. The heart will be set like a watch which goes not by other watches, but by the sun. It walks not by precedent, but precept. It regards not what is either its own, or other men's, but what is God's will. Its will and God's are like two strings of an instrument tuned in unison, if the one be struck and sounded, the other also stirs and trembles: when God's will is declared, the will of him that loves God moves accordingly. It is much more solicitous to understand duty, than to avoid danger. It desires to have a heart according to God's heart, to be moulded according to Scripture impressions; to love what God loves, and hate what he hates; to think and will the same with God.

(9.) It is a sociable love. It moves to the full enjoyment of God, as its centre. Converse with God is its element. The soul where this love is, debarred from prayer, hearing, is as the fish on dry land. It restrains not prayer from the Almighty. It walks with God. It sings in the absence of Christ, no more than did they in a strange land. It loves to have its bundle of myrrh all the night between its breast. It delights in every thing in which Christ may be seen; the word, sacraments, conditions, society, ministers; and the more these have of Christ's presence, the more it loves them: the closest, purest, most powerful, most sin-discovering, sin-disturbing preaching it loves best. The holiest and most exact walking saints it loves best. The sacrament or prayer wherein Christ smiles most sweetly it loves best. The condition, though outwardly bitterest, wherein it sees the face of Christ most clearly, it loves best. Chiefly is the sociableness of love discovered in longing after the second coming of Christ; in counting it best of all to be with him, Phil. i. 23; in loving his appearance, 2 Tim. iv. 8; in hasting to the coming of the day of God, 2 Pet. iii. 12. The unwillingness to have that day come, proceeds from a Christian's unrenewed part: so much soreness as is in the eye, so much loathness is there in a man to see the light, and proportionable to our love to sin is the disaffection to Christ's appearance; and the fear which is in a gracious heart of Christ's second coming, rather proceeds from a sense of its own unfitness to appear before Christ, than an unwillingness to have Christ appear to it; and more from a desire to be made meet for him, than to remain without him.

(10.) Lastly, It is an incessant love. A flame never to be quenched. The waters of affliction cannot drown it, Cant. viii. 7, but only, as they increase, elevate it. The very snuffers of death shall make it burn the more brightly. It unconquered outlives, as opposition, so its fellow graces, 1 Cor. xiii. 1—8. The faithful are rooted and grounded in love, Eph. iii. 17. They love God for himself, who fails not, and therefore love itself fails not, 1 Cor. xiii. 8. Hypocrites are uneven in their love: feigned things are unequal: appearing friends cannot dissemble so exactly, but that at one time or other their hatred will appear. In some companies or conditions they will show what they are. In the time of persecution they fall away, Matt. xiii. 21; like rotten apples, they fall off in a windy day. True love to Christ knows no holy-days; it ever has a rest of contentment, never has a rest of cessation.

2. I proceed to the properties of love to man.

(1.) It is a love unfeigned, 1 Pet. i. 22, without dissimulation, Rom. xii. 9. Φιλαδελφία ἀνυπόκριτη, love without hypocrisy. Love in deed and in truth, not in word and tongue, 1 John iii. 18; a love from the heart. It is not like the love of Joab and Judas, who outwardly kissed, and inwardly, at the same time, designed to kill. It contents not itself in giving, like Naphtali, "goodly words," Gen. xlix. 21. The apostle speaks of soundness in charity, Tit. ii. 2. Unsound charity is courtship, not Christianity. Of all things, dissimulation does worst in love, as most corrupting it, and contrary to its nature; and appearing love is nothing but Christianity acted, and religion painted: some sins scratch the face of love, but hypocrisy stabs it at the heart.

(2.) It is an expressive, open-handed love: though it arises at the heart, yet it reaches to the hand. Love is a fruitful grace; it bears not only the leaves and blossoms of words and promises, but the fruit also of beneficial performances. If love be in truth, it will also be in deed, 1 John iii. 18. Words, though never so adorned, clothe not the naked; though never so delicate, feed not the hungry; though never so zealous, warm not the cold; though never so free, set not the bound at liberty: our faith must work by love, Gal. v. 6. Love must be seen, felt, and understood: verbal love is but painted fire. Love is so beautiful a grace, that it is willing to be seen. The apostle saith, "Love worketh no ill," Rom. xiii. 10; it is a diminutive expression; there is more intended, even doing all the good the law requires, and therefore he adds, "Love is the fulfilling of the law."

(3.) It is a forward, cheerful love. It is not drawn or driven, but runs: it stays not till the poor seeks it, but it seeks for him. Onesiphorus sought out Paul diligently, 2 Tim. i. 17. It relieves not with an evil eye, Prov. xxiii. 6. It makes men given to hospitality, Rom. xii. 13: the water of bounty flows from it as from a fountain, and goes not out, as from a narrow-mouthed bottle, with grumbling. It is not like the sponge that sucks up the water greedily, but gives it not out unless it be squeezed. Ingenuous poverty rejoices in this forwardness of love as much as in the gift itself; for thereby not only its want, but bashfulness is relieved. It is a double beneficence when we give, and give cheerfully. The mind of the receiver is more refreshed with the cheerfulness of the giver, than is his body with the greatness of the gift. *Hoc ipso amplius gaudent pauperes, quum paupertati eorum consultum fuerit et pudori.* Leo. Serm. 4. *Duplex eleemosyna, et quia damus, et quia hilariter damus.*

(4.) It is an extensive, universal love. 1. Universal in respect of duties; it shuns no performance that may benefit the body, name, mind, or soul of another. Love is a Pandora, abounding in every good work and gift; it is therefore called the fulfilling of the law, Rom. xiii. 10. Love is the decalogue contracted, and the decalogue is love unfolded. Love is a mother; the ten commandments her ten children; and she forgets none, neglects none. 2. It is universal in respect of persons; it remembers the apostle's rule, to do good to all, Gal. vi. 10: even wicked men it loves, though not as wicked, yet as men; the men, not their manners. The love of the Colossians was extended to all the saints, Col. i. 4: wherever there is grace, love will follow, for grace is beautiful wherever it is. The ointment of love falls even upon the skirts of the garment, as well as the head. Love is set upon the brotherhood, 1 Pet. ii. 17, the whole fraternity of believers, not here and there upon one. Holy love regards grace in its working-day clothes, James ii. 1; upon a dunghill, in a prison; grace in the idiot, as well as in the scholar; in the servant, as well as the master. As all our delight must be in *Non peccatorem, sed justum in paupere nutrit, qui in illo non culpam, sed naturam diligit.* Gr. 3. past.

the saints, Psal. xvi. 3, so our delight must be in all the saints.

(5.) It is a religious and a holy love. It is from, in, and for holiness. From it: he that loves his brother, first loves God; first he gives his heart to God as a son, before he reaches out his hand to man as his brother. His love is said to be out of a pure heart, 1 Tim. i. 5. First he gives himself, then his. Secondly, in holiness, and holy ways: it joins not hands with any in a way of sin; for this is not unity, but faction: it has no fellowship with unfruitful works, but reproves them, Eph. v. 11: it makes a man most angry with the sin of him whom he loves most. He fears not only to be *fratricida*, but *fideicida*: he doth not so love a man as to be an enemy to religion. Thirdly, for holiness: this love is set upon holy ones, because they are so; not because they are great, but good. God's image in them is the loadstone of our love, 1 John v. 2.

(6.) It is a just and righteous love. It bestows gifts, not spoils; it hurts not some to help others; it buys not a burying-place for strangers with the blood of Christ; it is not bountiful upon any other's cost. The people of God must be blameless and harmless, Phil. ii. 15; not having in the one hand bread for one, and in the other a stone for another. We must not build God's house with Satan's tools: the poorest saint wants not our unrighteousness to help him.

(7.) It is a prudent, discerning love. It loves all, yet with a difference; it is most set upon those that are the fittest objects either for want or worth. It beats not the poor from the door, while it makes strangers drunk in the cellar. It is not like the oak, which drops its acorns to swine. It loves God's friends best; the wicked with a love of pity, the godly with a love of complacency. True Christians shall have a Benjamin's portion of love. It does good especially to the household of faith, Gal. vi. 10. Brotherly love is set upon brethren. Christ loved the young man, a Pharisee, by showing loving respect toward him, Mark x. 21; but he loved Lazarus, a godly man, with a dear, intimate love: the best men shall have the best love, John xi. 3; v. 11. There is a prudence also in the measure of expressing love, so to love to-day as we may love to-morrow. We sow not by the bushel, but the handful.

(8.) It is a mutual, reciprocal love. Hence it is that there is so frequent mention of loving one another, John xiii. 34; Gal. v. 13; Col. iii. 13; Gal. vi. 2; James v. 16; 1 Thess. v. 11. Giving and receiving benefits is by some compared to the game at tennis, wherein the ball is tossed from one to the other, and if it falls, it is his forfeit who missed his stroke. His disposition is very bad, who if he will not provoke, will not repay love: where affection, there gain is reciprocal. The pole sustains the hop, and the hop adorns the pole; the wall bears up the roof, and the roof preserves the wall from wet; the wise directs the strong, and the strong protects the wise; the zealous inflame the moderate, and the moderate temper the zealous; the rich supply the poor, and the poor work for the rich. Love must have an echo to resound and return.

(9.) It is a fervent, burning love. Ἀγάπη q. ἀγεῖν κατὰ τὸ πᾶν. Purity and fervency of love are joined together, 1 Pet. i. 22; and, 1 Pet. iv. 8, "Have fervent charity among yourselves." It must be a love to the utmost, not remiss and faint; not a love of courtesy, and civil correspondency, but of entireness, and holy vehemency; such a love as was between Jonathan and David, surpassing the love of women. The fervency of it must be so great, as that it may burn and consume all intervening occasions of hatred and dislike, by bearing with infirmities, covering of sins, construing men's meanings in the better part, condescending to those of lower parts and places; like the fire that fell from heaven upon Elijah's sacrifice, which licked up a trench full of water, 1 Kings xviii. 38. A love that overcomes the greatest difficulties for the good of others, and triumphs over all opposition.

(10.) It is a constant and unwearied love. A love that must abound more and more, Phil. i. 9. A love that must be like that of Christ's, who loved his to the end, John xiii. 1; xv. 12. Love is a debt always to be owed, and always to be paid: it is a debt which the more we pay, the more we have; and which herein differs from all civil debts, that it cannot be pardoned. When we have well chosen our love, we should love our choice, and be true Scripture friends, to love at all times; not fawning upon our friends when high, and frowning upon them when low; not looking upon them as dials, only when the sun of success shines upon them: we should love them most when they want us, not when we want them most.

This for the explication of the third and last blessing, "love," which the apostle requests for these Christians.

The observations follow.

Obs. 1. Love to God flows not from nature. God is not only the object, but the author of it, 1 John iv. 7. From him, for these Christians, the apostle desires it. The affection of love is natural; the grace of love is Divine. As love is the motion of the will toward good, it is in us by nature; but as it is the motion of the will toward such an object, or as terminated upon God, it is by grace. Love is one of the graces to be put on, Col. iii. 14; and we are no more born with it in us, than with our clothes on us. Wicked men are haters of God, Rom. i. 30, and that, as the word signifies, with the greatest abhorrence; they so hate him, as to desire he were not, that so they might live without the limits of his law, and the reach of his justice. God is only by them looked upon with fear as a Judge; and whom men fear as hurtful, they hate, and wish they were taken out of the way, Psal. cxxxix. 21; 2 Chron. xix. 2; 1 John iii. 13; John xv. 18, 20. Men's hearts, and God's holiness, are very opposite: "The carnal mind is enmity against God," Rom. viii. 7. The very reason of it, the best thing that is in corrupt nature, even Lady Reason herself, is not an enemy only, but enmity, and irreconcilable. There is in it an enmity against every truth, preferring before it human mixtures and traditions; and undervaluing God's mercy, and the way of obtaining it in his Son; misjudging all his ways as grievous and unprofitable; accounting all his servants base and contemptible; An enmity there is in affection against his word, wishing every truth which crosses its lust razed out of the Scripture; quenching the motions of the Spirit; refusing to hear his voice; rejecting the counsel of God: against his people, his messengers; hating them most that speak most of God, either with the language of lip or life. Enmity in conversation, holding the truth in unrighteousness; by wilful disobedience, forsaking the ways of God, to walk in those of nature; casting off his yoke, and refusing to be reformed. And all this hatred is against God, though man by it hurts not God, but himself; man being God's enemy, not by hurting his will, but resisting it. The consideration whereof should humble us for our folly and danger in hating so good and great a God. It should also teach from whom to beg renewed inclinations. Lord, whither should we go but to thee? and how, but by thee?

Θεοστυγεῖς Στυγέω, abhor. reo, unde Styx.

Obs. 2. Love is the best thing which we can bestow upon God. It is our all, and the all which the apostle desires these Christians may return to God, who had bestowed upon them mercy and peace. Love from God is the top of our happiness, and love to God the sum of our duty. It is that only grace whereby we most nearly answer God in his own kind: he commands, corrects, comforts, directs, pities, sustains, &c., in these we cannot resemble him; but he loves us, and in this respect we may and must answer, returning love for love. Love is the best thing that the best man ever gave his God. Love is a gift, in bestowing whereof hypocrites cannot join with the faithful: there is nothing else but they may give as abundantly as the most upright in heart; they may give their tongue, hand, estate, children, nay life, but love with these, or these in love, they cannot give. And the truth is, not giving this, they give to God, in his esteem, just nothing. The best thing that a hypocrite can bestow is his life, and yet Paul tells us, that though he gave his body to be burned, and had not love, he should be nothing, 1 Cor. xiii. 3; nothing in *esse gratiæ*, in point of truth, worth, and grace. Love is the beauty of our performances; their loveliness is love to God in doing them. Love Ἐχθροῦ δῶρον, δῶρον ἄδωρον. is the marrow of every duty. Love is the salt which seasons every sacrifice; the most exquisite service without it is but as a dead carcass embalmed. God delights in nothing which we give him, unless we give ourselves first. He more regards with what heart we give, than what we give. God accepts no duty when we do it because we dare not do otherwise, but when we do it because we love to do it, it is acceptable to God. He who wants love, though he do the thing commanded, yet he breaks the law commanding. He who loves keeps the command evangelically, while he breaks it legally.

Obs. 3. Love set upon other things beside God is wrong placed. The world must often be left and loathed; at the most but used, never loved. So to love it, as thereby to lessen thy love to God; so to love it, as to be excessive either in grief for wanting it, or joy for having it, and to be over-earnest in using it, and injudicious in preferring it before thy God; is to love it unduly and sinfully. If at any time the creature be beloved innocently, it is beloved in and for God; as a pledge of heaven, as a spur to duty. Among all the creatures there cannot be found a helper fit for man. Between the soul and them there can be no match with God's consent. He that is wedded in love to the creature, is married to one that is poor, base, vexing, false.

(1.) Poor. The whole world is but a short and unsatisfying good: the sieve in the water has something in it; pulled thence, it is empty: the creature apart from God is empty of all loveliness; it is a breast filled with nothing but wind. Should the whole world be cast into our treasury, it would hardly be a mite. Hagar out of Abraham's house found nothing but scarcity; and all plenty which is not God, is but penury. Earthly blessings, like to numbers, cannot be so great, but still we may reckon, and our desires reach some one beyond them. Men in their contentions for the world prove it a scanty thing, and that it cannot satisfy all. A lover of the world can endure no rivals, as knowing how scanty an object he contends for. So large a good is God, that he who loves him delights in company.

(2.) Base and ignoble. Whatsoever is below God is below our soul; it is as unfit to rule our hearts, as the bramble to rule the trees. What we love subdues us to itself, and we are always below it: to love these earthly, drossy comforts, is to make thy soul a vassal to thy vassal, a servant of servants. Love leaves the impression of the thing beloved upon the soul; if thou lovest the earth, thou hast the impression of vileness upon a noble soul. The impression gives denomination: a piece of gold is called a Jacobus, an angel, a serpent, a lion, according to the stamp it bears: if therefore earthly objects have by love set their impression upon thy soul, what is that golden, excellent, heaven-born creature, but a lump, a clod of earth? The earth should be under our feet, not upon our heart.

(3.) Vexing and unquiet love set upon the world has more of anguish than love; it ever wrangles with us for not giving it enough. Peace is the only product of the enjoyment of God. If Christ be not in the ship, the storms will never cease; nor can any thing but his presence bring a calmness upon the soul. Rest is peculiar only to God's beloved. Love never stings but when you disturb, anger it, and hinder it from resting in God; in him, its hive, it is always and only quiet and innocent.

(4.) False and inconstant. They are but lying and flying vanities. A soul that loves the world is matched to that which soon will break and run away; none are so foolishly prodigal as the covetous man, who assures all to that which can assure nothing, no, not his own, again to him. The world is like Absalom's mule, that runs away when its lovers most want relief; it is not able to love again those that love it most. The love of that which is inconstant and weak is the strength of our misery. The best of earthly blessings have their moth and their thief, Matt. vi. 20; they "make themselves wings, they fly away as an eagle towards heaven," Prov. xxiii. 5.

Obs. 4. God is an object very meet for our love to be set upon. Much he deserves it, even for what he is. His own lovely excellencies are so great, that even for these our hearts should be set upon him, although his hatred were set upon us. Goodness is more than beneficence. God is a bundle, a heap of all worth and perfections; all the scattered excellencies of the whole creation centre and meet in him: a flower he is, in which meet the beauties of all flowers. Suppose a creature composed of all the choicest endowments of all the men that were since the creation of the world, famous in any kind; one in whom were a meek Moses, a strong Samson, all the valiant worthies of David, a faithful Jonathan, a beautiful Absalom, a rich and wise Solomon; all the holy men of God eminent for any grace; nay, all the angels of heaven, with their understandings, strength, agility, splendour, spiritualness, and holiness; and suppose this creature had never known us, helped us, benefited us, yet how would our hearts be drawn out towards it in desires and complacencies! but this, alas, though ten thousand times more exquisitely accomplished, would not amount to a shadow of divine perfection. God had in himself assembled from eternity all the excellencies which were in time; and had not he made them, they had never been. If every leaf, and blade of grass, nay, all the stars, sands, atoms in the world, were so many souls and seraphim, whose love should double in them every moment to all eternity, yet could not their love be enough for the loveliness of our God. There is nothing in God but what is amiable: "He is altogether lovely," Cant. v. 16; nothing to cause loathing, fulsomeness, or aversion, though we enjoy him to all eternity. And it should much draw out love from us, to think what God does for us. Man does but little, and it is counted much; God does much, and it is counted little; and whence is this dis-

<small>Plus bonitas, quam beneficentia. Expiat infinita venustas omnem injuriam. Neiremb.</small>

tempered estimate? Must mercy therefore be undervalued, because it comes from God? Does water lose its nature because it is in the fountain, or heat because it is in the fire, and not in some other subject? Can we be thankful to a thief that spoiled us not of what we have, and not to a God that furnished us with what we have? Can we love a man that spared, and not a God that bestowed our life? Can we love him that supplied us when we had nothing, and not Him who made us when we were nothing? Is any want so great as to be nothing? or is any gift comparable to our very being? Children love their parents from whom they have their body, though they gave it not, but God by them. And what they did give was not for love of their children, but pleasure, and possibly they caused their children's beings unwillingly. It was not from any love in parents that these children were begotten rather than others, because it was not in their choice; but when it was in God's choice, seeing innumerable men, whom he could have made, he made these rather than others. What is it that shores and sustains our beings, but the prop of Divine manutenency? Did God make the house, and then leave it to stand alone? Has not the some power that set it up, held it up ever since? Has he taken off that hand of sustentation one moment since he built thee? Parents and friends have loved thee, but was not all their affection a drop of God's fountain? would not else their bowels have been flint and marble? and had not God bid them love thee, might they not have been upon choice, what some tender mothers are upon constraint, butchers instead of parents? The light of the moon and stars in the night is from the sun, though the sun be not seen; so every benefit afforded by man is from God, though God be not observed. And what save love itself was it that remade thee when thou wert worse than nothing? Surely the giving of Christ was the hyperbole of love, the highest note that ever love reached; a work that looks as if it were intended to draw out love from us. Fire in its sphere burns not, but in some solid matter; so God, though love itself, inflamed us not with love, but by coming to and becoming man. What immeasurable love was that whereby he was debased to our vileness, that we might be advanced to his majesty, and whereby he suffered even beyond measure, and was never prodigal of any blood but his own! A mercy for contrivance so peculiar to God's love, that angels could no more have invented it than infants; and for manifestation so appropriate to his love, that had not he discovered and tendered it, it had been blasphemy and sacrilege, saith one, once to have desired it.

How great a condescension of love is it for him to become a suitor to thee for thy love, to seek and beseech thee to be reconciled to him! Rom. v. 6, 8. What is thy portion, but poverty? what gets he if he gain thy love? what loses he if he miss it? what saw he in thy person, but deformity? what in thy affection, but impotency and antipathy? How long did love contend before it conquered thee! How witty wert thou to shift off happiness! How unlike to man's carriage towards man was God's carriage towards thee! Who ever heard before that abused patience should be turned, instead of fury, into affection. If the patience of him that unjustly offends, draws love from him who is justly offended, how much more should the patience of him that is justly offended, draw love from them who unjustly offend!

Obs. 5. A Christian's greatest service and work for God is most just and equal. Why? It is to love. And what more righteous? We are his creatures; if he had commanded a harder task, as to sacrifice our children, or burn our bodies to ashes, we ought to have done it. But, (1.) He asks no more than this at our hands, to love him. "And now, Israel, what doth the Lord require of thee, but to love him?" Deut. x. 12. Love is a ready, prompt, willing affection, which does all with ease, and is its own weight. (2.) Love is that which every one has; it is implanted in every soul. If God had required a child, the barren might have had a plea. If God had required our lands and money, the poor. If labour and travail, the sick might have had his plea of exemption: but every one hath love that hath a soul. (3.) This love which he requires he bestowed, and he calls for no more than his own: he does but gather the grapes of his own vineyard; the waters of his own fountain; the fruit of his own orchard: he requires no more than he first gives. (4.) If it be bestowed on him, he returns it much better than he received it. He purifies it, removes its pain and impurity; he slays nothing in it but the ram; he makes it like the rain, which though the earth sends up in thick and foggy vapours, falls down in pure and silver showers; or like to the waters which, though they come from the sea brackish and brinish, yet return thither again in sweet and crystal streams. God takes away the inordinateness, unholiness, and sensualness of our love; he quiets and appeases it, not emptying it of its honey, but only pulling out its sting. Love being never unquiet when in its centre, or stinging when in the hive, or vexing the soul when set upon God. (5.) In loving him we do no more than we have bound ourselves to do, Deut. xxvi. 17. We have chosen him for ours; for our Husband, Father, Master: he may challenge our love; we must not go back; we are baptized in his name. When we love not God, we rob him of ourselves; we are adulteresses, being married, not to love. (6.) In loving we can but repay him, (though with no proportion,) not prevent him: he loved us first, 1 John iv. 19. Loved our souls, in pitying, and pardoning, and renewing them; loved the body, in constant provision, protection, direction. Loved us in giving himself; loved us in giving his gifts. (7.) We must, if we love not him, love something else. And where can we find any other upon whom to bestow it? who among the gods is like to him? Exod. xv. 11; and what among the creatures is fit for us, that can satisfy our exigences, that will relieve us in distress, that will stay with us continually, that will love us again? (8.) In loving him we love one another; and love is the glue of the world, the cement of society; it thinks nothing too difficult for a friend; it makes us harmless and helpful. If twenty men love one another, every one as himself, every one is twenty, every one hath twenty hearts, forty hands, eyes, feet. Love unlocks every one's cabinet; making the one take out counsel, another riches, another strength, all something, for the good of one another.

Obs. 6. Wheresoever love to God is, there will love to man appear. The grace of love, as hath been opened, comprehends love to both: from the fountain of piety must flow the stream of charity. He who has not love enough for man, where will he find it for God? Love is the pulse of faith, and the breath of Christianity. "Faith works by love," Gal. v. 6: though love be not a hand to receive Christ, yet is it a tool in the hand to work for Christ, and that in working for Christians. The flames of zeal never consumed the moisture of charity. He who loves God for his own sake, will love his brother for God's. Add to your godliness (saith the apostle) brotherly kindness, 2 Pet. i. 7. He who shutteth up his bowels to a wanting brother, "how dwelleth the love of God in him?" 1 John iii. 17. The nearer the lines come to the centre, the nearer are they to one another. Our love to the godly increases with our love to God. The sunshine upon the dial moves, though not so swiftly, yet according to that proportion which the sun in the firmament moves; and our love to the people of God, though it be not so great as unto God, yet is it according to the measure of our love to God.

Obs. 7. It is a great discovery of God's goodness, in that with our loving him he joins our loving one another. He might have so challenged our love to himself, as thereby we might neither have had time, will, strength, or allowance to love one another. But behold his love, he will be served of us in our serving of man. He accounts this pure religion, "to visit the fatherless and widow," James i. 27. The serving of one another by love, he requires as a token of our serving him by faith, Gal. v. 13. So gracious is he, that he esteems what we do to our own flesh and blood as done to himself, and accounts himself a debtor to us for what we do for ourselves; he remembers it long, rewards it largely, and does both exactly: he has appointed charity as the most safe and gainful invention in the world, Prov. xix. 17; xxi. 13; Psal. cxii. 9; Matt. xxv. 40; Heb. xiii. 16; Luke xii. 33. It is a payment to the poor Christian in this place, who sends his bill of exchange, his prayer, to God, and he accepts the bill, and pays it for our use in heaven: we keep nothing as a mercy but what we are willing, and, one way thus, to lose. Death robs us by the way, if we think to carry our wealth to heaven with us; but if we send it by bills, we shall receive it safely. He who has laden himself with apples in the orchard, and is sure to be searched when he comes out of the gate, throws his apples over the wall to a friend, who keeps them for him. In this world we lade ourselves with gifts, death will undoubtedly search us when we go hence; but if while we are here we throw, by charity, our enjoyments into heaven, we have there a Friend that keeps them safe. He that denies to give this interest of his gifts by charity, forfeits the principal; and he that takes in his worldly commodities without paying God this custom, shall lose the whole.

Obs. 8. Prayer is a singular help to bring us to love God; it was here the apostolical engine in the text. When we cry for his Holy Spirit, the Spirit of love, he cannot deny us; he healed the lame when they cried. When thou criest, and sayest from the heart, I would fain love thee, but I cannot, will he not give thee legs to run after him? Prayer brings us into familiarity with God, and by converse (you know) love grows between men. God delights to show himself in his own way, and, as he did to Moses, send us down from the mount of prayer with souls shining with love. Prayer exercises our love; it blows up the sparks of love into a flame. Love is an especial gift of the Spirit, Gal. v. 22. We "are taught of God to love one another," 1 Thess. iv. 9. It is he that must warm our hearts with this Divine grace; and he being sought unto, and his power implored and acknowledged, will not deny it.

Thus much of the first particular, in this third and last part of the title, the prayer, viz. the blessings prayed for, "Mercy, peace, love." Hence follows,

2. The measure in which the apostle desires these blessings may be bestowed, "Be multiplied."

For the explication of which two things would be opened.

1. Wherein stands the multiplication of these blessings, or what it is that the apostle desires, when he prays for the multiplication of these gifts and graces.

2. Why the apostle makes this request, and prays not only for the bestowing, but the multiplying of these blessings.

1. What this multiplying is. The word in the original signifies, as to be multiplied, so to be increased, filled, enlarged; and it is in Scripture indifferently used to signify the multiplication of things in their number, and their augmentation in measure and greatness. Hence some render πληθυνθείη, *multiplicetur*, be multiplied; others, *adimpleatur*, be filled, or fulfilled, or filled up, or increased. It properly signifies to increase in number, and not in measure; and when it is applied to people, and the church, as it is oft in the Acts of the Apostles, vii. 17; ix. 31, &c., it is only used for an increase in number; but when it is spoken of sin, or graces, as Matt. xxiv. 12; 1 Pet. i. 2; 2 Pet. i. 2, and in this place of Jude, it may signify an increase in measure only. And so the apostle prays that the gifts and graces which these Christians had already obtained, might receive a further degree of augmentation, that believers might grow, abound, and increase in them more and more, Eph. iv. 16; 1 Pet. ii. 2; 2 Pet. iii. 18; Psal. lxxxiv. 7; 1 Thess. iv. 1; 2 Cor. xiii. 9. And thus, though the mercy of God, which was the first of the three blessings here desired by the apostle, as it is in itself, and as in God, cannot be increased, it being infinite; yet in respect of the effects and graces flowing from it upon believers, it may be increased.

More particularly, when the apostle prays that these Christians may have this increase and augmentation of grace, he comprehends in his request these several blessings.

(1.) That they may be sensible, and observing of their wants and deficiencies of grace. That they may often cast up their accounts, and see what they have gained, and wherein they are defective; that they may resent, as their gains with thankfulness, so their wants with humility. They who see not, can neither desire nor receive what they want. A Christian must be like a covetous man, *totus in rationibus*, much employed in searching and examining what he has not, as well as what he has; what he has lost, as well as what he has gained; what he has laid out, as well as what he has laid up; whether he stands, how he has fallen, how far he has gone; and though he must account no loss irreparable, yet none contemptible; and though no gain so small as to be unthankful for it, yet none so great as to be contented with, or proud of it.

(2.) That they make use of the helps, the food, and fuel which God has appointed for the increase of their grace, Luke xvii. 5; as reading, prayer, hearing, sacraments, meditation, 1 Pet. ii. 2; and he that neglects these, is not a strong, but a sick Christian. These are the marts and fairs wherein we trade for grace. A thriving Christian must keep constant traffic with heaven; sending thither, hearing thence: in the former, telling; in the latter, taking in what he wants. We must make growth the end of our feeding, and thriving of our trading: we must not trade, to trade; pray, to pray; hear, to hear; but to grow better thereby.

(3.) That they may proportionably answer the worth and length of those opportunities God afforded them for increasing grace. That they might not devour fat enjoyments, having meanwhile lean, and barren, or indifferent hearts. He is not an abounding, thriving Christian, who has but an ordinary growth under rich opportunities: we must abound in returning, as well as in receiving; we must not be like the kidney in the beast, lean in the midst of fatness; not heaths and wildernesses, under the showers of salvation, Heb. v. 12; nay, not content ourselves in being but as good as others, who haply enjoy less.

They who enjoy much from God, and yet are no better than those who enjoy less, are therefore worse because they are not better.

(4.) That they may forbear and avoid whatsoever hinders and keeps down the thriving and growing in grace. That they may take heed of secret ways of spending; that they may not privily delight in any known way of sin, or beloved lust, which makes the most glittering Christian abroad to be but a bankrupt at home. Christians must cut off the suckers that draw away their nourishment. Love of the world, pride, uncleanness, &c., cannot thrive with grace in the same heart; as the one goes up, the other goes down; as the spleen swells, the body decays.

(5.) That they may have an impartial increase in every grace, in one as well as another. That to one grace they might add another, 2 Pet. i. 5; loving every duty, and loathing every evil, Psal. cxix. 101. All graces have a concatenation, and an inseparability, a holy band, a divine league; and as every Christian has, so he grows in every part of the new creature. He fructifies in every good work, Col. i. 10: he labours to keep an equability in his courses; not strict in some things, and slack in others. He prefers not one before another, 1 Tim. v. 21; he has a pulse of grace that beats evenly and equally: he is neither a maimed person, who wants any limb, nor a monster, who has one limb so big that others want; but has a comely symmetry of part with part. No one of his graces stands at a stay, while the other grows: he does not go richly apparelled in some one piece of his apparel, and beggarly in the rest; all his nourishment is not conveyed to some one part, to the starving of the rest.

(6.) That they may multiply in grace to an exercise, acting and laying out of grace. That grace might be augmented into action; that the fountain full inwardly might overflow outwardly; that as it was, so it might appear grace; that they might be free as well as full, and fructify in every good work; that the hand as well as the heart might be filled with the fruits of righteousness. As grace will be increased in the pouring out, so must it be poured out when it increases. The running water, and the active Christian, are both the sweetest. The more a musical instrument is used, the sweeter is its melody. Graces, like garments, will be, the more we use them, the more free from the moth: the more we can, the more we should do; and the more we do, the more we can, we love to do.

(7.) That they may obtain a measure of grace suitable to their several and particular exigences and occasions. That they may not only have grace more than others, but enough for themselves; i. e. in some suitable measure to their own several conditions and employments. Some men have stronger temptations to resist, corruptions to subdue, greater burdens to bear, employments to go through, and these want more abundant graces than others. Some man may better keep house with a hundred pounds a year, than another who has a great family, and familiarity, can do with a thousand: a man who has great revenues, may yet be poorer than he who has less, if he have greater expenses.

(8.) That they may constantly abide and continue in the grace they had received. The further obtaining of what grace we want, necessarily implies a retaining and holding fast what we have. By the same reason that we desire to get more, we shall keep that which we have already gotten. Decay is ever inconsistent with growth. A Christian must not go aside, much less go backward; not lie still with the stone, nor creep with the snail, much less go back with the crab; not be a golden Christian in youth, a silver one in manhood, and a leaden one in old age. Our falls into sin must be but for a fit, not so our forwardness in Christianity; our goodness not like the morning dew, Hos. vi. 4; we must not turn back, deal unfaithfully, and turn aside as a deceitful bow, Psal. lxxviii. 57. It is hypocrisy to pretend that we are gone, or going, further in religion than others who are eminent, and yet be behind what ourselves once were, and that when we were beginners. If grace be not preserved, it cannot be augmented: fire cannot be made to blaze out, if it be not kept from going out. If the life of grace be gone, the growth will follow. If we continue not rooted in Christ, we cannot be built up in him, Col. ii. 7.

(9.) That they may be boundless and unlimited in the progress of grace; that they may be ever making additions to what they have, 2 Pet. i. 5. Christianity knows not enough: the degrees of a Christian's grace must be like numbers, the highest whereof being numbered, a higher than that may yet be named. Even those worthy Thessalonians had something lacking in their faith, 1 Thess. iii. 10. We must never cease growing till we be grown into heaven; we must forget what is behind, and press forward toward the mark, Phil. iii. 13, 14. If perfection be our pattern, proficiency is our duty. It is true, he that has least grace has enough to be thankful for; but he that has the most, has not enough to be idle. We are never gotten far enough till we are gotten home. He that is rich enough is nothing worth. He was never good, that desired not to be better; he is stark naught, that desires not to be as good as the best. Ubi incipis nolle fieri melior, ibi desinis esse bonus. Bern. Ep. 91.

(10.) Lastly, The apostle desires the multiplication of grace even to the sense, feeling, and apprehension of those who were partakers thereof; that those who had grace might know they had it. The people of God do not always know their own holiness and happiness: these are true, though not strong in grace. The perceiving of our grace is an additional happiness to our receiving it. In the light of God we must see light. It is a double and a very desirable blessing to have the company and comfort of grace at the same time.

This of the first branch of explication, What the apostle desired for these Christians when he prayed for this multiplication. Now follows,

2. Why he desired it.

This he did, (1.) In respect of God.
(2.) In respect of others.
(3.) In respect of themselves.
(4.) In respect of himself.

(1.) In respect of God. The more grace is multiplied, the more God is, [1.] Honoured, Matt. v. 16. Herein is my Father honoured, if ye bring forth much fruit, John xv. 8. If the servants of God do much work, God will be accounted a good, a bountiful Master, 2 Cor. iv. 15; Phil. i. 11. 1. In respect of the great reward men will think there is in his service, and some extraordinary benefit by it, that his servants are so laborious in it. And, 2. In respect of the great ability that he bestows upon his to be and do good. God will be admired in them that believe. If poor servants are so rich and glorious, what then, will men say, is the Master? if his servants be so holy, what then is he who keeps them? if there be so much in a drop, what is there then in the ocean? if he imparts so much to others, what then hath he in himself? The plenty of the crop is the praise of the husbandman. [2.] As God is honoured by the abounding of his servants in holiness, so is he likewise pleased. Fruitfulness upon earth Æstimari a cultoribus potest ille qui colitur. Salv. Chrysostomus existimat glorificationem hic poni pro exultatione. Gerh. in Johan xv 8.

is joy in heaven, Luke xv. 7. The husbandman is not only praised, but pleased by the fruitfulness of his grounds, the barrenness whereof is both his shame and his sorrow. The thriving of the child is the joy of the father. If we rejoice so much in holiness, that see it, and love it so little, what then must God do, who is holiness itself! How angry was God with his barren vineyard! Isa. v. 6. If God be best pleased with holiness, he must needs be best pleased with them who are most holy.

(2.) The apostle desired this multiplication of grace in respect of others; that they might not only speak good of God, but get good to themselves. The whole country fares the better for a rich Christian; he keeps open house; the more he has the more he gives; he labours to make all such as himself, his bonds only excepted, Acts xxvi. 29. There is nothing more covetous or prodigal than grace. A saint ever loves to be receiving from God, and imparting to others. From Jerusalem round about to Illyricum Paul preached the gospel, Rom. xv. 19. He who was so abundantly rich himself, made it his work to make others so, 2 Cor. vi. 10. What an encouragement is it to young beginners in grace, to see that they who once were as poor, and had as little to begin with, as themselves, have attained to such a plentiful spiritual estate! What a joy is it to the strong Christian, whose love of complacency is set upon the excellent ones, and whose crown of rejoicing it is to see the honour of God propagated!

(3.) The apostle desired this multiplication of grace in respect of themselves, and that, [1.] In respect of their duty; they could never be too abundant in goodness for Him, from whom they were, and had, and did whatever was good. How could God dwell too much in the house of his own building? How could the vineyard and garden of his own planting be too fruitful? the well of his own digging be too full? In their creation they received souls, bodies, faculties, senses, with parts and members from him; in him also they lived, and moved, and had their being; and could they do him too much service? In their redemption the delivery not only from condemnation, but from vain conversation, 1 Pet. i. 18, and from the service and corruption of sin, was aimed at by God; and not only a preservation of them to heaven, but in holiness. In their profession, they were Christians, and followers of Christ; and how could they walk too exactly, who had such a Guide? They had in the word precepts, promises, threatenings, examples; and how could they be too precise, who had such a rule? [2.] For their dignity. Holiness is a Christian's greatest honour, and therefore the greatest degree of holiness, the highest degree of honour. Grace is called glory, and the more grace, the more glory, 2 Cor. iii. 18. It is that which has the most of Scripture commendation. What an honourable mention does Paul make of the Romans, for having their faith spoken of throughout the world! Rom. i. 8. Our Saviour, who contemned the glorious buildings of the temple, when his disciples showed him them, admired a strong faith more than once, Matt. viii. 10; xv. 28. [3.] For their further peace and comfort in this life. There is no abundance, but that of grace, which can content the possessor; the more holiness, the more enjoyment of Him in whose presence is fulness of joy. Whence is a saint's trouble, but from the deficiency of his graces? what is it that pinches him, but the scantiness of these spiritual garments? the larger they are, the greater is his ease. He that has true grace may go to heaven certainly, but he who has strong grace only goes comfortably. A weak faith, a small degree of love, patience, humility, will not carry a man joyfully through great troubles. [4.] For their future crown and further felicity in the next life. If any shall follow the Lamb in whiter and larger robes of glory than others, they are those whom he hath adorned most with the robes of grace here. If any shine brighter than others in heaven, they shall be those who have been brightest in grace upon the earth. Though glory be not bestowed for any merit in grace, yet I see no inconvenience to hold that it is bestowed according to the proportion of grace. If the more grace a saint has, the more he is fitted for glory, Col. i. 12; then the more grace he has, the more, it is likely, he shall be filled with glory. The more the soul is widened with grace, the more capacious will it be of glory: the heaviest crowns are fittest for the strongest heads.

(4.) Lastly, The apostle desired this multiplication of grace upon these Christians in respect of himself. The holiness of the people is the crown of the minister; and the greater their holiness, the weightier and more glorious is his crown. The apostle John had no greater joy than to see his spiritual children walk in the truth. The thriving of the child, is the comfort and credit of the nurse; the fruitfulness of the field, the praise and pleasure of the husbandman; the beauty of the building, is the commendation of the artificer; the health, fruitfulness, and good plight of the flock, is the joy of the shepherd. Ministers are husbandmen, nurses, artificers, shepherds, in Scripture phrase. Nothing more troubles a godly minister than to see his multiplied pains answered with a scanty proficiency; and his double labour, with scarce a single return of holiness. A gainsaying people is the grief of a minister that all the day long stretcheth out his hands; although it may be a sweet mitigation of that grief, to consider that God will not reward his ministers according to their success, but their sincerity and industry.

This for the explication of this second particular in the apostle's prayer, The measure in which he desired these gifts and graces may be bestowed.

The observations follow.

Obs. 1. Great is the folly of those whose whole contention is for worldly increase, and multiplication of earthly blessings. In worldly things, their desires have an everlasting *et cætera*; they will lay house to house, field to field, like the widow, who, when she had filled all her vessels with oil, yet calls for another vessel. Ahab to his kingdom must add Naboth's vineyard: the rich man (Luke xii.) had his barns full, yet he must enlarge them. Many live as if God had sent them a voyage into the world to gather cockles and pebbles, whereas he employed them to trade for pearls. Where is the man that envies not him who has more wealth, and yet who is he that with a holy emulation looks upon him who has more grace than himself? Where does the best sort of earth deserve to lie, but at the apostles' feet? What has the man who goes Christless? What has he laboured for all his days, but that, not only without which he might have gone to heaven, but that with which he cannot get thither? What folly to lose a crown for a crumb; a kingdom, a soul, a God for a trifle! How vain is it to multiply that which in its greatest increase is but nothing! The truth is, earthly comforts are not capable of multiplication. Did men look upon the world with Scripture spectacles, and not with Satan's multiplying glass, it would appear in its greatness but a small thing. The world has two breasts; they who suck at the best of them, draw nothing but wind and vanity; they who suck at the other, draw woe and vexation.

Obs. 2. Great is the impiety of those that hinder

people from increasing in grace; who are the pullbacks, damps, and quench-coals of the companies where they converse. The holiest men pray that grace may be multiplied; what then are they who labour to have it extinguished? Elymas the sorcerer had one of the bitterest and severest expressions of detestation from the apostle that was ever bestowed upon any by a good man; the apostle calls him one full of subtlety and all mischief, a child of the devil, an enemy of all righteousness, Acts xiii. 10; and why? but because he sought to turn away the deputy from the faith. They who take away the key of knowledge, stop the mouths of ministers, cause a dearth of spiritual food, and cannot endure the preaching of sound doctrine, and the spreading of holiness, would haply account such expressions as these of Paul to be bitter; but I hardly see how they deserve milder.

Obs. 3. It is the height of impiety to hate people because God has multiplied grace in them. How hateful is it to hate where and because God loves! yet some there are, who, like gardeners, snip those most who are tallest sprouts in holiness. It is observed by some, that there is most admiration and highest respect bestowed by the professors of all false religions in the world, upon those that are most precise and exact in observing those religions. What an amazement is it, that professors of the true religion alone should most bitterly hate those that make the furthest progress in it! It is a commendable thing among men for one to be excellent and exquisite in his trade and occupation which he professes; and must it alone be a disgraceful thing that men should excel in the best of mysteries and callings? Yet what more common than to see the most thriving Christian to become the obloquy, nay, prey of the times? and those who are most illuminated, to have that Æolus of hell sending out his winds of opposition most against them? Heb. x. 32. And who has not observed the zealous and sincere Christian persecuted, when the time-serving and lukewarm formalist is not only spared, but preferred? and what trees are so cudgelled and battered as those who are most fruitful? If hatred be hellish because it is set against godliness, then certainly that hatred is most hellish which is set against most godliness.

Obs. 4. They who are ashamed of being exact and forward in religion, are ashamed of their greatest glory. Men commonly love to excel in every thing more than in that which is true excellency; they think that a little godliness is enough, and that abundance of wealth is but a little. In getting riches, they love to lead; in going toward heaven, they will hardly follow. So much religion as will preserve their estates and reputation, so much as will not cross their interest, or hinder their preferment, they will embrace; but they love not to follow religion too close, for fear of being dashed. They herein resemble some students of the law, who study that science, not to be exact in it, but only so far as they may be able another day to keep their estates. Men commonly love that much, which when they do so, it is hard not to love too much; but they are but remiss in that, in which it is impossible to be excessive; they making it their study to take heed of that of which there is no danger, viz. too much preciseness in the ways of holiness. Christianity in our times is like our buildings, much more slight than of old. Till I hear of one man, from the creation of the world to this day, that ever repented him when he came to die of being too holy while he lived, I shall desire to be no man of the times.

Obs. 5. God is most free of his best gifts; he gives his people leave and command to multiply spirituals, when often he impairs their temporals; he bestows a crown, where he sometimes denies a crumb: those whom he makes poor in the world, he at the same time makes rich in faith. He deals with his people when they are too heavy laden with the luggage of worldly enjoyments, as men do that are weighing their commodities in a pair of scales; they never leave taking, and taking away from that scale which is too heavy, till the other is as weighty or weightier than it. And God does justly and mercifully impoverish the body to enrich the soul. There is nothing good which hinders us from enjoying the chiefest good; which is not *vehiculum*, but *vinculum*; not a furtherance, but a fetter. How gracious is God to choose our comforts for us! we should ever take the worst part, should he leave us to our own skill: he loves to relieve us for our profit, not for our lust; we naturally love the contrary.

Obs. 6. The Christian whose grace multiplies, is neither careless of the helps, or fearless of the hinderances of grace. He dares not omit any duty, or slight any ordinances, which God has appointed to make him spiritually prosperous. He is rowing up a river that runs with a strong current, and he knows if he rest his oars, he shall fall down the stream; he delights to pray continually, 1 Thess. v. 17: he who has grace in plenty, will have prayer in fervency. Prayer woos grace to come, and wins it to tarry. Grace ever sets us upon praying for grace: the alms of grace will be begged for, and God gives it to the prayer of the humble, James iv. 6. Growing men have good stomachs. It is as possible at the same time to grow in the love of grace and decay in love to ordinances, as to increase the fire by withdrawing the fuel. The sprouting Christian sits under the dew of heaven: they who forsake the assembling of themselves together, will never hold fast the profession of the faith without wavering, Heb. x. 23, 25. As grace is not given *nolenti*, to him that continues unwilling to receive it; so neither is it increased *negligenti*, to him that doth not labour to improve it. Apostles, pastors, and teachers were given by Christ for our growth up to the measure of stature of the fulness of Christ, Eph. iv. 13. The forsaking of these is ever with a decreasing of grace. As a Christian abates in his appetite, he will decay in strength; and with his strength his stomach will return. They who have no spiritual hunger, are far from spiritual health; and never had God a working, who was not a feeding servant. He is but the picture of a Christian, who grows not, who feeds not. Nor can growth in Christianity consist with the love of poison, any more than with the forbearance of food. They who thrive hate the ways of inordinate spending. Sin is a waster of our graces and our comforts. The Spirit of God is a tender and delicate thing, nor will it stay with those that admit of company so contrary to it as is sin. Every beloved lust is as a worm at the root of a flower. He who has so excellent a jewel as grace, must keep it under the lock of the fear of sin: while sin comes in at one door, grace goes out at the other. The ark could not stay with the Philistines, nor grace with the love of the smallest sin. The least sin is terrible to the greatest saint; he makes not light of it, but well knows that a long thread of iniquity may be let in with a small needle.

Obs. 7. Decays in grace are most repugnant to a Christian's welfare. Decreasing in spiritual blessings directly thwarts the apostle's petition. It is uncomfortable to see the days grow shorter, to see a man grow behindhand in the world, to see a withered and a blasted field, a man in a lingering consumption. Naomi's condition moved pity, when she went out full, and returned empty, Ruth i. 21; but what pity does a decaying soul require from us! To consume heavenward, to be plundered of grace, to lose our first love, Rev. ii. 4, to be declining from God, is a misery indeed, a soul-misery, the misery of every misery. It is better for thee that God take away all than himself from thee. David was more fearful of losing God's Spirit than his kingdom, Psal. li. 11. It is the most sorrowful alteration in the world, after the enjoyment of it, to be forsaken by it.

Obs. 8. A saint allows not himself in any deficiency of grace. He desires to be perfect in every good work; to "grow up in Christ in all things," Eph. iv. 15; to be "full of goodness and knowledge," Rom. xv. 14; to be "throughly furnished to all good works," 2 Tim. iii. 17; and to have grace in all the powers of the soul, as his blood is in every vein of the body; to "perfect holiness in the fear of God," 2 Cor. vii. 1. His imperfection is a trouble to him as well as his pollution. He sees no grace in another, but he covets it; no ornament, but he admires it; no spot, but he abhors it. He ever wants as much of contentment as he does of grace: he never saith, I have as much as another has; but, I have less than I myself should have: he labours to furnish his house all over; he prizes every command, delights in every duty, sees a beauty in every way of God, and the weakness of his grace is the strength of his trouble. They who need nothing are indeed defective in every thing, Rev. iii. 17.

Obs. 9. A fruitless conversation is inconsistent with grace multiplied. A fruitless tree is little better than a log; there is a small difference betwixt a dead stock and a barren tree. True Christianity suffers not Christians to content themselves with bare hearing the word; or, as one calls it, with mere auricular profession. Wherever grace grows, others may see it. Men cannot discern the growing of it, or how it grew, but they can discern that it is grown when it is grown. The profiting of a saint, with Timothy's, "appears to all," 1 Tim. iv. 15. Growing grace, like corn, will appear above ground. The thriving of a child will be known by its looks; its colour and complexion will speak it. The thriving of Daniel, and the rest, was known by the looking upon their countenances, Dan. i. 13, 15. He who thrives in holiness, will have his visage altered, his outward carriage and complexion amended; he is like a grown man, who for some time has been absent, he is so grown that he can hardly be known. The voice of a grown Christian is much altered from that which it was when he was a child; he speaks now not vainly, but profitably. Hence it is that wicked men wonder at him as at a strange sight, 1 Pet. iv. 4.

Obs. 10. Lastly, The increase of grace, as well as the beginnings of it, is from God. The apostle here prays even for multiplication of grace. It is grace that must make us multiply in grace: the plantation and the accretion are from the same hand. When God at first made all living creatures, he bestowed on them their *crescite*, a blessing, as well as a being. He who makes us good must make us better. He who makes us come to him, must also keep us from going from him. He who begins the good work in us, must also perform it, Phil. i. 6. God is both the "author and finisher of our faith," Heb. xii. 2. If our graces be only put into us by God, and not kept in, they will soon go out. God it is that must not only set us up, but keep us up. Grace is like a top, or a bell; if God do not continue the impressions of his strength upon us, and keep us up, as well as raise us up, we shall soon go down. The strongest child in God's family cannot go alone. He

<small>Qui operatur ut accedamus, idem operatur ne discedamus. Aug. de Bon. Pers. c. 7.</small>

it is who enables us to take the first and every step we take toward heaven; we live in a constant dependence upon him; he is not only the term of our journey, but our way, our guide, our keeper in it. If God should give us a stock of grace, and then leave us to ourselves to trade, we should never thrive. Adam himself became a bankrupt, and so should we; but blessed be God, our happiness is held by a better tenure, even by Christ, the supplies of whose Spirit alone continue and multiply our graces.

This for the second particular in the third part of the title; viz. The measure in which he desired those blessings. Now follows,

3. The persons upon whom he prays that these blessings may be in this measure bestowed; "Unto you."

The apostle's desire of these blessings, and the multiplication of them, agrees to the persons for whom they are desired in two respects.

(1.) In respect of their forementioned privileges, sanctification, preservation in Christ, calling.

(2.) In respect of their after-mentioned dangers by seducers, who were crept in among them.

(1.) In respect of their forementioned privileges, of sanctification, &c., and so the apostle desires this multiplication of grace for them. [1.] Though they were sanctified, they were not so fully sanctified, and had not been so long preserved and called, but that they still wanted a further multiplication of grace; they still stood more in need of the effects of mercy, more inward peace and love; they had not yet attained their full measure, Phil. iii. 13. [2.] To all that are sanctified, preserved, &c. Though they were many, he wishes that every one might have a child's portion; that blessings might be multiplied to the whole multitude of saints; that there might not be one barren among them; that as God had a full hand, and was rich in mercy, so that his bounty might be dispersed to them all. [3.] To them only who are sanctified. They only who had grace, were capable of having grace multiplied; to these only who had, the apostle wishes that more might be given. There is no growth where there is not a truth of grace; nor can these distinguishing blessings of mercy, love, peace, be desired at all for wicked men, upon the supposition of their resolution to continue and proceed to be such. [4.] To them, because they were sanctified, preserved, called. How suitable was it for them who had formerly received these privileges, to multiply and increase in holiness; for them to thrive who had a stock of sanctity; for them who were preserved by Christ, to be kept from hurt by sin; for them who were called, to be holy in all manner of holy conversation, as he who called them was holy! 1 Pet. i. 15.

(2.) This desire of the multiplication of these blessings agrees to the persons to whom it is desired, in respect of their after-mentioned danger by seducers, who were crept in among them. It is observable that both Jude and Peter salute the Christians to whom they wrote with this prayer, for multiplication of these spiritual blessings; that since these Christians had more enemies, they might have more armour than others, and that their graces might be multiplied with their dangers.

Obs. 1. The sanctification of none is in this life so complete, but it admits of multiplication. Mercy, peace, love, even to you (saith the apostle) be multiplied. There is no plenary perfection on this side heaven; the highest saint in this life is not come to the fulness of his measure, Eph. iv. 13. Blessed Paul thought not himself to have apprehended, Phil. iii. 13. The most perfect Christian is perfectly imperfect when he begins, imperfectly perfect when he ends; when we have done all, we are unprofitable servants. The fullest vessel may have more wine poured into it, without any fear of bursting; none must bid God stay his hand. They who think they have need of nothing, have truly received nothing. Till the sabbath comes, we must daily be gathering manna: he that rests in the time of labour, shall labour, though in vain, in the time of rest. A Christian is not like a top, that moves by going round, and not by going forward: not like the sun in Hezekiah's time, that stood still; but like the sun in its natural course, that goes forward to the perfect day. We must go from strength to strength, till we appear before the Lord in Zion, Psal. lxxxiv. 7. Where there is no growing, there is some decaying. While we neglect to gain, we spend upon the stock. Sin is continually making breaches in our graces, and we must be daily making them up; our garment has daily rents, and therefore it wants constant mending; the dust daily falls in our houses, and therefore they want frequent cleansing; our hearts are like to children's faces, after every washing, they soon grow foul again. Sanctification is nothing but a return to our first estate, to which we cannot attain till death. When the sting of sin is gone, the stain cleaves close, and we had need wash seven times daily to get it out.

Obs. 2. God has enough grace for every one of his children. Grace is afforded and multiplied indifferently to one as well as to another; though all have not grace equally, yet all truly, and according to their particular exigences. As every good and perfect gift is from God, so (in a due proportion) upon every saint. None so hath all grace, as that every one hath not some. Christ is a Head that sends influence into every member, Eph. iv. 16. "Of his fulness we have all received," John i. 16. He is an overflowing fountain of grace, which though it may be imparted, yet is not impaired. The receiving of grace by one, does no more hinder the receiving thereof by another, than one man's seeing the sun hinders another from seeing it also. God is a rich Father, he gives, though not alike, yet sufficient portions to all his children. Our elder Brother had a double portion; he was anointed with the oil of gladness above his fellows, Psal. xlv. 7, but the ointment poured upon the Head fell down upon every member. He who had holiness for Abraham, Moses, David, Peter, will not suffer the least child in his house to be totally destitute. They all drank of that Rock which flows toward us, 1 Cor. x. 4. If we had but their thirst, here is as much water still as ever there was. The people of God should neither envy one another for their fulness, nor upbraid one another with their emptiness; but admire the wisdom, and bless the bounty, of him who gives to all, though differently. The whole company of saints is like to a well-tuned instrument, the strings whereof, though not all of one note, but some higher, some lower, yet all together make a sweet harmony, nor can the loudest be without the smallest. In what grace one is defective, in that let another labour to supply. In what one abounds, let another labour to imitate and excel; but let all adore and delight in Him, whose are the scattered excellencies bestowed upon all the saints in the world.

Obs. 3. Where God has begun grace, he is not weary of bestowing more. Mercy be multiplied to you sanctified ones. To him that hath shall be given, Mark iv. 25. God loves not to set up a foundation without a wall, nor walls without a roof. He perfects what concerns his people; and the work of the Lord is perfect, Deut. xxxii. 4. And he doth his whole work upon Mount Zion, Isa. x.

12. How good is God, not only to do good because he will do good, but because he has done so! to make one grace a kind of obligation upon himself to bestow another! God herein resembling some magnificent king, who when he has set his love upon a favourite, afterward is in love with his own choice of and bounty on him, and loves him for these very favours which he has given him. "Every branch that beareth fruit, he purgeth it, that it may bring forth more fruit," John xv. 2. Greater things, saith Christ to Nathanael, thou shalt see, John i. 50. He who kills one lust, shall kill another; he who is conscientious in one duty, shall be enabled to another. He who has the grace of desire, shall have grace bestowed on his desire; and he who has grace to do a little, shall have grace to do more. God is never weary of giving. He has oil enough for every vessel, and still asks when he hath filled all our vessels, as that woman in the story, "Bring me yet a vessel," 2 Kings iv. 6. The meditation whereof, as it should comfort us against our spiritual deficiencies, because we know where to have more grace; so should it incite us to proceed in holiness, and never to think we have enough, or to answer, as he did, "There is not a vessel." In the best things there is no excess.

Obs. 4. Only sanctified ones have the blessing of spiritual multiplication. As first God gave the word of creation, before he gave the word of benediction; so does he still spiritually. "Whosoever hath not, from him shall be taken away even what he hath," Matt. xiii. 12. If there be not *essentia* there cannot be *incrementum*; if no truth, no growth of grace. A stake that is merely thrust into the ground, having neither root nor life, grows in nothing but in rottenness: and this speaks the misery of one not in Christ and enlivened by the Spirit of regeneration; nothing does him good; he devours fat ordinances, but has a lean soul; he is by the showers of every sermon and sacrament made meeter for the axe, and fitter fuel for hell.

Obs. 5. Our beginning in holiness is an engagement upon us to go on. Sanctified, preserved, called ones, must multiply grace. The beginning in the Spirit must be a caution to us, that we end not in the flesh. If saints be barren, the trees of God's orchard, where can increase be expected? A fruitless tree in the field may haply be borne with, not such a one in the garden. They who are planted in the house of God, should flourish in the courts of our God, still bring forth fruit in old age, be fat and flourishing, Psal. xcii. 13, 14. It is an unanswerable dilemma, If the ways of God were bad, why did you begin in them? if good, why did you not proceed? They who are holy must be holy still, Rev. xxii. 11. It is a great disgrace for religion to be disgraced by her children, to be forsaken by her followers. The dispraise of any by a friend, is easily believed by every one, especially by an enemy to the dispraised: when sanctified ones grow loose and remiss, sanctity is stabbed; by the reproaches of others, it is but scratched. It is excellent counsel of the apostle, that we "lose not the things which we have wrought," 2 John 8. As the vigilancy of Satan is to take from sanctified ones, so their care must be to keep what they have gotten, and to get what they want, Luke xxii. 3.

Obs. 6. God affords graces suitable to all the exigences of his people; multiplied grace to those who are in multiplied difficulties and temptations. My grace," saith God to Paul, " is sufficient for thee," 2 Cor. xii. 9. Whenever God gives a burden, he provides a shoulder. He never requires brick from his people, without giving them straw. He will either multiply grace, or diminish the temptation. He bids his people up and eat, if he sends them a long journey. Those saints of his whom he has employed in winter seasons, he has ever clothed with winter garments: commonly the best men have lived in the worst times, and God's stars have shined brightest in the darkest ages. The faithful have been more than conquerors in conflicts, both with persecutors and seducers, Rom. viii. 37. And truly, grace multiplied is much better than temptation either assuaged or removed.

Verse 3.

Beloved, when I gave all diligence to write unto you of the common salvation, it was needful for me to write unto you, and exhort you that ye should earnestly contend for the faith which was once delivered unto the saints.

We have finished the first part of this Epistle, viz. the title. The second follows, the body and substance of the whole Epistle, wherein the apostle's scope is to incite these Christians to embrace a seasonable exhortation, to the 24th verse of the Epistle.

In it there are four principal parts, two of them contained in this third verse.

1. The reasons of the apostle's sending this exhortation to these Christians, or what it was that put him upon this profitable performance, of exhorting them in these words, "Beloved, when I gave all diligence to write unto you of the common salvation, it was needful for me to write unto you."

2. The exhortation itself, in these words, "And exhort you that ye should earnestly contend for the faith which was once delivered to the saints."

3. Sundry weighty and unanswerable arguments, to move the Christians to follow and embrace this excellent exhortation, from the 3rd to the 17th verse.

4. Several apt and holy directions, to guide and teach these Christians how to follow and observe the exhortation, which he had backed with the former arguments, to the 24th verse.

I begin with the former, The reasons which put the apostle upon sending this following exhortation: "Beloved, when I gave all diligence to write unto you of the common salvation, it was needful for me to write unto you;" and the reasons are these three.

I. The first is drawn from the dear love which the apostle bore to them; they to whom he wrote were "beloved."

II. The second is drawn from the care and diligence of the apostle for doing them good, and furthering their salvation; "When I gave all diligence to write unto you of the common salvation:" wherein consider,

1. With what mind and disposition he endeavoured their good, or how he was affected in endeavouring it; he gave all diligence.

2. In what work he was employed for their spiritual good, or by what means he endeavoured it; by writing.

3. The weightiness and great concernment of that subject about which he wrote; "the common salvation."

III. The third reason is taken from their need of having such an exhortation sent to them; "It was needful for me to write unto you."

I. The first reason is taken from the love which the apostle bore to them; they were "beloved."

For the explication whereof two things are briefly to be opened. What the word "beloved" imports, and what is contained in it; and, Why the apostle here bestows this title upon them, calling them "beloved."

1. For the first, The word ἀγαπητοί, beloved, notes two things. (1.) An amiableness and fitness for, and worthiness of, love in the thing beloved, which can and does commend itself to our love. It imports more than ἠγαπημένοι, *diligendi*, they who are to be loved; for that word comprehends every one, even the wicked, and our enemies: but ἀγαπητοί, beloved, properly respects those who have something of excellency to draw out our love towards them; and therefore it is in Scripture only attributed to the faithful. (2.) The word ἀγαπητοί, beloved, denotes a very intense, dear, tender, vehement love to the thing beloved; and therefore it is in Scripture not only the title of some most dear friends, Rom. xvi. 5; viii. 9, 12; Col. i. 7; iv. 7, 14; Philem. 1, 2; 3 John 1; but of brethren, James i. 16; Eph. vi. 21; Col. iv. 9; 1 Cor. xv. 58; of children, Eph. v. 1, and sons, 1 Cor. iv. 14; 2 Tim. i. 2; nay Christ, who was the Son of God by nature, who was his only Son, that his Son in whom he was well pleased, is also called ἀγαπητός, his beloved Son, Matt. iii. 17. The word ἀγαπητός is by Greek authors attributed to an only child: the Septuagint with this word interpret that phrase, only son, Gen. xxii. 2, "Take thy son, thine only son;" they translate, Take thy son, thy beloved one. And Zech. xii. 10, "They shall mourn for him as one that mourneth for his only son," they translate, as one that mourneth for his beloved one: and others attribute this word to an only eye; as when a man hath but one eye, they call it a beloved eye. [Vid. passim.]

2. For the second, Why the apostle bestoweth upon them this title of "beloved." He did it for two reasons.

(1.) To show what was his duty, not only as a man, in which respect love is a debt due to all, Rom. xiii. 8; or as a Christian, it being the duty of Christians peculiarly to love Christians, John xiii. 34, the household of faith, brethren, the members of one body, &c.; but especially as an apostle and minister, 1 Cor. iv. 14, 15; 1 Thess. ii. 7, 8. What more suitable than for a father, a nurse, to love their children, a shepherd his flock? The apostles were spiritual fathers, nurses, shepherds, John xxi. 15—17.

(2.) To gain their love by this affectionate compellation, "beloved;" that they by observing his love to them, might both love him, and thereby more readily embrace the following exhortation. He is very disingenuous, who if he will not provoke love from an enemy, will not repay love to a friend. Even publicans love those who love them, Matt. v. 46. The stone wall reflects heat when the scorching sun shines upon it. Love must be reciprocal; if we are to love those who are friends to our bodies, estates, names, &c., are not they to be beloved much more who are our soul friends? Nor was it more the duty of these Christians, than their benefit, to love this holy apostle. How much would their love to him forward their love to his ministry! Though the message should not be embraced for the messenger, yet it is not so easily embraced unless the messenger be beloved. That minister who is beloved, has a great advantage above another; he stands upon higher ground for doing good; and this is the main reason that the apostles so frequently call those to whom they write, beloved, 1 Cor. iv. 14; Gal. iv. 19; 1 Pet. iv. 12; Phil. i. 8; iv. 1; ii. 12; Rom. xii. 19; 1 Cor. x. 14; 2 Cor. xii. 19; Heb. vi. 9; James i. 16, 19; 1 John iii. 2, 21. They did not desire to insinuate themselves into the hearts of the Christians for their goods, but for their good; not to set up themselves, but Christ; they did not woo for themselves, but for the Bridegroom, they being his friends; they did not seek to advance themselves, but their message, and their Master.

Obs. 1. Piety is no enemy to courtesy. Christianity forbids not sweet compellations. Religion does not remove, but rectify courteous behaviour. (1.) By a flat prohibition of the act of dissimulation, and of sinful serving men's humours. (2.) By a moderation of excessiveness in our expressions which seem courteous. (3.) By preserving affection pure, from being made the instrument of profaneness and wantonness, that the pure seeds of religion may spring up in the terms of affability.

Obs. 2. The work and labour of a minister should proceed from love to his people. The apostle loved them, and therefore he wrote to them. Love should be the fountain of ministerial performances. First Christ inquired of Peter's love, and then he urged Peter to labour, John xxi. 15—17. A minister who speaks with the tongue of men and angels, and hath not charity, is as sounding brass, and a tinkling cymbal; though he have the gift of prophecy, and understand all mysteries, and all knowledge, and hath all faith; though he bestow all his goods to feed the poor; nay, though he give his body to be burnt; and have not charity, he is nothing, 1 Cor. xiii. 1—3. God will not reward ministers according to what they have done, but according to what they have done in loving to do. Love is the marrow, the soul of every service. All performances without love are but ciphers without a figure; in God's account they stand for nothing; they are sacrifices without fire.

Obs. 3. People should study to be fit for the love of their pastor. To encourage him to love them; to be *diligibiles,* such as these Christians were whom the apostle called "beloved." A painful minister should not only be put upon loving his people by conscience of this duty, but by encouragement to this duty. Ministers are often wrongfully complained of for want of love. All kind of love must not be afforded to all kind of people; a love of intimacy and complacency must only be set upon the godly among his people. If a faithful minister be not such to his offensive, unprofitable hearer as he would, it is because this man is not such to God and his own soul as he should. How unworthy a part in any is it to make a faithful minister spend that time in weeping, complaining, reproving, which he had much rather spend in sweet complacency, familiarity, and commendation!

Obs. 4. The love of a minister must not be slack and remiss, but vehement and ardent. Ministers are to imitate *him* in love, whose love was the most earnest, who was the chief Shepherd, and had the chief care of his flock, who "purchased it with his own blood," Acts xx. 28, who was nothing but love covered over with our flesh. As he was the precedent of ministers' love, so gave he earnest and frequent precepts to ministers to testify this love, John xxi. 15. Love alone can facilitate the difficulties of a minister's calling. Many things must be borne, as the hatred, frowardness, dulness, weakness of people. There must *ubera* be given, though *verbera* be returned; the breast must give its milk, though it be struck at. Sometimes lawful liberties must be forborne. A minister must be like indulgent mothers, or nurses, who forbear to eat such meats as they love, for fear of hurting the child which they are breeding, or nursing. Paul was such a one, who rather than he would offend a weak brother, would eat no flesh while he lived. A minister must be lowly in doctrine and life, patient, laborious; and nothing but love can make him be so. Every thing will be difficult to him that loves not. The object of a minister's love is the soul, the heaven-born soul, the precious immortal soul. What would it profit a minister to gain the whole world, and lose his peoples' souls? The beast, the name, the body of a man must be beloved; much more his soul. The winning of souls is the wisdom of a minister. A minister should say of his ease, profit, and pleasure, as the king of Sodom to Abraham, "Give me the souls, and take the goods to thyself," Gen. xiv. 21.

[marginal note: Ministri proferant ubverbera. non Bern.]

Obs. 5. Loving a minister's person has a great influence upon loving his doctrine. The apostle knew this when he desired that these Christians should know that he loved them. It is the folly of people not to love the word, whoever be the speaker. The message has not its commendation from the messenger, but the messenger from the message. Yet rare is it to find that Christian, who thinks well of that counsel which is given him by a counsellor who is not beloved; and therefore it is Satan's policy to asperse the minister, thereby to cause a dislike of his ministry. And great is their sin, who by their unamiable carriage often make their ministry abhorred, who either by profaneness, or unfit austerity, confute with their life what they persuade with their lip. Some offend by profaneness, preaching perhaps so holily in the pulpit, as some may almost think it pity they should ever come out of it; yet when they are out of it, showing so much levity, sloth, worldliness, looseness, as any would almost think it pity they should ever go into it. Others offend by unmeet moroseness, not considering that a minister must neither be all bait without hook, nor all hook without bait; as he must not by his flattery soothe, so neither by austerity affright his people. A minister must not be a flashing comet, but an influential star; not a storm or a tempest, but a sweetly dropping, bedewing cloud.

Obs. 6. The aim of a minister in being beloved of his people, should be to benefit their souls. The apostle desires to be beloved by these Christians, that he might have the greater opportunity to further their salvation. He robs Christ who improves not the interest he has in the hearts of his people for the honour of Christ. It is not service, but sacrilege, to desire the termination of people's love in ourselves. It is better, could it be without sin, that all should hate us, than that they should love us for ourselves; for if all should hate us, we should have but what is our own; if they should love us for ourselves, we should usurp what is Christ's. A minister's design in being beloved by his people, should be but to raise up seed to his elder Brother; all his services must be but scaffolds to erect a building of glory to Christ. Ministers should labour to be good for their own benefit, and to be accounted good for the benefit of others. They should not do good to get a good name, but they should labour for a good name, that they may be the more able to do good.

Obs. 7. The love of a minister to his people should procure love again from his people. The apostle in professing of love to these Christians, expected that they should love him again. Love must be the echo of love. It is often seen that they who love their people most, are beloved of them least. In a spiritual sense it is likewise true, that love descends more than it ascends. And ordinarily beggary, or at least poverty, is all the requital which is returned for the jewel of plain-dealing. People love not an eradicative, but a palliative cure of their spiritual distempers. Spiritual flatterers are commonly more respected than spiritual fathers. People and their lusts are so near together, that a godly minister cannot be an enemy to the latter, but he is esteemed such to the former. It is spiritual frenzy to rage against the physician of thy soul. A minister should requite such unkindness with the revenge of pity and prayer; and a holy resolution still to love, though he be the less beloved; endeavouring to do people good, though against their will. As Job's record, so such a minister's recompence, is on high.

This for the first reason of the apostle's sending the following exhortation to these Christians; they were "beloved." Now follows,

II. The careful diligence of the apostle to further their spiritual welfare; "When I gave all diligence to write unto you of the common salvation." And in that,

(1.) With what mind and disposition he endeavoured their good, or how he was affected in endeavouring to do them good; "I gave all diligence," πᾶσαν σπουδὴν ποιούμενος.

In the explication whereof I shall give the force and meaning of the words, diligence, and all diligence; and gather from thence what kind of diligence, and how qualified this of the apostle here was. The apostle expresses the forwardness of his mind and disposition in furthering their good by two words, by his giving diligence—all diligence.

Diligence, σπουδὴν. The Vulgate here translates it, *solicitudinem*, solicitude, or carefulness. Beza, *studium*, study, or earnest intention of mind. Our new translation renders it diligence, as it does also the same word, Rom. xii. 8; 2 Cor. viii. 7; Heb. vi. 11; 2 Pet. i. 5. Sometimes again it renders it carefulness, as 2 Cor. vii. 11; and forwardness, as 2 Cor. viii. 8; and earnest care, as 2 Cor. viii. 16; and haste, as Mark vi. 25; Luke i. 39. The Greek word comprehends all these significations; for it signifies an earnest and serious bending, application, and intention of the mind about the things which we are doing; and this is study. It imports also such a serious bending of the mind, as is with a fear of the future event; and this is care, carefulness, or solicitude. It also signifies a speedy and cheerful putting a thing in execution; and this is diligence, and festination, forwardness, haste.

Σπουδὴν, studium, solicitudo, diligentia, festinatio.

The other word, all, πᾶσαν, which the apostle uses to express his forward disposition to do them good, increases and enlarges the former. He gave not some part of, but all, or his whole diligence. For the apostle here, as the Scripture often elsewhere, puts all for whole, πᾶσαν, for ὅλην, as Rom. x. 18; 2 Tim. iii. 16; his whole diligence was bent this way, and other things, in comparison of this, he neglected. In this channel ran, as it were, the whole stream of his diligence.

From this force and meaning of the words it may plainly be collected what kind of diligence this of the apostle here was.

[1.] It was a solicitous, careful diligence. He resented the danger of these Christians, and feared their spiritual loss and hurt by Satan and his instruments. The care of these faithful ones was upon him, as upon holy Paul was the care of the churches. Paul was afraid of the Galatians, of whom he travailed in birth till Christ was formed in them, Gal. iv. 19, 20. Love is ever solicitous, doth its best, and fears the worst. Titus had an earnest care for the good of the Corinthians, 2 Cor. viii. 16; and among them none was offended but Paul burned, 2 Cor. xi. 29.

[2.] It was a studious and an intentive diligence. It set his head and heart working to do them good. There was an earnest and vehement application of both to this employment. Faithful ministers are laborious; they are peculiarly called labourers, and they labour in the word and doctrine. Paul laboured more abundantly than they all. Timothy was to show himself a workman. All their titles, as fishers, soldiers, watchmen, labourers, &c., bestowed upon ministers, commend Jude's diligence.

[3.] It was a cheerful, willing diligence. This he fully discovers, both by the word diligence, and giving diligence. He was not forced to this employment. Paul, 1 Cor. ix. 17, tells us his reward came in a way of willing doing. Jude had the constraint of love upon him; his service was not like honey pressed, but of itself dropping. His feeding the church was his meat and drink. This good work was not done with an ill will.

Studium est animi vehemens ad aliquam rem magna cum voluptate applicatio. Bez.

[4.] It was a speedy, ready diligence; it was with a holy haste. The seducers were already entered among these Christians; there was now no room for delays. The beginnings of this mischief were to be crushed. While ministers are lingering and doubting, Satan is devouring. They are soldiers, and victory loves to fly upon the wing of expedition.

[5.] It was his whole, utmost, entire diligence. Such a diligence as Paul professes he used, when he said, "As much as in me is, I am ready to preach the gospel," Rom. i. 15. This work he made his business, and to it he gave himself; in comparison of this his diligence for other things was but negligence. For three years he warned every one night and day with tears, Acts xx. 31. Nay, he was glad to spend and be spent, 2 Cor. xii. 15. He was fervent in spirit, but in serving the Lord, Rom. xii. 11.

Obs. 1. Greatest diligence is always to be used about the best things, about matters of greatest concernment. The custom of the world is to use substantial endeavours about circumstantial, and circumstantial endeavours about substantial employments. A holy remissness befits our care about the things of this life. A Christian should keep his sweat and industry for the things of heaven; when he uses the world, it should be as if he used it not. He should not pray or hear, as if he heard or prayed not. It is madness to make as great a fire for the roasting of an egg, as for the roasting of an ox; to follow the world with as much fervency as we do holiness; and about trifles to be employed with vast endeavours. It is impossible to be too diligent for heaven, and difficult not to be over-diligent for the earth.

Obs. 2. All that ministers, even the best of them, can do, is but to be diligent, to take pains and endeavour. Paul can but plant, Apollos waters, God it is that gives the increase, 1 Cor. iii. 6. It is our part to be diligent, it is God that blesses that diligence. *Aliud est docere, aliud flectere.* One thing to preach, another to persuade. The organ-pipes make no music without breath. He that teaches the heart sits in heaven. God must have the praise in the successfulness of the ministry; his glory must not cleave to our fingers, nor must ministers be discouraged in the want of success; God never required that at their hands. He accepts of their willing mind; nor does God reward them according to people's proficiency, but their own industry.

Nostrum est dare operam, Dei dare operationem.

Obs. 3. Diligence in duty is the commendation of ministers. The light of knowledge without the heat of love, speaks him not excellent. A golden key that opens not, is not so praised as a wooden one that opens the door. The shining, prancing, and trappings of a steed commend him not, but his serviceableness. Ministers are not made for sight, but for service. Nothing more unsuitable than for him to live without care, who hath gotten a cure. "Pray the Lord," saith Christ, "to send forth labourers into his harvest."

Ministers must labour for the pulpit, and in the pulpit; there must be the labour of study before we speak, the labour of zeal and love in speaking, the labour of suffering must be borne after preaching, always the labour of praying before and after. Their plainest performances must be painful. There must be a diligence even in their seeming negligence. "Cursed is he that doth the work of the Lord deceitfully," Jer. xlviii. 10. No danger is so great as spiritual, nor must any care be so great as ministerial. A godly minister must be careful for those that do not, and careful with those that do care for themselves. He should not only eat his bread in the sweat of his brows, but his sweat, his labour, should be his meat and drink, John iv. 34. Love to Christ and souls should constrain him. His life is short, and his reward is eternal. Short seasons require quick services. The nearness of Peter's departure made him diligent, 2 Pet. i. 13, 14. Seldom does the kingdom of heaven suffer violence under a remiss ministry. A sleepy preacher cannot expect a waking auditory. It is uncomely to see a minister weary himself in the world, in the family, in the field, in courts of justice. He must take his leave of other employments. He must not leave the word of God to serve tables, Acts vi. 2. He is a warrior, and must not entangle himself in the affairs of this life, 2 Tim. ii. 4. They who sweat in worldly employments, are commonly but cold in the pulpit.

Obs. 4. People who partake of the minister's diligence, must take heed of negligence, a double negligence. 1. They must not neglect themselves; nor, 2. Their minister. 1. Not themselves, their own souls; they must carefully gather up that spiritual manna that rains upon them in this wilderness; they must not play with that meat which the painful minister has been long preparing. If he take pains to do them good, what should they to do themselves good? They must give all diligence to make their calling and election sure, 2 Pet. i. 5, 10; in this their day knowing the things of their peace; walking while they have the light: they must be swift to hear, James i. 19, "fly as doves to the windows," Isa. lx. 8, delight in the word. Alphonsus, king of Naples, read the Bible over forty times in his lifetime. The Bereans "received the word with all readiness of mind," Acts xvii. 11. First they must seek the kingdom of God; not labour for that bread which perisheth, but for that which endureth to everlasting life. It is not meat on the table, but in the stomach, that nourishes. A minister's care without their own, will be but their curse. 2. They must not neglect their minister. Double diligence deserves double honour. If the minister consume his strength, they must labour to restore it. It is a shame that people should lay out more upon brooms to sweep their kennels, than upon a ministry to cleanse their souls. If ministers bring them venison, their souls must bless them. It was a saying of a holy man now with God, but his speech died not with him, London loves a cheap gospel. If ministers spend their oil, people must supply it. They must administer of their temporals. Alas, they give but pebbles for pearls. Since the ministry was so slighted, godliness never thrived.

Dr. Stoughton.

This for the first particular considerable in the second reason, why the apostle sent the following exhortation; viz. With what mind and disposition the apostle endeavoured the good of these Christians; he gave all diligence. Now follows,

(2.) In what work he was employed for, or by what means he endeavoured their good; viz. by writing: he gave all diligence; and it was to write.

And why would the apostle choose to further their salvation by means of writing? what was the advantage of a performance of that nature? His writing was sundry ways eminently advantageous.

[1.] It was helpful and advantageous to the absent; he could not speak, and therefore he writes to them, 1 Cor. v. 3; 2 Cor. ii. 3, 4; vii. 12. "Being absent," saith the apostle, "I write to them which heretofore have sinned," 2 Cor. xiii. 2. Writing is an invention to deceive absence. The use of epistles is, that even the separated by distance of place may be near to one another in affection, that there may be among the absent a resemblance of presence. The pen is an artificial tongue, the relief of the dumb and the distant; by it the former speaks plain, and the latter aloud. The tongue is as the pen of a ready writer, and the pen is as the tongue of a ready speaker.

[2.] The apostle's writing had the advantage to be diffusive of good to many. He was covetous of benefiting as many as he could, and his writing scattered holiness. Writing, as it reaches farther, so more than the tongue. It is like a little leaven that leaveneth a great lump, even whole countries, nay, after-ages. Paul's Epistles are ours, though not in their inscriptions, yet in their benefit. Augustine was converted by reading part of that to the Romans, xiii. 13, 14. The pen has the greatest auditories.

[3.] The apostle's writing had the advantage of authority and esteem. Often the contemptibleness of bodily presence, by reason haply of defects in utterance, aspect, life, rank, &c., damps the spirit, and diminishes the esteem of the worthiest speaker. Many are famous for their writing, who have been less esteemed for their speaking. Paul's adversaries objected to the weakness of his bodily presence, when they confessed his "letters were weighty and powerful," 2 Cor. x. 10. Writing abstracts the work from sundry prejudices against the workman. Many there are who build the tombs of the prophets, and garnish the sepulchres of the righteous, who publish, allege, adorn the books, those monuments of the memories, of holy fathers, and others, whose persons, had they lived in their times, they would have as much persecuted and opposed, as they now do those who are guided by the same Spirit, and walk in those holy ways in which those saints of old did. Many, but meanly esteemed of in foreign countries, by reason of their common and contemptible society, are most eminently and deservedly esteemed among us for their writings.

[4.] The apostle's writing had the advantage of permanency and continuance; it was a standing, lasting monument of his love and their duty. Words pass away, and are forgotten, when writing remains. Every new tide blots out a writing on the sand, and every new sermon makes the former forgotten; but writing deceives even death itself. It is a kind of image of eternity. Some by idleness have been dead while they lived; others by their labours have lived when they have been dead. Peter endeavoured that the Christians might be put in remembrance even after his decease, 2 Pet. i. 15. "This shall be written," saith the psalmist, "for the generation to come," Psal. cii. 18.

Obs. 1. The desire of ministers should be to benefit as many as may be. To help in the way to heaven, not their present, but even their absent friends; nor the age only in which they live, but even succeeding generations; like a great fire, they should heat those who are a great way off. The world should smell of the sanctity and holy labours of a godly minister, even when he is removed out of it. He should, like Zisca, who commanded that a drum should be made of his skin to terrify his enemies, even after his death be serviceable. Though the prophets live not ever, Zech. i. 5, yet their labours should. Some of the ancient worthies, like Samson, have thus done more good by their deaths than by their lives.

Obs. 2. God by giving us the constant and standing rule of a written word, shows our great readiness to leave him and swerve from him. As we could not have found out, so neither could we have kept in, the right way, without a written word. We have *ingenium erraticum*, we love to wander, and should, without this light shining in a dark place. In the infancy of the church, and while it was contained in narrow bounds, God manifested his will without the written word, by dreams, visions, and audible voice; but error and profaneness increasing in after generations, men must have God's will committed to writing: without it we can neither find nor keep our way to heaven. The pope, unwritten traditions, the sun, moon, and stars, reason and revelations, are all erring guides.

Obs. 3. Great is the goodness of God, who would have his will committed to writing, giving us a sure, a more sure word of prophecy, 2 Pet. i. 19; that upon which we may more safely build, than upon the voice which came from heaven when Christ was transfigured. How full of love is Christ, to send epistles to his spouse the church in his absence from her! Great is His care who hath safely transmitted an uncorrupted canon to every age of his church, and set up a light which the rage and subtlety of Satan can no more blow out, than can a man the sun with a pair of bellows. God provides not only light in heaven, but light to heaven. He teaches us in the school of Scripture. He has not dealt so with every nation, Psal. cxlvii. 20; the heathen have but the school of creatures: the Jews, though our careful library-keepers, yet understood not this written word.

Obs. 4. The great impiety of those who neglect and undervalue the written word. "I have written" (saith God) "the great things of my law, but they were accounted a strange thing," Hos. viii. 12. The written word is undervalued by some practically; their lives are visible confutations of it; they live crooked lives, though they have a straight rule. They commit the sins of darkness in a land of light, and they do their work worse under this glorious light, than those who lived in darkness. Others disgrace the written word doctrinally. Papists say it is not necessary for the church, calling it by way of contempt, *Atramentariam theologiam*, a dead letter, a divinity made of ink and paper; preferring before it the scripture which is made in the pope's breast. To these may be added the sectaries of our times, who peremptorily write, that no writing whatsoever, whether translations or originals, is the foundation of Christian religion. And to prove it, they borrow the popish arguments, whereof this is the prime; Religion was founded before the Scriptures, therefore the Scriptures cannot be the foundation of religion. They never remembering what is truly answered by our divines, Chamier, Rivet, Whitaker, &c., the latter whereof tells them, that though of old time, when God familiarly made known himself to the fathers, and by himself manifested to them his will, the Scriptures were not necessary; yet after God changed the course of teaching his church, and would have his word written, the Scriptures were a necessary foundation.

<small>Alb. Pighius. Costerus in Euchirid. Ecclus. Bailius, p. 1. Bellar. de Verb. Dei, l. 4. c. 4.</small>

<small>John Goodwin. Yo. Eld. p. 32. Vid. Blind Guide guided, p. 47.</small>

<small>Patribus olim Deus se familiariter ostendit, atque iis per se voluntatem suam patefecit, et tum Scripturas non fuisse necessarias fateor : at postea mutavit hanc docendæ ecclesiæ rationem, et scribi suam voluntatem voluit, et tum necessaria esse Scriptura cœpit. Whitak. de perfec. Scrip. cap. 7.</small>

Obs. 5. The misery of those times and places where writing is made an engine to advance the devil's kingdom. It is pity so useful an invention should be employed for any but for God, and that it should be used as a weapon against him. Heretical and profane writings kill souls at a distance, leaven a whole kingdom with sin, and propagate impiety to posterity. Satan hath prevailed more with his pen than his sword against the church. Far be it from a Christian commonwealth to suffer weekly advocates to write for Satan; to take away the pen from Jude, and to put it into the hand of the seducers against whom he desires to write. We put not a sword into the hand of our own, may we never put a pen into the hand of God's enemies.

This for the second particular in the second reason of the apostle's sending this following exhortation, namely, By what kind of means he endeavoured the good of these Christians; viz. by writing.

(3.) The excellency and weightiness of that subject about which he was to write; "the common salvation." Wherein he expresses

The nature thereof; it was salvation: and

Its property; it was common.

1. The kind and nature of that subject about which he wrote, "salvation." The word σωτηρία, here rendered salvation, properly signifies a deliverance from danger and distress, as also a preservation of a thing in a condition of safety; such a preservation or safety, without which a thing would be lost and destroyed; and by which it is perpetually preserved, and kept safe from all danger and evil whatsoever, 1 Sam. xiv. 45; xix. 5; Isa. lix. 11; Jer. iii. 23. <small>Chemnit. Har. in Luc. 1. Cameron. in Myroth. Evang.</small>

But salvation is taken in Scripture sundry ways.

[1.] First, For deliverance from temporal miseries and calamities. "Stand still, and see the salvation of the Lord," Exod. xiv. 13. And, "To-day the Lord wrought salvation in Israel," 1 Sam. xi. 13.

[2.] For the power and providential care of God, whereby he lets not his people want what is fit for them. When they desired food, "they trusted not in his salvation," Psal. lxxviii. 22.

[3.] For the garments of joy and feasting, which they were wont to wear upon occasion of public victories and deliverances. "I will clothe her priests with salvation," Psal. cxxxii. 16. And, "He will beautify the meek with salvation," Psal. cxlix. 4.

[4.] For the author of salvation, whether temporal or spiritual. "The Lord is my light and my salvation," Psal. xxvii. 1; Isa. xii. 2. And, "Mine eyes have seen thy salvation," Luke ii. 30.

[5.] For the entrance into the estate of blessedness, John iv. 22; Heb. ii. 3; 2 Cor. vi. 2; and so the means of salvation, the gospel, as, "Salvation of God is sent to the Gentiles, and they will hear it," Acts xxviii. 28: and the embracing of those means by faith, together with holiness of life, are called salvation; "This day is salvation come to thy house," Luke xix. 9. So Eph. ii. 8; Rom. xi. 11.

[6.] For our blessedness and glorification in heaven; whereof there are two degrees. The first, At the time of our death, when the soul being loosed from the body, is carried into the third heavens. The second, At the day of resurrection, when body and soul shall be received up into heaven by Christ. "Now is our salvation nearer than when we believed," Rom. xiii. 11. And, "Heirs of salvation," &c. Heb. i. 14.

[7.] For our blessedness, as comprehending both our entrance into it here, and the perfection of it hereafter. "If we neglect so great salvation," Heb. ii. 3. "The gospel of your salvation," Eph. i. 13. "Account that the long-suffering of the Lord is salvation," 2 Pet. iii. 15. In this last sense I take it in this place. The apostle gave all diligence to write unto them, so of the means, way, and entrance of salvation in grace, that they might happily at length enjoy and partake of it in glory; and so of the fulness thereof in glory, that they may not neglect the entrance into it in grace. And deservedly is the happy estate of the faithful, both *in semine* and *in fructu*, in the first fruit and full crop, in grace and glory, called salvation. For,

First, It is an estate of deliverance from the greatest enemies. All the most cruel, oppressive enemies in the world are nothing to the fury of the great God, Heb. x. 31, the wrath to come, 1 Thess. i. 10, the defiling and destroying power of sin, the curse of the law, and slavery to Satan.

Secondly, It is a deliverance of the soul, the precious eternal soul, Matt. x. 28. What triumphs have been kept for deliverance of bodies from slavery! What trophies, pillars have been erected to those who have saved our estates, and liberties, and country! These were but the shadows of saviours.

Thirdly, It is a deliverance from every adversary, to be sure, from adversity by every adversary. A complete deliverance. Nothing hurts the delivered by Christ; they are delivered from all that hate them, Luke i. 71. No sin, no devil, nor cross, nor death, shall hurt them. They are all conquered enemies.

Fourthly, It is a deliverance from every enemy fully. Christ is a horn of salvation, Luke i. 62, and able to the full to save all them that come to him (Heb. vii. 25) from the guilt and condemnation of sin, Rom. viii. They are fully justified in this life; "There is no condemnation to them who are in Christ;" their iniquities are blotted out as a cloud; they are forgotten and forgiven, thrown into the bottom of the sea, and subdued, Mic. vii. 19. Though they be sought for, yet can they not be found. And from the defilement and presence of sin they are fully saved in the next life: no spot, or wrinkle, or any such thing shall there be in glory, Eph. v. 27; no mixtures of sin with grace. Nothing that defiles shall enter into the New Jerusalem, Rev. xxi. 27. Here the people of God are *perficientes*, perfecting; there *perfecti*, perfect. They shall let their mantle of corruption fall when they go up to heaven.

Fifthly, It is a perpetual deliverance, everlasting salvation, not for a few years, as were the deliverances of Israel by their saviours. It is a happy security, and a secure happiness. The saved by Christ shall never fall, never fall totally into sin, or for sin. They "are kept by the power of God through faith unto salvation," 1 Pet. i. 5.

Sixthly, It is a positive deliverance; a preservation not from evil only, but to good also; a preservation in grace, and unto glory. Paul calls it a preservation to a heavenly kingdom, 2 Tim. iv. 18; "to an inheritance incorruptible, undefiled, that fadeth not away," 1 Pet. i. 4, where the perfection of all delights in the fruition of a soul-satisfying good shall make us forget all our troubles. Heaven is an eternal triumph over all our former adversaries and adversities.

Obs. 1. The faithful have many enemies. What need else of this salvation? Satan's design is their destruction, either for sin, or by sin, or both. He lies most in wait for the soul enriched with holiness, and like the thief in the house, takes most care to find the jewels. Let not the faithful be secure, or discouraged: not secure; though Christ saves, yet our hearts betray us; and Satan is a waking enemy: not discouraged, for Christ is a waking Friend, a powerful Saviour.

Obs. 2. They who are out of the way of salvation, out of Christ, and without holiness, are without safety. Secure they often are, but never safe. Sometimes they are kept from bodily dangers, and preserved by the general providence and the universal care of God extended to all his works; but, alas, this amounts not to Jude's salvation, it is rather reservation than preservation. All the care of God toward the wicked, is but as the provision that a jailer bestows upon his prisoner, to keep him alive against the day of execution; so that a sinner's preservation is not only common, but cursed. A sinner's security is not from want of danger, but discerning. If the command of God be not a hedge to keep thee from being a straying sheep, his care shall be no hedge to keep thee from being a devoured sheep. Was it dangerous for them of old to be shut out of the ark, and the city of refuge, and to be without blood upon their door-posts? and is it not dangerous to be without Jesus to deliver us from the wrath to come? 1 Thess. i. 10. They who will not be preserved from Satan as a seducer in their life, shall never be preserved from him as a destroyer at their death. Of this more before.

Obs. 3. The salvation of the faithful is begun in this life. Here they are saints, and here they are saved. Heaven is but the flower of salvation blown out; here in this life salvation is in the bud. Saints are here saved from the power of their corruptions; they are here in the suburbs of heaven; they here sit together in heavenly places in Christ, Eph. ii. 6. They here have salvation, not only in their desires and expectations, but in its cause. They have an entrance into the everlasting kingdom of Christ, 2 Pet. i. 11. They are by faith united to that Head which is already in heaven. They are freed, though not from the company of, and contention with, yet from conquest by all their enemies; and there is always the certainty of this salvation in respect of itself, the object, though not in respect of us, the subject.

Obs. 4. The people of God are safe, and saved, even while they are in dangers. Their enemies are but nominal. The Keeper of Israel never slumbers nor sleeps, Psal. xc. *per tot*. Though they are tempted, sick, persecuted, banished, yet never unsafe; and whenever God brings them into these conditions, it is because they are the safest for them. Their graces are alway safe, their souls, their comforts safe, because Christ their Head, their hope, their all is safe. The poorest saint has his life-guard. He who provided a city of refuge for those who killed men, will much more find out a city of refuge for thee when men shall labour to kill thee. Of this more before.

Obs. 5. Our dangers and enemies in this life should exceedingly commend heaven to us. The tempest commends the haven; the pursuit of the enemy, the city of refuge; the storms, the shelter. We are never fully safe till we arrive at eternal salvation. It is strange that saints should long no more to get into the bosom of Christ in glory; that they should be so unwilling to leave the lions' dens, and the mountains of leopards, Cant. iv. 8. *Mundus turbatur, et amatur.* We love to handle the world, though God makes it a bundle of thorns: what should we do if it were a heap of roses?

Obs. 6. God has appointed the holy writings for our salvation. Jude writes to further the salvation of these Christians. The Scriptures are able to make us wise to salvation, 2 Tim. iii. 15. Eternal peace is only upon those who walk according to this rule, Gal. vi. 16. The Scriptures tell us not only what we shall find heaven to be when we are there, but how we should find the way thither. They are the pillar and cloud in our wilderness; the light which shines in a dark place for our guidance. Let us labour to have salvation furthered by them. "How shall we escape, if we neglect so great salvation?" Heb. ii. 3. How sad is it to carry these letters of heaven about us only as Uriah carried David's, for his own destruction!

Obs. 7. The furthering of the salvation of others should be the end of our writing. "To write the same things to you," saith Paul, "is safe," Phil. iii. 1. "I have written," saith Peter, "exhorting, and testifying that this is the true grace of God wherein ye stand," 1 Pet. v. 12. "My little children," saith John, "these things I write unto you, that ye sin not," 1 John ii. 1. We must not write to show our learning, much less to obscure the truth. Nothing should be written but what the reading of the best should commend. The best thing that many do by writing, is to make paper dear, but which is worse, they make their reader worse; it were well that either they would not write at all, or else write a book of retractations. But among us, sectaries after conviction write with more rage instead of retractation. If these will not amend, readers are to take heed of buying their books, lest they embrace their errors; and rather to dig in the mine of the Scriptures for gold, than to wallow in the mire of the books of sectaries and seducers.

Videtur quicquid literis mandatur, id commendari omnium eruditorum lectione debere. Cicero 2 Tusc. quæst.

This for the first, the nature of that subject about which the apostle was to write, "salvation."

2. The property of it, Common; "common salvation." Wherein by way of explication we may show two things.

In what respect salvation is called common, and why the apostle in this place calls it so.

Common cannot be here taken according to the usage of the word sometimes in the Scripture, as it is opposed to holy, and as importing as much as profane, or that which every one may use, or belongs to every one: as 1 Sam. xxi. 4, that bread which was not consecrated to God, or hallowed, and of which any might eat, is called common. So Acts x. 14, 28; xi. 8, meats forbidden by the Levitical law are called common and unclean, because the profane Gentiles commonly used those meats, which the Jews, being a holy people, might not eat. And so those apostates are said to account the blood of the covenant a common or unholy thing, Heb. x. 29; esteeming the blood of Christ no more than if it had been the blood of some ordinary person, or of some wicked or guilty one. Nor is common here to be taken unlimitedly, for that which is common universally to every one, as if none were excluded from this salvation. Origen is charged as if he held that those who lived and died the most flagitious sinners, nay, that the devil himself, and his angels, after a thousand years' torments, should be saved.

Aug. de Hæres. cap. 43.

But common is here taken in a limited sense; this salvation being common only to the faithful, who all have an interest in the same; it belongs to one of them as well as to another; the meanest are not excluded it. Christ loseth none of his, John xvii. 12. It is a salvation for Jews and Gentiles, rich and poor, honourable and ignoble, bond and free, learned and illiterate, Rev. vii. 9; Acts i. 8; Rom. i. 16; Acts x. 35.

And thus it is common salvation sundry ways.

[1.] In regard of the meritorious Purchaser of this salvation. There is one common Saviour, the Saviour of the body, Eph. v. 23. Every member thereof has influence from this Head. There is "one Lord," Eph. iv. 5; there is this "one Mediator between God and man." They of old all drank of the same spiritual Rock, Christ Jesus, 1 Cor. x. 4. "Of his fulness we have all received," John i. 16. He is the Sun that gives lustre and light to every star, the Well that filled every pitcher, the only Foundation laid by all, 1 Cor. iii. 11.

[2.] It is common salvation in regard of the rule and way by which we are guided thither. There is but "one faith," Eph. iv. 5, called also catholic. God calls all his people with one voice. There is but one way to heaven, the good old way; there is one rule prescribed to all; sometimes it has been more plainly, sometimes more obscurely discovered, but yet the way has ever been the same. Our light now may be new for the degree, not for the kind of it.

[3.] It is common salvation, because faith both in the Purchaser and doctrine of salvation is common to all true Christians. They all have the same spirit of faith, 2 Cor. iv. 13. And faith is called common, Tit. i. 4. They all build upon the same personal and doctrinal foundation; and though, like the boughs of a tree, they cross one another in some things, yet they all grow upon the same root, and agree in that. Christ and Scripture are precious to all.

[4.] It is common salvation in regard of the earnest of it. The holiness of the Spirit is common to all the faithful. They all have the earnest of the purchased inheritance, Eph. i. 14; 2 Cor. i. 22; some have more, some less given them in earnest, yet it is in all of the same kind, and all have some, Eph. iv. 7. Without holiness none shall see God, Heb. xii. 14.

[5.] The waiting, the longing for this salvation is common to all believers. They all love the appearance of Christ, 2 Tim. iv. 8; Tit. ii. 13. They all are made to look upwards. Heaven has ever been their centre.

[6.] The profession of an interest in, and the hope of this salvation, is also common to all believers. They have all professed themselves strangers here below, and they have ever shown that they seek a country above, Heb. xi. 13, 14. They have all had heaven in their tongues, in their lives; they have not been ashamed to confess Christ before men; and have rather chosen to lose their lives than the end of their living; to part with what they had in hand, rather than what they had in hope; with their possession, rather than their reversion.

[7.] It is common salvation in respect of the term; the place of blessedness, to which all the faithful shall at length arrive. In heaven there shall be a general assembly, not one missing: "Whosoever believes shall have everlasting life," John iii. 16. God knows and loves all his children, as if he had but one. "I will," saith Christ, speaking of all believers, "that they whom thou hast given me be with me where I am, that they may behold my glory," John xvii. 24. Of all that thou hast given me, saith Christ, I have lost none, ver. 12. Christ's own glory would be incomplete in heaven, if any one believer should be wanting. The poor partakes of the same heaven with the rich. Lazarus and Abraham met together in heaven. The wife is an heir of the grace of life with the husband, 1 Pet. iii. 7. The servant shall reign in heaven as well as the Master. One heaven shall hold Jew and Gentile, bond and free, Col. iii. 11. It is the place where we shall all meet.

2. Why doth the apostle here call this salvation "common," writing to these Christians?

[1.] Some conceive that by showing it was common to him as well as to others, the surmise of his unfitness to write of so weighty a subject might be cut off. Jude would (according to this opinion) show that he writes to them of no other salvation, but what he himself in part understood, loved, expected with themselves; and therefore he being an experienced doctor, they ought the more readily to follow him.

[2.] Others, as I apprehend more fitly, conceive that the apostle calls this salvation common, to prevent the self-exemption of any particular Christian from embracing the following exhortation and directions, which belong to the salvation of all: q. d. I write of the things which all have followed that ever heretofore obtained salvation, and all must follow who would not incur their own ruin; therefore let every one embrace them.

Obs. 1. God is most free of his best blessings. He affords salvation in common to all his people. He gives honour and riches but to few of them; he gives Christ and heaven to them all. God sometimes denies a crumb, even to him on whom he bestows a kingdom. There are many things that a child of God cannot promise to himself, but heaven he may reckon upon. There is no famine where there is bread, though there be no plums and apples. And if God give salvation, though he denies these worldly toys, there is no fear of famine. God gives those things but scantily which often hinder from heaven. He keeps nothing from his people but what they may well be without. When the poorest saint looks upon the greatest emperor in the world, he may say, Though I have not the same worldly glory and wealth, yet I shall have the same heaven with him; only with this difference, I go not thither with so much luggage on my back. It is reported of the duke of Hereford, when he was banished out of the kingdom by Richard the Second, that he should say, Well, yet I shall have the same sun to shine upon me that he has who banishes me.

Obs. 2. Christ and heaven are full and satisfactory; they are enough for all. Salvation is imparted, but not impaired; the happiness of one is no diminution to the comfort of another. Christ and heaven cannot be praised hyperbolically; they are common fountains, and yet never drawn dry. The world is conscious of its insufficiency, when men are wary of having rivals in any enjoyment. Worldly comforts are like a narrow table-cloth upon a broad table; those on both sides pull to themselves, and on neither side have they enough. Christ and heaven always call and invite, and rejoice in comers. The world altogether denies most, satisfies none at all.

Obs. 3. None should be willing to be saved alone. Heaven was made for a common good. It is angelical to rejoice when men are brought to heaven, and, as I may say, hyper-angelical to bring them thither. Christians, but ministers especially, should be a common good; like the conduit that serves for the use of a whole city, blessings to a whole nation, compelling every one to the marriage-feast. Our gifts should be called common, not only because God commonly bestows them, but because we commonly use them. If heaven be large, our hearts should not be strait. How common a good was blessed Paul, who wished that all who heard him were such as he was! Acts xxvi. 29. This is a holy, honest covetousness.

Obs. 4. They who teach others the way to salvation, should be in a state of salvation themselves. He who has sailed into foreign coasts, discourses more thoroughly and satisfactorily than he who has only map knowledge. Then is the word likely to grow, when the piety of the preacher waters the seed of the sermon. He who loves not salvation himself, can hardly make others in love with it. Ministers must not only teach *facienda*, but *faciendo*. They must teach by doing what they teach to be done. He who teaches another should teach himself. He who comforts another, should labour to do it with that comfort wherewith God hath comforted him, 2 Cor. i. 4.

Obs. 5. The commonness of salvation to all believers, should be a great inducement to every one to labour particularly for salvation, and that they may not miss of it themselves. It is our trouble upon earth, when we see others obtain riches and preferments, and we ourselves go without them. We urge our friends with this argument, that they did such a kindness for such a one, and such a one, and therefore we hope they will not exclude us. "Hast thou," said Esau to his father, "but one blessing? bless me, even me also." O go to God, and say, Lord, thou hast salvation for such and such a friend, have it also for me, even for me also, O my Father. It may be thou hast a godly father or mother, a brother or sister, be not content that they should go to heaven without thee.

Obs. 6. There is but one way to heaven. There are many nations, more men, only one faith. The Jews shall not be saved by the law of Moses, Gentiles by the law of nature, and Christians by the gospel. It is true, "The just shall live by his faith;" but then it is as true, that the object of his faith is the object of every one's faith who is saved, although the special application thereof be his alone. The apostle Peter calls faith, " like precious faith," 2 Pet. i. 1.

Obs. 7. The partakers of this " common salvation," who here agree in one way to heaven, and who expect to be hereafter in one heaven, should be of one heart. It is the apostle's inference, Eph. iv. 3, 4. What an amazing misery is it, that they who agree in common faith, should disagree like common foes! that Christians should live as if faith had banished love! This common faith should allay and temper our spirits in all our differences. This should moderate our minds, though there is inequality in earthly relations. What a powerful motive was that of Joseph's brethren to him to forgive their sin, they being both his brethren, and the servants of the God of his fathers! Gen. l. 17. Though our own breath cannot blow out the taper of contention, O yet let the blood of Christ extinguish it.

This for the second reason why the apostle sends the following exhortation, drawn from his care and diligence to promote their happiness.

III. The third follows, taken from their present need of having such an exhortation; in these words, " It was needful for me to write."

Ἀνάγκην ἔσχον, *necesse,* or *necessitatem habui,* I had necessity, word for word; or, I held it needful. Here we translate it more agreeably to the English expression, " It was needful for me;" elsewhere, as Luke xiv. 18, " I must needs;" and (spoken of a third person) Luke xxiii. 17, " Of necessity he must;" and 1 Cor. vii. 37, " having necessity."

The word ἀνάγκη, here translated needful, signifies in Scripture a threefold necessity. 1. A necessity of distress and tribulation, as Luke xxi. 23; 1 Cor. vii. 26; 2 Cor. xii. 10; vi. 4; 1 Thess. iii. 7. 2. A necessity of coaction, or constraint; such a force as opposeth one's liberty, and which makes one do a thing against his will, as Philem. 14, it is opposed to willingly; " That thy benefit should not be as it were of necessity, but willingly." κατ' ἀνάγκην, κατ' ἑκούσιον. And, " Feed the flock of God," &c., " not by constraint, but willingly," 1 Pet. v. 2; " not grudgingly, or of necessity," 2 Cor. ix. 7. 3. A necessity upon supposition of some cause, ground, or reason whereby it becomes necessary or needful that such or such a thing should be or be done. And thus Christ saith, " It must needs be that offences come," Matt. xviii. 7; namely, because of the power and malice of the devil, the weakness and perverseness of men. Likewise Paul and Barnabas told the

Jews, "It was necessary that the word of God should first have been spoken to you, Acts xiii. 46; namely, because of the covenant which God had made with them above others. In this respect, he saith, "To abide in the flesh is more needful for you," Phil. i. 24; namely, upon supposition of the benefit you may receive from me, and the want you will have of me. And 1 Cor. ix. 16, "Necessity is laid upon me, and woe unto me if I preach not the gospel!" And this was the necessity which Jude intends, namely, that whereby it became needful and necessary for some weighty causes to write to these Christians. And so it was needful in three respects.

1. In respect of his great care towards them. His diligence for their good, and desire of writing, being so great, as that it would not suffer him to be silent; and so Erasmus interprets this necessity.

2. It was needful for him to write, in respect of his own duty, principally as he had the office of an apostle, which he received to further their spiritual welfare: so others.

3. But thirdly, as Calvin, Beza, and the most interpret this necessity, It was necessary for him to write in respect of their danger; their faith being in such hazard by false teachers and seducers. Of himself he was forward and diligent to do them good, but he was further put upon this service of writing by the very exigence and necessity of their present condition, they being in so much danger by false teachers and seducers. And their danger by seducers made it needful for him to write in sundry regards.

(1.) Because of the destructiveness of those doctrines and practices which the seducers brought in among them. They turned "the grace of God into lasciviousness;" they denied "the only Lord God, and our Lord Jesus Christ;" they despised dominions; they walked after their own ungodly lusts. These were not slight, but pernicious evils. Peter, in 2 Pet. ii. 1, 2, calls them "damnable heresies, pernicious ways;" not scratching the face, but stabbing the very heart of religion. The eternal salvation of their precious souls was hazarded.

(2.) Their danger by seducers made it needful for him to write, because of their subtlety and cunningness in propagating their impieties. The devil made not use of the ass, but the serpent, to tempt them. The seducers had craftily crept in among them; they did "by sleight and cunning craftiness lie in wait to deceive," Eph. iv. 14; they had feigned words to make merchandise of souls, 2 Pet. ii. 3, pretences of gospel liberty, &c.

(3.) Because of the great readiness even of the best to give way to seducers. Our natures are like tinder, ready to take with every spark. There is in the best a corrupt principle, that inclines to error in judgment, and impiety in practice; which, were they not kept by the power of God to salvation, would soon prevail. One who is diseased may more easily infect twenty that are sound, than those twenty can cure that one infected person. Rusty armour soon makes bright armour rusty by lying near it, whenas the bright armour imparts to the other none of its brightness.

Obs. 1. The written word is needful as the rule of faith and manners. Jude, upon the entrance of the seducers with their errors, tells the Christians it was needful to write this Epistle to regulate and direct them. They who deny that the written word is necessarily required to be the rule of faith, must necessarily give way to the overthrowing of faith. There is no truth in the Scripture can be proved or believed with a Divine faith, unless the *ratio credendi,* or ground of such believing, be the revelation of God in writing. "These things are written," saith John, "that you may believe that Jesus is the Christ," John. xx. 31. And, "These things have I written unto you, that ye might believe in the name of the Son of God," 1 John v. 13. "We have a more sure word of prophecy," saith Peter, "to which ye do well to take heed, as unto a light that shineth in a dark place," 2 Pet. i. 19. Without this light the way of truth cannot be found. The Bereans searched the Scriptures, whether those things they heard were so, Acts xvii. 11. The doctrines of faith have been ever by Christ and his apostles proved, and errors which oppose them have been ever by them confuted, by the written word, Luke xxiv. 25, 27; Acts xiii. 33; Rom. xiv. 11. They who build not their faith upon the written word, must needs go to enthusiasm, the pope, or reason for a foundation.

Obs. 2. The helping forward the good of souls is the most needful employment. Paul (as Jude here) tells us that necessity was laid upon him to do this work, 1 Cor. ix. 16. A saving ministry is that which we cannot be without. "We can better spare the sun in the firmament," (as it was once said of Chrysostom,) "than the preaching of a faithful minister." The word in its ministry is compared in Scripture to the most needful things, bread, salt, water, physic, armour, &c. Bread and salt are always set upon the table, whatever the other dishes are. Let our condition be what it will, the word is always needful. The life of the soul is the dearest, and the famine of the word is the sorest. Places, though never so rich and glorious, are but *magna latrocinia* without the word; dens of thieves, not dwellings for men. The removal of the gospel is a soul judgment, and the soul of judgments. It is foolish to account the falling of the salt upon the table ominous; but it is our duty to lament the falling of them whom Christ calls "the salt of the earth," Matt. v. 13. They who are weary of the word, are weary of heaven, weary of God. Ministers, for performing so necessary a work as is that of saving souls, should hazard themselves. What father would not burn his fingers to pull his child out of the fire? It is not necessary a minister should be safe, but that he should be serviceable, and that a soul should be saved.

Obs. 3. The opposing of seducers is a needful part of our ministry. It was this that made Jude account it needful to write to these Christians. It is the minister's work to defend, as well as to feed people; to drive away the wolf from, as well as to provide pasture for, the flock. The mouths of deceivers are to be stopped, and gainsayers must be convinced. They subvert, saith the apostle, whole houses, Tit. i. 9, 11. Cursed be that patience which can see it, and say nothing. I know not how it comes to pass, but among many the opposing of seducers is either accounted bitter, or needless; and it is still the policy of Satan not to suffer a sword in Israel. But if there be "damnable heresies," 2 Pet. ii. 1, I see not but there may be a damnable silence in those who should oppose them. Every one must give account for his idle words, and a minister for his idle silence.

Obs. 4. Ministers should preach such doctrine as is most needful for the places and people with whom they have to do. The physician administers not one kind of physic to all distempers. Some patients require one, some another. Some places abound most with profaneness, others more with errors. Some places are infamous for drunkenness, others for pride, others for covetousness, others for weariness of the gospel. The minister must suit his preaching to their exigences. It is not enough in war for a soldier to discharge his musket, though it be well charged with powder and bullet, unless also he aim well to hit the enemy. He who delivers good doctrine and reproofs, but not suitable to the people whom he teaches, discharges up into the air. God commands the prophet to show the people their sins, Isa. lviii. 1; not to show one people the sins of another, but their own. Some observe that Christ in his doctrine always set himself most against the raging impiety of the times wherein he lived. We find his vehemency expressed more against the secret, subtle hypocrisies of the Pharisees than against other sins, which in some times and places would have deserved most severe reprehension. And the truth is, the preaching of seasonable and needful truths is that which creates so much hatred to the faithful ministers. People can be content to hear us preach of the sins of our forefathers, but not of the sins of the present times. People will not take honey out of the lion unless he be dead, nor taste sweetness in that preaching which is lively, and roars upon them in their way of sin. A good heart considers not how bitter, but how true; not how smart, but how seasonable a doctrine is. It desires that the word may be directed to it in particular. It sets its corruptions in the forefront of the battle when God's arrows are flying, and patiently suffers the word of exhortation.

This for the third and last reason which put the holy apostle upon sending the following exhortation to these Christians, namely, The needfulness of sending such an exhortation to them, "It was needful for me to write;" and so I pass from the first part considerable about the apostle's exhortation, viz. The reasons why he sent an exhortation.

The second follows, viz. The exhortation itself, in these words, "And exhort you that ye should earnestly contend for the faith once delivered unto the saints."

In the words the apostle sets down, 1. The way or manner of his writing, which was hortatory, or by way of exhortation. 2. The matter or subject of the exhortation, or to what it was he exhorted them, viz. "Earnestly to contend for the faith once delivered unto the saints."

The first shows us what the apostle did. The second what these Christians ought to do.

First, Of the way or manner of the apostle's writing, which was by way of exhortation; "And exhort you."

In the explication I shall, 1. Show the force and meaning of the word exhort. 2. Show from thence what manner of exhortation this of the apostle's was.

1. For the former: the word in the original, παρακαλῶν, here translated exhorting, properly signifies to call to one, or vehemently to call out to another upon some urgent occasion; but it is in Scripture translated several ways, according to the nature and circumstances of the place where, and the thing about which, it is used.

Sometimes it is rendered to pray, entreat, beseech, 2 Cor. v. 20; Philem. 9, 10; so it is used 1 Cor. iv. 13, "Being defamed, we entreat." And Matt. viii. 5, "There came unto him a centurion, beseeching him." And ver. 31, "The devils besought him." So ver. 34; and chap. xiv. 36; xviii. 29.

Sometimes it signifies to exhort, as Luke iii. 18, John exhorting, preached. So Acts xi. 23, and xiv. 22, "Exhorted them with purpose of heart," &c.; and, "Exhorting them to continue in the faith." So Heb. iii. 13, "Exhort one another daily." Also chap. x. 25, &c.; and so in this place of Jude.

Sometimes it signifies to comfort and encourage, as 1 Thess. iv. 18, "Comfort one another." Acts xx. 12, "And were not a little comforted. Rom. i. 12, "That I may be comforted together with you." Matt. v. 4 "Blessed are they that mourn, for they shall be comforted." And λογὸς παρακλητικὸς is a consolatory speech, Zech. i. 13.

2. The word having these significations, shows what manner of exhortation it was which the apostle here useth. As,

(1.) It was a mild, sweet, and gentle exhortation; it had not the imperiousness of a lofty command, but the gentleness of a Christian entreaty. And thus the apostle Paul tells Philemon, ver. 8, 9, though he might be much bold in Christ to enjoin him, yet for love's sake he did rather beseech him. This is also suitable to that gentleness which Paul prescribes to Timothy, 2 Tim. ii. 24, 25, "The servant of the Lord must be gentle, apt to teach, patient, in meekness instructing," &c. And 2 Tim. iv. 2, "Exhort with all long-suffering." And the apostle tells us not only his practice, that he was gentle among them, as a nurse cherisheth her children, 1 Thess. ii. 7; that he warned the Ephesians night and day with tears, Acts xx. 31; that he charged every one as a father doth his children, 1 Thess. ii. 11: but expresses also his pattern, "I Paul beseech you by the meekness and gentleness of Christ, who was the copy of meekness," 2 Cor. x. 1. Both he and his servants gave the lamb, not the lion, for their emblem; pitying the defects and weaknesses, resenting the dangers, and tenderly handling the sores of every soul.

(2.) It was an ardent, earnest, and vehement exhortation. Though it were sweet, yet it was not slight; though with all his meekness, yet also with all his might: and this was the right temper of an apostolical spirit, neither to be incompassionate when zealous, nor remiss when gentle; ever to be driving the flocks, though not to over-drive them. Paul's advice to Timothy in 2 Tim. iv. 2, was, to be instant in season, out of season, to exhort, &c. Paul was an excellent orator, and all his oratory was employed to persuade men to be saved. Never did malefactor so plead to obtain his own life, as did blessed Paul plead with men to accept life: he was a wooer of souls to Christ, and he would take no denial. Though the more he loved, the less he was beloved; though the more he sued to them, the more he suffered from them; yet he suffers all things for the elect's sake. He labours abundantly; he becomes all things to all men, that he might by all means save some, 1 Cor. ix. 22. What importunate beseechings are his Epistles filled with! he seems to besiege souls with beseechings. "I beseech you by the mercies of God," Rom. xii. 1. "I Paul myself beseech you by the meekness and tenderness of Christ," 2 Cor. x. 1. "I the prisoner of the Lord beseech you," Eph. iv. 1: never did a poor prisoner so earnestly beg at the grate for bread. "We beseech you by the coming of our Lord Jesus Christ," 2 Thess. ii. 1.

(3.) It was an encouraging, animating, strengthening, establishing exhortation; such a one as is used to faint-hearted soldiers in battle: he raises up the spirits of these Christians to withstand seducers. Such a lion-like leader would even make an army of harts courageous, and put life into dead men. It is a great comfort to men going to fight, to see themselves regarded even by those who cannot help them, to hear men with loud voices calling to them, wishing them good success, and encouraging them with hopes of victory; a greater, when men will engage with them. Such was Jude in his present exhortation: such was the apostle Paul, who was set for the defence of the gospel; whose bonds made the brethren confident; who so often bids the faithful to quit themselves like men, to be of good comfort, to watch, to stand fast in the faith, to be strong, to be strong in the Lord, to

Davenant, in Col. ii. 2.

stand fast in the Lord, 1 Cor. xvi. 13; Phil. iv. 1; 1 Thess. iii. 8; Eph. vi. 10. Such was Barnabas, who exhorted the brethren that with full purpose of heart they should cleave to the Lord, Acts xi. 23.

Obs. 1. Gentleness and meekness is necessary for every exhorter. We live not among those who are perfect; and their defects should make us meek, as well as their duty make us earnest. Meek persuasions most take with ingenuous spirits. Men will rather be led than drawn; the cords wherewith we draw others should be the cords of a man. Ministers should rather delight in the optative than in the imperative mood. Indeed, the temper of the exhorted is much to be observed. Some are more sturdy, others more tender; and there is a difference to be put between an iron vessel and a Venice glass in the cleansing of them. But all gentle means are first to be used; we should choose to be gentle, and rather to drive away than shoot the bird.

Obs. 2. No persuasions or entreaties should be so vehement as those which are for the good of souls. It is hard not to be too importunate when we desire any thing for our own good; impossible to be so when we request others for their own souls. "Knowing the terror of the Lord," saith the apostle, "we persuade men," 2 Cor. v. 11. It is a holy impudence to be impudent in calling upon people to regard their souls. It is a sinful modesty to prefer courtesy herein before Christianity. The conscience of the most gainsaying sinner will commend an importunately exhorting Christian, although his lust be angry with him. That which can never be learned enough, can never be taught enough. That which men can never avoid enough, they can never be warned of enough. It is very good manners in Christianity to stay, and to knock again, though we have knocked more than three times at a sinner's conscience.

Obs. 3. The best Christians often stand in need of quickening by holy incitements. The strongest arms, like those of Moses, want holding up: the ablest Christian may now and then have a spiritual qualm. He who is now, as it were, in the third heaven, may anon be buffeted with the messenger of Satan, 2 Cor. xii. 7. Grace in the best is but a creature, and defectible; only the power of God preserves it from a total failing. Corruption within is strong, temptations without are frequent, and all these make exhortation necessary. A Christian more wants company as he is a Christian than as he is a man, though much as both. The hottest water will grow cold, if the fire under it be withdrawn.

Obs. 4. Holy exhortation is an excellent help to Christian resolution. It is as the sharpening of iron with iron; it is a whetstone for the relief of dulness. Jonathan in the wood strengthened David's hand in God, 1 Sam. xxiii. 16. They who fear the Lord must often speak one to another, Mal. iii. 16. The want of communion is the bane of Christian resolution. When an army is scattered, it is easy to destroy it. The apostle, Heb. x. 23, 24, joins these two together, the holding "fast the profession of our faith without wavering," the provoking one another to love and good works, as also the exhorting one another.

Obs. 5. Christians must "suffer the word of exhortation," Heb. xiii. 22. They must be entreated. If importunity overcame an unrighteous judge to do good to another, how much more should it prevail with us for our own good! Let not ministers complain with Isaiah, " I have spread out my hands all the day to a rebellious people," Isa. lxv. 2. Heavenly wisdom is easy to be entreated. Men want no entreaty at all to do good to their bodies. Whence is it that when we want no precept, and therefore have none, to love ourselves, all precepts and exhortations are too little to persuade us to the true self-love?

This for the way or manner of the apostle's writing, it was by exhortation.

The second follows, The apostle's expressing to what he exhorted these Christians, viz. "Earnestly to contend for the faith once delivered to the saints."

In which words I consider two things:

What it is which the apostle here commends to them carefully to maintain and defend; "The faith once delivered to the saints :" and, The means whereby, or the manner how, he exhorts these Christians to maintain and preserve that thing; which was by earnest contention; "Earnestly contend."

1. What thing it is which the apostle here commends to these Christians to maintain and preserve; viz. "The faith once delivered to the saints." This thing the apostle here first specifies, calling it "the faith;" secondly, amplifies three ways : 1. It was faith given, or delivered. 2. To the saints delivered. 3. Once delivered.

(1.) He specifies the thing which these Christians were to maintain and defend, "faith," πίστις.

The word faith in the Greek, πίστις, is derived from πείθω, *doceo*, and *persuadeo*, to teach, concerning the truth of a thing which we persuade men to believe; and it is in Scripture taken either properly or improperly.

[1.] Properly; and that either, 1. In its general notion, for that assent which is given to the speech of another. Or, 2. In its different sorts and kinds; and so it is either human or Divine : human, the assent which we give to the speech of a man; or Divine, the assent which we give to Divine revelation.

This Divine faith is commonly known to comprehend these four sorts.

Historical faith, called also by some dogmatical, which is *nudus assensus*, that bare assent which is given to Divine truth revealed in the Scripture, without any inward affection either to the revealer or to the thing revealed. Thus, "The devils believe," James ii. 19; and this is called dead faith, ver. 17.

Temporary faith, not so properly called a different kind of faith from the former, as a further degree of the same, which is an assent given to Divine truths, with some taste of, and delight, though not applicative and prevalent, in the knowledge of those truths for a time; he endureth for a while, Matt. xiii. 21; for a while they believe, Luke viii. 13.

Miraculous faith is that special assent which is given to some special promise of working miracles : and this is either active, when we believe that miracles shall be wrought by us, as 1 Cor. xiii. 2; Matt. vii. 22; or passive, when we believe they shall be wrought for and upon us, Acts xiv. 9.

Justifying faith, which is assent with trust and affiance to the promise of remission of sin, and salvation by Christ's righteousness, Rom. iii. 26; Gal. ii. 16; Luke xxii. 32; Acts xv. 9; Rom. iv. 5, &c.

[2.] Faith is considered improperly, and so it is taken in Scripture four ways especially.

For fidelity, and faithfulness. And so faith is attributed to God; "Shall their unbelief make the faith of God without effect," Rom. iii. 3. And to man; "Ye have omitted the weightier matters of the law, judgment, mercy, and faith," Matt. xxiii. 23. This is, as Cicero saith, *Dictorum conventorumque constantia*, the truth and constancy of our words and agreements. So we say, He breaks his faith.

De hac fide nunc loquimur quam adhibemus cum alicui credimus, non ea quam damus cum alicui pollicemur; nam et ipsa dicitur fides; sed aliter dicimus, non mihi habuit fidem; aliter, non mihi servavit fidem. Illud est, non credidit quod dixi; hoc, non fecit quod dixit; secundum hanc fidem qua credimus, fideles sumus Deo; secundum illam vero qua fit quod promittitur, etiam Deus est fidelis nobis. Aug. lib. 6. de sp. et lit. cap. 31.

For the profession of the faith, Acts xiii. 8; xiv. 22. "Your faith is spoken of throughout the world," Rom. i. 8.

For the things believed, or the fulfilling of what God hath promised. "Before faith came, we were kept under the law, shut up unto the faith which should afterwards be revealed," Gal. iii. 23; and ver. 25, "But after that faith is come." Here faith is taken for Christ, the object of faith.

For the doctrine of faith, or the truth to be believed to salvation; and more peculiarly, for the doctrine of faith in Christ. "A great company of the priests were obedient to the faith," Acts vi. 7. "Do we make void the law through faith?" Rom. iii. 31. "He heard him concerning the faith in Christ," Acts xxiv. 24; Rom. xii. 3. "He now preacheth the faith which before he destroyed," Gal. i. 23. So 1 Tim. iv. 16; Gal. iii. 2. So here in this place of Jude, "faith once delivered," is to be understood of the faith of heavenly doctrine, the word of faith, which the apostle saith God had delivered to them, and they were to maintain against the opposite errors of seducers. This holy doctrine being called faith,

Nomine fidei censetur, et illud quod creditur, et illud quo creditur. Lomb.

1. Because it is the instrument used by God to work faith. The Spirit by the word persuading us to assent to the whole doctrine of the gospel, and to rest upon Christ in the promise for life. In which respect faith is said to come by hearing, Rom. x. 17; and "the gospel, the power of God," &c. "to every one that believeth," Rom. i. 16. The faith to be believed begets a faith believing.

2. Because it is a most sure, infallible, faithful word, and deserves to be the object of our faith and belief. The author of it was the holy and true, the faithful and true Witness, God, who cannot lie, Rev. iii. 7, 14; Tit. i. 2. The instruments were infallibly guided by the immediate direction and assistance of the Holy Ghost, 2 Pet. i. 21. The matter of it an everlasting truth; the law being a constant rule of righteousness; the gospel containing promises which shall have their stability when heaven and earth shall pass away; and of such certainty, that if an angel from heaven should teach another doctrine, he must be accursed. It abounds also with prophecies and predictions most exactly accomplished, though after hundreds, yea, thousands of years. The form of it, which is its conformity with God himself, shows that if God be faithful, needs must his word be so; it is powerful, it searcheth the heart, Heb. iv. 12; it is pure and perfect, true and faithful, Psal. xix. 7, 9, and all this in conformity with the power, omniscience, purity, perfection, truth of God himself. The end of it is to supply us with assured comfort, Rom. xv. 4.

Obs. 1. The word of life is most worthy of assent and approbation. No word so much challenges belief as God's; it is so true and worthy of belief that it is called faith itself. When in Scripture the object is called by the name of the habit or affection, it denotes that the object is very proper for that habit or affection to be exercised about. Heaven is in Scripture called joy, to show it is much to be rejoiced in; and the doctrine of salvation is called faith, to show that it is most worthy of our faith. Infidelity is a most inexcusable and incongruous sin in us, when the faithful and true God speaks unto us. It is impossible for God to lie, Tit. i. 2; Heb. vi. 18; and yet, "Who hath believed our report?" Isa. liii. 1, may be a complaint as ordinary as it is old. How just is God to give those over to believe a lie, who will not believe the truth! How miserable is their folly who believe a lie, and distrust faith itself!

Obs. 2. Deplorable is their state who want the doctrine of salvation. They have no footing for faith; they have, they hear nothing that they can believe. Uncertainty of happiness is ever the portion of a people who are destitute of the word. He who wants this light knows not whither he goeth. The fancy of the enthusiast, the reason of the Socinian, the traditions of the papist, the oracles of the heathens, are all foundations of sand; death shakes and overturns them all.

Obs. 3. The true reason of the firmness and stedfastness of the saints in their profession: they lean upon a sure word, a more sure word than any revelation; a word called even faith itself. Greater is the certainty of faith than that of sense and reason. It is not opinion and scepticism, but faith. "The Holy Ghost is no sceptic; it works in us not opinions, but assertions, more sure than life itself, and all experience." The more weight and dependence we place upon the word, so firm a foundation is it, the stronger is the building. None will distrust God but they who never tried him.

Obs. 4. Our great end in attending upon the word, should be the furthering of our faith. The jewel of the word should not hang in our ears, but be locked up in a believing heart. It is not meat on the table, but in the stomach, that nourishes; and not the word preached, but believed, that saves us.

The apostle having specified the thing which they were to maintain, "faith;" he amplifies it, and that three ways.

1. He saith it was delivered. The word in the Greek, παραδοθείση, here translated delivered, signifieth to be given, or delivered from one to another several ways, (in Scripture,) according to the circumstances of the place where and the matter about which it is used.

Sometimes it imports a delivering craftily, deceitfully, or traitorously, in which respect the word παραδίδωμι is often rendered to betray, as Matt. xxiv. 10; xxvi. 15, 16, 21, 23—25, 45, 46, 48.

In some places it signifies a delivering in a way of punishment and suffering, as Matt. iv. 12, Jesus heard that John was delivered up. So Matt. v. 25; x. 17, 19, 21; xvii. 22; Acts vii. 42, &c.

In other places it signifies a delivering in a way of committing something to one's trust, to be carefully regarded and preserved, as Matt. xi. 27; xxv. 14, 20; John xix. 20; 1 Pet. ii. 23. And thus it frequently signifies a delivering by way of information, or relation of doctrines and duties from one to another, to be kept and observed: and that both from God, first by the speech, and afterward by the writing of holy men for the use of his church, as 1 Cor. xi. 2; 2 Thess. ii. 15; iii. 6; 2 Pet. ii. 21; and also from men, who often deliver doctrines to others, not written in the word, Matt. xv. 2; Mark vii. 9, 13, but invented by men.

In this sense the delivering here mentioned is to be taken; namely, for such an information or relation of God's will, as they to whom it is delivered are bound to preserve and keep as their treasure: in which respect the delivering of this faith, or doctrine of salvation, comprehends, first, God's bestowing it; secondly, man's holding and keeping it.

1. God's bestowing it; and in that is considerable, In what ways and after what manner God delivered it; and, What need there was of this delivery of the faith by God.

(1.) In what ways God delivered the faith. The Scripture tells us he hath delivered it either extraordinarily, as immediately by himself, by angels, by a voice, by a sensible apparition to men; sometimes when they were awake, at other times when they were sleeping, by dreams, and sometimes only by inward inspiration, Numb. xii. 6, 8; Heb. i. 1, &c. Or ordinarily; and so he delivers the doctrine of faith, 1. To his ministers, whom he has appointed to be stewards thereof to the end of the world; partly, by qualifying them with gifts and ministerial abilities; and partly, by appointing and setting them apart for the ministry by those whom he hath authorized thereunto. 2. To his people, by the ministry of his forementioned servants, who have instructed the faithful, sometimes by preaching with a lively voice, and afterward by committing the doctrine of faith to writing. And ministers shall to the end of the world be continued to deliver this doctrine of faith to the church, for their edification in holiness. And among those people to whom ministers deliver this faith externally, some there are to whom it is delivered also effectually, by the internal revelation of the Spirit, which so delivers this doctrine of faith to all the elect, that they themselves are delivered into it, Rom. vi. 17; their understandings being savingly enlightened to see that excellency in it, which by the bare ministry of it cannot be perceived; and their wills persuaded to embrace it, as that rule of life according to which they will constantly walk.

(2.) What need there was of the delivery of this faith.

[1.] In regard of the insufficiency of all other doctrines or prescriptions in the world to lead to life. Only this doctrine delivered is the rule of faith and manners. Peace internal and eternal is only afforded to them who walk according to this rule, Gal. vi. 16. God brings to glory only by guiding by these counsels. All other lights are false, are fools' fires, which lead to precipices and perdition. This is the light which shines in a dark place, 2 Pet. i. 19; to which whoever gives not heed can never find the way to heaven. Learned ethnics never wrote of eternal happiness in their ethics. "The world by wisdom knew not God," 1 Cor. i. 21.

[2.] In regard of the total insufficiency of man to find out this doctrine of himself. The things delivered in this doctrine are mysteries, supernatural, and depending on the mere will and dispensation of God. The incarnation of the Son of God, expiation of sin by his death, justification by faith, could never have entered into the mind of man, unless God had revealed them, Col. i. 26. They depend not upon any connexion of natural causes. Though there be a kind of natural theology, yet there is no natural Christianity. Also the understanding of man is so obscured by the darkness of sin, that in spirituals it is purely blind. The natural man perceives not the things which are of God, 1 Cor. ii. 14.

2. This delivering of faith comprehends the keeping and holding it by those to whom it was delivered. This is done therefore, 1. By ministers. 2. By every Christian.

(1.) This duty is incumbent on ministers, who must keep the truth, hold fast the faithful word, Tit. i. 9, and be tenacious, ἀντεχόμενοι, holding it, as the word signifies, against a contrary hold, with both their hands, with all their strength; holding it in their understanding, in their affections, in their preaching and delivery, in their life and practice, not parting with it for fear or favour, either to sectaries or politicians, rather parting with their lives than their sword.

(2.) The faith is kept by every Christian, by persevering in the knowledge, love, and practice of it. Every saint must keep it in his head, in his heart, in his hand; this he must do, though for keeping the truth he lose his life. It is not having, but holding the truth, which is a Christian's crown, Rev. ii. 13. He who lets it go never had it truly and effectually in the love of it, nor shall ever enjoy it in the recompence of it. Of this more afterward.

Obs. 1. God was the author of the doctrine of life; though by men, yet from him has it always been delivered; it is his word and revelation. "The word of the Lord," and, "Thus saith the Lord," is the Scripture stamp and superscription. When the patriarchs and prophets preached it, it was from him; when holy men of old time wrote it, it was from him; though he has spoken in divers manners, yet it was he who spake. When the doctrine of life was committed to writing, he commanded it. He moved and inspired holy men to write, 2 Pet. i. 21; 2 Tim. iii. 16; Exod. xvii. 14; xxxiv. 27; Isa. viii. 1; xxx. 8; Jer. xxxvi. 2. They were his organs and instruments of conveying his mind to the world. "The Spirit of the Lord," saith David, "spake by me, and his word was in my tongue," 2 Sam. xxiii. 2. And, "The Holy Ghost spake by Isaiah," Acts xxviii. 25. And the Spirit of Christ in the prophets foretold his sufferings, 1 Pet. i. 11. These and the other holy men were the scribes, the pens, the hands, the notaries of the Spirit. They wrote not as men, but as men of God. When any book is called the Book of Moses, the Psalms of David, the Epistle of Paul, it is in respect of ministry, not of the principal cause. Quicquid Christus de suis dictis ac factis, nos scire voluit, ipsis scribendum tanquam suis manibus imperavit. Aug. l. 1. de cons. Evang. c. 35.

Obs. 2. Great is the necessity of Scripture. The doctrine of life could never without a Scriptural delivery have been found out; without it indeed this doctrine was between two and three thousand years preserved by the delivery of a living voice; but afterwards, when their lives who were to deliver the word grew short, men numerous, memory frail, the bounds of the church enlarged, corruptions frequent, and therefore tradition an unfaithful keeper of the purity of doctrine, as appears by Terah's and Abraham's worshipping of other gods, the idolatry in Jacob's family, &c., Josh. xxiv. 2; Gen. xxxv. 2, God appointed that the doctrine of life should be committed to writing; and upon supposition of the will and pleasure of God, whose wisdom hath now thought fit to give us no other rule and foundation of faith, the written word is now necessary, as the means of delivering faith to us. Had not the faith therefore been delivered in Scriptures, whence should it have been found, how retained? The written word is the cabinet, wherein lies the jewel of faith; the star which shows where the Babe lodges; the light which discovers the beauty of salvation; a book of Apocalypse, or revelation of Christ. Apostoli quod primum præconiaverunt, postea per Dei voluntatem in Scripturis nobis tradiderunt, fundamentum et columnam fidei nostræ futuræ. Iren. lib. 3. adv. Hæres. c. 1.

Obs. 3. Strong is the engagement upon us to be thankful for God's discovering to us the doctrine of faith. It was above the compass of reason and nature ever to have found it out by their own inquiry: neither men nor angels could have known it without Divine revelation. It was a mystery, a great, a hidden mystery, which was kept secret since the world began, Rom. xvi. 25; Eph. i. 9; iii. 9. How much to be adored is God's goodness to us, to whom the faith is delivered, though from others it was hidden! Deut. vii. 6, 7; Matt. xi. 25, 26. This faith, without the knowledge whereof there is no salvation, and which could never have been known but by revealed light, was not given to us rather than to others, who lived and died in the utter ignorance thereof, for any preceding difference and disposition thereunto in us, but only out of the mere love and free grace of God.

Obs. 4. The great impiety of those who obtrude a

faith upon people invented by men, not delivered by God; who erect a building of faith upon the foundation of philosophical principles. Schoolmen and papists fasten many things for articles of faith upon the people, which they never received from divine delivery, but from the discourse of blind reason: what else are their errors concerning worship, free will, inherent righteousness, the merit of works, &c., but streams which flowed from the ethics of philosophers, not the Epistles of Paul? Human reason is deceitful, when it goes beyond its bounds. A philosopher, as such, is but a natural man, and perceives not the things of God. Blind men cannot judge of colours, beasts order not human affairs; nor must human reason determine of heavenly doctrine. The principles of reason are a sandy foundation for the conclusions of divine doctrine. Hagar must be ejected, if she submit not to Sarah. Reason must be subdued to faith.

Obs. 5. Great is the dignity of a minister's office. The end of it is the delivering of the faith to people. Ministers, though earthen vessels, yet carry a treasure; though torn caskets, yet they contain jewels, 2 Cor. iv. 7. A faithful minister is God's steward, to dispense his blessings. He is a star for light and influence; a cloud to distil down showers of plenty upon God's weary heritage; a nurse, a father, a saviour, a common good. Joseph's office in delivering out of corn to the people in the famine made him honoured; how worthy an employment is it then to deliver to souls the bread of life!

Obs. 6. It is a great sin to part with the faith delivered to us. It is a heinous sin either in ministers or people. In the former, when they shall either give it away, or suffer it to be taken from them. For the defence of the gospel they are set, Phil. i. 17; they must be men made up of fire in the midst of a field of stubble of errors; though holily patient when their own interest, yet holily impatient when the interest of Christ is endangered. They must not be dumb dogs when thieves attempt to rob the house of God, the church. Though they must not bite the children within, yet neither spare the thief without. Nor is any Christian exempted in his station from the duty of keeping faith: they must not sell the truth, Prov. xxiii. 23; not patiently suffer sectaries and persecutors to bereave them of it; not for the love of their swine suffer Christ to go, much less send Christ out of their coasts; not part with the faith by keeping their money. In a word, they must keep the faith by perseverance in the love and profession of it, by taking heed of error and profaneness, lest being led away with the error of the wicked, they fall from their stedfastness, 2 Pet. iii. 17.

2. Jude saith in the amplification of this faith, that it was delivered to the saints, τοῖς ἁγίοις. It may here be inquired, 1. Who are holy and saints? 2. Who the saints are to whom this faith was delivered?

Men are called holy in two respects. (1.) In respect of the holiness of destination, separation, or being set apart from common uses and employments to the holy service of God: thus the Greeks apply the word ἀφορίζω, to separate; and thus not only men, but the temple, vessels, sabbath, tabernacle are called holy, 2 Chron. vii. 16; Isa. xiii. 3; 1 Kings ix. 3. The first-born God commands Moses to sanctify, Exod. xiii. 2; which he explains, "Thou shalt set apart to the Lord," &c., ver. 12. Thus the prophets and apostles are often in Scriptures called holy; and Jeremiah was sanctified from the womb, Jer. i. 5, in regard of this holiness of separation and dedication; and all visible professors and their children are called holy, 1 Cor. vii. 14, as likewise may the whole body of a visible church.

(2.) In respect of their having holiness really and properly put into them; which is done by the Holy Spirit, whence it is read of the sanctification of spirit, it abolishing their native pollution and unholiness, and bestowing upon them graces and holy qualities by the renovation of God's image in them, 2 Thess. ii. 13; 1 Pet. i. 2; 1 Cor. i. 2; Exod. xix. 6. And the Holy Spirit makes them holy in two respects. 1. Of not holy privatively; and so man that had lost totally his holiness is made holy by regeneration or effectual vocation. 2. Of less holy; and so God's children are sanctified, by being enabled to exercise an actual mortifying of sin, and living in holiness, with proceeding in both.

2. Who the saints are to whom the faith was delivered?

(1.) Some by saints here understand those holy prophets, apostles, and other ministers, who are holy by peculiar office and employment, to whom God delivered the doctrine of faith, either of old, in an extraordinary, or since, in an ordinary way, that they might be his ministers in delivering it unto others; and these in Scripture are called holy: "He spake by the mouth of his holy prophets, which have been since the world began," Luke i. 70. And Acts iii. 11, the same words are again used. "Holy men of God spake as they were moved by the Holy Ghost," 2 Pet. i. 21. "The words spoken before by the holy prophets," 2 Pet. iii. 2. "Ye holy apostles and prophets," Rev. xviii. 20. "The Lord God of the holy prophets," Rev. xxii. 6. And these in a peculiar manner had the doctrine of faith delivered to them. "Ye" apostles "shall be witnesses to me both in Jerusalem, and in all Judea, and Samaria, and unto the uttermost part of the earth," Acts i. 8. These had commission to teach all nations, Matt. xxviii. 19. By these the great salvation was confirmed, Heb. ii. 3. Paul tells the Corinthians, he had received from the Lord that which he delivered to them, 1 Cor. xi. 23. And, "I delivered unto you first of all that which I also received," 1 Cor. xv. 3. And, "A dispensation of the gospel is committed to me," 1 Cor. ix. 17. "God hath committed unto us the word of reconciliation," 2 Cor. v. 19. "The gospel of uncircumcision was committed to me," Gal. ii. 7. "The glorious gospel of the blessed God was committed to my trust, 1 Tim. i. 11. "O Timothy, keep that which is committed to thy trust," 1 Tim. vi. 20. He principally means the gospel with which God had intrusted him. So Tit. i. 3, &c.

(2.) But, not excluding the former, by the saints to whom the faith was delivered, I understand all the people of God to whom it was delivered by the forementioned servants of God. And as some of these were saints in regard only of visible profession and dedication, and others were made saints in respect of true and saving sanctity; so the faith was delivered unto these differently: to the former, by way of outward administration and visible dispensation; to the latter, who were made true saints, by way of saving and effectual operation. They who were and continued to be only visible and external saints had the faith delivered unto them, as the common sort of Israelites had, to whom God wrote the great things of his law, and yet they were accounted a strange thing, Hos. viii. 12; and to whom were committed the oracles of God, Rom. iii. 2, and yet they believed not, Isa. liii. 1; contenting themselves in the retaining the letter of the law, declaring God's statutes, and taking his covenant into their mouth; in the mean time never regarding to have the law written in their hearts, but hating instruction, and casting the word of God behind them, Psal. l. 16, 17, &c. They who had the faith delivered unto them by way of effica-

F

cious and saving operation, did not only hear, but believe the report of God's messengers, and the arm of God was revealed to them, Isa. liii. 1; to whom it was given to know the mysteries of the kingdom of God, although to others it was not given, Matt. xiii. 11; and for whose sake alone the faith is delivered to others, who got no good at all thereby, but only an estimation for members of the visible church.

Obs. 1. The word is to be laid out and delivered to, not to be laid up and kept from others. The saints are to be the better for it. The ministry is in Scripture compared to light; what more diffusive? to seed; it must be scattered: to bread; it must be broken and distributed to every one according to their exigences: to salt; it must not be laid up in the salt-box, but laid out in seasoning the flesh, that it may be kept from putrefaction. He who hides truth buries gold. Ministers must rather be worn with using than rusting. Paul did spend, and was spent. The sweat of a minister, as it is reported of Alexander's, casts a sweet savour. His talents are not for the napkin, but occupation. How sinful are they that stand idle in a time of labour! how impious they who compel them to stand so!

Obs. 2. They who retain and keep the faith are saints. Visibly those are saints, and that is a church, which keep it by profession and ministerially. That is a church which is the pillar and ground of truth, 1 Tim. iii. 15; to whom the oracles of God are committed, as Paul speaks of the Jews, Rom. iii. 2. None are so to complain of the defects of our church, for what it wants, as to deny it a church, considering what it has. It holds forth the truth of all doctrines which serve both for the beginning and increase of faith. It is one of Christ's golden candlesticks wherein he hath set up the light of his word; and though sectaries do not, yet Christ walks in the midst of them. I must be bold to fear, that because our adversaries cannot rationally deny, that while we hold forth the truth we are a true church, they labour by their errors to extinguish the truth, that so we may be none.

Obs. 3. How much is the world beholden to saints! They have kept the faith, the word of life, for the ungrateful world ever since it was first delivered. Were it not for them, we had lost our truth, nay, lost our God. These are they who have in all ages with their breath, nay, with their blood, preserved the gospel, kept the word of Christ's patience, Rev. iii. 8, 10. And rather than they would nor keep the faith, they have lost their lives. They profit the world against its will, they are benefactors to their several ages; like indulgent parents, they have laid up the riches of faith for those who have desired their deaths. It is our duty, though not to adore them, yet to honour their memory. Satan knows no mean between deifying and nullifying them. Imitation of them is as unquestionably our duty, as adoration of them would be our sin.

Obs. 4. Unholiness is very unsuitable to them to whom the faith is delivered. It is delivered to saints in profession, and they should labour to be so in power. They should adorn the doctrine of God, Tit. ii. 10. How sad a sight is it to behold the unsanctified lives of those to whom this faith has been long delivered! How many live as if faith had banished all fidelity and honesty, or as if God had delivered the faith, not to furnish their souls with holiness, but only their shelves with Bibles! Books in the head, not in the study, make a good scholar; and the word of faith, not in the house or head, but in the heart and life, make a Christian. O thou who art called a saint, either be not so much as called so, or be more than called so; otherwise thy external privilege will be but an eternal punishment. If God have delivered his faith to thee, deliver up thyself to him.

Obs. 5. The fewness of faith's entertainers is no derogation from faith's excellency. They are a poor handful of saints by whom the faith is preserved, and to whom it is delivered in the world. The greatest number of men and nations have not the faith delivered unto them ministerially, and of them the far greater part never had it delivered efficaciously. It is better to love the faith with a few, than to leave it with a multitude. Numbers cannot prove a good cause, nor oppose a great God.

Obs. 6. The true reason of Satan's peculiar rage against saints, is because they have that faith delivered to them which is the bane and battery of his kingdom; that word which is an antidote against his poison; that doctrine which discovers his deeds of darkness. Satan's policy is to disarm a place of the word when he would subdue it; he peaceably suffers those to live who have not the weapons of holy doctrine; he throws his cudgels against fruitful trees; he lays wait as a thief for those who travel with this treasure. They who are empty of this treasure may sing and be merry when they meet with him; he never stops them. Others who have the faith he sets upon and annoys. "I have given them thy word," (saith Christ,) "and the world hath hated them," John xvii. 14.

3. Jude saith, in this amplification, the faith was once delivered, once, ἅπαξ.

Three things may be touched in the explication.
1. The meaning of the word once.
2. The agreement thereof with the delivery of faith, or how faith may be said to be once delivered.
3. Why the apostle adds this expression, "once," to the delivery of faith, amplifying it this way.

For the first, The word " once" is taken two ways in Scripture and ordinary usage.

(1.) As it is opposed to inconstancy, deficiency, cessation, or uncertainty of continuance; and so once is as much as firmly, constantly, irrevocably, always. Thus God saith, " Once have I sworn by my holiness that I will not lie unto David," Psal. lxxxix. 35; that is, my oath is irrevocable, nor is there any danger of inconstancy. What I have sworn shall surely be accomplished.

Nulla reparabilis arte læsa pudicitia est, deperit illa semel. Ovid.

(2.) Once is taken as it is opposed to reiteration, repetition, or frequency, either of the being or doing of any thing; and so once is as much as once, and no more; once for all; once, and not again; once, and only once. When a thing is done so fully and perfectly, that it need not, or should not, or cannot be done again. Thus "Christ was offered once to bear the sins of many," Heb. ix. 28. And we read of "the offering of Christ once for all," Heb. x. 10. And Abishai desired to smite Saul once, promising that he would not smite him the second time, 1 Sam. xxvi. 8.

2. For the second, Both these significations agree most aptly and suitably to the delivery of the doctrine of faith. For,

(1.) The faith is once delivered, as once is opposed to deficiency, or cessation, that is, firmly and irrevocably delivered. It shall ever be, it shall never be quite taken away from the church, it endures for ever, 1 Pet. i. 25. As the habit of faith shall never cease in the soul, so the doctrine of faith shall never cease in the world. It is a candle that all the winds of hell can never blow out, a flame that all the waters of trouble can never extinguish. Thus it is called the eternal gospel, Rev. xiv. 6, never to be destroyed; it shall ever be in the Scripture, ministry, hearts, and profession of a number of men. "My words" (saith God) "shall not depart out of thy mouth, nor out of the mouth of thy seed, nor out of the mouth of thy seed's seed, from henceforth and for ever," Isa. lix. 21. Christ promises to be with his ministers to the end of the world, Matt. xxviii. 19. The servants of Christ shall trade in the spiritual merchandise of faith till he come, Luke xix. 13. The people of God in the use of the Lord's supper shall set forth "the Lord's death till he come," 1 Cor. xi. 26. And the work of the ministry, with the edifying of the body thereby, shall continue till we all meet, &c., Eph. iv. 13. That the doctrine of faith shall ever continue in one place, is not asserted; but that it shall ever in some place, is certain. It is not for the dignity of Christ, the King of his church, ever to suffer his sceptre to be wrested out of his hands. It is not consistent with the safety, integrity, health, life, &c. of the church, in this her condition of constant exigence, to be deprived of the doctrine which is given her for armour, a rule, medicine, food. It is as easy for enemies to pluck the sun out of the firmament, as this faith out of the church. The whole power and policy of hell have been employed for that purpose sixteen hundred years. Could it have been done, it had been done long before now.

(2.) The faith is once delivered, as once is opposed to frequency or reiteration; it is once and no more, once for all, once, and not again to be delivered; in respect it shall never be delivered again, with any change or alteration which it is to receive. It is a work done so well that it need not be done again, because it cannot be done better. And thus the doctrine of salvation may be said to be once or unalterably delivered, both in respect of the matter of it, and the present manner of administering it.

Semel traditam doctrinam dicit quæ nunquam sit posthac immutanda. Beza in loc.

[1.] In respect of the matter; it never was, nor ever shall be changed. The same Saviour of man, and Mediator between God and man, hath unalterably been afforded: "Christ Jesus the same yesterday, and to-day, and for ever," Heb. xiii. 8. He was "the Lamb slain from the foundation of the world," Rev. xiii. 8. There never was any other but his name by which salvation at any time was bestowed, Acts iv. 12. All, even those before and after Christ, have drank of the same spiritual Rock, 1 Cor. x. 4. Christ is "the Lamb of God that taketh away the sin of the world," John i. 29; not he the sin of some ages, and another of other ages of the world. "He is the Saviour of the whole body," Eph. v. 23. No other gospel can be preached but the glad tidings of life by Christ, Gal. i. 7. "Other foundation can no man lay than that is laid, which is Jesus Christ," 1 Cor. iii. 11. As Christ, so the doctrine of life by Christ, is the same yesterday to Adam, the patriarchs, and prophets, to-day to the apostles, and for ever to all following saints. It is a testament wherein all the legacies of grace and glory are bequeathed; and therefore (as the apostle argues) it is unalterable, Gal. iii. 15. The rule of life, the holy law of God, is a standing and unalterable rule. Whatsoever is a sin against the moral law now, was a sin always; duties required now by it, were duties always. Peace is the portion now, and it was ever the portion of them that walked according to it. The ransom from death, and standing rule of life, were ever one and the same.

[2.] The doctrine of salvation is once, i. e. unalterably delivered now, in respect of the present manner of administration; namely, by ministers, preaching, and sacraments, &c. No other form or manner of exhibiting the benefits by Christ can be introduced. In respect of this manner of administration and exhibition of the benefits of the gospel, without legal types, shadows, and sacrifices, it is called the new testament; and it is called new because it is to be always new, and never grow old, as the former did. Should there ever be another manner of administration admitted, it must be called the new testament; and so either this must be called old, and then there must be two old testaments, the former and this, or this must still be called new, and so there should be granted two new testaments. Besides, this last way of administration of the benefits of the gospel being instituted by Christ himself, it should much derogate from the dignity of Christ, if another way should afterward be thought more excellent and perfect. God in these last times hath spoken (saith the apostle) by his Son, and therefore delivered his will more excellently and worthily than ever before, Heb. i. 2. After Christ comes none. The condition also of the times of the gospel is such, that they are called "the last days," Heb. i. 2, and after the last comes no time. So that faith shall never, in respect of the matter delivered, or manner of delivering, receive a new edition, for enlarging, correcting, or amending the former.

3. Why does the apostle add this expression "once" to the delivery of faith? It is used as a most invincible argument to prevail with these Christians to preserve the faith and themselves from the wicked and destructive errors and practices of seducers; and so it is a strong argument several ways.

(1.) It is an argument from the possible, nay, sure successfulness of the work of contending, they being to contend for a faith that was once delivered, that was always to remain, that should never be totally removed; against which the power of hell should never prevail. What soldier would not willingly fight for the party that doth prevail, and is ever sure to do so? when it is not a desperate battle, but there is a certainty of success?

(2.) It is an argument *ab honesto*, from the seemliness of it, and that two ways. 1. It is a faith once delivered, and but once; once delivered, and unchangeably the same which their holy predecessors, patriarchs, prophets, and apostles embraced and defended, and therefore to be preserved and maintained. Who will not carefully preserve the inheritance which belonged to his ancestors? God forbid, saith Naboth, "that I should give the inheritance of my fathers unto thee," 1 Kings xxi. 3. If the ancient landmarks be not to be removed, much less the faith-marks, Prov. xxii. 28. A ring, a jewel which belonged to our father or predecessors of old, how precious is it! 2. It is a faith once, and so always and perpetually to be delivered; and therefore by preserving it to be left as a legacy to posterity, to be laid up as a precious *depositum* or treasure for children and successors, we should endeavour that the generation which is yet to come may also serve the same God, and enjoy the same Christ and gospel. How desirable is it to put, as it were, a fallacy upon death, by doing good, and living when we are dead; to communicate religion to posterity; to be like musk, of which the box savours when it is emptied of it!

(3.) It is an argument *a periculoso;* it is a faith once delivered, i. e. without reiteration and alteration; and therefore the errors of seducers are not this faith: q. d. If you let it go for that pretended faith of these seducers, you part with a pearl for a pebble, a rich conveyance, not of an earthly, but of a heavenly inheritance, like children, for a doll. The living child by the seducers is taken away, and the dead one laid in its room. The faith is unchangeable, and therefore the faith which sectaries would fasten upon you is not faith, but fiction. Either this faith once delivered or none must be your faith. Hence Paul tells the Galatians, that the other gospel which seducers had obtruded upon them was not another, i. e. was none at all, Gal. i. 7. Now, how impossible is it in this wilderness to travel to Canaan without a guide, a cloud, a pillar! How dangerous to walk in a dark place without a light, and to follow a false, a fool's fire, which leads unto bogs and precipices!

Obs. 1. The sin and folly of those is evident who conceive they can live without and above this doctrine of faith. If it be once and perpetually to be delivered, it is perpetually to be embraced, and we stand in perpetual want of it. This manna must rain till we come to Canaan. We must be fed with the spoon of the ordinance while we are in this age of childhood, as the apostle calls it, 1 Cor. xiii. Certainly, the way of ordinance-forsakers is their folly; not their strength, but their weakness, their sickness; if ever they recover their health, they will fall to their food. A standing dispensation of faith is both promised and commanded, till we all meet "in the unity of the faith," Eph. iv. 13; and how that commanded dispensation of faith is consistent with a commendable despising thereof, I understand not.

Obs. 2. The doctrine of faith is perfect. Whatever truth or doctrine is needful to life and salvation, is fully and perfectly delivered in it. It needs not another delivery, because it cannot be made more perfect. "The law of the Lord is perfect, converting the soul," Psal. xix. 7. By the law is meant all heavenly doctrine. And St. Paul, Rom. x. 18, accommodates that psalm to the preaching of the apostles. The word is a perfect platform of righteousness. The gospel of salvation is Christ's testament; it contains therefore his whole will, and must not be disannulled or changed. The doctrine of faith is a canon, a rule; and if a rule be not perfect, it is no rule, Gal. vi. 16. It is able to make us wise to salvation, throughly furnished to every good work, 2 Tim. iii. 15, 17. It is propounded as a motive by Christ, that the Jews should search the Scriptures, because in them they thought to have life eternal, John v. 39. "These things are written," saith John, "that ye might believe that Jesus is the Christ, the Son of God; and that believing ye might have life in his name," John xx. 31. The Scripture accepts of no supplement from traditions. Papists, with all the heretics of old, are necessitated to fly to traditions, as the refuge of their heresies, though they can never with any show of certainty prove that their traditions were received from Christ or his apostles; many whereof are known to be lately devised fables; and all of them, when received as a rule of faith, are impious, and oppose the perfection of the Scripture. "In vain do they worship God, teaching for doctrines the commandments of men."

Obs. 3. Ministers have no liberty to deliver any new doctrine to their hearers. They must neither add nor diminish. Their doctrine is committed to them, not invented by them. They must preach what they have received, not cogitated. If they preach after a new manner, yet they must not preach new things. They must proceed in the faith, not change it. Timothy is commanded by Paul to keep that which is committed to his trust, 1 Tim. vi. 20. Ministers are stewards, not masters of the mysteries of the gospel. They must proclaim, not contrive laws for the conscience. Were they angels from heaven, people must not hear them delivering another gospel.

Obs. 4. Infinite is the power of God to preserve the faith perpetually and unalterably. The doctrine of faith is a torch burning in the midst of the sea; it is a Moses's bush, burning, not consumed. All oppositions are by God turned into victories on its side. The smutchings which heretics cast upon it, are but to make it shine the brighter. Naked truth will vanquish armed error.

Obs. 5. This delivering of the faith once, regulates the notion of new lights. If we understand by new light, a new and further degree of knowledge to understand what is unchangeably delivered in the Scripture, new light is a most desirable gift; but if by it we understand pretended truths which are new to Scripture, varnished over with the name of new light, they are to be shunned for false lights, which lead to perdition. After Christ hath spoken the word, we must not be curious; it is bastard doctrine which springs up after the Scripture. This one thing believe, that nothing but Scripture doctrine is to be believed.

Obs. 6. God's unchangeable, perpetual delivery of the faith, is a singular encouragement to expect his blessing in the delivery of it. It may encourage ministers and people. He who has promised a gospel to the end of the world, has also promised to be with the deliverers of it to that time. He who will continue a gospel to us, if sought, will also continue his grace to it. He who bestows the doctrine of faith, will not deny the grace of faith, if we duly ask it. When the Lord bestows the seed of his word, be encouraged to expect the showers of his blessing. If he sticks up his candles, comfortably hope that he will put light by his Spirit to them.

Obs. 7. It is a great comfort to the saints, that in all their changes and losses their best blessings shall never be altered or utterly removed. In an impure world there shall ever be kept up a pure word. This light shall never be put out till the Sun of righteousness arise at the last day. God will keep his stars in his right hand. They who will go about to remove the stars in his right hand, shall feel the strength of his right hand. Of the ministry it may be said, as Isaac said of Jacob, God hath blessed them, and they shall be blessed. The saints shall have a golden gospel, though they live in an iron age.

Obs. 8. It must be our care to be stedfast in the faith, and to shun heretical additions and superstructures. We must beware, lest being led away by the error of the wicked, we fall from our stedfastness, 2 Pet. iii. 17. To this end, (1.) We must be grounded in the knowledge of the truth. Ignorant and doubting people will easily be seduced. Silly women, ever learning, and never coming to the knowledge of the truth, will easily be led away, 2 Tim. iii. 6. Children in knowledge will soon be "tossed with every wind of doctrine," Eph. iv. 14. They will, like water, be of the same figure with the vessel into which it is put. They will be of their last doctor's opinion. (2.) We must get a love to the truth. Many receive the truth for fear of loss, disgrace, &c., or hope of gain, preferment, &c., or because others do so; and as hounds, who follow the game, not because they have the scent of it, but because their fellows pursue it. Those who embrace the truth they know not why, will leave it they know not how; and by the same motives for which they now embrace the truth, they may be induced to forsake truth and embrace error. God often sends to those strong delusions that they should believe a lie, who received not the love of the truth, 2 Thess. i. 11. (3.) Nourish no known sin. The jewel of faith can never be kept in a cracked cabinet, a crazy conscience. He who puts away a good conscience, concerning faith will soon make shipwreck, 1 Tim. i. 19. Those silly women laden with sins, may easily be led captives, 2 Tim. iii. 6. Solomon, by following strange women, soon embraced strange and idolatrous practices.

Demas having "loved the present world," soon forsook Paul, 2 Tim. iv. 10. Seducers through covetousness will make merchandise of souls, Tit. i. 11; 2 Pet. ii. 3. Pride will also hinder from finding and keeping wisdom, Prov. xiv. 6. God giveth grace to the humble, and resisteth the proud. The garment of humility is the soul's guard against every spiritual mischief. It is prudent counsel to be "clothed with humility," 1 Pet. v. 5. A humble soul will neither hatch nor easily be hurt by heresies. (4.) Labour to grow in grace. "Beware," saith the apostle, "lest being led away with the error of the wicked, ye fall from your own stedfastness;" the remedy is immediately subjoined, but "grow in grace." They who stand at a stay will soon go backwards.

This for the first part of the duty to which the apostle exhorted these Christians; viz. What the thing was which he commended to them to maintain, "The faith once delivered to the saints." Secondly, The means whereby he exhorts them to defend the faith; by an earnest contending for it, "That you should earnestly contend."

Two things offer themselves in the explanation.

1. To show what the force and importance of that word is which is translated "earnestly contend."

2. More fully, what the apostle here intends by earnest contending for the faith, and wherein this earnest contention consists, as it is employed for the faith.

Decerto. Bez. Superceto. Vulg. 1. The compound word in the original, ἐπαγωνίζομαι, which our English words "earnestly contend" answer, is only used in this place throughout the whole New Testament. All the several translations thereof by interpreters, speak this contention to which Jude exhorts these Christians to be eminent and extraordinary. The word ἀγωνίζομαι out of composition (though then it imports *'Αγωνία proprie* not so notable a contention as it does *dicitur de æstu-* here in composition) is rightly trans-
atione animi in eo lated, to strive, to fight, and that as *qui in certamen* for the mastery, to labour fervently,
descensurus est. John xviii. 36; Luke xiii. 24; 1 Cor.
Accipitur pro lucta in morte. ix. 25; Col. i. 29; 1 Tim. vi. 12; 2 Tim.
Gerh. Harm. iv. 7; and signifies that vehement fighting and striving which was wont to be among wrestlers in their solemn games, with sweat, pains, and trouble; but it being so compounded as in this place, it imports a more renowned and famous contention than ordinary. It is not agreed by all wherein the force of the composition ἐπί consists. Some conceive that thereby the apostle intends they should add one kind of contention to another, as possibly an open professed to an inward and secret contention. Others, that the apostle would have them after one battle to double and reinforce the fight again with new supplies. Others, best of all, that Jude exhorts these Christians to put to all their strength and utmost force in their contention, as those who fought for their lives, nay, that which was dearer than life itself, even the life of their souls: and so great is this contention, that no one English word is able to express the Greek; to contend with all their strength, extraordinarily, beyond measure, most earnestly, scarcely render the meaning of the word. More particularly, this extraordinary and most eminent contention imports five things. (1.) A serious and weighty cause and ground of contention. Men account not trifles worth any, much less vehement strife. The thing about which they contend earnestly, is either weighty, or so esteemed. (2.) It imports a considerable enemy to strive with; not one who is contemptible, but who requires a great power to contend with him. (3.) Some strength and force whereby to deal with him. A child is not only unable to conquer, but even to contend with a giant. (4.) A putting forth of strength against the enemy. Though a man be never so strong, yet if he stands still, and puts not out his strength, he contends not. (5.) And lastly, the contending after such a manner as is conducible to a victory, and prevailing over the enemy with whom we contend, even the using of our utmost, best, and choicest endeavours; not a slight, but a serious and victorious contention.

2. From hence we may gather what this earnest contention comprehends, which is here to be employed about this faith.

(1.) It imports that the forementioned faith is a serious and weighty ground, and a most considerable cause upon and for which to contend. What does the Scripture more hold forth to be our duty, than to buy the truth, and not to sell it, Prov. xxiii. 23; to "strive together for the faith of the gospel," Phil. i. 27; to be fellow helpers to the truth; to keep the word of God's patience, Rev. iii. 10; to be valiant for the truth; to justify wisdom, &c.? Matt. xi. 19. Most precious is this faith to be contended for! First, even God himself was the Fountain and Founder of it, the Sun from which this ray of faith was darted, the mine whence this faith, more to be desired than the finest gold, was taken, Psal. xix. 10. All the princes of the world, with all their combined bounties, could never have bestowed this faith upon the world. How precious is it, secondly, in regard of the price of it, the death of Christ, without which not one promise of the word of life would ever have been made, or made good to our souls! How precious, lastly, in regard of the benefit of it! it does all for us that God does, Psal. xix. 7—9; John xvii. 17. For God affords by it direction in our doubts, consolation in our troubles, confirmation in our fears, sanctification in our filthiness, guidance to glory. In sum, "it is the power of God to salvation," Rom. i. 16. It is not then a slight and trivial, but a most weighty and considerable cause, for which these Christians were so earnestly to contend, it being for the maintaining of the faith.

(2.) It implies and presupposes a considerable and strong adversary to contend with, in contending for the faith. The enemies with whom these Christians were to strive were sectaries, and soul-destroying seducers; and Satan is the ringleader, instructor, and assistant both of these and of all other forces raised against faith. "We wrestle not against flesh and blood," saith the apostle, "but against principalities and powers. We wrestle not with flesh and blood," Eph. vi. 12, as it is in itself, weak and frail, but as set on work, assisted, and guided by Satan. Flesh and blood are but Satan's instruments, he sets them on work; he tempted Eve, not the serpent, Gen. iii. 1; he winnowed Peter, when the man and maid made Peter to deny Christ, Luke xxii. 31. Satan hindered Paul from coming to the Thessalonians, though by the persecuting Jews, 1 Thess. ii. 18. Satan cast some of the Smyrnians into prison, when men did it, Rev. ii. 10. The false prophets, with whom these Christians here were to contend for the faith, are called the ministers of Satan; he is "the spirit that worketh in the children of disobedience," 2 Cor. xi. 14, 15; Eph. ii. 2; iv. 27; Acts v. 3. Satan has a hand in soliciting us to sin, either by our own lusts, or by the enticements of others. In all combats, either against our own corruptions or others, persecutors, or seducers, if we can drive away the devil, flesh and blood will not much annoy us. If the captain be conquered, the common soldier will yield. It is Satan who seduces in seducers. Paul was afraid, lest as the serpent beguiled Eve, the mind of the Corinthians "should be corrupted from the simplicity that is in Christ," 2 Cor. xi. 3. He is the enemy that soweth tares among the wheat, Matt. xiii. And had not these Christians in contending for the faith a considerable enemy? How could the seducers want subtlety to creep in among these Christians by their persons, and into them by their opinions, into whom Satan the serpent had crept before; nay, who now had the advantage of being the old serpent? Rev. xii. 9. How easily could he flatter each humour, propound suitable lusts to every palate, clothe and colour every heresy and lust with plausible titles, Christian liberty, new lights, rare notions, oil and butter over wicked practices, and do much with sweet words, and cunning and doubtful expressions! What powerful adversaries were these seducers, who had the prince of power, the strong man armed, the god of this world, to help them! Eph. ii. 2. How could they want malice and cruelty, who were assisted by the enemy of souls, the destroyer, the roaring lion, the red dragon? How could they want diligence and activity, who had the devil to drive them; him to instigate, whose motion in sin is his rest; who walketh about, seeking whom he may devour?

(3.) This earnest contention imports a considerable strength, whereby to contend for the faith against so potent an adversary. Every one's strength is in itself but weakness; the strongest are not of themselves able to stand before the weakest temptation. Our strength is then from our Head, our Captain, Jesus Christ, who bestows upon us such supplies of grace, as that we are never fully and finally foiled, but in and with him overcome all, as the persecuting, so the enticing world. More particularly, he affords this strength to us two ways. On his part, he sends his Spirit to bestow upon us; and on our parts, he enables our faith to receive from him the supplies of his strength.

[1.] On his part, he bestows his Spirit to strengthen us. His Spirit does this two ways: 1. By working. 2. By strengthening our union with Christ. In the former, the Spirit conveys a principle of spiritual life and holiness, puts into us a seed that shall never die, 1 John iii. 9, and infuses a habit of holiness never to be lost or overcome. In the latter, it affords those continued supplies of grace, whereby we are more and more strengthened with might to resist all temptations, Eph. iii. 16; vi. 10; to go through all conflicts; to find preservation and direction in every danger and doubt; to walk in daily detestation of every sinful way; to call and cry for grace which is wanting; and in a word, enabled to do all things through him who strengtheneth us, Phil. iv. 13.

[2.] On our parts, he enables our faith by his Spirit to receive from him the supplies of his strength. This he does by giving a power to faith, 1. To unite us unto, and to incorporate us into him, as the branches are in the tree, the member in the body, or the house upon the foundation. We lay hold upon him for ours by our faith, as he lays hold upon us for his by his Spirit; whereby the union is complete and reciprocal. 2. To improve this union for our assistance, by drawing daily influences of grace and strength from Christ, who is a fountain of fulness, John i. 16, as the root does from the soil, or the branches from the root, John xv. 1, 5, or the pipe from the fountain. Hence it is that we live by faith, Gal. ii. 20; it being the instrument that fetches virtue from Christ to sustain us in all our wants and weaknesses; it being not only in, but drinking of the fountain; it not only uniting us as members to the Head, but supplying us as members from the Head, with all virtue necessary to the preservation of grace, both from the filth of sin within us, and the force of temptations without us; and hence it is that faith makes use of all ordinances but as the conduit-pipes, or water-courses, to convey from Christ that grace and strength it wants; it esteeming ordinances without Christ, but as a vial without a cordial, or a pipe without water. Faith also having united us to Christ, helps us to expect through him that abundant reward which will infinitely more than countervail for all the combats and contentions for him against his enemies. Moses saw him that was invisible, he had an eye to the recompence of reward, Heb. xi. 26, 27. "We faint not," saith the apostle, "while we look not at the things which are seen, but at the things which are not seen," 2 Cor. iv. 16, 18. And herein consists principally the strength of Christians in this earnest fight and contention.

(4.) This earnest contention by which the faith is maintained, implies a putting out and forth of this strength against the enemy with whom we contend for the faith. He who has strength contends not, if he stands still and acts not.

Sundry ways is strength to be put forth in contending for this faith.

[1.] Magistrates must put forth their strength, 1. By commanding their subjects to submit to the faith. Their edicts and injunctions should be like those of Asa and Hezekiah, who commanded Judah to seek the Lord, 2 Chron. xiv. 4; xxix. 5, 30; xxxiv. 33. They must engage men to be true and faithful to God, by precept and example; their commands must not so savour of state policy, as to be regardless of Scripture purity. It is not reason of state, but ruin of states, to be remiss in enjoining piety. The laws of man should be a guard to the law of God, Neh. xiii. 19. They who reign by God, should reign for him. How unreasonable is it that people should be lawless only in religion! Shall it not be indifferent whether men will pay a tax? and shall it be indifferent whether they will ever hear a sermon? It was a commendable decree of Artaxerxes, though a heathen, and that for which the faithful servant of God blessed God, That whosoever would not do the law of God, judgment should be executed upon him, to death, to banishment, to confiscation of goods, or imprisonment, Ezra vii. 26, 27; and of Darius, who decreed that in every dominion of his kingdom men tremble and fear before the God of Daniel, Dan. vi. 26.

2. By repressing the perverters of the faith. Restraining heretics and seducers, removing the impediments of religion, whether persons or things. Nebuchadnezzar, a heathen, made a decree that none should speak any thing amiss against God. Asa took away the sodomites, idols, and removed Maachah an idolatress from being queen, 1 Kings xv. 12, 13. Hezekiah removed the high places, and brake the images, and cut down the groves, 2 Kings xviii. 5. So Josiah defiled the high places, and brake them down, 2 Kings xxiii. 8. Thus likewise Jehoshaphat "took away the high places and groves out of Judah," 2 Chron. xvii. 6. Thus also Manasseh "took away the strange gods, and the idol out of the house of the Lord, and all the altars that he had built," 2 Chron. xxxiii. 15. To these may be added zealous Nehemiah, in repressing sabbath-breakers, Neh. xiii. 21. And the apostle saith, "Rulers are a terror to wicked works," Rom. xiii. 3.

3. By providing and maintaining a faithful ministry to dispense the doctrine of faith. Thus did Jehoshaphat and Hezekiah, 2 Chron. xvii. 8; 9; xxxi. 4. That magistrate cannot contend for the faith, which contends against the ministers thereof. Satan knows no mean between the pampering and famishing of the ministry: double labour must not be requited with scarce a single maintenance. Minis-

ters should not labour for, and yet not without a comfortable recompence. They ought not to be left to the courtesy of those, who though they account enough for themselves but a little, yet they account a little for the ministry too much. It is not enough for faithful ministers to be kept from being battered and stormed by cruel persecutors, unless also from being starved by the common protestants.

[2.] Ministers must contend for the faith, principally two ways.

1. By preaching the word of faith. They must preserve the pattern of wholesome words, and speak the things which become sound doctrine, 1 Tim. vi. 3; Tit. ii. 1. They must take heed of their own mixtures, and not adulterate the doctrine of faith to please men. The beauty of heavenly truths wants not the paint either of human or heretical additions. The babes of Christ must be fed with sincere milk; and the soreness of men's eyes must not hinder the lights of the church from shining.

2. By confuting gainsayers and heretics. The apostle commands Titus "by sound doctrine to convince gainsayers," Tit. i. 9. Ministers must not only have a voice to call their sheep, but to drive away wolves; one to establish truth, another to oppose error: one of his hands must work, and the other hold a weapon. Christ confuted the corrupt glosses of the Pharisees, and Paul confounded the Jews, by proving that this is the very Christ, Acts ix. 22; and Apollos mightily convinced the Jews, and that publicly, showing by the Scriptures that Jesus was Christ, Acts xviii. 28. A minister's breast should be a storehouse of spiritual armour. He must be furnished both with skill in Scripture, in which he should be mighty, and in writings of men, even of heretics themselves, to beat them with their own weapons. He that will be but a looker-on while his fellow brethren contend, shall never be more than a looker-on while they are crowned.

[3.] Every Christian should contend for the faith. Every child of Wisdom should justify their Parent. Saints must strive together for the faith of the gospel. And this they must do sundry ways.

1. By praying for the success of the faith against error. They must pray that God would send forth labourers into his harvest, Matt. ix. 38. That utterance may be given to ministers, that they may speak boldly as they ought to speak, Eph. vi. 19. That God would open unto them a door of utterance, Col. iv. 3. That the word of the Lord may run and be glorified, 2 Thess. iii. 1. That Christian who can prevail with God, shall conquer heretics. Prayer hath got as many victories as disputation.

2. By holy example; confuting wickedness and heresy by the language of their lives. Christians must be blameless, harmless, the sons of God, without rebuke, in the midst of a crooked and perverse nation, among whom they should shine as lights in the world, Phil. ii. 15. The error of the wicked must not cleave to them. They must not walk by example, but by rule. They must live what their faithful minister preaches, strive and swim against a stream of impiety, being and doing best when the times are worst.

3. By encouraging those against whom Satan bends his greatest force and fury in this conflict about faith. They must know those who labour among them, esteeming "them very highly in love for their work's sake," 1 Thess. v. 12, 13. When the service of ministers grows hottest, the love of people must not grow coldest. What proportion does money bear to faith? what is gold but dung to religion? How just is it that they who will not part with their money for the truth, should part with money and truth too! and that they who will not pay the Scripture sessment, to honour God with their substance, to buy truth, &c., should have all swept from them by oppressors! No soldiers deserve so much to have the oil of love dropped into their wounds, as those who received them in contending for the faith: no scars are so honourable as those gotten in this conflict. Never did kissing better become an emperor, than when Constantine kissed the hollow of holy Paphnutius's eye; whose war having been so holy, made his scar honourable.

4. By mutual exhortation. Christians must incite one another to the spiritual conflict, "speak often one to another," Mal. iii. 16; Heb. x. 24, for the strengthening of their resolution, and the whetting of their zeal; for the blowing up their love to God. In the primitive persecutions Christians wanted the bridle, but they now want the spur.

5. By confession of the faith when called and examined about it. It is not enough to have faith in the heart, without confession in the tongue, Rom. x. 10. If the fire of faith be in the heart, the flames of confession must be in the tongue. He who believes must speak. It is our faith which justifies our persons, but our confession must justify our faith. A dumb faith is not a Divine faith, but the faith of devils. Hypocrites will confess Christ in times of encouragement, but not of contradiction. A Christian has no cause to be ashamed of his name, of his livery, or of his Master, 1 Pet. iii. 15, 16. He who will confess Christ when most deny him, shall be confessed by Christ when he shall deny most, Matt. x. 32. This is the only holy kind of boldness; and cursed is that modesty which makes us ashamed of our Master. Maledicta sit humilitas quæ huc se demiserit. Luth.

6. By suffering for the faith. A Christian is never so like a soldier or himself, as when he confesses the faith he has, and suffers for the faith he confesses. He that saves his life, and forsakes the faith, never lived comfortably; but thousands that have lost their lives, and kept the faith, have died joyfully. Would saints but betray the faith, all Satan's contests with them would be at an end, but then God's would begin; and though God be the sweetest friend, yet is he the sorest enemy. How kindly does God take it when we hold fast his name, and not deny his faith in the days wherein Antipas is slain! Rev. ii. 13. How honourable is it to follow our Captain through mud and blood! How unsuitable is delicateness to sanctity and soldiery! Every Christian must change his warm coat into a coat of mail; he must not expect rest, but tumultuous clamours; not to sleep in the shadow, but sweat in the scorching sun; and to have all the militia of hell to fight against him. But here is his comfort, he fights a good fight, wherein God is the Judge, the Holy Ghost the principal Ruler, and the eternal crown of glory is the reward of his fighting. Nemo miles ad militiam cum deliciis venit; de umbra ad solem, et sole ad cœlum, de tunica ad loricam, de silentio ad clamorem, de quiete ad tumultum, bonum agonem subituri estis, in quo agonothetes Deus vivus est, xystarches Spiritus sanctus, corona æternitatis bravium. Tert. lib. ad Martyres.

(5.) This earnest contention imports the putting forth our strength, or contending after such a manner as is conducible to a victory and prevalency over the enemy with whom we contend; not any putting forth of strength will serve the turn, but doing it to the purpose, eminently, with all our ability of power and skill.

[1.] We must contend resolutely and valiantly, 1 Cor. xvi. 13. Danger must be despised, difficulties adventured on, terrors contemned, fears suppressed, cowardice vanquished, Christian generosity and a holy manhood must be ἀνδρίζεσθε.

put on. There must be a manhood in bearing strokes, in assailing strikers; the former is as the back, the latter the edge of Christian valour. Blessed Paul, who fought a good fight, tells Timothy that he knew his purpose, faith, long-suffering; and Barnabas exhorted the Christians, that with full purpose of heart they should cleave to the Lord.

Fortitudo in ferendo et feriendo. Hoc gero titulum; Cedo nulli. Luth. Per charitatem flexibiliores arundine, per fidem simus duriores adamante. Luth.

[2.] We must contend vigorously, fervently, vehemently, with all our might, 2 Tim. iv. 5, 7; Acts xi. 23. A lazy, slender, slight contention will not serve the turn. Lukewarmness neither pleases our Captain, nor prevails over our adversary. Zeal is the beauty of Christian undertakings; slightness and lukewarmness are unsuitable to the Captain that leads, who sweat in his conflict, the enemy that assails us, the cause for which we contend, the crown that rewards us. Holy fervour is never so seemly as in contending for a holy faith. It is storied of Scanderberg, that in fighting against the Turks, he was so earnest that the blood would often start out of his lips. Indifference better becomes our worldly contentions between man and man, than spiritual contentions between men and devils.

[3.] We must contend for the faith unanimously, and with one consent. How easily will error prevail, when faith's champions are divided among themselves! How shall they adventure their lives one for another in war, who will not do so much as love one another in peace! Excellent is the counsel of the apostle, "Stand fast in one spirit, with one mind striving together for the faith of the gospel," Phil. i. 27.

[4.] We must contend for the faith against error universally, impartially, for every doctrine of faith, and against every opposite error. We must contend for discountenanced, disowned, persecuted faith, and take it into our doors when the most would have it laid in the streets, and give it entertainment when it is death to harbour it. Nor ought we to spare preferred, favoured error. The snake of error must be struck at, though in the field of a king.

Quo major est Princeps, eo minus ferantur ejus vitia. Nomina potestatum metuenda, sed vitia contemnenda. Luth.

[5.] We must contend for the faith constantly. We must never give over our conflict as long as one enemy is left. We must continue in the things we have learned, and hold fast the name of Christ, 2 Tim. iii. 14. It is not contention, but constancy therein, which crowns. We must be faithful to the death, if we expect a crown of life. It is easier once to persevere than often to begin, Rev. ii. 13. No Christian is too old to go out to fight in this spiritual warfare. As soon as we cease to fight, we begin to fly. Christianity knows no cessation of combating. We must take heed of losing the things which we have wrought and fought for, 2 John 8. It is as great a virtue to hold what we have, as to get what is worth holding. If the faith be bad, why did we begin? if good, why did we give over our contention for it?

[6.] We must contend prudently and with judgment. Christian prudence is not inconsistent with Christian fervency. Sundry ways must a Christian show his prudence in this contention. 1. He must oppose those enemies most that most oppose the faith, the greatest errors with greatest zeal, and place most forces where there is most danger; not being (as some) fervent against disciplinary, and superficial against doctrinal errors. The former do but scratch the face, the latter stab the heart of truth. 2. He must contend for the faith soberly, not passionately. God wants not the besom of passion to sweep down the cobwebs of error. Soft words and strong arguments are good companions. We may at the same time spare the person, and yet be merciless to his error. 3. We must contend for the faith orderly, not extravagantly. The minister must not contend like the magistrate, by politic government; nor the people like the minister, by public preaching. Every soldier in this war must keep his rank. Never did more contend against the faith, than in the times wherein all are suffered to contend how they will for the faith. 4. We must contend for the faith preparedly, not weakly. Faith deserves not obloquy, but victory. A weak judgment often hurts the faith as much as strong passion. An able mind is more needful in spiritual, than an able body is for worldly wars. What a pity is it that a good cause should have a feeble champion!

Obs. 1. The goodness of any cause and course exempts it not from opposition. What more precious than faith, and what more opposed? Hatred is ever the companion of truth. As that which Satan opposes must needs be good, so that which is good must needs be by him opposed. A good man once said, "He much suspected his own faithfulness in delivering that sermon for which he got not some hatred from wicked men." "Hatred" (as one saith) "is the genius of the gospel." "I have given them" (saith Christ) "thy word, and the world hath hated them," John xvii. 14. Wicked men's rage should rather make us thankful than discouraged. "I am proud," (saith Luther,) "because I hear I have an ill name among bad men." "I bless God" (said Jerom) "that I am worthy of the world's hatred."

Odium genius Evangelii. Luth.

Superbus fio, quod video nomen pessimum mihi crescere; gaudeo rebellis dici. Luth.

Gratias ago Deo, quod dignus sum quem mundus oderit. Hier.

Obs. 2. The best things require most contention for them. Not trifles, fancies, or fables, but doctrines of faith, deserve our earnest contention. How poorly are most men's contentions employed! How happy were we, could we but as earnestly contend for Christ, his cause, faith, and our own salvation, as wicked men do for riches, honours, interest, nay, for hell, by striving to outsin one another! How unsuitable is it that a greater fire should be made for the roasting of an egg than for an ox! that men should be more contentious for bubbles than blessedness!

Nostra impatientia non est pro reculis, honoribus, &c. sed pro contemptu verbi, et pertinacia impietatis, ubi anathema est esse patientem. Luth.

Obs. 3. Satan will fight, though he cannot prevail. Though he conquer not, he will yet contend. Though he be unable to overcome, yet he will oppose the faith. Such is the height of his malice, that rage he will, be it unsuccessfully. If he cannot disappoint the saints of their end, he yet pleases himself in disturbing them in their way. Satan's rage should not dismay us. His furious onsets do not prove his endeavours successful; rather his great wrath speaks his time short. And if he fight, who knows he shall be foiled, how earnestly should they contend, who know they shall both conquer and be crowned!

Obs. 4. Satan labours most to spoil us of the best things, those whereby God is most glorified, and we most benefited. If he may have our faith, heavenly things, from us, he cares not to leave earthly blessings behind him. Hence it is that the apostle saith, Eph. vi. 12, "We wrestle against spiritual wickedness," (ἐν τοῖς ἐπουρανίοις, in heavenlies; i. e. as I humbly conceive,) for heavenly things: see Heb. viii. 5: whereby is noted the cause of Satan's contention, which is, to bereave us of blessings of a heavenly nature. In tempting Eve, he aimed at bereaving our first parents of their

Chrysost. Musculus, Perkins.

happiness, and God's image. It was Peter's faith he sought to winnow. He blinds men's eyes, that the "light of the glorious gospel of Christ should not shine unto them," 2 Cor. iv. 4. In the troubles of Job, Satan aimed at a greater matter than bereaving Job of his temporal estate; namely, denying God, and blaspheming him to his face, Job i. 11. The excellency of the thing for which we contend, should strengthen and quicken our resolutions in contending. It should be a greater motive to our valour when Christ our Captain tells us we fight to preserve the faith, than if he had told us we fight for our lands, children, wives, lives; for what are these to grace, to glory, to our souls, to our God, all which we lose in losing the faith! What Satan in malice most assaults, we in wisdom must most defend.

Obs. 5. Of ourselves we are too weak for spiritual conflicts. All our strength is from another. He who is barely by profession, not really, united to Christ, will soon give in, and turn his back in a day of battle; he will be a soldier for show, not for service. He who is not built on the rock, cannot oppose the floods, Matt. vii. 27. Painted profession will not endure the washing. Things which are not strongly joined, but loosely put together, will part when thrown into the water; so will Christ and the hypocrite in sufferings.

Obs. 6. Moderation is not always commendable. Moderation in bearing the chastisements of God, in enjoying worldly comforts, in enduring private injuries, are all most Christian and commendable; but moderation which hinders a real and an earnest contending for faith, is no better than loathsome lukewarmness. I fear there is much time-serving, neutrality, sinful halting, and indifference gilded over with the name of moderation. Accursed is that moderation whereby men will lose the faith to keep their estates, and crack their consciences to save their skins. The policy of such I never admired, and their happiness, I trust, I shall never envy. How soon learned is the wisdom of shunning troubles, of self-preservation, and tame silence, when religion is endangered! How easy is it to swim with the stream, to hold with the strongest! and how easily, but, alas, how falsely, is this called moderation!

Obs. 7. The war of Christianity is laborious and dangerous. It will soon try our valour; and not only the truth, but the strength of our graces. Religion is like cold weather, good for those who are sound, bad for rotten hypocrites. They who go on to this sea for recreation, will soon come back in a storm. The more dangerous our conflict is, the greater is that strength by which we are supported, and the firmer should be our dependence upon it. If Satan cease from fighting with us, it is a sign he has conquered us. It is our wisdom when we have passed over light skirmishes, to prepare for greater. They who had endured a great fight of affliction, had still need of patience, Heb. x. 32, 36. Though we must never despair of conquest, yet also never presume of quietness, nor expect to be delicate members under a thorny head.

Obs. 8. A Christian should be best when the times are worst, and get good by others' sins. When others contend most against, we should most contend for the faith. Of the opposition of the truth by others, we should make a spiritual advantage. As God suffers nothing whereby he gets not glory, so a Christian should observe nothing whereby he gets not some good. As the faint and lukewarm assistance of friends, so the fierce and furious opposition of enemies, should make his contention for the truth the more holily vehement. It was not only the expression of a gracious heart, but of such a one in a very gracious temper, that because the wicked had made void God's law, therefore did he love his commandments above gold, Psal. cxix. 127.

Obs. 9. It is the duty and wisdom of Christians to observe directions for their spiritual conflict. Who contends with a potent adversary without considering how to encounter him? To this end, (1.) Let us get a love to the cause and Captain for which and whom we fight; not fighting for fear of his wrath or love of his wages, but affection to his interest. A soldier of fortune will turn to that side where he shall be best paid, but one to whom love is wages will keep to one side. The Christian who seems now to fight for, but yet loves not the truth, will soon either leave it, or fight against it. (2.) Let us not entangle our affections in worldly enjoyments. Bid earthly comforts farewell when you go on your spiritual expedition. It is a pity to lose a victory for regarding the bag and baggage, yet the love of the world has made many a Christian lose both his courage and his crown. (3.) Let us not go forth in our own strength against our enemies. A proud Christian will soon turn a coward. A limb, though swollen and big to sight, is but weak and lame for service. If God breathe not a spirit of valour into us, we shall faint. Spiritual soldiers must fight upon their knees. It is from God we fight, of ourselves we can do nothing but fly. (4.) Let faith consider its encouragements. Our cause is righteous and honourable; our Captain wise, valorous, bountiful; our supplies great and near; our friends in all places, if fighting, prevailing, and if not fighting, praying for us; our victory certain and sudden, our reward massive and eternal.

VERSE 4.

For there are certain men crept in unawares, who were before of old ordained to this condemnation, ungodly men, turning the grace of our God into lasciviousness, and denying the only Lord God, and our Lord Jesus Christ.

HERE our apostle enters upon the third main part in the exhortation, viz. The propounding sundry arguments, or reasons, to enforce the embracing of the forementioned exhortation of contending for the faith against seducers. The arguments or reasons used by him are reducible to these two heads:

The first is the dangerousness of the company of these seducers to the Christians to whom he wrote. This is set down in this 4th verse. The second is the downfal and overthrow of these seducers, amplified and proved from the 4th to the 17th verse.

The dangerousness of the company of these seducers to the Christians, expressed in this verse.

In this the apostle describes,

I. The entrance of these seducers into the company of the Christians.

II. The impiety of these seducers who had thus gotten entrance.

I. He describes their entrance into the society of the faithful, and that four ways.

1. From their nature; they were "men."

2. From their indefinite number; "certain men."

3. From their subtlety and sliness in getting in; they "crept in unawares."

4. By clearing and vindicating their entrance from the exceptions or objections which the Christians might have raised against God's suffering them to enter among them; he saith, they "were before ordained to this condemnation;" he thereby teaching,

that God was neither regardless and unmindful of the church, nor indulgent to the false teachers, or their false teachings.

II. In setting down the impiety of these seducers,

1. He expresses it more generally, saying, they were "ungodly."

2. More particularly he shows wherein that ungodliness appeared: (1.) In their abusing the grace of God, "Turning the grace," &c. (2.) In their opposing the God of grace, "Denying the only Lord," &c.

I. The apostle describes the entrance of the seducers among the Christians. And,

1. From the nature of the parties entering; they are "men," ἄνθρωποι. The apostle seems for two reasons to note the nature of these seducers, calling them men:

(1.) To aggravate the sin of the seducers. One man should be helpful, not hurtful to another. Man is a word used to denote goodness. "I drew them with the cords of a man," saith God, Hos. xi. 4, to express his gentleness toward the people. And in our ordinary expression humanity is used for kind and helpful carriage. Cruelty to the body is more beseeming beasts, but cruelty to the soul is fitter to be used by devils than by men. The nearer any one is to us, the more heinous is the injury which he offers us, or we him. *Natura nos cognatos edidit,* Senec.; Nature hath made us near of kin. To be cruel and hurtful to others, is to put off the man as well as the Christian.

<small>Riv. in loc. Melius sentiunt qui per hominis funes intelligunt omnem humanam et amabilem tractationem, qualis solet esse hominum erga homines. Homines hominum causa generati sunt, ut ipsi inter se alii aliis prodesse possint. Cic. l. 5. Offic.</small>

(2.) To amplify the danger of these Christians. Men like ourselves may most probably prevail over us by their seducements. Were they devils or beasts they might affright, but being men they allure. As it is the wisdom of God to send us holy men to instruct us, and win us to himself, so it is the subtlety of Satan to send wicked men to seduce and draw us from God. None hurt so unexpectedly and unavoidably as those who are near and suitable to our nature. Seducers are Satan's decoys to fetch men in to him by multitudes.

Obs. 1. Sin has made even man a hurtful creature. Not only man hurtful to beasts, and beasts to man; but man to man. Even man, who should be instead of God, a keeper, a defender, is by sin made a wolf, a destroyer of man. Man, till sinful, was never harmful. Before he sinned, he, naked, neither feared nor offered wrong. His sinless state will ever be known by the name of a state of innocency, or hurtlessness; and when the lost image of God is again restored, he is made a lamb, a dove, a harmless, Phil. ii. 15, or, as the word in the original signifies, a hornless creature.

<small>'Ακέραιοι, sine cornibus, non feriens cornibus.</small>

But how much more than brutishly cruel has sin made man become! witness not only the vast multitude of men destroyed in all ages by men, and the incredibly exquisite tortures, as rackings, sawings, burnings, &c., against man, invented by man, as if sin had set up a hellish inquisition in man's nature; but even the murders committed by seducers and heretics upon the souls of men; it being now as much against corrupt nature to go towards hell alone, as to walk in the ways of heaven at all. Oh that we could contemplate the odiousness of sin in this glass of its harmfulness!

Obs. 2. We should not content ourselves in being mere men. He who is and continues no more than a man, had better never have been so much as a man. A man altogether without grace, though otherwise never so exquisitely accomplished, is but a tame devil, and often most hurtful. How restless should we be till the Divine nature (2 Pet. i. 4) is bestowed upon us! The natural man, or the man who has no more than a rational soul, natural abilities and perfections, as he cannot receive, so he can and will oppose the things of the Spirit of God. Satan can as easily enter as assault a man merely natural. And many who have had religious education, and made hopeful beginnings, yet having never been by a saving change of heart more than men, have soon shown themselves as bad almost as devils. Nature elevated to the highest pitch by its most exquisite improvements, is still but nature; it may thereby be coloured over, but grace can only change it.

Obs. 3. We should beware of those who are but mere natural men, and have nothing more or more excellent than human nature. It is the command of Christ, to beware of men, Matt. x. 17. Beware of them, (1.) Lest they betray your liberties, lives, or external welfare. Christ committed not himself to man, because he knew what was in man; and let not us commit ourselves to them, because we know not what is in them. Nature is a slippery thing, and, unless backed by grace, will prove but unsteady. How oft have I seen, found, I had almost said, that the love of acquaintance merely natural, ends, upon a change of times, either in persecution, or at the best in cruel compassion, in persuading to self-preservation by wrecking conscience, and offending God! (2.) Especially let us beware lest they betray our souls by seducing them from God and truth. Follow no man further than he follows God. Look upon every man as a rule ruled, not as a rule ruling. Captivate thy understanding to none but God. Take equal heed of receiving the word of God as the word of man, and of receiving the word of man as the word of God. The error of the master is the temptation of the scholar. Love no man so much as to follow that of his which is not lovely; in that sense call no man master. We must never believe error when he speaks it, nor truth because he speaks it.

Obs. 4. Satan is wont to make use of such instruments as may most probably do his work. He loves to put upon himself the most taking and insinuating shape when he comes to tempt us. He employed the most subtle creature to convey his temptations to our first parent. Ordinarily he makes use of men, and most commonly of the fittest, either for parts, or seeming piety, to work upon men. He also has his apostles and ministers to pervert the world, "transforming themselves into the apostles of Christ, and the ministers of righteousness," 2 Cor. xi. 13, 15. But how unworthy is it for men to suffer Satan to use their parts and wits against their Maker! And never should we more suspect Satan's poison, than when he offers us to drink in a golden cup; never more fear his seducements, than when he uses men, and men whose plausibilities are most taking.

2. The apostle describes the entrance of these seducers, by the indefinite and uncertain expressing of their number that had entered among them. He neither names who they were, nor determines thereby how many they were, but only saith they were τινες ἄνθρωποι, "certain men." It is here demanded, Why the apostle mentions not their names, or who they were? (1.) It was possible (though not likely) their names might be altogether unknown to him. (2.) It is by various conceived that the apostle knew them by name. Thus Œcumenius, Aretius, and others; the former whereof tells us himself some of their names, as Nicholas, Valentinus, Simon, and Marcion. But it is conceived that the apostle forbore to name them, though he knew them,

[1.] To show how much he disdained them; as if

he apprehended them to be such vile persons as were not fit and worthy to be named among Christians, or by him distinctly, but confusedly to be bound up in this bundle, τινες ἄνθρωποι, "certain men." And this some, who conjecture that the discourse of Christ concerning the rich glutton is a history, conceive to be the reason why our Saviour gives us the poor man's name Lazarus, not so much as vouchsafing to name the rich epicure, calling him only "a certain rich man," as if it were unfit his name should be left to posterity, Luke xvi. 19. And this conjecture concerning these seducers in the text seems to be strengthened, not only by the consideration of their detestable practices and opinions, which deserved that their founders should be buried in forgetfulness; but also by the apostle's expressing their base and contemptible manner of entrance in the very next word, by creeping in unawares, as if he had set himself to slight them.

"Ανθρωπος τις πλούσιος.

[2.] It is thought the apostle forbears to express the names, and thereby to determine the numbers of these seducers, to make these Christians more wary and vigilant in their carriage and conversing, they living among seducers, and yet not knowing who they were. That there were sundry, many of them, he intimates; who, or how many, he conceals, that so they might be the more circumspect in taking heed of all who might any way seduce them. And thus the apostle exhorts the Christians to "try the spirits, because there are many false prophets gone out into the world," 1 John iv. 1. If a man converse among persons infected by the plague, when he is uncertain which of them or how many have that disease, he will be the more wary of every one. Our not knowing all those who are erroneous, should make us try what we hear even from those who are soundest.

Obs. 1. How much are heretics and seducers deceived, who expect to grow famous and honoured by being patrons of ungodly and erroneous opinions! Heresy never was a foundation of honour to the contriver, though the hopes of gaining honour is a furtherance to become heresiarchs. While the pure lights of the church have burnt sweetly, and shined brightly even to after-ages, there is nothing remaining of old heretics, notwithstanding all their new and pretended light, but stink, and smoke, and snuff. However they may be for a time respected in the world, yet as even at first the Scripture proclaims their infamy, and discovers their impostures to some, so shall posterity, by the advantage of time and Scripture study, reckon their sometimes-adored names among the notes of greatest disgrace. So that even those who through the love of error embrace their opinions, shall through the love of honour be ashamed of their names. Seducers love to call their books and companies by their own name, but their names are not up in God's book.

Obs. 2. False teachers are wont to be many and numerous in the church of God. In St. John's time many, though, as here, he names not how many, false prophets were gone out into the world, 1 John iv. 1. And he saith also, "Many deceivers are entered into the world," 2 John 7. And Paul tells Titus, that there were many deceivers, Tit. i. 10. The prophets of Jezebel were four hundred. Satan's emissaries are sent out by troops; what they want of weight, they make up in number. The goodness of any cause cannot be judged by the number of its patrons. There may be a hundred false prophets to one; and if there were a hundred true ones to one false, that false one may possibly have a hundred friends for one that truly loves the hundred who are true. Should religion be carried only by vote, heresy would oft prevail. *Argumentum pessimum turba.* The most are usually the worst. Numbers are but a slight argument to a heart that resolves to follow Scripture. It is better to go to heaven with and after a few, than to hell with and after the throng. Multitudes neither warrant in the way, nor comfort in the end.

Obs. 3. Christian vigilancy is most needful in days of heresy. "Beware of false prophets," saith Christ, Matt. vii. 15. "Beware," saith Peter "lest ye be led away with the error of the wicked," 2 Pet. iii. 17. The cunning craftiness (Eph. iv. 14) of false prophets in deceiving, our readiness to be deceived, and our hurt in being so, call aloud for the duty of circumspection. Seducers are crafty, error is catching; and being embraced, injury to the soul is certain. How sad is it to see so many wary men in trading for the world, and so many childish and simple in negociating for heaven! Most men invert the apostle's advice; for in malice they are men, in knowledge children. Should all be reckoned children, as indeed they may, who know not their right hand from their left in religion, where should we find a man? "The wisdom of the prudent is to understand his way," Prov. xiv. 8. Old Scripture preservatives should much be used in times of heretical infection: in ways wherein there are many turnings, it is safe often to inquire. The word is the way, the Spirit is the Guide; humility, prayer, vigilancy, excellent helps to walk in the one, and to follow the other.

3. The apostle describes the entrance of these seducers into the company of these Christians, from the subtlety and sliness of their entrance; they "crept in unawares," παρεισέδυσαν. Two things offer themselves in the explication. The first, The sense and force of the word. Secondly, The agreement of it to these seducers in their entrance among these Christians.

(1.) The meaning of the word. The word comprehends two things: 1. It implies a fact brought about and accomplished, which is obtaining a thorough entrance, and getting into some place or company, noted in the preposition, εἰς, in, or into. 2. It mainly intends the manner of accomplishing it, or the course taken and used to effect and bring that entrance about, which is by sliness and subtlety, close and cunning carriage, and entrance unawares: the single and simple verb δύω, or δύνω, signifies, *subeo, mergo, ingredior*, to dive, sink, to go in, to go under; and it is used concerning the setting of the sun, as Mark i. 32; Luke iv. 40, &c., because it seems then to sink or dive into the sea. And the apostle speaks of some who crept into houses, 2 Tim. iii. 6, adding only the preposition ἐν, in, to this verb δύνω, which Beza translates *qui irrepunt*, others, *qui immergunt*, who subtlely, silently slip in, and dive, as it were, to the bottom, to search and understand the affairs of houses, as Jesuits do in states and kingdoms. But the principal emphasis lies in the preposition παρὰ, which, added to the former verb, signifies a more secret and subtle, close and deceitful manner of seducers' entrance, than the simple word will bear; and it imports their entrance in a by-way, at a back-door, thievishly, by little and little, clandestinely, unawares, creepingly, a winding in by stealth, obliquely; beside the way of any real worth and fit qualifications of integrity and piety to further the spiritual welfare of the church; and beside the intentions of the faithful, who not knowing what manner of men these seducers were, but conceiving

Ἔδυσαν ὥς μόλιβδος, ἐν ὕδατι. Exod. xv. 10.
Δεδυκότος τοῦ ἡλίου. Deut. xxiii. 11.
οὐ γάρ δύσεται ὁ ἥλιός σοι. Isa. lx. 20.
Δύτης, urinator. Herodot.
Δύνοντος τοῦ ἡλίου. Luke iv. 40.
Ἀπὸ ἀνατολῶν, καί δυσμῶν. Matt. viii. 11.

ἐνδύνοντες.
Vulg. qui penetrant, i. e. qui penitus intrant. Scire volunt secreta domus, atque inde timeri. Subreperunt. Bez. Subintroierunt, Vulg. Furtive se inshnuare. Latenter et furtive ingredi. Obiter subrepere. Oblique se ingerere, et tanquam aliud agentes in gredi.

them, by reason of their painted and specious appearances of godliness, to be worthy of admission, gave them entrance before they were aware. And this is the force of the preposition; παρεισάξουσι, they shall privily bring in heresies, 2 Pet. ii. 1; that is, subtlely, deceitfully, and so as the church should not be aware of them, they bringing in their errors under the notion and appearance of truth. The same force has the word παρά, Gal. ii. 4, in two words in that one verse, where the apostle speaks of false brethren, παρεισάκτους, unawares brought in, who παρεισῆλθον, came in privily. They crept into the company of the faithful by fraud, and such cunning artifices, specious and plausible pretences, that the faithful never went about to keep them out; for though in both these places of Jude and Galatians their coming in might not be unawares, that the faithful knew not at all of their coming in; yet it was unawares, that they knew not what manner of persons, how unworthy and heretical, &c. they were, when they did come in among them.

(2.) The second thing to be explained, is the agreement of the word thus opened to the seducers in their entrance among these Christians.

[1.] It agrees to them, because they had already gotten in, they were fully entered by their artifices, they had obtained footing in the church. And the apostle urges these Christians by this motive, of the nearness of these seducers to them, and their presence among them, that they should be the more strenuous in contending against them. God had suffered them to obtain entrance, that those Christians who were approved might be made manifest. The sincerity of the faithful was discovered by the apostacy of hypocrites. When a city is altogether in peace, all the inhabitants are accounted faithful and loyal; but when seditions and commotions arise, they who are faithful to the prince are then discovered from the rest. And when heresies and persecutions for the truth arise, the sincerity of the faithful is manifested by the defection of those who in times of peace seemed haply as good as the best. "Thou shalt not," saith God to his people, "hearken to the words of that prophet, or dreamer of dreams; for the Lord your God proveth you, to know whether you love the Lord your God," &c. And by the entrance of these seducers, the faithful were more excited to search after and to defend the truth. Both the sincerity of believers, and the truths to be believed, were made more evident. Nothing is so certain, as that which out of doubtfulness is made certain. The sun of truth breaks most clearly out of a cloud of errors. The clashing of the faithful and erroneous, like the striking of flint and steel, sends forth the brightly shining sparks of truth. Yea, further, God by the entrance of these heretics made both them and their hypocritical followers manifest to the world, that so they might at once both *patefacere* and *pudefacere*, as Pareus speaks on 1 Cor. xi. 19, discover and disgrace themselves before all men, who hereby might know and shun them. By the entrance also of these seducers the faithful saw that this world was not a place of local separation from all wicked ones, and were incited to long for that place where good and bad shall be perfectly parted.

Pet. Molin. in Epist. dedic. ad Enodation. Languesceret fides non irritata, et ex judiciorum conflictu, quasi ex collisione silicum, emicant veritatis scintillæ, quæ tandem victrix perrumpit obstantia. Debemus Pelagio et Cœlestio, Aureolos tractatus Augustini, de prædestinatione, de natura et gratia, et perseverantia. Pravum hæreticorum acumen viri sancti acuebat industriam. Aug. de Ver. Rel. c. 8. Hæretici plurimum prosunt, non verum docendo quod nesciunt, sed ad verum quærendum carnales, et ad verum aperiendum spirituales catholicos excitando.

[2.] The word here used, of creeping in unawares, agrees to these seducers, because of the manner of their entrance, which was close, subtle, hypocritical, and unawares; without any fitness in themselves to enter, or any intention in the faithful to admit them; they only using many sly and sinful artifices, to bring both their persons and opinions into reputation among the faithful, by reason of which both were suffered unawares to enter, although indeed both deserved to be kept out before, and thrown out after their entrance.

This practice of insinuating, creeping, and winding unawares into the society and estimation of the faithful, has been used both by these and all other seducers; and therefore Paul calls these false apostles "deceitful workers," 2 Cor. xi. 13; Satan using them for his instruments to beguile, as sometime he did the serpent, which beguiled Eve. Likewise, Paul saith that they "deceive the hearts of the simple," Rom. xvi. 18. And, that they draw many disciples after them, Acts xx. 30. By these the ἐν κυβείᾳ, ἐν πανουργίᾳ πρὸς μεθοδείαν πλάνης. Galatians were bewitched, Gal. iii. 1. These would have beguiled the Colossians, Col. ii. 18. They have their "sleight and cunning craftiness, whereby they lie in wait to deceive," Eph. iv. 14. They "creep into houses, and lead captive silly women," 2 Tim. iii. 6. They are seducers, and deceiving, ver. 13. "False teachers, privily bringing in damnable heresies," 2 Pet. ii. 1. And they make merchandise of people, ver. 3. And they "allure those who were clean," &c., δελεάζουσι. ver. 18.

But more particularly, the by-ways in which they go, the subtle artifices and insinuations by which they creep into the company and good opinions of the church, and deceitfully enter unawares, are such as these:

1. They conceal their opinions, especially at their first entrance. Either they totally forbear to deliver errors, or else they deliver them so darkly, cloudily, and ambiguously, as that they may find Vid. Aug. contr. subterfuges, and places for retreating, Pelag. l. 1. whenever they are charged with them. liberum sic confitemur arbitrium, They love to know, but are wary in ut dicamus nos being known; like moles, they labour semper indigere Dei auxilio; ita to spoil the ground by keeping under hominis laudamus ground. It is often harder to find them, naturam, ut Dei semper gratiam than to overcome them. Their words addamus auxilium. Anathema and phrases have divers senses; the qui docet gratiam Dei, per singulos same sentence shall speak both truth and actus nostros, non falsehood, so that their disciples shall esse necessariam. Diligenter est interrogandus Pelagius quam understand them one way, and the ingenuous hearer shall hope that they dicat gratiam meant another; by reason of which deceit qua fateatur homines adjuvari, they resemble some light-fingered &c. Mihi pæne persuaserat hunc dealers, who can steal even from those illam gratiam, de qua quæstio est, who look upon them. Augustine was confiteri. Aug. de sometime almost well persuaded concerning gra. Christ. c. 37. In fraudem nominem Christi circerning Pelagius; so seemingly orthodox cumferunt. were his expressions about grace.

2. They utter some real and wholesome truths. Their custom is to mix something true with much that is false, that thereby they may put off one with another. The false apostles taught Christ, joining some other thing with him in the cause of salvation; and so the papists at this day. Their doctrines, like that cake which Hosea saith was not turned, Hos. vii. 8, are neither raw nor baked, i. e. neither altogether true, nor altogether false; or like a picture which seems beautiful on the one side, and deformed on the other; or like the commodities of some deceitful chapmen, the top, the uppermost of the bag is good and vendible, but the wares which are under are corrupt and unsound; or as that image, the head is of gold, but the feet of iron and clay, Dan. ii. 38, 41. Error would never be honoured before the people unless it were seen in the company of truth.

As a man who is often taken in a lie is not believed when he speaks the truth; so he who is often observed to speak truth is not mistrusted, though he sometimes utters what is false.

3. They preach doctrines pleasing to corrupt nature, 2 Pet. ii. 18; Isa. xxx. 10; such as are most delightful to flesh and blood. They know that naturally people cannot endure sound doctrine, 2 Tim. iv. 3, desire not to have right things prophesied to them, but smooth things, and deceits: and therefore they corrupt and deal deceitfully with the word, καπηλεύοντες, 2 Cor. ii. 17; like deceitful vintners, who, for gain, mix water with their wine: mere truth they know would be bitter truth, and therefore they are more desirous to be sweet and unsound, than harsh and wholesome; suiting their doctrines, as some fable of the taste of the manna in the wilderness, to the pleasure of every palate. Hence it was that the false apostles preached up circumcision, and others abrogated observations, because they knew such doctrines only would be savoury to Jewish palates. And hence it was that these seducers preached doctrines of liberty, 2 Pet. ii. 19, and licentiousness, and such as turned "the grace of God into lasciviousness," Jude 4, making the narrow way to heaven seem broader than God ever intended it; holding before people's eyes the spectacles of carnal liberty, whereby, in their passage over the narrow bridge of Christianity, they, adventuring upon a supposed breadth, tumble down into the waters of perdition.

4. They deliver such doctrines as savour of novelty. The subjects of which they treat must be represented as rare and unusual: to accomplish which, either they put upon them a new dress, a new shape, and fashion of words and expressions; or they deliver either that which is false and against Scripture, they choosing rather to be erroneous than not to be rare, and often venting for new truths old errors new dressed, or that which is nice, and very uncertainly grounded upon Scripture, they preferring a doubtful before a common way, well knowing that usual truths will not suit with itching ears. If the doctrines which they deliver are old and ordinary truths, they often, as men use to do by old stuffs, water them over with new expressions, strange and new-minted phrases, not savouring of Scripture simplicity, or agreeable to the pattern of wholesome words.

5. They labour to work the godly and orthodox ministers out of the affections of their hearers, 2 Cor. x. 10. They erect a building of honour for themselves upon the ruins of the reputation of such who deserve to stand when they are ruined. Well they know, as long as the messenger is loved, the message is not like to be loathed. They had much rather stand in the people's light, than that a godly minister should stand in theirs. The greatest enemies to true have ever been false teachers. Thus it was of old; Micaiah and Jeremiah had the one a Zedekiah, the other a Pashur, to smite them. And as the practice of smiting, with the tongue at least, still continues, so doth the pretence of that practice. Hence it is that faithful ministers must be represented as the disturbers and troublers of church and state, Amos vii. 10; though the true reason why turbulent practices against the peace of both may by false prophets condemned, is, that they may get all the practice to themselves, while the peaceable servants of Christ are only suspected. I mislike not the vessels, good words, but ill wine offered in them by drunken teachers. Nor did any so subtlely undermine blessed Paul as the false apostles; his great labour in some Epistles being the vindication of his apostolical reputation. If the eminence of a godly minister for piety and parts be so evident, as that they dare not bring any downright accusation against him, then these creeping seducers will ordinarily either doubt of or deny his calling, or else will mention his commendations with a *but* of their own framing, or else so slightly and lukewarmly commend him, (as thus, perhaps, He is a good honest man, a well-meaning man, a pretty man,) as that it shall almost amount to a discommendation.

<small>Non accuso verba tanquam vasa pretiosa, sed vinum quod in illis propinatur ab ebriosis doctoribus. Aug.</small>

6. They affix the highest commendations imaginable to their own opinions and persons. (1.) Their opinions they represent as the ways of God, the glorious beamings out of light, the only paths of peace and sweetness, the liberty of the gospel, and with other such like "good words and fair speeches they deceive the hearts of the simple," Rom. xvi. 18. Like mountebanks, who despairing that any will buy their oils and medicines for any good they find by them, are wont themselves to commend their virtue to the ignorant throng. (2.) Their own persons they represent as the most eminently qualified, for grace and learning, of any the mere sons of men. They trumpet out their own godliness, humility, and meekness, though Christ tells us they are wolves in sheep's clothing, Matt. vii. 15. And experience proves them, with Montanus, Arius, Novatus, Pelagius, Arminius, to be but Satan's ministers, transformed as the ministers of righteousness, 2 Cor. xi. 14. They pretend themselves to be the only ministers, though herein they do but imitate their predecessors, who said they were apostles, but were not, Rev. ii. 2; "transforming themselves into the apostles of Christ," 2 Cor. xi. 13. Their rare and raised parts, their unparalleled abilities, and deep insight into gospel truths, they proclaim to all the world, using great swelling words of vanity, in imitation of him who gave out that himself was some great one, that so he might be said to be the great power of God, Acts viii. 9, 10; and all because they know the fond multitude is ever more ready to judge of faith by the person, than of the person by his faith.

Obs. 1. The presence of wicked men in the church is no sufficient ground of being offended at the church. Mixtures of good and bad men have ever been in the best societies; nor is it to be expected, till the harvest, that tares and wheat can be parted perfectly, Matt. xiii. 30; neither the godly nor God's ordinances are therefore to be forsaken because the wicked are mixed. Needless society with the wicked, much more society with them in their wickedness, is to be avoided; but not such as from which we have no warrant from God to separate, or wherein we join not in sin, but in that which is in itself holy, saving, and commanded. As God does not, so neither must man punish the innocent, whether himself or another, for the nocent. I fly from the chaff, lest I should be also such, saith Augustine. I forsake not the floor lest I should be nothing. And though God does not account evil to be good, yet he accounts it good that there should be evil. And that good we shall find, could we, as we ought, be more watchful, zealous, humble, fervent in prayer, longing for heaven by the necessitated company of wicked men.

Obs. 2. Satan uses sundry sorts of attempts to hurt the church. Sometimes he creeps and crouches, at other times he roars and rages. He has several shapes, and often changes his habit, though he never lays aside his hatred. One while he openly acknowledged that Christ was the Son of God; afterwards he stirred up his instruments to destroy Christ, "because he made himself the Son of God," John xix. 7. Satan (like a highway robber) frequently changeth his apparel, that so the unwary passenger may not discern him; he seldom appears in the same habit twice together. In some ages of the church he is a red dragon, in others an old serpent; sometimes he uses his sword, at other times his pen. He commonly proceeds from one extreme to another, from endeavouring to overthrow the church by persecution under heathens, to hurting it more by promotions and seducings under papacy. In one age, he advances superstition; in another, profaneness: in one, nothing shall be lawful; in another, every thing. None shall preach at one time, every one at another. We cannot therefore judge that a way is none of Satan's, because it differs from that which was sometimes his, but because it agrees with that which is always God's.

Obs. 3. Satan is most hurtful to the church, when he opposes it by subtlety and creeping; when he comes not as an open enemy, but an appearing friend. He is never so much a devil, as when he appears in white, and transforms himself into an angel of light. He does more hurt by creeping into, than breaking into the church. False apostles and seducers in the church have been more hurtful to it by fraud, than bloody and paganish persecutors by force. *Serpit putrida tabes hypocrisis per omne corpus ecclesiæ, omnes sunt amici et omnes inimici, omnes necessarii et omnes adversarii, omnes domestici et nulli pacifici. Ecce in pace amaritudo mea; amara prius in nece martyrum, amarior post in conflictu hæreticorum. Bern. ser. 33. in Cant.* Satan has gained more victories by using the one as sunshine to dazzle the eyes, than by raising the other as wind to blow in the faces of the faithful. For his subtlety rather colours vice, than openly contends against virtue. Under the resemblance of those graces for which saints are most eminent, he draws to those neighbour vices which seem to have most affinity with their Christian perfections. He colours over superstition with religion, carnal policy with Christian prudence, cruelty with justice, toleration with mercy, indiscreet fervour with zeal, pertinacy with constancy. And never does sin so much prevail against us, as when it lies in ambush behind appearances of piety. Nor is Satan's subtlety less hurtful in using the ablest and most refined wits to devise and defend impious novelties against the orthodox faith; as Arius, Sabellius, Pelagius, &c. of old; and of late Servetus, Socinus, Arminius, &c. Satan fits every actor with a part agreeable to him, and carves his Mercury on the most promising pieces. Those whom God has furnished with the best weapons of parts and arts, have commonly given his cause the deepest wounds. It is our duty with prudence to countermine subtlety; to steer our course by the card of Scripture; to mislike no good way of God because Satan makes it seemingly deformed; to love no way of sin, though he makes it seemingly amiable; to build our faith upon no eminency of man, and ever to be more forward to examine than to admire what he saith or is.

Obs. 4. The best Christians may sometimes be mistaken in seducers. The advice of Christ to "beware of false prophets," Matt. vii. 15, shows how possible it is to be overseen. The shape into which they transform themselves, namely, the apostles of Christ, and the ministers of righteousness, shows the difficulty of discerning them. The very apostles were deceived in him whom some conceive to be the heresiarch, Acts viii. 13, and one from whom these seducers sucked their poison. God will alone have the prerogative of trying the heart; the doctrines we must, 1 Thess. v. 21, their hearts God only can search. And the difficulty of understanding who are seducers, should cause in the faithful diligence in trying what their best teachers deliver, 1 John iv. 1. The seduced most call for our pity, who with good meanings, though, alas, with bad success, follow their blind leader; whose misery that we may avoid, we must examine all we hear by the word, taking nothing upon trust, not loving doctrines for men, but men for their doctrine, and it for its consonancy to Scripture, which should, like a sword of Paradise, keep errors from entering into our hearts. Be not like little children, to gape at and be ready to swallow whatever the nurse puts to the mouth. If seducers appeal to Scripture, to Scripture let them go; and if they cannot endure the light of that sun, reject them as spurious, and their meeting-places as infected houses, and schools of impiety. "Sit not among vain persons," Psal. xxvi. 4. Let not Satan take thee among his own, lest he make thee one of his own.

Obs. 5. Sin loves not to be seen in its own colours. These seducers having in them no real goodness and worth, or fit qualifications of piety and integrity, but intentions by their entrance to seduce others, appeared not to be what indeed they were, but cunningly they seemed to be what they were not, that so the faithful might admit them unawares, not knowing who they were. Sin is a deed of darkness, not only because the sinner's portion will be utter darkness, but because his practices he loves to conceal in the dark. Sin's deformity makes not a sinner desire that it should not be, but only that it should not be seen. Aaron covered over his sin with the wickedness of the people, Exod. xxxii. 22. Saul coloured over his sin of sparing Agag and the cattle, with pretended resolutions to sacrifice to the Lord, 1 Sam. xv. 21. Carnal will ever has carnal wit attending upon it. Love to sin refines the invention for concealing it. No sin has beauty enough in its own complexion to win the affection of the fondest spectator, unless its wrinkles be filled up with the paint of religious pretences. Sinners have a false conceit of God, they think he cannot see through their coverts; like little children, because they shut their own eyes, they think they are in the dark to all others. How much is holiness honoured by its enemies, who even when they hate the having of it, love to appear to have it! How unable is a hypocrite to shun the dint of this dilemma, If holiness be bad, why doth he so much as appear; if good, why doth he no more than appear holy? In a word, how slight and childish will all hypocritical varnishings prove at the last day! Paint will not endure the fire of wrath, nor can hidden wickedness be concealed in the day of Divine disquisition.

Obs. 6. Seducers, with other sinners, are modest in the beginning of sin. When these seducers first entered, the faithful thought them not such as afterward they found them. They were like a deceitful gamester, or dice-player, who playing with one who is ignorant and wealthy, seems in the beginning of the game to be altogether unskilful, till, at length, by degrees, he puts forth his craft, and cheats him of all he has. And never has Satan been so dangerous an enemy, either to churches or persons, as when he has been hurtful insensibly, gradually, and creepingly. He can hardly tempt men at one leap to get up to the top of impiety, but by several steps. As, 1. By an evil motion. 2. By some kind of approbation. 3. By determination to embrace it. 4. By a vicious action. 5. By an evil habit. 6. By defence and justification of sin. Till, 7. There be a glorying and boasting in it. Satan dyes not a man a purple or a scarlet sinner at the first, but after divers tinctures, that so at the last he may take the deepest dye. He windeth not up his treble to the highest pitch hastily, but strains it up by little and little to the desired height: at the first he makes men adventure upon actions questionable, whether sinful or not; then he presses them forward to sins undoubted, yet small; and then he easily draws men from making little account of small sins, to make small account of great sins. How dangerously, because gradually, did Satan bring idolatry into the church! First, images and pictures of saints were used in private for memory, history, or ornament only; afterward, in Gregory's days, they were brought into the church, but with an express prohibition of worshipping them; in the next age, the worshipping of them was enjoined, yet not for themselves, but in respect only of what they represented; but since the council of Trent, it is the tenet of the Roman church, that images are to be worshipped for themselves; and further the heathen go not in their idolatry. The great seducer of the nations, the pope, was he not creeping and modest in his beginnings to get into his present height of tyranny? First he contends for a bare primacy or order; after he pretends to a little more, the receiving the last appeal from the other patriarchs. In the time of Boniface the Third, he puts in for the title of universal bishop; and in his next successor's time, to give spiritual laws to the whole church; and after him, in Pope Hildebrand's time, to give temporal laws to kings and princes. Satan is like a deceitful tradesman, who first by fair-dealing gains customers, that so afterwards by foul-dealing he may gull them. Teachers must not speedily be admitted. It is good to know before we take or trust them. And people should take heed that they forsake not their old approved ministers, who have been throughly made manifest to them in all things, 2 Cor. xi. 6, to embrace such strange doctors, whose design is in time to bring in strange doctrines. The mother's milk is most wholesome for the child. The ministry that begat thee spiritually is fittest to nourish thee. They who oft change their masters, are seldom good scholars. Please not thyself in the parts or abilities of thy minister, but labour to find the experimental working of his ministry upon thine heart, that thou mayst be able to answer seducers, when they suggest that thy minister is antichristian, thus: He has not been antichristian to me; for sure I am, he was the instrument of forming Christ in my heart.

Ut in se considerantur, non tantum ut vicem gerunt exemplaris. Bel. De Imag. Sanc. l. 2. c. 21.

Plat. in Bonif. 3.

This of the third particular in the description of the entrance of these seducers, viz. Their subtlety and sliness in getting into the society of the faithful.

4. The fourth and last thing by which he describes their entrance, is by clearing and vindicating it from the objections which the Christians might possibly raise against God, as if he were regardless of the welfare of his church, and indulgent toward the wickedness of the seducers in suffering them to enter; and against godliness, when they observed that they who pretended to be the most eminent in the church for religion turned apostates. And this he does in these words, "who were before of old ordained to this condemnation:" q. d. Although they have entered so cunningly, as that the church was not aware of them, yet was not their entrance unawares to God, but he foresaw it, and therefore will see that they do his church no harm; and though now God seems to spare them, yet are they in a state of condemnation; and though they formerly seemed such eminent professors of religion, yet God foresaw they would prove as they are; nay, for their sins ordained them to this condition into which they are now fallen.

In which vindication of God's care of his church, and justice against the seducers, their punishment is two ways considerable. In its severity, it was "this condemnation;" and, In its certainty, they "were before of old ordained to" it.

(1.) The punishment of the seducers considered in the severity of it, "this condemnation."

But what was this condemnation of which the apostle here speaks? and why is it called condemnation?

The word here importing condemnation, is taken various ways in Scripture. *κρῖμα· judicium, damnatio, condemnatio.*

[1.] And most properly, for the sentence pronounced by the judge, or rather a judiciary sentencing, or condemning; and so it is used Rom. ii. 2, where the apostle saith, "We are sure the judgment," τὸ κρῖμα, "of God is according to truth;" and Matt. vii. 2, "With what judgment," ἐν ᾧ κρίματι, "ye judge, ye shall be judged."

[2.] For administration of government toward those who are under it, whether by judgment or mercy; and it is spoken of God's providence ruling and ordering the affairs of the world, as Rom. xi. 33, "How unsearchable are his" κρίματα, "judgments!" also of Christ's government of that kingdom which his Father gave him, in the salvation of humble, and condemnation of proud sinners, John ix. 39, εἰς κρῖμα, "For judgment am I come into this world;" that is, for discharging the office of a king, or a judge, in adjudging to every one his due recompence. In which respect judgment is taken for the whole judiciary proceeding of Christ in the great day of judgment toward the good and bad, in regard of his discovering, and sentencing of, and executing sentence upon all at that day. "He reasoned," περὶ τοῦ κρίματος τοῦ μέλλοντος, "of judgment to come," Acts xxiv. 25; Heb. vi. 2.

[3.] For a cause or controversy discussed, judged, and determined by judges. So 1 Cor. vi. 7, κρίματα ἔχετε, "Ye go to law one with another," ye have causes and controversies among yourselves.

[4.] For the wrath, vengeance, damnation, and punishment, Mark xii. 40; Luke xx. 47; xxiii. 40; Rom. ii. 3, executed upon men for wickedness, as Rom. iii. 8, ὧν τὸ κρῖμα, "whose damnation is just." And 1 Cor. xi. 29, 34, "He that eateth and drinketh unworthily, eateth and drinketh" κρῖμα, "damnation to himself." So Matt. xxiii. 14, "Ye shall receive the greater" κρῖμα, "damnation." And Rom. xiii. 2, "They that resist, shall receive to themselves" κρῖμα, "damnation." And 1 Tim. iii. 6, "Lest he fall" εἰς κρῖμα, "into the condemnation of the devil." So 2 Pet. ii. 3, "Whose" κρῖμα, "judgment now of a long time lingereth not." And thus I take it in this place. The apostle Jude here by τοῦτο τὸ κρῖμα, "this condemnation," intends that punishment by God inflicted upon seducers in this life for abusing the grace of God, whereby they did not only themselves turn backsliders and apostates, but become opposers of the truth, and perverters of others; hereby making way for their own eternal condemnation. A punishment made up of many poisonful ingredients, and that has in it a complication of many spiritual woes, which, as the Scripture testifies, belonged to these seducers, and to others who were in the same condemnation with them: as,

Judicium vocat vel damnationem, vel reproborum sensum, quo feruntur, ut pietatis doctrinam pervertant; neque enim id quisquam facere potest nisi suo exitio. Calv. in loc. Potest hoc judicium intelligi justa derelictio, qua propter peccata præcedentia permissi fuerunt pati naufragium fidei, et variis errorum fluctibus abripi, ita ut etiam fierent errorum magistri, tandem judicium illud gravissimum æternæ damnationis subituri. Estius in loc.

1. A voidness of spiritual judgment and understanding, an inability to judge between good and bad, things that differ; an insufficiency to approve of any thing which is excellent, Phil. i. 10; whereby they put bitter for sweet, and sweet for bitter; spake

evil of the ways of grace, which they understood not, 2 Pet. ii. 12; and of the gospel, in which they saw no beauty, it being hid to these lost ones, 2 Cor. iv. 3, who contemned and slighted it; were delivered up to a reprobate sense, Rom. i. 28; and because they loved not what they knew, were not able to know what to love, Rom. i. 21—23.

2. Another woe in this condemnation is, a spirit of benumbedness, insensibleness, cauterizedness, under all the most awakening administrations of God's word or rod; a judgment which the Scripture puts for all the misery and condemnation of the reprobate, and that which differenceth them from the elect. "He hath mercy on whom he will have mercy, and whom he will he hardeneth," Rom. ix. 18. And having spoken of the elect, he saith, "the rest were hardened," Rom. xi. 7. Of seducers, Paul speaks of some who had "consciences seared with a hot iron," 1 Tim. iv. 2, whom nothing awakens but eternal burnings, though too late, to a serious sensibleness of their estate. These seducers fed "themselves without fear," Jude 12.

3. A third woe in this condemnation is, incorrigibleness, and unreformedness under the means of salvation. All the dews of salvation fall upon them as showers upon the barren wilderness; and they are by God compared to drossy silver, which all the art and pains of the silversmith cannot refine; and therefore called reprobate silver, Jer. vi. 30. These seducers in God's orchard were trees without fruit, "twice dead, plucked up by the roots," Jude 12.

4. A fourth woe in this condemnation is, God's giving them up to strong delusion; a delighting in error and false doctrine, with believing it; and thus seducers are said not only to deceive, but to be deceived, 2 Tim. iii. 13; and those who received not the love of the truth, had strong delusion sent them from God, and upon them the deceivableness of unrighteousness takes hold, 2 Thess. ii. 10; and thus God suffered a lying spirit to deceive Ahab and his prophets, 2 Chron. xviii. 18—22.

5. A fifth woe in this condemnation is, a stumbling at and a quarrelling with the word of life, 1 Pet. ii. 8, and Christ the Rock of salvation. Thus Paul speaks of some who were contentious, and obeyed not the truth, Rom. ii. 8; and of seducers who resist the truth, 2 Tim. iii. 8. Like these in Jude, who contended so much against the faith, that all which Christians could do, was little enough to contend for it against those who made the gospel a plea for licentiousness.

6. A sixth woe in this condemnation is, progressiveness in sin, and, as the apostle speaks of seducers, a waxing worse and worse, 2 Tim. iii. 13; a walking so far into the sea of sin, as at length to be over head and ears; a descending to the bottom of the hill; a daily "treasuring up wrath," Rom. ii. 5; a proficiency in Satan's school; a growing artificially wicked, and even doctors of impiety.

7. Which, lastly, will prove the great and heavy woe, not to be contented to be wicked, and to go to hell alone, but to be leaders to sin, and to leaven others with impiety; and thus Paul saith, that seducers were deceiving, as well as deceived, 2 Tim. iii. 13. And Peter, that "many shall follow their pernicious ways," 2 Pet. ii. 2. And certainly, impiety propagated shall be condemnation heightened.

Secondly, Why is this punishment of seducers called condemnation? Κρίμα for κατάκριμα, the cause for the effect. I grant condemnation is properly the sentence or censure condemning one to some punishment; and though in this place it is used for the very punishment itself, yet the Spirit of God fitly sets out this punishment of wicked men by a word that denotes a sentencing them thereunto; and that, 1. Because a sentence of condemnation is even already denounced against them. 2. Because it is such a punishment as by judiciary sentence is wont to be inflicted upon guilty offenders.

(1.) It is really and truly denounced, &c. For besides God's foreappointing the wicked to this condemnation, as it is the punishment of sin, and the execution of his justice, wicked men are in this life sentenced to punishment, 1. By the word of God, which tells them that "God will render to every man according to his deeds; to them who do not obey the truth, but obey unrighteousness, indignation and wrath," &c., Rom. ii. 6, 8. And that "he who believeth not is condemned already," John iii. 18. 2. By their own conscience, which accuseth and condemneth as God's deputy, and here tells them what they deserve both here and hereafter. "If our hearts condemn us," &c., 1 John iii. 20, &c. 3. By the judgments of God manifested against those who have lived in the same sins, the wrath of God being revealed against all unrighteousness, Rom. i. 18. 4. By the contrary courses of the godly: the practices of saints really proclaiming, that because the ways of the wicked are sinful and destructive, therefore they avoid them; and thus Noah sentenced the old world, by being a practical preacher of righteousness, 2 Pet. ii. 5; Matt. xii. 41, 42. And all these sentencings of wicked men do but make way for that last and great sentence to be pronounced at the day of judgment, to the punishment both of eternal loss and pain, Matt. vii. 23; xxv. 41.

(2.) It is such a punishment as by judiciary sentence is wont to be executed upon guilty offenders; and so it is in two respects: 1. Because it is righteous. 2. Severe.

[1.] Righteous. These seducers were not spiritually punished without precedent provocations; "as they did not like to retain God in their knowledge, God gave them over to a reprobate mind," Rom. i. 28; and God sends them justly strong delusions, that they should believe and teach a lie, because they received not the love of the truth, 2 Thess. ii. 10, 11; and because they would not be scholars of truth, they justly become masters of error.

[2.] The punishment of wicked men is such as is wont to be inflicted upon offenders by a sentence, because of its weight and severity. It is not παιδεία, or ἔλεγχος, not a paternal chastisement, or a rebuke barely to convince of a fault; but it is κρίμα, the judge's sentence, condemning to punishment the guilty malefactor. It is not medicinal, but penal; not the cutting of a surgeon, but of a destroyer: the happiness of correction stands in teaching us, but this punishment is the giving of sinners up to unteachableness; and what is it indeed but a hell on this side hell, for God to withdraw his grace, and to suffer men to be as wicked as they will, to be daily damning themselves without control, to be carried down to the gulf of perdition, both by the wind of Satan's temptation, and, which is worse, by the tide of sinful inclination! for God to say, Be and do as bad as you will, "be filthy still," Rev. xxii. 11, sleep on now, and take your rest, I will never jog nor disturb you in your sins. How sore a judgment is it to be past feeling, so as that nothing cooler than hell-fire, and lighter than the loins of an infinite God, can make us sensible, though too late!

Obs. 1. The condemnation of the wicked is begun in this life. As heaven, so hell is in the seed before it is in the fruit. The wicked on this side hell are tunning and treasuring up that wrath, which hereafter shall be broached and revealed, Rom. ii. 5. The wicked have even here hell in its causes. The old bruises which their souls by sin have received in this life, will be painful when the change of weather comes, when God alters their condition by death. When thy lust asks, How canst thou want the pleasure? let thy faith answer by asking another question, How can I bear the pain of such a sin? Put sin into its best dress, and it is but gilded condemnation.

Obs. 2. Spiritual judgments are ever the sorest. In God's withdrawing his grace, and delivering up to a reprobate sense, there is something of condemnation. The soul of a judgment is its seizing upon the soul. The greatest misery which can befall the body, is but for the soul to leave it; and what proportion bears this to the misery of God's leaving the soul! The death in death is the miscarriage of the soul. If a man be not heart-sick, though otherwise distempered, he is not feared; and if not soul-sick, and the union between God and him weakened, there is no danger. Bodily miseries are but appearing and opinionative, and there is a vanity in outward troubles as well as enjoyments. The apostle makes the greatest suffering of the body to be but as such, rather a dream than a reality of suffering. The poorest saint never had a drop of condemnation in a sea of calamity. His affliction is not *laniena*, but *medicina;* not butchery, but surgery; nay, the end of God's chastening is, that he may not be judged, 1 Cor. xi. 32. How different is the condemning of a malefactor from the reprehension of a son, the father's rod from the executioner's axe! If we endure chastening, the Lord deals with us as with sons, Heb. xii. 7. Strive not so much to get the rod taken off thy back, as to get it into a Father's hand. How madly merry is every obstinate sinner in all his worldly enjoyments! How unsuitable is thy music when thou art sacrificing that which should be dearer to thee than thy dearest child, and celebrating the funeral of thy precious soul! Who would not commiserate his mirth, who goes dancing to his own execution, whose only strife is to double his misery by shunning the thoughts of that which he cannot shun? Be not taken with what thou hast in gift, but what thou hast in love. In receiving every mercy imitate Isaac's jealousy, and say, Art thou that very mercy, that mercy indeed which comes in the blood of Christ? Art thou sent from a Father, or a Judge? What do I receiving, if I shall never be received? It is infinitely better that God should correct thee so as to awaken thee, than by prospering to let thee sleep in sin till it be too late to arise. It was better for the prodigal to be famished home than furnished out.

Obs. 3. These condemned ones should warn us that we incur not the like condemnation with them. Saints should be examples of imitation, and sinners of caution. A good heart will get good even by bad men, and take honey out of the carcass of a lion. These seducers were mentioned and stigmatized by Jude with this black mark, not only to show that God was righteous in punishing, but that we might not be unrighteous and wretched in imitating them. And that we may not, (1.) Neglect not, undervalue not the truths of the gospel. Shut not thy eyes, lest God suffer Satan to blind them; Rom. i. 28; 2 Thess. ii. 9—11. How severely did God punish the heathens for opposing the light of nature! and will not Christ, when clearly discovered, and unkindly neglected, much more heighten thy condemnation? If Christ be not a rock of foundation, he will be a stone of stumbling. Fruits which grow against a wall are soon ripened by the sun's heat, and so are sins which are committed under the sunshine of the gospel. The contempt of the gospel is the condemnation (John iii. 19) of the world, it brings swift destruction, 2 Pet. ii. 1. (2.) Preserve a tender conscience. Tremble at the first solicitations of sin, which make way for eternal, by taking away spiritual feeling. The deluge of impiety in which these seducers were drowned began with a drop. Many knots tied one upon another will hardly be loosed: every spot falling upon the clothes makes a man the more regardless of them; and every sin defiling the conscience makes a man the more careless of it. He who dares not wade to the ancles, is in no danger of being swallowed up in the depths. Modest beginnings make way for immodest proceedings in sin. The thickest ice that will bear a cart, begins with a thin, trembling cover that will not bear a pebble. As these seducers crept in by degrees into the church, so did Satan by degrees creep into them; they increased to more ungodliness, 2 Tim. ii. 16. They went down to this condemnation by steps; and after they had begun, they knew not where or whether they should stop. (3.) Take heed of turning the grace of God into wantonness, of abusing his goodness, either to soul or body, to impiety. Take not occasion to be sinful because God is merciful, to be long-sinning because God is long-suffering, to sin because grace abounds, to make work for the blood of Christ, to turn Christian liberty into unchristian libertinism. This must needs incense even mercy itself to leave and plead against thee; and what then will justice do? They who never enjoyed this grace of God, go to hell; they who have it and use it not, run on foot to hell; but they who abuse and turn it into wantonness, gallop or go to hell on horseback.

This for the first way in which the punishment of these seducers was considerable, viz. Its severity, "this condemnation." We now observe,

(2.) Its certainty, they "were before of old ordained to" it.

In this two things require explication. What this ordination is, of which the apostle here speaks; and, In what respect it is said to be "before of old."

For the first, The word προγεγραμμένοι, here translated ordained, properly signifying, forewritten, enrolled, billed, booked, or registered. It seems, say some, to be a metaphor taken from records in courts, wherein things are set down for an after-remembrance of them; or, according to others, from books of remembrance, wherein for the greater sureness of doing any thing, men write down what they purpose to do, and desire not to forget. Calvin draws the allusion from Scripture, in which the eternal counsel of God, wherein the faithful are elected to salvation, is called a book. Sure we are, it is a metaphorical speech; and by none of our protestant divines, as I remember, is that interpretation embraced which is given by some papists, who, haply, to wave the doctrine of reprobation, expound this forewriting here mentioned, to be the predictions by writing which went before in the Scriptures concerning these seducers. Nor can this writing here mentioned so be attributed to God, as if either he could properly be said to have a memory, or to remember any thing, or had any defect or weakness of memory, or had any material books wherein he wrote any thing at all; but this writing or booking is spoken concerning him ἀνθρωποπάθως, by way of resembling him to man, who, what he purposes exactly to remember, or certainly to do, he books and writes down beforehand. And the Scripture speaks of four metaphorical books or writings which God has. 1. The book of his providence, or God's knowledge and decree of all the particular persons, things, and events that ever were or shall be in the world; and in this book were written all the members of David, Psal. cxxxix. 16; and all the tears of David, Psal. lvi. 8. 2. The book of the last and universal judgment, which is the perfect knowledge that God hath of the actions of all men, good and bad, according to which at the last day he will give judgment: thus it is said, "The judgment was set, and the books were opened," Dan. vii. 10. And, "I saw the dead, small and great, stand before God; and the books were opened," Rev. xx. 12. It is a term taken from public judgments here among men, wherein are produced all the writings of informations, depositions of witnesses, &c., to show that God's omniscience shall discover and rehearse all actions, and his justice proceed accordingly. 3. "The book of life," Rev. xx. 12; xxii. 19; called also "the Lamb's book of life," Rev. xiii. 8; xxi. 27; which is God's eternal decree to bestow grace and glory upon some; and in this are set down the names of the elect: of these it is said often, Their names are written in the book of life, Phil. iv. 3; Luke x. 20; and at the last day this book is said to be opened, because it shall then be manifested to all who are elected. 4. This writing here mentioned by Jude, namely, that black bill, or the catalogue of those whom God hath appointed unto wrath, 1 Thess. v. 9, ordinarily considered as the positive or affirmative part of reprobation, wherein God decreed justly to damn some for sin. For reprobation is considerable in a double act. First, negative; which is that of preterition, or passing by of some, and God's will not to elect them. Secondly, positive; which is God's ordaining them to punishment for sin. And in both these acts there is a double degree.

In the first, the negative act, 1. God's denying his grace in this life. And, 2. His denying them glory and salvation in the next life.

In the positive or affirmative act, 1. God's ordaining the wicked to blindness and obduration here. And, 2. Eternal condemnation hereafter. And upon Holy Scripture are both these acts, and both the degrees of each of them, evidently grounded. 1. Concerning the negative act speaks the Spirit of God, John x. 26, "Ye are not of my sheep." And Matt. vii. 23, "I never knew you." Matt. xiii. 11, To them it is not given "to know the mysteries of the kingdom." And Matt. xi. 25, "Thou hast hid these things from the wise and prudent," &c., "for so it seemed good in thy sight." And Rev. xiii. 8; xx. 15, there are some mentioned "whose names are not written in the book of life." 2. Concerning the positive or affirmative act, speaks the Spirit of God in 1 Pet. ii. 8, where the apostle mentioning those that stumbled at the word, and were disobedient, saith, "They were appointed thereunto." And Rom. ix. 18, "Whom he will he hardeneth." And ver. 21, he speaks of vessels made to dishonour. And ver. 22, of "vessels of wrath fitted to destruction." And John xvii. 12, Judas is said to be a "son of perdition." And here Jude saith that these seducers were written down, and "appointed to this condemnation," which was their abode among the faithful, with an obstinate opposing of the truth and faith of Christ, making way to their own eternal condemnation; a doctrine (I confess) not more distasteful to the bad, than hard to be understood by the best. It is no where, as Pareus remarks, when treating upon it on Rom. ix., perfectly apprehended but in that eternal school. I profess my greater desire to study than discuss it. I did not seek it, nor dare I altogether shun it; ever remembering, that though we must not rifle the cabinet of the secret decree, yet neither bushel the candle of Scripture discovery; the former being unwarrantable curiosity, the latter sinful ingratitude. Briefly therefore,

For the second, in what respect this ordination is said to be "before of old." The word πάλαι, of old, is sometimes applied to a thing done a little time before: Pilate asks of Joseph, who came unto him to ask the body of Jesus, whether he had been πάλαι, any while dead. The word, as Dr. Twiss observes, does not signify any definite time. It is applicable even to eternity. And though, as he remarks, the signification of the word is not extended to eternity by any force in itself; yet from the matter whereof the apostle treats, viz. the ordination or decree of God, which is eternal, it ought to be so extended. The denial of the eternity of God's decree was one of the prodigious doctrines of Vorstius. As the Ancient of days was before there was a day, so this "of old" was before there was an age. Which as it refers to the forementioned ordination, comprehends, in the judgment of many learned and godly divines, as well,

The independency and absoluteness, as the immutability and unchangeableness, of this ordination.

1. This ordination, according to some, was absolute, from all causes in the creature; "of old," before these seducers were, before their sins were, in respect not only of their actual existence, but even of their prevision also and foresight of their futurition or coming to pass hereafter. And in delivering their judgment herein, they consider reprobation, with Aquinas and other schoolmen, either in respect of the act of God reprobating, God's willing and decreeing; or in respect of the effect thereof, the things willed or decreed, as God wills that one thing should be for another. ^{1. q. 23. Art. 5.}

(1.) As to reprobation in respect of the act or decree of God's reprobating, or God's willing or decreeing; they say, the sins of the creature cannot be assigned as the cause of reprobation; and herein they agree with Aquinas and the sounder schoolmen. They conceive that the decree of reprobation was not without the foresight of sin; yet that the sight of sin was neither in order of nature or time, before reprobation, nor after it; but purely, evenly, and equally accompanying it. That God's decree to permit sin, from whence comes prevision of sin, and to condemn for sin, were not the one subordinate to the other, or of a diverse order; as if the one were the end, and the other the mean; but coordinate, and of one and the same order and means, both accommodated to one and the same end: God neither condemning that sin may be permitted, nor permitting sin that he might condemn; but permitting sin, and condemning for sin, that the glory of his justice might be manifested; the glorious manifestation of his justice being not advanced only by permission of, or only by condemning for sin, but by both jointly, or together; according to which apprehension, sin foreseen could not be the cause of reprobation. They conceive, that God not depending upon any condition in the creature, no other way foreknew the futurition of sin, than by his own decree to permit it. And they further urge, if consideration of sin were before God's decree of reprobation, then the decree of permission of sin should have been before the decree of reprobation; and so God should intend the permission of sin before he intended the damnation of man for it; and then it would follow, (in regard that what is first in intention is last in execution,) that damnation for sin should ^{Non est assignare causam divinæ voluntatis ex parte actus volendi. Aquin. ubi supr.}

be in execution before the permission of sin, for which men are damned. And this is the argument oft urged by Dr. Twiss; to which he sometimes adds, that whatsoever is first in intention, has the nature of an end in respect of that which follows it; but the permission of sin cannot be considered as an end in respect of the damnation of men, it being impossible that men should be damned to this end, that sin should be permitted. And they of this opinion assert, that if because God decreed that condemnation shall only be for sin, it follows that sin is a cause of that decree, it will also unavoidably follow, because God hath decreed that salvation shall only be in a way of good works, that good works are a cause of that decree; they conceiving that though good works do not go before salvation with the same efficacy wherein sin goes before damnation, good works being only dispositive causes of the one, and sins meritorious causes of the other, yet that they go before it with the same order of necessity. And they add, that the apostle removes both from the election of Jacob, and the reprobation of Esau, the consideration of all works either good or evil, as well in respect of their prevision as actual existence; to the end that he might show that the purpose of God, according to election, was not according to works, but of him that calleth; and so by the same reason, that the decree of the reprobation of Esau was not of evil works, but of Him that calls and leaves whom he will.

(2.) As to reprobation in regard of the effect, or rather consequent thereof, the things decreed and willed, or as God wills that one thing should be for another, it is not doubted, albeit God's eternal volitions or decrees depend not upon any temporal object or causes, as the prime motives thereunto, but that God by his eternal decree ordained, that this or that event in the temporal execution shall not follow but upon this or that going before; as, that in those of years, the actual bestowing of eternal life shall depend upon believing, repenting, and persevering, and that the actual punishing with eternal death shall depend upon final unbelief and impenitency. This is not to make the eternal decrees of election and reprobation dependent upon the foreseen contingent acts of man's free-will, but to make temporal events, acts, or things one to depend conditionally upon another, for their being or not being in time.

And yet, (1.) The cause of reprobation, in respect of denying of grace, external, whether in regard of the outward means; or internal, either common or saving; is the will and pleasure of God. As it is the mere will and pleasure of God whereby in time men are reprobated from grace, was from eternity; for as God does or does not in time, so it he purposes to do or not to do from all eternity. Now, that in time the denial of grace is from the will and pleasure of God, is most evident from Scripture, which teaches that God calls to grace, and gives the very means of salvation to whomsoever he will. The Spirit suffered not Paul to preach at Bithynia, Acts xvi. 7. To you it is given (saith Christ) to know the mysteries of the kingdom of heaven, and to them it is not given, Matt. xiii. 11; Deut. xxix. 4. And because it seemed good in his Father's sight, he hid these things from the wise and prudent, Matt. xi. 25. Tyre and Sidon would have made better use of the means of grace than the Jews, yet God bestowed those means not upon the former, but upon the latter.

But, (2.) The cause of reprobation, in regard of God's denial of glory, is not merely from God's will and pleasure, but from the pravity and sin of men. God in time denies glory in regard of men's impiety, and therefore he purposed to deny it for that. "Depart from me," will Christ say only to the "workers of iniquity," Matt. vii. 23. "There shall enter into the New Jerusalem nothing that defileth." "The unrighteous shall not inherit the kingdom of God."

And, (3.) The cause of reprobation, in regard of blindness and obduration in sin in this life, and eternal damnation in the life to come, is from man's impiety. God decreed that condemnation should not be but for sin, nor hardening but for preceding rebellion, nor that the wages of death should be paid without the work of sin. No man is ordained to a just punishment but for some sin; but the withdrawing of grace, the blindness and obduration of sinners, are the punishments of preceding sin, as appears, Rom. i. 27, God gave them up, &c. that they might receive the recompence (ἀντιμισθίαν) of their error which was meet. To crown or to damn is an act of judiciary power, and proceeds according to the tenor of the revealed gospel. The eternal decree of the damnation of the very devils, was never determined to be executed otherwise than for their own misdeeds.

2. This expression "of old" notes the immutability and unchangeableness of this ordination; the τὸ ἀμετάθετον τῆς βουλῆς αὐτοῦ, the immutability of his counsel; that which is eternal is unalterable. This ordination is like such a booking and writing down of a thing as shall unfailingly be performed. Nor can this book or writing of God, as a man's book may, be lost or burnt, but it continues irreversibly and inviolably to be performed; he who wrote it wants not skill, nor will, nor power, to bring to pass whatever he hath written in it. What God hath written he hath written; and though sometimes he changes his denunciations, yet never his decrees: "I am the Lord, I change not," Mal. iii. 6. "The Strength of Israel is not man, that he should repent," 1 Sam. xv. 29. "His counsel shall stand," Prov. xix. 21. "The Lord hath purposed it, who shall disannul it?" Isa. xiv. 27. The number of those appointed to wrath, 1 Thess. v. 9, is determined as well *materialiter*, who, as *formaliter*, how many they are. God's appointments are peremptory, not depending upon the variable will of man, as if God had determined certainly concerning none, but only as he sees they will believe or not believe; for how suits it with the wisdom of God, so to work as to determine nothing of the end of his work? to make man, and not to appoint what shall become of him? How with the love he bears to his own glory, to have creatures more beholden to themselves than to their Maker? to hear them using this language, That we may escape hell, if we will, we thank God; but that we do, we thank ourselves, who by the use of our free-will made that possibility beneficial to ourselves?

Obs. 1. Groundless are the exceptions which corrupt minds raise against delivering this doctrine of reprobation, and weak are the calumnies with which they load it.

(1.) For the first, God cannot be charged with cruelty in any man's reprobation. It is no cruelty in God to deny him grace to whom it is not at all due, but an act of just liberty and free power, Rom. ix. 21; nor can it be cruelty, but vindicative justice, for God to appoint men to punishment for sin, Rom. ix. 22. This will be more clear, if we consider that by reprobation all grace is not denied, but only that grace which is peculiar to the elect. That which is afforded by the administration of common providence, either under the law of nature, or the dispensation of the gospel, being not

De ratione æternitas est immutabilitas. Aug. Cons. l. 12. c. 15.

Ea gratia quæ per communis providentiæ administrationem sive sub lege naturæ, sive sub gratia Evangelica hominibus vario dimenso dispensatur, per

taken away, God leaves the reprobate to their own free-will under his common providence, and in it affords to them those benefits which in the state of innocency were sufficient to salvation, and which in this state of corruption, especially under the gospel, make men altogether without excuse before God. And God never decreed to leave and harden any in sin, but such who by their own free-will leave God, harden themselves against his ways, and abuse his abundant mercy extended towards them. God never appointed that any should stumble at the word but for their contempt of it. From falling into which impiety the elect are prevented, and it is to be attributed to the free-will or mercy of God, extended indeed to them, but due to none.

hunc præteritionis actum non adimitur, sed potius præsupponitur. Synops. pur. Theol. p. 290.

Deus nunquam indurat, nisi habito respectu ad præcedentia peccata. Riv. disp.

(2.) Nor secondly, by decreeing the reprobation of sinners can any conclude that God is the cause of the sins for which the reprobate are damned. Although by reprobation God puts forth no act whereby man is made holy, yet neither is any thing done by it whereby man is made wicked. It is true, sin is a consequent of God's decree, or that which follows upon it, as its antecedent; but no effect flowing from the decree as its cause. It follows not, because God gives not, that therefore he takes away repentance from sinners; and that he throws down, because he raises not up. The sun cannot be said to be the cause of darkness, although darkness necessarily follows the withdrawing of it; nor is reprobation the cause of sin, although sin infallibly follows reprobation. It is God's bounty whereby we are preserved from falling, our own unstableness whereby we fall unless we are preserved. Predestination is an effectual cause in the producing of all salutiferous actions, but reprobation is no effectual cause in the producing of wicked actions; and neither the one nor the other implies any compulsion or forcing unto actions, whether good or evil. True it is, that God decreed not only privatively and permissively, but also with an energetical working will, to be conversant about sinful actions; as, 1. That he would give to the sinner at the very time when sinful actions are committed, the power and use of understanding, and free-will, without which he could not sin. And, 2. That he would concur *ad materialem actionem peccati*, to the matter of the action itself, which otherwise could not come into act or being. 3. That he would deny all such means as would have prevented the sinner's sinning. 4. That he would lay before sinners those occasions, and possibly stir up in them those cogitations, which he knew they would abuse to the committing of sin. 5. That he would so limit and order their sins, that they should break forth in no other measure, at no other time, upon no other persons, than himself hath foreappointed. 6. That all their sins should turn to his own glory, and the good of his elect: but any energetical operative will of God which so hath a working in sinful actions, as that it is the cause *quod talis actio fit cum tali defectu*, or that it should work the contrariety and repugnancy of the sinner's will to the law of God, or that there should be any influence sent into the wills of men from the decree to cause this, we utterly deny and disclaim. The liberty of the will is not at all extinguished by the decree of God; but freely and upon deliberate choice wicked men do as they do, having not only *potentiam in se liberam*, but *liberum usum potentiæ*, and the dominion of free agents over their actions, which ever are the productions of their own frail and defiled free-will. The decree of reprobation never

Deo reprobante non irrogatur aliquid quo homo sit deterior, sed tantum non erogatur quo fiat melior. Aug. Inter antecedens et consequens non intercedit causalitas.

shows itself by any such influx or impression as instils any malicious quality into man's will, or forces it to any malicious action.

(3.) Neither can this doctrine of reprobation justly be charged to be a means of driving men to despair; rather granting the truth of this Arminian conceit, that all were reprobated who were not foreseen believing and persevering, with much more dreadful advantage may Satan fasten temptations on poor wretches to despair; the tempted person knowing there is not one of many who either believes or perseveres; that he for his part has hitherto resisted the motions of the Spirit, and started aside from all inclinations to good; and finding also by his own experience, and now by Satan's arguing, who at last in part turns orthodox, that by his own power he can no more believe than carry a mountain. But the opinion which makes God's decree absolute, arms a man against temptation to despair, and gives him cause to bless God, as it has made thousands do, that their salvation depends not upon foreseeing what good courses out of their own free-will they would take and continue in, that the bending of men's hearts to believe and persevere are the supernatural fruits of God's eternal decree, and not the natural fruits of man's depraved and frail free-will. And though he is uncertain of the eternal will of God, yet is he more uncertain, as Augustine saith, of the strength and stability of his own. Nor do I at all understand, but that by the same reason whereby Arminians argue, that the absolute decree tends to drive men to despair, they must also grant, that the decree does the like, as founded upon the prevision of man's impenitency; for the Divine eternal prescience of future actions and events as much infers their absolute certainty and necessity, as the decree of absolute reprobation. And therefore, as it is commonly observed, the schoolmen are as much troubled (and Cajetan, though a learned man, confesses himself to be at a loss) in resolving whether the prescience of God, as well as predestination, imposes a necessity on future events.

Incerta est mihi de meipso voluntas Dei. Quid ergo tuæ tibi voluntas de teipso certa est, nec times? Aug. de præd. Sanc. c. 11.

In ignorantia sola quietem invenio. p. 1. q. 22. a. 4.

(4.) Nor is this doctrine of reprobation injurious to a godly life. It hinders not the use of the holy endeavours which God requires of those who expect happiness, and would shun wretchedness. Man's industry must not cease about things or ends determined by God's absolute unrevealed decree. Though our endeavours do not make the end otherwise *quoad eventum*, than God foredetermined it, yet it was so determined by God, as that it should never be acquired without the use of our endeavours. God does not by the absolute decree of election absolutely determine to save us, whether we believe or not believe, repent or not repent; and therefore faith and repentance are not to be rejected: nor does he by the absolute decree of reprobation determine to damn any, whether they believe or not believe, repent or not repent. Such absolute decrees (saith a learned man) are the absolute mistakings of the Arminians. We may truly say to every man in the world, elected or not elected, as God to Cain, "If thou doest well, shalt thou not be accepted?" Gen. iv. 7. And to every one that worketh good shall be glory, &c. Rom. ii. 10. Never did God make any decree to damn any man, though he should believe and live righteously; yea, God hath published a quite contrary decree, "Whosoever believeth shall have everlasting life," John iii. 16. And "there is no condemnation to them that are in Christ Jesus, who walk

Bishop Davenant.

Cum prædestinatio ad finem includit media, non potest hunc sperare, qui ista negligit. Prid. lec. 1.

not after the flesh," Rom. viii. 1. From a godly life we may conclude we are no reprobates, and may "make our calling and election sure," 2 Pet. i. 10. So that this doctrine is so far from quenching, that it quickens holy endeavours, seeing none but the unholy are ordained to condemnation, and that we are as well ordained to the works of grace, as the reward of glory. Wilt thou not fear reprobation, as Paul spake of fearing the civil magistrate, do that which is good, fear to do evil; but if thou wilt, upon hearing the doctrine of God's absolute decree, conclude that holiness is vain and fruitless; by the same reason resolve, because the length of thy life is certainly decreed by God, therefore thou wilt never either eat or drink to lengthen out thy life. If but one man in the world were elected, thou shouldst use the means appointed to life. If but one man in the world were reprobated, thou shouldst shun the ways which lead to death.

Obs. 2. In regard of God, there is no chance, nor any event by fortune. All which ever was, is, or shall be, was written before him as in a book. In regard of men, nature may seem to have many mischances, but we who know the true God should acknowledge, instead of chance, only his Divine providence. That blind goddess Fortune holds her deity only by the tenure of men's ignorance. Infinitely too weak is the axletree of fortune for the least motion of the world to be turned upon it. Punishments directed by God's providence are not to be entertained as the pastimes of fortune. That which is casual to us, is ordained by God.

Obs. 3. The faithful should not be surprised with wonder at the disturbance of the church by seducers. The opposition of the truth by such as would be and have been accounted its greatest maintainers, is oft to Christians the most unexpected evil. It may make an honest heart not only fear its own apostacy from the truth, but even question whether ever heretofore it embraced the truth or no. This foreordaining of many glistering professors to this condemnation, should be a preservative from such a distemper. Alas! God not only saw through them, when they were in their fairest appearances, but foresaw what they would prove, before they either were men, or were appearing Christians. Church disturbers are no men of yesterday. He that foresaw would have prevented their entrance into the church, had he not intended not only the preservation of his elect from them, but the benefiting of the elect by them, Matt. xxiv. 24.

Occurrere periculo voluit Judas, ne quos rei novitas turbaret. Calv. in loc.

Obs. 4. There is no judging of any one's reprobation. We are commanded to read over God's oracles, but we are not so much as admitted to look into his rolls. Who is "before of old ordained," written down, shall never be known till the books be opened. There is a peradventure of God's giving repentance even to opposers, 2 Tim. ii. 25. Censure thou mayst their actions, but not determine their end. Many a saint recollecting how far himself was suffered to go before he returned, may truly say, I will never despair of any; for surely, Lord, there never will be a baser heart than mine for thee to deal with. Sinners must have thy pity, not thy despair. That the end of their ways will be death, it is thy duty to declare; that the end of those, who for the present walk in those ways, will be death, it is thy sin, thy danger to determine. Least of all despair of thine own salvation. This conclusion, I am one of the reprobates, ought to be repelled as a temptation not more groundless than dangerous.

De nullius hominis salute desperandum, quem Dei patientia sinit vivere; de sui ipsius minime omnium. Tanquam caput omnis noxiæ tentationis repellatur ab animo Christiani, hæc mortifera conclusio,: Sum ex reprobis. Aug.

Obs. 5. Whosoever is exempted from this appointment to condemnation, is engaged to be eminent and singular in his love to God. No motive to love is so effectual as to be prevented by love: God's love to the elect was early, eternal. They were chosen by God before they could choose God. How due a debt is love to him when we were, who loved us without due debt before we were! We ought to love him more than others, who is incomparably more lovely, and who loved us more than others when we were no more lovely than others. Should not we single him out for our God, who infinitely excels all, and who singled us out for his people when we were no better than any? What was it beside election, that made saints by grace of sinners by nature, and (as I may say) white paper of the foulest dunghill rags? what but this went between the holiest saint and the most flagitious sinner? both were cut off from the same piece, and formed out of the same clay.

Justus quis est nisi qui amanti se Deo, vicem rependit amoris quod non fit, nisi revelante spiritu per fidem homini æternum Dei propositum super salute sua futura. Bern. Ep. 107.

Obs. 6. The faithful may be strongly armed against temptations to despair. The decrees of God depend not upon the pleasure of man's, but God's will, Luke xii. 32. The angels, and Adam, who fell from integrity, plainly show what would become of man, who (now) hath the treachery of sin within him, and the battery of temptation without him, if Divine predestination were removed, Rom. viii. 33, 35, &c. Forbear, then, wretched Pelagian, to make the supposed dependence of predestination upon man's will a ground of courage, and the certain dependence of man's will upon predestination a ground of despair. Proud potsherd! expect not happiness without more humility. Lord, how soon should I embezzle my happiness, and prove a beggarly prodigal, shouldst thou give me my portion into mine own hands!

An timendum est ne tunc de se homo desperet, quando spes ejus ponenda demonstratur in Deo, non autem desperaret si eam in seipso superbissimus et infelicissimus poneret. Aug. de Bon. Pers. l. 2, c. 22.

Obs. 7. This ordination of the wicked to condemnation should incite the best to humility. He who fares best has no cause of insultation over him who speeds worst. The least mercy deserves thankfulness, the greatest allows not pride. The reading of what the worst are and shall be, should instruct us what the best had been and should be without free grace, which alone makes the difference. Humble tenderness is the badge of election; as the elect of God, put on bowels, Col. iii. 12. Grace found the richest saint but a beggarly sinner, and grace makes the richest in possession to be poorest in spirit, Matt. v. 3. "God hath chosen the weak to confound the mighty," 1 Cor. i. 27, not the mighty to domineer over the weak. Every receipt is an alms, and the best furnished Christian only proclaims that he has been oftenest at the door of mercy. The taller thou art in grace, the more need thou hast to stoop, wouldst thou enter into the meditation of thy present estate without danger.

Obs. 8. Forbearance of punishment is no argument to the finally impenitent of their total immunity from punishment. They are billed and booked by God, and at length God will call in his debts; and, the longer he stays, with the more interest. The judgments of God are sure, if they be late. With God, delay wears nothing out of memory, nor is any thing gained by protraction. All things to the Ancient of days are present. How fruitless is a sinner's league with hell! The Lord laughs at him, for he seeth that his day is coming. Grudge not to see impenitency and prosperity go together. What is all a sinner's mirth, but a little unpunished wickedness? The thunder-clap of wrath will soon make his wine of mirth sour. He who now goes on so pertinaciously in sin, must either undo or be undone. His cheer may seem excessive, but there is a reckoning coming, which though it be the last, yet is it as sure as any part of the entertainment.

Obs. 9. Ministers ought not to propound to the people a reprobation absolute from the means. Reprobation is not so to be preached, as though men were to be damned whatsoever they do, but so as that it may be manifested that destruction is the fruit of impiety. It is possible a minister may preach what is true concerning God's absolute decree to save and reprobate men, and yet not in that due manner in which he ought to speak. For example, should a minister preach thus to his people; Whatsoever you do, ye shall be such as God decreed ye should be, &c. This is indeed a true doctrine, but it seeming to separate the end from the means, it is so true, that withal, as Augustine saith, it is most inconvenient and pernicious, because it is not wholesomely applied to human infirmity. Now it is the part of an unskilful or deceitful physician, so to apply a good plaster, that either it shall do no good, or do hurt. Therefore Paul speaking of the reprobates, "whose end is destruction," adds, "whose God is their belly, whose glory is their shame," &c.; and here Jude having said that these seducers were "ordained to condemnation," subjoins, "ungodly men," who "turn the grace of God into lasciviousness." To the handling whereof I now proceed.

Dolosi vel imperiti Medici est, etiam utile medicamentum sic alligare, ut aut non prosit, aut obsit. Aug. de Bo. Pers. l. 2. cap. 21.

This for the first part of the first argument to move the Christians earnestly to contend for the faith. The argument is the dangerousness of the company of these seducers. The first part of which was a description of their entrance.

The second follows, a description of their impiety, they having got entrance. Two ways the apostle describes it. More generally he calls them ungodly men. More particularly he shows wherein their ungodliness appeared; they "turn the grace of God into lasciviousness, and deny the only Lord God, and our Lord Jesus Christ."

I. The apostle expresses the ungodliness of seducers more generally, calling them ungodly; "Ungodly men."

For explication. I shall first express more briefly and generally what the apostle here intends by the term ungodly; and then more fully and particularly explain wherein that ungodliness of which he speaks consists, or what it is to be ungodly.

1. The word ἀσεβής, ungodly, is compounded of a word which signifieth to worship, or be devout, and of a particle which denotes a negation or denial of that thing with which it is joined. So that the word made up of both, properly signifies one who is indevout, or worships not, who yields no adoration, honour, or reverence to God, but casts off his service, or, as we say, is a profane man, and one of no religion. For godliness is properly the same with religion, and religion is a spiritual bond: not only a Divine impression, whereby we are possessed with most high and peerless thoughts of God, and rapt with admiration of that excellency which shines in him; but it is also a binder, a golden belt or girdle, that ties, and confederates, and clasps our souls to God. The faithful by religion are God's bundle made upon earth to be carried to heaven; men tied together, by being tied to God. Godliness is this gentle manacle and bond of love tying us by gratitude to God's mercy, by faith to his word, by fidelity to his covenant, by hope to his promises: godliness lays a most sweet and easy yoke upon all the parts of man, voluntarily resigning themselves to draw all together in the service of God; and so it ties the head from wicked imaginations, the heart from evil cogitations, the eyes from vanity, the tongue from profaneness, the hand from violence, the feet from running into sin. And though both religion and godliness in their largest extent comprehend the whole duty of man, to God and man, even holiness and righteousness; yet properly and primarily they denote piety, and the observation of duties belonging immediately to God himself, 1 Tim. vi. 6. And so though ungodliness be often used in the largest sense, as importing all kind of wickedness committed against God and man, as Rom. iv. 5; 1 Tim. i. 9, &c., yet always properly, and (as I conceive) in this place principally, it is to be understood of wickedness immediately done against God himself, in denying him that reverence and honour due, and abusing that worship and service given to him, Rom. i. 25. The apostle by the word ἀσεβεῖς, ungodly, at once discovers both the hypocrisy of these seducers, whose great endeavour was to be accounted in the highest form of religion, and also the root of all that following wickedness wherewith he charges them.

Hier. ad. Am. c. 9.

a and σέβομαι. 1. Σέβομαι, σεβόμενος, used indifferently of true and false worship, Acts xviii. 13; xiii. 50; xvi. 14.
2. Εὐσεβέω signifies to worship God aright, and duly.
3. Ἀσεβής noteth one who is of no religion, who worships not at all.

Dictam esse religionem, quòd quasi in fascem Domini vincti, et religati sumus.

2. More particularly, to consider what it is to be ungodly, or wherein ungodliness consists. I shall open it in three particulars.

(1.) The denial to God the honour which is due to him.

(2.) The attributing of the honour which is due to him to something else beside him.

(3.) The giving to God his honour after a wrong manner.

(1.) To be ungodly is to deny that honour to God which is due to him; and that sundry ways, as, [1.] To deny God his honour by not knowing him, and acknowledging his providence, presence, justice, mercy, power. "The fool hath said in his heart, There is no God," Psal. xiv. 1; he knows no such God as the true God is, no omniscient, just, merciful, powerful, &c. God. He who denies any attribute of God denies God himself: thus the sons of Eli "knew not the Lord," 1 Sam. ii. 12; and thus he, spoken of Psal. l. 21, who thought that God was altogether such an one as himself: thus likewise the ungodly, who say, How doth God know? can he judge through the dark cloud? Thick clouds are a covering to him, that he seeth not, Job xxii. 13, 14. This piece of atheism is the foundation of all the rest. He who knows not his landlord, cannot pay his rent. [2.] Not to honour God by believing him. Ungodly men totally distrust God's promises, though he seals them with an oath. It is impossible that God should utter a lie to them, Heb. vi. 18, and that ungodly men (while such) should do any other than give the lie to God. They make God a liar, 1 John v. 10, the greatest dishonour imaginable! an evil heart departs from, depends not upon the living God, Heb. iii. 12. [3.] Not to honour God by loving him. Ungodly men are haters of God, Rom. i. 30; and it is not for want of poison, but power, that they express not the greatest hatred against him, even the taking away of his very being, Psal. lxxxi. 11. Hence it is that some have called an ungodly man a deicide, though they meant him not such in regard of execution, but of affection, Isa. xxx. 11. It is true, God himself is out of the reach of an ungodly man, but what of him they can obtain, as his pictures, his image in his children, ordinances, they endeavour to destroy and abolish: like thieves, who wish the judge were dead or hurt, the ungodly desire that God might cease to be God, that he had lost the hand of his justice, the arm of his power, and the eye of his knowledge, Job xxi. 14. [4.] Not to honour God by fearing to sin against him. Ungodly men sometimes presume, sometimes they despair, but never do they reverentially fear him, so as to keep themselves from sin; they fear not an oath; they fear hell, they fear not God; they say not, How can we do this great evil, "and sin against God?" Gen. xxxix. 9; they fear sin for hell, not as hell. [5.] Not to honour God by obeying his word, Jer. xliv. 16. Ungodly men cast off the yoke, they are sons of Belial. They "slide back as a backsliding heifer," Hos. iv. 16. They will none of his ways. They desire not the knowledge of them, Job xxi. 14. They hate instruction, and cast the word of God behind them, Psal. l. 17. In their works they deny God, Tit. i. 16. They will never have Christ for their Ruler, nor his word for their rule, Luke xix. 14. [6.] Not to honour God by bearing his stroke. Ungodly men are not as children under the rod, but as wild bulls in a net, they had rather be able to tear than willing to kiss the rod. Like chaff, they fly in the face of, and not like the solid grain, fall down before, him that fans them. They accept not of the punishment of their iniquity, nor wait for deliverance from their punishment, 2 Kings vi. 33; they either faint under, or rage against, or take no notice of the hand of God when it is lifted up against them. [7.] Not to honour God by regarding his worship. The ungodly "call not upon the Lord," Psal. xiv. 4. Only the godly man is made like a man to look upward. The other in their wants go to Baalzebub the god of Ekron, or the witch of Endor, to earthly and sinful shifts; rather howling through the sense of their wants, than praying in the belief of receiving the blessings they desire. In obtaining comforts, they "sacrifice to their net, and burn incense to their drags," Hab. i. 16; and are as sensual in their enjoyments, as unsubmissive in their wants. They can neither pray when they are afflicted, nor sing psalms when they are merry: instead of praying, they despair; instead of singing psalms, they revel: when they are in want, they are as distrustful as if God could never help them; when they abound, they are as secure as if God could never hurt them. In a word, they account not the holy duties of prayer, hearing, or the sacraments, to be their privileges, but their drudgery. They are not "joyful in the house of prayer," Isa. lvi. 7; the sabbath is not a delight, Isa. lviii. 13; the word of the Lord is a burden; and when they are in holy performances, they are like a fish upon the dry land.

(2.) Ungodliness consists in giving the honour which is due to God to something else beside God. And this ungodly men do two ways.

[1.] Inwardly, in the soul, will, and affections, and the whole inner man; as, 1. When they place their trust and confidence upon something besides God, and so place it in the room of God, making flesh their arm and support, Jer. xvii. 5. Thus one ungodly man depends upon his wealth, making it his hope and confidence, Job xxxi. 24; another upon his strength, resting upon man, putting his trust in horses and chariots, Psal. xx. 7; another upon his wit and policy, which in a moment God is able to turn into foolishness, Prov. iii. 5. They will not take the word of a man who has once or twice deceived them, but they will rely upon the broken creature, which always fails fond expectation, and is no other than a lying vanity, Jonah ii. 8; hereby not only disappointing themselves, but dishonouring Him who alone requires and deserves our trust and affiance, Psal. lxii. 8. 2. When they set that love and delight upon other things which is due to God, who is to be loved with all the heart and soul: and thus sundry there are who love their pleasures more than God, 2 Tim. iii. 4, "whose belly is their God," Phil. iii. 19; others there are whose gain is godliness, and who are fitly therefore by the apostle called idolaters, Eph. v. 5. That which a man most loves is his God. Ungodly men set their hearts (Psal. lxii. 10) upon that which was made to set their feet upon; with unbounded eagerness they follow the world. Moderation holds not the reins of their earthly industry, in which they are not carried with the gentle gales of indifference, but the furious winds of violence. They will be rich, though they lose their souls and their God, and are drowned in perdition, 1 Tim. vi. 9. 3. When they bestow that fear upon the creature which is only due to God; when man, not God, is their fear and their dread, Isa. viii. 13. If outward troubles or troublers approach, they shake like "the trees of the wood," Isa. vii. 2; if man threaten a prison, they tremble more than when God threatens hell, Isa. li. 12, 13; fearing him more that can kill the body, than him who can throw both body and soul into hell: whence it is that they are insnared by the unlawful commands of superiors, "willingly walking after the commandment," Hos. 11; and "falling down before the wicked, become like a troubled fountain, and a corrupt spring," Prov. xxv. 26; serving, instead of the Lord, the times.

[2.] Outwardly, ungodly men give the honour to the creature which is due to God; and that they do by outward religious worship, when they worship and "serve the creature more than the Creator, who is God blessed for evermore," Rom. i. 25; before whom religiously we must only kneel and bow down, Psal. xcv. 6. How unlike are ungodly men to Him who was God and man! Christ refused to bow to the devil, not only because he was a devil, but a creature, Matt. iv. 10; denying to him not only inward devotion, but outward reverence. And how unlike to the three godly men, who tell the king commanding them to bow to his image, that they will not serve his gods! Dan. iii. 18. What do they but make a lie, when they make an image of an uncircumscriptible infinite God, Isa. xl. 18, 25, and show themselves as blockish as the block they worship, which is no better than that which even now they burnt? Isa. xliv. 19. Poor is their pretence, who, to exempt themselves from this ungodliness, plead, though they present their bodies at religious worship, yet they preserve their souls for God; for why could not Christ, for a whole world, with all his wisdom, find out such a piece of policy, and make not body and soul one man, that must have but one God, one worship? Are not our bodies the Lord's as well as our souls? or can she be accounted a chaste spouse, which gives the use of her body to a stranger, upon pretence of keeping her heart to her husband?

(3.) Ungodliness consists in giving honour to God after a false and an undue manner. As, [1.] When it is given unwarrantably, and not according to his revealed will; when tradition and human invention put the Scripture out of place. This is to worship God in vain, Matt. xv. 9. μάτην σέβονται. Nothing is more counterfeited and disfigured than religion. Men, through natural unsubmissiveness to the purity and simplicity of Scripture commands, through love of their own conceits, novelty, carnality, are prone to make many golden calves. People, like the Lacedemonians, who were wont to dress their gods after the fashion of the city, love to dress their devotions after their own humours, being zealous, but not according to knowledge; and like bats, converting the humour of their eyes to make their wings large. These give not God that "reasonable service," Rom. xii. 1, for the performance of which they must produce a word, a Scripture reason. Man's work is to keep laws, not either to be or make a law for himself or others. [2.] Honour is given to God after an undue manner, when it is not given him obediently; when, though what is done be commanded, yet it is not done because it is commanded, or in obedience to a precept. The hand must not only be at work, but the eye must also be upon the word. It is very possible for a work commanded to be an act of disobedience, in respect of the intent of the performer. [3.] When it is not given him inwardly, heartily, Col. iii. 23; when men are eye-servants, and do not the will of God from the heart, nor serve him in the spirit, Rom. i. 9. Ungodly men rather act a service than yield a service; they rather compliment God than serve him. They bring a bone without marrow. They glister, but they burn not; like some men who, lifting with others at a burden, make as loud a cry as the rest, but yet they put to it no strength at all. In God's account, they who do but appear godly, are nothing at all but ungodly, Matt. xv. 7, 8; 2 Tim. iii. 5; Ezek. xxxiii. 31. [4.] When honour is not given to God impartially. Ungodly men pick out one work, and reject another; choose an easy, and forbear a difficult work; serve and honour God so far as they may not disserve and dishonour themselves; engaging no further than they may safely come off. Whereas nothing should come amiss to one who rightly serves this Master. One piece of his service must not be preferred before another. We must answer to every call. We must not examine what the service is which is commanded, but who the Master is that commands, Psal. cxix. 6, 128; 1 Tim. v. 21. [5.] When honour is not given him cheerfully. Ungodly men do the will of God against their will; it is not their meat and drink; it goes not down as their food, but as a potion; not upon choice, but constraint; hence their services are neither easy to themselves, nor acceptable to God, whose service is as much our privilege as our duty, Psal. xl. 8; 2 Cor. ix. 7. [6.] When he is not honoured constantly. Ungodly men will have their rest from labour before they die. The honour which they give to God is full of gaps. Their heart is not stedfast with God, Psal. lxxviii. 37. Ungodly men want a fountain, a principle from whence their services should issue, and therefore, like a standing water, they will in time dry up. They are not friends, and therefore they love not at all times. The honour they give to God is like the redness of blushing, soon down; not like the ruddiness of complexion, abiding, Hos. vi. 4. [7.] When honour is not given to God fervently, and diligently, with all the might and strength. Ungodly men honour not God as a God, as the best, the greatest, but without cost, slightly and coldly. The heart has no love, and the hand has little labour. When the spleen swells, all other parts decay; and those who nourish any lust, will honour God but with lean and thin services. A divided heart will be a lazy heart. [8.] When honour is not given to God with single aims and sincere intentions. Ungodly men propound not to themselves glory-ends; God is not honoured by them for himself. They love not the lesson wherein there is not some toy of pleasure or profit; they seek themselves, and not God, and therefore they lose God and themselves too, remaining ungodly here, and unrewarded hereafter, 2 Kings x. 28, 29.

Obs. 1. It is possible for men to attain the highest estimation for godliness, and yet be inwardly at the same time ungodly. Men may be accounted the godly party, and yet not have a dram of true godliness in them. Had not these seducers been seemingly godly, they had never been admitted by the church; and had they not been really ungodly, they had never been by the Spirit of God called so. Ungodliness is a close, a secret evil; it may creep into our profession, participation in ordinances, and church communion, undiscerned. An ungodly heart may be in a glistering professor, even in those who have a form of godliness, 2 Tim. iii. 5. Judas, Simon Magus, the Corinthian teachers, were not without their estimation from men for piety, nor without detestation from God for hypocrisy. Christians should not, like some tradesmen, live altogether upon credit. What does a good name help a rotten heart? How poor an advantage to a dying man is it for one to come and say, Sir, I am glad to see you well! Truth of grace is alone beyond the reach of hypocrites. Shape may be pictured, life cannot. The magicians imitated Moses, till God discovered his own finger in the miracles. True godliness is God's handiwork: of this the most specious pretender falls short. O Christian, put not off the soul alone with shadows. Labour to be what thou seemest, and then seem to be what thou art.

Obs. 2. Ungodliness is the root of all lewd, irregular, and licentious practices. The apostle places the ungodliness of seducers in the forefront of all that wickedness wherewith he charges them. A man who has no care of God's honour, will make no conscience of any sin. Where God is not served, man will not be obeyed. Abraham rightly collected, that they who feared not God, would not fear to take away his life, Gen. xx. 11. "By the fear of God men depart from evil," Prov. xvi. 6; viii. 13. Religion in the heart is the best means to order the hand. Education, exigence of condition, resolutions, human laws, shame, fear, may for a while curb, but they cannot change a sinner; they may cloak, not cure sin; they may work a palliative, not an eradicative cure. All they can do, till the heart be changed, is but to sew a piece of new cloth to an old garment, new expressions, professions, to an old disposition, which will but make the rent the greater. How imprudent are those parents, who expect obedience to themselves from their children, who are ever suffered to be disobedient to God! How little policy do those magistrates express, who only care to make men subjects to them, willingly suffering them to be rebels to God! I confess, Satan loves to lay the brats of wars, treason, and rebellion, &c. at the door of religion. But as truly may politicians utter those words as ever they were uttered, O religion, if thou hadst been here our nation had not died. And if that death may be attributed to the absence of religion, how little are people beholden to them, who hinder it from coming to the nation to cure it!

Obs. 3. Eminent, if mere, profession will end in eminent profaneness. A fiery hypocrite will grow from being lukewarm in religion, to be stone-cold in irreligion. The seeming piety and glorious appearances of these seducers in advancing Christ, grace, and Christian liberty, was soon followed with the utter rejection of godliness. What profane, and even godless persons, and how purely neglectful of all Divine worship, did they prove! The higher the building is which wants a foundation, the greater will be its fall. No water is so cold as that which after greatest heat grows cold. A tradesman who breaks, having traded much, and been trusted much, makes a great noise when he breaks. The hypocrite who flies the highest pitch of religion, is most bruised with falls into profaneness. Are there any who so much scorn the ministry of the word, and all holy duties, nay, who so much deny and profess they can live above ordinances, as they who have heretofore been the most forward to run after them, though, alas! unfruitful under them when they did so? Who can with tearless eyes or a sorrowless heart observe, that many who have given golden hopes in their youth for godliness, and whose holy education was followed for a while with most pious appearances, should afterwards turn such loose libertines, so atheistical and irreligious, as if now they studied only to make up their former restraint and forbearance with a greater profuseness in all ungodliness? How much better therefore is a drop of sincerity than a sea of appearing sanctity! A land-flood which rolls and swells to-day will be down and gone, when the fountain will have enough and to spare. Study therefore, O Christian, to lay the foundation deep, before thou raisest the building high. And study first to get into Jesus Christ by a humble diffidence of thyself, and fiduciary recumbence upon him, and to evidence it by the thorough work and practice of mortification, and a hearty love to holiness.

Obs. 4. Every one should tremble to be branded deservedly with this black mark of ungodliness, which the apostle here sets upon the worst of men. To this end consider, (1.) Ungodliness crosses the end of our election. We are "chosen before the foundation of the world, that we should be holy," Eph. i. 4. Godliness is the eternal design which God had upon every one set apart for happiness. (2.) It opposes the end of Christ in redeeming us; which was, that we should be holy and without blemish, Eph. v. 27; Luke i. 75, and be presented holy and unblamable in his sight, Col. i. 22: wherever Christ justifies, he renews the ungodly. (3.) It is opposite to our profession. The name atheist we all disclaim. We have renounced ungodliness in our baptism, wherein we took an oath of allegiance and fealty to God; and which is not a sacrament of obsignation of the benefits, unless of obligation to the godliness of a Christian. We have taken God for our God, who is a holy God, and whom we profess to follow. (4.) It is opposite to the end of God's discovering his gospel, which hath appeared, to teach us that we should deny ungodliness, Tit. ii. 11, 12. "Let me go," said the angel to Jacob, "for the day breaketh;" much more should Christians bid farewell to all ungodliness, the day of the gospel so gloriously appearing. (5.) It opposes the acceptance of all our persons and services. God sets apart only him that is godly for himself, Psal. iv. 3: godly men alone are his treasure, his portion, his jewels: an ungodly man, though never so rich and honourable, is but a vile person. Morality without piety is but glistering iniquity. "The sacrifice of the wicked is an abomination to the Lord," Prov. xv. 8; Mal. i. 10. God looks to the person before the gift. Holy and acceptable are put together, Rom. xii. 1. Without godliness our performances are provocations. (6.) It opposes our comfortable enjoyment of every benefit. All the comforts of ungodly men are curses. Godliness makes loss to be gain; ungodliness makes gain to be loss, 1 Tim. vi. 6. It matters not what things we enjoy, but what hearts we have in enjoying them. Unto the defiled nothing is pure, Tit. i. 15. An ungodly man taints every thing which he touches. (7.) Ungodliness opposes our eternal blessedness; nothing but godliness stands in stead in the great day; then shall we fully discern "between him that serveth God, and him that serveth him not," Mal. iii. 18. "Seeing these things shall be dissolved, what manner of persons ought we to be in all holy conversation and godliness?" 2 Pet. iii. 11. An ungodly man is as unsuitable to the work as he is unworthy of the wages of heaven. If you expect glory, exercise, train up yourselves to godliness, 1 Tim. iv. 7, γύμναζε; labour to be expert therein, by believing that the promises of God in Christ shall be made good, by observing his presence in all your actions, by acknowledging his providence over all events, by casting from you whatever offends him, by taking upon you the yoke of obedience active and passive, doing and undergoing his pleasure cheerfully; and lastly, by fervent prayer for the blessings which you want, and sincere thankfulness for those which you enjoy.

This for the first and more general expression of the impiety of these seducers, the apostle saith they were "ungodly."

II. The apostle shows wherein their ungodliness appeared; and that, 1. In their abusing the grace of God, in these words, "Turning the grace of our God into lasciviousness."

In the words we may consider, 1. What these seducers abused, or their enjoyment, "the grace of our God." 2. How they abused it, or their misimprovement of that enjoyment, they turned it "into lasciviousness."

In their enjoyment we may take notice, 1. Of the nature of their enjoyment, "grace." 2. Of the owner thereof, "God;" with the propriety which the faithful have in him, he being called "our God."

1. Of the kind or nature of that enjoyment which these seducers abused, it was "grace."

Two things I shall briefly here show by way of explication. What thing it is which the apostle here intends by the name of "grace;" and, Why that thing is so called.

1. Not much to enlarge upon this first thing. Grace in its proper notion signifies that free goodness, favour, or good will whereby one is moved to benefit another, as both the Hebrew and Greek words manifest. But it is not only taken in Scripture in that primary and proper sense, but among sundry other acceptations, for the benefits and good things themselves which of free favour and good will are bestowed; and in this sense, as it often in Scripture denotes the benefits, alms, and beneficence which we receive from man, 1 Cor. xvi. 3; 2 Cor. viii. 4, 6, 19, so in a multitude of places, the gifts and benefits freely bestowed by God; and among them, as redemption, life eternal, the gifts of sanctification, &c., so the very gospel of salvation, and the revelation of the mysteries of redemption, and the free pardon of sin through Christ, Rom. vi. 14, 15; 1 Pet. iii. 7; John i. 16. And this last way it is taken Acts xiv. 3; xx. 32, where the gospel is called the word of grace; called also "the gospel of the grace of God," Acts xx. 23; and grace itself, 2 Cor. vi. 1; Tit. ii. 11, "We beseech you that ye receive not the grace of God in vain." And, "The grace of God hath appeared." In this last signification I take it in this place; wherein what the apostle had called the faith in the foregoing verse, for which the Christians should contend, he calls the grace in this, which seducers abused and opposed.

2. Why is the doctrine of the gospel called by the name of grace?

(1.) Because it is a gift of grace, and it was only God's free good will that bestowed it. These questions, Why it was ever bestowed at all? or why one age or place of the world should receive it rather than another? why God should discover the "mystery that was kept secret since the world began," Rom. xvi. 25, 26, to those who were sinners of the Gentiles, who served dumb idols? why God should be found of them who sought him not, and made manifest unto them who asked not after him? Isa. lxv. 1, can only be answered by that reason which Christ gives of God's hiding these things from the wise and prudent, and revealing them to babes: even so, Father, because it seemed good in thy sight, Matt. xi. 25, 26.

(2.) Because the subject-matter of the gospel, even all the benefits discovered in it, flowed merely from free grace, whether blessings without us or within us. Without us, election is the election of grace, and "according to the good pleasure of his will," Eph. i. 5: our vocation was "according to grace," 2 Tim. i. 9. Regeneration was of "God's own will," James i. 18. Faith the "gift of God," Phil. i. 29. Justification is "freely by his grace," Rom. iii. 24. And a "free gift," Rom. v. 15, 18. "Forgiveness of our sins according to the riches of grace," Eph. i. 7. "Eternal life is the gift of God," Rom. vi. 23. Even the life of glory is the grace of life, 1 Pet. iii. 7. Christ himself was a token of free love sent to mankind. And as his whole work was to love, so his whole love was free. The portion which he expects is nothing but poverty. Would we purchase any benefit of him, we must be sure to leave our money behind us, Isa. lv. 1. There is not one soul that ever he loved, but was poor and empty, sick and impotent, unamiable and filthy, regardless of him and ignorant, opposite to him and unkind, and often unfaithful to him and disloyal. And may not the gospel which discovers this goodness well be called grace?

(3.) As the gospel discovers and reveals, so it instrumentally imparts and bestows, these benefits of free grace. The gospel is not only light to discover them, but an invitation to accept them; not only a story, but a testament. The language of the gospel is, "Come, for all things are now ready," Luke xiv. 17. Nor has it only an inviting, but a prevailing voice with some. It is made powerful (Rom. i. 16) to overcome the most delaying, disobedient sinner, by him who does not only ordain, but accompany it, Acts vi. 7; 2 Thess. i. 8. This grace brings salvation, Tit. ii. 12; it brings it to us, not to look upon, but to take.

Obs. 1. What a happy difference there is between the law and the gospel! The law affords not a drop of grace; it bestows nothing freely. The language of the law is, Do thou, and live; if not, die; no work, no wages: but in the gospel, the yoke of personal obedience is translated from believers to their Surety; there is nothing for them to pay; all that they have to do, is to hunger and feed. Their happiness is free in respect of themselves, though costly to Christ, who by his merits purchases for them whatever they would obtain, and by his Spirit works in them whatever he requires.

Obs. 2. How shall we escape, if we neglect the salvation which the gospel of grace brings! If they are unexcusable who pay not their own debts under the law, what are they who will not do so much as accept of free pardon and a Surety under the gospel! Gospel grace neglected is the great condemnation of the world. How mindful should we be of the apostle's counsel, "Receive not the grace of God in vain!" 2 Cor. vi. 1; not "only in word, but in power," 1 Cor. iv. 20; as it is a quickening spirit, or spirit and life, not begetting only a form of profession, but as changing and transforming into the image of God, and altering the inward disposition of the heart, 2 Cor. iii. 6, 18. If the grace of the gospel make a stop at restraining, it only advantages men, *ut mitius ardeant,* not to save them.

Obs. 3. The sin and folly of those is great, who, though poor, are yet so proud that they submit not themselves to the freeness of the gospel; who will not feed upon the supper of evangelical benefits, unless they may pay the reckoning; who mix at least their own merits with Christ's, expecting justification for their own obedience. Alas, what is our rectitude, but crookedness! what our righteousnesses, but filthy rags! How fond an undertaking is it to go "about to establish our own righteousness!" Rom. x. 3; what is it but to endeavour ἰδίαν δικαιοσύνην στῆσαι. to make a dead carcass to stand alone? How just is the issue, that rich ones should be sent empty from the supper! A proud heart can no more be filled with evangelical grace, than can a vessel with water poured upon its convex outside. It is better to be a humble sinner than a proud justiciary.

Obs. 4. How cheerful, free, and forward should all their service be who partake of the grace of the gospel! If God have removed the insupportable yoke of legal satisfaction, how Jugum Christi non deterit, sed willingly should we take upon us the honestat colla. easy yoke of evangelical obedience! Bern. Though saints be exempted from bondage, yet not from service. Christians, though they serve not God by the compulsive power of the law, yet they ought by virtue of the Spirit renewing the soul. Their spirits should be free and willing, even when strength and power fail them. They should delight to do the will of God, Psal. cx. 3; xl. 8. If gospel grace be free, then it is most unsuitable that gospel service should be forced. The evangelical bond to obedience is strong, though it be silken.

Obs. 5. Every one should covet to be interested in the benefits of the gospel. They are freely bestowed. It is easy to know a house where alms are freely distributed, by the crowding of beggars: when money is freely thrown about the streets at the king's coronation, how do the poor thrust and tread one upon another! There is no such crowding about a tradesman's shop: why? here poor people must pay for what they have. But, alas, men act quite contrary in a spiritual respect, they throng after the world, which makes them pay for what they have dearly, and neglect Christ, who offers all they want freely. Why is it that the kingdom of heaven suffers not more violence? The world is not bread, and yet it requires money; Christ is bread, and requires nothing but a stomach! Pity those who, for lying vanities, forsake their own mercy. Call others to partake of this grace with thee; eat not thy morsel alone. Say, as those lepers did, This is a day of good tidings, and we hold our peace. Hast thou received this grace? wish all men were like to thee, thy sins only excepted. When beggars have fared well at a rich man's door, they go away, and by telling it, send others: tell to others how free a housekeeper thy God is; so free that he most delights in comers and company.

This for the kind or nature of the enjoyment which these seducers abused, "grace."

2. The owner thereof, whose grace it was, called here by the apostle "our God."

In the explication, I shall briefly show two things. What it is for God to be "our God," or what these words "our God" import; and, Why the apostle here mentioning the grace abused by seducers, calls it not simply the grace of God, but "the grace of our God."

(1.) What it is for God to be "our God." In this three things deserve a large explication, which I (to avoid tediousness) shall but touch. 1. Wherein the the nature of this propriety consists, or what kind of propriety it is. 2. What there is of God in which the faithful have an interest and propriety. 3. How suitable and beneficial a good this God is to those who have this interest and propriety in him.

[1.] For the nature of this propriety in God. God may be said to be ours, and we may be said to have a propriety in him, by a threefold right. 1. By a right of creation; and thus he is the God of heathens, of devils, of all creatures; they being all the work of his hands, having from him life, being, and motion, Acts xiv. 17, 18; xvii. 28, 29. 2. By a right of external profession, or federal sanctity; and thus God is often called the God of Israel; and in respect of this, the Jews are said to be the children of the kingdom. 3. By peculiar grace and saving interest through Christ; and thus only believers who are really united to Christ by faith have a propriety in him, with whom God hath covenanted that he will be their reconciled Friend and Father, pardoning their sin by Christ, putting his law into their inward parts, and writing it in their hearts, that he will be their God, and that they shall be his people, Jer. xxxi. 31.

[2.] For the second; the faithful have a propriety in all of God they can want or wish. Particularly, 1. In all the three Persons of the Godhead. The Father accepts them for his in his Beloved, Eph. i. 6; nay, he gave them to Christ, John xvii. 11, and chose them "before the foundation of the world," Eph. i. 4. The Father of Christ is their Father, to provide for, pardon, and govern them, and to afford them all things which pertain to life and godliness. The Son is their Mediator, 1 Tim. ii. 5, their Head, Col. i. 18, their Brother, Rom. viii. 17, their Husband, 2 Cor. xi. 2; they are his by the Spirit, and he theirs by faith; he delivers them from all the evil they fear; he obtains for them all the good they desire. The Holy Ghost is theirs, to direct and teach them, to purify and cleanse them, to furnish and adorn them, to support and comfort them, John xiv. 16. 2. They have a propriety in the attributes of God. In his omniscience, he knowing whatsoever they want or hurts them. In his wisdom, to teach and guide them. In his power, to protect and defend them. In his love, to delight in, pity, and provide for them. In his righteousness, to clear and judge their cause, Psal. iv. 1. In his all-sufficiency, to supply and furnish them with all needful blessings, according to every want, Psal. lxxxiv. 11; xxiii. 1; Rom. viii. 32. One God answers to all exigences. 3. They have a propriety in his promises, "great and precious promises," 2 Pet. i. 4, wherein all they want, and infinitely more than they can conceive or desire, is assured to them; grace, glory, mercies for the throne and the footstool; nay, God himself, in whom all blessings are summed up and centred; all being as certain as if already performed; and for the accomplishment whereof they have God's oath, wherein he has, as I may say, pawned his very being; and the seal of the blood of Christ, that being the blood of the covenant, and he the Mediator of the covenant, in whom all the promises are yea and Amen, Heb. vi. 17; xii. 24; 2 Cor. i. 20. 4. They have a propriety in the providences of God, whereby whatsoever may hurt them is withheld from them; not a hair of their head suffered to perish, Matt. x. 30; and they, though poor, persecuted, sick, dying, yet ever safe; nay, whereby whatever befalls them shall be beneficial to them; every stone thrown at them made a precious stone; every twig of every rod sanctified; the issue of every dispensation made sweet and beautiful. In a word, whereby they are enabled to be, and do, and bear whatever God either commands or imposes; and they relieved with whatever may do or make them good.

[3.] For the third; how suitable and beneficial a good God is to those who have a propriety in him! 1. He is a spiritual good, John iv. 24: drossy and earthy comforts suit not with a spiritual soul; nor are they such food as the soul loves. Thy soul is no fitter for gold to be put into it, than are thy bags to have grace put into them. 2. He is a living good. The creature is a dead, lifeless, lumpish, inactive thing; it may be said of it as it is of an idol, It must be borne, because it cannot go, Jer. x. 5—7. We rather uphold it than it upholds us. Like Baal, it is not able to plead for itself. It helps us not in distress of conscience, or in the day of wrath. Like Absalom's mule, it goes from under us, and leaves us in our distresses; but God relieves the soul, and affords strengthening consolation, Heb. vi. 18. He is a present help in the needful time of trouble; and ever either preserves us from or sustains in adversity. 3. He is an absolute, independent good, Isa. lix. 16. He is self-sufficient. If he be hungry, he will not tell thee, Psal. l. 12. He depends no more upon the creature than the fountain upon the stream. He is not hindered from helping us by any deficiencies of the creature. He has sometimes complained that he has had too many, never that he has had too few to deliver by. How safe is it to depend upon Him who depends upon none! 4. He is an unmixed good, and has nothing in him but goodness. He is an ocean of sweetness, without a drop of gall. He is altogether lovely, and a beauty without any shadow, Cant. v. 16. There is nothing in him that the soul could spare, or wish were absent. Every creature is a bitter-sweet, and so poor a comfort, that its bitterness is necessary to the very being of its sweetness; for had it not a bitterness, its sweetness would be fulsome: but though God is altogether delightful, yet he never cloys; but the more he is enjoyed, the more he pleaseth the enjoyer. 5. He is a never-failing good, Luke xii. 33; a fountain which the hottest summer dries not, a treasure never emptied, one whose perfections never leave himself, and one who never leaves any that ever truly enjoyed him. 6. Lastly, He is a most full good, and that in two respects. (1.) In respect of the comprehensiveness, or the fulness of the object. In one God is every thing. He is a bundle of all perfections. All the dispersed excellencies in the world are assembled in him. When he saith, "I will be thy God," there is as much said as can be said. And as we can have nothing better than God, so of good we can have nothing more. (2.) He is a full good in regard of contentment, or fulness of the subject: whoever has an interest in him, has that ἀφθονίαν, that abundant plenty, which, observed, will not suffer him to envy the most prosperous sinner. God can fill the vast, capacious soul, like those waterpots of Galilee, up to the very brim. He has enough for himself, and needs must he then have enough for us. The water which can fill the sea, can much more fill a cup. "My people shall be satisfied with my goodness, saith the Lord," Jer. xxxi. 14. "My God shall supply all your need," Phil. iv. 19. The tongue, the wish, the conception, all fall short of God. In heaven, though we shall comprehend as much as we want, yet not so much as he is.

(2.) The second branch of explication was, Why the apostle, here mentioning the grace abused by these seducers, calls it "the grace of our God." This he does to make the fact of these seducers in abusing it the more odious among these Christians. Dishonour offered to God deeply affects the soul of one who has a propriety in God. Our own child, servant, house, nay, beast, or a poorer thing, if it be our own, we suffer not to be wronged; and much more does our propriety in God make every thing which dishonours him hateful to us. And that upon two grounds: 1. As he is our God who loves us, takes us into covenant, and owns us. Holy ingenuity will constrain us to love that grace which saved us, that God who loved us freely when we were unlovely, who loved us abundantly, bestowing his very self, and in himself all things, and who continues thus to love us eternally. 2. As he is our God whom we have taken by covenant to be ours, to love and serve for ever. Now it is both against fidelity and inbred generosity, to suffer that thing to be abused which we have undertaken to serve. This neither agrees with honesty nor honour; it is not only a sin, but a shame. Hardly is any servant so low-spirited as to think it consistent with his credit to serve an abused, a disgraced master; but especially are all people tender of the honour of the God whom they have undertaken to serve. The Philistines tread not on the threshold upon which their god Dagon fell. They who have taken God for their own, cannot endure that his glory should suffer from themselves or others.

Obs. 1. Great is their folly and misery who content themselves in a common propriety and interest in God. It is a false consequence, to say, because God made thee, or because thou art reckoned to belong to God by common and visible profession, that therefore God will save thee, Isa. xxvii. 11. A man is not contented to be the king's subject, he desires to be his favourite. They who have not God for their God in Christ, have him so for their God, as they have him also for their enemy. Men think it not enough to have an opinionative, esteemed, unless they have also a real, a legal, propriety in their lands; and why should they not also labour to have their interest in God without cracks and flaws?

Obs. 2. Sin is the greatest evil in the world. It parts between us and the greatest good. "Your iniquities have separated between you and your God," Isa. lix. 2. We may be poor, persecuted, disgraced, and yet have God for ours; but living in the love of any sin, we cannot. There is more evil in a drop of sin, than in a sea of suffering.

Obs. 3. They who have God for theirs, may contentedly want all other comforts; they have enough besides. They may answer Satan when he offers worldly glory and preferments, as that woman did the prophet, I live among mine own people, 2 Kings iv. 13. I have enough: "The Lord is my shepherd; I shall not want," Psal. xxiii. 1. When a saint see all worldly vanities, he may say, How many things are there that I want not! Their names I will not take up into my lips, saith David; "the Lord is my portion," Psal. xvi. 4, 5. The people of God are as some countries, which can live of themselves without being beholden to others. A saint, like a rich man, may spare and spend for a good conscience as much in one day as a poor worldling would count his utter undoing to part with. And this is the reason why God cuts his people short of outward comforts, they have enough in having God; and never does God more delight to let out himself into the soul, than when he deprives of temporals. Joseph, when he manifested himself to his brethren, caused all to go out of the place where he did it.

Obs. 4. It is a false way of valuing one's worth by any worldly enjoyment. Gains or losses are to be estimated by enjoyment of more or less of God. The titles of substance, profits, goods, are abusively given to riches: without an interest in God, they are but shadows, losses, evils. They are only full (like the sieve in the water) when they are enjoyed in God; empty, when without him.

Obs. 5. The true reason of all the wrangling and unquietness of the soul with and in men, is because their soul has no real interest in God. Lord, thou hast made us for thee, and we are unquiet till we come to thee! Great is their folly, who, like the child that cries for want of sleep, and yet will not go to bed, cannot be quiet without God, and yet are most unwilling to have him. If men loved themselves in loving God, man might hate, and troubles approach, but not hurt, not disquiet them.

Obs. 6. It should be the grand design of all those who are without God, to obtain this propriety in him. To this end, (1.) Be sensible that you are by nature indigent, Godless creatures, broken off from God by the breach of the first covenant, and without God, hating and hated of God, Eph. ii. 12; alienated from his life, and from his love, Eph. iv. 18; children both of disobedience and wrath, Eph. ii. 1, 2. Judge yourselves for your former rebellion and unfaithfulness in breaking covenant, unworthy that ever God should own you, and that you stand at his mercy, either to be your God or your Judge. (2.) Make a Friend, who may make up the former breach and disunion between God and you. No readmission is to be expected without a Mediator. God will not be yours, if Christ be none of yours. A Christless soul is a Godless soul; an absolute God is a consuming fire. God will never be satisfied but by the mediation of a sacrifice; nor can we ever be taken into covenant without the blood of the covenant, Exod. xxiv. 8; Psal. l. 5. The blood of Christ is the only cement of reuniting and knitting God and man together. (3.) Break your league with sin. Expect not a propriety in God, if you continue to love that which first disunited you from him. God and sin draw contrary ways; there can be no accommodation between them, Matt. vi. 24. If God be ours, sin must be none of ours. They are like two balances, if one goes up, the other goes down. A man cannot look heavenward and earthward at the same time. God may take many of us for his, we can take only him for ours. (4.) Let the propriety be mutual. Expect not that God should be engaged to you, and that you should be loose from God. "Yield yourselves to the Lord," serve him, and give the hand to him, 2 Chron. xxx. 8. When he makes the strictest commands, be as willing to say, Lord, we are thine; as to say, when he makes the sweetest promises, Lord, thou art ours, Cant. vi. 3. Receive from him the law of your life. Let him make the conditions of the covenant and the articles of agreement after his own mind. Never startle at the proposal of any service. Consecrate, resign yourselves to him, and quit any interest in yourselves, 1 Cor. vi. 20. (5.) Observe his condescending willingness to become yours. How he beseecheth us to accept him for our God; and woos us, though he wants us not: he makes the first motion to every soul. He that cometh to him he will in no wise cast out, John vi. 37. All sight of sin which makes the soul distrust God's promise, is a sinful sight of sin. Say, Lord, though I am unworthy to be beloved, yet thou art worthy to be believed. Take hold of the covenant, and commit thy soul to God's offer; verily thou shalt not be rejected, Isa. lvi. 6.

Obs. 7. They who have a propriety in God should express and show it. And that, (1.) By depending upon him for supplies in all straits, Psal. xxxvii. 5, 7. He who has given himself, what can be withhold? he who has given a kingdom will not deny a staff to walk thither. Let them fear want who have not a God for their portion. Faith fears no famine. In one God is every thing. All who have this God, shall have what they want, if not what they would, Psal. lxxxiv. 11. (2.) By promoting the honour and service due to him. Propriety is the foundation of true obedience. All that we are, all that we do, all that we have should be his. His honour we should propagate, and make it our only plot and business to make him great, and to leaven the world with holy obedience to him. His honour we should preserve, enduring nothing that eclipses or impairs it. He who toucheth that should touch the apple of our eye. The reproaches of them that reproach him we should look upon as falling upon ourselves; mourning for that dishonour offered to him which we cannot redress, and hating all that unholiness in the world which we cannot help, Psal. lxix. 9.

This for the enjoyment under which these seducers lived, viz. "the grace of our God." The second particular, their misimprovement thereof, follows; they turned it "into lasciviousness."

Three things are considerable by way of explication: What the apostle here intends by lasciviousness; How the grace of God was turned into lasciviousness; and, Wherein appears the sinfulness of "turning the grace of God into lasciviousness."

1. For the first. Ἀσέλγεια, lasciviousness, is derived from the particle α and σέλγη, Selge; which Selge was a city between Galatia and Cappadocia, whose inhabitants, say some, were most modest and temperate; and these make α to be a note of privation of modesty and temperance, and importing the lasciviousness of these seducers by their being unlike the people of Selge, even destitute and void of all modesty and temperance. Others, upon better ground, say, that this Selge was a most dissolute and lascivious place, where the inhabitants were given to all manner of luxury and unclean profuseness; and these make α to be intensive, dilating and increasing the sense, and so importing the lasciviousness of these seducers by their being most like the people of Selge, namely, violent and unbridled in all lust and filthiness. The word, as all agree, denotes a monstrous open profusion, and pouring out, and spending oneself without measure, in lasciviousness and obscene lustful practices: it is translated, Rom. xiii. 13, wantonness, and it is joined with rioting, drunkenness, chambering. And 1 Pet. iv. 3, with lusts, excess of wine, revellings, banquetings.

Cives istius oppidi ut vires amissas recuperarent, nervosque debilitatos confirmarent, invenerunt oleum nervis utile, quod de nomine illorum Veteres appellaverunt Selgiticum: cujus meminit Plinius, l. 15. Nat. Hist. c. 7.

Ἀσελγέστεροι τῶν ὄνων. Lucian.

This word lasciviousness is, 2 Cor. xii. 21, joined with uncleanness and fornication. And in Gal. v. 19, with adultery, fornication, uncleanness. And Eph. iv. 19, this lasciviousness is expounded by the working of all uncleanness with greediness. And 2 Pet. ii. 7, the word here translated lasciviousness is put for all the filthiness of Sodom. Lot was vexed with the filthy, or lascivious, conversation of the wicked. And that apostle, ver. 18, speaking of seducers, (the same kind of men of which Jude here speaks,) mentions this lasciviousness as the bait with which they baited their hook of error. They allure, saith he, those who were clean, &c., through wantonness, or lasciviousness; which was that encouragement which they gave to people to exercise carnal lusts, under the pretence of Christian liberty. By comparing these places, it is conceived that this sin of lasciviousness properly imports all kind of carnal defilements and fleshly pollutions, as also all outward obscenity and filthiness expressed in men's behaviour, either by shameless words or gestures; and denotes the prosecution of these unclean courses with impudence, petulance, defence, violence, and contempt of all opposition or observation from men. It is a manifest wickedness. They who are guilty of it do not blush at it: they declare their sin as Sodom, Isa. iii. 9: they are not like the harlot, that wipes her lips; but like Absalom, that spreads his incestuous pallet on the roof, and calls the sun a blushing witness to his filthiness. They glory in their shame. Their hand is the organ of wickedness, and their mouth the trumpet: they outsin all shame; they crown uncleanness with garlands of honour. Their sin abandons secrecy; and admonition to it is as a pouring of oil down the chimney. Thus Rev. ii. 14, some there were who taught fornication. Simon Magus taught that women might indifferently be used; the prodigious impurity of whose followers, ecclesiastical writers tell us, would astonish any sober hearer, and is such as no modest man can either write or speak without offence. The Gnostics, who arrogated that name to themselves for their pretended excellency of knowledge above all others, were called, for their filthiness, Borboriti, or the dirty, miry sect. They used all kind of uncleanness as the fruit of the grace of God. And they declared that all holy and righteous courses commanded in the law of God were antiquated, and taken away by the preaching of the grace of God. Carpocrates taught men how to speak filthily and uncleanly, and how to live lewdly. And although by lasciviousness is properly understood the open profession and ostentation of incontinency, yet must it here be taken more generally, as the following description of these seducers declares, for a licentious, profane kind of living in and liberty of sinning.

2 Cor. xii. 21, ἀκαθαρσία, πορνεία, ἀσέλγεια. Gal. v. 19, μοιχεία, πορνεία, ἀκαθαρσία, ἀσέλγεια. Eph. iv. 19, tradiderunt seipsos τῇ ἀσελγείᾳ, εἰς ἐργασίαν ἀκαθαρσίας πάσης. 2 Pet. ii. 7, ὑπὸ τῆς τῶν ἀθέσμων ἐν ἀσελγείᾳ ἀναστροφῆς. Ἀσελγὴς usurpatur pro lascivo, qui petulanter indulget libidinibus. Ἀσέλγεια, proterva lascivia. Complectitur omne genus obscœnitatis, quando procacitas verbis et gestibus interior libido proditur. Gerh. in 1 Pet. iv. 3. Perkins saith, it is an open ostentation of incontinency, in Gal. v. 19.

Simon docebat turpitudinem indifferenter utendi fœminis. Aug. de Hæres. cap. 1. Eusebius, Irenæus, Epiphanius, Augustinus, Danæus. Τὰ δὲ τούτων, &c. Τὸν πρῶτον ἐπακούσαντα ἐκπλήσσεσθαι, καὶ θαμβωθήσεσθαι, &c. Ὡς μὴ μόνον μὴ δυνατὰ εἶναι παραδοθῆναι γραφῇ ἀλλ' οὐδὲ χείλεσιν αὐτὸ μόνον ὑπερβολὴν αἰσχρουργίας, &c. Euseb. Hist. Eccl. l. 2. c. 12. Gnostici, qui a nonnullis vocati sunt Borboriti, quasi cœnosi, propter nimiam turpitudinem, &c. Aug. Ib. Menandriani omnem turpitudinem libenter amplexi sunt, tanquam gratiæ Dei erga homines fructum; bonos etiam et sanctos mores, qui lege Dei præscribuntur, per gratiæ Dei prædicationem, ut jam inutiles et vanum studium tolli et antiquari sentiebant. Aug. de Hæres.

Carpocrates docebat omnem turpem orationem, omnemque adinventionem peccati. Aug. de Hæres.

2. For the second, How grace is said to be turned into lasciviousness.

The word in the original, by which the apostle expresses this turning, is μετατιθέντες, which signifies properly, the transposing or removing of a thing from the place of its ordinary abode to some other; but it is used to denote the alteration or removal, (1.) Of persons from former opinions or practices which they have embraced; and thus the apostle tells the Galatians, Gal. i. 6, "I marvel that ye are so soon removed (μετατίθεσθε) from him that called you." And, (2.) Of things, both from their former uses and ends; and thus the apostle saith, Heb. vii. 12, μετατιθεμένης ἱερωσύνης, "the priesthood being changed," or translated, there was μετάθεσις, a translation, or change of the law; and thus Jude saith, these seducers translated or removed the grace of God from its true and appointed to a false and wrong use and end. The end and use of the doctrine of grace, and justification by faith in Christ, was the serving of God without fear, in holiness and righteousness, Luke i. 75, the denying of ungodliness and worldly lusts, and the "living soberly, righteously, and godly in this present world," Tit. ii. 12; but these seducers transposed and removed this evangelical grace from the ends and uses appointed by God, unto such as were contrived by themselves; they teaching that Christ had fulfilled the law, and freed Christians from it, that so they might have a liberty to live as they list, and be freed from the law, not only as a covenant, which cursed those who broke it, but as a

Μετατιθέντες, μεταποιοῦντες, παραποιοῦντες. (Ecum. Heb. xi. 5, Ἐνὼχ μετετέθη. Acts vii. 16, μετετέθησαν εἰς Συχέμ.

rule also, prescribing the good to be done, and the evil to be avoided.

And thus the grace of God may be said to be abused and perverted to a wrong end and use sundry ways; five especially.

[1.] When men abuse this grace of God to an empty, bare profession of it; to a resting in the mere outward show of enjoying that grace, and the benefits of the gospel; never labouring for a true and real interest in the benefits themselves; herein resembling such bondmen, who, being made free, think it enough to be accounted free, and to be out of their time, to be such as may put on their hats, and wear a gown; but never care for setting up or falling to their trades, that they may thrive. Thus there are many who only care to have a name to live, Rev. iii. 1; who "receive the grace of God in vain," 2 Cor. vi. 1; and are mere titular Christians, never really thriving in godliness, and as very slaves to sin as ever: but they who here profess vainly, shall hear God profess severely, "I never knew you; depart from me," Matt. vii. 23.

[2.] When men abuse grace to the disobeying of authority. A sin to which our natures are too prone. And it is clear by the context of 1 Pet. ii. 16, that when the apostle forbids the Christians to use their liberty as a cloak of maliciousness, he intends by maliciousness disobedience to the lawful commands of the magistrate: and this was one way whereby these seducers perverted the grace of God; namely, by despising of dominions, and speaking evil of dignities, Jude 8; as if, because Christ had taken away our thraldom to sin and Satan, he had disannulled duty to all superiors; as if grace were violated by human laws. In a word, as if, because Christ bestows a heavenly, he takes away earthly crowns. Thus the papists pervert the grace of God, who turn his grace, in giving to his church the power of the keys to open and shut heaven, into an instrument of rebellion against lawful magistrates, deposing them, and freeing subjects from their allegiance; whom they stir up to seditions and conspiracies, though obedience for conscience' sake be a Divine command, and resistance of lawful authority have a Divine commination, and that no less than damnation. Thus the Anabaptists, from the grace of the New Testament, and our freedom purchased by Christ, teach the unlawfulness of magistracy, and of obedience to it; pretending that it infringeth the liberty of our consciences, which are only subject to God; whereas the bond of conscience consists not in the particular laws of men, but in the general command of God; the conscience being bound to obey God's command of obeying magistrates.

<small>Docent, Christianum magistratus partibus omnino non posse defungi, nulliumque se in Ecclesia magistratum agnoscere quam Christum. Colloqu. Emdan. Act. 112. §1. Non licet Christianis tolerare regem hæreticum, &c. Bel. lib. 5. de Rom. Pon. c. 7.</small>

[3.] When the grace of God, in the liberty which it affords, is abused to the offence of the weak consciences of our brethren, 1 Cor. viii. 9. When we remit nothing of the extremity of that right and power we have in things of indifferent nature, to please our neighbour for his good unto edification, Rom. xiv. 19. Although we must not be the servants of men, 1 Cor. vii. 23, yet we must by love serve one another, Gal. v. 13; yea all, that by all means we may (with the apostle) win some, 1 Cor. ix. 22. We should be persuaded with the persuasion of faith that all things are lawful; and yet we should resolve for charity' sake to forbear the use of many things, if we find them inexpedient; and as well consider what is useful for others, as lawful for ourselves.

<small>Omnia libera per fidem, omnia serva per charitatem. Luth.</small>

[4.] When the grace of God is abused in the excessive, immoderate enjoyment of things in themselves lawful. When men think they are limited to no measure in the enjoyment of a lawful comfort; suppose recreation, diet, apparel, &c. As if, because the thing is lawful to be used, therefore all use of that thing is lawful; as if lawful things could not be used unlawfully. He who always goes as far as he may, sometimes goes further than he should. Satan never falls upon us so much to our disadvantage, as when he lies in ambush behind our lawful enjoyments.

[5.] When the grace of God is abused to the casting off our obedience to the law of God as a rule. When men will discharge themselves from duty to, because God discharges them from condemnation by, the law; and because grace frees from sin, therefore they will sin freely: as if because God prohibits the opinion of works, therefore he dispenses with the performance of works. That we are by nature apt scholars to learn this hellish sophistry, it is plain by Paul's supposition, that some would conclude from the doctrine of free justification by Christ, that they might continue in sin, to the end that grace might abound; and that evil might be done, that good might come of it: that there are some who are forward to teach it, is clear from Peter's description of seducers, who allure people through much wantonness, promising them liberty, 2 Pet. ii. 18, 19. Conformable to whom are, (1.) The Antinomians, who from the grace of God in mitigating the law, would infer an utter abrogation of the law; denying that it has a directive, regulating power over a believer. True it is, the law is abrogated, 1. In respect of justification; believers expecting acceptance from God, not for what they are or do, but by relying upon Christ. 2. In respect of condemnation, Christ having been made a curse for them. 3. In respect of compulsion by terror, so far as they are regenerate, there being in them a delight in the law. 4. In respect of rigid and perfect obedience; imperfect, if sincere, obedience being accepted through Christ, though by the law we are obliged to that which is perfect. 5. In respect of the irritation and increase of sin by the law, it not stirring up, but subduing corruption in believers, who partake of sanctifying grace: but yet as a rule of life it ever continues, even to believers. That the ceremonial law vanisheth, decayeth, waxeth old, is broken down, changed, disannulled, abrogated, the Scripture testifies; Phil. ii. 24, 25, λύσας and καταργήσας; Heb. vii. 12, μετάθεσις; ver. 18, ἀθέτησις; Heb. viii. 13, παλαιούμενον, and γηράσκον; but not one of these words are used concerning the moral law. And of what does the Spirit of God more frequently admonish believers, than not to refuse obedience to the law, under pretext of Christian liberty. Use not your liberty as an occasion to the flesh, Gal. v. 13, not taking a rise, as the word signifies, from your deliverance from the law, to <small>εἰς ἀφορμήν. Noli libertate abuti ad libere peccandum. Aug. Tr. 41. in Johan.</small> the satisfying of your lusts. And 1 Pet. ii. 16, Use not your liberty as a cloak of maliciousness; i. e. abuse not your liberty by grace to cover licentiousness in sin. In a word, if disobedience to the law be still a sin in the believer, the power of the law is not abolished; for there can be no sin unless it be a transgression of a law. (2.) The papists abuse the grace of God to a rejecting of the law; who from the doctrine of absolving repenting sinners, plead for a power in the pope to give licences and indulgences to the greatest of sins; who for his corban forgives sins both past and future, and sends his briefs to be left in as many countries as he pleases, for granting liberty to sin for many years to come, the price whereof is set by the Court of Faculties in Rome; which fills up the measure of Europe's sins, by exhausting Europe's revenues. How great a wantonness must this produce! Why should any rich man now care how he live or die, seeing all shall be well with him for a little money?

3. For the third, Wherein appear the sinfulness of turning this grace into lasciviousness.

(1.) It comprehends the sin of hypocrisy. Sin is the fouler for receiving a cover. To do that which is in itself evil, must needs offend God; but to do evil by appearing to do the contrary, comprehends both the sin itself which we endeavour to hide, and a sinning by endeavouring to hide it. To the sin itself is added a practical lie, by speaking in our practice that we are and do contrary to what we are or do. As God is a God of pure eyes, he hates all sin; but as he is a God that loves a pure heart, of all sins, he most hates hypocrisy. All murderers sin heinously, but none so heinously as those who employ a man's own hands to kill himself. A hypocrite labours to destroy religion by religion.

(2.) As it is hypocrisy to cover lasciviousness, so is it even heightened profaneness to cover it with the grace of God. Will no cheaper stuff than grace serve to clothe lasciviousness? The excellency of any thing adds to the fault of abusing it. To make a king's son lackey to a beggar, to make hay with the sceptre royal, to dig in a dunghill with a golden spade, to stop an oven with the robes of an emperor, are all actions of greatest unworthiness, and wild unsuitableness; but to make religion a stirrup to profaneness, and the grace of God a credit to lasciviousness, is a presumption of a higher and far more insufferable degree. This is to make God accounted a patron of impiety, and the Judge of all the earth to seem the greatest malefactor, and to profane his holy name, Ezek. xxxvi. 20.

(3.) This "turning the grace of God into lasciviousness" argues the grossest folly; it is a forsaking of our own mercy, a receiving the grace of God in vain. What is, if this be not, to neglect the great salvation; to be prodigal of blessedness; to ravel out and to wanton away the offers of Christ himself? Who would not heartily chide himself, that by toying, trifling, or unnecessary lingering in the way to the exchange, misses a bargain by which he might have gained a thousand pounds? Foolish sinner! Lasciviousness under grace is the loss of glory; and the loss of heaven can never be redeemed with the tears of hell.

(4.) Grace turned into lasciviousness is the top of all ingratitude. What greater unkindness than to be evil because God is good? If it be a sin for thee to have an evil eye against another, because God is good to him; what is it to have an evil eye against God, because he is good to thee! If it be a sin to reward a man evil for evil, what is it to return to God evil for good! To be lascivious because God is gracious, is to fight against God with his own weapons, to wound God with that arm which he has cured, Hos. vii. 15, to kill and crucify Him who has freed us from death; in a word, to make that a pillow for presumption which God appointed for an antidote against despair.

(5.) By grace to grow lascivious, is destruction even to desperate irrecoverableness. No poison is so deadly as the poison extracted out of grace. Abused mercy pleads against a sinner most persuasively. If that which was appointed for a sinner's rising and standing makes him fall, how irrecoverable must his falling be! If mercy be his foe, how should justice ever be his friend! Lamentable was the death of Zimri who was burnt by the flames of that house which was for his safety. Grace is the sweetest friend, but the sorest enemy. Lead, of itself, is very cold and cooling, but nothing so scalding, if it be thoroughly heated. The lowest place in hell is provided for those who have been lifted up nearest to heaven. Grace discovered and abused is *the* condemnation. Out of him who lavishly spends riches of grace, God will recover riches of glory. God will not lose by any.

Obs. 1. Great is our natural propenseness to grow wanton against God by his goodness. Seldom is God provoked so much by any, as by those who most deeply partake of his indulgence. It is very hard for God to smile, and for us not to be wanton. How frequently does God complain of the unkind requitals returned for his love! "Do ye so reward the Lord, O foolish people?" Deut. xxxii. 6. "Jeshurun waxed fat, and kicked;" who, because laden with fatness, therefore forsook God that made him. And Isa. i. 2, "I have nourished children, but they have rebelled against me." It is pity, as we say of fair weather, that the goodness of God should do any hurt; but we are commonly not more unsubmissive under corrections, than wanton under comforts. God's severity restrains from that impiety which his indulgence draws forth, by meeting with a sensual heart that turns the favours of God into the fuel of lust. It is much easier to walk steadily in a path of deep dirt, than of slippery ice. How just, nay, how good is God to abridge us of that comfort, either inward or outward, which we abuse; to turn us, like sheep, into short pasture, if there we thrive best; and rather to deny us mercies in mercy, than to bestow them in wrath!

Obs. 2. The best and choicest of outward administrations cannot better a bad heart. Even grace may be received in vain. The best preaching and preachers in the world have not seldom been sent to a gainsaying people, Rom. x. 21. Neither Moses and the prophets, nor one raised from the dead, Luke xvi. 31, nay, nor the preaching of Christ himself, can of themselves work upon the heart. Moral suasion comes far short of effectual grace; and the word of grace much differs from the grace of the word. Warm clothes and strong waters cannot fetch life into a dead man. The most plentiful showers leave the heath unfruitful. Nature, after all imaginable improvements, is still but nature till supernaturally renewed. How happy were we, if men would attribute the unreformedness of the times under the gospel of grace, more to the strength of their own lusts than the weakness of the ministers' labours; and if, instead of glorying, I had almost said of placing religion, in the parts of ministers, they would humbly and ardently seek God for that blessing, without which, the fattest ordinances devoured, leave but lean souls.

Obs. 3. The most holy and happy enjoyments are not without their snares. There is danger in enjoying the best things, even the grace of God. Men ordinarily conceive that there is danger in wanting the ordinances, in sinning, in being in sinful company, and using worldly comforts; but they consider not that even their graces, their good works, their comforts, every ordinance and duty, have their snares accompanying them. Our very graces may occasion us to be proud, and our very comforts to be secure. Luther was wont to advise men to take heed of their good works. There are no services so holy but Satan creeps into them, and when he cannot hinder the external, he endeavours to spoil the spiritual performance of them. He labours to wind himself even into paradise, and loves

Diabolus surgit armis quibus dejicitur. Cave non tantum ab operibus malis, sed etiam a bonis. Luth.

to stand among the sons of God. How oft does he show men the beautiful buildings of their late performances to a worse end than the disciples did Christ the buildings of the temple! And how rare is it to find that Christian, who by self-debasing leaves not, as it were, a stone upon a stone which he casts not down by having low thoughts of high services! Thou must not only keep thy foot from entering into places of vanity, but also keep thy foot when thou enterest into the house of God, Eccl. v. 1; not only take heed that thou neglectest not hearing, but also take heed how thou hearest. How oft have the servants of God been humble and hungry in the want of those tokens of grace, under the enjoying of which they have been proud, unprofitable, and, the sin of these seducers being natural, almost lascivious!

Obs. 4. An unholy heart sucks poison out of the sweetest and holiest enjoyments. Even the grace of God he abuses to his own perdition. "Unto them who are defiled and unbelieving is nothing pure," Tit. i. 15. They taint every thing they touch. Their best services are "abomination to the Lord," Prov. xv. 8; xxviii. 9. Their prayers are turned into sin. The word is to them the savour of death, and the grace of God pernicious. The sacraments are poison and damnation; Christ is a stumbling-stone. Their table snares to them; their prosperity slays them. Whatever we have, till Christ be ours, cannot be enjoyed profitably: the guilt of the person must be removed, before the comfort of the gift can be enjoyed. Out of Christ, all comforts are but like a funeral banquet, or the prison provisions of him who is fed against his execution. And a sinner is as far from returning any enjoyment by love to God, as he is from receiving it in love from God. His heart is the heart of an enemy, even under the dispensations of grace. And what are all blessings, till the heart be changed, but furniture to oppose God, and fuel to increase sin? O Christian, instead of boasting how good thy enjoyments are in themselves, labour to find them good to thee. It matters not what the things are which thou receivest, but what thou art who dost receive them. The same promise which purifies a saint, through thy sin pollutes thee. The same breath which warms him cools thee; he being near, thou far, from Him that breathes. Till grace savingly work upon thee, thou art but a wanton under grace.

Obs. 5. Corrupt nature can cast even upon foul and lascivious courses the cloak and colour of a religious pretext. The murderous contrivances of Absalom and Jezebel, 1 Kings xxi. 13, the disobedience of Saul, 1 Sam. xv., the devouring of widows' houses, Matt. xxiii. 14, the maliciousness spoken of by Peter, 1 Pet. ii. 16, had their several cloaks and covers. The unloveliness of lusts in themselves, and the love of sinners to them, put sinners upon this covering of them: by reason of the former, this covering is required; by reason of the latter, it is contrived. But of this more before.

Obs. 6. God is gracious even unto them who abuse his grace. He affords the means and offers of it to them who turn it into lasciviousness. He holds the candle to them who will not work by, but wanton away the light. He calls men though they will not hear, and woos them who will not be entreated. Certainly, God does not only show himself a God in powerful working, but even in patient waiting upon the wicked; none but a God could do either. O sinner, how inexcusable wilt thou be in that great day, when God shall say, "What could I have done more?" Isa. v. 4; or how couldst thou desire me to wait longer for thy good? Certainly, thine own conscience shall be God's deputy to condemn thee. If thou shalt give an account for every idle word which thou thyself hast spoken, how much more for every unprofitable word which thou hast made God speak to thee! For the Lord's sake, Christians, take heed of receiving the grace of God in vain. And how should this goodness of God put us, especially ministers, upon imitating him! though sinners be wantons under grace, yet let not us be weary of dispensing it. Let us wait, if peradventure at any time God may give sinners repentance, 2 Tim. ii. 25. Ministers are spiritual fishers; and fishing, we know, is a tedious work to him who has no patience. The catching of one soul will make amends for all our waiting. Our patience cannot be so much abused as is God's.

Obs. 7. The doctrine of grace is warily to be handled by ministers. It is hard to set up Christ and grace, and not to be thought to destroy the law. Christian liberty is to be propounded as giving no allowance to libertinism. Satan has in no one point more drawn teachers to extremes. Because he could not keep them in popery, by the doctrine of satisfying the law as a covenant, he labours to drive them to Antinomianism, by the doctrine of casting off the law as a rule; because they have rejected the merit of works, he labours to make them cast off the obedience of works. But the man of God should observe the methods of the devil. The apostle Paul having at large proved the doctrine of free justification by Christ, Rom. v. 1, 2, subjoins, and that twice in one chapter, Rom. vi. 1, 15, a most vehement denial, by way of interrogation, of any liberty to sin by grace; "Shall we continue in sin, that grace may abound?" and, "Shall we sin, because we are not under the law, but under grace?" The like he had expressed before, chap. iii. 31, "Do we then make void the law through faith?" To all which he answers with a $\mu\grave{\eta}$ $\gamma\acute{\epsilon}\nu o\iota\tau o$, God forbid, words of defiance and detestation. What though ministers, for their preaching holiness of life, be represented as those who preach not Christ? And what though their names be crucified between the slanders of the papists and Antinomians; the former calling them libertines, for defending the doctrine of justification by Christ; and the latter legalists, for urging the law as a rule? yet let them hold fast the faithful word against both, Tit. i. 9; and remember, that as Jesus is to be preached in opposition to the former, so is Christ as an anointed King in opposition to the latter; and that, as there was a resurrection of the body of their crucified Master, so shall there be a resurrection of the crucified names of his servants; and that it is their duty to preach the Lord's Christ, as Simeon calls him, and not the drunkard's, the libertine's, the Antinomian's Christ.

Obs. 8. No expressions of God's grace or goodness of any kind ought to be abused and perverted to sin.

(1.) Not the temporal gifts and worldly blessings which God bestows.

[1.] We must not abuse the gifts of outward estate, whether riches or honours. (I.) Riches must not be abused to covetousness; the possessors of them should not be possessed by them. They should rather be refreshments than employments; rather used as steps to raise us towards, than stops to hinder us from heaven; rather as those things without which we cannot, than for which we do live. Only such things must be loved much which cannot be loved too much. (2.) Riches must not be abused to creature-confidence. Gold must not be our hope; we must not trust in uncertain riches, lying vanities, mammon of unrighteousness, Job xxxi. 24; 1 Tim. vi. 17. Riches never deceive us but when we trust Non fallitur qui them. The creature may be used as a nullifidit. staff to walk with, not to lean upon. (3.) Nor must they be abused to prodigality. Abundance requires sobriety. They who walk in slippery and dirty ways, had need to gird up their loins, 1 Pet. i. 13. Men should not feed upon, but only taste pleasures; like Jonathan, who did but dip the end of his rod in the honey-comb. 2. Honours must not be abused to pride. Height in place requires lowness in opinion. There is no advantage comes by having honour from men, but only the having thereby an opportunity of honouring God. It is sacrilege and idolatry to accept of honour to God's dishonour.

[2.] Nor must the gifts of the body, as strength, and beauty, be abused. 1. Strength must not be abused, (1.) To luxury. It must not be given to wine and women, Prov. vii. 26. (2.) Nor to the wronging and oppressing of the weak; nor be a weapon of any unrighteousness: nor, (3.) Be abused to boasting, Jer. ix. 23. If God withdraw his manutenency, the most strongly built body drops into the grave; and he who cannot be overcome by others, may by God be suffered to be his own executioner. 2. Beauty must not be abused to the enticement of others to sin, or the contempt of others who want it, or to a sinful mending, or rather marring, of God's wise handiwork, by paintings and spottings; as if the form bestowed by God should be reformed by the devil: or to a neglect of that true beauty of the soul, by being transformed from glory to glory by the Spirit, 2 Cor. iii. 18; as if the house were more to be regarded than the inhabitant, and the casket more to be prized than the pearl.

[3.] We must not abuse the gifts of the mind. Parts, wit, understanding, must not be employed against God, to plot against or oppose Christ and his truth. The edge of wit must not wound religion. Men must not be wise to do evil, Jer. iv. 22; or as Pharaoh, deal wisely against God's people, Exod. i. 9. Parts are never used aright but when they are engines to set up a building of glory to Christ, and when employed, as once the ass was, to exalt their Master.

(2.) But especially should we take heed of perverting spiritual favours.

[1.] How pernicious is that abuse of the decrees of God to a liberty in sin, by concluding, that if we be elected, a wicked life shall not hurt, and if we be reprobated, godliness shall not help us! Whereas, he who has elected to salvation, has likewise ordained those means whereby salvation shall be obtained, and that we shall walk in the way which leads to the same, Eph. i. 4; Rom. viii. 30.

[2.] We should fear to pervert the patience and long-suffering of God to a presumption and a delaying of repentance. This being a despising that goodness which leads to repentance, and a treasuring up wrath by God's forbearance, Eccl. viii. 11; Rom. ii. 4. God intended mercy to be prized, not despised; and He who has made a promise to repentance, has not made a promise of repentance when we please; nay, how justly may God punish the contempt of his grace with final impenitence! Heb. iii. 7, 11, 12. Repentance delayed till death is seldom unto life.

[3.] Take heed of perverting the Scriptures to countenance thy sin, either in opinion or practice. Wrest them not, 2 Pet. iii. 16, rack them not, to make them speak that which they never intended; bring not the Scriptures to thy opinion, but thy opinion to the Scripture; and every doctrine that cannot endure to look upon that sun, cast it down as spurious. Take not occasion by Scripture to be sinful in practice; Scripture was written that we should not sin, not that we should sin, 1 John ii. 1. Let not the idle person be prompted from Matt. vi. 34, "Take no thought for to-morrow," &c., to neglect his calling; nor the covetous, from 1 Tim. v. 8, "If any man provide not for his own, he is worse than an infidel," to be immoderate in following it; let him as well remember, that as he is worse than an infidel who is defective in regarding his own, so likewise that he imitates the Gentiles, who seeks after all these things more than he should, Matt. vi. 32. Take not liberty from the record of the infirmities of saints in Scripture to follow them in sin; rather let the falls of the stronger be the fear of the weaker; and the punishments which saints brought upon themselves by their sins, be the terrors of those who have nothing of sanctity in them. The falls of holy men set down in Scripture are like stakes fixed in a pond, not to call us, but to caution us.

[4.] Let us be eminently careful, lest our deliverances obtained by Christ from the curse be perverted to looseness of life, Tit. ii. 12; Luke i. 74, 75. Let that which was a pledge of his love be a spur to our duty. Though some abuse this grace to a wrong end, let us use it to a right end. To this end, 1. Admire and study the excellency of this grace, (1.) In its fulness and sufficiency: abuse not that which is so able to help thee. Who but a madman would throw away a cabinet filled with the richest pearls and purest gold? But we were not redeemed with such "corruptible things, but with the precious blood of Christ," 1 Pet. i. 18, the blood of God. (2.) In its freeness. God's bestowing it upon thee when thou didst not deserve it, when thou hadst no other merit but misery to call for it, aggravates thy sin in abusing and contemning it. Thankfulness becomes the distressed rather than scornfulness. 2. Get an experimental taste of this grace. Grace has no enemy but the ignorant. They who abuse it, show they never found benefit by it. A notional professor may be wrought to a contempt of that grace which an experimental partaker will highly esteem. Grace is never good in the soul's valuation till it be possessed. Those who love it they know not why, will soon disrespect it they know not how.

This for the first particular expression of the ungodliness of these seducers, their perverting the grace of God. The second follows, viz. their denying of the God of grace, "Denying the only Lord God, and our Lord Jesus Christ."

In the words I consider,

I. The description of his dignity whom they opposed; "The only Lord God, and our Lord Jesus Christ."

II. How they opposed him, or wherein that opposition stands; they denied him.

I. The description of his dignity.

I conceive with Beza and the best interpreters, that it is not to be understood partly of God the Father, and partly of Christ, but altogether of Christ; and that not so much because it seems to be parallel with that place of Peter, "denying the Lord that bought them," 2 Pet. ii. 1, as because in the original the prefixing of only one article to all these titles seems to require this reading; The only Lord who is God, and, or even our Lord Jesus Christ.

In this description of the dignity of Christ, that I may avoid tediousness and repetition, I shall not speak of his person and offices as they are held forth in these latter words, "Jesus Christ;" but I shall principally consider from these words, "The only Lord God,"

Our Saviour's dignity, 1. In respect of his place and authority; so he is called "the only Lord."

2. In respect of his Divine nature and essence; and so he is called "God."

1. In our Saviour's dignity in respect of his place and authority, he is "Lord," Δεσπότης; which title is set out by the peculiarity of it to himself, "The only Lord."

In the explication of Christ's dignity in this first respect, I shall briefly show in what respect he is called "Lord," and then "the only Lord."

The title given to Christ is Δεσπότης, Lord.

Δεσπότης is a word betokening a private right to rule; such as is exercised in guiding and governing a family, and most properly signifies a master, ruler, or governor over servants, who are bound to him. And such a Lord and Ruler is Christ; whether we consider, His title to this rule and dominion, or, His exercise of it.

(1.) His title to it: and a title he has to it,

[1.] By a right of creation: "All things were made by him, and without him was nothing made that was made," John i. 3. "By him were all things created," Col. i. 16. And this his creation of all things the apostle makes the argument of his dominion; "To us there is but one Lord Jesus Christ, by whom are all things, and we by him," 1 Cor. viii. 6.

[2.] Of sustentation and preservation: "By him all things consist," Col. i. 17. If he withdraw his Divine power and manutenency, they all fall into nothing. He is a Being by his own nature, but all others have their beings by their participation of essence from him, and his continuation of that action whereby he gave them being: "Upholding all things by the word of his power," Heb. i. 3.

[3.] By a right of ordination, designation, and appointment from God: "God hath made him Lord and Christ," Acts ii. 36. God hath given his elect to Christ, that he should be their Lord and Head; that they should be his possession, John xvii. 6. God hath given him power over all flesh, Psal. viii. 6; he hath the right and prerogative of the first-born, to be the Lord of all, Acts x. 36. God hath given all things into his hand, Matt. xxviii. 18; John iii. 35; he hath ordained him to be Judge, Acts x. 42; he hath appointed him over his own house, Heb. iii. 2, 6.

[4.] By a right of unction, and reception of that furnishment and fulness of the Spirit of grace, whereby he was abundantly meet to be the Head and Lord of his church. He had as much of grace as there was of grace. All fulness dwelt in him, Col. i. 19; and he received not the Spirit by measure. He had not the fulness of the vessel, but of the fountain: all others had only a measured fulness, and for themselves; Christ had a fulness of redundancy for the whole church, Luke i. 15; Acts vii. 55; 1 Cor. xii. 11; John i. 16; Isa. lxi. 1.

[5.] By a right of redemption. He is our Lord, because he has delivered us from the hands of our enemies, Luke i. 74, 75; and when we were bondslaves to sin, Satan, and death, paid our ransom. The ransomer of a bond-slave was wont to be his lord. No bondage so great as ours was, no price so great as that which Christ paid; and therefore no service so great as that which we owe, Tit. ii. 14; 1 Pet. i. 19; Rom. xiv. 7, 8; 1 Cor. vi. 20.

[6.] Lastly, by right of covenant he is the Lord of Christians. We promise to take him for our Lord, both, 1. By a marriage covenant; so we take him for our Head, Guide, Governor, and Protector. And, 2. By a covenant of hiring, and binding out ourselves to his service; not only baptismally and visibly, but by an effectual and saving resignation of ourselves to all the works of new obedience.

(2.) Christ is a Lord, if we consider his exercise of dominion: and this he puts forth,

[1.] By giving laws to bind his servants to obedience. None but Christ can give laws, and there are none of Christ's servants but receive laws from him. Only Christ can ordain laws to bind the conscience: man's laws bind not as they are man's, but as they are backed by Christ; nor can any beside Christ so give laws to which we should be obedient, as to make us obedient to the laws which he gives. Human laws can make men cover sin, but not make them cast off sin. Christ only can write his laws in the heart. Nor are there any servants of Christ, but so far as they are such, receive laws from him. Christ's servants are no sons of Belial. Every one must have a yoke upon him, though it be made by the Spirit sweet and easy. By becoming servants of Christ, we do not cast off, but only change, our yokes.

[2.] Christ exercises his dominion by appointing officers in his house, Eph. iv. 11, 12. These he furnishes with gifts suitable to their places. He makes them able ministers, 2 Cor. iii. 6, and appoints them to be his stewards, 1 Cor. iv. 1, to distribute to every one in his family their due proportion, by way of feeding and governing, Luke xii. 42. The carriage of these stewards is not arbitrary, but appointed. They are all accountable to their Lord, for and from whom they rule.

[3.] By finding his family with all necessaries for body and soul. His servants shall want no good thing, Psal. xxiii. 1; lxxxiv. 11. They shall neither pine for want, nor surfeit with abundance; they shall never have so much or so little as to make them unfit for service. Christ loves to keep them in working case. Even of outward necessaries they shall have what they want, if not what they would. Christ gives them "all things that pertain to life and godliness," 2 Pet. i. 3; he encourages them, he assists them in their work; he gives them "exceeding great and precious promises," 2 Pet. i. 4; he feeds them with his own flesh and blood, he clothes them with his own righteousness, he directs them with his own Spirit.

[4.] By protecting his family from all dangers. There is no safety but in Christ's family: never are his servants in danger but when they go out of it. He is the Keeper of his Israel peculiarly, 1 Sam. ii. 9. Though he sometimes suffers evils to touch, he never suffers evils to hurt them, Psal. cv. 14, 15; he visits them in and delivers from all their troubles; he suffers not kings to hurt any of his servants. He takes the wrongs offered to his servants as offered to himself.

[5.] By correcting it for its miscarriages. Judgment commonly begins at the house of the Lord, 1 Pet. iv. 17. His servants are safe, but must not be secure; he suffers the world to do that which he will not endure in his own family. His servants will never be faithful to him, nor find him faithful to them, if he did not sometimes chastise them. He judges them, that they may "not be condemned with the world," 1 Cor. xi. 32. And whensoever he chides, he does it not because he loves it, but because they want it.

[6.] By rewarding every servant according to his service. He is indeed the only Lord, but he has sundry sorts of servants. He is a good Master, but most that call themselves his servants are unprofitable, and only titular and complimentary, wearing his badge, but refusing his work; using the name of the Lord, and crying, Lord, Lord, but shunning the rule of their Lord. The reward of these is, to be "cast into utter darkness," Matt. xxv. 30, who heretofore were unprofitable under light. His good and faithful servants shall be rewarded with the joy of their Lord, even the presence of him whom they served faithfully in his absence, Matt. xxv. 21. Their labour of love shall not be forgotten by Christ, but all their former toil shall be forgotten. Their work, though never so great, is but small to their wages; nor is the weight of their labours comparable to that of their crown; Jesus Christ will pay them for every work which they have forgotten. Their services are all booked. He who formerly gave them abilities to work, will now give them a recompence for working.

2. In what respect is Christ called "only Lord?"

(1.) Not to exclude the Father and the Holy Ghost, to whom with the Son all outward works are common: and frequently to the whole Trinity of Persons is this name of Δεσπότης, or Lord, given in Scripture, Acts iv. 24; Rev. vi. 10. God the Father, John xvii. 3, is called "the only true God," not to exclude the Son; and God the Son is called "the only Lord," not to exclude the Father, who is represented in the natural glory of the Deity, as the Son in the voluntary office of a Mediator.

But, (2.) In respect of all creatures is Christ called "only Lord." "One Lord Jesus Christ," 1 Cor. viii. 6. "One Lord," Eph. iv. 5. And that,

[1.] To exclude the partnership of any other in the government with him. The rule is not shared between him and other lords. In government he has no copartner; he is God's only Vicegerent. "There is no other name under heaven given among men," Acts iv. 12. To him has the Father committed "all power in heaven and earth," Matt. xxviii. 18, as Pharaoh set Joseph over all the land of Egypt. God hath appointed him heir of all things, Heb. i. 2. And as Christ had no coadjutor in the work of redemption, so has he no partner in the glory thereof, Isa. lxiii. 3; lv. 10, 11.

[2.] To note his superiority and pre-eminency above all other lords. In which respect he is called "King of kings, and Lord of lords," 1 Tim. vi. 15; for,

1. He is the only absolute Lord. All other lords are subordinate to him, dependent on him, advanced by him, receive authority, laws, gifts from him, are responsible for the use and abuse of these to him, and are therefore punishable by him. The supreme of earthly lords are, in respect of him, inferior lords.

2. He is the only universal Lord. To him every knee must bow, Phil. ii. 10. The three kingdoms of heaven, earth, and hell never had any Lord but Christ: in the first of these, he eminently shows his glory and beauty; in the second, his power of ruling and directing; in the third, his strength and severity. Angels and glorified saints in heaven; saints, sinners, and every creature on earth; the damned and devils in hell; are all his subjects. "He is Lord of all," Acts x. 36.

3. He is the only Lord for power and might. "He is able to subdue all things to himself," Phil. iii. 21; and 1 Tim. vi. 15, he is called "the only Potentate." He made, and he can annihilate the world with one word. He can kill the soul, and throw both body and soul into hell. Happy we, that earthly lords, though never so tyrannical, cannot do this. He can subdue the hearts of men, even of his deadliest enemies, unto his love and obedience. Happy would earthly monarchs think themselves, if they could do thus. But he who only made can only mend the heart, Psal. cx. 1—3.

4. He is the only Lord for majesty and glory. All the glory of all the Cæsars, emperors, kings who ever were, combined in one heap, is but a black coal in comparison of the splendour of his glory. If "Solomon in all his glory was not arrayed like the lilies of the field," Matt. vi. 29, how much less was he like the Lord of the world! The glory of Agrippa and Bernice was but a great fancy, Acts xxv. 23, μετὰ πολλῆς φαντασίας. How easy and often doth Christ stain the pride of the glory of the greatest, and even cause shameful spewing to be upon it! The glory of kings is but a borrowed ray or spark from his majesty. When he shall appear in his glory, all the nightly glow-worms of worldly splendour shall be put out, and all worldly majesty shall be extinguished. Nay, the poorest saint shall appear with him in that glory, of which all the splendour of emperors is not so much as a shadow.

5. He is the only Lord in respect of his deportment toward his servants. (1.) He is the most discerning Lord and Master: no earthly masters are so able to observe the ways and works of their servants as he is; for the closest and subtlest among them cannot deceive him; he spies them in every corner, nay, every corner of their hearts in them. He now, in some measure, is absent, and yet he needs no informer, but knows what every servant does in his absence, and will manifest every one's work to all the world. His eyes are as a flame of fire, and clearer than ten thousand suns; all things are naked and open before him, Heb. iv. 12. Nor does he less observe the wants and troubles than the ways and works of his servants. He has an eye therefore as pitying as it is piercing, Exod. iii. 7. For, (2.) He is the most gracious Lord and Master. 1. No lord ever bought servants so dear, he having bought them from slavery by laying down his dearest and most precious blood for them. Never such a price! He has given not his money, but himself for them. 2. No lord ever fed his servants so highly and so plentifully. The servants of Christ have various and sumptuous dishes: first the word, after that the sacrament. The table of the Lord is furnished with the body and blood of the Lord to nourish the servants, not only to labour, but also to eternal life. 3. No lord ever clothed servants so sumptuously: their garments are made of that web which was woven out of his own bowels; they put on the scarlet of his righteousness, and the merit of his death; the fine linen of holiness and sanctification, yea, the beautiful robes of glory and immortality, which they shall change for the filthy rags of sin and mortality. 4. No lord ever used his servants so gently and mercifully. He puts them only upon honourable, safe, comfortable employments. He puts no more upon them than they can go through. He is not only their Lord and Master, but their helper and fellow worker: when they grow faint and weary, he strengthens them, Phil. iv. 13; when doubtful, he teaches them, Psal. xxv. 4, 5, 9; when slothful, sometimes indeed he corrects them, Hab. i. 12; yet not to kill, but quicken them; and not to destroy them, but their slothfulness; when they are sick, he pities and spares them; when old, he turns them not out of his service; but the longer they live in it, the more they love it, yea, the more able they are to perform it. In a word, when they die, he neither suffers them to lie still, nor sends them to seek another master; for then they change not their Master, for another, but their work for a better, or rather for their wages. For, 5. No master ever rewarded his servants so bountifully. As Christ gives more for, so more to his servants than any master. That happiness which Christ gives his servants in this life is unspeakable; their work seems to have more of wages than work: but in the next life their joy will be so great, as that it cannot so well be said to enter into them, as they to enter into it. For why? it is the joy of their Lord, Matt. xxv. 21, whose bosom is the hive and centre of all goodness, and that in which all the scattered parcels of blessedness are bundled up. Study, but yet expect not to understand either the comfort or condescension of that promise, made to the faithful servants of Christ, "He shall gird himself, and make them sit down to meat, and come forth and serve them," Luke xii. 37. Lord! did I not think that the cheer and the attendance were both one, I should say, the attendance were infinitely better than the cheer. Think what

it is for Christ himself to serve at the table. What is it but infinite delight for the guests to have him set himself to solace them, who is infinite, as in sweetness, so in knowledge, to make his sweetness please them! Nor will the dignity of those servants be less than their delight, who have Majesty itself to serve them! Certainly, in heaven there shall be as many kings as subjects.

6. He is the only Lord, for the duration of his dominion: Of his government there shall be no end, Luke i. 33. He is "the King immortal," 1 Tim. i. 17. "He only hath immortality," 1 Tim. vi. 16. To other potentates, though they be called gods, yet he who is the true God saith that they shall die like men, Psal. lxxxii. 7. Few earthly monarchs there are whose lives are not tyrannical, and their deaths untimely; who ruling by the sword, commonly die by it. And should they escape the poniards, the poisons, the powder-plots, bullets, axes, which have swept away the most, one disease or other will lay all their glory in the dust. In an evening, a midday, yea, perhaps a more early cloud, shall be the sunset both of their lives and reigns. But Jesus Christ is the same yesterday, to-day, and for ever; his throne is for ever and ever. Death itself, the king of terrors, and the terror of kings, is subdued by Jesus Christ; and that not only so as it shall never touch him, but also never hurt any of his servants.

Of our twenty-five monarchs since the Conquest, thirteen (taking in three who are thought to have been poisoned) are said to have had violent and untimely deaths.

Obs. 1. All our obedience to earthly lords must be only such as this only Lord allows, and only in the Lord. We must take heed of the sin of the Israelites, willingly to walk after the commandment, Hos. v. 11; and of that of the papists, blind obedience to any superior. The greatest lords in the world are but rules ruled; Jesus Christ is the only rule ruling.

Obs. 2. The greatest diligence and fervency of spirit is requisite in the service of this only Lord, Rom. xii. 11. We must not do the work of this great Lord negligently, nor offer him a female instead of a male. This only Lord must have, as it were, our only service. We must not serve him as if we served him not. Though the best servant of this Lord be but an unprofitable, yet the least must not be an idle servant. We must not offer to this Lord that which cost us nothing. The blind and the maimed are too bad for our ordinary lords: our only Lord must have our best, our hearts, our all, even the whole of our created abilities. This great Lord hath much more business than all the time and strength of his servants can bring about. If every hair of the head were a hand, we might have our hands full of work. Our Lord requires the service of thoughts, 2 Cor. x. 5; of words, Eph. iv. 29; of works, 1 Cor. x. 31; of body and spirit, 1 Thess. v. 23. A vast deal of diligence is requisite about honouring God, attending our own heart and ways, and helping and edifying others.

Obs. 3. How warily and conscientiously should all other lords govern! They are lords, but not only lords; they are but servants to this only Lord, and must as well be accountable to him for their commanding, as others must be responsible to them for their obeying. They must remember they have a Master in heaven, with whom there is no respect of persons, Eph. vi. 9; Col. iv. 1. The wrath of God in his creatures, fire, sword, sickness, makes no distinction between the greatest lords and the poorest slaves; how much less will Christ himself make, when all shall stand naked before his tribunal!

Obs. 4. Christ has power to do what he will with us or ours. This only Lord has no master to whom to give an account; and how far should any of his servants be from expecting that he should give an account of any of his actions to them! It should suffice them, that whatever befalls them, it is from the Lord: The Lord giveth, and the Lord taketh away, Job i. 21. Whensoever he removes any comforts, if we find ourselves too ready to say to instruments, as did the owners of the colt, What do ye loosing and removing it? we should be silenced, though not with that answer which was returned by the disciples to them, "The Lord hath need of it," Luke xix. 33, 34; yet with this, He sees it needful for us that thus it should be. Whenever he commands the hardest duty, or inflicts the smartest stripes, every servant of Christ should stop their murmuring mouths with this, The Lord will have it thus.

Obs. 5. The servants of this one and only Lord should be at unity among themselves, Eph. iv. 3—5. Fellow servants must not fall out and beat one another, Luke xii. 45. The servants of this one Lord should be of one mind. Though some may have higher, some lower employments in Christ's family, yet all are but servants to this only Lord, and all their services meet in this one end of glorifying him. In this respect the apostle saith, "He that planteth and he that watereth are one," 1 Cor. iii. 8. The servants of Christ should shun division because "Christ is not divided," 1 Cor. i. 13. They cannot forgive one another so much, or so often, as their Master has forgiven them.

Obs. 6. How careful and wary should we be in using the creatures! All the comforts which we enjoy are the goods of this Lord; we are but stewards of them. What we use must be used for, not against our Lord: learning, riches, honour, nay ourselves, are of and from him, and therefore should be for him. All our enjoyments are but borrowed, we must therefore use them well, not spot and stain, tear and cut them by sin, lest we be ashamed when we are to return them back to the owner.

Obs. 7. We should neither give nor receive ambitious and flattering titles of honour. Christ gives us the reason, one is our Lord and Master, even Christ, Matt. xxiii. 8—10. We should so acknowledge a superiority among men, as to be fearful of causing pride in men. The carriage of a servant to his earthly lord, must be such as that his lord may know himself not to be the only Lord. When they cried up Herod's voice for the voice of God and not of man, God would not bear it. He made him immediately to become worm's meat, Acts xii. 23, σκωληκόβρωτος, who but just now was men's idol.

Obs. 8. There is no possible escape for Christ's enemies. If they had another lord or potentate to match Christ in strength, they might fly to him to defend them from Christ; but Christ is the only Lord, and woe to them who have him for their only enemy! Can thy heart endure or thy hands be strong in the day when this Lord shall deal with thee? Ezek. xxii. 14; Isa. x. 3; Jer. iv. 13. Foolish sinner! who if thou wilt needs be contending, dost not choose one of thy fellow worms to contend with. But thou dost as vainly contend with thy Maker, as the smoke with the wind, the wax with the fire, the stubble with the flame, or the snow-ball with the sun, when thrown against it. "It is hard to kick against the pricks," Acts ix. 5. Thy greater wisdom is to "kiss the Son" with a kiss of sincere and hearty love, worship, homage, "lest he be angry, and thou perish from the way," Psal. ii. 12. There is no flying from him but by flying to him. All must, one way or other, be subject to him; either as servants, or as slaves; either under his grace, or under his wrath, Rom. xiv. 10, 11.

Obs. 9. All doctrines and practices are to be abhorred which derogate from the dignity of this only Lord. Doctrines; especially the popish, which deprave our redemption by this Lord with the doctrine of merits; the worship due to this Lord, by the doctrines of image adoration, and the pope's headship; the authority of this Lord, by the doctrine of saints' intercession, and the pope's pardoning of sins. Practices, of those who serve the times instead of serving the Lord; love their pleasures more than God; serve their bellies, Rom. xvi. 18, their lusts, themselves, as if they were their own lords; the humours of vile men, their father the devil, John viii. 44. Oh how many, how ignoble, how poor, how cruel are the lords of that man, who has not this one, this only Lord!

<small>Quam multos habet dominos qui unum non habet!</small>

Obs. 10. Great is the happiness of, and strong are the engagements upon, every servant of this only Lord. But of this largely before, pages 4, 5, ver. 1.

Thus much for our Saviour's dignity in respect of his place and authority, as he is called " the only Lord." We now contemplate,

2. His dignity in respect of his Divine nature and essence; he is called also " God."

For explication whereof, observe, this title is not here to be taken, (1.) Improperly, as it is, [1.] Given to false gods or idols, which are accounted gods in the depraved apprehensions of blind and seduced heathens, Acts xiv. 11, 12; 1 Cor. viii. 4, 5; Acts xvii. 29. [2.] To the devil, who is called "the god of this world," 2 Cor. iv. 4, because the wicked world obeys him, and fulfils his commands, as if he were a God, John viii. 44. [3.] To those things which men prefer before God, as the belly is called the god of some men; who serve their bellies, and not Christ, Rom. xvi. 18. [4.] To kings, princes, magistrates, Exod. xxi. 6; xxii. 8; Psal. lxxxii. 1, 6; cxxxviii. 1; John x. 34, 35, who are in the room and place of God, exercise the judgments of God, 2 Chron. xix. 6, and are ordained by God, Rom. xiii. 1. [5.] To the ark of the covenant, to which metonymically the name of God is given, the sign being often put for the thing signified, Numb. x. 35, 36; 2 Sam. vii. 6.

But, (2.) Properly, for God the Maker and Preserver of all things, though not, [1.] οὐσιωδῶς, essentially, and indefinitely, signifying the whole Trinity, the Divine essence, common to the Father, Son, and Holy Ghost, Matt. iv. 7, 10; John iv. 24, &c. But, [2.] ὑποστατικῶς, personally, and as signifying some one Person of the Trinity. Thus the Father is called God, Matt. xvi. 16; John iii. 16; Rom. vii. 25, &c. Thus the Holy Ghost is called God, Acts v. 4, compared with ver. 3, " Thou hast not lied to men, but to God; Satan hath filled thine heart to lie to the Holy Ghost:" 2 Cor. vi. 16, compared with 1 Cor. vi. 19. And thus the Son is called God: " The church of God, which he hath purchased with his blood," Acts xx. 28. " The great God, and our Saviour Jesus Christ," &c., 1 Tim. iii. 16; Tit. ii. 13: and this is the Person which is here called God. To whom are given,

1. The same titles which are given to God. Isa. ix.
<small>אֵל גִּבּוֹר
Numb. xiv. 22.
Psal. xcv. 8.</small>
6, he is called " The mighty God;" and chap. vi. 1, he is called Jehovah; for there Isaiah is said to see Jehovah sitting upon a throne, &c. And John xii. 41, this is expressly by the holy evangelist applied to Christ, of whom he saith that Isaiah saw his glory, and spake of him. Exod. xvii. 7, the people are said to tempt Jehovah; and the apostle saith, 1 Cor. x. 9, " Let us not tempt Christ, as some of them tempted." It is said of Jehovah, " Of old hast thou laid the foundation of the earth, and the heavens are the work of thy hands: they shall perish, but thou shalt endure," &c., Psal. cii. 25. And the apostle clearly testifies, Heb. i. 10, that these words are spoken of Christ. Zech. xiii. 7, Christ is called the Father's fellow. John i. 1, the Word, which in the beginning was with God, is expressly said to be God. And Rom. ix. 6, he is called " God blessed for evermore." And 1 Tim. iii. 16, " God manifested in the flesh." And 1 John v. 20, " The true God."

2. The same essential attributes and properties of the Godhead are ascribed to him; as, 1. Eternity: " The Lord possessed me in the beginning of his way, before his works of old," Prov. viii. 22. " Before Abraham was, I am," John viii. 58. " Glorify me with the glory which I had with thee before the world was," John xvii. 5. And ver. 24, " Thou lovedst me before the foundation of the world." " He is before all things," Col. i. 17. 2. Omnipresence: " Where two or three are gathered together in my name, there am I in the midst of them," Matt. xviii. 20. And chap. xxviii. 20, " I am with you alway, even to the end of the world." 3. Omniscience: " He knew what was in man," John ii. 25. He is also frequently said to know the thoughts, Matt. ix. 4; xii. 25; Luke v. 22; vi. 8; xi. 17; xxiv. 38; yea, to know all things, John xxi. 17. 4. Omnipotence: " All power is given unto me." " He is able to subdue all things," Phil. iii. 21. " What things soever the Father doth, these also doth the Son," John v. 19.

3. The same works which are peculiar to God are ascribed unto Christ. As, 1. Election: the elect are called his elect, Matt. xxiv. 31. 2. Creation: " All things were made by him," John i. 3; and ver. 10, " The world was made by him." " By him were all things created," Col. i. 16. 3. The preservation and sustentation of all things: " By him all things consist," Col. i. 17. " He upholdeth all things by the word of his power," Heb. i. 3. 4. Remission of sins: " The Son of man hath power to forgive sins," Matt. ix. 6. 5. Working of miracles, works either above or against the order of nature: He opens the eyes of the blind, John ix. 32. He raiseth dead Lazarus, John xi. Yea, he both raiseth from the grave of sin, John v. 21, 25, and raiseth all the dead, John v. 28, 29. 6. The bestowing of eternal life: " My sheep hear my voice, and I give unto them eternal life," John x. 27, 28.

4. The worship which is due to God alone hath been both given to and accepted by Christ. First, Inward worship: as, 1. Believing on him. Faith is a worship which belongs only to God, enjoined in the first commandment: and against the trusting in man is there a curse denounced, Jer. xvii. 5. But Christ bids us believe in him. " Believe in me," John xiv. 1. " He that believeth in the Son hath everlasting life," John vi. 47. 2. Loving him with all the heart; commanded above the love, nay, even to a hatred of father, mother, wife, children, yea, our own lives, Luke xiv. 26; and for the gaining of him, blessed Paul accounted all things but loss and dung, Phil. iii. 8. Secondly, Outward worship is due to Christ. 1. Dedication in baptism is in his name, Matt. xxviii. 19. 2. Divine invocation is given to him. Stephen calls upon the Lord Jesus to receive his spirit, Acts vii. 59. " All that in every place call upon the name of Jesus Christ," 1 Cor. i. 2. " God himself and our Father, and our Lord Jesus Christ, direct our way unto you," 1 Thess. iii. 11. Praises are offered to him, Rev. v. 9, 12. 3. Divine adoration is also given to him: " A leper worshipped

him," Matt. viii. 2. Though the wise men of the East, who saw Herod in all his royalty, worshipped not him, yet they fell down before Christ, Matt. ii. 11. Yea, not men only, but angels are commanded to worship him, Heb. i. 6.

Obs. 1. As groundless as blasphemous are all the cavils against the Deity of Christ. For though he be from and begotten of the Father, by an ineffable communication of the Divine essence to his person; yet if we consider his Deity and essence absolutely, he is God of himself, and has being from none, and he is only God of God, as we consider the Divine essence in the Son, and as it is under a certain and distinct manner of subsistence.

Though the Father is greater than the Son in respect of his manhood, John xiv. 28, yet the Son is equal with the Father in respect of his Godhead, John x. 30; Phil. ii. 6.

Though the Son be truly called the "image of God," Col. i. 15, yet he is as truly said to be very God. For when the apostle saith that he is the "image of God," this word "God" ought not to be taken essentially, but personally; and by it we are to understand not the Divine nature, but the person of the Father. Christ is the image of the Father, not of the Deity, and the person of the Son bears the image of the person of the Father, but the Divine essence in the Son is one and the same with that which is in the Father: "I and my Father are one."

Obs. 2. Inconceivable was the wisdom, justice, love, and humble condescension, manifested in God's becoming man. (1.) Wisdom. None but a God could have contrived it; and so far was man from inventing this plot of mercy, that it had been blasphemy, should it have entered into his thoughts before God had discovered it to him. The hypostatical union was purely a Divine invention: poor shortsighted man cannot conceive it now since it was, much less could he have contrived it before it was. Infinite was that wisdom which found out a way for God to begin to be what he was not, and to remain what he was: that the two natures should be united, 1. Ἀσυγχύτως and ἀτρέπτως, so as that there should be no confusion, mutation, commixion of them; but that both natures should remain distinct and entire in their properties, wills, and actions, without any change of one into the other. 2. Ἀδιαιρέτως and ἀχωρίστως, individually and inseparably, so as one nature should never be separated from the other, no, not by death; there never being two Christs, but one Son of God manifested in the flesh. How great was that wisdom which found out a way for the Mediator between God and man, to partake of the natures of both those parties between whom he mediates! and which contrived a reconciliation between God and man by the marriage of the natures of both! (2.) How eminent was that justice of God, that would be satisfied no way but by the Son of God assuming the nature of men, veiling his glory, emptying himself of majesty, and debasing himself "to the death of the cross!" Phil. ii. 8. So that God may seem more severe in sparing man this way, than if he had punished him without sending his Son thus to redeem him. (3.) How transcendent was the love of God to poor lost man, to weave the garment of his spotted and defiled nature anew in the virgin's womb! to become a new and living way over that gulf of separation which was between God and man, whereby God might be willing to come to man, and man able to go to God! to disrobe himself of majesty, and to clothe himself with the rags of mortality! Did ever love cause such a condescension as this? The thistle did not here send to the cedar, but the cedar comes to the thistle, to woo for a marriage. Let the deepest apprehensions despair to dive to the bottom of this humble undertaking. Angels themselves may stoop to look into it, 1 Pet. i. 12, and be students in this piece of divinity; but never can they be completely apprehensive what it is for the Maker of the world to be made of a woman; for the everlasting Father to be an infant in the womb; for majesty to be buried among the chips; for Him who thundered in the clouds to lie in the cradle; for Him who measured the heavens with a span to be a child of a span long.

Obs. 3. Any other saviours beside Christ are altogether needless and fictitious. If Christ be God, there is no other saviour, Isa. xliii. 11; Hos. xiii. 4; and he no more wants the help of men or angels in the redemption of the world, than he did in the creation. To an infinite power nothing can be added; and the strength of Christ to save is infinite. What brings the creature to God but wants and weaknesses? That which receives all its strength from God, adds no strength to God. There is none but God able to do the work and fit to receive the honour of a Saviour. The highest of all popishly-voiced saviours throw down their crowns at the feet of Christ, and with one voice acknowledge him their Saviour. The crown of purchasing our salvation is too heavy for any created head. Did those glorified spirits in heaven know how much honour is taken from Christ, by casting it upon them, some think that heaven would be no heaven to them.

Obs. 4. Divine justice is completely satisfied, and the sins of believers are perfectly removed. The merits of Christ are of infinite value: the least sin was a burden too heavy for all the created backs of men and angels to undergo. None but he that was God could perfectly satisfy God. Christ is "able to save to the uttermost," Heb. vii. 25; he "taketh away the sin of the world," John i. 29. Our iniquities are said to be subdued, thrown into the bottom of the sea, Micah vii. 19, "covered," Psal. xxxii. 1, washed away, "blotted out as a cloud," Isa. xliv. 22, utterly forgotten, Jer. xxxi. 34, and cast behind the back of God, Isa. xxxviii. 17. Believers have nothing to pay to justice. The payments of popish merits are not in current but copper coin, which will not go in heaven, but will certainly be turned back again. The sins of one believer are ten thousand times greater than Satan can represent, but yet the merits of the blood of God infinitely exceed all the sins of all men put together: "The blood of Christ cleanseth from all sin," 1 John i. 7. Christians, take heed of a sacrilegious ransacking of the grave of Christ, wherein he has buried your sins. If Christ be God, desperation is the greatest of sins. Is there any spot so deep, which the blood of God cannot wash out? any disease so desperate, which the blood of God cannot cure? any heart so faint, which the blood of God cannot revive? any debt so great, which the blood of God cannot satisfy? any burden so heavy, which the shoulders of God cannot bear away? O believer, let thy spirit "rejoice in God thy Saviour," Luke i. 47.

Obs. 5. How high is the advancement of human nature! He who has taken it into the unity of his person is true God. The seed of Abraham is now more highly dignified than the nature of angels, Heb. ii. 16. There is not a knee, either in heaven, in earth, or under the earth, but shall bow at the name of Him who is God and man in one person, Phil. ii. 10. Let us fear to debase that nature which Christ has magnified. There is nothing but sin that makes a man a vile person, Psal. xv. 4. How unworthy a condescension is it for that nature to stoop to devils which is advanced above angels! The Philistines tread not on that threshold upon which their idol Dagon fell, 1 Sam. v. 5; and shall man suffer lust and devils to trample upon and defile that nature which the Son of God assumed? O man, acknowledge thy dignity; and being made a companion of the Divine nature, be not so ungenerous as to become a slave to sin.

Obs. 6. How peculiarly dignified and blessed are all believers! Their Head, their Husband is very God. They have not only the common honour of all men, in the union of human nature with the Son of God; but a special privilege, in being united to him by his Spirit through faith. Man is advanced above other creatures in respect of the first, believers are advanced above other men in respect of the second union; and if thus we are united to him who is God, what influences of holiness, wisdom, power, shall flow to us from such a Head! A prince who has all the gold and ornaments of the world, will not suffer his wife to want necessaries; and certainly, the spouse of Christ shall have what she wants, if not what she would.

Obs. 7. Whatever it is that Christ, who is God, ordains and owns, deserves our highest estimation. The day instituted by Christ deserves rather to be esteemed holy than any days of man's ordaining; it should be accounted both a good day and a high day, having such an institutor. The ordinances of Christ should be preferred before human traditions: no institutions but his shall stand, nor should religiously be esteemed. I fear that the great and bloody controversies which Christ hath had so long with England, are about some ordinances of his which yet we will not take up, Luke xix. 27, and some traditions of our own which in stead thereof we will keep up. What is become of those men, and of their wisdom, whose wise work it was heretofore to invent and impose their own innovations for Christ's institutions? *Sapientes sapienter in infernum descendunt.* The servants and messengers of Christ should be more loved and honoured than the servants of any earthly potentate. They are the servants of God: we should love as he loves. It is more honourable to be a servant of God than a king over men. Our delight should be in those excellent ones, who bear the image and wear the badge of Christ, Psal. xvi. 3. The feet of his ambassadors should be beautiful, whether we regard their Master or their message, Rom. x. 15. Lastly, his word should be preferred before any other writings. "Let the word of Christ dwell in us richly," Col. iii. 16; let it be taken in, not stand at the doors, or lodge only in our books, or on our shelves; let it dwell there, not be turned out again; let it dwell richly in all that is within us, understanding, will, affections, memory; and richly in all that is of it, in its threatenings, commands, promises; it is the word of God, who hath strength to back it. In a word, take heed of opposing this great God in any kind. If God the Father be offended, Christ is our Advocate; but if Christ be provoked, who shall mediate?

Thus far of the description of the dignity of him whom they opposed. Next we must show,

II. How they opposed him, or wherein that opposition consists; they denied him.

Two things are here to be explained:

How Christ may be said to be denied; and particularly, what denial of him is here to be understood; and, Wherein the sinfulness thereof shows itself.

1. How Christ may be said to be denied.

"Denying," ἀρνούμενοι. Denial, properly, is verbal; it respects our words, and signifies the contrary to affirmation. Thus those envious rulers spake concerning the notable miracle of healing the lame man, that they cannot disaffirm or deny it, Acts iv. 16. Thus Peter denied openly before them all that he had been with Jesus, Matt. xxvi. 70; John xviii. 25, 27. Thus John denied not who he was, John i. 20.

But improperly, and figuratively, denial may be taken for such a renouncing or rejection of a thing as may likewise be expressed by the actions, and in reality; and thus Moses is said to deny or "refuse to be called the son of Pharaoh's daughter," Heb. xi. 24; and so some are said to have a form of godliness, and to deny, namely, in their course and carriage, the power thereof, 2 Tim. iii. 5. And,

Christ may be said to be denied, doctrinally, and by our words; and, really, and by our works.

(1.) Christ is denied doctrinally, and by our words; and thus Christ hath been denied, 1. In his person. 2. In his offices.

[1.] In his person; and thus, 1. The Jews deny his person wholly, or that he was the promised Messiah, Acts iii. 13, 14. And the followers of Simon Magus taught, as himself had taught them, that he was the son of God. The like is reported of Menander, Judas of Galilee, and he who styled himself Bencocab; all which, as credible stories relate, gave out that they were Christs and Messiahs; the latter, though he called himself Bencocab, the son of a star, applying to himself that prophecy of the Star of Jacob, was afterward by way of derision called Barcozba, the son of a lie. 2. Christ, in respect of his person, has been denied in either of his natures. In his Godhead, by the Ebionites, Cerinthians, Arians, Samosatenians, and of late by Servetus and his followers. In his manhood, by the Valentinians, Marcionites, Manichees, Apollinarists, and of late by some Anabaptists. 3. The person of Christ has been denied by those who opposed the hypostatical union of the two natures; and thus he was denied by Nestorians, Eutycheans, Sabellians; the first dividing Christ into two persons, the second confounding and mixing his two natures, the third mixing him with the person of the Father.
_{Epiphan. lib. 1. c. 21. Aug. de Hæres. cap. 1. Joseph. l. 2. c. 12. Tertul. lib. de Hæres.}

[2.] In his offices. 1. Christ in his prophetical office is denied by papists, who impose upon us a new scripture; (1.) By taking away from it, in denying the eucharistical cup to the people, 1 Cor. xi. 26; meats also and marriage, Heb. xiii. 4; 1 Tim. iv. 3; and, which is worse, in denying the food of life, the reading of the Holy Scriptures, to the common people, Col. iii. 16. (2.) By adding to it, in bringing in a second place for punishment after this life, the feigned fire of purgatory; by inventing five sacraments, and introducing their own unwritten traditions, which they equally esteem with and often prefer before the Scriptures, and by making a pope the infallible judge of the controversies of faith.

2. In his priestly office, Christ is denied, (1.) By Socinians, who teach that he died not for us, that is, in our place and stead; but only for our benefit and profit, to show us by his example the way which leads to salvation, 1 John ii. 2; Matt. xx. 28; Mark x. 45; Heb. x. 12, 14; 2 Cor. v. 21. (2.) By papists, who teaching that the mass is a propitiatory sacrifice, make the sacrifice of Christ imperfect; and by joining many other mediators and advocates with Christ, deny him to be the one and only Mediator. They mingle the blood of martyrs, yea, of traitors, with the blood of Christ; and teach that images are to be worshipped, angels invoked, and relics adored.

3. In his kingly office, Christ is denied by papists, who acknowledge the pope the head of the church, and teach that all power is given to him in heaven and earth, and that he can make laws to bind

the conscience, and is universal bishop, &c. In a word, the eastern Turk denies the person of Christ, and the western his offices.

(2.) Christ is denied really and by our works. And this denial, I conceive, the apostle here principally intends; for had these seducers in word denied Christ, the church would easily have espied them. In speech therefore they professed Christ, but in their deeds they denied him, Tit. i. 16.

Christ may be denied by men's works sundry ways. [1.] By a malicious and spiteful opposing Christ and his gospel, Heb. x. 29; of the truth and benefit whereof the Holy Ghost has so evicted a person, that he opposes the gospel even against the inward operation and supernatural revelation of the Holy Ghost. This, as I conceive, is the unpardonable sin, and was the sin of Alexander the coppersmith, 2 Tim. iv. 14, and of Julian.

[2.] By an open and wilful apostatizing from the faith, and profession of religion, haply for fear of persecution, and out of too much love of this world. This, I conceive, was the sin of Demas and Spira, 2 Tim. iv. 10.

[3.] By a politic and time-serving neutrality, a lukewarmness, and halting between two opinions, for fear or shame, when a man is oft on either side, but truly on neither. They on that side think him theirs, we on this side think him ours, his own conscience thinks him neither's. To hold our peace when the honour of Christ is in question, is to deny Christ, even to a mistaking of the end of our redemption. " Ye are bought with a price, therefore glorify Christ in your body and spirit," 1 Cor. vi. 20: Christ is not glorified when his name is concealed. John Baptist "confessed, and denied not," John i. 20. Whosoever does not openly confess Christ, does secretly deny Christ. Christ is not to be hid, as the woman hid the spies, in the deep well of our hearts, and covered over, as she did the mouth of the well with corn, for worldly concernments. If it be enough to believe in the heart, Rom. x. 10, why did God give thee a mouth? He denies Christ that does not profess himself a Christian. We are bound both *consentire* and *confiteri*, both to consent to and confess Christ, 1 Pet. iii. 15. If it be sufficient for thee to know Christ without acknowledging him for thy Lord, it shall be sufficient for Christ to know thee, but not to acknowledge thee for his servant. He who refuses to suffer for, denies Christ, 2 Tim. ii. 12. He who is not for Christ, is against him. There may be a sinful, a damnable moderation. Following Christ afar off in this life, is no sign that thou shalt be near to him in the next. No man will be afraid of being too professed a Christian at the day of judgment, or will think that he has lost too much for Christ when he is presently to lose all things by death. If the time wherein we live be a night of profaneness, it is our duty the more brightly to shine as lights, Phil. ii. 15, 16.

Christum deserit, qui Christianum se non asserit.

[4.] By despairing of salvation offered through the merits of Christ in the promise of the gospel. This is a thrusting from us the hand that would, and a casting away the plaster that should cure us. This sin makes God a liar, 1 John v. 10; changes his truth into a lie, and Satan's falsehood into a truth; and justifies the devil more than God. He that despairs of mercy, whatever he pretends, practically denies the faithfulness, sufficiency, and sincerity of the Lord Jesus, and asserts the faithfulness of him who is the father of lies.

[5.] Lastly, By a loose and profane conversation; and this kind of practical, real denying of Christ, I conceive, the apostle particularly charges upon these seducers. They walked after their own ungodly lusts, their lives being full of earthliness and epicurism, and their mouths of reproaches against holy obedience; they encouraged themselves and others herein, by perverting the sweet doctrine of the grace of God. They professed the grace of Christ, but led most graceless lives. Their practice gave their profession the lie. If they were not ashamed of Christ, yet were they a shame to Christ their Lord, who kept such servants: they walked not worthy of their Lord. They had the livery of Christ upon their backs, and the works of the devil in their hands. The merit of his redemption they acknowledged, but they denied the efficacy thereof, whereby he sanctifies and renews the heart, subdues sin, and quickens to new obedience. They acknowledged Christ a Jesus, but denied him as a Lord. Christ they took for their Saviour, but Satan for their master. They like it well to come to Christ for ease, but they will not take his (though easy) yoke upon them.

Ii qui sanguine Christi redempti fuerant, diabolo se rursus mancipantes, incomparabile illud pretium irritum faciunt. Calv. in loc.

2. Wherein appears the sinfulness of this denial of Christ.

(1.) It plainly comprehends the sin of atheism. There is none who denies this only Lord God in his life, but first denied him in his heart; and they who serve him not as the word commands, apprehend him not as the word discovers. They who are corrupt, and do abominable works, have said in their hearts, "There is no God," Psal. xiv. 1. Life atheism is but the daughter of heart atheism. All outward actions are the genuine productions of the inward man; they are (as I may say) the counterparts of the spirit, and so many derivations from that fountain. Now think, O Christians, what a heinous sin it is to deny that Being which thine own proves; nay, to hear, to speak of God, to plead for God, to pray to God, so frequently, and, in appearance, feelingly, and yet to deny that this God is.

(2.) The denial of this Lord as clearly contains the sin of unbelief and distrust. They who deny the service of this their Lord, truly think what that wicked servant in the gospel said; namely, that Christ, notwithstanding all his promises, is as a hard man, that reaps where he did not sow, Matt. xxv. 24; and that there is no profit in serving him. This evil heart of unbelief makes men depart from the living God, Heb. iii. 12. When men see no excellency in Christ, it is easy for them to be persuaded to reject him. He who believes not a jewel is precious, will easily part with it. He who denies Christ, plainly shows that he has no trust in him to receive any benefit from him. And how great a sin is this unbelief, whereby fulness itself is esteemed empty, mercy itself is reckoned cruel, gain itself deemed unprofitable, and all because faithfulness itself is accounted false!

(3.) The denial of Christ is notorious and unspeakable profaneness. It evidently shows that a man prefers other things before, and loves other things more than Christ. No man ever denies and leaves this best of masters, till he be provided with a master whom he thinks and loves better. But how great a disparagement and indignity do they, who set up any thing above Christ, offer to Him, who hath sent and designed Christ, John v. 23; xvi. 27, the master-piece of all his merciful and wise contrivements, and to Christ himself! for there is nothing which can come in competition with Christ, but is infinitely below him. All the combined excellencies of creatures, put into the balance with Christ, bear not so much proportion as a feather to a mountain. To forsake Christ for the world, or a lust, is to leave a treasure for a trifle; a mountain of gold, for a heap of dung; the pure, lasting fountain, for the muddy, broken cistern; eternity for a moment; reality for a shadow; all things for nothing. And therefore,

(4.) The denial of Christ is the height of folly, and the forsaking of our own mercy. Christ is the only remedy against death, Acts iv. 12; to deny the remedy, is to perish unavoidably: he who denies him who is the Saviour, nay, salvation, cannot be saved, no, not by salvation itself. No disease kills that soul who casts not away this physic; but he who refuses the means of recovery, concludes himself under a necessity of destruction. "How shall we escape, if we neglect this great salvation?" Heb. ii. 3. Other sins put men upon a possibility, the denial of Christ upon a necessity of damnation. They who deny Christ shall be denied by Christ. He often denies them in this life, by leaving them to serve and love those lords whom they have chosen instead of him, Psal. lxxxi. 11, 12; and by a denial of any power to them ever to return to Him whom they have renounced, 2 Thess. ii. 11, 12; Rev. xxii. 11; yea, by denying them to their own consciences, which oft flash in their faces the flames of hell, for the quenching of which they sometimes relinquish, though in vain, those trifles for which they denied Christ. But most assuredly will Christ deny these Christ-deniers at the last day; he will be ashamed of them, not know them, and banish them from his presence, notwithstanding their calling, Lord, Lord, and hypocritical claiming of former acquaintance with him, Matt. vii. 23. He that denies Christ, denies a Lord who will destroy all rebels, Luke xix. 27; he denies a Lord, not weak, titular, and mortal, but just, ever-living, and omnipotent.

(5.) The practical denial of Christ discovers a most rotten and unsound heart. What greater falseness imaginable, than to profess and deny Christ at the same time? to put on his cloak for security in sinning? to speak service, and live opposition, to him? to call him Master only to mock him, and to do the work of his enemies? not to serve him whom we do serve? to be in the skin a Christian, and in the core a heathen? Certainly, this mere outside, complimentary Christianity, that bows to Christ, and yet buffets him, shall one day be found to have had profession only for an increase of judgment. Oh how just will it be for those who never truly loved Christ, notwithstanding their professions, to hear Christ professing that he never knew them! The rotten professor is the fittest fuel for eternal flames.

(6.) The denial of Christ implies the greatest unthankfulness. If it be an unkind wickedness to deny a creature, a servant that fears thee; what is it then to deny that Lord whom thou shouldst fear? If to deny a father that begat the body; what is it then to deny God, that created the soul? If to deny a wife, with whom thou art one flesh; what is it to deny the Lord, with whom thou art one spirit? What evil have any found in him, to forsake, to renounce such a Master? How great was his goodness, to take such unprofitable servants as we are into the family of his church! What saw he in us more than in heathens, to reveal to us the light of his truths, and the mysteries of salvation? What an honour did he put upon us, when he took us for his by baptismal initiation! Were not the employments ever noble, safe, and sweet which he put upon us? is not the reward rich and bountiful which he hath promised? Must not our own consciences be our own accusers, when he requires of us the reason of denying him?

Obs. 1. Christ accounts a verbal, outside profession, contradicted by an unholy conversation, to be no better than renouncing him. The profession of the lip, without the agreement of the life, most dishonours God. How ready will the ignorant be to think that God allows the sins, or that he cannot punish the impiety, of those who profess profanely! Ezek. xxxvi. 20. How hateful to the God who loves truth in the inward parts, must he be who has nothing but falseness in the inward parts! God seeks none to serve him but such as serve him in truth. The service of the soul is the soul of service. The singleness of the intention is the sweet of a performance, and makes it even a sacrifice with marrow. All our professions and speculations without holiness are but profanations; and of him that hates instruction, God justly requires the reason of his taking his covenant into his mouth, Psal. l. 46. Profane professors are but wens upon the face of religion, which God will one day cut off. The higher the building is raised which wants a foundation, the greater will be its fall; and the more eminent men's appearances of religion are, the more shameful will be their apostacy, if they want the foundation of sincerity. A sincere professor, though he do not actually forsake all for Christ, is habitually prepared so to do, when Christ shall require. A mere formal professor, though he do not, as yet, openly renounce Christ, yet is prepared to do so, when his interest shall call him to it. <small>Sacrificium medullatum.</small>

Obs. 2. The excellency of any way or person is not to be judged by the regard it ordinarily finds among men. Christ himself cannot want a place by foolish men. If it be put to the vote, Barabbas will have more voices than Christ. The ways of Christ are never the worse because wicked men renounce them; rather their rejecting them speaks them holy. Let us not be offended at Christ because he is by most denied. Bless God if thou hast a heart to own him; and remember, it is a sign of a gracious heart, when the wicked make void the law of God, therefore to love his commandments, Psal. cxix. 126, 127.

Obs. 3. It is the great interest of Christians to take heed of denying Christ. To this end,

(1.) Deny yourselves. That man which sets much by himself, will never reckon much of a Saviour. He who has not learned to deny himself, when Christ and self come in competition, and meet on a narrow bridge, will endeavour to make Christ go back. He who does not account himself nothing, will soon esteem Christ so. Let the heart be taken off from any thing which may take thee off from Christ. Crucify every inordinate affection. Beseech God to alienate thee from thyself, and to annihilate in thee whatever opposes Christ. Reserve nothing in thee from his stroke, although the lot fall upon Jonathan; and resolve to part with thy dearest comforts for Christ, rather than deny him. Know nothing to be thine but himself.

(2.) Make a right estimate of the comforts which are to be enjoyed in Christ. 1. Account them realities, not notions; not imaginary, though invisible. Look upon them as substantial and indeed, John viii. 36. 2. Account them not as scanty, but abundant, so large that thou needest not go to other things for additions. Look upon Christ only as having enough for thee, and able to fill thy vast receptions to the brim. 3. View them as sublime, precious, not as low and vile; so excellent, that a holy generosity may be kindled in thee, and all these dunghill delights accounted unworthy thy stoop. 4. Account them useful and efficacious, not idle and unhelping; such as want not thee to uphold them, but as are able in all distresses to relieve thee, and will procure strong and strengthening consolations, Heb. vi. 18. 5. View them as thine, not another's. Christ is never good in the soul's account till it has a propriety in him. Nor can a soul be contented when it sees a parting from other things, unless it considers its propriety in Christ, who is far better. 6. View them as near and at hand, and always prepared to relieve the soul's exigences: let faith, as a prospective glass, make remote comforts appear hard by. 7. Lastly, view them as eternal, not as finite; such as are above the reach of thief and moth, and which alone triumph over time and enemies; and which shall live and last when all worldly enjoyments are dead and gone. Oh, who would deny such delights as these for a blast, a bubble, a nothing! What poor nothings of comfort are the sweetest delights which would allure us, what poor nothings of misery are the sorest sufferings that would affright us, from Christ!

(3.) Labour for an inward real implantation and rootedness in Christ. The advice of the apostle is to be rooted in Christ, Col. ii. 7. A stake in the ground may easily be plucked up, but a tree rooted in the ground stands immovable. They who are in Christ only by way of external profession may be pulled from Christ; and outward troubles will overcome a merely visible and outside professor; but they who are in Christ by way of real and internal implantation, will keep their standing. He who is but a visible Christian, may in a short time cease to be so much as visible. He who speaks for Christ only notionally, will soon be won to speak against him. From him who professes not Christ truly, may soon be taken away his very appearances. Please not yourselves with the form of religion. Realities are only durable. The colour of blushing is soon down, that of complexion remains longer.

(4.) Let no worldly comfort be beloved, but only so far as it is a pledge of Christ's love to thee, or an incentive of thine to him. Let not Christ content thee with any thing without himself. Love not thy enjoyments as gifts, but as mercies and love-tokens. Look upon every thing out of Christ as a sieve plucked out of the water, as a coal without fire, as a cipher without a figure. "Were it not that I regard the presence of Jehoshaphat, I would not look toward thee," said Elisha to Jehoram; and were it not for a taste of the love of Christ in our worldly comforts, we should not much regard them. Love nothing but as it is a step to raise thee up higher and more toward him, only as a phylactery and a remembrancer of thy Friend; as that which incites to him, not as that which bewitches from him. If Christians would study thus, by and in every comfort to taste Christ, they would not for gaining these comforts be willing to part with Christ.

(5.) Take heed of professing Christ for by-ends. Serve him not to serve your own turns. Make not religion a design. Let every interest be subservient to Christ. Be willing to set up a building of glory for him upon your own ruins. Learn to perish, that the glory of Christ may live. Let Christ be sweet for himself: love him for his beauty, not his clothes. In serving him, let nothing else be your scope; and then nothing will divert you: aim not at profit, so gain will not allure you; not at pleasure, so ease will not corrupt you; not at friends, so favour will not seduce you. Let none but Christ be your end.

(6.) Daily increase sweet acquaintance and humble familiarity with Christ. Stand not at a stay in taking in his comforts. Stint not communion with him. O labour to take in his sweetest consolations fresh and fresh every morning. If communion with Christ be but a while intermitted, the love of the world will soon be admitted. When the people were without their wonted converse with Moses, they began to think of a golden idol. The soul cannot live without some comfort or other. If it finds no sweetness in Christ, it will look out for it elsewhere; and if it taste nothing in his ways to whet and keep it up, it will be ready to go down, as the Israelites went down to the Philistines to sharpen their instruments, to earthly delights for relief. But if Christ be sweet, the world will be bitter. And if thine eyes have but looked stedfastly upon his glory, they will not suddenly behold beauty in any thing else.

Verse 5.

I will therefore put you in remembrance, though ye once knew this, how that the Lord having saved the people out of the land of Egypt, afterward destroyed them that believed not.

At this verse the apostle begins the second argument, whereby he proves it the duty of these Christians "earnestly to contend for the faith once delivered to the saints," and now opposed by the seducers of those times. The argument is taken from the certainty of the destruction of those seducers; the apostle, by the zealous prosecution thereof, declaring, that these Christians must avoid their doctrines, if they would not be involved in their downfal.

The apostle, in managing this argument,

1. Gives us several examples of God's severe wrath upon others in former times, for sundry heinous sins, to the 8th verse.

2. Declares that these seducers lived in the same sins which God had formerly punished in others, to the 11th verse.

3. Concludes, that they practising the same impieties, shall partake of the same plagues with those who were before them, to the 17th verse.

For the first of these, the apostle propounds three examples of God's most severe displeasure against the sinners of former times:

The first is of the Israelites, who were destroyed in the wilderness.

The second of the wicked angels, who are "reserved in everlasting chains under darkness."

The third of the Sodomites, who suffer the vengeance of everlasting fire. The apostle with admirable wisdom making choice of these examples, to prevent the plea which might be made for these seducers, from their privilege as visible professors, from their eminency for place, and from their reputation for sanctity: for though they had church privileges, yet so had the Israelites; though they were eminent for place and station, yet so were the angels; and though they were desirous to be accounted in the highest form of religion and sanctity, yet were they as filthy and guilty as Sodomites, a people as famous for God's judgments as they were infamous for their own impurities.

The first of these examples, that of the Israelites, who were destroyed in the wilderness, &c., is set down here in this fifth verse; wherein are two parts:

1. A preface prefixed.
2. An example propounded.

1. He sets down a preface before the example, in these words, "I will put you in remembrance, though ye once knew this." Wherein two things are expressed.

I. The duty of the apostle; or, what he would do: "I will therefore put you in remembrance."

II. The commendation of the Christians; or, what they had already done; "Though ye once knew this," namely, the following example of the Israelites.

I. For the duty of the apostle; "I will put you in remembrance."

For the explication of this, observe,

1. What the apostle means by this putting of them in remembrance.

2. Why he would put them in remembrance.

1. What he intends by putting them in remembrance.

Ὑπομνῆσαι, In memoriam revocare. Ὑπεμνήσθε ὁ Πέτρος. Ταῦτα ὑπομίμνησκε. Ὑπομίμνησκα αὐτούς. Ὑμᾶς ὑπομιμνήσκειν. Διεγείρω ὑμῶν τὴν διάνοιαν ἐν ὑπομνήσει.

The word in the original, here translated to put in remembrance, properly signifies, to recall a thing past to mind or memory: a thing, I say, though formerly understood, yet possibly almost forgotten, or at least, for the present, not duly considered or remembered; and thus it is used Luke xxii. 61, "Peter remembered the word of the Lord;" and 2 Tim. ii. 14, "Of these things put them in remembrance," &c.; and Tit. iii. 1, "Put them in remembrance to be subject," &c.; and 2 Pet. i. 12, "I will not be negligent to put you in remembrance," &c.; and 2 Pet. iii. 1, "I stir up your pure mind by way of remembrance." So that the word rather notes reminiscence than memory; a calling back of that which heretofore they had thought of, but for the present was not duly and thoroughly thought of.

2. Why did the apostle thus put them in remembrance? Great reason hereof there was, both in respect of,

The apostle who wrote, and the Christians to whom he wrote.

(1.) In respect of the apostle. It was his duty, not only once to deliver, but again to recall truths to their minds formerly delivered. Upon this duty the apostle puts Timothy, 1 Tim. iv. 6, "If thou put the brethren in remembrance of these things, thou shalt be a good minister of Jesus Christ." And sending him to Corinth, he gives him the same command, 1 Cor. iv. 17; and this was also practised by Paul himself, Rom. xv. 15, "I have written to you the more boldly, as putting you in remembrance." A course practised by Peter likewise, who tells the Christians that he thinks it meet to stir them up, by putting them in remembrance, 2 Pet. i. 13; and that his Second Epistle was written to that end, 2 Pet. iii. 1. Hence it is that ministers are called the Lord's remembrancers, Isa. lxii. 6, 7; not only for putting the Lord in mind of the people's wants, but also in whetting holy instructions upon the people, and putting them in mind of their duty to God.

(2.) In respect of those to whom he wrote, he puts them in remembrance. It was safe for the Philippians to have the same things written to them, Phil. iii. 1. Those eminent Christians, the Romans, to whom Paul wrote, and the saints who had pure minds, to whom Peter wrote, wanted this putting in remembrance, Rom. xv. 14, 15; 2 Pet. iii. 1; for,

[1.] The best are imperfect in their knowledge. The greatest part of those things which we know, is but the least part of what we do not know. The plainest and best known truths are not so well known, but they may be better known. The most experienced Christian may say of every truth, as a man says to his new friends, I would be glad of your better acquaintance. Our knowledge is but in part, even in respect of the plainest truths, 1 Cor. xiii. 9. We cannot name any number so high and great, but a man may reckon one still beyond it; and there may be always an addition to our knowledge. A Christian should grow in his head as well as in his heart; in his light as well as in his heat, Col. ii. 2; i. 9, 10.

It was a humble speech of Luther, I acknowledge myself a scholar even in the catechism. *Fateor me catechismi discipulum.* Every point of divinity has a vast circumference; every command is exceeding broad; and what one article of faith or precept of the law is there of which a man may say, There is nothing contained in it which I fully know not? Christians should often be reminded of the plainest truths, that they may conceive of them the better.

[2.] The memories of the best Christians stand in need of frequent remembrances. They are frail to retain the things of God naturally, Heb. ii. 1. The most precious truths laid up in our memories, are jewels put into a crazy cabinet. Memory is like a sieve, that holds the bran, lets the flour go; remembers what is to be forgotten, and forgets what is to be remembered: and like a sieve that is full in the water, but empty when taken out; the memory is full perhaps while men are hearing, but empty so soon as their hearing is ended. If we would have our garment hold its colour, it must be double-dyed; so, that a truth may take a deep impression, it must be pressed again and again. And this natural unfaithfulness of the memory is furthered by the temptations of Satan, who labours to steal away the most useful truths; like a thief, who robs a house of the best household stuff. In times of temptation to sin, how hard is it to remember the truths that should defend us! How far from Peter's memory was the speech of Christ, till the crowing of the cock reminded him! Luke xxii. 61. "Ye have forgotten," saith the apostle, "the exhortation," Heb. xii. 5. In every sin there is some kind of forgetfulness. When passion is violent, and temptation strong, the use of memory is commonly suspended. "Thou hast greedily gained of thy neighbours by extortion, and hast forgotten me, saith the Lord," Ezek. xxii. 12. And in all true obedience there is remembrance; working righteousness and remembering God are put together, Isa. lxiv. 5.

[3.] The best Christians are subject to abate and decay in spiritual fervency of affection to the best things. Now frequent remembrances not only recall truths to the mind, but quicken the heart to affect them. We are dull to learn what we should do, and more dull to do what we have learned. The sharpest knife grows blunt without whetting; the most honest debtor sometimes wants calling on. The apostle Peter puts the Christians in remembrance, to stir up even their pure minds, 2 Pet. iii. 1. The freest Christian sometimes wants the spur. Our very sanctified affections are like heated water, which of itself grows cold; but neither retains nor increases its heats, unless the fire be put under, and blown up. Good things in the heart lie as embers under ashes, and need daily stirring up.

Obs. 1. Great is the sin of those who contemn repeated truths. A Christian must not have an itching, but a humble and obedient ear. Sinful is that curiosity that despises a wholesome truth because it is common. Truths delivered of old may possibly now be freshly useful; and those delivered now may be helpful in old age, or on our death-beds. Who would neglect a friend that may stand him in stead hereafter? Every truth, like a lease, brings in revenue the next year as well as this. He that knows truth never so fully, knows no injury by it; nay, the more he knows, the more of worth he sees in it. How foolish are those Christians who count no doctrine good but what is new! who, as it is storied of Heliogabalus, cannot endure to eat twice of one dish! How just will it be for want to overtake the wantonness of these hearers!

Obs. 2. Christians must not only receive, but retain also the truths of God. Our memories must be heavenly storehouses and treasuries of precious truths; not like hour-glasses, which are no sooner full but they are running out. The commandments must be bound upon our hearts, and holy instructions (like books in a library) must be chained to our memories. "Keep these words in the midst of thy heart," saith Solomon, Prov. iv. 21. And, "I have hid thy word in my heart, that I might not sin against thee," saith David, Psal. cxix. 11. The slipperiness of our memories causes many slips in our lives. Peter forgot his Master, and then forgot himself: first he forgot the word of a Master, and then he forgot the duty of a servant. Conscience cannot be urged by that truth which memory does not retain. The same truths which being taken in begat our graces, being kept in will increase our graces. To help us in remembering heavenly truths, let us, (1.) Be reverent and heedful in our attentions, as receiving a message from God. He who regards not a truth in hearing, how shall he retain it afterward? (2.) Let us love every heavenly truth as our treasure: delight helps memory, Psal. cxix. 16, and what we love we keep. (3.) Our memories should not be taken up with vanities. A Christian should be most careful to keep that which Satan is most industrious to steal away; and he is like a thief breaking into a house, who takes not away earthen vessels, but plate and jewels: Satan empties not the head of worldly trifles, but of the most precious things. The memory which is filled only with earthly concerns, is like a golden cabinet filled with dung. (4.) Let instruction be followed with meditation, prayer, conference, and holy conversation; by all these it is hid in the heart the more deeply, and driven home the more thoroughly, Deut. vi. 6, 7; Psal. cxix. 97.

Obs. 3. There is a constant necessity of a conscientious ministry. People know and remember but in part, and as children; and till that which is imperfect be done away, we cannot spare ministerial remembrances. We shall want pastors, teachers, &c. till we all meet, &c. in a perfect man, Eph. iv. 12, 13. And there are none weary of the ministry, but they who love not to be remembered of their duty. Of this before.

Obs. 4. The forgetfulness of the people must not discourage the minister. A boat is not to be cast up and broken in pieces for every leak: the dullest and weakest hearer must not be cast off for his crazy memory, but pitied. The very lambs of Christ must be fed; the feeblest child in his house attended. Paul was gentle among the Christians, even as a nurse cherisheth her children. If the preaching of a truth once will not serve the turn, if it be not understood or remembered the first time, ministers must declare it more plainly the next time, and put people in remembrance again and again.

Obs. 5. The work of ministers is not to contrive doctrines, but to recall them. They should deliver what they have received, not what they have invented. Their power is not to make, but manifest laws for the conscience. "That good thing," saith Paul to Timothy, "which was committed to thee keep." Ministers are not masters, but stewards of the mysteries of God.

Thus much of the first part of the preface, The duty of the apostle. Now follows,

II. The commendation of the Christians, "Ye once knew this."

It may be demanded, why the apostle saith that the Christians "once knew this" following example of the Israelites, of which he puts them in remembrance.

The apostle mentions this knowledge of the Christians, that he may gain their good will and favourable respect to the truth of which he was now speaking, and that his arguing from these examples might the more easily find entertainment with them; for by saying that they "knew this," 1. He labours to win them to a love of himself by commending them, and acknowledging that good to be which he saw in them. He commends them for their knowledge and expertness in Scripture, and declares that he spake not to rude and ignorant, but to expert Christians. 2. He gains the reputation of certainty to the truths of which he was speaking, by appealing for this to their own knowledge, which was so clear herein, that he amplifies it, by saying, that they knew it "once;" * that is, certainly, unchangeably, and once for all, never to revoke and alter this knowledge: and both these insinuations Paul uses to the Corinthians, "I speak as to wise men; judge ye what I say," 1 Cor. x. 15; and to Agrippa, for gaining his favour to that cause which he there defended, "I think myself happy, that I shall answer for myself before thee," &c., "because I know thee to be expert in all customs and questions which are among the Jews," Acts xxvi. 2, 3. And ver. 26, "The king knoweth of these things, before whom I speak freely." 3. By saying that they knew this, he prevents the objection which might be made against what he was about to speak, in regard that it was old and ordinary; he insinuating, that of set purpose he produced a known and ancient truth, rather than a new and unheard of uncertainty.

Obs. 1. Knowledge is very commendable in a Christian. For this the Romans are commended, chap. xv. 14, "I am persuaded, brethren, that ye are full of goodness, filled with all knowledge." For this grace given to the Corinthians the apostle blesses God, 1 Cor. i. 5. The knowledge of the Scripture from a child, was the praise of Timothy, 2 Tim. iii. 15. True wisdom gives to the head an ornament of grace, and a crown of glory, Prov. iv. 9; it makes the face to shine, Eccl. viii. 1. When the apostle saith that some had not the knowledge of God, he spake it to their shame, 1 Cor. xv. 34. How little to the honour of others was that complaint of the apostle, that when for the time they ought to be teachers of others, they had need that one should teach them again which be the first principles of the gospel of Christ! Heb. v. 12. And as Paul speaks of some, "Ever learning, and never able to come to the knowledge of the truth," 2 Tim. iii. 7. The whole life of an ignorant person is an aberration from the rule, Gal. vi. 16; he sails by no chart. All his actions are wild and roving wanderings. His sacrifice is the sacrifice of a fool, and devout idolatry. He cannot pray, unless it be to the unknown God. He cannot believe; for only they can trust God who know his name, Rom. x. 14; Psal. ix. 10. Nor can he fear and love God, or desire Christ, John iv. 10. Wait therefore on the ordinances, O ye ignorant ones, with humble, hungry souls, Prov. viii. 34. Be Wisdom's clients. Purge your hearts of conceits of a Laodicean fulness. God teacheth only the humble, Psal. xxv. 9. Taste the sweetness of Divine truths, 1 Pet. ii. 3. Lay up what ye hear. Not he who gets, but he who saves much, is the rich man. Yield conscientious obedience to that of God's will which you know. Hold not the truth in unrighteousness. The more you practise what you know, the more shall you know what to practise. Knowledge is the mother of obedience, and obedience is the nurse of knowledge: the former breeds the latter; the latter feeds the former. And yet put not off yourselves with every kind of knowledge, labour for a soul-humbling knowledge, Job xlii. 5, 6. The more the light shines into you, the more you must see your

* Concerning the word "once," I have spoken largely before, p. 66, 67.

own imperfections. Every man is so much a fool as he thinks himself wise, 1 Cor. viii. 2. Let your knowledge be applicative, Job v. 27. If ye be wise, be wise for yourselves, Prov. ix. 12. Let not knowledge swim in the brain, but sink into the heart. Endeavour to possess for thine own the good of every threatening, command, and promise. Let your knowledge be influential in heart and life, Psal. cxix. 104; not informing only, but reforming, John xiii. 17; 1 John ii. 3; not as the light of torches, which scatter no influences where they shine, but as the light of the sun, which makes the earth and plants green and growing. He who is rich in knowledge must be plentiful in holiness; and not like the rich Indians, who have much gold in their possessions, and go naked and beggarly. In a word, let your knowledge be useful and helpful to others. Know not to know, that is curiosity; nor to be known, that is vain-glory; but to do good by your knowledge, that is Christian charity: knowledge increases in pouring out; and, as some have experimentally found it, the teacher learns more by the scholar, than the scholar by the teacher.

Obs. 2. Ministers ought to commend their people's proficiency in holiness. Jude here mentions the knowledge of the Christians to their praise. When people do what is commendable, ministers should commend what they do. If the former find matter, the latter should find words. "I am persuaded of you," saith Paul to the Romans, "that ye are full of goodness," Rom. xv. 14. And, "I praise you, brethren," saith he to the Corinthians, "that you remember me," &c., 1 Cor. xi. 2. A minister's prudent commendation wins that love to his person without which the best doctrine is often but unprofitable. Rare is it to find that Christian who embraces a message which is brought him from a messenger not beloved. A wise commendation will make a reproof go down the better. Constant chiding is like physic, which being too frequently taken, grows natural, and therefore proves not operative. Ministers should be wise in choosing a fit object for commendation: the commendable actions of every one must not be presently commended; some can less bear the sweetness of praise, than they can the bitterness of reproof. A little wine will turn a weak brain. Nor should we commend any to flatter, but to benefit them; to encourage the humble, not to content the proud. But truly, Christians, it were happy for ministers, if the time you make them spend in weeping and reproving, they might fill with encouraging and cheering you. The work and delight of a minister is, with the bee, to give honey; he puts not forth the sting, unless you by sin provoke him. Of this more p. 53.

Obs. 3. Every private Christian should be acquainted with the Scripture. It is sinful to clasp up the Scriptures in an unknown tongue. The end of writing the Scriptures, was the instruction of every one, Col. iii. 16; John v. 39; Rom. xv. 4. None are so much commended in Scripture as those who most diligently searched into it, Acts xvii. 11. To private Christians Paul writes sundry Epistles. The study of Scripture is useful and needful to people as well as ministers: illumination, conversion, direction, preservation from sin, belong to the one as well as to the other, Psal. xix. 8, 9; cxix. 24; and if for the abuse of Scripture, the use thereof should be denied to people, why would Christ and his apostles preach and write to those who perverted and wrested their doctrines? yea, why should not the reading of Scripture be denied, not only to ignorant monks and priests, but erroneous clerks and bishops, from whom by abuse of Scripture most heresies have proceeded? But whether Satan has not by his methods wrought us into the other extreme, when instead of general restraint from reading, he puts people upon a general liberty of preaching and expounding the Scripture, our present distractions sufficiently witness.

Obs. 4. The knowledge of truth is a strong engagement upon Christians to embrace and love it. The apostle, from their knowing the examples, hopefully expects that they will lay them to heart. Truth known and not loved is unprofitable. Not he who knows a trade, but follows it, grows rich. It will fare ill enough with the ignorant, worse with the obstinate; and many stripes are reserved for opposing much knowledge. But of this before.

Obs. 5. Ministers ought not to content the curiosity, but to consult the benefit of their hearers. They should rather deliver truths old and useful, than doctrines new and unprofitable. Their work is not to please the Athenian, but to profit the Christian. They are not cooks, but physicians; and therefore should not study to delight the palate, but to recover the patient: they must not provide sauce, but physic. If to preach the same things be safe, it matters not whether it be sweet or no. Jesus Christ has given us no commission to study the pleasure, but the preservation of our people. It is better that our people should be angry for not pleasing their lusts, than that God should be angry for not profiting their souls.

Obs. 6. The truths of the word are to be known unchangeably, stedfastly, once for all. Christians must not be removed from the truth, Gal. i. 6; they must labour to be men in understanding, and not be "children, tossed to and fro with every wind of doctrine," Eph. iv. 14. They must be known by the truth, as men say they will by the gift of a friend, many years after it is delivered. Holy instructions must be entertained with full assurance of understanding, and looked upon, not as opinions, but assertions, more sure than what we see with our bodily eyes, Col. ii. 2. A sceptical, doubtful, staggering Christian will soon prove a falling, an apostatizing Christian.* A Christian must be rooted and grounded in the love of the truth, Eph. iii. 17. *Si fidem scrutari hæsitando cæperimus, omnium patiemur jacturam. Theophylact. in Rom. i.*

Thus far of the first part of the verse; viz. The preface prefixed. I come now to the second, namely, The example propounded, in these words, "How that the Lord, having saved the people out of the land of Egypt, afterward destroyed them that believed not."

In the example I consider,

1. A famous deliverance; "The Lord having saved the people out of the land of Egypt."
2. A destruction following that deliverance; "Afterward destroyed."
3. The meritorious cause of that destruction, unbelief; those "that believed not."

1. A famous deliverance, contained in these words; "The Lord having saved the people out of the land of Egypt."

The greatness of this mercy in delivering the Israelites out of Egypt is frequently mentioned in Scripture. Besides the large history thereof in the Book of Exodus, it is prefixed briefly to the ten commandments, as a most prevailing motive to obedience; and often set down as one of the most famous deliverances that ever God bestowed upon his church, Deut. iv. 20; Lev. xxvi. 13; Psal. lxxvii. 15, 16, 20; lxxviii. 12—14, 41—54; cv. 23—39; cvi. 6—13; cxiv. 3, 5; Isa. lxiii. 11—13; Psal. cxxxvi.

---

* Helps hereunto, see p. 68.

9—17; Acts vii. 18—37. And indeed, so it was, if we consider,

I. What the Egyptians did to the Israelites in abusing them during their abode in Egypt.

II. What God did both to the Egyptians and Israelites, when he delivered the Israelites from the abuses of the Egyptians.

For the first: 1. The Egyptians offered many cruel injuries to the bodies of the Israelites. 2. By their heathenish idolatry they were great enemies to their souls.

The first of these the Scripture expresses in setting down,

First, The bondage and servitude of the Israelites, whereby their liberty and ease were taken away.

Secondly, The murderous edicts which were given out for taking away also their lives.

First. The cruel bondage of the Israelites was so great, that Egypt is called in Scripture "the house of bondage," Exod. xx. 2; and Egyptian bondage is even become a proverb. The Israelites were not more lovingly received by one Pharaoh, than they were cruelly retained by another. They who of late were strangers, are now slaves. With Joseph, died the remembrance of his love to Egypt, Exod. i. 6, 8—11. Thankfulness to him by whom under God the lives and beings of the Egyptians were preserved, is swallowed up in envy at the increase of his kindred and posterity. The great fault of the Israelites is this, that God multiplieth them. To pull them down, though by opposing God, and to make them as unfit for generation as resistance, the Egyptians make them serve with rigour, and make "their lives bitter with hard bondage in mortar and brick," Exod. i. 13, 14: every word denotes Egyptian cruelty. The word translated, to make them serve, עבדו Hanc habet vim præpositio κατά. signifies to oppress by mere force; and it is a word denoting properly a tyrannical abuse of power, and therefore translated by the Seventy καταδυναστεύειν, which signifies such a proud and cruel domineering as is used by tyrants. Nor is the word translated, with rigour, without an emphasis; it signifies, saith Cajetan, a making them to serve, even to the breaking of their bones. It is added, that the Egyptians made their lives bitter; a word transferred from the body to the mind, to note the grievousness and unpleasantness of a thing. The same word is used Lam. iii. 15, where the church מרה unde מרד saith, "He hath filled me with bitterness, he hath made me drunk with wormwood." And (as Lorinus thinks) Miriam the sister of Moses had that name given to her, which signifies bitterness, because she was born in those times. The Seventy, in their translation, express this imbittering of the Israelites' lives by a word which signifies the most sharp and cutting pains in childbearing. And doubtless this bitterness was much increased by the nature of the work in which the Israelites were employed, which was in mortar, dirt, and brick, and all manner of service of the field: they were put upon the most sordid and servile employment.

2. Antiq. c. 5. Philo and Josephus, with others, report, that the works of the Israelites were mere drudgeries, the most mean and dirty, as scouring of pits, the casting up of banks to keep out inundations, the digging and cleansing of ditches, and carrying the dung out of the cities upon their shoulders. And it is said, Psal. lxxxi. 6, "I removed his shoulder from the burden, and his hands were delivered from the pots." And that which yet made their servitude more extreme and bitter, was, that being in these dirty drudgeries of mortar and brick, the tale of the bricks is by the task-masters laid upon the people, though the straw wherewith to make brick is denied them, Exod. v. 18. The poor Israelites now take more pains to please, and yet please their cruel masters less than ever before. They are commanded to gather straw, and yet cruelly beaten, because while they were gathering straw, they were not making brick; that is, because they performed not impossibilities, and did not make straw as well as brick. Do what may be, is tolerable; but do what cannot be, is cruel. Hereupon the Israelites cry and complain to Pharaoh of their want of straw, and their plenty of stripes. In a word, all that they desire is, that they may but work; as for wages, they desire none. Instead of relieving them, he derides them, and with cruelly cutting scoff, and sarcastical insult, he wounds their very wounds, and tells them, against his own knowledge, they are idle, they are idle. Hereupon, the Egyptian rigour is continued, and the people of God, who after all their toiling received no other rewards but stripes and scorns, are worse handled than Egyptian beasts. So great was this cruelty, that, as Philo reports, if any Israelite, Philo, lib. 1. de vit. Mos. through sickness of body, abstained from labour, it was accounted a crime deserving death. Eusebius saith, that by reason of their excessive labour and heat, many were taken away by the pestilence. By this we may gather why the Lord tells them, "I brought you forth out of the land of Egypt, that ye should not be their bondmen; and I have broken the bands of your yoke, and made you go upright," Lev. xxvi. 13. Servitude is a kind of death; nay, by free people accounted worse than death; who have often chosen rather to die valiantly, than to live slavishly. Nor is it any wonder therefore to read of the groaning, sighing, and crying of the poor Israelites, yea, of their 'Ἀπὸ τῆς ὀλιγοψυχίας. Septuag. anguish, shortness and straitness of spirit, by reason of cruel bondage, Exod. ii. 23, 24; vi. 9.

Secondly. The second discovery of the cruelty of the Egyptians towards the Israelites, was in the bloody commands for the taking away of the lives of the male children, Exod. i. 15. This was a blow at the root. It was out of policy, not any tenderness of conscience, that this murderous command took not in the females also. The females did not constitute families; the taking away of the males would suffice to hinder the multiplying of the people. The females could not make war, join with the enemies of the Egyptians, or by force endeavour to depart from Egypt; and the sparing of some might make the murders less suspected. From bondage these Egyptians proceed to blood, and from slavery to slaughter. Women are suborned to be murderers, and those whose office is to help, must destroy the birth: the midwives were put upon this bloody work, because, as they had more opportunity of doing, so would others have less suspicion of them for doing the mischief. The male children must be born and die at once; and, poor babes, they must be killed for no other fault but for their stock and their sex, because they are Israelites and males: pure and downright bloodiness! Needs must the Hebrew women, contrary to all others, not joy, but mourn, when they saw men-children born. This device of employing the midwives not succeeding, the tyrant gives commission to all his own people to cast every son that is born into the river, ἐκθέτα τὰ βρέφη, Acts vii. 19. Josephus writes, that the command was given also to the Hebrews to kill their own children;* but most barbarous it was, although it were only given to the Egyptians. Pharaoh's cruelty smoked before, now it flames out.

* This seems to be opposed by Exod. i. 22.

He practised secretly in his commands to the midwives, he now proclaims it openly to all the world. No Egyptian now could be obedient, unless bloody; every man is made an executioner; the reins are laid upon the neck of cruelty. Every Egyptian may rifle the houses of the Israelites, and search for children as for prohibited commodities. How difficultly are these poor babes hid, and yet how dangerously found! They who had no armour but innocence and tears, are exposed to authorized rage. How poor a shelter is the arm of an indulgent mother against the command of a king, and the fury of his heathen subjects; whose vigilance and violence were so great, that as the mother of Moses was unable long to hide him, so was she more willing to trust him with the mercy of beasts and waters than of Egyptians! And how hard was it for the strongest faith of the best Israelite to bear up against this temptation! So long as the Israelites saw themselves increasing, though oppressed, their faith in God's promise of blessing the seed of Abraham might be comfortably relieved; but now this cruel edict of murdering their children, by whom the seed of Abraham was to be propagated, seems to cut off all hope, and to make void all the promises.

2. The Egyptians from whom the Israelites were delivered may be considered as heathen idolaters, and so enemies to the souls of the Israelites. Had the outward ease and prosperity of Israel in Egypt been never so great, yet eminent had been the mercy of being drawn out of such peril for the soul as was in idolatrous company. Joshua thankfully records the mercy of God to Abraham, in bringing him out of Ur of the Chaldeans, where his ancestors served strange gods. And how great this mercy was, appears by observing the forwardness of the Israelites to be infected by the contagion of Egyptian idolatry. The Egyptians were a most idolatrous people, whence it is that so often we read of the idols and gods of Egypt, Isa. xix. 1; Jer. xliii. 12; xlvi. 25; Ezek. xx. 7, 8. No people idolized so many and such vile creatures as did the Egyptians; the mole, the bat, the cat, the dung-fly, monkeys, birds, crocodiles; yea, leeks, onions, garlic, &c. were adored by them as gods. So gross was their superstition, that the heathens deride them for it. Pliny saith, that they were wont to deify and swear by their leeks, onions, and garlic. And Juvenal lashes them for adoring these garden gods. And from the vileness of those creatures, Sanctius supposes that the gods of the Egyptians are called abominations. It is evident also that the Israelites were too forward to worship the idols, although they were weary of the oppressions of the Egyptians. Hence it is that the prophet complains of their rebelling against the express prohibition of God, that they should not defile themselves with the idols of Egypt; and that they did not forsake those idols, Ezek. xx. 7, 8. And the same prophet, reproving Israel for their early adulteries, by which he means their idolatries, saith, that she committed whoredoms in Egypt in her youth, chap. xxiii. 3; i. e. when the Israelites were but a young and new nation. And that she left not her whoredoms brought from the Egyptians; "for in her youth they lay with her, and bruised the breasts of her virginity," ver. 8. Clear likewise to this purpose is that command of Joshua to the Israelites, "Put away the gods which your fathers served in Egypt," Josh. xxiv. 14. Nor are there wanting learned men, who conceive that the reason why the Israelites in the wilderness made them an idol which had the figure of a calf or an ox, Exod. xxxvi. 4; Psal. cvi. 20, was, because they had often seen the Egyptians, under that kind of image, worship either their greatly adored Apis, who had formerly been their king and benefactor, and whom now they esteemed their tutelary god; or else, as other learned men think, the river Nile, which by its inundation made the land of Egypt fruitful. And very probable it is, that God intended this bitter oppression of the Israelites by the Egyptians, partly as a punishment for joining with them in their idolatry formerly; partly as a remedy, to prevent in the Israelites that familiarity and friendship with the Egyptians for time to come, whereby they might easily fall again in love with their superstitions. For if after all the indignities and cruelties which the Israelites suffered in Egypt, they were desirous again, as they were, to return thither, Numb. xiv. 4, how forward would they have been, had the Egyptians always favoured and loved them! If they loved to be handling of thorns, how would they have delighted in roses!

And this may serve for the explication of the greatness of this deliverance from the Egyptians in this first consideration; namely, of what the Egyptians had done to the Israelites, in abusing them during their abode in Egypt.

II. But secondly, This deliverance will yet appear much more eminent, if we consider what God did, both to Egyptians and Israelites, in delivering the Israelites from the abuses of the Egyptians.

1. What God did to the Egyptians. He poured his plagues upon them; he made Egypt the anvil of his angry strokes. He punished them, powerfully; and, justly.

(1.) Most powerfully did God punish the Egyptians. For this cause did God raise up Pharaoh, to show in him his power, Exod. ix. 16. All the judgments which befell the Egyptians came as soon as God called them. At his command the waters run blood, the frogs, the lice, the flies, the grasshoppers, the darkness, the hail, the thunder, and all those wrathful troops of plagues obey the will of him who commanded in chief, and revenge the wrongs of their Maker. The most despicable of creatures, lice and flies, the weakest twigs of God's rod, shall fetch blood, when managed by the hand of Omnipotence. Nor was his power less conspicuous in setting a stint to the very flies, and making that winged army to acknowledge their limits, and to keep at a distance from Goshen. Yea, let but God speak the word, and frogs, and flies, and grasshoppers depart as readily as ever they came. And to show that he could plague without them, the greatest of Egypt's plagues is inflicted when they are gone. The strength of Egypt, their first-born, die, and are but worms and weakness to the Strength of Israel. All this was much; it was admirable strength which broke the backs of the Egyptians: but nothing but pure Omnipotence could break such rocks and oaks as were their hearts; but even these also are bowed and broken. None so forward now to thrust the Israelites out of Egypt, yea, to hire them to go, as they who even now tyrannically detained them. Their rich jewels of silver and gold are not too dear for them whom lately they spoiled of their substance. Glad they are now to pay them for their old work. Those who lately were detained as slaves, are now sent away as conquerors, with the spoils of their enemies. Still the power of God appears. No sooner were the backs of Israel turned to depart, but the warlike Egyptians, furnished with horses and chariots, pursue the feeble and unarmed Israelites; who hereupon give up themselves for

Per allia, cæpe, et porros jurant. Plin. l. 19. c. 6.
—Crocodilon adorat pars hæc: illa pavet saturam serpentibus ibim. Effigies sacri nitet aurea cercopitheci. Porrum et cæpe nefas violare et frangere morsu. O sanctas gentes quibus hæc nascuntur in hortis Numina.— Juv. Sat. 15. Sanctius in Ezek. xx. 7. Nauseas, Symmach. Inquinamenta, Aquila.

dead, and are now talking of nothing but their graves. They know not whether is more merciful, the sea before them, or the Egyptians behind them; but the sea retires and flies, and the Israelites put their feet into the way it has made them. Pharaoh thinks he may adventure as well as they; he marches smoothly, till he come to the midst of that watery trap, and would fain return when it was too late. The rod of Moses is now more powerful than the sceptre of Pharaoh. The sea is now again unbridled, returns in its force, and devours the late devourers of Israel. And therefore,

(2.) How justly did God punish the Egyptians! Was it not just that the bold blasphemer, who even now asked, Who is the Lord? should be made to know him by feeling him, and that this Lord should be known upon him to all the world? The river Nile, which by its inundations made Egypt fruitful, was by the Egyptians regarded more than Heaven, and worshipped for a deity; and how righteously are they punished by the blood and frogs of that which they make a rival with God! They had lately defiled the rivers with the blood of infants; see now their rivers red with blood, and they themselves are afterward overwhelmed in the Red Sea. He who had rather satisfy his own curiosity by the feats of magicians, than labour for humility under strokes, not more smart than miraculous, is at once both deluded and hardened. They who, to spare themselves, burdened and enslaved poor groaning Israelites, are now plagued when Israel is preserved. How justly does God distinguish, when they had done so before! They who are hardened, are at length broken by judgments. They who sinned by the removal, are justly punished by the renewing of plagues. They who so cruelly oppressed God's first-born son, his Israel, are now plagued in the destruction of their own first-born. They who lately made poor Israel drudge, and toil in dirt and mire, without allowing them any wages but scoffs and stripes, now pay them wages for their old work, with interest; and with their gold and silver bear the charges of that journey which all this while they were hindering the Israelites from taking. They who are not taught, justly stumble by the people of God. To conclude this, how just was it, that he who with his people hoped that the Israelites were so entangled and shut up in the wilderness and the sea, as they should not be able to make escape; that he and his (I say) should by this bait be drawn so far to pursue the Israelites, as neither to be able to go backward or forward!

2. The mercy of saving the people out of the land of Egypt will yet more fully appear, if we consider what God did to the Israelites. He "delivered them;" and this he did, most wisely; and, most graciously.

(1.) Most wisely did God deliver his people, in raising up Moses to be their deliverer. The mother of Moses brought him forth in a time wherein she could not but think of his birth and death at once, and hourly expect some cruel executioner to tear her tender and lovely babe out of those arms wherein she was as unable as she was willing to hold him. For fear of such a one, she puts him into an ark of bulrushes, and hides him among the flags of the river. God showed that he knew the place where Moses lay, by guiding thither even the daughter of Pharaoh to deliver Moses. She soon espies and causes the ark to be opened: the tears and beauty of the child move her compassions; which the sister of Moses observing, offers to procure a nurse for the babe, and fetches his mother. She who even now would have given all her substance for the life of her child, has now a reward given to her to nurse him. How admirably did the wisdom of God deceive the Egyptians! The daughter of him whose only plot was to destroy Israel, is made the instrument of saving Israel, by preserving him who was to be their deliverer, and the instrument of Egypt's destruction. The Egyptians also, who compel the Israelites to serve them without paying them wages, are compelled by God at the same time to pay for the nursing of him who shortly after overthrows the Egyptians. At length Pharaoh's daughter takes Moses home from nurse, and gives him as good breeding as the Egyptians' schools and court can afford him. Moses was not in more danger among the flags than among the courtiers; but God, who of late kept him from hurt by Egyptian cruelty, keeps him now as wisely from hurt by Egyptian courtesy. The honours of Egypt cannot make him either own a heathen for his mother, though a king's daughter, or forget his Hebrew brethren, though the king's bondmen. He observes their sufferings, and suffers with them. He having from God an instinct of magistracy, mortally, though secretly as he thought, smites an Egyptian who was unjustly smiting a Hebrew. The fact is known, and Moses, warned thereof by a churlish word which was intended to wound him, flies from Pharaoh seeking to slay him. In Midian God provides him a shelter. Moses has now changed his place, yet neither has he changed his Keeper and acquaintance, nor Israel lost their deliverer. In a strange land God appears to Moses, and calls him to this honourable employment of saving Israel. God confirms his faith by vision and voice: by the vision he taught him, that if the tinder of a weak and most combustible bush could overcome a flame of fire, that a poor Moses and an oppressed Israel might as easily prevail over cruel and armed tyranny; by the voice, which was the comment upon the vision, God, being moved by Israel's afflictions, and not hindered by Moses's objections, expresses his resolution, that Moses shall bring Israel out of Egypt. Whereupon Moses yields to undertake the employment. *Quid sibi vult ardere, et non exuri rubum? nempe Israelem Ægyptiis superiorem futurum. Theod. in loc.*

(2.) Most wisely did God deliver the people, in respect of the time of their deliverance. [1.] How wisely did God time this deliverance, considering the extreme and distressed lowness of Israel at that time wherein God began to work it! The darkness was very thick immediately before the day-break; the tide was at the lowest, before it began to turn; Moses himself was too faint to believe without the double support of a promise and a vision: now was Egypt's cruelty high, Israel's strength low; all their arms were toil and tasks, tears, and sighs, and groans, weapons which overcame him who overcame the Egyptians. For thus it faring with Israel, Moses the deliverer comes and serves Pharaoh with a warrant from God himself to let Israel go. But Israel is not yet fit, that is, weak enough to break out of Egypt. They must be required to make brick without straw; and, in effect, to make straw; and then God creates deliverance. The deliverance from their tasks of brick seems as impossible as was the fulfilling of these tasks; and they for very anguish are as unable to hearken believingly and patiently to God's messenger, promising deliverance, as they were desirous to receive it. Oh how did the desperateness of Israel's disease commend the skilfulness of Israel's Physician! [2.] How eminent was the wisdom of God in timing of Israel's deliverance, so as that they should be compelled by Pharaoh to depart that very day in which God had promised that they should depart four hundred and thirty years before! Pharaoh's choice of time for the departure of Israel meets with God's exactly; that very night when the four hundred and thirty years were expired Israel must go; God will have it so, yea, Pharaoh will have it so, who neither can nor can will to keep them any longer.

But, secondly, God delivered Israel out of Egypt as graciously as he did wisely. (1.) How tender was he of his Israel when his wrath was hottest against the Egyptians! He commands his plagues to distinguish between Egypt and Goshen. Israel was now like a man upon a high hill, that sees the dreadfully stately spectacle of a bloody battle, but is himself out of gun-shot. All Israel's work is but to behold and believe. (2.) Afterward in their departure, how good was God to give them furniture for their journey, at the voluntary charges of their late oppressive enemies! (3.) Further, how indulgent was God in having such respect to the infirmities of his people! as not to choose them the shorter, but the safer way; and to preserve them from war, whose late and long condition of slavery had made them unfit for soldiery; he intending them no fighting till after more preparation; and not suffering evils to be ready for Israel, till Israel were ready for those evils; dealing herein as gently with his people as the eagle with her young ones, the resemblance used by Moses, Deut. xxxii. 11; for the eagle turns not her young ones presently out of her nest, either for flight or prey, but first nourishes them, and then by little and little accustoms them to fly, by bearing them on her wings. (4.) Mercy still proceeds; it both chooses a way for Israel, and guides Israel in that way. In the day God appoints a pillar of a cloud to guide them, and not of fire, because the greater light extinguishes the less. In the night he erects a pillar of fire, because in the night nothing is seen without light. The cloud shelters from heat by day, the fire digests the rawness of the night. Day and night God suits himself to Israel's exigence. (5.) Yet more mercy; Pharaoh and his formidable army are now within sight of Israel, and Israel more fears Egypt than believes God. They charge Moses in their murmurings with not intending to deliver them from, but to betray them to, the Egyptians. And Josephus reports, that the unbelieving Israelites were about to stone Moses, and to yield up themselves again to their late cruel masters the Egyptians. God's patience is no less a miracle than their deliverance. (6.) But mercy stops not yet; the sea forgets its natural course, and stands still to wait upon the servants of the God of nature. The sea made them way, reared them up walls on both sides, and dares not stir till Israel have passed through it. That which Israel feared would destroy, now protects them from their late destroyers and present pursuers.

Obs. 1. The goodness of God to his Israel stirs up envy in the Egyptians. Because God's eye is good, theirs is evil. Joseph was envied by his brethren, because God blessed him with the love of his father. Saul envied David, because God was with him; Pharaoh the Israelites, because God multiplied them. It is a sign of a wicked heart, to look upon every addition to another's happiness as a diminution of its own: an envious man in one thing is worse than other sinners; for whereas others rage and fret, that the world, as they conceive, is so bad, the envious are angry it is so good. And wisely does God suffer his own bounty to be mixed with his enemies' envy, lest his people being too much glued to his footstool favours, should not enough look up to that place where envy shall be no more. Only in heaven is so much plenty that there is no envy.

<small>Uberior seges est alienis semper in agris. Vicinique pecus grandius uber habet.</small>

<small>'Αφθονία.</small>

Obs. 2. The kindnesses of God's Israel to Egypt are often but unkindly requited by Egypt. To Joseph, under God, did the king and kingdom of Egypt in the time of famine owe their preservation; but a new king and generation arising, old favours are forgotten. Had Joseph been an enemy to Egypt, it would have been well enough remembered; but as his brethren remembered not his afflictions, so the Egyptians remembered not his favours. Light injuries, like a feather, will easily swim upon the water; weighty favours, like a piece of lead, sink to the bottom, and are forgotten. The loyal love of Mordecai to Ahasuerus had been utterly buried, if the annals had not recorded it. Gideon, who had been that famous deliverer of Israel, is so far forgotten after his death by the Shechemites, that they slew his sons, Judg. viii. 35. God would have his people in all the good they do, not to seek the applause of men, but to eye his command, and to look to him, who registers the slenderest performance, even the giving a cup of cold water to any in his name; and with whom our reward is, and who will make our favours coals of fire to consume and destroy, if not to thaw and dissolve, our hardened enemies, Rom. xii. 20.

<small>Παλαιὰ εὕδει χάρις. Pind.</small>

Obs. 3. Affliction is the lot of God's Israel. The holy patriarch who had the name of Israel, had a life made up of sorrows. Affliction was his daily bread, and his constant diet drink. His brother threatens to kill him: his uncle, to whom he flies for refuge, is churlish and deceitful: his eldest son is incestuous: his only daughter ravished: two of his sons turned cruel murderers: his best beloved wife dies in childbirth, and his dearest child is given over for murdered: he and his family are soon after punished with a sore famine: in sending for food, he loses, as he thinks, Simeon: his days, by his own computation and confession, were few and evil, Gen. xlvii. 9. The posterity of Israel have afflictions left them for their legacy. Egypt, the wilderness, Canaan, Babylon, were the stages of Israel's tragedies. The spiritual Israel is in all the parts and ages of the world a distressed number. Witness that book of martyrs epitomised, Heb. xi. Of all people, God would have his Israel holiest, and he corrects them to make them partakers of his holiness, Heb. xii. 10. If he suffers weeds in the forest, he endures them not in the garden. Affliction is appointed for the consumption of sin. It is as fire to the raw flesh, to roast out the crudities and blood of our corruptions. It is poison to lusts, and food to graces. The sheep of Christ thrive best in shortest pasture; faith, humility, patience, prayer, heavenly-mindedness, in affliction, like spices under the pestle, are sweetly fragrant. How sweet is music upon the water! How heavenly are the prayers of a weeping saint! Affliction is God's touchstone, to difference between the precious and the vile; his fan, to sever between the wheat and the chaff; his waters, like those to which Gideon brought his soldiers, for the trial of their fitness for war, Judg. vii. 5; his furnace, to separate between the metal and the dross. Of all people, therefore, true Israelites should never promise to themselves outward ease. God sees it best for his people, like waters, to be in motion: should they stand still, they would soon putrefy. The rest of the people of God remains, Heb. iv. 9. It is too much to have two heavens. He who said he should never be removed, like Peter in the mount, knew not what he said. That saints may be always safe, they must never be secure. Of all people, those should be least censured who are most corrected; they may be, nay, are most like to be Israelites. The happiness of Israel is not to be

<small>Parisiensis.</small>

judged by outward appearances. The Israels, the princes of God, are in this world but princes under a disguise. This life is but the obscurity of their adoption. We see their combats, we see not their crowns; we view them in the tents of Kedar, not within the curtains of Solomon.

Obs. 4. More particularly, it is no new thing for Egypt to be unkind and cruel to Israel. Israelites and Egyptians are of contrary dispositions and inclinations; the delight of the one is the abomination of the other. Besides, it is the duty of Israel to depart out of Egypt. Israel is in Egypt in respect of abode, not of desire. Egypt is not Israel's rest. If Egypt were a house of hospitality, it would more dangerously and strongly detain the Israelites than in being a house of bondage. The thoughts of Canaan would be but slight and seldom, if Egypt were pleasant. It is good that Egyptians should hate us, that so they may not hurt us. When the world is most kind, it is most corrupting; and when it smiles most, it seduces most. Were it not for the bondage in Egypt, the onions and idols of Egypt would be too much beloved. Blessed be God, who will by the former wean us from the latter, and will not let us have the one without the other: far better that Egypt should oppress us, than we oppose God. Further, it is the endeavour of Israel to depart out of Egypt; and never was any known to forsake Egypt without persecution. This world loves its own, but it loathes them who show that they belong to another. To forsake the courses of the world is practically to speak our dislike of them; and therefore he that will not associate with sinners, shall be sure to smart by them. "They think it strange," saith the apostle, "that ye run not with them to the same excess of riot, speaking evil of you," 1 Pet. iv. 4. The wicked speak evil of saints, not for doing any evil against them, but only for not doing evil with them. I wonder not that Israel was either so courteously sent for and invited out of Canaan into Egypt, or so cruelly opposed when they offered to depart out of Egypt into Canaan. When thou art coming to Egyptians, they will love thee; when thou goest from them, they will hate thee.

Obs. 5. Judgment begins at God's Israel. God whips his children before he beats the servants, and corrects Israel before he kills the Egyptians, 1 Pet. iv. 17. First God performs his whole work upon Mount Zion, before he punisheth the fruit of the proud heart of the king of Assyria, Isa. x. 12. God ordinarily makes use of Egypt for the base and low service of punishing Israel; and the wisp must first scour the vessel before it be thrown on the dunghill. The building must first be erected before the scaffold be taken down. The corrupt blood must be drawn out before the leech fall off. The wicked in all their tyranny and lordship are but servants, the lowest, scullions to serve and scour the godly. They are spared and punished in order to the saints' exigence: and when wicked men are advanced, it is not for their own worth, but for the wickedness of the church; not because the wicked deserve to have such servants as the godly, but because the godly deserve such masters as the wicked. God sets them up, not out of love to their sin, but out of hatred to the sins of his people; and the best prognostic of the downfal of Egyptians, is the reformation of Israelites. Besides, God will render Egypt inexcusable when he comes to plague them. What can Egypt say for itself, when God hath dealt so severely with his own Israel before their eyes, yea, by their hands? so many crosses as befall Israel, are so many evidences against Egypt. If God do these things in the green tree, what will he do in the dry? Luke xxiii. 31. If he scourge the children with rods, he will whip the slaves with scorpions. "They whose judgment was not to drink of the cup have assuredly drunken; and art thou he that shalt altogether go unpunished? thou shalt not go unpunished, but thou shalt surely drink of it. I begin to bring evil upon the city which is called by my name, and should ye be utterly unpunished? ye shall not be unpunished," Jer. xlix. 12; xxv. 29. When Egypt has seen God so severe, and themselves so cruel against Israel, what can they say why judgment should not pass against themselves? Yet further, judgment begins first with Israel, that so they may be the more fitted to see judgment come upon Egyptians. Israel would not know how to manage the mercy of Egypt's overthrow, if God had not first humbled Israel. Too many sails are dangerous for a small vessel. The heart of Israel is so slight and giddy, that it would not be able to sail without the ballast of correction. Yet again, Israel would not so much rejoice in Egypt's after-overthrow, if God had not first corrected Israel; the people of God cannot be thankful in the downfal of their enemies, when they cannot tell but that judgments may afterward fall upon themselves. How can the throwing of the rod into the fire delight the child, whenas the child knows not but that the parent may throw it into the fire afterward? If a house be not finished, it will soon decay; if a sore be not thoroughly cleansed, it will break out again. If Israel be not well purged by corrections before the Egyptians be destroyed, punishments seven times worse may again return to Israel. And a new deliverance bestowed upon an old heart will but make the rent the greater. All this shows us the reason why Egypt still is unpunished; truly, Israel is not yet corrected, or at least not humbled and reformed by corrections sufficiently. The plaster falls not off till the sore be healed: the people of God are beholden to themselves for their lingering calamities. All times are not seasonable for Egypt's overthrow. Though the enemies of God may be high enough, yet the people of God may possibly not be low enough, for the accomplishment of such a work. *Præpostera celeritas. Calv. in Isa. x. 12.* We, poor creatures! have short thoughts; and, like silly children, are desirous to have the apple taken out of the fire before it be roasted enough: and, like them, we love green fruit; I mean, mercies before they are ripe; but green fruit breeds worms, and mercies bestowed before we are fit to enjoy them, make us but proud and unreformed.

Obs. 6. God often brings his Israel into such straits, as out of which they see no possibility of deliverance. So bitter was Israel's affliction, that they had as little patience to hear of their deliverance as to endure their bondage, Exod. vi. 9. God's people are sometimes brought into a condition so strait, that it is resembled to a prison; to denote, that they are so confined to and enclosed in their troubles, that they see no way of escape. David prays that God would bring his soul out of prison, Psal. cxlii. 7. The afflicted servants of God are called prisoners of hope, Zech. ix. 12. Abraham was in a great strait when God commanded him to sacrifice his only son Isaac, in whom the promises were to be fulfilled. David was greatly distressed when Ziklag was burnt with fire, and his wives taken captives, and his soldiers spake of stoning him, 1 Sam. xxx. 6. And in a great strait he was, when God, by the prophet, offered him his choice of plague, famine, and pursuit by the enemies, 2 Sam. xxiv. 14. Jehoshaphat was in a great strait, when at the approach of so vast an army of enemies, he said, We know not what to do, 2 Chron. xx. 12. Israel was in a great strait, when instead of deliverance which Moses had promised them, their tale of bricks was continued, and their straw taken from them," Exod. v. 8; and afterwards, when Pharaoh was pursuing them, and the sea was before them, Exod. xiv. 10. God's Israel would never be humble in, nor thankful for enlargements, if God did not sometimes bring them into distresses. How sweet is liberty after a prison! how pleasant is the haven after a storm, which brought the distressed mariner to his wits' end! Psal. cvii. 27. Israel would not so believe God in future distresses, if they had not been in them before. Israel might have gathered strength against their distress at the Red Sea, by considering God's delivering them from the distress of oppression. Their faith should also have been upheld against straits in the wilderness, by remembering their deliverance at the Red Sea. And their distrustfulness after deliverances from their distresses is oft recorded as their sin. The graces also of God's Israel are much manifested by encountering with and overcoming distresses. Their graces hereby are discovered both in their truth and their strength. Weak grace cannot go through strong temptation; but the distresses of an Abraham, a David, a Job, a Paul, prove in the end trophies of triumphant faith. And all the power of grace does but discover the power of God; who delights not that his saints should be distressed, but that the world and the devil should be vanquished by poor believers, and ultimately that himself should be glorified by all. Instead of murmuring under lesser trials, consider that these are nothing to the distresses of your betters. Remember, Christians, that if your drink be water or wormwood, some have drunk blood. Prepare for distresses. Christians, pray for increase of faith: the journey may be long, desire God to help you to feed heartily upon the promises, even again and again, as God bids Elijah, when he was to go to Horeb. By bearing lighter, labour to grow fit for heavier pressures. A delicate Christian will not endure to be a distressed Christian. He who by the daily practice of self-denial and mortification does not displease himself, will never endure that another should distress him. How fearful, further, should we be of censuring the most distressed! Abraham's distress, David's strait, Paul's viper, proved them neither wicked nor forsaken. Oh how much better is it to be a distressed saint than an enlarged sinner! to be in God's pound, than in Satan's champaign! If the one condition has more liberty, the other has more safety. Where God loves, there he corrects; and where he loves most, there he distresses. To conclude this; in distress, take heed of despondency; recollect former deliverances out of as great distresses, 2 Cor. i. 10. When you meet with such a strait, pinching Egyptian yoke which God cannot break, with burdens which he cannot take down, with a Red Sea which he cannot divide; when you are pursued by a Pharaoh which he cannot devour, and are in a distress which he cannot remove; then, and not till then, distrust him. Improve your interest in God, and, with David in distress, encourage yourselves in the Lord your God, 1 Sam. xxx. 6.

Obs. 7. God's Israel shall not be utterly destroyed, though it be in an Egyptian furnace of affliction. The church is supported even when oppressed. When Israel was afflicted, they multiplied, Exod. i. 12. Thus it was with the seed of Israel; yea, thus with the Saviour thereof. After his death, his name, his glory lived more vigorously than ever; and they who in his lifetime sought to destroy him, as unworthy to live, after his death sought to live by believing on him. This he foretold of himself, "If a corn of wheat die, it bringeth forth much fruit," John xii. 24. Thus was it with the ancient Christians. The more we are mown down, the more we grow up, saith Tertullian. <small>Plures efficimur, quoties metimur a vobis. Tert.</small> The church is in Scripture compared to things which, though weakest, yet are most fruitful, as doves, and sheep, the vine. The church, like the palm-tree, rises up the more men endeavour by weights to press it down. The Egyptian flames cannot devour the Israelitish bush; the gates of hell cannot prevail against the church. God's blessing overcomes all human opposition. If God saith, "Increase, and multiply," all the enemies of the church help it when they most endeavour to hinder it. It is neither from the weakness of the flames, nor the strength of the bush, that it is not consumed; but from the gracious presence of Him who dwelt in it; and his dwelling there he manifests, 1. By restraining the fire, and keeping in its fury. All the wrath of man which shall not praise God, shall be restrained by God, Psal. lxxvi. 10. 2. By strengthening the bush against it; if not by bestowing worldly, yet spiritual power to oppose it. How much was Pharaoh mistaken when, intending to oppress the Israelites, he said, " Let us deal wisely with them!" Exod. i. 10. The sun may as easily be blown out with bellows, and battered with snowballs, as Israel may be overthrown by opposition. But how great therefore is that folly which puts worms upon contending with the great God! What do the Egyptians in contriving against Israel, but besides the disappointment of their hopes, curiously weave their own woe, by torturing themselves with envy, and making way for Israel's deliverance by their own overthrow? Against the God of Israel there is no wisdom, nor understanding, nor counsel, Prov. xxi. 30. Oh how happy were we, if the time which we spend in fearing and shunning trouble, were only improved in hating sin and cleaving to God!

Obs. 8. Satan and his instruments then begin to rage most furiously, when God calls and stirs up instruments to help and relieve his church. Before Moses went in to Pharaoh for Israel's release, the Israelites were used unkindly; but afterward they were oppressed tyrannically. How cruel was Egyptian rage upon the entrance of Moses into his ministry! As soon as David was anointed king, how cruelly did Saul rage! In all ages of the church Satan endeavours to obscure the dawnings of the gospel with a bloody cloud of persecution. When God begins to cast the devil out of his hold, he deals with the church as with that man possessed by him, whom, when Christ was about to cure him, he did rend, and tear, and lay for dead. In the beginning of reformation antichrist filled all places with blood and slaughter. When God begins to heal his church, the antichristian humour of violence and persecution discovers itself, Hos. vii. 1. The cross follows the entrance of the gospel; hence we should be encouraged, and cautioned. Encouraged; for it is a good sign, that when Satan wars and rages, God is wounding and dispossessing him, and that his time is but short. We should also be cautioned: let us look for trials, even after Moses has promised deliverance. Commonly when God has given his church hopes of mercy, he seems to threaten inevitable disappointment of it. After God had given Abraham a son, in whose seed all the promised mercy was to be accomplished, God seems to put Abraham upon pulling down the foundation of all this happiness with his own hands. And we should take heed that we impute not our troubles to the reformation en-
<small>Promissam gratiam crux sequitur. Rivet. in Exod. p. 133.</small>

deavoured, but to that opposition which Satan and the distempered world put forth, and not to blame God's care of our recovery, but our own phrensy.

Obs. 9. No difficulties can hinder Israel's deliverance. God can command, yea, create deliverances for his people. When there is none left and shut up, when there is no force and might to relieve, he can deliver them alone, Psal. xxv. 22; xxxiv. 7; lxxi. 20; Isa. xliii. 13; Gen. xviii. 14. When there are mountains of opposition, he can level them, and make them become a plain. Jesus Christ comes skipping and leaping over them all. The wisdom, power, and malice of his enemies only make his strength triumphant; yea, the unworthiness and unkindness of Israel cannot stop the course of delivering mercy. So unexpectedly can he scatter difficulties, that his people have been like them that dreamed when mercy came, they thinking it too good to be true. Yea, their enemies have been amazed, and compelled to profess, that God hath done great things for his church. How strong must the forces of God's decree, power, love, wisdom, faithfulness, the prayers and tears of his people, needs be, when they are all united! And hence it is that, as the enemies of Israel have cause to fear, though they are high; so the true Israelites have cause to hope, though they are low. There is no defeat so great but faith has a retreating place. Means can do nothing without, much less against God; but God can do all things without, yea, against means. A saint abhors indirectly to wind himself out of any trouble; why? he has a God who can help in every strait: whereas a sinner who wants God, shiftingly betakes himself to any unworthy practice. O Christian, take shame to thyself, that every slight trouble should so dismay thee, having such a Deliverer; that the mountain should be full of horses and chariots, and thou shouldst not have thy eyes open to see and believe them, 2 Kings vi. 15—17. What is a Pharaoh, a house of bondage, a puissant army, a Red Sea? delivering mercy makes way through them all, and is a mighty stream that bears all before it, Psal. cxxvi. 4. It is infinitely stronger than the strongest blast of gunpowder to blow up all opposition. O Christian, fear not thy danger, but believe in thy Deliverer.

Fides in periculis secura est, et in securis periclitatur.

Obs. 10. God loves not to give deliverance till it be welcome. When the tale of bricks is doubled, then, and not till then, Moses comes. When Israel is parched with the heat of persecution, then comes the showers of deliverance. God is a help in the needful time of trouble. Then is it God's time to deliver, when there are no visible helps or hopes of deliverance. "For the oppression of the poor, and sighing of the needy, now will I arise, saith the Lord," Psal. xii. 5. In such a case it was that God said to Moses, "Now shalt thou see what I will do to Pharaoh," Exod. vi. 1. Times of extreme oppression are times of earnest supplication; and God loves to bestow mercies when they are by prayer desired. The cry of Israel must come up to God, before mercy from God comes down upon Israel. Further, where deliverance comes in a time of extremity, it will be entertained upon its own terms. Israel will part with any thing that offends their deliverer; they will submit to strict reformation, which before they would not hear of, and say with Saul, " Lord, what wilt thou have us to do?" Acts ix. 6; and with the Egyptians, who were pinched with the famine, " Buy us and our land for bread, and we and our land will be servants to Pharaoh," Gen. xlvii. 19. Lastly, when deliverance is afforded in the church's extremity, the glory of God's power, wisdom, and free goodness is most clearly discovered. God loves so to work for his people, as to gain most by them; he will have the tribute of praise out of every salvation. And this discovers the true reason why mercy is delayed; why God only, as it were, shows a mercy, and then pulls it in again: we are not yet so pinched by the want thereof, as to stoop to God's conditions, to accept of an exact universal reformation, to be willing that God should do with us what he pleases; and to those whom God has so fitted, mercy shall not long be delayed; nay, God has given to them the best of mercies, in bestowing a heart meet to enjoy them.

Obs. 11. God often proportions the punishment to the sin. The Egyptians encompass poor Israel with affliction, neither suffering them to go from or to remain in Egypt; and now they themselves can neither go backward or forward in the sea. The bloody rivers, and their destruction in the Red Sea, tell them their cruelty in drowning the Israelitish children. Sodom was inflamed with the fire of lust, and God consumes them with the fire of wrath. Joseph's brethren sell Joseph for a slave, and they themselves are detained as bondmen. Adonibezek cuts off the thumbs and great toes of seventy kings; and as he did to them, so did God requite him, Judg. i. 7. Haman was hanged upon his own gibbet. David's murder and adultery were followed with the death of his children, and the ravishment of Tamar. It is thy duty to trace sin by the foot-prints of punishment, and observe what sin thou hast lived in which bears most proportion to thy punishment. Art thou sick? consider whether thou hast not abused thy strength to sin. Doth God take away thy sight, thy hearing, thy tongue, thy estate? ask thy conscience whether these have not been employed against God. And if this direction seem to put thee upon an uncertain course of finding out thy beloved sin, imitate the example of Herod, who, that he might make sure work to kill our Saviour, slew all the children in Bethlehem. In like manner let us impartially destroy all our sins. If we know not which was the thorn that pricked us, cut down the whole hedge. If we know not which was the bee that stung us, let us throw down the whole hive.

Obs. 12. When the enemies of God labour most to oppose and frustrate, they accomplish and fulfil the will of God. Pharaoh studies to destroy Israel; but even then Pharaoh by his own daughter preserves and nourishes him who was to be Israel's deliverer. Pharaoh resolves to detain Israel in bondage; but even he shall shortly not only send them away, but compel them to go; yea, in that very night which God had four hundred and thirty years before set down and prefixed. Joseph's brethren sell him that his dream might prove false, and that they might not be brought to bow before him; but so did God order it, that therefore they came to do obeisance to him because they sold him. *Ideo veneratus, quia venditus.* The Jews killed Christ to extinguish his fame and glory, but by his death was his glory and fame advanced. Oh the folly of God's enemies! how can God want weapons to beat them, when he can beat them with their own? how impossible is it but God should prevail over them, when he does so by being opposed by them! How should this encourage the afflicted church of God! when his enemies most resist him, they are against their wills compelled most to serve him and his church.

Obs. 13. God is most faithful in keeping promise with his people. God misreckoned not his people one day, nay, not one hour in four hundred and thirty years. "All the paths of God are mercy and truth," Psal. xxv. 10. The faithfulness of God never fails, nor will he alter the thing which is gone out of his lips, Psal. lxxxix. 33, 34. The promises of God are called "the sure mercies of David," Isa. lv. 3; sure unto all the seed of David that are in covenant with God, as David was. They are yea and Amen, 2 Cor. i. 20. There shall not fail one word of all the good which God hath promised to do for his people, Josh. xxi. 45; xxiii. 14; 1 Kings viii. 56; Jer. xxxiii. 20; Isa. liv. 19. The promises of God are built upon the unchangeable purpose of God, which is a sure and unshaken foundation, 2 Tim. ii. 19. Hence it is that God is said to have promised eternal life before the world began, because the promises which are made in time are according to that purpose of God in himself. And Heb. vi. 17, the apostle grounds the truth of the promise upon the stableness of God's counsel; so that unless God's counsel and purpose change, the promise cannot fail. To assure us of the certainty of his covenant, God has given us the pledges of his oath, Psal. lxxxix. 3, 35; Heb. vi. 17; his seal of the blood of Christ, the Mediator, Heb. ix. 16, 17, the earnest of his Spirit, 2 Cor. i. 22. Let the true Israelites hence gather strong consolation. Christians, you are not worthy to be beloved, but God is worthy to be believed. The promises are as sure as they are great. Though all the world falter and deceive you, yet the promises of God are firm and stable. God will try your faith, but never disappoint it. Judge of his faithfulness, not by his providences, but by his promises. Of this more in the last part of the verse.

Obs. 14. The great God has all the creatures at his command. He commands in chief, and the creatures are his hosts; even from the least of the lice that crept upon the poorest Egyptian, to the most glorious angel in heaven. If he say to a plague, Go, it goeth; if, Come, it cometh; they all fulfil his word: the unruly sea tamely stands still, if God command it, Psal. cxlviii. 8; lxxvii. 16; yea, though of itself it be unkind and raging, it lovingly opens its bosom to entertain the Israelites. He can make the swift sun to stop its course, Josh. x. 12; yea, to go backward, Isa. xxxviii. 8. The greedy and cruel lions are muzzled up and grow gentle at God's command. If God speak unto the fish, it shall take, retain, and restore Jonah. How should this relieve the faithful in all their exigences! Their Friend, their Father, has all the world at his command to supply their wants, to deliver them from troubles, to destroy their enemies. Man roweth, but God bloweth. The Egyptians pursue, but the wind, the sea, the chariot-wheels shall all obey the God of Israel. Never need a true Israelite fear who has such a Friend. Never can an Egyptian be safe that has such an enemy.

Obs. 15. Wicked men grow not wise till it be too late. Why could not the Egyptians as well refrain from the pursuit of Israel, as endeavour a retreat? It had been better for them not to have entered into the sea, than to struggle to get out when once they were in it. They might with more wisdom have said, Let us not follow after; than have said, Let us fly from the Israelites. Wicked men do not believe their danger till they feel it. Satan suffers not their eyes to be opened till, with the blinded Syrians, they are in the midst of their enemies. O sinner! labour to be wise betimes; in this thy day know the things that belong to thy peace. It is easier to be warned of the wrath to come, than to wade out of it.

Obs. 16. God makes those conditions and employments easy to his people, when they are once in them, which before seemed impossible. Israel rather thought that the wilderness should have given them graves, than that the sea should have given them passage. They who feared that none could roll away for them the stone of the sepulchre when they came, found it rolled away to their hands. The works of God are sweet in the performance, which are unpleasant in their undertaking: the yoke of Christ is grievous to take up, but easy to bear and undergo. It is otherwise in the employments of sin; they are easy and delightful in the beginning, but bitterness in the end. The Israelites find the sea shut against them when they approach it, but it was open in their passage through it. The Egyptians found it open at their approach, but shut when they would return. The ways of God are narrowly broad; the ways of sin broadly narrow. Israel has nothing to do but to follow God, and to believe. For their way, if mercy do not find it easy, it will make it so.

The second part of this example of the Israelites is their destruction after their forementioned deliverance, in these words; "Afterward destroyed."

Two things may here be explained.

I. What this destruction was which befell Israel afterward.

II. Wherein the eminency and remarkableness of this destruction which was afterward, appeared.

I. For the first. The Scriptures record sundry destructions brought upon the Israelites while they were in the wilderness, after their deliverance from Egypt: as, 1. Some were destroyed after their idolatrous worshipping of the golden calf, by the command of Moses, to the number of three thousand men, Exod. xxxii. 28. 2. There was a destruction by fire which the Lord kindled, mentioned Numb. xi. 1—3: whether this fire brake out of the earth, or came from the pillar of fire which went before the Israelites, or was poured upon them from heaven, it is not expressed; certain it is, that it was a grievous burning; and therefore the place where it burnt was called Taberah. 3. Another destruction by the plague we read of in the same chapter, ver. 33, at Kibroth-hattaavah, after the people had impatiently and discontentedly lusted for flesh. 4. There is a destruction by fiery serpents, recorded Numb. xxi. 6; where, after their murmuring for want of water, it is said, "much people of Israel died." 5. Many of the Israelites were destroyed about the conspiracy of Korah and his accomplices, related Numb. xvi. 31; where, besides the swallowing up of sundry in the earth, and the consuming by fire of two hundred and fifty who offered incense, fourteen thousand seven hundred more were destroyed for murmuring and raging against the former judgments. 6. For committing whoredom with the daughters of Moab, and bowing down to their gods, we read, Numb. xxv. 9, of a plague by which died twenty-four thousand. 7. Besides the death of ten of the spies who brought up a slander upon the promised land, a discomfiture of the Israelites by the Amalekites and Canaanites is recorded, Numb. xiv. 45, for a rebellious attempt to invade it against the will of God. These destructions by violent death are the principal which are mentioned particularly in the sacred story. But though the destruction which is here intended by the apostle is not exclusive of these, yet is it to be extended beyond them, and to be understood of that more general destruction, which, Numb. xiv. 29, is threatened against all the Israelites from twenty years old and upward, whose carcasses for forty years fell in the wilderness, because of their rebellious and unbelieving murmurings against God, upon the evil report which the spies had brought upon the land of Canaan.

II. The eminency and remarkableness of this destruction; it was a dispensation compounded of severity, principally intended, and mercy, also comprehended, in the setting down of this example.

First, For its severity. This appears in,

The persons who were destroyed; and, The season when they were destroyed.

1. The persons who were destroyed are considerable, 1. In their quality and privileges. 2. In their quantity and number.

(1.) In their quality, noted in the word "them." They were "the seed of Abraham, the friend of God, Israelites according to the flesh." Not heathens, but a peculiar, a chosen people, privileged above all the people of the earth, to whom belonged the covenant, sacrifice, sacraments, worship; of which Christ came according to the flesh, 1 Cor. x. 3, 4; Rom. iii. 2; ix. 5. A people who so heard "the voice of God speaking out of the fire" as none other ever did, Deut. iv. 33; to whom God had "shown his statutes and his judgments," after which manner he "had not dealt with any nation," Psal. cxlvii. 20. In a word, a people whose privileges Moses thus admires; "Happy art thou, O Israel: who is like unto thee, O people?" Deut. xxxiii. 29. How conspicuous was Divine severity in destroying a people so near, so dear to him; and whom he only knew of all the families of the earth! "O Lord," saith Joshua, "what shall I say, when Israel turneth their backs before their enemies!" Josh. vii. 8. O smart severity, thus to fetch blood from a son, a first-born; to destroy not Egyptians, Canaanites, but even Israelites!

(2.) The persons destroyed are considerable in their quantity and numbers. The power and mercy of God were not more remarkable in the recruiting of seventy souls in two hundred and fifteen years to six hundred thousand, besides women and children, than in reducing so many hundred thousand in forty years to two persons, a Joshua and a Caleb. Oh how angry was their Father, to go round his family with his rod! yea, how just was their Judge, to ride such a large circuit with his sword!

2. The severity of this destruction is considerable in the season when they were destroyed, noted in the word "afterward;" after they were saved out of the land of Egypt; and so it was a severity which admits of a threefold amplification.

(1.) This destruction of the Israelites afterward, was a fall after an eminent advancement. The higher a place is from which a man falls, the more dangerously does he fall. How woeful is it to have been happy! It is a double mercy, to be raised up from a low to a high estate; and it is a double misery to be thrown down from a high to a low degree. "Thou hast lifted me up, and cast me down," saith David, Psal. cii. 10. And thus Job amplifies his misery with admirable elegance, Job xxix. *per totum*, and chap. xxx.: "Young men saw me, and hid themselves; princes refrained talking," &c. "But now they who are younger than I have me in derision, whose fathers I would have disdained to have set with the dogs of my flock," &c. Oh how glorious was Israel in their Egyptian preservation, their Red-Sea deliverance, their wilderness provisions and protections! being, as Moses in admiration of their happiness breaks out, a people to whom none was like, in being saved by the Lord. And if so, then was no people so miserable in being forsaken by the Lord.

(2.) This destruction of the Israelites afterward, was a miscarriage after vast cost and expenses laid out upon them. How angry is that father with his son, who casts him off after all his care and cost of education! How hateful is that house to the owner, which he pulls down after vast and immeasurable expenses about its structure and furniture! How much anger did God express in the destruction of the temple, when after all the cost which David and Solomon laid out upon it, the Babylonians burn it to ashes, and carry away all the gold and sumptuous monuments thereof! Was ever God at such charges with any nation as he was at with Israel? For their sake he turns Egypt upside down, he rebuked kings, he scattered and destroyed armies; the wild water waits upon them in a standing posture; the pillar of a cloud and fire conducts them; the heavens pour them down miraculous showers of angels' food; the rock splits itself into cups, and gives them drink; their garments continue fresh, and grow not old; and, which is infinitely beyond all this, God renews his covenant with them, and gives them a law from heaven, speaks out of the fire, and sends them an epistle to instruct them, written with his own hand: and after all this cost and care, how great must Israel's destruction be!

(3.) Yet further, this destruction of the Israelites afterward, was a sad disappointment of highest expectations. Israel was now cast away, as it were, in the haven. They who not long since were singing and dancing at the spectacle of floating Pharaoh and his followers; they who had passed through the furnace and the sea, and escaped both their oppressors and pursuers; they who had safely marched through a hot, howling wilderness, even unto the borders of the promised land, and were now safely arrived at the confines of Canaan; in a word, they who had nothing now (as they hoped) to do but to enter and take possession of a land flowing with milk and honey; are not only forbidden to enter it, but commanded back to the sandy and scorching wilderness, there to spend the residue of their few and evil days, Numb. xiv. 25, 29, 30. O sorrowful, stupendous disappointment!

Secondly, Even in this destruction of Israel the mercy of God was more remarkable than his severity. If Israel's scourge be compared with Israel's sin, they had no cause to complain. They might rather wonder at what did not, than at what did befall them; rather at the mercy which was left, than at what was removed. Well might Israel say with Ezra, "The Lord hath punished us less than our iniquities deserve," Ezra ix. 13; and with the church afterward, It is the goodness of the Lord that we are not consumed, Lam. iii. 22. Look upon Israel's provocations, in Egypt, at the sea, in the wilderness, their murmurings, idolatry, their unthankfulness for and forgetfulness of God's multiplied mercies, their rebellion against their godly governors; their hypocrisy, covenant-breaking, lingerings after their old Egypt, unreformedness under all the dealings of God with them; especially their distrust of God's power and goodness after frequent and abundant experience of both; look, I say, upon all these, and then wonder that this destruction should be,

1. So slow, and not more speedy.
2. But in part, and not total and universal.

1. It was a destruction mercifully mitigated, in respect of the slowness and deferring thereof. How much longer was God about destroying a handful of sinners, than he was in creating the whole world! Israel, a people that could not be kept from sinning, had a God that could hardly be brought to punish them. Had the fire of God's wrath been proportioned to the fuel of their sins, he would have destroyed them in a moment. "Forty years long was I grieved," saith God, "with this generation," Psal. xcv. 10; and so long endured he their manners in the wilderness, Acts xiii. 18; daily suffering that which he beheld, abhorred, and was able to have punished every moment in those forty years; instead whereof all that while he waited for their repentance, and was at the expense of supplying them with miraculous provision, direction, protection, feeding them, and attending them as ἐτροποφόρησεν. carefully as the nurse her froward infant.

2. The destruction of the Israelites was but in part, not total. For besides the sparing of Caleb and Joshua, who believed the promise of God, all who believed not were not destroyed; for all under twenty years were exempted from the forenamed destruction, and reserved, that God might still have his church among them, and that there might be of them a people left to possess the good land, according to the promise. And in this respect it was, that upon the prayer of Moses for the pardoning and sparing of the people, God answers, that he had pardoned them according to the word of Moses, Numb. xiv. 13—20. For although he spared not the persons of the elder and rebellious multitude, yet he spared the stock of Israel, remitting the punishment of present and universal death, and not blotting out their memory, lest the seed of Abraham being extinguished, his covenant should have failed and fallen to the ground. The distrustful refusal of the parents to accept of the promised land made not God unfaithful, for the blessing which they rejected was performed to their children; God reserving a seed to propagate his church, and tempering his severity inflicted upon some with mercy afforded to others, though deserved by none.

Non personis, sed generi data venia. Calv. in loc.

Obs. 1. The most numerous company of sinners are unable to withstand an angry God. He can easily destroy six hundred thousand persons in a few years, and a hundred fourscore and five thousand Assyrians in one night, 2 Kings xix. 35. "Though hand join in hand, yet shall not the wicked go unpunished," Prov. xi. 21. He to whom it is all one to save by few and by many, can as easily destroy many as one. Numbers are nothing with God. The whole old world of sinners are no more in the hands of God than a handful of worms. The greatest combination of sinners are but stubble to the flame, and but as snowballs to the sun. He can as easily cast down multitudes of sinning angels, as they can crush an ant upon a molehill. There is no proportion between created strength and uncreated Omnipotence. The powers of all the world are but borrowed of him, and as purely dependent upon him as the stream is upon the fountain, the beam upon the sun. How can that power be too hard for him who gave it, and can withdraw it at pleasure? Never let multitudes dare to oppose him, nor one poor weak saint fear to trust him.

Obs. 2. The worst cause commonly hath the most abettors. Had this been put to the question, whether will God keep his promise in giving to Israel the land of Canaan? Caleb and Joshua would have been overvoted by almost six hundred thousand Israelites; who nevertheless would have as much failed in their cause, as they exceeded in their numbers. The multitude is but a weak argument to prove a strong cause. The most have ever been the worst. Righteous Noah stood in a manner by himself, against the whole world of ungodly. The prophet Elijah was not the worse for being opposed by four hundred Baalites, nor they the better for having only one Elijah to withstand them. Let us walk by rule, not example. Numbers commonly no more please God than they can oppose him. It is better to go to heaven with a handful, than to hell in a crowd; and to enter in at the strait gate with few, than at the broad with many; to go into Canaan with Caleb and Joshua, than to fall in the wilderness with six hundred thousand.

Obs. 3. No privileges abused can exempt from punishment. The soul of God may "depart from Jerusalem," Jer. vi. 8; and Ariel, the city where David dwelt, has woe denounced against it, Isa. xxix. 1. God may forsake his tabernacle in Shiloh, "deliver his strength into captivity, his glory into the enemy's hand," Jer. vii. 12; Psal. lxxviii. 60, 61; and "pluck the signet from his right hand," Jer. xxii. 24. "With many of the Israelites God was not well pleased; for they were overthrown in the wilderness," 1 Cor. x. 5. To him that breaks the law, circumcision is made uncircumcision, Rom. ii. 25. Chorazin, Bethsaida, Capernaum, get nothing by the mighty works of Christ; and their elevation to heaven, but greater woes and falls, Matt. xi. 23. God delights not in outward privileges, but in inward purity. The new creature, worship in spirit and truth, a Jew inwardly, an Israelite indeed, circumcision and brokenness of the heart, only please the eye of God, John iv. 23, 24; Gal. vi. 15; and without these external service is but painted atheism. As the "pure in heart shall only see God," Matt. v. 8, so God only sees the pure in heart with contentment. God loathes sin wherever he sees it, but most of all when it is sheltered with appearances, professions, and privileges. A name to live, external ordinances, circumcision in the flesh, the temple of the Lord, commend us not to God. "I will punish," saith God, "the circumcised with the uncircumcised; Egypt, and Judah, and Edom, the children of Ammon and Moab; for all these nations are uncircumcised, and all the house of Israel are uncircumcised in heart," Jer. ix. 25, 26. The Bible in thy house, the word of grace in thy ear, will not avail, unless the grace of the word be in thy heart; and the former without the latter will but prove like Uriah's letters, which he carried for his own destruction: Paul accounted all his privileges as dung in regard of the knowledge of Christ. The means of salvation in word and sacraments must be used in faith and repentance. Otherwise, they being out of their holy use enjoyed, will turn to our destruction.

Obs. 4. God labours to win people by mercies, before he wounds them by judgments. Israel is first solicited by love; God destroys them not till afterward; and if his goodness had made them blush, his greatness should not have made them bleed. Oh how propense was that God to save his Israel! and how unwilling to destroy them! He gave them the honey of deliverance and provisions freely, and of his own accord; he put not forth the sting of punishment till he was provoked. Israel shall first have the cloud to guide them, the sea divided, Egyptians drowned, manna showered down, the rocks gushing them drink, and they by all left inexcusable, before they are destroyed. Oh that the long-suffering of God might be salvation, and lead us to repentance, and that by submission to mercy we may prevent a conquest by judgment; and not put the Lord upon a work more unpleasing to him than to ourselves, whose backs do not suffer so much as his bowels when we are beaten, Hos. xi. 8.

Obs. 5. Miraculous mercies do not benefit an unholy heart. After all the salvations that God had bestowed upon Israel, they were fit for nothing but destruction. Every step they took in the Red Sea, they trod upon a miracle of merciful preservation: every time they tasted a crumb of bread or a drop of water, they took in a miracle of merciful provision: every time they looked up to the heavens, they beheld a miracle of merciful direction; but none of these could work upon stubborn hearts: only he who commanded that more soft rock to give them water, could make their hearts obedient. They who will not be taught by the word, will not be bettered by the rod of Moses; and without the Spirit we shall be benefited by neither.

Obs. 6. Great deliverances abused make way for

severest judgments. Many times did God deliver Israel, but they provoking him with their counsel, were brought low for their iniquity, Psal. cvi. 44: the whole book of Judges is the comment upon this truth, a book made up of the vicissitudes of deliverance, provocation, and punishment. Sins committed against the love of a God, are committed most against the happiness of a people. Every deliverance is a bill of indictment against the unthankful. This makes God to call to the heavens and earth as witnesses against those children which he had brought up and rebelled against him; yea, to profess, that the owner of an ox, and the master of an ass, were more respected by their beasts than he was by his Israel, Isa. i. 2, 3. This makes God to profess, that he will consume his people after he hath done them good, Josh. xxiv. 20; and that he will deliver them no more, Judg. x. 13; and elsewhere, that he is weary of repenting, Jer. xv. 6. "After all that is come upon us," saith Ezra, "should we again break thy commandments, wouldest not thou be angry with us till thou hadst consumed us?" Ezra ix. 13, 14. Oh that England would, instead of murmuring at its present distresses, mourn for its abuse of former deliverances; and more fear, without a speedy reformation, that the mercies which still we enjoy shall be removed, than hope that those we want shall be bestowed!

Obs. 7. Sin disappoints the most hopeful expectations of mercy. It stifles it even when it seems to be come to the birth. "We looked for peace, but no good came; and for a time of health, and behold trouble!" Jer. viii. 15; xiv. 19. Who could have expected but that Israel, after so many miraculous mercies, being now upon the confines of Canaan, should instantly have entered? but, behold, their sin sends them back into the wilderness, there to linger and pine for forty years together. Sinners disappoint God's expectation, and justly therefore may God disappoint theirs. After all the costs bestowed by God upon his vineyard, "he looked that it should bring forth grapes, and it brought forth wild grapes," Isa. v. 2. Israel gives God appearances of holiness, and God gives Israel an appearance of deliverance. They flatter God with shows of that obedience which he deserved, and how justly does God disappoint them of those mercies which they desired! They fall short of promised duty, and therefore of expected delivery. Oh that we could condemn ourselves, and justify God in the sad disappointments of England's recovery! We made show at the first of a thorough reformation, but we soon faltered and made a halt; and why should God be bound, when we would needs be loose? Our goodness was as the early dew, and the morning cloud that goeth away, Hos. vi. 4; and justly therefore was our deliverance as a morning sunshine, soon clouded and overcast with unexpected troubles.

Obs. 8. Even in judgment God remembers mercy. God was good to Israel when he destroyed Israel. God in his smiles will be feared, and in his frowns will be loved; as it is said of Asher, that his shoes were iron and brass, and yet that he dipped his foot in oil, Deut. xxxiii. 24, 25; so does God ever mix the hardest and heaviest severities toward his Israel, with the oil of mercy and gentleness. He spared the children, when he overthrew the parents. He did as well remember his own covenant as their provocation. He cut off some luxuriant branches, but did not cut down the tree; he punished some for their sins, he punished not all, for his own glory. He wrought for his name's sake, Psal. cvi. 8. "I said, I would scatter them into corners, I would make the remembrance of them to cease from among men, were it not that I feared the wrath of the enemy," Deut. xxxii. 26. So good is God, that he raises arguments of pity toward rebellious Israel out of himself, yea, out of his enemies, when Israel affords him none. Though justice made him cast his church into the fire to be scorched, yet mercy made him pluck it like a brand out of the fire, lest it should be consumed, Zech. iii. 2. And a seed he reserves, a remnant, that his church may not be as Sodom, Isa. i. 9. In the vintage of a judgment, he leaves the gleanings of grapes upon the vine of his church. He never shakes his olive-tree so thoroughly, but he leaves at least "two or three berries in the top of the uppermost bough, four or five in the outmost branches," Isa. xvii. 6. Though I make a full end of all nations whither I have driven thee, yet "will I not make a full end of thee, but correct thee in measure; yet will I not leave thee wholly unpunished," Jer. xxx. 11; xlvi. 28. Let not Israel presume upon mercy, if they will sin; but yet let them not despair of mercy, though they suffer. "God will not cast off his people," Psal. xciv. 14. Though the destruction of his Israel be never so great, yet it shall never be total; and should many fall, yet all shall not; the cause, the interest of Christ shall not: and though possibly in a wilderness of common calamities, the carcasses of some of his own may fall among others, so as they may never live to enter the Canaan of a longed-for peace and reformation in this life; yet by faith ascending up to the Nebo of a promise, they may behold it afar off, and see it possessed by their posterity; they themselves, meanwhile, repenting of their unbelief and unworthiness, and so entering that heavenly Canaan, where they shall enjoy the fulness of that which here they could have enjoyed but in part.

The next branch of the example of the Israelites, is, 3. The cause of their destruction, viz. their infidelity, contained in these words, "That believed not."

For the explication whereof two things are to be considered.

I. In what respect these Israelites are here said not to believe.

II. Why they were punished for this their not believing, rather than for any other sin.

I. For the first. Unbelievers, 1. Are frequently in Scripture taken for pagans and heathens, 1 Tim. v. 8; 2 Cor. vi. 14, 15; 1 Cor. xiv. 23; who are always without the profession of the faith, and oft without the very offer of the word, the means of knowing that faith which is to be professed; and then it is termed an unbelief of pure negation. 2. Unbelievers are said to be such, who, though they profess the faith, and hear and know the word, yet deny that credence to it which God requires; and their unbelief, called an unbelief of evil disposition, is either a denial of assent to the truths asserted in the word, or of trust and affiance to the promises of good contained in the same; and both these are either temporary, or total and perpetual. Into the former sometimes the elect may fall, as particularly did those two disciples, who by their unbelief drew from Christ this sharp reproof, "O fools, and slow of heart to believe all that the prophets have spoken," Luke xxiv. 25. And for this Christ upbraided the eleven, when they believed not them who had seen him after he was risen, Mark xvi. 11, 13, 14. And of righteous Zacharias is it said, that he believed not those words which were to be fulfilled in their season, Luke i. 20. Into that unbelief which is total and habitual the reprobate only fall, John vi. 64, 65; of whom Christ speaks, "Ye believe not, because ye are not of my sheep," John x. 26; and afterward the evangelist, They believed not, nay, they could not believe, because that Esaias said, He hath blinded their eyes, &c., John xii. 37—39; as also Acts xix. 9. "Divers were hardened, and believed not." These abide in unbelief, and the wrath of God abideth on them, John iii. 36. This unbelief of the Israelites principally consisted in their not yielding trust and affiance to the gracious and faithful promises, made by God to their forefathers, and often renewed to themselves, of bestowing upon them the land of Canaan for their inheritance. These promises, upon the report of the spies concerning the strength of the Canaanites and their cities, were by the people so far distrusted, and deemed so impossible to be fulfilled, as that they not only wished that they had died in Egypt, but resolved to make them a captain to return thither again: see Numb. xiii. xiv. And probable it is, that the unbelief of the most was perpetual; but that others, even of those who at the first and for a time distrusted the faithfulness of God's promise, by the threatenings and punishments denounced against and inflicted upon them, repented afterward of their infidelity, and so believed that God was faithful in his promise, though they by reason of their former unbelief did not actually partake of the benefit thereof. However, this their sin of distrustfulness was their great and capital sin, that sin, like the Anakims which they so feared, much taller than the rest, and which principally was that provocation in the wilderness spoken of so frequently in the Scripture, Heb. iii. 8, 12, 16, 18; Psal. xcv. 8. And hence it is that God explains his provoking him, by not believing him: "How long," saith he, Numb. xiv. 11, "will this people provoke me? how long will it be ere they believe me?" And that it was their great stop in the way to Canaan is evident, in that the punishment of exclusion from Canaan was immediately, upon their unbelief, inflicted upon them; as also by the express testimony of the apostle, who saith that they could not enter in because of unbelief.

Certum est, complures fuisse pios, qui vel communi impietate non fuerunt impliciti, vel mox resipuerunt. Cal. in Heb. iii. 18.

Incredulitas malorum omnium caput. Cal. in Heb. iii. 18.

II. For the second, Why they were destroyed rather for their unbelief than for other sins.

1. Their unbelief was the root and fountain of all the rest of their sins. This evil heart of unbelief made them depart from the living God by their other provocations, Heb. iii. 12; Jer. xvii. 5. All sins would be bitter in the acting, if we believed that they would be bitter in their ending. Faith is the shield of every grace, and unbelief the shield of every sin. Faith purifies, Acts xv. 9, unbelief pollutes the heart. Unbelievers and disobedient, are in the Greek expressed by one word, $\dot{\alpha}\pi\epsilon\iota\theta o\tilde{\upsilon}\nu\tau\epsilon\varsigma$, 1 Pet. ii. 7, 8; Heb. xi. 31. What but unbelief was the cause of all those impatient murmurings of the Israelites? Numb. xiv. 27. Had they believed a faithful God, they would quietly have waited for the accomplishment of his promises; had they believed in him who is all-sufficient, they would in the want of all means of supply have looked upon them as laid up in God. The reason why they made such sinful haste to get flesh, was because their unbelieving heart thought that God could not furnish a table in the wilderness. What, but their not believing a great and dreadful Majesty, made them so fearlessly rebellious against God and their governors? What, but their not believing an all-powerful God, made them fear the giants and walled cities of Canaan? Faith went out, and fear and every sin got in. They believed God too little, and man too much; by their unbelief making God as man, and man as God.

2. God had afforded many helps and antidotes against the unbelief of the Israelites. God had given promises, first, to their fathers, and afterwards to these Israelites their posterity, of his bestowing upon them the land of Canaan for an inheritance, Gen. xii. 7; xiii. 15; xv. 18; xvii. 7, 8; xxvi. 4; Deut. i. 8; Exod. iii. 17; vi. 8. His promises, like himself, were faithful and true, and impossible it is that he who made them should lie. These promises were often repeated to their forefathers and themselves; and the very land of Canaan is called "the land of promise," Heb. xi. 9. And afterward Solomon professed, "There hath not failed one word of all God's good promise which he promised by the hand of Moses," 1 Kings viii. 56. All his promises are yea and Amen. The promises of giving to Israel the land of Canaan God had sundry times confirmed by oath, Gen. xxii. 16; xxvi. 23; Psal. cv. 9: the oath God followed with his seal of circumcision, Gen. xvii. 10, whereby was confirmed the promise of the earthly and heavenly Canaan. To all these God had added the abundant examples of those their holy forefathers, who openly professed their believing the promise, that their seed should inherit Canaan. Hence Abraham sojourned contentedly in the land of promise, where he had not so much room as to set his foot on without borrowing or buying, Heb. xi. 9; Acts vii. 5. Hence also he purchased a burying-place in that land, of which, though living, he had not possession, yet dying, nay dead, he showed his expectation. How holily solicitous was Jacob and Joseph, that their bodies after their deaths should be carried out of Egypt into that Canaan where their hopes and hearts had been while they lived! To all these examples God had given them, to prevent unbelief, their own multiplied and astonishing experiences of his former power and love. Could not He, who by the lifting up of the arms of one Moses destroyed an army of Amalekites, as easily overthrow the armies of the Canaanites by the hands of six hundred thousand Israelites? Could He who commissioned the very lice and flies to plague Egypt, and at whose command are all the hosts of heaven and earth, want power to deal with the sons of Anak? Could not He who made the weak and unsteady waters of the Red Sea to stand up like walls, as easily make the strongest walls of the Canaanitish cities fall down? But they believed not for his wondrous works, they remembered not his hand, nor the day when he delivered them from the enemy, Psal. lxxviii. 32, 42.

In terra promissa sibi emit sepulchrum, ut spem suam vel mortuus testaretur. Rivet. Exerc. 119. in Gen.

3. Their unbelief most of all robbed God of his declarative glory. It was a bold sin, it rifled his cabinet, and took away his chiefest jewel, even that which he saith he will not give to another, Isa. xlii. 8. (1.) It takes away the glory of his truth; it no more trusting him, than if he were a known liar, and as we say of such a one, No further than we see him, 1 John v. 10; Rom. iv. 20. It endeavours to make God in that condition of some lost man, whose credit is quite gone, and whose word none will take: now to discredit, is to dishonour a man. Unbelievers account it impossible that He should speak true, for whom to lie it is impossible. After all the promises of giving them Canaan, though repeated, sworn, sealed, Israel believed not God. (2.) The Israelites by their unbelief obscured the glory of God's goodness. They did not only labour to make their misery greater than God's mercy, but even his very mercy to appear tyranny. They often complained that he had brought them into the wilderness to slay them, Numb. xiv. 3; and they despised that pleasant land which God had promised them, Psal. cvi. 24; yea, as some note, in regard that the land of Canaan was a type of the heavenly Canaan, they believed not that God would

See M. Perkins on the place.

bring them to heaven, and give them inheritance in that eternal rest by means of the Messiah; so that they rejected at once both the blessings of the footstool and the throne, the earthly and the heavenly Canaan at the same time. (3.) Their unbelief blemished the glory of his omnipotence. They proclaimed by this sin, that He to whom power belongs, Psal. lxii. 11, and nothing is too hard, who can do all things but those which argue impotency, as lying, and denying himself; who made heaven and earth with a word, and before whom all the nations of the world are as the drop of the bucket, and the small dust of the balance, Isa. xl. 15; could not crush a few worms, nor pull down the height of those giants, whom by his power he upheld.

4. Of all sins, the unbelief of the Israelites most crossed their own professions. They voiced themselves to be, and gloried in being, the people of God; and they proclaimed it both their duty and privilege, to take God for their God. They sometimes appeared to believe him; but the unbelief of their hearts gave both God and their own tongues the lie. They professed that they believed the power of God, and remembered that God was their Rock; but at the news from Canaan, they showed that they believed that the Anakims and the walled cities were stronger, Psal. lxxviii. 34—37. They professed that they believed the mercy of God, and that the most high God was their Redeemer; but at the very supposal of danger, they thought that they were brought into the wilderness to be slain. They professed that they believed the sovereignty of God; they returned and inquired after him, and promised obedience to him; but upon every proof they showed themselves but rebels. So that by reason of their unbelief, and unstedfastness of heart in God's covenant, they did but flatter God with their mouth, and lie unto him with their tongues. How heinous a sin is it for God's professed friends to distrust him! How shall a stranger take that man's word, whom his most familiar friends, yea, his own children, will not believe? "Thine own nation," said Pilate to Christ, "have delivered thee unto me." Thine own people, may heathens say to God, will not trust thee, and how should we?

5. Of all the sins of the Israelites, unbelief was that which properly rejected the mercy which God tendered to them. Canaan was by him frequently in his promise offered; and though all the sins of the Israelites deserved exclusion from Canaan, yet they did not, as unbelief, by refusing the offer of it, reject the entrance into it. As the faith of the Ninevites overthrew a prophecy of judgment, so the unbelief of the Israelites overthrew the promises of mercy, Psal. lxxviii. 41, 42. The breasts of the promises were full of the milk of consolation, and yet these froward children refused to suck and draw them by believing; and instead thereof, struck and beat them away by unbelief and rebellion. Unbelief, as to the Israelites, cut asunder the sinews of the promises, so that they could not stir hand or foot to help them, and turned the promises into fallacies. Only unbelief concluded this people under the necessity of destruction, Heb. iii. 19. They must needs perish who cast away the means of recovery. What shall be a remedy for him who rejects the remedy? other sins are sores, but unbelief throws away the plaster. Every sin made Israel obnoxious to destruction, but unbelief made them opposite also to deliverance. This sin stopped, as it were, the spouts and passages of grace. Christ could do no mighty works because of their unbelief, Mark vi. 5. They who believe not, render themselves incapable of blessings, and lay impediments in the way of mercy, binding the hands of God lest he should help them. Other sins lay persons, as it were, in the grave, this of unbelief lays the gravestone upon them, and makes them rot therein. Upon them wrath abides, John iii. 18.

Obs. 1. Difficulties soon discover an unbelieving heart. Many seemingly believing Israelites, upon the news of the Anakims and the walled cities, believed not. Joram's profane pursuivant discovered his temper, when he said, This evil is of the Lord, why then should I wait upon the Lord any longer? 2 Kings vi. 33. Saul appeared to depend upon God, and sought to him in his troubles; but when God seemed to neglect him, and gave him no answer, then left he God, and sought to a sorceress. Rotten fruit will not hang upon the tree in a windy day. A shallow, a highway pool of water will soon be dried up in a scorching sunshine. One who is only a believer by a shallow, outside profession, will soon leave believing and professing. For a while he will believe, but in time of persecution he falls away. Wisely therefore God seems sometimes to disregard and reject his own children, to try the sincerity of their confidence in him, 2 Chron. xxxii. 31; Deut. viii. 2; xiii. 3; and whether they will cease to depend upon him, because he seems not to provide for them. They who depend upon God continually, depend upon him truly. God makes it appear to all the world, that his people serve not him to serve their own turn upon him, and that they are neither hirelings nor changelings. *Nec iratum colere destitit numen. Virtus fidei credere quod non vides, merces fidei videre quod credis. Aug. in Psal. cix.* It is the efficacy of faith to believe what we see not, and the reward of faith to see what we believe. How improvident are those mere professors and appearing Israelites, who please themselves with shows of believing and cleaving to God! their paint will not endure the washing, nor their refuge of lies keep out the storm: when sufferings, death, or judgment approach, their confidences will be rejected. Christians! labour for a faith unfeigned, yea, both true and strong; there may come times that will require it.

Obs. 2. In vain do they who live in unbelief pretend against their other sins. So long as that lives no sin will die, notwithstanding instructions or corrections. Sin may be brought to the place of execution, but it will not die, so long as unbelief brings it a protection; and while it is backed by this, it will but laugh at all the means used to mortify it. As faith quencheth the fiery darts of the devil, so will unbelief quench the holy darts of the Spirit. The sin which is armed with it, will not be wounded by the sword of the word; but will save its skin, much more its heart, till faith set it naked to the strokes of that sword. Our neglect of and coldness in holy duties, comes from our not believing a benefit that will bear the charges of fervency and frequency in performing them. Unbelief clips the wings of prayer, that it cannot ascend; and turns much praying into much speaking. Whence is all our trouble and impatience in adversity, but from want of that grace which comforts the heart in God, and makes us quietly to rest and trust on and in him? Whence are those base, indirect courses to get a living by lying and deceiving, to be made rich by a worse than the king of Sodom, but from not believing God to be an all-sufficient portion, that he will never leave or forsake us? From what but unbelief proceed all the temporizings, haltings, and sinful neutralities? In temptations to all these faith is our victory, and unbelief our defeat, which makes men unworthily render themselves prisoners to every promise and threat; causing them either to have two hearts, with the hypocrite, or no heart, with the coward. They who have little faith have much fear; and they who have no faith will be all fear; even slain, and not by the sword. Whence proceed all our carnal confidence, and trusting in an arm of flesh, but from this sin, which makes the heart depart from the Lord? Jer. xvii. 5. Whence come the unbrotherly breaches and divisions among brethren, but from the distance which by unbelief is between God and us? Christians being like lines, which come the nearer to one another as they come nearer to the centre. Unbelief lies at the bottom of all these sins. And all mortification of sin which comes not from a principle of affiance in God through Christ is imaginary. How short-sighted are they into their misery, who are troubled for their scandalous sins of drunkenness, adultery, and murder, but neither observe nor sorrow for their unbelief, the mother sin, the main sin, the nursery of all sins! The soul, saith Luther, is a hypocrite, that sees a mote in the eye of the flesh, but not a beam in its own eye; namely, infidelity, which is incomparably greater than all sins committed by the body.

Obs. 3. Great is our forwardness to fall into the sin of unbelief. God seemed to study the prevention of this sin among the Israelites, but it broke the bars that he put in the way to stop it. Covenants, oaths, miracles, plagues, were all as easily snapped asunder by this sin, as were the cords by Samson. Even Christ himself marvelled at the strength thereof, in opposing the power of all he had said and done, Mark vi. 6. We are carried unto unbelief, both by the tide of our own natures, and the wind of temptation. Our hearts, ever since we left God, crave and look for relief from sensible objects; and having forsaken the true, embrace even any opinionative God or good which has enough to flatter into expectation, though nothing to fill or to yield satisfaction. And so great is our natural pride, that we had rather steal than beg; rather rob God of glory by resting upon our own crutches, than go out of ourselves to depend upon another for happiness. The batteries of Satan are principally placed against faith. He would not care for taking away our estates, names, liberties, unless he hoped hereby to steal away our faith. He fans not out the chaff, but bolts out the flour. Satan, saith Christ to Peter, hath desired to winnow thee as wheat; "but I have prayed for thee, that thy faith fail not," Luke xxii. 32. Satan's first siege in Paradise was laid against the faith of threatenings. He knows that all our strength, like Samson's in his locks, is from laying hold upon another: if therefore he can make us let go our hold, which is our faith, he desires no more. Faith is the grace that properly resists him, and therefore he principally opposes it: unbelief befriends Satan, and therefore he most promotes it in our hearts. Oh that we might most fear and oppose that sin which is most difficultly avoided, and most dangerously entertained! Of all keepings, keep thy heart; and of all means principally use this, of keeping out unbelief.

Obs. 4. Nothing more displeases God than the forsaking of our own mercies. In the true loving of ourselves, we cannot provoke God. He is angry with Israel because they refuse that which might make them happy. God loves to be giving, and is pleased with them who are always taking in his goodness. Unbelief obstructs mercy, and God opposes unbelief. He delights in them who hope in his mercy. He has such full breasts, that he is most pained when we will not draw them by believing. The great complaint of Christ was, that people would not come to him for life. He was grieved for the hardness of their hearts, and incensed against those guests that would not come when they were invited to the feast of his gospel dainties. He is so abundant a good, that he wants nothing; or if he does, he wants only wants. If he be angry with us, how should we be displeased with ourselves, for rejecting mercy! It is the proud and unbelieving soul which God only sends empty away. They who will buy his benefits, must leave their money behind them. How inexcusable are they who perish! they starve and die in the midst of fulness. But, alas, we are the poorest of beggars, not only without bread, but without hunger. O beg that He who bestows grace upon the desires, would first give us the grace of desire.

Obs. 5. None are such enemies to unbelievers as themselves; nor is any folly so great as infidelity. The business and very design of unbelief, and all that it has to do, is to stop mercy, and hinder happiness. Every step which an unbeliever takes is a departing from goodness itself, Heb. iii. 12. And no wonder if such a one carry a curse along with him, if he "be like the heath in the desert, and see not when good cometh," Jer. xvii. 5, 6. Unbelief is like the unwary hand of him who, being without the door, pulls it too hard after him, locks it, and locks himself out. Faith is the grace of receiving, and unbelief the sin of rejecting, all spiritual good. How vainly does the unbeliever expect refreshment by going from the fountain; or gain, by leaving the true treasure! Distrustful sinner! who is the loser by thy incredulity, and who would gain by thy believing, but thyself? What harm is it to the cool and refreshing fountain, that the weary passenger will not drink? and what benefit is it to the fountain, though he should? What loseth the sun, if men will shut their eyes against its light? what gains it, though they open them? What good comes by distrusting God, unless the gratifying of Satan in the damning of thyself? How foolish is that disobedience that will not wash and be cleansed from a worse leprosy than Naaman's; that, like a man in a swoon, shuts the teeth against a life-recalling cordial; that will not open a beggar's hand for the receiving of a jewel more worth than all the world; that believes the father of lies, who cannot speak truth, unless it be to deceive; and will not trust the God of truth, nay, truth itself, to whose nature lying is infinitely more opposite than to our good! O unbeliever! either thou shalt believe before thou diest, or not: if not, how scalding will be this ingredient, among the rest of those hellish tortures which hereafter shall complete thy pain, to consider, that offered, sincerely offered mercy was despised! that the promise of grace and truth daily desired thy acceptance, but had nothing from thee but contempt! that thou, who art now crying eternally and vainly for one drop, hadst lately the offers and entreaties of the fountain, to satisfy thyself fully and for ever! If thou shouldst believe before thou diest, how great a trouble to thy heart, holily ingenuous, will it be, that thou hadst so long together such unkind thoughts of mercy itself, that thou didst deem truth itself to be a liar! How angry wilt thou be with thyself, that thou didst so slowly believe, and so hardly wert brought to be happy!

<small>Nullum genus insipientiæ, infidelitate insipientius. Bern. de Consid.</small>

Obs. 6. Our greatest dangers and troubles are no plea for unbelief. Notwithstanding Israel's temptation, their unbelief was a provocation. A howling wilderness and dismal tidings excused them not from sin in distrusting God. Even He who hides his face from the house of Jacob is to be waited for. When we sit in darkness, and see no light, we should trust in the Lord, and stay ourselves upon our God. Faith goes not by feeling and seeing, but should go against both; it must both believe what it sees not, and contrary to what it sees. Not outward props, but the stability of the word of promise, should be the stay of our faith; a foundation that ever stands, though heaven and earth should fail.

Verbum fidei pabulum. In thy word (saith David) I hope; and thou hast caused me to hope, Psal. cxix. 49, 114. The greatness of danger must not lessen faith. Dangers are the element of faith; among them faith lives best, because among them it finds most promises. When the world is most against us, then the word is most for us. Faith has best food in famine, and the fullest table in a time of scarcity. The very earth which we tread on should teach us: this so massy a body hangs in the midst of the air, and never stirs from its place, having no props or shores to uphold it but the bare word of God alone.

Cum rogo te nummos sine pignore, non habeo, inquis: Idem, si pro me spondet agellus, habes. Quod mihi non credis, veteri fidoque sodali; Credis coliculis arboribusque meis. Mart. Ep. 25. l. 12. God must be trusted upon his promise, without a pawn. A usurer will trust a beggar, a liar, a bankrupt, for his pledge; and shall we believe God no further? this is not at all to trust him, but his security. It is a lame faith that cannot go without crutches. He that cannot stand when his stilts are taken away, was held up by them, not by his legs. He whose faith keeps not up when outward comforts are removed, stood not upon the promise, but upon earthly props. The faith which Christ commends, is that which believes much, and sees nothing. "Blessed," saith Christ, "are they who have not seen, and yet have believed." This was the commendation of Abraham's and Stephen's faith, Rom. iv. 18—20; Acts vii. 5. Such a faith quiets the heart most, in testimony of its own sincerity, and against expectation of any threatened, and in the sustaining of any incumbent, difficulties. Oh how sweet a life leads that Christian who does all by another! who gets the blessing without hunting; and whose only work is to sit still and trust God; and, like Joseph's master, to leave all in the hand of another; to have all its comforts compendiously from one object, and not to take a wearisome circuit about the whole world for contentment; to sit at his Father's table, and not to beg for food from door to door! And such a faith honours God as much as it quiets the soul. It proclaims that God is ἀυτόπιστος, to be believed for himself; it desires not that the creature should be bound for God, though he seem never so backward to perform his promise, and accounts itself as rich in respect of what it has in hope, as what it has in hand. Yea, in the enjoyment of comforts, it places its trust only in God; and if God does not withdraw created props from it, yet it will withdraw its confidence from them; using them, indeed, in thankfulness to the Giver, not trusting them instead of the Giver. O noble, glorious life of believing! to draw our comforts thus out of the bosom of God himself; not to be beholden to the dunghill for our delights; not to live, with worldly men, upon mud and corruption, but upon the pure and heavenly breathings of the Spirit in the promise. A life emulating that of the angels; for though indeed believers use the world, feed and sleep, marry and are given in marriage, yet they only enjoy God, and their better part is wholly solaced with Him that shall suffice them in glory.

Obs. 7. It should be our principal care to get believing hearts; even such a holy affiance in the promises, as may shelter from that destruction which befell these unbelieving Israelites. To this end,

(1.) Truly, and upon the terms of the gospel, wholly and solely accept of him who is the Mediator of the covenant, and through whom alone every promise in it is made good to the soul, and is "yea and Amen," 2 Cor. i. 20. Out of Christ, promises are but mere speculations; nor can we, unless united to him by faith, challenge any blessing by virtue of a promise. A Christless person receives blessings as one that finds a piece of silver accidentally in the streets, and not as a man who receives a sum of money due upon covenant.

(2.) In relation to the promises to be believed, which are the element wherein faith lives, 1. Find them out, and lay them ready: find out a promise suitable to every exigence of thy condition. How can a man claim money upon a covenant, who knows not where that distinct bond is laid upon which he is to demand it? Go to the several promises for the supply of thy several wants. Mark what promises God has made for pardon, grace, direction, protection, provision, and ever make choice of some one or two of every kind which thou mayst run to with speed. A Christian should do in this case with the promises as one which is given to fainting fits, who carries his *aqua-vitæ* bottle always about him, and sets it constantly at his bed's head, that it may be at hand. 2. Ponder the promises: go aside, separate thyself, suck and hide their sweetness, dwell upon them. Dive in thy meditations into their freeness. Consider that promise has made God a debtor, and free grace made him a promiser. Into their fulness; there being enough to relieve the largest capacity, and greatest necessity; they having more oil than thou hast vessels, even enough to be revealed from faith to faith, Rom. i. 17. Into their stability; they being bottomed upon truth and strength itself, the Strength of Israel, who cannot lie; as sure as God's own essence, which is pawned by an oath for their accomplishment, for he swears by himself: they being further confirmed by the death of Him, who has bequeathed all the benefits of the promises by his will and testament; in which respect they are the sure mercies of David. 3. Be convinced by the promises to see the whole heart and meaning of God in them, and to be under the authority and evidence of them. Faith is an evidence, conviction, or a convincing demonstration. *Ἔλεγχος, Heb. xi. 1, significat ἐλέγχειν, convincere, et causam aliquam eo deducere, ut objici aut prætexi nihil amplius queat. Hyper.* Laban, when he saw how matters stood between the servant's message and the affection of Rebekah, said, "The thing proceedeth from the Lord; we cannot speak bad or good," Gen. xxiv. 50. The Lord having brought thee under the condition of the promise, and since thou canst not deny but that the promise has a stable foundation, say, Lord, I must needs yield, I am unable to gainsay thee, I confess myself overcome. 4. Consent, cleave to, clasp about the promises, as the ivy about the oak; roll thy soul, and rely upon it; concur with it, and be carried down the stream of it, against the motion of thine own rebelling heart. As Rebekah, convinced that the marriage was from God, being called to speak, answered, "I will go." 5. Plead the promises. In temptation and sense of unworthiness, strong unlikelihood of making them good may be represented to thee, but even then cling to them closely. The woman of Canaan would not be put off by silence and vilifying terms; she was called a dog, yet she held close to the word, that Christ was the Son of David: happy she, that in this she was like a dog, namely, in that she would not be beaten off. Thus Jehoshaphat pleaded with God by the promise made to Solomon, and so prevailed against the children of Ammon, 2 Chron. xx. 1—30.

(3.) Beware of giving way to the love of any one sin. The love of sin hinders believing. Sin will not act believingly, nor faith sinfully. It is the nature of sin to cause guilt and fear it; it expects not performances, but repulses from God. How can any one depend upon me for a courtesy, who knows that I am acquainted with his underhand and unkind contrivances against me? Besides, the love of any one sin hinders from yielding to the terms of the promise: it would be loose, and yet have God bound; whereas he never made his promises to gratify lust, but to engage us to holiness. Nor will faith act sinfully. Faith embraces the whole word of God, even precepts as well as promises, and respects the rule prescribed as well as the rewards promised; it works uniformly; and it trusts to God in the way of his commands, not in the precipices of sin: "Trust in him, and do good," Psal. xxxvii. 3. Besides, it acts warily, and in the eye of God, and therefore holily, and tells us, that if we must not tell a lie to promote God's cause, much less to procure our own comforts.

(4.) Limit not God for the way of accomplishing of his promise. This is the noted sin of Israel; "they limited the Holy One of Israel," Psal. lxxviii. 41; *Deum metiri suo modulo. Cal. in loc.* they circumscribed him for the way of bestowing mercy within the narrow bounds of their own apprehensions. Whereas, if he will work, who shall hinder him? Faith triumphs over difficulties, and measures not God by the narrow scantling of reason; knowing that things that are impossible with us, are easy with God. This was the excellency of Abraham's so much commended faith, that he considered neither the improbability of performing the promise of having a son when his body and Sarah's womb were both dead, Rom. iv. 19, nor the incongruity of performing the command of sacrificing his son, which seemed to destroy both God's faithfulness and his own expectations, Heb. xi. 17. And this is indeed the duty of believers, only to consider who promises, and who commands, and neither to question what is promised, though never so impossible, nor to forbear what is commanded, though never so unpleasing.

(5.) When God affords thee creature-props, trust not to them. Men would never be distrustful when the creature departs, if they did not confide in it when it stays. If we would not account ourselves the stronger for having worldly helps, we should not esteem ourselves the weaker for wanting them. Could we live upon God alone in the use, we might live upon him alone in the loss of the creature. It is a noble faith that depends upon God in the strength of means; like that of Asa and Jehoshaphat, the former of whom having an army of five hundred and fourscore thousand to rest upon, when Zerah the Ethiopian came against him, adventured not upon so feeble a crutch, but expresses himself thus in his prayer: Lord, we have no power, and we rest on thee, 2 Chron. xiv. 8, 11; and the latter, when his enemies made war upon him, though he had an army of eleven hundred and threescore thousand fighting men, 2 Chron. xvii. 14, 15, professing thus: "Lord, we have no might, neither know we what to do; but our eyes are upon thee," 2 Chron. xx. 12. He who will account God to be all when the creature is at the best and fullest, will surely account him so when the creature proclaims its nothingness.

(6.) Trust God in the serving of his providence, and in the use of such means as he has appointed and sanctified. He that will not do for himself what he can, may not trust that God should do for him what he would. Though man liveth not by bread alone, but by the word (of blessing) which proceedeth out of the mouth of God, yet that word is by God annexed unto bread, not to stones; and that man does not trust God, but tempt him, who expects to have stones turned into bread. If God has provided stairs, it is not faith, but fury, to go down by a precipice; thus David's trusting in the name of the Lord made him not to throw away his sling when he went against Goliath. Jacob's supplicating God made him not neglect sending a present to his brother. The fast of Esther made her not forget to feast the king. Second causes are to be used in obedience to God's order, not in confidence of their own help: the creature must be the object of our diligence, though not of our trust. Faith, while it causes us to be so diligent in the use of means, as if God did nothing for us, causes us so to withdraw our trust from the means, as if God were to do all for us. He who in observing the other rules has also added this, may quietly rest upon God for promised mercy; lay the matter before God, and humbly put him to the accomplishing part.

Verse 6.

And the angels which kept not their first estate, but left their own habitation, he hath reserved in everlasting chains under darkness unto the judgment of the great day.

In this second example of God's severity, which was expressed against the fallen angels, these two parts are contained.

I. The revolt and defection of the angels.
II. The ruin and downfal of the angels.

I. In the first, these three particulars are principally considerable.
1. By whom this defection was made.
2. From what this defection was made.
3. Wherein this defection was made.

1. It was made by "the angels."
2. It was from "their first estate," and "their own habitation."
3. It was, 1. In not keeping the former; and, 2. In leaving the latter.

II. In the second, are considerable these two parts.
1. The punishment which now they undergo in the prison; they being in that "reserved in everlasting chains under darkness."
2. The punishment which shall hereafter be laid upon them at and after their appearing at the bar; they being reserved, &c. "unto the judgment of the great day."

In the former, their punishment of the prison is twofold.
1. Reservation "in everlasting chains."
2. "Under darkness."

In the latter, their punishment is considerable,
1. In that to which they shall be brought, viz. to "judgment."
2. In the time when they shall be brought to judgment, viz. at "the great day."

I begin with the first part, their defection and revolt; and therein I consider,

I. The persons by whom this defection was made, viz. the angels.

The word ἄγγελοι, angels, is a term peculiar to the Scripture; profane writers among the Grecians express them by the word Δαίμονες, and those among the Latins, by the word *Genii*. It properly is a word which intends the office of angels, and signifies no more than messengers, or those who are sent at the command and by the commission of their superiors. And yet it comprehends and recalls to mind the essence of angels, which is considerable

Angelorum nomen sacræ scripturæ peculiare: profani Scriptores Græci per vocem Δαιμόνων, Latini Geniorum, fere exprimunt. Synop.pur.Theol. disp. 12. p. 117.

before the office, and without which the office is but a mere notion. Briefly therefore for the explaining thereof, I shall consider, 1. The nature and essence; 2. The office and employment of angels.

1. For their essence. Angels are spiritual and incorporeal creatures, subsisting by themselves. (1.) By the name of spirits the Scripture commonly expresses the essence and nature of angels; and it is used both to denote good and bad angels: of the former it is said, "He maketh his angels spirits," Psal. civ. 4; a place cited in the New Testament, Heb. i. 7. Of the latter it is said, There came forth a spirit to persuade Ahab to go to Ramoth Gilead; who afterward proved a "lying spirit in the mouth of all his prophets," 1 Kings xxii. 21, 22. And when they brought to Christ many who were possessed with devils, the evangelist immediately subjoins, that "he cast out the spirits with his word," Matt. viii. 16. And our Saviour plainly expresses that such persons who have not flesh and bones, and such are angels, are spirits, Luke xxiv. 39. Nor is it imaginable but that those are spirits, of whom a legion, that is, at least six thousand, according to Hierom, may be in one man; but this is clearly asserted concerning the devils, or evil angels, Luke viii. 30; where it is added, that many devils were entered into the man. Nor can any but spirits get entrance into bodies without moving or hurting them, and into prisons and other places when closely shut up, and most narrowly watched. It is true, angels have often appeared in human bodies and shapes. The Son of God, before his incarnation, as also the Holy Ghost afterward, did so; and yet it follows not hence that their essence is corporeal; as neither can it be evinced that souls are corporeal, because Moses appeared to the disciples in an outward shape. These their bodies might either be such only in show and appearance, or if they were true bodies, they were only joined to them for a time by God's power, and afterward resolved again into their own principles, as also were their garments, which the angels wore while they conversed with men. And whereas sundry of the fathers have asserted that the angels are corporeal, and have bodies of their own, they are to be understood commonly as speaking of them in comparison of God, as if though being compared with us they are spirits, yet compared with God they are bodies.

And certain it is, that angels are not spirits purely and altogether simple, as God is, who only is that most simple Spirit; and yet it is conceived by learned Zanchy, that their bodies are more refined, subtle, and pure than either bodies aerial or celestial, which were created out of the first matter, and that the substance of the bodies of the angels is very like to the substance of the heavens of the Blessed, or the empyrean, wherein (he saith) they were created, and which are of a corporeal substance, but far more excellent for their purity than the other heavens. From this spiritual nature of the angels flows their immortality, incorruptibility, or immutability; for since they are immaterial, and free from all contrary qualities, composition of matter and form, and the contrariety of qualities, being the causes of intrinsical corruption, they are rightly termed incorruptible. Indeed, only God is simply immutable, who is a being of himself, and not by participation; and every creature is mortal, mutable, and may be brought to nothing by Him who made it of nothing, should he only withdraw his sustaining power. But a thing may be said to be mortal and corruptible two ways, either by a passive power which is in itself, or by. an active power which is in another, and upon whom it depends: now although in the nature of angels there be no passive power whereby they are corruptible, yet in respect of the active power of God, upon which their being depends, they cannot simply be termed incorruptible, because if God withdraw his power, they would instantly perish, though denomination being from the nearest and internal cause, they may properly be called incorruptible. (2.) Angels are true subsistences, or substances by themselves and separately subsisting. The Sadducees of old, and the libertines of later ages, have held that angels are only certain inspirations, motions, and inclinations of the mind; and that the good of these are the good angels, and the bad of these the bad angels. But that they are vera ὑφιστάμενα, that they are substances, and truly subsist by themselves, is most clearly evinced, 1. From their creation: God created no accidents separately from their substances; accidents were concreated in and with their substances. But angels were created by themselves, and not in any subject. 2. From their actions: they praise God, they worship the Son, they are heavenly messengers, they assume bodies, defend the faithful, they have wrestled, eaten, been received as strangers, had their feet washed, &c., they shall gather the elect from the four corners of the earth, they shall come with Christ to judgment; none of which actions could be done, unless they were substances. 3. From their endowments: they have life, power, understanding, wisdom; they are immortal, they excel in strength: some things they know not, as the day of judgment. Some of them sinned, others abide in the truth. 4. From their happiness and misery: some of them behold the face of God, and are blessed and glorious, Matt. xviii. 10; others are punished "in everlasting fire, prepared for the devil and his angels," Matt. xxv. 41; Mark xii. 25. 5. From that likeness which we shall have to them in heaven, where we shall be as the angels: shall we there cease to be true substances? This for their essence.

2. The consideration of the office of angels follows, and this the word angels properly denotes, which is not a word expressing the nature, but the office of angels; and the words both in the Hebrew and Greek intend the same, importing messengers, or such as are sent. The word angels or messengers is applied in Scripture both to good and bad angels, Luke vii. 24.

(1.) To good angels most frequently, who are those ministering spirits spoken of Heb. i. 14, and are in Scripture more commonly called by a name of office than of nature, because God delights in their service, and they themselves are more glad of obeying God than of their very being. In regard of office, that Christ himself accepted the name, and is called the Angel of the covenant, Mal. iii. 1. They are by God sent forth for the good of his people. Hence they are called watchers, ministering spirits, Dan. iv. 17, &c. And for those who shall be the heirs of salvation they minister three ways.

[1.] In their life. 1. By defending them from their enemies. "Their angels," saith Christ, "always behold the face of my Father," Matt. xviii. 10. Michael and his angels fought in defence of the church, Rev. xii. 7; and the prophet Elisha spake of the angels, when he told his fearful servant that there were more with them than against them, 2 Kings vi. 16. The angels of the Lord pitch their tents about them that fear him, Psal. xci. 11; Dan. x. 20; Psal. xxxiv. 7. An angel it was that slew the army of the Assyrians, Isa. xxxvii. 36; that delivered Peter out of prison, Acts xii. 7; as also preserved Lot, Gen. xix. 15. 2. By comforting them. Thus an angel encouraged Jacob when he feared his brother Esau, Gen. xxxii. 1, 2; an angel it was who bid Mary not to fear, Luke i. 30; and who stood by Paul, and bid him be of good cheer, Acts xxvii. 24: when Daniel had fasted and prayed, an angel it was who said, "O Daniel, greatly beloved," &c.; and afterward, "Fear not," Dan. x. 19. The women at the sepulchre met with an angel, who comforted them, Matt. xxviii. 5. Yea, an angel appeared unto Christ, and strengthened him, Luke xxii. 43; the servant comforted the Master. 3. By inciting and stirring them up to holiness, and in furthering their salvation: they suggest nothing but what is agreeable to the will of God; they can no more suggest a doctrine contrary to that which is revealed in the Scripture, than they can be accursed, Gal. i. 8. The law was revealed by the disposition of angels, in respect of their service and attendance in the giving thereof, Acts vii. 53; Gal. iii. 19: by an angel was the incarnation of Christ foretold to the virgin, and by a multitude of angels was it proclaimed afterward, Luke i. 30; ii. 8, 13. These instruct the apostles concerning the coming of Christ to judgment, Acts i. 11, and forbid the worshipping of themselves as idolatrous, Rev. xix. 10. An angel leads Philip to expound the Scripture to the eunuch, Acts viii. 26; sets Peter at liberty to preach the gospel, Acts xii. 7; bids Cornelius send for Peter, to be instructed by him, Acts x. 3—6; and prays Paul to come over to Macedonia to help them, namely, by preaching the gospel, Acts xvi. 9.

[2.] In and after their death. An angel strengthened Christ when he was in his great heaviness of soul. Angels conveyed the soul of Lazarus into Abraham's bosom, Luke xvi. 22: he who, living, was licked by dogs, is, now dead, attended by angels. The glorious angels are as forward to carry the souls of the faithful to heaven, as every one is to share in the bearing the body of a great prince to the grave. The good angels, in this work of conveying souls, are thought to watch, for prevention of the bad, who always seek to devour the saints, living and dying. At the end of the world the angels shall be the glorious attendants of the great Judge, shall cite all to appear, and shall separate between the good and the bad; gathering the elect from the four winds, from one end of the heaven to the other; so that there shall not one be lost, Matt. xxiv. 31.

(2.) The term angels or messengers is also in Scripture bestowed upon the wicked and unclean spirits. Thus it is said that God sent evil angels among the Egyptians, Psal. lxxviii. 49; and of this the apostle speaks in that scripture, "Know ye not that we shall judge the angels?" 1 Cor. vi. 3; and 2 Pet. ii. 4, "He spared not the angels that sinned." And these evil angels are employed, [1.] In exercising the faithful with temptations, Job i.; Luke xxii. 31, which God always turns to their good: these angels stir up terrors against the faithful inwardly, and troubles outwardly. Satan sent his messenger to buffet Paul, 2 Cor. xii. 7. He casts the faithful into prison, Rev. ii. 10. He casts his fiery darts, sometimes tempting and alluring, at other times affrighting and dismaying. [2.] In being the executioners of God's displeasure against the wicked, whom, for their wickedness, God delivers up to these wicked angels, to blind, harden, and bewitch them with sin, 2 Cor. iv. 4; Gal. iii. 1, and then to drive them to despair for sin, Matt. xxvii. 5. Satan employs them as slaves in the basest work, and rewards them as slaves, with the smartest stripes; often

Diodat. Annot.

in this life, as in the case of Saul, and Judas, and Abimelech; always after it, both by dragging away those souls to punishment who have followed him in sin, and by being a tormentor afterward of those of whom first he was the tempter.

Obs. 1. How glorious a majesty is the God of angels! If the lowest of earthly creatures, if a blade of grass, a worm, an ant, speak his wisdom and power, how much more those glorious spirits who excel in strength and understanding! How pure and simple a being is that God who is the Father of all these spirits! How glorious he whom angels adore, and before whom principalities fall down! How strong is he who, with one word of his mouth, made so many thousands of those angels, one of whom overthrew a hundred fourscore and five thousand men in one night! How wise he who is the Father of all that light which angels have, and which is but one ray of his sun! Infinitely greater is the disproportion between one God and all the angels, than between all those glorious hosts and the least ant upon the molehill. How can that King of glory want forces, who has such a militia, so many thousands of such chariots to ride upon, such a heavenly host as all the millions of angels? Psal. lxviii. 7, 8. Wonder, O man, that this Majesty, who is furnished with the attendance of angels, should accept of the services of worms! that he, the beholding of whose face is the heaven of those blessed spirits, and who has their beauties constantly before him to look upon, and the sweetness of the exactly skilful and melodious music of a concert, a choir of angels to delight him, that this God should accept of the chatterings of cranes, the blackness of Ethiopians, the stammerings, the lispings of infants, the jarrings of our poor broken instruments, the bungling services of which even poor we ourselves are ashamed! What a word of condescension is that of Cant. ii. 14, "Let me see thy countenance, let me hear thy voice; for sweet is thy voice, and thy countenance is comely;" and John iv. 23, "The Father seeketh such to worship him!" Lord! thou dost not seek thus because thou wantest servants, but because we want work; not because thou art defective in attendants, but abundant in grace and rewards, and delighted with that of thyself which thou seest, wherever thou findest it.

Obs. 2. How highly advanced is he who is God and man! The excellency of angels speaks the greater excellency of him, who is above all principalities, and power, and might, and dominion, who hath a name above every name, Eph. i. 21; Phil. ii. 9, who is made better than the angels, whom all the angels are to worship, Heb. i. 4, 6, and unto whom angels, and authorities, and powers are made subject, 1 Pet. iii. 23. When Christ was upon earth, the angels were his ministers, Matt. iv. 11: angels proclaimed his entrance into the world. Yea, not only at his incarnation, but at his temptations, resurrection, ascension, angels attend him, serve him, worship him. Our King has not a guard of men, as the great princes of the earth, but a guard of princes; and not of princes only, but even of principalities and powers. Christ is the Lord of the holy angels. The eyes of the cherubim are fixed upon the mercy-seat, Exod. xxv. 20; the angels look upon Christ as their Master, expecting his commands. The vail of the tabernacle which covered the most holy, expressly signifying the flesh of Christ, which, hiding his Divinity, made way for us to heaven, was made of broidered work with cherubim, Exod. xxvi. 31; there being hereby noted unto us the service which the angels give to Christ as man. They are called the angels of the Son of man, Matt. xvi. 27. Christ took not upon him the nature of angels, and yet they undertake the service of Christ. Blush, O man, that angels should obey him, and that thou shouldst rebel against him. Oh, since he is come to his own, let them receive him. Let not Christ suffer for his condescension. If submission to Christ be the grace of angels, contempt of Christ is the sin of devils. O kiss the Son, subject yourselves to him, and so stoop to your own blessedness. And take heed of disgracing that nature by sin, and of making it lower than devils, which Christ has advanced above angels.

Obs. 3. How much below angels is poor mortal man! When David saw the moon and stars, he had self-debasing thoughts, Psal. viii. 3; how much more should we, when we contemplate angelical excellency! Even the best part of man, his soul, is lower than angels. An angel is a perfect soul, and a soul but an imperfect angel; for the angel is an entire, perfect, spiritual substance, but the soul is a spirit but imperfectly, and by halves, because it is the form of the earthly body, and hereby a part of a man. An angel is all spirit; man part spirit, and part flesh; partly like an angel, and partly like a beast: an angel is all gold; a man partly gold, partly clay. How childish, yea, brutish and dull is our understanding, in comparison of that of angels! What great pains man takes for a little knowledge, how is he beholden for it to his senses, and discourse from the effects to their causes; and after all industry, how doubtful, superficial, and staggering is he in his apprehensions! but angels behold things with one view, at once discern things, both effects and causes, and pierce into the substance as well as the accidents of things. As much difference between the knowledge of men and of angels, as there is between the sight of an owl and an eagle, an illumined doctor and a sucking child. How weak and impotent are the operations of the soul of man in comparison of those of an angel! The soul by the command of its will can only move its own body; and that, too, how slowly, how creepingly, and with what a dull progressiveness upon the dunghill of this earth! nor can it bear up this upon the water, in the air, and carry it whithersoever it will; whereas these spirits, with their alone force, can carry vast and heavy bodies upward, and whither they please. One angel wants no weapons, nay, no hands, to destroy a whole army. How far below the angels are we in habitation! The poorest pigeon-hole is not so much inferior to the ivory palaces of Solomon, or the blackest under-ground dungeon to the most magnificent mansions of a king, as is man's habitation to that of the angels. How glorious is that court which is adorned with the presence of the King of glory; and how blessed those attendants which ever behold his face therein! Poor man has no better lodging for his noble, heaven-born soul than a cottage of clay, and that too so frail and crazy, as were it not once or twice every day daubed over, it would fall about his ears; and whithersoever he goes he is forced to carry, to drag this clog, this clay, this chain with him: whereas angels, free from the shackles of flesh, can move from heaven to earth, from earth to heaven, even as swiftly as can our very thoughts! Poor man! wilt thou yet be proud? Oh that we were as low in heart as in condition! How uncomely a garment is pride for those who embrace the dunghill, when the glorious angels are clothed with humility! But, alas, as the height of heaven cannot make an angel proud, so neither can the lowness of earth, no, not of hell, make sinners humble. Oh that we might only have high thoughts of that condition, wherein we shall be equal to the angels! Luke xx. 36. Lord, though I beg that I may be more thankful for the mercies which I enjoy, than dejected for the troubles which I endure in this life; yet grant, till I come to be like the angels in the full enjoyment of thyself, that about the sweetest of earthly comforts I may rather be employed with patience than delight. ἰσάγγελοι.

Obs. 5. Angelical services require proportionable abilities. As angels excel in forwardness, so in sufficiency, to be God's messengers; they are wise, strong, swift. "Provide thou," said God, when he directed Moses what officers to choose for public employment, "out of all the people able men, such as fear God, men of truth," &c., Exod. xviii. 21. Not favour, money, seniority, &c., but grace, wisdom, and courage, must advance men unto rule. A steed is not commended for prancing and trappings, but for swiftness, and holding out: officers in church and state are not for sight, but for service. We judge not of a pillar by its beauty, but by its strength. Should the pillars of a building be all gilded and adorned, yet if within they were rotten and crazy, we should fear to abide within that building. It is better to be under a zealous, faithful John Baptist, though his raiment be hair and leather, than under a silken Diotrephes, who is all for pre-eminence, nothing for performance. Oh with what unworthy trash and rubbish have we, and still do we, put off the great King! In prelatical times, he that could but sing, and cross, and cringe; and since, he that can but make a noise, and has but boldness enough for an hour; was and is sufficient for that work which requires the abilities of an angel. Cursed be that deceiver, who hath a male in his flock, and sacrificeth to the Lord a corrupt thing, Mal. i. 14. And what but curses from God and man those will meet withal, by whose means such corrupt and contemptible services are offered to the great King, I do not understand. Is thy lame, thy sickly, thy dullest child, the refuse of all thy number, good enough to make a minister? Had Achish no need of madmen, and hath God need of idiots? 1 Sam. xxi. 14, 15.

Obs. 5. Angelical abilities require proportionable services. Angels excel in sufficiency, and they likewise excel in forwardness, to be God's messengers. They are wise, strong, swift; but they think not their best and greatest gifts too good, too great for Him that is the best and greatest. God expects his tribute out of all our receipts, and they should be all for him, as they are all from him: Where much is given, much again is required, Luke xii. 48. They who are full should be free, and pour out to others. We must return as we have received. They who have received the endowments of angels, should return their employments. He who hath ability to do better than others, and yet is but equal to them, does therefore worse, because he does not better. How unworthily do those deal with God, who are angels for taking in, and yet below the very brutes for laying out their abilities! even the very oxen are strong to labour. How bad, how hard a master is God proclaimed by such servants, who can, but will not work! How little is the place, the age wherein they live, beholden to them! David served his generation, and then fell asleep; but these fall asleep while they should be serving their generation, and rest from their labours even before they are dead. How just with God is it that those who will not give God the interest should forfeit the principal! and that they who will not use should lose what God hath given them! Gifts will not be augmented, unless acted; nay, how frequently, but sadly, have I observed, that they who have been even angels for their abilities, have by sloth and sensuality grown even below men, and lost the edge and smartness of all their parts; and, like unsavoury salt, been good for nothing but the dunghill!

Obs. 6. Greatly is that God to be feared who has all the angels at his command. Sinners are never safe when most securely sinning. If God speaks the word, angels will execute his pleasure upon them. Who dares to provoke a general who is at the head of a powerful army? The heavenly hosts only wait for the word, to destroy the enemies of their Master and Commander-in-chief. An angel smote proud Herod, who robbed God of his glory. How foolishly bold is that sinner who thinks to prevail against God by rebellion! The best policy is for us to cast down the weapons of sin, and to make him our Friend in Christ who is the Lord of all those glorious hosts; and if a king should consider whether he be able with ten thousand to meet another king coming with twenty, how should we consider whether our hearts can be strong in contending with that God, between whom and us there is an infinite disproportion, and as we are sinners, an infinite opposition!

Obs. 7. God's people are always safe. The angel of the Lord pitcheth his tents about them that fear him, Psal. xxxiv. 7. None are so nobly attended as saints; they have a life-guard of angels to encompass them about: angels are as careful of the faithful as a nurse of her sucking child; they bear them up in their arms, that they dash not their feet against a stone, Psal. xci. 11, 12. God at the birth of the faithful puts them, as it were, out to these to nurse; and at their death he makes these nurses bring home his children again. They keep them from receiving hurt from others, and offering hurt to themselves. The faithful are not to be judged by what we see of their danger, but what we read of their safety. Could they but open the eyes of their faith, they might see the mountains full of horses and chariots in all dangers, and more with them than against them.

Obs. 8. It is our duty to take the care of those who are below us. None can be so much under us as we are under angels. If those heavenly spirits attend upon a lump of earth, how regardful should we be one of another, as being in the body! Heb. xiii. 3. How unsuitable is it to hide our eyes from our own flesh! Isa. lviii. 7. The angels are not ashamed to serve us, though we smell of the earth and the dungeon; and more condescend than a prince in attending upon a man full of sores and vermin: let us "condescend to men of low estate," Rom. xii. 16, and account no work too low for us but sin.

Obs. 9. The higher the privileges are which any abuse, the greater shall be the punishment for abusing them. Angels were creatures placed in the highest form of the creation: for their nature, they are spirits; for their dignity, they are principalities and powers; for their employment, the messengers of the Most High, Rev. x. 1; in strength they excel, Psal. ciii. 20: the devil is called the strong one, Matt. xii. 29. Angels can break iron chains, open prison doors and iron gates; one can destroy whole armies, 2 Kings xix. 35. They are the hosts of heaven, God's militia, his chariots, Psal. lxviii. 17. For their wisdom, Dan. viii. 16; x. 14, they are termed by philosophers demons and intelligences: admirable is their knowledge, natural, experimental, revealed. The widow of Tekoah told David that he was wise according to the wisdom of an angel of God, to know all things on the earth, 2 Sam. xiv. 17; xix. 27. And when the Scripture attributes the highest praise to inferior creatures, the comparisons are borrowed from the angels. The king of Tyre is called an anointed cherub, Ezek. xxviii. 14. The most eminent among men are called angels, Matt. xi. 10; Rev. ii. 1. David admiring man's glory breaks forth thus, "Thou hast made him little lower than the angels," Psal. viii. 5. They saw the face of Stephen as if it had been the face of an angel, Acts vi. 15. If I speak, saith Paul, with the tongues of angels, 1 Cor. xiii. 1. If they had tongues, they would speak incomparably better than the most eloquent orator. "Man did eat angels' food," Psal. lxxviii. 25. But the higher the created excellencies of angels were, the lower sin pulled them down. Sin will make one who is an angel for perfections and privileges, become a devil for impiety and punishment. If an angel sins, he makes himself a devil; if he falls, he falls as low as hell. The more accomplished any one is with abilities, when that is wanting which should sanctify and season them, the more destructive their abilities become to themselves and others. The better the weapon is which a madman holds, the more dangerous is his company. Nothing more precious and beneficial than a unicorn's horn in the apothecary's shop, but nothing more deadly than it when used by the fierce creature to wound men. None have done the church of God so much hurt, or tempted so many to sin, as some whom we may call fallen angels; who, by their places, were the Lord's messengers, and for their knowledge, as the woman of Tekoah said of David, like an angel of God, 2 Sam. xiv. 17. Great pity that their abilities had so bad a lodging; and that either their heads should be so good, or their hearts no better. Whom has the devil used in all ages for heresiarchs, and ringleaders into heresy and profaneness, but fallen angels, popes, popish prelates, Jesuits, and men reputed, at least for subtlety, and often for piety? But the eminency of their abused parts and places makes a dismal addition to their wretchedness. None has God left to fall so irrecoverably; nor is the lost savour of this salt again to be restored; for what salt is there that shall season unsavoury salt? Nor hath God spared to throw some of them, the popish apostates, already on a dunghill of disgrace, and made them trampled on by all; and, without repentance, the present seducers must look for the same reward. In a public minister of church or state smallest sins are abominations, blasphemies. God will be sanctified in those who draw near to him in any eminence of employment. If a prince have servants in places remote from his person, he expects that they should not disgrace him by their carriage; but if they wait upon him at his table, then he expects more exactness of deportment from them. God looks for holiness in all his servants, but most of all in his angels, those whom he prefers to places of ministry and nearest service about himself.

The second particular considerable in the revolt of the angels is, from what they made their defection.

I. From "their first estate."

II. From "their own habitation."

I. For the explication of the former. These words "first estate" are in the Greek contained in one word, ἀρχή, which sometimes signifies principality; sometimes, and most properly, beginning. And hence it is that Œcumenius and some others conceive that the angels are here said to leave their principality, height, eminency, principal dignity which they had by creation above all the creatures; angels being by Paul called, Col. i. 16, principalities, ἀρχαί. This interpretation, saith Junius, seems too narrow, though not altogether, as Beza thinks, to be excluded. Others by this beginning understand God himself, who was the author of their first being; but this seems to be a harsh phrase and expression, to make the keeping of their beginning, or first estate, to be adhering to and acquiescing in God, who gave them their first being. The best interpretation, and that which is most agreeable to the scope both of these and other scriptures, seems to be that which makes this their first estate to be that original and primitive condition of angels, not as they are substances spiritual and immortal, (for such even the fallen angels are,) but as they were created with their original holiness, righteousness, or integrity of nature; in which respect the elect angels which were preserved from falling are called the angels of God, of the Son of man, holy, and such as behold the face of God. This "first estate" which Jude saith these wicked angels kept not, Christ expresses by this one word, "truth;" where he saith that the devil did not abide in the truth, and hath no truth in him, John viii. 44. By truth in this place is to be understood that righteousness and true holiness, holiness of truth, wherein stands the image of God, Eph. iv. 24; nor is it unusual in Scripture to express that rectitude of heart and life which is bestowed upon renewed persons by the word truth. "Remember," saith Hezekiah, "how I have walked before thee in truth," 2 Kings xx. 3. And fitly may holiness be called truth, because it neither deceives him in whom it is by false hopes, nor any other by mere shows. We must not think that angels were inferior to men. If man from the beginning was holy, why not angels? And as bodies cannot be said to fall, but from a higher place than that into which they fall; so neither can there be a fall of spirits, but from the height of some good which formerly they had; which fall from good is not so much in regard of local motion, as of their defection from righteousness to sin, of which their change of place is afterwards a punishment. And how can any but most impiously imagine, that He who is perfectly and absolutely good, and goodness itself, should create evil? And if God does righteously punish the sin of angels, then God did not create them sinful; for how can God punish for the being of that which he himself made to be? And it is by all the learned exploded for impious Manicheism, to hold that any creature is evil by a necessity of nature. It is plainly expressed, "God saw all that he had made, and it was very good." The creatures were good with a goodness of nature, and very good because to the goodness of every particular creature there was an accession of the goodness of that order, whereby they all harmoniously suited and agreed with one another for making up the beauty of the whole. And whereas some object that the wolf is by nature ravenous, and the fox subtle and deceitful, therefore that angels may possibly be subtle and cruel by nature; it is answered, that this is the dignity and excellency of intellectual nature, either angelical or human, that what is the nature of beasts is a sin in angels and man. To which may be added, that the forenamed qualities of cruelty and subtlety in angels and man would be against a law given to them; but this cannot be said of those beasts which are not capable of a law.

Holiness then it was which at first God bestowed upon the angels, and from this first estate of holiness they made a defection. A heinous offence! whither we consider what this holiness was bestowed upon them, and when it was bestowed. (1.) It was a conformity to the original pattern of purity and excellency. It was that by which they as much resembled the great and glorious God as creatures, yea, the best of creatures, could do; that whereby they who stood are still called the sons of God, yea, gods, Job i. 6; Gen. xxxiii. 10. To cast dirt upon, or to cut in pieces, the picture of a king is a heinous offence, but to trample upon and spoil the image of God is an infinitely more heinous indignity. We are wont to burn or openly disgrace the pictures only of traitors or eminent offenders; and we account that the dishonour of the picture is the dishonour of the person: the image of God in man was very excellent, but it was far more excellent in an angel, who was a subject more capacious to receive it, and wherein it might more gloriously appear. But, (2.) When was this holiness bestowed? It was bestowed upon angels at their creation. It was given to their nature; it was their "first estate." These angels were, as it were, crowned in the cradle. God was a Benefactor to them betimes. And what an impiety was it to trample upon so early a mercy! That land which comes to us by inheritance, with Naboth, we love to keep, though bequeathed by an earthly father; yea, a gift which is bestowed upon us as soon as we are born, we love to keep all our days; but these angels threw away a gift even born with them, as old as their beings, conveyed by God himself.

II. The angels forsook also "their own habitation." By these words τὸ ἴδιον οἰκητήριον, "their own habitation," some understand those heavenly places of happiness and glory in this sense, as if for their defection from their original holiness they were cast out, and compelled to depart from them; but because the punishment of their fall is subjoined in the second part of the verse, I conceive, with learned Gerhard and others, that by "their own habitation" we are rather here to understand that proper station and set office in heaven, wherein their great Lord and Master was pleased to fix them for serving him; the apostle comparing them to a company of fugitive soldiers, who leave their colours, and that station in the army where by their Commander they are placed. And this interpretation seems to be much favoured by these words τὸ ἴδιον, "their own," that place properly and peculiarly appointed, allotted, and set out for them by God; viz. to serve and honour him in; and this is the force of the word in other places of Scripture, when used either concerning persons or places. God in the beginning appointed several places for his creatures, wherein they were to perform their services unto him; and, like a master of a family who has sundry servants, distinct offices to all sorts of creatures. Heaven was the place of angels, and the melodious praising of God in heaven the work of angels: and, possibly, in heaven those glorious spirits might have their several parts peculiarly appointed to each of them, all of them together making up the celestial harmony; and because there are sundry titles of dignity given them in Scripture, it seems to follow, that there are sundry sorts of duties allotted to them; from which several duties, for in respect of their nature angels are all alike, some are simply called angels, some archangels, some powers, some principalities; though what the particular differences between these are, and what the offices of these, I confess, with Austin, I understand not. I conceive it is neither my duty to know, nor my danger to be ignorant of these things. The bold determinations of Aquinas and other schoolmen herein, are by the most learned and godly writers rather noted than liked. And this forsaking of "their own habitation" seems in a due and proper sense to be subjoined to the former expression, of the falling of these angels from their original holiness, and intended by the apostle to be its effect; as if, because they kept not their natural integrity, they therefore forsook their appointed duty and office wherein God had set them. For, as Junius well remarks, these angels having deprived their nature of what good was in it before, since it could not be idle, it did not now incline to and act in former, but contrary ways and employments; for that privation being put, the effects thereof must needs follow accordingly in the same kind; as a man being blind, suitable effects and operations will succeed. Hence it is that Christ, to this privation of holiness and not abiding in the truth, most fitly annexes the impotent inclination of the devil to sin in these words, "There is no truth in him;" and the action whereby he expressed that inclination, which was, in being a murderer. By reason of this defection then from his original holiness he became a liar, an adversary to God and all his, a tempter, a murderer, a spirit of uncleanness, a slanderer, a devil. So that from the former privative action of forsaking his primitive integrity, as from a fountain, flowed a voluntary and incessant acting suitable thereunto, and opposite to the duty which at first God appointed him.

Jun. in Jud.

And now for the high nature of this offence of the angels in leaving "their own habitation," it must needs be answerable to the forementioned cause, viz. the revolting from their original integrity. Bitter was that stream which came from such a fountain: how high a contempt of God was this!

1. To slight the place of his presence, in which is fulness of joy, and at whose "right hand there are pleasures for evermore," Psal. xvi. 11. If it be a heinous sin not to attain that presence when we are without it, how insufferable a provocation is it to despise it when we have it! The presence of God is heaven upon earth, and the heaven of heaven. The forsaking of this was the despising of all good at once, even of that which was able to satisfy all the desires and capacities of all the creatures to the brim. Nay, the glorious perfections of God satisfy God himself; and if they can fill the sea, how much more a little vessel!

2. Heinous was the impiety of these angels in leaving their own habitation, as it was forsaking that office and station wherein God had placed them. (1.) They were the creatures, nay, the sons of God, Job i. 6. He made them, and therefore it was their duty to serve him; the homage of obedience was due to God for their very beings. He gave them those hands which he employed; he planted in them those endowments of which he desired the increase. (2.) They were of the highest rank of all the creatures. If he expected work from the weakest worm, how much more might he do so from the strongest angel! If God required the tax of obedience from the poorest, how much more due was it from those richest, those ablest of creatures to pay it! And, (3.) As God had bestowed upon them the best of all created beings and abilities, so had he laid out for them the happiest, the most honourable of all employments. All creatures were his subjects, but these his menial servants; or, other creatures did the work without doors, these waited upon his person by an immediate attendance. This employment was both work and wages. What was their work, but to behold the face of the King of glory, and to praise the glory of that King? and what other happiness is desirable, imaginable?

Obs. 1. Holiness, the image of God, makes the difference between an angel and a devil. When an angel leaves his integrity, he becomes a devil. If he keep not his primitive purity, he parts with his primitive pre-eminence. The original holiness of the angels is set out by the word ἀρχή, which signifies dignity. Cut off Samson's locks, and he will be even as another man. Though never so many other accomplishments be left behind, as spirituality, strength, wisdom, immortality; yet if holiness be gone, the truly angelical part is gone. That which is to be desired in a man, yea, an angel, is goodness. All the stars cannot make a day. Should a whole sheet of paper be filled only with ciphers, they could not all amount to the smallest number; nor can the rarest endowments without grace make a person excellent. The righteous, not the rich, the honourable, the learned, is more excellent than his neighbour. There is nothing will have a lustre at the day of judgment but purity. Riches and honours, like glow-worms, in the dark, blind night of this world glister and shine in men's esteem; but when the Sun of righteousness shall arise in his glory, all these beauties will die and decay. How much are they mistaken, who shun and abhor Christians as devils, because they are poor, deformed, disgraced, though they keep their integrity! and how great their sin, who hate them because they keep their integrity! but the world will love its own. Black men account the blackest most beautiful. Would we look upon men with a renewed eye and Scripture spectacles, we would judge otherwise. The poorest saint is an angel in a disguise, in rags; and the richest sinner is, for the present, little better than a gilded devil. Holiness, though veiled with the most contemptible outside, is accompanied with a silent majesty; and sin, even in the highest dignity, bewrays a secret vileness.

Obs. 2. Truth and holiness can only plead antiquity. The first estate of the fallen angels was holy; sin came, or rather crept in afterwards: holiness is as ancient as the Ancient of days; and the essential holiness of God, the pattern of that which was at the first created in angels and man, is eternal and uncreated. Sin is but an innovation, and a mere invention of the creatures. A sinner is but an upstart. They who delight in sin do but keep alive the adventitious blemishes of their original, and the memory of their traitorous defection from God. Oh that we might rather remember from whence we are fallen, and in Christ recover a better than our first estate! To any who pretend the greatest antiquity and longest custom for error, or any other sin, it may be said, "From the beginning it was not so," Matt. xix. 8. And custom without truth is at the best but the antiquity of error. The old path and the good way are put for the same, Jer. vi. 16. If the removal of the ancient bounds and landmarks which our fathers have set be a sin so frequently prohibited, Hos. v. 10; Prov. xxii. 28, how heinous is the violation of the ancient boundary of holiness, which at the first was fixed by God himself! *Consuetudo sine veritate, vetustas est erroris. Tert.*

Obs. 3. The depravation of nature introduces all disorder in practice. When these angels had left their original purity, they soon forsake their original employment; and the devil abiding not in the truth, becomes a murderer. All the irregularities of life, are but derivations from unholy principles. The corrupt tree yields not good fruit, Matt. vii. 18. Out of the evil treasure of the heart are evil things brought forth, Luke vi. 45. The wheels of the clock going wrong, needs must the hand do so; the translation will be according to the original. We see at what door to lay all the prodigious impieties in the world, which are but the deformed issues of corrupt nature. How foolishly are men angry with themselves for outward and visible transgressions in their lives, when they tamely and quietly endure an unchanged nature! like men who manure and water the roots of their trees, and yet are angry for their bearing fruit. How preposterous, and how plainly begun at the wrong end, are those endeavours of reformation which are accompanied with the hatred of renovation! If the tree is bitter and corrupt, all the influences and showers of heaven cannot make the fruit good. When these angels had lost the integrity of nature, even heaven itself did not help them to it. How miserable, lastly, is he who has no better fountain than corrupt nature for issuing forth all his services! Even the best performances of an unrenewed person cannot be good, coming not from a pure heart, a good conscience, and faith unfeigned; they are but dead carcasses embalmed; and at the best but hedge-fruit, sour and unsavoury, till they who bear them are ingrafted into Christ, and partake of his life, Phil. i. 11; Eph. ii. 10.

Obs. 4. Corrupt nature cares not for the joys, joined with the holiness, of heaven. As soon as these angels had left their first estate of integrity, they forsook even that holy, though most happy habitation. Heaven itself was no heaven to them, when they became unholy. A sinner may not unfitly be compared to a common beggar, who had rather live poorly and idly, than plentifully in honest employment. How great is the antipathy of corrupt nature to heavenly performances, when they will not down though never so sweetened! The enmity of sin against God and holiness is not to be reconciled. How little are we to wonder that heaven is a place only for the pure in heart, and that Christ at the last day will say to the workers of iniquity, "Depart from me," Matt. vii. 23; since they not only in this life say to God, "Depart from us," Job xxi. 14; xxii. 17, but should they be admitted into that habitation of bliss with unholy hearts, they would be unwilling there to continue with him! Let it be our care to be made meet for the inheritance of the saints in light, if we expect to have, nay, to love, the joys thereof.

Obs. 5. How irrational is every sinner! There is no person in love with any sin but is indeed out of love with his own happiness. These angels, for a mere supposed imaginary happiness of their own contriving, part with the real blessedness of enjoying the satisfying presence of the blessed God. None can become a devil, till first he become a beast. A sinner can with no better plea of reason yield to any temptation of sin, than could Samson to that motion of Delilah, "Tell me where thy great strength lieth, and wherewith thou mightest be bound to afflict thee," Judg. xvi. 6. Wicked men are rightly called unreasonable, 2 Thess. iii. 2, or absurd, ἄτοποι. such whom no reason will satisfy; and brute beasts, led with humour and sense against all reason, Jude 10; Psal. xlix. 20. Who, that had not laid aside even reason, would lose his soul for a trifle, a shadow, and die (as Jonathan said) for tasting of a little honey? He who accounts it unreasonable to part with the poorest worldly commodity without a valuable consideration, much more to exchange a conveyance of a thousand pound *per annum* for a painted paper, is yet much more absurd in sinning against any command of God, which is backed with the very height of reason, both in respect of our duty to the Commander, and benefit by the command.

Obs. 6. It is a sin for any, even the highest, to exempt himself from service. Angels have their tasks set them by God, which they must not leave: there is no creature but has an allotment of duty. Though we cannot be profitable, yet must we not be idle. God allows the napkin to none upon whom he has bestowed a talent; nor has he planted any to cumber the ground, and only to be burdens to the earth. If we are all of him, we must be all for him. It is not consistent with the sovereignty of this great King, to suffer any subject within his dominions who will be absolute, and not yield him his homage; nor to his wisdom, to make any thing which he intends not to use. The first who adventured to cease from working was a devil, and they who follow him in that sin shall partake with him in the suitable punishments of chains and darkness. It is a singular mercy to have opportunities of service, abilities for it, and delight in it at the same time. It is the privilege of the glorious angels, to be confirmed in their work as well as in their happiness. God never is so angry with any, as those whom he turns out of his service.

Obs. 7. The glorified are in heaven as in a habitation. Heaven is in Scripture often set out by expressions importing it to be a place of stability, settlement, and abode; as, "everlasting habitations," Luke xvi. 9; a "Father's house, mansions," John xiv. 2; a "building of God, a house not made with hands, eternal in the heavens," 2 Cor. v. 1; "a city, a city which hath foundations," Heb. xi. 10, 16; a "continuing city," Heb. xiii. 14; "a rest," Heb. iv. 9. How suitable are fixed and immovable affections to this permanent and stedfast happiness! every thing on this side heaven is transitory. "The fashion of this world passeth away: here we have no continuing city." Our bodies are tabernacles and cottages of clay, which shortly shall be blown down by the wind of death; yea, their falling begins with their very building; and this whole world is a habitation which ere long will be consumed by fire. Let us love the world as always about to leave it; and delight in the best of earthly enjoyments only as refreshments in our journey, not as in the comforts of our country; only as things without which we cannot live, not as things for which we do live; not making them fetters, but only using them as furtherances to our place of settlement. Wicked Cain was the first that ever built a city, and yet even then the Holy Ghost brands him with the name of a vagabond. The godly of old dwelt in tabernacles; and the reason was, because they "looked for a city which hath foundations, whose builder and maker is God," Heb. xi. 9, 10. To conclude, let the sin of these angels in leaving this habitation make us fear lest we should fall short of it; let us be thoroughly sensible of our misery by nature, in being born without a right to it, and interest in it. Let us speedily get into, and constantly keep in, the way that leads to it. Christ is that way; let us by faith procure him, as one who has purchased it for us by the merit of his obedience; and in him let us continue, that he may prepare us for it by his Spirit of holiness. Let us profitably improve those ordinances which are the gates of heaven; let us content ourselves with no degree of proficiency by them, but proceed from strength to strength, till at last we appear before God in this habitation.

'Ἐκεῖ γάρ ἐστιν ὄντως ἡ μονή. Ἡ γάρ παροῦσα ζωή σκηνή ἐστιν εὐτελής σύνδρομον ἔχουσα τῇ συμπήξει τὴν κατάλυσιν. Isid. Pelus. l. 1. ep. 65.

The third branch of this first part of the text, containing the sin of these angels, is this, Wherein this defection of the angels was seen, and did consist. This is expressed two ways. 1. Negatively, They "kept not," &c. 2. Affirmatively, They "left their," &c.

1. Ἀποφατικῶς.
2. Καταφατικῶς.
Gerh. in 2 Pet.

The nature of the subject, and indeed the very expressions of the apostle, of not keeping, and leaving, require us to explain three particulars.

1. What was the original cause that these angels made a defection, or that they "kept not their first estate."

II. What was that first sin wnereby this defection was made, or their first estate not kept.

III. In what degree and measure it was made, it being here said they "kept not their first estate, but left their own habitation."

I. What was the original cause that these angels made a defection, or that they "kept not their first estate."

1. God, who is infinitely and perfectly good, and holy, the fountain of all goodness, and goodness itself, was not the cause of the sinful defection of these angels; nor had it been justice in God to have condemned them for that which himself had caused; or to make them fall, and then to punish them for falling. And whereas it is objected, that God might have hindered them from falling, therefore he was the cause thereof; I answer, 1. Not every one who can hinder an evil is accessory to it, unless he is bound to hinder it; but God was not here so bound.

Angeli et homines ex officio debent Deo. Deus nihil debet nisi ἐξ εὐδοκίας. Junius in loc. Nor owes he any thing to any of his creatures further than he binds himself. Angels and men are bound to God *ex officio*, by duty: nothing from God is due to them but of his own good will and pleasure, when freely and of his own accord he binds himself to them by his promise of grace. Angels and men owe to God all they are, all they have, all they have lost; they are debtors to God by nature, and even nature itself is owing to God.

Asserunt malam esse naturam,quæ immutari nullo modo potest. Aug. con. 2 Ep. Pet. 2. Nor, secondly, were the angels made to sin (as the Manichees fondly and falsely imagined) by some first evil cause, which (as they held) was the original and fountain of all sin; and whereby a necessity of sinning lay upon creatures from the very being of nature, which therefore could not be changed from being evil, but was so, unavoidably, unalterably.

3. Nor, thirdly, do I conceive that this sin of the angels proceeded from any error or ignorance in their understanding before their sin, as if their understanding first judged that to be good which was not, and therefore they afterwards sinned in willing and embracing that good; for this were to make them erroneous before they were unholy; miserable, before they were sinful; whereas the ignorance of that which ought to be known is a part of sin, and all misery is a fruit of sin. That ignorance or error, saith *Illa ignorantia sive error secundum quem omnis peccans ignorat et errat, proprie non est causa peccati, sed potius aliquid peccati. Peccat enim homo eo ipso, quod ratio prave judicat. Peccat inchoative, sicut consummative peccat, in eo quod voluntas male eligit. Nam omne peccatum quasi duabus illis partibus constat, &c. Error judicii non est separandus a peccato, sed in plena ejus ratione includitur. Estius in l. 2. Sent. dist. 22.* Estius, whereby he who sins is ignorant and erroneous, properly is not a cause of sin, but something of sin; for a man who judges amiss sins inchoatively; as he whose will chooseth wickedly, sins consummatively and completely; for all sin, he saith, as it were, consists and is made up of two parts, false judgment, and evil election; and the error of judgment is not to be separated from sin, but to be included in and involved under the sin itself of evil election, as something intrinsical to it; and that every one who sins, properly is said to err in that he sins, and improperly said to sin by or from error. And thus the soundest among the schoolmen answer the objection against the possibility of the fall of the angels, taken from this ground, that every sin proceeds from ignorance, which cannot (say they) be true of the sin of the angels.

4. Fourthly, I conceive that sin, being a defect, a privation of good, and a want of due rectitude, has not properly any cause whereby it may be said to be effected or made. Sin is not a nature or a being, for then it would be a creature, and appetible, every creature desiring its being, and by consequence good. Nor yet is it a mere negation of good, for then the bare absence of any good belonging to another creature would be a man's sin. But sin is a privation of that good which has been and should be in one. Now as sin is a privation and defect, Let none, saith Augustine, inquire after the efficient cause of an evil and sinful will, of this *Aug. de Civ. Dei, l. 12. c. 7.* there being not an efficient, but only a deficient cause; for to depart from that which is chief and highest, to that which is less and lower, is to begin to have an evil and a sinful will. To inquire therefore after the causes of that defection, when they are not efficient, but deficient, is as if a man would go about to see darkness, or to hear silence; both which, notwithstanding, are known to us; the former by the eye, the latter by the ear; and yet not by any species or representation, but by the privation thereof: darkness cannot be seen, unless it be by not seeing; nor silence perceived, unless by not hearing.

5. The original or beginning of the sin of these angels, was the defectibility and mutability of their own will; whereby, though for the present they willed that which was good, and might have willed to have persevered therein; yet, being mutable, they might also will evil, and so fall from God. Every creature, as it is made of nothing, may again, unless sustained by God, return to nothing; and in that respect it was that the intellectual creature might make a defection from him who created it, and deviate from the rule of Divine righteousness: for, (as St. Augustine observes,) the being of nature comes from hence, that it is *Vitio depravari, nisi ex nihilo facta, natura non posset: per hoc ut natura sit, ex eo habet, quod a Deo facta est; ut autem ab eo a quo facta est, deficiat, ex hoc quod de nihilo facta est. Aug. de Civ. Dei, l. 14. c. 13.* made by God; the defection of nature from hence, that it is made of nothing. If there be any creatures therefore which cannot sin, they have not this from the condition of nature, but from the gift of the grace of God. And Aquinas seems to argue rightly, that, according to the condition of nature, none is exempted from a possibility of *Non ex conditione naturæ, sed ex dono gratiæ. Aquin. par. 1. q. 63.* sinning but only God; because that sin being the declining of an act from the rectitude of the rule, it is only impossible for that act not to decline from rectitude, the rule of which is the very power and will of the agent: for, as he well illustrates it, if the hand of the artificer were the very rule of cutting a piece of timber, the artificer could not but cut the wood evenly and rightly; but if the rectitude of the cutting be by another, an external rule, the cutting may either be right, or not right. The Divine will is only the rule of his act, as not being ordained to any higher end; but the will of every creature has in its act no rectitude, but as it is regulated by the will of God, which is its ultimate end. And hence it is, that *Solum illum actum a rectitudine declinare non contigit, cujus regula est ipsa virtus agentis; si enim manus artificis esset ipsa re gula incisionis, nunquam possit artifex nisi recte lignum incidere; sed si rectitudo incisionis sit ab alia regula, contigit incisionem esse rectam, vel non rectam; Divina autem voluntas sola est regula sui actus, quia non ad superiorem finem ordinatur; omnis autem voluntas cujuslibet creaturæ rectitudinem in suo actu non habet, nisi secundum quod regulatur. Aquin. par. 1. q. 63.* notwithstanding the nature of the intellectual creature was good, yet evil is said to arise and proceed from it; and that Augustine so frequently, and others after him, assert, that evil has its original and beginning from that which was good. For though evil does not proceed from good, saith St. Augustine, *Vid. l. 1. cont. Jul. Pelag. c. 3.* as that good was made by God, yet it proceeded from good, as that good was made of nothing, and not of God. And whereas it is objected against this, that a good tree cannot bring

forth evil fruit; therefore evil could not arise from the nature of angels, and the angels could not sin of themselves: it is answered by the forementioned father, that though a good tree cannot bring forth evil fruit, yet good ground may bring forth evil plants; out of the same soil may grow both thorns and vines; and though from the good act of the will sin cannot arise, yet out of the same nature may sprout and arise a will either good or evil. Nor was there any beginning from whence at first a sinful will should arise, but from the intellectual nature which was created good. Nor does this defectibility of the intellectual creature at all countenance the profane cavils of those who hence would needs infer, that God might have made the world better than he did; and that he had done so, if he had made the intellectual creature free from all possibility of sinning. For, (1.) It is a question, (though perhaps too curious,) and by some learned among the schoolmen diversely maintained, whether it was possible for any creature to have been made impeccable by nature, or free from all possibility of sinning. Some of them indeed determine it affirmatively; but herein they oppose the fathers, Ambrose, Augustine, and Hierom. The two former of whom teach, that, because it is said that God only has immortality, it follows, that he only has immutability, and so by consequence, only by nature impeccability. The same argument is also used by the learned Junius, who denies that simply God could have made the angels better than they are by nature, because then they should have been most constant in their own perfect goodness by themselves, which can only be attributed to God. Also to the forecited fathers agree the schoolmen of the greatest note, among whom Estius asserts, that supposing that the angels had been from their beginning created such as they are now made to be by the grace of confirmation, yet even so they had not been impeccable, or free from a possibility of sinning by the condition of nature, but by the gift of grace; which although it may be termed natural, as given with and implanted in their nature, yet it might have been taken away and removed without the destruction of their nature. And he saith, It is no derogation from the power of God, that a creature cannot be made by nature impeccable; for the thing spoken of is not in the number of possibilities; and it is a contradiction to say, that a creature, that is, a thing made of nothing, should not be able to change; and that therefore God cannot make a creature by nature immutable, because he cannot make that a creature should not be a creature, which, as such, is defectible, God being always able to withdraw its being, or the operation of its being, or the rectitude of its operation. Whereby, saith he, it is manifest, that not by denying, but by granting that a creature may be impeccable by nature, we derogate from the power of God.

Johan. Major. in 2 ist. 23. q. Ambr. 3. de Fid. ad Grat. l. c. 2. Una sola substantia divinitatis quæ mori nescit. Anima moritur, nec angelus immortalis, &c. in angelis naturæ capacitas vitio obnoxia. Nec ex immortali natura habet, sed ex gratia, si se ad vitia non mutat. Hierom in 6. Gal. Aug. cont. Max. cap. 12. Jun. in Jud. Greg. de Val. q. 14. punct. 1. Aquin. 1. p. q. 63. Esti. l. 2. d. 7. Etiamsi ab initio tales conditi fuissent quales nunc per gratiam confirmationis facti nt, nec sic tamen ex conditione naturæ impeccabiles essent, sed ex dono gratiæ; quod etsi hactenus naturale dici posset, quia cum ipsa natura datum esset, et in natura insitum, eadem tamen natura, atque essentia salva, posset auferri. Solus Deus est qui non gratia cujuspiam, sed natura sua, non potest, nec potuit, nec poterit peccare. Aug. l. 3. cont. Max. c. 12. Res de qua agitur non est de numero possibilium. Includit enim contradictionem, ut quod creatum est, i. e. ex nihilo productum, deficere non possit. Ideo non potest Deus facere creaturam ex natura impeccabilem, quia facere non potest ut creatura non sit creatura. Siquidem eo ipso quo creata est, defectibilis est, Deo potente subtrahere vel esse vel operari, vel ipsius operationis rectitudinem, ex quo manifestum est, non negatione, sed positione creaturæ per naturam impeccabilis derogari potentiæ Dei. Est. in 2, Sent. dist. 7. § 9.

But, (2.) I answer with Aquinas, p. 1. q. 36. a. 2. that God appointing an inequality in the things which he created, hereby made the world after the best manner. The perfection of the whole requires that there should be an inequality in the several creatures, that so there might be all degrees of goodness made up: and this is one degree of goodness, that something be so good, that there should be an impossibility for it ever to swerve from its goodness; and another degree of goodness is, that some things should be made defectible, and in a possibility of leaving their goodness. And as the perfection of the world requires that there be not only incorruptible, but also corruptible creatures; so likewise that there should be some things defectible from goodness. If angels might have been made more excellent in themselves, yet not in relation to that goodly order and admirable beauty which God has caused in the world, by making them in that capacity wherein they were created. A captain, a colonel, are better than a common soldier in an army; but yet it is better, for the order and beauty of the army, that some should be common soldiers, and commanded, than that all should be officers and commanders. And God, as Augustine saith, thought it better to bring good out of that which was evil, than not at all to suffer evil to be. For he that is perfectly good would not suffer evil in his works, unless he were so omnipotent as to bring good out of that evil.

Aug. Ench. c. 11. 27. Melius judicavit de malis bene facere, quam mala nulla esse permittere.

II. What was that first sin whereby this defection was made, or this first estate of the angels not kept. And here sundry opinions offer themselves.

Some falsely expounding Gen. vi. 2, "The sons of God saw the daughters of men that they were fair, and they took them wives," &c., imagined that the angels being taken with the love of women, sinned by lust. Strange it is, that so many learned men among the ancients should embrace an opinion so flatly opposite to Scripture and reason. For, not to speak of the spiritual nature of angels, whereby they are incapable of carnal and sensible pleasures, or of the different nature of their, by some supposed, bodies from ours, theirs being, if they be at all, not compounded of the elements, but so pure and thin that it is impossible they should be fit for generation; the Scripture plainly teaches that the angels fell from their integrity before there were any daughters of men in being; besides, Christ tells us that the angels in heaven "neither marry, nor are given in marriage," Matt. xxii. 30. Others conceive that the first sin of the angels was hatred of God; the adhering of the angels to God being by love, their departure from God, they say, must needs be by hatred; but this opinion seems false, because hatred of God must needs proceed from inordinate love of something else, God being hated because he hinders the creature from something which it loves inordinately. Hatred therefore could not be the first sin, but the irregular affecting of something else, or some other sin.

Philo, Orig. Josephus, Irenæus, Justin Mart. in Apol. pro Chr. Clem. Alex. strom. l. 3. Tertul. l. de hab. mul. Lactant.

Odium omne ex amore est. Nascitur odium Dei tanquam prohibentis amantem ab eo quod inordinate amat. Est. in 2. l. Sent. dist. 6. § 2.

A third opinion is of those who hold, that the first sin of these angels was envying the dignity of man in being created after the image of God; but this is confuted by Augustine, who saith, that pride must needs go before envy; and that envy was not the cause of pride, but pride the cause of envy; for none can by envy hate another's excellency, unless by pride he first inordinately loves his own, which he apprehends to be impaired by another's.

Superbiendo invidus, non invidendo quisquam superbus est. Aug.

A fourth, to add no more, and the most probable opinion, is, of those who hold that the first sin of these angels was pride. And this is the opinion most received and commonly embraced by the fathers; and after them received generally by the schoolmen

THE EPISTLE OF JUDE.

and others. Aquinas seems strongly to prove that it could be no other sin but pride. *[Aquin. 1. p. q. 63. a. 2. Bern. in Cant. ser. 22. Greg. l. 34. Moral. c. 14. Ambros. in Psal. 37. Hierom in Es. 14. August. l. 12. de Civ. Dei, c. 6.]* A spiritual nature, and such is the angelical, can only, saith he, affect some spiritual object, as being that which is only agreeable to it: now there can be no sin in affecting spiritual objects, which in themselves are good, unless it be because in affecting them the rule of the superior is therein not obeyed; and this is the sin of pride. For the proper object of pride, saith Cajetan, is something exceeding that measure prefixed and limited by God. Now as spiritual things cannot be excessive, nor can we have too much of them in respect of themselves, because the more of them the better, it follows, that then they are sinfully desired when they begin to exceed, and to become incommensurate to the Divine rule and dispensation; the affecting them in which inordinate measure, namely, beyond the limits prescribed by God, was the sin of pride in the angels.

That this pride, then, or an affecting (as Augustine calls it) of some spiritual highness beyond the bounds of God's will, was the first sin, seems very probable by reason, but more than probable by that of Paul, 1 Tim. iii. 6, where the apostle gives this reason why a bishop must be no novice, " Lest," saith he, " being lifted up with pride he fall into the condemnation of the devil:" *[Quid est superbia nisi perversæ celsitudinis appetitus? Aug. de Civ. Dei, l. 14. cap. 13.] [Ne ob superbiam incidat in eandem damnationis pœnam cum diabolo. Est. in loc.]* in which place I do not understand why the apostle expresses the condemnation or punishment of the devil to deter from pride, unless the devil had fallen into condemnation for that sin, and unless the apostle had intended to show the danger of being proud, by setting down the punishment of Satan for that sin.

But more particularly, if it be inquired wherein this pride of the angels consisted, and what that highness was which they affected beyond their measure, I think the answer can be but conjectural and uncertain.

Some conceive that it was revealed to the angels soon after their creation, that the human nature should in time be hypostatically united to the Divine; that the Son of God, in human nature, should be the Head of men, yea, of angels; that hereby man's nature was to be exalted above the very angels, and that they were commanded to worship and submit to him, Heb. i. 6. Hereupon, say some, they desired that the dignity of this union with the Divine might be afforded to their own angelical nature. But, say others, they refused to consent and submit to God's pleasure in the former discovery: in this, say they, stood the pride of angels. *[Vid. Zanch. de op. Dei.]* And of this opinion is Zanchy, whose chief argument is taken from that deadly hatred which Satan has ever put forth against the doctrines of the person and offices of Christ, and his incessant opposition to believing and affiance in him.

Others conjecture, for indeed none on this point can do much more, that the angels desired to be equal with God, and that they aspired to the Divinity itself. And here they distinguish between a twofold will in the angels. 1. A will of efficacy, which others term a will of intention. 2. A will of delight and complacency. According to the former, they say that the angels did not desire to be equal with God, as if they had intended or used means to attain to Divinity; for this the angels knew was absolutely impossible: but according to the latter will of complacency, they say, the angels might desire to be equal to God; namely, wish it as a pleasing and delightful thing to them: as a sick, a dying man, who despairs of recovery, and desires health without using means to procure it, because he judges it impossible to be obtained, yet as a good and most pleasing benefit; and thus, they say, these angels had this will of delight, or a *velle conditionatum*, such a will, whereby, if it had been possible to have attained to the Divinity, they would have used means to have done it: and this was the opinion of Scotus, and after him of sundry others, *[Scotus in l. 2. Sent. dist. 6. Estius in dist. 6. § 6.]* who consider the temptation that Satan laid before our first parents, " Ye shall be gods;" and afterward, being blinded with pride, his endeavouring to have Christ worship him, and his propagating the adoration of himself among heathens, under the names of sundry gods.

The most probable opinion is that of Augustine, and after him Aquinas, Cajetan, and others, who think that the pride of the angels was in desiring and resting in their own natural perfection as their ultimate end. That as God is blessed by his own nature, having no superior from whom to draw his blessedness; so these angels desired to be, and would needs rest in the perfection of their own nature, neglecting that rule of their superior, whereby they were called to desire to attain supernatural blessedness by the grace of God. *[Sua potestate delectati, velut bonum suum sibi ipsi essent, a superiore communi omnium beatifico bono, ad propria defluxerunt. Aug. de Civ. Dei, l. 12. c. 1.]* Or, as some express it, this pride stood in staying within themselves, reflecting upon their own excellency, and by consequence, affecting an independence of any superior virtue in being and working, making themselves the first cause and the last end of their own motions; for since next unto God every reasonable created being is nearest unto itself, we cannot conceive how it should turn from God, and not in the next step turn unto itself. *[It seemeth that there was no other way for angels to sin, but by reflex of their understanding upon themselves, who being held with admiration of their own sublimity and honour, their memory of their subordination to God, and their dependency on him, was drowned in this conceit; whereupon their adoration, love, and imitation of God could not choose but be also interrupted. Hooker, l. 1. § 14.]*

III. The degree and measure of the defection of these angels. They fell finally, they "kept not," &c., they "left their," &c., they quite forsook God, his image, heaven itself, and that office therein assigned unto them. *[Nemo sanæ fidei credit apostatas angelos ad pristinam pietatem correcta aliquando voluntate converti. Aug. ep. 107. Prosp. l. 1. de vit. contempt. c. 3.]* And as the holy are confirmed in goodness, so the fallen angels are hardened in the love of that which formerly they chose. This is intended by Christ, in those words, "There is no truth in him," John viii. 44; they cannot so much as will to do well, but immovably cleave to wickedness. These trees, as they have fallen, so they lie. Angels went so far, that they never turn; they fell so low, they never arise. This is proved from their eternal misery, which the Scripture mentions in this verse, and elsewhere frequently; this everlastingness of their punishment including the perpetuity of their sinning; and such an eternal forsaking of them by God, that they shall never have righteousness repaired in them again. The schoolmen are too curious in inquiring into the ground of this total and final fall of the angels into sin. Aquinas and his followers hold that their obstinacy proceeds from the very nature of the wills of angels, according to which (say they) angels are so inflexible and immovable, that they can never hate that which once they have chosen, nor choose that which once they have hated; but, as I conceive, Valentia overthrows this opinion, by arguing, that if the immutability of the good angels from good to evil be not from nature, but from grace only, who with full deliberation chose that which *[Dæmones nec mala unquam possunt carere voluntate, nec pœna. Vid. Aquin. at 1. p. q. 64. a. 2.] [Angeli boni non habent ex sua natura, immutabilitatem ex bono in malum, sed ex sola gratia, qui tamen cum plena deliberatione, bonum eligerunt,] atque ita nec mali habent natura sua, immutabilitatem ex malo in bonum, sed ex sola privatione gratiæ. Greg. de Valent. Disp. 4. q. 15. punct. 2.*

was good, then the immutability of the evil angels from evil to good comes not from nature, but from the just and total privation of grace. Others of them assert, that God preserves in the wills of devils a hatred of himself, and that this preservation is an act of punitive justice, and that God causes that wicked habit in the wills of the devils, whereby they are necessarily inclined to sin; and this impious opinion is asserted by Occham, Biel, and Aureolus; which I note by the way, as wishing that while the papists behold a supposed mote in the eye of holy Calvin, they would observe those real beams which are in the eyes of their own most famous schoolmen, as to this point of making God the author of sin. But those who speak more modestly and piously than either of the former, give this reason of the obstinacy of the fallen angels; namely, the total and perfect privation of all holiness: which is considerable, (1.) On their part; and so it is that defective and depraved quality, as Junius calls it, that utter impotency to all good, intended by those words of our Saviour, "There is no truth in him," and flowing from that defection, as its fountain, called by our Saviour a not abiding in the truth; and here by Jude, a not keeping their first estate: which defection is so set down by Jude, saith Junius, as that this total impotency to, and privation of, all good in the angels is also comprehended. For (saith he) what they kept not they ceased to have, and were deprived of; and what they were deprived of they lost totally, ἐφάπαξ, as he expresses it, once for all, as those who deprived their very nature of it. And since the nature of these angels, though it cannot be holy, yet also cannot be idle, it inclines incessantly to the contrary of that of which it was deprived, there following effects of the same kind with this constant privation. (2.) On God's part, who has determined never to bestow upon the fallen angels relief and assistance for their recovery, which being denied to them, it is impossible that ever they should turn from their sin to God, but to deliver them totally up to the bent of their own depraved nature. God having so laid out their state, and ordered the nature thereof, that their fall should be the term of their being holy; and it is natural for every thing not to move when once arrived at its term, but there to stop; and that as the end of life is the term beyond which God will not offer to sinners his grace, so that the fall should even be the same to the angels as death is to man.

Qualitas defectiva.

Hoc est angelis casus, quod hominibus mors.

Obs. 1. The best of created perfections are of themselves defectible. Every excellency, without the prop of Divine preservation, is but a weight which tends to a fall. The angels in their innocency were but frail without God's sustentation. Even grace itself is but a creature, and therefore purely dependent. It is not from its being and nature, but from the assistance of something without it, that it is kept from annihilation. The strongest is but a weakling, and can of himself neither stand nor go alone: let the least degree of grace make thee thankful, let not the greatest make thee proud. He that stands should "take heed lest he fall," 1 Cor. x. 12. What becomes of the stream, if the fountain supply it not? what continuance has the reflection in the glass, if the man who looks into it turn away his face? The constant supplies of the Spirit of Jesus Christ are the food, the fuel of all our graces. The best men show themselves but men if God leave them; he who has set them up, must also keep them up. It is safer to be humble with one talent, than proud with ten; yea, better to be a humble worm than a proud angel.

Obs. 2. Nothing is so truly base and vile as sin. It is that which has no proper being, and is below the lowest of all creatures; its very nature stands in the defection of nature, and privation of goodness: what is it but the deflouring and fall, the halting and deformity, of the creature? So obscure is its extract, that there can be no being properly assigned to it as its original cause. It came not from nature as it was, but as it was of nothing. Sin alone debases and disennobles nature. What prodigious folly is it to be patient under it, much more to be proud of it! what generous, princely spirit can contentedly be a servant of servants? A slave to sin is guilty of a more unsuitable condescension; sin alone is the soul's degradation. We never go below ourselves but in sinning against God. They who glory in sin, glory in their shame; they who are ashamed of holiness, are ashamed of their glory. Sin removes from the highest, and therefore it must needs be a descending.

Omnis elongatio ab altissimo est descensio. Parisiens.

Obs. 3. In defection from God there is an imitation of Satan. He was the first who left his "first estate." Every backslider follows Satan, though every one goes not so far as he; all decays in holiness are steps towards his condition. Satan's chiefest industry is to pull others after him; he loves to have followers, and not to be sinful and miserable alone, Luke xxii. 31. If he can make men decline in grace, he can be contented to let them thrive in the world; he cares for no plunder but that of jewels; and being the greatest enemy, he studies to deprive us of our greatest happiness. Christians! of all decays, take heed of those that are spiritual. Better to lose thy gold than to lose thy God; to be turned out of thy house, than to part with holiness and heaven. He that loses all the comforts in the world can but be a beggar, but he who forsakes God becomes a devil. Of this largely before.

Obs. 4. It is difficult to be high, and not to be high-minded; to be adorned with any excellencies, and not unduly to reflect upon them. It is a natural evil to make ourselves the centres of our own perfections, to stay and rest in our excellencies. Men of power are apt to deify their own strength, 2 Kings xviii. 33, 34, 45; men of morality to advance their own righteousness, and to rely on their merits, Rom. x. 3; Phil. iii. 6, 9; men of wisdom to set up their own reason. How just is it with God to hinder the creature from encroaching upon his own prerogative; to make those low, who otherwise would not be lowly; and to let them know that they are but men! Psal. ix. 19, 20. God singles out such to be the most notable monuments of his justice, and their own folly, who vie with him in Divine prerogatives, Acts xii. 23. If God has appointed that we should go out of ourselves to things below for a vital subsistence, to bread for food, to clothes for warmth, &c., much more will he have us to go out of ourselves for a blessed and happy subsistence; more being required to blessedness than to life. It is the poor who commits himself to God, Psal. x. 14. Nothing will make us seek for help above ourselves, without an apprehension of weakness in ourselves, Zeph. iii. 12; Hos. ii. 7. The vine, the ivy, the hop, the woodbine, are taught by nature to cling to and to wind about stronger trees. Men commit themselves to the sea naked, and do not load themselves with gold, treasure, and rich apparel. How fearful should poor worms be of that sin which God allowed not in angels, and whereby they became devils! Let us "be clothed with humility," 1 Pet. v. 5. The adorned with this grace are only

Humiliatio humilitatis mater.

meet to attend upon the King of glory; even an archangel, Michael, has humility imprinted on his name. Humility is the ornament of angels, and pride the deformity of devils. If heaven will not keep a proud angel, it will keep out a proud soul. In all conditions of highness, we should take heed of high-mindedness. As, (1.) In the highness of worldly advancements: poverty and disgrace are the food of humility; riches and honour are the fuel of pride. I have read of a bird that is so light and feathery, that it always flies with a stone in its mouth, lest otherwise the winds should carry it away. In high conditions we shall be carried away with pride, unless we carefully keep our hearts. David and Asa were both lifted up in their outward greatness. It is hard to walk in slippery places of prosperity, and not to slip by pride: we commonly most forget God and ourselves when he remembers us most. (2.) In the highness of raised endowments, abilities, and performances. It is said of Nazianzen, that he was high in his works, and lowly in his thoughts; a rare temper! our very graces and good works not seldom occasion pride. I have heard of a man who having killed an elephant with his weapon, was himself killed with its fall. And nothing is more ordinary than for high services, possibly the conquest of some corruption or temptation, to usher in that pride which may hurt the performers. We should know our good works as if we knew them not. It is a rare *Magna et rara virtus, manifestam omnibus, tuam te solum latere sanctitatem.* and noble temper, when that worth which all others observe is only hid to him in whom it is. How few are there who hide their beautiful endowments by humility, as Moses's parents did their beautiful son for safety; and with Moses, when he spake with God, pull off their shoes, and hide their faces; uncover and acknowledge the lowness, the infirmities, and cover the beauty and comeliness of their services! When Satan spreads our gifts and graces, let us spread our sins, our weaknesses, before our eyes; and so the soul may have its ballast evenly proportioned, and on both sides. There is no poison hurts so dangerously, although delightfully, as the contemplation of and reflection on our seeming deservings. Scotus calls the sin of the *Scotus, dist. 6. q. 2. art. 2.* angels *luxuriam spiritualem*, a kind of spiritual luxury, whereby they were too much delighted with their own excellencies. It is only a Christian of strong grace that can bear the strong wine of his commendations without the spiritual intoxication of pride. It is as hard humbly to hear thyself praised, as it is patiently to hear thyself reproached. That minister, of whom I have heard, was a rare example of humility, who being highly applauded for a sermon preached in the university, was by a narrow observer soon after found weeping in his study, for fear that he had sought, or his auditors unduly bestowed upon him, applause. How heavenly was the temper of John the Baptist, when he said, Christ shall increase, but I shall decrease! It was a *Luth. pref. in Gen.* good fear of Luther, namely, lest the reading of his books should hinder people from reading the Scriptures. Would we account ourselves nothing, (and indeed in ourselves we are so,) we should think it as ridiculous a thing to be solicitous for our own, as for that man's honour who is not yet created.

Obs. 5. The better the persons are who become wicked, the more obstinate they are in wickedness. When angels fall into sin, they continue in it with pertinacy: the hottest water cooled becomes the coldest. They whose light of knowledge is most angelical, sin with highest resolution, and strongest opposition against the truth. The greater the weight of that thing is which falls, the more violent is its fall, and the greater is the difficulty to raise it up again. They who leave God notwithstanding their clear light, are justly left by God to incurable darkness. None should so much tremble at sin as those who are enlightened; obstinacy is most like to follow their impiety. It may be impossible to recover them. Seducers, saith the apostle, wax worse and worse, and do not only show themselves men in erring, but devils in persevering. But of this before, ver. 4.

Obs. 6. The happiness of believers by Christ is greater than that of angels merely as in the state of nature. These had a power to stand or fall, we by Christ have a power whereby we shall stand and never fall. By creation, the creature had a power either to abide with God, or to depart from him; but by regeneration, that fear of God is put into the hearts of his people whereby they shall not depart from God, Jer. xxxii. 40. And this power of not falling is in them indeed, but not from them. The faithful "are kept by the power of God through faith unto salvation," 1 Pet. i. 5. They are stablished, settled, strengthened, 1 Pet. v. 10. Created will has a power to will to persevere in that which is good, but it hath not the will itself to persevere, neither the act of perseverance, as the regenerate will hath. Of this before, p. 19, 21, 24, 25.

Thus far of the first part of this verse, viz. the defection of these angels. The second follows, namely, their punishment; and herein first, that of the prison is considerable; which is twofold. I. "Everlasting chains." II. "Darkness."

I. For the first, "Everlasting chains." It may here be inquired,

1. What we are to understand by these chains.
2. How and why these chains are everlasting.

1. What is meant by "chains." The word in the original is δεσμοῖς, in bonds, which bonds are not to be taken literally for those material instruments or bonds whereby things are bound, that they may stand firm and steady, or persons are hindered from acting what they would, or drawn whither they would not; but metaphorically, as are also those chains into which Peter saith these fallen angels were delivered, for that condition of punishment and woe wherein they shall remain like prisoners in bonds, 2 Pet. ii. 4. The metaphor being taken from the *Certus inclusos tenet locus nocentes, utque fert fama, impios supplicis vinclis sæva perpetuis domant. Senec. in Herc. Fur.* estate of malefactors, who in prison are bound with chains to hinder them from running away, that so they may be kept to the time of judgment and execution; or who by the mittimus of a justice are sent to the gaol, there to lie in chains till the sessions. And thus these angels are kept in chains or bonds of three sorts. (1.) They are in the chain of sin, bound by the bond of iniquity, as the phrase is, Acts viii. 23; and Prov. v. 22, the Σύνδεσμος ἀδικίαν. wicked are said to be holden with the cords of their sins: and deservedly may sins be called bonds or chains, they both holding sinners so strongly, as that without an omnipotent strength they can never be loosed, as also being such prison-bonds as go before their appearing at the bar of the last and dreadful judgment. The bonds of sin wherein wicked men are held, are often by the goodness and power of God loosed; but the bonds of sin wherein wicked angels are held shall be everlasting: there is, and ever shall be, a total inability in those cursed creatures to stir hand or foot in any well-doing; they are *in arcta custodia*, close prisoners in these chains of iniquity, staked down, wedged, wedded to sin, chained as it were to a block: hence it is said, 1 John iii. 8, that "the devil sinneth from the beginning;" whereby may be noted, not only how early he began, but also

how constantly he proceedeth in sin: for (as Bede well observes) it is not said he sinned, but he sinneth from the beginning; to note, saith he, that since he began, he never ceased to sin: he keeps no holy-days, makes no cessation from pride and other impieties; and as He sleeps not who keeps, so neither doth he who opposes Israel; he goeth about seeking, &c., 1 Pet. v. 8. To this purpose our Saviour saith, John viii. 44, the devil hath no truth in him, to note his utter impotency, saith Junius, to any thing of goodness and integrity; and "when he speaks a lie, he speaketh of his own," according to his custom and disposition; and when he speaks truth, he borrows it, to the end he may deceive. Satan cannot lay down his sinful inclination; he is *totus in mendaciis delibutus*, saith Calvin, stained and soaked in sin. In a word, this chain of sin, which he has put on, he never can or will put off.

(2.) These false angels are in and under the chains of God's power; the strong man is bound by a stronger than himself. The old dragon was bound for a thousand years, Rev. xx., and the chain which curbed him was the power of God: this power hinders him both from escaping the evil which he undergoes, and from effecting and causing that evil which he desires. Satan will for ever be miserable in sustaining what he would not, and in not obtaining what he would: the impossibility of his being happy necessarily follows his impotency to be holy, purity being the path to blessedness. All the forces of hell cannot scale the walls of heaven. There is a gulf fixed between fallen angels and happiness which they can never pass over; as they can never return to God so as to love him, so never so as to enjoy him. They are debarred from these joys unavoidably which they forsook voluntarily; nor is it a small matter of their punishment to be curbed against the bent and violent inclination of their own will, from stirring a hair's breadth for hurting any further than God lengthens their chains. How painful a vexation is it to Satan, that he cannot hurt the soul by affrighting, alluring, and seducing, nor our bodies by diseases and pains, nor our estates by losses, nor our names by disgraces, unless our God gives him chain! "Satan hath desired to have you," &c., saith Christ, Luke xxii. 31. And when Satan besought Christ not to torment him, Luke viii. 28, it is by many interpreted, that the torment against which he prayed was his ejection out of the possessed, whereby he was to be hindered from doing the hurt which he desired; it being immediately subjoined by the evangelist, "For he had commanded the unclean spirit to come out of the man:" and whereas the devils further desired Christ that he "would not command them to go out into the deep," ver. 31, Calvin, with others, refer this petition to the great desire of the devils to continue among men, to annoy and molest them. They grieved, saith Calvin, to think of being cast into the deep, wherein they could not have so much power and opportunity of doing harm to men, the destruction of men being the delight of the devil. And this seems further to be confirmed by the words of Mark, who saith the devils desired that Christ "would not send them out of the country," Mark v. 10; whereby they would want opportunities of doing harm to the souls and bodies of men. The chain of Divine power, which restrains the devil from hurting men, must needs be a considerable part of his torment, whose work is to go about, "seeking whom he may devour."

(3.) The fallen angels are in and under the chain of their own guilty consciences. These, by the tenor of God's justice, bind them over to destruction; they know they are adjudged to damnation for their sins. Let them be where they will, in the earth or air, these chains of guilty consciences bind them over to judgment; they can no more shake off these than leave themselves. In these the devils are bound like madmen; they must endure what they cannot endure. The devils fear and tremble, James ii. 19: horror is the effect of diabolical assent. How evidently did this guilty trembling appear, when they ask Christ whether he was come to torment them before their time! The sight of the Judge, saith Calvin on the place, made these guilty malefactors tremble at the thoughts of their punishment; their evil conscience told them, Christ being silent, what they deserved. As malefactors, when they are brought to the bar, apprehend their punishment, so did these devils at the sight of their Judge. The fallen angels shall ever contemplate what they have done, and how they have sinned; as also what they shall undergo, and how they shall suffer: and hereby, as God delivers the damned men into the hands of guilty angels, so he delivers guilty angels over to themselves to be their own tormentors. This fiery furnace of a tormenting conscience, which of all others is the most scorching and scalding, every devil shall carry in his bosom. This inward and silent scourge shall torment him, this arrow shall stick in his side, this vulture shall prey, this worm shall gnaw, and this hell shall he carry about him wherever he comes: though he may change his place, yet he never changes his state. As the happiness of the good angels is not diminished when they come to us, and are not actually in the heavenly place because they know themselves blessed; (as the honour of a king is not impaired, though actually he sits not in his chair of state;) so neither is the misery of the wicked angels lessened, when they are not actually in the very place of the tormented in hell, because they know that eternal woes are due to them; as the scorching distemper of one in a burning fever is not removed, though he be placed in a bed of ivory, or the most refreshing place.

2. The second particular to be explained is, How and why these chains are everlasting?

By the word in the original, ἀϊδίοις, which signifies always continuing, perpetual, is intended that the forementioned chains shall never be shaken off; and that these angels shall stand guilty for ever, expecting the last judgment, despairing, and without any hope of recovery and redemption, they having no Saviour, nor any means allowed them by God for their release. And if it be here demanded, why the fallen angels, rather than fallen man, stand guilty for ever without any deliverance or hope of recovery, it is by several differently answered.

1. Some say, Because man was seduced to sin; but the devil sinned merely by his own will, without instigation from any other; he fell alone, and must, if at all, rise alone.

2. Others say, Because in the fall of angels the whole angelical nature of angels perished not; but the first man sinning, the whole human nature had

perished, if the goodness of God had not afforded a remedy: "In Adam all die," 1 Cor. xv. 22.

<small>'Ανεπίδεκτος μετανοίαν ὁ ἄγγελος, ὅτι καὶ ἀσώματος, ὁ γὰρ ἄνθρωπος διὰ τὴν τοῦ σώματος ἀσθένειαν, τῆς μετανοίας ἔτυχε· ὅπερ ἐστὶ τοῖς ἀνθρώποις ὁ θάνατος, τοῦτο τοῖς ἀγγέλοις ἡ ἔκπτωσις. Damascen. l. 2. Orth. Fld. cap. 3 & 4. Gerh. in 2 Pet. ii.</small>
3. Others say, That the nature of the angels being more excellent and sublime, their fault was more damnable than that of man; and that so much the more ungrateful to God were they in their fall than man, by how much the more bountiful in their creation God was to them than to man. But I humbly conceive we may more safely say with Gerhard, It is better thankfully to acknowledge the love of God to mankind in affording him a recovery, than curiously to search into the depths of Divine judgments without the warrant of the word, Deut. xxix. 29.

Obs. 1. They whose course and trade of life is in sin most resemble Satan. Sin is a chain to the godly, to weary and trouble them; but it is a chain to the devil and wicked men, wholly to subdue them to its power and obedience. The holiest may sometimes fall into sin, but the ungodly only live and lie in sin. The godly are like a sheep, which sometimes may slip, and be tumbled into a dirty ditch; but the wicked are as swine, who tumble and wallow in the ditch. The former beat themselves with striving to get out, the latter are ready to beat and hurt any who labour to help them out. The former cry out of sin and sinning, as their torment; the latter, like the devil, when any go about to reform and hinder them from sin, cry out, What have we to do with you? are you come to torment us before our time? The godly sin, but the wicked are ἐργαζόμενοι, workers of iniquity, witty and skilful practitioners in impiety. Sin is the woe of a saint, and the work of a sinner: to the former, it is a thorn in the eye; to the latter, as a crown upon the head. In the former *sin is*, but the latter are *in sin:* a sober man may have drink in him, but the drunkard only is in drink. A saint, when he sins, is as a poor child when he falls into a pond of water; but a wicked man as a fish in the water, sports and swims in sin as his element; his *bibere* is his *vivere*, he drinks in sin as the fish drinks in water. A sinner performs good duties by fits and starts, but sin is his course and standing employment; a saint sins by fits, but holiness is his course, and he walks with God, though sometimes he is drawn away by a temptation. Oh that they who live in sin, cannot sleep unless they sin, who are sick, with Amnon, till they have satisfied their lusts; who can walk in sin from morning to night, week after week, year after year; yea, and if they had more lives, they would do so life after life; would consider who is their father, and whom they resemble, and never be at rest till they get from under the cruel slavery of sin into the service of Jesus Christ, which is the true and only liberty! And let them fear lest the Lord at length give them up to final obstinacy, and say in his wrath, Thou that art filthy, be filthy still, Rev. xxii. 11; my Spirit shall never more strive with thee; I will never give one blow more to knock off thy chains, but they shall be like the devil's, everlasting chains; and thou who holdest thy sin so fast here upon earth, shalt be held and bound by that chain for ever in hell.

Obs. 2. Torments cannot reform devils. Hellish horrors cannot change hellish hearts. Sinners will not be persuaded, either by the rising of one from the dead, or their own remaining among the damned. The braying of sinners in a mortar cannot make their folly depart from them. Outward troubles may break the back; only God, by his supernatural working, can melt the heart. Notwithstanding smiting, people may revolt more and more, Isa. i. 5. After all the repeated plagues upon Pharaoh and Egypt, their hearts were hard. And though God battered the Israelites with successive judgments, yet he testifies, they returned not to him, Amos iv. 8. Judgments move only by way of outward and objective persuasion, they cannot reach, really work upon, or turn the heart. The smartest outward poverty cannot make a man poor in spirit. The glorified angels are humble in the joys of heaven, the devils are proud in the torments of hell. It is not the inflicting, but the sanctifying of troubles that can benefit us. Whenever the Lord chastens us, let us beseech him likewise to teach us, Psal. xciv. 12; otherwise we shall continue unreformed.

Obs. 3. Restraint much differs from reformation. Devils may have a chain upon them, and yet no change within them. A necessitated forbearance of sin may accompany a devilish nature; Divine chastisements and human laws may hide sin, and hinder sinning; but it is only a principle of renovation whereby we hate sin. Let none please himself with such a conversion as that to which he is forced by his earthly superiors. They who only leave sin because men forbid it, will, upon the same ground, be brought to forsake any way of holiness. And yet what is the religion of the most, but a mere restraint? and hence it is that so many have proved apostates: constrained goodness is never constant. The fear of man's laws may make a good subject, it is only the fear of God in the heart that makes a good Christian.

Obs. 4. Satan can do nothing but by God's permission. God keeps him in a powerful chain. Wicked angels are potent, only a good God is omnipotent. When God gives way, one devil may overthrow a legion, a million of men; but till God lengthens out his chain, a legion of devils cannot hurt one man, nay, not a silly beast, Matt. viii. 31. God who made can ruin them; and would do so, were he not able to overrule them, and to advance his own glory against, nay, by all their endeavours, 1 Kings xxii. 21; Job i. 12. The consideration of this should both quiet and counsel us. (1.) Quiet us, because our worst enemy is wholly in the power of our best Friend. Satan takes out a new commission from God for every undertaking against us; and, as Christ told Pilate, he could have no power over us, unless it were given him from above. It was in the power of Satan to carry Christ up, but not to cast him down: he that fears God neither need nor will fear Satan. As the rage of men, so that of devils, shall also praise God, and the residue thereof will he restrain. (2.) Counsel us, to take heed of that heathenish error whereby men commonly give the honour due to God to conjurers and impostors; and of that common fault among Christians, in being more angry with the instrument than patient under the hand that smites them.

Obs. 5. Satan cannot hurt us, unless he gets us within the compass of his chain. If we go not to him, he cannot come to us. All the ways of Satan are deviations and swervings from the way and rule of the word. He who keeps in this way, and walks according to this rule, keeps himself from the destroyer, and peace shall be upon him. Satan was fain to beg of Christ to cast down himself; he cannot cast us down, unless we cast down ourselves; he can suggest sin to us, he cannot force us to sin. No man is hurt but from himself, and out of the voluntary inclination of his own mind to evil. The devil cannot infuse wickedness into us, but only stir up wickedness in us; he cannot bend the will as God does, who by his own absolute power works in a way of creation in us; who without ourselves, and <small>Non extorquet a nobis consensum, sed petit. Aug. Non potest vincere nisi volentem. Hieron.</small>

against ourselves, gives a new heart, and changes a heart of stone into a heart of flesh. Satan moves not our wills, either by any proper power which he has over them, or without our assent first gained to him, but by working upon the imagination; sometimes so presenting objects to the understanding, as that it apprehends evil in the colour of good; sometimes stirring up the corruption, passions, and lusts already in us, to darken the understanding, and incline the will. If Satan could hurt us without our will, he could never be resisted in any temptation. The devil is not so dangerous an enemy as our own sin; this slays us without him, he hurts us not without this. If Satan plough not with our own heifer, he can get no advantage. Many, having sinned, lay the blame on the devil, who, they say, owed them a spite; whereas it is their sin, not the devil, which pays it: had they not cast down themselves, the devil could never have done it. The thief indeed is to be blamed for stealing thy money, but it was thy fault and folly to leave thy doors open, and give him entertainment. Satan never beats us but with our own weapons. Though David was stirred up to number the people by Satan, 1 Chron. xxi. 1, yet when he came to see his folly, he thought not his sin less because Satan moved him to it, but took all the blame of sin to himself, and said, "I have done very foolishly." Let therefore the time we spend in blaming Satan when we have sinned, be spent in opposing Satan, that we may not sin, James iv. 7; let us not "give place to the devil," Eph. iv. 27, but resist him, 1 Pet. v. 9; by faith applying the victory of Christ, and viewing present assistances and future recompences; by prayer bringing God into the combat; by sobriety in the use of comforts, and watchfulness against all temptations to sin, continuing our allegiance and God's protection, Eph. vi. 13, 16. Adventure not within the chains of a mad dog; supply not their want of length by thy want of watchfulness. Our natures are tinder and gunpowder; we had need beware, not only of fiery darts, but the least spark.

Obs. 6. God can make an offender his own afflicter, a Magor-missabib, a terror to himself, and constantly to carry his own chains of terror and torment about him. That which makes us enemies to God, makes us enemies to ourselves; wickedness is its own vexation. A sinner, though he be truly a friend to none, yet never is he so great a foe to any as to himself. Powder which blows up the house cannot itself escape from burning. Such is the power of God's justice, that, without any trouble to himself, he can make a transgressor his own tormentor, industriously to fetch in matter of excessive horror to himself out of his own bosom; to gaze willingly into that false glass which Satan sets before him; to be led by that lying cruelty, which misrepresents to the sinner's affrighted imagination every gnat as a camel, every mote as a molehill, every molehill as a mountain, every lustful thought as a Sodomitical villany, every idle word as a desperate blasphemy, every angry look as a bloody murder, every transgression against light of conscience as a sin against the Holy Ghost. In this amazedness of spirit, God can cause a man to turn his own artillery, his wit and learning, upon himself, to argue with subtlety against the pardonableness of his sins, to wound his wounds with a conceit that they are incurable, to vex his very vexations with refusing to be comforted. In a word, to turn to his own torment, not only his crosses and temptations, but even the very comforts of his life; wife, children, gold, goods, honours, as that woeful Spira did. If God speak the word, the hand shall rebel and strike the head, the nails shall tear the skin, the teeth shall gnaw the flesh. Those who are made to take one another's parts shall become mutinous, like the Midianites, who sheathed their swords in their fellows' bowels. A man forsaken of God has least mercy for himself. Never let us please ourselves, or envy the enemies of God, in any sinful quietness, since God can make men self-destroyers. To conclude this, if ever you would be reconciled to yourselves, (1.) Labour to be reconciled to God in Christ. Never will conscience, God's deputy, speak peace, if God himself speak war; nor will God be at peace, but through Him who is our peace. (2.) Let us maintain a constant war with sin. Such is the cruelty of sin, that it always torments those who love it; and such is its impotency, that it cannot hurt those who hate it. (3.) Let us constantly walk in those ways which are called "peace," Prov. iii. 17; remembering that holiness troubles nothing but our lusts, which we should not only trouble, but destroy.

<small>quod non ille vel refelleret argutissime, vel eluderet callidissime, vel dissolveret promptissime. Sæpe intra meipsum cogitavi eum nequaquam fuisse ita perspicacem in judicio dogmatum, ita porro exercitatum in disputationibus theologicis, cum sanus esset. Hist. Fran. Spira, p. 120, 121.</small>

Obs. 7. There is no liberty to be found in forsaking of God's service. As soon as these angels had thrown off the yoke of obedience, they put on the chains of bondage; they were in bondage to sin, and for sin. Every sinner is a captive, he cannot stir hand or foot in heavenly employments. A saint only walks at liberty; the service of God alone is freedom. Where the Spirit of the Lord is, there is liberty, and a changing of the chains of slavery for a heavenly activity. None but saints can run the ways of God's commandments, and willingly wait upon their Master; and hence it is, that only they can perform duties either delightful to him or themselves. The ways of obedience, which are torments to a sinner, are the pleasures of a saint; that which the one counts his yoke, the other esteems his privilege, and knows not how to live without daily performing them. And how comfortable is their condition, in having their chains of guilt beaten off by Christ! As their services are, so their usage is, that of sons, not of slaves and captives. Their duties savour of the Spirit of adoption and filial ingenuousness. Their services are without fear; whereas others are all their life-long subject unto bondage. How are sinners mistaken, in thinking that liberty is inconsistent with sanctity! A saint loses nothing but his bonds and fetters by becoming holy; nor is holiness a chain to any, but those who know no other freedom than a house of bondage.

8. The pleasures of sin bear no proportion to the horrors thereof. Its pleasures are light and momentary, its chains are heavy, horrid, and everlasting. The act of sin is instantly ended, and the delights of sin soon fall off; but its chains are strong, and not to be broken; there is no *aqua-fortis* to eat them asunder. How happy were it that sinners would be but as wise in preventing, as they will be woeful in undergoing, the everlasting sorrows which follow their short sinning! Oh that when you say you know not how to forbear the breaches of the law, you would ask yourself whether you are able to bear or knock off the chains of the prison! Foolish sinner! say no more, as I have sometimes heard thee in thy fits of passion, I must speak, and then I have done: when thou hast done, God hath not done, he then begins; and should he, as thou deservest, once chain such a wild offender in that black dungeon of hell, he would not have done with thee to eternity. Look upon sin with Scripture spectacles: oh view the chain, the everlasting chain of guilt and horror, through every temptation. Let the meditation of

<small>Nihil potuit adeo apte proponi, nihil tam accommodate adferri,</small>

eternity damp and stop thee in thy sinful heats and fury. If thou canst not find a man who, to gain the world, would be compelled to lie bound upon a bed of roses a hundred years, how shalt thou endure the flames and chains of hell to eternity?

Obs. 9. How eminently is the goodness of God manifested to men more than to angels! The fallen angels continue under the chains of eternal guilt, helpless without, and hopeless of recovery. Man, who deserved no better, is loosed from those chains by a strong Redeemer, and by the blood of Jesus Christ they are broken asunder. How should so great mercy quicken our hearts to thankfulness! Wonder, O' man, that God should break in pieces, and throw on to the dunghill of hell to eternity, those golden vessels, the angels, beset with the most precious gems of most shining and glorious endowments, when they had contracted rust; and that he should cleanse the earthen pot, poor man, instead of breaking it, when the uncleanness of sin had defiled and eaten into it. I only add, that in one thing the sins of men admit of a greater aggravation than those of devils, they never sinned against the offers of a Saviour. Unbelieving sinner! the very devils will condemn thee. If all the examples in the world of ingratitude to God and unkindness to oneself were lost, they might be found again in thee.

Thus far of the first part of the punishment of these fallen angels in the prison, viz. their being in "everlasting chains."

II. They are "under darkness."

Two things may here needfully be opened.
1. What the darkness is under which they are.
2. What is their misery in being under it.

1. "Darkness" is in Scripture taken two ways. (1.) Properly, for the negation, defect, and privation of light, Gen. i. 2, 4; Isa. xlv. 3, 7, 19; 1 Cor. iv. 5; 1 Thess. v. 5; 1 John ii. 8; Rom. i. 21; ii. 19; 1 Thess. v. 8; 1 John ii. 11; Jer. xxiii. 12. (2.) Metaphorically: 1. For a secret, hidden, or private place: "What I tell you in darkness, that speak ye in light," Matt. x. 27; so Luke xii. 3. 2. For error and ignorance: "To turn them from darkness to light," Acts xxvi. 18. Having their minds darkened, Eph. iv. 18. Once were ye darkness, &c., Eph. v. 8. In which respect principally, sins are called the "works of darkness," Rom. xiii. 12; Eph. v. 11. 3. For great calamities and punishments. (1.) External: "When I looked for good, evil came unto me; and when I waited for light, there came darkness," Job xxx. 26. "If one look unto the land, behold darkness and sorrow," Isa. v. 30. "They shall look unto the earth, and behold trouble and darkness," Isa. viii. 22. "We wait for brightness, but we walk in darkness," Isa. lix. 9. "Get thee into darkness, O daughter of the Chaldeans," Isa. xlvii. 5. (2.) Internal. Thus Heman complains that God had laid him in darkness, Psal. lxxxviii. 6. "Who is there among you," &c. "that walketh in darkness, and seeth no light?" Isa. l. 10; Jer. xiii. 16; Ezek. xxxii. 8; Mic. vii. 8; Psal. cxliii.

Metaphorice, per tenebras, Scriptura horrendum mœrorem designat. Calv. in Matt. viii. 12.

3. (3.) Eternal, for the uncomfortable condition of the damned in hell, by reason of the absence of God's presence, Jude 12, 13. We read of some cast into "outer darkness," Matt. viii. 12; xxii. 13, i. e. without the kingdom of God, which is light, and a kingdom of light. This phrase of "outer darkness" some conceive is an allusion to the darkness which God sent upon Egypt, Exod. x. 23; that Egyptian darkness being without the habitations of the Israelites, in all which was light. Or, as Calvin conceives, to the darkness wherein they are, who are excluded in the night-time from places in which are suppers or feasts, where they set up many lights and lamps. Or, as others, to the darkness of prisons, which were oft wont to be without the city, Acts xii. 10. Whatever the allusion is, by this outer darkness is intended a state of the greatest remoteness and distance from the light of God's presence, the joy, yea, the heaven of heaven; for, as Brugensis well notes by the comparative note, ἐξώτερον, outer, may well be intended the superlative, utmost, or most without, furthest, or most distant from the kingdom of light, as 1 Cor. xiii. 13, the greater, i. e. "the greatest of these is charity." This eternal darkness, which stands in the withdrawing of the light of God's pleased and pleasing countenance, wherein is fulness of joy, and pleasures for evermore, is that here by the apostle intended to be the portion of these angels in their prison of hell. And most fitly is this their woeful estate of separation from God's presence called "darkness;" because, as the, though but deficient, cause of darkness is the departure of the light, so the separation from the favourable presence of God is the greatest misery of the damned; as the face and comfortable presence of God is the heaven of heaven, so absence from God is the hell of hell. It is not heaven to be in the place of heaven, but to be with God in heaven; and it is not hell to be in hell, but to be without God's loving and gracious presence in heaven.

Afflictus, vitam tenebris luctuque trahebam. Virg. Æneid 2.

Luc. Brug. in Matt. viii.

2. The misery of this condition of darkness, or separation from God's presence; and it may be amplified two ways.
1. Considering from what this separation shall be.
2. How the misery thereof shall be further heightened.

(1.) There shall be a separation from the favourable presence of God, which is, [1.] A full good, comprehending all good; that wherein all good things are assembled and combined. He who has Him who is all things, must needs have all things. To him there can be made no addition of goodness; in parting with him, the damned part with whatsoever is good. [2.] A filling, satisfying good, enough and sufficient for himself; and that which can fill the ocean, can undoubtedly fill the vessel. God satisfies all the wants and exigences of the soul. "My God shall supply all your needs." The favour of God is better than life. "The Lord is my shepherd; I shall not want." Every good besides God is but of a limited nature, answering but to this or that exigence; but one God answers to every want. Bread relieves hunger, water thirst, clothes nakedness, money poverty; God relieves in every want, and has infinitely more oil than we have vessels. Deservedly therefore is this punishment of loss frequently expressed in the Scripture as the great woe of the damned, Matt. vii. 23; Luke xiii. 27; Matt. xxv. 10, 41. The throne of iniquity shall have no fellowship with God, Psal. xciv. 20. Needs must hell be a dismal dungeon, where the sunshine of God's presence never comes.

Summa mors animæ est alienatio a vita Dei, in æternitate supplicii. Aug. lib. 6. de Civ. Dei, c. 12.

But, (2.) The misery of the loss of this blessed presence of God is further heightened, aggravated, and made intolerably tormenting; considering, [1.] The damned in hell know the incomparable worth of what they have lost; their understandings are clear, though they are not changed: their knowledge increases their sorrow. How happy (comparatively) would they be, if their understandings were taken from them, if they could but put out their eyes! Though they see not God so fully and clearly as do the blessed in heaven, yet they see enough of him to rend and grind them with inexpressible vexation for losing him. A company of wretched beggars, who in a dark night stand at the door of that house where there is a wedding-feast, though they see not the stately preparations, the furnished tables, the costly ornaments of the married couple and guests so fully and clearly, and though they hear not the sweet music within so distinctly, as the guests themselves who sit at table; yet by lights in the windows, the voices of mirth, and musicians, with the confused sound of instruments, the passage to and fro of attendants with their cheer, they cannot but observe enough to think themselves, being excluded, very miserable, in comparison of those who are attended at the table, and in the midst of all their mirth and plenty. Christ makes the application, Luke xiii. 25, 28; where he speaks of those who stand without and knock, &c., and shall see Abraham, and Isaac, and Jacob, and all the prophets, in the kingdom of God, and they themselves thrust out. The rich man sees Abraham and Lazarus, but afar off: see them he must, though he would not; get to them he must not, though he would never so fain. And certainly, the large vessel of an angel's understanding holds more matter of this torment than can more shallow capacities.

[2.] These damned spirits remember that this loss of the presence of God was a rod of their own making, a woe of their own most wilful procuring; the door which shuts them out of heaven was pulled to with their own hands. How much will it sharpen the edge of their horror, to consider that none forced them to sin; that the forsaking of God was the choice of their own will; that they had no enemies but themselves! The treasures of glory were not stolen from them, but voluntarily dissipated, and prodigally misspent with their own hands. How easily could they have prevented that loss which now is irreparable; and have kept their foot out of that snare, out of which they can never wind themselves! The arrow which falls down upon their heads, was shot up with their own hands; and the destruction which has caught them, was spun out of their own bowels.

[3.] They consider how poor a trifle and contemptible a toy it was for which they have lost the blessed presence of God. How does it cut them, to remember that they have lost all things for nothing; a massy crown, a weight of glory, for a bubble, a butterfly; the inheritance of heaven for a song! What proportion is between a notion, a fancy, and the satisfying fruition of a real good! How men blame themselves for lodging in a dear inn, where they are compelled to pay as much more as their entertainment is worth! How heartily have I heard men beshrew themselves for parting with great sums of money, for which they say they never drunk! A minute of pleasure, a poor, silly, slight, shallow nothing, may the damned say, was all I had, for have he cannot say, to show for myself, my blessedness, my God. O mad exchange! O amazing disproportion! deservedly miserable wretch that I am; I had but a dream of delight for heaven itself. Did ever any fool buy so dear, and sell so cheap?

[4.] They consider who it is that excludes them from this blessedness, even God himself, who is not only a God of power, and therefore able to hinder them from entering, for if he shuts, none can open; but a God of tender compassions, to some: this God, who made them, will not have mercy on them. Mercy itself is now made wrath. He now thunders in his fury, whose bowels once made a noise, which, though formerly tender, are now harder than flints. What shall open the door, when He who is goodness and love itself shuts it?

[5.] They are therefore hopeless, and utterly despairing ever to be admitted to the presence of God: the anchor of hope is now broken; the bridge of mercy is now drawn; the gulf of separation shall never be passed. The heaviest rock can as easily take wings and fly, and kiss the body of the sun, as can a damned spirit get up into the gracious presence of God. When the door is shut, it is too late to think of entering, Matt. xxv. 10. Knocking, weeping, entreating are altogether fruitless, Luke xiii. 25. How deeply did the departure of Paul pierce the heart of the Christians with sorrow, when he had told them that they should see his face no more! O dreadful word, never! the bitterest word, in comparison of it, is sweet.

Obs. 1. Separation from God is the evil indeed. It separates from the greatest good. Worldly evils hurt the skin, not the soul: it is possible they may be corrective, but the loss of God is destructive. God, in depriving men of his gifts, whips them; but in the final removal of himself, he executes them. Scourging is oft the lot of sons, but separation from God is the portion of devils. God may take away every thing in love, unless it be his love. Separation from God is a distinguishing judgment. How much are men mistaken in their estimations of misery! The most know no other hell but poverty, or some such worldly woe; whereas outward evils are but appearing, and opinionative, and all their deformity is in the eye of the beholder; if they drive us, as oft they do, nearer to God, they are good for us; and nothing is truly bad which separates not from the chiefest good. There is more bitterness in a drop of sin than a sea of suffering.

Obs. 2. How gross is the delusion of sinners! who, for the tasting of the slight and superficial pleasures of a temptation, will lose the soul-satisfying presence of the ever-blessed God! If all the delights of the earth cannot countervail one moment's loss of the light of God's countenance in this life, what proportion is there between a moment's taste of worldly pleasures, and the everlasting loss of the fruition of God in glory! Could Satan make his promise good, in saying, "All these things will I give thee," truly it would be but a slight performance in the esteem of that soul, who knows that the gain of the world would be followed with an eternal loss of God. The eternal weight of the loss of God infinitely more weighs down all momentary delights, than a mountain of lead does a feather. Could sinners part with God upon some valuable consideration, their folly were not so much to be pitied; but nothing can be given them in exchange for God, because God whom they lose is all things.

Obs. 3. The wisest care imaginable is that of enjoying the presence of God in glory. Show your care hereof, (1.) By observing and laying to heart your distance from God by nature, Eph. ii. 1, 2, 12; iv. 18. We all came into the world with our faces toward Satan, and our backs turned upon God; let no worldly enjoyments bribe your consciences into a false and feigned quietness while you so remain. If the poor Jews would not be made to sing in a strange land, let not sinners please themselves in this condition of estrangement from God. How have the saints mourned under the apprehension of God's departure! Their lamentations show what sinners must do, either here or hereafter. (2.) By making him your friend, who only admits us into the presence of God. Jesus Christ is that way whereby that gulf between God and the soul is only passed over. There is no seeing his face without bringing Christ along with us; nor can we more endure the presence of God without an interest in Christ, than can the stubble endure the flames. Every Christless soul is a Godless soul. The blood of Christ is the only cement which can join God and us together. (3.) By labouring to be made fit for his presence: holiness becomes all those who shall enjoy it. Heaven is no place for dogs; and without holiness no man shall see God. Heaven must first be in us, before we can ever get into heaven. God forbids his people to have fellowship with the works of darkness, and much less will he himself delight in such company. Sin hinders from enjoying God here, Isa. lix. 2, much more hereafter. Nor will heaven ever be sweet to that soul which here accounts not sin bitter. The light of glory would dazzle those eyes which only have been used to the darkness of sin: filthy garments may, undiscerned, be worn in the dark, but not in the light. It is the happiness of heaven, that all its inhabitants are of one mind. The company of sinners would spoil the harmonious concert of glorified spirits. (4.) By delighting in the presence of and acquaintance with God, while we are here upon earth. How shy are men of admitting strangers into their houses; and how readily do they open their doors to those with whom they are acquainted! No wonder if Christ bids those depart whom he never knew. Account those duties, conditions, companies to be but empty, in and by which thou enjoyest not something of God. Content not thyself with that prayer, sabbath, ministry, wherein God hath not discovered his humbling, quickening, strengthening presence to thee, in thee. Let no sacrifice please thee without fire. Love the ordinances because God meets thee in them. If God be not at home, think it not enough that his servants, his ministers, have spoken to thee. Let the society of saints be thy solace, and dearly esteem those in whom thou beholdest any resemblance of God. With the wicked, converse rather as a physician to cure them, than as a companion to delight in them. Let not thy heart be taken with any comfort, any further than thou beholdest the heart of the Giver in it, or findest thine own raised to serve and delight in him.

Obs. 4. No distress should dishearten those here, to whom God will not deny his presence hereafter; though God brings them into miseries, yet he will not exclude them with the miserable. If men cast them out of their company, yet Christ will never say to them, "Depart from me." If they want a house to hide their heads in, and a bed to rest their bodies on, yet their Father's house and bosom will supply both. Let men do their worst, they may send saints to him, not from him. How little do those rods smart, in striking with which the Lord takes not away his loving-kindness? What has that poverty more than a name, which is not accompanied and followed with the loss of God himself? In a word, though sometimes the saints sit in darkness, and see no light, yet is light sown for them; they shall not lie under darkness: but after the darkest night of desertion, shall arise to them that glorious Sun of God's presence, which shall never go down again, but make an eternal day.

Thus far for the first part of the punishment of the angels, viz. that which they undergo in the prison. The second follows, viz. that which shall be laid upon them at and after their appearing at the bar; and in that,

I. To what they are reserved, viz. "to judgment."

There are two things may here be inquired after. 1. What we are to understand by the judgment to which these angels are reserved. 2. How the angels which are punished already, are yet said to be reserved to judgment.

1. For the first. Though the word κρίσις, judgment, is frequently in Scripture taken more largely and improperly, for the cause of punishment, John iii. 19, for the government of the world, John v. 22, amendment or reformation, John xii. 31, &c., for the place of judgment; yet in this place it comes more closely to its own proper signification, according to which it imports a judiciary trial of and proceeding about causes. In which respect it is taken in this place, and oft in the New Testament, for the solemn action of the last and general judgment, Matt. x. 15; xi. 22, 24; xii. 36; Mark vi. 11; 2 Pet. iii. 7, where we read of the "day of judgment;" and Eccl. xi. 9, 12, 14; Luke x. 14; Heb. ix. 27; x. 27, where there is mention made of this judgment. Which judgment consists of three parts. (I.) A discussion and manifestation of the faults for which the prisoners were committed. (2.) A pronouncing sentence upon them for every crime discussed and manifested. (3.) A severe executing upon them the sentence so pronounced. *Veritas in inquisitione, nuditas in publicatione, serenitas in executione.*

(1.) In this judgment faults and causes shall be discussed and manifested; and judgment is sometimes in Scripture put for this discussion and discerning of causes, Acts xxiii. 3; xvi. 15; 2 Cor. v. 14. "Some men's sins are open beforehand, going before to judgment," &c., 1 Tim. v. 24, &c. And this knowledge of the cause is intended, Rev. xx. 12; where we have mention of those who "stand before God," of the opening of the books, and the judging "out of those things which were written in the books." For though at the last judgment God will make use of no books, properly so called, yet all the works of the judged shall be as manifestly known, as if God kept registers, rolls, and records of them in heaven; and at his coming he "will bring to light the hidden things of darkness, and will make manifest the counsels of the hearts," that the righteousness of his proceedings may appear to all, Ezra iv. 15, 19; vi. 2; Esth. vi. 1; Deut. xxxii. 34; Psal. lvi. 8; Hos. vii. 2; 1 Cor. iv. 5. These books of discovery are two; that of God's omniscience, and that of the creature's conscience. [1.] According to the former, every creature is manifest in his sight, and all things are opened unto his eyes, Heb. iv. 13; he has a "book of remembrance," Mal. iii. 16; he needs not that any should testify of man, for he knoweth what is in man, John ii. 25. As God hates sin wherever he knows it, so he knows it wherever it is, Jer. xxiii. 24. Men may hide their sins from men, from God they cannot, Mark iv. 22; Rom. ii. 5, 16. Men may, like foolish children, when they shut their eyes and see none, think that none sees them; but the light and the darkness are both alike to God; nor can any, by seeking deep to hide their counsels from the Most High, help himself, Isa. xxix. 15. Never has one sin since the creation of the world slipped from the memory of God's knowledge, though he has been pleased to put away the sins of some out of the memory of his vengeance; nor does he forget any sin out of necessity, but merely out of mercy. [2.] According to the latter, the book of conscience, the Lord will, in the general judgment, bring to every man's remembrance what he has done; he will set the sins of the wicked in order before them, Psal. l.; their consciences shall then be dilated and irradiated by the power of God. Here in this life conscience is bribed, and gives in an imperfect, but then it shall bring a full and impartial evidence against sinners, who shall be speechless, and have their mouths stopped: hence it is said, Jude 15, that God shall ἐξελέγχειν, "convince all the ungodly." Their faults shall be so demonstrated to them, that they shall have nothing to object, but shall be compelled to acknowledge all, both in point of fact and desert, *Deus nec fallitur, nec flectitur.* *Idem judex, reus, testis, tortor, flagellum.*

Isa. v. 3. That which before was almost imperceptible, shall, being held to the fire of vengeance, and the light of conscience, be made legible.

(2.) In this judgment to which these angels shall be brought, there shall be a decisive, definitive sentence; and frequently and most properly in Scripture is judgment taken for a decisive passing of sentence, Matt. vii. 1; John xviii. 31; Acts xxiv. 6; xvii. 31; Matt. xix. 28; 1 Cor. vi. 3; Acts iv. 19. To the former sentence, viz. that of their own consciences, shall be added that of the Judge, whereby they shall be adjudged to the punishment of loss and pain for ever. A sentence which shall be openly promulgated. Heretofore it was written down in the book, now it shall be pronounced before all the world. A sentence which shall be published soon after that of benediction has been uttered to the godly, that so the damned may grieve the more, to consider what they have lost; and the saved rejoice, to observe what they have escaped. A sentence, every syllable of which is more dreadful than ten thousand thunder-claps, roaring in their ears to all eternity. Wonder one may, that so much woe can be couched in so few words. In being sentenced to depart from God, what pleasure are they not adjudged to lose! In being sentenced to the flames, what pain are they not adjudged to feel!

(3.) In the judgment to which these angels shall be brought, there shall be an execution of the sentence denounced; and frequently in Scripture is judgment taken for punishment to which men are adjudged, Matt. v. 22; Mark iii. 29; John v. 24, 29; Acts viii. 33; 2 Thess. i. 5. The sentence shall not be an empty sound, as a report without a bullet, a noise without a sting; but it shall be executed without any exception, delay, reply, appeal. The sentence of malediction shall be a fiery stream proceeding from the throne of the Judge, and sweeping the condemned into hell. The wicked "shall be punished with everlasting destruction from the presence of the Lord, and the glory of his power," 2 Thess. i. 9; which place Beza expounds of their expulsion from the presence of the Lord by that terrible voice, "Go, ye cursed." Others thus interpret it, The glorious power and majesty of Christ's presence shall suffice to destroy the wicked. If the devils were unable to endure the presence of Christ upon earth, when emptied of glory, upon considering that hereafter Christ should be their Judge; crying out, and asking whether he was come to torment them before their time; how shall they abide his presence, when filled with dreadful majesty!

Jam. ii. 13, κρίσις put for κατάκρισις.

Expulsi a facie, hac terribili ipsius voce. Bez.

2. How the angels who are already punished, and therefore judged, can be reserved to judgment. We must not conceive (with some) that, because they are said to be "reserved to judgment," therefore for the present they are not punished; for if the good angels are, before the general judgment, in a state of happiness, διαπάντος, always beholding the face of God, then why should not the bad be in a state of misery? Besides, if the souls of wicked men are now tormented in hell, which nevertheless may be said to be " reserved to judgment," why may it not be asserted, that the angels who seduced men have been ever since their fall tormented, considering that the fall was that to the angels which death is to ungodly men? And further, if the fallen angels be in hell, a place of punishment, with the damned souls, then it is as certain they partake of the same punishment with them; as it is absurd to imagine that the holy angels should be in heaven with the souls of the blessed, and not be with them partakers of the fruition of God's presence.

Justin. in Apol. 1. Dæmones igni sempiterno nondum traditi sunt, sed in die judicii tradendi: Hanc opinionem amplectitur Irenæus, l. 5. cont. Hær. Lactant. lib. 3. Divin. Instit. cap. 28.

There is therefore a threefold judgment which the fallen angels incur: 1. That wherewith they were punished immediately upon their fall, when by God they were thrown into misery. Of this speaks Peter, " God spared not the angels which sinned, but cast them down into hell," &c., 2 Pet. ii. 4. 2. That whereby they are cast out of their dominion, and their power over us destroyed by the death of Christ, John xii. 31. 3. Their full and final judgment, to which they are here by Jude said to be reserved; in respect whereof, though they are in part punished already, yet by it there shall be a dreadful addition and accession to their present torments; in regard of ignominy, and of restraint.

(1.) Ignominy: for they being most proud creatures, cannot but deem it an unspeakable shame, [1.] To have all their malice and mischiefs that ever they committed since their fall manifested to all the world; whereby all who have heretofore honoured them as gods shall know their vileness, and look upon them as abominable deceivers, and never be brought, as formerly, to worship them. [2.] To have it publicly seen, that poor man, whose nature is so much inferior to theirs, has done that which they were not able to do, in embracing holiness, and honouring his Creator, and obtaining those mansions of glory which they have lost. [3.] To have it known to all the world how often they would have done evil when they could not, and how frequently even women and children have overcome their fierce and fiery temptations. [4.] To have judgment passed upon them, not only by Christ himself, but even by those formerly poor saints whom they so vilified and persecuted; even these shall judge the angels, 1 Cor. vi. 3. And that not only, 1. By having their practices compared to those of the damned, as the Ninevites and the queen of the south are said to rise up in judgment, Matt. xii. 41, 42; Luke xi. 31, 32. Nor, 2. Only by their consenting to and approving of the sentence which Christ shall pass upon the wicked. But also, 3. In regard of that *dignitas assessoria*, that dignity whereby they shall be advanced to an honourable assessorship with the Lord Christ, in sitting (as it were) with him upon the bench, or about the throne of judicature. As likewise, 4. They in that judgment being to appear with Christ manifest victors over all their enemies, by trampling upon all the pride, malice, and weakness of devils before the whole world; and holily insulting over them as vile, vanquished, and contemptible enemies: a greater punishment, undoubtedly, to those proudest of creatures, than was that to Bajazet, whose back famous Tamerlane used for a horseblock to raise him up to his steed, when he caused him to be carried up and down as a spectacle of infamy in all his triumphant journeys.

Dolet diabolus, quod ipsum et angelos ejus, Christi servus ille peccator judicaturus est. Tert. lib. de pœn. c. 7.

(2.) By the last judgment there shall be an accession of punishment to these angels in respect of their restraint, because then they shall be unable to seduce the wicked or to hurt the elect any more. Their chain, now more loose, shall then be so strait, that they shall never come near nor among the saints of God: a vehement vexation to those malicious spirits, whose element is mischief, and their torment restraint from doing hurt. They now deem it some lessening of their torment to be suffered to tempt men to sin: they think themselves hereby somewhat revenged on God; as he that defaces the picture of his enemy, when he cannot come at his person, eases his spleen a little; or as the dog somewhat breaks his rage by gnawing the stone, when he cannot reach the thrower. They now walk abroad, as it were, with their keeper; but then they shall be closely confined, yea, dungeoned: now they contain their hell, then their hell shall contain them. In short, as the punishment of wicked men shall be at the full, when their souls and bodies are reunited, and both cast into hell; so the torment of these angels shall be completed, when at the last day they shall be so fettered in their infernal prison, as that there will be no possibility of stirring forth. They are now entered into divers degrees of punishment, but the full wrath of God is not poured out upon them till the day of judgment.

Obs. 1. No secrecy can shelter sin from God's observation. He who will make sins known to conscience and all spectators, must needs know them himself. Sins are undoubtedly written in, if they be read out of the book. God need not rack, no, nor ask the offender, to know whether he has sinned or no; he searcheth the heart, he trieth the reins, Jer. xvii. 10; "his eyes behold, his eyelids try, the children of men," Psal. xi. 4. He compasseth (he winnoweth) our paths, and is acquainted with all our ways. Whither shall we fly from his presence? Psal. cxxxix. He understands our thoughts afar off; knows them long before they come into us, and long after they are gone away from us. All the secrets of our hearts are dissected, anatomized, and barefaced in his eyes. He who knew what we would do before we did it, must needs know what we have done afterwards. There is nothing existing in the world but was before in God's knowledge; as the house is first in the head before erected by the hand of the artificer. He made us, and therefore knows every nook, and corner, and turning in us; and we are sustained and moved by him in our most retired motions. How plainly discerned by him is the closest hypocrite, and every devil, though in a Samuel's mantle! We can only hear, but God sees hollowness. We do but observe the surface, but God's eye pierces into the entrails of every action: he sees not as man sees; man looketh on the outward appearance, but God looketh on the heart. How exact should we be even in secret walkings, we being constantly in the view of so accurate an Observer! We should set the Lord always before us. The eye of God should ever be in our eyes: the presence of God is the counterpoison of sin. Whenever thou art sinning, remember that all thou dost is booked in God's omniscience. Latimer being examined by his popish adversaries, heard a pen walking behind the hangings, to take all his words; this made him wary how he expressed himself: but more cause have we to fear sin, since God writes down every offence, and will one day so read over his book to conscience, that it shall be compelled to copy it out with infinite horror. God did but read one page, one line of this book, one sin, to the conscience of Judas, and the terror thereof made him his own executioner.

Obs. 2. How foolish are sinners, who are so despairing at, and yet so fearless before, the pronouncing of the last sentence! Most irrational is that resolution, "Because sentence against an evil work is not executed speedily, therefore the heart of the sons of men is fully set to do evil," Eccl. viii. 11. How wise were it to argue contrarily, Because the sentence is deferred, therefore let us labour to have it prevented; and to say with the apostle, "What manner of persons ought we to be!" 2 Pet. iii. 11. The deferring of judgment is no sign of its prevention; the speedy repentance of sinners would be a much more comfortable prediction. Wrath, when it is to come, may be fled from; when once it is come, it is unavoidable. Christians! be as wise for your souls as the Egyptians were for their cattle; who, fearing the threatening of hail, took them into houses: faith in threatenings of judgment, may prevent the feeling of judgments threatened. For your souls' sake, be warned to get your pardon in the blood, if ever you would avoid the sentence of the mouth of Christ. If the Judge give you not a pardon here, he will give you a sentence hereafter. It is only the blood of Christ which can blot the book of judgment. Judge yourselves, and pass an irrevocable sentence upon your sins, if you would not be sentenced for your sins. Repent at the hearing of ministers in this your day; for if you put off that work till God speaks in his day, repentance itself will be unprofitable. If you harden your hearts here in sin, the heart of Christ will be hardened hereafter in his sentencing, and your suffering. The great work of poor ministers is the prevention of the dreadful sound of the last sentence: knowing the terror of the Lord, they warn you. All the hatred we meet with in the world, is for our loving plainness herein; but we will not cease to warn you with tears, as well as with sweat: we can better bear your hatred here, than either you or we bear God's hereafter; and we had rather your lusts should curse us here, than your souls to all eternity. If our voice cannot make you bend, God's will make you break: if you will not hearken, is it not because the Lord will slay you?

Obs. 3. Great is the sinfulness of rash judgment. It is a sin that robs Christ of his honour, whereby a man advances himself into Christ's tribunal, and which takes the work of judgment out of Christ's hand; and therefore the apostle, Rom. xiv. 10; 1 Cor. iv. 5, strongly argues against it from the last judgment. Christians commit this sin, both by a curious inquisition into the ways of others, for this end, that they may find out matter of defamation; and principally, by passing of sentence, or giving of censure, against the persons and practices of others without necessity, and not according to the law of charity, which binds us to judge the best of others, so far as may stand with a good conscience and the word of God. Judgment may either be of persons, or their practices: in persons, their future or their present state is to be considered. All judgment of men's future state is to be forborne; God may call the worst as well as thee. Three things, saith Augustine, are exempted from man's judgment; the Scriptures, the counsel of God, the condemnation of any man's person. For men's present state; if we see men live in whoredom, drunkenness, swearing, we may judge them wicked while continuing in this state, and that they shall be damned if they repent not. We may judge the tree by the fruit, and this is not rash judgment, because it is not ours, but the judgment of the word of God. Practices are either good, bad, indifferent, or doubtful. Good actions are to be commended. If actions be evil, judge the facts, not the persons; yet study withal to excuse the intention, if thou canst not the fact. Indifferent or doubtful actions are to be free from censure; Christian liberty exempts our neighbour from censure for the former, charity allows us not to be censurers of the latter. If it be doubtful whether a thing were spoken or done, or no; or being certain to be done, whether well or ill; in charity judge the best. If a man lay with a betrothed damsel in the fields, the man was only to die, because it was in charity supposed that the damsel cried; the best being supposed in a thing doubtful, Deut. xxii. 25, 27. In matter of opinion, if it be uncertain whether an error or no, suspend thy judgment till thou know more certainly; thy brother may see as much and more than thyself into that which is doubtful. Our ignorance as men, though never so knowing, should be a strong bar from rash judgment. Besides, who are we that judge another man's servant? this is to reproach God himself for receiving him. We are fellow servants with our brethren, not fellow judges with God; we must love, not judge one another; our Master's house is to be ordered by our Master's will. He who by rash judgment destroys the good name of another, is, by some, termed the worst of thieves, in stealing away that which is better than riches, and can never be restored; and the worst of murderers, in killing three at once, his own soul in thus sinning, his neighbour whose name he ruins, and the hearer who receives his slanders. And yet, take away this sinful censuring from many professors, there will nothing remain to show them religious; whereas a just man is a severe judge only to himself.

Obs. 4. How happy are they who shall be able to stand in the judgment! I know it is doubted by some, whether at the last judgment the sins of the saints shall come into the judgment of discussion and discovery; Scripture seems to many most to favour the affirmative, Rev. xx. 12; Matt. x. 26; but that they shall escape the judgment of condemnation, it is not doubted. That sun which discovers the sins of the wicked, shall scatter those of the godly. "There is no condemnation to them that are in Christ Jesus; who shall lay any thing to their charge?" Rom. viii. 1, 33. The greater their sins are, the greater will their deliverance appear. The more punishment they deserved, the more they escape. The sins of the saints will prove, as the matter of their songs, so the trophies of victorious mercy. The wicked shall have judgment without mercy, and the godly shall have mercy in a day of judgment, 1 Cor. xi. 32. How contentedly may they here undergo that chastisement whereby they escape judgment! It is better to hear the reproofs of a father, than the sentence of a judge; and the correction of a son is much lighter than the condemnation of a malefactor. It matters not what shall ever be said or done against them, to whom Christ shall never say, "Depart from me." "Do with me what thou wilt," said Luther, "since thou hast pardoned my sins."
<small>Vid. Aquin. q. 87. suppl. Est. in l. 4. Sent dist. 47.</small>

Obs. 5. The greatest enemies of God will be but contemptible creatures at the last judgment. What underlings then shall those appear and be, who now are principalities and powers! Satan, who has had so many followers, adorers, who now is the prince of the air, yea, the god of this world, shall then openly appear to be a trembling malefactor at the bar of Christ. As once Joshua's soldiers set their feet upon the necks of the Canaanitish kings, so the poorest saint shall at the last judgment trample upon these fallen angels. Death speaks the impotency of men, but judgment even that of angels. Legions of angels shall no more oppose Christ, than can a worm all the angels of heaven. Methinks even all the crowned, sceptred, adorned, adored monarchs of the world, if enemies to Christ, should tremble at the approach of judgment. The greatest safety and honour, even of a king, will then be to be a subject to Christ, and what the emperor Justinian was wont to call himself, the meanest servant of Christ. Robes will then fall off. The dimmer light of human glory will be obscured when the Sun of righteousness shall appear. Let us neither fear nor admire the greatness of any but of Christ, much less that which is set against Christ. How great is the folly of Satan's subjects! they serve a master who is so far from defending them, that he cannot defend himself, from judgment.
<small>Ultimus Dei servus.</small>

Obs. 6. The reason why Satan rages is, he knows that his time is but short; and after this last judgment his furious and spiteful temptations shall be ended: and he labours to supply the shortness of his time with the sharpness of his assaults; like the besiegers, who having often stormed a town or a castle, make their last onset the most resolute and terrible. A traveller who desires to go far, will go fast if the sun is setting. The shortness of Satan's season occasions his swiftness in wickedness; besides, he is in a state of desperation, he knows there is no possibility of his recovery; and as faith is the furtherer of holiness, so is despair of all impiety. It was the logic of despair which argued thus, "Let us eat and drink, for to-morrow we shall die." I wonder not that these last are the worst and the most perilous times. Satan now strives to add to his number, to seduce and pervert souls, because after his judgment he shall never be suffered to do so any more. At all times holy vigilancy over our hearts and ways is needful; but in these times, wherein Satan's judgment draws so near, it should be our care more than ever to keep our hearts with all diligence, to beware of seduction and atheism, and of "being led away with the error of the wicked, lest we fall from our own stedfastness." If Satan double his rage, let us double our guard. Doctor Taylor reports of a noble lord, who was wont to say, "That he never would go without a sword so long as there was a papist about the court." Never let us lay off our spiritual weapons, till Satan be taken from us by judgment, or we out of his reach by death. Let us, even taught thus much by our adversary, make the shortness of our time a motive to lay out ourselves the more for God: short seasons require speedy services. The nearer we come to judgment, the fitter let us labour to be for it. Let the sweetest part of our lives be at the bottom, and, as Samson's, let our last prove our greatest goodness. To conclude this, let those poor souls who are daily buffeted by Satan, consider that his judgment is approaching; that all conflicts with him shall then be at an end; and that the fury of his assaults prove not their success, but the shortness of continuance.

Thus far of the first particular considerable in the punishment of these angels at the bar, viz. that to which they are reserved, "to judgment."

II. The time when they shall be brought to judgment, viz. at the "great day."

Two things for the explication of this season.
1. How the word "day" is here to be understood.
2. In what respect it is called a "great day."

1. For the first. There are three opinions. (1.) Some take the day here spoken of precisely and properly, as if the day of the last judgment should not exceed that space and proportion of time. (2.) Some conceive that by the "day" is meant a thousand years, because some are said to sit on thrones, and have judgment given unto them, (that is, power of judging,) and to live and reign with Christ a thousand years, Rev. xx. 4. But I conceive that this judgment and reign of a thousand years cannot be understood of the last judgment, because death, the last enemy, shall, in the resurrection, be destroyed: now after the end of the thousand years mentioned by St. John, Satan shall be loosed out of prison, and the nations deceived by him shall compass the camp of the saints about, and the beloved city, and fire shall come down from God out of heaven and devour them. (3.) Others seem more safely to apprehend that the day here mentioned is to be taken improperly, for time indefinitely, it being in Scripture very ordinary to put a day for time: "In an acceptable time have I heard thee, in a day of salvation have I succoured thee," Isa. xlix. 8. "If thou hadst known in
<small>Per quot dies hoc judicium extendatur, incertum est: scripturarum more diem poni solere pro tempore nemo nescit. Aug. l. 20. de Civ. Dei, cap. 1.</small>

this thy day," Luke xix. 42. "Your father Abraham rejoiced to see my day," John viii. 56, &c. There must be a day wherein that great work of judgment shall begin, but its duration is to be measured by the nature of the thing, and the counsel of God. With Augustine, I determine nothing peremptorily concerning the continuance of the last judgment-day.

2. For the second, the greatness of this day. The titles given it in the Scripture speak it great; it being called "that day," Matt. vii. 22; Luke xxi. 34; 2 Tim. i. 12, 18; iv. 8; the "last day," John vi. 39, 40, 44, 46, 54; "the day of judgment, and perdition of ungodly men," 2 Pet. iii. 7; the day of God the Lord; "the day when God shall judge the secrets of men," Rom. ii. 16; a day wherein "he will judge the world in righteousness," Acts xvii. 31; "the day of wrath, and revelation of the righteous judgment of God," Rom. ii. 5; the day of the Lamb's wrath, Rev. vi. 17; "the day of Jesus Christ," Phil. i. 6, 10, &c. More particularly, this day of judgment is called "great" in respect of the Judge, the judged, and the properties of the judgment.

(1.) The Judge, who is Jesus Christ. And herein two particulars are considerable.

[1.] That Christ shall be Judge.

[2.] Wherein his being Judge shall make the day "great."

The first is evident, 1. From the frequent and express mentioning him as Judge in Scripture, Acts x. 42; Phil. iii. 20; iv. 5; 1 Tim. vi. 14, 15, which assures us that "God shall judge the secrets of men by Jesus Christ," Rom. ii. 16; that "Jesus Christ shall judge the quick and the dead," 2 Tim. iv. 1; that "the Lord Jesus shall be revealed from heaven," 2 Thess. i. 7; that "the Son of man shall come in the glory of his Father," Matt. xvi. 27; that "they shall see the Son of man coming in the clouds of heaven, with power and great glory," Matt. xxiv. 30; that "the Son of man shall come in his glory," Matt. xxv. 31; that hereafter we "shall see the Son of man coming in the clouds of heaven," Matt. xxvi. 64; that the same Jesus who is taken into heaven, shall so come in like manner as he was seen to go into heaven, Acts i. 11; that "he cometh with clouds, and every eye shall see him," Rev. i. 7. In which respect the day of judgment is called, "The day of the Lord Jesus Christ," 1 Cor. i. 8: so chap. v. 5; 2 Cor. i. 14; Phil. i. 6, 10; ii. 16. And the seat of judgment is called, "The judgment-seat of Christ," Rom. xiv. 10; 2 Cor. v. 10. And some understand that place, Heb. iv.12, "The word of God is" κριτικός, "a discerner of the thoughts," concerning the hypostatical Word. Nor is the Old Testament destitute of testimonies of this kind, though somewhat more obscurely expressed. Abraham speaks to the Son of God, when he said, "Shall not the Judge of all the earth do right?" Gen. xviii. 25. And the Father spake to the Son, when he said, "Thou shalt break them with a rod of iron; thou shalt dash them in pieces like a potter's vessel," Psal. ii. 9. And that of Isaiah xlv. 23, "By myself have I sworn, Unto me every knee shall bow," which the apostle, Rom. xiv. 11, applies to Christ, and thence proves that we shall all stand before his judgment-seat. 2. By God's appointment of him, and giving him authority to judge: "He is ordained of God to be the Judge of quick and dead," Acts x. 42. "He will judge the world by that man whom he hath ordained," &c., Acts xvii. 31. "The Father judgeth no man, but hath committed all judgment to the Son; he hath given him authority to execute judgment," John v. 22, 27. And all power is given him in heaven and in earth. 3. By his former state of humiliation. As he emptied and humbled him-

Humilitas carnis nostræ throno judicatoris honorata est. Cypr.

self according to his human nature, so in that he is to be exalted. "He humbled himself, and became obedient to death," &c., "wherefore God hath highly exalted him," Phil. ii. 8, 9. And as Christ in his human nature was unjustly judged, so in that nature shall he justly judge. "Christ was once offered to bear the sins of many, and he shall appear the second time without sin," Heb. ix. 28. 4. By reason of the necessity of the visibility of the Judge and judicial proceedings at the last day. He executes judgment "because he is the Son of man," John v. 27, and every eye shall see him. The Judge is to be beheld and heard by the judged. "God will judge the world by that man," &c. In respect of the judicial process, a man must be our Judge; for God is invisible, and the Judge shall so appear, as to be seen both of those whom he shall crown, and of those whom he shall condemn. Nor can it be but that God will be the more justified, and men without all excuse, having one who is bone of their bone, and flesh of their flesh, to be Judge between God and them. Notwithstanding all which immediate, audible, visible administration of the last judgment by the Second Person, this judgment belongs to the other Persons in Trinity, κατ' αὐτοκρατορίαν κριτικήν, in respect of authority, dominion, and judiciary power, though to the Son only κατ' οἰκονομίαν, in respect of dispensation and office, and external exercise.

Sedebit judex qui stetit sub judice, damnabit veros reos, qui factus est falsus reus. Aug. Homil. 150.

Talis apparebit judex, qualis pos sit videri ab iis quos coronaturus, et ab iis quos damnaturus est. Prosp.

[2.] For the second, viz. Wherein the Judge makes the day of judgment "great."

He makes it a great day, 1. As he is considered in himself. 2. As he is attended and accompanied by others.

1. As we consider him in himself; and that either, as God, or man.

(1.) As God. He who shall be the Judge is the mighty God; it is Jehovah, to whom "every knee shall bow," Isa. xlv. 23. Hence the apostle calls the appearance of this Judge, who is God, glorious, in those words, Tit. ii. 13, "The glorious appearing of the great God." If the great God be Judge, the day of judgment must needs be a great day. How great is the day of an earthly judge's appearance, a man, a worm, dust and ashes! one who, though he can give, yet cannot avoid the sentence of death; and one who has scarce a faint reflection of that majesty with which this King of glory is adorned: think then, and yet thoughts can never reach it, what it is for God, before whom the whole world, though full of judges, is as nothing, and less than nothing, and vanity, to come to judge the world. God is a Judge omnipotent, and therefore one whose voice, as the living who are distanced so many thousands of miles shall hear and obey, so even the dead shall hear, being quickened, and shall at his beck come and stand before his judgment-seat. He shall come with great power; and the wicked "shall be punished with everlasting destruction from the glory of his power," 2 Thess. i. 9. Nor shall he use the ministry of angels for necessity, but majesty. God is an omniscient Judge, infinitely, only wise; his eyes are clearer than ten thousand suns; one who will, in the day wherein the brightness of his omniscience shall shine in its full lustre, bring every hidden work to light, and tell to all, as the woman of Samaria said, all that ever they did; one who does not, as earthly judges, only know what to ask, but what every one will answer; who wants no witnesses; nor needs he that any should testify of man, for he knows what is in man. God is a true and a just Judge. The apostle, 2 Tim. iv. 8, calls him "the Lord, the righteous judge;" he will render to every one according to his works. The apostle proves the righteousness of God from his judging the world, Rom. iii. 6; and Abraham's question asserts it strongly, "Shall not the Judge of all the earth do right?" Other judges may do righteously, but God cannot do otherwise. The wills of other judges must be regulated by righteousness; but so righteous is God, that righteousness itself is regulated by his will, which is the root and rule of all righteousness.

(2.) This Judge shall make the day great as he is man. Greatly amazing and dismaying must his appearance as Judge in man's nature needs be to sinners who have denied him, persecuted, crucified, and put him to an open shame; all whose designs have been to crush and keep him under. With what horror shall the Jews then see their delusion, who would not heretofore believe him to be the Messiah! Needs must they and others who would not have this man to reign over them, to whom he was a stumblingstone when low and small, contemptible in his former discoveries upon earth, now find and feel him a rock to fall upon them from heaven, and crush them to powder. Greatly comforting and refreshing must the appearance of this man be to believers, who shall not only behold him to be the great Judge of the whole world, who has taken upon him their nature; but who has also given to them his Spirit, whereby, through faith, they are mystically united to him as their Head and Husband; upon whom they have fixed all their hopes and expectations of happiness; for and with whom they have so long suffered from the world; whom they look upon as their treasure, their portion, and for whose coming they have so longed, and sighed, and groaned. In a word, how greatly glorious shall his appearance in our nature be both to good and bad, when in it he shall be decked and adorned with majesty, and clothed with unspeakable glory above all the angels, as he will "come in the glory of his Father," Matt. xvi. 27, "with power and great glory!" Matt. xxiv. 30. The glory of a thousand suns made into one will be but as sackcloth to that wherein Christ shall appear in man's nature that great day. The glory of the sun scatters the clouds, but from the glory of Christ's face the very earth and heaven shall fly away, Rev. xx. 11. The beams of his glory shall dazzle the eyes of sinners, and delight the eyes of saints. The wicked "shall be punished with everlasting destruction from his presence, and the glory of his power," 2 Thess. i. 9; and "when his glory shall be revealed," the saints shall be glad with exceeding joy, 1 Pet. iv. 13.

2. The Judge shall make this day of judgment great, considering him, not only in himself, but as he is attended by others; and so he will make the day great, if we consider by *whom*, and by *how many*, he shall thus be attended.

(1.) By whom. They shall be creatures of great glory and excellence. The glorious angels shall be Christ's attendants at the great day; in which respect Christ is said to "come in the glory of the holy angels," Luke ix. 26; and in Matt. xxv. 31, it is said that "the Son of man shall come, and the holy angels with him;" and Luke xii. 9, that Christ will deny some before the angels of God; and 2 Thess. i. 7, that "the Lord Jesus shall be revealed from heaven with his mighty angels." These angels that excel in strength are his heavenly hosts, his ministers, to do the pleasure of Christ their great Lord and Commander. If at the time of his nativity, Luke ii. 13, temptation, passion, resurrection, ascension, they readily gave Christ their attendance; how much more shall they do it at the great day, when all the glory of Christ shall be revealed! If at the promulgation of the law upon Mount Sinai angels waited upon him, Gal. iii. 19; Deut. xxxiii. 2, how readily will they serve him when he shall come to judgment for the execution of that law! What glory shall be in that day, when the very servants of the Judge, who shall wait upon him, run at every turn, and upon every errand; who shall blow the trumpet, summon the world to appear, bring the prisoners before the bar, and take them away again; when even these waiters, I say, shall be angels of power, 2 Thess. i. 7; the heavenly host, every one being ἄγγελοι δυνάμεως. stronger than an earthly army; holy angels; creatures of unspeakable agility and swiftness; glorious angels, who as much exceed in glory the greatest emperor in the world, as the sun in the firmament does a clod of earth, Matt. xxiv. 31; Psal. ciii. 20. Nor can it be but the day must be very illustrious, if we consider that the saints shall appear also with Christ in glory, Col. iii. 4, that they shall "meet the Lord in the air," 1 Thess. iv. 17, and be witnesses for, nay, assessors with Christ in judgment, and partakers of that victory which in the last day he shall have over all his enemies; that all the enemies of Christ and his church shall stand before the saints to be justly judged, whom they in this world have judged unjustly; and in a word, that every one of these saints shall in their spiritual bodies shine as the sun, Matt. xiii. 43, when it appears in its perfect lustre.

But, (2.) Christ as attended will make the day great, if we consider by how many he shall be attended. At that great day there shall be a general assembly, a great number, even all his servants waiting upon him, both saints and angels; hence, 1 Thess. i. 13, is mentioned the "coming of the Lord Jesus with all his saints;" and Eph iv. 13, the meeting of all. In this glorious concourse there shall not be one wanting. If Christ will raise up every saint from the grave, then doubtless shall every saint appear in glory at the last day, John vi. 39. He will not lose his cost laid out upon them. But if he bestows new liveries upon his servants, they shall all, when adorned with them, wait upon him. Nor shall there be one angel but shall glorify him in that day. If all the angels of God are commanded to praise and worship him, Psal. cxlviii. 2; Heb. i. 6, then undoubtedly will they perform this duty at that day wherein the glory of Christ shall be so eminently manifested: all the holy angels shall come with the Son of man, Matt. xxv. 31. And if all the angels and saints must wait on Christ, the number must needs be vast, and the multitude exceeding great: of angels there must be an "innumerable company," Heb. xii. 22, myriads, ten thousands of saints, Dan. vii. 10, or holy ones, Jude 14 (a definite number being put for an indefinite). And "about the throne" are said to be "ten thousand times ten thousand, and thousands of thousands," Rev. v. 11, ten thousands of saints. An innumerable company of angels attended the solemn delivery of the law at Mount Sinai, Deut. xxxiii. 2, in allusion to which the triumphant ascension of Christ into heaven is described, Psal. lxviii., to be with "twenty thousand chariots, even thousands of angels;" and of those who "stood before the throne, clothed with white robes, and having palms in their hands, there was a great multitude, which no man could number," Rev. vii. 9. Now if the glory of one angel was so great, that those who of old time beheld it expected death thereby, Judg. vi. 22; xiii. 22; and if for fear of an angel, whose countenance was like lightning, the keepers "did shake, and became as dead men," Matt. xxviii. 4; how great shall be the glory of all the millions of angels and saints at the great day, when

God shall let out his glory unto them, and fill them as full of it as they can hold, that he may be admired in them! Who can imagine the greatness of that day, wherein the Judge shall be attended with so many millions of servants, every one of whom shall have a livery more bright and glorious than the sun? The splendour of this appearance at the great day will ten thousand times more surpass that of the attendance of the greatest judges and kings in the world, than theirs excels the sport and ridiculous acting of their more serious solemnities by children in their play.

2. This day of judgment shall be great, in respect, as of the Judge, so likewise of the judged; and the judged shall make the day great, as they fall under a fourfold consideration, or in four respects:

1. In respect of the greatness of their company and number.
2. The greatness of their ranks and degrees.
3. The greatness of their faults and offences.
4. The greatness of their rewards and recompences.

(1.) In respect of the greatness of their numbers. When many persons are tried and judged, many prisoners cast and condemned, we ordinarily say that the assizes or sessions are great, though the number of the persons judged are not so great by a hundred parts as the number of those who stand by to hear the trial. How great then shall the day of judgment be, wherein all shall be tried and judged! It was of old prophesied by Enoch, that the Lord would execute judgment upon all. Before the throne of the Son of man all nations shall be gathered, Matt. xxv. 32. And in 2 Thess. ii. 1, the day of judgment is called the time of our gathering together unto Christ. "We must all appear before the judgment-seat of Christ, that every one may receive the things done in the body," *πάντες παραστησόμεθα.* Rom. xiv. 10; 2 Cor. v. 10; Acts xvii. 31. "He cometh with clouds, and every eye shall see him," Rev. i. 7. He is called the Judge of the whole earth, Gen. xviii. 25. All men are divided into two sorts or ranks, living and dead, 2 Tim. iv. 1; 1 Pet. iv. 5; Rev. xx. 12; and both these shall Christ judge, Acts xvii. 31; who hath power over all flesh, John xvii. 2; who "shall reward every one according to his works," Matt. xvi. 27; and to whom God hath sworn "every knee shall bow," Isa. xlv. 23; Rom. xiv. 11. So that if there should but one be exempted from appearing before Christ at the last day, the oath of God would be broken, which is impossible. If God number all the hairs of our head, Matt. x. 30, how much more all the persons whose those hairs are! If he number all our steps, how much more all those who take those steps! Psal. lvi. 10. And whereas it is said that believers shall not come into judgment, and that the wicked shall not stand in the judgment, Psal. i. 5: the former is to be understood of the judgment of condemnation, as it is translated, or rather expounded, saith one, in John v. 24; the latter of prevailing in judgment, by receiving a judgment of absolution. *Causa cadent.* Men may hide themselves, and fly from men's courts and tribunals, but the judgment-seat of Christ cannot be avoided. It will be in vain to call for the rocks and mountains to fall upon them and hide them, for the mountains shall melt like wax at the presence of the Lord. There is no flying from this Judge but by flying to him; and death itself, which prevents judgment among men, shall give up its dead to this great judgment.

(2.) The day shall be great in respect of the judged, as they are considered in the greatness of their ranks and degrees. Among men, not the judging of every mean, contemptible person, but of noblemen, princes of the blood, or great monarchs, makes the day of their judgment great. How solemn in this world is the judiciary trial of a king! But how glorious and magnificent shall be the arraignment of great and small persons, of all ranks and degrees, at that great day! Rev. xx. 12; angels and principalities as well as men, good as well as bad. "Watch and pray always, that ye may be accounted worthy to stand before the Son of man," Luke xxi. 36. "He that judgeth me is the Lord," 1 Cor. iv. 4; and, "Every one of us must give an account of himself to God," Rom. xiv. 12; they who have been high and mighty, emperors, as well as the poorest outcasts. The tallest cedar, the stoutest oak, must bend, yea, break, at that great day. Christ, he shall "strike through kings in the day of his wrath," Psal. cx. 5. The grave and the judgment-seat put no difference between monarchs and vassals. The grave-dust of a queen smells no sweeter than that of a beggar: none can distinguish between the ashes of an oak and those of a humble shrub. There will be no other crowns worn at that day than the crowns of righteousness; no other robes than those washed in the blood of Christ; and these will better fit the head and back of a Lazarus than a rich glutton. True greatness, goodness I mean, will be the only greatness at that truly great day. The glorious sunshine of this day will extinguish the candle of worldly glory. O great day! wherein majesty shall lie and lick the dust of the feet of Christ; the stiffest knee bend before his majesty, and the strongest back of sinners break under his wrath; when the great swordmen and emperors, the Alexanders, the Cæsars, who once made the earth to tremble, shall now tamely tremble before him!

(3.) The day of judgment shall be great in respect of the judged, if we consider them as great offenders. When men are tried before human judicatories for common crimes, as for pilfering or stealing some small or inconsiderable sum, the day of their trial is soon forgotten, and not greatly regarded; but when they are arraigned for such horrid and heinous offences as the ears of the hearer tingle to hear, and his heart trembles to think of, some sodomitical villany, wilful murder of some good king, the blowing up of a parliament, &c., the day of their judgment is great, and greatly observed: there is great wonder at their boldness in sin, great indignation against them for it, great joy when they are sentenced, and greater when they are executed. How great then shall this judgment-day be; for how great at that day shall every sin appear to be! Sin can never be seen to be what it is, or in its due dimensions, but by the light of the fire of God's wrath. In the dim and false light of this world, it is nothing, it is nothing, a trick of youth, a toy, a trifle; but at the appearing of the light of Divine disquisition, when conscience shall be searched with candles, and all paint, pretexts, and other refuges swept away, the least sin will appear infinite. The cloud awhile since no bigger than a man's hand, will overspread the face of the heavens. The least breach of a law infinitely holy, and the smallest offence against a God infinitely just and powerful, will then appear inconceivably more heinous than any breaches of the peace, or offences against the greatest of men: there is nothing little which, as sin does, kills and damns the soul; yea, *omne peccatum est deicidium*, the least sin will then be looked upon as striking even at God himself. But how great shall that day be made by the judging of those prodigious abominations, the commissions whereof the earth groaned to bear! scarlet, crimson transgressions, at which even natural conscience is affrighted, as blasphemies, murders, open oppressions, unnatural uncleanness! How greatly shall the justice of God be magnified in punishing them! How great the joy of the saints, when the enemies of that God whom they so dearly love, and highly admire, shall be sentenced! against whom the souls under the altar have so long prayed, Rev. vi. 9; when every devil, who has here so often tempted them; and every adversary, who for their profession of Christ has so cruelly persecuted them; shall be condemned!

(4.) Lastly, This day shall be great in respect of the judged, if we consider the greatness of their rewards and recompences. The sentencing to a slight punishment, as that of a small fine, a few stripes, burning in the hand, &c., is not regarded greatly, even by the sufferers or spectators; but the sentencing to a loss of all, even of life itself, a terrible death, as burning, pressing, rending limb from limb, starving, hanging in chains, makes the judgment great. The sentence whereby a man for a while is reprieved, recovers a little loss, or has small damages given, is little regarded, and soon forgotten; but that whereby a man has his life, and with that his estate and liberty, and all that is dear and desirable, granted unto him; this his sentence and judgment, I say, is great, and makes the day wherein it is passed deservedly to be accounted such. What are all the losses sustained by, or fines imposed on any, in comparison of the loss of God's presence? He who loses God, has nothing besides to lose. He who is doomed to the pains of those fires prepared for the devil and his angels, has nothing left him more to feel. The torments of the body are no more comparable to those of the soul, than is the scratch of a pin to a stab at the heart; nor can there possibly be an addition made to the blessedness of those who shall be sentenced to enter into the joy of their Lord, whose presence not only is in, but is even heaven itself; in a word, there is nothing small in the recompences of that great day; great woe or great happiness; and therefore it is a great day in either respect.

3. This day of judgment is great in respect of the properties of it. As,

(1.) It is a certain day. Were it doubtful, it would not be dreadful; were it fabulous, it would be contemptible. [1.] Natural conscience is affrighted at hearing of a judgment-day. Felix trembled when Paul preached of it, Acts xxiv. 25; and though the Athenians mocked when they heard of a resurrection of the dead, yet not at the hearing of the day of judgment. The reason why men so much fear at death, is because they are terrified with the thoughts of judgment after death: were it not for that supreme and public tribunal, the inward tribunal of conscience would be in vain erected. [2.] The justice of God requires that every one shall receive according to his works. In this life the best men are of all men most miserable, and sinners oft most happy. All things fall alike to all, Eccl. ix. 2. "The wicked," saith Habakkuk, "devoureth the man that is more righteous than himself," Hab. i. 13. There must come a time therefore when the righteous Judge will, like Jacob, lay his right hand upon the younger, the more despised saint, and his left hand upon the elder, the now prosperous sinner. There is now much righteousness and oppression among magistrates, but it would be blasphemy to say that injustice shall take place to eternity, Gen. xviii. 25; Job xxxiv. 10—12; Isa. iii. 10, 11. Every unrighteous decree in human judicatories must be judged over again, and from the highest tribunal upon earth the saints of God may joyfully and successfully appeal to a higher bar. The day of judgment shall set all things straight and in right order: "It is a righteous thing with God," saith Paul, "to recompense tribulation to them that trouble you; and to you that are troubled rest with us, when the Lord Jesus shall be revealed," &c., 2 Thess. i. 6, 7. To conclude this, the Scripture is in no one point more full and decided than in assuring us that this day shall certainly come, Matt. vii. 22; xxv. 31, 46; x. 15; 2 Cor. v. 10; Rom. xiv. 10; Luke xxi. 34; ix. 26; 2 Pet. iii. 9; Tit. ii. 13; 1 Pet. iv. 5; and if the other predictions in Scripture, particularly those concerning the first coming of Christ, have truly come to pass, why should we doubt of the truth of Christ's second appearance? and if the mercy of God were so great that he would repent of the evil intended against the wicked, yet even that mercy of his would make the judgment so much the more necessary for the good of the elect.

(2.) The judgment of this great day shall be sudden. Christ will come as a thief in the night, who enters the house without knocking at the door. The judgment will come upon the secure world as the snare does upon the bird, Luke xxi. 35. The greater security is at that day, the greater will the day and the terror thereof be to sinners: the noise of fire is neither so usual nor so dreadful as in the night. The approach of the bridegroom at midnight increased the cry of the foolish and sleeping virgins, Matt. xxv. Sudden destruction, or that which befalls them who cry peace, is destruction doubled.

(3.) The judgment of this great day shall be searching, exact, and accurate. There shall be no causes escape without discussion, notwithstanding either their multiplicity or secrecy, their numerousness or closeness. The infinite swarms of vain thoughts, idle words, and unprofitable actions, shall clearly and distinctly be set in order before those who are to be tried for them, Psal. l. 21; Matt. xii. 36. " God shall bring every work to judgment, and every secret thing, whether it be good, or whether it be evil," Eccl. xii. 14; 2 Cor. v. 10. " He will bring to light the hidden things of darkness, and make manifest the counsels of the heart," 1 Cor. iv. 5.

(4.) It shall be righteous. As every cause shall be judged, so rightly judged, Psal. lxxii. 2; Acts xvii. 31. Christ is a " righteous Judge," 2 Tim. iv. 8. " In righteousness doth he judge," Rev. xix. 11. " The sceptre of his kingdom is a right sceptre; he loves righteousness," Psal. xlv. 6, 7. The day of judgment is a " day of the revelation of the righteous judgment of God." Righteousness shall be the girdle of his loins, it shall stick close to him. This Judge cannot be biassed by favour; there is no respect of persons with God, Rom. ii. 11; 2 Chron. xix. 7; Psal. lxxxii. 2; Job xxxiv. 19. The enemies of Christ justified him in this particular, that he " regarded not the persons of men," Matt. xxii. 16. Kindred, friendship, greatness, make him not at all to warp and deviate from righteousness. He is not mistaken with error; " he shall not judge after the sight of his eyes, neither reprove after the hearing of his ears," Isa. xi. 3. This Judge shall never be deluded with fair shows and outsides, or misled by colourable but false reports, as earthly judges may be, because they cannot pierce into men's hearts to discern their secret intentions as Christ can, whom no specious appearance can deceive; he shall never acquit any who is in truth faulty, or inwardly unsound, nor upon any flying report or forged suggestion proceed to the censure of any. He shall never be in danger of being misinformed, through untrue depositions, but he shall always proceed upon certain knowledge in passing his own sentence upon any,

Tò ἔνδον βῆμα. Nazian. Sua quemque fraus, sua audacia, suum facinus, suum scelus, de sanitate, ac mente deturbat; hae sunt impiorum furiae, hae flammae, hae faces. Cicer. in Pison.

John vii. 24; 2 Cor. x. 7; Jer. xvii. 9, 10; Gal. vi. 7.

(5.) This judgment shall be open and manifest. "There is nothing hid but shall be revealed." Sinners shall be openly shamed, their secret sins, their speculative impurities, their closest midnight impieties shall be publicly discovered, and their feigned hypocritical appearances shall then be unmasked. Then saints shall be openly honoured; the good which they have done in secret shall be divulged; from their sins, against which they have mourned, prayed, believed secretly, they shall be acquitted openly and honourably; from all the censures, suspicions, aspersions, and wrong judgments upon earth, before all the world of men and angels, they shall be publicly cleared. In a word, as the Judge *is* righteous, he will be *known* to be so; and therefore not only his sentence, but its equity, shall be manifestly known. Every tongue shall confess to God the just proceedings of that day; and Christ shall be clear when he judges, and justified when sinners are condemned.

(6.) This judgment shall be immediate. Christ will not any more judge by man. They whom he has intrusted with judicature, have often miscarried in the work; acquitting where they should condemn, and condemning where they should acquit; now therefore he will trust others with the work no more, but take it into his own hands. Judgment here among men is the Lord's mediately, but the great judgment shall be his immediately. Sinners might hope to escape while saints were their judges; saints might fear cruelty while sinners were their judges. In a word, when frail, sinful man is judge, he, like the unjust steward in the gospel, who cut off fifty in the hundred, punishes malefactors by halves, and with him wicked men can tell how to deal; but can their hearts endure, or can their hands be strong, in the day wherein the Lord shall deal with them? Ezek. xxii. 14. When Gideon commanded young Jether to slay Zebah and Zalmunna, he feared to draw his sword against them, being but a youth, but Gideon himself arose and fell upon them, and as was the man, so was his strength, for he instantly slew them, Judg. viii. 20, 21. And God commands those who should resemble him in righteousness, to cut down sin, and cut off sinners; but, alas, they are oft either unwilling or afraid to draw the sword of justice, and therefore the Lord himself will come and take the sword into his own hands, and as is he, so will his strength be found and felt to be, infinite. The mountains and hills will be but light burdens to fall upon sinners, in comparison of this mighty God.

(7.) This judgment shall be the last judgment. The sentence that there shall be pronounced, is the final, conclusive, and determinating sentence. The day of judgment is frequently called "the last day," John xi. 24; xii. 48: "the last day" and the "great day" are sometimes put together, John vii. 37. Wicked men have had in this world many days of judgment by the word, by temporal troubles, by the examples and warnings of the saints; but now their last day, their last judgment, is come, after which there shall be no more trial. Former judgments might be reversed upon repentance, but this last is irrevocable. Repentance will not move the Judge to repent of his sentence; repentance will be hid from his eyes, Jer. xi. 7—9. From his sentence there can be no appeal, nor is there any judicatory above or after it.

(8.) This judgment is called eternal, Heb. vi. 2. How great are those days wherein an earthly judge sentences to a temporal punishment of a few minutes! but Christ sentences to an eternal state; the effect of his judgment shall last for ever. An earthly judge allows men to put the sentenced to death out of their pain, at their execution; but this shall be the bitter ingredient in the sentence of the great day, namely, that the sentenced shall be executed, but never die. "Depart from me, ye cursed, into everlasting fire:" departure for loss, and fire for sense, are the greatest punishments; but this "everlasting" is that which makes both insupportable. Dreadful sentence! Without this "everlasting" departure hell would not be hell. This "everlasting" burns hotter than the fire, or rather is the heat of the fire in hell; and oh the bottomless ocean of sweetness in this word "ever," when joined with being with the Lord! this is that which, like the faggot-band, binds all the scattered parcels of heaven's blessedness together, and keeps them from dropping out; in a word, this stability of happiness is that which makes it happiness. Great day! wherein there is a sentence to no estate shorter than eternity.

Obs. 1. Great is the vanity of all earthly greatness. While we are in this world, troubles and comforts seem far greater than they are; the former we think too great to bear, the other too great to forsake. How men groan under small burdens, and how they admire the poor enjoyments of the world! but when this great day is come, neither of these will seem great. How small will former disgraces be esteemed by those who shall be honoured before all the world! How contemptible shall poverty be in the thoughts of those, who shall ever be enriched with the satisfying enjoyment of God himself! How slight, yea, forgotten, will the few bitter drops of pain be to those who shall be filled with rivers of pleasure! What poor trifles will all the profits and revenues of the earth be esteemed, when all the stately edifices and the richest treasures upon earth shall be consumed in the flames! What a bubble, a shadow, will all worldly honour and dignities appear, when the faint candle-light of the earthly glory of the greatest monarchs shall be swallowed up in the glorious sunshine of the appearance of the King of kings, and Lord of lords! How will sentencing to the everlasting flames of fire and brimstone blast those former dreams of pleasure in cool and pleasant arbours, costly perfumes, and sumptuous banquets! To those who so admire earthly enjoyments, I say, as Christ to his disciple, when he showed him the buildings of the temple, "Seest thou these great buildings? there shall not be one stone left upon another," Mark xiii. 2; the flame of that day will devour them, as easily as the fire from heaven consumed the stones and the sacrifice, and licked up the water about Elijah's altar.

Obs. 2. Boldness in sin is no better than madness. The great judgment-day is by the apostle called "the terror of the Lord." And though it may be our sin to be affrighted at men's judgment-days, and to be afraid of their terror; yet is it our folly not to fear this great day of the Lord, and a great punishment of sin not to fear the punishment of sin. What judge would not be incensed, if, when the prisoners were warned of his solemn approach, they grew more licentious and madly merry! Against that servant, saith Christ, who shall say in his heart, My Lord deferreth his coming, and shall eat and drink with the drunken; shall his Lord "come in a day when he looketh not for him, and cut him in sunder," &c., Luke xii. 45, 46. Although Gaal and the Shechemites, while fortifying the city against Abimelech, were eating, drinking, making merry, and cursing him, and at the approach of Abimelech's army were told by Zebul that they saw the shadow of the mountains as if they were men; yet when his

Magna peccati pœna metum futuri judicii perdidisse. Aug. ser. 120. de Tem.

Judicium humanum est vix alphabetum illius ultimi. Luth.

army drew near, he who had before deluded now terrified them. "Where," saith Zebul to Gaal, "is thy mouth wherewith thou saidst, Who is Abimelech, that we should serve him?" Judg. ix. 38. Wicked men, who now sport in sin, and look upon judgment at a distance, make a mock of it, and the devil tells them that all the terrifying sermons they hear concerning the day of judgment are but the shadows of the mountains, and the dark productions of the melancholy fancies of some precise minister; but at the nearer approach of this great day, when judgment is at the door, and the armies of vengeance rushing in upon them, how will their mouths be stopped, their false confidences be rejected, and how great will their folly appear in being so weak, and yet presumptuous at the same time! O sinner! more fear of this great day would better become one that has no more force to resist it. The way to be fearless hereafter, is to be fearful here: happy is that fear which prevents future trembling.

Adventum æterni judicis tanto securiores quandoque videbitis, quanto nunc districtionem illius timendo prævenitis. Greg. Mor. l. 14. c. 30.

Obs. 3. Our meditations of this great day should be deep and serious. Great things are greatly observed, and make deep impression. Though feathers and cork being cast upon the water are wont to swim, yet lead and iron sink into it; though slighter thoughts become matters of less concernment, yet serious things should be seriously regarded, and thoroughly admitted into our meditations. It is said of the wicked, that the judgments of God are far above out of his sight, Psal. x. 5. Let not trifles expel out of the mind the thoughts of the eternal judgment, as the eye is sometimes hindered from viewing an object of vast extent by putting that before it which is not bigger than a single penny.

Obs. 4. Great should be our desires and longing after this great day. Christians only sin in seeking those things that are falsely and appearingly great; but the blessings to be enjoyed at this great day are truly great. We should love the appearance of Christ, and look for and haste to the coming of the day of God, 2 Pet. iii. 12. If we would approve ourselves for the spouse of Christ, let our note be, Come, oh why is his chariot so long in coming? *Res dulcis, mora molesta,* the sweeter the enjoyment, the stronger the desire. Be ashamed, O Christian! that the day should be so great, and thy desires so small; that a spouse should so desire the day of her marriage, a prisoner his liberty, a malefactor his pardon, a labourer his rest, an heir his inheritance; and that thou shouldst be so sluggish and remiss in regarding that day which removes every sorrow, supplies with every comfort!

Non potest esse verus Christianus, nec recitare orationem dominicam, qui non toto corde hunc diem desiderat. Luth.

Obs. 5. Our chief care should be that this great day may prove a good day to us, even as good as it is great. The judgment-day cannot be a good day to those to whom the Judge is not good. "There is no condemnation to them that are in Christ Jesus," Rom. viii. 1. The comfort of a Christian at the judgment-day will be, to be one with the Judge, and to be found in him by faith, not having his own righteousness, Phil. iii. 9. The Judge will not endure that they who are his own members should be cut off. He who hereafter shall be the Judge, is now the Advocate of believers. It can never be a good day to those who are in love with that which makes it and every day evil. They who love sin must needs fear judgment. If sinners cannot endure the light of the word in the ministry, how shall they endure the light of Divine disquisition at the day of judgment? Men who have taken in smuggled goods, or prohibited commodities, cannot desire the company of the searchers, who are appointed to open their packs. The packs of every sinner shall be opened at the great day; the hidden things of dishonesty shall be discovered, and every conscience ripped up. Empty your hearts of the love of every secret sin, if you would not fear a searching. Sins unthought of will then seize upon the wicked unawares. At this great day, the purity of the heart will more profit than subtlety of words, and a good conscience than a full purse. How happy were it that men would by repenting here prevent repenting hereafter! It cannot be a good day, if the enjoyments of this world be accounted the chief good. He who has no other paradise but his gardens, no other mansions but his beautiful buildings, no other God but his gold and possessions, cannot delight to see those flames which shall consume them. He will certainly cry out as a man does who has laid up all his treasures in a house set on fire, I am undone, I am undone. Covetousness proclaims both the world's old age, and its nearness to and the unwelcomeness of its dissolution. Wares laid up in a low, moist room will be corrupt and rotten; but those laid up in a high loft will be kept safe: and if we lay up our treasures only in this world, they will corrupt and come to nothing; but those which we treasure up in heaven will be ever safe and sound, Matt. vi. 20. It cannot be a good day to them who are overtaken with it, upon whom it comes as a snare upon the birds, who are taken as the old world was with the flood, whose wine was turned into water, and whose drunken security was swallowed up in a devouring deluge, Luke xvii. 26. Lastly, it can be a good day to none but to those who do good, who in the general are persons of a holy conversation, Tit. ii. 12, 13; 2 Pet. iii. 11. "To him who ordereth his conversation aright will God show his salvation," Psal. l. 23. Christ will bless people, not by the voice, when they shall say they are Christians; but by the hands; he will handle and feel them, 1 Cor. xv. 5, 8; 1 John i. 1. And more particularly, it is a good day to those only who have done good to the afflicted friends of Christ. No good duty is acceptable to Christ if we reject works of mercy. How cheerfully may he look upon the Judge, who has saved the lives of the Judge's wife and children! The saints are tied to Christ in both relations, Matt. xxv. 40; 2 Cor. xi. 2; Psal. xvi. 3; 2 Thess. i. 1; Eph. v. 1. What can cruelty and oppression expect from Christ at that day, but the measure which Zebah and Zalmunna found from Gideon, who were slain by him for slaying his brethren? If not relieving the saints deserves a curse, what shall robbing them do?

Multa peccata tum proruent ex improviso quasi ex insidiis. Bern.

Obs. 6. Great should be the consolation of every friend of Jesus Christ in thinking of this great day. It shall be to them a good day. A day *of clearing from all undue imputations.* Moses being charged with ambition in taking too much upon him, comforted himself with the thoughts of the morrow: To-morrow (saith he) shall the Lord show who are his, Numb. xvi. 5. When the counsels of the heart shall be manifest, every one shall have praise of God, 1 Cor. iv. 5. When a Christian is called a dissembler and a hypocrite, he may say at the great day, The Lord shall show whether it be so or no. All slanders and defamations shall fall off from the saints, as drops of water from an oiled post. The weight of their glory shall weigh down all their light and slight disgraces. *In all the wants and losses* of the faithful for Christ in this life, how great may be their consolation! Great shall be their reward in heaven, Matt. v. 12: none shall be losers by Christ that are losers for him. The day of judgment shall be the day of restitution of all their comforts. God takes away nothing but what he gave, and what he will again restore, yea, for which he will restore a thousand-fold. This great day should relieve us against the *length of our troubles,* and the slowness of deliverance. Though God asks day for the rewarding of his children, yet the greatness of the recompences of that great day shall infinitely more than countervail for the slowness of bestowing them. In all *obscurity and contempt* how may the saints rejoice, to consider that at the great day they shall appear with Christ in glory, and shine as the sun in the firmament! When a master is absent from a school, the scholars are mingled together; those who are of the highest form are perhaps standing amongst those of the lowest; but when the master comes into the school, every scholar takes his right place; so at the last day every one shall have their due place allotted them, though now there appears nothing but confusion. This great day may comfort saints *in their greatest distances.* In this world they are oft far from one another, both in respect of places, opinions, and affections; at this great day they shall all meet, yea, and " in the unity of the faith of the Son of God," Eph. iv. 13. *In all the cruelties* and unkindnesses of wicked men. It is the duty of the saints in this life to be patient among, but it shall be their privilege hereafter to be freed from the company of the wicked; they shall neither be troubled with sin, nor sinners, nor sorrows: the day of judgment shall be a "day of redemption," Luke xxi. 28; Eph. iv. 30, of refreshment, Acts iii. 19. The thoughts of this day may support them *in their absence from Christ.* At that great day they shall meet with their Redeemer, their Spouse, their Head. How shall not Christ save those from death, for whom he has suffered death? Who shall come to judge the saints, but he who came to be judged for them?

<small>Quomodo Christus cum damnabit quem propria mors redemit. Ambros. lib. de Jacob. cap. 6. Quis venturus est judicare te, nisi qui venit judicari pro te? Aug. in Psal. cxlvii.</small>

VERSE 7.

Even as Sodom and Gomorrha, and the cities about them in like manner, giving themselves over to fornication, and going after strange flesh, are set forth for an example, suffering the vengeance of eternal fire.

This verse contains the third example of God's severe displeasure against the sinners of former times, and it is that of "Sodom and Gomorrha," which the apostle sets down by way of comparison, noted in these words, "Even as;" the former part, or proposition of which, is in this verse, and the reddition, or second part, in the two next following.

In this example I observe four parts.

I. The places punished; "Sodom and Gomorrha, and the cities about them."

II. The deserving cause of their punishment; "In like manner, giving themselves over to fornication, and going after strange flesh."

III. The severity of their punishment; "Suffering the vengeance of eternal fire."

IV. The end and use of their punishment; they "are set forth for an example."

I. The places punished; "Sodom and Gomorrha, and the cities about them."

Four things may be by way of explication inquired into.

1. What places these cities of "Sodom and Gomorrha" were.

2. What were these "cities about them."

3. Why Sodom and Gomorrha are rather named than those cities about them.

4. Why these places are rather named than the persons and inhabitants thereof.

1. What places these cities of Sodom and Gomorrha were. We read, Gen. xiii. 10, upon occasion of Lot's choice of the plain of Jordan for the place of his habitation, that all that plain " was well watered every where, before the Lord destroyed Sodom and Gomorrha, even as the garden of the Lord, like the land of Egypt, as thou comest unto Zoar." The river Jordan beginning from the mountain Libanus, and rising, say some, out of two fountains, called Dan and Jor, which joined together make the name Jordan, after it has run, saith Pererius, about fifteen miles, falls into the lake Samechonitis, the same which is called the waters of Merome, Josh. xi. 7, then passing along by Chorazin and Capernaum, falls into the lake Gennesareth; and so having continued a current of a hundred miles in length, it falls into the lake Asphaltites, <small>Hoc cave cum Lyrano referas ad proxime dictum, de Egypto, quasi Ægyptum velit esse feracem maxime, qua ex ea venitur ad Segor; Id non vult, sed cum remotiori jungendum; Erat inquam illa Jordanis planicies irrigua qua itur in Segorem. Mercerus in locum. Hanc lectionem amplectuntur Musculus, Mercerus, Pererius, Willetus.</small> or the Dead Sea, where these cities of Sodom and Gomorrha stood, and with its most pleasant streams enriches and adorns the plain through which it passes with such great fertility and pleasantness, that it is compared to the garden of God. This expression, "the garden of God," as some think, is given to these places after the manner of Scripture, wherein things which are eminently great and goodly are attributed to God; all excellency both being from and for him; and that these places being so great, it might seem, if God himself would dwell upon earth after the manner of men, he would make choice of them as the spot for his mansion or garden. Luther rejecting this interpretation as judaical, thinks, though according to my observation without company, that this place of Sodom and Gomorrha was Paradise itself, or the garden of Eden. I rather conceive with Augustine, Calvin, Mercer, Rivet, and others, that the place in which Sodom and Gomorrha stood, for its wonderful delightfulness, is compared to that garden of God, properly called Paradise; or that garden of Eden, called "the garden of God," because planted by God himself, in which Adam was first placed, and whence afterward he was expelled for sin; the rather, because, as in the description of the pleasantness of the garden of Eden it is expressly said, that " it was watered with a river;" so in this place the watering of this plain with Jordan is particularly mentioned as that which made it so fruitful and delightful; and thus we are in other places to understand this adage of "the garden of God;" as Isa. li. 3, "He will make her wilderness like Eden, and her desert like the garden of the Lord." So in Ezek. xxviii. 13, it is said of the king of Tyre, that he had "been in Eden, the garden of God." <small>ὡς παράδεισον κυρίου. Sept.</small> And that these places where formerly Sodom and Gomorrha stood, are compared to that same ancient Eden in which Adam was placed, I am yet the more inclinable to believe, because Egypt, mentioned in the next branch of the comparison, is a place properly so called; this plain, wherein dwelt the Sodomites, being also said to be like the land of Egypt; a country whose fruitfulness, by reason of the overflowing of the Nile, was so great, that it was commonly called the granary of other nations, the Egyptians themselves sowing almost every month; in consequence of which <small>Horreum cæterarum regionum. Riv. in Gen. Dicuntur Ægyptii sæpius in anno serere, imo singulis pene mensibus. Riv. in Gen.</small>

<small>Cogito ego hunc ipsum locum fuisse Paradisum. Luth. in loc.</small>

when other countries were afflicted with famine, the Egyptians had not only corn sufficient for their own use, but also for the relief of their neighbours. Nor was Sodom unlike to Egypt in respect of this plenty of bread, the fulness whereof is expressly said to be "the iniquity of Sodom," Ezek. xvi. 49. And probably because of the plenty, pleasantness, and pride of the cities of the plain, Chedorlaomer forced them into subjection to himself. When they afterward rebelled against him, Chedorlaomer, assisted by three other kings, attacked them, and becoming victorious, they "took all the goods of Sodom and Gomorrha," Gen. xiv.

2. It may be inquired what these cities about Sodom and Gomorrha were, which (Jude saith) were destroyed. In Scripture we read but of two, besides Sodom and Gomorrha, which were overthrown, viz. Admah and Zeboim. Of these we have frequent mention in Scripture, as Deut. xxix. 23, where we read only of the overthrow of Sodom and Gomorrha, Admah and Zeboim; as also Hos. xi. 8. Lyra, Theodoret, and Suidas think that Zoar was also involved in that calamity after Lot's departure from it, mentioned Gen. xix. 30; but it seems rather that Zoar was spared at the intercession of Lot, Gen. xix. 21, "I will not overthrow this city for which thou hast spoken;" and long after Sodom and Gomorrha were consumed, Zoar is mentioned in Scripture, as Deut. xxxiv. 3; Isa. xv. 5. Jerom saith, that Hier. de loc. Heb. of all the five cities, only Zoar was spared, and that in his time it stood between the Dead Sea and the mount of Engedi. Nor must the Sap. x. 6. author of the Book of Wisdom, when he speaks of the fire that fell down upon the five cities, necessarily be understood to speak of the five cities severally; but the word Pentapolis may be taken jointly for the region wherein the five cities stood, and of them so called. Strabo mentions the overthrow of thirteen cities by fire, of which, he saith, that Sodom was the metropolis. Others speak of a greater number, and these possibly the more boldly mention so considerable a number, on account of the largeness of the sulphureous lake, or the Dead Sea, which covers that region where the Plin. l. 5. c. 16. cities stood. Pliny saith, that this sea Jos. l. 5. de Bel. is above a hundred miles in length, and Jud. c. 5. twenty-five miles in breadth; but Josephus, who better knew, gives it but five hundred and eighty furlongs in length, that is, seventy-two miles, and somewhat more; and a hundred and fifty furlongs in breadth, that is, nineteen miles, or thereabouts.

3. Why are Sodom and Gomorrha named rather than the other cities of the plain. It is not only observable in this, but in most of those places where the sin and destruction of these cities are mentioned: see Isa. i. 9, 10; xiii. 19; Jer. xxiii. 14; xlix. 18; l. 40; Amos iv. 11; Zeph. ii. 9; Matt. x. 15; Mark vi. 11; Rom. ix. 29; 2 Pet. ii. 6. It is not doubted but that, (1.) These two were the principal of all those cities which were destroyed; the kings of Sodom and Gomorrha are eminently mentioned above the rest of the five kings, Gen. xiv. 10; and though every one of the five cities had a king peculiarly belonging to it, Gen. xiv. 2, 8, yet Sodom was the metropolis, or chief city; hence we read so frequently, Ezek. xvi. 46, 48, 49, 53, 55, &c., that the other cities which God overthrew are called the daughters of Sodom; and it is probable that Gomorrah was next to Sodom in dignity. (2.) These two cities were the most infamously and eminently wicked. Hence it is that great sinners are called the inhabitants of Sodom and Gomorrha, Isa. i. 10; Jer. xxiii. 14; Matt. x. 15, &c. And Jerusalem is called the sister of Sodom, Ezek. xvi. 46. And a wicked life is compared to the vine of Sodom and Gomorrha, Deut. xxxii. 32. The cry of the sins of Sodom and Gomorrha is peculiarly mentioned, Gen. xviii. 20. When God expressed how much he abhorred the prophets of Jerusalem for sin, he saith, they were to him as Sodom and Gomorrha. When he sets forth the impiety of the rulers and people of Jerusalem, he calls them, The rulers of Sodom, and people of Gomorrha, Isa. i. 10. The seat of antichrist is called spiritual Sodom, Rev. xi. 8. And it is observable, that the sin for which these cities were so infamous receives its denomination from Sodom, rather than from any of the rest of the cities, it being to this day called Sodomy. These cities then being more wealthy, were also more wicked than the rest, and from them, as from the head, there came a defluxion of sin upon the rest. In Jonah i. 2, it is said that Nineveh was a great city, and the wickedness thereof came up before the Lord.

4. Why these places and cities are named rather than the persons and inhabitants thereof. To note, that their overthrow was universal and total; they were all and utterly ruined. God has made them cease from being a people; not only cutting off some branches, but plucking them up by the root; not only executing the rebels, but demolishing their fortifications, and at once both firing the bees and the hive. The overthrow of Sodom was total, both in respect of the inhabitants and the place itself. For the former, only one Lot was excepted from this destruction, Luke xvii. 29; 2 Pet. ii. 7. Hence the prophet saith, Isa. i. 19, " Except the Lord of hosts had left unto us a very small remnant, we should have been as Sodom, and like unto Gomorrha." Had there been ten righteous, all should have been spared; but there being but one righteous, there was but one delivered. The punishment was as universal as the provocation; " From the sole of the foot even to the head there was no soundness in them." And in Scripture a general calamity is proverbially expressed by the overthrow of Sodom and Gomorrha: concerning Edom and Babylon, it is said, " As in the overthrow of Sodom and Gomorrha, no man shall abide there, neither shall a son of man dwell in it," Jer. xlix. 18; l. 40. Total also was the destruction of these cities in respect of their place. To this purpose speaks Peter, God turning their cities into ashes, condemned them with an overthrow, 2 Pet. ii. 6. Hence we find that the plain wherein they were seated was overthrown with the cities, Gen. xix. 25, "and that the whole land is brimstone, salt, and burning; it is not sown, nor beareth, nor any grass groweth therein," Deut. xxix. 23. The salt or Dead Sea has not only overwhelmed the place itself where the cities stood, but, as may be gathered from Deut. xxix. 33; xxxii. 32, the grounds which bordered upon them are spoiled; their fruits, if there be any, are Poma oculis temost loathsome and unsavoury; as Jo- nus, contacta cinesephus, Solinus, Strabo, and also Ter- rescunt. Tert. tullian and Augustine, report, who say Forinsecus matura, instrinsecus of the apples which grow there, that fumea. Aug. de in appearance they are apples, but C. Dei, l. 21. c. 7. being touched, they fall into ashes; and that when they seem ripe, they are within only smoky; that an outward rind keeps in the filthy embers. And hence in Scripture a total and irrecoverable subversion is compared to that of Sodom and Gomorrha: " The cities," saith Jeremiah, " which the Lord overthrew, and repented not," Jer. xx. 16. " Moab," saith Zephaniah, " shall be as Sodom, and the children of Ammon as Gomorrha; even the breeding of nettles, and salt-pits, and a perpetual desolation," Zeph. ii. 9.

Obs. 1. With what admirable wisdom has God ordered that there should be such variety of places for man's habitation! Sodom and Gomorrha were seated in the fruitful valley, the country near it was more barren and mountainous. Some countries are high, and thirsty, and barren; others low, and watered, and fruitful. God could have made the whole earth to have been alike in all places, and not so variously ordered; but this singular diversity excellently praises the wisdom of his providence. They who live in barren mountains, which are only watered by the showers of heaven, are compelled to acknowledge that they owe all their increase to a blessing from above. They who inhabit the fruitful valleys enriched with fountains and rivers, are admonished of the bounty of God's providence to them above others, in the plenty of their supplies. They who live in mountainous and barren places, show the goodness of God in sustaining them even in such places of scarcity, and that it is not necessary for man's preservation to live delicately; those who fare more hardly often living more healthfully than those who swim in great abundance. In a word, by this variety, places are made helpful and beneficial one to another; some places abound with the blessings of one kind, some with those of another; the mountains with health, the valleys with wealth; the mountain wants the valley for supply of food, the valley is beholden to the mountain for strength and defence. Every place enjoys not every comfort, but is necessitated to crave supply from a neighbouring country. The city cannot live without the food of the country, nor the country without the coin and commodities of the city; the poor wants the rich, and the rich the poor: the one is helpful by his labours, the other by his rewards; the one by work, the other by wages. *Pauper rogat, dives erogat.* True is that of Solomon, The rich and the poor meet together, and the Lord is the Maker of them all, Prov. xxii. 2; who by this variety both advances the honour of his own wisdom, and provides for the good of human society.

Obs. 2. God often affords the richest habitations and the greatest earthly plenty to the greatest sinners. Sodom for wealth and fertility is compared to the garden of God, and yet God bestows it upon the worst of men. Egypt and Babylon, abounding with waters and plenty, are given, not only to those who are *without* the church, but who are enemies *of* the church. In these countries God made his people slaves and captives; and truly it is safest for Israel to meet with most woe in places of most wealth. God gives his enemies their heaven, their portion, their all in this life, Psal. xvii. 14; they here receive their good things; and have all in hand, nothing in hope; all in possession, nothing in future reversion. *Babylon irrigua, et fertilis. Ægyptus irrigua, et amœna; et tamen utraque quasi carcere usus est Dominus ad castigandum Israelem: sic exposcit humani ingenii corruptio, ut locis amœnioribus utatur Deus, non ad delicias, sed ad tristem servitutem et castigationem populi sui. Musc. in Gen. xiii.* By this distribution of earthly plenty, God would have us see how slightly and meanly he esteems it. He throws the best things that this world affords upon the worst and, as Daniel speaks, the basest of men. Who but the Nimrods, the Nebuchadnezzars, the Alexanders, the Cæsars, have ordinarily been the lords of the world? These have fleeted off the cream of earthly enjoyments, when the portion of saints has been thin, and lean, and poor. Some observe, that Daniel expresses the monarchies of the world by sundry sorts of cruel beasts; to show, that as they were gotten by beastly cruelty, so enjoyed with brutish sensuality. The great Turkish empire, said Luther, is but as a crust which God throws to a hungry dog. God sometimes indeed, lest riches should be accounted in themselves evil, gives them to the good; but ordinarily, lest they should be accounted the chief good, he bestows them upon the bad; oftener making them the portion of foes than of sons. What is it to receive, and not to be received; to have nothing from God but what he may give in hatred; to have, with Sodomites, a garden of God upon earth, with the loss of the true Paradise! in a word, to have no other dews of blessing but such as may be followed with showers of fire!

Obs. 3. The plenty of places oft occasions much wickedness and impiety. Commonly where there is no want, there is much wantonness. The rankness of the soil occasions much rankness in sin. Sodom, which was watered with Jordan, and fatted with prosperity, was a nursery of all impiety: she had fulness of bread, and therefore abundance of idleness; "neither did she strengthen the hands of the poor; and they were haughty, and committed abomination before me," Ezek. xvi. 49, 50. "Jeshurun waxed fat, and kicked," Deut. xxxii. 15. "The drunkards of Ephraim were on the head of the fat valleys," Isa. xxviii. 1. Wealth unsanctified is but as oil to nourish the flame of lust. How deceitful an argument of God's love is worldly abundance! Not the having, but the holy improvement of wealth, is the distinguishing mercy. God cuts his people short of bodily supplies in much love to their souls. His Daniels thrive best with the diet of pulse. I never yet heard or read that prosperity occasioned the conversion of one soul. Cyrus, they say, would not suffer his Persians to change a barren soil for a fruitful, because dainty habitations make dainty inhabitants. Rich cities have ever been the stoves of luxury. Men have natural inclinations according to the genius of their country; and it is rare to see religion flourish in a rich soil. In the scantiness of earthly enjoyments, want restrains and stints our appetites; but where there is abundance, and the measure is left to our own discretion, we seldom know what moderation means. Islands are the richest soils, and islanders are held the most riotous people: we in this city lie in the bosom of an indulgent mother; we live in as dangerous a place for prosperity as Sodom; and as the fattest earth is most slippery for footing, we had need of special grace at every turn, and of that watchfulness whereby in the midst of abundance we may not want temperance. How hard is it, with holy Paul, to know how to be full, and to abound! How holy is that man who can be chaste, temperate, heavenly in Sodom! Let us not only be content to want, but even pray against those riches which may occasion us, full, to deny God, Prov. xxx. 8, 9. *Nullos esse Deos, inane Cœlum, affirmat Selius, probatque quod se factum, dum negat hæc, videt beatum. Mart. l. 4. Epig. 21.* It is a most unwise choice, with Lot, to leave Abraham to inhabit Sodom; and an ill exchange, to go with Jacob, from Bethel, the house of God, to Bethlehem, though a house of bread and plenty. They who, for worldly advantages, betake themselves to places only of outward accommodations, soon find, with Lot, the recompence of their inexcusable error. How much more commendable was the choice of holy Galeacius, who forsook all the wealth and honours of Italy, to enjoy God in the purity of his ordinances in poor Geneva! It is much better to travel to Zion through the valley of Baca, than to pitch our tents in the plains of Sodom.

Obs. 4. Sinners are not bettered by premonition. They commonly remain unreformed, notwithstanding the bitter foretastes of judgments. How soon has Sodom forgot that she was spoiled and wasted by Chedorlaomer and the other kings! But sinners grow worse by afflictions, as water grows more cold after heating. If that wicked city had been warned by the sword, it had escaped the fire. But now this visitation has not made ten good men in those five cities. And as they leave not sinning, so God leaves not plaguing them, but still follows them with a succession of judgments. There is no greater sign of final overthrow than misimproving judgments. Oh that the time which we spend in an impatient fretfulness under them, because they are so great, we would more profitably employ in a humble mourning for our unprofitableness under them, lest they be the forerunners of greater!

Obs. 5. The greatest, the strongest cities cannot keep off judgment. Nor are they shot-proof against the arrows of vengeance. Great sins will overturn the foundations of Sodom and Gomorrha, and the cities about them. Nothing can defend where God's justice will strike, as there is nothing can offend where his goodness will preserve. The height of a city's proud towers may hold the earth in awe, but they cannot threaten heaven; and the closer they press to the seat of God, the nearer they lie to his lightning. The bars of our gates cannot keep out judgments. What is the greatness of Sodom, though the mother city, compared with the greatness of the Lord of hosts! The lands of Alcibiades, in the map of the whole world, could not be espied. "The nations are as the drop of a bucket, as the small dust of the balance; he taketh up the isles as a very little thing: all nations before him are as nothing, and less than nothing, and vanity," Isa. xl. 15, 17; Jerusalem was the perfection of beauty, and the joy of the whole earth, Lam. ii. 15; yet how were her gates sunk into the ground, her bars broken! Zion was so desolate, that the foxes ran upon it, Lam. v. 18. Her strength was such before, that the inhabitants of the world would never have believed that the enemy would have entered Jerusalem, Lam. iv. 12. Greatness of sin will shake the foundations of the greatest cities upon earth: if their heads stood among the stars, iniquity will bring them down into the dust. Even of Babylon the great, that spiritual Sodom, shall it be said, It is fallen, Rev. xviii. 2. Ammianus Marcellinus called Rome, *Urbs æterna*, The everlasting city; but even she shall see the day when the eternity of her name, and the immortality of her soul, wherewith she is quickened, which, saith a learned man, is the supremacy of her prelates, above emperors and princes, shall be taken from her; and as Babylon has left her the inheritance of her name, so shall it leave her the inheritance of her destruction. In vain do we build, unless the Lord lay the first stone; or plant, unless he say, Let it grow. Blessed is the city whose gates God bars up with his power, and opens with his mercy; otherwise Sodom's plenty and power cannot secure its inhabitants. It is said of Tyre, that her merchants were princes, and her traffickers the honourable men of the earth; yet how doth God deride her greatness at the time of her overthrow! Is this that glorious city? "her own feet shall carry her far off to sojourn. The Lord of hosts hath purposed it, to stain the pride of all glory, and to bring to contempt all the honourable of the earth," Isa. xxiii. 7, 9. Sodom, Babylon, Jerusalem, Constantinople, have felt the weight of God's power, and their own impieties. God once asked Nineveh whether she was greater than No, Nahum iii. 8. Let me ask London, whether she is greater than those cities which, for sin, God has made small, yea, brought to nothing. He who in former great plagues has made grass to grow in the streets of London for want of passengers, is able again to "stretch out upon it the line of confusion, the stones of emptiness," Isa. xxxiv. 11, and to turn the glory of our dwellings into ploughed fields. The fear of God is the strongest refuge, and righteousness a stronger bulwark than walls of brass, Prov. x. 25.

How great is the folly of the greatest city, to be at the same time sinful and secure! There is no fortification against, no evasion from the Lord. There is no way to fly from him but by flying to him; by making him, in Christ, our friend; by becoming enemies to sin, and by reforming.

Obs. 6. Sin brings a curse upon every thing that belongs to man. The sin of Sodomites overthrew them, their houses, their cities, their children, yea, their plain, and all that grew upon the earth, Gen. xix. 25. The curse of thorns and briers grew out of the soil of sin. The punishment of Amalek reached even the infant and suckling; yea, the ox and sheep, the camel and ass, 1 Sam. xv. 3. That which was made and bestowed for man's comfort, may justly be destroyed for man's wickedness. Who wonders to see the children, the followers, the palaces, and gardens of a traitor to droop and decay; and the arms of his house, and the badge of his nobility, to be defaced and reversed? That which is abused by man to the dishonour of God, may justly be destroyed by God to the detriment of man. How deservedly may God demolish and dismantle those fortifications, and break in pieces those engines, in and by which rebellious man fights against his supreme Lord and Sovereign! How profitably may we improve all the miseries which we behold dispersed upon the whole creation! How fruitful a meditation may we raise from the barrenness of the earth! A fruitful land turneth he into barrenness, for the wickedness of them that dwell therein, Psal. cvii. 34. All the monuments of ruin, the demolished monasteries, and overthrown abbeys, and subverted cells of sodomitical and lazy friars, full fed and unclean inhabitants, are but the scratches that sin hath made upon the fair faces of nations. Oh that England would look with Scripture spectacles upon all its fired towns and razed mansions, and say, and believe, If sin had not been, these had not lain here; and that these demolitions are but the *Vestigia peccati.* foot-prints of sin; that so having found out sin, we may voice it, and deal with it as the Philistines did with Samson, who, said they, was the destroyer of their country! Judg. xvi. 24. Certainly, that which wants reason is by God ruined, that we who have reason may thereby be reformed. We should say in the destruction of the creatures, as David in the death of his subjects, I and my father's house have sinned; "these sheep, what have they done?" and we should look upon God's taking away of abused comforts as stoppages in our way of sin, and the withdrawings of the fuel of lust; God as it were firing our ships, and breaking down our bridges, lest by these we should depart from him.

Obs. 7. Great is the difference between God's chastising his people and punishing Sodomites. The universality of Sodom's ruin followed the community of its sin. The church of God is never destroyed utterly, but in it he always leaves a number: "Except the Lord had left us a seed," saith Paul, "we should have been as Sodom, and like unto Gomorrha," Rom. ix. 29. Though a householder spend and sell the greatest part of the corn of the harvest crop, yet he will be sure to reserve a little seed-corn to sow his ground for a new crop. Though Sodom be utterly consumed by fire, yet Jerusalem is as a brand plucked out of the burning, Amos iv. 11. God makes a light account of whole cities full of sinners, he takes away the ungodly of the earth like dross, Psal. cxix. 119, which is put into the fire to be consumed; his own people being like gold only, put in to be purged. A man, when his house is on fire, more regards a small box full of jewels than a great room full of ordinary lumber. God having intimated to his people that they deserved to be made as Admah and Zeboim, Hos. xi. 8, the two cities that were destroyed with Sodom and Gomorrha, he subjoins, ver. 9, "I will not return to destroy Ephraim:" by not returning to destroy, he means he will not utterly destroy; he will not be like a conqueror, who, having overcome a city, and in the heat of blood destroyed all with whom he met, at length gives over, but afterward returns to make a total destruction thereof: though God make a full end of all nations, yet he will not make a full end of his people, but correct them in measure, yet not leave them altogether unpunished, Jer. xxx. 11; xlvi. 28; he will ever have some to serve him, and to be monuments of his mercy, Zech. iii. 2. God will deal with his people as he enjoined them to do in gathering their grapes at vintage, Lev. xix. 10, the gleaning of grapes he will leave in it, and as the shaking of an olive tree, two or three berries in the top of the uppermost bough, Isa. xvii. 6; vi. 13; x. 22. God will have evermore some of his people above the reach of their enemies. This indulgence of God should both teach us humility, considering what we deserve; and thankfulness, considering what we escape, it being the Lord's mercies that we are not utterly consumed.

Vid. Rivetum in loc.

This for the first part of this seventh verse, viz. the places punished. Now follows,

II. The deserving cause of their punishment, expressed by the apostle in these words; "In like manner, giving themselves over to fornication, and going after strange flesh."

Wherein he sets down, 1. The sin of some; namely, of the cities about Sodom and Gomorrha, which was to sin "in like manner."

2. The sin of all the cities destroyed.

Wherein I consider, (1.) Into what they fell; viz. uncleanness; yea, one of the most odious sorts of uncleanness, Sodomy, or pollution with "strange flesh."

(2.) The degree or measure of their embracing this sin; they gave themselves over to the one, they went after the other.

In the explication of this second part, viz. their sin, three things principally are considerable.

1. What we are to understand by this sinning "in like manner."
2. What by "fornication and strange flesh."
3. What by this "giving themselves" to the former, and "going after" the latter.

For the first. These words, "in like manner," in the original, τὸν ὅμοιον τούτοις τρόπον, some refer not to the cities of Sodom and Gomorrha, but to the Israelites and angels of whom the apostle spake in the foregoing verses; as if he had intended, that these cities about Sodom and Gomorrha sinned after that manner in which the Israelites and angels sinned; and their only reason is, because the gender is changed in this word τούτοις, which (say they) cannot be referred to the cities of Sodom and Gomorrha, but to those Israelites and angels of whom he spake before, and who sinned, though not by that bodily uncleanness which Jude afterwards mentions, yet by spiritual whoredom, in making defection from God. But I conceive, with Beza, Calvin, and Estius upon the place, that Jude intends that these cities about Sodom and Gomorrha sinned after the same manner with these greater cities, whose steps and examples they followed, and therefore were involved in their punishment. We never find in Scripture that the Israelites sinned in following strange flesh, nor can we either according to Scripture or reason attribute this sin to angels;

Hoc non ad Israelitas, et angelos, sed mutuo ad Sodomam et Gomorrham refero. Nec obstat quod pronomen τούτοις masculinum est; nam ad incolas potius, quam ad loca Judas respexit. Calv. in loc. Vid. etiam Bezam; et Estium in loc.

and as for the change of the gender in the word τούτοις, by a metonymy of the subject, the Scripture often puts the city for the inhabitants of the city, as Matt. viii. 34, "The whole city went out to meet Jesus," &c.

2. We are to inquire what the apostle here intends, 1. By "fornication;" and, 2. By "strange flesh."

First, "fornication," I take not properly and strictly for that act of uncleanness committed between persons unmarried; but as in Scripture it is put for μοιχεία, adultery, where Christ saith, "Whosoever shall put away his wife, saving for the cause of fornication," &c., Matt. v. 32; so is it here to be taken for all sorts of carnal uncleanness, and as comprising all breaches of chastity.

Παρεκτὸς λόγου πορνείας.

The impure pens of those more impure penmen, the Jesuits, and among them of Thomas Sanchez, in his Treatise of Matrimony, have in their casuistical discourses treated this subject fit for those whose father, his unholiness the pope, invites to the public profession of fornication. Rivet observes, they utter such things as scarcely Satan himself with all his study would have suggested, examining not only the kinds and several sorts, but even every manner, object, subject, circumstance of this sin so exactly, that chaste readers cannot read them without blushing and abomination. To mention therefore only the principal sorts of carnal uncleanness, and such as we find (though with sacred modesty) set down in Scripture. This sin, if practised with a man's own body, according to the opinion of some, is called μαλακία, and ἀκαθαρσία, effeminateness and uncleanness, for which God slew Onan, Gen. xxxviii. 9; 1 Cor. vi. 9; Col. iii. 5; if with a beast, it is bestiality, a sin forbidden and severely to be punished by God's law, Lev. xviii. 23; xx. 13; if with mankind unwillingly, the party patient not agreeing, it is called ravishing, Exod. xxii. 19; Gen. xxxiv. 2; 2 Sam. xiii. 14; if the parties agreeing be males, they are called ἀρσενοκοῖται, and their sin, to the perpetual infamy of Sodom, is called Sodomy, Rom. i. 27; 1 Tim. i. 9; 1 Cor. vi. 9. The parties being of a different sex, and if the sin be committed with more, there being a pretext of marriage, it is called polygamy; there being no such pretext, whoredom, or uncleanness, transported to the abuse of many. If uncleanness be committed by parties between whom there is consanguinity or affinity in the degrees forbidden by God, it is incest; if by parties not so allied, when both or either of them is married, it is adultery, Lev. xviii. 20; Prov. ii. 16, 17; v. 7, 8, 20. If the female be a virgin, and not married, it is *stuprum*, or deflouring her; if she be retained peculiarly to one, she is a concubine, Judg. xix. 1; if the act be oft repeated, it is called luxury; and he who sets himself after it, a whoremonger. Nor is it impossible but that uncleanness may be between married couples, when the use of the marriage bed is in a season prohibited, or in a measure not moderated, or in a manner not ordained, or to an end not warranted. To all which may be added the sin called *lenocinium*, when a female is prostituted to the lusts of another, either for gain or favour; forbidden, Lev. xix. 29; with which some join the toleration of uncleanness, either in private families or in public states, as in Rome that spiritual Sodom. As also all those things which incite, dispose, or provoke to actual uncleanness; as immodest kisses, embraces, glances, filthy speeches, impure books, amorous songs, mixed dancings, and lascivious attire. And lastly, the concupiscence, boiling or burning lustfulness of the heart, out of which "proceed evil thoughts, murders, adul-

Talia, quæ vix Diabolus ipse, studium omne adhibendo, suggerere posset. Non solum genera, species, sed et modos omnes, subjecta, objecta, minutatim examinant. Rivet in Decal. p. 245.

teries, fornications," Matt. xv. 19; called 1 Cor. vii. 9, burning; and Col. iii. 5, "evil concupiscence."

It is most probable that these impure Sodomites at first began at some of the less heinous of the forementioned sorts of uncleanness, and that they went through most, if not all, of them before they became such hellish proficients and practitioners in their villanies, as to abuse themselves with mankind; the heinousness of which abomination swallows up the mention of the rest. They left the natural use of the woman, and burnt in lust towards one another, and, as Jude saith, followed "after strange flesh." Musc. in Gen. p. 464.

Briefly, though suitably to this branch of explication, I shall add to the discovery of the sorts of uncleanness a touch of the peculiar odiousness of this sin. (1.) It is a close and cleaving sin, much cherished by corrupt nature. It bears, as a reverend divine notes, the name of its mother, which is called in general lust, or concupiscence; it has the name of its kind, and therefore it is lust eminently; it lies near the heart, and sleeps in the bosom. (2.) It is an infatuating sin, Hos. iv. 11, taking away the heart; even David was led with a stupor of spirit for a whole year together after his uncleanness. How did this sin beset Samson! It blunts the edge, not of grace only, but even of reason also; even Solomon himself could not keep his wisdom and women at once. (3.) It is an injurious sin to others. It loves not to go to hell without company. An adulterer cannot say, as some other sinners may, that he is his own greatest enemy. How many, besides those whom it kills in soul, does it wound in body and name at one shoot! and for this wound there can be no salve of restitution or recompence. (4.) It is an attended sin; not only inducing others to sin, but it brings on other sins with it; it is like the needle which draws the thread after it; idolatry, perjuries, murders, riot, defrauding even of nearest relations. The apostle joins fornication and wickedness, πορνεία and πονηρία, together, Rom. i. 29. An unclean person runs down the hill, and cannot stop his course in sin. (5.) It is a dishonourable sin to the body, and peculiarly said to be against the body, 1 Cor. vi. 18. The unclean person makes himself a stigmatic; he brands his body, and leaves upon it a loathsome stain. Other sins comparatively are without the body, by it, not in it; this both, it being a more bodily sin, and requiring more of the body for perfecting it. (6.) It is a sacrilegious sin; it takes away from God that which is his own: he made our bodies, and curiously wrought them like a piece of tapestry, and he will not have them spotted, Psal. cxxxix. 15. Our bodies are the members of Christ our mystical Head, united strongly, though spiritually. If it were heinous for David to cut off the skirt of Saul's garment, what is it for any to divide between Christ and his members, and that by making them the members of an harlot! Our bodies are the temples of the Holy Ghost, 1 Cor. vi. 15, 16, 18, 19; dedicated, therefore not to be profaned. (7.) It is a heathenish sin. Gentiles walk "in the lust of concupiscence," 1 Thess. iv. 5. And a sin before conversion; "Such were some of you," 1 Cor. vi. 11. A sin of night and darkness, Rom. xiii. 12, wherein men care not how much their apparel is spotted or torn. A sin not to be named among Christians; in a word, a sin not of saints, but of Sodomites; who,

2. Are specially taxed with the breach of chastity in pollutions by "strange flesh." The words in the original are σαρκὸς ἑτέρας, properly signifying another flesh. Whereby the apostle intends, such a flesh as was another, or different from that which was afforded to their natural use by the law of nature, or a flesh that was made by God to another use and end than that unto which they abused it. Or, as Œcumenius thinks, that flesh which they followed may be called another, or strange, because God never appointed that male and male, but only that male and female, should be one flesh; in which respect, the flesh of a male must always be another flesh. And Chrysostom well observes on Rom. i. 27, that whereas by God's ordinance in marriage two became one flesh, both sexes one, by Sodomitical uncleanness the same flesh is divided into two.

Of this sin of pollution with strange or another flesh, in Scripture two sorts are mentioned: the one, carnal joining with a beast, which is of another kind, prohibited Lev. xviii. 23, and punished with death, Lev. xx. 15, wherein it is observable, that the very beast is also appointed to be slain, by which was manifested the detestableness of that sin, in that it pollutes the very beasts, and makes even the unclean creatures more unclean, and the beast below a beast, and not worthy the living the very life of a beast; but especially (as Calvin notes) the Lord would show how much this sin displeased him, when he commands that even the harmless beast, neither capable of nor provoking to the sin, was punished with death. (2.) The other sort of pollution by strange flesh was that which is properly termed Sodomy, committed when persons defile themselves with their own sex. Ad ipsum innoxium animal pœna transit. Calv. Πάθη ἀτιμίας. Βδέλυγμα. Nefas, de quo ne fari licet; of which it is not lawful to speak, or, as Varro deriveth it, as though they who committed it were ne farre digni, not worthy to eat bread. Vid. Willet in Lev. p. 504. The sin which the Gentiles committed when "God gave them up to vile affections," or affections of dishonour and ignominy, whereby men with men wrought that which was unseemly, Rom. i. 27; whereby, as they had left the author, they were also suffered to leave the order of nature. A sin called an abomination, Lev. xx. 13, sending an abominable savour unto the Lord. Incest with the daughter-in-law is called confusion; with the mother and daughter, wickedness. This sin of Sodom is called βδέλυγμα, abomination. The ἐβδελυγμένοι, abominable, are numbered among the "fearful, unbelievers," &c., who "shall have their part in the lake which burneth with fire and brimstone:" by abominable, many learned men understand those who are given to this sin against nature, as if abomination properly belonged to it. In adultery, violence is offered to marriage; in incest, to affinity; but in this sin, as Tostatus observes, infamy is offered to the whole human nature. And Pererius notes, because it is said these Sodomites were sinners before the Lord, the word being Jehovah, that it is signified they sinned against the right and light of nature. Infamiæ irrogatur toti humanæ naturæ. Ex eo quod relatione ad Deum sub nomine tetragrammaton, dicuntur valde mali et peccatores, significatur eos contra jus naturæ valde peccasse. Per. in Gen. xiii. And it is called, as Gerard notes, Sap. 14. 26, γενέσεως ἐναλλαγή, a changing of birth. The unsavoury sulphur that was mixed with the flames of Sodom, and (if travellers may be believed) the still continuing stench of that sulphureous lake where Sodom once stood, seem to be comments upon the abhorred unsavouriness of this sin. By the law of Theodosius and Arcadius, Sodomites were adjudged to the fire. Among the Athenians the offender was put to death, and the sufferer was debarred from all office. In the council of Vienna, the Templars who were found guilty of this sin were decreed to be burnt. Among the Romans it was lawful for him who was attempted to that abuse to kill him who made the assault; and thus C. Lucius did, who, as Tully saith of him, had rather do dangerously than suffer Probus adolescens facere periculose quam turpiter perpeti maluit. Orat. pro Milon.

shamefully. In short, against this sin of Sodomy no indignation, as Lactantius speaks, is enough. The greatness of the sin overcomes the office of the tongue. Tertullian brings in Christianity triumphing over paganism, because this sin was peculiar to heathens, and that Christians neither changed the sex, nor accompanied with any but their own wives. This and such like, as Tertullian speaks, are not so much to be called offences as monsters; and not to be named without holy detestation by saints, though they be committed without shame by Sodomites.

Qua indignatione tantum nefas prosequar? Vincit officium linguæ, sceleris magnitudo. Piget dicere. Lact. l. 6. c. 23. de vero cultu.

Non delicta, sed monstra. Tertull. de pud. Κίναιδος, quasi κενὸς αἰδοῦς, quia vacat pudore. Justinian in 1 Cor. vi. 9.

Thus having in the second place spoken of the "fornication" of these Sodomites, and their pollution by "strange flesh," it remains that briefly, in the third place, we should inquire what was their "giving themselves over" to the former, and their "going after" the latter. Both these are contained in a double expression in the original; the first is the preposition ἐκ, being in composition in the word ἐκπορνεύσασαι, by the addition whereof the signification of the word saith Gerard, is dilated, enlarged, increased; as also are the significations of other words by the same preposition. The second is in the words ἀπελθοῦσαι ὀπίσω, &c., "going after," &c., whereby is intended more than the accepting or embracing, even the prosecuting the motions of their unnatural uncleanness. In sum, I conceive by these expressions of their " giving over themselves," and " following after strange," &c., here is noted, besides the original root and fountain both of uncleanness and all other lusts; I mean, that *fomes innatus*, that inbred occasion of sin; as also, besides the arising of unclean motions in the heart, the delighting in such motions, the consent to those motions so delighted in, the actual performance and execution of those motions so consented to; I say, besides all these, which are supposed in these expressions of the apostle, there is intended the more hideous height and prodigious eminence of this Sodomitical uncleanness; and that in sundry respects. As,

(1.) Of their making provision, and in projecting for their lusts. Both by spending their time, pains, cost in fetching in and laying on its fuel; the constant providing and pouring on of oil to keep in and increase the flame, by fulness of bread, and excessive eating and drinking; and also by listening after, relating of, and laying out for such objects as seemed to promise most satisfaction to their unsatiable lusts, which appeared by the sudden notice and shameful resentment of the arrival of Lot's beautiful guests.

(2.) The excessiveness and exuberancy of their lust, even to the consuming, wearing, and wearying themselves by uncleanness; the boiling over of their strength and lusts together, though with difference, the former being hereby impaired, the latter increased ; and in a word, their becoming hereby their own destroyers and Satan's martyrs. And this the apostle Peter intends clearly in that word, ἀσέλγεια, 2 Pet. ii. 7, where he speaks of the ἀναστροφή ἐν ἀσελγείᾳ, the filthy conversation of the Sodomites; the word ἀσέλγεια comprehending not only all kinds of lust and obscenity, but also a monstrous profusion, a violent spending oneself without measure in all lasciviousness, even the greatest "excess of riot," 1 Pet. iv. 4.

ἀνάχυσις τῆς ἀσωτίας.

(3.) Their impudence and shamelessness in sinning, whereby they feared not to own their impurity before all the world. These Sodomites were not only practitioners and proficients in, but also professors of, their black and hellish art of uncleanness. Hence it is (say some) that the men of Sodom are said to be "sinners before the Lord," Gen. xiii. 13; that is, publicly and shamelessly, without any regard of God's eye or observation. Hence likewise, Isa. iii. 9, the prophet reproving boldness of sinning in the Jews, saith that they "declared their sin as Sodom," whose inhabitants hid not their filthiness in corners, but by their countenance, carriage, and words proclaimed it to all spectators. This impudence was noted by the heathen historian as the height of wickedness in Caligula, one of the worst of men; but in Sodom behold a city full of Caligulas. The sin of these miscreants abhorred secrecy; they blushed not, though the sun was a blushing witness of their filthiness. They gloried in their shame because they had outsinned all shame. Their hands were the organs, and their tongues the trumpets of wickedness. Would any but a company who had more of monsters than men in them, have made such a demand in the open streets, as is mentioned Gen. xix. 5, "Bring them out to us, that we may know them?"

Tostatus in loc. *Potest idem significare quod palam et publice.* Perer. in loc. *Nihil magis in natura sua, laudare se dicebat quam ἀδιατρεψί-αν.* Suet. in Calig.

(4.) Their obstinacy and pertinacy in sinning. The late bloody war, the spoiling and plundering of their city, the preaching of Lot's life, the persuasions of his tongue, their plague of blindness, could not reclaim them, but they are by these rather exasperated than amended; like violent streams, that when they are resisted by flood-gates, swell over the banks. After they were smitten with blindness, it is said "that they wearied themselves to find the door," Gen. xix. 11; upon which place Musculus well notes, that such was their obstinacy in sin, that even after their blindness they were as mad upon their lust as before, even to weariness of body. What were all the means used to amend them, but like pouring oil down the chimney? By a hellish antiperistasis they become more hotly furious by calm and cool opposition; and all that Lot could gain by his meek and earnest dissuasion from abusing his guests was but a scoff for becoming a judge, and a threat that they would deal worse with him than with them. Were not these possessed with the unclean spirit of lust, who could break in sunder all the chains of reproof and persuasion? Were they not thoroughly scorched with the heat and thirst of lust, thus to break through armies of opposition to draw the stolen waters of unnatural and poisonous pleasures?

Quamvis obcœcati essent, ostium tamen ad fatigationem usque frustra quærebant. Mus. in loc.

Obs. 1. Wicked men agree in sinning. Sodom and Gomorrha, and the cities about them, sinned in like manner. The inhabitants of several cities were inhabited by the same sins; in opposing of God they join hand in hand. However the wicked may disagree in secular conditions and interest, yea, and may have their private quarrels among themselves, yet in offending God they are unanimous; and though it be possible that they may agree with the people of God in civil concernments, yet in the matter of holiness they will ever differ. There may be many grudges and quarrels between the soldiers of the same army among themselves, who yet all consent to oppose the common enemy. The heads of Samson's foxes were turned contrary ways, but the foxes met in the tail and the firebrand. The heads, the policies of sinners, may be divided, but in their lusts they are united. They are acted by one spirit, and agree in that which is natural, though they differ in regard of what is accidental. How good is God to his people, to divide sinners among themselves in their worldly interests! to order that by the contests between the Pharisees and Sadducees Paul should find favour, and by the conflicts between Saul and the Philistines David should escape! yea, how just is it, that they who agree against God should disagree with one another! and that they who sin should also suffer after the like manner; that they who are unanimous in the same sin of filthiness, should also be swept away in the same shower of fire!

Obs. 2. Great is our proneness to follow corrupt example, and a multitude to do evil; to sin " in like manner." We are apt scholars in sinful lessons. How easy is it to be, nay, how hard not to be, carried down the stream, when at once we go with the wind of example and the tide of nature! The diseases of the soul are very catching; and when the times are corrupted, the soul is more endangered than is the body by the corruption of air. One proctor for Satan shall have more clients than a hundred pleaders for Jesus Christ. Rusty armour laid near that which is bright infects it with rustiness, but the bright imparts not its brightness to that which is rusty. The finer bread in the oven partakes of the coarser, but seldom does the brown take away any of the white. How great should be our care to be holy in bad times and companies! It was the failing of righteous Lot to live in Sodom, but it was his greater commendation to be righteous in Sodom. Though these cities about Sodom sinned in like manner, yet so did not Lot, though Sodom and Sodomites were round about him. It showed that his holiness was of a strong complexion, to retain its healthfulness in so corrupt an air. He is a star that can shine in a dark night. If we can do the wicked no good, it is our unhappiness; but if they do us hurt, it is our sin. Noah was upright, and walked with God, even when all flesh had corrupted their way. How kindly Christ takes it, when we will " shine as lights in the midst of a crooked and perverse generation," Phil. ii. 15, and sail against the wind of example! It is no commendation to be good in good company. A swine may for a while possibly be clean in a fair meadow; the difficulty is when the mire is presented to abhor wallowing in it. As it is a great sin to be bad among the good, so it is a high commendation to be good among the bad, to continue a lily among thorns, and to have a fire of zeal for God, the more hotly burning, by how much the cold of profaneness is the more increased; but as this shows the strength of grace, so yet doth that grace the greatness of God's power. Instead of imitation, let us bewail the sins of the times, and what we cannot bear down for the good of others with a stream of power, let us for our own overcome with a flood of tears.

Sicut gravioris culpæ est, inter bonos bonum non esse; ita immensi est præconii, bonum inter malos extitisse. Greg. l. 1. Mor. c. 1. *Non mediocris titulis virtutis est, inter pravos vivere bonum, et inter malignantes innocentiæ retinere candorem, versari inter spinas et minime lædi Divinæ potentiæ est, non virtutis tuæ.* Bern. ser. 48. in Cant.

Obs. 3. Corrupt greatness is very influential upon and into inferiors. The lesser cities sinned after the same manner with Sodom and Gomorrha. Jeroboam the son of Nebat made Israel to sin. "Ephraim walked after the commandment," Hos. v. 11. When the sin which we love is joined with that greatness which we admire, needs must it be very drawing. All the world wondered at the beast which had received power and authority, Rev. xiii. 3. Let those who are powerful in place, take heed lest they be strong to sin; for if they improve their power against God, they shall be powerfully punished by God. "Whoso causeth the righteous to go astray in an evil way, he shall fall himself into his own pit," Prov. xxviii. 10. Without the sins of others our own would be insupportable, if unpardoned; and it is too much to be so much as a follower in sin. The examples, yea, the injunctions of the best, the greatest, are limited and bounded by the pleasure of a greater. The midwives of Egypt, and the three servants of God threatened with the fiery furnace, are standing monuments of religious disobedience. Fear God is put before that of honouring the king. Our earthly is below our heavenly Father: he who begat us is to be beloved, but he who created us is to be preferred. The greatest, the richest cannot put in security to save us harmless at the day of judgment for following their example; even their followers shall be punished. Admah and Zeboim, the daughters of Sodom, sinned and smarted in like manner with Sodom.

Amandus est generator, sed præponendus est Creator. Tert. l. 1. de Idol c. 12.

Obs. 4. How fitly is the title of spiritual Sodom bestowed upon Rome! Sodom has now met with her match. Not to speak of that cloistered crew, the leprosy of whose sin had eaten so deeply into the walls of their monasteries in England, that the justice of God both pulled down them, and plucked up their foundations; but look upon their holy fathers, and their purple cardinals, their mitred prelates, and you shall find a second Sodom raised out of the ashes of the former. My pen is ashamed to write what I read concerning the two Juliuses, the second and third, Sixtus the Fourth, Paul the Third, and Leo the Tenth. Prodigious was that impure monster John Casa, archbishop of Beneventum, and legate apostolical, who wrote a book in commendation of the sin of Sodomy, and printed it at Venice; and by the licence of Julius the Third were other books set forth in praise of that villany. Perpetual will be the infamy of Johannes Imperialis, a popish writer, who published a book in commendation of this archbishop Casa, and others of the same stamp, wherein he writes, " That when Pope Paul the Second," observe his holiness, " endeavoured to advance the said Casa to the dignity of a cardinal, he was by some persons enviously upbraided, and blamed for lasciviousness." Nor will Rome ever be, or be accounted, other than as Sodom, a mother of harlots, and a stable of uncleanness, (a fit place for the seat of the beast,) so long as her laws for prohibiting marriage and permitting whoredom are in force.

Vid. Speed's History.

Bale de act. Rom. Pont. Bishop Jewel defens. Apol. p. 354. Sleid. Commen. ad annum 1550. Joh. Imperialis Musæum Historic. pag. 27. *Tolle de ecclesia honorabile conjugium, nonne replebis eam concubinariis incestuosis, masculorum concubitoribus?* Bern. Cant. ser. 66. *A lupanari ad missam unus tantum passus.* Rivet.

Obs. 5. How hellishly black is the depraved nature of man! The fountain surely was filthy and poisonous that sent forth such streams of Sodomitical uncleanness. Sodom's lake of brimstone is not half so unsavoury as were their streams of fornication; nor were these so filthy as that spring of polluted nature from which they issued. Who reads without horror and amazement the overflowing of this sin of Sodom into the lives of those accounted the best of heathen, and the wisest of philosophers, to whom that which might be known of God was manifest, Rom. i. 19; who professed themselves wise, and yet burned in lust one toward another? Tertullian and Gregory Nazianzen charge this foul abomination upon Socrates himself, and others upon Aristotle, Zeno, and Periander; but most of all upon Plato, how unworthy the name of divine! Who might not be more than amazed to read that Solon and Lycurgus should make laws, as they did, according to Chrysostom, for the toleration of this sin? To the fountain of this heathenish filthiness we are led by the apostle, when he declares that

Ταῦτα μὲν πολλῷ τιμώτερα τῆς Σόλωνος ἀπληστίας, &c. καὶ τῆς Σωκράτους φιλοκαλίας (ἀίδιομαι γὰρ εἰπεῖν παιδεραστίας). Greg. Naz. Orat. 1. contra Jul. pag. mihi 78. Laert. in vita Platonis. *Lego partem sententiæ Atticæ in Socratem, corruptorem adolescentium, pronuntiatam.* Tert. Apol. cap. 46.

this uncleanness was "through the lusts of their own hearts," Rom. i. 24. What cause of humility have the best, when they consider they were born with the nature of the blackest Sodomites! And how greatly should they praise and admire that *love* whereby, and *laver* wherein, they were washed and sanctified! To conclude this, what is there in the world for which tears and blushing seem to be made, but for the pollution of that nature which is the same with that of a Sodomite?

Obs. 6. Nor yet should the most deeply defiled, either in nature or practice, despair. Even Sodomites returning shall be accepted; and washing in the fountain, set open even for their uncleanness, shall be cleansed, Zech. xiii. 1. The blood of Christ can wash from the sins of Sodom. Even a people as bad as Sodomites have been invited by and unto mercy; for, Isa. i. 10, the prophet calls the Jewish princes the princes of Sodom, and their people the "people of Gomorrha;" that is, such princes and people as matched Sodom and Gomorrha in wickedness; and yet he invites them to repentance, with proffer of mercy and promise of pardon; and though their sins were as red as scarlet, yet he saith that he would make them as white as snow, ver. 18. The apostle tells the Corinthians that some of them had wallowed in this sin of Sodomy; but, saith he, "Ye are washed, and sanctified," 1 Cor. vi. 9, 11. The gospel refuses to pardon no sin for which the soul can be humbled. Free grace can bring those to heaven whose sin equalized theirs who were thrown into hell. The least sinner has cause of humility, nay, in himself, of despair; the greatest has, by closing with Christ, ground of hope. If it be the glory of God to pardon great sins, it is his greatest glory to pardon the greatest sinners. There is no spot so deep which the blood of God cannot wash away. The argument which David used for the pardoning of his sin could only be prevalent with God; "Pardon my sin, for it is great," Psal. xxv. 11. There is infinitely a greater disproportion between the blood of Christ and the greatest number of greatest sins, than between the smallest pebble and the ocean.

Obs. 7. The toleration of some places of uncleanness is no means to prevent the spreading of this sin. Sodom had liberty enough of sinning, but their lust increased with their liberty. The cause of Sodom's sin against nature was not the penury, but the ordinariness of fornication. Lust is insatiable and excessive, nor will any liberty seem enough to it; indulgence makes it insolent; it will not be persuaded by fair means, nor must this nettle be gently touched, but roughly handled and nipped, if we would not have it sting. If the flood-gate of restraint be pulled up, lust keeps no measure in its pouring forth: the more we grant to it, the more it will desire from us. To prevent sin by permitting it, is to quench fire with oil, to make the plaster of poison, and to throw out Satan by Satan. Improvident and impure is that remedy used in the papacy for preserving people chaste; I mean the toleration of places of uncleanness. But if the Roman pander may fill his own coffers with the tribute, he can be indulgent to sin.

In rebus humanis non peccat magistratus si meretricibus certum locum urbis incolendum attribuat, quamvis certo aciat eo loco ipsas non bene usuras. Potest enim permittere minus malum, ut majora impediantur. Bel. l. 2. de amis. gr. et stat. pec. c. 18.
Romana scorta in singulas hebdomadas Julium pendent pontifici, qui census annuus nonnunquam viginti millia ducatos excedit, adeoque ecclesiæ procerum id munus est, ut una cum ecclesiarum proventibus, etiam lenociniorum numerent mercedem. Agrip. de van. scient. c. 64.

Obs. 8. Corrupt nature delights in that which is strange to God's ordination. In the room of male and female, which was appointed by God, Sodomites go after strange flesh. Marriage was ordained by God, Gen. ii. 22, but nature being depraved forsakes that way, and embraces the forbidden bosom of a stranger, a strange woman not standing in the former relation, Prov. v. 20. The marriage of one man and one woman was the ordination of God; but instead thereof man's corruption has brought in polygamy. Nor is the depravation of man's nature less opposite to religious ordinations. God appointed that he alone should be worshipped, but corrupt nature puts man upon serving "strange gods," Jer. v. 19, called also "strange vanities," Jer. viii. 19. The true God has appointed the manner of his worship, and strictly forbids the offering of "strange incense," Exod. xxx. 9; but the same corruption which put the Sodomites upon following "strange flesh," puts Nadab and Abihu upon offering "strange fire," Numb. iii. 4. Man hath found out many, and goes a whoring after his own inventions, and delights only in deviating from God's way. The wicked go astray from the womb. How justly may our crooked natures be charged with what was unjustly imputed to the apostles; namely, the turning of the world upside down! All the breaches of ranks, all the confusions and disorders upon earth, proceed from our distempered hearts. How comely an order would there be upon the face of the whole world, if sin did not meddle!

Obs. 9. Little do they who allow themselves in sin know where they shall stop. Once over the shoes in this puddle, rarely will Satan leave till he have by degrees got them over head and ears. The modest beginnings of sin make way for the immodest and irrecoverable proceedings. The sin of the Sodomites, which began at the unclean motions of the heart, at length arise to a prodigious tallness of impudency and obstinacy. The smallest spark may be blown up to a flame; the flame upon the hearth may, if not quenched, fire the chimney. None provide so wisely for themselves as they who kill sin in the cradle. How easily do we proceed from one degree of sin to another; and how ordinarily does God punish one degree of sin with another! He who allows himself in speculative filthiness, may at length arrive at Sodomy. He who now gives way to sin, may shortly be given over to sin.

Obs. 10. Sinners prosecute their lusts most laboriously. The Sodomites weary and spend themselves in uncleanness, and painfully pull down a shower of fire and brimstone upon their heads. Ἐκπορνεύσασαι. Incomparably greater is the labour of sinners in damning, than of saints in saving themselves. The sinner is the only true drudge, sin the only true slavery, and therefore much greater than any other, because they who are in it delight to be so, and are angry with the offer of a release. Lusts are many and opposite, and yet one sinner must be servant to them all, and they all agree in rending and tearing the soul; they are cruel, instead of wages giving only wounds and scourges, and that to the tenderest part, the conscience. Nor does the body escape the tyranny of lust; envy, intemperance, wrath, luxury, have had more martyrs than ever had holiness. Such is the goodness of God, and the sweetness of his service, that it is beneficial even to the body; but through how many troubles and woes do wicked men pass to greater! Woeful had the life of a Sodomite been, though the fire and brimstone had never fallen. Great should be the grief of God's servants, that Satan's slaves should do more for him that will shed their blood, than they can do for Him who shed his blood for them; that the former should give themselves over to uncleanness, and the latter not more willingly yield themselves to the Lord.

Obs. 11. By viewing the odiousness of this sin in the Sodomites, it is our duty to avoid it ourselves. To this end,

(1.) Labour for a sorrowful sensibleness of that inward corruption of nature, from which alone arises the flame of uncleanness. Lay the foundation of mortification deep. Throw the water at the bottom of the flame, stop the fountain; the hating of some outward acts of this sin may exist without any abhorrence of that which is the principle and fountain thereof. David began at the right end, when he abhorred and confessed that poison wherewith his mother had warmed him in the womb, Psal. li. 5. Actual abomination comes from the natural pollution. Inbred concupiscence is the body; that outward is but a toe or a finger of that body. The inward dunghill, if unremoved, will steam forth into a thousand adulteries: till this be healed, thy cure will be but palliative, not eradicative. Tertullian holily derides the folly of the heathen Democritus, who, to prevent lust, would needs put out his eyes. The Christian, saith he, can safely look upon a woman, being mind-blind to lust. Lay thy mine under the foundation; silence that bosom orator which pleads for uncleanness. *Christianus salvis oculis fœminam videt; adversus libidinem cæcus est. Tert. Apol. c. 46.* The bird which gets loose from the stone or stick to which it is tied, if flying with the string about its leg, is entangled in the next bough. Though some courses of actual uncleanness be for the present escaped, yet if the entangling inclination be still entertained, it will insnare upon any after occasions and temptations.

(2.) Banish unclean contemplations and ideal uncleannesses. Cleanse the thoughts; stifle them when they begin to plod and plot, and contrive uncleanly; let not thy spirit be their thoroughfare: "Cleanse your hands, ye sinners," James iv. 8. Satan, when he inflames with lust, throws his fireballs into the thoughts. Fill these table-books with holy contemplations, that there may be no room in them for the impression of unclean injections.

(3.) Beware of plausible excuses for extenuating uncleanness. Abhor the aprons of fig-leaves, of nature, constitution, allurements, example. Look upon this sin as it is, not as it is coloured; behold it with Scripture spectacles; consider its true complexion under the falseness of paint; and contemplate it as tumbling in the mire of its own filthiness, and in the blood of thy precious soul.

(4.) Fear God. He who fears God can never find a place dark enough to offend. Joseph knew that all the favours of his Egyptian mistress, or of Egypt itself, could not buy off the guilt of this one sin. Dream not of impunity; "whoremongers and adulterers God will judge;" secrecy, power, can never carry it away from omniscience or omnipotence: what a silly shelter is closeness! Thou canst never shake off thy punishment, unless thy being, thyself. It is easy for God to make thee terrible to thyself, and thine own tormentor; yea, more desirous to utter thy sin openly for thine ease, than ever thou wast to act it secretly for thine honour.

(5.) Fear thyself; renounce all self-confidence, and venturousness upon thine own strength. The Lord is as truly the keeper of the heart as of the city. Rather fear than scorn snares, 1 Cor. x. 12. The best way never to fall is ever to fear.

(6.) Take heed of feeding the humour of lust. 1. Keep thyself from being fit ground or meet mould for the devil to cast in his seed; whether, 1. By gluttony; or, 2. By idleness: both these were Sodom's sins, Ezek. xvi. 49.

[I.] Gluttony, saith one, is the gallery that lechery goes through. Luxurious living, saith Jerom, quickly disposes a man to lust. Swine love not to tumble in dry dust, nor does the spirit of uncleanness delight in a body exercised to fasting: though the body is not to be starved, yet neither to be pampered; the body must be kept down, that lust grow not impertinent, 1 Cor. ix. 25. The right way to put out the fire of lust, is to withdraw the fuel of excess: a pampered horse is hard to rule; a servant delicately fed will be cheek-mate with his master; the flesh too much cherished will kick against the soul: keep under the beast by taking away the provender. *Venter est molestus cliens.* The stomach is an unpatient suitor; but having food and raiment, let us therewith be content. They who have taken the measure of man's throat, say it is less than in other creatures of answerable proportion, to teach us temperance. Satan chooses to enter into the greedy swine; Esau was a greedy eater and a fornicator. Looking upon the wine when it is red, and giving its colour in the cup, and looking upon strange women, are put together, Prov. xxiii. 31, 33. Paul allows even weak Timothy but a little wine, 1 Tim. v. 23.

[2.] Idleness, another of Sodom's sins, is also a feeder of uncleanness. Chambering, or lying in bed, is joined with wantonness, Rom. xiii. 13. Our sleep, saith Jerom, must not be the burial of one suffocated, but the rest of a wearied man. *Non sepultura suffocati, sed requies lassati. Hier.* The standing pool will gather filth, and be full of toads and vermin. Labour is a good remedy against lust. The same servant is called slothful and wicked, Matt. xxv. 26. Slow bellies are called evil beasts. Israel was safer in the brick-kilns of Egypt, than in the plains of Moab. Lust conquered good David, when he was idle and at ease. In troubles, when he prevented the morning watch, he was innocent and holy; but when Satan finds him indolent, he thinks him fit for a temptation. Lust can be no stranger to an idle bosom. While we work not ourselves, Satan works on us. The sitting bird is the fowler's mark. The heavens that are ever in motion are always pure. By how much the greater I am, (saith one,) by so much the more I labour; by how much the more I labour, by so much the greater I am. *Quo major sum, magis laboro; et quo magis laboro, major sum.*

(2.) As we must keep ourselves from being meet mould or fit ground for the devil to cast in this seed of lust, so must we also beware of those objects and allurements which water concupiscence. Set a watch before thy senses. The sons of God looked on and lusted after the daughters of men, Gen. vi. 2. The eye of David and Joseph's mistress led their hearts, 2 Sam. xi. 2. Thamar desiring to be unclean with Judah, "sat," as we translate it, "in an open place;" but it is in the Hebrew, "in the door of the eyes," Gen. xxxviii. 14. Sin gets in at the senses, like the wind at the crevice. The order of sin is the same with that of Achan; I saw, I coveted, and took. Looking upon a woman and lusting after her are put together, Matt. v. 28; and we read, 2 Pet. ii. 14, of "eyes full of adultery," or the adulteress. *Tu otiose spectas, otiose non spectaris. Tu spectas curiose, spectaris curiosius. Bern.* But willingly neither be nor behold a provocation of sin. God will preserve thee in thy ways, not in thy wanderings. Dinah was not safe out of the woman's orb, the house: only to see is not sufficient warrant to draw us to the suspected places. What wise man will go to a house infected with the plague only to see the fits of the visited? It is good to keep temptation at the stave's end, and not to let it into the grapple; for though possibly we may fight and conquer, yet it was our fault that we were put to fight. The project of Balaam was too prosperous; had the Moabites sent their strongest soldiers to persuade the Israelites to idolatry, they had been returned with contempt: but as God fetches glory to himself out of the worst actions of men, so men often undo themselves by the fairest works of God.

Thus far of the second particular considerable in this example of Sodom, viz. the cause of their punishment. Now follows,

III. The severity of their punishment, their "suffering the vengeance of everlasting fire."

The punishment being set out, 1. More generally; so it is called "vengeance."

2. More particularly; so it was a vengeance manifested by "eternal fire;" wherein is considerable,

(1.) By what they were punished; by "fire."

(2.) In what measure or how long they were punished; the fire is "eternal."

I shall here inquire what we are to understand by "vengeance," and the fire here called "eternal."

1. The word δίκη, here translated vengeance, is of a signification belonging to the proceedings of courts of justice; and it is taken several ways. (1.) Properly it signifies right or justice; in which respect, among the heathens, the goddess of just vengeance, Nemesis, was called δίκη, justice, or vengeance, Acts xxviii. 4: "No doubt," say the barbarians of Paul, "this man is a murderer, whom, though he hath escaped the sea, yet ἡ δίκη, vengeance suffereth not to live." (2.) It is taken for the sentence of condemnation given by the judge, as Acts xxv. 15, where it is said that "the chief priests and elders desired to have δίκη, judgment, against Paul." (3.) For the punishment itself inflicted after the passing of sentence: thus, 2 Thess. i. 9, the apostle saith the wicked shall be punished, δίκην τίσουσι: and thus it is taken in this place by Jude, who fitly expresses the punishment inflicted by God upon the Sodomites by this word, because it was most justly, and according to the merit of the offence and offenders, executed by the Judge of all the world, who is righteous in all he brings upon sinners; yea, is righteousness itself; whose very judgments, even because they are his, are just and righteous. And as to the case of Sodom and Gomorrha, so eminent was the righteousness of God's judicial proceeding, that he would go down to see whether they had done altogether according to the cry of their sin, Gen. xviii. 21; where he speaks after the manner of men, who ought not to condemn any before an accurate examination of the cause. But of this, by occasion of the words (judgment, and the great day) much hath been spoken in the foregoing verse.

Non dubito quin sicut plurimis locis κρίνω accipitur pro κατακρίνω, et κρίσις pro κατάκρισις: sic etiam δίκη ponatur hoc loco, pro καταδίκη. Bez. in Act. xxv. Δίκη comprehendit seriem totam judicii, usque ad executionem. Lorin. in Act. xxv.

2. The fire wherewith these Sodomites were punished.

They burnt with a threefold fire. (1.) The fire of lust (both sin and punishment). They burned in their lust one toward another, and God gave them up to uncleanness, and to vile affections, 1 Cor. vii. 9; Rom. i. 27.

(2.) The fire which was rained down from heaven upon them, Gen. xix. 24, the remarkableness of which punishment by fire appears in sundry respects. It was, [1.] A miraculous fire, out of the course of nature. Brimstone, to which some add salt, and all that vast quantity of fiery matter, were never produced by natural causes; God it was who provided the matter for so great a flame, the fall whereof also he ordered for time and place. Hence it is said that the Lord rained brimstone and fire from the Lord; that is, by an elegant Hebraism, from himself, the noun being put in the place of the pronoun, as 1 Sam. xv. 22; 1 Kings viii. 1; 2 Tim. i. 18, &c., to show that the raining there mentioned was not from the strength of natural causes, nor after a natural manner, but immediately from the Lord himself, and by the putting forth of his own omnipotent arm. [2.] It was an abundant fire, of a vast quantity; and hence it is said to be rained down; it was not a sprinkling, but a shower; here were not sparks, but flakes, sheets of fire, rivers of brimstone. [3.] It was a sudden fire. It came not by degrees; when the morning arose, or at break of day, there were no tidings of destruction; till then Lot was in Sodom; and yet when the sun arose, fire was rained down; and early in the morning Abraham beheld the smoke of the country, Gen. xix. 24, 28; perhaps the work was done in a quarter of an hour: "Sodom was overthrown as in a moment," Lam. iv. 6. [4.] It was a tormenting fire. The execution by fire has ever been accounted one of the most afflictive to sense, and therefore imposed upon the greatest offenders. How great is the torment when the skin is puckered, the sinews cracked, the blood scalded! Famine, the greatest of punishments, is but a kind of fire, whereby the natural moisture is dried up; nay, fire lends a resemblance to the torments of hell. [5.] It was a destructive fire, utterly consuming all upon which it fell; cities, inhabitants, the plain, and all that grew upon it, Gen. xix. 25; and, as Brochardus reports, so far as the vapour arising out of the lake of Sodom is carried by the wind, it makes all places dry and barren, destroying all fruits, grass, plants, and whatever the earth yields, Deut. xxix. 23. And so poisonous is that brimstone lake which is now in the place where Sodom stood, that it is called the Dead Sea, having neither fish nor any living creature therein. And this is confirmed by the prophet, who foretelling how these waters should be healed by the waters running out of the sanctuary eastward, on which side this lake is situate, and that then the creatures should live therein, that there should be a multitude of fish, and that the fishers should stand upon it from Engedi even unto Eneglaim, the two cities at either end of the lake, hereby implies, that for the present, before this healing, the waters were dead, that no fish nor any creatures lived therein, and that no fishermen frequented the same, as they did the lake of Gennesareth and other places through which the river Jordan run, Ezek. xlvii. 8. [6.] The punishment by this fire is lasting, everlasting, a standing monument of God's displeasure; in Moses' time it was so, Deut. xxix., and the Lord never repented him of this overthrow. It is under a perpetual destruction, recorded by authors of great credit and reputation, and it shall continue as long as the world shall last, or there shall be any time or age; in allusion whereunto, when the enemies of the church are destroyed, it is foretold that their "land shall become burning pitch. It shall not be quenched night nor day, the smoke thereof shall go up for ever."

Called also the salt sea, John iii. 16.

Olet adhuc incendio terra. Tert. Apol. c. 40. Perpetuo poenas luere videtur. Brocard. 1. p. c. 7.

Strabo, Solinus, Tacitus, Josephus Plinius, Tertul. c 40, Augustin de C. D. c. 21, Adrichomius, Brochardus.

His verbis significatur quod praeter naturalem rerum cursum, miraculum operatus est, ponendo iniquos; ad differentiam enim naturalium casuarum materiali ordine occurrentium ad generandum sulphur et ignem, adjunctum est illud a Jehova. Cajetan. Sic quoque Perer. Calv. Musc. Rivet, &c.

(3.) The fire of hell; and this (some think) the apostle only here intends, because he calls it eternal fire. I acknowledge that these Sodomites were punished with the eternal fire of hell. God's dealing with some infants or aged I dare not determine; but it is sure their children were part of their parents' enjoyments, by nature the children of wrath, and that God is an absolute Lord; and the Lord saith concerning Sodom remarkably, I took them away as I thought good, Ezek. xvi. 50. Christ saith "it shall be more tolerable for Sodom and Gomorrha in the day of judgment than for Chorazin," &c.; but a more tolerable condition in regard of degrees, takes not away, but implies the kind of the condition: the temporal punishment of the impenitent Sodomites was but a degree to the eternal, and in regard of the suddenness of their destruction, they might want time of repentance. Notwithstanding all which, with submission to better judgments, I conceive that the apostle does not in this place intend primarily, much less solely, the destruction of these Sodomites by hell-fire. Inclusively and secondarily I suppose he does, as the fire of hell was typified by that which fell upon them from heaven. Nor do I clearly understand how these cities can be set forth as an example to sinners by suffering the punishment of hell-fire, when of that the history of Genesis does not speak at all, and the example (saith Estius) should be taken from the history, which sinners may read and hear. And although it is said the fire wherewith these Sodomites were punished was eternal, yet is it not necessarily to be understood of hell-fire; for even that fire which consumed these cities may be called eternal, [1.] Because the punishment by this fire is irreparable, to last to the end of the world, these cities being never to be restored; and in this sense eternal is often taken in Scripture, where we read of the eternal hills, Deut. xxxiii. 15; perpetual desolations, Psal. lxxiv. 3; that the land of Canaan was given to the seed of Abraham for an everlasting habitation, Gen. xvii. 8, and for ever, Gen. xiii. 15; that the Levitical ceremonies are for ever, Lev. vi. 22; Heb. v. 6; vii. 17. [2.] Because these cities suffering the punishment of fire and brimstone described in Génesis are a type or figure of everlasting fire, and of the eternal punishment of wicked men therein. And this some learned men seem to make good out of the text, reading these words, as referring eternal fire to example, thus, "are set forth for an example of eternal fire, suffering vengeance;" not as our translators do, who refer eternal fire to vengeance, thus, "are set forth for an example, suffering the vengeance of eternal fire:" by which construction they gather, that the fire which irreparably has destroyed Sodom, was a figure or type of that eternal fire reserved for wicked men in hell, and by which sinners ought to be warned. And, as learned Paget, in his treatise called Meditations of Death, observes, hell is denominated from the similitude of this place, The lake of fire burning with brimstone. And of the great whore it is said, "Her smoke rose up for ever and ever." "And God," saith he, "has made a visible hell in that great lake which had once been a pleasant plain." And Brochardus, who spent ten years in viewing the country, saith, "That the Dead Sea is always black, smoking, and the very face of hell."

Nor yet do I conceive, because in these words "eternal fire" Jude may also include the punishment of the Sodomites in hell-fire, that therefore they are there tormented with material or bodily fire: it is sufficient that the torments of the damned are set out by the pains of fire, than which no creature is accounted by men more tormenting; so that undoubtedly they are unconceivably greater, and more exquisite, than are any which can be caused by material fire; and they are more tormenting in sundry respects. Hell-fire burns the soul; Christ bids us fear none but soul torments, Matt. x. 28; and, indeed, if we can bear them least, we should fear them most. Hell-fire, though it burns, yet it consumes not; the wicked shall be its perpetual fuel, and it shall be a living death preying upon them, not making an end of them. Hell-fire cannot, as ours, be relieving or refreshing; they who are in it shall never say, "Aha, I have seen the fire," Isa. xliv. 16; but, Oh, " I am tormented in this flame," Luke xvi. 24. Hell-fire is blown, not as ours, by the breath of man, or any other created blast, but by God himself, whose breath is both the fire and a stream of brimstone, Isa. xxx. 33, and the bellows. A powerful God powerfully punishes; as is he, so is his strength. How unsupportable must needs be the pains inflicted by angry Omnipotence! Hell-fire cannot be extinguished, Matt. xxv. 41, 46; nor tears nor time can put it out. The many thousands of years that the effect of Sodom's fire lasts upon earth, are but a faint resemblance of the true everlastingness of hell-fire. Nor yet is God unjust in punishing those eternally who have sinned but a little time: he measures the punishment by the greatness of the offence, not by the time of doing the crime. Treason or murder may be committed in an instant, but the punishment may last for scores of years; nay, when men punish by death, there is a removing of the malefactor from the society of men for ever: and if the offence committed against God be infinitely heinous, why may not the punishment be infinitely lasting? besides, how ordinarily do men sell away their possessions by bargain, or refuse an offered gift in a moment, which thereby they part with for ever! and how justly are sinners deprived of true blessedness, (and that is not less than eternal,) which in a short time they refused and sold away for the satisfying of their lusts! Nor can it be unjust with God to punish those in his eternity who have sinned against him in theirs, who, if they had to eternity been allowed to live, would have improved it altogether in sin; yea, and who dispositively, and in respect of their inclination, did so.

Obs. 1. The sin of uncleanness is remarkably followed with vengeance. As pleasure is that which the unclean mainly expect, and which this lust principally promises, so woes and pains are afterward by God constantly inflicted: fornication and vengeance are by Jude joined together.

(I.) Spiritual vengeance attends upon this sin. It *insnares* and captivates the soul; God oft justly saith to the lovers thereof, "He that is filthy, let him be filthy still." It is both an inlet to all impiety in the world, (a lustful man hesitating at no sin that may bring him to enjoy his impure pleasure,) and also a lust which so binds down a sinner, ingulfs him in, and engages him so deeply to the love of itself, that notwithstanding the longer he lives in it the more he is afflicted and weakened by it, yet the more unable and unwilling he is to leave it: it lies down with sinners in the dust. Seldom is this sin found in the way of repentance: "A whore is a deep ditch," Prov. xxiii. 27. Few are the foot-prints of returners from this den, and they too have escaped very narrowly. Instead of repentance, it labours concealment; and men rather study to hide it than to turn it out of doors; to cover it with a rag of secrecy, than to cure with the plaster of repentance. Nor doth this sin less *disquiet* than captivate; it wastes both the strength of the body and the peace of the conscience: its pleasures are short, its terrors are lasting: by how much the sweeter Satan makes it in the mouth, by so much the more bitter God makes it in the stomach. The fall into this sin brake David's bones, Psal. li. 8; the deep impression of its stain, and the communicativeness of its guilt and defilement to others, are standing troubles to the conscience, when once it is awakened.

(2.) This sin is pursued with external vengeance.

1. Upon the name; a dishonour is gotten, and a reproach that shall not be wiped away, Prov. vi. 33. Though the sore may be healed, yet the scar abides, although repentance should be the plaster. Though Samson and Solomon were pardoned, as to their own execution, yet were they burnt in the hand, and branded in the forehead, for a warning to others. Such was the hatred of God against this sin, that God hath not left it a blank, but a blemish, in David's story; nay, so deep was the spot of dishonour which cleaved to this sin, that the bastard issue of the adulterer was shut out from the congregation to the tenth generation, Deut. xxiii. 2. 2. Upon the body. It makes a man the devil's martyr. This sin is the seed of diseases; and though it loves to lie hid in the shop, yet the distempers bewray it which are laid in open view upon the stall. The noisome breath, the unclean botches, the inflamed blood, the consumed flesh, Prov. v. 11, the speedy age, the short life, of many, are some of the most favourable productions of carnal uncleanness. The penalty inflicted by the law of God upon adultery was death by stoning, as it is generally thought; and for some other excesses in this sin, death by burning, Lev. xx. 10; Deut. xxii. 22. The woman suspected of adultery, drinking those waters of jealousy which (if she were guilty) plagued her with the rotting of her belly and thigh, was a clear testimony of the heinousness of this sin, Numb. v. 27; and if these instances suffice not, remember the death of twenty-four thousand Israelites at Peor. 3. Upon the estate. Lust is a flame that has burnt down whole families, cities; it spoiled David's posterity of the greatest part of his kingdom; it gives rags for its livery; and though it be furthered by the fulness, yet it is followed with a morsel, of bread, Prov. v. 10; vi. 26. It is a fire (saith Job) that consumes to destruction, and roots up all increase, Job xxxi. 12. It is a secret canker and moth in the substance of the wealthiest: witness the destruction of many noble families and irreligious houses in England.

(3.) Eternal vengeance follows this sin. Whoremongers and adulterers God himself will judge, Heb. xiii. 4. God returns flames for flames, and revenges the hell of this fire in the heart with the fire of hell. The strange woman lodgeth her guests in the depths of hell, Prov. ix. 18. Nor shall dogs be admitted into the new Jerusalem, nor the unholy see the face of God, Rev. xxii. 15. How great then is their sin who account this carnal uncleanness no sin; who drink down this pleasant poison of stolen waters, and never think of its certain operation; and throwing this firebrand into their beds, their bodies, families, revenues, say they are in sport! What prodigious heaven-daring impudence is it to glory in this both sin and shame! What are those bold enticers to it, by paint, speeches, naked breasts, (fire and brimstone shall one day cover them,) but the devil's decoys, the emissaries and factors of hell, the stratagems of Satan, the increasers of transgressors? Prov. xxiii. 28. Let it be too much for Rome to suffer it to set open shop by toleration: why do we punish the stealing of a piece of silver with death, if we connive at these whose theft flies higher, even at estate, health, honour, life, nay, the soul itself? In brief, how nearly does it concern those who have burnt in these impure flames of uncleanness, and thereby have also kindled the flames of God's wrath, to labour to cool and quench them with the blood of Jesus Christ, which alone can allay the heats of sin in them, and wrath in God; as also to cast their tears of godly sorrow into the flame; because they have not been pure-hearted Josephs, to become broken-hearted Davids! while for the future they carefully avoid all those objects whereby their lust has too frequently been, and is too forward again to be inflamed.

Obs. 2. God punishes sinners in a way of judiciary process, even with the greatest equity and righteousness. His vengeance even upon Sodom was δίκη, a vengeance of justice. In his proceedings with our first parents after their sin, as also with Cain and the Babel-builders, first he accurately examines and inquires into the fact, and afterwards he pronounceth sentence, Gen. iv.; xi. 1—9. As the word "vengeance," here used by Jude, has righteousness included in its signification; so in the work of vengeance, as related in Genesis, righteousness is as openly displayed as wrath. The cry of Sodom's sin was no uncertain rumour, requiring that God should go down and see, for his better information, whether they had done altogether according to the cry thereof, Gen. xviii. 21. He who knew the secret sins of the heart, could not be ignorant of the proclaimed sins of Sodom; nor was any proper descension consistent with his omnipresence, nor information with his omniscience; but hereby he would become exemplary to judges, who ought to take heed of their precipitancy in judgment, and never proceed to condemnation without accurate examination. In Sodom's punishment there was a map of hell, a sea of wrath, not a drop of injustice. Sin can make God angry, not unrighteous; though sometimes he may destroy his creatures, yet never deny himself. How contented should this make us to be under the smartest providences! A gracious heart will justify God when God sentences him. "Thou art just" (saith Nehemiah) "in all that thou hast brought upon us; for thou hast done right, and we have done wickedly," Neh. ix. 33. That we are spared, it is mercy; that we are punished, cannot be injustice. Could we have harder thoughts of sin, our thoughts of God's dealing would be more honourable.

Obs. 3. Great is the patience and long-suffering of God even toward great sinners. God overthrew not Sodom till they gave themselves over to fornication; till they were impudent in sin, and it became crying: God did not show that he heard it till they proclaimed it to every one. He puts not his sickle into Sodom till it was ripe. He goes down to see "whether they had done altogether according to the cry of it;" altogether, or, as the Hebrew has it, whether they had made a consummation, i. e. whether their iniquities were full; God hereby showing his purpose to spare them till it was so. He loves to clear his justice before man, as well as to execute it upon man: he shows how mercy pleases him, even when he puts forth justice. There is no judging of God's love by our impunity, or having the space without the grace of repentance. God bears with the wicked, but yet not that they may be so. The longer the sinner is spared, the more the sin is aggravated. Sinners are beholden to God for their being spared so long, to themselves for their being spared no longer. Unless Sodom's sin had cried importunately, God had not answered it. Even by this expression of the crying of sin (saith Salvian) God shows how unwilling he is to punish sinners; and that mercy persuades him to spare them, did not the cry of sin constrain him to punish them. Misericordia mea mihi suadet ut parcam, sed tamen peccatorum clamor cogit ut puniam. Sal. de Prov. l. 1.

Obs. 4. The justice of God is not abolished by his mercy. So good was God in his gracious condescension even to the lowest step of Abraham's request for Sodom, to such a measure did God suffer the sin of unpunished Sodom to swell, that justice seemed to be laid aside; but though it had woollen and leaden, silent and slow feet, yet had it also iron hands, which at length the Sodomites felt to their cost. Justice may be dormant, and yet not cease to be; it may be said of it, as once Christ did of Lazarus, It is not dead, but sleepeth. God is long-suffering, not ever suffering. The rising of the sun in the morning was no sign that fire and brimstone should not fall upon Sodom before the evening. God's forbearance to strike shows not that he will always spare, but that we should now repent. If we will sin by his long-suffering, we shall smart by his severity. "These things hast thou done, and I kept silence; and thou thoughtest I was altogether such an one as thyself; but I will reprove thee," &c., Psal. l. 21. When God comes to exact the punishment, he will require interest for his forbearance; and indeed God is never more angry than when he suffers men to go on securely and uninterrupted in sin by sparing them. Let not the indulgence of God make us presume, but let us understand the language of love, that we may not undergo the load of his wrath. These Sodomites, notwithstanding their sin, were so securely asleep in their delights of eating, drinking, buying, selling, planting, building, Luke xvii. 28, that nothing could awaken them but the fire which destroyed them. This point should also be improved for imitation. To spare all offenders is cruelty, equal to a sparing of none. Asher's foot was dipped in oil, yet his shoes were iron and brass, Deut. xxxiii. 24, 25.

Obs. 5. Nothing is so dreadful as the wrath of God. Sodom's fire and brimstone showered down in a sweeping and overwhelming plenty, are but shadows of the wrath of God incensed. "Our God is a consuming fire," Heb. xii. 29; his wrath is the fire, yea, the very hell of hell. When God Almighty sets himself to torment, and to show what he is able to do against a worm; God, (I say,) who can marshal and draw into a body all the forces of the creation together, and then can draw forth all their virtue and vigour, and, which is more, set on every degree of that force and vigour according to the strength of his own all-powerful arm, yea, and create infinitely more and greater torments than we can either oppose or apprehend; how sorely, how unsupportably, shall his wrath rack and torment the creature! How great and how inexcusable is the stupidity of every sinner! The fire on earth is but painted and imaginary, in comparison of God's wrath. If he who cries Fire, fire, at midnight, at once both wakens and affrights us, how amazingly should they affect us who know and denounce the terror of the Lord! Who knoweth the power of his anger? even according to his fear, so is his wrath, Psal. xc. 11. What interest have we in the world comparable to that of making him our friend in Christ? he is the severest enemy, but the sweetest friend: "When his wrath is kindled but a little, blessed are all they that put their trust in him," Psal. ii. 12. Greater is the disproportion between the pleasure and pains of sin, than between a drop of honey and an ocean of gall. Consider, O sinner, when thou art bathing thy soul in the fire of lust, how thy soul shall burn in the flames of hell; and remember that fire and brimstone lie under the skin of every Sodomitical apple, and are in the belly of every lust. Meditate, O saint, of the love of Christ in delivering thee from this eternal fire, this wrath to come, in becoming a screen between that flame and thy soul, in cooling thee, though by scorching himself. To conclude this, if he has delivered us from this eternal, how patiently should we endure any trying fire, and how cool should we account the hottest service in which God employs us in this life! All is mercy besides hell. And how should we pity and pull back those who are posting, and that laboriously, toward these pains of eternal fire!

Obs. 6. God's anger changes the use of the creatures; it turns helps into plagues. The fire which God appointed to warm and purify, shall, if God be our enemy, consume and burn us to ashes; the air shall poison us; our houses shall be prisons to keep us for execution by flames; the sun shall hold, or rather be, the candle to give light to our slaughter, as in Joshua's time; the earth, which should bear, shall devour us; the seas, which serve for conveyance, shall swallow us up; the stars, which at some times are sweetly influential, shall, if God be angry, fight in their courses against Sisera; the heavens, which are wont to afford their fruitful drops, shall shower down fire and brimstone, and by both barrenness. The most useful creatures of God, if he bid them, shall go upon errands of destruction, in obedience to their Commander-in-chief, who can commission and empower for services of severity and revenge, not only his chief officers, the glorious angels, but even his common soldiers, the poorest of creatures. If he be our foe, even those shall hurt us from whom we have formerly received and now expect most friendship. Our greatest comforts shall become our greatest crosses. The wife of the bosom, the children that came out of our loins, may become our butchers and traitors; yea, God can make ourselves our own deadliest enemies. Let none be secure in their freedom from enemies till God be their friend; nor in the multitude of friends, so long as God is their enemy. God can punish unexpectedly, even such a way as we never dream of. Jerusalem, saith the prophet, "came down wonderfully," Lam. i. 9; and what Sodomite ever heard before of a shower of fire? but unheard-of sins procure unheard-of punishments.

Obs. 7. Most heinous is the sin of contempt of the gospel. These Sodomites were sinners and sufferers even to amazement. Sodom was a hell for sin, and typically a hell for punishment; and yet Christ saith, "It shall be more tolerable for the land of Sodom and Gomorrha in the day of judgment, than for the city" which is guilty of this sin, Matt. x. 15. Unbelief is worse than Sodomy. Of all sins, gospel sins damn most unavoidably. The pollutions of Sodom defile not so deeply as doth the refusing of that blood which should cleanse us. How dangerous is the condition of that man who, pleasing himself in a civil conversation and freedom from those sins which bring him within the compass of man's law, allows himself in that one which concludes him under the curse of the law of God!

Obs. 8. God often proportions the punishment to the sin. Sodom's sin was against the light and use, their punishment against the course, of nature; they fetch up hell to the earth, and God sends hell out of heaven. Their sin was notorious, and proclaimed in the face of the sun; their punishment was, nay, yet is, visible to all the world. Their sin was universal, and the raining of "fire and brimstone," saith Christ, "destroyed them all," Luke xvii. 29. Their sin was a flame of lust, and their punishment a flame of fire, Exod. xxi. 24. Their sin was filthy, not, without abominating it, to be named; their punishment, as by fire, so by brimstone, was so unsavoury to the smell as not to be endured. How happy were it for us, if, as our sins lead God to inflict such a kind of punishment, so that punishment may lead us back again to find out the sin! But of this before, ver. 5.

Obs. 9. Great is God's care of man's safety and human society. How angry was God with the Sodomites for a sin committed against their own bodies, and the honour of one another! God has appointed and executed punishments for and upon any that shall abuse poor sinful man; and with whom is God so angry as with those who hurt themselves most? How strong a hedge has he set about man's welfare in his ten commandments! in them he distinctly provides for man's authority, life, chastity, estate, name, and generally in them all for his soul. All the rebellions, murders, rapes, oppression, defamations, &c. in the world, whereby men suffer from men, are from hence, that God is not obeyed by men; and all the violences among men proceed from the violation of the law of God, which, were it observed, what a face of calmness and comeliness would be upon the whole earth! God is infinitely better to us than we are to ourselves, to one another. How observable is the difference between those places where the fear of God sways and others, even in respect of civil, comely, and honest behaviour! To conclude, though God might have enjoined us the worshipping and serving of himself, without any regard to our own benefit, yet such is his love to man, that as no command hinders, so most are intended for the furthering of man's outward welfare. How strong an engagement lies upon us to be studious of giving him that honour which we owe, who is so careful to make that provision for us which he owes us not!

Thus far of the third particular, the severity of the punishment inflicted upon the Sodomites, viz. "the vengeance of eternal fire."

IV. The end and use of that punishment, in these words, "are set forth for an example."

Two things must here be explained.

1. What kind of example these Sodomites were set forth to be.

2. Why any example of this kind was thus set forth.

For the first. The word example in the Greek is δεῖγμα, and it signifies not only that which is openly shown, and pointed at, Mark xiv. 15; John ii. 18, and exactly to be observed; as Matt. viii. 4, Christ commanded the leper, whom he had cleansed, to go and show himself to the priest; so Mark i. 44; Luke v. 14. But also a showing by way of exposing to open infamy and disgrace; and thus it is said, that Christ "having spoiled principalities and powers, ἐδειγμάτισε, made a show of them openly;" where the word signifies, saith Zanchy, a leading, a showing them in the public view of all spectators, to their perpetual infamy, as captives were wont to be led with their hands tied behind them; the compound word παραδειγματίζω signifying to set an offender before others as a public spectacle of shame and infamy, for the warning of all the beholders; in which sense this word δεῖγμα is to be taken in this place, as also is that word ὑπόδειγμα, used in 1 Pet. ii. 6, parallel with this of Jude, and translated also example; it also signifying the setting before the eye, or subjecting something to a man's view or sight, not only for caution and warning, (saith Gerhard,) as in that place of Peter, but even for imitation also, as John xiii. 15; James v. 10; and sometimes it signifies a type or figure of something, as Heb. viii. 5; ix. 23.

Δεικνύω sive δείκνυμι, ostendo, indico. Δειγματίζω, Traduco palam, ostento. Col. ii. 15. Significat aliquem, per publicum coetum spectantium, ducere, sicut olim Romani victores, hostes victos, manibus retro devinctis, in conspectum hominum, ad perpetuam illorum ignominiam ducere solebant. Significat spectandum omnibus proponere. Vide Laurent. in 2 Pet. ii.

These punished Sodomites, then, were set forth for an example, not of imitation, their courses thus described and punished requiring rather our detestation; nor, therefore, of God's mercy and compassion, as Paul saith of himself, that in him Jesus Christ showed forth all long-suffering πρὸς ὑποτύπωσιν, for a pattern and example to them who should hereafter believe.

But, (1.) For an example, by way of pattern, type, and figure of those who are tormented in hell with fire truly eternal, in which respect some read the text not with a comma after the word δεῖγμα, example, as our translators and most interpreters do, who read the words thus, "are set forth for an example, suffering the vengeance," &c.; but with a comma after the word fire, thus, are set forth for an example or figure of everlasting fire, suffering vengeance: though when I consider that parallel place in Peter, where it is said that they are made an example to those that afterwards should live ungodly, I conceive we should rather keep the ordinary reading, viz. are made "an example, suffering," &c. It is nevertheless plain, from what was said before, that the fire wherewith the Sodomites were punished was a type of hell-fire, and that the Sodomites are set forth as punished with fire from heaven, that they who afterward should live ungodly might be cautioned and warned to shun that eternal fire in hell, whereof the Sodomitical fire was a type. And therefore,

Ipsa verba, πρόκεινται δεῖγμα πυρὸς αἰωνίου δίκην ὑπέχουσαι, vel legi possunt cum commate post vocem δείγμα, ut sit sensus, propositæ sunt exemplo; vel cum commate post vocem αἰωνίου, propositæ sunt exemplo ignis eterni: prior tamen lectio magis congruit cum loco Petri, et communiter prohatur interpretibus. Laur. in 2 Pet. ii.

(2.) And principally, these Sodomites were set forth as an example of caution, warning, or admonition, that sinners for time to come might, by their plague, take heed of their sin. The philosophers of old (as Gellius saith) thought there were three causes of punishing offences. *Noct. Attic. l. 6. c. 14.*

1. That which is called νουθεσία, when punishment was inflicted for the amendment of the party punished for the time to come. The second they called τιμωρία, when any were punished for the preservation of the honour of him against whom the offence was committed, lest indulgence should occasion contempt of his dignity. The third they called παράδειγμα, when an offender was punished for example sake, that so others might be deterred from the like practice: this was the end (here mentioned by Jude, and before by Peter) of the judgment of these Sodomites; God dealing with them as a judge with some notorious murderer, whom he sentences to hang in chains by the way-side, to warn others by his suffering; or as a pilferer or thief is set forth upon the pillory in some public place of the city, with his crime written and pinned upon his breast. And that in this punishment of Sodom God intended a special example of caution seems evident, because no one judgment of God upon sinners is so frequently in Scripture recalled to the minds of sinners as this, repeated even above twenty times; is also because God has made the signs and effects of Sodom's overthrow to continue to this very day, as historians unanimously report, as if he intended the laying forth or public placing of this standing monument of his wrath before the eyes of men as a warning to all the world, Deut. xxix. 23; xxxii. 32; Isa. i. 9; xiii. 19; Jer. xxiii. 14; xlix. 18; l. 40; Lam. iv. 6; Ezek. xvi. 46; Hos. xi. 8; Amos iv. 11; Zeph. ii. 9; Matt. x. 15; xi. 23, 24; Luke x. 12; xvii. 29; Rom. ix. 29. Nor are these examples of caution strange in Scripture. "Go ye now unto my place which was in Shiloh," (saith God unto the Jews,) "where I set my name at the first, and see what I did to it for the wickedness of my people Israel." God commands, Deut. xiii. 10, that the enticer to idolatry should be put to death, to which he immediately subjoins, in ver. 11, "And all Israel shall hear, and fear, and do no more such wickedness as this is among you." And the apostle tells the Corinthians that the destructions of the Israelites in the wilderness happened unto them "for ensamples; and they are written" (saith he) "for our admonition, upon whom the ends of the world are come," 1 Cor. x. 11. "And these things were our examples, to the intent that we should not lust after evil things, as they also lusted," 1 Cor. x. 6; and he warneth the

Hebrews to take heed of falling "after the same example of unbelief," Heb. iv. 11; as likewise doth Christ his disciples by remembering Lot's wife, Luke xvii. 32.

2. Why the Lord would show forth such an example of caution. Hereby he would show,

(1.) Our natural forwardness to sin in like manner. He who saith, Take heed of such a practice, shows a likelihood, without care, of doing the very same. The natural inclination of our hearts answers to that of the greatest sinners, as face answers face in the glass. Their practices are but expositions upon our natures. It is a proverb, What fools speak, wise men think; I am sure it is a truth, To that which the worst man acts, the heart of the best man, without grace, inclines. And though the godly are not companions with the wicked in sin, yet should they be humble for the very sinning of the wicked.

(2.) His constant abhorrence of sin. Examples of caution speak both God's hatred of the sin of those who went before, whose punishments are the monuments of his vengeance, as also his equal dislike of it in those who succeed, against whom (if they will sin) he is prepared to do what he has done against the former. Though God's forbearance towards some shows that sometimes he can spare sinners, yet his punishing others shows that he never loves sin.

(3.) The aptitude of examples to prevent sin. Greater is our forwardness to be affected with what we see executed, than with what we hear denounced: "My eye," saith the prophet, "affecteth mine heart." Examples, either of imitation or caution, work more on us than doctrines. The rod has a louder voice than the word; a man's word will not be so soon taken as his hand and seal: God has not only set seals to his promises, but to his threatenings also; and such seals as are examples. "Israel saw that great work which the Lord did upon the Egyptians; and the people feared the Lord, and believed," Exod. xiv. 31. "When thy judgments are in the earth, the inhabitants of the world will learn righteousness," Isa. xxvi. 9. "When a scorner is punished," saith Solomon, "the simple is made wise," Prov. xxi. 11. At the death of Ananias and Sapphira "great fear came upon all the church," Acts v. 11. "If one went from the dead," said that tormented glutton, "they will repent," Luke xvi. 30.

(4.) His merciful willingness to prevent our ruin. The Lord gives us to see, that so we may not be examples; and lets us read the stories of others, that so we may not be stories to others. Such is the goodness of God, that he had rather we should be driven away from than destroyed in sin. Oft does God recall to the minds of Israel the sins and punishments of their forefathers, and his plagues upon the Egyptians. It had been as easy for God to have destroyed them with as warned them by others, had not mercy pleased him. *Quot vulnera, tot ora;* every wound of another is a mouth that calls upon us to repent.

(5.) The inexcusableness of sinning after setting examples before us. This was the great aggravation of Belshazzar's pride, that he humbled not his heart, though he knew the judgment which God had laid upon his father for the very sin of pride, Dan. v. 22. Thus likewise the prophet heightens the impiety of Judah, in that notwithstanding Judah saw the idolatry which Israel had committed against God, and what judgments God had laid upon Israel, yet "Judah feared not, but went and played the harlot also." How just is God in hitting those to whom he had said before, Stand off! They who sin against examples sin presumptuously, and even to a contempt of all God's attributes, his immutability, power, righteousness, long-suffering, &c. They cannot sin at so cheap a rate as those who never were warned. He who will ride into the depth of the river, notwithstanding the stake, deserves irrecoverably to be drowned. That thief offends obstinately, who will rob in that place where his fellow hangs in chains.

Obs. 1. The works of God, especially his judgments, have a language as well as his word. Examples of judgment are visible sermons, and speak the pleasure of God. When God forbears to punish, he is said to keep silence. "Then shall he speak unto them in his wrath," saith the psalmist, "and vex them in his sore displeasure." A word is significative, and God is not only known by his word, but even by his works also, and particularly by his "judgment which he executeth," Psal. ix. 16. A word is not more easily uttered than the greatest work is performed by God. There is nothing done by God but, as a word is *filia mentis,* produced by the mind, was first determined before in his secret counsel. There is no word so diffusive and scattered among so many as the works of God are, "there being no speech nor language where their voice is not heard." In short, no word or speech requires so much attention as the works of God do observation. It is a shame for us that God has spoken so often, and so loud, so long, so plainly by them, and that we will not hear. If that voice be not loud enough, and if he has stood too far to be heard, he will speak more loudly, and come nearer to us, to our cost. Entreat the Lord to open the ear as well as to speak the word, and to teach as well as to speak, Psal. xciv. 12.

Obs. 2. Great is the excellency of the word in point of purity. It sets not forth sins by way of mere relation, much less by way of imitation, but by way of caution. As in it the filthiest of sins are spoken of modestly and purely, so they are mentioned as punished severely. Sodom's filthiness is set forth in Scripture, but so likewise are Sodom's flames, and both to warn us, not to allure us. The Scripture mentions the scourge as well as the sin of the holiest man, the medicine as well as the malady. How groundless is their impiety who take liberty to sin from reading the sins, especially of good men, in the word! what is this but to read it with Satan's spectacles, who, as he cites, so always shows Scripture by halves? To sin without examples of caution is bad, to sin against them is worse, to sin by them is worst of all; the first is to walk, the second to run, the third to fly to hell.

Obs. 3. Public and notorious offenders ought to be open examples. Sodom is not afraid to declare their sin, and God declares it to make others afraid. Though punishment should reach but a few, yet fear should reach all. Secret punishment is a plaster not broad enough for an open, a scandalous fault. God threatens, even his otherwise dear David, that he who had made "the enemies of the Lord to blaspheme," should be punished "before all Israel, and before the sun," 2 Sam. xii. 12. Private corrections for open crimes are not plasters to cure, but only to cover the sore. If sin be impudent, reproof and correction should not be bashful. If a minister sees that error and profaneness seek no corners, he should not hide truth in a corner. Public offences are like a bag of poison thrown into a common fountain, serving for the use of a whole city; and the end at which God aimed in the punishing of offenders, was that all Israel should "hear, and fear, and do no more any such wickedness," Deut. xiii. 11. The Syrians cared not to fight with small or great, but with the king of Israel, and magistrates and ministers should principally strike at reigning sins. All the reproofs of the prophets and Christ were bent against the impieties of their times. I verily believe that one main sin whereby God is provoked to make public officers in church and state so contemptible as they are, is their fear to oppose public and spreading sins so freely as they should.

Obs. 4. In this our present condition we want as well the affrightments of fear as the allurements of love to keep us from sin. The burnt Sodomites should make us fear the fire. The overthrow of the Israelites are examples to saints under the New Testament. And "let us" (saith the apostle) "therefore," he means by the example of the unbelieving Israelites, "fear, lest, a promise being left us of entering into his rest, any of you should seem to come short of it." "I am," saith holy David, "afraid of thy judgments," Psal. cxix. 120. "Who," saith Jeremiah, "would not fear thee, O King of nations?" Jer. x. 7. And, "Who shall not fear thee, O Lord, &c.; for thy judgments are made manifest," Rev. xv. 4. Fear him, saith Christ, who is able to cast soul and body into hell. Faith is as truly due to threatenings as promises; and holy fear is the proper effect of that faith: "By faith Noah being warned of God, moved with fear," &c. Nor is it possible or profitable, so long as we have such an eager proneness to sin, to want a stoppage by fear. So unwilling are we to be weaned from the forbidden breasts of sinful pleasures, that we daily need to fear the wormwood and aloes wherewith the Lord imbitters them; and all little enough: only heaven perfects love and casts out fear.

Obs. 5. There is a proneness to sin in every age of the world. Why should God make Sodom an example of caution to succeeding ages, if these were not forward to make Sodom an example of imitation? Peter saith expressly that these overthrown cities were made an "example to those who after should live ungodly." The world always was, is and will be the world, saith Luther. *Mundus semper fuit, est, et erit mundus. Luth.* The several ages of the world have differed in their other fashions, but sin was never out of fashion. Look over all times and places, and it will be found true in both, "the whole world lies in wickedness;" and of all times, so true was that prediction of the apostle, the last days are the most perilous. We now live in the sink, the dregs of time; Satan now labours to do much mischief, and posts the faster because he shall not long have day-light. Men likewise by long practising, and by the sinful experiments of former times, are now grown, as in other things, so in sin, greater artists than heretofore. How careful should we be that God may have some, even in these worst of times, who may love holiness when most leave it; control, if not conquer sin; who may shine as lights in the world; and who, if they can do no good to others, yet may get no hurt from others! To conclude this, though evil times should not damp our zeal, yet neither should they make us impatient. The tares and wheat will grow together till the approaching harvest. Meanwhile, none is so much provoked as that God who is most patient. Nor should we forget that all foregoing ages have abounded with those sins and difficulties, which much imbittered the lives of holy men who lived in them; in which respect we may wisely make use of that counsel of Solomon, "Say not thou, What is the cause that the former days were better than these?" Eccl. vii. 10. Errors and impieties were in former times, and are now, but newly acted over; and let us rejoice, that though the sins of the times should make us mourners for them, yet they cannot make us followers of them.

Obs. 6. In all ages God is the same. He hates the same sins in after-times which he hated in the former. Sodomy is now as abominable in his sight as heretofore; "He is the same yesterday, and to-day, and for ever;" in him there is no shadow of change; he loves the same holiness now which he ever loved. How great a terror is this to those who live in those sins against which God has formerly declared his wrath! God will not go out of his way to gratify their lusts; no, it is the duty of the sinner to change: "If he turn not, he will whet his sword," &c., Psal. vii. 12. Much may this comfort those who walk in the steps of former saints. Paul was a pattern to those who "hereafter should believe," 1 Tim. i. 16. They find God as ready to accept them as any heretofore. This comforted the psalmist, "Our fathers trusted in thee, and thou didst deliver them," Psal. xxii. 4. We are forward to entertain hard thoughts of God, if he continue not the same favours to us which he afforded to others; we think he changes, whereas we alone are to be blamed. It is not the shore which moves, but the boat. If we will turn to God, we know where to have him; our prayers and repentance will make a change in us, and make us fit to be accepted, they make no alteration in him at all; as they who being in a ship, and pull at a rope fastened to a rock, move not the rock to them, but themselves to the rock.

Obs. 7. God is gracious even in his greatest severity. Even when he was punishing Sodom with fire and brimstone, he had thoughts of preventing similar punishment upon others for the time to come. He warns even when he wounds, and punishes a few that he may spare many; he takes occasion by the sin and punishment of Sodom to do good to following ages; his justice magnifies his mercy. God lays up manna with the rod, and is not forgetful to feed us even when he smites: in his smiles he will be feared, in his frowns he will be loved; in the midst of judgment he remembers mercy. If God be so sweet in his bitter administrations, how sweet will he be when he is altogether employed in the ways of grace! We should herein look upon the Lord as our pattern; severity should not make us forget and throw off tender-heartedness. We should have merciful ends in our severest punishing of offenders, and not wound like murderers, to destroy, but like surgeons, to cure, and to prevent the spreading of sin, yea, of punishment.

Obs. 8. It should be our great desire, by all our own sufferings for sin, to prevent the like sin in and sufferings of others. We must not be like those that have the plague, who love to infect others with it. A gracious heart rather desires to hear of converts by his falls and woes, than to have companions in either. They who have been by sin examples of imitation, should pray that by their sufferings they may become examples of caution. How rare is this heavenly temper in sufferers! Most Christians, when they are in troubles, only desire the removal of them, perhaps the sanctifying of them to themselves; but who prays for the sanctifying of them to others? It is ordinary for men under their sufferings to have thoughts of impatience against God, and of revenge against the instrument of their troubles; but unusual for men to have aims of benefiting beholders by their troubles. If the Lord would thoroughly affect us with love to his glory, and hatred to sin, we should be willing to have the house pulled down upon our own heads, so that sin may be destroyed in others; and hereby we may do more good at our death than we have done throughout our whole lives.

Obs. 9. Sinners of these latter times sin more heinously than they who lived in former ages. The sins committed by those who have others for an example are greater than those committed formerly, though they are the same for kind. He who falls by stumbling at the same stone at which he dashed who went before him, falls without apology. We in these times stand upon the shoulders of those who lived of old, and therefore ought to see further; we may behold by what means they stood, where also and how they fell, and how by either they sped. More exactness in working and walking becomes us who have more light to guide us. How happy were we if as we strive to excel our forefathers in other arts, we did not come behind them in that heavenly art of a holy life, though their helps were fewer than ours! It is a common observation concerning our buildings, that though they are of more curious contrivance, yet less substantial and durable, than those of old time: I fear this may be more truly said of our religion than of our buildings. It will be more tolerable at the last day for those who lived in the times of Sodom, than for sinners in these days, upon whom the ends of the world are come. "Unto whomsoever much is given, of him shall be much required." Surely, as we pay dearer for our worldly commodities, we must pay much dearer for our sinful pleasures, than our forefathers have done. We had better never have heard of Sodom's ruin, than not to mend our lives by the example.

Obs. 10. It is our duty to make a holy improvement of the worst things which fall out in the world. Even Sodom and Gomorrha were our examples, and we should make lye to cleanse us of their ashes. A good man should sail, as they say of skilful mariners, with every wind, and, as Samson, take honey out of the carcass of the lion. Vespasian raised gain out of an excrement; the ostrich digests iron. Even the waters of jealousy, which rotted the bellies and limbs of some, made others healthful and fruitful. The sins of the worst should, and sometimes do, teach the godly to walk more closely and humbly with God. Were we not wanting to ourselves, the sin of Sodom might be to us *felix culpa*, a happy fault. But, alas, most men more imitate than shun the sins of others; nay, which is much worse, they rather take occasion to oppose, deride, and so get injury by seeing the holy strictness of the godly, than grow more watchful and holy by observing the sinful looseness of the wicked. But here is the excellency of grace, to make a man, like David, therefore to love the commandments of God, because wicked men make void the law, Psal. cxix. 127.

Obs. 11. It is our wisdom to learn how to behold the examples of caution which God has set forth, especially in Scripture, with most advantage to our souls. Against that which God shows we must not shut our eyes. To this end,

(1.) Let us give our assent to the truth of examples as delivered in Scripture, which not only relates the judgments themselves, but their causes also; the supreme, God; the deserving, sin. Faith takes into its vast comprehension every part of God's word. It has been the devil's policy to strike at the truths of Scripture stories, either by denying or adulterating them. Porphyry, to overturn the miraculousness of the Israelites' passing through the Red Sea, saith, that Moses took the advantage of a low ebbing water, and so went through safely, which the Egyptians not understanding, were drowned by the flowing of the water. Strabo likewise perverts the truth of this story of the destruction of Sodom and Gomorrha by attributing it to natural causes, and reporting that these cities were seated on a soil sulphureous, and full of holes, from which, fire breaking forth, consumed them. Examples of the most dreadful aspect will never affright us from sin, when we look upon them in the devil's dress.

Prophani quidam ex schola Porphyrii ut miraculum elevarent, confinxerunt Mosem peritissimum naturæ, observasse fluxum et refluxum maris Erithræi et, refluente illo, suos traduxisse. Riv. in Exod. *Græci scriptores Sodomam cum vicinis civitatibus eam ob causam incendio perlisse sentiunt, quod regio illa cavernosa esset et sulphurea, atque ita hujusmodi exitio* obnoxia. Muscul. in 19. Gen.

Let us not sport at examples, and make them our play-fellows. Read not the example of Lot's wife as the poetical fiction of turning Niobe into a stone. What judgment thou readest believe, though never so severe, never so far beyond thy apprehension.

(2.) Look upon examples with deep and diligent observation. They must sink into us; we must set our hearts to them, steep our thoughts in them, and ponder them in their certainty, causes, severity. Posting passengers cannot be serious observers of any place. How profitable is it sometimes to dwell in our meditations upon these monuments of Divine justice! Assent must be followed with consideration: transient thoughts become not permanent examples.

(3.) Look upon these examples with an impartial examination. Inquire within whether such a one whom vengeance overtook was a greater sinner than I am. Ask thy conscience that question which the prophet put to the Israelites, Are there not with me, even with me, the same sins against the Lord? Ransack thy soul to find out the traitor; hide not that in secret which hath made so many public examples.

(4.) Behold examples in a way of particular application; not with self-exception, but as bringing thee tidings of thine own ruin. Without repentance, never say, What is this to me? unless I repent, I shall likewise perish. Most hearing of examples of God's judgment, say to themselves as Peter to Christ, These things shall not be to us. Look not upon any outward thing as able to ward off the blow, or privilege thee from punishment. Wealth cannot raise a ransom, power cannot prevail, wisdom cannot contrive, secrecy cannot shelter one from wrath. God has as many arrows in his quiver as he had before ever he began to shoot any. We have no protection against the arrest of justice. Outward privileges, nay, saving grace itself, can give thee no dispensation to sin.

(5.) Look upon examples with an eye of prudent prevention. Fly from that wrath of which thou art now warned; it is easier to keep out than to get out of the snare; even beasts will avoid the places where they see their fellows have miscarried. Happy would they, who are thy examples, think themselves, had they the opportunities of preventing that which they now feel. While the enemy is in the way, agree with him; while judgment is approaching, consider whether thou art able with thy ten to meet him that cometh against thee with twenty thousand. O weak sinner, while he is (as yet through his forbearance) at some distance send an embassage, and desire conditions of peace, in the way of sincere turning to the Lord. All the armies and examples of vengeance which compass thee about in the world shall retire from thee, if thou wilt throw the head of Sheba over the wall, the sin that God struck at in others.

(6.) Look we upon examples with humble thankfulness; not as rejoicing in the sorrows of others, but as blessing God for his mercy towards ourselves. How happy were we, and how cheap our schooling, to have all our learning at the cost of another! Admire that free grace which made a difference between us and the filthiest Sodomites: our sins have some aggravations which neither these nor the sins of thousands in hell admitted. It was the mere pleasure of God that Sodomites were not in our room, and we in theirs, and that we should not equalize those in punishment whom we have exceeded in sin.

Verse 8.

Likewise also these filthy dreamers defile the flesh, despise dominion, and speak evil of dignities.

Here Jude sets down the second part of the second argument, which he brought to incite these Christians earnestly to "contend for the faith" opposed by the seducers: the argument was taken from their certain destruction. In the managing of which, having first mentioned sundry examples of God's judgment upon the offenders of former times, he now in the second place adds, that these seducers lived in those sins which God had punished in others; and this he prosecutes in the eighth, ninth, and tenth verses.

In the eighth verse two parts are considerable.
I. The faults with which these seducers are charged.
II. The fountain from which these faults issued.

I. For the first, the faults, &c. We may consider, 1. Their specification. 2. Their amplification.

1. Their specification: (1.) Defiling of the flesh. (2.) Opposing of authority, set down by the apostle here in two branches: [1.] Their despising of "dominion" inwardly. [2.] Their speaking "evil of dignities" outwardly.

2. Their amplification, in these two words, "Likewise also." (1.) They sinned both as the former sinners had offended, and although they knew they were punished.

(2.) The fountain from which these their faults issued, viz. their spiritual security and delusion, both contained in the word "dreamers."

Concerning the explication of the first fault specified in these seducers, their defiling the flesh, which was the abuse of their bodies by fornication and carnal unchastity, even as Sodom had done before them, I have at large spoken in the foregoing verse; and therefore, that I may forbear needless repetitions, I shall now pass it over, only I shall make three observations, and then proceed to their next fault.

Obs. 1. Sins of carnal uncleanness are peculiarly against the body or flesh of men. In many, if not all other heinous sins, the thing abused is without the body, as in murder, theft, &c., but in this the body itself is abused, 1 Cor. vi. 18. The body not only concurs, but suffers by this sin more than any other, both by dishonour and diseases. Dishonour, in the staining and defiling that noble piece of workmanship, curiously wrought by the finger of God himself. By diseases; this lust being not only a conscience-wasting, but a carcass-wasting enemy. Sensual men kill that which they pretend most to gratify. Wherein are the enslaved to this lust wiser than Samson, in his discovering to Delilah where his strength lay? though that impudent harlot plainly told him she desired to know it to afflict him. I have heard of a drunkard that said, having almost lost his sight by immoderate drinking, he had rather lose his eyes than his drunkenness; and of an old adulterer, who was so wedded to, and yet so weakened by his lust, that he could neither live with or without his unclean companion. Were not these slaves? Truly such sinners are no better than the devil's hackneys, meeting with nothing but stripes and drudgery; and when they can do no more, the filthiest ditch, even hell itself, is their receptacle. Our bodies never cost Satan any thing; and he, like the harlot who was not the mother of the child, pleads indeed vehemently to have them for his own, but yet withal cares not if they are cut in pieces. The worshippers of Baal slashed their poor carcasses for a god that was not able to hear them. Idolaters have not thought their own dear children, themselves repeated, sacrifices too dear for Moloch. How do papists tear and macerate their bodies in their will-worship! among them the *fratres flagellantes*, who once, as Hospinian reports, for thirty-three days together went up and down slashing their carcasses with whips, till they had almost whipped themselves to death, expressed more madness than mortification. Superstition neglects and punishes the body, Col. ii. 23. How different from these, how gentle and indulgent even to the poor body, are the services of God! he calls for honourable services and merciful sacrifices; nay, mercy, and not sacrifice. Chastity, temperance, &c. are severe only to those lusts which are cruel to us; even fasting itself, which seems one of the sorest services, furthers the health of the body. God might, and yet mercifully too, have appointed, since the body is such an enemy to the soul, that, like medicines given to those that are troubled with contrary diseases, the services which are beneficial to the one, should have been hurtful to the other; but so meek and indulgent a Master is the Lord, that his commands are profitable to both.

Obs. 2. Sins of unchastity are peculiarly defiling. Besides that spiritual uncleanness wherewith every sin defiles, carnal unchastity defiles with that which is bodily. All sin in general is called uncleanness, but fornication is the sin which is singled out particularly to be branded with that name. Some think that adulterers are especially compared to dogs, unclean creatures. The hire of a whore and the price of a dog are put together; and both forbidden to be brought into the house of the Lord, Deut. xxiii. 18. And when Abner was by Ishbosheth reproved for defiling Rizpah, he answers, " Am I a dog?" The child begotten in adultery is, Deut. xxiii. 2., called *Mamzer*, which some learned men derive from two words, signifying another man's spot or defilement: how foolish are they who desire to have their dead bodies embalmed, and their living bodies defiled! There is a peculiar opposition between fornication and sanctification: "This is the will of God, even your sanctification, that ye should abstain from fornication," 1 Thess. iv. 3. The saints of God should have a peculiar abhorrence of this sin : " Fornication and uncleanness," &c., " let it not be once named among you, as becometh saints," Eph. v. 3; they should cleanse themselves from all filthiness of flesh and spirit, 2 Cor. vii. 1. A man who is of a cleanly disposition loves to wear clean garments. The body is the garment of the soul, and a clean heart will preserve a pure body. Remember, Christians, by what hand your bodies were made, by what guests they are inhabited, to what head they are united, by what price they are purchased, in what laver they have been washed, and to whose eye they shall hereafter be presented! Consider, lastly, whether Delilah's lap be a fit place for those who expect a room in Abraham's bosom.

<small>Weems on the Seventh Commandment.</small>

Obs. 3. The love of lust makes men erroneous and seducers. They who make no conscience of ordering their conversation will soon be heretical. These seducers who opposed the faith were unclean, and flesh-defilers. The fool said in his heart that there was no God, and the true ground thereof immediately follows, " they are corrupt, and have done abominable works," Psal. xiv. 1.

They who put away a good conscience, concerning faith will soon make shipwreck, 1 Tim. i. 19. The lust of ambition and desire to be teachers of the law makes men turn aside to vain jangling, 1 Tim. i. 7. Diotrephes' love of pre-eminence puts him upon opposing the truth, 3 John 10. The lust of covetousness did the like. They who supposed that gain was godliness quickly grew destitute of the truth, 1 Tim.

vi. 5; while some coveted money, they erred from the faith, 1 Tim. vi. 10; Micah iii. 5. They who subverted whole houses, and taught things which they ought not, did it for filthy lucre's sake, Tit. i. 11. The blind watchmen and the shepherds which understood not, were such as could never have enough, and looked every one for his gain; and they were dumb, because greedy dogs, Isa. lvi. 10, 11. The lust of voluptuousness produced the same effect; they who caused divisions contrary to the doctrine which the Romans had learned, were such as served their own belly, Rom. xvi. 17. They who led captive silly women laden with divers lusts, resisted the truth, were men of corrupt minds, and reprobate concerning the faith, 2 Tim. iii. Wine and strong drink made the prophets err and go out of the way. The heretics of old, the Gnostics, Basilidians, Nicolaitans, &c., were so infamous for carnal uncleanness, as Epiphanius, Augustine, and others report, that a modest ear would even suffer by the relation thereof. Nor have the papists and Anabaptists of late come far short of them. The lusts make the affections to be judges; and where affection sways, judgment decays. Hence Alphonsus advised that affections should be left at the threshold when any went to council. We are prone to believe that to be right and lawful which we would have to be so. Lusts oppose all entrance of light which opposes them. Repentance alone makes men acknowledge the truth, 2 Tim. ii. 25. "How can ye believe," saith Christ, "who receive honour one from another?" Sensual men taught that the resurrection was past, because it troubled them to think of it, 2 Tim. ii. 18. The consideration of a resurrection, a hell, a heaven, disturbs them, and therefore they deny these. If the light be too much in men's eyes, they will either shut their eyes, or draw the curtains. Lusts will pervert the light which is brought in, making men instead of bringing their crooked lives to the straight rule, to bring the straight rule to their crooked lives; and instead of bringing their hearts to the Scripture, to bring the Scripture to their hearts. Hence it is that wicked men study the Scripture for distinctions, to maintain their lusts; and truly a carnal will is often helped by Satan to a carnal wit. Lastly, God in judgment gives up such who will not see to an inability and utter impotency to discern what they ought, and to a reprobate mind: they who will not be scholars of truth, are by God justly delivered up to be masters of error. And because men will not endure sound doctrine, God suffers them to heap unto themselves teachers after their own lusts, to turn away their ears from the truth, and to be turned unto fables; because that when the very heathen extinguished the light of nature, and "knowing God, did not glorify him as God, professing themselves wise, they became fools, and God gave them up to uncleanness and vile affections;" much more may God send those who live under the gospel, and "receive not the love of the truth, strong delusions, that they should believe lies," 2 Thess. ii. 10, 11. Wonder not therefore at that apostacy from the truth which abounds in these days, and the opposing of those old precious doctrines which heretofore men have embraced in appearance; some unmortified lust or other there was in them; some worm or other of pride, licentiousness, &c., in these beautiful apples, which made them fall from the tree of truth to the dirt of error: instead therefore of being scandalized at them, let us be careful of ourselves; if we would hold the mystery of faith, let us put it into a pure conscience. Let us keep no lust *in deliciis*; love we no sin if we would leave no truth. Let us love what we know, and then we shall know what to love; let us sincerely do the will of Christ, and then we shall surely know the doctrine of Christ: "I understand more than the ancients," saith David, "because I keep thy precepts," Psal. cxix. 100. The Lord will teach such his way, and guide them in judgment. "Evil men," saith Solomon, "understand not judgment: but they that seek the Lord understand all things," Prov. xxviii. 5. If we will turn from our iniquities, we shall understand the truth, Dan. ix. 13. Who is wise, and he shall understand these things.

Having treated of the first specified fault wherewith these seducers were charged, viz. their defiling the flesh; the second follows,

(2.) Their contempt of magistracy; and in that, first of the first branch thereof, viz. They "despise dominion" inwardly.

Three things I here propound by way of explication.

1. What we are here to understand by "dominion."
2. What by despising that dominion.
3. Upon what ground Jude here condemns them for despising it.

In the first we may consider two things. [1.] To whom this dominion is attributed. [2.] What it is, and wherein it consists.

[1.] The word in the original κυριότης, dominion, is the same with that mentioned in 2 Pet. ii. 10, and translated government. Κυριότητος καταφρονοῦντες. And though it properly signify lordship, domination, or government in the abstract, the power and office of magistracy, or any ruling over others, yet must it necessarily comprehend the persons themselves governing, or in the place of authority. Government without governors is but a notion; and were it not for governors, there would be no hating of government. Paul, by "higher powers," Rom. xiii. 1, understands both the power or authority itself, as also the persons vested with that power and authority. And when Peter commands the Christians to love τὴν ἀδελφότητα, the brotherhood, 1 Pet. ii. 17, he intends the whole company of the brethren, as we understand by the nobility of the land, the nobles themselves; and yet here Jude names in the abstract, rather dominion and authority itself, than those who were placed therein, to show what it was which these seducers opposed and struck at, namely, not at officers so much as at their office; not at magistrates, but at magistracy; they loved not this same ruling over others, and such a difference among men. They aimed at anarchy, as Calvin remarks upon the place; being proud, they could not endure superiors; and being licentious, they were impatient of restraint. Some by this dominion of which Jude speaks understand the dominion and authority of the Lord Christ received from his Father; and so refer this despising of dominion to that sin of ungodliness mentioned ver. 4, where these seducers are said to be ungodly, and to deny "the only Lord God, and our Lord Jesus Christ." They "despise dominion," that is, saith Lyranus, Christ himself, who is not only called Lord in the concrete, but even dominion in the abstract, because of the excellency of his dominion. But though it be true that Satan has ever endeavoured to overthrow the domination of Christ by heretics, who have denied his natures sometimes, his offices at other times, and have indeed showed themselves antichrists, 1 John ii. 4; yet under correction, I conceive, that the dominion and dignities whereof Jude here speaks, are to be referred to the civil magistrate. The word κυριότης, or dominion, is never attributed to Christ in the New Testament, but always either to angels or magistrates, Eph. i. 21; Col. i. 16; and it is only agreeable to the scope of this place to interpret it of the magistrate. Even they who by these words understand the dominion of Christ, yield that the next words, "despise dignities," are to be understood of magistrates. And the apostle in this verse, as is conceived, compares these seducers, as for uncleanness, to Sodomites; so for contempt of government, to the Israelites, who rebelled against Moses; most suitably also subjoining this sin to the former of uncleanness, because the love of their lusts, and dissoluteness of life, made them hate that government which was appointed to restrain them.

[2.] For the second, What this dominion and power is that is attributed to the magistrate, and wherein it consists.

1. More generally, it stands in superiority, pre-eminence, and supereminence above others, as is evident, (1.) By those names by which it is set forth in Scripture, as "power, authority, rule," Rom. xiii. 1; 1 Tim. ii. 2; Tit. iii. 1. (2.) By those titles which are given to magistrates, as "kings," and such as "exercise authority," Luke xxii. 25; "they that are great," Matt. xx. 25; "rulers," Rom. xiii. 3; "powers," in the abstract, Rom. xiii. 1; "magistrates," Luke xii. 11; "governors," Luke xx. 20; and elsewhere "nobles," 2 Chron. xxiii. 20; Jer. xiv. 3; "dukes" or mighty ones, Exod. xv. 15; Ezek. xxxi. 5; "great men," 2 Sam. iii. 38; "captains," 1 Sam. ix. 16; "princes," Psal. lxxxiii. 11; Ezek. xxxii. 9. With sundry metaphorical names also; as "gods," Exod. xxii. 28; Psal. lxxxii. 1; cxxxviii. 1; "children of the Most High," Psal. lxxxii. 6; "the sons of the mighty," or of the gods, Psal. lxxxix. 6; "fathers," tender fathers, as the word may be, and, according to Jerom, is to be rendered, Gen. xli. 43; David calls Saul "father," 1 Sam. xxiv. 11; Deborah is called a "mother in Israel," Judg. v. 7; "heads," Numb. xiv. 4; Judg. xi. 8; "mountains," Micah vi. 1; "anointed," 1 Sam. xxiv. 6; "shepherds," Numb. xxvii. 17; Isa. xliv. 28, &c.

Κυριοτης, δυναμις, εξουσια, υπεροχη, αρχη, δοξαι, 1 Cor. xv. 24; Tit. iii. 1; Luke xii. 11. οἱ ἐξουσιαζοντες, Luke xxii. 25. οἱ μεγαλοι, ἀρχοντες, Matt. xx. 25. κυβερνητης, Acts xxvii. 11. Οὐδὲν διαφέρει ἀρχων ἀγαθος ἀγαθου πατρος. Xen.

2. More particularly, this dominion or power consists in three things. (1.) In *ordinando*, in ordaining laws for the good of the subjects. This is called *potestas νομοθετική*, the legislative power. Laws are like the line and plummet of the architect, without which there is no right working; and they are to a commonwealth what the sun is to the earth; without them people would not see whither to go, what to do, and all places, as is usual in darkness, would be filled with filthiness and violence; they are the cords of the tent, which, being cut, it falls to the ground. Laws are the best walls of a city; without them even walled cities want defence; they are as physic to the body, both for preventing and removing diseases; nay, they are as the soul to the body, without them the commonwealth would neither have beauty nor being. Laws have been ever esteemed so necessary, that no commonwealth under any form could ever be without them. Nor do these positive laws derogate at all from the perfection of the law moral, or of nature, but only discover the depravation of man's nature; in whose heart, though that ἔργον νόμου, that work of the law be written, which inclines all to some kind of natural goodness; yet by the fall is the knowledge of the law of nature so obscured, and the force of inordinate affection so prevalent over reason, that there is need of positive laws, for directing, restraining, encouraging. And, indeed, positive laws are but rivulets derived and drawn from the law of nature, and particular conclusions formed out of its universal principles. The law of nature only in general prescribes what is to be done or avoided, not descending to particulars: now all being not able from those general principles to deduce that which is to be practised in particular cases, which admit of innumerable variations, according to circumstances, positive laws for the good of subjects are necessarily to be suited to the condition of every commonwealth. Nor can it justly be alleged by any that dominion may be committed as well to men alone as to laws, for the law is the voice of God, being a deduction from the law of nature, whereas a man is a servant of affections, and apt to be biassed by hatred, anger, fear, friendship, foolish pity; by reason whereof it is (as a learned man once said) easier for one wise man to make, than for many to pronounce law. It was a wise speech of Solon, "That only that commonwealth could be safe, where the people obeyed the magistrate, and the magistrates the laws." And of Plato, who said, "That city cannot be far from ruin, where the laws are not above the magistrate, but the magistrate above the laws." And if against this it should be argued, that the law must needs be defective, speaks generally, and cannot come up to sundry contingent and special cases and circumstances, which it cannot foresee and determine, I answer, let conscientious prudence supply the unavoidable defects; and that we may not set the magistrate and law at variance, let the law have power to hinder the magistrate from transgressing by the force of affection, and let the magistrate have power with rational and religious regard of circumstances to explain and apply the law. This power of the magistrate serving to make a happy temperature of *jus* and *æquum*, strict justice and Christian equity, and being as necessary as it is for a physician to have one eye to the rules of his art, and another to the condition of his patient; not suffering himself so to be bound up by the precepts of the former, as by laying aside his own prudence to endanger the life of the latter. And that God has given to the magistrate this legislative power is most evident, because dominion without such a power would be in vain, and never obtain its end, either in advancing godliness or the public peace, Numb. xi. 16; good laws made and executed being the direct means to promote both. As also because God has given the magistrate the prudence and power requisite to making laws; and all the commands given by God to people of being obedient would be void, and to no purpose, unless the magistrate might impose laws. And yet he must remember that the matter of his laws must be possible, else they cannot obtain their end; profitable also to the commonwealth, and just or righteous, for else they destroy their end. Nor can that be said to be a law, but rather anomy, or a breach of the law, which commands any thing against God's law.

L. 4. de Leg.

(2.) The power and dominion here spoken of consists in *administrando*, in jurisdiction, by way of execution or administering of justice to the people, according to the forementioned good laws. A law without execution is neither of force nor fruit. Miserable is that commonwealth whose manners have brought their laws under their power, and miserably confined and nailed them to the pillar. This jurisdiction or execution of the laws is twofold.

Omnia judicia, aut distrahendarum controversiarum aut puniendorum maleficiorum causa reperta sunt. Cic. pro Cecin.

The first is seen in judgments, or the determinations of civil controversies between parties according to the rules of the law: that this is part of the magistrate's power is evident, 1. From God's ordination and command: "By me kings reign, and princes decree justice," Prov. viii. 15. "How long will ye judge unjustly," &c. ? "do justice to the afflicted and needy," &c., Psal. lxxxii. 3. And, "O king of Judah, that sittest upon the throne, thou and thy servants, execute ye judgment and righteousness, deliver the spoiled," &c., Jer. xxii. 2. And, "O ye house of David, execute judgment in the morning," Jer. xxi. 12. 2. From the direction which God gives to people to seek judgment at the hand of the magistrate: "For all manner of trespass, whether it be for ox, for ass, for sheep, for raiment, or for any manner of lost thing which another challengeth," &c., "the cause of both parties shall come before the judges; and whom the judges shall condemn," &c., Exod. xxii. 9. And, "Both the men, between whom the controversy is, shall stand before the Lord, before the priests and the judges," Deut. xix. 17. 3. From the use and necessity of judgments. [1.] Truth often lieth in the bottom, and falsehood lurks in corners. A prudent magistrate brings both to the light; the one because it seeks it, the other because it shuns it. [2.] Good men, by reason of their fewness, weakness, and meekness, are often great sufferers, and the wicked are numerous, potent, and oppressive. The public judgment of the magistrate is in this case to the former "a hiding-place from the wind," Isa. xxxii. 2, and as a wind to scatter the latter, Prov. xx. 8. And without these public judgments what would places be, but as mountains of prey, dens of wild beasts, and habitations fitter for Cyclops than Christians! God hath not by grace given to any a right in another's estate, nor taken away from any an orderly and regular love of his own welfare; and nature in the best dictates and desires; and the God of nature, by these public judgments, has granted helps for self-preservation from injury and oppression. Only it must be here heeded, that these suits and judgments are not transacted unduly, either by the judged or the judges. First, By the judged. 1. They must not desire judgments out of envy, revenge, covetousness, or a desire of contending. 2. The matter about which judgment is desired must not be slight and frivolous. 3. The remedy of the law must not be desired till after patient waiting and Christian endeavours to compound differences, and to procure an amicable reconcilement. 4. The parties who differ must not manage their contestation with bitter and unchristian animosities, railings, briberies, or false accusations. *Sic certent causæ, ut non certent pectora. Judex q. jus dicens. Var. Νόμος ἔμψυχος.* 5. The end of desiring judgments must not be the undoing or defaming of our adversary, but the preserving of ourselves, and the administration of justice, the welfare of others, Zech. vii. 9; viii. 16.

Secondly, The judges must not wrongfully transact these judgments, they must give every one his due. Justice, justice, or "that which is altogether just, shalt thou do," Deut. xvi. 20. And Moses saith he charged the judges to hear the causes between their brethren, to "judge righteously between every man and his brother," Deut. i. 16. "Execute judgment in the morning," Jer. xxi. 12. Justice is the soul of judgment. An unjust judge is a solecism, a contradiction. A judge should be the law enlivened: to this end, judges must be godly. Righteousness will not stand without religion. Jethro's advice to Moses was, Choose men fearing God, Exod. xviii. 21. "Let the fear of the Lord be upon you," said Jehoshaphat to the judges, 2 Chron. xix. 6, 7. The Ethiopians apprehended that the angels attended on all judicatories, and therefore, as I have read of them, they left twelve chairs empty in the judgment-place, which they said were the seats of the angels; but judges must believe that a greater than the angels is there. 2. Impartial: he must "not respect the person of the poor, nor honour the person of the mighty," Lev. xix. 15; and he must "hear the small as well as the great," Deut. i. 17. There must no man's condition be regarded in judgment, nor must the judge behold the face of any one's person, but the face of his cause. God "accepts not the persons of princes," Job xxxiv. 19. A judge will be a sun of righteousness, shining as well upon the beggar as the noble. 3. A master of his affections. Anger, hatred, pity, fear, &c., the clouds of affection, will hinder the sunshine of justice. The Athenian judges used to sit in Marsstreet, to show that they had martial hearts. Constantine is termed a man-child, for his courage, Rev. xii. 5. He who will go *So Brightman.* up to the mount of justice, must leave his affections, as Abraham did his ass and servants, at the foot thereof. Love and wisdom seldom dwell under one roof, and the fear of man is a snare. A coward, we say, cannot be an honest man, nor will a fearful and flexible judge be able to say in justice, Nay. 4. Deliberate. In the case of information about false worship, Moses directs to this deliberation before sentence be given: "If it be told thee, and thou hast heard of it, and inquired diligently, and, behold, it be true, and the thing certain," &c., "then shalt thou bring forth the man," &c., Deut. xvii. 4, 5. What plenty of words are here to prevent precipitancy in judicature! It much commended the integrity of Job, who professes, "The cause which I knew not I searched out," Job xxix. 16. Both sides must be heard, the small as well as the great. Though a judge's sentence be right, yet he is not right in giving it, if he give it before either party be heard. *See the example of the heathen Festus, Acts xxv. 16. Qui statuit aliquid parte inaudita altera, æquum licet statuerit, haud æquus fuit. Sen. in Med.* 5. A lover of truth. A man of truth, Exod. xviii. 21. Hating lying, "executing the judgment of truth," Zech. viii. 16. His heart must love, his tongue speak the truth; nor will the hand without go right, if the wheels within go wrong. 6. Incorrupt; hating bribes, because hating covetousness. "A gift blindeth the wise, and perverteth the words of the righteous," Exod. xxiii. 8; Deut. xvi. 19. Of whose hand, saith Samuel, have I received any gift "to blind mine eyes therewith?" 1 Sam. xii. 3. A judge must neither take money to be unjust, nor to be just. Righteousness is its own reward. The Thebans erected the statues of their judges without hands. The gain of bribes is summed up, "Fire shall consume the tabernacles of bribery," Job xv. 34. 7. Sober and temperate. He that follows the pleasures that attend on majesty, will soon neglect the pains which belong to magistracy. It was a prudent instruction of Lemuel's mother, "It is not for kings, O Lemuel, it is not for kings to drink wine, nor for princes to drink strong drink; lest they drink, and forget the law, and pervert the judgment of any of the afflicted," Prov. xxxi. 4, 5. "Whoredom and wine and new wine take away the heart," Hos. iv. 11. Some understand those words, "Execute judgment in the morning," Jer. xxi. 12, properly, as if they should perform acts of judgment early, before they were endangered by abundant eating or feasting, to render themselves less able to discern of causes.

The second branch of jurisdiction which belongs to the magistrate, consists in the distribution of rewards and punishments. 1. Of rewards to those who keep; 2. Of punishments to those who break the laws.

1. Of rewards. Of this the apostle speaks, "Do that which is good, and thou shalt have praise," Rom. xiii. 3. Of this the supreme Lord gives an example, who joins "showing mercy to thousands," with "visiting the iniquities of the fathers upon the children," Exod. xx. 6. Nor must a magistrate be a sun only for lustre of majesty, but also for warmth and benignity.

2. Of punishments. These are of sundry kinds. Some concern the name, as degradations; some the estate, as pecuniary mulcts; some the body, and these are either capital, or not captital, as mutilation of some part, &c. Evident it is from Scripture commands, that it is the magistrate's duty to punish: "The judges shall make diligent inquisition. And thine eye shall not pity, but life shall go for life," Deut. xix. 18, 21. (2.) From his function: "He beareth not the sword in vain," Rom. xiii. 4. Governors are for the punishment of evil-doers. (3.) From the benefit of these punishments. To the punished, who may grieve for what they have done; to the spectators, who may be warned from doing the same, Prov. xix. 25. Sinful indulgence silently, yet strongly, invites to a second wickedness. *Indulgentia flagitiorum illecebra.* Even capital punishments are enjoined by Scripture: "Whoso sheddeth man's blood, by man shall his blood be shed," Gen. ix. 6; Exod. xxi. 12; Lev. xxiv. 17, &c.; a law which, being before the erection of the Mosaic polity, shows that the laws which afterward commanded capital punishments, did not simply and absolutely, but only, in respect of some circumstances, concern the Israelites. The capital punishment of malefactors by the magistrate was dictated by the law of nature. And as the force of the foresaid command was before, so it continued after Moses; Christ himself, even from it, drawing an argument to dissuade Peter from shedding of blood, Matt. xxvi. 52. Nor do I understand but that, if all punishments of malefactors by the sword be now unlawful, as Anabaptists dream, it must necessarily follow, that all defending of the subjects by the sword against an invading enemy is unlawful also; the public peace being opposed by the one as much as the other; nay, may we not argue, that if the power of the sword belong not to the magistrate to defend the commonwealth, that it belongs not to any private man to defend himself against the violent assaults of a murderer?

In sum, capital punishments may be inflicted, but sparingly, slowly. It is observed by some, that God was longer in destroying Jericho than in making the whole world. As many funerals disgrace a physician, so many executions dishonour a magistrate. The execution of justice should, like thunder, fear many, and hurt few: let all means be tried before the last be used. A magistrate must not be bloody when he sheds blood: the master bee alone is (they say) without a sting. If a butcher may not be of the jury, much less may he be a judge. In a doubtful case, it is better to spare many nocent than to punish one innocent; nor must vehement suspicion, but clear evidence, satisfy a judge. Punishment delayed may afterward be executed; but being once executed, cannot be recalled; and even when the malefactor is condemned, the man should be commiserated; though as an offender his blood be debased, yet as a man it is precious.

Thus we have explained the first thing considerable in this part, "dominion."

2. What is to be understood by despising dominion.

Proprie significat aliquid suo loco ut indignum amovere. Bez. in 6 Mar. 26. The word αθετοῦσι, saith Beza, properly signifies to remove something out of the place, as unworthy any longer to remain therein; and it is in Scripture either spoken of persons or things: when of persons, it is declared most fitly by disdain or contemn, as Mark vi. 26; Luke x. 16; 1 Thess. iv. 8; and it is spoken of things properly, which being removed from their place, are accounted of no value, effect, or force; and thus it is declared by rejecting, Luke vii. 30, disannulling, Gal. iii. 15, casting off, 1 Tim. v. 12; and here, because we reject that which we despise, it is rendered "despise."

Now these seducers did not reject, disannul, cast off governing, so as to make it cease, that was not in their power; but in their judgment, desires, insinuations, and as much as in them was, they laboured to make it accounted void, abrogated, and of no value or force. And their pretence for this practice was the liberty which was by Jesus Christ purchased for them, with which they taught that obedience to magistrates was inconsistent. This seems to be plain by that more general sin which the apostle lays to their charge, of turning the grace of our God into wantonness, ver. 4, i. e. the goodness of God in bestowing liberty by Christ into libertinism. And hence it was that these seducers allured their poor seduced followers, under the pretence of liberty obtained by Christ, 2 Pet. ii. 18, 19, to all manner of wickedness and licentiousness of life; bearing them in hand, that as they were not now bound to any holiness of life, so particularly that Christ having redeemed them, they were free from all subjection and obedience to others. A doctrine which, as it is very taking with flesh and blood, so is it frequently by the apostles Paul and Peter opposed, who grant indeed a liberty wherewith Christ hath made a Christian free, but yet add, that this liberty is spiritual, a liberty from the law, sin, death, and hell, Gal. v. 13; not an immunity from civil obedience, and therefore not to be used for an occasion to the flesh, or for a cloak of maliciousness, 1 Pet. ii. 16. Nor indeed is any thing further from truth, than that because of spiritual liberty Christians should be free from civil subjection. For as this liberty exempts us not from obedience to the commands of God, (for, as the apostle saith, Rom. vi. 18, "Being made free from sin, we became the servants of righteousness;" and ver. 22, "servants to God,") so neither doth it exempt from obedience to the magistrate ordained by God. Yea, so far are the godly commands of a magistrate from opposing spiritual liberty, that they rather advance it; for true liberty stands in the choosing of good, and the rejecting of evil, and this is furthered by the righteous commands of superiors. Licentiousness is not liberty, but slavery, and makes sinners love their own insensible bondage.

3. Lastly, we shall inquire upon what ground the apostle condemns them for despising dominion. Of this briefly.

(1.) This was a sin against an ordinance of God: "By me kings reign," Prov. viii. 15. "There is no power but of God: the powers that be are ordained of God." And though magistracy is an ordinance of man in regard of the subject, it being borne by man; the object, it being employed about men; the end also, the good of men; the kind or sort thereof, left unto the choice of several nations: yet not in regard of the invention or institution thereof, which is only from God. *Quamvis in acquisitione et usu potestatis potest esse deordinatio; tamen in ipso ordine superioritatis in quo consistit Dominium, non potest esse deordinatio, sicut ordo non potest esse deordinatus. Vid. Durandum de Origine Jurisdictionum. Aug. de C. D. l. 5. c. 21. Et. qu. ex vet. Test. c. 35. Aug. Tr. 116. in Joh. Gerh. in 2 Pet. ii. Pareum in Rom.*

In it are considerable also, the power itself, the acquisition thereof, and the execution of it. The acquisition may be from the devil, by bribery, fraud, cruelty, intrusion, invasion. The execution, or manner of using this power, may be from him likewise, as when superstition is set up instead of religion, and cruelty for equity, by those who govern. But authority itself, dominion, principality, are from God, though not tyranny. Riches gotten by usury, extortion, &c., cease not to be good in themselves; yea, and the gifts of God: and as the owner of these unjustly procured riches may be said to be a rich man;

and he who has learning, though procured by unlawful means, may be said to be a learned man; so the possessor of a most unjustly obtained authority may be said to be a magistrate, and in authority, 1 Kings xv. 27; xvi. 2, 7; xiv. 14; Dan. iv. 17, 25; Prov. viii. 15.

(2.) This sin of the seducers was a sin against the welfare and happiness of the public. They being weary of magistracy, were weary of all the comforts and blessings of peace; and in being desirous to throw down the pillars, they endeavoured to pull down the building upon their own and others' heads. What would nations be without government, but the dens of wild beasts! "Judah and Israel dwelt safely every one under his vine and fig-tree all the days of Solomon," 1 Kings iv. 25. Even Nebuchadnezzar was a tree under which beasts of the field had shadow, in whose boughs the fowls of the heaven dwelt, and of which all flesh was fed, Dan. iv. 12. The funerals of a political parent millions of children will celebrate with tears. Over Saul, who was wicked and tyrannical, doth David bid the daughters of Israel to weep, who clothed them in scarlet, 2 Sam. i. 24. Nor was it, according to some, any of the best of kings who is called " the breath of our nostrils," Lam. iv. 20. And it is observable, when God threatens the taking away of the staff of bread, and the stay of water, he adds, as no less a judgment, the taking away "the judge and the prophet, the prudent and the ancient," &c., Isa. iii. 2.

(3.) By this despising of government, they were in an especial manner their own enemies, and sinned against their own happiness. The overturners of lawful magistracy shall find their calamities to arise suddenly, Prov. xxiv. 22. "He who breaketh a hedge, a serpent shall bite him," Eccl. x. 8. "An evil man seeketh only rebellion, therefore a cruel messenger shall be sent against him." It has been observed by some, that most, if not all, those whom the Scripture mentions as opposers of magistracy, have been punished by violent death, God not vouchsafing them so much as a reprieval to a death-bed. Korah and his company, Athaliah, Absalom, Zimri, Joab, Sheba, Adonijah, with many others, will prove this; and besides the vast supply which foreign histories afford, how hath vengeance pursued all the rebellious mentioned in our English Chronicle! Who has not heard of Becket, Montfort, Mortimer, the Percies, Tyler, Warbeck, the saltpetre saints, with sundry others, whom God made marks of vengeance for removing the ancient land-marks set for order and propriety in the nation? Nor do I remember that ever God suffered any one godly man, mentioned in Scripture, to put any lawful magistrate out of, or indirectly to put himself into, government. I say, I remember no instance of either.

Obs. 1. How provident is God for man's peace and welfare! Without dominion we should be worse than beasts: it is the breath which so many thousand creatures draw; take it away, and none can say, This is mine. If the magistrate were not a god to man, man would soon prove a wolf, nay, a devil to man. There is no creature which so much wants a ruler as man. We may say of all other creatures, *Nascuntur artifices*, they are born craft-masters, they were apparelled and armed by nature, they are their own cooks, physicians, builders, even at their first entrance; only man came in without strength, weapon, clothes, or skill. How good is God to provide protectors for him! Violent and bloody men fear not hell so much as the halter; like beasts, they are more afraid of the flash of powder than the bullet; and though their fear of the magistrate saves not their souls, yet many a time has it saved our lives. Without magistracy robbery would be a law, and men (like dogs) try all right by their teeth: where there is no ruler, every one will be a ruler; he who has no ruler over him, will be a tyrant over another. When there was no king in Israel, every Micah had a house of gods, and the Levites went begging, Judg. xvii. 6; xviii. 1, 14. It is just with God that they should feel the curse of anarchy who never were thankful for regular dominion.

Obs. 2. God is highly provoked by sin, when he suffers magistrates to be burdensome to a people, and dominion to be abused; when their deliverers and saviours become their destroyers, and they, like Ephraim, oppressed and broken even in judgment. It was threatened as a sore judgment, "I will give children to be their princes, and babes to rule over them." For the sins of a people, many and bad are the princes thereof, Prov. xxviii. 2. And God often sets up wicked governors over people, not because they are worthy to rule, but these worthy to be so ruled. God may give a king in his anger. He speaks often of princes who were wolves ravening to the prey to shed blood, Ezek. xxii. 27; Micah iii. 1—3; Zeph. iii. 3. How righteous was God in making Abimelech a scourge to the Shechemites, who had made themselves the stirrup to his ambition! And undoubtedly if God may suffer the prophets of a people to be fools, and the spiritual men to be mad, to delude and misguide the people "for the multitude of iniquity, and the great hatred," Hos. ix. 7; he is not hindered from suffering the princes of people who refuse to be reformed, to be Jeroboams to their souls, and Rehoboams to their bodies, pernicious to both. Oh that people would spend more time in blaming their sins, and less in complaining of men, and but sadly and impartially examine their hearts, whether the parting with the gospel and ministry would ever fetch a quarter so many complaints from them, as an inconsiderable sessment; or whether sin startle them so much as a tax! and if they find their consciences to give in verdict for God, let them adore his righteous severity.

[margin: Secundum merita subditorum dis-ponit corda præ-positorum.]

Obs. 3. God is much seen in causing men's subjection to magistrates. All naturally love to excel in worldly greatness, and like not superiority in others. Every one, saith Calvin on 1 Pet. v. 5, hath in him the mind of a king: that one therefore should keep millions of men in order, restrain, constrain, correct, command; how could it be but that God himself has imprinted the characters of Divinity upon him? and but that there is a Divine constitution in a human person? It is thou, O Lord, that subduest my people under me, saith David, Psal. cxliv. 2. And Psal. lxv. 7, the stilling the noise of the seas, the noise of the waves, and the tumult of the people, are put deservedly together, the latter manifesting the power of God as much as the former. How did David allay the fury of those furious spirits, who so eagerly desired to take away the life of Saul, but by this, "He is the Lord's anointed?" And hence princes should gather, when people cast off subjection and despise their dominion, that they themselves have despised God, provoked him to pour contempt upon them; and to make them, for cutting off their lock of loyalty to God, to become even as other men; and hence also people should learn to whom to return the praises of their peace and safety, not only to the power and policy of their governors, but principally to the ordination of that God by whom kings reign.

Obs. 4. The power given by God to magistrates should be improved for the Giver. Their dominion should advance that of the chief Lord: the greatest kings are his vassals. The highest earthly powers shall give an account to a higher hereafter, and must therefore be regulated by, and serve for, promoting a higher for the present. The king is commanded to write him a copy of the law, and keep all the words thereof, Deut. xvii. 18. When the crown was put upon the head, the testimony was also put into the hand of Joash, 2 Kings xi. 12. The first table should be first in the magistrate's care. Even kings and rulers must kiss the Son, Psal. ii. 12, and advance his kingdom; and provide that their subjects may not only live under them in peace and honesty, but also in godliness. If this must be the end of the subjects' prayers, it must be the end of the magistrates' government. These "shields of the earth" should protect God's glory, Psal. xlvii. 9. The "fat upon the earth" must worship Christ, Psal. xxii. 29, and "all kings fall down before him," Psal. lxxii. 11. The church, infant-like for weakness, must be nourished and nursed, yea, and that by kings and queens, Isa. xlix. 23. How unsuitable is it for them who are called gods, to cast off all care of the honour of God! and for them who are called shepherds, to take no care that their subjects should have the pastures of wholesome doctrines! to suffer them to wander in the ways of sin and hell, without any care to reduce them; and to give leave to grievous wolves, seducers, to devour them! They who make all the care of the magistrate to concern the worldly welfare, without any regard of the souls of people, make him like an ox-herd, who thinks he does enough in providing fat pasture for his cattle, suffering them willingly to be carried by droves to the shambles. And why political as well as natural parents should not take care that their children are "brought up in the nurture and admonition of the Lord," Eph. vi. 4, I understand not. Ample testimony is given to David, Solomon, Asa, Jehoshaphat, Hezekiah, Josiah, of their zeal for religion. Nor ever is the contrary mentioned in any of the other kings, but as their great sin and infamy. Nor ever will the names of Constantine, Theodosius, Justinian, cease to be precious for their care of the church of Christ. Even the heathens, Aristotle and Plato, acknowledge that the chief care in a commonwealth should be about religion; the most beautiful structure of a civil government is erected upon the sand, unless religion be the foundation.

In sum, though the power of the magistrate, as such, in the holy things of God, is not formal, intrinsical, and spiritual, so that he should administer therein, as if Christ had committed the keys to him, yet it is objective, to be employed about ecclesiastical causes, though politically, and to provide for the benefit of the church; and that by removing the impediments of religion, by preserving its maintenance, by convening assemblies for reformation, &c., and by taking care that matters ecclesiastical be duly managed by those who administer therein. Though the magistrate himself exercise not the art of physic, yet he takes care that none shall abuse that art, or exercise it hurtfully, 2 Kings xv. 14; 1 Cor. ix. 14; 2 Chron. xxxi. 3; xxix. 4; 2 Kings xxiii. 1, 2.

Obs. 5. The enemies of godliness soon become opposers of civil dominion. The apostle had told us that these seducers denied the only Lord God; and here he saith, they despised dominion. They who fear not God, will not be afraid to "speak evil of dignities." The despisers of Saul were the sons of Belial. Good men will not be bad subjects, nor will bad men conscientiously be good subjects. The fear of God is the best foundation of obedience to the magistrate. Remarkable is the order of obedience prescribed by the apostle, "Fear God, honour the king," 1 Pet. ii. 17; and by Solomon, "My son, fear thou the Lord and the king," Prov. xxiv. 21. Men may from a principle of policy forbear opposing magistracy as a danger, but only from a principle of conscience can they abhor it as a sin. The fear of man is but a weak bond, and as easily broken as were the cords by Samson. What a noise leave these words, "Submit to every ordinance of man for the Lord's sake," in a religious ear! Whatever interest or reputation dictates, the declaration of God's will to a gracious heart is the end of all strife. The discovery that such or such a course has a sin against God in it is enough for a saint; no more disputes then: the threats of a thousand hells are not so dissuasive. Human laws may make men hide, only God's laws can make men hate, disobedience. A mere man is firm and steady in no relations. The greatest interest of magistracy is to advance religion. If they provide for the keeping of God's laws, the observation of their own will follow of course. David discovered himself to be a good man, both in sparing Saul in the cave, (oh how well was it for Saul that he fell into the hands of a David!) and a wise man in setting his "eyes upon the faithful of the land," and in taking the perfect in their way to serve him, Psal. ci. 6. The way for the magistrate to bring men under his subjection is to plant the gospel, and to make them subject to Christ. The power of the word in the consciences of people binds more strongly to obedience than the power of the sword over the bodies of the people. And if God always restrain people from rebelling against governors, who shall tolerate in people all sorts of rebellion against God? What means that of 1 Sam. ii. 30, "Them that honour me," &c., "and they that despise me shall be lightly esteemed?" _{Christianus inimicus nemini, multo minus imperatori. Tert.}

Obs. 6. Christianity does not destroy, but strengthen magistracy. The seducers and libertines are here by Jude condemned for despising dominion. One ordinance of God does not abolish another. The laws of Christ in his church bring not in lawlessness into the commonwealth; nor is God a God of order in the first, and the author of confusion in the latter; yea, contrarily, he maintains government in the commonwealth for the good of his church, that it may find a harbour therein; and keeps up the pole of civil dominion, that the weak hopbine, the church, may be sustained. The spiritual authority of Christ divides not civil inheritances; his sceptre swallows not up, as did Aaron's rod the other, the sceptres of worldly monarchs; nor does He who came to give heavenly, take away earthly crowns. The weapons of Christ's kingdom are not carnal. He who, when he had a right, would not be made a king, gives no liberty to those who have none to put out those who have. It is the labour of Satan to persuade civil governors that Christ's kingdom is the greatest enemy to theirs. Thus Haman represented the Jews to Ahasuerus as a people that would not obey the king's laws, Esth. iii. 8. Thus the courtiers of Chaldea accused the three companions of Daniel of rebellion against the king's edict, Dan. iii. 12. By this fetch likewise the enemies of the Jews hindered the building of the temple, Ezra iv. 13. How often was Paul accused for sedition among the Jews! Acts xvii. 18. Nay, Christ himself was accused and executed for an enemy to Cæsar, Luke xxiii. 2. Thus papists seek to wash themselves by throwing dirt upon the servants of Christ. Were ever accusations more senseless than for Harding to say that Luther animated Munzer in his rebellion, which was by that man of God so zealously opposed? But the whore of Babylon loves to lay her own brats at her neighbours' doors. In short the weak ground of this imputation of rebellion to the godly, has been their refusing to obey such commands of magistrates as they apprehended sinful. And truly, in this case, when Christ calls another way, I neither owe burial to my dead, nor obedience to my living, though political, father. And, as Tertullian holily descants upon those words of Christ, "Render to Cæsar the things which are Cæsars, and to God," &c., "It is well added, 'and to God the things that are God's;' that is, give the image of Cæsar to Cæsar, which is on his coin; and give the image of God to God, which is in man; so as Cæsar may have thy money, but God thyself." And, according to the civilians, we must not give obedience to him that gives law out of his own territory, so neither obey man when he goes beyond his bounds in commanding against the word; and in this the apostles, Acts v. 29, and the three servants of God in Babylon, have been our examples.

Tert. lib. de Idol. c. 15. Extra territorium jus dicenti impune non paretur.

Obs. 7. Lust opposes restraint, is an enemy to dominion, loves not to be bridled. Libertines "despise dominion," and reject magistracy, because thereby their licentious humour is restrained, Acts xix. 27. The mad upon lust, like the mad dog, are the more enraged by the chain which curbs. They who run to excess of riot in this their pouring forth, if they meet with opposition, like the stopped stream, swell the higher, and overflow the banks. This opposing of restraint goes along with every lust, but especially with that of carnal uncleanness; they who defile the flesh reject dominion. The sons of Eli were lustful, and withal disobedient to the command of the magistrate, 1 Sam. ii. 22, 25. The Gibeonites were as refractory to the message of Israel as they were addicted to filthiness, Judg. xx. 13. The Sodomites were at the same time both set upon their uncleanness and enraged against Lot's counsel. The Anabaptists of Munster were grown to that height of uncleanness, that they openly taught men might marry as many wives as they pleased; and John of Leyden, their king, upon a pretended revelation from heaven, presently married three; and they who were most bold in this kind, and took most wives, were accounted the best men, and most commendable. But the fruit of this doctrine was, their teaching that before the day of judgment, Christ had a worldly kingdom, and in that the saints only had dominion; that this kingdom was that of the Anabaptists newly begun, wherein magistracy was to be rooted out; and although Christ and his apostles had no civil government, yet that they had committed the same, with the power of the sword, to those who after them should teach in the church. Nor is it possible but that lust should vehemently oppose restraint, considering its propensities and motions are natural, and therefore strong, as also furthered by all the helps which a powerful and impure spirit can invent and apply. False then is the pretence of libertines, who would be thought only to oppose the irregularities of magistracy or ministry, when it is clear that their lusts are most offended at the existence of their offices, and the conscientious discharge of them. And much should this comfort those who are thus conscientious, in the midst of all the rage and reproach with which they are followed for their faithfulness. It is a sign they have disquieted men's lusts; and, as Luther once said, when Satan roars, they have given him a full blow. Nor yet should the unquietness and troubles of the world be laid at the door of restraint and dominion. If religious opposition draws out men's rage, it does it by labouring to keep it in, or rather to take it away. From men's lusts are wars, in that they will not stoop to God, who will not lay aside his dominion to gratify licentiousness. In a word, we may hence gather the insufficiency of human laws, nay, any external means, to change the heart from a love of sin; they may possibly restrain and curb, and frequently irritate and enrage sinners, it is only the power of grace at once to take away the disobedience of the life, and the despising of the heart. To conclude, we may hence learn the direct way to avoid the sin of these seducers: oppose lusts, these put people upon opposing magistracy; such are, (1.) Covetousness, when men desire to set the nations on fire, that they may steal away the goods; and to have states wrecked, that the goods may be cast upon their coasts. (2.) Discontentedness with our condition. The trees in Jotham's parable pleased themselves in their own station, of privacy and usefulness; and she was a wise woman who contented herself with her abode among her own people. (3.) Ambition and affectation of superiority. It is better to be fit to rule, than to rule and not to be fit. He is only worthy of honour of whom honour itself is unworthy, and to whom it even sues for acceptance. Absalom aspired to be high in his life, and he was in his death as high as the boughs of the tree; a fit reward for his ambitious climbing. (4.) Envy at the height of others, whereby men look into the failings of magistrates to blemish them, and will not see the gifts and graces of their superiors, but only with repining; grieving, not because things go ill, but because they go no worse: a cursed temper! (5.) Self-conceitedness, whereby, with Absalom, men think themselves fitter to sit at the stern than any placed there already. (6.) Implacableness, whereby private injuries are retained with a watching of all occasions of revenge, though to the involving of multitudes in the copartnership of their own sedition and destruction. In a word, so long as we love lust, we cannot conscientiously obey magistrates; and yet so long as we have lust, we cannot be without magistrates. The Lord fit us for that condition wherein we shall not be troubled with the former, nor stand in need of the latter.

The second argument brought by our apostle to incite these Christians earnestly to contend for the faith opposed by the seducers, is taken from the certainty of the destruction of those ungodly men. This argument he handles from the fourth to the seventeenth verse. In managing which, having first mentioned sundry examples of God's judgments which befell the great sinners of former times, ver. 5—7; he now secondly adds, that these seducers lived in the very same sins which God had punished in those sinners of old; and this he prosecutes in the eighth, ninth, and tenth verses. And then thirdly, from ver. 10—17, he infers and amplifies this conclusion, Woe to them, ver. 11; q. d. Therefore these seducers shall likewise perish.

This eighth verse, then, is part of that second branch, wherein the apostle shows that these seducers lived in the same sins which God had punished in others.

Having treated of opposing authority in its first branch, viz. the despising dominion, I now proceed to speak of it in the second branch, contained in these words, they "speak evil of dignities."

By way of explication, I shall inquire into these two particulars:

1. Why the apostle calls magistrates, or persons in authority, "dignities?"

2. What was the sin of speaking evil of those dignities?

1. For the first. The apostle calls them "dignities," in Greek, δοξάς, glories, because of that glory and excellency wherewith God is pleased eminently and peculiarly to adorn them, whereby they raise in

the minds of people a singular admiration and veneration to themselves, joined with fear. To this purpose speaks the prophet concerning Nebuchadnezzar: "The most high God gave Nebuchadnezzar majesty and glory: and for the majesty that he gave him, all people, nations, and languages trembled and feared before him," Dan. v. 18, 19. And more particularly, this dignity or glory appears,

(1.) In those glorious titles wherewith magistrates are dignified and adorned above others. Hence they are called "kings," Luke xxii. 25, "princes," Matt. xx. 25, great men, "rulers," Rom. xiii. 3; Gen. xli. 43, "powers," Luke xii. 11, "governors," 2 Chron. xxiii. 20, "nobles," Jer. xiv. 3, "mighty ones," Ezek. xxxi. 11, "captains," 1 Sam. ix. 16, "children of the Most High," Psal. lxxxii. 6, "the sons of the mighty," Psal. lxxxix. 6, fathers, anointed, saviours, and, as the upshot of all, gods, because they are from God, and ought to be for God: they are appointed by him, and to be employed for him; they stand in the place of God, and are his vicegerents on earth, and have a particular charge and power of executing the judgments of God among men. "Ye judge not," saith Jehoshaphat to his judges, "for men, but for the Lord," 2 Chron. xix. 6.

(2.) In those endowments and qualifications wherewith God has adorned them for executing their offices; God never bestowing employments without endowments. Saul being chosen king, is said to have another heart given him, 1 Sam. x. 9. He had those heroic gifts and kingly abilities of wisdom, valour, &c., infused into him, which enabled him to discharge his place of government. He who formerly sought asses, now spent his thoughts about preserving his kingdom. When David was anointed king by Samuel, it is said that the Spirit of God came upon him, 1 Sam. xvi. 13, which furnished him with gifts, as of sanctification, wherewith though formerly endowed, yet possibly not in so great a measure as now, so of regimen and government; and, it may be, of prophecy and poetry, Numb. xi. 17; 2 Kings ii. 15; Exod. xviii. 21; Deut. i. 13.

(3.) In that due respect or honour which is yielded to them. This is, first, Internal; consisting, 1. In an honourable opinion and high estimation of them. Despising and thinking evil with the heart, will make way for despising and speaking evil with the tongue: the people thought David worth ten thousand of them. It was Korah's sin to think, for else he had not said as he did, that Moses and Aaron were no more excellent than the rest of the people, Numb. xvi. 3. 2. This internal honour stands in a reverent and awful fear of them; a duty which we owe to our parents, either by nature or analogy, Lev. xix. 3.

Secondly, External; as, 1. To rise up when the person of the magistrate is in presence, Job xxix. 8. 2. As in most countries, to uncover the head. 3. To bow the body, 2 Sam. xxiv. 20; the knee, Gen xli. 43. 4. To stand, Exod. xviii. 13; 2 Kings v. 25. 5. To be silent when he speaks, and to attend, Job xxix. 9, 10. 6. To use words of submissiveness, as Gen. xlii. 10, they call Joseph, My lord, and themselves his servants, ver. 13. 7. To obey, Josh. i. 16, though in the Lord, Eph. vi. 1. 8. To pray for the magistrate, 1 Tim. ii. 1, 2.

(4.) Lawyers and politicians mention sundry *jura majestatis*, or rights belonging to majesty; as, 1. The giving of laws. 2. The exercise of supreme jurisdiction, beyond which there is no appeal. 3. The power of the militia. 4. Receiving tribute of lands, custom from the sea, subsidy of goods. 5. The liberty of hunting. 6. A propriety in such things as have no rightful owners to claim them. 7. The deriving of honours. 8. The coining of money. To which may be added that state or port suitable to their places, in respect of attendance, diet, apparel, buildings, &c., Gen. xli. 41, 42.

2. We inquire what was the sin of speaking evil of dignities?

These words, "speak evil," are in the original one word, βλασφημοῦσι, they blaspheme. It signifies properly to hurt one's name by defamation or slander. And though it be now appropriated to a dishonour offered to God's name, yet frequently in Scripture it is used for defaming or evil speaking against man; as 1 Cor. iv. 13, Being defamed, evil spoken of, (βλασφημούμενοι,) blasphemed, we entreat; and 1 Pet. iv. 4, "Wherein they think it strange that ye run not with them to the same excess of riot," βλασφημοῦντες, blaspheming, or "speaking evil of you." So Rom. iii. 8, καθὼς βλασφημούμεθα, "as we be slanderously reported." And here in this place the word is spoken concerning defaming, or speaking evil of persons in authority; a sin with which the seducers are in this place charged; they being such, who, because they could not by the power of their hand remove and displace magistrates, would do their utmost to blast and abuse them by the poison of their tongue.

This sin of speaking evil of dignities may be several ways committed. Sometimes more secretly, by whispering only, or libelling, for fear of censure: scandals of governors have seldom any fathers; they kill, and make no report; they steal away reputation. Sometimes more openly, and before any, promiscuously: and both these ways of evil speaking may be in a way either of murmuring, or of mutinying. Of murmuring. When the people are in any distress, oft the first stone of complaint is thrown against the magistrate. The Israelites want water, and they pray not to God, but murmur against Moses, as if he had made the waters bitter, and the wilderness dry. It is a kingly condition to deserve well and hear ill. If men prosper never so much, they only applaud themselves; if they suffer never so little, they murmur against their rulers. Of mutinying. Sometimes men so speak evil of magistracy, as to raise up evil against them. Murmurers offend out of impatience, mutineers out of envy: by the former, governors are taxed for not taking enough; by the latter, for taking too much upon them, Numb. xvi. 3. Though Moses's command was a burden to him, yet was it an eyesore to others, Korah and his company. This sin offends both by uttering against rulers things false and evil: thus Absalom unworthily traduces his father's government, by telling the Israelites that there was no man deputed of the king to hear them, 2 Sam. xv. 3; and Shimei cursed and reviled David, by calling him a bloody man, and a man of Belial, 2 Sam. xvi. 7. And by uttering things true and good, falsely and evilly, as sometimes, though reporting, yet lessening, extenuating, and detracting from their good actions, or depraving them as done of bad intents, for bad ends, or in hypocrisy; by uncovering their secret infirmities, by amplifying and aggravating their faults; affirming that miscarriage to be deliberately done, which was done rashly; or presumptuously, which was done weakly, &c.

The sinfulness of this evil speaking appears several

ways. (1.) By its notoriously thwarting and opposing the evident commands of Scripture.* "Thou shalt not revile the gods, nor curse the ruler of thy people," Exod. xxii. 28; Eccl. x. 20; a text cited by Paul himself, Acts xxiii. 5, who there, as I humbly conceive, apologizes for himself for his sudden and unadvised expression, in calling the high priest a whited wall; the words οὐκ ᾔδειν not signifying, I knew not, absolutely; but, I wist not, I considered not, I heeded not, I took not sufficient notice how he was the high priest: q. d. In my haste I termed him whited wall, which term, I confess, might well have been spared, not because it was false, but not fit, nor consonant to that which is written. "Honour the king," 1 Pet. ii. 17. "Render to all their dues," &c., "honour to whom honour," Rom. xiii. 7. The will of God, against all pretexts imaginable, should be the end of all strife. (2.) Because the speaking evil of dignities is the speaking evil of God himself, who ordained them. If he who mocketh the poor, then much more he who revileth the ruler, reproacheth his Maker, Prov. xvii. 5. In the contempt of magistrates God accounts himself contemned: "They have not," saith God to Samuel, "rejected thee, but they have rejected me," 1 Sam. viii. 7. And this was the true cause why God was so angry with Miriam and Aaron, who spake against Moses: "Wherefore were ye not afraid to speak against my servant Moses?" Numb. xii. 1, 8. To speak against him whom God appointed and set on work, is to speak against a great one indeed. (3.) By the punishments inflicted upon such revilers, which are evident in the example of Miriam, Absalom, Korah, &c. All princes are not like Titus, the delight of mankind, who said, None can reproach me, because I do nothing that can be reprehended; and those things which are spoken of me falsely, I altogether neglect: for Tiberius, when Paconius had scattered reproachful verses against him, wrote to the senate to appoint severe punishment against him; and although many princes have remitted the injury as offered to their own persons, yet as prejudicial to the good of the commonwealth, they have, and that deservedly, punished them. And however princes themselves have spared such railers, yet God would not suffer them to go unpunished, as in the case of Shimei, whom, though David spared, yet God spared not. (4.) This speaking evil of magistrates is a spreading evil, hurtful to others: the reviler kills many with one shoot; himself, speaking wickedly; the ruler, whom he accuses unjustly; his hearer, who listens to him credulously. A reproaching tongue, being, though worst to himself, yet hurtful to those who hear him: and who knoweth how great a fire the tongue of one reviler may kindle? Seldom such a pedlar opens his pack of wares but some or other will buy. No music is so sweet to most, as to hear well of themselves and ill of their rulers. People's hearts and ears are commonly tinder and touchwood, presently taking fire when any spark of defamation flies from the fire of a reviler's tongue; and how great a flame such a spark may kindle, we may see in the cases of Absalom and Sheba.

Imaginem Dei rex gestat, idcirco colendus et amandus est; si non propter se, saltem vocationis et functionis suæ causa.

Deliciæ humani generis. Nemo me insequi contumelia potest, propterea quod nihil ago quod reprehendi mereatur: ea vero quæ false de me dicuntur, prorsus negligo. Dio.

Lev. xix. 16, "a talebearer." רכיל signifieth a trafficker up and down.

Obs. 1. Great is the audacious extravagancy of an unmortified tongue. James, chap. iii. 6, calls it a "fire;" and here we see it aspires like fire, and moves upward, and fastens upon such things as were much above it. Peter saith these seducers "are not afraid to

Μεγαλαυχεῖ. Jam. iii. 5.

* See p. 175, concerning the sin of despising dominion.

speak evil of dignities," 2 Pet. ii. 10: the tongue set on fire by hell below, fires even upon those which are called gods, and are in the highest and most eminent degree. "The tongue speaketh proud things," Psal. xii. 3. "In the mouth of the foolish is the rod of pride," Prov. xiv. 3. In which place the fool's tongue may either be termed a rod of pride, which for proud speaking shall whip the fool himself; or else a rod which by the fool's proud speaking whips and lashes any other. The Septuagint read it, The fool's tongue is βακτηρία ὕβρεως, a rod of reproach; and some conceive in using the word חטר Gr. ῥαβδίον, (according to some,) Solomon alludes to the custom of magicians, who by their rods were wont to do their magical exploits and false miracles of transforming, metamorphosing, and changing the shapes of things, Exod. vii. 12; as if these proud railers by the rods of their tongues, their revilings and slanderous reproaches, laboured to metamorphose and transform men, making the honourable to appear base, the learned most illiterate, and the upright most dishonest. The pride of the heart is most frequently discovered by the tongue. Rabshakeh threatened he would make them "eat their own dung." The tongue threatens God himself: "I will ascend into the heavens, I will exalt my throne above the stars of God," Isa. xiv. 13. "Talk no more exceeding proudly," saith Hannah, 1 Sam. ii. 3. "They set their mouth against the heavens, and their tongue walketh through the earth," Psal. lxxiii. 9. "Our tongues are our own; who is lord over us?" Psal. xii. 4. The tongue, though small, opposes the greatest. It was a gracious care of David to take heed to his tongue, Psal. xxxix. 1. Man's glory, his tongue, must not be employed against God's glory, or the magistrate's, here called glories. The tongue, of which we had not the use till we had the use of reason, was never appointed to be used without reason, for pride and passion. He who made the tongue soft and pliable, all flesh, without a bone in it, teaches us that it should not be harsh, rugged, and proud in its expressions: the double rail or hedge of the teeth and lips shows that this wild beast is very unruly, James iii. 8, and that it ought to be kept in. The best way to keep the fire from breaking out at the chimney, is to quench the coals upon the hearth: a cool and humble heart will abate the heat of the fiery tongue.

Leviter volat sermo, sed graviter vulnerat; leviter transit, sed graviter urit; leviter profertur, sed non leviter revocatur; facile volat, atque adeo facile violat charitatem. Bern. Serm. de trip. cust.

κακὸν ἀκατάσχετον.

Obs. 2. Dignities lie open to the lash of the tongue. The more eminent the person, the more censured is his action: the highest towers are most frequently blasted with lightning; nor power, nor innocency can protect from imputations. The fire of the tongue dares touch even laurel, which lightning (they say) never blasts: the sword of the mouth will adventure even upon the mouth of the sword. When Saul was chosen, and carried and lifted up with highest acclamations, the sons of Belial despised him, 1 Sam. x. 27. It is a vain ambition to expect the good word of all. It is an equal weakness to be proud of the applause, and impatient under the reproaches of the multitude: the care of all, especially of governors, should be rather to be worthy of honour than to receive honour, rather to be honourable than honoured; and not so much to seek quiet abroad, as in themselves and the conscience of their upright and sincere endeavours. It is better to deserve well, and to hear ill; than to deserve ill, and to hear well.

Obs. 3. Magistrates should take heed of blemishing their dignity, and losing their glory. The apostle here calls them dignities or glories. And to maintain their glory, it is not enough to be magnificent and outwardly pompous in their attendance, apparel, diet, buildings, &c., but let them show themselves dignities in their entrance into their places, and in their deportment when they are entered. (1.) For their entrance, let it not be sordid and unworthy, in the way of suing by friends, money, &c. Such should be preferred, not as would have places, but such as places would have. Olives, vines, fig-trees refuse their honours; brambles catch hold on preferment. Saul's modesty in hiding himself when chosen king, detracted not from his dignity when he accepted it. It was a high commendation of Theodosius the emperor, that when he had done all that could make him worthy to rule, he would do nothing that he might rule. The worthiest to govern, are they often who think themselves unworthiest. Let Christ herein be the pattern, who humbled himself; but he left his exaltation to his Father. How is dignity debased, when they are advanced, not who deserve best, but bid fairest! when money makes the magistrate, and shall provide preferment for him who is not at all fit for that! What wonder is it to see that they who buy their places dear, should afterward sell justice dear also? (2.) In their deportment when they are entered. Let magistrates keep up their glory, [1.] By wisdom and understanding; if no Christian, much less must a magistrate, be a child in understanding: a fool cannot be harmless. A king in our English expression imports as much as cunning, or knowing, from the old Saxon word koëning. Wisdom makes a man's, especially a magistrate's, face to shine: wisdom and magistracy cast a reciprocal lustre upon one another. Solomon's wisdom made him more glorious and sought to than his wealth. It was a notable speech of our Henry the First, A king without learning is but a crowned ass: that creature is but contemptible under the richest ornaments. If a ruler's calling hinders him from the study of many commendable parts of learning, yet let it put him upon such studies as are necessarily requisite to the understanding of government: "The wisdom of the prudent is to understand his way," Prov. xiv. 8. To preserve dignity, a magistrate in his place must carry himself, [2.] Courageously. Solomon's throne was beset with lions, not with apes. They who oppose vice, had need of heroic spirits: cowards are fitter to be slaves than rulers. A magistrate in his own cause should be as flexible as a reed; in the cause of God, as stiff as an oak. A timorous ruler is a hare in a lion's skin: all dare meddle with him, who dares meddle with none. And it is just with God, that he should suffer by the subjects, who dares not make their sins suffer by him. [3.] Let dignity be upheld by the hatred of covetousness, base and filthy lucre. How unseemly is it for a golden spade to dig in a dunghill! for the robe of an emperor to stop an oven! Let not those who are called gods grovel in the earth: what is not cheap to him, to whom money is dear? How unfit is it for a magistrate to soar high in respect of his place, and at the same time, like the kite, to have his eye fixed upon the dunghill, or carrion! It is the judgment of God against covetousness, that they who follow gain as their god, shall yet account another a base miser for doing so. It was a noble speech of Themistocles, who seeing a precious stone upon the ground, bid another take it up; For thou, said he, art not Themistocles. [4.] To preserve dignity, let magistrates carry themselves usefully, industriously, for the public good. There is a near conjunction between dignity and duty. The shadow of honour attends upon the body of service. It was a true speech of the wise old counsellors to Rehoboam, "If thou wilt be a servant to this people," &c. "they will be thy servants," 1 Kings xii. 7. The tree which is most deeply rooted flourishes and spreads most; and the person who is most deeply and lowly engaged in service, shall best flourish and spread in renown. Empty are those titles which are only obtained by birth, retinue, and favour, &c. The titles of most illustrious, excellency, right honourable, &c. bestowed upon an unprofitable governor, are but nicknames and upbraidings for his not being what he should, and is said to be; and as unduly given him, as the names of wholesome drugs are put upon empty boxes in the apothecary's shop. [5.] Let dignity be upheld with piety. Holiness is the lustre of all other accomplishments, and the most lasting foundation of honour: "They that honour me will I honour." If religion at the bar make the profane magistrate to tremble, much more may religion on the bench dismay a profane offender. When the lusts of wicked subjects make them willingly reproach religious rulers, their consciences shall make them unwillingly honour them. Never did those magistrates long preserve their own names, who suffered God's to be profaned. The greatest potentate on earth cannot be loose and ungodly by authority; their place will not bear them out in it. Religion is no disparagement to magistracy. How needless, how unsuitable is it for great ones to fear nothing more than to have a name to fear God!

Obs. 4. How highly is God provoked, when he makes these dignities and glories unglorious! It is no small offence that puts the Lord upon pouring contempt upon princes; that makes him stain the pride of their glory, and cover it with shameful spewing. When Manasseh shall be fettered, Jehoiakim be a broken idol, " buried with the burial of an ass," and the signet upon the right hand plucked thence, and thrown on the dunghill, Jer. xxii. 19, 24, Nebuchadnezzar turned into a beast, &c.; when the Lord deals thus with rulers, they should look beyond a rebellious, headstrong people: they have *negotium cum Deo:* their work is to look inward and upward, to study what their sin has been which has incensed God to debase that which he commands all others to honour. If the Lord suffer people to cast off the yoke of their obedience to princes, surely princes first cast off the yoke of obedience to God. " They who despise God shall be lightly esteemed," 1 Sam. ii. 30. If it be the Lord who subdues the people under princes, Psal. xviii. 47, it is he that subdues princes under their people. It is God who "stilleth the noise of the seas, and the tumult of the people," Psal. lxv. 7. If he remove the banks and bounds of his protection, the proud waves both of seas and popular tumults will overflow the highest mountains. If at any time princes are overborne by such an overflowing scourge, let them examine themselves whether they have not transgressed the bounds of God's commandments; whether if God deal with them as with Saul, Manasseh, Nebuchadnezzar, Zedekiah, Jehu, Jeroboam, they have not, with them, been disobedient, idolatrous, proud, and oppressive. The alterations of governors and governments peculiarly belong to God's prerogative royal. He " ruleth in the kingdom of men, giveth it to whomsoever he will, and setteth up over it the basest of men." And the putting of proud princes and people upon a holy and humble consideration hereof, which can never be, unless not only his bare permission, but even his positive working, and such as flows from his effectual ordination, be acknowledged, is clearly intimated in Scripture to be one main end of the severe dispensa-

Cum omnia faceret ut imperare deberet, nihil faciebat ut imperaret.

Eo dignior erat quo magis se clamabat indignum. Hier. in Epitaph. Nepot.

tions of providence, in pulling down governments and debasing dignities, Dan. iv. 17.

Obs. 5. It is lawful for magistrates to preserve their authority by a certain external, though decent and moderate, pomp and majesty. They may lawfully use and receive titles of honour, and have attendance, apparel, buildings, diet, suitable to their dignities; the Spirit of God here calls them dignities, or glories. Paul gave to Festus the title of "most noble," Acts xxvi. 25. God himself has cast upon rulers a beam of his glory; honour and majesty hath God laid upon them, Psal. xxi. 5. "The most high God," saith Daniel, "gave Nebuchadnezzar a kingdom, and majesty, and glory, and honour," Dan. v. 18, 19. Faithful and godly Joseph, when advanced, was adorned with Pharaoh's ring and a gold chain, arrayed in vestures of fine linen, riding in the second chariot which Pharaoh had, they crying before him, "Bow the knee," Gen. xli. 41, 43. Jude here puts dominion and dignities together. Magistracy decked with dignity, is oft hated and envied; and stripped of dignity, is always scorned and contemned. The fomenters of anarchical confusions well know this, who endeavour to overthrow dignities that they may thereby destroy dominions. Nor yet ought magistrates to please themselves with titles and dignities, empty of that goodness and worth which should accompany and adorn greatness; they should not so affect the title, as to neglect the thing and work of which their titles admonish them. Glorious titles and dignities, contradicted by a wicked and undue deportment, proclaim equally both the sin and shame of those upon whom they are cast. To conclude, though rulers should be honoured, yet not adored; they should so endure to be acknowledged the people's superiors, as to fear to be accounted God's equals. Soon was Herod the food of worms when he patiently endured to have his voice cried up for the voice of God. Historians mention the sacrilegious impiety of Domitian, who would be called by the people, The lord our god. To these may be added the proud usurpations of the pope, who exalts himself above all that is called God, who pretends to pardon sin, and to be the head of the church; and of those princes that have taken the title of most mighty, most invincible, &c.

<small>Prohibiti sunt maledici, non jussi sunt sacrificiis honorari. Aug. q. 86. in Exod.</small>

<small>Suet. in vita Dom. cap. 13.</small>

Obs. 6. It is our duty to be cautioned against flattering governors. They are dignities and glories, but should not dazzle our eyes into a sinful winking at their sins. Though they are not to be reviled, yet neither soothed when they offend God. What ill have governors deserved at our hands, that we should, instead of friends, be their flatterers? and that they only of all the men in the world should be without friends, that is, reprovers? We must honour them instead of, not against God: "Say unto the king and queen, Humble yourselves," Jer. xiii. 18. More than once we read that Samuel reproved Saul, 1 Sam. xv. 28; nor did Nathan spare David, 2 Sam. xii. 1—14; or Elijah Ahab, 1 Kings xviii. 18; or Isaiah Hezekiah, Isa. xxxix. 6; or the Baptist Herod, Matt. xiv. 4. The danger of flattering rulers reaches beyond themselves. The soothing of such in sin is the casting of a bag of poison into a common fountain serving for the use of the whole city. Nor yet ought the reprehending of public persons to be practised without much prudence, lest by it the disease be rather irritated than cured. Singular was the wisdom of Nathan to draw the sentence of David against himself out of his own mouth, 2 Sam. xii. 5—7; 1 Kings xx. 39. Nor do all sorts of faults require

<small>Honor quo præditi sunt non est vitiorum integumentum.</small>

the same severity in reproving: some sins are warts, others are ulcers; some are secret, and then the plaster should not be broader than the sore, the reprehension more open than the offence. Care is to be had lest reprehension degenerate into sedition; preachers for conversion should have another aim. In short, in every reproof, difference is to be put between the person and office of the magistrate; the dignity of the office should not suffer for the vices of the person, nor should the vices of the person be spared for the dignity of the office.

This for the specification of the faults of these seducers, which was the first branch in the first part of the text. The second branch of this first part of the text follows, viz. the aggravation of these faults, in that the apostle saith, that these seducers sinned "likewise also." In which two words the apostle expresseth a twofold aggravation of their sins.

The first stands in the harmony or consent between the sins of these seducers and the wickedness of those who went before them; they sinned "likewise."

2. The second stands in the obstinacy of these sinners in their impieties, they sinning "also," or, as Beza reads it, notwithstanding they knew the forementioned severe judgments which had befallen the former sinners for their impieties.

<small>Similiter tamen.</small>

I shall but briefly touch upon both these by way of explication, the difficulty not being great, although the matter contained in them profitable.

1. The harmony or consent of these seducers with former sinners in their wickedness is expressed in this word ὁμοίως, likewise; a word importing as much as those words in the seventh verse, where the apostle saith that the cities about Sodom and Gomorrha did ὅμοιον τούτοις τρόπον, in like manner give themselves, &c. If it be demanded wherein that agreement or consent which was between these seducers and former sinners consists; it is answered by some, that the apostle did not intend that these seducers walked precisely in the same particular sins in which the forementioned sinners, the Israelites, angels, Sodomites, had lived; or that they traced them κατὰ πόδα, step by step, in every several sort of wickedness, but only that they were in general very grievous and heinous sinners, as those of old were, giving themselves with them over to all manner of impiety.

But comparing the practice of these seducers with the sins wherewith the Israelites, angels, Sodomites were charged, as also considering the word "likewise" most properly imports such a connexion of this verse with the former, as is intended that these seducers imitated those former sinners in those very sins which were before by the apostle mentioned, ver. 5—7; I conceive it may be best answered, that the agreement here mentioned by Jude between the former and latter sinners, was an agreement in the same sins for sort and kind; and that he intends, as the Israelites and angels proudly refused to yield due obedience and subjection to God; the former rebelling against God who governed them immediately, the latter despising that government which he exercised over them by his servant Moses; and as the Sodomites sinned by sensual filthiness and carnal uncleanness, in like manner did these seducers "defile the flesh, and despise dominions," &c. And yet I doubt not but the apostle in this word "likewise" insinuates a further agreement between these former and latter sinners; and that was in the same punishment which was likewise to fall upon those who lived in the same sins for which they of old were punished.

<small>Videtur Judas indicare Gnosticos Sodomitis fuisse similes, quasi eorum improbitatem imitarentur. Vid. Justinian in loc.</small>

The second aggravation of the wickedness of these

seducers is taken from their obstinacy in sinning, contained in this expression, μέντοι, "also," or notwithstanding; noting that these seducers sinned, although they well knew what judgments of God had befallen the forementioned sinners for the very same sins of which they were guilty. These angels, Israelites, Sodomites had been whipped (as it were) before their eyes; God had laid them before them for a δεῖγμα, as Jude spake before, an example to them who after should live ungodly, ver. 7. These judgments were as a buoy before the anchor, to prevent the dashing of future generations against the same destruction. Yet these seducers sinned notwithstanding these judgments of God upon those of old, Rom. i. 32; like a thief, so mad upon cutting a purse, that he commits that offence even under the gallows whereon one was newly hanged for the same fault.

Obs. 1. Great is our proneness to follow corrupt example. Of this before, p. 160.

Obs. 2. There is a proneness to sin in every age of the world. Israelites and Sodomites before, and these seducers afterward, provoke God. A doctrine that puts the godly both upon a holy contention against, and contentation under the iniquity of their times; they should be both patient and zealous: patient, to show their submission to God's providence; zealous, to preserve their own purity; they must shine as lights in the midst of a crooked generation, Phil. ii. 15. Even the godly are as ready to savour of the follies of their generation, as waters to receive a twang from the earth through which they run.

Obs. 3. The wicked agree in sinning; they run together into the same excess of riot, 1 Pet. iv. 4. Hand may join in hand against holiness. This unity is but conspiracy, it is against unity. God's people should be ashamed of their divisions even by the example of sinners.

Obs. 4. Greatest severities are in themselves insufficient to work upon sinners. These seducers sinned notwithstanding the punishing of the same sins formerly. What a calamitous catalogue of judgments do we find mentioned by Amos, chap. iv.! and though all of them had been inflicted upon the people, yet did not the punished return to the Lord. They turn not, (saith the prophet,) "to him that smiteth, neither do they seek the Lord of hosts," Isa. ix. 13. And Lev. xxvi. 39, it is not threatened only as a judgment, that the people should be carried into their enemy's land, but, which is far worse, that there they should pine away in their iniquities; though their liberties, estates, lives were consumed, yet their sins outlived them, and remained. Their iniquities did not pine away in them, but they in their iniquities. The prophet Hosea compares them to a foolish child, that stays in the place of breaking forth of children, Hos. xiii. 13. Men may be in troubles, and yet rather die there than seek by repentance to be delivered; like as the prophet in that passage uses the comparison of a foolish child, which though in a dark, stifling womb, there continues, though to the destruction of itself and mother. There is an insufficiency in all outward dispensations to change the disposition of the heart: the back may be broken, and yet the heart remain unbroken. Though devils be thrust down into and tormented in hell, yet they ever continue proud and unreformed. Ahaz trespassed the more the more he was distressed, 2 Chron. xxviii. 22: judgments may irritate, not remove sin; they may make us fret and rage by stopping us in a way of sin, as a dam makes the torrent the more to rise and swell, but they cannot turn or dry up a stream of corruption. Resistance occasions it to break forth afterward with the greater violence. Great wounds cannot work in us good wills: unless grace inwardly renews us, as well as troubles outwardly restrain us, there will be no true turning to God. The more God stopped Baalam in his way, the more mad he was to be going on. A man who is stopped in the street with a cart, is not made thereby out of love with his journey, but the more resolved to go on the faster afterward. It is a singular mercy when an affliction is wrought into us: if God has a mind to do us good, he will make us good by all our troubles. This is the depth of misery, for God to say, Let him that is filthy, notwithstanding his washing, continue so still. Consider in every trouble thy work is with God, and that not only to observe him sending it, but to beg his blessing upon it. Beseech him that no wind may go down till it has blown thee nearer thy haven, to take off no plaster till thy sores are healed; pray not so much with Pharaoh, to have the frogs, as with David, to have thy sins, taken away. Calamities are then removed in mercy, when sanctified before they are removed. Love me not, Lord, said Augustine, with that love wherewith thou puttest one out of the way, but reducest him that is wandering. *Non quo extrudis de via, sed quo corrigis devium.*

Thus we have explained the first part of this verse, viz. the faults wherewith these seducers were charged, both in their specification and aggravation. Now follows,

II. The fountain from which these faults issued, intended in this expression, "filthy dreamers."

In the explication of which I shall show in what sense the apostle here gives these seducers this title, and the sin and misery in being such as this title imports.

The word here interpreted "filthy dreamers," in the Greek is ἐνυπνιαζόμενοι, signifying properly such who are dreaming in sleep. *Ἐνυπνιαστὴς somniator.* Beza renders the word *sopiti*, such who are fast or sound asleep, in a deep, dead sleep. Erasmus and Vatablus, *delusi in somniis*, such who are deluded in dreams. The Vulgate wholly omits the translation of the word; *Ἐνυπνιάζει τῶν ζώων μάλιστα ὁ ἄνθρωπος. Arist.* but the word properly signifies such who in their sleep are dreaming; and thus Joseph is called ἐνυπνιαστής, a dreamer; and in Acts ii. 17, it is said, "your old men" ἐνύπνια ἐνυπνιασθήσονται, "shall dream dreams," importing likewise thus to dream in sleep. And these of whom our apostle here speaks may be termed dreamers in sleep, either in a proper or in a metaphorical sense. If, (1.) In a proper sense, then these seducers were dreamers in their natural and bodily rest and sleep: thus they, mentioned Acts ii. 17, dreamed dreams in their natural sleep; and thus Gagneius, Vatablus, Salmeron understand this place; as if the apostle had intended, that these impure seducers put forth and expressed their filthy lustfulness in their very dreams, when they were asleep. *Redundat effusior libido usque ad nocturnas inter dormiendum pollutiones. Vatab.* Thus likewise our own learned interpreters understood this dreaming in sleep, as is plain by their rendering the word ἐνυπνιαζόμενοι, by "filthy dreamers," as conceiving that these seducers in their unclean dreams had defiled and polluted their bodies when they were in their natural sleep; not that the word ἐνυπνιαζόμενοι admits of the interpretation of filthy dreams by the force of its own signification, for in Acts ii. 17 it is used in a good sense, namely, of holy and pure dreaming; but the foresaid interpreters were pleased so to refer this word to the following expression, viz. "defile the flesh," that they interpreted it of that dreaming in sleep wherein these seducers defiled their bodies by nocturnal pollutions, Lev. xv. 16. A strong inducement hence may be gathered for every one to hate that odious and, I fear, too common a sin of self-pollution, and to keep their hearts with all diligence from those impure thoughts in the day-time, which may otherwise make them filthy dreamers in the night; and when they go to sleep, to beseech God to keep the key of their imagination, that it may not run out into dreaming impurely.

But secondly, others, and those the most, better interpret this dreaming of which Jude speaks metaphorically, or in a borrowed sense; conceiving that the apostle here in calling these seducers dreamers in sleep, compares them to such; and that,

In respect of sleeping, and of dreaming in sleep.

1. In respect of sleeping, these seducers may be compared to dreamers in sleep; they were spiritually drowned, overwhelmed in a deep, sound sleep of sin; such a deep sleep as the prophet mentions, "The Lord hath poured upon you the spirit of a deep sleep," Isa. xxix. 10, a dead and midnight sleep. "Let us not sleep as do others," 1 Thess. v. 6. "While the bridegroom tarried, they all slumbered and slept," &c., Matt. xxv. 5. This spiritual sleep in sin is threefold, as divines observe. (1.) That natural sleep whereby every one is overtaken, and is both unable and unwilling to move himself to the least supernatural good till God awake him by his Spirit, and effectually say unto him, Awake, thou that sleepest, and stand up from the dead. (2.) That slumber, or the remains of that natural sleep in the godly, continuing in them even after they are awakened out of their dead sleep of nature; they being hereby oft overtaken with spiritual slumber, by reason of the relics of sin still abiding in them. This the spouse acknowledges, "I sleep, but my heart waketh," Cant. v. 2. (3.) The third is a judicial and penal increase of that natural sleep, and that deadness of heart, by the custom and continuance in sin. This is properly that forementioned deep sleep, Isa. xxix. 10, poured upon the impenitent Jews; and this last is that which is here attributed to these seducers. And in two respects may such sinners be compared to men in a deep sleep; in regard of the causes, and the effects of sleep.

[1.] The causes of sleep. 1. The sleep of the body comes from obstruction and binding up of the senses by vapours which arise out of the stomach; so the spiritual fumes of worldly cares and desires obstruct the senses of the soul; therefore our Saviour speaks of being oppressed, or overcharged, with surfeiting and drunkenness, Luke xxi. 34. Prosperity is a vapour, which if it overcome not, yet weakens the brain, as strong waters do. This was the cause of David's, Solomon's, and Asa's sleep. 2. Sleep ariseth from weariness and want of spirits; and there is a weariness causing spiritual sleep, namely, that which arises from too much expense of the strength of the soul upon other matters, impertinences that concern not its true happiness and welfare. 3. Oft sleep comes from want of exercise; and when there is a cessation from spiritual exercises, prayer, hearing, sacraments, meditation, there follows a spiritual sleep: these are the fuel of grace; and he that will not exercise himself to godliness, 1 Tim. iv. 7, shall never keep himself long awake. 4. Sleep may come from sleepy yawning and slothful company; the company of spiritual sluggards causes spiritual sleep. Cold, formal persons cast a damp upon the heat of others; frozen company derive a spiritual iciness into the souls of those who converse much with them. 5. Some are made to sleep by singing and music; and many by the flatteries and sinful soothing of false doctrines, of libertinism, or Arminianism, &c., and by the unfaithfulness of those who dare not reprove for, but soothe in sin, are cast into a spiritual sleep.

[2.] Sinners may be compared to men in a deep sleep, because of the effects of sleep; and that in respect, 1. Of their want of shame and bashfulness in sin; they who are asleep, though naked, yet blush not: these seducers proclaimed their sin like Sodom. They could not blush, saith the prophet, Jer. viii. 12: a blushing colour is not the colour of such impudent ones. 2. Of their unarmedness and liableness to danger. In sleep, the most precious thing men carry about them may be taken away without resistance; they suffer that to be loose which they held fast before, be it ever so rich a jewel. Sisera was slain in his sleep, and Ishbosheth upon his bed, and in spiritual sleep men suffer the precious jewel of truth, and the profession thereof, to be wrung from them, and may be robbed of all that good which they had. There is no temptation, sin, or judgment but a sleeping Christian is exposed to; he is a field without a fence, a city without a watch, he hinders no invader, he is ruined without resistance. In the approach of judgments, he is naked; he makes not the name of the Lord his strong tower, he cannot act faith to close up himself in the wounds of Jesus Christ. The people of God in the midst of troubles are above them, whereas wicked men, though without trials, are ever exposed to them; they fence their estates, families, &c., not their souls. 3. In respect of unactiveness, and being without motion. Men in a deep sleep are without sense and motion: wicked men act not, move not holily; what they do they do without delight; they are summer-sluggards, harvest-sleepers; though the work be great, there is no working. A sleeping sinner works not out his salvation, he offers no violence to the kingdom of heaven, he strives not to enter the strait gate, he wrestles not in prayer, he lives as if he had nothing to do in the world; heaven is not his business: he is, but he lives not; he is a spiritual drone, a mute, a cipher, a nullity, a superfluity in the world; like Jeremiah's rotten girdle, or bad figs, Jer. xiii. 1—12; xxiv. 1—10; or like Ezekiel's vine branches, weak and unfruitful, good for nothing but the fire, not fit to make beams or rafters of, Ezek. xv. Such a kind of rest as this to a saint would be his greatest unquietness; unserviceableness is a kind of hell upon earth to a godly man. 4. In respect of unwillingness to be disturbed, stirred, or disquieted. Men disposed to sleep desire to be alone; they who are spiritually sleepy avoid such company as would rouse them from their sloth; they compose themselves to rest, draw the curtains, put out the candle, are afraid to be disquieted by the light; they are loth to do what they know, and to know what either they do or should do. "They that sleep," saith the apostle, "sleep in the night," 1 Thess. v. 7; they are angry with the word and ministers, because they will not let them sleep quietly in sin: such as will let them alone in sin, and never disturb them, are the quiet, honest men; they will not endure wholesome words, sound doctrine. 5. And especially in respect of insensibleness, stupidity, blockishness. Men in a deep sleep feel nothing that is done to them. This I conceive Jude principally aims at, for "likewise also," or notwithstanding, saith he, they knew the judgments of God upon others, yet still they sinned, they slept: so senseless and stupid were they! their consciences were "seared with a hot iron," 1 Tim. iv. 2, "past feeling," Eph. iv. 19, bound up by a deep benumbedness caused by custom in sin: this was that deep sleep poured upon them by God, like that which befell Adam, whereby though a rib was taken out of him, yet he perceived it not; like that also of Saul, Sisera, and Jonah. The apostle expresses it by that significant word κατάνυξις, Rom. xi. 8; we translate it "slumber:" it signifies, say some, midnight sleep, which is the time when men are most thoroughly asleep. But by this word, say others better, is imported such a sleep as out of which all the pinching, wounding, pricking, cannot raise a man; or such a sleep as whereby a man is so fastened and nailed down to his sloth, that he and his sloth cannot be parted; the word κατάνυξις properly signifying pricking, or compunction: "They were pricked," &c., Acts ii. 37. And so great is the spiritual stupidity and insensibleness of sinners in their sleep of sin, that, (1.) They are insensible of the greatest dangers; these they prevent not, yea, foresee not: they go on, and are punished; they fear nothing; feeling only troubles them, and that too when it is too late; they are like drunken men on the top of a mast. (2.) They are insensible of the loudest noises; severest denunciations do but deafen their ears; nor do voices lifted up like a trumpet make them prepare for a battle. (3.) They are insensible of the stirrings and joggings given them in their spiritual sleep, the most faithful admonitions of friends. A rebuked scorner hates both rebukes and rebuker; though oft reproved, he hardens his neck. (4.) They are insensible in this their sleep of being uncovered and stripped of their clothes; yea, of being wounded and maimed by God's severer strokes and bloody stripes. Though the water-pot and spear be taken from the bolster, yet they stir not. Like the hen, which loseth now one, by and by another, then a third chicken, till the kite have almost snatched away all her brood; and yet she follows her scraping and picking as eagerly as ever. They regard not the works of God; when the hand of the Lord is lifted up, they will not see. Though grey hairs be upon them, they know it not. 1. They are insensible who wounds, they think not of the hand of God in the miseries that befall them, they consider not they have *negotium cum Deo*, to do with God, when men hurt them; all their study is how to avenge themselves upon or reconcile themselves to the instrument. 2. They are insensible why they are wounded, of sin the deserving cause; they, neither looking upward nor inward, are not driven by what they feel to consider what they have done; no man saith, What have I done? They search not after the Jonah when any storm arises: every thing shall be blamed sooner than sin; though there be many a foot-print of punishment upon them, they trace not the foot, the sin that made it. 3. They are insensible of the way to cure their wounds; they turn not to the Lord their God for all this. They are like a foolish child, that stays "long in the place of breaking forth of children," Hos. xiii. 13. They had rather stifle themselves in the womb of sin and punishment, than come forth by repentance. They turn not to him that smites. They use every way to remove punishment but the right, so that they "pine away in their iniquity," Lev. xxvi. 39; and though their books were torn, yet their lessons are not learned.

2. These seducers are compared to dreamers in sleep, in regard of their dreaming; that is, their vain, false, empty imaginations, dotages, doctrines, which, in the end, like dreams, deceived themselves and their followers. A dream, when a man sleeps, seems to have truth and reality in it; but when he awakes, it quite vanishes away. He who utters his own foolish conceits and vain delusions, is, in common speech, said to dream, and to speak his own dreams; and thus these seducers, instead of the truths of God, vented their own fables and groundless fictions, fancies, and dreams. In this sense Epiphanius understands the apostle Jude, when he calls these seducers "dreamers:" Jude speaks not, saith he, of them who dreamed in bodily sleep, but of such as utter their words like them who dream, and not like those who speak with the sobriety of such as are awake. To the same purpose speaks Irenæus likewise, lib. 1. cap. 20. They put off, saith he, their own dreams for Divine oracles. And such have been the dreams of enthusiasts, and of the Anabaptists in Germany; one of whom, as Sleidan reports, cut off his own brother's head in the presence of his parents, pretending that he did it by an immediate revelation and command from God. The false prophets are in Scripture oft called dreamers, because they delivered not the truths of God, but the vain figments of their own deluding and deluded fancies. As Deut. xiii. 3; Jer. xxiii. 25, where the prophet who saith, " I have dreamed, I have dreamed," is by Jeremiah said to be a prophet of the deceit of his own heart, ver. 26. These seducers of whom Jude speaks, being asleep in sin, deceived themselves and hearers with doctrines, vain opinions, and especially false hopes of pleasure and liberty in sin, though when their consciences awaked, they found themselves miserably deluded by Satan and their own sensual hearts. Thus Zophar speaks, Job xx. 8, that the hypocrite shall fly away as a dream, that is, as the good dreamed of, or the joy of a dream, which is short, vanishing, and deceiving. So Psal. lxxiii. 20, " As a dream when one awaketh; so, O Lord, when thou awakest, shalt thou despise their image." And thus the prophet compares the temper of the people under all the judgments of God to that of a deluded dreamer, who pleases himself with dreaming of food and fulness, and when he awakes, instead of a furnished table and a filled stomach, finds and feels himself more indigent and nearer famishing than ever he was before, Isa. xxix. 8. Thus the fond sinner is dreaming of a kingdom when he is going to execution, and when Jael's nail is nearer his temples than a crown; he blessing himself in his heart, and saying that he shall have peace, though he live in a way of warring against God. And sundry ways may sinners delude themselves like dreamers by their vain and groundless deceits; as in dreaming of their persons, and of their actions.

(1.) Sinners delude themselves in dreaming of their persons. [1.] Dreaming that they are not so bad as others, because they abstain from gross, apparent, and notorious abominations; thus the Pharisee deluded himself, Luke xviii. 11. Some dream that they have not such and such corruptions, because God restrains them from outward acts of sin; as if the rest and silence of corruption always came from the renovation of the spirit; whereas it comes not from the want of a mind disposed to sin, but of an object proposed to draw forth corruption. Others dream that if they had lived in the days of Christ, the prophets, and martyrs, they would not have persecuted them; though they bitterly oppose those in whom the image of Christ shines, (and they who cannot endure that spark of holiness in a saint, how could they have loved that flame which was in Christ?) and hate those most in whom the piety and zeal of the holy martyrs and saints of old is revived.

[2.] Sinners delude themselves in dreaming that they are in a good and happy estate before God, being indeed miserable and bad, Rev. iii. 17; Gal. vi. 3. Thus some dream that God loves them because he gives them worldly prosperity, whereas the prosperity of the wicked is their ruin; and God oftenest gives it in wrath, and denies it in love, Psal. lxix. 22; Heb. xii. 6. Some dream that their condition is happy because they are civilly honest in the world, whereas their irreligious honesty is as bad as unhonest religion; and "except your righteousness exceed," &c., Matt. v. 20. Others dream they are happy because they have been born in the church, and enjoy its privileges; whereas a barren fig-tree is nearer cursing than a bramble; and they who received sacraments every meal were destroyed in the wilderness, 1 Cor. x. 5; Matt. vii. 22, 23. Some dream of happiness because they have some kind of knowledge, faith, repentance, obedience; whereas their knowledge transforms them not; it is light without heat. Their faith applies, in a manner, Christ to them; not themselves to Christ, but to their lusts: their repentance respects the punishment of sin, not the sin to be punished; they hate sin for hell, not as hell; and in their tears sin is rather bathed than drowned; their obedience is not serving God, but themselves upon God, they serve God for by-respects; and in their obedience they aim not at obedience, Hos. i. 4.

(2.) Sinners delude themselves in dreaming concerning their actions that they are good, because done with a good intention; not considering that a work may be good in a man's own eyes, and the issues thereof the ways of death, 2 Sam. vi. 7; Prov. xvi. 25. Or that they are warrantable because of the example of the multitude, whereas the most are the worst, and "the whole world lies in wickedness." Some dream that small sins are as none, as vain thoughts, idle words; whereas the least sin is the breach of a great and royal law, and an offence against a great God; and thoughts and words shall be both brought into judgment. Some dream that the outward works of the law are sufficient, whereas the law in every command is spiritual, and binds the heart as well as the hand; and they who made their philacteries broad, made the expositions of the law too narrow. Some dream that their actions are good because followed with success, whereas the goodness of the action is not to be judged by the goodness of the success, but the goodness of the success by the goodness of the action: plenty could not justify sacrificing to the queen of heaven, Jer. xliv. 17. Some, because of the corruption of their natures, dream of excusing their actions; they are but men, say they; whereas they deserve damnation both for the corruption of nature, and the fruits thereof. Also some dream because the faults of the godly are mentioned in Scripture, they make that an argument of boldness in sinning, which should be an argument of fear to sin. Some, because they are ignorant and not book-learned, whereas ignorance, though simple, only somewhat extenuates, but it excuses not sin, and keeps not from hell, but only from such a degree of torment as that of unfruitful knowledge; and wilful (now the common) ignorance increases both sin and punishment, as showing that men will willingly suffer the damage of ignorance to enjoy the freedom of sinning. Some dream that the employments of their callings may excuse them for the neglect of holy duties, as if callings were made to call us away from God, or as if eternity were to give way to trifles. Others fondly dream that outward temptations, the counsels or commands of others enticing them to sin, shall sufficiently excuse them; whereas the outward temptation could do nothing without the compliance of the inward corruption; and the disobeying of God for man's command, is a disobedience with a greater disparagement to God than if man had said nothing. Endless it would be to mention all those spiritual dotages and deluding dreams of sinners about their actions; as that they may sin because they dream some places of Scripture will give them allowance, or that much good will ensue of their sin; that they may take liberty, though excessive, in things because lawful; that they may do evil because they make account to make amends for it afterward, or upon pretence that they do it only for trial to learn the vanity of sin; or that the necessity of their living urges them, or upon presumption of God's mercy, or by the painting of sin with the colour of virtue. To these may be added a sinner's dreaming that good duties may be omitted because they are difficult, or because of their many other important occasions, or because there is a purpose of doing them hereafter, or in respect of their troubles threatened, or because they have done enough good already, or more than others, or by reasoning from predestination; as if being ordained to salvation, though they live never so wickedly, it shall never disadvantage them. All which, with many more, are the vain dreams and delusions of sinners, whereby, with these seducers, they take liberty to offend God, and thereby to overthrow themselves.

Obs. 1. Spiritual judgments are the sorest. Insensibleness in sin and self-delusion were judgments which made these seducers miserable; they are judgments which seize upon the soul. No blessings so sweet as soul blessings, and no judgments so sore as soul judgments. The soul is the excellency of a man: the body is a body of vileness; the soul is precious, excellent every way, but only as depraved with sin. It is noble in regard of its origin, functions, endowments. If all be well with the soul, all is well with the man, though the body be never so miserable: if it go ill with the soul, the man is wretched, let the body be never so happy. The funeral of a nobleman is much spoken of. When a prince dies, all lay it to heart; when his page dies, it is never regarded: the body, the soul's page, is not to be lamented, from which the soul parts; but the soul, from which God himself parts. And further, the distempers which befall the soul are of all others hardest to remove. There is no herb in the garden, no receipt from the physician, no medicine in the shop, that can cure the soul: men are only parents and physicians of the body; he that made the soul can only mend it: the Father of spirits is the only Physician of spirits. It is omnipotent strength that recovers a sin-sick, and raises and rouses a sleeping soul. Man can cast thee into thy sinful sleep, only God can awaken thee: outward helps cannot cure the inward man; he that sits in heaven can only touch and teach the heart. And further, the distempers of the soul uncured are of all others the most deadly and destructive. A scratch on the finger we call a slight wound, but a wound that reaches to the heart is deadly. Whatever befalls the body is comparatively slight, and to be slighted. The worst things which befall the body may be sent in mercy; they part between us and contemptible enjoyments; yea, oft they make way for enjoying the best blessings; but they which befall the soul sever from Him in whom all blessedness is laid up: spiritual comforts or miseries are true, real; the temporal of either are but opinionative. "Fear not him," saith Christ, "that can kill the body, but fear him that can throw both body and soul into hell." To conclude, spiritual judgments are always inflicted in displeasure, in the last place, as the sorest of all, as a reckoning for all other faults, when all other chastisements are despised: when God is showing mercy, the last mercies are the best; and the further he goes in mercy, the sweeter he is: and when he is punishing, the last punishments are the sorest; and the further he goes, the more bitter he is: the judgment of pining away in iniquity is the last of all that dismal catalogue, Lev. xxvi. 39. The spirit of a deep sleep is contiguous to hell itself. "He that is filthy, let him be filthy still," is the last judgment we read of, befalling in this life, in all the New Testament, Rev. xxii. 11; yea, the more God inflicts it, the more he is provoked to inflict it: outward punishments move God to pity; but this being a sin as well as a punishment, the more it lies upon man, the more it offends God.

Obs. 2. All the sinful sleepiness of saints differs much from that of the wicked: "I sleep, but my heart awaketh," saith the spouse, Cant. v. 2. The godly have ever in them a regenerate principle, that is waking when they seem to be most sleeping, and that is contending against natural self. The godly, as one speaks, are more pained and laborious in their sleep than in their waking; it more troubles them to be idle than to do their Lord's work; their souls yield not to that slothfulness wherewith their senses are overtaken. Sensual sinners sleep all at once, all in them and of them sleeps; but the saint keeps his heart watchful. The very business of the wicked is but vanity and dreams, but the sleeps of the godly are busy and vigilant: the wicked sleeps and trifles when he is most serious to work his wickedness; but when the righteous sleeps, his heart rises and works upwards toward God, in whom only he finds rest when thus employed. The wicked man sleeps and loves to sleep, lays himself to sleep, shuts the door, draws the curtains, puts out the candle, charges that none wake him; but a saint is like a man overtaken with sleep against his will, who is surprised with it as with an armed man; and being never so sound asleep but he is between sleeping and waking, he always even then fears he sleeps, and wishes he were awaked, and would be glad if any would take the pains to rouse him, though by making the loudest noise, and giving him the most violent jog; yea, will gladly accept of the smartest blows, and the bloodiest stripes, that the Lord lays upon him, if by all he may be awakened from his slothfulness. He complains of himself, and he is sensible of his sleeping. "I sleep" (saith the spouse); and so far as she saith she sleeps, she did not sleep. To conclude this, she wakes in her heart, though the outward man sleep; but the heart of a sinner sleeps (as we say of one sometimes, His heart is asleep) even when he is awake. Sometimes a Christian under a temptation may be brought so low as that his spiritual life runs all to the heart, and the outward man is left destitute; as in war, when the enemy has won the field, the people run into the city; and if beaten out of the city, they run into the castle: the grace of God sometimes fails in the outward action, the field, when yet it retires to the heart, in which fort it is impregnable. From all which I gather that as the wicked should not flatter himself, so neither should the godly be disheartened by spiritual sleeping; and the reason is, because their sleeps are so unlike one another.

Laboriosius dormiunt quam vigilare potuerunt.

Obs. 3. Self-soothing, delusion, flattering, are very dangerous and destructive, as being the foundation of the wickedness and woe of these seducers, these dreamers; nothing against which we are more cautioned in Scripture. "If a man think himself to be something, when he is nothing, he deceiveth himself," Gal. vi. 3. "Be ye doers of the word, and not hearers, deceiving your own selves." "Be not deceived, God is not mocked," Gal. vi. 7. James speaks of those who by seeming to be religious deceived their own hearts, James i. 26. "Ephraim said, Yet am I become rich, I have found me out substance: in all my labours they shall find no iniquity in me that were sin," Hos. xii. 8. Because he was wealthy, he soothed himself in his sin. Laodicea flattered herself that she was "rich, increased with goods, and had need of nothing," Rev. iii. 17. "He flattereth himself in his own eyes," Psal. xxxvi. 2. "If we say that we have no sin, we deceive ourselves," &c., 1 John i. 8. "Let no man deceive himself," 1 Cor. iii. 18. Nothing can be so dangerous as when one so near as oneself becomes false and flattering, 1 Cor. vi. 9; xv. 33; Obad. 3; Isa. xliv. 20; Job xv. 31. When the centinels and guards of a city are treacherous, how great and unavoidable is its destruction! when he who should be his own preserver becomes his own destroyer, how sore and sure a destruction he incurs, and how great is its indignity! There is nothing under which men are so impatient, and which they can less bear, than to be deceived and circumvented by others; and yet how unworthily patient are men in being deceived by themselves, or rather by the deceitfulness of sin! Nothing is accounted so great a disgrace as to be deceived in those things which ought to be best known and most familiar to a man; and what should be so well known to thyself as thyself? In nothing are men so fearful of being deceived as in matters of greatest moment; and what business in the world of so weighty concernment as the salvation of thy own soul? Nor does the most dreadful judgment fall upon any so dreadfully as upon the self-flatterer and deluder; the same judgment which befall him with others, makes him more miserable than others, because he expected to be more happy than others. How woeful is that hell into which a sinner falls by presuming of heaven! It is a hell upon earth for sinners to dream that they are going to heaven. An imaginary happiness in sin occasions a doubled woe and misery for sin. When our natural dreams are false, it is better they should be of bad than good, of fearful things than of joyful. It is better for a king to dream himself to be a beggar, than for a beggar to dream that he is a king; for when the king wakes his grief is gone, and his joy is doubled, he then seeing the vanity of his dream; but when the beggar wakes his former grief is increased, and returns the fiercer, by reason of the false joy of his dream. And thus it is in the deceitful dreams and dotages of the heart: far better is that deceit whereby a son of God thinks himself a slave of Satan, than that whereby a slave of Satan dreams himself a member of Christ. Better it is for Nebuchadnezzar being a man to think himself a beast, than for a beast to think himself a man. A man's false conceit of misery when indeed he is happy does not make him miserable, but rather occasions his happiness; but a man's false apprehension of happiness, he being miserable, is so far from making him happy, that it makes him doubly miserable. To conclude this, as nothing is so calamitous as to dream of happiness when we are in misery, so nothing is more common. It is natural for men to think too well of themselves, to nullify others, and to deify and omnify themselves. There is nothing so easy as to be deceived, to dream of false delight, and to neglect true danger; men are naturally witty in nothing but in deluding, and thereby in damning their own souls; like a man who, having to pass over a narrow bridge under which is a deep river, puts on a pair of false spectacles, through which he adventures upon a supposed and imaginary breadth, falls into the water, and so is drowned.

To prevent then this self-flattery and delusion, (1.) Be much in conversing with that faithful discoverer and friend the word of God. Let it be the man of thy counsel, and dwell richly in thee. A man has many flatterers, and but this one friend. This is an impartial glass, that will represent to a king, as well as to a beggar, his spots. It is quick and powerful, piercing even to the dividing asunder of soul and spirit, discerning the thoughts of the heart, and making manifest the intents of the heart, Heb. iv. 12. When Ahab inquired of his false prophets concerning his going up to Ramoth-gilead, Jehoshaphat asks, whether there was not a prophet of the Lord, that they might inquire of him also. When thou hearest the flatterings of thine own false heart, rather fear than follow them; at least suspend thy belief till thou hast inquired of the word of God. (2.) Search thoroughly and diligently into the grounds and reasons upon which thy heart would needs persuade thee of thy happiness. He that has to do with cheaters, will not easily believe all they say. The simple believeth every word; but the wise man, as he ponders his own words before he utters them, so the words of another before he credits them. Let not thy heart persuade thee of thy good condition, by laying before thee common marks, which may agree even with hypocrites; as external profession, an orthodox judgment, opposing error, pleading for the truth, attending upon ordinances, freedom from scandalous sins, some sweet and sudden motions of heart in holy duties; but ever build upon such marks as will necessarily infer sincerity and a principle of saving grace in the heart; such as have some singular excellency in them which a hypocrite cannot reach, a τὶ περισσὸν, as Christ speaks, something more than others ordinarily attain, things which always accompany salvation, Heb. vi. 9. (3.) Possess thy heart with an apprehension of God's presence. Set thyself as in his eye: consider though thou mayst baffle thy conscience, yet not the eye of God's omniscience. Never think thou art out of the reach of his hand, or the view of his eye. Tell thy conscience (as the church speaks) there is no dealing falsely; for shall not God search it out, who knoweth the secrets of the heart? Psal. xliv. 17, 21. Would not a malefactor speak truly at the bar, if he knew the judge had windows to see into his breast? (4.) Look not upon thyself through the spectacles of self-love. A man that is in love with any thing, thinks the blemishes and deformities of the thing beloved are beauties and ornaments. Self-love makes shadows to be substances, and molehills to be mountains. Let not affection bribe or throw dust into the eye of thy judgment. The more thou lovest thyself, the more thou wilt desire to appear amiable, and adorned with a specious and seeming goodness. Joseph loved his brother Benjamin, and he gave him five changes of raiment. Till thou deniest thyself, and puttest off the person of a friend, thou wilt never put on the person of a just judge. Study to know thyself as thou art in thyself, not as thou art partially represented to thyself. Be not like limners, who so as they can make a man's picture gay and gaudy, care not to draw it so as to resemble him. The want of true humiliation and denial of ourselves, is the ground of all self-flattery and heart delusion. Gold must be melted and dissolved before it can be purged of the dross. Bodies full of vicious humours must be cleansed, before they can come to a healthful state. Crooked things cannot be made straight without the wringing and bowing of them by the hand. The greater our humiliation, the greater our integrity.

Vitia nostra, quia amamus, defendimus; et malumus excusare illa quam excutere. Sen. Ep. 116.

Obs. 4. It is our wisdom to take heed of spiritual sleeping in sin. For which purpose,

(1.) Make much of a stirring ministry. Love that preaching most which is most exciting. The word preached is both light and noise, both which disquiet sleepers. A still, easy minister makes a sleepy, drowsy people. Ministers must stir those who sleep in sin, though they stir them up to rage. They must be sons of thunder against sinners, not sweet singers and pleasant musicians. No employment requires so much holy vehemency and fervour as the welfare of souls. Cry aloud, (saith God to his prophet,) and lift up thy voice as a trumpet: and people should be so far from blaming the loudness of the sound of the word, that they should only blame the depth of their own slumber. They should ever take part with the word against their lusts, and entreat God that his word may be an awakening, though it be a displeasing voice; as also, that he would cry in the ears of the soul by the voice of his own Spirit, and to stir it in the ministry with his own arm; for indeed otherwise ministers shall rend their own sides, before they rouse their people's souls.

(2.) Labour for a fruitful improvement of sufferings. Beseech the Lord that no affliction may blow over without benefit to thy soul. None sleep so soundly as they who continue sleeping under the greatest joggings. Physic, if it works not, is hurtful to the patient. If thou art so close nailed to thy sin, that afflictions cannot part it and thee, it is a provocation to God to leave thee, and an encouragement to Satan that he shall keep thee, Isa. i. 5. God is never more displeased than when he takes away judgments in judgment; than when he punishes by delivering thee from thy trouble, and delivers thee up to thy own heart. O beg earnestly of God, that the blessed opportunities of suffering times may never leave thee as bad as they found thee; for if so, they will leave thee worse; and that no wind may go down till it have driven thee nearer thy haven.

(3.) Endeavour for a tender, trembling heart at the very beginning of the solicitations of sin. That which makes way for eternal, takes away spiritual feeling. Men sleep by little and little, from slumber they fall to sleeping. Every sin neglected is a step downward to a deep sleep. A deluge of sin is made up of several drops. Many knots tied one upon another will hardly be loosed, Prov. v. 22. Every sin repeated, and not repented of, binds down the soul in insensibleness and sloth. Every sin suffered to defile the conscience makes it the more regardless of itself. Sin is of an encroaching nature; like a small river, it grows in going; like a gangrene, it creeps by degrees. The deceitful modesty of sin, by asking little at first, quickly entices us to more. Small beginnings usher large proceedings. One bit draws down another. As every good work increases our ability for obedience, so every sin leaves upon the soul a readiness for further disobedience. The not resisting the first inclination to sin, makes way to stupefaction by sin. He who dares not wade to the ancles, is in no danger of being swallowed up.

Dum servitur libidini, facta est consuetudo; et dum consuetudini non resistitur, facta est necessitas. Aug. Conf. l. 8. c. 5.

(4.) Labour for faith in threatenings. Restrain not belief only to what God has promised. Let faith comprehend all truths in its vast bosom, and overcome all the improbabilities that seem to keep away judgment, as well as those that seem to keep away mercies. Noah was not drowned in a deep sleep of sin, and in a deluge of waters, with the old world; and the reason was, faith taught Noah to fear, and fear, that watchful grace, prevented feeling, Heb. xi. 7. Faith makes a man solicitous for a while, and safe to eternity. Naturally we are more moved with fear than stirred with hopes.

(5.) Vigorously and constantly exercise thyself in godliness. Never think thou hast done enough. Think not thy work is ended till thy life is ended. Take heed of remissness in holy duties. Fervency of spirit is by the apostle joined with serving of the Lord, Rom. xii. 11. Let the tempter ever find thee employed. "The night comes when no man can work," John ix. 4; but as long as the day lasts no man must loiter. As sleep causes idleness, so idleness causes sleep. Strive to attain to the highest pitch of grace, and yet ever be working as if thou wert at the very lowest: " Forget those things which are behind," Phil. iii. 13. Take heed of turning thy spur into a bridle, namely, of making that former practice of holiness, which should be an inducement to thy further active progress, a hinderance from proceeding therein. All the steps we have taken are lost, if we give over before the race is run.

(6.) Keep company with waking Christians; such as neither dare sleep in sin themselves, nor suffer any to sleep who are near them. In the sweating sickness they say, that they who were kept awake by those who were with them escaped; but their sickness was deadly if they were suffered to sleep. The keeping one another awake is the best fruit of the communion of saints. The apostle speaks of provoking one another to love and good works, of exhorting or calling upon one another, Heb. x. 24, 25.

(7.) Watch over thyself in the use of such things as are in themselves lawful. In lawful things there is least fear, and therefore most danger. More perish by meat than by poison; because every man takes heed of the hurtfulness of the latter, and fears not any harm by the former. Satan lies in ambush behind our lawful enjoyments. Christ was once lost at a feast, and oft since in worldly abundance. Prosperity never waked any out of sin. It is as hard to be full and watchful as to be empty and contented. Sobriety and vigilance are put together. Take heed lest the vapours of sensual enjoyments overwhelm thee, Luke xxi. 34. Let the things of this life be thy *solatia*, not thy *negotia*; thy refreshments, not thy employments; use them as the things, not for which thou dost live, but without which thou canst not live. They who are inclined to be gross in their bodies should use much exercise; and they who have abundance in the world should take much pains with their hearts, lest while they get the world they lose their God.

VERSE 9.

Yet Michael the archangel, when contending with the devil he disputed about the body of Moses, durst not bring against him a railing accusation, but said, The Lord rebuke thee.

THESE words contain an aggravation of that heinous sin wherewith our apostle had charged these seducers in the foregoing verse; their crime was, their speaking evil or blaspheming of dignities: the greatness of this sin the apostle evidences and evinces by comparing it with the contrary meek and humble carriage of the "archangel," even towards the worst of creatures, the "devil" himself.

This comparison the apostle first propounds, ver. 9, wherein he describes the meek and humble carriage of the archangel towards the devil in his contending with him; and secondly, he accommodates and applies it to these seducers, ver. 10.

I. In the comparison propounded in ver. 9, there is intimated a threefold amplification of the sin of these seducers, by comparing it with the deportment of the archangel.

1. In respect of the persons compared: and this branch of the comparison is double. (1.) Between a chief angel and vile men. If Michael an angel, an archangel, durst not rail, how impudent and proud are men, dust and ashes, to adventure to do so! (2.) Between magistrates and the devil. If he did forbear to revile the devil himself, the enemy of God and his church, the worst of evil ones, and one who was his inferior, how great was their sin who would speak evil of magistrates, called gods, and set up by him, as those to whom they ought to be in subjection!

2. The second branch of the comparison whereby their sin is amplified, was from the different cause about which the angels and these seducers were employed. The cause for which the archangel contended was good, clear, and righteous; namely, the burial of "the body of Moses;" a work very good, whether we consider the authority of him who enjoined it, God himself, or the end of the injunction, the preservation of the people from idolatry. But the cause which these seducers had undertaken was wicked and sinful, considering that it was the blaspheming of that order which was instituted and ordained by God himself, and by his special command to be highly honoured and esteemed, Tit. iii. 1; Rom. xiii. 1; 1 Pet. ii. 17.

3. The third branch of the comparison, whereby the apostle heightens their sin, was the different carriage and deportment of the archangel towards the devil from that of these seducers toward magistrates. The archangel reasons humbly, and disputes; the seducers peremptorily determine the question, pass sentence, and give judgment. The angel commits his cause to God, and appeals to him for redress and relief; the seducers are judges in their own cause, break their bounds, detract from God's authority, and usurp his throne. The angel in the fervour of contention, when most highly provoked, was patient and humble; these, provoked by none, rage and revile. These are the particular branches of the comparison set down in this verse.

If it were needful, before I handle the several parts of the verse, to premise any thing by way of vindication of it, and the whole Epistle, from the exception of those who allege that the Epistle is not canonical, because the contention about "the body of Moses" is not mentioned in Scripture, but was only a tradition; I might answer,

1. With learned Junius, the substance of this history is mentioned in Scripture; therein we finding that the Lord buried Moses, and that "none knoweth of his sepulchre unto this day," Deut. xxxiv. 6; so that it is plain that the body of dead Moses was buried by God, i. e. either by his own immediate power, or by the instrumental power of an angel, as seems from this place most probable, and also that the particular place of his burial was altogether unknown to men and devils. It is true, the Scripture mentions not circumstances, either a contention of Michael with the devil, or the carriage and expressions of either party in that contention. But therefore,

2. Though these passages here set down by Jude are not expressed in the sacred story, yet it is sufficient for us that they are now by the apostle, who was led by the Spirit of God, inserted into holy writ. Possibly, as Rivet notes, this story was not delivered to the apostle by tradition, but revealed to him by the Holy Ghost. Some indeed say it was taken out of a certain (uncertain) book, called the Ascension of Moses, περὶ ἀρχῶν, l. 3. c. 2.

and mentioned by Origen. Others, that it was handed by tradition from generation to generation. But granting either of the two last, is the Divine authority, either of this passage or of the Epistle, therefore to be doubted? By the same reason sundry other places of Scripture must be questioned. Frequently the Spirit of God in the Scripture sets down that as done in former stories, which was not at all there mentioned, as Jannes and Jambres withstanding of Moses, 2 Tim. iii. 8; Jacob's worshipping on the top of his staff, Heb. xi. 21; Moses saying that the sight upon the mount was so terrible, I exceedingly fear and tremble, Heb. xii. 21; that Joseph's feet were hurt with fetters, and that he was laid in irons, &c., Psal. cv. 18. Yea, how ordinary is it for the penmen of Scripture to make use of sentences taken out of heathen poets! as that of Menander, 1 Cor. xv. 33, "Evil communications corrupt good manners." Of Epimenides, Tit. i. 12, "The Cretians are always liars, evil beasts, slow bellies." Of Aratus, Acts xvii. 28, "In him we live, and move, and have our being." The Spirit of God, which could sanctify passages taken out of heathens, and make them canonical, might do the like by this relation or tradition, if it were so, of the archangel's contention with the devil, and by inducing the apostle to insert it give it the stamp of Divine authority, and so render it to us most certain and infallible. By this we at once answer both those who reject this Epistle, because Jude brings an example from tradition, no where recorded in Scripture; and likewise the papists, who offend in the other extreme of excess, from hence pleading for a liberty in the church to join traditions with the holy Scripture: whereas they can neither prove that the apostle had this story by tradition; for why might not the Spirit of God reveal to the apostles what had been done before in ages past, as it did to the prophets what should be done afterwards in ages to come? nor that it is lawful for us to do all that the apostles might, who, as Rivet well notes, did many things by a singular and peculiar right, wherein none either ought or is able to imitate them. This premised briefly, I come to the words of the verse, wherein we have three parts considerable.

Riv. in Isa. p. 474. Apostoli multa singulari jure usurpārunt in quibus nemo debet aut etiam potest eos imitari.

I. The combatants; "Michael the archangel," and "the devil."

II. The strife and contention itself; set down,
1. More generally; so it is said they contended.
2. More particularly; and so it was a disputation about the body of Moses.

III. The carriage of the archangel in this contention, which was twofold:
1. Inward, in respect of his disposition, set down negatively; he "durst not bring a railing accusation."
2. Outward, in respect of his expression, set down affirmatively; he said, "The Lord rebuke thee."

I. The parties contending, "Michael the archangel," and "the devil."

In the explication whereof, we shall consider, First, "Michael the archangel," who is described two ways, or from a double name. 1. Of his person, and so he is called Michael. 2. Of his office and place, and so he is called an archangel.

The name of his person is Michael. This name signifies, who is as, or like, or equal to God. But who this person should be, learned men agree not. Some conceive that the Son of God, the second person of the Trinity, is here called Michael: others, that a holy and created angel is here by Jude intended by the name of Michael; and that as by the name of Gabriel, so likewise of Michael, a certain angel is to be understood. And that this latter is the true opinion, seems to me undeniable for these reasons. 1. Because Michael, Dan. x. 13, is called one of the chief princes, that is, of the chief angels or archangels; but how this can fitly be spoken of Christ, I understand not, whom we must not account one of the number of the angels, but one without, or rather infinitely above that number or order, even the omnipotent Creator of angels as well as men, Col. i. 16. 2. An angel, ver. 21 of the forenamed chapter, describing the difficulty of his work, tells Daniel that there was none that held with him or strengthened him but Michael. But this expression (as learned Gomarus notes) seems to be unfitly applied to Christ, because there can be no greater strength named than that of Christ, whose power is infinite. To say, There is none with me but the Son of God, seems a harsh expression; he who has the Son of God to stand by him wants no other. 3. Jude calls this Michael an archangel: but as we never read in Scripture that Christ is called an archangel, or a chief, or the chief angel; so, 1 Thess. iv. 16, we find that Christ and the archangel are manifestly distinguished, the apostle saying that "the Lord shall descend from heaven with the voice of an archangel." 4. It seems also to be very unmeet to say of Christ, that he durst not bring against the devil "a railing accusation," Christ being the Lord and Judge of devils, and whom he shall at the last day condemn to eternal punishment. Yea, we find that he passed judgment upon him, and pronounced him a murderer, one that has no truth in him, a liar, and the father of a lie, John viii. 44; a sentence which the angel, here disputing with the devil, though he had just cause, yet durst not utter, he only saying, "The Lord rebuke thee." 5. The apostle Peter speaking of this very matter, and aggravating the sin of these seducers by this humble carriage of their superiors, plainly speaks not of Christ, but of the holy angels; he saying thus, "Whereas angels, which are greater in power and might, bring not a railing accusation," &c., 2 Pet. ii. 11.

Inepta et filio Dei indigna oratio. Gom. de Nom. Mich. Tom. 1. p. 107. & Tom. 2. p. 217.

Nor does the argument drawn from the signification of the name Michael, prove that by Michael we are here to understand the Son of God. This word Michael, by interpretation, (say some,) is *qui sicut Deus;* and, according to them, imports one that is as, or equal to, God, a name which cannot agree to any creature. But it is answered, that the particle מ in the Hebrew is not here to be taken relatively, as signifying one who; but interrogatively, who is? and it is ever in Scripture so taken, when used in expressions wherein the name of God is celebrated; as Exod. xv. 11, "Who is like unto thee?" &c. So Psal. xxxv. 10, "All my bones shall say, Lord, who is like unto thee?" So Psal. lxxi. 19; lxxxix. 8; Isa. xliv. 7; Jer. xlix. 19; l. 44. And thus the giving of this name Michael to the creature, is no dishonouring of God, by making it equal to God; but rather an advancing of God, by a humble confession or acknowledgment of the matchless majesty of that glorious God whom none can equal. And hence, as the name Micaiah is imposed upon one who was a holy prophet, so this name Michael is in Scripture frequently found to be imposed by the people of God on their children, Numb. xiii. 13; 1 Chron. v. 13; yea, Jehoshaphat gave this name to one of his sons, 2 Chron. xxi. 2; perhaps in token of thankfulness for that glorious victory which in his reign God bestowed upon him and all Judah, 2 Chron. xx. And possibly for the zeal of this angel in vindicating the glory of God was this name Michael given him.

Est confessio majestatis Dei, non alienatio illius a Deo. Gomarus.

Fieri potest ut ob divinæ gloriæ zelum, nomen id impositum sit isti angelo. Lor.

2. This first party contending is described by the

name of his office and place, and so he is called the archangel. It is here demanded, 1. Whether he was the only archangel, the chief of all the rest of the angels, or only one of the archangels, or chief angels? 2. Wherein this principality and superiority stands? Questions whereof the Scriptures, and therefore we ought to, speak sparingly.

For the first. The Scripture speaks not any where of archangels in the plural number, nor of more than one archangel. "The Lord himself shall descend from heaven with the voice of the archangel," 1 Thess. iv. 16. Some conceive, that as there is one chief of the evil angels, called the "prince of the devils," who are called "his angels," "the devil and his angels," Matt. xxv.; so likewise that there is one chief or principal among the good angels, and that he is this Michael; and thus they understand that place of Rev. xii. 7, where "Michael and his angels" are mentioned as fighting with the devil and his angels. And divers of the popish schoolmen account this "Michael the archangel" to be superior to all those three hierarchies and nine orders of angels, one whereof, they say, is that of archangels, which they boldly affirm to be in heaven.

(2.) The second question, Wherein the superiority and pre-eminence of this archangel stands? is more difficult to resolve than the former. The schoolmen following Dionysius, Gregory, and others, groundlessly assert that the angels are distributed into three ranks and hierarchies; and that each of these three contain three several orders. The first of the three ranks and hierarchies, they say, comprehends cherubims, seraphims, and thrones; the second, dominions, principalities, and powers; the third, mights, archangels, and angels. Nor do they only show their boldness in ranking and dividing them thus into these three hierarchies and nine orders; for how can they precisely assert that they should be thus marshalled in rank and file, distributed and divided after this manner, and that there are just so many and no more orders of angels? but they presume to tell us the reasons of all these several appellations, and to set down the several properties and offices which are allotted to all these orders of angels whereby they are distinguished among themselves. The seraphims, they say, are so called because they are inflamed, and inflame others, with extraordinary and ardent love to God. The cherubims are named from their excelling in the light of knowledge. The thrones are those who contemplate and adore the judiciary equity and righteous judgments of God. And the angels, those who are contained in this first *classis* or order, are never sent forth (a bold assertion, and contrary to Scripture, which saith, "They are all ministering spirits, sent forth to minister for them who shall be heirs of salvation," Heb. i. 14) upon any ministry or employment, but their work is only to wait immediately upon God. In the second rank and hierarchy they tell us, that dominions are those that govern and order all the offices of the other angels. Principalities, such as are set over people, and provinces, nations, as their keepers and princes. Powers, such as are to restrain and keep under the powers of devils. For the third rank, they dictate, that those upon whom they put the title of mights, have the working of miracles for their employment; that archangels are messengers employed by God in matters of greater and weightier concernment, and angels in lesser business. How audacious the vanity of these assertions is, how much without, yea, against the warrant of Scripture, it is evident by the naming of them. Where find we in Scripture that seraphims are either a certain or the first order of angels, and that they are so called from their ardent love of God?

Or might, δύναμις, Eph. i. 21.

There is nothing attributed to these seraphims in Isa. vi. 2, where they are mentioned, which may not agree to all the rest of the angels; nor can it thence be proved that they are called seraphims from their ardent love to God. The word seraphim in the Hebrew signifies ἐμπρηστὰς, *incensores*, such who set on fire. It is a name given to the fiery serpents, Numb. xxi. 6, 8; and it is much more probable that they are so called, not from their office or inward gifts, but from the external likeness in which they appeared. As Ezekiel, i. 13, speaks of the living creatures, that their appearance was like burning coals of fire, and like the appearance of lamps. Nor can it be proved from the signification of the word cherubim, that they are so called from their great knowledge; for though some (indeed) say the word cherub signifies, as a multitude (which yet must be far fetched, to import the abundance of their knowledge); yet others more probably conceive that it signifies, as young men, or intimates their appearance in a winged shape; and so indeed by the command of God they were shadowed out, Exod. xxv. 18. Nor are they less mistaken in making the overseeing and ruling of provinces the work of principalities; for if any such thing belong to any angels, it may be with more probability attributed to the archangel Michael, who, according to some learned men, is said to be, under Christ, the prince of the Jews. This opinion they found on Dan. x. 21, where he is called "Michael your prince." It is generally conceived by our more learned and modest interpreters, that those several expressions of thrones, dominions, principalities, powers, Eph. i. 21; Col. i. 16; Eph. iii. 10, do not signify purely the same thing, but divers orders and ranks of angels; and this they prove from the disjunctive particle or, put between thrones, dominions, principalities, powers; and also from that place of Dan. x. 13, where Michael is said to be one, or the first, of the chief princes; likewise from the title of an arch or chief angel. Lastly, because there is an order among the devils which they lost not with their integrity at their fall. But what and wherein this order among the angels should consist, and how they differ, they modestly profess they dare not determine; that it is curiosity to inquire into, and rashness to define this secret; that this is a learned ignorance: and herein Augustine joins with them, who saith, How those names of angels differ let them speak who are able, if yet they are able to prove what they speak; I profess my ignorance herein. And this by way of explication of the first party here contending, "Michael the archangel." It follows that we speak of the second, who is here said to be "the devil."

From כרב sicut multitudo.

Quid inter se distant hæc vocabula, dicant qui possunt, si tamen possunt probare quod dicunt. Ego me ista ignorare confiteor. Enchirid. c. 58.

2. Of the word devil, in the Greek διάβολος, I meet with sundry interpretations among the learned. Some, as Gerson and Bonaventure, say that the word signifies falling, and tending downward; and the devil, say they, not being able to keep up in his former height of glory and excellency, but compelled to descend from it, is not to be moved from his malice. Others also, with more wit than strength, say that the word *diabolus* comes from *dia*, which they say is as much as two, and *bolus*, signifying a draught taken up in a fisher's net, because when the devil draws man into his net, he makes of him, as it were, a double draught, by destroying both body and soul. The ordinary and true derivation of the word is from διαβάλλω to slander, calumniate, and falsely

c. Deorsum fluens. Gerson Tr. in Magnificat. Bonavent. l. 2. Sent. dist. 5. q. 1. Dictus est diabolus, quia deorsum fluxit, et ex hoc in sua malitia firmatus est. Diabolus non valens conscendere, sed compulsus descendere, odit Deum justum, et invidet excellentiæ ejus.

to accuse; and hence the appellative name of devil is often in Scripture used for any false accuser: thus Judas is called devil, " One of you," saith Christ, " is a devil," John vi. 70. The wives of deacons must not be διάβολοι, slanderers, 1 Tim. iii. 11; and the apostle speaks of some who are treacherous, false accusers, or devils, &c., 2 Tim. iii. 3. So Tit. ii. 3, concerning the aged women he saith, that they must not be false accusers, or devils; in which sense some understand that command of Eph. iv. 27, Give not place to the devil, or to any false accuser, or slanderer, who shall come with slanderous reports against another; the apostle giving that precept as a direction to the observing of what went immediately before; namely, that the sun should not go down upon our wrath. False accusers being makebates and kindle-coals between persons, are to be opposed and resisted. More especially, the word devil is taken for an evil spirit, or angel, Matt. xiii. 39; Luke viii. 12; Acts x. 38; xiii. 10; 1 Pet. v. 8; 2 Tim. ii. 26, &c.; and yet more especially the term devil is attributed to the chief or prince of devils, called so by way of eminence. He tempted Christ, Matt. iv. 1. He and his angels fight with Michael and his, Rev. xii. 7. See Matt. xxv. 41. Thus it is taken here. And clear reason there is why Satan should thus be called a slanderer or false accuser. Some say, because of his accusing of God to man, and that principally by that first accusation, wherein he accused God of falsehood, by saying, notwithstanding what God had threatened, that they should not die; and of envy, by telling them that God knew that in the day they did eat thereof they should be like gods. And this is the opinion of Justin Martyr, in that excellent exhortation of his to the Greeks: The Scriptures (saith he) call that enemy of mankind the devil, from that first slander or calumny which he brought to man. And thus he is still a slanderer, laying his accusations sometimes against God's justice, persuading sinners that God allows them in their sins, so driving them to presume; sometimes laying them against his mercy, persuading those who are humbled that their sins are greater than can be forgiven, so driving them to despair; sometimes against his faithfulness, omniscience, &c., frequently against his providence, making men believe that God has no care of the ordering and governing of things in the world; the good are miserable, and the wicked happy. When Christ was on earth, he was accused by the devil to be an impostor, that cast out devils by the help of Beelzebub, &c. Falsely did he accuse God to Christ, by clipping his word, and perverting the Scripture to a pernicious sense.

Ἀπὸ τῆς πρώτης αὐτοῦ πρός τὸν ἄνθρωπον διαβολῆς. Justin in Paræn. ad Græc. p. mihi 21.

2. He is (according to others) called an accuser for accusing man to God. This is the opinion of Lactantius. The devil, saith he, is called an accuser, because for those very faults to which he tempts and allures us he accuses us, by laying them before God. "The accuser of the brethren is cast down, which accused them before our God day and night," Rev. xii. 10. He objects things before God for the disgrace and hurt of the godly. Thus he accused Joshua the high priest for his sins noted by filthy garments, Zech. iii. 1, 3. As also Job, for self-seeking. Satan spies the least sins in them, these he aggravates, and for them pleads their unworthiness of the least mercy: the sins which in them are weaknesses, he represents as wickednesses; the sins which they condemn in themselves, and for which they condemn themselves, he lays before God to have him also condemn them for them, claiming the justice of the law, and the execution of the curse, against

Diabolum criminatorem vocamus, propterea quod crimina in quæ ipse allicit, ad Deum defert. Lact. lib. 2. Instit. cap. 8.

and upon them. This accuser diminishes, wrests their best actions, as if performed to a wrong end, and hypocritically; thus he accused Job of serving God only for wages, hereby representing all his services to be void of sincerity. In nothing is the malice of Satan so clearly discovered as in accusing the godly before God. For, (1.) Hereby he shows his desire to do them the greatest hurt, which is to bring them out of favour with God, to separate them from their only friend, by being a talebearer and slanderer: "He accused them before our God," Rev. xii. 10. And, (2.) Such is his malice, that he will endeavour that which he can but endeavour, and never effect; yea, in the undertaking whereof he is sure to miscarry. Oppose them he will, though hurt them he cannot, and is sure to hurt himself; putting forth his poison, though he have no power; accusing saints before a God who sees the falseness of his accusations, whose power, justice, and mercy ever makes him rebuke the accusing devil, and pity the accused saints, Zech. iii. 1—3. And in respect of this accusing the faithful to God, I conceive that Satan is principally called our adversary, 1 Pet. v. 8, in the original, ἀντίδικος; a word that properly signifies an adversary, pleading or contending against another before a judge in judgment; in which sense it is used Matt. v. 25, "Lest thy adversary," ἀντίδικος, " deliver thee to the judge," &c.: so Luke xii. 58, "When thou goest with thine adversary," μετὰ τοῦ ἀντιδίκου, "to the magistrate;" so that when the apostle calls the devil our adversary, he intends that he is our adversary by way of accusing us before the Judge of heaven and earth. And very fitly may this our accuser be called an ἀντίδικος, or adversary in judgment, because he who contends with another before a judge commonly labours to pervert his cause by slanders and false accusations, which (as hath been said) aptly agrees to this our adversary; and hence it may be, that when the Septuagint meet in the Old Testament with the Hebrew word Satan, an adversary, they translate it by the Greek word διάβολος, a false accuser, 1 Chron. xxi. 1; Job i. 6; Zech. iii. 1.

ὁ κατηγορῶν αὐτῶν.

שטן

3. Our enemy is here called the devil, or false accuser, because he accuses one man to another; stirring up hereby strife and contention between man and man: and as sometimes he accuses the godly to one another, as plain-hearted Mephibosheth to David (his devilish stratagem in these times); so most commonly he accuses the godly to the wicked. Thus he accused Joseph of incontinency, David of treason, Daniel of disobedience, Elijah of troubling Israel, Jeremiah of revolting, Amos of preaching against the king, the apostles of sedition, rebellion, alteration of laws; Paul was accused as a pestilent fellow, and one that taught against the law of Moses; Christ himself was accused of gluttony, sorcery, sedition. And how skilful a master he is in this hellish art of false accusation, appears in that he accuses the faithful, though never so innocent, devising what he cannot find, Jer. xviii. 18; nay, not only though they are, but even because they are holy; for the matter of their God, for praying, hearing, fasting, keeping sabbaths, preaching the truth. He accuses them oft by those who are tied to them by dearest relations; David of injustice by Absalom. He accuses all the godly for one man's offence, "Thus they are all," &c.; nay, for a personal failing in one or two he accuses the whole religion itself; railing against the sun because one has stumbled in the sunshine. He has an art to accuse for that of which he and his are most guilty; thus he accused Joseph of incontinence, Elijah of troubling Israel, Christ of being an enemy to Cæsar; yea, of that to which the accused are most

contrary, as in those instances appears, accusing even the sun of darkness. And God hereby makes their integrity more apparent, either here or hereafter. Slanders are but as soap, which though it soils for the present, yet it makes way for whiteness. The sun of their good fame shall break out gloriously from under the cloud of slanders; God will "bring forth their righteousness as the light, and their judgment as the noon-day," Psal. xxxvii. 6; yea, which is the greater advantage, the smutchings of slanders shall brighten the graces of God's people, their humility, peace, watchfulness, faith. The tongues of sinners are but as brushes or rubbers to fetch off the dust which is but too ready to fall upon the graces of saints. The devil is Satan, and therefore he is a devil; he is an adversary to Christ, to holiness: what will not malice say? Now Christ is gone beyond Satan's reach, he throws the dirt of slanders upon his pictures, and on them most which are fairest and most resemble him. He loves to trouble them in their way whom he cannot hinder of the end. The devil is a serpent, and therefore he is an accuser; he has subtlety to invent, as well as malice to utter his slanders. He is the god of the world, and has the tongues of wicked men at his command; if he saith to one, Go, it goeth, &c. He has found the successfulness of this engine of accusation, he has murdered thousands with it, and thereby ever brought religion into suspicion and disgrace; he has many receivers, he will therefore thieve away the names of saints; his calumnies easily enter, and hardly depart.

4. This adversary may here be called a devil, an accuser, because he accuseth a man to himself, and that in two respects: (1.) He makes a man think better of himself than he should; tells him he is going to Dothan, when he is going to Samaria; that the way to hell is the ready way to heaven. As Absalom told the people flatteringly, "Thy cause is good;" so he, Thy case is happy; strangling them oft with a silken halter. (2.) He makes men think their estate worse than it is, by stretching the sins which he has drawn them to commit beyond all the measure of mercy and possibility of pardon, to bring the sinner to despair. Thus he dealt with Cain and Judas. He who once told men they might repent when they would, and it would be time enough hereafter to call for mercy, now affrights them with apprehensions that the day of grace is at an end, and that it is too late to make their peace with God. He who was of late a tempting is now a tormenting devil.

Hitherto of the explication of this first part, the parties contending; the observations follow.

Obs. 1. The higher our eminence is, the greater should be our humility. The more glorious any one is for endowments, the more humble should he be in beholding them. This eminently glorious angel, this archangel, has humility stamped upon his name; by it he does not ask, Know you not who I am? or, Who is so great as I? but, *Quis sicut Dominus,* Who is like the Lord? The more thou art above others in the height of place, the more shouldst thou go beyond them in the grace of humble-mindedness. Humility is an angelic grace. No creature so high as an archangel, no creature so humble as he; and the highest is the humblest angel. None so low as the devil, and none so proud as he: the devil tempts Christ to worship him; the archangel worships Christ. We must, though high, take heed of high-mindedness. When we shine most with outward glory, we must not know it; know it we must, so as to be thankful, not so as to be proud. What have we that we have not received? The more we have received, as, the greater shall be our account, so the greater should be our acknowledgment. They who partake of most gifts do but proclaim, like beggars, that they have oftenest been at the door of mercy. When any great performance has been wrought by us, we should fear to arrogate the praise thereof to ourselves; herein imitating Joab, who when he had as good as taken Rabbah the royal city, sent messengers to David to come and complete the conquest by taking it fully, lest the city should be called after his name, 2 Sam. xii. 27, 28. He knew the jealousy of kings in point of honour; he wisely might remember, that attributing more thousands to Saul than to David, though but by female singers, had almost cost David his life. God is jealous of his honour, he will not give it to another, nor might any one take it to himself.

Obs. 2. The highest dignity is to be much in duty. In this word archangel here is equally both comprised superiority and service: an archangel is in English but a high and supreme messenger or waiter. The service of God is the glory of the highest angel. How poor a creature would Michael have thought himself, had he not been a messenger to Christ! It is well observed by some, that angels are more frequently called by their name of office than of nature; oftener angels than spirits; as if they more delighted in their being dutiful than in their very being. And a saint is as thankful that God will deign to be his master, as a sinner is proud that he can make men to be his own servants. Theodosius, the good emperor, esteemed this the highest of all his titles, *Ultimus Dei servus,* The lowest servant of Christ. A person is truly so honourable as he is useful. Paul's glory was not that he had ruled and domineered, but laboured, more than they all; yea, in the meanest services for Jesus Christ; not in planting of and preaching to churches, or in governing them only, but in stripes, prisons, journeys, weariness, perils, hunger, thirst, cold, nakedness, 2 Cor. xi. 23—25. The meanest service about a king is honourable. Many think the glory of a minister or magistrate consists in great revenues, fat benefices, large incomes, shining retinue; but ask an archangel, and he will say it is in being a servant, a messenger. How unglorious is a man in scarlet, purple, gold, crowns, nay, with the most eminent and angelical parts, if he serve not Christ by all! He is at best but like a small letter in the midst of a great embellishment; where there is, though much flourish, little benefit, much hinderance to the reader. Oh how happy we, if among us every one in eminence laboured to join the arch and the angel together! otherwise, he who is most eminent in dominion may but prove an arch-tyrant; eminent for riches, an arch-usurer; eminent for learning, an arch-heretic.

Obs. 3. The sovereignty and dominion of God extends itself even to the highest of created beings. Even from the lowest worm to the highest, the archangel, all are at the beck of the great God; as every soul must be subject to the higher power, so every soul and power must be subject to him who is the highest; he who excepts himself deceives himself. The greatest are at God's disposal; they must either be voluntary servants or involuntary slaves. God is the God of the mountains as well as the valleys. He is indeed the God of the valleys to fill them, but the God also of the mountains so as to be above them, to level and pull them down. No proud Pharaoh must say, "Who is the Lord, that I should let Israel go?" Angels are great and high, but God is greater. Angels excel us, but God even them in strength, infinitely more than do they the lowest worm. If one angel can slay a hundred fourscore

Qui se excipit, se decipit. Bern. ad Eugem.

and five thousand, what can the God of angels do? This lessons both high and low; the highest adversary to take heed of opposing the high God: are they stronger than he? If he was a fool who thought himself wiser than Daniel, Ezek. xxviii. 3, much more is he such who thinks he is stronger than God. The proudest Pharaohs, Nebuchadnezzars, must either break or bend; God will either be known of them or on them. The great design that God had in sending Nebuchadnezzar from his Babel among the beasts, was, that he might learn this lesson, that the Lord "ruleth in the kingdom of men, and giveth it to whomsoever he will," Dan. iv. 17. This is his controversy with us still, and never will it end till he has prevailed over us, and is seen to have the better of us. This subjection to God is that lesson which sooner or later every one must learn. The true interest and wisdom of the greatest potentates is to learn it here in the way, lest they perish from it. It teaches also the poorest saints: as in all their privileges God will yet be known to be their [Lord as well as their Friend, and therefore will be served with holy fear; so in all their sufferings from their proud enemies, they may say with Solomon, "There be higher than they," Eccl. v. 8. "The Lord on high is mightier than the noise of many waters, yea, than the mighty waves of the sea." The great God is their good friend; he who has the service of angels, has goodness and protection for them. When the strongest servant in the house beats and abuses them, the weakest child of God may say, I will tell my Father: he can and will redress every saint's injury.

Obs. 4. Great is the comeliness of order. Even angels have and love it. There are angels, and there is one (at least) archangel. In heaven, even among the creatures where God immediately manifests his presence, there are thrones, dominions, principalities, powers; what the difference is, we know not; that there is a difference, we know: nay, the devil, who is the great enemy of order and government on earth, observes and upholds a kind of order and rule in hell. Even there is a prince of devils, and the devil and his angels. Though it is true, the most powerful devil is the most powerfully wicked; nor heaven, nor hell allows of a parity; though there is no good, yet there is some order in hell. Holy angels are no friends to levelling. They are mistaken, fanatic spirits, who think it a point of perfection to be without superiors: would they be more perfect than the glorious angels? The truth is, they cry out for this liberty that they may be in slavery to their lusts, which government curbs; and not so much that they hate government, the love of which is implanted in all by the light of nature, as because they hate those hands in which it is; they would fain get it into their own; and could they once do so, though none could govern so ill, yet none would govern so much as themselves who most cry down ruling. They who most oppose government in others, most desire the government over others. Evil angels, who will not be subject to God, are most tyrannical over men. Satan, who would not continue in the worship of God, tempted Christ to worship him. Order is the beauty and safety of places. They who are weary of it are weary of their own happiness.

Obs. 5. The devil is a hurtful spirit. His work is to do mischief; his name devil speaks him a destroyer and wounder of names; and all his names import mischievousness. He and his angels are called cacodemons, evil angels, frequently in Scripture evil spirits; not evil only in regard of the bad which is in them, but also of the hurt which is done by them. The devil is Abaddon, perdition, Rev. ix. 11; he is perdition or destruction itself; not only passively, but even actively also: and as we call a wicked man *scelus*, wickedness, for most wicked; so is the devil called perdition or destruction itself, because he is the chief, cruel, skilful, industrious destroyer, seeking whom he may devour; compassing the earth, as a fowler does the tree where the bird sits; or as besiegers do a city, to plant murdering engines. He seeks not whom to scratch, bite, or wound; but whom to destroy, devour, swallow up, (καταπίῃ,) 1 Pet. v. 8. To Abaddon is added his name in the Greek, whereby he is also noted to be a cruel destroyer, Apollyon, Rev. ix. 11. He is in Scripture called a murderer, an old bloody one, such from the beginning. Compared also to a lion, a serpent, a dragon, a red, bloody, fiery dragon, Rev. xii. 3. He is bloody in being thirsty after and imbrued in blood, in all the blood of the saints since the beginning of the world. His works prove him more hurtful than his names. Hurtful he is to the bodies of men; these he has often possessed, counting the tormenting of them all his pleasure, and ejection out of them his torment. These he has thrown into fire and water; cutting also and wounding them; rending them when compelled to leave them; by his instruments, wicked men his weapons, martyring, mangling, and murdering them, from Abel till now; afflicting them with noisome and destructive diseases. Hurtful to the estates of men, by tempests, winds, fires, as appears by his dealing with Job, whom he made, both in body and estate, his very anvil, upon which he laid all his angry and cruel strokes. Hurtful he is to the souls of men, either tempting to, corrupting in, or else tormenting or affrighting them for sin. Hurtful to the name he is by slanders and false accusations. They who are freed from consuming by the former, shall not escape totally from singeing by this latter. Where he cannot devour with the mouth of the sword, he will wound by the sword of the mouth. Where he cannot strike with his hand, he will spit with his mouth, and bite with his teeth. And lastly, the properties of his hurtfulness show it more than its workings; for he is anciently hurtful; he began many thousand years ago with the first man. How hurtful do we account that thief and murderer who has been mischievous for some few years! No murderer so old a one as Satan. He is maliciously hurtful, not being so by accident, or beside his intention, but aiming to be so. He kills none by chance-medley, but his murders are wilful: it is his meet and drink, his recreation, his only ease, if he could be said to have any. His hurtfulness is incessant, his trade, his work, as well as his recreation. He cannot give over this employment; it is his element; nor can he any more live without it than a fish out of the water. He is restless in sin. When he is not in places where he may do much hurt, he is said to walk through dry places, a barren, uninhabitable wilderness, and there he finds no rest: his only rest is a hurtful motion. A sinner sleeps not till he sin; but the devil always sins, and never sleeps; he is a vigilant dragon; he never rested one moment since the beginning of the world. As he never wanted, so he never would have rest: he has no holidays: he goes up and down continually, seeking whom he may devour. Upon the sabbath as much as, nay, more than other days: and he never does more hurt than when he seems to do least; nay, when he seems to do most good. He is universally hurtful in respect of the object; he is hurtful, in intention at least, to all mankind; to good and bad, to his enemies, yea, to his friends: to the former, because the less he can, the more he would do. The more God loves, the more he hates and labours to hurt, as in all the forementioned respects. He had rather find one pearl than a thousand pebbles. Oh how sweet to him is the fall of a Peter, a David, a Noah! the blood of a Stephen, a Paul, a godly minister! He winnows the best wheat most, and beats the tree most that bears the best fruit: our great Lord himself must not go without his marks. Nay, he is hurtful to his own greatest friends. Those he hurts most who serve him most: a cruel master, that wounds and starves all his slaves! wounds the conscience, wears out the body. Sinners are his hackneys, whom he whips and spurs all the day of life, and at night he lodges them worse than in the day he used them. Never suffers he them to feed upon one morsel of the bread of life; gives nothing but wind and wormwood, vanity and vexation. Lastly, he is skilfully hurtful; he is skilful to destroy, and has an equal mixture of the lion and the serpent. He has seven heads, Rev. xii. 3, and many devices in them all. Elymas, full of all subtlety and mischief, is aptly therefore called the child of the devil, Acts xiii. 10. Our worst enemy sometimes comes to us as our best friend. He disguises his person, like the Gibeonites, that so he may get within us. He seemed to Eve to be more friendly than God himself. He oft seems to compassionate the sinner; to the profane, he propounds an easy, loose religion; to the proud, he suggests the unfitness of suffering himself to be trampled on, &c. He never kisses, but to kill; and this crocodile never sheds tears but to shed blood. He chooses his fittest times for his temptations; as in time of conversing in bad company, so he set upon Peter; in time of solitariness, so he set upon Christ and Joseph. In times of trouble of conscience, then he suggests we are hypocrites; like Simeon and Levi, who killed the Shechemites in their soreness. In times of security and ease, so he set upon David: like enemies who fall upon one another's quarters in their midnight sleep. If he cannot hinder from good, he can blemish it by sinful means; an undue manner, a bad end. He can by a thousand arts disparage a holy duty to those that behold it, if he does not mar it in the performance. This hurtfulness of the devil shows whom they resemble, who are never well themselves but when they are doing something that may make others bad, or do them hurt; whose only work is to pull down and pluck up, to tear and rend; to lay gins and snares, not for beasts, but men; to search out iniquities, and to accomplish a diligent search; who are skilful to destroy, but ignorant how to build up. How unlike are these to him who went up and down continually doing good! It likewise discovers the goodness and power of God, in stopping this hurtful creature, in bounding him within his limits, in binding him in chains of restraint; so that though he wills to do what, nay, more than he can, yet he shall never do what he will, nor often what he can. It teaches us to make him our Friend who only has care and goodness to countervail the devil's cruelty. Oh miserable they whose souls do and shall ever dwell among lions, in a Godless, Christless, shepherdless state! Lastly, it instructs that better is the suffering of him who is hurt, than the solace of him that is hurtful; the former is conformed to Christ, the latter to the devil.

Obs. 6. Saints must expect slanders, but not be afflicted with them. So long as there are devils there will be false accusers. We oft say, upon hearing false and infamous reports, we wonder who should raise them: but wonder not; there is a mint constantly going in hell, and there is a mint-master, whose work it is to coin calumnies; and though they are men who circulate them for him, yet this coin bears his stamp. It is a good sign thou pleasest not Satan when thou canst not have his good word. He does no more against thee, than he has done against all thy brethren, whose accuser he has ever been: count not this trial by his fiery tongue strange; nay, count it strange when this tongue is not fired upon thee. The Son of God himself was in this fire before thee, nay, is in it with thee. If the flame be hot, remember the company is comfortable and cooling. Had it been enough to have been accused, there would never have been one innocent. God indeed suffers this fire to burn thee, because thou art not pure enough; but the devil kindles it because thou art not impure enough. It is a sign that thy tongue vexes Satan, when his tongue vexes thee. Remember that thy name is bright in God's sight, and like the sun, glorious heavenward when most clouded earthward. God takes a greater care of his servants' names than they do of their own. "Wherefore were ye not afraid to speak against my servant Moses?" saith God to Aaron and Miriam, Numb. xii. 8. Besides the accidental good which slanderers do thy soul for the present, by making thee humble, watchful, self-searching, there will come a time wherein they shall make restitution in specie of all thy stolen reputation. They stole it from thee in secret, but they shall restore it before men and angels, and that with interest. Thy innocency may be hid, but not extinguished; and he that willingly detracts from thy name, though unwillingly, adds to thy reward. <small>Quisquis volens detrahit famæ meæ, iste nolens addit mercedi meæ. Aug.</small>

Obs. 7. To censure every one that is accused is to condemn the innocent. It is not ground enough for thy censure that they are accused, for Satan may cause that; but, if called, thoroughly sift the accusation; "judge righteous judgment," John vii. 24; and look not only upon the outside, but enter into the bowels of the cause. Bare accusation makes no man guilty: commonly the slanders of wicked men speak the person, and often the cause also good. Be slow of belief; hear both sides; let both thy ears, like balances, take in equal weight. It is true, charity believeth all things, but they all are good things; it also hopeth all things, 1 Cor. xiii. 7. There is no harm in suspending thy belief till proof comes. If thou shootest thine arrow too soon, thou mayst haply hit a Jehoshaphat, dressed up by Satan in Ahab's attire. It is better to acquit many guilty, than to condemn one innocent. In doubtful cases hope the best. God went down to see, when the cry of Sodom came up to heaven, though he saw before he went down. It is good to be forward in accusing thyself, and by that time that work is well done, thy censorious credulity will be cooled when thou hearest reports of others.

Obs. 8. How harsh and cruel a master does every wicked man serve! The devil puts his servants upon sin against God, and then accuses them for those sins to God, themselves, and others. He that at the first allured Saul to disobey God by sparing Amalek, afterwards drive him to despair, by representing his sin and God's wrath when he appeared in the shape of Samuel. The sins which his temptations represent but as tricks and trifles, his accusations will aggravate even to a mountainous proportion. He that in the former saith, Thy sin is so small, thou needest not fear it; nay, perhaps tells thee is a great good; will afterwards make it appear so great an evil that thou canst not bear it. Though at the first he tells thee it is so small that God will not see it, yet at last he suggests it so great that God will not forgive it. The time thou now spendest in hearing his accusations, would have been better spent in opposing his temptations. Who would serve such a master, who, instead of standing by his servants for their diligent service, will stand up before God and man against them? While they are serving him, he is quiet; when they have done, he pays them with terrors, and persuasions that they are damned wretches: and yet this is the prince of the world, who has more servants than Jesus Christ; though he, instead of accusing for, covers sin. Oh that sinners were so wise, as in time to look for a new service, and to stand astonished at this amazing folly, that they should more delight to serve him who sheds their blood, than Him who shed his blood for them!

Obs. 9. Great should be our care to prevent false accusations, to stop Satan's mouth, and the mouths of sinners, which are so ready to be opened against us; to take heed that they speak not reproachfully and truly at the same time.

(1.) It ought to be our care to make straight steps to our feet, seeing we shall be sure to hear of the least halting: we ought to walk circumspectly, Eph. v. 15. If wicked men will make faults, at their own peril be it; let them not find them made to their hand: though we may account such or such an error to be but small, yet the slanderous beholder will look upon it with an old man's spectacles, and to him it will appear great. The sharp weapons of slanders must be blunted by innocency. Let the matter, manner, and end of every action be good, and then God will justify, if Satan slander.

(2.) Never leave integrity, to remove infamy. He that will part with a good conscience to get a great name, shall lose name and conscience too.

(3.) Defend and plead God's cause against false accusation. If we be shields to his, he will defend ours.

(4.) Let us be as careful of the names of others as of our own. Let us not receive, believe, laugh at the slanders cast upon others. Our name will be entertained at our neighbour's houses as his is at ours. We must open our mouths for the dumb, the absent, the innocent.

(5.) Be willing the godly should reprove thee. He who will not hear a just admonition, may justly hear an unjust accusation: the smitings of friends will prevent the stabbings of enemies. Godly rebuke embraced will preserve thee from reproach and being a by-word.

(6.) Accuse thyself before God, humble thy soul for whatever thyself and others can allege. Be more vile in thine own than thou canst be in the thoughts or mouths of others; and thereby fly to Jesus Christ, who will answer all accusations within or without thee; the clefts of that Rock being the best refuge against the pursuit of slanderous tongues. Oh how sweet is it to say in the midst of slanders, Well, yet, my soul, God has nothing to lay to thy charge!

Obs. 10. False accusers imitate Satan, they are the devil's first-born, and bear his name. Their tongues are set on fire of hell: but of the greatness of their sin I shall have clearer occasion to speak in the third and last part of this verse, as also of the helps against it.

This for the first part of this verse, the parties contending; "Michael the archangel," and "the devil." Now follows,

II. The strife or contention itself; "Michael contending with the devil, disputed about the body of Moses."

In the explication of this contention, I shall speak, 1. Of this combat, as it is described more generally; so here it is said that Michael contended. 2. As it is set out more particularly, in the particular case and cause in which he contended; "Michael disputed about the body of Moses."

1. More generally. It is said that Michael contended, διακρινόμενος. The word, saith Justinian, is borrowed from courts of judicature, and belongs to judgments; διακρίνεσθαι δίκη, is to contend in judgment. *Vox διακρινόμε νος forensis est, et ad judicia spectat. Justiniani in loc.* The word in Scripture is used several ways, and often signifies to hesitate, and stagger, or doubt, Rom. xiv. 23; Matt. xxi. 21; Rom. iv. 20. And the word imports a doubting with a contention: he that doubts or hesitates in a business, being by different opinions drawn several ways, finding a struggling and a contention, as Budeus notes, within himself, as unresolved what course to take. *Qui hæsitat, altercantibus sententiis, secum quasi litigat et disceptat. Bud. in comment.* The apostle speaks of doubtful or contentious disputations, or (as the word signifies) contentions of disputations, Rom. xiv. 1. They of the circumcision (διεκρίνοντο) contended with Peter, Acts xi. 2. *Διακρίσεις διαλογισμῶν, altercationes disputationum. Beza.*

It may here be demanded, What are those contentions between good and bad angels? It is answered, that they are either about things, 1. Of temporal; or 2. Of spiritual concernment.

(1.) About temporals, and so they contend, the good angels for, and the bad against, the outward welfare of the people of God. The good angels, like soldiers, pitch their tents about the godly, Psal. xxxiv. 7, to protect them, where Satan pitches his forces to destroy them. Evil angels strive to drive men into places of danger; the devil would have had Christ leap from the top of the pinnacle; but the good angels keep us in all our ways, and bear us up in their hands, Psal. xci. 12; Matt. iv. 6. When Elisha was beset, the mountain was full of horses and chariots, 1 Kings vi. 17. The devil, who stirred up Daniel's enemies to destroy him by the lions, was disappointed by that good angel, who shut the lions' mouths, Dan. vi. 22. The angels of God defended Jacob from the fury of his brother Esau, into whose heart Satan had put it to contrive Jacob's death, Gen. xxxii. 2. Satan endeavours the destruction of people and countries; but good angels fight for their safety. When Satan prevailed with David to number the people, he left him fewer to number by seventy thousand, 2 Sam. xxiv. 15. Michael the chief of the chief princes protected the Jews against the tyranny of the Persians, Dan. x. 13. And an angel smote a hundred fourscore and five thousand which came to destroy Judah, 2 Kings xix. 35. An angel went between the Israelites and the army of Egyptians, Exod. xiv. 19. When Satan stirred up Jezebel to seek and vow the death of Elijah, persecuted Elijah was fed and preserved by a good angel, 1 Kings xix. 5. Devils labour to destroy the families and estates of the godly, as in the case of Job; the angels of God are their guard, when it is for their good, to protect them, and encamp about their persons and habitations.

(2.) The contentions of good and bad angels are about spiritual things. Jesus Christ, who is the spiritual Head and Husband of the church, was by evil angels with deadly hatred opposed; good angels admire, adore, advance him. When Christ was in the womb, Satan would have had his mother suspected of uncleanness, so that her husband was "minded to put her away;" but the good angel affirms, that what was conceived in her was "of the Holy Ghost." The devil sought to murder him in his infancy; the good angels appeared in multitudes praising God at his nativity, and one directs Joseph to carry Jesus into Egypt for his preservation from Herod's cruelty. The devil tempts Christ, and tosses him from place to place, Matt. iv.; the good angels, when he was afterward faint and weary, came and ministered to him. The devil, through the whole course of his life, stirs up persecution and raises slanders against him, enters into Judas to betray him, and into the Jews falsely to accuse and crucify him; but as one good angel appeared from heaven in his agony strengthening him, so would more than twelve legions of such, had God but given a commission, have waited upon him, and rescued him from his enemies. The devil's malice against Christ died not with him; but to baffle the glory of his resurrection, he suggests the aspersion of his disciples, their stealing away his body by night. The good angels attest the glory of his resurrection to those who came to the sepulchre, and afterward his ascension to those who looked toward heaven; assuring them also of his return to judgment. Nor is the contention of good and bad angels less about the church of Christ. The good angels rejoice at the enlargement of Christ's kingdom, the conversion of one sinner; and it is a pleasure to them to be present at the public ordinances, and to look into the mystery of the gospel, 1 Cor. xi. 10; Eph. iii. 10. As impossible it is they should preach another gospel as to be accursed, Gal. i. 8. They further the gospel, and preserve the true worship of God, forbidding the worship of themselves. The law was given by their ministry, Gal. iii. 19. The angel directs Cornelius to send for Peter, Acts x. 1—7. The angel brought Philip to instruct the eunuch; invited the apostle to come to Macedonia, and help souls to heaven; delivered Peter out of prison to preach the gospel; carried the soul of Lazarus to heaven; resisted Balaam in the way wherein he came forth to curse Israel, &c. "Michael and his angels" fight for the defence of the church against all the injuries of the devil, Rev. xii. But the devil is the grand adversary of souls. Evil angels labour to stop the passage of the gospel; they put forth their power in Jannes and Jambres to resist Moses in his ministry. The devil offers himself to be a lying spirit in the mouth of all Ahab's prophets. He stands at Joshua's right hand to withstand him in his office, Zech. iii. 1; he soweth tares in the field, where the good seed of the word is sown, Matt. xiii. : false doctrines are the doctrines of devils, 1 Tim. iv. 1. Satan hindered Paul once or twice from his journey to the Thessalonians to confirm their faith, 1 Thess. ii. 18; he raises persecution against the church; he "cast some into prison," Rev. ii. 10. And where he cannot hinder powerful preaching, he contends to make the word sundry ways ineffectual: some he holds fast in unbelief and contumacy; from careless hearers he snatches the word; those who hear attentively, he hinders from practising; and of some kind of practisers he often makes apostates.

2. The strife and combat between Michael and the devil, set forth more particularly in the particular case and cause thereof; the archangel "disputed about the body of Moses." And here,

1. What he did; "he disputed."
2. About what he did it, or the subject of that disputation; "the body of Moses."

(1.) "He disputed," διελέγετο. The word signifies a contest by argument and reason; besides which manner of strife there is no other, say some, after which spirits can strive and contend one with another. I shall not dispute the truth of that assertion, the *mos angelicus*, the manner of angelical disputation, being to us so dark; nor shall I now inquire how angels represent their minds and apprehensions one to another in their disputations; but sure I am, that as the arguments which this holy archangel produced against the devil to justify his action were strong and cogent, as being drawn from the revealed will of God, so the practice of disputing for convincing the adversaries of the truth, or stopping their mouths by arguments grounded upon that foundation, was frequently used by the apostle Paul, and to be imitated by us; who, were our words softer, and our arguments stronger, might more convince the adversary against whom, and credit the cause for which, we contend, Acts xvii. 17; xviii. 4, 19; xix. 9; xx. 9; xxiv. 12, 15.

If it be here demanded, Why this archangel would dispute with an incorrigible adversary? it is answered, He disputed not with hopes to recover his adversary; but, [1.] To credit his cause. It was a righteous cause, and was worthy of a strong advocate: though the adversary against whom we reason deserves neglect, yet the truth for which we argue deserves our contention.

[2.] To apologize for himself. He might have been looked upon as one who resisted and opposed Satan upon bare resolution and self-will, and would effect his desire by bare force, had he not disputed the equity of his proceedings with the devil.

[3.] To render the devil the more inexcusable. Though he was so far from being bettered or amended by all the disputation and reasoning of Michael with him, that he was the more enraged against the truth; yet he must needs be more clearly convinced that he opposed the righteous and holy will of God.

(2.) For the subject of this disputation, it was (saith Jude) "about the body of Moses." The principal doubt in this branch is, what should be the cause of this contention and disputation between Michael and the devil about the body of Moses. Various causes are by sundry interpreters mentioned. I shall rehearse some of the most probable, and cleave to that which I conceive to be the true one. Some affirm that the body of Moses is here to be taken figuratively, not for that body which was buried on Mount Nebo, but for that holy priesthood about which Satan resisted Joshua, Zech. iii. 1; because this priesthood, as a shadow, was to be restored at the return of the captivity, and to be in Christ truly fulfilled, whom the apostle calls "the body," Col. ii. 17, that answered the shadows of the law. Others also, making this place of Jude to refer, though after a different manner from the former, to that of Zech. iii. 1, conceive that by the body of Moses we are here to understand the synagogue or church of the Jews; the delivery whereof from the captivity of Babylon Satan, say they, opposed, and Michael contended for.

Opinio mystica est, ut corpus Mosis fuerit synagoga; ac synagogam liberari prohibuerit diabolus de captivitate Babylonis. Lorin. in loc.

But besides the arguments which have been brought already to prove that this Michael here mentioned by Jude was not Jehovah, as was he who is mentioned Zech. iii. 1, it seems a harsh expression, and no where used, to call either the Mosaic priesthood as fulfilled by Christ, or the synagogue and church of the Jews, "the body of Moses." Some conceive that this contention about the body of Moses was from Michael's endeavouring, and the devil's opposing, the honourable burial of Moses; to whom, say they, the devil would have had burial denied, because of his slaying the Egyptian in his lifetime; and that the devil contended that the body of a murderer belonged to him to dispose of. But this opinion seems false, both in regard of the great distance of time which was between the slaying of the

Egyptian and this contention; as also that the devil knew either that the slaying of the Egyptian was no true murder, or, if it were, that it was forgiven by God, who sundry times after it manifested tokens of signal love to his servant Moses. It is therefore lastly and most truly asserted by others, that Michael therefore "contended with the devil about the body of Moses," because the devil endeavoured, contrary to the express will of God, that it might be buried in some open and well-known place, that the Israelites, who were always too prone to idolatry, might thereby be drawn to give Moses Divine adoration. Michael, in zeal to the honour and obedience to the will of God, opposed the devil, and contended that the body of Moses should be buried in a secret place, where no man might know of his sepulchre, Deut. xxxiv.

<small>Vid. Chrysost. Hom. 5. in Mat. August. To. 3. p. 731. Ambr. Offic. c. 7.</small> 6. This last is the opinion of most, if not of all, modern writers, both protestant and popish, and of many of the ancients.

The most think that Satan in his contention aimed at stirring up the people idolatrously to worship the very dead body of Moses; and some affirm, though I suppose without ground, that after his death his face retained its former shining lustre: and to prevent the idolizing of Moses's rod, they conceive that Moses took it away with him when he went to die; it being that rod whereby he had wrought so many miracles, and which was called "the rod of God." Others rather think that Satan intended to have put the Israelites upon the idolatrous worshipping of Moses's soul, or ghost, by the discovery of his sepulchre: this opinion seems to me very probable. I know not that the worshipping the relics of dead men's bodies was an idolatry used in those times. I suppose it will not be denied but that it was the practice of the heathens to worship the ghosts or souls of the dead, who in their lifetime had been eminent for their greatness and beneficence; hence Jupiter, Mercury, Æsculapius were counted deities after their deaths for that good which their survivors had received from them while living; and heathens used this their idolatry by having among them the tombs and sepulchres of the deceased. Thus the Cretians worshipped Jupiter for their god, whose sepulchre they boasted they had among them. And <small>Quomodo potest deus alibi esse vivus, alibi mortuus; alibi habere templum, alibi sepulchrum? Lactant. l. 1. c. 11.</small> hence Lactantius holily and wittily derides them for honouring a god, who (as they thought) was in one place living, in another place dead; who in one place had a sepulchre, in another a temple.

The Roman emperors, after their deaths, were deified at the burning of their bodies; which being burnt, their souls were worshipped by the name of *manes*; and upon their sepulchres they engraved <small>Diis manibus.</small> these words, To the gods, the ghosts or souls of the departed; blindly believing that the souls of the departed resided about, or were present at, the places where their bodies were buried. These souls of the departed, heathens were wont to worship and consult at their graves and sepulchres; a practice which from heathens was received by the Israelites also. Hence we read of the idolatrous Jews, "who remained among the graves, and lodged in the monuments," Isa. lxv. 4; namely, to consult with the spirits of the dead; as is clear from Isa. viii. 19, where the prophet reproves the people for consulting for the living with the dead, i. e. with the souls or ghosts of those who were dead and departed. And at these graves and sepulchres of the dead were idolaters wont idolatrously to feast and banquet with those sacrifices which they had offered to the honour of the dead. Hence we read of the great idolatry of the Israelites, in eating "the sacrifices of the dead," Psal. cvi. 28. This idolatrous custom of seeking to the dead at their tombs or sepulchres the devil invented, that these deluded idolaters, who expected to consult with dead men, might indeed and really receive answers from, and so worship him; for though he persuaded his vassals that they who were dead gave them their answers, yet indeed those answers came from him. And to this practice the devil might easily have brought these Israelites, could he have obtained the discovery of Moses's sepulchre; which, containing the remains of so famous a lawgiver, and one so eminent above all the men in the world for acquaintance with God, would in probability upon all exigences have drawn idolaters to it for the adoration of and consultation with Moses; (especially considering the great and constant need of direction in which the Israelites stood while they were in the wilderness for their passage to Canaan;) though indeed the name of Moses was to have been but a stirrup, to have advanced the adoration even of the devil himself; who, as he was the sole contriver of this idolatry, so would have been pleased most with it, and honoured only by it; it being as much beyond the power of idolaters or devils to deal with a true, since dead, Moses, as it ever was against the will of Moses to have any such dealing with them. If it be here objected, that the Israelites did not worship at the sepulchres of Abraham, Jacob, Joseph, and the other patriarchs, and therefore that neither they would have idolatrously worshipped Moses, if they had known the place of his burial; it is answered, that there was far greater likelihood and danger of their idolizing Moses than any of the forementioned patriarchs; and that both for the honour which Moses had received from God, and also for that good which the Israelites had received by Moses. [1.] In respect of the former, none of the godly ancestors of the Israelites were so illustrious as was Moses for working miracles, and so many renowned performances, both in Egypt and after the Israelites came out of it; none by the testimony of truth itself being like Moses, whom God knew face to face; none who had the reputation of being so frequently and long with God, and of being a lawgiver to the people, and a mediator between God and them, to fetch them laws from God, and to carry their desires again to God; to be taken up, that he might converse with God, to the top of a flaming mount, the foot whereof no other person might touch upon pain of death; to have a face so gloriously shining, upon descent from God, as if God had imparted to him a kind of ray of Divinity; in a word, to have God say of him, as he did to and of Moses, "I have made thee a god," a speech not yet forgotten by Israel, to so great and puissant a monarch as Pharaoh. [2.] In respect of the great benefits that God bestowed upon the Israelites by Moses; never did they receive the like by any other instrument in any age; who ever was there besides Moses by whom God sent so many miraculous plagues upon their enemies? by whom (at the holding up of a rod) he divided the sea, and sent six hundred thousand men through it dry-shod, and afterwards caused it to return upon and swallow up their enemies; by whom he split the rocks into cups, and gave them water in a scorching wilderness, and fed them with miraculous showers of bread from heaven, &c. It is therefore probable that one so eminently honoured of God, and beneficial to Israel, as was Moses, had his grave been known, would after his death have been idolatrously worshipped, and perhaps, too, consulted as their guide in the remainder of their journey into the land of Canaan. Yea, <small>Hæres. 55.</small> Epiphanius reports, that in Arabia,

Moses, for the miracles wrought by him, was accounted a god, and that there his image was worshipped.

And whereas it may be said that the Israelites could not be so blockish as to have worshipped a dead Moses, his mortality being so pregnant a confutation of their idolatry and his divinity; it is answered, idolatry is a sottish sin; spiritual as well as carnal whoredom taking away the heart. It is just with God, that they who lay by his rule, should also lay off their own reason. Nor yet would the known zeal of Moses, while living, against such a practice as this, have, in probability, kept the Israelites from this idolatry, had the body of Moses been discovered; considering not only their proneness to that sin, and their forgetfulness of holy instruction; but also, that they might haply impute the unwillingness of Moses to be worshipped in his lifetime, and while he was among them, rather to his modesty and humility, than to his disallowing of such a practice after his death, when he should be both absent in body and glorious in soul. In short, needs must that be bad which that evil one is so violent in contending to have effected; nor certainly would Satan much have regarded Moses's body, had it not been to injure the Israelites' souls; and he who by his subtlety had once before with so much success drawn the people to idolatry, and almost to destruction, by the company of the Midianitish women, was much more industrious and hopeful, by this means, which had a face of greater plausibility, and would have proved far more hurtful, to have effected the same again.

Obs. 1. The opposition between sin and holiness is universal; they never meet but they fight. This enmity flies higher than men, it reaches even to angels also. It is in the heart, between a man and himself; outward, between men and men, between men and angels, between God and both, between angels and angels. Holiness and sin are irreconcilable; their opposition is reciprocal. Holiness can never tamely endure sin, nor sin quietly endure holiness. These antipathies can never be reconciled. Such is the opposition between them, that they cannot brook one another, notwithstanding all the plausible and rarely excellent qualifications that may be mixed with either. A saint cannot love a sinner, nor a sinner a saint, as such, though either be never so beautiful, affable, noble, learned. The devil meeting with holiness, and Michael with sin, though both in an angel, fight and contend with one another. It is in this case as with the dressing of some meats, though the sauce, the mixtures, be never so pleasant, the dressing never so cleanly and skilful; yet if such or such an ingredient be put in, the food will be loathsome to some stomachs, and will not be tasted. Such a one were a good man, saith a wicked person, were he not so precise and pure; and such a one were an excellent companion, saith a saint, were he holy and heavenly. Between the wolf and the lamb there is an antipathy of natures. Even their entrails, (say some,) made into lutestrings, will never sound harmoniously together. If they live quietly, (as is prophesied, Isa. xi. 6,) it is because the nature of the one is changed. They who act from contrary principles, by contrary rules, for contrary ends, must needs thwart one another. The people of God may hence be both cautioned and comforted. Cautioned, not to expect to be altogether quiet if they will be holy. Their legacy left them is, in the world to find hatred and trouble, John xvi. 33. They must be men of contention, though angels for their endowments. Cautioned also they should be that they leave not their holiness; for then, though man's contending

Sir Fr. Bacon's Nat. Hist.

with them should end, yet God's would begin; and the world's friendship is bought at too dear a rate, when with the loss of God's favour. Cautioned, lastly, not to hate the person of any under pretence of hating his sin: abhor not the body, but the sore. Zeal must not be destroying, but refining, fire. No man is so good, as for all things to be beloved; no man so bad, as for any thing but sin to be hated. The people of God may hence also be comforted: when they meet with most contention from men, it is but what angels have met with from devils; nay, what Christ has met with from men and devils. As Christ is our Captain, so angels, yea, archangels, are our fellow soldiers, nor shall we any more miscarry than either. The world's bad word is no bad sign. Two things declare what a man is, the company that he keeps, and the commendation which he receives. Wicked men cannot speak well of them who cry down their sin; nor is their discommendation any disgrace.

Pax cum viris, bellum cum vitiis.

Obs. 2. Satan is overmatched in his contentions. Michael an archangel, a good angel, contends with him. Although all the angels are equal by nature, and created with equal power, yet was the power of the fallen angels [much impaired by and for their apostasy; and as the holy angels exceeded them in other qualifications, so likewise in this of power. Good angels, though they are not omnipotent, yet had they not that chain put upon them which was put upon the bad immediately after their fall, whereby they are both restrained from what they would, and oft from what they can. This subjection of the bad angels is manifested by Augustine, from that order which God has placed among the creatures. The bodies (saith he) which are more gross and inferior, are ruled in a certain order by the more subtle and superior. All bodies are ruled by a spirit of life, and the irrational spirit of life by the rational; and that rational spirit of life which fell and sinned, by that rational spirit of life which is holy and righteous; and this holy spirit by God himself. Nor do we ever in Scripture read of any contention between the good and evil angels, wherein the good had not the victory. The devil and his angels fought, and prevailed not, Rev. xii. 8; and ver. 9, "He was cast out unto the earth." The devil never fights, either himself or by his instruments, but he is foiled, but he falls. Besides, the good angels ever contend for and by a great God, under a glorious and victorious Head and Captain, Jesus Christ; against a cursed, yea, a captivated enemy, who cannot lift up a hand further than the Captain of the good angels pleases; in a good cause, for the honour of God, and the welfare of the church: should they ever be foiled, their Captain would lose the most glory. How good is God, to order that the best creatures should be the strongest! How happy saints, in that they have, though an invisible, yet an invincible life-guard, an army of angels to pitch their tents about them, Psal. xxxiv. 7, whose safety thereby can be no more than shadowed by mountains full of horses and chariots of fire! If any thing sometimes befall them afflictive to their sense, yet nothing can befall them destructive, nay, not advantageous to their souls. How great is our interest to continue our guard! These holy spirits are driven away by our filthy conversation, like doves that cannot endure noisome places. They will protect none whose protection draws not allegiance to their great Lord and Master Jesus Christ. O give not the good angels cause to say of us, as David of Nabal, Surely in vain

Corpora crassiora et inferiora per subtiliora et potentiora quodam ordine reguntur; omnia corpora per spiritum vitæ; et spiritus vitæ irrationalis, per spiritum vitæ rationalem; et spiritus vitæ rationalis desertor et peccator, per spiritum vitæ rationalem, et pium, et justum, et ille per ipsum Deum. Aug. de Trin. l. 3. c. 3.

have we kept all that they have, &c., 1 Sam. xxv. 21. A man without angels is not without devils. Miserable is it for the poor sinner to be like a lamb in a large place, exposed to the cruelty of the wolf, instead of being defended by the care of the shepherd. Miserable (lastly) is the condition of every enemy of Christ and his church, who joins with that head, and fights under that leader, which is sure to be foiled; that walks "according to the prince of the power of the air;" that wars against the angels of God, yea, with him, the God of those angels. And how can they expect, who have fought for Satan against Michael in their lifetime, that Michael should contend with Satan for their souls at their deaths?

Obs. 3. In all contentions our care should be that our cause be good. Michael contended in a righteous quarrel. It is commonly seen, the hottest contentions are bestowed upon the unholiest causes. Idolaters cry out louder and longer for Diana of the Ephesians, wicked men more strenuously strive for promoting the devil's kingdom, than the saints do for advancing Christ's. How loud did Baal's priests cry to their god for help, and how cruelly did they gash their bodies when the reputation of their dumb and deaf deity was hazarded! 1 Kings xviii. 26, 28. How eager were the men of Ophrah that Gideon might be put to death for throwing down the altar of Baal! Judg. vi. 28. But what a shame is it, that blind zeal should be more eager and active than that which is enlightened! The goodness of that for which we contend only commends the greatness of our fervour in contending for it. The more fiery and furious a horse is which wants eyes, the more dangerous to himself and others is his career. The higher and stronger the winds are which drive the ship upon the sands and rocks, the more destructive and inevitable will be the wreck of the ship. We must first be sure we have a clear, a Scripture way, and then how sweet and suitable a connexion is it to be fervent in spirit when serving the Lord! Rom. xii. 11. We should mistrust and fear our course is wrong, when we find our hearts most eager and impetuous; and when we are sure our course is right, we should be ashamed that we are so faint and sluggish.

Obs. 4. Satan contends with the strongest, even with the strongest angel. No excellency can exempt any one from his onsets. He adventured upon Christ himself, Matt. iv. The most famous worthies mentioned in Scripture, Job, David, Peter, &c., could not escape the devil's encounter. This serpent set upon our first parents in their innocence. He commonly singles out the leaders for combat; and they often meet with the sharpest assaults. That Christian which is most angelical shall find Satan most diabolical. The devil's malice being most against God, is most against them who have in them most of God; in them he labours to be revenged on him; in the servants he strikes at the Master. And God in wisdom so orders it, that they who have most strength should be most exercised, to make his graces the more manifested to all beholders. God was not delighted that Job should be assaulted and tempted, but that thereby Satan should be overcome. And such is the devil's malice, that he will trouble those most in the way, whom he knows he can least hinder of the end. He contends, though he conquers not. Where he cannot destroy our grace, he will labour to disquiet our peace. Satan's assaults are no sign of God's hatred, nor should they be any occasion of our censures. If we be not so fiercely set upon as others, instead of censuring them for having no grace at all, let us rather think that they have more than ourselves. They whom Satan least troubles commonly least trouble him. In short, what need have weaklings of watchfulness, when the devil fears not an archangel! A weak Christian, when watchful, is in less danger than the strongest when secure. He who sets upon an angel's strength, will not fear human weakness. If he comes upon those who have nothing to help forward his conquest, he will come with a courage upon those who bring him weapons. In the best of us there is a strong party for Satan to join withal.

Obs. 5. The more God advances any in gifts and employment, the more Satan molests them. If this archangel were not, though some think he was, employed about the burying of Moses's body, yet sure we are he was here employed in contending for God; and that he was a choice, if not the chiefest, of all the servants that God kept in this great family of the world; the great minister and messenger of God to perform his Master's pleasure in matters of highest concernment. Persons of public employment are most fiercely assailed by Satan; they who are set apart to offices, whereby God is most glorified and his church relieved, are set upon by Satan the enemy of both. We never read that Moses, David, Paul, &c. were molested by the devil, till they were appointed to be God's archangels, as it were, his messengers, in delivering, governing, teaching the church. God never employs any in service but to oppose Satan's kingdom; and the higher their service is, the hotter is the opposition which they make; and whoever disturbs Satan shall be sure to hear of him: the more watchful any one is to do his duty, the more watchful is Satan to do him hurt. Commonly, God shows his servants in their entrance into duty what they are like to meet with in its continuance; and thereby he gives them such proof of his faithfulness in supporting them, that all the rage of hell afterward shall only prevent security, not overthrow faith; awaken, not dishearten them. And ever as the servants of God are afflicted, so are they fitted for his service; God is but training them to a due expertness in high employments. The more any one contends for God, the more let him expect to contend with Satan. They who most stop the devil's mouth, least stop his malice. Reckon upon Satan's wrath, if thou goest about God's work: they deceive themselves who expect to be quiet and serviceable at the same time; such groundless apprehensions are but the inlets to apostacy, and make us forsake our duty, because we cannot perform it with our outward ease. To conclude, Satan's opposition should not discourage us from duty, nay, we should look upon it as a hopeful sign of the conscientious discharge of our duty. Let us be sure that we are employed by God in his work, and that we labour to perform it after his mind; and then let us account opposition our encouragement and crown, as being that which almost only meets us in a good cause.

Obs. 6. Decent burial belongs to the bodies of the departed. God himself buried Moses; nay, (as most think,) the grand argument whereby Satan disputed with the archangel for *Vid. Jun. in loc.* the publicness of Moses's sepulchre, was the known fitness of bestowing a comely burial upon the bodies of God's servants; nor did Michael at all contend that Moses might not be buried, but that the devil might not be at the funeral, or not have the interring of him. Nature itself teaches a decency of burial. The very heathens readily entertained Abraham's motion to sell him a burying-place; yea, they had it in their own practice; "In the choice of our sepulchres bury thy dead," Gen. xxiii. 6. And want of burial is so hateful, that some have been more restrained by the fear of not being buried than of dying. Abraham was buried in the same cave with Sarah, Gen. xxv. 9, 10; after him, Isaac, Gen. xxxv. 29; Jacob, Gen. xlvii. 30; Joseph, Gen. l. 25; there also was Rebekah bestowed, Gen. xlix. 31. And when the kings and judges of Israel are recorded, their burials, with their places, are also mentioned; of which there are three ranks: 1. Some deserving ill, only buried in the city of David, the upper part of Jerusalem, wherein was the temple and David's palace, but not in the sepulchre of their fathers: thus was Jehoram, 2 Chron. xxi. 19; Joash, who fell to idolatry, 2 Chron. xxiv. 16; and Ahaz, 2 Chron. xxviii. 27. 2. Others, who were good kings, were buried in the city of David, and in the sepulchres of their fathers. And, 3. Some of the highest merit were buried in the city of David, in the sepulchres of their fathers, and in the upper part of the sepulchres of the sons of David; as Hezekiah, 2 Chron. xxxii. 33. Nor was it a small judgment that God inflicted upon Baasha and Jezebel, that they should be buried in the dogs, 2 Kings ix. 37; that Jehoiakim should be buried with the burial of an ass, Jer. xxii. 19, dragged out by the heels, and cast into a ditch; and that the king of Babylon should not be joined with the kings in burial, Isa. xiv. 20. Neither was it a slight imprecation which fell from David, Let them be a portion to foxes, Psal. lxiii. 10; nor a small threatening, that the bones of the kings, priests, and prophets should be taken out of the grave, and laid open to the sun and moon, Jer. viii. 1, 2. Hence David highly commended the burying of Saul, though a bad man, for a good work, 2 Sam. ii. 5. As of a sore judgment the church complains, The dead bodies of thy servants have they given to be meat to the fowls of the heaven, &c.; there was none to bury them. Suitable it is, that so choice and curious a piece of God's workmanship as man's body should not be carelessly laid aside, Psal. cxxxix. 14—16; yea, it has been repaired, redeemed, as well as made by God, Gal. iv. 4, 5; partner in redemption with the soul, and bought with the precious blood of Christ, Eph. i. 7; 1 Cor. vi. 20. The body also God hath sanctified, it is his temple. The ointment of sanctification rests not only upon the head, the soul, but diffuses itself to the body, the skirts also, 1 Thess. v. 23. The chair where the King of glory has sat should not be abused. With the bodies of our deceased friends we had lately sweet commerce. The body of the wife was lately entertained with dear embracement; the body of our child, a piece of ourselves: the body of a dear friend, what was it, but ourself divided with a separate skin? the body of a faithful minister, an earthen conduit-pipe, whereby God conveyed spiritual comforts to the soul. The body, when living, was a partner with the soul in all her actions; it was the soul's brother twin: what could the soul do without it? Whatever was in the understanding was conveyed by the sense. The soul sees by the body's eyes, hears by its ears, works by its hands, &c.; yea, even now still there is an indissoluble relation between the dust in the grave and the glorious soul; as the union of Christ's dead body to the Deity was not dissolved in the time of its lying in the sepulchre. Burying-places were not, among the Jews, called the houses of the dead, but of the living. The body is sown, not cast away; it is not dead, but sleepeth. The grave is a bed, and the churchyards sleeping-places. In short, the glory of the body's future state challenges the honour of burial. All the precious ointments bestowed upon the dead of old had been cast away, had it not been for the hope of a resurrection. A great heir that shall hereafter have a rich inheritance is regarded, though for the present he is in rags. And this decent burial of the dead discovers the more than heathenish barbarousness of papists, who not only deny, but recall the granting of burial to the dead bodies of the saints, digging them up again, as they did at Oxford and Cambridge, in Queen Mary's time; herein worse than heathens, as testifies the greater humanity of allowing interment, in Alexander, to the body of Darius; Hannibal, to that of Marcellus; Cæsar, to Pompey. The comfort of saints is, that the happiness of their souls is not confined to the burial of their bodies. "Precious in the sight of the Lord is the death of his saints," Psal. cxvi. 15, who carefully keeps every one of their bones: and as he left not one out of his book when he made them at first, Psal. cxxxix. 16; so, to be sure, neither shall one be missing when he will remake them; their very bodies being the members of Christ, and part of that lump whereof he was the first-fruits, 1 Cor. xv. 20. To conclude this, the care of a dead body should not be comparable to that of a living soul. What profit is it for the body to be embalmed and entombed richly, and the soul to be tormented eternally? As great a folly is, respecting the vile body, joined with neglecting the precious soul, as for a frantic mother only to lament the loss of the coat of her drowned child. Nor, lastly, ought this care of the bodies of the departed, though formerly never so holy, amount to a superstitious reverencing of their relics. Some think that the prevention of this sin was the ground of Michael's contention with the devil. But sure we are, though the devil could not obtain a licence for this sin of Michael, he has obtained command for it from the pope. It is hard to name that martyred saint who has not left some limb behind him to be adored: to name this folly is to confute it; for beside its idolatry and derogation from the merits of Christ, it is injurious to the saints themselves, giving their bodies only *insepultam sepulturam*, keeping them from their honour of rest, and bringing them into the compass of a condition threatened as a curse, Jer. viii. 1, 2. Yea, lastly, this popish foppery of adoring relics is ridiculous, Isa. xliv. 14—16. The very popish historians tell us that the bones of the worshipped have proved afterwards to be the relics of thieves and murderers; and common observation proves, that the cross of Christ, the milk of the virgin, and the relics of saints, are increased to such a proportion, as makes them more the objects of derision than adoration. The best reverence we can give to the departed, is to respect their spiritual relics, their holy lives and example.

Obs. 7. Satan's aim in every contention is to draw to sin. The body of Moses Satan regarded not any further than to hurt the souls of the Israelites. All his contentions with Christ were purposely to win him to sin. If ever Satan desired any thing which was good, yet it was after an ill manner, or to a wrong end. He would not contend against your estates, lives, liberties, were it not to get advantage against your souls. As God in all his contentions with us aims at advancing our holiness, so Satan propounds this as his end of every contention, the drawing us to wickedness. He would not have contended against Job's children, goods, body, &c., had he not aimed to drive him to distrust and impatience. He had not winnowed Job of worldly comforts, but for the winnowing him of his grace. "Satan" (saith Christ to Peter) "hath desired to have you, that he may sift you as wheat; but I have prayed for thee, that thy faith fail not," Luke xxii. 31, 32. The drift of the devil was to sift out Peter's faith. All the storms he raises against godly ministers and Christians, are not so much against their persons, as to hinder from holy performances. When he casts some into prison, disgraces, impoverishes, kills them, his aim in all this is that he may hinder the doing of good. He will allow all worldly enjoyments, if thereby he may the better accomplish the end of drawing to sin. He is a spiritual and a malicious enemy; spiritual, and therefore spiritual morsels are only suited to his palate; grace, like that herb called *morsus diaboli*, is that which he nibbles at; throw him this head over the wall, and, with Joab, he will soon raise his siege. He is a soul adversary, and no blood is so sweet to him as the blood of souls. Give me thy soul, saith he, and keep thou, nay, I will give thee, thy goods. Our enemies are spiritual wickednesses ἐν ἐπουρανίοις, in heavenlies, i. e. heavenly things, Eph. vi. 12. He is a malicious enemy, and well he knows that the greatest hurt he can do is to take away the greatest good; as he most strikes at the best men, so most at the best things in men; their grace, their soul; he is truly a murderer that aims at the heart. God deals with his people in a way of chastisement, the devil deals with them for destruction; he contends not to take away our gold, but our God. It is the most diabolical disposition to endeavour to put people upon sin, not to be willing to be miserable alone; nay, not only to be willing to follow and go along with others to hell, but to make them follow or go with us: what a trueborn progeny of hell did those papists show themselves, who drew timorous Christians to recant, and then put them to death, that so they might be murderers of soul and body at once! and who daily by the Jesuits, Satan's factors, compass sea and land to make proselytes! Let it be the greatest fear of every Christian, lest others should be so much as occasioned by them to sin: grieve much when any sin; most, when by thy means; pray that none may be confounded for thy sake, Psal. lxix. 6. Our greatest contention should be to advance holiness. All the good which Satan does to the body is to hurt the soul; so all the hurt which any do to the bodies of others, should be for the good of their souls; as Satan's lenitives are poisonous, so our very corrosives should be salubrious.

Obs. 8. Satan can bring colourable reason for the foulest practices. Even for that which he intended should be the sin and idolatrous snare of Israel he can dispute, and that with an archangel. It is probable he here argued for the fitness of burying Moses's body in a known place, from the eminence of the man's piety and worth while living; from the great unseemliness, that so faithful and public a servant of God should be buried in obscurity. What! might he say, shall not the just be had in everlasting remembrance? Psal. cxii. 6. Is not an obscure funeral the way to obscure all that ever Moses did, and at once to make the people forget God's works with Moses's name? As the worst courses may be coloured over by specious pretences, so there is none so skilful at this art as the devil; he is an expert logician, and showed himself so in this disputation; he can make the beautifullest grace seem deformed, and the most deformed sin seem beautiful. He puts the colour of sin upon grace, and the colour of grace upon sin. Never could the true Samuel have spoken better than did this counterfeit to Saul at Endor; in deluding Saul, he took the help of Samuel's prophecy: "The Lord hath done even as he spake by me," 1 Sam. xxviii. 17. He often kills men (as David Goliath) with their own sword; winding himself into them, and them into sin, by that which is the only preservative against sin, the Scripture. He can allege something good to hinder from any thing good; he can overthrow duty by duty; he draws the fairest glove over the blackest hand, and seems to make the worst cause without all danger or absurdity. He had that to say which the Son of God himself could not refuse; he disputed against him (though fallaciously) with scripture arguments, Matt. iv. 6: had he had a Psalter, he would have shown Christ the very place; nor is there any sinner whom he cannot furnish with a scripture to defend his lust; and such a scripture as the deluded novice has neither skill nor will to answer. The truth which Satan speaks ever tends to destroy truth. In alleging Scripture, he both colours himself and his motion, and frames himself according to the disposition of the parties with whom he deals. He knows the authority of Scripture always sways in the school of the church. It is our safest course to hold up against Scripture light all the plausible reasons or scriptures which Satan brings for any opinion or practice; to ponder, with prayer and study, every allegation, and to consider whether in their scope and end they are not against other direct scriptures, and the principles of religion; for God's Spirit never alleges Scripture, or propounds arguments, but to lead us into the knowledge and practice of some truth. This was the rule of Moses, Deut. xiii. 1, to try a false prophet by his scope. If any scripture or reason be alleged to put us upon sin, though the text be God's, yet the gloss and allegation is the devil's.

Obs. 9. In dealing with our greatest adversaries, we must do nothing wilfully, but with the guide of reason. Michael did not, though he could have done it, here shake off his opponent without answer or a rational disputation, though he deserved none; but to show that he did not withstand Satan's motion merely of a wilful mind, but upon just ground, he answers him, and disputes the case with him. Christ himself did not put off this very adversary of Michael without an answer, Matt. iv.; and when he refused the most unreasonable request of the sons of Zebedee, he gave a just reason, "It is not mine to give, but it shall be given to them for whom it is prepared," Mark x. 40. It is good, though our adversaries are stubborn, yet to manifest the ground of all those opinions and practices wherein we oppose them: our courses should be so good as to deserve to be justified, though our adversary may be so bad as not to deserve to be answered; and we shall hereby, though not recover him, yet both acquit and quiet ourselves, and possibly preserve others from being infected with that sin, which rather our reason than resolution is likely to prevent.

Obs. 10. Satan delights to put people upon giving that honour which is only due to God to something else besides God. He here contends for the servant against the Master, and for the worship of Moses against the worship of God.

Satan makes people give that honour to the creature which is due to God two ways; inwardly and outwardly. (1.) Inwardly. 1. By making people put their trust and confidence in something besides God, to make flesh their arm, to put confidence in man, to trust in horses and chariots, Job xxxi. 24; Psal. xx. 7; Prov. iii. 5. 2. By making people set their love and delight upon other things more than God; to love their "pleasures more than God," 2 Tim. iii. 4; to make gain their godliness; to be idolaters by covetousness, Eph. v. 5; to set their heart on that which was made to set their feet upon, Phil. iii. 19. 3. By making them bestow that fear upon the creature which is only due to God, Isa. viii. 13; to fear man's threats more than God's, Isa. li. 12, 13, and him who only can kill the body more than Him who can throw both body and soul into hell; to walk willingly after the (though wicked) commandment, Hos. v. 11.

(2.) Outwardly. Satan makes people give the honour to the creature which is due to God two ways. 1. By worshipping that for God which is not; thus the heathen worship false gods, Mars, Jupiter, Diana, Dagon, Baal, Moloch, Mahomet; and thus papists give Divine worship to relics, stocks, stones, a breaden god. 2. By worshipping God by other means, and after another manner, than he has appointed. That cannot be God's worship which is devised by another, the manner prescribed by himself being refused: the worshipping of God according to man's devices and traditions shall be as far from acceptance as ever it was from his institution. He best knows what he loves best.

Nor is it a wonder that Satan thus opposes God's worship, not only because he is an adversary to God, and strives to break asunder those bands of allegiance whereby the creature is tied to the Creator, and to deprive God of his homage; as also because an adversary to man, whom he endeavours to draw into God's displeasure; but by the making men to worship the creature instead of God, he aims to advance his own honour and worship in the room of God's. If men come once to be children of disobedience, and sons of Belial, such as will not submit to God's will, and bear his yoke, they "walk according to the prince of the power of the air," Eph. ii. 2; he is their "father," John viii. 44; "prince," John xiv. 30; "god," 2 Cor. iv. 4, both in regard of his own usurpation and their acceptation. In all divine worship, whatsoever is not performed to God is performed to the devil, Acts xiii. 10, there being no mean between them in worship. God and Satan divide the world of worshippers; for although in the intention of the worshippers the devil be not worshipped, yet worshipped he is in respect of the invention of the worship, which was Satan's device and appointment; and hence it is that we meet in Scripture such frequent mention of the worshipping of devils. The Gentiles, 1 Cor. x. 20, yea, the Jews, sacrificed to devils, Psal. cvi. 37; Lev. xvii. 7. And the truth is, Satan's contention that the people might find the way to Moses's sepulchre, was but that they might lose the way to God's service, and find the way to his own; as was more fully shown in the explication. Oh how lamentable is it that so bad a master should have so much service! that he who sheds our blood should be more willingly and frequently served than He who shed his own blood for us! To conclude, if holy Michael here contended that others might not worship any other than God, let us more contend that we ourselves may not do so. If Satan throw us down, yet let us not cast ourselves down. We have another, a better Master, his will let us study; the voice of his word and Spirit let us hear. Be above all those baits wherewith Satan allures to the adoring of any thing instead of Christ. Know nothing great or good but the service of Christ.

Obs. 11. Satan's great design is to make the holiest persons the greatest occasions of sin. He had much rather that a Moses, who had so zealously opposed idolatry, should be idolized, than one who had himself been an idolater. The devil loves to wound religion in the house of her friend, and with her own hands and weapons; to make Cromwell, a protestant, to sentence a godly Lambert to death. Oh how it delights him to overcome Scripture by alleging, not of the Alcoran, but the Scripture! And as he here dealt with the body, so he still deals with the books and writings of God's Moseses, the men of God: for as he fain would have made him who was the greatest enemy in the world to idolatry while living, to have been the greatest occasion of it when dead; so still he contends by heretics, that they who have been the renowned opposers of heresy in their lifetime, should be accounted the greatest patrons of it when dead. Thus the papists contend that the fathers, Augustine, Ambrose, &c., are theirs, and for their opinions. Thus the Pelagians of our time, that Augustine, Bucer, Ball are for free-will. Vid. John Goodwin, Sion College visited. But he much more contends, and had rather that a living than a dead Moses should be a stumblingblock to others. If one who is holy may, thinks he, be useful to me by his dust and relics, how much more by his falls, his scandals, his corrupt examples! Of all others, let those who fear God take most heed of giving advantage to Satan. When without their knowledge or consent they are by Satan only made advantageous to him, it should be their sorrow; but when they make themselves so, it is their great sin.

Obs. 12. The worst persons are oft compelled both to have and express a high opinion of God's faithful servants. Even Moses, one who was a great opposer of and greatly opposed by the devil, is yet secretly by this cursed enemy greatly honoured. Yea, the people who in Moses's lifetime would have stoned him, would, and Satan knew it too, after his death have idolized him. Our blessed Lord, when he was murdered by his enemies, was by some of them lauded as a just man: the young man calls him "Good Master," Luke xviii. 18; even bloody Herod reverenced the Baptist, Mark vi. 20; and Felix trembles at the preaching of Paul, Acts xxiv. 25. Wisdom shall sometimes be justified, not only by her children, but even by her sworn enemies. The father of lies, when he alleges Scripture to overthrow it, strongly argues that it is the strongest weapon, and has greatest power over the conscience. God delights to put a secret honour upon his saints and ways, and to make even those who love them not praise them. Many lewd livers strictly enjoin their children to be more religious. Every saint may be encouraged in holiness. God will often make its greatest opposers extol it; and when in their words they revile it, in their consciences they shall commend it. The praise of an enemy is equivalent to a universal good report. In short, let sinners seriously consider how they can answer this dilemma at the last day, If the ways and people of God were bad, why did you so much as commend them? if good, why did you not more imitate them also? If Christ were not a good Master, why did the young man call him so? if he were, why did he not follow him?

Obs. 13. The greatest respect that wicked ones manifest toward a godly Moses is when he is dead. While Moses was living, he was in danger of being destroyed; now dead, of being adored, by the Israelites. Joram, when Elisha was living, opposed him; but when dead, laments over him in that pathetical speech, "My father, my father, the chariots of Israel, and the horsemen thereof," 2 Kings xiii. 14. Saul disobeys and rejects Samuel when living, but when dead he with great pains, though no profit, endeavours to recall, to inquire of him. They build and garnish the sepulchres of the prophets when dead, whom, living, their fathers, led by the same spirit, destroyed, Luke xi. 47. God often makes the worth of his servants to be known by the want of them; and shows when they are gone, that they who in their lifetime were accounted the plagues and troublers, were indeed the preservers and peace-makers, of Israel. They shall then know, saith Ezekiel, that they have had a prophet among them, chap. xxxiii. 33. And it is a work of little cost, and of much credit, to extol the dead. The wicked are not troubled and molested in their ways of sin by departed saints. Samson could take honey out of that dead lion with which he fought when living, and which he slew because it roared upon him. The living, who roar and lift up their voices against men's sins, and labour to rend them from their corruptions, shall be persecuted; but when dead, exalted, to advance the reputation of those who praise them, for sweet and blessed men of God. The papists and many common protestants, who speak highly of Christ, and call him their sweet Saviour, had they lived in his days, and heard him preach against their lusts, would have hated him as much as, nay, more than now they hate those who have but a drop of his fountain of holiness. And, indeed, if a Moses, a servant of God, in his lifetime please wicked men, it is commonly because he is too like a dead man, not so quick and lively against their lusts as he should. It is not idolizing, but imitating the saints, that shows our love either to God or them.

This for the second part of this verse, the strife or contention itself. Now follows,

III. The carriage and deportment of the archangel in this combat. And first to speak thereof as it is set down negatively, in respect of his inward disposition; he "durst not bring a railing accusation."

Two things are here to be considered in the explication.

1. What it was which Michael did forbear; viz. to "bring a railing accusation."

2. Why it was that he did forbear it; he "durst not bring" it.

For the first, the thing forborne is here said to be "a railing accusation." The Greek hath κρίσιν βλασφημίας, an accusation of blasphemy, of railing; and Peter, 2 Pet. ii. 11, calls it κρίσιν βλάσφημον, a railing, or blasphemous judgment, or accusation; both places are rendered by these words, railing accusation; a judgment or accusation of railing, by a Hebraism, importing the same in Jude which a blasphemous judgment or accusation does in Peter.

Κρίσιν βλασφημίας per Hebraismum idem valet apud Judam, quod apud Petrum κρίσις βλάσφημος. Piscat. in Jud. Judicium maledicum. Piscat. Maledictionis judicium. Bez. Execrabile judicium. Vulg. in Pet. Judicium blasphemiæ. Vulg. in Jud.

In the opening of which,

(1.) I shall show you what is meant by this κρίσις, here rendered "accusation" or judgment.

(2.) What the apostle intends by a "railing accusation," or the railing of the accusation.

(3.) Wherein consists the sinfulness of that "railing accusation" from which this holy angel here abstained.

(1.) For the first. The word κρίσις, here translated "accusation," properly signifies a sentence or judgment passed upon a person, as appears by sundry places of Scripture; and therefore this accusation must needs be such a charging of another with some heinous crime, as whereby we judge and sentence him to be guilty of the crime, and, by reason thereof, of punishment. So that here the archangel, notwithstanding Satan's person, cause, and carriage were wicked, did forbear to bring any charge against him, whereby he might appear to judge or sentence him as guilty of punishment. Nor do we find in Scripture, and here in this place the contrary is clearly manifested, though holy angels were often employed as the messengers and ministers of God against the wicked to withstand them, and to execute upon them God's judgments, that they at all censured them, but ever they left the judging of them to God; a practice suitable to a gracious person, and acceptable to God, who, though he requires public, yet forbids private judgment. When he calls and ordains any to judge others, and to pass sentence upon them for their offences, it is their duty to perform his pleasure, though with the displeasing of any; but when he calls them not, they must not judge others for pleasing themselves. Public judgment is required by God of magistrates for the suppression of injustice, and the protection of the innocent; but private judgment passed upon others, being without any lawful call from God, merely out of private revenge and personal hatred, is frequently in Scripture forbidden, and here by Michael forborne. His work was a work of service, not of judicature. He was fellow creature with this, though evil, angel, not a fellow judge with God. Michael and the devil were now both pleaders before God, and God only was to pass sentence. Michael opposed the practice and attempt of the devil, and might judge it evil; but he censured not his person, a work which he left to God: though the devil deserved to be judged for his sin, yet God deserved not to be robbed of his glory; and Michael would not do a work which God never commissioned him to perform; nor would he, to show his hatred to the devil, show himself disobedient to God. God wants not our wickedness to do his own work, nor the besom of our passion to sweep his house.

(2.) What the apostle intends by "a railing accusation," or by this railing here, with the accusation forborne. The word is βλασφημία, and signifieth properly, hurting one's name by evil-speaking; and it is used in Scripture either for evil-speaking against God or the creature: the first is principally called blasphemy; which is committed three ways: 1. When that is attributed to God which is repugnant to his nature; as to say, that it is possible for God to sin, or that he is corporeal. 2. When that is denied to God which to his nature and excellency belongs to him; as omnipotency, omniscience, &c. 3. When that is attributed to the creature which is due to God; as to say that any creature is omnipotent, created the world, or can forgive sin; a sin which God commanded should be punished with death, Lev. xxiv. 16, 23.

But here, as in other places, it is used concerning the creature, and is most aptly added to the former word judgment, or accusation, because both in sinful judgment there is a speaking evil, or a hurting the name of another; and also, in evil-speaking there is a passing of judgment. He that judges or sentences another, must needs do it for some evil which he lays to his charge; and he who lays that evil to his charge, judges him thereby to deserve punishment. And this sin of evil-speaking is committed against man, either in his absence or in his presence.

1. In his absence; so it is called detraction and backbiting: of this evil-speaking some reckon six sorts. [1.] The publishing of the secret faults of others. [2.] The relating of what evil we hear, with increasing and aggravating it. [3.] The accusing them of false crimes. [4.] The denying of those good things which we know either to be in others, or to be done by them in secret. [5.] The diminishing of that good which is manifest. [6.] The perverting or turning of good spoken by another into evil. Others reduce all these to three heads. They say the sin of backbiting or detraction is, 1. By uttering things against others which are false and evil; and that first, when we speak evil of them by accusing them for that which we know is false, and which they never did. Thus Ziba spake evil of Mephibosheth, by informing David that he went not out to meet David, but staid at home expecting to be made king of Israel, 2 Sam. xvi. 3. 2. When we speak evil of others upon bare suspicion, slight reports, or any insufficient ground. Thus the princes

of Ammon charged David's servants with deceit, and caused them to be abused upon suspicion that they were spies, 2 Sam. x. 3.

This sin of evil-speaking by detraction is committed by uttering against others true things after a sinful and evil manner; and that several ways. As, 1. In the way of searching into and blazing of secret infirmities; uncovering that which ingenuous humanity would conceal, and making the house-top a pulpit to preach of what was done in the closet. "A talebearer revealeth secrets, but a man of a faithful spirit concealeth the matter," Prov. xi. 13. 2. When we amplify the offences of others beyond their due proportion; when for fifty we set down a hundred, and hold spectacles before faults of a small print, to make them seem greater than they are, representing that as done presumptuously which was done weakly, or as done unconscionably which was done carelessly, or as done deliberately which was done rashly. 3. When we speak good of another, but either lessen or deprave it, as done with a bad intention, in hypocrisy, for bad ends; and so relate the truth, but with wicked and false insinuations and collections of evil. Thus Doeg spake the truth to Saul concerning David, but falsely insinuated that David and the priests conspired against him, 1 Sam. xxii. 9, 10. 4. When in speaking of a thing truly done or spoken, we destroy the sense, and pervert the meaning. Thus the Jews spake evil of Christ, when they witnessed against him, that he said, He would destroy the temple, and build it up again in three days.

We may commit this sin of evil-speaking against others by detraction, even by others; and that both, 1. By suborning those who will accuse and speak evil of them; as Jezebel did against Naboth, and the Jews against Christ and Stephen, Acts vi. 11. And, 2. By receiving of evil reports against them from others, when, instead of driving away a backbiting tongue with an angry countenance, as the north wind driveth away rain, Prov. xxv. 23, we encourage and cherish evil-speakers, by our receiving what defamations they bring us, still to steal from the good names of others; when, though we set not our neighbour's name on fire, yet we stand and gladly warm our hands by it when we see it set on fire.

2. The sin of evil-speaking may be in his presence, or to his face; and then it is either mocking or railing. 1. Mocking is when a disgraceful taunt or gird is given to another; as Gen. xxxvii. 19, the brethren of Joseph scoffingly called him dreamer; the children called Elisha baldpate, 2 Kings ii. 23; and so in Babylon, they mock at the Israelites for their Hebrew songs, Psal. cxxxvii.

Σκῶμμα.

Λοιδορία. 2. Railing is properly when any sin or wickedness is objected, as murder, uncleanness, sedition: thus Shimei called David a bloody man, and a man of Belial; and the heathens called the Christians incestuous enemies to the state, &c.

(3.) Wherein consists the sinfulness of that "railing accusation" from which this holy angel abstained. And this appears,

1. In regard of God. It is a wickedness eminently injurious to him, and strictly prohibited by him, Matt. vii. 1; Lev. xix. 16; Col. iii. 8; Eph. iv. 3; James iv. 11; severely threatened and punished, 2 Kings ii. 23. It audaciously invades the seat and room of God himself, taking his office out of his hands, who is the Judge of heaven and earth; and from our standing before the judgment-seat of Christ, the apostle argues strongly against the judging of others, Rom. xiv. 10. "Judge nothing before the time," 1 Cor. iv. 5. And what hath any man to do to judge another man's servant? When we speak evil against any for his holiness, we most of all speak evil against him who is the Author of that holiness. Yea, this sin of reviling and evil-speaking is contrary to the course and carriage of God, who approves of the ways of his people, highly esteems their graces, accepts and rewards their weak endeavours; he pleads for his saints, acquits them, answers accusations brought against them, and pronounces a righteous sentence upon them; he calls Nathanael a true Israelite, Paul an elect vessel, &c.

2. In regard of those who hear these evil-speakings. Hearers commonly both willingly and hurtfully hear others defamed. It damps and destroys in them the love of their brethren: it is a draught, though of sweet, yet of deadly poison, given in at the ear: it lays a stumblingblock before the blind, by abusing, and falsely or unduly informing the ignorant, to whom the defamation is reported. It has separated chief friends.

3. In regard of the party who is guilty of evil-speaking. This sin speaks his madness and folly: if he may destroy his neighbour's name, he adventures to damn his own soul; if he may make others think ill of him whom he hates, he cares not how deeply he himself incurs the wrath of God; if he may but kill one by defaming him, he cares not, though in the doing thereof he destroys thousands by infecting them. He is like one who will blow in a heap of dust, though thereby he puts out his own eyes. Truly said Solomon, "He that uttereth slander is a fool," Prov. x. 18. True religion cannot consist with such a course. "If any man seem to be religious, and bridleth not his tongue, that man's religion is vain," James i. 26. A good man cannot be an evil-speaker.

This sin of evil-speaking is the disgrace of the evil-speaker. It is a practice of the old man, unbecoming and to be put off by Christians, that profess new life, as sordid rags, Col. iii. 8. An evil-speaker is the devil's eldest son, he bears his name; his mouth is the devil's vessel, which he fills with the water of cursing; he is the devil's tooth to bite men; he is a pedlar, furnished with wares by the devil to vend in the world for him; he scatters perfumes to delight him; he tells tales to make him merry; he more defiles his own heart and tongue than his neighbour's name. He is by some not unfitly compared to a butcher's dog, taught by his master not to touch the good and choice pieces of flesh in the shop, but the filthy offal he greedily and eagerly devours: by others to swine, who if they come into a garden, in one part whereof grow a thousand sweetly fragrant flowers, and in a corner whereof is laid a heap of manure, delight more to be grovelling in the manure than smelling the flowers; or who go not to the flowers to smell, but to root them up. They rake in the faults and infirmities of others; their graces they abhor as much to observe as they do to imitate; like owls, in the dark they see, in the sunshine they are blind.

Detractores diabolo thurificant. Pera. d. p. 320.

This evil-speaking is a soul-disquieting sin; it wears out, whets out the heart with vexation. Envy, the mother of calumny, is the saw of the soul: an evil-speaker is his own scourge. Miserable is his life who places his content in another's unhappiness, instead of his own happiness.

Invidia animæ serra.

To conclude, it is a God-provoking sin; punished frequently in this life by defamations, (a payment in its own coin,) troubles, law contentions, loss of estate, and often life; as appears in the death of the forty-two children, 2 Kings ii. 23, of Shimei, the leprosy of Miriam, &c. He who casts up the stones of reproaches will crack his own crown. But certainly, without repentance, destructive eternally, excluding from the kingdom of God, 1 Cor. vi. 10. God will reprove in his wrath if we reproach with our words, Psal. l. 20, 21: when we have done with our speech, our speech has not done with us.

4. In respect of him who is spoken against. Evil-speaking is a sin of the greatest cruelty; it takes away that which is better than honour, riches, yea life; and such a good stolen away cannot be recompensed, because its worth cannot be estimated. Evil-speaking buries the dear and precious name, the throat of the evil-speaker being an open sepulchre. At the best, it deals with men as the Ammonites with David's servants, it takes away half their names, cuts their reputation off at the midst; and commonly, they who are defamed in one respect, are suspected and slighted upon every occasion: one fly mars the whole pot of ointment. And one defamation will be sooner believed, though reported but by one never so unworthy of credit, than a commendation, though confirmed by the joint suffrages of a hundred faithful witnesses. The reviler lives upon man's flesh and blood as his meat and drink; nay, upon something better, the name being better than life. By a good name many have done good after their death; by the loss of it, many have been rendered useless while they lived. The former have lived when they were dead, the latter have been dead while they lived. Evil-speaking is more cruel than hell, for hell only devours the bad, but the hell of the tongue the good and bad too.

This for the explication of the first branch, namely, what the archangel did forbear, viz. to "bring a railing accusation." Hence follows,

Secondly, why he did forbear it; he "durst not bring" it. Wherein two things are to be opened. 1. What is meant by this not daring. 2. Why he was not daring.

1. For the first. The words are οὐκ ἐτόλμησε in the original, and the word τολμάω, here expounded by daring, has a double signification in Scripture; sometimes it signifies to endure, bear, sustain, or to be able and fit to undertake or undergo such a difficulty; and thus it is taken Rom. v. 7, One dare, or will endure, to die for a good man: and so the sense will be this, Michael durst not, that is, could not endure, was not able to give a railing accusation. But it more frequently signifieth to be bold, or to dare to do, or to adventure upon a business, as not being dismayed with any dangers. Thus it is taken Phil. i. 14; Mark xv. 43; John xxi. 12. And thus it is to be understood in this place, Jude intending that the archangel durst not be so bold, or was holily afraid to bring against the devil a railing accusation. And thus the difference between the seducers and the archangel, by whose contrary practice the apostle aggravates the sin of the seducers, will appear more clear and evident; the apostle telling us, 2 Pet. ii. 10, that these bold libertines were presumptuous, and not afraid to speak evil of dignities; but the archangel durst not, &c.

Τολμᾷ ἀποθανεῖν, Mori sustineat. Beza.

2. Why was the archangel thus far from daring and adventuring? There are three grounds of fear to adventure upon any way or course propounded to us. (1.) A natural desire of our own preservation, causing a dread of any thing which may endanger it. This in itself is no sin, it having been, not only in the holiest men, but in Jesus Christ himself, who prayed, that if it were possible the cup of death might pass from him. (2.) That corruption of nature whereby the creature fears nothing but the smart of punishment, and shuns it only as it is afflictive to sense, not at all as it is offensive to God; the party thus fearing having a heart only filled with guilt and self-accusation, and empty of that faith which worketh by love. Thus the devils believe and tremble. (3.) That principle of grace whereby persons fear sin as its opposite, and displeasing to God, whom they dare not offend; not only because he sets himself against sin, but principally, in the first place, because sin sets itself against God: this was the holy fear of David, "My flesh trembleth because of thee, and I am afraid of thy judgments," Psal. cxix. 12. First he feared God, and then he stood in awe of his judgments. This is indeed to fear sin as hell, and not only to fear it for hell. This is that fear commended by Solomon, for causing us to "depart from evil," Prov. xvi. 6; a fear that proceeds more from sense of duty enjoined than of danger threatened, and whereby we more respect God's will than our own woe. In a word, a fear which therefore is regardful of God's wrath, because it proceeds from a faith which reposeth itself on his mercy.

Obs. 1. Purity of affection should accompany angelic illumination. Michael had the holiness as well as the wisdom of an angel; he had not only ability to dispute, but care to keep from sin in disputing. A head full of knowledge, with a heart forward to sin, agree indeed with an angel, but it is an angel of darkness. An archangel given over to wickedness is an arch-devil. Great knowledge, without holiness, is but a great temptation; knowledge (saith the apostle) puffeth up. Sanctity in a child is better than all the understanding of devils. A clean heart is better than a clear head. If thou desirest, saith one, to understand like an angel, why art thou not more desirous to will as doth God? The great Diana of worship in the world is brain knowledge, and estimation of an acute and reaching apprehension; whereas holiness is esteemed but as a dull, contemptible qualification: but the glory of Michael here in the text was to keep himself from sin. It is a pity that a good head and a good heart should not ever be companions, or that the notional perception of truth should at any time go along with the practical refusal thereof. Wicked angels or ministers, who by their doctrine teach people how to be saved, do by their lives teach God how to damn themselves. If the Lord has given thee integrity of heart, though thy parts be but mean, bless him; he has truly shown thee the more excellent way, afforded thee an angelic excellency.

Si velles intelligere, ut angelus, quod non potes, cur non vis velle, ut Deus, quod potes? Nieremb. de Ador. in Sp. et Ver.

Obs. 2. It is a high commendation, to shun sin when we are necessitated to converse with sinners. Michael disputes with the devil, but yet holily and angelically. He got no infection from his devilish carriage. The devil sets upon our blessed Saviour more than once, yet Christ gathered no soil from this unclean spirit. It is a sign of a good constitution to continue healthful in a bad and infectious air. The truth of grace should show itself in its care, not only to avoid the company of sinners, but the contagion by sinners: perhaps we cannot shun the former, yet we should, and by holy watchfulness may, escape the other. If we cannot do the wicked good by conversing with them, we must take heed lest they do us hurt. It is a justly suspected goodness which can only hold up in good company: he who will then be bad rather overtakes sin than is overtaken by it; but he who keeps the spark of holiness alive in the midst of damps and quench-coals, though he may with holy David bewail his condition in respect of bad company, Psal. cxx. 5, yet may he withal rejoice in the hopes of his own integrity.

Obs. 3. It is our duty to learn this angelical lesson of forbearing to bring railing accusations. To this end, (1.) Be much and serious in accusing thy sinful self. In this duty it is hard to be severe enough. Put not thy eyes into thy pocket when thou art alone at home. It is a sign that they who desire to sacrifice their brethren's names, are, as Pharaoh charged the Israelites, but too idle; I mean, they labour not about their own hearts: every enemy, by how much the nearer, by so much the more hateful is he to us; our own sins are our nearest, and should be our most hated enemies. (2.) Envy not the worth of any: the very word (*invidia*) envy may either be derived from looking into, or not looking upon another at all; the envious are guilty of both, they will not look at all upon what is truly excellent; they love to look through and through, when they think they have found any thing culpable; in both respects they are occasioned to be evil-speakers. When they only are on the dark side of the cloud, it is no marvel that they stumble into slanders. (3.) Look upon every action of another with the spectacles of love. The apostle tells us that love thinketh, and it is as true that it speaketh, no evil, 1 Cor. xiii. 5. Malice (we say) never spake well; it ever makes, if it finds not faults, and puts a false gloss and a wrested interpretation upon the text of every action. Love covers a multitude of faults where they are, malice creates them where they are not. (4.) Keep a watch before thy mouth. Pray that thou mayst have God's aid. Resolve with David, before thou enterest into any company, not to offend with thy tongue: check thyself when thou perceivest thy proneness to offend; "return not evil for evil; being defamed, entreat; bless, and curse not," Rom. xii. 14; 1 Cor. iv. 13. Lock the door of thy lips so fast that the strongest provocation may never be able to pull it open. Strike not the second blow. Let the ball of contention go down on thine end. Instead of reviling revilers, commit thy cause to Him that judgeth righteously; herein thou followest Christ. When thou hearest another reviled, be as a stone wall; when thou hearest thyself reviled, be as a soft mud wall; in the former respect show thy opposition, in the latter thy patience; in the former carry not the devil in thine ear, in the latter carry him not in thy tongue. (5.) Deal with another's good name as thou wouldst have him deal with thine, if it comes in his way; they who handle the names of others most rudely, are most delicate when they themselves are touched. But nothing is more just with God than to suffer others to open their mouths against those who will open their own against their neighbours.

Obs. 4. There is no cowardice in not daring to sin. The lowest of all the holy angels has more magnanimity than all the presumptuous sinners on earth; yet, lo, here the chiefest, as some suppose, of all that heavenly host durst not sin in reviling. True valour stands in opposing, not in stooping to sin. It is not magnanimity, but madness, to damn thy soul, and to fight with the Lord of hosts. Men of greatest courage in Scripture have ever been most fearful of sin. David, who had shed the blood of so many thousands, yet waters his bed with tears for his sin. He who had overthrown so many armies is himself laid flat by one poor prophet. Josiah was stout-hearted, and yet tender-hearted also. The greatest cowardice is to yield thyself a captive to any lust: the audacious swearer is the coward, not he who fears an oath. The world ridiculously extols for valorous the great pretenders to valour; I mean, bloody duellists, or single combatants: of all sorts of sinners in the world these are the truest dastards, in being so excessively fearful of reproaches, who, suspecting they shall be pursued by the report of cowardice, fly they know not whither; even as far as hell, before they dare look back. They who fight with others are overcome of their own lusts. They who dare not fight with an enemy, either with tongue or hand, for fear of displeasing God, overcome their lust, which is a greater discovery of valour than to vanquish a city. It is not courage, but fool-hardiness, to go boldly to hell, proceeding from an ignorance of danger; sinners therein being like American Indians, who press upon the mouth of the musket, because they know not its force.

Obs. 5. The fear of God is the bridle of sin. Not daring to sin is a preservation against sin. This fear stopped the archangel from giving the devil a railing accusation. This holy fear made him contemn Satan's reproaches, and will make any despise all the difficulties of shame and sorrow which may be met with in the way of holiness. The greater fear expels the less; the fearing of Him who can destroy the soul, abolishes the fear of them who can only touch the body. If God be our fear, we shall not fear man's fear; he who fears God, fears nothing but him, Isa. viii. 13; he had rather be mocked for holiness than damned for sin; he is not like children, that fear an ugly vizard which cannot hurt them, but fear not the fire that may consume them; he is not such a fool as to be laughed out of his happiness, and to hazard the loss of his soul because he will not be mocked. Abraham thought if the fear of God had been in that place, Gen. xx. 11, that they would not have slain him for his wife's sake. How (saith Joseph) shall I do this great evil, and sin against God? Gen. xxxix. 9. "The fear of God," saith Solomon, "is to hate evil," Prov. viii. 13; it causes us not only outwardly to abstain from sin, but inwardly to abhor it; not only binding the hand, but also changing the heart: the fear of man will make us hide, the fear of God even hate sin also. Fear is the daughter of faith, and faith assents to the truth of the word, as promising, and commanding, and threatening, Heb. xi. 7. The worth of God's fear will be known to eternity. That which keeps from sin keeps from the only evil; they who fear the word shall not feel the rod. "I trembled," saith Habakkuk, "in myself, that I might rest in the day of trouble," Hab. iii. 16. If we would not fear with a servile, distrustful fear hereafter, we must fear with an awful, child-like fear for the present. If we fear wisely, we shall not fear vainly. In short, we hence learn the true reason of all the wickedness and woe in the world. Had the fear of God been here, sin had not been here, and punishment had been prevented; that which is now woe had then been watchfulness.

Timeamus prudenter, ne timeamus inaniter. Aug.

Thus far in this third part of this verse, of the first, the negative, branch thereof; "Durst not bring against him a railing accusation." The second, the positive, follows in these words; "But said, The Lord rebuke thee."

Two things for the explaining of this second branch of the third part:

1. What Michael here intends by the Lord's rebuking of Satan.
2. Why he uses this imprecation, and desires the Lord would rebuke him.

1. For the first. The word "rebuke" in the original is ἐπιτιμῆσαι; the Vulgate renders it *imperet*, The Lord rule thee; Beza and Erasmus, *increpet*, The Lord chide or rebuke thee; and the word signifies both to charge or command, by way of severe commination or threatening, to prevent disobedience in the commanded; as also (and most properly) to chide or reprehend, so as a servant is rebuked

ἐπιτιμάω, increpo, interminor. Significat increpare cum potestate, et objurgatione imperare, et ab incepto deterrere. Justinian in Jud. Increpando imperare, et imperando increpare. Lap. in 3. Zec.

Interdicere, et imperare, additis minis. Lor. in loc.

by his master, who both by his charging with threats, and chiding or rebuking, shows, as his authority to command, so his strength and ability to punish, in case the party whom he threats and chides is not deterred from going on in his begun enterprise. And because the commands, threats, and rebukes of God are not verbal, but efficaciously put forth in their effects, this word ἐπιτιμάω, here used by Jude, is used by the evangelist to express the authority and power of Christ, in stilling and calming the winds of the sea, ἐπετίμησε τοῖς ἀνέμοις, he "rebuked the winds," Matt. viii. 26; and in casting the devil out of the possessed, ἐπετίμησε τῷ πνεύματι, &c., "he rebuked the foul spirit," Mark ix. 25; and in healing Simon's wife's mother of the fever, ἐπετίμησε τῷ πυρετῷ, "he rebuked the fever," Luke iv. 39. So that this imprecation here used by the archangel of rebuking Satan, (1.) Presupposes Satan's bold readiness to oppose, and resolution to overthrow, the pleasure of God, unless he were hindered by the force of God's threats and rebukes, and the slavishness of Satan's fear, who forbears and gives over any wicked attempt merely for fear of punishment, and by a powerful restraint from God. And, (2.) It more properly intends the sovereign authority of God over the highest of wicked creatures, and his power, whereby, without any pains, easily, even as by the uttering of a rebuking word, he quells the devil; yea, the putting forth of his authority and power in the curbing and restraining of his impudent malignancy, whereby he resisted the will and pleasure of God concerning the body of Moses.

Divinum imperium efficax.

2. Why Michael in this hot contestation with the devil interposed this imprecation or desire of God's rebuking him. I answer, hereby he expressed, 1. His confidence in God. 2. Zeal for God. 3. Submissiveness to God.

(1.) Hereby he would show his confidence that God was able to maintain that righteous cause wherein he was now employed, viz. his opposing of Satan; the holy angel manifesting, that He whose will and pleasure it was that the sepulchre should be concealed, could easily curb and restrain this evil spirit from accomplishing, though he suffered him to attempt, its discovery. His carriage herein agrees to his name; for as his name Michael signified, Who is like or equal to the Lord; so by saying, "The Lord rebuke thee," he expressed that Satan's contestations against so great a God were all but in vain, he being a great and powerful Lord, and the devil, though a wicked and rebellious, yet a weak and timorous slave and underling, the Lord being able to chide all the devil's undertakings and contentions into nothing, even with one word or rebuke of his mouth.

(2.) Hereby Michael discovered his zeal for God. Though this holy angel was not so sinfully hot as to revile Satan, yet was he so holily zealous as to plead, yea, to imprecate for God. He who was holily patient in his own, was holily impatient in God's cause and quarrel. He prays not here in his own, but in God's behalf, that the foul mouth which had disputed against and blasphemed the holy God, might by that God be stopped. Angels are zealous for God's glory. Some think that the name of seraphim is therefore given to some of them for their burning zeal. As God takes the dishonour offered to any of his angels and messengers as offered to himself, so should they more sadly resent the dishonour offered to God, than if it had befallen themselves. Michael here, seeing the devil's carriage impudently derogating from God's glory, could no longer refrain, but zealously prays, "The Lord rebuke thee."

(3.) Hereby he shows his holy and humble submissiveness to God, and forbearance to be his own or his adversary's judge; he remits and refers revenge to God, desiring that God would take up the controversy: "The Lord" (saith he) "rebuke thee." The holy angel besought God to be mediator between him and the devil in this disputation: he knew well that vengeance belonged to God, and therefore he desires that God would deal with him as seemed best to himself. He repays not evil for evil, neither in affection or expression and speech. God being the righteous Judge, he expects the sentence only from him, who best knew what punishment the devil deserved, and how to vindicate the glory of his own name, and from whose hand the archangel well knew that the devil was not able to make an escape. In short, the devil's sinful opposing of Michael, yea, of God's glory, by contending for the discovery of Moses's sepulchre, was no warrant for Michael to offend God by expressing any undue desire of revenge; he therefore remits the matter to God's determination, "The Lord rebuke thee."

Obs. 1. Satan's forbearance of or desisting from any way of wickedness, is purely from God's threatening rebuke, and his powerful chiding him. The archangel saith not, The Lord mend, change, reform thee; but, The Lord hinder, stop, and by his power effectually rebuke thee. Satan may be driven away from some act of sin by God's power, not drawn by God's love; like a dog, he fears the whip, not loathing that which he is compelled to leave. The devil is held in an everlasting bond of sin; he is wedged and wedded to sin; he "sinneth" (as it is said, 1 John iii. 8) "from the beginning;" since he began, he never did nor shall cease from the love, although he may be forced to forbear the outward act of sin. There is in him an utter impotency to any good, nor can he lay down his unholy inclination; he may be curbed, he shall never be changed. It is ever a torment to him, not a delight, to forbear any wickedness: when he besought Christ not to torment him, Luke viii. 28, the torment against which he prayed was his ejection out of the possessed, whereby he was hindered from doing that hurt which he desired; it being immediately added by the evangelist, "For he (Christ) had commanded the unclean spirit to come out of the man." Satan came to tempt Christ of his own inclination, but he went away by Christ's powerful command. He ceased to molest Job, when he had vexed him as much as he could obtain leave to do: when he gives over any enterprise, he changes not his nature, but constrainedly leaves his exercise; he goes, but it is when he can stay no longer, when his commission is expired. Every commanded performance or forbearance is not a sign of grace. That which is incident to the devil argues no grace in man. Balaam was forbidden to curse the people of God, and he forbears, but forcedly, against his will. Let not men content themselves with the devil's obedience. To leave sin for fear of hell may go along with the love of it more than heaven. When Moses's parents exposed him to the waters, they loved him as much as or more than ever. To leave sin for want of a body to commit it, is not to leave our affection to it; the leaving of sin at our deathbeds is seldom true, ever suspicious. God loves a living Christian: any one will be a Christian dying. Duties without must flow from a gracious forwardness within. Join that in thy obedience which the devil hath divorced, inward subjection to outward services. It is one thing to be hindered from, another thing to hate sin. The rebukes of our superiors may cause the former, a principle of inward renovation can only produce the latter.

Obs. 2. God's power limits Satan's. Though the

will of Satan shall never be changed, yet his power is by God often curbed; when he is most violently running on in any way of opposition to God or man, God can stop and chide him back. With what a holy fearlessness may the godly go on in duty! The wicked are willingly serviceable to a master who cannot protect them from God's wrath: O let us serve Him cheerfully, who is able and willing to keep us from the devil's rage; we see likewise to whom we owe our preservation, only to Him who rebukes devils.

Obs. 3. How easily God prevails over his greatest enemies! It is but (as it were) a chiding and rebuking them, and even in their greatest fury they are mute, and dare not, cannot answer. What more easy than for a master to give a word of rebuke? a word of God's mouth is enough to make the devils tremble; they are all underlings to God, they are before him as nothing: the greatest mountain of worldly strength and opposition shall be before God but a mountain of chaff. If God do "but arise, his enemies are scattered," Psal. lxviii. 1; yea, He who sits in heaven "shall have them in derision," Psal. ii. 4; he derides them sitting: the fire does not so easily consume the stubble, the wind dissipate the smoke, the rod of iron break in pieces a potter's vessel, as God overthrows his enemies. With a word did God make the creature, with a word he moves it, with a word he stops it, with a word he destroys it; in all these "his word," as the psalmist speaks, "runneth very swiftly," Psal. cxlvii. 15. How vain are they who think that worldly greatness, their wealth, their strength, their youth, can shield them from the stroke of God's power, whetted with his wrath! The scythe can get as well through the green grass as the dry stubble. He who has but faith enough to believe himself a creature, may be cautioned against security in sin. The most glittering monarch is but a gilded potsherd; in nothing so mad as to think itself safe in contending with its Maker. Nor is it a less excusable folly to be swallowed up of fear by reason of the worldly greatness of any of God's enemies. Who art thou that art afraid of man that shall die, and the son of man, that shall be made as grass, and forgettest the Lord thy Maker? Isa. li. 12, 13. At the rebuke of God his and our enemies shall flee and fall. How great is that folly whereby men slight the great God, and fear a silly worm! All the peace and forbearance that God expresses towards his enemies proceeds not from his want of power, but from the greatness of his patience; a strong inducement to us, who are weak worms, to be patient under injuries which we cannot repel; since God is so full of forbearance, who is both infinitely provoked by, and infinitely powerful to be avenged of, his strongest enemies.

Obs. 4. The holiest persons are most offended with practices that oppose God's glory. When Satan dishonours God, the holy angel cannot refrain from praying that God would rebuke him. Michael does not only dispute for God, but he desires God to plead for himself. It would have been below Michael to have been affected with any thing a creature should have said or done, unless the honour of God had been concerned: nothing is little whereby God's name, or man's soul, suffers. The more any one knows the excellencies in God, or has tasted of the love of God, the less can he endure any thing either done or said against God. Angels, who continually behold the beauty of God's face, most abhor that which blemishes or disparages it. These sons of God endure not any thing whereby the honour of their Father suffers. Heaven itself would be no heaven to those glorious spirits, should they be constrained to behold God's name polluted. No mere man ever had on earth so clear a glimpse of God's glory as had Moses; nor was ever any so holily impatient when he apprehended a blemish to be cast upon it. The broken tables, the Israelites, which this meekest of men caused to be put to the sword, yea, his request that himself might be "blotted out of the book of life," rather than any blot should be cast upon God's honour, sufficiently prove that he who touched it touched the apple of his eye. How unlike to angels are they who put up no injuries with such a tame contentedness as those which are offered to God's name! who never say to any, The Lord rebuke you, but to those who dishonour themselves; yea, are ready to rebuke themselves whensoever they stumble upon any act of zeal! Surely the fire of such men's zeal is not angelical and heavenly, but culinary and smoky. What likelihood that they shall ever inhabit the place who are such strangers to the disposition of angels?

Obs. 5. It is unsuitable to a gracious temper to recompense evil for evil. Michael here commits his cause and remits revenge to God; suitable to whose carriage is the command of Scripture against private revenge: "Say not thou, I will recompense evil," Prov. xx. 22; and, "Say not, I will do so to him as he hath done to me; I will render to the man according to his work," Prov. xxiv. 29; and, "Recompense to no man evil for evil," Rom. xii. 17; and, "Avenge not yourselves, but rather give place to wrath," ver. 19. Revenge opposes the mind of God, and both disturbs and expels the spirit which would abide in the soul, and is the spirit of peace and dovelike meekness; and lets in and gives place to the devil, who is the father and furtherer of war and revenge. It divests God of his office. God alone knows how to punish our enemies without passion and inequality. It makes him, instead of a judge, only an executioner. It takes the sword out of God's hand, and drives him from his dominion. What difference makes it between the party provoking and provoked, save that the last is last in the offence against God? both are equally displeasing to him, whose law is by both broken; and supposing that our enemy has deserved to be hated, has God deserved to be disobeyed? Nor does revenge less oppose our own welfare than God's pleasure. The devil by this sin bereaves a man of his reason, and, like a bird of prey, which seizing upon a dead carcass, first pecks out his eyes, he blinds his understanding, and then leads him into what wickedness he pleases. By revenge we lose all that good which we might get, even by injuries. Holy patience turns every injury thrown at us into a precious stone, and makes it an addition to our crown. He who has received an injury, if wise to improve it, has received a favour, a reward; and it is against the rule of justice to return evil for good. What madness is it, because our enemy has done us wrong, to do ourselves more! because he has hurt our bodies, to damn our souls! that we may kill our enemy's ass, his body, to kill ourselves! that we may tear his garment, to lose our own lives! What unmanly folly is it to hate those in their sickness or madness, whom we love in their health! to hate those wronging us, whom we would love when they do us good! When our enemies are most unkind, they show more distemper in themselves than they do hatred to us; and therefore deserve more pity than opposition. What greater cruelty than to cut and wound one who is dead, I mean spiritually! What more ridiculous, than because one has taken away something from us, therefore to throw away all that is left behind! because he has stolen

Qui injuriam patitur, magis debet de peccato injuriantis, quam de injuria sibi allata.

away our cloak, or twenty pounds, therefore to throw our coat or whole inheritance into the sea! When one has taken from us the cloak of our good name, or a little of our worldly estate, how wild a folly is it therefore to throw away by revenge the beautiful garment of our innocence, yea, the inheritance of heaven! It is ridiculous, for the hatred of him that hurt us, to cast away that which never hurt, will always be helpful to us; and because we are bereaved of something which we had, our goods, therefore to throw away all we are, our souls. What madness comparable to that, whereby in our prayers we daily pour forth curses against, instead of requests for ourselves! Who would not think him weary of his life, who being struck by one whom he knows to be full of leprosy and plague sores, will spend his time in grappling and contending with him again? None can avenge himself upon another without spiritual defilement and infection; and, which is most inexcusable, that malice for which he is so much enraged against another he loves in himself. The empty, transitory, though reproachful, expression of his brother he lays to heart; but the sword of revenge, with which the devil endeavours to kill him, he contemns and disregards. In a word, what temper is more childish than that of revenge, whereby, like children, men desire and delight to strike that thing which hurt them! It is folly to beat the instrument which wounded us; our wisdom is, to labour that the wound which is given us may be healed and sanctified. Yea, there is more of brutishness than manliness, when we are kicked to kick again. Nothing more honours a man than overcoming revenge. He who can master his own revengeful heart, has a spirit truly noble, and fit to govern others. Upon David's sparing Saul, wisely did Saul say thus to David, "The Lord hath delivered me into thy hands, and thou killedst me not: and now, behold, I know well that thou shalt be king," 1 Sam. xxiv. 18, 20. He only has something supernatural in charity who requites evil with good, who loves his enemies, does good to them that hate him, wearies them with patience, and writes after a heavenly copy, Matt. v. 14.

Ridiculum est, odio nocentis innocentiam perdere. Senec.

Obs. 6. The consideration of our having a God to whom we may commit our cause, is the best means to make us patient under wrongs. Michael was a servant to a great Lord, and to him he appeals, and lays the controversy before him: "The Lord rebuke thee." There would be more bearing in the world, were there more believing. Did we look more upon him that is invisible, we should less regard the evils which we see and feel. "Walk before me," saith God to Abraham, "and be perfect." Nothing, either of pleasure or pain, will seem great to him, in whose eye there is this great Lord. The greatest prop in opposition is to have a God to fly to. The greatest loss for him shall be made up again by him. When David considered that God was his portion, he abhorred to go to other subterfuges, Psal. xvi. 4, 5. They who believe they have a God to right them, will not wrong themselves so much as to revenge their own wrongs. God, they know, will do it more equally, and more beneficially. And the true reason why there is no more willingness, either to forbear any sin, or to bear any sorrow, is because we think not of this great Lord, so as either to fear or trust him. They who can call God Father, may with Christ pray concerning their enemies, "Forgive them." They who can see heaven opened, and Christ at the right hand pleading for them, may with Stephen plead for their enemies, and pray, "Lord, lay not this sin to their charge."

Verse 10.

But these speak evil of those things which they know not: but what they know naturally, as brute beasts, in those things they corrupt themselves.

In this verse our apostle accommodates and applies the comparison of Michael the archangel, or further shows wherein the holy and humble carriage of Michael made the sin of these seducers appear more sinful and abominable. The angel was a creature, not only of the greatest created might and power, but also of wisdom and understanding, and knew what the devil was, namely, a wicked creature, and destined by God to eternal perdition; accurately also he understood that the cause wherein he contended with the devil was just and righteous, knowing the pleasure and will of God concerning the hiding of Moses's sepulchre; but these, saith he, speak evil of what persons and things they know not; are outrageous, though ignorant; active, though blind. And this want of due wisdom and understanding, in not knowing what they spake against, the apostle illustrates, by showing what that kind of knowledge was which was left in these seducers; namely, such as was merely brutish and sensual, and such as whereby they corrupted themselves: so that, as they sinned in what they hated and opposed, because they knew it not; they sinned also in what they embraced and loved, because they knew it, but after a natural, beastly manner, viz. for the satisfying of their sensitive appetites. Our apostle with admirable artifice subjoins this second, their natural brutish knowledge, to the former, their ignorance; because thereby he amplifies most wisely both those sins mentioned in ver. 8, viz. their defiling the flesh, and despising of dominions; though (as Junius notes) by a *hysteron proteron*, he amplifies the ὕστερον πρότερον. latter, their despising of dominion, in the first place.

The words contain principally these two parts: 1. The malicious ignorance of these seducers, in speaking evil of what they knew not. 2. Their sensual knowledge, in corrupting themselves in those things which, like brute beasts, they knew. In the former they showed themselves no Christians, in the latter scarce men.

1. Their malicious ignorance; "These speak evil of those things which they know not." Wherein I consider, 1. Their act; βλασφημοῦσι, they "speak evil," or blaspheme. 2. The object of which they speak evil, and which they blaspheme; "those things which they know not." To the first of these I have before, on ver. 8, and ver. 9, spoken. Of the latter I now treat.

Three things here are to be opened.

1. What the things are which these seducers are here said not to know.
2. What kind of ignorance, or not knowing of those things, it was wherewith they are here charged.
3. Wherein appears this sin of speaking evil of those things which they knew not.

1. What the things are which these seducers are here said not to know.

Some conceive (as Œcumenius and others) that the things of which these seducers were ignorant, and spake evil, were sundry doctrines and points of faith, and mysteries of Christian religion. The doctrines of Christianity surpassed their reason, nor could they be perceived by the power of nature. These seducers were such as were "ever learning, and never able to come to the knowledge of the truth," 2 Tim. iii. 7; and having swerved from the faith, turned aside to vain jangling; and desiring to be teachers of the law, understood not what they said, nor whereof they affirmed, 1 Tim. i. 7. They were blind leaders of the blind, not knowing the Scriptures, Matt. xv. 14. In a word, they consented not to wholesome words, even the words of our Lord Jesus Christ, and to the doctrine which is according to godliness, but were proud, knowing nothing, but doting about questions and strife of words, 1 Tim. vi. 3, 4. And particularly, they were ignorant of that main, fundamental, gospel truth, viz. that the grace of God teaches us to deny ungodliness; holding that they were by that grace freed from all holiness of life, and that all were thereby left at liberty to live as they pleased; so that their lusts, like the dust, put out the eyes of their understanding.

Others conceive, more probably, that though the apostle here uses an indefinite expression, in saying ὅσα, those things, yet he here intends principally, that these seducers were ignorant of the nature, institution, and end of that dominion, those dignities which they so much despised and reviled, ver. 8, that they knew not that magistracy was appointed by God, and to continue, even in the time of the gospel, notwithstanding the liberty which Christ hath purchased for us; in short, they were ignorant of the great utility and benefit of civil government in and to the world; that it defends justice, opposes vice, preserves public peace, relieves the oppressed, and is that tree under the shadow whereof we quietly and safely sit, and are sheltered.

2. For the second, What kind of ignorance it was with which the apostle here charges the seducers. There are three sorts of ignorance. (1.) A happy and profitable ignorance, viz. not to know those things the knowledge whereof proves hurtful; thus it had been good for Adam not to have known evil experimentally. It had been good for the Jews if they had never known the corrupt and idolatrous fashions of the heathens; and, in some respect, it had been good for apostates if they had never known the way of righteousness, 2 Pet. ii. 21. (2.) There is a knowledge of mere and simple negation; as Christ knew not the day of judgment, and as illiterate mechanics know not sundry arts and sciences, as physic, astronomy; and this is without sin. (3.) There is an ignorance of evil disposition, and this is twofold. 1. Of frailty, when we are ignorant, and naturally indisposed to the knowledge of those things which we ought to know; but yet we are holily sorrowful for it, mourn under it, and pray against it. Thus even the godly are ignorant. 2. Ignorance of evil disposition may be supine, gross, or affected; when men like themselves well enough in their ignorance, and their ignorance in themselves; and this is not only *non profligata*, an ignorance not fought against and opposed, but also *affectata*, affected and loved, by men who refuse instruction, that so they may sin the more freely, and prosecute evil the more without controlment. This sort of ignorance is not barely *nescire*, a nescience, and not knowing either of the things which we are enjoined to know and bound to know; but a *nolle scire*, a conceited, contracted, contented ignorance, which thinks it knows what it knows not, and desires to unlearn what it knows: the former is the cause of sin, but of the latter sin is the cause; that ignorance whereby men desire not the knowledge of the ways of God, know not (as the psalmist speaks) nor will understand, our will, but walk on in darkness, Psal. lxxxii. 5. In brief, this ignorance wherewith our apostle charges these seducers is not only that *qua nesciunt*, whereby they discern not; but *qua respuunt*, whereby they

<small>Non est consequens, ut continuo erret, quisquis aliquid nescit; sed quisquis se existimat scire quod nescit. Aug. c. 17. Enchir.</small>

despise things needful to be known, approve not the things that are excellent, delight in error, quarrel with and resist the truth, and, as Peter speaks of this very sort of men, are willingly ignorant, 2 Pet. iii. 5. The heathen are said not to like to acknowledge God; their blindness was natural, and they also voluntarily chose their superstition before the knowledge of God, Rom. i. 28.

3. Briefly for the third, Wherein appears the sinfulness of their speaking evil of those things which they knew not.

(1.) It is a sin discovering the grossest folly. Not to understand is a man's infirmity, but to speak what, and evilly of what, he understands not is his folly. If folly be discovered in speaking much, even of what we know, more is it manifested in speaking any thing of what we know not. If an ignorant speaker, much more is an ignorant reviler, his own enemy; he shoots up arrows, which, for aught he knows, may fall upon his own pate; he speaks that in his fury which he cannot unsay, and for which he may be undone in his sobriety. "He that answers a matter before he hears it, it is a folly and a shame unto him," Prov. xviii. 13. "The heart of the wise teaches his mouth," Prov. xvi. 23.

(2.) To speak evil of what we know not is greatest injustice. If he speaks unjustly who utters what is good and just in a cause which he knows not, because it is more by hap (as they say) than by honesty; how much greater is his injustice, who speaks that which is evil and unjust of what he knows not. It is unjust to speak evil of any without a call, though we do know it; much more when we do not know it. How unequal is it that another should suffer for my ignorance, much more from myself! It is the happiness of him who suffers, but the sin of him who offers the injury, that the former has no fault but the ignorance of the latter. Though David will ever be reckoned among good men, yet his act of ignorant censuring Mephibosheth, unheard Mephibosheth! will ever be reckoned among his unjust actions. The like may be said of Potiphar's doing evil to Joseph before he knew his cause, and Eli's censuring Hannah for drunkenness before he heard her.

(3.) To speak evil of what we know not argues the height of malice. He may be malicious who speaks the evil he knows, much more he who utters that which he knows not. It is from want of love, to discover the sin we find in another, but it is the excess of malice to make that sin which we could not find. If love makes us believe that good which we know not in another, 1 Cor. xiii. 7, then must it be malice which makes us believe and report that evil of which we are ignorant. To conclude, it is a malicious rejoicing in evil, 1 Cor. xiii. 6, to delight in uttering an evil which we really behold in another. But how great a pleasure does he take in another's evil, who rejoices in his very fancying and imagining that evil against another which he frames in his own thoughts!

(4.) To speak evil of what we know not discovers impudence in wickedness, and a sinful immodesty as well as maliciousness: such an evil-speaking argues that a man has sinned away shame as well as love. What greater impudence than for a man to outface at once the common observation of hearers, who haply can contradict foolish slander, and also the danger that false accusation incurs among men; yea, conscience checking, and representing God himself both observing and threatening ignorant and evil speaking.

Obs. 1. None are so ready to speak as the ignorant. They who know least speak most and oftenest. A fool is hardly discerned when silent; his picture is best taken when he is speaking; if he holds his peace, he is accounted wise; he is, by Solomon, called "a prating fool:" "A fool," saith he, "is full of words," and is known thereby, Eccl. x. 14; v. 3: empty vessels sound. A wise man has something to do before he speaks, and besides speaking; namely, to consider, and let down the bucket of his tongue into the well of his reason, before he pour forth words. A fool's work is only to speak; no wonder then if he does it with greater speed than a wiser person; and if he, like Jacob in his hasty providing of meat for his father, more suddenly presents the hearer with a kid of the goats than another shall with venison; and more easily brings what comes next hand, and is at the tongue's end, than another does that for which he has laboured: and yet deluded hearers, to whom such a present of empty words is tendered, commonly, like blind Isaac, bless and applaud the bringers thereof sooner and more than those whose words are more weighty, and prepared with greater pains. Their backwardness to learn of others has made them so forward to teach others; and because they were fruitless scholars, they are forward and fruitless teachers. And yet these empty speakers, that they may be commended by the ignorant for knowing, care not if they are condemned by those who are knowing for ignorant. It is good counsel of the apostle, to be slow to speak, James i. 19, and to take heed of coveting, with Ahimaaz, to be messengers before we have tidings ready, 2 Sam. xviii. 22; and with the empty and ambitious bramble, of desiring to be erected over others as their instructors, when, having never been instructed, we can administer nothing to the hearer but fruitless words, empty leaves, and unsavoury discourses. The faulty in this kind may well give good measure, for they give but bad weight, and may sell that cheap which costs them nothing. It is inverted order to be teachers before we are scholars. The apostle commands that a bishop be not διδάσκαλος only, a teacher; but διδάκτικος, fit, or meet, or apt to teach, 1 Tim. iii. 2; and that he attend to reading as well as speaking, 1 Tim. iv. 13. As without the blessing of God no means are prevalent, so without the use of means no blessing can be expected. It is only suitable, that his tongue only should be the pen of a ready writer, whose heart has first been inditing a good matter, Psal. xlv. 1. Nor should the hearer be less careful to discern, than the speaker is to indite, a good matter, Prov. xviii. 15. How few hearers have we that can yet difference between matter and words! it suffices the most, if the hour be filled up with an empty noise, without any solid instruction: how rare is it to find, though we run to and fro in the streets of London, a man, I mean, in understanding!

Obs. 2. Ignorance is the cause of opposing the ways of God. "They speak evil of those things which they know not." The opposing and crucifying of Christ himself proceeded from ignorance. "Had they known," saith the apostle, "they would not have crucified the Lord of glory," 1 Cor. ii. 8. "I wot that through ignorance," saith Peter to the Jews, "ye did it," speaking concerning the killing "the Prince of life," Acts iii. 15, 17. Christ himself testifies of his murderers that they knew not what they did. "And these things," saith Christ, speaking of the unkindness and cruelties of sinners against his servants, "will they do unto you, because they have not known the Father, nor me," John xvi. 3. "If thou knewest," saith Christ to that poor Samaritan, "the gift of God, and who it is that saith to thee, Give me to drink, thou wouldest have asked of him, and he would have given thee living water," John iv. 10. The reason why those profane ones refused God's service, and asked what profit they should have if they prayed to him, is plainly implied to be their ignorance; they desired not the knowledge of his ways; and, Who, say they, is the Almighty? &c., Job xxi. 14, 15. The reason why the heathen did not call upon God, is said to be this, they knew him not, Psal. lxxix. 6. "There is none that understandeth, that seeketh after God," Rom. iii. 11. Ignorance made the Gentiles strangers from the life of God, Eph. iv. 18. It is a sin which never went single; it ever walks in company, and is an inlet to all impiety. Although the prayer of Christ for his ignorant enemies, showed that God might take occasion from their ignorance to forgive them, yet it plainly implies that the sin to be forgiven them took its rise from their ignorance; their doing was from their not knowing what they did. An unregenerate man's practice is a fashioning himself according to lusts in his ignorance, 1 Pet. i. 14.

Did men either see the deformity of sin, or the beauty of holiness, they would neither delight in the former, nor dislike the latter: when there is no knowledge of God in the land, there is neither "truth nor mercy," but "swearing, lying, killing, stealing, committing adultery," Hos. iv. 1, 2. The foundation of obedience must be laid in knowledge, which, in a sort, is the root of other graces: "Grace be multiplied unto you through the knowledge of God," 2 Pet. i. 2. See also ver. 3. The will and affections are led by the understanding, which sits at the stern in the soul: all the sins of the people are called errors, Heb. ix. 7. As Eve, so others since, are drawn to sin by being deceived, 1 Tim. ii. 14.

The first work of grace is to reform the understanding. Be ye changed by the renewing of your mind, Rom. xii. 2. And, "The new man is renewed in knowledge," Col. iii. 10. The imaginations and thoughts of the mind are by the apostle called those strong holds and high things exalted against the knowledge, and to be subdued " to the obedience, of Christ," 2 Cor. x. 4, 5. How dangerous then is ignorance! He who wants the right knowledge of God is still under the dominion of Satan, who is called "the ruler of the darkness of this world," Eph. vi. 12. This ruler of darkness takes up his throne in dark hearts; none are turned off the ladder but such whom he first blinds. "I send thee," saith Christ to Paul, "to turn them from darkness to light, and from the power of Satan unto God," Acts xxvi. 18. Ignorance is the beaten path to hell: My people perish for want of knowledge, Hos. iv. 6. Whomsoever God will have to be saved, he will bring "to the knowledge of the truth," 1 Tim. ii. 4. They who have not known God's ways, shall never, if we may believe God's oath, enter into his rest, Psal. xcv. 10, 11. Foolish are they who boast of their good minds and meanings, and yet continue ignorant. Without knowledge the mind is not good, Prov. xix. 2. Many cry up practice and good meaning to cry down knowledge: ignorant devotion is but feet without eyes, which the farther and faster they carry us, the greater is our deviation and danger.

To conclude this point. How excellent is every way of God, of which only ignorant ones speak evil! besides the ignorant, heavenly learning has no enemy. There is none who know it, as we say of some men, but love it. All the children of wisdom justify her, Matt. xi. 19; nor was she ever condemned but by those who never would hear what she could say for herself. How patient should every saint be under all the reproaches which he meets with for holiness from blind sinners, whose tongues are in this no slander! A blind man cannot judge of colours. Much more deserve they our pity and prayers for their want of eyes, than our wrath for their abusing their tongues. Let all our revenge be, to labour to make them know and speak better. He who strikes his friend in the dark, will be most offended with himself when the light discovers his mistaken unkindness.

Obs. 3. How great is the sin of speaking evil of those things the worth whereof we do know! If to speak ignorantly and evilly against what is good be a sin, then to speak knowingly and evilly against it must needs be a greater sin. If they may sin who think they do God service in speaking against a person; how heinous is their sin who know that they do God disservice, and the devil service, in such speaking! All sin against light, especially reviling against light, borders upon the sin against the Holy Ghost, and adventures to make too near an approach unto it. To speak evil even of what is not good, may be bad; to speak evil of what is good, is worse; to speak evil of what is good, though we know it to be so, is much worse, and within one step of speaking evil against it because we know it to be so. Such sins more stupify and benumb the conscience than others, and keep it from sensibleness; and therefore it will want a deeper wound (and possibly such a one as shall never be cured) to make it sensible. How deservedly solicitous therefore was holy David in his prayer to be kept from sins of contumacy and presumption! Psal. xix. 13; sins which, as they are more ordinarily committed in days of light and much knowledge, so can they not be committed at so easy and cheap a rate as those which are caused by ignorance.

Obs. 4. We should speak against known evils, and for what we know to be good. If the wicked fear not to speak evil of the good which they know not, how unsuitable is it for saints to be afraid to speak against those evils which they know to be such! As it is a sinful forwardness to speak at any time of the things which we know not, so it is oft sinful backwardness not to speak the things which we do know: "Knowing," saith the apostle, "the terror of the Lord, we persuade men," 2 Cor. v. 11. "We speak that we do know, and testify that we have seen," saith Christ, John iii. 11. Shall not sinners forbear to revile holiness, and shall others refrain to withstand impiety? How inexcusable is it that ignorance should be more active in a wrong than knowledge in a right way! When men oppose holiness, they fight without eyes; and shall light produce lukewarmness? What a shame is it that Satan should have more confessors and martyrs than Jesus Christ! If sin and error fear no colours, and covet no corners, should grace and truth do either? the fool-hardiness of sinners may justly reprove the faintness of saints. It is our duty to be valiant for the truth, and to give the glory of God reparations, as it were, by wiping off the blemishes cast upon it by foolish and ignorant men. When we have upon grounded deliberation chosen our love, we should zealously express the love of our choice. Sinners, as they say of young men's thoughts of old, think that saints are foolish, but saints know that sinners are so. Let not their prosecution of sin be more zealous than thy reprehension of it; nor their opposition of any way of God be more hot than thy contention for it. Let thy fire have more purity than theirs, but let it not be inferior in its fervour. The Christian's serpent must not devour his dove. How good a Master do the godly serve, who requires no duty but such as he warrants in and rewards after the doing! Satan's servants are sceptics, and he puts them upon such employments, in the doing whereof they cannot know they do well; and afterward they shall know they have done ill, and that to their cost.

Obs. 5. Corrupt affections blear and darken the judgment. These seducers hated the ways of God, and delighted to oppose them, and therefore they did not, would not know them. He who will be disobedient in heart, shall soon have a dull head. They who love sin will leave the truth. Lust opposes the entrance of the light. Repentance makes men "acknowledge the truth," 2 Tim. ii. 25. "Every one who doeth evil hateth the light," John iii. 20. Men love not to study such truths as will hinder them (being known) from going on in some gainful wickedness. It is from unrighteousness that men imprison truths. They who thought believing the resurrection would hinder their course in sin, taught that the resurrection was past, 2 Tim. ii. 18. Lust perverts light, and makes men, instead of bringing their hearts and lives to the Scripture, to bring, to draw the Scripture, by carnal and wittily wicked distinctions and evasions, to both, Prov. xxviii. 5. Knowledge is the mother of obedience, and obedience the nurse of knowledge; the former breeds the latter, and the latter feeds the former. *Ποιοῦντες μανθάνομεν.*

Obs. 6. It is our duty to forbear speaking against any thing which we understand not. "He that answereth a matter," saith Solomon, "before he heareth it, it is folly and shame unto him," Prov. xviii. 13. As men are not to be commended, so neither to be condemned, before the knowledge of their cause. As he causes a harsh and unmusical sound who strikes and plays upon the strings of an instrument before he has tried and tuned them; so he must needs pass a foolish and absurd sentence upon any cause, who passes that sentence before he has seriously heard and weighed the cause to which he speaks. Herein Eli manifested his fault and folly, 1 Sam. i. 14, rashly and weakly charging Hannah with drunkenness. Thus also David discovered his folly in giving credit to the information of flattering and false-hearted Ziba against good Mephibosheth, before he had heard what Mephibosheth could allege for himself, 2 Sam. xvi. 3, 4. Potiphar likewise showed himself as unjust as his wife showed herself unchaste, by an over-hasty heeding of his wife's false and forged accusation against righteous Joseph, Gen. xxxix. 19, 20. To these may be added the ignorant censure of those scoffers who derided the apostles, filled with the Holy Ghost, as if filled with new wine. Doubtful cases are to be exempted from our censure. The wheat and coarser grain (saith Jerom) are so like one another, when newly come up, and before the stalk comes to the ear, that there is no judging between them, and therefore the Lord, by commanding that both should be let alone till the harvest, admonishes that we should not judge of doubtful things, but refer them to the judgment of God. Even God himself, who clearly discerns the secrets of the heart, and needs not examine any cause for his own information, determines not by sentence till after examination, that so he might teach us by his example the method of judging, Gen. xviii. 21; which is, to know before we censure. They who, to make a show of what they have not, a quick understanding and nimble apprehension, will take off a speaker in the midst of his relation, and make as if they knew all the rest of his speech which is

Qui, prius quam chordas exploraverit, omnes simul inconcinne percutit, absonum et absurdum strepitum reddit; sicut judex, qui singulas litigatorum causas non pulsavit, nec audivit, stultam plane et absurdam sententiam pronuntiet, necesse est. Petrarc.

Inter triticum et lolium, quamdiu herba est et nondum culmus venit ad spicam, grandis similitudo est, et in discernendo, aut nulla, distantia. Præmonet ergo Dominus ne, ubi quid ambiguum est, cito sententiam proferamus, sed Deo judici terminum reservemus. Hieron. *Ut nobis exemplum proponat ne mala hominum ante præsumamus credere, quam probare.* Gr. Mor. l. 19. c. 23.

to follow; and others, who though they will hear the whole speech out, yet not clearly understanding it, scorn to have it repeated again, lest they might be thought slow of apprehension; by their foolish and ill accommodated answers often grossly betray their ignorance and folly. And this speaking of any thing ignorantly should principally be avoided by magistrates and ministers. By magistrates, because their passing a sudden and over-hasty answer is accompanied with the hurt of others; and withal, by so much the more should they take heed of this folly, because when they have once passed, though a rash and unjust sentence, yet so great a regard must be had to their honours, by themselves already dishonoured, that seldom or never will they be induced to retract or recall any unrighteous censure, when once they have uttered it. Which sinful distemper appeared not only in those heathen governors, Herod and Pilate, in censuring of John and Christ, but in that holy man David, in the case of Mephibosheth. By ministers likewise should this speaking ignorantly and doubtfully of any thing be avoided, whose work being to direct souls, and that through greatest dangers, to the obtaining of greatest happiness; they cannot be blind leaders and ignorant teachers without the infinite hazard of their followers. How unlike are they who will be teachers before they themselves have been taught, and affirmers of what they understand not, to Him who spake only what he knew, and testified only what he saw and heard! John iii. 11, 32.

Vid. Cartw. in Prov. xviii. 13.

Thus of the first part of this verse, their malicious and unchristian ignorance; "They speak evil of what they know not." Now follows,

2. What kind of ignorance, or not knowing of those things, it was wherewith they are here charged; "What they know naturally, as brute beasts, in those things they corrupt themselves."

In which words two things are mainly considerable: The sensuality of their apprehensions, and of their conversations.

(1.) The kind or nature of their knowledge, "What they know naturally, as brute beasts."

(2.) The effect of that their knowledge, "In those things they corrupt themselves."

The first is, 1. Propounded and specified in these words, "What they know naturally."

2. Expounded by and compared to the knowledge of the brute beasts, "As brute beasts."

Three things here require explication in this second part of the verse.

1. What the apostle here intends by knowing naturally.

2. Why he compares them for this knowing naturally to brute beasts.

3. In what respect by this knowing naturally, as brute beasts, they are said to "corrupt themselves."

1. For the first. By this knowing naturally, in the Greek φυσικῶς, is to be understood a knowing only by the guidance of nature, merely by their senses, by touching, tasting, seeing, &c.; a knowing whether a thing please sense or no, without any other teaching, or any judgment and reason at all; and it respects those things which belong to the sensitive appetite, as meat, drink, sleep, &c.; and hence it might possibly come to pass that Gagneius conjectured, though without ground, that ἐπίστανται, they know, is put for ἐφίστανται, they desire, or have an appetite. This word "naturally" is opposed to reason and judgment; these sensual

Naturaliter nórunt; i. e. ipsa duce natura, nullo adhibito magistro. Ut sunt ea quæ sensu percipiuntur, tactu, viz. et gustu. Justinian in loc. Naturaliter, solis sensibus, absque judicio rationis, ac si essent bruta animalia, cognoscunt, viz. quæ pertinent ad appetitum sensitivum, qualia sunt potus, cibus, somnus, veneris usus. Gerh. in Pet.

persons only knew things as carried to their outward senses. The force of nature only ruled them; reason never guided them. Œcumenius expresses it very aptly: Whatever, saith he, with natural force or desire, without putting difference, as irrational creatures, they know, they violently follow, as lustful horses or swine. Junius explains it thus, To know naturally is to know without counsel, human reason, or the light of God's Spirit, and with the blind force of nature and bestial motion, only following natural appetite and outward senses.

Ὅσα δὲ φυσικῇ ὁρμῇ, ἀδιακρίτως, ὡς τὰ ἄλογα ἐπίστανται ζῶα, ταῦτα μεταδιώκουσι, ὡς ἵπποι θηλυμανεῖς ἢ χοῖροι. Œcum. Scire naturaliter, est scire non consilio ullo, non ratione humana, non Spiritus Divini luce, sed cæco naturæ impetu, et belluino more. Junius in loc.

2. Why Jude compares them to brute beasts. The apostle exegetically explains by an apt comparison, what he intends by this knowing naturally; he saith they know things as brute beasts, in the Greek, ἄλογα ζῶα. The word ἄλογα, brute, signifies either mute, or irrational and brute, either without speech, or without reason. There being no irrational creature but is also mute; that is, though not without a voice, so as fish are said more properly to be mute, yet without speech, which none but man useth naturally. Now this knowledge which belongs to brute beasts, is that which arises from the instinct of nature, consisting in the senses; and by the benefit of it brute beasts discern between the food which is suitable and that which is unfit, between that which is beneficial and that which is hurtful; unto which is joined a natural appetite toward such things as tend to their preservation. Of this knowledge speaks the Scripture: "The ox knows his owner, and the ass his master's crib," Isa. i. 3. And, "The young lions roar after their prey, and seek their meat from God," &c., Psal. civ. 21. And, "They wait upon thee, that thou mayest give them their meat in due season. That thou givest them they gather: thou openest thine hand, and they are filled with good," ver. 27, 28. And, "The range of the mountains is the pasture of the wild ass, and he searcheth after every green thing," Job xxxix. 8. And, "The eagle abideth on the rock," &c., "and from thence she seeketh the prey," ver. 28, 29. And, "Behemoth eateth grass as an ox," Job xl. 15: "The mountains bring him food," ver. 20. Yea, "The ants prepare their meat in the summer," Prov. xxx. 25.

Acts xxv. 27. Ἄλογον, præter rationem, sine ratione. Animantia rationis expertia. Bez. Animalia muta. Vulg. O mutis quoque piscibus, donatura cygni, si libeat, sonum. Horat. Car. lib. 4. O. 3.

And by this knowledge of irrational creatures is that of these sensualists here by Jude set forth for sundry reasons.

(1.) In their knowledge of things naturally, they desired sensual objects violently and impetuously. They laboured not for them with a holy submissiveness to and dependence upon God, but followed them with a brutish fierceness. They were like the lion roaring after his prey; when they see what they love, there is no holding them in with the reins either of reason or religion; they ran greedily after reward, subverted whole houses, and taught any error for filthy lucre's sake, Tit. i. 11. They were greedy dogs.

(2.) They received no enjoyments thankfully, not considering the Giver; they drank of the river, taking no notice of the fountain; filling their vessel with it, and then turning their backs upon it. They received gifts, but regarded not the hand which bestowed them. Their bellies were filled with treasures (to them) hidden. Like swine feeding on acorns, which though they fall upon their heads, never make them look up to the tree from which they come. When God opened his hand they shut their hearts, denying the tribute of praises which God expects for all his blessings.

(3.) They pleased themselves with the gifts solely, never regarding the love of the Giver. Beasts care not with what affection any thing is given to them so that they have the thing which they want. These sensualists desired not that the gifts which they enjoyed might be turned into mercies; not considering that the love of God is the fulness of every enjoyment: in this worse than some beasts, who suspect a snare when provision is most plentiful. These never caring whether the heart of God were toward them or no, so as his hand were opened; and using the gifts of a Creator, not regarding the affection of a Father; not questioning whether their provisions were bestowed upon them as children, with love; or whether as condemned prisoners, to keep life in them against the day of execution: and in short, like beasts, as the apostle saith, they were made to be destroyed, 2 Pet. ii. 12; they so knew these sensitive objects, as not knowing whether they were fatted by them for slaughter.

(4.) They knew these things so brutishly, as not to know how to improve them; they cared not to be fitted by them for service. Brute beasts only live to eat; and so these made their sensual pleasures the end of their living, never referring them to glory-ends; not making them *vehicula*, chariots, to carry them faster, and to raise them up higher to God in a way of love and duty; but *vincula*, bonds, to keep and bind them down to the satisfaction of sense. They used not their comforts as wings, to make their thoughts and affections mount up to heaven; but as birdlime to their wings, and hinderances from all heavenly both desires and services.

(5.) They knew no measure in using these things. They, like swine, wallowed over head and ears in the mud of sensual enjoyments, being themselves gulfs of them, and ingulfing themselves in them; and not tasting them, but even bursting with them. Like some horses, they had rather break their wind than their draught. Their hearts were overcharged with surfeiting, Luke xxi. 34. They ran to excess of riot. Instead of cheering, they clogged nature, turning Christianity into epicurism; they made their belly their god, and they served it, Rom. xvi. 18; Phil. iii. 19. Their sensual appetites were boundless and unlimited; they rather pampered than fed themselves.

(6.) They so brutishly knew these things, as not to know instruction or any restraint; growing untamed and impatient of the yoke, like a backsliding heifer. They would not endure admonition; and he, saith Solomon, who hateth reproof is brutish, Prov. xii. 1. Like Jeshurun, they waxed fat, and kicked, Deut. xxxii. 15. Hence they despised and opposed all dominion and government, like the wild ass, which snuffing up the wind, is not to be caught, Jer. ii. 24; Hos. viii. 9. A brute beast fed to the full endures not to be beaten; these seducers resisted the truth which opposed their lusts, 2 Tim. iii. 8, and quarrelled with the word of life; like brute beasts, which though never so sick, will strike at those who let them blood, or give them wholesome drink. It was as easy to catch a hare with a tabret, as to make them hear reproof in their sensual enjoyments. They who are in a harvest of worldly pleasures commonly have harvest ears, not at leisure to hear what may regulate them in their sensual prosecutions.

(7.) They knew these things so brutishly, as never to consider of a removal of them, or the approach of the hatchet; they were sensually secure, like the beast, feeding themselves without fear; they mocked at the denunciations of judgment, as Peter speaks, 2 Pet. iii., drinking away sorrow; like the old world, eating and drinking though the flood were approaching, and never considering that their wine was soon to be turned into water.

(8.) They so brutishly knew these things, as not to know how to part with them. A beast knows no other woe but want of provender, nor sensualists any other penalty but the parting with sensual objects: these never learn, with Paul, how to want, and how to abound; or with Job, to bless God when taking away as well as giving. They so addict themselves to sensitive delights that they cannot be without them; and so are they fastened to them, and their heart so set upon them, that the pulling them away is the pulling off their very flesh. When they enjoy them, they are so secure, as if God could never remove them; when they want them, they are so impatient, as if God could never restore them.

3. In what respect by their knowing naturally they are here said to "corrupt themselves." The words "corrupt themselves" are contained in one word in the original, φθείρονται, which signifies properly so to spoil and deprave or mar a thing, as that it loses its former worth and excellency, or is unfit for that use to which it should be employed. Among profane writers it is often used to note the violating and abusing of the body by unchastity; and so it is commonly said, that a virgin or her virginity is corrupted or violated. *Juvenis corruptor, Virgo corrupta.*
And thus Epiphanius understands it in this place, who saith that the Spirit of God by Jude shows these seducers to be φθειρομένους καὶ φθείροντας, corrupted, and corrupters, in respect of their lasciviousness. But the Scriptures use the word to express any other kind of violation or abuse of a thing. So 1 Cor. xv. 33, "Evil communications corrupt good manners." And Eph. iv. 22, the old man is said to be corrupt, according to deceitful lusts. And 2 Cor. xi. 3, the apostle uses it to express the corruption of the mind, &c. And in this larger sense I take it in this place; as noting not only bodily, but even spiritual and eternal corruption. And the word φθείρονται includes that other word, "themselves;" it being not altogether of the passive form, but of the active and passive together, answering to the Hebrew conjugation *Hithpael*, which notes the action of any one toward or upon himself. And this the apostle Peter plainly expresses, 2 Pet. ii. 12, when he saith, they utterly perish in their own corruption; they rush into their own ruin, and go of themselves headlong to destruction, as the fish, seeing the bait, into the net, and then more and more by sin entwisting and entangling themselves to an utter overthrow and perdition. *Vide Junium in loc.*

And more particularly, by their sensual knowledge of carnal objects they incurred a fourfold corruption:

(1.) They corrupted themselves with a natural corruption; in bringing upon their bodies sundry kinds of diseases, by their luxury and intemperance, making themselves old before their time, and hastening their death. As vermin haunt those places where there is much food; so diseases abound in those bodies which are used, or rather abused, to excess of riot. More (saith one) are drowned in the cup than in the sea; and gluttons are said to dig their graves with their teeth. *Immodicis brevis est ætas, et rara senectus.*

(2.) They corrupted themselves with a civil corruption; overthrowing their families, and wasting their substance, to maintain their intemperance, bringing themselves to a morsel of bread. Sensual and intemperate persons swallow their estates down their throats. "The drunkard and the glutton shall come to poverty," Prov. xxiii. 21. Diogenes once said of a drunkard whose house was to be sold, I thought he would ere long vomit up his house, alluding to his vomiting in drunkenness. The prodigal wasted his portion upon harlots. These corrupters are worse than infidels, nay beasts, who by the light of nature provide for their young.

(3.) They corrupted themselves inwardly and spiritually. And that, 1. By clouding their reason and understanding; drunkenness being (as one wittily saith) an interregnum of the mind, which for the present loses the use of reason, whereby a man should be governed. Many have drunk away their wit and wealth too. When wine gets in, wit (we say) goes out. Wise men are seldom excessive. Wine and women take away the heart, Hos. iv. 11. 2. By hindering the spiritual, heavenly, and supernatural actings of the soul, making it unfit for holy services, prayer, hearing, meditation, &c. Hence the apostle opposes being drunk with wine to being filled with the Holy Ghost. Excess in sensual hinders spiritual pleasures. Hence it was a good rule of Ambrose, So to rise from table as to be fit for prayer. How can he have his heart in heaven, who, as they say of the fish called the ὄνος, or the ass fish, has it in his stomach? Grace is starved, while the flesh is pampered. Meat is to be used as our medicine. Feasting days are soul-starving days, and fasting days are soul-fatting days.

Anima sicca, anima sapientissima.

(4.) They corrupted themselves eternally; destroying themselves soul and body, by the loss of those pleasures at God's right hand, Psal. xvi. 11, to which here in this life they preferred the pleasures of sin for a season. Sweetly bitter pleasures! sweet in the palate, bitter in the stomach; bitter to the soul and body for ever! How dismal a retribution will a river of brimstone be for a cup of wine! Drunkards are in the catalogue of the excluded from the kingdom of God. They who are here drowned in profuseness, shall hereafter be drowned in perdition; yea, here they begin to be so.

Obs. 1. How great a confusion and disorder has sin made in this little world, man! He whose reason was once wholly subjugated to God, and whose appetite was guided by and submissive to his reason, has now an understanding which has cast off the government of God, and an appetite which has cast off the guidance of his understanding. In the state of innocence, the sensitive appetite of man was ruled by the golden sceptre of reason; the sensitive powers were not factious, but were willingly subject to the higher powers, to the intellectual. The first bubblings of the soul (as one saith) were pure and crystalline, and streamed out freely, without any murmuring or foaming; but now, alas! the soul is full of insurrections. The master waits, and the servant is master. The knowledge of the understanding is made a vassal to this natural knowledge. That leading faculty in a man, his understanding, is now a page to wait upon the sensual appetite, or the knowledge of the senses; and all the contrivances and inventions of the former are referred to the service of the latter. The master not now leads his horse, but the horse drags and hurries the master, even as a beast sometimes draws a condemned malefactor to the place of execution. All the confusions we see in the world are but derivations from this. Reason casts off religion, and then sense and carnal appetite cast off reason. All the errors in doctrine proceed from the former, and the irregularities of practice flow from the latter. The servant casts off the master in the state, because it has first cast him off in the soul.

Cognitio sui intellectus, licet præstantior sit, quavis cognitione brutorum, referunt eam ad exercitium operum sensualium, at satisfaciant appetitionibus carnalibus. **Lor.** in loc.

Obs. 2. They who oppose spiritual knowledge, justly lose even that which is reasonable. They grow, with these seducers, mere sensualists; not admitting the former, deservedly they part with the latter. These seducers opposing the truth of the gospel, denying the Lord Jesus Christ, and becoming enemies to supernatural knowledge; now what they knew, they knew but naturally, and only with the knowledge of the outward senses. They would not be real saints, and they came to be not so much as visible. They would not be saints, and at length they ceased to be men. The heathens by opposing even the faint light of nature, were by God given up to uncleanness, to dishonour their own bodies between themselves, to vile affections, and a reprobate mind, Rom. i. 21, 24, 26, 28. He who will put out light revealed, shall justly extinguish light implanted. It is righteous with God to leave them to sense, who will not be guided by grace. From him who hath not, shall be taken away even what he hath: even appearances of goodness shall be taken away. Brass but silvered over, will at length plainly appear to be but brass. A face only beautiful with paint, shall, when wrinkles grow deep, be destitute not only of complexional, but even fictitious beauty also. How exquisitely do these days of ours comment upon this truth! Oh that we could not say, that hundreds, whose eyes have seemed to be fixed upon the stars, themselves pretending to a seraphical pitch of knowledge, have yet fallen into a ditch of beastly sensuality! None so shamefully beggarly as he who breaks after much trading and trusting. Christians, beg of God that your grace may be true and supernatural, and then it will be growing; but if it be only appearing, and not arising to true sanctity, it may soon arrive at sensual bestiality.

Quia nolunt intelligere quæ sunt gratiæ, amittunt sapere quæ sunt naturæ.

Obs. 3. The light of reason is too weak to contend with sensual appetite. When these seducers had bid adieu to spiritual light, notwithstanding their rational light, they grew sensual and brutish. Should the sky be furnished with millions of torches, they all could not, as one sun, bestow those influences upon the earth whereby it could be made green and fruitful. The light of grace is only influential upon the heart and life; that of reason produces no fruit truly savoury. That which it draws forth is but like the fruit which, requiring a hotter soil and sunshine, when men sometimes plant it in our colder countries, never comes to perfection, and has hardly half heat enough to concoct it. The greatest (if a mere) scholar in the world knows nothing as he ought to know, and therefore loves nothing as he ought to love. He sees not, without renewed light, in any way of God that prevailing transcendent excellency which outbids the bravery of every other object. The light of reason in the most knowing heathen that ever was in the world was but a candle-light, notwithstanding which he was yet in the night; it scattered not the works of darkness; nor did he, as one saith well, warm his hands at this candle: notwithstanding this, famous moralists have been cold in their devotions, and dissolute in their practices. The wisest heathens, (Rom. i.,) how sensual and impure were they, notwithstanding their most refined reason!

Obs. 4. Outward enjoyments make no man excellent. He may, yea, unless he be more than a man, he will become a beast by using them. The four monarchies of the world were represented to Daniel under the similitudes of beasts, not of men, because they were neither erected nor exercised in a way of reason, but of brutish sensuality.

Quatuor imperia ostensa sunt Danieli, sub similitudine bestiarum, non hominum, quia non insurrexerunt per viam rationis, sed inpetu sensualitatis. Durand. de Orig. Jurisd. A man may be laden with gold, and yet be as a brute. His being changed from poor to rich is but a poor change, unless he be changed from natural to spiritual, from an old to a new man. Even the wealthy is called a fool, and a brutish person, Psal. xlix. 10; and ver. 12, "Man being in honour abideth not; he is like the beast that perisheth." Nero was a lion, Herod a fox, the princes of Israel wolves, kine of Bashan, notwithstanding worldly glory. Outward ornaments make no inward alteration. Hence see what is the true standard of honour. Lust is the soul's degradation, even in all earthly abundance; only grace makes us excellent; it destroys not, but elevates nature. Sensual objects do not elevate, but corrupt us.

Obs. 5. Sensual appetite is deceitful. When these seducers knew things naturally, with sensual knowledge, they were led to corruption. An ignis-fatuus leads men into bogs and precipices. Natural knowledge carries men, like silly beasts, into a snare: "If the blind lead the blind, both must fall into the ditch." The lusts of the sensitive appetite are foolish, 1 Tim. vi. 9, and therefore foolish because they make men fools who are led by them; and Eph. iv. 22, the old man is said to be "corrupt according to deceitful lusts," κατὰ τὰς ἐπιθυμίας τῆς ἀπάτης. As man shows his infection with original pollution principally by his lusts, so those lusts principally discover themselves in their deceitfulness. When they tempt a man to sin, they promise pleasure and contentment; they perform nothing less, but leave the poor seduced sinner spoiled of his happiness, and corrupted both inwardly, outwardly, and eternally. Sensual delights strangle *Latrones quasi latrones; viatoribus amice se quasi συνοδῖται adjungunt, ut incautos eo facilius grassentur.* with a silken halter, kill a man in embracing him, and, like thieves, will ride friendly and pleasantly with the passenger, that so unawares they may the more easily destroy him. St. James saith a man is drawn away of his own lusts, and δελεαζόμενος, enticed. They bait over every hook. Oh that when a man saith, How can I forbear the bait? he would ask himself, How can I endure the hook? Oh, will the comfort countervail the corruption; the spoiling, not only of my body, of my goods, but the loss of my soul, my grace, my heaven, my God, my all? Consider the bitter farewell of all sinfully sweet morsels; view them with a Scripture prospective; look upon them as going away as well as coming. Behold their back, their black side; they are *venenatæ deliciæ,* poisoned pleasures. It is easier to pass by than get out of the snare. "If thou be a man of appetite, put a knife to thy throat," Prov. xxiii. 2. Lust betrays with a kiss. All carnal delights go out in a stink, and commonly it is that of brimstone. As we cannot walk in this life by sight in respect of glory, so should we not in respect of sensuality. As we are absent from heaven in regard of sense, and present there in regard of love; so though we are present among earthly enjoyments in respect of sense, yet should we be absent in regard of affection. To conclude this, consider the difference betwixt spiritual and sensual pleasures: the former are good in harvest, the latter only in seed-time; ("He that soweth to his flesh shall of the flesh reap corruption; but he that soweth to the Spirit shall of the Spirit reap life everlasting," Gal. vi. 8;) the former are bitterly sweet, the latter sweetly bitter; the former turn water into wine, the latter wine into water. In that which a man knows spiritually, and to which he is led by the guidance of the Spirit, in that he preserves himself. And it is observable how the apostle opposes "the deceitful lusts" to "the truth in Jesus," Eph. iv. 21, 22. Christ is truth; lust is vanity and deception. Christ gives true happiness, and more than was ever expected; lust deludes, disappoints, corrupts.

To end this needful point: In all worldly pleasures wisely draw off thy soul, by comparing such sordid puddles with the crystal rivers of eternal joys. Let moderation and heavenly discourse be two dishes at every banquet. A soldier supping with Plato, who had provided nothing but green herbs, said, He who sups with Plato shall be better the next day. Tertullian said of the primitive Christians, that they did not *tam cœnam cœnare, quam disciplinam.* One would have thought they had been at a sermon, not at a supper. Oh that spiritual delights were more tasted! He who lives at the table of a king despises scraps; and such are all worldly pleasures esteemed by him who has tasted how sweet the Lord is. The more pleasant any thing is to us, the more suspected let it be by us. Satan lies in ambush behind our lawful enjoyments. As the body is the temple of the Holy Ghost, so is Christian temperance the *ædituus,* or keeper of that temple. *Tertullian.*

Verse 11.

Woe unto them! for they have gone in the way of Cain, and ran greedily after the error of Balaam for reward, and perished in the gainsaying of Core.

At this verse, and so on to the seventeenth, our apostle prosecutes the third part of that second argument, whereby he puts the Christians upon contending for the faith against seducers.

That second argument was taken from the certainty of the destruction of those seducers, and is prosecuted from the fourth to the seventeenth verse of this Epistle. In managing which the apostle first set down several examples of God's wrath upon others in former times for their sins, from the fourth to the eighth verse. And secondly, declared that these seducers lived in the same sins which God had formerly punished in others, from the eighth to this eleventh verse.

He now, thirdly, concludes, that these who practise their impieties, shall partake of their plagues. And this conclusion he prosecutes throughout this eleventh verse unto the seventeenth. In handling which the apostle concludes their destruction,

1. By propounding;
2. By expounding it. Or,
1. By a denunciation; and,
2. By a delineation thereof.

1. By propounding and denouncing it in those words of this eleventh verse, "Woe unto them!"

2. By expounding or delineating it in the following expressions of this and the other verses to the seventeenth; and he expounds it by a mixed description of their sin and misery; and he mixedly describes their sin and miseries (the effects of their sins) three ways:

(1.) From the suitable examples of Cain, Balaam, Core, in this eleventh verse, whom he rather mentions than any others, because of their great injury to the church by cruelty, seduction, and sedition, they being the types and forerunners of these seducers. *Nominat hos tres præ aliis, quia hi tres fuere Dei, hostes, ac fideles seducere, et ecclesiam perdere voluerunt; unde fuerunt Simonis, Gnosticorum, et hæreticorum typi et prodromi. Cor. Lapide in loc.*

(2.) From sundry elegant comparisons, ver. 12, 13.
(3.) From the certain and infallible prophecy of Enoch, propounded and amplified ver. 14—16.

This eleventh verse, then, consists of these two parts.

1. A denunciation of woe and judgment.

2. An amplification thereof, from the three examples of Cain, Balaam, Core.

1. The denunciation of judgment, in these words, "Woe unto them!"

It may be demanded in what sense the words, "Woe unto them!" are here used, and how to be understood.

The uttering of this word "woe," denoting in Scripture grievous calamities and miseries, either present or approaching, is used three ways:

Væ condolentis, imprecantis, prædicentis.

(1.) There is *væ dolentis*, and *condolentis*, when woe is used as an exclamation of grief, pity, and commiseration; and then it imports as much as if the apostle had said, Alas, how am I grieved, in consideration of their approaching ruin, for these wretched sinners, who are running to their own destruction! And thus the word woe is often taken in Scripture; as Micah vii. 1, 2, where the church resenting the general corruption of the times, and her small number, cries out, "Woe is me! for I am as when they have gathered the summer fruits, as the gleanings of the vintage. The good man is perished out of the earth; and there is none upright among men." Thus also the prophet Isaiah, chap. xxiv. 16, laying to heart the wickedness of the people, and the judgments which were to follow, expresses his holy sympathy in these words, "Woe unto me! the treacherous dealers have dealt treacherously." Thus the same prophet again, chap. vi. 5, "Then said I, Woe is me! for I am undone; because I am a man of unclean lips: for mine eyes have seen the King, the Lord of hosts." So Jer. iv. 31; vi. 4; xiii. 27; xlv. 3; Lam. v. 16. Now though it cannot be denied that the faithful do and ought with holy commiseration to lay to heart the miseries of others, yet I understand not this expression of woe in this place in this sense; for besides that Jude knew that these seducers were ungodly men, and appointed to this condemnation, his scope was not to express his sorrow for them, but to warn the church of them, by discovering the judgments of God against them.

(2.) There is *væ imprecantis*, a woe of cursing and imprecation, used sometimes by godly men against the implacable and irrecoverable enemies of God. Thus the prophet Habakkuk utters it against the Chaldean, who wasted the church, Hab. ii. 6, 9, 12, 15, 19. Thus David prays for the destruction of his enemies, Psal. cix. 6—9, &c.; xl. 14, 15. That the apostles had this power of cursing the incurable enemies of the church, whose destruction the Lord had extraordinarily revealed to them, and that they used it, is very evident. Paul prays that the Lord would "reward Alexander the coppersmith according to his work," 2 Tim. iv. 14. And it is hard to deny that Jude in this place puts forth that power against these seducers. Sure I am, Paul prays that the false teachers might be cut off who troubled the church, Gal. v. 12; and He who enabled the apostles to foreknow the ruin of seducers certainly, without error, might help them to desire it holily, without revenge. And never did either Christ or his apostles express so much heavenly vehemency against any, as against those who hindered the eternal salvation of souls: witness the woes eight times repeated by Christ against the scribes and Pharisees, Matt. xxiii.; as also Paul's carriage towards Elymas the sorcerer, Acts xiii. Some (indeed) of this impious rabble, who were not so obstinate, malicious, and subtle as others, Jude might spare; he desiring the Christians afterward, that on some they should have compassion, putting a difference.

Non dicit apostolus, ἀποδώσει, reddet: sed ἀποδώη, reddat. Sunt vota imprecantis, non verba prædicentis. Rivet. in Psal. xl.

And if it be here demanded how the apostle could lawfully say, "Woe unto them!" I answer,

1. He expresses not this "Woe unto them" in respect of his own cause, but the cause of God; not as they were his, but God's enemies.

2. He directs not his imprecations against persons curable, but incurable; and he might know them to be so by some extraordinary inspiration.

3. His affections herein were not carnal, but divine and spiritual, stirred up purely by zeal to God's glory and the safety of the church. In a word, if this woe here pronounced by Jude were a woe of imprecation, he was carried to the uttering thereof by the same Spirit by which he penned the Epistle.

(3.) There is a *væ prædicentis*, a woe of prediction and denunciation, whereby imminent and impendent evils are foretold and denounced against others; and in this sense it is commonly used and uttered in Scripture, Eccl. iv. 10; x. 16, and most commonly by the prophets: "Woe unto the wicked! for it shall be ill with them," Isa. iii. 11. "Woe unto them that join house to house," &c.! Isa. v. 8. And, "Woe to them that rise early in the morning, that they may follow strong drink," ver. 11; Isa. xxviii. 1; xxx. 1; xxxi. 1; Hos. ix. 12. "Woe unto them that are with child, and to them that give suck in those days!" Matt. xxiv. 19. And this sense, though some learned men exclude not that which was last mentioned, we may safely admit in this place; our apostle concluding, that undoubtedly they who were as bad as the worst of former sinners in respect of sin, should be as miserable as they were in regard of punishment.

Obs. 1. Spiritual and eternal woes are the true woes. To be woeful indeed is to be under the wrath of God. This is the woe here by Jude denounced against, and by God inflicted upon, these seducers. Whatever woe comes without God's wrath, may have more of weal in it than of woe. Other woes touch the skin, these the soul. Other woes part between us and our estates, names, worldly comforts; but these between us and God, in whom is laid up all happiness. How foolish is every sinner to fear the name, the shadow, and not to tremble at the thing, the reality of woe! like the beast, who is more affrighted with the flash of the fire, and the noise of the report which is made in shooting off the gun, than with the fear of the bullet. Eternal woes come with less noise, and therefore with more neglect than others. They kill, though they do not affright. The fear which Christ commands is of Him who kills the soul. What proportion of misery is there between the soul's leaving the body, and God's leaving the soul? Bodily miseries are but opinionative and appearing. There is not a drop of true woe in a deluge of outward troubles which befall a saint.

Obs. 2. Wickedness ends in woe. Sinners may see nothing but wealth in the commission, but they shall find nothing but woe in the conclusion of sin. Every lust, though it kisses, yet betrays. "The end" (as the apostle speaks) "is death," Rom. vi. 21. It is the truest wisdom to consider whether, when we find it difficult to overcome the present temptation, it be not more difficult to undergo the following woe. Oh, could we but look upon the blackness of the back of sin, how little should we be allured with the fairness of its face! How far from wisdom will it be for the deluded sinner hereafter to say, I did not think it would have been thus with me, that hell was so hot, that God's wrath was so heavy! The mirth of every secure sinner that goes dancing to hell is no better than madness. How bitter should that drop of pleasure be to us, which is answered and overtaken with a sea of pains! There is no judg-

Amara sint omnia gaudia quibus respondent æterna supplicia.

ing of our future, either woe or happiness, by what appears at present. The portion of the cup of God's people is to have the best, and of the wicked to have the bitterest, at the bottom; and yet the top of the cup seems to promise the contrary to both.

Obs. 3. Scripture imprecations and cursings must not be used as our examples. We may, indeed, pray against the wicked practices of others, (1.) That God would stop and hinder them; with David, that God would turn the wisdom of Ahithophel into foolishness. (2.) It is lawful for us to pray for temporal afflictions to befall the wicked, to the end, that they, being sensible of God's anger against sin, may be brought to repentance, and so to salvation. But, (3.) Prayers for the eternal confusion of others are not absolutely to be put up to God. They who will imitate the Scripture in imprecations against others must be sure they imitate those holy men who uttered them, in being led by the same Spirit, both of infallibility in discerning of men's persons and estates; and also of purity, or freedom from those corrupt affections wherewith our zeal for God's glory is ever too much mixed, and therefore to be suspected. This counsel Christ gave his disciples, who, asking whether (after the example of Elijah) they should pray that fire might come down from heaven to consume the Samaritans, were answered by Christ, that they knew not what spirit they were of, Luke ix. 55. Our Master's precept was, "Bless them that curse you," Matt. v. 44; yea, bless and curse not: and his pattern left us is, "When he was reviled, he reviled not again," 1 Pet. ii. 23. The time of prayer, saith Chrysostom, is the time of meekness. And he, saith Augustine, drives away God from himself, who would turn him away from others; he being injurious to God, in making him the executioner, and himself the judge. <small>Ideo Deum a se expellit, qui illum a proximo avertit; et facit Deo injuriam, quia seipsum judicem constituit, et Deum tortorem. Aug. Ser. 4. de Sanc.</small>

Obs. 4. God warns of woe before he sends woe. He takes not sinners at the advantage, as he might, in the act of sin, but he foretells the woe before he inflicts it. He usually cuts men down by the mouth of his ministers, before he cuts them off by the hand of executioners; by the sword of his mouth, before he does it by the mouth of the sword. God's method is to give premonition before he inflicts punishment. The two destructions of Jerusalem by the Chaldeans and Romans came not till foretold by the prophets and Christ. Of the two general destructions of the world, the past by water, Gen. vi. 3, and the future by fire, 2 Pet. iii. 7, sufficient warning has been given. God hereby speaks himself gracious, and the wicked inexcusable. He threatens that he may not smite; and he smites that he may not slay; and he slays some sometimes temporally, that they may not be destroyed eternally. God foretells ruin that it may be prevented. Jonah's prophesying of Nineveh's overthrow, was, as Chrysostom saith, a kind of overthrow of the prophecy. And hereby the wicked are proclaimed inexcusable. They cannot say in their greatest suffering but that they had premonition. Even the enemies of God shall justify him when he condemns them. They cannot but excuse God from desire of revenge, the desirers whereof are not wont to give warning. Christians, take heed of turning the denunciations of woe into wantonness. It is neither for want of sin in man, nor strength in God, that instead of wounding he only warns. His hand is not weakened that it cannot strike, nor his arm shortened that it cannot reach us; he has not lost his power, but he exercises his patience, and he exercises his patience <small>Venturum se prædicat, ut cum venerit, quos damnet non inveniat. Greg.</small> <small>Professa perdunt odia vindictæ locum. Sen. Medea.</small> <small>Non ille potentiam perdidit, sed patientiam exercet.</small> in expecting our repentance. Let us prepare to meet our God, even when he is coming toward us, before he come at us. Let us despatch the messengers of prayer and reformation to meet him, and make peace with him while he is yet in the way, and afar off. Though God's patience lasts long, it will not last ever. If we will sin, notwithstanding a woe threatened, we shall be punished, notwithstanding a mercy promised. He who is long before he strikes, strikes heavy. The longer it is ere woe comes, the heavier will it be when it comes. No metal so cold as lead before it is melted, but none more scalding afterward. <small>Patientiam exercet suam, dum, pœnitentiam expectat tuam. Aug.</small>

Obs. 5. Ministers must denounce woes against the wicked. Jude describes the fierceness of seducers, and exhorts the Christians to compassion; and yet his meekness abolished not his zeal. The regard of God's glory, and the souls of the saints, draws forth this severe denunciation against the enemies of both. He is as bold to foretell their woe as they to proclaim their wickedness. The like spirit we may behold in the holy men before him: Moses so meek, that when he was with God, though he pleaded the cause of the people with prayers, yet when he was with the people, he pleaded the cause of God with the sword. The prophets after him, Samuel, Elijah, Isaiah, Jeremiah, were cold and calm in their own cause, but full of heavenly heat in God's cause. Their denunciations of woes, like lightning which smites the highest towers, spared not the greatest, if enemies to God. Prophetic zeal struck at sin wherever it found it; witness all those numerous threatenings scattered in every leaf of their prophecies. The apostles had their rod as well as the spirit of meekness, and partook of that Spirit which was represented as well by fiery tongues as by the shape of a dove. Paul strikes Elymas blind, and cursed Alexander. Christ himself, whose mouth was so full of beatitudes, Matt. v., no less than eight several times denounced woes against the enemies of God. It is the disposition of saints to be holily impatient when God's glory suffers; and, though never else, then to esteem anger seemly: disgraces against their Father they cannot endure, these injuries they cannot concoct. Their commission likewise requires this temper: "Cry aloud, spare not, lift up thy voice like a trumpet, show my people their transgression, and the house of Jacob their sins," Isa. lviii. 1. "Whatsoever I command thee, that thou shalt speak: be not afraid of their faces," Jer. i. 7, 8. A dumb dog is good for nothing but the halter. Though the children in the house must not be bitten, yet the thief either without or within must not be spared: sinful silence and flattery most oppose a minister's function. If sinners will be bold, let not ministers be bashful. The most zealous ministers have lived in the worst times; and they who are most hated for their holy vehemency, can better endure the hatred of people for the discharge of duty than the wrath of God for its neglect. He that reproves shall have favour at the last both of God and man. And even here a zealous reprover is honoured when he is hated; and the cause (saith one) why God makes the world so bitter to ministers by sufferings, is because they are no more bitter to the world by reprehensions. To conclude this, let none, no, not the greatest, be angry with ministers for their faithfulness in reproving. If there were physicians or surgeons only provided for the poor, and not for the rich, the rich would be accounted of all the most miserable; and truly they were much more miserable for their souls, if they only were de- <small>Causam populi apud Deum precibus; causam Dei apud populum gladiis allegavit. Greg. Exod. xxxii. 27.</small> <small>Chrysost.</small>

barred from reproofs, the physic of the soul. There is no greater sign of a gracious heart, than to be both holily patient in taking, and wisely zealous in giving a reproof.

Crudelis est eorum mollities, quibus molesta est nostra vehementia. Calv. in Matt. xiii.

Thus of the first part of this verse, the denunciation of judgment, "Woe unto them!" Now follows,

2. The amplification thereof, from three examples, of Cain, Balaam, and Core; and first that of Cain, "They have gone in the way of Cain."

Four things here are to be touched by way of explanation.
1. Who this Cain was.
2. What his way was.
3. Why it is called a way.
4. How seducers are said to go in his way.

1. Who this Cain was. The holy story relates his birth, and the imposition of his name.

(1.) His birth is described Gen. iv. 1, where it is said that Adam knew Eve his wife, and that she conceived and bare Cain. This Cain was the first-born of the first parents in the world, and so elder brother to all the sons of men; and Moses, to show the common and constant way of the multiplication of mankind, fully declares his generation; hereby manifesting, that Cain was neither formed out of the earth, as was Adam; nor of the rib of the man, as was Eve: that he came not of Adam alone without Eve, nor of Eve alone without Adam; but that there was a conjunction of both. And withal, in this relation of the birth of Cain, Moses discovers the corruption of our first parents descending to all their posterity by ordinary generation; so that whoever is now naturally begotten, has not a holy and pure nature, as had our first parents before they sinned, but a nature depraved and corrupted, as they had after they had sinned. Particularly in relation to Cain, he shows that Adam, a sinner, and of a corrupt nature, knowing Eve, who was infected also with sin, and she conceiving and bringing forth Cain, it is no wonder that this their first-born was of so wicked and corrupt a disposition, since he was conceived and born of the seed of sinful flesh: nor is it to be thought that Abel, a holy man, had his holiness derived to him from his parents, as if he had not with Cain been conceived in sin; but that by the mere and singular grace of God he had that integrity bestowed upon him, of which Cain was destitute.

Creavit ex terra; procreavit ex legitimo conjugio. Pareus.

(2.) The imposition of Cain's name. The word Cain is derived of Cana, which signifies a possession; for his mother Eve giving him that name, said she had gotten, obtained, or possessed a man from the Lord. It is disputed by learned men what Eve intends, by saying, "I have gotten a man," את־יהוה as we render it, "from the Lord." Sundry conceive, because the preposition *eth* is commonly a note of the accusative case, that Eve's words are thus to be read, *Acquisivi virum Jehovam,* I have gotten a man who is the Lord; as if she had thought that this her first-born was that promised Seed, the Messiah, which God had promised should break the head of the serpent, and redeem mankind from sin and misery: but the preposition *eth* is oft in the Scripture a note of the ablative, and imports as much as from, with, by, &c.; as, "Enoch walked" את־האלהים "with God," Gen. v. 22. The children of Israel who came, *eth,* with Jacob into Egypt, Exod. i. 1. "When they were gone" את־העיר "out of," or from "the city," &c., Gen. xliv. 4. Some there are who take *eth* here for the note of the dative ל, and then the meaning of the words is, I have gotten a man to the Lord; that is, who after our death shall in our stead serve and worship the Lord. But the best expound *eth* (as I said) by with, from, by, &c., and so the meaning is, I have gotten a man σὺν Θεῷ; that is, by the favour, help, and blessing of the Lord, as his gift, by ratifying his blessing of multiplication, chap. i. 28, and that both blessing my conception of a child, and also my childbirth, without the assistance of a midwife. This may well be the meaning of the place, and Eve's thankful acknowledging God's bounty in giving her a son; as it is suitable to those expressions of Scripture, Gen. xxxiii. 5; Psal. cxxvii. 3, where children are said to be a heritage and gift of the Lord. Thus it is agreeable to the carriage of holy persons in other times, who have praised the Lord for their children; though Eve, besides the common apprehension and acknowledgment of God's blessing and bounty herein, probably expected some extraordinary comfort and relief by this her son, to sweeten that afflicted state into which they had brought themselves, and particularly, she had brought both her husband and herself by sin.

Certum est particulam eth, ut plurimum esse notam accusativi casus, quem verba transitiva regunt; sed tamen accipi non raro pro a, ex, de, cum, præpositionibus: et exempla adferunt ex scriptura grammatici ubi particula illa juncta verbo intransitivo, aut Hithpahel, accipitur pro ל*, Gen. v. 22;* Exod. i. 1, pro מ a, vel abs. Gen. xliv. 4. Riv. in Gen. Jun. Trem. Rivet. Mercer.

2. What Jude here intends by the way of Cain.

The word way in Scripture is frequently mentioned, and is oft used as a metaphorical expression of a man's course and manner of living, carriage, or conversation in the world, whether good or bad.

(1.) Good, called the way of the righteous: "The Lord knoweth the way of the righteous," Psal. i. 6. "That thou mayest walk in the way of good men," Prov. ii. 20. Samuel's sons walked not in the ways of their father, 1 Sam. viii. 3. So ver. 5. Josiah walked in the way of his father David, 2 Kings xxii. 2. The good way: Samuel saith that he would teach the people the good way, 1 Sam. xii. 23. So Jer. vi. 16, "Ask for the old paths, where is the good way." Job xxii. 3; Psal. ci. 2, 6. "The right way," 1 Sam. xii. 23. And of these seducers it is said that they "have forsaken the right way," 2 Pet. ii. 15. Also it is called the "narrow way," Matt. vii. 14, because grievous and unpleasing to the flesh. Also "the way of understanding," Prov. xxi. 16; ix. 6; Isa. xl. 14. "The way of wisdom," Prov. iv. 11. "The way of peace," Rom. iii. 17. "The way of righteousness," Prov. xvi. 31; Matt. xxi. 32. "The way of light," Job xxi. 13. "The way of holiness," Isa. xxxv. 8. "The way of truth," Psal. cxix. 30; 2 Pet. ii. 2. "The way of salvation," Acts xvi. 17.

Nec prece, nec pretio, nec gratia, nec periculo, nec simultate, a via recta deduci oportet. Cicer. Rhet. l. 3.

(2.) Bad, called the way of the wicked: "The way of the ungodly shall perish," Psal. i. 6. "The way of the wicked he turneth upside down," Psal. cxlvi. 9. "The way of the wicked is as darkness," Prov. iv. 19. "The way of the transgressors is hard," Prov. xiii. 15. "The way of the heathen," Jer. x. 2. The way of one's own heart, Eccl. xi. 9; Isa. lvii. 17; Acts xiv. 16. An unequal way, Ezek. xviii. 25, 29; xxxiii. 17. "A way that is not good," Psal. xxxvi. 5; Prov. xvi. 29. "An evil way," Prov. xxviii. 10; viii. 13. "The way of a fool," Prov. xii. 15. "Of the froward," Prov. xxii. 5. A way of pain or grief, Psal. cxxxix. 24. A stubborn way, Judg. ii. 19. A broad way, Matt. vii. 13. A way of darkness, Prov. ii. 13. "A way not cast up," Jer. xviii. 15. Under this evil and wicked way falls the way of Cain, here mentioned by Jude, which is not so largely to be taken, as for the whole sinful course and carriage of Cain throughout his life, but for some particular course of his, for which in Scripture he is most condemned and punished by God, and in which he was by these seducers most imitated; and that way might be made up of three principal parts:

Abel obtulit præstantius sacrificium, non id intelligi debet ratione materiæ aut quantitatis, sed animi offerentis et fidei. Rivet. in Gen. iv.

Ex fide obtulit non solum ex mandato Dei, sed etiam fiducia promissionis; certo statuens non opere operato hujus ritus, se aliquid mereri, sed propter victimam Messiæ significatam hac victima, se recipi in gratiam Dei. Pareus in Gen.

[1.] The way of hypocrisy. Cain indeed offered a sacrifice to the Lord, and perhaps, though some deny it, every way as good and costly, in respect of the outside thereof, as was that of Abel; yet he sacrificed in a faithless, hypocritical manner, as is clear from the reason why Abel's sacrifice was better, and better accepted with God, than Cain's. The apostle declares, Heb. xi., Abel offered in faith; by which faith, he offering a better sacrifice, and better accepted, it is plain that Cain sacrificed not in faith; he performed a good work, but with a rotten and hypocritical heart; not in spirit and truth worshipping God. The faith of Abel in offering his sacrifice stood principally in two things. 1. In eyeing the rule and command of God obediently, who had enjoined it. 2. In expecting acceptance from God for the merit, not of his work, but of Christ, who was signified by his sacrifice. Of both these Cain, though sacrificing, was destitute, neither offering because he believed the command of God was to be obeyed, nor looking to find acceptance for his person and performance through Christ; but profanely, customarily, and proudly doing the thing which God commanded, but disregarding the manner commanded in doing it.

[2.] A second way of Cain, and that principally, as I conceive, here intended by our apostle, was the hatred and murder of his brother, ἀδελφοκτονία. 1. He slew a man, herein sinning against the common nature of mankind. 2. He slew one that was his subject, and obedient to him, whom he ought therefore to have defended against all injury and violence.

Hoc nomine non simpliciter homicida, aut servicida, sed fratricida. Musc.

3. He destroyed not a slave, and a common subject, but his own brother; and some think that Cain and Abel were twins. 4. A just and good man did not slay an unjust and wicked man, but a wicked and ungodly slew a just and innocent man. 5. He did not slay him for any fault of his, but for his holy and sincere worship of the true God. 6. He slew him, not stirred up by any sudden rage, heat, or commotion of mind, or by imprudence, but out of settled hatred, and in premeditation to take away his life. 7. This murder was committed by Cain after God had admonished him to take heed of that sin. 8. And after he had made a show of friendship and reconciliation to his brother, Gen. iv. 8. Cain talked in a friendly and familiar manner with his brother, and then slew him. Hence this inhuman murder is that sin for which, by the apostle John, Cain is said to be of that wicked one, 1 John iii. 12. In short, first he inwardly hated and envied his brother, because his sacrifice was better accepted than his own; and then he expressed this hatred by his cruelty in killing him. His hatred was murder begun, and his murder was hatred perfected. He who cared not how he served God, regarded not how he used his brother. Cain begins with sacrifice, and ends with murder. There were in the whole world but two brothers, and the one was a butcher of the other: Abel was the first martyr, and Cain the first murderer; and the same cause that moved Satan to tempt the first man to destroy himself and his posterity, moves the second man to destroy the third. Groundless envy! what injury did God's accepting Abel do to Cain? what help against God's rejecting Cain could be brought by Abel? It should have been Cain's joy to have seen his brother accepted; it should have been his sorrow to have seen that himself deserved a rejection. Could Abel have stayed God's fire from descending? or should he, if he could, reject God's acceptance to content a brother? Cain was envious because God or Abel is not less good: he envied that good in his brother which he neglected in himself. In short, Cain's envy made him bloody; and indeed, as one aptly expresses it, such is this sin, that if it eats not another's heart, it will eat our own.

[3.] A third way of Cain was manifested in complaining of his curse: "My punishment" (saith he) " is greater than I can bear," Gen. iv. 13. The words in the original admit of a double reading. Some understand them to be words of despair of mercy, and read them thus, *Major est iniquitas mea quam parcere*, (so Arias,) My sin is greater than that I should ever obtain pardon. Others think they are words aggravating his punishment, and complaining of its severity; and they read them thus, *Major est punitio mea quam ut feram*, My punishment is greater than I can undergo. And this interpretation seems to be most favoured by the following words, "Behold, thou hast driven me out this day from the face of the earth, and from thy face shall I be hid, and I shall be a fugitive," &c. According to this interpretation, he does not so much confess the greatness of his sin, as complain of the grievousness of his punishment; and seems not to be so solicitous of reconciliation with God, as of the preservation of his life. But nothing hinders us from taking the words properly, as words of despair of pardon; for those which follow may be an exaggeration of his calamity, as if he had said, I am not only, wretch that I am! without hope of pardon from God, but banished also from my dear parents, and compelled to wander about in the world. And these different interpretations were occasioned by the different significations of the two words in the original, עוני and מנשא. The former imports both iniquity and the punishment of iniquity. The latter, both taking away or remitting, and also bearing and sustaining. There is no danger in reading the words either way; for as the words allow either reading, so his impatience and despair imply each other; his despair of taking away his sin being the true cause of his accounting his punishment greater than could be borne, for it is sin only that makes punishment heavy; and the complaining of the intolerableness of the punishment a true sign of his despair of the pardon of his sin; so that it matters not much which way we take. It is plain that he rather accused God of cruelty against himself, than himself of cruelty against his brother; so that he added to the taking away of his brother's life the denying of God's nature, in making his own sin greater than God's mercy: horrid, heinous either to speak or think! In short, hereby Cain showed that he could keep no mean; from security in sin he fell into despair after sin.

Iniquitas, pœna iniquitatis. נשא Ferre, remittere: verbum nata frequens est in significatione portandi: sed quia ferre et tolerare, etiam apud Latinos, significationem habent parcendi, ideo est in voce ambiguitas. Rivet. in Gen. p. 218.

3. Why this course of Cain is here called a way. Take it in these following considerations.

(1.) A way is that wherein there are sundry passengers. Out of a way passengers or travellers are not to be expected, but in a way persons ordinarily pass to and fro. There is no way of sin, though it be even Cain's, but some, yea, many traverse it. The worst courses find most imitation. "Wide is the gate, and broad is the way, that leadeth to destruction, and many there be that go in thereat," Matt. vii. 13. The way of sin is most trodden and beaten. Sinners go to hell in multitudes; and it is as much against their nature to go to hell alone, as to go in the way to heaven at all. They encourage one another in an evil way. They wonder at those who go not with them, and reproach them, thinking them mad for going out of the way: "Wherein they think it strange that you run not with them to the same excess of riot, speaking evil of you," 1 Pet. iv. 4.

(2.) This sinful course is a way, in respect of the expertness of those who walk in it. When men are out of the way, they often understand not where they are, and whither they are going; but in a way which they have often beaten, they go on skilfully and expertly. Hence every one is esteemed expert and believed in his way. He who has been long used to a way will undertake to go in it blindfold; he knows every turning, town, mark, mile's end. The wicked are witty in sin, they are workers of iniquity, ἐργαζόμενοι, Matt. vii. 23, curious contrivers of wickedness, wise to do evil; though to do good they understand not, but are sottish children. When in sin, they are in their element, and wiser in their generation than the children of light. Put them out of their way, and they are presently at a loss. How lefthanded are they in holy duties! how untowardly do they discourse of and act for God! they are children in understanding.

(3.) In respect of progressiveness. When a man is in a way, he stands not still, and takes not only one or two, but many steps, goes on step by step. Wicked men proceed in sin; they grow worse and worse; they know where they began, but not where they shall end. Cain proceeded from formality in God's service to hatred against his brother; from hatred to dissimulation; from thence to murder; from thence to despair. His way was made up of several stages. Every step he took left a stronger engagement to go on. The child of God, by the frailty of the flesh, may slip, step into sin; but he does not stand, go on, keep a course in that way. They are the wicked who "stand in the way of sinners," Psal. i. 1. They make a trade of sin. A sinner falls into sin as the fish, the saint as a child, does into the water. In the latter sin *is*, but the former is *in* sin.

(4.) In respect of its period and term. The longest way has an end. The longest course of sin, though of a thousand years' continuance, terminates in destruction. The full point of every sinful way is damnation; the end, though not of the worker, yet of the work, is death; that is the wages of sin. The way of sin is broad in the entrance, but narrow in the conclusion; it "is the way to hell, going down to the chambers of death," Prov. v. 5; vii. 27. Foolish sinners in good duties separate the means from the end, accounting exactness needless: in sinful ways they separate the end from the means, thinking torments fabulous; although Scripture equally prescribes the former, and foretells the latter. God's method is first to bring into a wilderness, and then to Canaan; Satan contrarily leads from Canaan into a wilderness. God's way is right, and may seem rugged; Satan's smooth, but false. Cain never left travelling in his way of hypocrisy, envy, murder, till it ended in despair.

4. How these seducers went in this way of Cain.

(1.) They went in this way of Cain's formality and hypocrisy. They partook of the same ordinances and privileges with true saints: in name, in the skin, they were Christians; in the heart, at the core, they were unholy; they pretended to the highest pitch of religion; but all this while, as the apostle calls them, they were but ungodly men. While they sacrificed outwardly with Cain, they had inwardly the spirit of Cain; like those of whom St. John speaks, who went out from, but never were truly of us. Their impure life was a practical confutation of their verbal profession. In words they professed Christ, but in their deeds they denied him, though the only Lord.

(2.) They went in the way of Cain in respect of their hatred and malice against the faithful. None so much envied and opposed faithful pastors and teachers as they did. False teachers were Paul's standing antagonists; they were like Jannes and Jambres, who withstood Moses. The scribes and Pharisees of all others most hated Christ. "Pilate knew that for envy they had delivered him." Seducers hate those most who hurt them most. The faithful minister who shines with the light of pure doctrine these thieves most strike at. The leaders of God's army they principally fight against. The magistrate, whom God appointed for the restraining of sin, they bitterly hated and envied; and it was not for want of poison, but power, that they did not destroy and pluck up magistracy by the very roots. These seducers were likewise murderers with Cain, the worst of murderers, soul murderers. Their work was to draw men into perdition. They were deceived and deceiving, blindly leading their blind followers into the ditch of destruction. They denied Him who is the way, the truth, the life. Their sacrificing was with a murderous intent; and though, with Cain, who spake most kindly to his brother when he was inwardly most cruel, they utter fair and sweet expressions, yet all to deceive the hearts of the simple. Under every bait of good words there lay the hook of error and heresy. They gave their poison in a gilded cup, and ever came with a hammer and a nail when they presented butter in a lordly dish; nor ever were they so much the ministers of Satan, as when they transformed themselves into angels of light.

(3.) They went in the way of Cain in regard of his complaint and despair. They who walked in Cain's wickedness could not escape Cain's woe. Jude here denounces it against them, and tells us they were "before of old ordained to this condemnation;" they were beasts, made to be taken; they corrupted themselves; they languished and pined away in their filthiness. There was a ditch followed their blind leading; and though the grace of God was turned into lasciviousness by them, and abused as an occasion to sin, yet how glad would they have been in the end for one drop of those streams of grace, which once they paddled in and trampled under feet! They who formerly taught that by reason of grace men might sin, afterward felt that for want of grace they and their seduced followers were sure to smart. They who once preached nothing but grace, afterward felt nothing but wrath; a just recompence, since with Cain they account the greatest sin in the commission so small that they need not fear it, in their afterdespairing confession find it so great that they are not able to undergo it; and besides all this, with Cain, to be marked with infamy and dishonour to all posterity.

Obs. 1. Privileges of nature commend us not to God. We find not seldom in Scripture that the eldest child proves the unholiest. Abel, the younger, was a saint; Cain, the elder, was a murderer: Cain excelled Abel in the dignity of primogeniture, and further, in the expectation of his parents. Cain, if he were not (as some think) deemed by them to be the promised Seed of the woman, and their Saviour, is yet called a possession obtained of God, as one by whom they expected to reap much good and com-

Abeli nomen inditum fuit a vanitate, ut significa- retur humanam conditionem meram esse vanitatem; ideoque He- brœi, הֶבֶל appel- lant oris halitum qui cito evanescit. Kiv. in Gen. Exerc. 42. Qui clarus erat nativitate carnis et charus existi- matione paren- tum, respuitur a

fort. Abel, according to his name, is deemed unprofitable and vain. And yet he who was so eminent, both for his birth and his parents' estimation, is rejected; and he who was, saith Musculus, accounted as vain, and nothing worth, and unprofitable, is accepted by God; who, though he refuses not, yet neither receives any for outward prerogatives: he is no respecter of persons. Jacob, the younger, was a godly man, and beloved; Esau, the elder, a profane person, and hated of God. David, the youngest of Jesse's sons, was he who, of them all, we find to be according to God's own heart. Reuben, the eldest son of Jacob, was incestuous, Simeon and Levi cruel and bloody, Judah adulterous; Joseph, one of the youngest, only eminent for sanctity among them all. If the privileges of nature had been any thing worth, the first-born of the sons of men had not been a reprobate; but God will have his grace known to be free: he neither sees nor loves as man, because he finds a lovely object; but he of his own free bounty makes a person lovely, and then loves him: with God, the first are often the last, and the last first. When the lots were given forth for choosing an apostle, though Joseph called Barsabas, who was surnamed Justus, was the brother or near kinsman of Christ, yet the lot fell upon Matthias. "Not many wise men after the flesh, not many mighty, not many noble, are called; but God hath chosen the foolish things of the world to confound the wise; and weak things of the world to confound the things that are mighty," &c., 1 Cor. i. 26, 27. "Thou hast hid these things," saith Christ to his Father, "from the wise and prudent, and hast revealed them to babes; for so it seemed good in thy sight." How groundlessly do any conclude that God loves them from worldly pre-eminence!

Deo; et qui habebatur abjectus et nullius momenti, respicitur et probatur. Respuit igitur Deus primogenitos et omnes eos qui chari sunt parentibus? non colligimus istam consequentiam, sed id annotamus, non morari Deum hasce carnis prærogativas, vel quamcunque aliam excellentiam secularem magis quam spiritualem. Musc. in Gen.

It is not any gift without us, but something of peculiar grace wrought within us, that can evidence the favour of God toward us: not the first-born, but the new-born; not the eldest, but the holiest; that may say, I know, Lord, that thou lovest me. To conclude; it is the duty of those who have received more favour from God than others, to acknowledge that God has done more for them than for others; and that it was only his mere love that he did not more for others than them; and to cry up free grace with heart, tongue, pen, life.

Ut intelligamus eum, qui humano judicio præfertur, esse inferiorem apud Deum.

Obs. 2. Though grace may be repaired in ourselves, yet is sin propagated to ours. The clearest grain being sown, sends forth that chaff from which it was fanned. Cain was too like his father in that, wherein both were unlike God. Adam might see his own sinful nature in Cain, not that grace whereby he had laid hold upon the promised Seed, nor the fruit of his care in training up his children in religion. Before Adam fell, holiness was natural, and sin would have been adventitious; but now since the fall, sin was natural, and holiness adventitious. The corruption of nature is that legacy which Adam leaves to every one of his sons: grace is not native, but donative; not by generation, but regeneration.

After sin, corrupt, mortal Adam begets a corrupt, mortal Cain; for although Adam through the grace of God was renewed by faith and repentance, yet his son naturally begotten of him was such as his father became by sin. "That which is born," saith Christ, "of the flesh, is flesh," John iii. 6: where the begetter and bearer are a lump of corruption, the birth is no whit better. When God looked down upon Adam's sons, they were all corrupt; not one who in himself was of a more pure, refined condition, or free from a depravedness and disorder of the whole man, Psal. xiv. 3; Rom. iii. 12; Eph. ii. 2, 3. "Who can bring a clean thing out of an unclean?" "Adam begat a son in his own likeness," Gen. v. 3. That which is required to convey original sin, is, that a man by true generation descends from Adam. God at the first set Adam as a public person, representing the person of all mankind, with this condition, that if he retained his integrity, the blessing of multiplication once given, should be sanctified to him for the bringing forth of a posterity righteous and holy like himself; but if he fell away from his obedience, that the blessing should be turned into a curse, and should be a means of multiplying a corrupt and sinful generation. He who conveyed his nature to his posterity, conveyed also the pollution thereof. In the first man, the person corrupted the nature; in every other man, nature corrupts the person: whoever is a man by the propagation of Adam's nature, is also a sinner by the derivation of Adam's corruption. Before we can partake of renovation by grace, we must know our pollution by nature. Pride caused, and humility should follow, our degenerate estate: the ancient house, the many descents, the coat, the crest of a born leper, should not make him proud. Happy we, if the corruption derived from the first drive us to the Second Adam: this latter also has a posterity who bear his image. The church comes out of Christ's side, in the sleep of his death. Let us labour to be ingrafted into him, to draw from him a spiritual life, to bear the image of the heavenly, as we have borne that of the earthy, 1 Cor. xv. 49. Whatever the first Adam brought into the world by sin, the Second carries out by righteousness, Rom. v. 12, 14. In a word, how due and suitable a recompence is it for every parent to labour to bring their children into a state of grace by education, whom they have made sinners by propagation!

Obs. 3. Our expectations in earthly blessings often disappoint us. Eve names her eldest son Cain, a possession, and her second son Abel, which signifieth vain or unprofitable: she showed, as some think, hereby the preposterousness of her affection, and that she esteemed the worst most. Her Cain (she was not herein unlike carnal parents among us) was her jewel; her Abel was vain and unprofitable in her thoughts. She who mistook, saith one, the fruit of the garden, mistook also the fruit of her own body; her hope deceived her in both. God often crosses us in those comforts from which we look for most contentment. He whom Eve called a possession destroys the best part of her possession. Absalom, called The father's peace, proved his greatest disturber. If thou makest any earthly enjoyment thy possession, God may make it thy murderer; and that thy trouble, which thou expectest should be thy rest. If the Lord loves us, he will not suffer us to love any thing more than himself; and it is our wisdom to set our hearts upon nothing but that which is above the reach of danger and disappointment, and to love nothing much but what we cannot love excessively.

Fallitur augurio spes bona sæpe suo.

Obs. 4. It is the duty of parents to be thankful, as Eve was, for their children. "Children are an heritage of the Lord: and the fruit of the womb is his reward," Psal. cxxvii. 3. God will be known to have the prerogative of opening the heavens, the grave, the heart, and the womb. These are the children, saith Jacob, which God hath given me. It is vile ingratitude to murmur at the numerousness of our offspring: to rejoice when our cattle multi-

Clavis cœli, sepulchri, cordis, et matricis in manu Dei.

ply, and repine when our children increase; and to despise a present of God's preparing and sending, so curious a piece of workmanship, wrought with that incomparable and stupendous artifice in the "lowest parts of the earth," Psal. cxxxix. 15. It is heathenish distrustfulness, to fear that He who has provided children for us will not provide necessaries for them. He who has given mouths will give bread, and often provides better for the poor children than for the repining parents. The Israelites in the wilderness, who with sinful solicitousness cried out that their little ones should be starved for want of food, were themselves destroyed in the wilderness for want of faith, their children meanwhile being reserved for Canaan, Numb. xiv. 31. Nor yet is it enough to take our children cheerfully at the hand of God, but to dedicate them to him thankfully, and to part with them contentedly. Men are not born into the world only that the world should not be empty, but that the church should be increased, and God more served. If we ought to honour God with our dead, Prov. iii. 9, much more with our living substance, and to take care that a generation may serve the Lord when we are gone, Gen. xviii. 19; that, as we live, as it were, after our deaths in the persons, so God's glory may live in the services, of our children. Adam instructed his sons, both in the works of their calling, and in the worship of God. And for parting with our children; he who gave, or rather lent, or rather put them to nurse to us, may peaceably be permitted to require them again when he pleases, and he should never lose a friend of any of us for calling for his own.

Obs. 5. Cains please not God in the performance of holy services. "To Cain and his offering God had not respect;" he was in his way of sin even when he was sacrificing. The prayer of the wicked is an abomination, Prov. xxviii. 9; God delights not in their services; he demands, Who hath required them? he cannot away with them; his soul hates them; they are a trouble to him, Isa. i. 11—14; he is weary of them, despiseth them; he will not accept nor smell their offerings, Amos v. 21. "He that killeth an ox is as if he slew a man; he that sacrificeth a lamb, as if he cut off a dog's neck; he that offereth an oblation, as if he offered swine's blood; he that burneth incense, as if he blessed an idol," Isa. lxvi. 3. The wicked perform holy services from an unholy heart. The spicing and embalming a dead carcass can put no beauty or value upon it: "They who are in the flesh cannot please God," Rom. viii. 8. All the fruit of an evil tree is evil fruit, Matt. vii. 18. The works of natural men want a holy principle, the Spirit of Christ, the law of the Spirit of life. A beast cannot act the things of reason; nor can a man, unless sanctified by the Spirit of God, do any good work. Till a man be ingrafted into Christ, and partake of his fatness, he is but a wild olive. All the works of unregenerate men are sin as they come from them. Without the Holy Spirit there is no holiness. Zaccheus was too low of himself to see Jesus; he was fain to go up into a tree. We are too short to reach to any good work; it is above our reach till the Spirit of God lift us up. All the services of a natural man are but the works of nature; he does every spiritual work carnally. "Without me," saith Christ, "ye can do nothing," John xv. 4. All the works of a Christless person are like the children of a woman never married, spurious and illegitimate; they are not done through a power received from Christ.

Wicked men perform no duty to a right end. Their fruits are not fruits to God, Rom. vii. 4; Phil. i. 11. As they are not from him, so neither for him. He is neither their principle nor their end, Zech. vii. 5, 6. Vain-glory is the worm that breeds in the best fruit of the wicked. The flame of Jehu's zeal was but kitchen fire, and therefore his reformation but murder in the sight of God, Hos. i. 4. "The godly," saith a learned man, "in doing good works, are like the silk-worm, which hides herself, and is all covered over while she works, within the curious silk which she works." At the day of judgment they know not the good works which they did. *Her motto, Operitur dum operatur.*

The outward acts of obedience of the wicked are works of disobedience: he does not what he does because God enjoins it, *Cum intuitu voluntatis Divinæ.* His sanctification, such as it is, is not endeavoured like that 1 Thess. iv. 3, "This is the will of God, saith the apostle, "your sanctification." He proves not what is the good and acceptable will of God, Rom. xii. 2. One may do a good work in obedience to his lusts, and that which God bids him do, because his lust bids him do it. "Where no law is, there is no transgression;" and where no respect to the law, no obedience.

The best performances of the wicked are but the gifts of enemies, proceeding not from love, which is the sauce of every service, making it delightful both to the servant and the master, and the principle of the saint's obedience. By nature we are enemies, doing our works, not with the affection of a child, but out of bondage, Gal. v. 6. None have been greater enemies to Christ and his servants and service, than many who have been most exact in outside performances; as Paul, who in the midst of his zeal was a persecutor.

Lastly, The wicked neither have the guilt of sin taken away from their persons by the merit of Christ, nor the pollution of it from their services by the intercession of Christ. Till faith have fastened us to Christ neither persons nor performances can be acceptable. Good works go not before, but follow justification. We are not justified by doing good works, but being justified we then do good, Eph. ii. 8—10. Abel's person was accepted before his sacrifice. Works are rather justified by the person of a man, than his person by the works; and it is a vain thing to look for justification from that which thou must first justify. A man till justified is a leper, and every thing he touches he makes unclean to himself. As a small thing which the righteous hath is better than great possessions of the wicked, so a small thing that the righteous does is better than the greatest performances of the wicked. Till a man takes Christ by faith, his sacrifices have no golden censer to perfume them, no altar to sanctify them, nothing but his own evil heart to consecrate them upon. Upon which considerations, though a wicked man may do what is good morally in the sight of men, by way of example, or by way of edification to others, yet not divinely in relation to religion, or in order to God, so as to please him. And though God sometimes be pleased to reward the works of wicked men, yet do not those works please him. The works of Nebuchadnezzar, Jehu, Ahab, &c., he did, I confess, reward temporally; but, alas! it was but temporally. They give him services which please not him, and he benefits which profit not them. They give him services, but not with their heart; and he them blessings, but not with his heart; and that little he bestows upon them is not to recompense hypocritical, but to encourage sincere obedience. God often, as Calvin saith on Jer. xxxv. 19, rewarding the shadow, to show how the substance of virtue would please him. Wicked men are hence, (1.) Cautioned not to leave holy duties undone. The certainty of their sinning in performing them must not, cannot abrogate the law of God, which enjoins them. Nor is our duty impaired with our power to serve the Lord. When a thing done is evil, not in its substance, and because it is done, but because of our irregular manner of performing of it, we ought still to do it, notwithstanding the defects cleaving to it. (2.) They should likewise hereby be made willing to go out of themselves to Jesus Christ for his Spirit and merit. Till Paul saw all that he could do to be but dung and dross, he never could duly esteem the excellency of the knowledge of Christ. Till we account our own righteousness to be but filthy rags, we shall never esteem Christ to be a beautiful robe.

Simon Magus was commanded to pray, Acts viii. 22.

Obs. 6. Envy is a pernicious, and yet a groundless and foolish wickedness. It was the entrance of Cain's way, and the inlet of his murder. It is a sin that breaks both tables at once; the first by discontent with God, the latter by injuriousness to man. Who is able to stand before envy? It is, as jealousy, cruel as the grave: it is a calamity without a remedy. Some understand that request of the rich glutton, that Lazarus might be sent to him with water to cool his tongue, to proceed from envy; he desiring rather that Lazarus should be tormented with him, than himself eased by Lazarus; and he craving not that he should be carried to Lazarus, but that Lazarus should be sent to him. It was the cruelty of envy that sold innocent Joseph, and that sought the destruction of good David. From envy it was that the devil overthrew our first parents; and by it he puts Cain upon killing his innocent brother, and the Jews upon murdering the holiest person in the world. Plainly also does this envy of Cain discover the groundlessness of this sin. The fault of Abel was not that he had hurt Cain, but that God accepted Abel. Truly is envy therefore said to be worse than covetousness: the covetous is only unwilling to distribute his own goods, but he loves to see others communicate theirs; but the envious neither will do good himself, nor is willing that others should do so: he is angry that God is so bountiful. It is worse than hatred and anger; for these in desiring the hurt of another have their rise from the offence which is offered by him; but envy has its rise merely from its own malignity. And in some respect it is the worst of all sins; for when the devil tempts to them, he draws men by the bait of some delight; but the envious he catches without a bait; for envy is made up of bitterness and vexation. Other men's welfare is the envious man's wound. To him the vine brings forth thorns, and the fig-tree thistles. Nothing but misery pleases him, nor is any thing but misery spared by him. Every smile of another fetches a sigh from him. To him bitter things are sweet, and sweet bitter. And whereas the enjoyment of good is unpleasant without a companion, the envious had rather want any good than that another should share with him. A certain prince (they say) promised an envious and a covetous man that he would give them whatsoever they desired of him, upon this condition, that he who asked last should have twice so much as he who asked first: when both were unwilling therefore to ask first, the prince commands the envious man to ask in the first place, and his request was, that one of his own eyes might be put out, that so both the other man's eyes might be put out also. How contrary is envy to charity, which without my labour makes all the happiness of another mine own! Hence envy is said to take away from every man his neighbour. It is said that God turned the heart of the Egyptians to hate his people, Psal. cv. 25; which God did, as Augustine interprets it, not by making the Egyptians evil, but by bestowing upon the Israelites those good things for which the wicked were ready to envy them.

Cant. viii. 6. Calamitas sine remedio est, odisse felicem. Cypr. lib. de zelo et Livore.
Adhuc divitem malitia non deserit, quem jam possidet pœna, qui non se ad Lazarum duci postulat, sed ad se Lazarum vult deduci. Chrysol. Ser. 122.

Nusquam melius invidos torquere poteritis, quam virtutibus et gloriæ serviendo. Aug. Ser. 18. ad frat. in Erem.

Sola miseria invidia caret.

Nullius rei possessio jucunda sine socio. Senec.
One seeing an envious man very sad, said, I know not whether this man hath received some hurt, or another some good.

Superbia mihi aufert Deum; invidia proximum, ira meipsum. Hug. de S. Vict. August. in loc. Non illos malos faciendo, sed istis bona quibus mali facillime possent invidere, largiendo, incitasse dicitur ad odium.

To conclude, envy is its own punishment; a saw, a scourge, not so much to him upon whom it is set, as to him in whom it is. It is a moth which breeds in us, and corrupts us. It is a natural sin: "The spirit that dwelleth in us lusteth to envy." Saints have been overtaken with it; Peter, John xxi. 20, 21; Joshua, Numb. xi. 29. Let us labour against it. To help us herein, let us love such good things which one, yea many, may have without the detriment of others, which may be enjoyed by and be distributed to every one without diminution; and withal, beat down the love of ourselves, and the apprehension of our own excellency. Could we understand our own baseness and unworthiness, we should not envy those who are above us, but wonder that any should be below us.

Qui faucibus invidiæ carere desiderat, illam hæreditatem appetat, quam numerus possidentium non angustat. Greg.

Obs. 7. There is no measuring of God's love by outward events. Wicked Cain stands over bleeding Abel, whose sacrifice was first accepted, and now himself sacrificed. Death was denounced as a curse for sin, yet behold it first lights upon a saint. No man knows love or hatred by any thing which befalls the outward man, Eccl. ix. 1. We cannot read or understand God's heart by any thing he dispenses outwardly with his hand. He oft suffers an Abel to be killed in love, and a Cain to survive in hatred. Prosperity and impunity often slay the sinner, when slaying and death shall benefit the saint. Worldly enjoyments are given us that we by them should testify our love to God, not by them to get assurance of God's love to us. Oh how slender an evidence of heaven is that with which ordinarily men go to hell! Thou canst only understand that the heart of God is set upon thee, by finding that thine is set upon him. The least dram of grace is an earnest of heaven. The greatest sum of outward enjoyments amounts not to the least part of payment, or pledge of happiness.

Obs. 8. They who are corrupt in their judgment go in the way of cruelty. Not to intimate what some have said of cruel Cain, that he was the first heretic, sure I am he was after the devil the first murderer; and these seducers were as full of hatred as they were of error; they went in the way of Cain. They were cruel to souls, which by their errors they poisoned and destroyed; cruel to the names and dignities of their superiors, of whom they speak evil. They were, as the apostle speaks afterward, ἄγρια κύματα, fierce and "raging waves," ver. 13, such as uttered "hard speeches" (ver. 15) against the godly, especially ministers, who opposed them in their way of sin. Not to speak of the cruelty of idolaters recorded in the Old Testament, as of Pharaoh, Haman, Ahab, Jezebel, Manasseh, Nebuchadnezzar, Antiochus; nor of the heathenish emperors, within the first three hundred years after Christ, by which tyrants the apostles suffered violent death, and whosoever made profession of their doctrine were cruelly murdered; of Nero, Domitian, Trajan, Antoninus Verus, Hadrian, who crucified ten thousand Christians in one mount; of the last of the ten persecutions, wherein, in the space of one month were slain seventeen thousand martyrs. I say, to pass by these, what lively expositions upon this text and the cruelty of Cain have the bloody actions of those been who would have been counted of the church, nay, the only church, and friends and brethren to the members thereof, as Cain was brother to Abel!

I might here relate what ecclesiastical history mentions concerning the cruelty of the Arian heretics, their banishing and false accusing Meletius and Eustatius bishops of Antioch, and Athanasius of Alexandria; the latter of whom hardly escaped with his life; for the cruel Arians, finding that they could not destroy him by false witness, purposed by violence to tear him in pieces: the banishing and deposing Paulus from Constantinople by the Arian emperor Constantius; and, at last, the cruel murdering of him by the bloody Arians: not to mention with these the vast number of examples of Arian cruelty, recorded in ecclesiastical history; Socrates, Theodoret, Sozomen, &c. consent in this, that the Arians banished, imprisoned, cruelly whipped, mocked, tore with nails, burnt, and exercised the cruellest punishments against the orthodox; and that they were more cruel against them than the heathens who tyrannised in those times. Athanasius saith, The inhumanity of the Arians exceeded all expression.

Theod. l. 1. c. 29.
l. 5. c. 21. Socrat. l. 2. c. 7. 16.
Socrat. l. 4. c. 22. Theod. l. 4. c. 21. Sozom. l. 6. c. 19. Vid. Centur. Magd. p. 79. Cent. 4. Οὐκ ἔστιν οὐδὲ λόγῳ φράσαι, νίκωσης τῆς ὠμότητος αὐτῶν τὴν ἐκ τῶν λόγων διήγησιν. Epist. ad Solit.

I might likewise mention what Augustine in sundry epistles relates of the Cain-like cruelty of the Donatists of his time, who pretended to so much purity, as that they held that the church was no where in the world to be found but in that corner of Africa where they dwelt. In his fiftieth epistle he tells us, that the masters stood in fear of their servants that were gone over to the Donatists; that no man durst demand the money which his debtors owed him, for fear of clubs and fire; the houses of any that offended them were burnt or pulled down; and they pulled out the eyes of the ministers, and put them out with chalk and vinegar, cut off their hands, pulled out their tongues, cruelly whipped and slew them, and then tumbled them in the mud, and then carried them about afterward in derision. And though these sectaries pleaded frequently for toleration and liberty of conscience, yet when under Julian the apostate they had gotten power, who can declare (saith Augustine) what slaughter they made of the orthodox? All Africa was filled with blood and desolation; men were rent, matrons dragged, infants slaughtered, women with child miscarried, none were secure in their houses.

Epist. 50. Quis non Dominus servum suum timere compulsus est! Quis quem libet poterat exigere debitorem! Quorundam oculi extincti sunt. Cujusdam episcopi manus et lingua præcisa est; taceo crudelissimas cædes. Epist. 68. Conclericos nostros plagis immanissimis quassaverunt. Quendam immaniter cæsum, et gurgite cœnoso volutatum, &c. Nos fustibus quassant ferroque conciduut. In oculos extinguendos, calcem, mixto aceto incredibili excogitatione sceleris, mittunt. Epist. 166, 159. Lacerati sunt viri, tractæ sunt matronæ, infantes necati, abacti sunt partus, nulli licuit securum esse in possessionibus suis. Optat. cont. Par. L 23.

But if ever the spirit of Cain breathed in any since his time, or if ever any wrote after Cain's copy in letters of blood, certainly they have been those of the papacy: how deservedly may their head and father the pope be called a Cain in chief, as he is called the son of perdition! as being not only appointed to perdition, but the author of perdition and destruction. How evidently is his antichristian cruelty set forth by being drunk with the blood of the saints, and with the blood of the martyrs of Jesus! Rev. xvii. 6. It is said by some that there is no day in the year which might not be dedicated to a hundred- several martyrs, whose blood has been shed by the papal power. (1.) Papal cruelty spares not, pities not any degrees, sex, order, age, condition of men opposing their religion. Alphonsus Diazius, another Cain, barbarously killed his own brother, John Diazius, because he was a protestant. With what inhuman cruelty have protestants been compelled to discover for slaughter their dearest relations, parents, children, brethren, wives, to carry faggots to burn their godly and painful pastors! and, which might surpass belief among heathens, children have been constrained to set fire to their own fathers. And Thuanus reports, that a certain woman, having fled to a secret place to shun the rage of her enemies, being drawn out of it by them, was in the sight of her husband shamefully defiled, and then was forced, by some of them who ordered her hand, to give her husband his death's wound with a drawn sword. Horrid was that spectacle of the child which sprang out of the womb of a woman burnt at Guernsey, which being saved out of the fire, was by the bloody executioner cast in again, because it was a young heretic. A child of eight years old was by them scourged to death for religion, and a boy under twelve years condemned for the six articles; yea, popish cruelty forbears not either to bury the quick, as one Marion was condemned to be buried alive, or to unbury the dead, by violating their graves, digging out the bodies and burning them; thus they dealt with the bodies of Bucer, Fagius, Wickliff. How frequently has papal power made kings and princes wolves and tigers one against another! and sent forth cut-throats and villains with pardons, to stab and poison kings and potentates of the earth! their lives by any art (they hold) may be taken away, if the pope hold them excommunicate. Emanuel Sa affirms it lawful for one to kill a king, if the pope have sentenced him to death, though he be his lawful prince. But Mariana gives direction how it may be done with the best convenience; he thinks poison to be the best way; but yet, for the more secrecy, that it be cast upon the saddles, garments, chairs of the prince. And he further tells us, that if they who kill such kings shall escape, they ought to be looked upon and received as long as they live as great and noble worthies; but if it fall out otherwise, that they lose their lives in the undertaking, that then they are a sweet-smelling sacrifice to God and man, and that their names shall be illustrious to all posterity.

Act. and Mon. p. 814, 751, 874, 710, 766.
Act. and Mon. p. 1864, 1879.
Act. and Mon. p. 816.
Lata sententia quisque potest fieri executor. In Aphor. de Rege et Regis Instit. l. 1. c. 6. Quod si evaserint, instar magnorum heroum in omni vita suscipiendi: si vero secus accidat, gratam hominibus, gratam superis hostiam cadere, nobili conatu ad omnem posteritatis memoriam illustratos judicabimus. Marian. l. 1. de Reg. c. 7.

This book of Mariana was approved by the gravest and most learned of the Jesuits' order; and so with a special commission from Claudius Aquaviva their general, with their approbation, and other solemn privileges, it was printed at Toledo and Mentz, and lastly inserted in the catalogues of the books of their order. It is not lawful, saith Bellarmine, for Christians to tolerate an heretical king, if he labours to draw his subjects to his heresy; and (saith he) it is lawful for the spiritual power to restrain the temporal by all means and ways; and when the pope has passed sentence upon a king, then after this public sentence, they generally affirm it lawful for any to kill a king. So Bellarmine, Gregory de Valentia, Tolet, Suarez, Molina, Lessius, &c.

Non licet Christianis tolerare regem hæreticum, si conetur pertrahere subditos ad suam hæresim. Bellar. l. 5. de Rom. Pont. c. 7. Potestas spiritualis debet coercere temporalem omni modi et via. Id. l. 5. c. 6.

Nor, (2.) Doth popish cruelty less discover itself in the numbers, than in the ranks and degrees of those whom they destroy for religion. These popish Cains destroy multitudes of Abels. Infamous is the cruelty of that savage Minerius, the pope's champion, in his bloody enterprise against the Merindolians; he destroyed twenty and two towns, and murdered the inhabitants, whether they resisted or not; and when the men of Merindol, flying from his army, left behind them their tender wives and children, this popish bloodhound practised all manner of villany and cruelty upon them. The town of Cabriers, upon condition that he would use no violence against them, was yielded into his hands, but he falsified his promise, hewing thirty men in pieces in one place; putting forty feeble women, some pregnant, into a barn full of straw, caused it to be set on fire at the four corners, and those who got out he caused to be cut in pieces. In this one town were thus mercilessly murdered above a thousand protestants. To these I might add the cruel murdering of about eight hundred protestants in two towns in Calabria, fourscore whereof had their throats cut one by one, yet so as that every one was left but half dead by the executioner. And the French massacre, wherein in thirty days were thirty thousand slain. Not to speak of that incredible effusion of blood which the Spaniards have made among the poor Indians, under pretence of converting them to the faith; they having in the space of forty years slain seven and thirty millions of people; famishing in three months seven thousand children; at one time massacring two thousand gentlemen; and murdering with such cruelty, that, to avoid it, poor men would hang themselves, with their wives and children. Lastly, and principally, this bloody disposition of Cain discovers itself in the cruel and savage manner of murdering. Minerius (forementioned) cut off the paps of the poor mothers of sucking children, and the children looking for suck from their dead mothers were starved to death. It has been their practice to hold men in death so long as they could, inflicting, as it were, a thousand deaths in one, and making them so to die as to perceive themselves to die. What should I speak of their burning men by piece-meal, and that with brimstone, pitch, and tar, &c., with barrels of pitch and tar dropping upon their heads? Joannes de Roma, a monk, having got a commission to examine the Lutherans, used this torment to force them to accuse themselves: he filled boots with boiling grease, and put them upon the legs of those whom he suspected; and tying them backward to a form with their legs hanging down over a soft fire, he examined them.

<small>White, Way to the Church, Digr. 50.</small>

<small>Farnesius vowed to ride his horse to the saddle in the blood of Lutherans.</small>

<small>Moriatur, ut sentiat se mori. Acts and Mon. p. 869, 805, 860.</small>

To this Cain-like cruelty of the erroneous papists, I might add that of the Anabaptists in Germany, who were as bitter and bloody enemies to the reformed party as were the papists; and more opposed God and orthodox Christians than they did the papists themselves; they always declaring Luther to be worse than the pope. I shall not mention the bloody uproars made by Munzer, John Mathias, John Becold, Knipperdolling, John Geles, Henry Goethlit, James of Kemp, &c., with their followers, at Wormes, Augsburg, Bazil, Shafhuse, Berne, Munster, Amsterdam, &c., filling all places with blood and slaughter; murdering their own natural brethren, yea, their wives, and pursuing the doctrine of the gospel, and the professors thereof, especially the godly ministers, with cruel fury. It will be more than sufficient to set down the words of one concerning this savage crew, who has taken much pains in examining their doctrines and practices; his words are these, The spirit of Mahomet was not so hellish in making an open trade of bloodshed, robbery, confusion, and catholic oppression, through the whole earth, as the spirit of Anabaptism.

<small>See Sleidan. Bullinger, Heresbachius, Hortensius, &c.</small>

<small>Mr. Bayly.</small>

Nor need we think it strange concerning the fiery cruelty of those who embrace and follow false doctrines. The erroneous in their judgment, may be left of God to apprehend so much truth, and weight, and worth in their errors, that even that thing, conscience I mean, which by its light and tenderness hinders others from sin by discovering it to them, and troubling them for it, may, being depraved by error, put people upon sinful injuriousness to others, and to think that they do God the best service, when they are most cruel to his best servants. And, as it is commonly observed, no feuds are so deadly, no contentions so bitter, as those upon which conscience puts men; conscience urging more strongly than interest: and as a good conscience is a thousand witnesses to comfort and excuse for what good we have done; so may an erroneous conscience be a thousand weights to induce us to what evil we have not done.

And further, such is man's natural enmity against the way of truth, which opposes his lust and advances God's will, that if the white horse go forth, the red horse will follow him at his heels; and they who carry the light of truth, shall be sure to be maligned and pursued. Hence the idolatrous Ephesians cried out with maddest rage, "Great is Diana," Acts xix.

And as the tide of man's inclination, so likewise is the wind of all Satan's endeavours, set against the truth. He who is an old serpent is also a red dragon; yea, therefore a dragon red and cruel, because a serpent false and deceitful. He did not abide in, nor can he abide, the truth. As a serpent, he made and was the father of lies; as a dragon, he shields and is the defender of lies.

To conclude: The wisdom and power of God is in nothing more manifested, than in overthrowing error by the weight of its own cruelty and rage, and in making the professors of truth increase by dying; in making every martyr a stone to break the teeth of those mad dogs who bite them, and to overcome by being overcome. The professors of truth, then, have as little cause to be secure, as the patrons of error have to be cruel. Never did the light shine but the wicked barked at it. If righteous Abel was murdered when there was but one Cain, what may he expect when Cains so abound both in wrath and numbers! Martyrdom came into the world early: the first man that died, died for religion. And how careful should Christians be that they leave not the truth of God, to avoid the wrath of men! It is better to die fighting for it than flying from it. How much sorer an enemy is the great God than a silly worm! And they who leave the love of truth will soon leave their love to the professors thereof. Every apostate is in the high-way to become a persecutor.

Lastly, It may be a word of comfort as well as caution to all persecuted Abels. Cains do not so much strike at them as at truth in them, and professed by them. "I have given them thy word," saith Christ, "and the world have hated them," John xvii. 14. God will vindicate his own cause. Though the enemies are red with the blood of truth's champions, yet their great Captain will one day appear in garments made red with the blood of their enemies, whom he will tread in the wine-press of his wrath; and the blood of every Abel cries with a loud voice for vengeance, which will never give rest to the righteous Judge, till all those who will not become the friends of his truth, become his footstool for rising up against it.

Obs. 9. Great is the difference between the sinning of the godly and wicked. The sin of the wicked is his way; he delights, proceeds, is skilful in it; sin is a sport to him; he is a curious artificer and cunning worker of iniquity; he goes on, and proceeds from one degree of wickedness to another. When he performs any good duty, it is not his way; he rather steps into it, or stumbles upon it, than chooses it, or walks in it. Cain's sacrifice to God is not here called his way, but his sacrificing of his brother. God accounts of men by the constant tenor and bent of their hearts and lives. The godly may fall into sin, but he lives not, rests not in sin; he may, like the sheep, be thrown into the mire, but he does not, like the swine, tumble, and wallow, and delightfully snort therein. He sins not with full consent; there are some contrary votes in his soul against every sinful suggestion. He sleeps, but his heart wakes. Holiness is his way, and whenever he is drawn out of it by some deceitful lust, or by some seducing temptation, he cries out with David, "I have gone astray like a lost sheep; seek thy servant," Psal. cxix. 176. He never leaves calling and inquiring till he has got into the right way again; and when he is so, he walks more humbly, watchfully, evenly, and mends his pace; he gains ground by his stumbling; he does not, as wicked men, wickedly depart from God, 2 Sam. xxii. 22. A saint falls, and cries, I fall, as a child that falls into the fire. A sinner falls, and loves to fall, and is like a stone that falls to the centre. As there is much difference between the suffering, so between the sinning, of the good and bad: as sufferings are on the saints, and not on them; so sin is in them, and not in them. The sufferings of the godly are on them as afflictive to sense, not on them as penal for sin, so as to sink and destroy them; but the wrath of God abides on the wicked, and falls upon them as upon its proper place, to remain and dwell upon them: so when the godly sin, they are not swallowed up of sin, grace works them out again; but the wicked lie soaking in their sin, and, as God speaks, Lev. xxvi., pine away in their iniquity; and if God should give them to live in the world to eternity, they would live it in sin. A godly man is like a pure fountain into which dirt is thrown, though it be thick and muddy for the present, yet at length it works it out; whereas a sinner is like a standing water, into which when dirt is thrown, at the best, it does but settle and fall to the bottom; and when it appears clearest, the dirt is not wrought out, but there abides, and upon every stirring discovers itself. A saint lives not, walks not in sin; wickedness is not his way: whenever he sins, he looks upon himself as in his wandering, not as in his way. If thou wouldst try thy sincerity, examine the bent of thy heart, and whether sin be thy delight, thy way; or thy trouble, thy disallowed aberration.

Obs. 10. Despair is the period of presumption. The contempt of grace ends in the despair of grace. God graciously warned Cain; he sins, and despairs, having sinned. These seducers live in sin, notwithstanding grace, and are overwhelmed in woe, and deprived of grace. No poison is so deadly as that which is extracted out of grace. Abused mercy pleads against a sinner most persuasively. Oh that they who are so fearless when they sin, would consider how fearful they shall be when they have sinned! they who when they are tempted fear no wrath, no death, afterward will be ready to say with Cain, Every one who meets us will kill us. The way to be bold when the wicked shall be afraid, is to be afraid when the wicked are bold. He who is afraid of sin shall not feel punishment.

Obs. 11. They who most plead for liberty exercise most cruelty. None would rule so much, and so bloodily, as they who deny others to rule altogether. These seducers who despised dominions, and spake evil of dignities, for all that, walked in the way of Cain. They who would have all others to be ciphers, to do nothing, would themselves be Cains, to do too much. Their little finger was heavier than the magistrate's loins. They who shall peruse the writings of Austin concerning the Donatists, and among them the Circumcellious, as also the relations of others concerning the Anabaptists of Germany, shall find both these sects to be bloody commentators upon this truth. They who abrogate the law of God, will endure no law but that of their own making: though they have cried out of persecution, and complained of restraint, when they have been under the power of others; yet they have most tyrannised over the spiritual and civil liberties of others, when they have gotten the power into their own hands. And it is impossible that they should rule gently and meekly, who are themselves ruled and ordered by Satan, that cruel one. They who are not delivered from the hand of this enemy will neither serve God in righteousness and holiness themselves, nor suffer others to do so. Nor will any be so unwilling that others should have liberty in holiness, as they who most love and allow liberty in sin.

This for the amplification of the wickedness and woe of these seducers from this first example, viz. of Cain.

2. I come to speak of the error of Balaam; "And ran greedily after the error of Balaam for a reward."

Three things are here to be opened.

1. Their guide, "Balaam."

2. The example he set before them, erring for reward.

3. The manner of their following this example, set forth in their running greedily after the same.

1. Their guide was Balaam. Concerning his practice and punishment, it will be more proper to speak in the following part. Touching his country, parentage, and office, I shall speak briefly in this.

(1.) His country: we read that it was Mesopotamia, and that the town or particular place of Mesopotamia where he resided was Pethor, Deut. xxiii. 4; and of himself he saith, "Balak the king of Moab hath brought me from Aram, out of the mountains of the east," Numb. xxiii. 7. This Mesopotamia, and Aram, or Syria, are used indifferently, sometimes the one for the other; and not only because some small part of Syria is Mesopotamia, properly so called, but because the greatest part of Syria is called Mesopotamia, or the region lying between those two great rivers, Tigris and Euphrates. Some have thought that this Balaam was a Midianite; and their reason is, because it is said that he was slain with the Midianites when the Israelites destroyed them, Numb. xxxi. 8; Josh. xiii. 22. Of this opinion is Masius, one of the most learned among the pontifician expositors. Pineda in his comment upon Job seeming also inclinable to it. For though the Scripture tells us that he was of Aram or Mesopotamia, yet, say they, under the name of Aram or Mesopotamia, largely taken, is contained so large a tract of countries as takes in Midian; and some conceive that he speaks himself to be of Aram, to gain the more honour and credit to himself, because the Aramites and Chaldeans were in those days most famous for divining and astrology. But whether his abode among the Midianites was because Midian was his country; or whether he took the Midianites in his way homeward from the king of Moab, to give them counsel to draw Israel to sin; or whether he returned to them again from his country of Aram or

Mesopotamia to receive his wages; I determine not: sure I am it was a most just retribution of Providence, that he should be among the Midianites when they were destroyed; their counsellor in sin deserving to be their partner in punishment, Numb. xxxi. 16.

(2.) The parentage of Balaam. The Scripture tells us that he was the son of Beor, Numb. xxii. 5; Micah vi. 5: and 2 Pet. ii. 15, he is called "Balaam the son of Bosor." How could both be true? The Vulgate translation renders the place, *Balaam ex Bosor*, Balaam of Bosor, as if Bosor were the name of a place where Balaam lived. But the words in the original, Βαλαάμ, not ἐκ τοῦ, but, τοῦ Βοσόρ, will not bear that interpretation, but must necessarily denote, not the place, but parent of Balaam, as some of the papists themselves, notwithstanding their zeal for their translation, are forced to grant. And whereas the father of Balaam is called Beor, Numb. xxii. 5; Micah vi. 5, not Bosor, it is conceived by some that he was διώνυμος, had two names, viz. Beor and Bosor, this bestowing of two names on one man being frequent in Scripture: thus the wife of Esau is called both Bathshemath and Adah, Gen. xxvi. 34; xxxvi. 2; the son of Zerah is called both Zimri and Zabdi, Josh. vii. 1; 1 Chron. ii. 6; Mephibosheth is called Merib-baal, 1 Chron. viii. 34; Ishboshcth is called Eshbaal, 1 Chron. viii. 33; Jerubbaal, Jerubbesheth, Judg. vi. 32; 2 Sam. xi. 21. Others answer, that the word Beor is here put for Bosor, which mutations of proper names are frequent: so Tiglath-pileser is called Tilgath-pilneser, 2 Kings xv. 29; 1 Chron. v. 6; Ram is called Aram, 1 Chron. ii. 9; Matt. i. 3; the place where Joshua was buried is called both Timnath-heres and Timnath-serah, Josh. xxiv. 30; Judg. ii. 9.

Quia Græce dicitur Balaám τοῦ Βοσόρ, significatur Balaam fuisse filium Bosor; licet Num. xxii. dicatur filius Beor, et aut hic positus est vox Bosor pro Beor, aut utroque nomine vocabatur. Salmer.

(3.) The office of Balaam: he is called both a prophet and a soothsayer, or diviner. A prophet he is expressly called by Peter, 2 Pet. ii. 16; and in the story of Balaam set down by Moses, there is frequent mention of his receiving messages and words from Jehovah: "I will bring you word," saith he to Balac's messengers, "as the Lord shall speak unto me," Numb. xxii. 8. And, "The Lord refuseth to give me leave to go with you," ver. 13. And, "I cannot go beyond the word of the Lord my God," ver. 18. And Moses saith, that "the Lord put a word in Balaam's mouth," Numb. xxiii. 5, 16. He uttered a prophecy concerning Christ by Divine inspiration: "There shall come a Star out of Jacob, and a Sceptre shall rise out of Israel," Numb. xxiv. 17; to which prophecy he prefixes this solemn preface, "He hath said, which heard the words of God, and knew the knowledge of the Most High, which saw the vision of the Almighty." Even the worst men (as here Balaam) have sometimes foretold future things by a spirit of prophecy. God inspired Pharaoh with a prophetic dream: "God hath showed unto Pharaoh," said Joseph, "what he is about to do," Gen. xli. 1, 25. The like may be said of Nebuchadnezzar, Dan. ii. 47. Some of the wicked who shall be sentenced to depart from Christ at the day of judgment, shall be able to say, "Have we not prophesied in thy name?" Matt. vii. 22. Caiaphas the high priest, a bloody, unrighteous man, prophesied that "Christ should die for that nation," John xi. 51. Possibly Balaam uttered not his prophecies, as understanding their force or genuine sense; his heart was not holily affected with what his tongue uttered; which some conceive to be intimated in that expression, of putting a word into Balaam's mouth, a phrase never used concerning the inspiring any of the holy prophets. And whereas Balaam is called a soothsayer or diviner, Josh. xiii. 22, the word which we translate soothsayer is a word of a middle signification; for in Scripture it is not only taken in the worst sense, for one that uses divination, or is a soothsayer; but in a good construction, for one that prophesies or foretells things to come, as Micah iii. 11. And some there are, who think that Balaam is here called a soothsayer only in regard of his ambition and covetousness, and of his ends and aims in all he did, which were not God's glory, or the love of the truth revealed to him, or of his people whom he blessed, but his own advancement, and the wages and reward of divination, according to the manner of wicked soothsayers. But I rather conceive that Balaam, out of desire of gain, made use of devilish arts and unlawful divinations for the cursing of Israel. It is said that "he went not, as at other times, to seek for enchantments," Numb. xxiv. 1. Whereby it may be evidently collected, saith Ainsworth, that all his former altars, sacrifices, and consultations with the Lord, were by the wicked art of enchantment, or observing of fortunes, such as the prophets and diviners of the nations used, Deut. xviii. 10, 14, which he now left, as seeing them not available for his purpose. His serving of God was mixed with his old superstition, in the number of altars and sacrifices, in their site or posture towards the points of heaven, in his gestures and set form of words.

Deut. xviii. 10.

Mic. iii. 11. Sept. Μάντιν, Vatem, reddiderunt.

See English Annot. on Josh. xiii.

Annot. in Numb. xxiv.

Vid. Ames. in 2 Pet. p. 272.

This for the explication of the first particular, viz. whom these seducers followed, or their guide.

2. The example which he set before them, viz. his [Balaam's] "error for reward." In the Greek the words are πλάνη τοῦ Βαλαάμ μισθοῦ.

Two things are here to be opened.

(1.) What that error was which they followed.

(2.) How it was for reward.

(1.) What that error was which they followed. The word πλάνη, here translated error, properly signifies an aberration, or wandering from a right path or course wherein a traveller should walk; and therefore more fully Peter explains this error of Balaam, and these seducers who followed him, to be a going astray, and forsaking the right way, 2 Pet. ii. 15. But more particularly, the error whereof the apostle here speaks is differently expounded. 1. Some learned men conceive it to be that whereby both Balaam and these seducers were deceived in their expectation of reward and wages, honour, pleasure, profit, &c., by their sinful endeavours; and no doubt in this respect their way might be fitly called error or deceit, for Balaam in propounding to himself the wages and reward which Balak promised him, in case he would curse the Israelites, was himself clearly deceived; he being not only disappointed of what he looked for, viz. honour and gain, but also bringing upon himself that which he looked not for, a violent death by the sword, and, most likely, the eternal destruction of his soul: instead of receiving his reward from Balak, he received it from God, Numb. xxxi. 8; Josh. xiii. 22. As also did these seducers draw to themselves, instead of worldly advantages, which they aimed at, swift destruction and condemnation, as the apostles speak, both of soul and body. Others, as I conceive, more suitably to the scope of the apostle, and to the construction of the other words immediately going before and following, understand this error to be the swerving, wandering, or deviation

Πλάνη, πλανάω, hinc planeta, a planet or wandering star.

Vid. Aug. Trac. 49. in Joh.

of Balaam (imitated by the seducers) from the way of God's will and commandment, both in regard of their practice, and especially their doctrine, or what they taught others, whereby they made them to err and wander from the right way; for Balaam's practice was an erring and wandering from the plain and express precept of God, in that he went to Balak, and that with a desire to curse the people. His way was perverse before the Lord, Numb. xxii. 32; he was out of God's way when he was in the way of his journey. For his teaching of others, he taught Balak to err, in counselling him to build altars and offer sacrifices for enchantments, and to entice the Israelites to adultery and idolatry by the company of the daughters of Moab; and it is as plain that he made the Israelites to err from the way of righteousness, by teaching Balak to cast a stumblingblock before them, to eat things sacrificed to idols, and to commit fornication, Rev. ii. 14; that thus they sinning might be afterward destroyed.

As touching these seducers, it is most evident that they in their own practice wandered from the way of righteousness, and left the way of truth in their doctrines; that they were ringleaders to error; blind guides, who made many follow them into the ditch; deceivers, false prophets, bringing in damnable heresies, many following their pernicious ways, 2 Pet. ii. 1, 2; and that hereby (as Peter speaks) they went astray, and forsook the right way, viz. the way of truth. A great sin, 1. Because error is a deviating from, and an opposing of the way and word of truth. Errors (as Tertullian speaks) arise *cæde Scripturarum*, by the fall of Scripture. The erroneous resist the truth, 2 Tim. iii. 8. The least error disposes the heart to reject the greatest truth. And as in nature darkness destroys light, blindness puts out sight, sickness removes health; so errors undermine and destroy truth. None are such enemies to Scripture as the lovers of error; they ever oppose it, either by denying it or perverting it. 2. Errors are deviations from holiness; they oppose grace as well as truth. They overthrow the faith of people, and also eat up godliness. An erroneous head and a godly heart will not meet. Error makes men deny the power of godliness, 2 Tim. iii. 5, and is an inlet to profaneness. Every text in Jude's Epistle is a comment on this truth. The apostle calls false teachers evil workers, Phil. iii. 2. They whose minds are defiled are reprobate to every good work, Tit. i. 15, 16. Truth reforms as well as informs. Antichrist is called the man of sin, 2 Thess. ii. 3. The corrupting of the judgment is the casting poison into the spring. 3. Error is catching and diffusive. The erroneous have many followers; nor do they go to hell alone. Every error meets with a complying party in our natures. Truth is hardly entertained; error readily admitted. And seldom is any one erroneous, but withal he endeavours to propagate his opinion, and that violently and subtlely. 4. Error, by departing from truth and holiness, opposes the peace of the church. From men's not consenting to wholesome words, come envy, strife, and reviling, 1 Tim. vi. 3, 4. "I would they were cut off" (saith Paul) "that trouble you," Gal. v. 12. Error turns men into devouring dogs, Phil. iii. 2; "grievous wolves," Acts xx. 29. Witness Arians, Donatists, Papists, Anabaptists. To conclude, error is pernicious, damnable, a shipwreck, a gangrene, creeping from joint to joint till it eats out heart and life, and destroys all truth, grace, peace, salvation.

(2.) Error for reward. The word in the Greek is $\mu\iota\sigma\vartheta o\tilde{v}$. Our learned divines observe against the papists, that though $\mu\iota\sigma\vartheta\grave{o}\varsigma$ sometimes signifies a reward due and deserved, or hire due to a workman for his work; yet it is at other times a word of a middle signification, noting a free and gratuitous, as well as a due and deserved reward; and plainly it signifies a reward of mere grace, Rom. iv. 4, not a hire or wages; and the force of the word implies only a reward due by the covenant of him who gives it, to him to whom it is given, whether his work deserves it or no. The penny given to those who had wrought but only one hour, and that in the cool of the day, is as well called by this word of reward, as the penny given to them who had borne the heat and burden of the whole day, Matt. xx. 8, 14, 15. In this place it denotes the wages or recompence which Balaam and these seducers aimed at and expected for their error; for I read not $\mu\iota\sigma\vartheta o\tilde{v}$, reward, as relating to the word $\pi\lambda\acute{a}\nu\eta$, error, (as some learned men do,) thus, They ran greedily after the error or deceit of the reward or wages of Balaam: but I rather refer the word $\mu\iota\sigma\vartheta o\tilde{v}$, reward, to the word $\grave{\epsilon}\xi\epsilon\chi\acute{v}\vartheta\eta\sigma a\nu$, ran greedily, thus, They ran greedily for reward after Balaam's error; that is, as Balaam toiled, journeyed, took pains, went from place to place, from altar to altar, &c., to speak perversely, to curse Israel, and give wicked and pernicious counsel; and all this for filthy lucre or base gain, and to get reward from Balak; so these seducers care not what heresies they utter, what pernicious and damnable doctrines they preach, or errors they broach, so as they may but gain reward and wages from poor deluded people. And our last English translation intends this sense. Thus likewise Œcumenius, Montanus, Justinian, with sundry others. And as this interpretation of their running greedily for reward after error is most apt and elegant, and seems best to answer the original word $\grave{\epsilon}\xi\epsilon\chi\acute{v}\vartheta\eta\sigma a\nu$, in regard of its composition; so it is most agreeable to those other places of Scripture which mention the end which false teachers propound to themselves in venting their errors, and which tell us "that they serve their own belly," Rom. xvi. 18; "that their gain is godliness," 1 Tim. vi. 5; that they err from the faith while they covet after money, 1 Tim. vi. 10; that they "teach things which they ought not, for filthy lucre's sake," Tit. i. 11; that through covetousness they make merchandise of people, with feigned words, 2 Pet. ii. 3; that "they have a heart exercised with covetous practices," 2 Pet. ii. 14. Cyprian, writing of Novatus, that mischievous heretic, saith that he was *avaritiæ inexplebili rapacitate furibundus*, beyond measure, and even to madness, covetous. The covetousness of heretics is the companion, fuel, mother, nurse (saith Amesius) of their heresies.

Now the sinfulness of following "error for reward" appears in two things especially.

[1.] In its profaneness. What more profane and godless course imaginable, than for an instructor of souls to be a vassal to dross! Covetousness is iniquity in all men, but blasphemy in a teacher of souls. His titles, Master, office, doctrine, are all heavenly; how insufferable is it then for him to be earthly! How shall he take off men's affections from the world, when he follows that as most precious which he tells others is most superfluous? The birds of the air which fly next heaven neither sow, nor reap, nor carry into the barn; and how unsuitable is it, that

[Margin notes: Mercedis nomen passim in sacris Scripturis accipitur pro constituto quidem præmio, sed eo tamen gratuito. Bez. in Matt. vi. — Deceptione mercedis qua deceptus fuit Balaam, effusi sunt. Beza, Erasmus, Vatablus, Pagnin. Errore Balaam mercede effusi sunt. Vulg. Montan. Melior sensus, quod effusi sunt propter mercedem, seu mercedis gratia, ita ut in $\mu\iota\sigma\vartheta o\tilde{v}$, suppleatur $\chi\acute{a}\rho\iota\nu$ vel $\acute{\epsilon}\nu\epsilon\kappa a$. Sic Œcumenius. Κέρδους χάριν. Errantes, sicut illi lucri et quæstus gratia, dogmata prava annunciaverunt. Lorin. Præpositio $\grave{\epsilon}\xi$, quæ est in $\grave{\epsilon}\xi\epsilon\chi\acute{v}\vartheta\eta\sigma a\nu$ poscit genitivum. Lapid. in loc. Nonnulli perperam reddunt deceptione mercedis qua deceptus, &c. Multo elegantius aptiusque vocem $\mu\iota\sigma\vartheta o\tilde{v}$, Græcanica scholia ad subsequentia referunt, ut sensus sit, Gnosticos Balaami errorem secutos esse mercedis cupiditate, ut subaudienda sit vox ἕνεκα, &c. Justinian in loc. — Avaritia est plerumque hæresium comes, fomes, mater, nutrix, &c. Ames. in 2 Pet.]

they who by their vocation are next heaven, should yet in their deportment be farthest from it! that they should be like foxes, dissuading the beasts from that booty which they intend to make their own; and that they, bidding men look upward, should cast their own eyes only downward! "Thou, O man of God," saith Paul, speaking of covetousness, to Timothy, "flee these things," 1 Tim. vi. 11. A man of God must not be a man of the world, a slave to mammon, a mere muckworm, or rather a moving muckheap. A star of heaven, nay, an angel, must not degenerate into a clod of earth. What likewise more profane than to barter away precious souls, heaven, Christ, God himself, for base pelf, filthy lucre! to make merchandise for a piece of earth of Christians and Christianity! How unsuitable and disproportionable a price is silver, when for it that soul is sold for which Christ died! In short, how impious is it to sell that truth for dung which we ought to buy with our blood!

[2.] In its hypocrisy and dissimulation. Who ever broached or taught an error professedly for gain, nay, without a pretence of advancing truth, and of aiming at God's glory and the good of souls? What cozenage so vile as that which seems pious? All deceit is abominable, and that most which shrouds itself under the wing of religion; for gain to be the meaning, and godliness the cloak. Is not this as bad as for Jacob's sons to hide their cruelty against Shechem with circumcision? for Abner to cover his revenge against Ishbosheth with the Divine oracle? or Absalom his treason with a religious vow? or Jezebel her murder with a fast? This odious dissimulation of these seducers made them like the kite, eyeing the prey on the dunghill, gain, when they seemed to soar up to the clouds in instructing souls. It is most unsuitable for Satan's servants and mammon's drudges to be cloaked with Christ's livery, to deliver doctrines for gain, and yet to pretend conscience, religion.

Quærunt discipulos quos pecuniis emungere possunt, non quod salutem animarum procurare curabunt. Mont. App. Sec. 28.

3. After what manner they followed the error of Balaam for reward. Jude saith, ἐξεχύθησαν, they "ran greedily after" it. The word properly signifies, they poured out themselves, it being a resemblance taken from the pouring out of water. And according to this resemblance, taken from the pouring forth of water, the word may note either,

(1.) A pouring forth in point of destruction, dissolution, and overthrow; such as whereby, in regard of their total and irrecoverable ruin and perdition, these seducers, with Balaam, became utterly lost, as water poured out. Thus the psalmist, as a type of Christ, describing his extreme debilitation and approaching dissolution, complains that he was as water poured out, Psal. xxii. 14. So the woman of Tekoah, setting forth a desperately lost estate, saith, "We must needs die, and are as water spilt on the ground." In this sense it is said, when the Israelites were smitten before the men of Ai, that "the hearts of the people melted, and became as water," Josh. vii. 5; and thus also I understand that expression of Jacob concerning Reuben, whom, though in respect of what he might have been by the right of primogeniture, he calls his might, "the beginning of his strength, the excellency of dignity, and the excellency of power," Gen. xlix. 3; yet in regard of what he was to be in the loss of this power and dignity, Jacob saith that he was unstable, or poured forth as water; that is, was to be weak, brought low, and so emptied of strength, that nothing great and heroic was to be expected from him. How fitly this dissolution and lost estate agreed to Balaam and these seducers, that sought deinceps sit expectandum magni et heroici. Rivet in Gen. xlix. to heighten and strengthen their condition by error and unrighteousness, who sees not? their sin could not be a stable and solid foundation of greatness, but it made them vanish and perish like water poured forth; they perished in their names, estates, bodies, souls. And therefore the Arabic renders this place, in *mercede exaruerunt*, in their reward they dried up or decayed, as after the pouring forth of water there follows dryness in that thing out of which the water is poured.

Qui robore exce.lens eras, aut esse debueras, factus et debilis et attenuatus, viribus omnibus destitutus. Ita aptissime quadrat oppositio. Qui eras principium roboris mei, effusus es sicut aqua, liquefactus es, exhaustus viribus, ita ut nihil a te

(2.) Or this pouring forth as water may import a pouring forth in respect of the forwardness, force, violence, and impetuousness of these wicked men, in the sinful prosecution of their lusts; and thus this resemblance of pouring forth as water is ordinarily used in Scripture; as, "I will pour out my wrath upon them like water," Hos. v. 10. "Let judgment run down as waters, and righteousness as a mighty stream," Amos v. 24. Jude then here intends that these seducers put forth themselves, in the prosecution of their lust, like water poured out. As a forcible swelling stream breaks down the banks, and violently bears down all before it; so these were so mad upon their Sic dicimus effundere se in libidine, in questus, lachrymas, vota; effundere furorem, iram, minas, querelas, rabiem, vires, vocem, honores in mortuum. Lor. in loc. gain that they could not be restrained, but violently broke down all the banks and bounds which were set to keep them in. And probably the apostle may here refer (in his setting down the violent eagerness of these seducers upon their reward) to that furious march and impetuous progress of Balaam, when he journeyed to Moab upon promise of wages, whom neither God's prohibition before he began his journey, nor the crushing of his foot, nor the speaking of the ass, nor the drawn sword of the angel in his journey, nor the ineffectualness of all his enchantments afterward, could hinder from pursuing his covetous design; but early in the morning up he gets, breaks the bounds of God's command, begins his journey, furiously strikes, madly answers his ass, wildly lays about him, breaks through all difficulties, at length comes to Balak; and then runs from altar to altar with enchantments; and in a word, would not give over till the sword which he saw drawn before his eyes was sheathed in his bowels.

And this violent impetuousness put forth by Balaam, these seducers, and other wicked men, this running greedily in the prosecution of their lusts, is notably set forth in Scripture, and that principally by these two considerations:

[1.] The means used for hindering and reclaiming them have not stopped and hindered them: like the man possessed with devils, no chains are strong enough to hold them. Hence the prosecution of lust is sometimes compared to the effusion, rushing out, foaming, or boiling of the sea, Isa. lvii. 20; sometimes to the swiftness of a "dromedary traversing her way," Jer. ii. 23; sometimes to the rushing of a horse into the battle, Jer. viii. 6; also the backsliding of a heifer, which will endure no yoke, nor be kept in any bounds, Hos. iv. 16; to the unbridled unruliness of the wild ass, which is and will be alone by himself, and will not endure any man to come near him to bring him under government, Hos. viii. 9. "Who," saith God, "hath sent out the wild ass?" &c., "he scorneth the multitude of the city, and regardeth not the crying of the driver," Job xxxix. 5; that is, who but I (God) hath manumised or set free the wild ass from all service of men, and set and kept him loose from those bands to which other cattle are subject, 1 Pet. iv. 4, ἀνάχυσις.

whereby they serve in the cart or for the saddle? If drivers should offer to urge him to work, as they do tame beasts, he would scorn it, and show them a light pair of heels. If a whole city should seek to scare him, and bring him to work, he would not regard it: an exact emblem of a man pursuing his lust, who will not endure to hear of a master, but will be a stranger to discipline, knows no other law but his lust, will be a son of Belial, without a yoke; yea, the vehement impetuousness of the wicked in prosecuting their lusts is set out by the violence of a wild ass, in her occasion none being able to turn her away, or willing to weary themselves therein, Jer. ii. 24. The wicked "set their hearts on their iniquity," Hos. iv. 8. "The heart of the sons of men is fully set in them to do evil," Eccl. viii. 11. More particularly, (1.) The word and will of God hinders not sinners in their courses of lust; they break the yoke, and burst the bonds, Jer. v. 5. They break bands asunder, and cast away cords from them. When the prophet had exhorted the people to turn from their evil ways, they tell him plainly, "There is no hope," Jer. xviii. 12; ii. 25; that is, It is to no purpose to speak to us, there is no possibility of reclaiming us, we are resolvedly bent upon our courses which we have pitched upon, and firmly fixed to live as we list ourselves. I spake unto thee in thy prosperity, and thou wouldst not hear, Jer. xxii. 21. Though Joshua stopped the sun, that swiftly running creature, in its course; yet by severest threats, and strictest prohibition, he could not hinder Achan from his covetous attempt. Though Samuel told the Israelites the manner of their king that was to reign over them, and foretold them their many and certain calamities which should thereby ensue; yet they refused to hear Samuel's voice, and said, Nay, but there shall be a king over us. The Levites in their confession acknowledge that their fathers hardened their necks, dealt proudly, hearkened not to God's commandments, refused to obey, were disobedient, rebelled against him, cast his law behind their backs, sinned against his judgments, withdrew the shoulder, would not hearken, Neh. ix. 16, 17, 26, 29.

θηλυμανεῖς ἵπποι. Clem. Alexandr.

Jesus qui potuit solem sistere ne procederet, avaritiam hominum non potuit sistere ne serperet: ad vocem ejus sol stetit, avaritia non stetit. Sole itaque stante confecit Jesus triumphum, avaritia procedente pene amisit victoriam. Ambr. l. 2. de Offic. cap. 26.

Fuit hoc gentilitium ac genuinum vitium Judæorum, ut nihil minus crederent quam quod a prophetis traderetur. Mendoz. in 1 Sam. viii.

So obstinate was Judas in his sin, that the admonishing of the traitor, and mentioning of the treason, by Christ himself, could not work upon him. Though Cain was forewarned of God to take heed of hurting his brother, yet would he not be stopped from the murder, Gen. iv. 7. The preaching of righteousness to the old and obstinate world by Noah, who by the language of his tongue in speaking to them, and hand also in building the ark, a work wherein he spent a hundred years, foretold them of their approaching deluge, could not reclaim them from their lusts, 2 Pet. ii. 5; Heb. xi. 7; Gen. vi.; yea, the slow proceedings of God in raining upon the earth forty days, Gen. vii. 12, could not work upon those obstinate sinners, but as they lived, so they died, in their contumacy. The like may be said of the Sodomites, who would not be dissuaded from their unclean practices by all the arguments that righteous Lot could use, Gen. xix. 9. The Jews would not, by the most clear and convincing miracles of Christ, be reclaimed or convinced.

Yea, (2.) So great is a sinner's contumacy, that the greatest of God's judgments cannot reclaim him. "Thou hast stricken them," (saith the prophet,) "but they have not grieved; thou hast consumed them, but they have refused to receive correction: they have made their faces harder than a rock," Jer. v. 3. And, "Every one turned to his course, as the horse rusheth into the battle," Jer. viii. 6. The most visible and apparent threatenings of death cannot stop the horse from running into the battle, nor a sinner from proceeding in his course of wickedness. Such was the resolution of the Egyptians in pursuing the Israelites, that they would rush into the sea, which they knew could not be divided for their sakes, and enter the jaws of death, rather than think of a seasonable retreat. Rather than sinners will not satisfy their unlawful lusts, they will spend and profusely cast away their dearest enjoyments. Some think that Aaron being required to make gods for the Israelites, demanded of them their golden earrings, which were in the ears of their wives, their sons and daughters, to try whether he could suppress that idolatrous desire, by calling for those things which were so dear and costly; and yet the people were so obstinately bent upon idolatry, that notwithstanding these difficulties, they took Aaron at his word, and gave their most precious ornaments for making a golden idol; and Abulensis thinks that these earrings were taken away from the younger sort, their sons and daughters, against their wills, and with such violence, that their ears were torn and bloody, before the earrings were pulled from them. Jeroboam, by the rending of the altar, and the drying up of his hand, was not reclaimed from idolatry, 1 Kings xiii. 33. Esau, rather than he would not satisfy his sensual appetite, for a mess of pottage sold his precious birthright. But that which is the most astonishing wonder of all is, that the idolaters were so pertinaciously set upon their idolatry, that they spared not their dearest children, but offered the fruit of their loins and wombs to idols, to devils. And who can sufficiently admire that sottish and sinful pertinacy of Ahaz, who as he trespassed yet more against God in his distress, so he expressed it by sacrificing to the gods of Damascus which smote him! being more desirous in the worshipping of devils to be scourged, than in serving the true God to be crowned; and, that he might satisfy his lust, more willing to be trampled under Satan's feet than to be taken into God's embraces. See further for this Amos iv. 6, 8, 9, 10, &c., the prophet's repeating "Yet have ye not returned," &c. And Isa. ix. 13, "The people turneth not to him that smiteth." Nor can the vanity, unsuccessfulness, and apparent ineffectualness of all the endeavours of sinners, no, nor yet their weariness, weakness, and inabilities, take them off from their lusts. Hence God speaks concerning the Jews, in the pursuing of their idolatrous courses, "Thou art wearied in the greatness of thy way, yet saidst thou not, There is no hope," Isa. lvii. 10. Though she was tired out with the length of her journeys in sending to idolaters, and saw that all her toiling and tiring out herself was in vain, yet she would not give over, but went on still desperately in that toilsome and chargeable course; though all her endeavours were fruitless and unsatisfying, yet she never said, Why should I weary myself any longer? Though sinners observe that nothing which they do profits them, Isa. xxx. 5, 6; Jer. ii. 36, 37; vii. 8; that all their cisterns are broken, and will hold no water, Jer. ii. 12; that they sow the wind, and reap the whirlwind, Hos. viii. 7; that their chariot wheels are broken off, and all their bridges broken down; that whatever they labour to lay hold

Quod Aaron jubet inaures demi ab auribus uxorum, &c. non absurde intelligitur, difficilia præcipere voluisse, ut hoc modo eos ab illa intentione re vocaret. Aug. q. 141. in Exod. Abulens. q. 10.

Verberari a dæmone mallebat quam a Deo coronari. Illa flagella adorabat, hæc dona fastidiebat. Mallet sub diabolicis plantis crudeliter tundi, quam inter divinas ulnas molliter foveri. Mendoz. in 1 Sam. viii. 22.

on flies away from them, as did Joseph from his mistress when she took hold of his coat: in short, notwithstanding the ineffectualness of all their labours, they yet are like those Sodomites, who though they were smitten with blindness, yet wearied themselves in feeling for and finding of Lot's door, and were as full of unclean rage as ever. Though the bodies of sinners may grow weary, and thereby the services of their bodies fail and languish, yet their lusts are as vigorous and green as ever; like a furious rider, never wearied by the length of his journey, though the poor beast under him be tired and worn out. The carcass may be worn and wearied out, but lust is never tired: lust outlives its faculties, and never grows crazy in the oldest body. If the faculty could, lust would still rise up early, lie down late, pursue unclean objects, lade itself with thick clay.

[2.] Sinners, instead of being stopped or hindered in the prosecution of their lusts, by the means used to restrain them, become thereby the more violent and outrageous in their courses. The longer the priests of Baal continued unanswered, and the more Elijah derided them, the more they leaped, the louder they cried, and the more they cut and gashed themselves, 1 Kings xviii. 22. "Why should ye" (saith the prophet) "be stricken any more? ye will revolt more and more," Isa. i. 5. Ahaz in his affliction trespassed yet more, 2 Chron. xxviii. 22. The worshippers of Diana, when their idolatry was opposed, cried out with the more vehement rage, "Great is Diana of the Ephesians," Acts xix. 28. Jerusalem being called of God to weeping and mourning, in opposition to God, fell to all expressions of joy, in slaying of oxen, and killing of sheep. The rebellious Israelites, who, when Caleb persuaded them to go up to Canaan, refused the undertaking; when Moses forbade them, desperately and obstinately, to their own destruction, adventure upon it. The wicked in the land of uprightness, where his wickedness is discovered and reproved, will deal the more unjustly, Isa. xxvi. 10. When Christ had so clearly convinced the Jews of their sin and his own innocency, that they could hold dispute no longer with him, they run from arguments to stones and railings; "Thou art a Samaritan," (said they,) "and hast a devil," John viii. 48. When he had wrought a miracle on the sabbath day, and justified his action, they were the more filled with madness, Luke vi. 11. When Stephen had reproved the Jews of their hypocrisy and cruelty, "they were cut to the heart, gnashed upon him with their teeth, stopped their ears, ran upon him, and stoned him," Acts vii. 54, 57. When Peter (though a holy man) was charged to be one of Christ's company, he denies it with oaths and cursings of himself. When the prophet told Asa of his folly in making a league with the Syrians, it is said that he was in a rage, and imprisoned the prophet, 2 Chron. xvi. 10. When God sent to the Israelites by his prophets to make known to them their sins, they mocked and misused them, and despised the word which they delivered from God, 2 Chron. xxxvi. 16. As the prophets called the Israelites, "so they went from them," Hos. xi. 2. They would have nothing to do with them or their doctrine. When God would have healed Israel by his word, mercies, and judgments, when he tried to cure the sins of his people, their secret wickedness manifested itself; all the means which he used, instead of healing them, did but stir and provoke the evil humours, and being rubbed on their sores, they kicked and raged the more, Hos. vii. 1. The rage of the mad dog is the more increased by the chain; the swelling of the stream, by the stopping thereof; and they who are hindered in their passage in the street by carts go on the faster afterward. The more rubs and stops Balaam met with in his journey, the more was his fury and violence increased. Nor did the Sodomites ever rage so much as when they were opposed by the gentle admonition of Lot, and the suitable and seasonable punishment of blindness.

Cum cœli januæ aperirentur, ipsas Judæi mentes claudebant. Aug.

Καταναθεματίζειν. Matt. xxvi. 74.

Nor will this violence and fury seem strange, if we consider, that in the prosecution of lust, wicked men are carried on, both in the way of their own natural propensions and inclinations, and also by the strong and vehement impulse of that powerful and impure spirit the devil. The violent and propense motions of a person to any sin are set out in Scripture by the word spirit, because they are naturally seated in the spirit, and furthered by a bad spirit; stirred up in and by an unholy spirit; so we read of the "spirit of a deep sleep," Isa. xxix. 10; "a perverse spirit," Isa. xix. 14; "the spirit of whoredom," Hos. iv. 12.

The natural propensity alone has very much in it to cause a vehemence and swiftness in motion; but when seconded and set forward by the force of an outward agent, the vehemence of that motion is much increased. A stone thrown and hurried downward moves the swifter, because the natural weight thereof is improved by an accessory impression; and the natural motion of a person in sin, is made much more eager and impetuous by the impulsions of Satan: sinners then in following their lusts are both carried down the tide of their own nature, and withal vehemently driven by the winds of Satan's instigations; and how swift a passage must needs be made by both conjoined!

Besides, wicked men follow their lusts, and endeavour their satisfaction as their chief end and good, and they have no other god: gain was Balaam's god, and advantage was the godliness of these seducers. And whatsoever, saith Aquinas rightly, any one propounds to himself as his chief end, he seeks and prosecutes without measure. Every man endeavouring to obtain that with his best and greatest industry, which he apprehends as the best and greatest good. *Quicquid proponitur tanquam finis, quæritur nulla adhibita mensura. Aquin.*

To conclude: Lust knows no enough, no satisfaction, it always desiring more; ever needy, and therefore ever greedy; ever empty, and therefore ever earnest; lust can find no centre or term, and therefore it will be eager in motion. Sinners are said to drink "iniquity like water," Job xv. 16; not only in regard of the easiness of drinking, drink being more easily and speedily taken down than meat, but in regard of the excessiveness, men drink water without measure, because without the bridle of fear to restrain them: fear of drunkenness may restrain men from drinking much wine, but men care not how much water they take in, fearing no danger. The apostle speaks of working uncleanness ἐν πλεονεξίᾳ, "with greediness," Eph. iv. 19, or, as the word properly signifies, with having more. There is enough in the objects of lust to entice it, not enough to content it; there are reserves of desire in the soul, fresh supplies of lustings new raised, whensoever the old are cloyed or foiled: no more is lust satisfied with its objects, than the fire is with wood, than the grave with carcasses; the more we give it, the more it will demand; and if by lading it with courtesies we think to oppress it, the more it is thus oppressed, like the Israelites in Egypt, the more it will grow.

Obs. 1. Satan makes use of the meetest and ablest instruments to advance his designs. Balaam, a prophet, he deems of all other the fittest to curse Israel. He oft employs refined wits to defend error as Arius,

Sabellius, Pelagius, Socinus, Arminius: he carves his Mercury on the most promising pieces. He uses those to pervert the world, who transform themselves into the apostles of Christ, and the ministers of righteousness, 2 Cor. xi. 13, 15; he speaks by those who know how to use fair speeches, wisdom of words, sleight, cunning craftiness, and can lie in wait to deceive, Eph. iv. 14. Satan knows that his cause is bad, and therefore he employs those in managing it who are able to make the best of a bad matter: rotten stuffs want most watering, and wrinkled faces most painting; and error and impiety the most skilful pretences, subtle evasions, fairest glosses, and most cunning insinuations. Tertullus is fittest to plead against Paul; soothsayers to oppose Moses; a Simon Magus to deceive the whole city. Besides, Satan is most hurtful to the church when he opposes it by subtlety and seduction. Balaam did more hurt to the Israelites by his counsel, than the Moabites could by their courage: the daughters of Moab by tempting to adultery and idolatry destroyed twenty-four thousand; the sons of Moab could not overcome one: they whom God hath furnished with the best weapons of arts and parts, have oft given his church the deepest wounds. Men of great ability should labour to be men of good abilities and great integrity. There is no eminency, either of outward power or inward parts, but Satan labours to make useful and subservient to his own ends and interest, and a stirrup to lift him up into the saddle. How great a pity is it that a good, a clear head, should be accompanied with a bad, an unclean heart! Tremble to think that any of thy accomplishments should be ornaments to beautify Satan; that thy voice should make him music; that thy wit, eloquence, strength, authority, should be weapons to fight for him against thy Lord, and their Donor. O let not Satan drink the wine of that vineyard which he never planted, or draw out of that well which he never digged, inhabit that house which he never built. O let all thy endowments be engines employed for the Giver. Thy abilities never have their due improvements but when they advance Christ. Never had the ass so rich, so precious a burden, as when Christ sat upon it.

Diabolus cupit abs te ornari.

Obs. 2. God often gives excellent endowments to wicked persons. Balaam, famous for his prophecies, was infamous for his profaneness: they who are workers of iniquity may prophesy in Christ's name, work miracles, and " cast out devils," Matt. vii. 22; both Judas and Caiaphas prove this point. God is a very bountiful Master, some bones and crumbs he lets fall even to dogs: God's bounty is so full a cup, that though it be filled for his children, some drops run over upon the wicked. And by the endowments of the worst of men God often does good to his church: gifts are *ministrantia*, not *sanctificantia*, beneficial to others, not to the owners; for edifying, not sanctifying; they are (as it were) God's shipping, to convey his treasure of grace upon the shore of his people's souls. God oft gives men excellent parts and abilities to benefit others, as some rich or noble man, who causes the nurse to fare daintily for the good of his child, not out of love to herself. The Israelites were enriched even by gold that was Egyptian: they who preach Christ out of envy, may yet preach Christ to the benefit of hearers. A raven brought Elijah food, and wicked men may sometimes profitably dispense the food of life; the dull whetstone may sharpen the knife; the deaf bell may give a sound to the ears of others; a sweetly-sounding lute, not itself delighted with the music, may yet recreate, yea, almost ravish others. An unskilful serving-man may open the gate for his master, and let it shut to again before he himself can get through. Balaam's mouth uttered an excellent prophecy of Christ and his church for the good of others, his own heart (meanwhile) being untouched, untaught; God put the word of prophecy but into his mouth. And further, God will have a tribute of glory even from his enemies. Balaam, in the midst of his rage and covetousness, praised God; he can extract water out of the rock, and raise children out of stones; it is not so much glory for God to take away wicked men, as to use their evil to his own holy purposes; as the heart of Balaam cursed against his tongue, so his tongue blessed against his heart. God makes wicked men to serve him when they think most to resist him; and that which is not, nay, is contrary to the end of the worker, he makes the end of the work. Lastly, God will render wicked men inexcusable even by their own carriage: they who preach and praise the ways of God to others, can have no apology for not practising them themselves; let none then please himself with parts and gifts of edification without the power of godliness; these are but like Uriah's letters, which cut the throat of him that carried them. A drop of grace is worth a sea of gifts: he that can shed one tear of godly sorrow, presents a more acceptable gift to God than all the silver and gold of Solomon's temple. Light may make a good head, only heat can make a good heart. The devil knows more, and can speak as good a sermon as any man, and yet he is still a devil. Rejoice not therefore in gifts without grace; not (as Christ said) that the devils are subject unto you; but in this, that your names are written in heaven. Labour for that which never was nor can be bestowed upon an enemy; the Spirit may be assisting, where it never is inhabiting; God may speak to an enemy, he only speaks peace to a friend. Grace is the proper and genuine effect of the Spirit, gifts are but (as it were) the outward artificial effects thereof; and as much difference is there in the Spirit's production of these two, as between a man's possessing his child and making a house. Gifts are dead graces, but graces are living gifts. The greatest ministering gifts expel no lust, mortify no inordinate affection, cleanse no heart. When gifts are in their eminency, sin may be in its prevalency. In that man who is the fullest of them, there may be as much room for Satan to dwell as ever. A man may be a great scholar, and yet a great sinner; yea, (unless sanctified by grace,) the greater scholar, the greater sinner and enemy to God; and so the more gifts, the more condemnation: as it is with a sinking ship, the more it is laden with gold, the deeper it sinks; so the more a man is laden with gifts, without graces, the deeper he sinks into hell. Indeed gifts may beautify grace, but grace only sanctifies gifts; as the gold beautified the temple, but the temple sanctified the gold. To conclude, as there may be a gracious heart who never had these gifts, so they who have them are not certain always to enjoy them: the least drop of saving grace shall grow to a river; but the greatest flood of gifts may decay to less than a drop. There is nothing that God bestows upon us but he may repent of the giving thereof, unless it be grace.

Obs. 3. It is both great impiety and ignominy to be a ringleader in sin, like Balaam, to mislead others. The greatest seducer, who has a double portion of wit to teach others error and heresy, obtains no more by this than to become *primogenitus diaboli*, Satan's eldest son. It is honourable to lead others to heaven, to teach men the way to happiness, to be an Abraham, a Joshua, a David, to instruct our families, to bring our house with ourselves to serve the Lord, to teach sinners in the way; but to be a Jeroboam, an Elymas, a Balaam, how disgraceful, how destructive is it! Have not men sins enough of their own, unless they make the sins of others their own also? How deeply shall they be plunged into hell, who are crushed both with their own and other men's sins also! By every one whom thou hast made wicked, shalt thou, without repentance, hereafter be made woeful. Some think that the reason why the rich glutton desired that his brethren might not come into that place of torment with him, was because the coming of those whom he had induced to sin, would have been an addition to his torment. Seldom will princes pardon the ringleaders of a rebellion; and rarely is it seen but that the teachers of others to sin have been eminent either for repentance or ruin. Korah, Dathan, and Abiram, who were ringleaders in the rebellion, smarted accordingly. And think, though God peradventure should at any time give thee repentance, how many fresh bleedings and renewed troubles of soul will, nay, should be stirred up in thee by the recollection of thy former putting those upon sin, who, though sinning with thee, it may be, never repented with thee, and so were either by thy counsel or example sent to hell. It was not the least part of Paul's aggravation of his sin, nor of his trouble, even when he was converted, that he had formerly compelled men to blaspheme. If thou hast led others to hell, God will not, without deep repentance, bring thee to heaven. And upon none lies there so strong an engagement as upon thee, of doing good to others' souls for time to come. Paul, converted, was as earnest to draw men to Christ, as formerly he was industrious to drive them from Christ.

Of a wolf he became a shepherd.

Obs. 4. Love of lust makes men erroneous. Balaam's love to reward made him say any thing. Of this largely before, page 171.

Obs. 5. Desire of gain will carry a man upon any wickedness. It neither fears nor forbears any sinful course for attaining its end. "They that will be rich fall into temptation and a snare, and into many foolish and hurtful lusts," 1 Tim. vi. 9. They meet with many enticements to sin, and they will not fear to embrace any enticement. They are, as Chrysostom expresses it, as a city without walls, on every side beset with besiegers, and unable to resist any assault. "The love of money," saith the apostle, "is the root of all evil, 1 Tim. vi. 10. Take this away, saith Chrysostom, and thou takest away all wickedness, fraud, rapine, war, heresy, theft, lying, and contention. A covetous man, saith he, knows no friend, nay, no God. The love of money gives nourishment to every sin, as the root does to the whole tree. And Aquinas conceives, that though pride, in respect of intention, is the root of sin, as it is the scope and end at which the sinner looks in his sinning; the end of obtaining all temporal good things being that a man thereby may get a kind of singular perfection and excellency to himself; yet that covetousness is the root and beginning of sin, in respect of execution, as it is that which furnishes a man with matter to act and commit sin, and gives opportunity to fulfil all the desires of sin. Agreeable to this is that declaration of Solomon, "He that maketh haste to be rich shall not be innocent," Prov. xxviii. 20; and, "Labour not to be rich," Prov. xxiii. 4. He that desires more than enough, will not know where to stop, will break all bounds. To desire beyond the bounds of sufficiency, is to

Avaritia est plus velle quam sat est. Aug. de lib. Arb. l. 3. c. 17.

Hom. 13. in Act.

Dicitur radix omnium malorum, ad similitudinem radicis arboris, quæ alimentum præstat toti arbori. Aquin. part 2. q. 84. Art. 1. Ex parte intentionis, superbia, quæ est appetitus excellentiæ, est initium omnis peccati; sed ex parte executionis, est primum id quod præbet opportunitatem adimplendi omnia desideria peccati. Art. 2. ubi supra.

seek for more than man may pray for. No sooner does a man step over this hedge, but he is presently in the wide, wild, and boundless champaign of covetousness; and being once there, he has no limits to keep him in. Achan's taking the accursed thing; Ahab's violent and injurious snatching away of Naboth's vineyard; Judas's selling his Master; Gehazi's, Ananias's, and Sapphira's lying; Demetrius's contention for idol Diana; Saul's disobeying God in sparing the cattle; and Jehu's halt in reformation; sufficiently prove this truth. The covetousness of the scribes made them devour widows' houses, Luke xx. 47; for it the priests made the temple a den of thieves, by admitting money-changers, &c. They cared not with what corruption they filled the temple, so that they might fill their own treasuries. Popery has hewn the principal pillars of her superstition out of this rock of covetousness. It is a religion wholly compacted and contrived for gain, not only gotten from the living, by pardons, masses, confessions, offerings, pilgrimages, worshipping of saints, indulgences; by making a money matter of the most crying abominations; of witchcraft; of murder of father, mother, child, wife; of incest, sodomy, bestiality, &c.: but also from the dead, who pay large tributes by means of their purgatory; a toy which they cry not up at all for truth, but merely for traffic. Silver is in the sack's mouth of every popish error. Covetousness swallows down any equivocation, oath, lie, perjury. This sin makes the sabbath *sabbatum Tyri et Bacchi*, a marketing and junketing, a selling and drinking day, Neh. xiii. 16; Amos viii. 5; that stupifies nature, and makes men without natural affection toward dearest relations, desiring their deaths, instead of preserving their lives. The thirst after gain makes them thirsty after blood, as Balaam, Ahab, and Judas were both covetous and bloody. If the hands be not defiled with blood, it is the law, not conscience, that keeps them clean. Many have violated their matrimonial faith and chastity, and the covenant of their God, allured more with the adulterer's purse than his person. And what are all the thefts, false dealings, oppressions, usury, but the issues of this sin? Jer. vi. 13. Judas was covetous, and therefore a thief. Theft and covetousness are joined together, 1 Cor. vi. 10. Whence come false accusing, pleading for an unrighteous cause, making the conscience a very hackney, flattering men in sin, and having their persons in admiration, but from love of advantage? Covetousness damps holiness, as the damp of the earth puts out a candle. A covetous heart, like places where most gold is, is most barren. Christians, think not to be free of any one, if you will embrace this one sin. To overcome it,

Multo æquanimius decem millium animarum ferunt jacturam quam decem solidorum. Nicol. Clemangis de Pontif.

(1.) Overcome the unbelief of thy heart; the root of this root of all evil is distrust of God's promise and providence. Sinful care comes from small faith. "Let your conversation," saith the apostle, "be without covetousness; for he hath said, I will never leave thee, nor forsake thee," Heb. xiii. 5. He who has God for his, in him finds his gold, and all things else. "The Lord is my Shepherd," saith David; "I shall not want," Psal. xxiii. 1. "If thou return to the Almighty," &c., "then shalt thou lay up gold as dust," &c.; "yea, the Almighty shall be thy defence," Job xxii. 23—25; or gold, or choice gold, *aurum lectissimum*, as Junius reads it. He that by faith makes God his gold, shall never through covetousness make gold his god.

(2.) Rectify thy opinion of riches. The earth is the lowest of creatures, and made to be trampled under our feet; and the primitive Christians laid the price of their possessions at the feet of the apostles, Acts iv. 34—37. Gold and silver are fitter to set our feet than our hearts upon. It would be against nature for earth and heaven to join together; what an incongruity is it then for our souls, purer than the heavens, to be glued to the clods! To have much is not to be rich. God is called rich in Scripture, not for money, but for mercy, Rom. x. 12. True riches stand more in doing than in receiving good. Worldly enjoyments have but the name, the show of riches. Nothing but opinion makes them excellent. The common names given to riches are bestowed but abusively. They are not gain; by them and for them men oft lose their souls. Not goods; they neither make us good, nor are they signs of goodness. They are not substance; they are but shadows, nor can they so much as shadow the excellency of those which are true. They are not means conducing to the chief end, happiness; indeed they are means to damn and undo many a soul: they are nothing. Solomon saith, they are not, i. e. in point of duration, satisfaction, efficacy, and usefulness, when we are in distress.

Quodam cordis itinere divitias tuas sequere. Sequatur totum nostrum, quo præcesserit aliquid nostrum. Aug.

(3.) Study the excellency of riches indeed, true riches; of being rich to God, rich in faith, rich in heavenly treasures, 1 Tim. vi. 11; Matt. vi. 19. Look upon him that is invisible; view the sun, and then thy eyes will be so dazzled, that in other things thou wilt behold no beauty. Consider thy crown, and contemn the dunghill. Our Head is in heaven; let Head and heart be together. Let thy soul take a journey every day by faith to thy country, thy treasure, thy Christ.

Obs. 6. The power and goodness of God are seen in turning the violent propensities of the heart from any way of sin toward himself. His power; for what but the power of grace can turn the tide and stream of nature? Human laws can curb us from the act and exercise of sin, but only the law written in the heart can command and change the heart, and destroy in it the love and propensity to sin. We may apply that apostrophe of the psalmist, "What ailed thee, O thou sea, that thou fleddest? thou Jordan, that thou wast driven back? ye mountains, that ye skipped like rams; and ye little hills, like lambs?" The answer is, "Tremble, thou earth, at the presence of the Lord," Psal. cxiv. 5—7. Who but God can stop the sun in its career, and make it go backward? Who but he can stop a Saul in his journey, and make him go back as well in heart as in body, and become more earnest in praying than he was in persecuting? The church complaining that she was "as a bullock unaccustomed to the yoke," aptly adds, "Turn thou me, and I shall be turned," Jer. xxxi. 18. The giving of a clean heart is a work of creation; Create it in me, saith David. Nor is the goodness of God herein less observable than his power. How great is that love which doth us good against our wills, and turned us when we were running greedily to our own destruction! when we regarded the persuasions of men no more than the wild ass (as Job speaks) does the cry of the driver! Job xxxix. 7; when all the means which friends, parents, ministers could use to reclaim us, were lost upon us! nay, we became worse, like the woman in the Gospel by going to the physician. Then what love was it for Christ to teach, to touch the heart, and to turn us, when we had run even to hell-gates! Nor was the smartest dispensation, the most unpleasing stop, the most thorny hedge, any other than an unspeakable mercy, which hindered thee from finding thy way to hell, and running greedily to thine own damnation. How much better was it to be diverted than damned!

Obs. 7. They who strive to hinder sinners in their course, are likely to meet with unkind returns of opposition. Till God turns their hearts, how angry are men with stops, and vexed that bridges are broken down, when they are running greedily, and marching furiously! All the hatred which ministers meet with, is because they would stop sinners in their way to hell, and will not suffer them to be at peace, when they are going on to eternal pains. Never did any meet with so many cruel and bloody contradictions from sinners, as He who in his life, and doctrine, and death most opposed sin. "Am I therefore become your enemy, because I tell you the truth?" saith Paul. He who was sent to turn people from Satan to God, had all the rage of people and Satan turned against him. Hatred, saith Luther, is the genius of the gospel. Saul's javelin followed David's music. It is very likely, that he who is quiet among sinners, suffers them to be quiet in sin. We should pity sinners, though, nay because, they oppose us; if we turn them, they will love and thank us; and whenever they come to be their own friends, they will be ours. However, the Lord will reward even unsuccessful faithfulness; and to be sure we can much better bear hatred from the wicked for doing, than from God for neglecting, our duty.

Obs. 8. The best way by which to try our sincerity, is willingness to be stopped in any way in which our lusts would make us run most greedily. If sinners run greedily and violently after their lusts, then none but saints can rejoice when they are stopped in the prosecution of them, and bless God, as David did for Abigail's counsel, when they are hindered in any sinful career. God promises to his elect a thorny hedge, Hos. ii. 6, if they will be gadding; and they look upon it as a singular mercy, if thereby they are turned back to their first Husband. Only the people of God love that preaching which most opposes their lusts, and that angel or messenger of God most which stands with the drawn sword of the word to hinder them in their unlawful journey. The patient and thankful enduring of stops and strokes when we are sinning, is a very noble, though a bloodless martyrdom; a true note of true grace.

Obs. 9. Men have most cause to suspect their courses are bad when swift; when they run greedily, that they run wickedly; when they run fast, that they run wrong. When we are in any way of God, commonly we do but go, or rather creep; but in the way of sin, after the error of Balaam, we are ready to run, and that greedily too; we are here carried with wind and tide, our own inclinations and Satan's impulsions: the Jews cried out against Christ, but not so much as whispered against Barabbas. It was misguided zeal, when the disciples desired that fire might come down from heaven. Whenever we are furious in any march, we should fear that we are in Balaam's journey; I mean, we ought to suspect the goodness of that undertaking wherein we are most violent, and to doubt that we are sailing to a wrong port, when with a full gale and a strong tide. A smooth, if a false way, should not delight us; nor should a rugged, if a right way, dishearten us. It is no sign thou pleasest God, or speakest the truth, because men do not oppose thee in what thou doest or sayest. We must be wiser than either Christ or his apostles, if we have got the skill to please the most in doing that which is best. The peaceableness of sinners is but impiety not opposed. Rather should I hope that what I do is right, when wicked men most rage and roar against me for doing it. When the devil roars, saith Luther, it is a sign I have struck him right: that is good which Satan hates.

To conclude this. Embrace no opinion because

it is maintained with multitudes and violence. Fire and faggot of old were but weak arguments to prove the truth of transubstantiation. As strong passions destroy a good, so do they not seldom discover a bad cause. Paul resolved to know not the speech, but the power of them who were puffed up, 1 Cor. iv. 19. The worship of Diana is cried up with more rage, than that of the true God is advanced with zeal.

Obs. 10. They who run down the hill little know where they shall stop. These seducers poured forth themselves to the utmost. Who knows in what a sad agreement the very parley and treaty with any lust may end? The more modest motions which it makes at first, may end in excessive, immoderate pouring forth, and a profuse spending of what we have and are, our time, estates, yea, strength of body and soul, and all which is in our power to bestow upon it. Men foolishly may think, that when they have gone thus or thus far, they will go no further, and stop at their pleasure, and that their lusts will grow dry; as he in the fable, who having a mind to go over a river dry-shod, and seeing it run with a fierce stream, hoped that within a little space it would run itself quite dry; but after all his waiting and expecting, the river ran with as full a stream as ever: and so though men think that their lusts will at last grow dry, and that they shall easily step over them unto God, yet the sinful desires of the heart will grow stronger and stronger. They are like to be safest who kill lust in the cradle. He who gives way to it now, may justly be given over to it hereafter. He who will, against God's command, step up to the ancles, justly may, beyond his own expectation, wade till he be over head and ears, and so swallowed up. And hence we may gather the desirable safety of those ways wherein there can be no immoderateness, and which cannot be loved excessively, though never so earnestly.

Expectat dum defluat amnis, at ille,—Labitur et labetur. Horat.

Obs. 11. It is from a Divine hand that wicked men are hindered from greatest outrages. Balaam's running was so greedy, and his march so furious, that he had cursed the people, had not God stopped him. It is an arm of Omnipotence that pulls the wicked back from those courses to which their heart stands. No thanks to them that their worst undertakings are not successful. Whence is it that the world is not overrun with evil, but from this, that men cannot do so ill as they would? When we consider the impure propensities of nature, we ought to be thankful that every man is not a devil to his neighbour. It is God that puts a stop to the sinner, as well as to the sea. Whatever rage of his enemies breaks not forth, is bridled in by God, תחגר Psal. lxxvi. 10. It is not for want of poison in the hearts, but power in the hands, of the wicked, that the people of God are not both cursed and crushed at once. How should we both admire the power and praise the goodness of that God, who hinders the fell and fierce nature of wicked men from venting itself upon the poor unarmed church! who bridles up and sets bounds to that proud sea of sinners' rage, which is so much higher than the poor humble earth, the church in her low estate! and to sing after all our deliverances, in the tune of the thankful psalmist, " If it had not been the Lord who was on our side, when men rose up against us; then they had swallowed us up quick," &c.; then the waters had overwhelmed us, the stream had gone over our soul; then the proud waves had gone over our soul," Psal. cxxiv. 2—5. "The floods lifted up their voice, the floods lifted up their waves; the Lord on high is mightier than the noise of many waters, yea, than the mighty waves of the sea," Psal. xciii. 3, 4.

Obs. 12. God is never more offended with men, than when he gives them most scope and liberty in sin, that they may run greedily. Balaam and these seducers were appointed to destruction, and God lets them run greedily in the way that leads to it. The after permission which God gave Balaam to go to Balak, was worse than the former denial. God suffers some things with an indignation, not because he gives allowance to the act, but because he gives a man over to his sin in the act. It is one thing to like, another thing to suffer. God never liked Balaam's journey, yet he displeasedly gives way to it; as if he had said, Well, since thou art so hot on thy journey, be gone; and thus Balaam took it: else, when God after professed his displeasure for the journey, it had been a ready answer, Thou commandest me; but herein his silence argues his guilt. Balaam's suit and Israel's quails had one fashion of grant, in anger. How much better is it to have gracious denials than angry yieldings! to have our way in sin stopped up with thorns than strewed with roses! God is never more angry than when he is not angry. Never are men in such likelihood of snaring and strangling themselves, as when God gives the greatest length of line. Seldom does God suffer men to be their own carvers, but they cut their own fingers. God, in granting sinful desires, hates, and in denying them, loves, the petitioners. I had rather, said Augustine, have that mercy whereby I am whipped into the right way, than suffered to wander out of it.

Obs. 13. How shameful is it to be sluggish in our race toward the eternal reward! Balaam runs greedily toward a false, we remissly toward a sure, reward: he rose up early, and saddled his ass; the night seemed long to his forwardness; he needed neither clock nor bell to awake him, his desires made him restless. Where is the Christian that deserves not to be condemned even by the lost? Who presses " toward the mark for the prize of the high calling," &c.? Phil. iii. 14. Who offers that holy violence to the kingdom of heaven, knocks, seeks, asks, with half that industry for spiritual blessings, for heaven, for life, which wicked men put forth in labouring for their own destruction? I have heard of a philosopher, who, living near a blacksmith, and hearing him up every morning at his hammer and his anvil before he could get out of his bed to his book, professed himself ashamed, that such an ignoble employment as that smith followed should be more diligently attended than his more serious and excellent studies. Blush, O Christian, when thou seest wicked men sweat in their worldly, and thyself grow cold in heavenly, employments. Surely, were the sweetness, the honourableness, the vastness, the profitableness of God's service seriously considered, holy duties would find hotter affections in us. What a shame is it, that worldlings should be more laboriously busied about rattles and trifles, than we about the kingdom of heaven and eternity!

This for the amplification of the sin and woe of these seducers from the second example, viz. of Balaam. Now follows,

3. The example of Core; "And perished in the gainsaying of Core."

Two things here are principally to be explained.
1. Whom they followed, Core.
2. Wherein they followed him. (1.) In his gainsaying. (2.) In perishing therein.

1. Whom they followed, Core. Here it may be inquired who this Core was.

Besides his sin and punishment, the Scripture mentions his pedigree, his employment, and his posterity.

(1.) His pedigree: he was of the tribe of Levi;

his father's name was Izhar, the brother of Amram, who was father to Moses, Exod. vi. 18; 1 Chron. vi. 2; so that Korah and Moses, whom he opposed, were brothers' children, or cousins-german: the nearness of this relation could not hinder him from attempting the downfal of those who better deserved to keep than he to get the government.

(2.) His employment (with that of the rest of the Levites) is mentioned, Numb. xvi. 9, to be honourable, they being separated by God from the congregation of Israel to be brought "near to himself to do the service of the tabernacle, and to stand before the congregation to minister unto them." The Levites were brought nearer to God than the other tribes, though not so near as the priests. Aaron's sons, the priests, served in the sanctuary in praying for the people, and offering incense and sacrifice, Numb. xviii. 3; 1 Chron. vi. 49; but the rest of the tribe of Levi were not to come nigh the altar upon pain of death, Numb. iii. 10, but served in offices inferior to theirs, Numb. i. 49, 50. Their work was, [1.] To attend the service of the sanctuary, according to the command of the priests, Numb. iii. 6—8; iv. 2, 3; vii. 5; xviii. 6. When the tabernacle was movable, they were appointed to take it down, carry, set it up, and to keep all the instruments thereof, and also with the priests to carry the ark of the Lord; "to wait on the sons of Aaron for the service of the house of the Lord, in the courts, and in the chambers, and in the purifying of all holy things," 1 Chron. xxiii. 28, 29; Deut. x. 8; 1 Chron. vi. 48; ix. 28, 29; 2 Chron. xxvi. 18. Their work was to watch about the tabernacle, and afterward the temple, to defend it, 1 Chron. ix. 27. They also were to have the oversight of the shew-bread, meat-offerings, unleavened cakes, and of all manner of measure and size; they had to see that all measures, both of dry and moist things, which were used in God's service, might have their just proportion, and that there might be a due length and breadth of all things measured by the meteyard. All manner of just measures for the things belonging to the house of God were to be tried by the measures and sizes which the Levites kept, and these were called the "measures of the sanctuary;" whether the Levites had the ordering of civil measures and sizes or no is uncertain. [2.] The work of the Levites was to sing praises to God; and they praised him both by singing holy songs and hymns, and also by musical instruments, 1 Chron. xvi. 4; xxiii. 30; 2 Chron. viii. 14; xx. 19; xxx. 21; Neh. ix. 5. [3.] The Levites were to teach the people the law, according to the good word of the Lord, 2 Chron. xxx. 22; xxxv. 3; and this employment was common both to the priests and Levites, Deut. xxxi. 9—13; 2 Chron. xvii. 7—9; Ezra vii. 10, 11; Neh. viii. 7, 8; ix. 4, 5. [4.] To the Levites it also belonged, with the priests, to take cognizance, and to judge in causes about holy things, 2 Chron. xix. 8, 10, 11. So that the priests and Levites were the two ecclesiastical orders in Israel employed about holy things, the Levites making the lesser, the priests the greater and higher order, and yet both called "brethren," Numb. xviii. 6. And in process of time, by the appointment of God, when the worship of God was to be stationary and fixed in one place, David divided the Levites into sundry orders and ranks, according to their families, for discharging their several functions and ministries, having their several courses of waiting and charges allotted to them. See 1 Chron. xxviii. 13; xxii.; xxv., &c.; 2 Chron. viii. 14; xxxv. 4, 5, 10. The reason of separating the Levites to the worship of God is plainly mentioned in Scripture: "I have" (saith God) "taken the Levites from among the children of Israel instead of all the first-born, because the first-born are mine; for on the day that I smote all the first-born of the land of Egypt, I hallowed unto me all the first-born in Israel," Numb. iii. 12, 13; viii. 16; Exod. xii. 23. The first-born then were God's by a particular right of redemption as well as creation, and therefore were in an especial manner to serve him. In other creatures the first-born were to be sacrificed to him, if they were clean beasts; and if they were not, to be ransomed at a price for the maintenance of the tabernacle. Now, instead of taking the first-born of mankind to his service, he appointed that the Levites should be particularly set apart for it; and he chose to be served by one tribe, rather than by a number of first-born taken out of many tribes, as learned interpreters conceive, to prevent confusion, discord, and division in holy services; and by the tribe of Levi rather than any other, for their zeal of his glory in revenging the indignity done unto him in worshipping the golden calf, Exod. xxxii. 26, 28. To conclude; as Israel was separated from all other people to be the Lord's peculiar, Lev. xx. 26, so were the Levites separated from the sons of Israel to be the Lord's, Numb. viii. 14. And the employment of the Levites, of which this Korah was a chief, and among whom he was famous, was, though inferior to the priests, who were nearer to God in their attendances, very honourable. And therefore from the high honour thereof doth Moses argue against the ambition of this rebellious Korah, whose desire it was to invade the priestly dignity also: "Seemeth it," saith he, "a small thing unto you, that the God of Israel hath separated you from the congregation of Israel, to bring you near to himself to do the work of the tabernacle?" Numb. xvi. 9. If it be an honour for the greatest subject to have the meanest employment about the body of an earthly prince, how much greater is the advancement of the highest sons of men to have the lowest degree of peculiar service to God! and truly David, though a king, went not an inch below his state in not disdaining the office of a door-keeper in the house of the Lord, and in putting on a linen ephod.

(3.) The posterity of this rebel Korah, we find in Scripture, were spared and exempted from this destruction of their father, and afterward they were employed by God in his service, which some of them holily discharged.

[1.] That they were spared is expressed Numb. xxvi. 11, "The children of Korah died not;" neither did the fire from heaven, nor the opening of the earth, hurt them. Whether they were in their father's rebellion, and were spared by the prerogative of free mercy, or for God's care of his ministry; or whether they consented not to the sin of their father, as is most likely; or whether they repented upon the warning given by Moses, Numb. xvi. 5; I determine not, the Scripture being silent. Nor will it be needful here to relate that fabulous invention of the Jews, by whose relation God wrought as great a miracle in saving Korah's children, as he did in destroying Korah himself; for they write, That when the earth opened and swallowed up the father, the children were taken up in the air, and there remained hanging till the earth closed up again. What way they were saved it matters not, spared they were; and their names were Assir, Elkanah, and Abiasaph. God is so just, as to be feared in the midst of his smiles; and so merciful, as to be beloved in the midst of his frowns; his goodness makes him remember mercy in the midst of judgment, although our sins sometimes stir him up to remember judgment in the midst of mercy.

[2.] It is evident that afterward they were employed by God as Levites in several services. They were "keepers of the gates of the tabernacle," 1 Chron. ix. 19. Their fathers had been over the host of the Lord; namely, those Levites who encamped about the tabernacle, the host of Israel compassing it like the king's tent, Numb. i. 50; ii. 17. Some of this family " were for the outward business over Israel," 1 Chron. xxvi. 29; namely, such things as in the country were to be done, gathered, and prepared for the house of God, and for the service thereof, as all manner of provision, fuel, oil, wine, tithes, firstfruits, &c. Some were, possibly, teachers in the law, and judges in causes ecclesiastical and civil; for the Israelites being governed by the judicial laws, and the Levites being best exercised therein, they were sent abroad among the several tribes to be judges, Deut. xvi. 18; 2 Chron. xix. 8; xvii. 9. But the eminent employment to which those of Korah's family were designed, was singing in the house of the Lord; they were "set over the service of the song in the house of the Lord," 1 Chron. vi. 31; and "they ministered with singing," ver. 32. And Heman, a Korahite, who is said to be "the king's seer, and to lift up the horn," 1 Chron. xxv. 5; that is, say some, a musical instrument; was the chief musician, 1 Chron. vi. 39, 44, and had his fourteen sons under him, " for song in the house of the Lord, with cymbals, psalteries, and harps," 1 Chron. xxv. 6, 7; and they are said, with their fellows, to be "instructed in the songs of the Lord," and to be cunning. Many psalms (as xlii. xliv. xlv. xlvi.) have in their title, "For the sons of Korah;" and some conceive that some of the psalms were penned by them, particularly that the 46th was their thanksgiving for their escape at their father's destruction, the title saying, of, or "for the sons of Korah;" to which mention of the sons of Korah the Chaldee paraphrast adds, By their hand was it spoken in prophecy at the time their father was hidden from them, but they were delivered, and uttered this song; a conjecture which was occasioned by those words in the second verse, "We will not fear, though the earth be removed," &c. I rather conceive that the psalm might be indited by David, and that it was appointed for them to set a tune to it. It is generally held that the 88th Psalm was penned by the forementioned Heman; if so, it speaks him a very humble, godly son (though) of a wicked, rebellious forefather, 1 Chron. vi. 33, 37. How free God is in dispersing his grace, and how gracious he was in preserving Korah's posterity, is much more manifested, in that Samuel, a man so eminent for being a holy man, God's favourite, and Israel's judge and happy preserver, was one of Korah's offspring, 1 Chron. vi. 27, 28.

Thus, by way of explication, we have seen whom the seducers followed, Core.

2. Wherein did they follow him; Jude saith, " in gainsaying," and in perishing therein.

(1.) In this gainsaying, [1.] I shall show wherein it stood. [2.] How great the sin of it was.

[1.] For the first. The word in the Greek, ἀντιλογίᾳ, signifies contradiction, or gainsaying, either verbal or real.

Verbal: "Without all contradiction," χωρὶς πάσης ἀντιλογίας, " the less is blessed," &c., Heb. vii. 7; and the Sadducees are called οἱ ἀντιλέγοντες, those who deny that there is any resurrection.

In some places the word principally imports real contradiction or opposition, though not excluding the verbal. Thus, Heb. xii. 3, where it is said of Christ that he endured the " contradiction," ἀντιλογίαν, " of sinners;" and I understand it in this place to be a contradiction, as by words, so (chiefly) by works. More particularly, this contention, opposition, or contradiction which Korah expressed, and is at large described, Numb. xvi., was that insurrection and sedition which he enterprised against Moses, whom he gainsayed, and against whom he stood up, to throw Aaron out of, and to gain to himself, he being of the tribe of Levi, the office of priesthood, wherein Aaron was placed by Divine appointment. This real was accompanied and coloured over with that verbal gainsaying, wherein Korah charged Moses and Aaron with usurpation and ambition, in taking too much upon them. That this gaining of the priesthood was the design is plain from the words of Moses, ver. 9—11, where he thus expostulates; " Seemeth it a small thing to you, that the God of Israel hath separated you from the congregation of Israel, to bring you near to himself?" &c. "And seek you the priesthood also? for which cause both thou and all thy company are gathered together against the Lord: and what is Aaron, that ye murmur against him?" For accomplishing this rebellious design, he not only joins to himself a great company of the chief Levites to throw Aaron out of his office, but incites Dathan and Abiram, who were of the tribe of Reuben, in regard of their primogeniture before Moses, they being of the eldest tribe, to depose Moses from the civil government, and to assume it themselves at the same time. In this work he also joined with them, well knowing, that if Moses continued to enjoy the government of the commonwealth, he should never be able to carry on his design of getting to himself the priesthood.

As for these seducers, against whom our apostle here writes, I dare not peremptorily assert that the apostle only intends that they imitated Korah in disturbing the order and rule of the church; I doubt not but Korah opposed both civil and ecclesiastical order. It is plainly stated, Numb. xvi. 3, that he, with Dathan and Abiram, and their followers, gathered themselves together both against Moses and against Aaron. And supposing that Korah only had opposed Aaron, by labouring to invade the priesthood; yet, as Gerard well notes, this example of Korah in opposing church order might well be accommodated to Jude's purpose, were his purpose only to show that these seducers were enemies to civil order and superiority; for although the sin of Korah and these seducers had different objects, yet they both agree in resisting superiors. But it is most probable that Jude intends that these seducers, by comparing them to Korah, opposed all order and superiority in church and state, not only despising and speaking evil of civil dignities and dominions, as we have formerly showed, but opposing and disturbing the state of all ecclesiastical order. None were such bitter enemies to the faithful apostles and ministers of Christ, who were the shepherds, guides, governors, and overseers, by Christ set over the flock and family of his church. None laboured so much to pour contempt upon them and their doctrine, prating against them (as John speaks of Diotrephes) " with malicious words," 3 John 10, that they, with Korah, might have the pre-eminence, and be looked upon, as Simon Magus their master, as the only great ones; commending themselves, boasting of things without their measure, glorying after the flesh, drawing disciples after them, Acts viii. 10; 2 Cor. x. 13; xi. 18; and labouring, by winding into the church, to work the faithful ministers out. In a word, as Œcumenius speaks, though they were never so unfit, though uncalled, yet their main study was to snatch all authority of teaching to themselves. And (as Tertullian speaks

Potest hoc exemplum accommodari ad propositum apostoli, etiamsi objecta peccatorum sint diversa. Gerh. in 2 Pet. p. 257.

Cum Core pereunt, propterea quod sicut ille, docendi auctoritatem sibi prærīpuerunt. Œcum. Hoc est negotium hæreticorum, non ethnicos conver tendi, sed nostra evertendi: nostra suffodiunt, ut sua ædificent. Tert.

of heretics) their work was not to convert heathens, but to overturn the labours of faithful teachers, and to pull down them to build up themselves. Augustine defines a heretic to be one who for any worldly benefit, especially for glory and pre-eminence, either frames or follows new opinions.

de Præscrip. Hæreticus est qui alicujus temporalis commodi, et maxime gloriæ principatusque gratia falsas et novas opiniones gignit vel sequitur. Cont. Ep. Parm. c. 3.

2. The great sinfulness of this "gainsaying" appears sundry ways. It was made up of,

(1.) Contempt of God's ordination. Moses and Aaron were both placed in their governments by God's appointment, both immediate and express, Prov. viii. 15; Rom. xiii. 1. God was more opposed than these his servants; and therefore truly Moses tells them, that this their gathering together was "against the Lord," Numb. xvi. 11. Though Dathan and Abiram, Reubenites, had the right of natural primogeniture, yet they vainly challenge pre-eminence where God hath subjected them. If all civil honour flow from the king, how much more from the God of kings! His hand exalts the poor, and casts down the mighty from their throne. How insufferable a presumption is it for dust and ashes to attempt to mend his work, and to subject his ordination to their own humour!

(2.) Regardlessness of the public. They cared not what ruin and woe they brought upon the whole company of Israel, by the loss of their lawful, godly, and able governors, so that they might accomplish their own private designs. They were desirous to raise themselves upon the destruction of thousands; and their endeavour was to remove away Israel's shelters and shields, their saviours, shepherds, and pillars; yea, and at one blow to behead six hundred thousand men; to turn God's garden into a wilderness, God's well-governed family into a den of thieves; and to hasten the death of their political parents, though thousands of children would have celebrated their funerals with tears.

(3.) Hypocrisy and falsehood. The rebels pretend that all the congregation was holy, and that Moses and Aaron lifted up themselves, Numb. xvi. 3. Every word was a falsehood. Israel was as holy as Moses and Aaron were ambitious: God lifted them up over Israel, and they dejected themselves; and what holiness was there in so much infidelity, idolatry, mutiny? What could make them unclean, if this were holiness? The Israelites had scarce wiped their mouth since their last obstinacy, but these flatterers tax their governors, and flatter the people; and yet all this not out of love to these fond and flattered people, of whom they intended to make no other use but to be stirrups to advance themselves into the saddle of government. They pretend that all the people, in respect of their holiness, might make as near approaches to God as their governors; but their design was hereby to appropriate all administrations into their own hands, and to wipe the poor people of that which now they laboured to take away from their governors, namely, all power.

(4.) Discontentedness with their present condition. While they looked upon the few rulers that were above them, they never thought of the many thousands of people who were below them. They so discontentedly looked upon the difference between the Levites and the priests, that they considered not the difference between the Levites and the people; and their thankfulness that they were above so many, was drowned in discontentment that one or two were above them.

(5.) Envy at and repining against the due advancement of their faithful governors. "They envied Moses also in the camp, and Aaron the saint of the Lord," Psal. cvi. 16. Had Moses and Aaron been but fellows with the rebels, none had been better beloved; but now they are advanced, the malice of these rebels is not inferior to the honour of their governors. Their fault was, that God had set them up, not that they had ever opposed God, or hurt Israel; so that the trouble of the rebels was not the badness of their governors, but the goodness of God. The cursed humour of plain downright envy, which is not troubled that things in the world go ill, either in point of sin or sorrow, but that they go so well, or no worse.

(6.) Pride and ambition. They aspired to a dignity in which God had placed others, and for and to which they were neither called nor fitted. Their ambition to be above the people, made them desirous to be likewise above God who had put others into that dignity: they who were not fit for the oar desire to sit at the stern. Though the thing they desired was good, yet their desiring it out of God's way was wicked. If they who are fittest to govern should not accept of rule unless they are drawn, then they who are unfit should not run to take it. Should ambitious Korahs get power by running, they would not be honoured by their great place, but their place dishonoured by them.

Si ille qui virtutibus pollet, invitus debet accedere, quid de illo qui vitiis sordet! Perald.

(7.) Infection and contagion dispersed among others. Korah draws in two hundred and fifty into the conspiracy, "famous in the congregation, and men of renown." The plague-sore in this one Korah infects a great part of Israel. The contagion was worse than the act; his wickedness was diffusive. He would neither be alone in woe nor wickedness. His abode was so near to the Reubenites, that he soon infuses his poison into Dathan and Abiram: he errs not without many followers. Surely his sin and woe had been sufficient, though he had not drawn in partakers in both; but it is the constant guise of sinners, both to forbear labouring after happiness themselves, and to hinder others; to run into ruin themselves, and to carry others with them; though they shall dearly find hereafter that it is not in this case, the more the merrier, every sinner being but a bundle of fuel to make the fire of wrath burn the hotter against any who led him into sin.

(8.) Great ingratitude to God and their governors for all that care and cost which they laid out upon them. How unkind a requital was this to God and his servants for the many miraculous protections, directions, provisions, which primarily from him, and secondarily from them, they had received! What did Moses gain by the troublesome government, but danger and despite? Who but Moses would not have wished himself rather with the sheep of Jethro, than these wolves of Israel? How full of care was Moses that these rebels might be secure! Magistracy is like an upper garment, which a man puts on when he rides in wet and dirty weather; though magistracy be uppermost, and all the dirt and ashes fall upon it, the under garments are meanwhile kept dry and clean.

(9.) Boldness and obstinacy in sin. What a presumptuous wickedness was it for Korah and his accomplices to take the censers and to offer incense! Had they had the least drop of God's fear, their hands would have shaken, and the censers would have fallen out of them. Though Korah had lately seen the judgment of God upon Nadab and Abihu, yet his contumacy would not be checked. The mentioning of the holy censers and incense should have made him dread his own destruction, by intermeddling be-

Si qua fuisset residua in illis gutta timoris Dei, repente e manibus excidissent acerræ. Se vulgi favore munire tentat contra Deum; ac si, objecto fumo, vellet solis lucem extinguere. Si ambitiosis ap-

yond his calling; but, as Calvin well notes, by the favour of the people he banished the fear of God, and so opposes God, as if he would have put out the sun with smoke.

plaudit mundus, inebriantur exitii ali fiducia, ut in nubes ipsas conspuant. Calvin. in Numb. xvi.

2. The second thing wherein they followed Korah, was in perdition; noted in these words, and perish, or "perished," ἀπώλοντο, "in the gainsaying," &c. The time both past and present is often put for the future; to import and signify the great and undoubted certainty that a thing shall come to pass; that it is as sure to be as if it were already accomplished. And thus the apostle is to be understood, in saying that these seducers perish, or perished, in Korah's gainsaying. The word ἀπώλοντο denotes not only a bare dying, as in its best signification, but a dying by some miserable means; as by hunger, Luke xv. 17. Sometimes a destruction by hell, 2 Thess. i. 9; in which respect Judas is called the son of perdition and destruction, John xvii. 12; and the devil is called a destroyer, Rev. ix. 11. And Paul calleth the man of sin "the son of perdition," 2 Thess. ii. 3; he being such both actively and passively. The word, saith Gerard in Harmon. is used to denote temporal, spiritual, and eternal destruction. The simple word ὄλλυμι signifies to destroy; but the compound, and such is this here used by Jude, is not without an additional emphasis.

Concerning the destruction of Korah we read at large in Numb. xvi. It is much controverted by learned men what kind of destruction this of Korah was. Some think that he was swallowed up in the earth with Dathan and Abiram, thus referring the words of Moses, "If the Lord make a new thing, and the earth open her mouth, and swallow them up," &c., ver. 30, to all three, Korah, Dathan, and Abiram; and it being said, Numb. xxvi. 10, "the earth opened her mouth, and swallowed them up" (meaning Dathan and Abiram) "together with Korah, when that company died, what time the fire devoured two hundred and fifty men." And that Korah also was swallowed up, Ambrose, Richelius, Lorinus, with some others, conceive. Others think that Korah was not swallowed up with the rest; that though all his substance and tents were destroyed by that punishment, and also all that appertained to him, his children only excepted, yet they think that Korah himself was consumed with fire from heaven with "the two hundred and fifty men that offered incense," ver. 35. Of this opinion are Cajetan, Oleaster, Haimo, Perkins, Tremelius, Diodate. And their reasons are,

(1.) Because it seems by several passages in the history that Moses spake concerning Dathan and Abiram only, and those which belonged to them, when he said, "Hereby ye shall know that the Lord hath sent me," &c., "if the earth open her mouth, and swallow them up," &c., Numb. xvi. 25, 27—30.

(2.) When Dathan and Abiram are expressly said to be swallowed up, mention is made, ver. 32, only, in relation to Korah, that "all the men that appertained to Korah, and all their goods," were swallowed up; Korah himself being not named, as are the other two.

(3.) They say that when in other places this destruction is rehearsed, as Deut. xi. 6; Psal. cvi. 17, there is mention made only of the swallowing up of Dathan and Abiram, with theirs, not of Korah at all.

(4.) Some are much confirmed in this apprehension, from that command of God, that the brazen censers of those who were burnt should be made broad plates to cover the altar, for "a memorial that no stranger come near to offer incense before the Lord, that he be not as Korah and his company," Numb. xvi. 38—40. From which command they conceive that Korah was, with the rest, burnt with fire: 1. Because he joined with the rest of the company in offering incense, as is plain, because others were to take warning by his punishment not to offer incense; and ver. 6, Moses saith, "Take you censers, both Korah, and all his company;" and ver. 17, "Take every man his censer; thou also, and Aaron," &c. Now, say they, it is probable that Korah sinning by fire was also punished by fire; and that joining in the same sin, and being present when the fire devoured the rest, which was immediately after their offering incense, he was also joined in the same punishment. 2. When Moses speaks here of the offenders, he joins them together in the punishment; he calls them Korah and his company, in these words, "That he be not as Korah and his company." 3. The censers which were to be plates for the altar are called, The censers of those which were burnt: now Korah's censer was among those which were plates for the altar; because the reason why they were to be plates for the altar was their offering them before the Lord, and their being hallowed, ver. 38, which agree to Korah's censer as well as to the censer of any other. 4. God's command to make plates of the censers of those who were burnt being followed with this reason, that others "be not as Korah and his company," seems to import that others by looking upon the censers of those who were burnt should take heed of being as Korah and his company, namely, burnt as they were. And whereas it is said that "the earth opened her mouth, and swallowed them up, together with Korah," &c., Numb. xxvi. 10; some understand that place not of Korah's person, but of his substance, goods, and retinue; and therefore Tremelius reads it, *absorpsit eos, et quæ erant Korachi;* the earth swallowed them up, and those things which appertained to Korah, as we find, Numb. xvi. 32. Others conceive that Korah is joined here with the other who were swallowed up, because he was a confederate in the same wickedness, and was punished by a miraculous death at the same time. But, to leave the further discussion hereof, sure we are that Korah was also destroyed. Jude here tells us that he perished. And it has been observed, that most, if not all, those whom the Scripture mentions as opposers of lawful authority, have been punished by violent death, God not vouchsafing them so much as a reprieve to a death-bed; several instances have I set down. God makes them marks of vengeance who remove the ancient land-marks, set for order and propriety in a nation; and, as Chrysostom notes, they who durst open their mouths against Moses and Aaron, making their throats an open sepulchre to bury their dignities, were justly punished when the earth opened her mouth and swallowed up such rebels.

Obs. 1. The great misery and disgrace to be a ringleader in sin. Korah is here only mentioned by Jude; he was the great wheel of the rebellion. It is thought that he exasperated Dathan and Abiram, by the pretence of their primogeniture before Moses. It is too much to follow in wickedness; but to lead, it is inexcusable, insufferable. The rebels that opposed Moses and Aaron are called Korah's company, Numb. xxvii. 3, and the rebellion itself is called the "matter of Korah," Numb. xvi. 49. He who was higher than the rest in sin, is principally branded in Scripture story with perpetual infamy.

Obs. 2. Bad parents may have good children. Jeroboam, Amon, Ahaz, and here Korah, are pregnant proofs hereof. God is free in his gifts of grace. He disperses them where and to whom he pleases. They who have nothing in themselves or parents to commend them to God are received by him, to show that the foundation of all God's love is in his own bosom, and that the privileges of nature commend us not to him. God also will hereby show the excellency of grace's original; that it is not by generation, but regeneration; not native, but donative; not by the first, but second birth. The bad parents of a godly child proclaim that their child has a heavenly Father, and that good which they never bestowed upon it; as the wicked child of godly parents proclaims that they who contributed a natural, could not afford a spiritual being. Yea, further, hereby God will manifest the power of his grace, which in a sort gathers grapes of thorns, and figs of thistles, and can bring pure water through a filthy and polluted channel; and that the power and poison of natural and sinful example cannot hinder the irresistible strength of his own Spirit. How wisely doth God hereby beat Satan, and batter his kingdom with his own weapons, and strike him through with arrows taken out of his own quiver! How should the consideration hereof engage the godly children of Godless parents, (1.) To love, admire, and serve that God who has transplanted them out of Satan's nursery into his own orchard; who made white paper of dunghill rags! If Judas said, Lord, why wilt thou manifest thyself to us, and not to the world? well may a godly child say, Lord, why wilt thou manifest thyself to me, and not to my father and mother? (2.) To be humble in considering the rock out of which they were hewn, and the fountain from which they flowed, and the poorness and impurity of their beginning, even when they are in the midst of their highest proceedings in holiness. To pity likewise, and to labour to do good by a spiritual στοργὴ, or natural affection spiritualized, to the souls of their poor unregenerate parents, that they may study to requite them for being the causes of their natural being, by procuring their parents' spiritual birth; and truly, no way but this can that maxim be confuted, The child can never recompense the parent. _{Deo et parenti non redditur æquivalens.}

Obs. 3. Great is our proneness to follow corrupt example. Hundreds here run after one rebel.

Obs. 4. Corrupt greatness is very influential on inferiors. Let but an eminent Korah go before, and the rest will follow. Great men seldom sin alone; witness Absalom, Jeroboam, Simon Magus.

Obs. 5. Ambition knows no bounds. A high condition seems but low to a high spirit. Korah was a Levite, and his privilege and dignity thereby was not small: "Seemeth it a small thing to you," saith Moses, "that the God of Israel hath separated you from the congregation of Israel, to bring you near to himself?" yet his ambition made it seem contemptible, because he had not the priesthood also. Absalom, though a king's son, and his father's beloved son, and newly taken into favour, yet because he had not the kingdom, could not be content. Haman, though the greatest favourite of the greatest monarch in the world, yet because he had not the obeisance of poor Mordecai, accounted all his preferments worth nothing. The greatest honours only widen and enlarge the ambitious man's desires; they entice, but not content a man. The subjects whom kings have advanced to highest dignities, have ever been forwardest to oppose and depose those who have exalted them, and all because they have thought that they could never be high enough; witness the conspiracy of the nobles exalted to highest English honours in the reign of William the First, and that famous example of the great Stanley, in the reign of Henry the Seventh, who, though the greatest peer in the realm, and laden with many favours and great offices, yet was a man of that exorbitant and unbounded ambition, that nothing would please him but a preferment which used to go to the king's eldest son. _{Vid. Daniels's History of William I. p. 40. and Sir Francis Bacon's History of Henry VII.} No rewards can clear accounts with them that overvalue their merits. Though Pelion be laid upon Ossa, and one mountain of greatness upon another, yet will an ambitious mind look upon them all as too low. Kingdom added to kingdom, and, could it be so, world to world, would but be a drop to the stomach of the elephant, ambition. The best way to satisfy the thirst of one in a fever is, instead of giving him drink, to cure his distemper. Let us not think to satisfy our lusts by making provision for them; it is Christian wisdom rather to study to kill than content inordinate desire; and more to bring our hearts to our condition, than our condition to our hearts. Let us look upon that station of life wherein God has set us as the best for us. A garment which fits us is better for us, though it be plain, than one which is gaudy and three or four handfuls too big. God best knows how to order our estates. Should we be our own carvers, we should often cut our fingers. Let us also compare our receipts with our deserts; and though the former seem small when they stand by themselves, yet if we set them by the latter, they will appear of a large size, and a tall stature.

Obs. 6. A mere man is firm and steady in no relation. Natural relations, unless backed by grace, are very slippery and unstable foundations of friendship. Korah, a wicked man, though a near kinsman to Moses, proves his greatest adversary. _{Naturæ bonitas nisi pietate confirmetur, facile illabescit. Cart. Harm.} Abel's brother, Joseph's brethren, David's son, could not be kept from murder and treachery by the bond of nature. A sinner will as easily break the bonds of nature, as Samson did his cords, till his locks (his lusts) be cut off. It is not the alliance, but the renovation of nature, that can establish friendship. No natural man accounts his own brother that lay in the same womb with him so near to him as the lust that lodges in his heart. He provides friends most wisely for himself, who either finds or makes them friends to God. An enemy to God will not long be a friend to thee. Natural love oft ends in an unnatural hatred. A bad man will not conscientiously be a good husband, son, brother. Grace doth not slay, but sanctify; not annihilate, but elevate nature; turns water into wine, and spiritualizes carnal affection. How just with God is it, that he whom thou dost not desire to make God's friend shall prove thy foe! that thy child which is most indulged by thee in sin, should afterward prove the greatest grief to thy heart! God suffering, to thy sorrow, him to rebel against thee, whom thou hast suffered and seen without sorrow to rebel against God.

Obs. 7. Innocence is no shelter from opposition. The goodness of no person or cause can exempt either from hatred. No man meeker than Moses, none better beloved than Aaron, none more beneficial to Israel than both; no cause more righteous than holding a government, to which they were appointed by God himself; yet neither the persons nor their cause could be free from the conspiracies and contests of sinners. Jesus Christ himself endured their contradictions and gainsayings, Heb. xii. 3. It is no sign of a good man to have few opposers, nor of a good cause to have many abettors. He who is not opposed by the stream goes with it. The world will hate where God loves. So far is holiness from exempting the godly from the ill-will of sinners, that it draws it forth. Let other qualifications of learning, amiableness, birth, never so much abound, yet grace mars the taste of all these in a carnal palate.

Antipathies can never be smothered or reconciled. The meekest Moses, will he be a Moses, shall be gainsayed, notwithstanding his meekness. The wicked rise up against the faithful, not for doing any evil against, but for not doing evil with them. If in our keeping close to God we meet with unkindness from the wicked, let us not wonder; if with love, let us be thankful; but yet withal suspicious of ourselves that we do, or at least cautious that we do not, sinfully correspond with them.

Obs. 8. Instruments of public good often meet with unkind requitals. Moses and Aaron, Israel's deliverers and defenders, were gainsayed by an unthankful people. Israel owed to these faithful governors, under God, their provision, peace, and protection; but for this the tribute which they paid was conspiracy and rebellion. Nothing is so easily forgotten as the benefits we enjoy by governors. The lightest injuries are easily remembered, and are like feathers that swim on the top of the water: weighty favours, like a piece of lead, sink to the bottom, and are forgotten. Gideon had been a famous deliverer of Israel; but the benefits which that unthankful people enjoyed by him were so neglected, that they slew his sons, Judg. ix. 5. Though Jehoiada was the renowned restorer of Israel's government and peace, yet was his son destroyed by them, who, next to God, owed all that was dear to them to his faithfulness and wisdom, 2 Chron. xxiv. 21, 22. It is a kingly honour, to meet with unthankful returns from those to whom we do much good. The mother's breast gives milk to the froward infant that strikes it. God would have all, especially public officers, in all the good they do, eye his glory and command, and not the applause of men. No opposition must discourage us in the faithful discharging of our places, nor chase us from the station wherein God has set us.

Obs. 9. Excellency and superiority are the marks of envy. Though Moses and Aaron cannot be opposed for their sin, yet they may be envied for their power. As equals are envied because they are such, and inferiors lest they should be our equals; so principally superiors, because we are not equal to them. Joseph was envied because he was higher than his brethren in his father's favour, and dreamed that he should be higher than they in his worldly condition; the Israelites likewise were envied because they increased more than Egyptians; David by Saul, because the women ascribed more thousands to him than to Saul; Moses by Miriam and Aaron, because advanced by God above them; and here Moses and Aaron by Korah and his accomplices, because of their superiority. The object of hatred is oft the sin of others; but of envy, always the excellency of others, either real or seeming, of body, mind, estate, or fame, the cause being pride, or an inordinate self-love; the envious ever deeming his own excellency to be diminished and obscured by another's happiness. Thus the elder brother, Luke xv., deemed himself wronged by the love which his father showed to the younger; and by reason of envy against his brother, he forgets his father's bounty to himself; and he who had received all his father's inheritance, denies that ever his father had given him a kid. Of all sinners, the envious is most his own scourge and torment. He had rather suffer misery than see others in prosperity; as some have noted of the Philistines, who could hardly be brought by the smart of their own distresses to send the ark back to Israel. It is said, that God turned the heart of the Egyptians to hate his people, Psal. cv. 25; but, as Augustine well notes, not by making the heart of the Egyptians evil, but the estate of the Israelites prosperous. What a moth to the soul, saith Cyprian, is envy, to turn another's good into our own hurt, to make another's glory our own punishment! The meditation of this cursed distemper of the envious may provoke us to contentment in a low condition. They are high towers upon which the lightnings of envy fall. It is oftentimes a mercy to be in misery. How many righteous and well-deserving persons have been made faulty and guilty only for their being wealthy and honourable! How abundantly does the sweet safety of a retired life recompense for all that obscurity which seems to debase it! How oft have I known those who have lived in envied honour, to envy those who have lived in safe obscurity!

Paternæ largitatis memor non est, qui est fraternæ immemor charitatis : hœdum sibi datum negat, qui tantam substantiam accepit. Chrysol. Ser. 4.

Non illos malos faciendo, sed

istis bona quibus mali facillime possunt invidere largiendo, incitasse dicitur ad odium. August. in loc. Cypr. de Zel. et Liv.

Obs. 10. Heretical seducers are commonly turbulent and seditious. They here followed Korah in his opposing authority. They who deny the only Lord God, as these seducers did, will make nothing of despising dominion. They who oppose God's dominion will never regard man's. Impious men will not be obedient subjects. The order of obedience prescribed by the apostle, is first to "fear God," and then to "honour the king," 1 Pet. ii. 17. "My son," saith Solomon, "fear thou the Lord and the king," Prov. xxiv. 21. The Romish offspring of antichrist, who throw off and deprave the law of God, will not submit to civil authority. They openly teach that the clergy are exempted from the power of the magistrate. So long as the arch-heretic the pope lives, Korah and these seducers will never die. In one pope are many Korahs, seducers, rebels, libertines. He usurps a dominion over all the princes in the world; he makes himself the sun, and from him, as the fountain of light, he pretends that all civil governors, as the moon, borrow their light: to himself he saith is given all power in heaven and in earth; and as profanely he applies that passage, Psal. lxxii. 8, "He shall have dominion from sea to sea, and from the river unto the ends of the earth;" and that of Prov. viii. 15, "By me kings reign." And when he speaks concerning the distribution of empires and kingdoms, he imitates his father in these words, They are delivered to me, and to whomsoever I will I give them. It would be endless, and in some respect needless, as having touched upon this sad subject before, to relate the many bloody machinations and murderous enterprises of the pope's emissaries against the persons of Christian princes. Under the wing of this whore of Babylon, in the nest of the pope's chair, have been hatched those stabbings, poisonings, powder-plots, and, which is worse, the defence of all these by his janizaries, the Jesuits, in their writings in blood, which have filled the ears and hearts of true Christians with horror and amazement. Nor would it be unsuitable to the present subject, to mention the seditious turbulence of the heretical crew of Anabaptists of late years, who, to all their other erroneous tenets, add this, that before the day of judgment Christ should have a worldly kingdom erected, where the saints only are to have dominion, and magistracy is to be rooted out; and with what an inundation of blood these idle, and at first neglected, dreams and opinions have filled Europe, the histories of the last age have related to us, and the Lord grant that we who have read and not been warned by them, may never ourselves become a history to the age which shall come after us.

Cunctus totius orbis clerus imperio magistratus civilis exemptus. L. 2. Decret. Tit. 2.

Imperator quod habet, totum habet a nobis ; in potestate nostra est, ut demus imperium cui volumus. Hadrian, in Epist. ad Archiep. Treu. Mögunt. & Colon.

Obs. 11. It is a sin for those who are uncalled to

thrust themselves into the office of the ministry. Korah's sin was his endeavour to invade the priesthood: "Seek ye the priesthood also?" saith Moses to him, Numb. xvi. 10. And because all the Lord's people were holy, as Korah alleges, ver. 3, therefore he pretends that others had as much right to discharge the office and function of Aaron as Aaron himself had; and that since the people had a holiness by vocation to grace, whereby the Israelites where distinguished from other nations, there needed no holiness of special consecration to distinguish the priest from other Israelites. Now that this sin of Korah, which was an invasion of the priest's office, may still be committed in the times of the New Testament, is clear, because the apostle reproves it in these seducers. And that it can be no other way committed in the times of the gospel, but by intrusion of uncalled persons into the ministry of the gospel, is, say some, as plain, because there is no other office which these seducers could invade, answering to that of the legal priesthood, but this office of the evangelical ministry. From all which it will unavoidably follow, that they who shall enter into the office of the ministry only upon pretence of inward abilities, without receiving a commission and authority from God, and a particular separation to that office, are guilty of sin against God, and that no light and slight one, Korah's sin. The receiving then of a power by way of authority, external mission, and commission, from those whom God has appointed to confer it, is requisite for those who will enter upon the ministerial function, which no man may undertake but by power lawfully thus conferred. That private Christians in a way of Christian charity may, yea, ought to confer with one another, by way of information, admonition, and consolation, 1 Thess. iv. 18; v. 14; Heb. iii. 13; 1 Pet. iii. 1, and so communicate their gifts for their mutual edification, is not denied or envied, but granted, yea, earnestly desired. It is yielded also, that in some cases of urgent necessity befalling the church, when it is not fully planted, formed, or when it is scattered and dispersed by persecution, and so hindered from the ordinary and orderly course of ministration which it enjoys in times of peace and settledness, private Christians may publicly instruct others; yet this cannot be alleged against the course which the Scripture has established for sending forth of ministers, Rom. x. 15; Heb. v. 4, 5; Acts xiii. 1, 2; xiv. 22, 23; Tit. i. 5; 2 Tim. ii. 2. The great eminence and commonness of gifts in the church of Christ in the times of the apostles, which were bestowed upon many who were not ordained and set apart for the ministry, were no hinderances to conferring ministerial power on them, by setting them apart to the ministerial employment, 2 Tim. i. 6; 1 Tim. iv. 14; v. 22. Timothy was a man of much holiness, and of excellent parts, and yet these hindered not his after-separation to his holy function by the presbytery. The command of the apostle, that Timothy should "lay hands suddenly on no man," clearly argues, that they on whom he did lay hands, were before to be men gifted with internal qualifications, for the trial whereof Timothy was forbidden to be too sudden in ordaining, 1 Tim. v. 22. And most clear is that of 2 Tim. ii. 2, where, for a succession of teachers, Timothy is commanded to commit the things which he had heard of Paul to faithful men, able to teach others; whereby it is evident that they were to be able and faithful before Timothy committed those things to them. There is not only a meetness for, but an inauguration into, the office of the ministry required of those who are to enter it; and gifts are not sufficient to make ministers, without the ordinary call and mission settled in the church by Christ. Every Israelite or Levite able to offer incense was not admitted to offer; none but the sons of Aaron, who were particularly set apart thereto, had that honour; nor can any under the times of the gospel, who have never so much inward furniture of gifts, be right ministers or officers from Christ, where there is not a right commission and patent given in his name by due ordination. As it is treason for the ablest statesman or lawyer to undertake the office of an ambassador or judge before he is made such by those who only can confer that power, so it is an insufferable affront offered to Jesus Christ, for any to pretend the doing of that in his name which is done without his declared will and consent.

Obs. 12. How ready are men to be weary of enjoying those things which they most impatiently desired when they wanted them! What would not these rebels have given for a Moses and an Aaron, to deliver them out of their Egyptian bondage! how welcome were the first tidings of God's appointing them to be the instruments of so great a mercy! And yet now they have a while enjoyed them, and tasted the benefit of their government, how weary are they of both, and therein of their own happiness! The people who with passionate and sinful earnestness cried out for a king, after the manner of other nations; so soon as God had gratified their desires therein, a great part of them were weary of what they so ardently wished, despised their king, "brought him no presents," and muttered their unthankful discontentedness in these words, "How shall this man save us?" 1 Sam. x. 27. And long before that, the same people who would have been glad of the coarsest pulse in a starving wilderness, murmured because they had no better commons than bread from heaven, angels' food; herein in a sort resembling David, whose soul longed for the water of Bethlehem, and yet when his three worthies, with the endangering of their lives, had brought that water to him, he poured it out on the earth, and would not drink thereof, 2 Sam. xxiii. 15—17. How righteous is God in denying us many a comfort, notwithstanding our earnest and impetuous craving, he knowing that when he gives it us, we shall either unthankfully despise it, or rather profanely abuse it! How willingly should we justify God in all his deferrings and denials of creature-enjoyments! for though we think that the want of them will undo us, yet he knows that the having of them would both hurt us and dishonour him.

Obs. 13. God opposes the opposers of lawful authority. They are enemies more to themselves than to those whom they are enemies; they perish in their gainsayings with this Korah. "An evil man seeketh only rebellion; therefore a cruel messenger shall be sent against him." "My son," (saith Solomon,) "fear thou the Lord and the king: and meddle not with them that are given to change: for their calamity shall arise suddenly; and who knoweth the ruin of them both?" Prov. xxiv. 21, 22. Some interpret this passage of Solomon to be a command, that fear and obedience should be yielded to the king in a way of subordination and subjection to God; as if Solomon had said, Be sure thou fear God in the first place, and the king only in the second; so that when the commands of God and the king seem to cross one another, let God rather be obeyed than the king; that is, fear and obey the king in the Lord. And the next words, "meddle not with them who are given to change," they understand of the changing of that order of obeying God in the first place; as if he had said, meddle not with them that would change, or invert that order, Nequaquam mores illorum consectari velis, qui ordinem istum invertunt, et regi primum, deinde Deo deferendum esse honorem existimant. Salas. in Prov. xxiv. Sic et Aug. de Verb. Dom. Serm. 6.

here enjoined by God; and would persuade thee to obey the king in the first place, and God after him: a very pious, but I question whether a proper interpretation. Others therefore better understand this rule of Solomon, of obedience to kings for God: q. d. Show thy fear of God by fearing the king; thy fear of God should put thee upon fearing the king, who is the minister of God, and in his stead. By those words, "which are given to change," I conceive we are to understand a brief character of those who are seditious, who, out of a desire of alterations and change in political government, shake off their due and former obedience to the magistrate. He adds, "Their calamity shall arise suddenly;" that is, their conspiracies and machinations shall speedily and unexpectedly be discovered, and God and the king will both set themselves with their power against him. And lastly, by those words, "Who knoweth the ruin of them both?" some understand "of them both" to mean of God and the king; as if Solomon had said, Who knoweth what that ruin or perdition is, which both God and the king will bring upon the rebellious? taking ruin here actively, of God and the king's ruining them. Others better, by "the ruin of them both," understand the ruin which shall befall both the party given to change, and him who shall meddle with him; that is, shall be though but a partaker, or accessary, or drawn in to join with him. A scripture, the explication whereof I have the more willingly touched upon, because it is so clear a comment upon the present instruction.

It has been observed by some, as I have noted upon the eighth verse, page 176, that the calamity of no sinners ordinarily arises so suddenly, unavoidably, and certainly, as that of the seditious. We rarely, if at all, meet with any in Scripture who opposed authority but have been punished eminently in this life, to the observation of others; and scarcely do we read of any seditious person who was not taken away by a violent death; witness the examples of Korah and his accomplices, Absalom, Sheba, Joab, Adonijah, Zimri, Baasha, Athaliah. And it is observable, that of these seducers, Jude here saith that they perished, to note the speediness, certainty, and irrecoverableness of their destruction. I need not mention the numerous examples of God's severity against seditious persons recorded in our own histories. They who have read of Becket, Montford, Mortimer, the Percies, Tyler, Warbeck, Wyat, the gunpowder traitors, Squire, Lopez, Campian, &c., will easily acknowledge the severity of God against the tribe of traitors. Nor seems there to be so much wrath put forth by God against them without extraordinary cause. Opposing lawful authority being both an open affronting and resisting the ordinance of God, and a pulling down and demolishing his very image and representation in the world; an indignity insufferable, were it only offered to men, as also a crossing of that merciful provision of God, whereby he will have human society, and thereby his church, upheld and propagated in the world; treasons and seditions being the pulling down of the pillars, and the plucking up the foundations, as it were, of the world's edifice. In a word, how just is it with God that they should restrain others from sin unwillingly, by being made examples, who will take away those who should restrain others from sin willingly by their place and office! and that they should be made marks of vengeance, who will attempt the removing of the ancient land-marks set by God for order and propriety in nations! How the consideration hereof should make us thankful to God our supreme Protector, and show us how deeply God is offended with a people when their alterations, conspiracies, and kingdom-quakes are frequent; and engage magistrates in duty and allegiance to God, who receive so much protection from God; and make us loathe and leave those lusts which are the greatest enemies to government!

Obs. 14. How merciful is God even in judgment! God spared Korah's posterity, when the father was destroyed. God in his severity will be loved, and in his indulgence feared. He mixed his smartest dispensations with sweetness. Mercy it was that Korah's posterity should be preserved from death; more, that God should make so holy an offspring come of so unholy a parent; most of all, that one who had been rebellious against God should have a seed so eminently serviceable to God. In the destructions of the parents in the wilderness he spared the children. He cut off some luxuriant branches, but did not cut down the tree. God lays up manna with the rod: he ever shows that mercy pleases him, though sometimes he is compelled to use judgment. How should this goodness of God teach us both thankfulness and imitation! Thankfulness in his severest dispensations; we may in the midst of them say, "He hath not dealt with us after our sins." Even in our greatest rebellions we may see him indulgently and undeservedly sparing us or ours. If he have suffered our forefathers to be covered with the darkness of superstition and ignorance, he has dealt more graciously with us their posterity, who live to praise him, like Korah's children, for that goodness which we no more deserved than our forefathers did. If the fire of his displeasure burn against us, who knows but our children may live to have better hearts, and to see better times, and to be the more humble and holy seed of rebellious parents? Hence we learn imitation likewise: when we are employed in works of greatest severity, we should not throw off tender-heartedness. We should remember that gentleness becomes us in punishing the worst, who have ever something to draw out our pity; and to be sure, less to draw out our severity to them, than we had to deserve God's toward us.

VERSE 12.

These are spots in your feasts of charity, when they feast with you, feeding themselves without fear: clouds they are without water, carried about of winds; trees whose fruit withereth, without fruit, twice dead, plucked up by the roots.

THE apostle having amplified the sin and misery of these seducers from sundry examples, now further illustrates the same by sundry apt and elegant comparisons, in this and the following verse. Three of these similitudes, whereby he describes their estate, are set down in this verse, and two in the next. In this verse they are compared,

Hanc conclusionem duobus comparationis generibus exornat, unum est in exemplis rerum ante gestarum positum : alterum in exemplis elegantissimis rerum naturalium. Jun. in loc.

I. To spots; "These are spots," &c.
II. To "clouds without water, carried," &c.
III. To decayed trees; "Trees whose fruit withereth."

I. To spots; in these words, "These are spots in your feasts of charity, when they feast with you, feeding themselves without fear."

Four things are here to be explained.

1. What these seducers are here called, or the name affixed to them; "spots."

2. Where they conversed, or to what company these spots cleaved; "in your feasts of charity."
3. What they did there: 1. They feast. 2. They feed themselves.
4. How they feasted and fed; viz. "without fear."

1. They are called "spots," σπιλάδες. The word has a double signification, very congruous to the present scope and drift of the apostle.

1. The word σπιλάδες, here interpreted spots, signifies rocks, such as in the sea are not discerned and shunned by mariners, may easily cause shipwreck. And in this sense Œcumenius understands the word in this place; as if these seducers in their meetings with the Christians were as pernicious to their souls, as are rocks in the sea to those ships which, by the unwariness of the mariner, unexpectedly dash against them. Others conceive that they are compared to rocks near the shore, which, being hollow, contract and gather the filth and mud which the sea casts up into their holes; as if the apostle would note them to be a *colluvies*, sink, or common receptacle of all filth and wickedness. But, 2. I conceive the word is here more fitly rendered spots than rocks; for the word spots, σπίλοι, 2 Pet. ii. 13, is of the same derivation and signification, and used upon the very same occasion with this; and there it is joined with the word μῶμοι, which imports blemishes, or any thing in the body or actions which may render either liable to disgrace and reproach. They are, saith Peter, σπίλοι καὶ μῶμοι, (*labes et maculæ*, Bez. *coinquinationes, et maculæ*, Vulg.) spots and defilements, or blemishes. And the words σπίλος and σπίλας, a spot, among profane writers, betoken defilement and deformity, and are used either to signify any speck, mole, or wrinkle on the face, or any stain on the garment by the dropping of wine or oil upon it, very often done in feasting; which notion, saith Lorinus, is most agreeable to the apostle's purpose of speaking concerning there being spots in feasts: and by way of resemblance it is used concerning the spots and stains of the soul; namely, sins which render him who was made after God's image defiled and deformed; hence the apostle speaks of the church, washed and cleansed by Christ, as not having spot, σπίλον, or wrinkle, but as being holy, and ἄμωμος, without blemish, Eph. v. 27. Nor is it without a singular emphasis that the apostle expresses them, who were themselves so defiled, and ready to spot and defile the Christians, by a word in the abstract; calling them not such as defile and bespot, but even very spots and defilements; and thus abstractly speaks the Spirit of God in other scriptures, when it would increase and intend the signification. We have found this man a pest, a very plague, Acts xxiv. 5. Once were ye darkness, but now are ye light, Eph. v. 8. And most deservedly are these impure seducers called spots, both in regard of their deformity and defilement. 1. Of their deformity: (1.) They (like spots) cast a deformity, disgrace, or blemish upon their Christian profession. What heathen, who never heard of Christ, but would have thought, by seeing these beastly epicures, that their Christ was a Bacchus, and these love-feasts, as profaned by them, Bacchus's feasts? the worship and worshipped being judged of according to the worshippers. They have profaned, saith God to the Jews in captivity, mine holy name, (among the heathen,) when they said, "These are the people of the Lord, and are gone forth out of his land," Ezek. xxxvi. 20; xliii. 8.

(2.) They were spots of deformity to the meetings whereinto they came; they were blemishes to the faces of the Christian assemblies. As one or two brass shillings in a sum of money make all the rest suspected, so by the unholiness of some the rest suffered. Wicked men look upon spots among and upon saints with a multiplying glass, and as with old men's spectacles, making a great letter in a small print: heathens seeing these among Christians, might say, Such are they all. Hence it was that Irenæus writes concerning the Carpocratians, that they were men sent by Satan to defame the name of God and the church; that men observing their wickedness, and thinking that we all were such, might turn away their ears from the preaching of the truth. To the same purpose likewise speaks Epiphanius, These men (saith he) were sent forth by Satan to be a disgrace to the church, putting upon themselves the name of Christians, that, for their sakes, the nations might abhor to get any good by the church of God, reject truth preached, and think that all who are in the church are like them, and for the wickedness of a few reproach all the rest; and therefore wherever any of them come, the Gentiles will have nothing to do with us.

(3.) They were spots of deformity to themselves; they disgraced not only their professions, but their very persons, and blemished even human nature itself; they turned themselves into beasts, and caused in themselves an interregnum of reason; making reason, the prince, to be a lackey; and sense, the servant, to ride, and be exalted: if ever any deserved to be called brute beasts, dogs turned to their vomit, or sows wallowing in mire, 2 Pet. ii. 28, they were these impure Borborites.

2. They were spots of defilement.

(1.) Carnally, they defiled themselves, their own bodies, their flesh, (these "defile the flesh," ver. 8,) by drunkenness, and especially by uncleanness. I tremble to English what Epiphanius reports of these impurities among the Gnostics; and Clemens Alexandrinus, and Minutius Felix, among the Carpocratians at their meetings. That sins of unchastity are peculiarly defiling, has been shown before, p. 171.

(2.) They defiled one another spiritually; they were pitch, and it was hard to touch them and not to be defiled; they were leaven, plague-sores, gangrenes, lepers, diffusive of sin, infectious to others: the devil conveyed his puddles through these pipes. The contagion of these infected the sound, but the soundness of the healthful recovered not the infected. That Christian had need be of a very hale constitution indeed, who, conversing with such pestilential persons, contracts not their sickness. Every sin (as we say of some diseases) is catching. Any root of bitterness springing up may defile many, Heb. xii. 15.

Thus we see the first thing opened, viz. the name which the apostle affixes to them; he calls them "spots."

2. For the second, the places where these spots cleaved, or the meetings and companies which these seducers frequented, are expressed in these words, "your feasts of charity," ἐν ταῖς ἀγάπαις ὑμῶν: though

the word ἀγάπη in the singular number signifies love, or charity, yet the word ἀγάπαι being in the plural, is seldom or never taken in that sense, but for feasts, or banquets of love; whence Erasmus is by some reprehended for turning these words, ἐν ἀγάπαις, in charitatibus, in your charities: and as deservedly do Beza and Gerard correct the Vulgate, which reads this place *in epulis suis*, in their feasts, viz. of love, as if the apostle intended that these seducers were spots in their own feasts; whereas these love-feasts were the brotherly meetings of the church, into which these sensual epicures intruded, and unto which, like spots, they cleaved. And therefore our apostle, in this word συνευωχούμενοι, to which some copies add ὑμῖν, tells the Christians that these impure companions did feast with them, and manifested their lewdness. The institution of these love-feasts was founded on the custom of the church, which immediately before the celebration of the Lord's supper used to have a feast, to testify, continue, and increase brotherly love among themselves; as also to the poor, who hereby were relieved; whence they had their name ἀγάπαι, charities, as if they were so intended for love, that there could not be so fit a name by which to call them as by love itself. Of these feasts speaks the apostle, when he saith that "every one taketh before other" τὸ ἴδιον δεῖπνον, "his own supper," 1 Cor. xi. 21; as also 2 Pet. ii. 13, where he speaks concerning the feasting of these seducers with the Christians; and frequent mention is made of these feasts among the ancients. Tertullian speaks most fully of them in the 39th chapter of his Apolog., where he tells us, that the name of those feasts manifested their nature, they being called by a name which signifies love. In them (saith he) our spiritual gains countervail for all our worldly costs; we remember the poor; we ever begin with prayer. In eating and drinking, we relieve hunger, but show no excess. In our feeding at supper, we remember that we are to pray in the night. In our discourse, we consider that God hears us. As soon as water for our hands and lights are brought in, any one sings, either out of the Scriptures, or, as he is able, some meditation of his own, and by this he shows how temperate he was at supper time. Prayer is the first and last dish of the feast; with this it began, and with this it ends; and when we depart, our behaviour is so religious and modest, that one would have thought we had rather been at a sermon than at a supper. And Tertullian writing to the martyrs in prison, relates how they were relieved *per curiam ecclesiæ, et agapen fratrum*, by the care of the church, and the charity of the brethren at their love-feasts. Of these also speaks Cyprian, in his third book to Quirinus, where he saith that these feasts of charity and brotherly love are religiously and firmly to be exercised; so that the ground of those ancient love-feasts was provision for the poor brethren, the preserving of mutual love among themselves, and the expressing by both their thankfulness to God for bestowing his Son upon them; in which respect they thought it most fit to celebrate them immediately before their receiving the Lord's supper; though in a short time, in the church of Corinth, these feasts of charity grew to be corrupted and abused by divisions, the excluding of the poor Christians from them, as also by riot and luxury, 1 Cor. xi. 21.

Some conceive that these feasts of charity were by the Christians, converted from heathenism, brought into the church to retain something like the customs of the heathens, who were wont at the time of their sacrificing to their gods to have public feasts of joy, which feasts Paul calls "the cup of devils, and the table of devils," 1 Cor. x. 21. Others think they were introduced in imitation of the Jews, who, by God's appointment, were wont to join feasting to their offering of their eucharistical sacrifices, and their peace-offering; as Deut. xxvii. 7, "Thou shalt offer peace-offerings, and shalt eat there, and rejoice before the Lord thy God." So Exod. xviii. 12, Jethro having taken "burnt-offerings and sacrifices for God, Aaron came, and all the elders of Israel, to eat bread with him before God." See likewise Deut. xiv. 23; xii. 7; xvi. 11. And though God bids Moses ask Pharaoh that Israel might go and sacrifice in the wilderness, Exod. iii. 18; yet Moses desires Pharaoh that they might hold a feast unto God in the wilderness, Exod. v. 1. And Calvin thinks that this both Jewish and heathenish custom of joining sacrificing and feasting together was imitated by the Christians in these feasts, they being almost ever wont, saith he, so to correct and reform the viciousness of superstitious rites and customs, as yet to retain a resemblance to them. Estius, with others, think that these love-feasts, being before the sacrament, were used in imitation of Christ, who instituted the holy sacrament immediately after the ordinary supper. An opinion which seems most probable, both in regard of the great likelihood that the Christians would imitate their Master rather than heathens, as also because the Jewish and heathenish feastings were after their sacrificing; whereas the love-feasts of the Christians were before the sacrament, as the best interpreters observe on 1 Cor. xii. 23.

3. The third thing to be explained is, what these seducers did in these meetings of the Christians; set down in these two expressions:

(1.) They feast with you.
(2.) They feed themselves.

(1.) They feast with you, συνευωχούμενοι. The word εὐωχοῦμαι, which signifies to feast or banquet, though Eustathius derives from ὀχή, food or nourishment, yet Athenæus rather thinks it to come of εὖ and ἔχειν, because it is said to be well with them, or they fare well, or live merrily, who are feasted and entertained with banquets. Hence Clemens Alexandrinus said that ἐνωχία, the true feast or banquet, is only in heaven. Some think the word signifies to feast or banquet publicly; which may aptly agree to this place, the love-feasts being public meetings. And Peter states them to be riotous in the day-time, openly and in the light, not seeking to shelter their luxury in darkness and corners. According to others it notes a feasting or banqueting, riotously and luxuriously. Thus it is used in Lucian, who tells us of one Gorgias, who being a hundred and eight years old, and being asked by what means he had lived to so great an age, answered, that he had reached those years because he never could be induced συμπεριεχθνεῆναι ταῖς ἄλλων εὐωχίαις, to go about to any feasts or banquets, to which by his friends he was invited. And this signification of riotous banquets is most suitable to this place, where these voluptuous epicures are said to feed without fear, the bridle of excess: these served their belly, and made it their god. Peter saith that they "count it pleasure to riot," 2 Pet. ii. 13, being given up to and swallowed up in voluptuousness: "Lovers of pleasure more than lovers of God." Pleasure was the fruit which they expected by sowing all their heresies.

And when the apostle tells these Christians, not only of the riotous feasting of these epicures, but of this their feasting with them, they being not only εὐωχούμενοι, but συνευωχούμενοι, that they had crept into their companies, and sat among them, he discovers to them their danger of being seduced by their company to their errors and sensualities; he wisely insinuates that these seducers did not come charitably into their feasts of charity, but to gain occasion to delude and insnare them by error; and therefore Peter saith, that while they feasted with these Christians, they sported themselves with their own deceivings.

(2.) The apostle saith they were feeding themselves, ἑαυτοὺς ποιμαίνοντες. The word ποιμαίνοντες, here translated feeding, is properly such a feeding as belongs to the office of a shepherd, or one who feeds cattle. Some translate it ruling or governing: the word indeed may bear that signification, being not only applied to teachers, 1 Cor. ix. 7; 1 Pet. v. 2, &c.; Acts xx. 28, but also to kings: " A Governor that" ποιμανεῖ, "shall rule my people," Matt. ii. 6 ; and Rev. xix. 15, ποιμανεῖ, "He shall rule them with a rod of iron." It is also used by the LXX., Psal. ii. 9, where we translate it rule. It comprehends besides feeding other parts of a shepherd's office, as leading, seeking, reducing, defending, healing his sheep; though, according to the notation of the word, it imports as much as ἐν τῇ πόᾳ μένειν, to remain or continue in the pasture, viz. where the sheep are which the shepherd is to attend. Of old, a king or ruler was called, as particularly Agamemnon by Homer, ποιμὴν λαοῦ, the shepherd or ruler of the people, it being his office to regard them as a shepherd does his flock; and hence it is that the Arabic turns this place, *gubernant seipsos sua virtute,* as if they would be under no government but their own ; Pagnin, Erasmus, and Vatablus, *suopte ductu arbitrioque viventes;* ordering and guiding themselves according to their own will and pleasure. But, as our learned divines have noted concerning this word against the papists, who interpret it to rule, in order to establish the pope's rule, a word of double signification is to be understood according to the subject-matter spoken of. This being spoken of a spiritual pastor, cannot be meant of ruling as a king; and, in this place, of those who were employed about feeding their bodies, and feasting, and, as Peter has it, who counted it pleasure to riot and fare deliciously; I conceive it is better translated feeding; and so Beza and the Vulgate render it, *pascentes.* And some think the apostle made choice of this word, ποιμαίνοντες, which oft signifies a shepherd's feeding his flock, to aggravate the fault of these cormorants, and secretly to tax their hypocrisy, who, boasting and pretending to be the only eminent shepherds and feeders of the people, took no other care but to fill themselves ; and instead of feeding their sheep, did ποιμαίνειν ἑαυτοὺς, feed themselves; but did indeed fleece and feed upon them, neither feeding their souls nor their bodies, but poisoning the former, and riotously wasting upon their own sensual appetites that which was appointed at the charge of the church for feeding the latter. The apostle, as some conceive, alludes to that threatening uttered against the shepherds, "Woe be to the shepherds of Israel that do feed themselves! should not the shepherds feed the flock ?" Ezek. xxxiv. 2. For my part, I conceive the apostle here uses the word ποιμαίνοντες, which oft signifies the feeding of sheep or other cattle in pastures, to note the brutish and beastly sensuality of these epicures, who fed more like cattle in a fat pasture, than Christians at a feast of holy sobriety; and where they should, as Tertullian speaks, rather feast upon holy discourse than full dishes. So that when the apostle saith these seducers were εὐωχούμενοι, and ποιμαίνοντες ἑαυτοὺς, he notes,

[1.] They feasted and fed immeasurably, beyond the bounds of Christian moderation, more like beasts than either saints or men; their hearts were oppressed with surfeiting, their souls were lodged like bright candles in the filthy, greasy lanterns of their bodies, and by eating made so dull and sluggish, that they were unfit for holy services; like the Sodomites, they offended in the fulness of bread, they were drowned in delights, 2 Pet. ii. 13.

[2.] The apostle notes by these expressions that they feasted and fed upon delicates; they loved to fare very well, to feed high and deliciously; plain dishes would not serve the turn; like the Israelites, manna without quails would not content them. The sin likewise of Eli's sons, who, not content with what portion God had allowed them, viz. the shoulder, the breast, the tongue, nor to eat the flesh sodden, according to the law, caught at what came to hand; and they would have it raw, that they might cook it to please their taste, 1 Sam. ii. 13, 14.

[3.] The apostle notes they fed greedily and earnestly; so intent and eager they were upon their feeding, that they never thought of giving thanks, either before or after. Their eyes were upon the table, like those of swine upon the acorns, so that they never looked up to the hand that shook down their plenty. Like the people, Exod. xxxii. 6, "They sat down to eat and drink ;" they rather did raven and devour, than eat or feed. They resolved all the powers of their mind upon their meat. This was Esau's sin, who was so greedy after meat that he had no regard of his birthright. They went to their food with the violence and eagerness of brutes which cannot be kept off.

[4.] It may also be intended that they feasted and fed injuriously, both with and upon the Christians; not only forgetting the poor Christians, whom they suffered to fast when they were feasting, but misspending and wasting the contribution belonging to the maintenance of the poor, and, as some conceive, of the ministry ; and if so, they feasted and fed sacrilegiously also. The surfeiting of these gluttons was accompanied with the starving of Lazarus.

[5.] They feasted and fed impurely and lustfully; making the plenty which God bestowed upon them but fodder and fuel to nourish their lusts of uncleanness. Like fed horses, they neighed after their neighbours' wives. Eli's sons were gluttons and adulterers; Esau was sensual in feeding, and also a fornicator.

4. Our apostle saith that this feeding of themselves was ἀφόβως, without fear. These words, without fear, may be referred either to the word συνευωχούμενοι, feasting with you, or ποιμαίνοντες ἑαυτοὺς, feeding themselves. Œcumenius seems doubtful which of

these to embrace; but, as Lorinus saith, *ad rem nostram nihil interest*, it matters not which way we take, both aiming at the same scope, which is to show the security and impudence of these gluttons in their sensual pleasures. And without fear they may be said to feed themselves, either in respect of God, or the church with whom they feasted, or of themselves; neither fearing God *metu* nor *timore*; neither fearing his wrath to punish them, nor reverentially fearing to displease him by sin; they being likewise touched with no reverence of that holy society with which they sat, nor yet at all with any mistrust or jealousy of the slipperiness and sensuality of their own hearts; and this their fearlessness they showed two ways.

<small>Convivantes sine timore, sive quia intrepide sese fidelibus convivantibus miscent, sive quia liberius gulæ ac genio indulgent, &c. Justin. in loc.</small>

(1.) In their entrance into the meetings and assemblies of the church. They never took any heed to their feet when they went into those places where the saints assembled. With the same unholy, unprepared, irreverent disposition of heart they undertook these religious banquets with which they were employed about earthly business; they feared not to go to these feasts, and after (as Augustine thinks) to the eucharistic banquet, without their wedding-garment of holiness. They trembled not with unwashen hands to touch those *tremenda mysteria*, those mysteries which might have struck terror into the hearts of any but such secure and impudent sinners.

(2.) They showed their fearlessness in their carriage when they were entered into the assembly. [1.] They were not afraid of lascivious gestures. Their eyes were then adulterous; for so the apostle, 2 Pet. ii. 13, 14, to these words, "while they feast with you," presently adds, "having eyes full of adultery," or the adulteress. They were not afraid of unclean looks and glances. [2.] In their meetings (probably) they were not afraid to utter unseemly expressions and erroneous conceits; whereby, as Peter goes on, they defiled and beguiled unstable souls. They showed themselves spots and blemishes ἐν ἀγάπαις, in the love-feasts, by sporting themselves ἐν ἀπάταις, in their deceivings. They went into the assemblies to fish for proselytes. There was no way so likely for these to prove themselves spots, σπιλάδες, in these feasts, as by their words. The tongue, saith James, is σπιλοῦσα, bespotting and defiling, not only our own body, by engaging it to and involving it in sin, but others also, by communicating and suggesting evil to others; and a full stomach at a feast is commonly, among those who are more modest than these impure libertines, accompanied with an unbridled tongue. [3.] And especially in these feasts of charity they were not afraid of feeding excessively and riotously. Peter tells us they counted it pleasure to riot; they ingulfed themselves in the waters of fulness and excess, and never feared drowning either their souls or bodies by their intemperance; they would observe no stakes set up in those waters, nor set any limits to their lusts; they took no heed lest their hearts might be oppressed by surfeiting, nor did they at all care how ill accommodated mansions their souls lived in by pampering their bodies, nor how unfit they made themselves for performing holy duties. The impairing their health, the digging their graves with their teeth, the being felons of themselves, never troubled them; much less did they fear lest they might (instead of kings) be tyrants and torturers of the creatures; they feared not the wronging of the poor, whose goods they devoured; in short, they feared not that God would punish them with want for this their wantonness, or with eternal pains for these their short and sensual pleasures; but like beasts, to which they are compared, 2 Pet. ii. 12; Jude

<small>Vide Clem. Alex. pæd. l. 2. c. 1, 2.</small>

19, when they were in the fat pastures of riot and sensuality, they never feared the shambles or slaughter-house, though they were made to be taken and destroyed, and perished in their own corruption.

Obs. 1. Sinners are deformed creatures. As a spot, so sin, is the deformity of a person; yea, it makes him to be and become a very deformity: sin is a blemish cast upon God's image. The very angelical nature was by sin made deformed; by it angels became devils. Though never so many other accomplishments of spirituality, wisdom, strength, and immortality were left behind, yet, upon their fall, they lost their beauty. No endowments without holiness can make any person truly excellent. The greatest potentates in the world (while living in sin) are but (like Naaman) noble lepers. Every wicked man is a naked person, not only because without a shelter, but an ornament also. Sinners are both shelterless and shameful. The people after their idolatry were naked, " for Aaron had made them naked to their shame," Exod. xxxii. 25. Holiness is both a soul's and church's ornament. "Can a maid forget her ornaments, or a bride her attire? yet my people have forgotten me," &c., Jer. ii. 32. Holiness (as the ark was to Israel) is the soul's glory, and when the Philistines have taken it away, the true glory is departed, it is but an Ichabod. The most golden Israelite, notwithstanding all his privileges, in God's esteem had but an Æthiopian skin; a Jew, an Egyptian, an Edomite, an Ammonite, and a Moabite in God's account are all one, if without the circumcision of the heart, Jer. ix. 26. Wicked men are in their best dress but vile persons, the very blots and blemishes of their societies. Sin is that not only of which the people of God are afterward ashamed, but that of which even sinners themselves are ashamed when most they love it; and therefore even the worst of men, yea, devils, have loved the appearance of holiness; the rottenest sepulchres have loved painting; the filthiest harlot, a wiped mouth; the profanest heart, a dress of religion. The clothes of sin are of more worth than its whole body. Even Satan delights to appear like an angel of light, and is ashamed of his own colours. All the performances of wicked men are but deformities; their prayers an abomination; the calling of their assemblies is iniquity; when they spread forth their hands, God hides his eyes, Isa. i. 13—15. How incompetent a judge is a blind man of colours, or a sinner of beauty! The black, they say, thinks the blackest face most beautiful, and wicked men laud wickedness as the greatest comeliness. Jesus Christ himself had no beauty or comeliness in the eyes of unbelieving sinners, Isa. liii. 2. Holiness is an inward, a hidden beauty, Psal. xlv.; a carnal eye can neither see it or esteem it. If grace be, as with sinners it is, a scar, it is a scar of honour, not uncomeliness: riches and worldly dignities, like glow-worms, only shine in the dark night of the world; but there is nothing will have a lustre at the day of judgment but holiness. The poorest saint is a prince, and the most glorious sinner a beggar, both in a disguise. Holiness, though veiled with the most contemptible outside, carries with it a silent majesty; and sin even in highest dignity bewrays a secret vileness. That which is to be desired of a man is his goodness. "The righteous is more excellent than his neighbour," Prov. xii. 26. The poor saints are called the glory of Christ, 2 Cor. viii. 23, who presents them without spot or wrinkle, or any such thing. Sinners are spots, saints are stars and jewels; as jewels, the stars of the earth; and as stars, the jewels of heaven. Though saints have not a herald to emblazon their arms, yet the Scripture sufficiently sets forth their dignity: the rottenest stuffs are oftenest watered, and, among men, sinners most glorious, but yet in Scripture they are but spots.

Obs. 2. Sinners are filthy and defiling. They are spots for defilement as well as deformity: sin and uncleanness are put together, Deut. xxxii. 5. The filthiest of beasts are scarce filthy enough to set forth the filthy nature of sinners; swine, the dog, the serpent, the goat, the neighing horse. The filthiest things are used in Scripture to set forth sin, as dung, vomit, mire, leprosy, scum, pitch, plague-sores, issues, ulcers, dead carcasses, the blood and pollution of a new-born child, the noisome exhalations breathing from a sepulchre, Rom. iii. 13, spots. A sinner is called, that which defileth, Rev. xxi. 27. Sinful gain is filthy lucre. Unholy speech is filthy and rotten communication; whoredom is called uncleanness; gluttony turns the temple of the Holy Ghost into a dunghill; and drunkenness common sewers of filthiness, the drunkard is a walking quagmire. The covetous wretch that loads himself with thick clay is but a moving muckheap, a speaking dunghill; his riches are but dung, good when they are spread abroad by charity, but stinking and useless when heaped. Pride is but a swelling botch. Sinners are the children of the filthy and unclean spirit; they are of their father the devil, like Joab's posterity, therefore all filthy and leprous; their natural parents were naturally all unclean; and who did ever bring a clean thing out of an unclean? Job xiv. 4. "That which is born of the flesh is flesh," John iii. 6. Their greatest hatred and enmity is set upon purity and holiness; clean and sweet objects are death to them, as they say that roses kill the horse-fly; the gospel is to them a savour of death. And this filthiness and pollution of sin has two properties which may render it very hateful. 1. It is a spreading pollution: (1.) Over all of a man, flesh and spirit, soul, body, understanding, thoughts, conscience, memory, will, affections, eyes, hands, tongue, Tit. i. 15, 16. (2.) All done by a man: even the best things, the prayers of polluted sinners, are abominations; their incense stinks, their sacrifices are unclean, their mercies cruel, their profession of godliness a form, their plausiblest performances no better than embalmed carcasses, Isa. i. 13, 14. (3.) It spreads even unto others, and infects them, by encouraging, teaching, seducing, constraining them to sin. It oft is diffused from the wicked even to the godly themselves; nothing more difficult than to be familiar with, and not to be infected by sinners: the error of the wicked sometimes cleaves to them, and the example of sinners entices them. The sons of God saw the daughters of men, and were polluted. What an insensible deadness of spirit and decay of grace conversing with sinners brings upon saints! (4.) Yea, this contagion of sin spreads even to the good creatures of God about us, even into them it puts (as the apostle speaks) vanity, groaning, bondage, consumption, mourning; and at length it will bring combustion and dissolution upon the whole frame of nature, 2 Pet. iii. 10. 2. It is a deep and indelible pollution, Jer. xvii. 1, of a scarlet and crimson dye, Isa. i. 18, compared also to an Ethiopian's blackness, a leopard's spots, Jer. xiii. 23, not to be washed away with nitre and much soap, Jer. ii. 22. Hell-fire shall not be able to eternity to take out the stains of the smallest sins from man's nature; yea, the greatest measure of grace received in this life by the best of men does not wholly abolish this defilement: the best have their sores, and stand in need of curing and daily cleansing: "Who can say, I have made my heart clean?" All the legal washings, purifyings, and cleansings of the filthiness of the flesh, were but faint representations of our need of and purity by being washed in the blood of Christ. And oh that sinners would be as unquiet as they are unclean, till they wash in that fountain which is set open for sin and for uncleanness! It is only the blood of God which can wash away the filthiness of sin; no other laver can take away that spot. Not only look, but go into it, wash thyself all over, Jer. iv. 14; Rev. vii. 14; 1 Cor. vi. 11. Cry out, O sinner, "Unclean, unclean." See thy spots in the glass of the law. Be weary of thy defilement as well as thy deformity. Being washed, keep thyself pure; take heed of spotting places and persons. Though upon a conscience uncleansed, like an old spotted garment, a sinner cares not what filth he suffers to drop, yet, O saint, keep thy new clothes white, clean and pure; sin, like a mired dog, when it fawns upon thee, fouls thee. A spot will easily be seen upon thee; trifles in thee are accounted blasphemies. Be not troubled at the spots upon thy name, so as thou keepest a pure conscience; not that wicked men make them, so long as they do not find them. Wash thyself in thine own tears; be troubled that thy justification is so complete, and thy sanctification so imperfect; that thou art at once both without spot or wrinkle, and yet so full of both. In short, labour to be spotless in a spotting and spotted generation; in foul streets to walk with clean garments. Let not the error of the wicked cleave to thee. If thou canst not cleanse them, which is most desirable, let not them defile thee.

Obs. 3. The Lord's supper is a love-feast. "In your feasts of charity." The reason why these feasts of charity, whereof Jude here speaks, were annexed to the Lord's supper, 1 Cor. xi. 21, 22, and also why those ancient Christians in these feasts expressed so much love one to another, was because they were about to celebrate that sacrament, which expressed as great a token of God's love towards them, as deserved unfeigned and fervent affections in them toward one another. The sacrament of the Lord's supper then promotes and testifies, confirms and contributes, to the mutual love which ought to be among Christians. The passover, but a shadow of the Lord's supper, tended to increase the love of the receivers, Exod. xii. 1. It was to be one whole lamb. 2. Not one bone of it was to be broken. 3. It was a joint action, wherein every one was to communicate; and therefore to be performed with joint affection. 4. It was to be eaten in one house, to show that there was to be among those who ate a unity and harmony of hearts and affections. One house will not hold those who are at jars and dissensions, and divided in affection. 5. The eating of the passover was to be done at one and the same time, month, day, hour, and that in the evening, when they were all in their cold blood, the injuries and offences of the day forgotten and forgiven, the sun being not to go down upon our wrath, when their affections were as calm and quiet as the evening. 6. The partakers of the passover were all to be regulated in receiving it by one law. There was but one law for the stranger and the homeborn; both submitted to the same rule, and consented to the same direction. 7. It was to be eaten without leaven, whereby, as the apostle expounds it, was noted the keeping the feast without the leaven of maliciousness and wickedness, 1 Cor. v. 6—8. And when Hezekiah restored the passover, it is expressly said, that to all Judah was by the good hand of God given one heart, and that they met at one time and in one place, and that they kept the feast of the passover with great joy, 2 Chron. xxx. 12. But if we look from the shadow to the substance, we shall see this love and unity of the faithful more clearly manifested.

1. When our Saviour was about to ordain this sa-

crament, he gave all his disciples an example of Christian and loving condescension, even to the washing one another's feet, John xiii. 4—14. After this institution, he presses upon them the commandment of love, as the chief commandment, and their principal duty, both by the precedent and precept of love, showing that his supper was a communion of love, John xiii. 34, 35.

2. Consider the appellations of this sacrament. It is called the communion, the table of the Lord, the Lord's supper; a word not noting the time of, but fellowship in eating; *cœna, ἀπὸ τοῦ κοινοῦ*. Eating together was ever held a token of friendship. Joseph's love to his brethren was testified by feasting them. David's love to Mephibosheth, by causing him to eat bread at his table continually, 2 Sam. ix. 7. David calls his familiar friend "one that did eat of his bread," Psal. xli. 9. The eating at one rack hath bred peace between savage beasts. And that hatred which was between the Jews and Egyptians could no way be more fitly expressed than by their mutual abominating to eat bread one with another. Men by nature are directed to express their love and reconciliation by feasts and invitations; and this communion which by eating and drinking the faithful have one with another, the apostle tells us comes from their partaking of one Christ. "The cup of blessing which we bless," saith he, "is it not the communion of the blood of Christ? The bread which we break, is it not the communion of the body of Christ? For we being many are one bread, and one body: for we are all partakers of that one bread," 1 Cor. x. 16, 17; that is, we partaking of the same Christ, and having communion in his merits and benefits, have thereby communion also one with another in the Lord's supper. And we all partaking of that one bread, broken and divided into divers parts, are made "one body and one bread," though we are never so many. The faithful then partaking all of one Christ, and every one of them having communion in his body and blood, have also communion among themselves: nor can this but be a communion of much dearness and nearness, which arises from partaking of this one Christ, and all his benefits and merits; for hereby,

(1.) They are all children of the same Father. We are all the sons of God by faith in Christ, Gal. iii. 26; and "to as many as received him, he gave power to be the sons of God;" and what nearer bond than to be the children of the same father? In the Lord's supper the faithful sit like olive branches round about their Father's table. " Love as brethren," saith the apostle. " How good and how pleasant it is," saith the psalmist, " for brethren to dwell together in unity!"

(2.) By partaking of this one Christ the faithful are all members of the same body, and they grow up into him who is the Head, Eph. iv. 15, and from him receive life and grace; being as members animated with the same Spirit, and incorporated into his mystical body, and therefore the apostle speaks of drinking into one Spirit in the Lord's supper. Now what can more aptly express the near union, dear affection, and tender sympathy between Christian and Christian than this, being fellow members of one body; one member counting the woe and welfare of another as its own?

(3.) By partaking of one Christ in the sacrament, they profess themselves to be of the same faith and religion; to expect life and happiness the same way, for Christ is the way; and this sameness of religion has bound those who have been of false religions very strongly together. Now that by feeding together in the Lord's supper there is professed a communion in the same religion, the apostle strongly proves, 1 Cor. x. 18, from the practice of Israel after the flesh, that is, the Jews who descended from Jacob or Israel. These carnal Israelites who lived in his time, and denied Christ, were, saith the apostle, by eating of the sacrifices "partakers of the altar;" that is, professed themselves to be of the Jewish religion and worship, and to approve of the same.

(4.) By partaking of one Christ at the Lord's supper, the faithful profess themselves to be the servants of one Lord and master. Fellow servants must not fall out and beat one another, Luke xii. 45. The servants of this one Lord should be of one mind. If Christ be not divided, his servants should shun division.

(5.) Hereby they profess, that they are to be pardoned by the same blood, "shed for many for the remission of sins," Matt. xxvi. 28. And what inducement stronger to move us to forgive a few pence, who have been forgiven so many pounds! What will quench hatred, if the blood of Christ will not!

(6.) Hereby they profess both that they all live in the same family here, where they feed at the same table, serve the same Master, own the same Father; and that they shall live together in the same habitation for ever, partaking of that meritorious blood which is the purchase of the same inheritance, and having all thereby the same key to open paradise withal. They who receive Christ, as communicants profess to do, shall be received. One saint may truly say to another, You and I must be better acquainted. And what an engagement to love is this, for us to consider we shall for ever live and love together in heaven! Oh how should Christians begin to do that here, which they shall never be weary of doing to all eternity! If one house, then one heaven, calls for one heart. Thus the appellations given to the sacrament, the table of the Lord, the Lord's supper, the communion, &c., show it to be a love-feast.

3. The outward elements, bread and wine, used at the supper, evince the same. Separated and several grains and grapes make one and the same bread and wine. They who are severed and disjoined from one another, not only by sea, habitation, trades, but in heart also and affection, are, by the receiving of Christ in this sacrament, reunited into one spiritual body, as the elements, though originally several, are into one artificial mass. "We being many," saith the apostle, "are one bread." How necessary, then, is the Lord's supper in these times, when love so much decays! If the Christians in their summer season, when love was burning hot, so often laid on this fuel, what need have we then to do so in this winter season, when the love of most grows so cold! Confident I am, that the withdrawing of this sacrament that feeds and foments love, has much tended to its decay among us. And further, this discovers the great policy of Satan, not only in hindering from the sacrament, which was appointed to strengthen love, but in breaking love by this very sacrament. Who would ever have expected to have heard of a sacramentary war? How many valiant champions lost their lives in this land, in their Smithfield fights, about the controversy of transubstantiation! and how subtlely hath the murderer of souls mixed his poison with the sacramental bread, and stolen away the cup in the papacy! What fierce contests have there been between Calvinists and Lutherans about consubstantiation! Who remembers not the prelatical fury, in imposing superstitious for sacramental gestures? And oh that the flames of these unchristian quarrels about the sacrament did not blaze and spread even at this very day! Oh the unbrotherly breaches between brethren about the admission and

qualification of communicants! Consider, dear Christians, whether Satan is not likely to prevail, when he turns that artillery whereby we should batter his forts upon ourselves, and makes his strongest weapons of war of olive branches, ensigns and emblems of peace; and is not love in danger of death when its food is daily poisoned? Who warms his hands at these flames of contention, but only our adversary? Satan, as they say of the lawyer, will be the only gainer, when you fall out, like unkind brethren, about your Father's will and testament. The Lord humble us for all those unworthy receivings which have made us so unkind and quarrelsome about receiving this feast of love, the Lord's supper; and make us for the future, in all our opinions about and participations of it, to be men in understanding, and children in malice.

Obs. 4. Spotted and spotting sinners are unfit guests at holy feasts. The apostle, by saying these seducers were spots in the feasts of charity, notes the unsuitableness of such blemishes to assemblies that should be clean and Christian; these spots casting an uncomeliness upon those holy meetings, which made those spots appear and set off with the more ugliness and uncomeliness. The mixture of scandalous persons in church fellowship is here by the apostle blamed; and if their meeting at these feasts of charity be reprehended by the apostle, if at these feasts these spots appeared so black and deformed, how much more reprovable was their meeting at the Lord's supper, which is an ordinance of Christ wherein approaches to him are more near, and ought to be more holy, than in those feasts of charity. Spots and blemishes, as Mr. Perkins well spake of his times, ought to be washed off by ecclesiastical discipline from the face of holy assemblies at the Lord's supper, because they pollute it. True it is, that, 1. There are two sorts of pollution of the Lord's supper; the one, that which makes the sacrament no sacrament, but a common or unhallowed thing, to those who receive it, as if it were given by those who are no ministers, or to those who are no church, or without the blessing and breaking of the bread; the other sort of pollution of the sacrament is, that which makes its administration to be sinful, and those who administer it to be guilty of doing that which is contrary to the revealed will of God. This latter kind of pollution is by admitting spotted and scandalous sinners. 2. It is granted, that the mixture of the scandalous pollutes not the sacrament to those who have used all the lawful means against it, who, being officers, have discharged their duty by exercising church discipline, and being private Christians, admonished the offenders, and petitioned those who have the authority to restrain them from the sacrament: in that case, though the scandalous partake of the sacrament, yet officers and worthy communicants partake not of their sin. But otherwise, the admission of scandalous persons to the sacrament is a pollution of that ordinance. "Give not," saith Christ, "that which is holy to dogs, neither cast ye your pearls before swine," Matt. vii. 6. By that which is holy, I understand, though primarily, yet not solely, the word; but consequently the sacraments, prayer, and Christian admonition. Christ does not speak of one holy thing only, nor does he say, the pearl; but he saith, that which is holy, and pearls. And by dogs and swine are not only to be understood infidels, heathens, open apostates, and persecutors, which, like dogs, bite, bark, and contradict; but also such who, like swine, profane, trample these pearls under their feet, and by an impure, swinish life show how much they despise holy things. And needs must the sacrament be profaned, when in its use not grace, but sin is increased, because hereby the main end of the sacrament, which is to be food to nourish grace, and poison to kill sin, is perverted; but no grace is nourished in any profane, impenitent sinner, he being spiritually dead, and so without the life of grace. And further, his hand is strengthened in sin; for by his receiving the sacrament his conversion is much more difficult than that of a sinner who has been kept back from the sacrament altogether; and by joining in the highest act of church communion an impenitent sinner entertains a good opinion of his spiritual happiness, and so trusts in lying vanities. And again, the giving of the sacrament to those who are known to live in gross sins without repentance, is a contradiction to, and a confutation of, the word, which denounces condemnation against them that eat and drink unworthily; and in the faithful delivery thereof we pronounce the wrath of God to such as live impenitent in sin: the word saith, "Be not deceived, neither fornicators, nor idolaters, nor adulterers," &c., "shall inherit the kingdom of God." And do we not, by giving the sacrament to these, give the lie to the word? do we not in the sacrament absolve those whom we condemn in the word, and open the kingdom of heaven in the sacrament to those against whom we shut it in the word? for is not the sacrament a seal of the covenant, the righteousness of faith, and the promises of the gospel, as is evident by those sacramental phrases, "This is my body, This is my blood," which denote a spiritual obsignation and exhibition of the benefits of Christ's body and blood? and doth not Christ say to those to whom he delivered the sacrament, This is my body which is given for you, and this is my blood which is shed for you, and for many, for the remission of sins? Matt. xxvi. 28; Luke xxii. 19, 20. Do not they, then, who consent to wicked and scandalous persons taking the sacrament, acknowledge the children of the devil to be the children of God, and the enemies of God to be in covenant with him, and so partake of the benefits of the covenant from him? Further, is it not a profanation of the sacrament of baptism, to baptize a Jew or a pagan professing a resolution to turn Christian, who yet is an openly profane and wicked liver, and continues under the power of visible and abominable sins, although he be able to make a sound and orthodox confession of faith? And shall a scandalous living in adultery, swearing, lying, keep a man from entering into the visible church by the door of baptism, and shall they not as well hinder him from being welcomed at the table, in the house, as a child and friend? Yet, again, is the sacrament profaned by admitting infants and idiots, who can make no good use of it; and is it not as much, if not more polluted, by admitting those to it who will make a very bad use of it? Also may not one man by ignorance, drunkenness, defence of sin, and heresy, lie under a sinful contracted disability to examine himself, and so to be an unfit communicant, as another man may lie under a natural disability? and is not a man more blamable for the former than the latter? Further, holy things under the Levitical law were polluted and profaned by wicked and profane persons: "They have defiled my sanctuary," &c.; "for when they had slain their children to their idols, they came the same day into my sanctuary to profane it," Ezek. xxiii. 38, 39. And in that question, "Who shall abide in thy tabernacle?" Psal. xv. 1, the prophet shows by those offences for which men were excluded from the sanctuary, what it was which should keep men from

Hæc enim Dei voluntas non erit in æternum, ut ecclesia Christianam, alicui gratiam Christi et remissionem peccatorum, annunciatione verbi divini denegret, et eidem exhibitione sacramentorum spondeat? Ursin. judicium de discipl. Ecclesiast.

eternal life; and why that moral unholiness, for of such he speaks, which made men unfit to go into the sanctuary, which had a sacramental signification of Christ, should not as well exclude them from the sacrament, I understand not. Were not the sacrifices of old polluted by profane and morally unholy persons offering them? "So," that is, unclean, "is this people before me; so is every work of their hands, and that which they offer therein, unclean," Hag. ii. 14. Where it is plain that the moral unholiness of the persons defiled holy ordinances; the people and their works being evil, the Lord for that cause accounted their sacrifices to be unclean. If morally profane persons defiled the sacrifices of old, they may surely be charged with defiling our sacraments now, Psal. l. 16.

Obs. 5. Such things as are given for the public benefit of the church, are not to be consumed in or converted to any other uses. These feasts of charity, which were appointed for the relief of the poor Christians and the ministry, were profanely wasted by these seducers. This sin is commonly called sacrilege, which by some is thought to be so called, q. *sacræ legis, vel rei læsio,* the hurting, spoiling, or violation of a holy law or thing. Others better consider it q. *sacra legere,* to gather holy things; and they define it to be a taking away of things consecrated and devoted to the Lord. This is mentioned in Scripture to be done either ignorantly or knowingly; if ignorantly, it required, according to the law, 1. Restitution of the principal, with an addition of the fifth part over and above, as a forfeiture for the offence, and a caveat against the like in future time. 2. Reconciliation or atonement; the priest making an atonement with the "ram of the trespass-offering," Lev. v. 16, 17; xxii. 14, to note the greatness of the offence against God. If this sin were committed of knowledge and wittingly, that which was taken, and all that the taker had, was for the Lord as a sacrifice for restitution, and he with his whole family stoned and burnt for purgation. This judgment of God upon Achan for taking that to his own use which was devoted to God is largely related, Josh. vii.; as also the punishment inflicted upon Ananias for changing that which was dedicated to a holy to his private use. And in this latter instance the word ἐνοσφίσατο, which we barely translate kept back, properly signifies a nimming or purloining, and so is the word rendered, Tit. ii. 10. "It is a snare," or destruction, "to the man," saith Solomon, "who devoureth that which is holy, and after vows to make inquiry," Prov. xx. 25; that is, to apply or take that to his own use which was appointed to God's, yea, to go about to do it by inquiring how the vow might be made void. For that may be called holy which is not such only by creation, as angels and the first man, but also by dedication and separation; and that whether this separation were by God's command, or by man's free and voluntary bestowing it. In the old law, tithes and first-fruits were holy; so now in the times of the gospel, those things which are either appointed by law, or bestowed by the liberality of men, for maintaining the worship and service of God, and Divine uses; and the taking away of these is the devouring of holy things; a sin so much the more heinous in these times, by how much the more bounty has been exercised by those who lived in times of blind superstition for maintaining idolatry. How unseemly is it that men should live as if all their light seemed to show them how to delude God; as if faith had banished all fidelity; as if any worship better deserved maintenance from men than his who gives men both their own maintenance and worship; yea, as if the more they saw into religion, the more they saw in it which deserves starving and overthrow! This sin, which some divines make to be a breach of the eighth commandment, "Thou shalt not steal," must needs be of thefts the worst, because it is a robbing of him who is the best, even God himself. "Will a man rob God? yet ye have robbed me," Mal. iii. 8.

Sic usurpatur a LXX. in casu sacrilegii. Josh. vii. 1; 2 Mac. iv. 32. Vid. et Est. in loc. Aug. de Verb. Ap. Ser. 25. p. mihi 378. et Hieron. Ep. 8. p. mihi 55.

It is a sin to wrong our beast, yea, our enemy's beast, Prov. xii. 10; a greater to wrong man: and if no injury may be offered to man, no, not our enemy, much less to our brother, 1 Cor. vi. 6; and if not to our brother, much less to our superior, to a king, 2 Sam. xvi. 9; and if not to an earthly king, far less to the King and Lord of heaven, who is our superior in the highest degree, who is our Father and Benefactor, our Maker, and Feeder, and Father. When Joseph had feasted his brethren, then to steal his cup! what greater injury? "God forbid" (say they) "we should do this thing," Gen. xliv. 7. And aptly does Solomon call the devouring of holy things a snare, because it is a sin alluring us to overthrow; there is in it a bait to cover the hook, and somewhat scattered to draw us into the net. To a foolish sinner, the gain appears very beautiful and beneficial. The wedge of gold, and the Babylonish garment, seemed to Achan at first great enticements; but the garment clothed him "with shame and dishonour," Psal. xxxv. 26, and the wedge of gold was a wedge to rive his soul and body asunder. How severely does God threaten those of Tyre and Sidon for their sacrilege in ransacking the temple, and in taking away the gold and silver appointed for his service, and carrying it into their idol temples, Joel iii. 4, 5. If it were not lawful for Ananias and Sapphira, having consecrated the whole price of their own land to God, to keep away part thereof; then it is much more unlawful to keep away any part thereof from the church, which we never gave, it being the church's possession before we were born; such alienation not being made in case of extreme necessity for maintaining the commonwealth, and preserving life, or for the church's greater benefit and conveniency, Lev. xxv. 23; Ezek. xlv. 4. Satan knows that the outward worship of God and religion cannot be continued without a ministry, nor a ministry without ministers, nor ministers without such goods as should sustain them; and hence he instigates profane men to violate and steal church goods, that thereby the ministry, God's worship, and the salvation of souls may be overthrown. The alienation of church goods has been prohibited by the decrees of sundry ancient councils. If our forefathers by the injury of their times, mistaking the truth, gave aught superstitiously to Romish priests to religious uses, it is fit their general purpose should be kept, with amendment of their particular error.

Synod Ancyr. circa ann. 308. Synod Arelateus. 2. ann. 326. Synod Antioch. ann. 344. Concil. Carthag. 4. ann. 401. Concil. Tolet. 2. ann. 529. Concil. Syn. 9. ann. 656.

Obs. 6. The godly in this world are never totally freed from the company of the ungodly. It was the lot of these Christians to have these wicked men with them. The godly must never love, but yet they will always have the company of the wicked; though they should not feast together, yet they will always live together. They who will be quite freed from the company of the wicked, "must," as Paul speaks, "needs go out of the world," 1 Cor. v. 10. Our delight should only be in the godly, but it will be our condition to be among the ungodly; and God thus disposes of the outward estate and condition of his people for sundry causes. Hereby they are made more watchful over their hearts and ways: the greater their danger is, the less is their security; the more dirt and defilement they see, the more they labour to keep their garments pure, and to gird up their loins. When enemies approach our cities, we double our watch. In times of infection, we most mind our preservatives. "Save yourselves from this untoward generation," said Peter to the new converts, Acts ii. 40; he means not so much by leaving the places, as by taking heed of the impurities, wherein the wicked live. By this abiding likewise among the wicked, the godly are more put upon loving and cleaving to one another. It is noted, Gen. xiii. 7, 8, upon the mention of the Canaanite and Perizzite being in the land when the strife was between the herdmen of Abram and Lot, that Abram desired there might be no strife between them. Countrymen in a strange country should beware of contention; the common foe should make disagreeing brethren unite; dissension will be both their ruin and their reproach, and will both disgrace and destroy them. If a Herod and a Pilate could be made friends, should not saints join together when Christ is struck at? Sometimes God makes his people by the presence of the wicked more zealous against wickedness; the nearness of contraries strengthens their opposition; the eye increases grief and hatred: nor have any saints so much set themselves against sin, as they who have been most compelled to see sin: the best men have oft lived in the worst times; the hottest fire is in the coldest winter, the brightest stars in the darkest night. In the midst of a crooked and perverse nation the godly shine as lights, Phil. ii. 15. Lot's righteous soul was vexed with the unclean conversation of the wicked, and David's eyes ran down with rivers of tears when he saw God's law broken. What a work of power is it, that a sea of ungodliness should, instead of damping, redouble the heat of a saint's love to holiness! Further, God will hereby either better the wicked, or render them inexcusable; either their living among his people shall change or condemn them; either the holy conversation of saints shall turn the hearts, or stop the mouths of sinners; they shall not be able to plead ignorance of their duty, when they have been instructed by the language of lip and life. Though Noah by preparing the ark saved his own house, yet he condemned the world, Heb. xi. 7. To conclude, by the company of wicked men, God makes his people more prize communion with himself, long for heaven, where there shall be neither sin nor sinner to molest them, where they shall no longer sojourn in Meshech, nor dwell in the tents of Kedar, nor their souls with them which hate peace, Psal. cxx. 5, 6. Heaven would not be sweet, if the world were not bitter; nor the company of saints in glory be so desirable, were it not for the unkindness of and vexation by sinners on earth. Oh how sweet will that condition be, where all the society shall be of one mind! How melodious that choir, which shall ever sing without any jarring, any discord! Till which condition, let us, whatever our times, wherever we abide, neither impatiently complain of God, nor sinfully comply with the ungodly, but account it our duty to do the wicked what good we can, if we cannot do them what good we would; to be careful that they may not, and comforted that they cannot, do us that harm they would; but contrarily, both by their company, yea, and unkindnesses, that good they would not.

Obs. 7. Feasting is not always unlawful. The Christians here are not blamed for their cheer, but warned of their guests. The holiest men, in Scripture we read, have made feasts, as Abraham, Lot, Isaac, David, Solomon, Gen. xix. 3; xxi. 8; xxvi. 30; 2 Sam. iii. 20. Nehemiah also and Ezra commanded the people to "eat the fat, and drink the sweet, and send portions unto them for whom nothing was prepared," Neh. viii. 9, 10. And more than once I read of our Saviour's honouring a feast with his presence, Luke v. 29; John ii. 1—11. God has provided not only for our necessity, but also lawful delight; and his bounty reaches not only to our being, but honest solace; nor does it only give us naked lives, but lives clothed with many comforts, that we may more than live, even live cheerfully. When Christ's mother told him they had no wine, he turns water into wine, even to a very great proportion; he thought it not enough that they should have water to quench their thirst, he gives them also wine to cheer their spirits; and it being at a feast, that quantity which at another time had been superfluous, was now but necessary. A man may be angry so he sin not, and take lawful delights so he surfeit not: why has God given man such choice of earthly delights, but for his use? Some observe, that God has made more creatures serving for the delights of man than for his necessity; and certainly he has made nothing in vain. The whole earth, full of his goodness, is a well-furnished table; if we altogether fast, we show ourselves but sullen guests: some indeed have run from the world, and, to avoid the danger of pleasure, have changed places of plenty for solitary and barren mountains and deserts; but may not the world be in a desert? a boiling desire in a neglected body? Did not Jerom find Rome in his heart, when only rocks and bushes were in his eye? But God has appointed a better way than this; the wise man will be a hermit at home; and it is a much more Christian practice, to turn the world out of ourselves, than ourselves out of the world: we may distinguish between the love of pleasure, and the use of it; we may warm ourselves in the sun, without worshipping it; we may be merry without being mad; and get crucified affections to our lawful and delightful comforts: and without this inward mortification upon the heart, notwithstanding our leaving outward enjoyments, we shall be snared; as the bird, which though getting loose from the stone to which she was tied, yet flying with the string about her leg, is in danger to be entangled in every bough. But yet,

Obs. 8. Gluttony is a great sin. It was here the sin of these seducers; they fed themselves, though among men, yet not like men, but beasts; and all their food was but fuel for their lusts: Peter joins their feasting and their eyes full of adultery together, 2 Pet. ii. 13, 14. Several ways is the sin of gluttony committed.

(1.) When men offend in the quantity of what they eat; when they eat and drink in too great abundance: it is lawful sometimes to exceed in provision, but never to exceed the bounds of moderation. We are forbidden to be among riotous eaters of flesh, Prov. xxiii. 20: the feasting of the ancients was called but eating of bread; and Christ bids us to take heed lest our hearts be overcharged with surfeiting and drunkenness, Luke xxi. 14. That proportion of meat, I confess, surcharges the stomachs of some, which perhaps is not enough to satisfy the hunger of another; as that quantity of rain will make a clay ground drunk, which will scarcely quench the thirst of a sandy country; but this I fear not to assert, that we offend in the excessive quantity of our food, when at any time we eat so much as to be disabled to perform the service which we owe to God, either in our general or particular callings. Fulness of bread was one of Sodom's sins. Moderate showers refresh the earth, immoderate drown it. Nor yet are men only gluttons by overcharging their stomachs, but also by overcharging their estates, spending that in superfluity which they should use for necessity.

(2.) When we offend in the quality of our food.

And that, 1. When our meat is too costly. What we eat is put into a vessel that corrupts it. Necessaries are fitter for the body, the soul's servant, than delicacies. Manna had been better for the Israelites than quails, Numb. xi. He was a glutton who fared sumptuously. And here also is caution to be used; as some men's stomachs and estates require more food, so others in both respects may have that which is more costly. 2. In quality of our food we offend, when our meats are incentives to sin. Our enemy, the flesh, is too strong for us, though we take away his armour, and fight against him. We need not put weapons into his hand, and send him ammunition. We need not, should not, help the flesh; the better part is much in danger of being overmatched, though we make not the sensual part two to one by affording it auxiliaries. Our own corruption wants the bridle more than the spur. And some to these add, 3. The unlawfulness of eating such meat as is too young. And they say the prohibition of eating that which wants age is contained in that command, "Thou shalt not seethe a kid in his mother's milk," Exod. xxiii. 19. The creatures are condemned to die for us, and they expect, though not our pardon, yet our reprieve.

<small>Palatum tuum fames excitet non sapores. Sen.</small>

(3.) When we offend in the manner of eating. As, 1. Say some, when we eat too soon, too hastily; namely, before the time of eating, without any necessary cause: "Woe to them that rise early in the morning, that they may follow strong drink!" Isa. v. 11. Woe to the land whose "princes eat in the morning!" Eccl. x. 16; a time wherein the stomach is not to be filled, but the heart ordered, and the mind fed with holy meditations. The tavern is a place never very seemly for a Christian, but in the morning very unseemly. If princes should eat in due season, much more ordinary people. If a master, as Christ speaks, gives not his servant leave to sit down at meat till he have first waited upon him, we should not suffer the soul's page and servant, the body, to feed till it have first attended upon the soul in its spiritual repasts of prayer and meditation. 2. When we eat studiously, making it our work to provide and prepare for the stomach, to invent and study pleasing dishes, strange meats, foreign sauces; when men live to eat, meditating upon nothing but the trencher. As some men by intemperance overthrow the nature of man; so others by this sinful studiousness, and exactness in feasting, overthrow the nature of their meat; when things are prepared with so much art that the nature of the creature is lost, and the eater knows not what he eats. Oh how unworthy is it for a Christian to be always plodding and contriving his meats! to lock up his soul in the kitchen, which should be walking in heaven! 3. When we eat with a vehement appetite, and greedily: thus men may be gluttonous in feeding upon the coarsest fare. David, though he earnestly desired the water of Bethlehem, yet instead of drinking it greedily, poured it upon the ground. Gluttons rather devour than eat their meat, and rather indeed are eaten up with it. They drink of the stream, and forget the fountain; their greediness swallows up their thankfulness; and as soon as ever they have filled their bucket, they turn their backs upon the well. 4. When we feast without any difference of times. How unseasonable was it for Joseph's brethren to eat bread when their brother was in the pit! or for the Israelites to eat "the lambs of the flock, and the calves out of the midst of the stall," to "drink wine in bowls," &c., and not to be "grieved for the affliction of Joseph!" to slay oxen, kill sheep, &c., when

<small>Animalia ruminantia, ruminant post sumptionem cibi, sed gulosus, ante. Perald. de Gula.</small>

God called to weeping and mourning, &c.! When the church drinks blood and tears, we should not drink wine in bowls; we should rejoice with trembling, and feast as if we feasted not. It is God's goodness that he calls us to feast any day, our own licentiousness if we will feast every day. He who fared sumptuously every day shall be in eternal want of so much as one drop. 5. When we feast uncharitably; feasting the rich, never thinking upon the poor. "When thou makest a dinner or a supper, call not thy rich neighbours, but call the poor," &c., Luke xiv. 12. Lazarus must not starve at the gate. We must not be like oaks, who with their acorns only feed swine. 6. When we feast with too much expense of time in feasting; when we dine all day, and sup all night; when our supper shall tread upon the heels of our dinner. "Woe to them that continue until night, till wine inflame them!" Isa. v. 11. This expense of time is worse than our expense of meat and money. The former may be regained, not the latter. And yet how frequently do men complain that they have spent too much money, how rarely that they have spent too much time at feasting! Prodigality of time is the worst.

If the opening of the nature of this sin does not sufficiently discover its odiousness, let us a little further look upon it by other dissuasive considerations.

(1.) Gluttony is an enemy to all holiness of life. It hinders a man from doing himself any spiritual good. It blunts the understanding with blockishness and stupidity. "Whosoever is deceived by wine" (saith Solomon, Prov. xx. 1) "is not wise." Wisdom is not "found in the land of the living," Job xxviii. 13. The Vulgate reads it, *in terra suaviter viventium*, in the land of those who live in delights and pleasures. "Whoredom, wine, and new wine," saith the prophet, "take away the heart," Hos. iv. 11. The four children, Dan. i. 16, 17, who lived upon a frugal diet, were most eminent for learning and wisdom. Wine in feasts, and the not considering of the operations of God's hands, are put together, Isa. v. 6. Jerom and Ambrose observe, that as Moses received the tables of the law when he was much in fasting, so he broke the tables when he saw that the people had been eating and drinking; as thinking that after feasting the people were unfit to hear the law. How can an impure glutton lift up in prayer pure hands? Surfeiting oppresses the heart, and suffers it not to lift up itself toward heaven; it is the birdlime of the soul's wings. It is a weight which presses us down in our race; yea, rather the ungirding of the loins of our minds, our affections, which, like long and loose garments let down into the mire of sensual pleasures, hinder and stop us in our spiritual progress. Oh how unfit a mansion is a beastly epicure for the Holy Spirit to dwell in! Being drunk with wine is opposed to being filled with the Spirit, Eph. vi. 18. The voluptuous sensualist is only a sty for Satan to lodge in. The unclean spirit finds no rest in dry places, in those who are sober and temperate in worldly enjoyments; but like the swine, not delighting in such dust, he loves to wallow in a sensual and impure glutton, as in a slough or quagmire. Gluttony is the sepulchre of the living, and a kind of spiritual drowning of a man.

<small>Mente recta uti non possunt multo cibo et potu repleti. Cicer. Tota ebriorum vita insomnium quoddam, rationis naufragium.</small>

<small>Tabulas legis quas accepit abstinentia, conteri fecit ebrietas. Ambr. cap. 6. de Helia. et Jejun. Sciebat Dei sermonem non posse audire temulentos. Hier. l. 2.; contr. Jov.</small>

<small>Loca arida sunt homines temperate viventes, in quibus diabolus non invenit requiem. Parisiens.</small>

(2.) This sin profanely denies God his service, and opposes him, not only notwithstanding, but even by, his bounty turns the temple of the Holy Ghost into a kitchen, and makes (as the apostle speaks) a god even of the base, filthy belly. How unseemly is it "for a servant," says Solomon, "to have rule over princes!" Prov. xix. 10. The reigning of a servant is reckoned to be the first of the four things which the earth cannot bear, Prov. xxx. 22. Gluttony makes the prince, the soul, to serve the belly, of all the soul's servants, viz. the parts of the body, the basest and filthiest. The apostle speaks of some who serve their own belly, Rom. xvi. 18; Phil. iii. 19. O miserable servitude! Besides the baseness of serving such a master, it is also very cruel; it makes a man a servant to all those meats and drinks which serve his gratification; it is a slavery to a master who is never pleased, who will have the best provisions brought him, and, having taken them, is presently calling for more; his work is never done; he puts his servants upon drudging for him as long as they live; several times every day making men labour in filling a trunk, sometimes three or four score years together; requiring and exacting his supplies so imperiously and rigorously, that his servants oft take thought to the cutting of their hearts, and pains to the cracking of their sinews, for getting his provisions; and yet when all is done, no service is so vain and unprofitable as this belly service. What is it but daubing and propping a rotten cottage, which will, notwithstanding, in a short time crumble away and tumble down; the delicate feeding of a condemned malefactor, who must die, and whose strength by all his provisions serves him but to go to execution? yea, what is it but preparing a banquet for the worms, for whom the leanest carcass is even fat enough?

Multis servit, qui corpori servit. Sen.

(3.) This sin of gluttony uses and abuses that part most in its service, which of all the rest is so noble, and should be most employed for God, and filled with his praises, the mouth.

(4.) It is a sin which most unsuspectedly surprises us, as lying in ambush behind our lawful enjoyments, and which is most like to insnare us in those ways wherein we most walk, and such a one whereby even Adam in innocency was caught.

(5.) This one is an inlet to all sin. He who is overcome with this is not able to overcome any sin. Having possession of the gate of man, his mouth, it lets easily into him the whole troop of vices. It is Satan's bridle, which he puts into the mouth of a sinner, and turns him any way at his pleasure. When the iron is hot, the smith can fashion it how he will. A gluttonous person is earth so tilled, manured, and moistened by Satan, that it is fit to receive any seed which he shall cast into it; cruelty, uncleanness, security, profaneness, all grow in that soil, Luke xii. 45.

(6.) Gluttony is the source and nurse of all diseases. It must needs be unhealthful to carry a fen within one. Temperance is the noblest physic. The inordinate life is not patient enough to stay for sickness. Our food becomes by gluttony, instead of a plaster, a wound. The glutton digs his grave with his teeth, and is a self-destroyer. They who most follow, most fly from pleasure: having taken their leave of an hour's pleasure, they oft meet with a year's pain. The temperate person only enjoys the sweetness of the creature.

(7.) This sin is the ruin and hazard of men's estates. The very word ἀσωτία, luxury, from α and σώζω, properly signifies not preserving, or keeping the good which we enjoy. How many have swallowed their estates down their throats! "The drunkard and the glutton," saith Solomon, "shall come to poverty," Prov. xxiii. 21. The philosopher asked of the frugal citizen but a penny, but begged of the prodigal a talent; because he thought of the one he might beg oft, of the other, who spent so fast, he was like to receive but once.

(8.) It is a sin most injurious to the poor. The glutton's superfluity causes and increases the scarcity of the poor. As the spleen grows, so the other parts decay; and as the riotous abound, so the poor wants; and none are so willing to let Lazarus starve at their gate, as they who fare sumptuously every day.

(9.) It makes way for eternal emptiness and scarcity. He who has here been unprofitably a gulf to devour God's blessings, shall hereafter be thrown into a gulf of misery, wherein there is no drop of mercy. How poor is that plenty which makes way for eternal penury! O woeful receipts, which are only in this life, and not followed with being received! Sinful pleasures are by some compared to those locusts, the crowns upon whose heads are said to be only as it were such, or such in appearance, and like gold, Rev. ix. 7; but it is said there were, not as it were, but "there were stings in their tails," ver. 10. The pleasures of sin are seeming and appearing, the pains true and real.

Obs. 9. In feasting we are too prone to cast away holy fear. These seducers fed themselves without fear. In doing those things which are lawful, we are too ready to be fearless both of God and ourselves. Job feared that his sons had sinned by this want of God's fear in their feasting, Job i. 5. It is an easy matter to sin, when the thing we are about is not sinful. Our lawful comforts, as trading, sleeping, marrying, feasting, are oft occasions of what is unlawful. The old world was very fearless of sinning when they eat, drank, bought, sold, Luke xvii. 27, 28; so fearless, that nothing would awaken them but feeling. Most people are drowned in the shallows of lawful enjoyments. The meat and drink which in themselves are wholesome have killed a thousand times more than poison ever did, because the former are not feared as is the latter. Men startle at evident and known sins, whereas in lawful and allowed delights they are oft overtaken without suspicion. Besides, as feasting is a lawful, so it is a full condition. And when we have most fulness, we commonly have least fear. Men who most abound in enjoyments, are most bold in wickedness. "Jeshurun waxed fat, and kicked," Deut. xxxii. 15. "When thou shalt have eaten and be full; then beware lest thou forget the Lord," Deut. vi. 11, 12. Agur's prayer was against riches, upon this ground, lest being full he should forget God, Prov. xxx. 9. In slippery paths we are most ready to fall; and in a condition of greatest abundance we soonest are overturned. A full condition is commonly but fuel to lust; nor can our sensual hearts easily feed upon pleasing objects without surfeiting. The drunkards of Ephraim were on the head of the fat valleys, Isa. xxviii. 1. It is a rare thing to see religion flourish in a rich soil. Where the soil is richest, there the inhabitants commonly are most riotous. And if it be thus, then worldly abundance is a weak argument to prove God's love; and we should be content to want, yea, pray against, and shun those delights which will occasion us, being full, to deny God. And we should particularly feast with holy fear, which will keep us from sin in our feasting, from falling in such a slippery path. This fear of God and ourselves we shall show,

(1.) By propounding holy ends in our feasting. As, 1. The refreshing of our bodies; not living to eat, but eating to live, and to keep our frail cottages in meet reparations. 2. We should aim at glorifying God, at delighting in the Giver by and above his gifts; being more firmly tied to him with every cord of love. A godly man has a heavenly end in doing every earthly employment; and though he does the same thing which he was wont to do, yet now he does it for a higher end, and would account a feast but a dry morsel, if thereby he might not see it come in love, and be enabled to return it again to love.

(2.) By acknowledging God's attributes. In our feasts meditating, 1. On God's fulness and sufficiency, who with the opening of his hand fills every creature, and is the great Householder of the whole world. 2. On his goodness, in causing so many creatures to die for us who deserved death most of all, and are less than the least of all God's mercies.

(3.) By observing Divine rules. [1.] The rule of piety: 1. In praying for a blessing, and particularly for a heart to be thankful for the receiving, holy in the using, and fruitful in the improving every gift. 2. In using holy discourse: this box of ointment we then should bring and break, like that good woman, Luke vii. 36. Bread and salt are necessary at every feast; our discourse must both feed and season others. [2.] The rule of charity in remembering the poor, whose wants our compassions should make us feel, though our conditions do not; and, to show that our bowels are not shut up, our hands should be open. [3.] The rule of temperance: sometimes we should fast, never be gluttonous. If thou art, saith Solomon, a man of appetite, put a knife to thy throat, Prov. xxiii. 2. Nature seems to dictate thus much, by giving to man a smaller mouth, and a narrower throat, than any other creature of his size hath. We should rise from the greatest feast fit to pray.

This for the first resemblance whereby the apostle describes the state of these seducers.

II. He compares them to "clouds without water, carried about of winds."

Two particulars are here to be explained.

1. From what sort of creatures he draws the resemblance, viz. from "clouds."

2. From what sort of clouds, viz. 1. From empty clouds. 2. From unstable clouds.

1. From what sort of creatures the resemblance is drawn. Two things are considerable.

(1.) What we are to understand by clouds.

(2.) Why the apostle made choice of such a resemblance, taken from these clouds.

(1.) What we are to understand by clouds. The word is νεφέλαι, clouds, derived, as some think, from the Hebrew word נחל which signifies to drop; or, as others, from נפל to fall, or descend. And a cloud (such as the word νεφέλη properly imports) is "a moist vapour drawn up by the heat of the sun unto the middle region of the air, where, being by the coldness of that place knit together and congealed, it continues until, being dissolved and melted by the warmth of the sun, it is turned into rain." So that the property and use of clouds is to carry water and rain for the use of the earth; they water the garden of the earth like a garden-pot; they are the treasuries of rain, and, as one saith, rain condensed or congealed, and rain is a cloud dissolved. And therefore, as the learned Junius on this place notes, when our apostle adds ἄνυδροι to νεφέλαι, saying that these clouds are without water, he rather uses *ratione populari*, a popular and vulgar kind of speech, than agrees with philosophical accuracy; for those clouds which are without water Aristotle and other philosophers call not νεφέλας, nubes, but ὁμίχλας, nebulas, thin dispersed vapours, which indeed obscure the face of the heavens, but have within them no rain for the thirsty earth at all; so distinguishing them from νεφέλαι, rainy clouds, Psal. lxxvii. 17; Isa. v. 6; 1 Kings xviii. 41—46.

Zanch. de Op. Dei, l. 3. c. 6. p. 381.

Illud hoc loco, tum plerique allis observari necesse est, scripturam non uti accurationis philosophorum, sed ratione populari in nominandis rebus, ὁμίχλαι distinctionis ergo, a philosophis nebulae appellantur, quae ἄνυδροι sunt et ἄγονοι, ἔστι γὰρ ἡ ὁμίχλη νεφέλη ἄγονος. Arist. Met. l. 1. c. 9. Jun. in Jude.

The naturalists who write concerning watery meteors, inquire how it can be that a cloud should contain so vast a bulk and quantity of heavy waters, and not violently and at once fall to the earth; heavy things naturally descending or tending downward. Several causes are assigned; some say that they are kept up by the natural and inbred warmth included in them, and by the heat without of the sun and stars; others say by their motion which they have from the winds; others by reason of their spungy hollowness, which receives and takes in the thin air: but philosophers in this are like little children that cannot speak plain, at least to my dulness: the safest way, according to the best divines, is to resolve this by the Scripture, which represents the holding up of the clouds as the work of God's power, and teaches us that God has given his command in the creation that the clouds fall not: "He established the clouds above," Prov. viii. 28. "Let the firmament," that is, as Zanchy largely and strongly proves, the air, in respect of the middle region, "divide the waters from the waters," Gen. i. 6; namely, those which are drawn up, and made clouds for rain, from those which run below. And in Job xxvi. 8, it is expressly said that God "bindeth up the waters in his thick clouds, and the cloud is not rent under them:" he hath bound these waters in a garment, Prov. xxx. 4. The waters above the heavens are recorded among the things which God has established for ever, and for which he has made a decree that they shall not pass, Psal. cxlviii. 4, 6. It is his power that enables so weak a cobweb to hold, as it were, a strong man prisoner; it is that alone which lays up even a sea of waters in the thin sieve of a cloud, which, till he pleases, shall not let go one drop, and then rain shall come, as through a sieve or strainer, not in floods, but in drops. Or rather, as Zanchy that divine naturalist speaks, he makes his clouds spunges; till he press and squeeze them with the hand of his providence not a drop shall fall out of them: he presses these spunges not too hard, but gently, that so they may moderately, and by little and little, distil and drop upon us, and not overwhelm us, as they did the old world, when he wrung these spunges hard upon them. He whose word is a dam to hinder the proud waves from flowing over the face of the earth, has a word likewise which, as a stopper, shuts up the bottles of his clouds, and keeps them from running out. In a word, he who hangeth the earth upon nothing, is in the next words deservedly said to bind up the waters in his thick clouds.

Aer, sua media regione, dividit aquas quae sursum evehuntur, ab iis quae infra fluunt. Zanch. de Op. Dei, l. 2. c. 1. p. 277.

Sunt nubes, ut spongia quaedam aquarum plena. Deus autem manu sua providentiae, spongiam hanc comprimit, non totam simul, et quantum potest, sed paulatim, ut molliter descendant aquae. Zanch. de Op. Dei, l. 3. c. 6. p. 383.

(2.) Why the apostle made choice of a resemblance taken from these clouds. He saith these seducers were νεφέλαι, clouds, which according to the notation of the word, and common usage, signify such as have in them water for the refreshment of the earth: and I conceive that our apostle hereby intends either, 1. To show their duty, which was, as the ministers of Christ, to be watering clouds, to afford to people the sweet and refreshing showers of wholesome doctrines; or rather, 2. Their great boastings, hypocritical shows and appearances, seeming and pretending to be clouds full of water, as the holy prophets and apostles were; whereas indeed they were, though appearing full, yet really and truly empty; unprofitable and waterless, like the boaster of a false gift, of whom Solomon speaks, Prov. xxv. 14, that he is as clouds without rain, though by reason of his great promises he seemed to be full of water and benefits: as if the apostle had said, These seducers are clouds full of water of holiness and heavenly doctrine, if you will believe their own expressions and appearances; but if you come to try or use them, you shall find no benefit, comfort, or refreshment from them. And I conceive that the apostle by calling them clouds, intimates their proud and hypocritical pretending to resemble the worthy and profitable instructors and teachers of the people of old, who are oft and elegantly in Scripture compared to clouds, and whose doctrine is resembled to dropping; as Isa. v. 6, where God (according to some) threatening to take away the prophets and their ministry from the people, saith, "I will command the clouds that they rain no rain." And frequently in Scripture is prophesying or teaching called a dropping: "My doctrine" (saith Moses) "shall drop as the rain," Deut. xxxii. 2. "Son of man, drop toward," &c., "and prophesy against the land of Israel," Ezek. xxi. 2. And, "Prophesy not against Israel, drop not thy word against the house of Isaac," Amos vii. 16. "Son of man, drop toward the south, and prophesy," &c., Ezek. xx. 46. And, "Prophesy" (or drop) "not, say they to them that prophesy," Micah ii. 6. And in ordinary speech we say, The clouds drop, and when it begins to rain, It drops. "His clouds drop down the dew," Prov. iii. 20. And clouds are a most lively resemblance of faithful ministers: (1.) In respect of the cause of both: the supreme, highest cause is God, Prov. viii. 28; Psal. cxlvii. 8; clouds are frequently in Scripture called his clouds, Job xxvi. 8; Psal. xviii. 12; Prov. iii. 20. Ministers are his; they are from him, for him, kept up by him; he gives the word, and great shall be the company of those who publish it, Psal. lxviii. 11; he sends forth labourers: the natural cause of clouds is the sun drawing up vapours; Christ, the Sun of righteousness, he calls, appoints, gives gifts to ministers. (2.) In respect of the condition of clouds; they are carried from place to place, tossed to and fro with the winds: ministers are oft removed by God from one place, in anger for its unfruitfulness, to another, and tossed by the winds of persecution hither and thither, the church nevertheless by their dispersion gaining moisture and spiritual benefit. (3.) In respect of their situation: clouds are above us; ministers are dignified by God, over us in the Lord, and they, as clouds, ought to be nearer heaven, and having their conversation there more than others, Phil. iii. 20. They are not clods, but clouds, yea, stars, yea, angels. (4.) Clouds they are in respect of sustentation, upheld by the powerful word of God's providence; else, as clouds under their loads, they could never be upheld; they are as dying, yet behold they live; stars in the right hand of Christ. (5.) In respect of fulness, usefulness, and benefit. A cloud is both *umbrifera* and *imbrifera*, bringing shadow and moisture to the earth: a faithful minister cools and refreshes a scorched conscience by preaching the righteousness of Christ; he is a messenger, an interpreter, "one among a thousand to show unto man his uprightness," Job xxxiii. 23; his feet are beautiful, Rom. x. 15, as welcome to a scorched conscience as the rain to the parched earth: these spiritual clouds drop down the fruitful showers of heavenly doctrine. Good ministers are apt to teach, 2 Tim. ii. 24. (6.) Like clouds, they spend and consume themselves in dropping on others; like salt and torches, they melt themselves to benefit others; like silkworms, they weave out their own bowels to cover others' nakedness.

2. From what sort of clouds does our apostle draw a resemblance to suit with these seducers?

(1.) From empty clouds, "without water."
(2.) From unstable clouds, "carried about," &c.
(1.) From empty clouds; they are νεφέλαι ἄνυδροι, "clouds without water." Here two things ought to be explained.
[1.] What it was to be "without water."
[2.] When it was a sin to be so.
[1.] For the first: as in Scripture the prophets and ministers are compared to clouds, so their heavenly doctrine to water or rain showered down from those clouds: "My doctrine," saith Moses, "shall drop as the rain, my speech shall distil as the dew, as the small rain upon the tender herb," Deut. xxxii. 2. "As the rain cometh down, and the snow from heaven, and returneth not thither, but watereth the earth, and maketh it bring forth and bud," &c.; "so shall my word be that goeth forth out of my mouth," &c., Isa. lv. 10, 11. "The earth drinketh in the rain that cometh oft upon it, and bringeth forth herbs," &c., Heb. vi. 7. And most fitly may the word be compared to rain, 1. For its original. God gives rain: "Are there any among the vanities of the Gentiles that can cause rain? or can the heavens give showers? art not thou he, O Lord?" &c., Jer. xiv. 22. "I will give you the rain of your land, Deut. xi. 14. "I will give you rain in due season," Lev. xxvi. 4. God can only give us a word; it is called "the word of the Lord." He appoints what ministers should preach, and he teaches them how to preach; and he makes the word effectual.

2. Rain is of a searching, insinuating nature, soaking to the roots. The word searches the heart, pricks the heart, and purges it, Acts ii. 37; Heb. iv. 12.

3. Rain cools and refreshes the earth and plants. The promises of the word delight the soul, the chapt, gasping, thirsty soul, Isa. xliv. 3.

4. Rain softeneth the earth, though hard like iron. The word makes the heart tender, pliable, and obedient, Jer. xxxi. 33; Ezek. xxxvi. 26, and fit to be moulded according to God's mind.

5. Rain causeth the earth to be fruitful. The word makes us fruitful in every grace and good work; it is an instrumental cause of spiritual growth, 1 Pet. ii. 2; Psal. i. 3; 1 Pet. iii. 16. So that these seducing teachers were clouds, (1.) Without the water of holiness, and sanctification of heart, life, and example; they made show to be the only sublime saints, and Christians of the first magnitude, and that others, in comparison of them, were but in the lowest form of godliness; yet these ungodly men had not in them a drop of true sanctity; they only had "a form of godliness, but denying the power thereof," 2 Tim. iii. 5; and these waterless wells, as Peter calls them, had nothing in them but the mud and filth of sin, not to cleanse, but pollute and defile. (2.) They were without the water of true knowledge. They pretended to be the only knowing persons, that they only had two eyes, and all others but one. They assumed to themselves the title of *Gnostici*, for their great pretended insight into the doctrines of faith; they looked upon others as the Pharisees upon the people, who (they said) knew not the law, and were accursed; or as Caiaphas upon the other priests, he telling them that they knew nothing; and yet for all this they were empty, and without the water of saving knowledge and instruction. Their doctrines were but wind, chaff, and idle speculations, vain janglings, contentions about words, not profiting them who are exercised therein, improving no soul heavenward, making it after all their empty discourses no further admitted into communion with Christ, cleansed from sin, in love with

holiness, fitted for death; in a word, their verbal triflings never made a proselyte to Jesus Christ, but only to an opinion. They had perhaps the wisdom of words, but not the words of wisdom. They left the Scripture, and only regarded dreams and fables. They were blind leaders of the blind, and erred from the right way; desiring to be teachers of the law, they understood neither what they said, nor whereof they affirmed, 1 Tim. i. 7. And instead of being clouds that bedewed their hearers with the drops of heavenly instruction, they were clouds only to darken their mind with error, and to hide from them the sunshine of truth. (3.) They were without the water of consolation and refreshment for those who expected benefit and relief from them. "Whoso boasteth himself of a false gift, is like clouds and wind without rain," Prov. xxv. 14. All the glorious promises of peace and liberty which they made to their misled followers were empty and deceitful: "While they promise them liberty, they themselves are the servants of corruption," 2 Pet. ii. 19. They pretended that they had found out a nearer way to heaven than any before them had done, and that people might, without fetching such a compass of mortification and holiness, go straight on to peace and blessedness. But their poor deceived disciples found them herein to be but clouds without water, such who could not make good these promises, and that there was no peace in impurity. Peter calls them "wells without water," 2 Pet. ii. 17, elegantly describing their disappointing those who expected relief and refreshment for their souls from them, being like the waters or wells in a hot summer, that in Jer. xv. 18 are said to lie or fail; or a brook that is deceitful, Job vi. 15, disappointing the thirsty who go to them for refreshment. They who trusted to what these seducers promised by their doctrines, being like to those little ones, who, being sent to the pits, found no water, "returning with their vessels empty, ashamed and confounded, covering their heads," Jer. xiv. 3.

[2.] For the second, Wherein it was a sin for these seducers to be as "clouds without water."

1. It argued profane presumption; namely, in undertaking a holy function for which they had no fitness; they had no worth, either of piety or sufficiency; they had lips, but not such as could preserve knowledge; they polluted the holy things of God with their unmeetness to manage them: had they been persons of greatest abilities, the work of teaching and instructing souls would have deserved and taken them all up; the shoulders of an angel would have been weak enough for the weight of such a service: "Who is sufficient for these things?" 2 Cor. ii. 16. A mortal man would have scorned to be put off with such performances as they thought good enough for the great God. These cursed deceivers offered to God not a male, but a corrupt thing. The God who is the best and greatest requires the best and greatest of our abilities. But these offered that to God which cost them nothing.

2. It argued the sin of unprofitableness; they could not give what they had not; they had no worth, and they did no work. They had no water, nor did they pour down any. They were wicked and slothful, and therefore wicked because slothful, Matt. xxv. 26. These false teachers knew not what labour meant. They were spent not with cutting, but rusting. They were loiterers in the time of harvest; and they were neither faithful nor labourers. If they perspired at all, it was not with working, but feeding. They were not as clouds that spend themselves in watering the earth. They were not impaired by service, but sensuality. If a private person must be a public good, then must not a public person be a private good? They lived to themselves, and cumbered their places to no purpose in the world. When men went secure to hell, they quietly suffered them to do so. Their cruelty was great because it was soul cruelty, they starved souls.

3. In their sin was delusion and hypocrisy; as they neither had worth nor did good, so in both they opposed their profession. They praised themselves as the only able instructors; but as the waterless clouds delude the expecting husbandman, so did these their fond followers. They pretended to be spiritual nurses, and though they expected full payment, they gave the children but empty, windy breasts. Their deluded disciples spent their money for that which was not bread, and their labour for that which satisfied not. Had these seducers appeared to be what they were, empty, they had not been called clouds; or had they been what they appeared to be, they had not been called "clouds without water." Under a glorious title there lodged a base and unworthy temper.

It is a great sin to be confutations of our professions. Injustice is not so inexcusable in any as in a judge; blindness is not so blamable in any as in a guide, a seer; silence in none is so hateful as in a preacher; dryness no where so unexpected as in a well, a cloud.

It was not the barren oak or elm, from which fruit was never expected, but the fig-tree, whose kind was fruitful, that Christ cursed for unfruitfulness. Nor did the damage of their hypocrisy only redound to themselves. As by reason of their emptiness they did good to none, so in regard of their seeming fulness they did hurt to many. How easily might their misguided followers spend their time in a vain gaping after these empty clouds of error and presumption for the water of life and happiness, and meanwhile neglect the rain of heaven, a soul-saving ministry! these erroneous guides, though hereby aggravating their own, yet not excusing their followers from damnation.

2. Our apostle, to set forth the instability as well as the emptiness of these seducers, draws a comparison to suit these seducers from clouds, as carried about with the winds; he saith, they are ὑπὸ ἀνέμων περιφερόμεναι.

Two things I shall here touch by way of explication.

1. What the apostle here intends by their being carried about.

2. What those winds were by which they were carried about.

1. What the apostle intends by their being carried about. Περιφερόμεναι, driven this way and that way, not abiding or resting in any one place, like any light matter, feathers, stubble, dust, &c., which are at the courtesy of every blast and puff of wind. And hereby is intended the unstableness and unsettledness of these seducers in their Christian course; expressed likewise by the same word, Eph. iv. 14, "children tossed to and fro, and" περιφερόμενοι, "carried about with every wind of doctrine;" and, μὴ περιφέρεσθε, "Be not carried about with divers and strange doctrines," Heb. xiii. 9. If one wind comes, the cloud is carried this way; if another, that way; sometimes to one quarter of the heavens, at other times to a quite contrary: so was it with these unsettled souls, who, wanting the ballast and solidity of grace in their heart, were unstable, unconfirmed in their opinions, affections, and practices. For the apostle may hereby intend a threefold instability and unsettledness, or their being carried about in three respects.

(1.) In respect, principally I conceive, of opinion

and judgment; they were not settled in the truths of religion, like those who "halted between two opinions," 1 Kings xviii. 21. They continued not "in the faith, grounded and settled," Col. i. 23; they were not placed upon a firm foundation, nor were they seated as a man in a seat, from which he cannot easily be removed. It is frequently observed, that the erroneous are never firm either to the truth or their own opinions. They forget what they have been, understand not what they are, and know not what they shall be. Augustine tells us how frequently Pelagius altered his opinions concerning grace; and Hilary reports of Arius, that he had for every month a sundry faith, as if he had swallowed moons; that he was never consistent to and with himself: before the council, he held for the Divinity of Christ; among his companions, otherwise. Thus the apostle complains of the Galatians for their being " so soon removed unto another gospel," Gal. i. 6, and warns his Ephesians that they should not be carried about, Eph. iv. 14; and Peter, 2 Pet. ii. 14, mentions "unstable souls." Oft from Brownism men wander to Anabaptism, from thence to Arminianism, thence to Socinianism and Arianism, and then they become Seekers, or rather indeed losers of themselves, just nothing; as a thin, empty cloud, they are tossed so long up and down by winds, that at length they come to nothing. Their heads are like inns, and their opinions like travellers, which oft lodge not above one night in them; like wax, they take any new impression. It is hard to say whether they are pluralists or neutralists in religion, and as hard to please them in any opinion as to make a coat that should constantly fit the moon. They know they shall die, but in what faith they know not. One error is ever a bridge to another. They are called unlearned and unstable, and therefore such as wrest the Scriptures, 2 Pet. iii. 16; whence it is plain that by unstable he means such as were not grounded in the faith and learning of the truth. Hymeneus and Philetus, who once held the truth concerning the resurrection, afterward erred concerning the faith, saying that the resurrection was past already, 2 Tim. ii. 18.

(2.) They might be carried about and unstable in respect of their affections, the goodness whereof was only by fits and pangs; sometimes they were fire-hot in religion, soon after stone-cold; their heat, like that in the fit of an ague, is not from nature, but distemper, and therefore, though violent, yet not permanent; they resemble the mariners of whom the psalmist speaks, that at one time are mounted up to heaven, and presently fall down again into the depths, Psal. cvii. 26: like David, who in his youth was full of spirits and vigour, but in his old age grew cold and chilly, these who sometimes seemed fervent in spirit, ζέοντες τῷ πνεύματι, now are cold in their affections, and come to a state of indifference and neutrality, and frame to themselves such a moderation as will just serve the times. They were, they say, forward and foolish in the heat of their youth to oppose sin, but now they see their error, and admire their present staidness, and the golden mean which they have attained. Thus it was with those unsettled Galatians, who at first could have pulled out their eyes for Paul, soon after counted him an eyesore, their enemy, for telling them the truth, Gal. iv. 16. The church of Ephesus had left her first love, Rev. ii. 4. Thus Alexander, who, as some think, for his zeal against Diana, the heathens' idol, or, as others, for his noted love towards Paul, was like to have been torn in pieces as a martyr; afterwards, as Calvin thinks, became Paul's deadly adversary, 2 Tim. iv. 14, and would have martyred him.

<small>Qui martyrio propinquus erat, perfidum et sceleratum apostatam factum videmus. Cal. in Acts xix., formidabile exemplum.</small>

John's hearers rejoiced in his light for a season. Affections raised upon no true grounds will soon fall; and as much greater will the fall be, as the higher the building was. They who have been sometimes more than Christians in their fervour for, afterwards have proved worse than heathens in fury against, the truth.

(3.) They might be carried about and unstable in their practices; very strict and precise in their carriage at the first, very loose and profane afterwards. Seducers grew from better to worse, or, as the apostle speaks, "worse and worse," 2 Tim. iii. 13; golden professors haply in their youth, silver in their middle age, leaden in their old age. They set out well, but did not hold out at all; appearing so conscientious at the first, that the very appearances of sin were shunned; so really wicked at last, that the greatest abominations are not scrupled; and they are grown so strong, that their stomachs can digest those impieties, with the very sight of which heretofore they seemed to be sick. How frequently has the glorious, the morning beginnings of Christian profession been overcast with the darkness and gloomy cloudiness of profaneness before the evening! Many who have been elevated to a high pitch of profession, have fallen like clouds into some dirty lane, or slough of uncleanness and looseness. They begin in the flesh, and end in the flesh, Gal. iii. 3; though they seemed to have escaped the pollutions of the world, and to be washed from their filthiness, yet they return with the dog to their vomit, and with the sow to their wallowing in the mire, 2 Pet. ii. 22.

2. By what they were carried about and unsettled, viz. by the winds, ὑπὸ ἀνέμων: the word ἄνεμος signifies any blast which blows in the air, but Peter, 2 Pet. ii. 17, saith they are ὑπὸ λαίλαπος ἐλαυνόμεναι, carried with a tempest; the word λαῖλαψ properly signifying a whirlwind, not one wind, but a conflict of many winds. It is used by the evangelists in describing the tempest miraculously appeased and calmed by Christ, Luke viii. 23; Mark iv. 37. There were several sorts of winds and tempests wherewith these seducers were carried about.

<small>Plurium conflictus ventorum. Lorin. Impetuosus turbo. Gerh.</small>

(1.) The wind of strange doctrines: this is noted by the apostle, Heb. xiii. 9, where he warns the Christians that they "be not carried about with divers and strange doctrines," διδαχαῖς ποικίλαις καὶ ξέναις μὴ περιφέρεσθε, and Eph. iv. 14, "with every wind of doctrine," παντὶ ἀνέμῳ τῆς διδασκαλίας. Every doctrine which was new was by them entertained as true. They had itching ears, delighted with novelty, not obedient ears, attentive to profitable truths; whence it was that every new doctrine carried them a different way, and that meeting with several new doctrines they were hurried round as in a whirlwind, and knew not where to rest. The devil pleased them, like children, with change of toys. The true gospel was neglected for another, as Paul speaks, Gal. i. 6; they were of the same mind with him who taught them last; they were mere movables in the church; like the water, ever of the same figure with the vessel into which it is put; like a company of ciphers, which signify just the figure which is put before them.

(2.) Seducers are carried about with the wind of fear; to save their skins, they cared not what they held, taught, or did; they were impatient of persecution. Thus speaks the apostle of these seducers, "They constrain you to be circumcised; only lest they should suffer persecution for the cross of Christ," Gal. vi. 12. That which they entertain merely for fear, they present to others as a doctrine of faith. These are reeds that bow and hang according to the standing of the winds; such a reed shaken with the winds was not John Baptist, but rather an oak, which will sooner be broken than bend by the winds; by a holy antiperistasis, his zeal was doubled by opposition. These false teachers were like a man that goes to sea for pleasure, not for traffic; if a storm arise, he will come back, or put to the next shore. Like that ship, Acts xxvii. 15, they bear not up to the wind; "they are not valiant for the truth," Jer. ix. 3; nor hold they "fast the faithful word," Tit. i. 9, but let it go if enemies contend to pull it away.

(3.) They were carried about with the wind of pride and ambition. They gaped after the breath of applause. Old truths are of no reputation among the giddy sort; hence it was that these were carried to teach that whereby they might be cried up for some rare men, dropped out of the clouds, and seeing further than all the rest of their times. They could not tell how to get above others, unless they taught something different from others: truth was counted but a dull, stale business, and therefore they chose rather to be accounted such as excelled by being erroneous, than such as were only equal to others by delivering the truth. The wind of pride is the life and soul of error, it is the element wherein it moves and breathes. Seducers were puffed up vainly by their fleshly minds, Col. ii. 18. A humble soul will not easily either teach or follow an error. It has ever been the property of seducers to follow the people's humour with errors, that so the people might follow them with applause.

(4.) They were carried about with the wind of earthly-mindedness. They taught any false doctrine for filthy lucre's sake, 1 Pet. v. 2; they would rarely be carried with any wind but such as blew them some profit; they steered their course by the compass of gain; their religion began at their pursestrings; they served not the Lord Jesus Christ, but their own bellies, Rom. xvi. 18. This was that wind which carried Balaam about from country to country, from altar to altar; he and his followers loved to be of the king's religion. Thus Erasmus said, that one poor Luther made a great many rich abbots and bishops; he meant, that by preaching against him they were wont to get their great livings and preferments: Demas forsook truth to embrace the present world.

Obs. 1. The want of the showers of a faithful ministry is a singular curse and calamity. Conscientious ministers are clouds, and their doctrine rain. As no rain is so useful and profitable as the rain of the word, so neither is it so great a misery to be deprived of any as of this. God often in Scripture promises showers and teachers as great blessings: "The Lord shall open unto thee his good treasure, the heaven to give the rain," &c., Deut. xxviii. 12. "Rejoice in the Lord your God, for," &c. "he will cause to come down for you the rain," &c., Joel ii. 23. And for instructors, see Jer. iii. 15, "I will give you pastors according to mine heart, which shall feed you with knowledge and understanding." "Though the Lord give you the bread of adversity, and the water of affliction, yet shall not thy teachers be removed into a corner any more," Isa. xxx. 20. God also threatens the keeping away of rain, and the taking away of instructors, as dismal curses: "The heaven that is over thy head shall be brass; thy rain shall be powder and dust," Deut. xxviii. 23, 24. "I will make your heaven as iron, and your earth as brass," Lev. xxvi. 19. "Upon them shall be no rain," Zech. xiv. 17. Never was a greater plague on Israel, than when in three years and a half it rained not on the earth in Ahab's time. And concerning the prophets, the Lord saith, "They shall not" (Heb. drop) "prophesy," Micah ii. 6; and God threatens his vineyard, that he will command his clouds, his prophets, "that they rain no rain upon it," Isa. v. 6. God threatened a great judgment in great displeasure against the people, when he told Ezekiel that he would make his tongue cleave to the roof of his mouth; and that he should be dumb, and no reprover to them, Ezek. iii. 26; and when he threatened that he would remove away the candlestick of Ephesus out of its place, Rev. ii. 5. The want of spiritual is a much greater woe than the want of natural rain. The withholding of showers from heaven can but produce a famine of bread: the want of a faithful ministry brings a famine of the word of the Lord, Amos viii. 11. And this famine of the word of the Lord is a soul famine. And,

(1.) Opposes not natural, but spiritual life. The separation of the soul from the body is but the shadow of death; true death stands in the separation between God and the soul. "Where there is no vision, the people perish," Prov. xxix. 18. "My people are destroyed for lack of knowledge," Hos. iv. 6. Salvation and life eternal stand in knowledge, John xvii. 3; 1 Tim. ii. 4.

(2.) Bodily famine takes away our natural strength and vigour, whereby we perform our ordinary and worldly actions; but a soul famine destroys that spiritual strength, whereby we are enabled to heavenly employments, praying, repenting, believing, holy walking.

(3.) Bodily famine makes the outward man look pale, deformed, lean, unpleasing; soul famine brings a leanness into the soul, deformity and profaneness into the face of our conversation. Who observes not in congregations from whence the word is taken the miserable change of men and manners? In Eli's time sin abounded, and the reason is set down 1 Sam. iii. 1, "The word of the Lord was precious in those days."

(4.) Bodily famine, as other external judgments, may be a help to bring men to God, by causing repentance and bettering obedience, as in the prodigal; but the famine of the word puts men farther from God, and by it men grow more obdurate in sin.

(5.) Bodily famine may be recompensed and made up with spiritual food. "Though the Lord give the bread of adversity," Isa. xxx. 20, yet he countervails that loss, by giving them to see their teachers; whereas spiritual famine cannot be recompensed by having bodily food, because when God takes away the food of the soul, he takes away himself, the tokens of his presence and grace; and what can be given in exchange for God himself?

(6.) Of bodily famine people are sensible, they cry and labour for a supply; but the more soul famine rages, the more people disregard their misery, and slight their wretchedness; by fasting, forgetting how to feed, and with their food losing often their stomachs too. How much then are they mistaken, who account spiritual showers their greatest plague, and complain of these dews of grace as if they were a deluge of woe; to whom the word of the Lord is the greatest burden; who cry out, The land cannot bear it! A church without a preacher, is as a ship sailing in a dark night on a rough sea without a pilot. Never was Christ more moved in compassion toward the people, than when he saw them scattered as sheep without a shepherd. They who would be rid of the word, would also be without pardon, peace, holiness, happiness; it being the word of faith, the word which sanctifies, the gospel of peace, the word of life, the power of God to salvation. Ministers are saviours, watchmen, labourers in the harvest, nurses, guides, builders, sowers, seers, light, salt, clouds, &c. What then are places destitute of saving instruction, but unsafe, spoiled, starved, waste, blind, wandering, unsavoury, barren? and yet how commonly do many curse the preaching of the word, as the people who live under the torrid zone do the rising of the sun! To conclude, what apparent enemies are they to the souls of people who hinder the preaching of the gospel! who will not suffer it to run and be glorified; who revile and abuse the faithful dispensers thereof! an act, no doubt, of greater unthankfulness, than to wrong and abuse a man who in a time of famine should open his garners for the relief of a whole country.

Obs. 2. The greatest commendation of a minister is industry for, and usefulness to, the souls of others. Clouds are not appointed for themselves, but to water the earth; and in doing so they consume themselves: like silkworms, ministers wear and weave out themselves. It is a sin for any, much more for a minister, to be an unprofitable servant. He must not go to sea in his ministerial calling for pleasure, but employment. He must say, with Pompey, who, having to sail over the seas with corn to relieve distressed Rome, and being told by the pilot that it would prove a dangerous voyage, answered, It is not necessary we should live, but that we should sail. Πλεῖν ἀνάγκη, ζῆν οὐκ ἀνάγκη. The excellency of the sun is not so much in respect of its glory and splendour, as its influences and beneficialness; and he who expects hereafter to shine like the sun, must here run like the sun. They who preach the Sun of righteousness, must be like the sun who cometh forth of his chamber like a bridegroom, and rejoiceth to run his race. The clods of the earth may be of a more dull and sad temper, rest and lie still; but the clouds of heaven must be in a perpetual motion. Ministers must, like the cherubims, which give attendance in the presence of God, have wings for expedition in the execution of his will. They are called labourers and workmen; they labour in the word and doctrine. Paul's glory was not that he was more advanced, but that he laboured more abundantly than they all. "As much as in me is," saith he, "I am ready to preach the gospel." He made preaching his business; therein he was glad to spend, and to be spent, 2 Cor. xii. 15. Knowledge without industry speaks no man excellent. None is accounted good for the good he hath, but the good he doth. A wooden key that opens the door, is a better one than a golden one that cannot do it. Greatest industry is always to be used about the salvation of souls. Daring importunity is in no case so commendable as in this. Paul was an excellent orator, and all his oratory was to persuade men to be saved. Never did malefactor so plead to obtain his own life, as did Paul beg of men to accept of life. He was an importunate wooer of souls, and he would take no denial. Ministers must rather be worn with using than rusting. The sweat of a minister, as it is reported of Alexander, casts a sweet smell: his talents are not for the napkin, but occupation; not to be laid up, but to be laid out. They who are full clouds should be free in pouring out, returning as they have received. How unworthily do they deal with God, who are all for taking in, and nothing for laying out! How little is the age and place wherein they live beholden to them! How just is it with God, that they who will not give him the interest of their abilities by improving and using them, should lose the principal by ceasing to have and retain them! "The manifestation of the Spirit is given to every one to profit withal," 1 Cor. xii. 7. Standing water soon putrifies. Musical instruments which are most used sound most melodiously. If Solomon observed it to be a great vanity, that some men had riches who had not power to use them, Eccl. vi. 2; how much greater is the vanity of having great intellectual abilities, and yet to have no power to make use of them for the good of others! In short therefore, ministers must remember that they are not appointed for sight, but service and usefulness. We account not a pillar to be good because it is sightly, but strong. We should fear to sit under that structure, the pillars whereof are, though curiously gilded and painted outwardly, yet crazy and rotten within. It is better to be under a disgraced, persecuted Paul, than under a silken Diotrephes, who is altogether for worldly glory and pre-eminence, nothing for duty and performance.

Obs. 3. Ministers of the gospel must be full and watery clouds; able and apt to teach; gifted and fitted for their ministry. As ambassadors, they must be sure to have their instructions with them; and to be "able ministers of the new testament," 2 Cor. iii. 6, "for the perfecting of the saints, for the work of the ministry," Eph. iv. 12. Able to impart spiritual gifts, "bringing forth out of his treasure things new and old," Matt. xiii. 52; being "workmen that need not be ashamed, rightly dividing the word of truth," 2 Tim. ii. 15.

(1.) Able they must be to open the Scriptures. They must have the water of knowledge, and be able to unlock the cabinet of the word, fit to feed the people with understanding; to roll away the stone from the mouth of the well for the watering of the flocks of Christ. He who calls for a reasonable sacrifice, will not be content with an unreasonable sacrificer. Ministers must teach every one in all wisdom, Col. i. 28.

(2.) They must have ability to "convince gainsayers by sound doctrine," Tit. i. 9. A minister's breast should be a spiritual armoury, furnished with spiritual weapons for overcoming opposers. Apollos mightily convinced the Jews; so Paul disputed against the adversaries of the truth, Acts ix. 29; xvii. 17.

(3.) The gift of working upon the affections, and quickening to duty. Ability not only to enlighten the understanding, but to warm the heart. "I think it meet," &c., saith Peter, "to stir you up," 2 Pet. i. 13. Paul, "knowing the terror of the Lord, persuaded men," 2 Cor. v. 11. The minister's lips, like Isaiah's, must be "touched with a live coal," Isa. vi. 6; and he must partake of that Spirit which came down in the likeness of fiery tongues, to fire the affections of his hearers, and to make their hearts burn within them with love to holy duties. It was said of Basil, that he breathed as much fire as eloquence.

(4.) The gift of comforting the distressed conscience; of speaking "a word in season to him that is weary," Isa. l. 4; of declaring to man his uprightness; of binding up the broken heart, and of pouring oil into its wounds; of dropping the refreshing dews of the promises upon the parched conscience. In a word, of giving every one his portion, like a faithful and wise steward.

(5.) Lastly, They must have the water of grace and sanctification. Of this their hearts and life should both be full. If a beast was not to come to the mount where the law was delivered, much less may he who is a beast deliver the law. The doctrine of a minister must credit his life, and his life adorn his doctrine. Dead doctrine, not quickened with a holy life, like dead Amasa, lying in the way, stops people, that they will not go on cheerfully in their spiritual warfare. Doth God require that the beast which is offered to him should be without blemishes, and can he take it well that the priest who offers it should be full of blemishes?

He then who will win souls must be able and wise. A minister must be thoroughly furnished, as Paul speaks, 2 Tim. iii. 17. There is some wisdom required to catch birds, fish, and vermin; how much more to catch souls! The best minister may blush to consider how unfit he is for his calling; and when he has gotten the greatest abilities, he should beg pardon for his inability, and pray and study for a further increase of his gifts. They are none of Christ's ministers who are not in some measure gifted for their work. "He that sendeth a message by the hand of a fool, cutteth off the feet, and drinketh damage," Prov. xxvi. 6; he is sure to suffer for it, it being as if he should cut off a man's legs, and then bid him go on his errand.

To conclude; how unworthy and profane are they who bestow such of their children upon the ministry, as are the dullest and most unfit of all their number! who say, that when a child is good for nothing, he is good enough to make a preacher! whose children (as Doctor Stoughton speaks in allusion to his speech who called Basil, Πυρετοῦ δῶρον, The gift of an ague, he being preserved from the violence of an Arian emperor, because he recovered his son of a dangerous ague) may be called the gift of some lameness, infirmity, deformity! "Offer it now to thy governor; will he be pleased with thee?" Mal. i. 8.

Obs. 4. Ministers are sustained and upheld in their work by the mighty power of God. It is much to be wondered that the natural, but more that the spiritual, clouds are kept from falling. It is God who bindeth up the waters in the cloud, so that it is not rent under them, Job xxvi. 8; he that established and made a decree, which shall not pass, for the waters above the heavens, Psal. cxlviii. 4, 6. It was God who preserved Elijah when Jezebel had vowed his death; God delivered Paul out of the mouth of the lion; he kept Isaiah in his ministry during the reign of four, and Hosea during the reign of five kings; he continued Noah a hundred and twenty years, against the opposition of the old world. Jeremiah, notwithstanding all his enemies, was upheld in his work till the captivity. God promises the church that their teachers should not be removed into corners, but that their eyes should behold them, Isa. xxx. 20. A minister of Christ may say, as Christ of his working miracles, I preach the word to-day and to-morrow, Luke xiii. 32, and do the world what they can, they shall not hinder me, till that day be come that Christ hath appointed. The ministers are stars in Christ's hand. So long as there is any one soul which these lights are to guide to heaven, all the blasts of hell can never extinguish them. God sets them, and God keeps them up; he erects, he upholds, he gave, and he continues their commission during his good pleasure; they are ambassadors, 2 Cor. v. 20, whom he calls home when he pleases. Let not the servants of Christ fear man in the doing of the work of their Lord. He who hangs the earth upon nothing, and keeps the clouds from being rent under the burden of the waters, can uphold them under all their pressures. Their times are in God's hand; they are neither in their own, nor in their enemies'. "They shall fight against thee," said God to Jeremiah, "but they shall not prevail against thee, for I am with thee," Jer. i. 19. Let faithful ministers fear none but their Master, and nothing but sin and unfaithfulness. Not outward evils, because he sleeps not who preserves them; but inward evils, because he sleeps not who observes them. Let ministers undauntedly make their faces hard against the faces of the wicked. In their own cause let them be as flexible as a reed; in God's, as hard as an adamant; who can powerfully say to the strongest enemies of his ministers, "Do my prophets no harm;" and who will turn the greatest harm which they receive for his sake into good, and make even a fiery chariot to carry his zealous Elijahs into heaven. Hence likewise people are taught how to have their faithful ministers continued; namely, by making God their friend, who at his pleasure removes and continues them. How careful were they of Tyre and Sidon to be at peace with Herod, "because their country was nourished by the king's country," Acts xii. 20. It is doubtless greater wisdom to make God our friend, by whose care and providence our country is nourished spiritually, and supplied with those who should break the bread of life unto us. If people would keep their ministers, let them keep and love no sin. Upon the repentance of the Jews, God promised them that his sanctuary should be in the midst of them for evermore, Ezek. xxxvii. 26. Let them bring forth likewise the fruits of the gospel. The husbandman lays his ground fallow when he perceives it will not repay his charges. The kingdom of heaven, saith Christ, shall be taken from you, and given to a nation which will bring forth the fruits thereof, Matt. xxi. 43.

Lastly, let them be importunate with God in prayer to uphold his ministers. Importunity held Christ with the disciples when he was going away, Luke xxiv. 29. Say, Lord, thou shalt not go till thou hast blessed me with more spiritual blessings and grace by the means of grace. O lay hold upon God, as Galeacius's children hung about his legs, when their father was going from them to live at Geneva. The prophet complains that none stirred up himself to take hold of God, Isa. lxiv. 7. Say, "O thou the hope of Israel, why shouldst thou be as a stranger in the land, and as a wayfaring man that turneth aside to tarry for a night?" Jer. xiv. 8. When Peter was cast into prison, prayer was made without ceasing of the church unto God for him; and their prayer broke open the prison doors, and knocked off Peter's chains. When Paul was a prisoner at Rome, he tells Philemon, "I trust that through your prayers I shall be given unto you," Philem. 22.

Obs. 5. Ministers must not in this world expect a settled, quiet condition.

They are clouds, and they must expect to be tossed and hurried by the winds. The most faithful servants of Christ have ever been opposed, when they were opposers of the sinners and sins of the times in which they lived. They are light, and therefore thieves and tender eyes cannot endure them. They are soldiers, and if they, like Ishmael, will draw their sword against every one, every one's sword shall be against them. They are the salt of the earth, and therefore smart and biting; fishers, and therefore they shall be tossed as upon the sea. "Which of the prophets," saith Stephen, "have not your fathers persecuted?" Acts vii. 52. "So persecuted they the prophets," Matt. v. 12. Saith Christ, "I send unto you prophets," &c. "and some of them ye shall kill," &c. "and persecute," Matt. xxiii. 34; Luke xi. 49. So long as ministers will not suffer wicked men to be quiet in their lusts, they will not suffer ministers to have quiet lives. Satan does not so much oppose any of the soldiers in Christ's army as he does the commanders; nor does that wolf any way so much endeavour to devour the sheep as by removing the mastiffs. By the persecuting, likewise, and scattering his ministers, God wisely provides for the relief of his church: God waters the several parts thereof by dispersing these clouds into several quarters. "They who were scattered abroad," οἱ διασπαρέντες, (saith Luke,) "went every where preaching the word," Acts viii. 4. Unless the seed be scattered, there can be no crop expected, and the scattering of the sowers makes way for the scattering of the seed. The scattering of Simeon and Levi in Israel dispersed the knowledge of the law. By carrying the Jews into captivity the truth was made known among the heathen. In the primitive persecution, the more martyrs, the more Christians were made. By the irruption of the Goths and Vandals the persecutors themselves became Christians. The persecution of the truth is its propagation. The sufferings that happened to Paul fell out to the furtherance of the gospel, Phil. i. 12; a consideration which should sweeten the bitterness of a minister's persecution and unsettlement. God does not only thereby make them more pure, but his church more numerous; they ought to prefer service before safety, and account that condition to contribute most to their good, which they may make most become good.

In tantum Deo places in quantum hominibus displices. Ruat cœlum et terra, potius quam aliquid Christo discedat. Luth. To conclude this, let ministers take heed, lest they abate in their zeal and faithfulness for God to gratify a sinful world. If I please men, saith Paul, I am not the servant of Christ. It is much easier to bear the wrath of men for the conscientious discharge, than the wrath of God for the neglect of our duty.

Obs. 6. People should sit under the ministry of the word as under the rain distilling from the clouds. They should be as the dry and parched soil, not in regard of barrenness under, but thirstiness after, heavenly doctrine and the dews of grace; like those of whom Job speaks, who waited for him as for the rain, Job xxix. 23; gasping after the word as the chapt earth opens its mouth in its clefts for the showers, every cleft whereof is, as it were, a tongue to call to the clouds for rain. People should be athirst for God, yea, the living God, panting after Christ in his promises "as the hart after the water-brooks," Psal. xlii. 1, 2. "Open thy mouth wide," saith God, "and I will fill it." The reason why we come not to the word, drink not, relish not, digest not, is, because we thirst not after it. This thirst must be, (1.) An inward, hearty, sincere thirst: "My soul followeth hard after thee," Psal. lxiii. 8; my heart saith, "Thy face will I seek." "The desire of our soul is to thy name," Isa. xxvi. 8. Our desires must not be, as they say of some spices, hot in the mouth, cold in the stomach; not only the expression of the tongue, but accompanied also with the sincerity of the heart. Christians must not be like some hounds, which, following the game, open very loud with the rest for company, when they have not the scent of that beast which they pursue. We must thirst with the inward savour of that good which is in the word. (2.) It must be a vehement, ardent thirst, like that of David, "My soul breaketh for the longing it hath," &c., Psal. cxix. 20, with the whole heart, ver. 10. "My soul fainteth for thy salvation," Psal. cxix. 81. "My soul longeth, yea, even fainteth for the courts of the Lord." All the sweetness is put into the benefits of the gospel which God could put into them, and all the desire must be set upon them which thy soul can set upon them: all the vehement propensities wherewith things are carried to their centres in their courses can no more than shadow out spiritual desires. If a rock should fall from the clouds, it would break any intervening impediment; the sun cannot be stopped in its course; gunpowder bears all away that would hinder its force. (3.) It is a predominant thirst. No power of nature is so importunate and clamorous for satisfaction as tasting; a thirsty man much more ardently desires water, than another does beautiful prospects, sweet odours, or melodious music. Wanting these things a man can live, not so without water: those a man would have, this he must, he will have. A spiritually thirsty soul desires nothing much, but him whom it cannot desire too much.

A greater fire is made for roasting an ox than an egg; and greater is the flame of desire after the great and vast benefits of the gospel, than after these inconsiderable things below; in comparison of Christ they are dung, dross, loss; a Christian will step over them, and kick them away, when God requires; lay them down as sacrifices, or hate them as snares. Christ gives himself wholly to the soul, and so does a soul deal with him. The greatest worth that it sees in any thing beside Christ is this, that it may be left for Christ. (4.) It is an industrious thirst; not a lazy wishing, but a desire which take pains for the thing desired; it suffers not a man to sit still, but makes him, as the Scripture asserts, seek, knock, ask, cry, call, sell all, wrestle, strive; it offers violence to, and makes a holy riot upon heaven. It is like fire that will not be smothered. It saith, as Elijah to Obadiah, "As the Lord liveth, I will show myself." It stands not for any cost, it turns every stone; like the arrow drawn to the head, it flies apace. It is not like the desire of the slothful, which slays him, because his hands refuse to labour, Prov. xxi. 25. (5.) It is a resolved, waiting, permanent thirst: hence we frequently read of waiting for the Lord, and his salvation and consolation, Luke ii. 25. It stays the Lord's leisure, and will not away though the Lord seems to deny. No waters of discouragement shall quench it. It does not cast off hope because it cannot presently find comfort: "It is good" (saith the soul) "that a man should both hope and quietly wait for the salvation of the Lord," Lam. iii. 26: like one who goes to a house to speak with one much his superior, the spiritually thirsty soul will tarry the Lord's leisure for his coming to it. (6.) It is a thirst determined and limited to that one thing upon which it is set; nothing else will serve its turn, nor will it be bribed or put off with any thing instead thereof: "Whom," saith the psalmist, "have I in heaven but thee? and there is none upon earth that I desire beside thee," Psal. lxxiii. 25. "One thing have I desired of the Lord, that will I seek after," Psal. xxvii. 4. What have I, said Abraham, so long as I go childless? Gen. xv. 2; and what have I, saith the soul, so long as I go Christless? Land, riches, honours, children, &c., are good, but yet they are not Christ. A bag of gold will not serve him who is perishing with thirst instead of a cup of water. (7.) It is a returning, progressive thirst; never fully satisfied on this side heaven; it puts upon craving and seeking again and again. The earth desires not rain once only in a year, but a return of showers, the latter as well as the former rain; nor does refreshment with drink to-day, make a man regardless thereof to-morrow. David's desire was to "dwell in the house of the Lord for ever," Psal. xxiii. 6; xxvii. 4. The least degree of spiritual relief satisfies and stays a Christian's stomach to the world; but the greatest takes not away its further desires of Christ. (8.) It is a thankful thirst; it blesses the Lord for every drop of grace, with the psalmist, "My soul shall be satisfied as with marrow and fatness; and my mouth shall praise thee with joyful lips," Psal. lxiii. 5. Oh, saith the soul, Lord, who shall praise thee if I do not? A soul satisfied with mercy is a spiritual psalm sung out in the praises of God, Psal. ciii. 1—3. "Blessed be the God and Father of our Lord Jesus Christ, who hath blessed us with all spiritual blessings in heavenly places in Christ," Eph. i. 3. As soon as ever Paul had said, "Christ came into the world to save sinners," whereof he was chief; he adds his doxology, "Now to the King immortal," &c., 1 Tim. i. 17. What a delightful fragrance comes from, and what a face of freshness, greenness, cheerfulness is upon, the face of the parched grass and plants after a shower of rain! Oh what a spiritual freshness of joy is upon him, what sweetly breathings of praises issue from that soul which God has relieved with his spiritual showers of love and favour! The soul's greatest trouble is now, that it brings not forth more fruits of new obedience after those showers, and it is now as boundless in duty as heretofore it was in desires.

Obs. 7. Seducers are wont to make great appearances of worth in themselves and their doctrines. These seducers seemed to be watery clouds, who were filled with the rain of instruction and holiness; but, for all this, the apostle tells us they were clouds without water. Heresy is compared to leaven, Mark viii. 15, and, among other reasons, for its puffing and raising the dough. This spiritual leaven puffs up men with an undue and excessive opinion of their own parts and graces. The Pharisees "trusted in themselves that they were righteous, and despised others," Luke xviii. 9. "No doubt," think they, "we are the people, and wisdom shall die with us," Job xii. 2. They are "vainly puffed up by their fleshly mind," Col. ii. 18. The ministers of Satan desired to be accounted the ministers of righteousness. False apostles commended themselves; measured themselves by themselves, and compared themselves among themselves, 2 Cor. x. 12. They measured and esteemed themselves according to their own mind and judgment, and not according to their real worth or excellency. They also never considered the excellency of others, who were much beyond them in worth, but only such who were of the same pitch with themselves; or, as some understand the place, they commend and receive praises from one another, and among themselves. And whereas the apostle saith that he would not boast of things without his measure, ver. 13, he intimates that these seducers boasted beyond all the bounds or measure of their gifts and calling, or (according to some) that they boasted of their labouring in the gospel beyond the measure and term of Paul's labour; Theophylact and Œcumenius conceiving that these seducers falsely boasted that they had propagated the gospel to the ends of the earth, and that, according to the psalmist, "their line was gone out through all the earth, and their words to the end of the world," Psal. xix. 4. Arius vainly gloried that God had revealed something to him that was hidden from the apostles themselves. Montanus boasted that he was the Paraclete or Comforter himself. Simon Magus, the father of these heretical seducers, boasted that he was the mighty power of God. Heretics boldly intrude into things which they have not seen; they profess knowledge falsely so called. The disciples of Basilides valued themselves only to be men, and all others to be swine and dogs, saith Epiphanius; and Nazianzen tells Eunomius that he was, he means in his own conceit, a beholder of things which to all others are invisible, a hearer of things which it is not lawful to utter; that he was taken up to heaven as was Elias; that he had seen the face of God as had Moses; that he was rapt up into the third heavens as was Paul. Thus the papists style some of their schoolmen, angelical, seraphical, irrefragable, most subtle, illuminate: the consideration of all which should make us more wary of being led away with the big words and high expressions of these titular worthies. Let us consider what the power is which goes along with their words; and instead of admiring the flourishing titles of every vain dogmatist, examine what is the consonance between the Scriptures and their opinions. Who honours a mere titular, nominal prince? Let us not be taken with the glory of the doctor, but search into the bowels of the doctrine. Fools indeed, who take money, may be put off with brass coin because it glitters; but a wary man tries it by the touchstone. Try all your doctors and doctrines by the word, and ever be more ready to suspect than admire either.

Obs. 8. It is a great and inexcusable sin to make show of that goodness of which we are wholly void, and to which we are opposed.

Sinful was the pretending of these seducers to be watering clouds, large and black, accompanied with emptiness and dryness. The sin of the church of Sardis was, resting in a bare name and show of holy life. A Christian must look after both name and thing. The prophet charges the Jews with swearing "by the name of the Lord, and making mention of the God of Israel, but not in truth and righteousness," with contenting themselves to be called "of the holy city," &c., Isa. xlviii. 1, 2. Nor will this impiety seem small, if we consider either God, others, or ourselves.

(1.) The sinfulness hereof appears in respect of God. It pollutes and profanes his name. What greater profanation thereof imaginable, than to put it upon an unholy, hellish heart? Is it not more insufferable than to clothe a swine with the robes of a prince, and to put the crown and sceptre of a king upon the head and into the hand of a dunghill-raker? Is any disgrace to an emperor greater than for a base-born slave to state himself his son, and heir to his crown? This is that pollution of God's name with which God charged the people, Ezek. xxxvi. 20.

(2.) In respect of others. It hardens the wicked, who when they see the mere profession separated from the reality of holiness, applaud themselves, and think their own estate very blessed, and that religion is a mere notion and nullity; deride also at it, as did the heathens at those hypocritical Israelites: "These are," said they, "the people of the Lord, and are gone forth of his land," Ezek. xxxvi. 20: q. d. These are your saints, your Israelites, that came out of the holy land. And what more damps the goodness of young beginners, than the falseness and emptiness of those who have made great shows of forwardness in holiness? thereby one hypocrite pulls them back more than a hundred sincere ones can urge them forward. At the best they set up their staff before they are gone half way, and are made like the people, who seeing the body of Amasa lie dead by the way-side, stood still. In short, what are these bare pretenders to holiness, but deluders of others, gins and pitfalls in religion, dunghills covered over with snow, reeds that run into the arms of those who lean upon them, and such who do not only by their faithlessness deceive those who trust them with their estates and worldly concernments, but also much more dangerously misguide and delude the souls of those who follow their empty doctrines and crooked lives?

(3.) The greatness of this sin appears principally by considering them who live in it. For, 1. All their glorious appearances are purely unprofitable unto them. The report of a man's being wealthy adds nothing to his estate, or that of full feeding to one who is hunger-starved. God tells the hypocritical Jews that they trusted "in lying words," Jer. vii. 8, when they only trusted to their outside shows. "I will declare thy righteousness, and thy works," (said God to that false-hearted people,) "for they shall not profit thee," Isa. lvii. 12. 2. Shows without reality of holiness are very hurtful. [1.] Appearing goodness makes men furthest from being and becoming really good. Religion is a very serious, real business; yea, it is very reality, and called in Scripture truth itself. As the privileges, so the practices, of godliness

---

Vide Danæum in descriptione arboris. Hæres.
Ἡμεῖς ἐσμεν οἱ ἄνθρωποι, οἱ δὲ ἄλλοι πάντες ὗες καὶ κύνες. Epiph. Hær. 24.

Τῶν ἀθεάτων θεάτης, τῶν ἀρρήτων ἀκροατής, ὁ μετὰ Ἠλίαν μετάρσιος, καὶ ὁ μετὰ Μωυσέα θεοφανίας ἠξιωμένος, καὶ μετὰ Παῦλον οὐράνιος. Naz. in Orat. 33.

are in deed and in truth, and by nothing so much opposed as shadows and falseness. [2.] They who please themselves with appearances will never labour for the reality of holiness, nor truth in the inward parts; they are seldom reproved by others, nor is it so easy to fasten a reproof upon them as upon those who are void of all shows of religion; and so they go on in a miserable quietness and uninterruptedness to their own destruction. [3.] They who barely appear holy are of all others the most impudent, not blushing to be accounted such as their own consciences tell them they are far from being. Naomi was ashamed of herself, when the men of Bethlehem said, "Is this Naomi? Call me not," said she, "Naomi, call me Marah; for the Almighty hath dealt very bitterly with me," Ruth i. 20. But these say, Call us Christians, though they are no better than heathens; call us saints, though they are inwardly but rotten sepulchres; account us to be in the highest form of religion, though they have not as yet stepped over the threshold of religion's school; esteem us to be full, although we are altogether empty. True saints are ashamed of commendation, though they are full of worth; hypocrites glory in being commended, though they have nothing in them commendable. When men have not the thing, it is most unreasonable that they should have the name. When God gave Abram the name of Abraham, he told him there was a reason why he should be called by that name; "Thy name shall be Abraham, for a father of many nations have I made thee," Gen. xvii. 5. Abigail said concerning her husband, "As his name is, so is he; Nabal is his name, and folly is with him," 1 Sam. xxv. 25; and if Christians be our name, true Christianity should be with us. Lastly, such clouds without water, appearing professors, render themselves of all others most inexcusable. If religion were bad, why did they so much as profess it? if good, why did they not more, even love it also? If they took upon themselves the title and trade of God's servants, why would they not do his work? If God be a Master, where is his fear? if a Father, where is his honour? If they would not be his servants, why would they be called so? If they would be called his servants, why would they not be so? How fearful should we then be of putting our souls off with shadows of goodness! Labour for that truth in the inward parts, which all the expressions of the outward man are not able to reach; and remember that hereafter all paint must fall off which is not laid in the oil of sincerity; and hypocrites shall be discovered and unmasked both to their own consciences, and the judgments of all others.

Obs. 9. The empty are also unstable. These "clouds without water" are, by the apostle, said to be "carried about of winds." The apostle, 2 Pet. iii. 16, joins the unlearned and unstable together; and Heb. xiii. 9 he mentions the establishment of the heart with grace. A heart empty of saving knowledge and true holiness is soon unsettled; and needs must it be so, being not firmly united to and set into Christ by faith: unbelief and distrust make a man carried up and down like a meteor. He who is not built upon the rock can never stand: if a reed be not tied to some stronger thing, it can never be kept from bending and shaking : where grace, the fruit, is not, there Christ, the root, is not; and where there is no root, there is no stability. Further, where there is a total emptiness of holiness, there is an emptiness of peace and contentment: "There is no peace to the wicked." And he who wants true contentment, will ever be looking out for it where it is not to be had. Without joy life is no life; and if it is not gotten one way, another will be tried. "Who will show us any good?" is the language of natural men; they have still hopes to be better; and like men in a fever, they toss from one side of the bed to the other, in hope to find coolness and refreshment: but a soul that exercises itself in the ways of holiness tells every temptation, You would draw me away to my loss. Yet again, a heart void of grace is divided in the service of God, and therefore an unsettled heart; it is not united to fear God's name; it serves not the Lord without distraction; all its love, fear, joy, runs not one way; but having inclinations not wholly bestowed upon God, and several ways of the heart's outgoing from God being allowed, it is never safe and certain. When the scales are even in weight, they tremble and waver; sometimes one is up, sometimes another: they who will serve two masters, God and the creature, and are double-minded, and will divide their hearts between them, will often be wavering, and show themselves sometimes for religion, sometimes for the world; grace fixes and weighs down the heart for God and to God, and chooses him only. Here is the true reason then, in general, why men are so tossed and carried away from the truth of the gospel, they are empty of the truth of grace; they go from us, because they were never of us; they are a land-flood, a cistern only receiving from without, and void of an inward living principle and fountain.

Obs. 10. Christians should beware of unstedfastness, of being carried away with any winds from their holy stedfastness in the truth. "Continue in the things which ye have learned," 2 Tim. iii. 14. Be not as children tossed to and fro with every wind of doctrine. To this end, (1.) Let the word of Christ ballast your souls; store them with the knowledge of saving principles of religion. Empty table-books are fit to have any thing written in them, and a soul empty of the knowledge of wholesome truths is a fit receptacle for any error. Ye do err, saith Christ, because ye know not the Scriptures, Matt. xxii. 29. Stones will easily be removed, unless fixed upon a foundation. He who buys commodities without either weighing or measuring them, may easily be deceived; the Scripture is the measure and balance of every opinion. How easily may he be cheated with errors instead of truth, who buys only in the dark! Ignorant Christians are like infants which gape, and take in whatever the nurse puts to their mouths. (2.) Labour to get your hearts fastened to the truth by love, as well as your heads filled with the truth by light. He who never loved truth, may easily be brought to leave truth, and to embrace error. He who embraced truth he knew not why, will forsake it he knows not how; the heart which has continued deceitful under truth, may soon be deceived by error; a literal, without an experimental knowledge of the truth, may quickly be drawn to error: from that wherein we find neither pleasure nor profit we may easily be enticed. But when once we feel the truth both enlightening and delighting, unloading its treasures of glory into our souls, quieting our consciences, quelling our lusts, changing us into the image of the Lord, quickening our graces, seducers will not be able to cheat us of this jewel, because we know they can bring us nothing in exchange for which we should barter it away. (3.) Let there not be any one lust allowed within thee to loosen thee from the truth. They who are not sound in the fear of God, may easily become unsound in the faith of God. A remiss heart will close with remiss principles. The mystery of faith must be held in a good conscience, which some, saith the apostle, having cast away, have made shipwreck of the faith, 1 Tim. i. 19; he compares conscience to a ship, and faith to a treasure therein embarked, which must needs miscarry if the ship be cast away, any corrupt affection entertained: the soul, like an unwalled and unfenced city, lies open to the rage and rapine of and ruin by any enemy. If seducers suit their bait to the unmortified lust of a sinner, he is easily made their prey, Prov. xxv. 28. Particularly, [1.] Beware of pride; the proud Christian, like a light, puffed bladder, will easily be puffed any way of error: a bird of a very small carcass, and of many feathers, is easily carried away with the wind. Pride is the mother of heresy; it is the proud man who consents not to " wholesome doctrine, but dotes about questions," 1 Tim. vi. 3, 4. Humility is the best fence against error; a humble man is so small in his own eyes, that the shot of seducers cannot hit him; and lies so low, that all their bullets fly over him. God teaches the humble, but the proud person is Satan's scholar. [2.] Fence thy soul against worldly-mindedness; a worldly heart will be bought and sold at every rate. The truth can never be safe in the closet of that heart which error can open with a golden picklock. The covetous both make merchandise of others, and will be made merchandise by others. The hook of error is easily swallowed down by a worldly heart, if it be baited with filthy lucre. Take heed of being a servant of truth for gain, for if so, thou wilt soon be a slave unto error for more gain. [3.] Keep out of the wind of seducing doctors and their doctrines. " Mark them who cause divisions, and avoid them," Rom. xvi. 17. If it be dangerous to be tempted by, what is it then to be tempters of the devil! Turn away from such as creep into houses, and lead souls captives, 2 Tim. iii. 5, 6. Eat not of the banquets of him who hath been found to mix poison in his dishes; let holy zeal, in this respect, hinder civility. If these seducers come to you, yet neither receive them into your houses, nor bid them God speed. Shun the meeting-places of error as the schools of impiety. Beware of false prophets, who put on a sheepskin profession over a wolfish purpose, "deceitful workers, transforming themselves into the apostles of Christ," 2 Cor. xi. 13. The devil never deceives in his own likeness. Feed not like silly sheep upon rotten grass because it is sweet and luscious. Polycarp would entertain no acquaintance with Marcion, but termed him the first-born of Satan; and, as Irenæus states, the apostles and their disciples were so full of holy fear, that they would not communicate with heretics in the world who had adulterated the word. Let not Satan take us among his own, lest he make us of his own.

<small>Polycarpus Marcioni aliquando occurrenti sibi, et dicenti, Cognosce nos; respondit, Cognosco te primogenitum Satanæ. Tantum apostoli et horum discipuli habuerunt timorem, ut neque verbo tenus communicarent alicui eorum, qui adulteraverant veritatem. Iren. l. 3. c. 3. pag. mihi 171.</small>

Thus much for that second comparison, whereby the apostle describes the sin and misery of these seducers, viz. " clouds without water."

III. He compares them to "trees whose fruit withereth, without fruit, twice dead, plucked up by the roots."

Two things principally are here considerable in this resemblance taken from bad and corrupt trees.

Their badness in consideration, 1. Of their fruits. 2. Of the trees themselves.

1. In consideration of their fruits; so our apostle expresses,

(1.) The decay and withering of their fruits ; " whose fruit withereth."

(2.) Their cessation from and privation of their fruit; their fruit was none; " without fruit."

2. Their badness in consideration of themselves, the trees, which, (1.) Were irrecoverably dead; "twice dead." (2.) Deservedly therefore "plucked up by the roots."

So that four particulars we shall here explain in this similitude borrowed from bad trees; the lost estate and the spiritual misery of these seducers being set down by a fourfold gradation, or by four steps, each one rising to a further degree of wretchedness than the other, and the lower making way for the higher.

1. When they seemed to have fruit, at the best it was decaying, withering.

2. This withering fruit proved no fruit; "without fruit."

3. This ceasing from fruit, or this no fruit, was joined with a total want of life in the trees ever to produce any more fruit; "twice dead."

4. This total want of life made an easy way for the loss of place and ground to continue in.

1. When they seemed to have fruit, at best it was decaying and withering. The apostle saith that they were "trees whose fruit withereth." The word whereby he expresses it is φθινοπωρινά, which, according to the different apprehensions of interpreters, has several interpretations affixed to it. The Vulgate renders it *autumnales*, autumn trees, or trees of autumn, from φθινόπωρον, which sometimes signifies autumn; and such trees, say some, the apostle calls these seducers, because when trees at that time of the year begin to put forth and make show of bearing fruit, they bring not their fruit to perfect maturity, it being too late in the year, and men judge it to be a sign that the trees themselves also are withering, and shortly after will die. Others, rather explaining than opposing this interpretation, conceive that these words, δένδρα φθινοπωρινά, intend *arbores ultimi, finientis, extremi, senescentis autumni*, trees of the latter end of autumn, or that part which is next to winter, because φθινόπωρον properly signifies the ending, far-spent autumn, it being called so, παρὰ τὸ φθίνεσθαι τὴν ὀπώραν, *a finiente autumno*, from the going out or wasting away of autumn: and this, say they, may be the meaning of the apostle, that as at the end of autumn, toward the beginning of November, the fruit and leaves of trees fall off, and the trees themselves seem to wither and die; so these seducers, what show soever they made formerly, were at last empty and destitute, not only of fruit, all true worth and goodness, but also even of all appearances thereof; but this seems rather to be intended in the last branch, "plucked up by the roots." Others think that by δένδρα φθινοπωρινά the apostle means *arbores frugiperdas*, such as spoil and destroy fruit, from φθίνειν and ὀπώραν, which they make to be the same with ὀλλύειν τὸν καρπὸν, as if the apostle had intended that these seducers aimed by all they did and brought forth only to corrupt and spoil the church, even as fruit being rotten and putrified easily corrupts and infects that fruit which lies near it: but this seems not to be an apt beginning to that following gradation, of their being without fruit; it being worse to hurt others than not to be good ourselves. Others conceive that the word φθινοπωρινά respects not here that time of the year which we call autumn, but only the nature of the fruit which these trees brought forth; namely, such as are withered, and altogether unprofitable, as if these trees were called φθινοπωρινά, *scil.* ὧν φθίνει ἡ ὀπώρα, or παρὰ τὸ φθίνεσθαι τὰς αὐτῶν ὀπώρας, as bringing forth no fruit but what was corrupt and withered; the apostle hereby intending, that though these seducers seem to promise and make a show of good and wholesome fruit, yet wanting the vital moisture and inward vigour of faith, could bring nothing forth to maturity and perfection, but all their fruits were withered and corrupt. This interpretation of the withering and corruptness of their fruit, I conceive most genuine and suitable to the scope of

the apostle, though he should, as many learned men think he does, compare these seducers to autumn trees, the fruit of such trees being mostly but withered and immature, and not coming to its perfection.

More particularly, two things are here further to be opened.

(1.) What that fruit was which these seducers might have, and what kind of fruits these trees might bear.

(2.) What was the withering of that fruit.

(1.) What that fruit was which they might bear. There are three sorts of metaphorical fruits mentioned in Scripture which men, compared to trees, are said to yield.

1. The fruits of the sanctifying Spirit of God, (graces and works,) brought forth in the hearts and lives of the saints; called fruits, because they come from the Spirit of God as fruit from the tree, and are as pleasing to him as the pleasantest fruit is to us. Thus we read of "the fruits of the Spirit," Gal. v. 22; and "fruits of righteousness," Phil. i. 11. "Fruits meet for repentance," Matt. iii. 8. All comprehended by Paul, Eph. v. 9, where he saith, "The fruit of the Spirit is in all goodness, and righteousness, and truth." Goodness being that quality contrary to malice or naughtiness, whereby a sinner is evil in himself. Righteousness opposed to injustice, whereby one is hurtful and injurious to others. Truth opposed to errors, heresies, hypocrisy, &c.

2. There are fruits which in themselves and their own nature are bitter, corrupt, poisonous, put forth not only by a corrupt tree, but by it as such, evil *propter fieri*, in themselves and their own nature; such fruits by which the false prophets were known, and whereby men may be known to be wicked men, grapes of gall, and bitter clusters, Deut. xxxii. 32; such works of the flesh as Paul mentions, "Adultery, fornication, uncleanness, lasciviousness, idolatry, witchcraft, hatred," &c., Gal. v. 19.

3. There are other fruits which are not evil in themselves, unlawful or intrinsically evil in their own substance and nature, *propter esse* and *fieri*, because they are, or are done; but because they grow upon such trees, by reason whereof something which should make the production of them good is omitted, and sundry defects cleave unto them, and they have evil cast upon them by the agent.

And sundry fruits of this sort and rank there may be upon such trees as Jude speaks of. As,

(1.) The fruits of gifts, parts, and abilities in matters of religion, as preaching, praying, utterance. Of these speaks Christ, Matt. vii. 22, "Many shall say in that day, Lord, have we not prophesied," &c. And 1 Cor. xii. 1, they are called spiritual gifts, wrought by the Spirit; but are not *sanctificantia*, but *ministrantia*; not so sanctifying him in whom, but helping those for whom they are; as a rich man may bestow good and dainty diet upon a poor woman that nurses his child, not for her own sake, but that his child may be nourished: such fruits as these, indeed, may beautify grace, but yet grace must sanctify them. These may make us profitable to men, not acceptable to God.

(2.) The second sort of these fruits which these trees might bear is a temporary faith, orthodox or sound judgment, assent to that which is the very truth of God's word; that there is a God, infinite in all his glorious perfections; that there are three Persons; that Christ was God and man, &c., and that all who believe in him shall be saved. Thus some unconverted are said to believe for a while, Luke viii. 13; thus Simon Magus and Demas believed. These fruits are good in their kind, and without them there can be no holiness of life, nor happiness after death, and yet they are not good enough; not purifying the heart, but only perfecting the understanding; poured only on the head, not running down, like Aaron's ointment, to the heart and other parts; though making a man protestant in doctrine, yet leaving him to be a recusant in his life; carrying him out to believe the word as faithful, but not to embrace it as worthy of all acceptation; to shine with light, but not to burn with or work by love.

(3.) A third sort of these fruits might be some heated affections, sweet motions, "receiving the word with joy," Matt. xiii. 20; a finding some sweetness in the ordinances. Ezekiel was to his hearers as a lovely song of one that hath a pleasant voice, chap. xxxiii. 32. They who shall be cast into utter darkness may for a season rejoice in the light, John v. 35, and may have sorrow and grief about sin, Matt. xxvii. 3. The Israelites were oft deep in their humiliations; they sought God and returned, inquired early after God, Psal. lxxviii. 34: Ahab humbled himself, 1 Kings xxi. 17—29. And yet these fruits are not the best, they may spring up from a root not good; the pleasantness or sadness of the matter of any doctrine may cause suitable affections of joy or sorrow; the novelty or rarity of a doctrine may much delight; or the dexterity and ability of the deliverer; the suitableness of a clearly discovered truth to a hearer's understanding: the apprehension of the goodness of spiritual things may stir up some desires; thus they cried out, "Lord, give us evermore this bread;" thus Balaam desires to "die the death of the righteous;" yea, as some have observed, corrupt lusts in men, such as pride and self-seeking, may produce great affections in holy duties. The desire of applause may make men in public administrations enlarged in their affections. The more excellent a prayer or sermon is, the more carnal the heart of the performer may be; the stronger the invention is, the weaker the grace may be; and as ground full of mines of gold is oft barren of grass, so a heart full of grace may be barren of the ornaments of words and expressions.

(4.) A fourth sort of fruits, borne even by these afterward apostates, might be external appearances of conformity to the law of God, in avoiding all open and scandalous courses, and in performing the visible and outside acts of obedience: thus the Pharisee was not an extortioner, unjust, an adulterer, Matt. xviii. 11. Paul, touching the law, was blameless, Phil. iii. 6. The young man professed he had kept the law, in the letter of it, from his youth. The Pharisees paid tithes exactly, abhorred idolatry, made long prayers and frequent, were strict in the outward observation of the sabbath, professed chastity, temperance, &c. Thus it is said of these very apostates, that they had escaped the pollutions of the world, 2 Pet. ii. 20, and that they had been washed, ver. 22. And these fruits of outward conformity to the law of God are highly commendable; sincerity of grace can neither be nor be known without them; by them it resolves, as Elijah said, 1 Kings xviii. 15, to show itself; they are commanded by God, who, though he commands not the godly to fulfil the law perfectly, yet permits them not to break it wilfully; and though by the presence of external obedience we cannot conclude salvation, yet by the absence thereof we may conclude damnation to follow: these honour God, benefit others. Though our righteousness satisfies not justice, yet in our unrighteousness we cannot be saved without injustice; nor is any man called a good man for the good which he has, but the good which he does: outward obedience strengthens true grace where it is, and is necessary to preserve a justified estate, though not as deserving it, yet as removing that which would destroy it. And yet all these fruits, the acts of external obedience, are not the best; they may be a shape without a soul, appearances without an inward principle of life; they might be with a despising of the righteousness of Christ; they might be performed only for want of temptations to the contrary; God's glory might never be aimed at, in performing them, as their end, nor his word eyed as their rule. These things commanded by God might be done in obedience to lust.

(2.) What was the withering of their fruits.

1. They were withering fruit for their deformity and unpleasantness to the eye, and their sourness and unsavouriness to the taste of God. The fruits of righteousness are only pleasant fruits, and the trees of righteousness only pleasant plants. A withered apple is not sweet and delightful. The best performances which grow upon a wicked man, are not acceptable as they come from him: goodness of being is before that of working. The tree must be good before the fruit can be pleasant: "They who are in the flesh cannot please God." The meanest duty of a saint is more amiable than the most gilded performance of a sinner; the stammering of a child is more pleasing to a parent than the best oratory of a beggar. If the vine be a vine of Sodom, and of the fields of Gomorrah, the grapes will be grapes of gall, and the clusters bitter, Deut. xxxii. 32.

(2.) This fruit might be said to be withered fruit, for ceasing to grow bigger, and not proceeding to perfection. Withering fruit grows not, and these stood at a stay; their fruit found no new degrees; their faith went not from assent to adherence, and from thence to assurance; they brought not forth fruit to perfection, Luke viii. 14. They added nothing to that which was lacking; they did not abound more and more in the work of the Lord. Their last works were not more than their first, Rev. ii. 19. They soon knew enough in Christianity. They did not press forward towards the mark, Phil. iii. 13, 14; nor were they like the sun, rejoicing to run its course, and increasing more and more to the perfect day. They went not "from strength to strength," Psal. lxxxiv. 7, nor studied exactness in Christianity. Most love to excel in every thing more than in that which is true excellence; though they think that abundance of wealth is but a little, yet they live as if a little godliness were enough. They have their *maximum quod sic*, beyond which they move not; and say of spiritual good things, as Dives of his temporals, Soul, take thine ease, thou hast much goods laid up for many years. They desire not to have more cubits added to their stature. He who has only a form of godliness, and is but the picture of a Christian, not having the life thereof, will never grow; he is still upon the same hinges where he was; he goeth on in a circle of duties, prays and hears as he did of old.

(3.) Their fruit might be called withering, as it decayed, languished, and grew less and less.

They were so far from obtaining that grace which they wanted, that they did not retain that grace which they had; they lost their first love, and grew worse and worse; they were so far from getting more, that they kept not what they had already gotten. They did not so much stand at a stay as go backward; the bitterest of their life was in the end thereof. The sap of abilities which once they had now decayed; all life in holy duties and speeches was withdrawn; yea, their leaves fell off; they could not speak of holy things with so much holy savour as they were wont. God withdrew his Spirit from them: thus the Spirit of the Lord departed from Saul, and all his gifts vanished: and, indeed, this follows upon the former, where there is no increasing, there is some decaying; while we neglect to gain, we spend upon the stock. A boat going up a river that runs with a strong current, falls down the stream if the oars rest but never so little. Decays in spirituals deserve most of our pity. It is not so uncomfortable to see a man decay in his health or estate as in his grace, and to lose heavenward, to lose his first love, to decline from God.

(4.) As the cause of all the former, their fruit was like withered fruit, as it wanted spiritual life, juice, and nourishment from the tree to feed and supply it; they had not spiritual life, and therefore had not spiritual growth, and had spiritual decays. Only to them who have is more given. There is no growing where there is no living. If a snowball be rolled up and down, and thereby made larger, yet it does not grow, because it is by *extra* addition, not by *intra* reception. A vital principle is the foundation of growth, either natural or spiritual: "He that abideth in me, and I in him," (saith Christ,) "the same bringeth forth much fruit; for without me," or severed from me, "ye can do nothing," John xv. 5. The picture of a child will never come up to be a man, because in it there is no life. They who only have a name of Christianity, and receive not efficacy and power from Christ, are as withered fruit, without union to and life from him, there being no Christian increase. We are God's "workmanship, created in Christ Jesus unto good works," Eph. ii. 10. Till the Spirit of God be put into us, there is no walking or proceeding in his ways, Ezek. xxxvi. 27.

This for the opening of the first gradation whereby the apostle sets forth the loss of these seducers; they were trees whose fruit withered.

2. This withering fruit proved no fruit; ἄκαρπα, "without fruit."

But how can the apostle say here that they were without fruit, when in the foregoing words he had said that they had withering fruit?

(1.) Possibly he may here in these words represent them as having cast and lost their withering fruit. We know fruit that withers quickly and easily falls off from the tree; trees which have withering fruit will soon be without fruit. Wanting that which only can make us good for the kind, a good root, and a renewed principle of life, we must needs want that which should make us good for continuance, namely, internalness and sincerity. Out of Christ there can be no perseverance, only union to him makes us permanently holy. And it is most just with God, that they who would not bear better than, should not bear so much as withering fruit; that they should cast off the very appearances of fruit, and even their outside profession; that they who never regarded the truth and reality of holiness, should from hypocrisy fall to profaneness, and from a bare form of godliness to ungodliness, and from paint to deformity. But this open and plain discovery of their hypocrisy, I rather conceive is contained in the last branch of the verse, in these words, "plucked up by the roots."

(2.) Therefore I understand, with Mr. Perkins and others, that these words, "without fruit," are (as it were) a correction of the former, as if the apostle had said, they are "trees whose fruit withereth," or rather without fruit altogether, the fruit which they bear not deserving so much as the name of fruit; as trees that bear no other than withering fruit are esteemed no better than unfruitful trees: and thus, notwithstanding their withering fruit, they may be said to be without fruit in sundry respects.

[1.] They were without fruit, because all their forementioned fruits were not produced by the inward life and vigour of the Spirit of sanctification in their souls; their fruit grew upon a corrupt tree, and proceeded from an unclean, bitter root. They were not the issues of a pure heart and faith unfeigned, but the streams of an unclean fountain. The fruitfulness only of sloe-bushes, crab-trees, and brambles cannot make the year accounted a fruitful year. "A corrupt tree," saith Christ, "cannot bring forth good fruit," Matt. vii. 18. How can ye that are evil speak good things? Their best fruits were but fruits of nature, coming from an unregenerate heart. That fruit which before his conversion Paul accounted as precious as gold, he after esteemed as base as dung.

[2.] They were without fruit, because their fruits were not brought forth to a Divine end; they were directed to no higher an end than themselves. "Israel," saith God, "is an empty vine," though bringing forth fruit; for it follows, "he bringeth forth fruit to himself."

I am not ignorant that some interpreters expound not that text concerning the fruit of works, though yet they grant the place may be by consequence drawn to take in them likewise. As these fruits were not fruits of righteousness, so neither were they to the praise of his glory, Phil. i. 11. "If thou wilt return, O Israel," saith God, "return to me," Jer. iv. 1. They returned, (saith the psalmist,) but not to the Most High. The pipe cannot convey the water higher than the fountain-head is from whence it comes; and these fruits being not from God, were not directed to him. Fruits brought forth to ourselves are rotten at the core; they are not for his taste who both looks into and tries the heart.

[3.] They might be without fruit, as not producing works in obedience to the rule. The doing of the thing commanded may possibly be an act of disobedience. God looks upon all our works as nothing, unless we do the thing commanded because it is commanded. This only is to serve him for conscience sake. A man may do a good work out of obedience to his lust. As it is possible for a man to believe, not because of Divine revelation, 1 Thess. iv. 3; v. 18; so is it possible for a man to work, and not upon the ground of Divine injunction. "Be not unwise, but understand," saith the apostle, "what is the will of God," Eph. v. 17. Man's wisdom is to understand and follow God's will.

[4.] Without fruit as to their own benefit, comfort, and salvation. The works of hypocrites are not ordained by God to have heaven follow them; at the last day all they had or did will appear to be nothing; and when the sun shall arise, then the works which here have shined like glow-worms shall appear inglorious and unbeautiful; of all that has been sown to the flesh shall nothing be reaped but corruption: God crowns no works but his own, nor will Christ own any works but those which have been brought forth by the power of his own Spirit.

[5.] Lastly, Without the fruit of any goodness in God's account, because without love to God. Love is the sweetness of our services. If I have not love, saith Paul, "I am nothing," 1 Cor. xiii. 2, 3; and as true is it, without it I can do nothing: the gift of an enemy is a gift and no gift. As love from God is the top of our happiness, so love to God is the sum of our duty. There is nothing beside love but a hypocrite may give to God with God's people; it is the kernel of every performance: God regards nothing we give him, unless we give ourselves also. It is love which makes a service please both the master and servant. Now wicked men in all they bring forth, though they may have bounty in the hand, yet have no love in the heart; they have not a drop of love in a sea of service.

This for the explication of the second aggravation, or gradation, of the sin and misery of these seducers; they were "without fruit."

3. This fruitless state is joined with a want of life in the trees; "twice dead."

These words I take to express a further degree of their spiritual wretchedness, under the continued metaphor of trees. It was bad to have withering fruit; worse, to have no fruit at all; worse yet, to be not only without all fruit, but even altogether without life, "twice dead."

Two things are here to be explained.
1. In what respect these trees may be said to be "dead."
2. How to be "twice dead."

1. How these trees are dead. Death is, (1.) Temporal and corporal; that which is a privation of life by the departure of the soul from the body.

(2.) Spiritual; befalling either the godly or the wicked. [1.] The godly are said to be dead spiritually three ways. 1: "Dead to sin," Rom. vi. 2; 1 Pet. ii. 24; the corruption of their natures being by the Spirit of Christ subdued and destroyed. 2. Dead in respect of the law ceremonial: "Dead with Christ from the rudiments of the world," Col. ii. 20. Moral: so Paul saith, he was "dead to the law," Gal. ii. 19; and, "Ye are dead to the law," Rom. vii. 4; it not being able to make them guilty who are in Christ, nor to terrify their consciences, nor to irritate them to sin. 3. Dead to the world: so Paul was crucified to the world, Gal. vi. 14, either because the world contemned and despised him as a dead man; or else because the world had no more power to entice and allure him from Christ, than the objects of the senses have to work upon a dead man. [2.] Spiritual death befalls the wicked and unregenerate, they being without the Spirit of Christ to animate and quicken them, which Spirit enlivens the soul supernaturally, as the soul does the body naturally. Hence they are said to be "dead in sins," Eph. ii. 1, 5; Col. ii. 13; and "dead," Matt. viii. 22; Luke ix. 60; Rom. vi. 13; John v. 25; and to remain in death, 1 John iii. 14. Hence their works are said to be dead, Heb. ix. 14. As the immortality of the damned is no life, but an eternal death; so the conjunction of the souls and bodies of wicked men is not properly life, but *umbratilis vita*, a shadow of life, or rather a very death, they being without spiritual feeding, growth, working, all vital operations, and lying under the deformity, loathsomeness, insensibleness, in a spiritual sense, of such as are dead; or, according to the resemblance here used by our apostle, which is that of trees dead, they are spiritually dead, because without and severed from that root of every good tree, the Lord Christ. The old Adam is the root upon which they still stand, and therefore they are without all spiritual and supernatural life. As from the root flows life into all the branches of the tree, so from Christ all who are united to him by the Spirit through faith, have by those means the life of holiness imparted to them. As in Adam, the first root, who has now lost the moisture and vigour of holiness, and is become a dried root, all die; so in Christ shall all, and only, they who are really united to him live. Hence it is, that as they are without the root, and therefore without life, so without all spiritual growth and fruitfulness; the inward principle of life being wanting, the effects that flow from that principle, all vital operations, must needs be wanting likewise; for though abiding and living by Christ we bring forth much fruit, yet severed from him we can do nothing, John xv. 5. It is true, that as the wicked have something from Christ like the Spirit of life, so thereby they bring forth something like good and spiritual fruits, Heb. vi. 4; 1 Cor. xii. 6, 7; I mean, those forementioned fruits of gifts, assent to the truth, sweet affections, acts of external obedience: but though in the producing these the Spirit helps them, yet it never changes the nature of the trees, but they still retain the natural sourness of their roots; and though God gives them the Spirit to edify others, yet not to sanctify themselves; though Saul had another spirit, and sundry prophesied and cast out devils, Matt. vii. 22, yet all these were but works of ministration, not renovation; though the Spirit works as an outward efficient cause, breathing on them, and is in them as *in organis*, instruments and ministers, yet not as *in domiciliis*, as in habitations and members; for as the soul works not as a form to any part that is not united to the body, so neither does the Spirit of Christ work savingly but in the body of Christ. In the wicked it may be *Spiritus movens*, a moving Spirit; in the godly it is only *Spiritus inhabitans*, an inhabiting, indwelling Spirit. The Spirit of God in a hypocrite is like an angel appearing in some outward shape; of which he is only an assisting, not an informing form; for which cause his assumed body has neither life nor nourishment; but the Spirit of God in the godly is like the soul in the body, not only assisting, but informing and working in them spiritually vital and supernatural operations. And notwithstanding the best workings of the Spirit of God in the wicked, they are oft left more fleshly, self-confident, less poor in spirit, and sensible of their want of Christ, than before. And thus these seducers were spiritually dead.

Or, (3.) Death is eternal, the effect of the former; which eternal death is that most miserable condition of the reprobate after death, wherein they are deprived of all the blessedness and glory of heaven, standing in the enjoyment and unitive vision of God; it is indeed the spiritual death continued and perfected. As heaven or eternal life in the enjoyment of God by Christ, is begun in this life, and completed in the next; so is hell or eternal death in the loss of God begun in this, and consummated in the next world. The presence of God is the heaven of heaven, the joy of heaven, the life of heaven, and of all who shall come thither.

2. In what respect these seducers may be said to be "twice dead."

The word twice, δὶς, is taken two ways; sometimes indefinitely, or as a definite put for an indefinite, a certain for an uncertain number. Thus Job xxxiii. 14, "God speaketh once, yea twice, yet man perceiveth it not;" that is, God does by his gracious ways and means sufficiently, abundantly, and frequently acquaint man with his will, although man be so stupid and senseless, as not to understand what the meaning of God is therein. So Psal. lxii. 11, "God hath spoken once; twice have I heard this, that power belongeth to God;" that is, God has abundantly, oft, several times, or sundry ways, by his word and works, asserted and discovered that he is eminently and transcendently powerful. Thus the apostle commands, that the elders that rule well should be accounted worthy *duplici*, that is, *multiplici honore*, double, much, manifold honour, 1 Tim. v. 17. So the prophet prays that his enemies may be destroyed with a double destruction, Jer. xvii. 18, i. e. with a severe, thorough, total destruction. So Elisha desired that a double portion, that is, a large, abundant portion, of the Spirit might be upon him, 2 Kings ii. 9. Thus some take the word twice in this place, as if by the signification of the very word the apostle intended that these dead trees were finally dead, and past all hopes of recovery, such as could never be bettered by all the pains and cost, digging, dunging, &c. that could be laid out upon them. That our apostle here intends that these seducers were like trees irrecoverably and totally dead I easily grant; but withal because trees may be said to be twice dead in respect of their dying twice, or a second time, this word twice seems to import in this place a definite certain number, and to intend a double or twofold death of these seducers, who are here compared to trees in their dying twice, as well as in all the other three respects, viz. their having withered fruit, their being without fruit, and being plucked up by the roots.

Trees then are said to be twice dead thus: the first time, a tree is said to be dead when in the former spring it decays, fades, withers in its leaves, blossoms, or newly-formed fruit: from this decaying or dying, for a dying it is, as to leaves and fruit, a tree is oft by pruning and dressing recovered; but if in autumn or the latter spring, which is the critical or climacterial time of trees to discover whether their disease be mortal or not, the tree fades again; if then the leaves, or whatever it bears, wither, the bark grow dry, and be, as they say, sick; the fault is then *ab intra*, the root is rotten, and the very substance of the tree is inwardly corrupt, no more labour or cost is now bestowed upon it, it is now dead twice, or the second time, and therefore totally and irrecoverably: and, as I have understood from those who are exactly skilled in the nature of trees, it has been oft known that trees which have seemed to die in the former spring, have afterward been recovered; but never did they know that any languishing in the former spring, and then, after some overtures of reviving in the latter spring, fading and decaying again, ever were recovered and restored afterward. In like manner, these seducers of whom Jude speaks had a double death, or were twice dead; first they were dead in respect of their natural condition, by being, as are others, born in sin; and so, as the apostle speaks, Eph. ii. 1, "dead in sin;" from this they were so far recovered, as that they seemed to live, and, as Peter speaks, 2 Pet. ii. 20, to have escaped the pollutions of the world, and by visible profession to flourish, and to give fair hopes of bearing good fruit: notwithstanding this first death, they were not given over as irrecoverable, but their latter death, which was by apostacy from the faith of Christ, by re-entangling themselves in the pollutions of the world, and returning to their vomit and wallowing in the mire, brought them into such a hopeless, deplorable condition, that our apostle no more expected their recovery than the restoring of a tree dead twice, or the second time.

Indeed there is an apostacy of impotency of affection, and prevalency of lust, a recidivation or relapse into a former sinful condition, out of forgetfulness and falseness of heart, for want of the fear of God, to balance the conscience, and to fix and unite the heart to him. This was the frequent sin of Israel in breaking their covenants, Psal. cvi. 7—9, 12, 13; and this falling from our first love, and returning again to folly, though it be exceedingly dangerous, yet God is pleased sometimes to forgive and heal it, as he promises to some, Hos. xiv. 3. But there is another kind of apostacy, which is proud, wilful, stubborn, malicious; and whereby, after the taste of the good word of God, and the powers of the world to come, men set themselves to hate and oppose godliness, to do despite to the Spirit of grace, to rage against the word, to trample upon the blood of the covenant, and when they know the spiritualness and holiness of God's ways, the innocency and piety of his servants, they set themselves against them for that very reason, though under other pretences: this speaking against the Spirit, this opposing, persecuting the doctrine, worship, ways, servants of Christ; so as that the formal motive of malice against them is the lustre and holiness of that spirit which appears in them; and the formal principle of it, neither ignorance nor self-ends, but very wilfulness and immediate malignity, is that daring height of enmity against godliness which shall never be forgiven in this world, nor in the world to come, Matt. xii. 32; i. e. say some, neither in this life by justification, nor in the world to come by public judiciary absolution; or rather, as others, shall be plagued and punished in this life, and in that which is to come; in the former spiritually, in the other eternally; and God leads those who thus offend forth with the workers of iniquity, as cattle are led to slaughter, or malefactors to execution. And hence it was that Peter said their latter end is worse than their beginning, and that "it had been better for them not to have known the way of righteousness, than, after they have known it, to turn from the holy commandments delivered to them," 2 Pet. ii. 20, 21. Nor is the irrecoverableness of such backsliders any wonder. (1.) This their apostasy in the formal nature of it is quite contrary to faith and repentance: by faith we come to Christ, cleave to him, John vi. 37, prize Christ as infinitely precious; but by this apostasy we draw back, depart from him, let it go, vilify, set him at nought, and after covenant entered into with God, fling up the bargain, and deal with our sins as the Israelites did with their servants, dismiss them, and then take them again; and in a word, so repent of our former, that our heart is incurably hardened against future repentance. (2.) And further, such of all sinners most provoke God to beat them with many stripes, Luke xii. 47; a much sorer punishment do they deserve than did those who died without mercy: they sin wittingly and willingly, not out of ignorance, but against knowledge; not only against light, but love also; and trampling upon the blood, and spurning against the bowels, of Christ, even mercy itself becomes their enemy; and pardoning grace frequently tendered, and seemingly received, but truly rejected, now condemns them: so that they cannot sin at so cheap a rate as they who never had the knowledge of Christ. (3.) Besides, their foreheads are now steeled, and they are made impudent in sin. The oftener a thief is imprisoned, the less he blushes: custom in sin makes the heart insensible, and seared as with a hot iron; lust causes custom, and custom contracts necessity, and every return to sin makes the sinner more unable to resist it. When a disease first meets with a strong constitution, it finds an enemy to grapple with; as it weakens the body so the body weakens it; both their forces spend together one upon another, and they fight upon some terms of equality. But suppose the body gets the victory, and the disease departs, yet if a new adversary, a new sickness, soon sets upon it again, here is great odds; the one is fresh, the other quite out of heart; it is not now strong enough to bear the means of recovery, but altogether lies at the mercy of the disease. In the first estate of sin, the soul perhaps did grapple with sin; and if it were foiled, yet not without reluctance, it could endure reproof, and suffer the word of exhortation; but sin returning upon it again, the soul is so weakened that it makes no resistance, sin entering as an enemy upon a weakened and depopulated country. When Satan returns to his house, saith Christ, he finds it empty, Matt. xii. 44; that is, empty of the Spirit of God, and the power thereof which might oppose him; as well as "swept and garnished," i. e. adorned with all those unbeautiful and deformed beauties which please him. All the former profession of an apostate serves but to make him take the deeper dye in sin; and no colour

Ex perversa voluntate facta libido: Dum servitur libidini, facta consuetudo; Dum consuetudini non resistitur, facta necessitas. Aug. l. 8. Conf. c. 5.

is so lasting as when profaneness is laid upon appearing holiness.

Lastly, Satan's re-entry is with more fierceness and resolution than was his first entry; when he returns to his house from whence he came out, as he finds the house empty and swept, &c., so he brings seven spirits with him worse than himself. After he was compelled to go out of the man, he found no rest, saith the text; yea, all the while he was banished out of him he was as a man living in a dry and desert wilderness, for such is every habitation to Satan in comparison of man's soul: now, then, how great must his resolution needs be the second time, both to assail and hold his former possession! If ever the jailer catch the prisoner who, through indulgence showed him, broke prison, he will be sure to secure him fast enough: he that before had no shackle, shall be bound with two chains for failing; before he was in *libera custodia*, had the liberty of the prison, now he is in *arcta custodia*, cast into the dungeon; before he had but one keeper, now he hath seven worse to captivate and enthral him. They who have escaped in profession the servitude of Satan, and seem to cleave to a new, a better Master, should they again revolt from Christ, and be reapprehended by their old jailer, how irrecoverably will he make them his own, how watchful will he be to keep them in hold, and his hold in them, by hardening their hearts, searing their consciences, following them with temptations, and even hindering them from all the very appearances of holiness! And that brings me to the last branch of explication.

Quamdiu domicilium in hominibus non inveniat, omnia loca, vel cultissima, squalidas solitudines existimat. Cartw. Harm.

This for the explication of the third gradation of these seducers' misery; they were "twice dead."

4. Their loss of life occasioned their loss of place; "plucked up by the roots."

It was bad for these trees to wither, to be without fruit, to be dead, twice dead, though having still the place and appearance of trees; but to be without growth, fruit, life, and place also, makes the loss and woe complete.

"Plucked up by the roots," ἐκριζωθέντα; rooted up as plants they might be said to be in two respects.

(1.) In respect of removal from their former place wherein they stood.

(2.) In respect of the discovery of the rottenness and unsoundness of the root by that removal; the manifesting what was at the bottom of the tree, the turning of the inside outward.

(1.) In respect of removal, the apostle must speak by way of prediction, for according to it they were plucked up by the roots; either, 1. Out of the soil of the church, by being removed at first out of the affections and prayers of the church, and afterwards by excommunication quite cast out of the church; it being denied to such unsound trees any longer to stand in such a garden. Or, 2. Plucked up by the roots out of the soil of the world, and out of the land of the living; and this plucking up was by death, which plucks up not only the withered, dead, but even the most green, flourishing, deeply and strongly rooted tree in the world.

But I understand the apostle to speak of a plucking up, in point of discovery of all that unsoundness or secret rottenness which was at the root of these trees, and the manifestation of them by their abominable errors and profaneness, to be such as never had any vital influence from Christ. Trees may be withered fruit, be without fruit, and twice dead, and yet he who passes by them, and beholds them among the rest of trees, may possibly be ignorant, especially at that time of the year when other trees also are without leaves and fruits, that these trees are utterly and irrecoverably dead; but when he sees them plucked up by the roots, then their privation of life is made evident and manifest to every one: haply most thought they were dead before, but now all know they are dead. Other trees which yet stand perhaps they may suspect to be dead, but these which are plucked up by the roots they evidently and certainly behold to be so. Nor is it any wonder that these dead trees should also lose their place, and plainly appear to be altogether dead, if we consider,

1. How unable dead roots were long to bear and hold up the trees. How could that tree stand constantly which wanted a living root to supply and feed it? A dead root bears not a steady tree. As without a vigorous and living root the tree cannot be kept from withering in its fruit, so neither from its ceasing to stand: out of Christ there can be no perseverance. He who sets us up, only keeps us up. He who laboured to make his picture stand alone, quickly saw the vanity of his endeavour, when he considered, as he said, that something, life he meant, was wanting within. As the hope, so the holiness of the hypocrite is like the spider's web. Union by profession will not serve the turn to make us persevere; no, to that there must be added union by real implantation. If the heart be not set right, the spirit will not be stedfast with God, Psal. lxxviii. 8. They who stand loose from Christ will never stand long; a hypocrite and his very profession will part in a temptation: he who believes not will never be established.

2. How just it was of the owner to pluck up those trees. Most just was it with God to pluck up these trees by the roots, for, [1.] Punishing their hypocrisy. These seducers, (of whom Jude speaks,) who would never endure to be more than, are now suffered not to be so much as, hypocrites; they never cared to be better than visible, and now they are not so good as visible professors; they who would not have the life of trees, shall not now have the room and place of trees; they who were inwardly corrupt, are now openly profane; they regarded not the reality, and they retain not the appearances of sanctity; they who formerly feared not to appear unholy in the sight of God, are afterward discovered justly to be unholy in the sight of man. Heretofore they disdained to be scholars of truth, and they now are left to be masters of error. In a word, they who once were deemed to be something when they were nothing, now neither are nor appear to be any thing; and, as Christ said, from them who had not, even that which they seemed to have is taken away. [2.] Justly does God pluck up these trees by the root to punish them for their unfruitfulness: as a fruitless soil, so a fruitless tree, is "nigh unto cursing," Heb. vi. 8. If Solomon (a type of Christ) have a vineyard, he must have a thousand pieces of silver, and the keepers thereof (but) two hundred; the chief gain was to come to Solomon, Cant. viii. 11, 12: he that planteth a vineyard should eat of the fruit of it; and there is no plant in God's vineyard but God will either have glory from it by its bearing fruit, or glory on it by its burning in the fire.

Obs. 1. Even corrupt trees bear some fruit. These trees had fruit, though it were but withered fruit: most men go to hell in the way of religious appearances; they who shall be excluded out of heaven, will pretend many good works, prophesying, miracles, Matt. vii. 22, 23. Outside services are cheap, and cost but little. Good words, we say, are good cheap; they may procure much credit, though they ask but little cost. Besides, natural conscience will not be put off with a total laying aside of duty; and if Satan can cheat poor souls with putting a pebble instead of a pearl into their hands, he thinks it as cunning as if he put nothing into their hands at all: nothing so dangerously hinders men from happiness, as putting off themselves with shadows and appearances of that which is really and truly good. He who is altogether naked, may be sooner brought to look after the getting a garment, than he who pleases himself with his own rags wherewith he is already clad. A man who is smoothly civil, and morally honest, is in greatest danger of being suffered to go to hell without disturbance; he snorts not in his sinful sleep to the disturbing of others, and he is seldom jogged and disquieted, nay, perhaps he is highly commended. Christians, please not yourselves in the bare profession and appearances of Christianity; that which is highly esteemed among men may be abominable before the Lord; let not the *quid*, but the *quale*, not the work done, but the manner of doing it, be principally regarded; examine yourselves also concerning the principle whence your actions flow, the righteousness whereby they are to be accepted, the rule by which they are regulated, the end to which they tend; and, as the apostle speaks, let every one examine his own work, and consider whether his duty be such as will endure the Scripture touchstone.

Obs. 2. Withering and decaying in holiness is a distemper very unsuitable, and should be very hateful to every Christian. It was the great sin and woe of these seducers, and should be looked upon as such by us, and that upon these following considerations.

(1.) In respect of God. Decays in our Christian course oppose his nature, in whom is no shadow of change. "I am the Lord," saith he, "I change not," Mal. iii. 6. He is eternally, "I am," and ever the same; his "years are throughout all generations," Psal. cii. 24: and what has inconstancy to do with immutability? how unlike to the Rock of ages are chaff and stubble! no wonder that his soul takes no pleasure in those who draw back, Heb. x. 38, and that they only are his house, who hold fast the confidence and rejoicing of the hope firm to the end, Heb. iii. 6. If a frail, weak man will not take a house out of which he shall be turned within a few years, how unpleasing must it be to God to be so dealt with! (2.) Spiritual decays and witherings are unsuitable to the works of God. "His work is perfect," Deut. xxxii. 4; he completed the work of creation, he did it not by halves. "The heavens and the earth were finished, and all the host of them," Gen. ii. 1. God finished the building of his house before he left. His works of providence, whether general or special, are all perfect; he never ceases to provide for and sustain the creatures; the doing hereof one year is no hinderance to him from doing the like another and another: nay, the day, week, month, year, generation, end; but God's providential care still goes on, he upholds every creature, nor is the shore of providence in danger of breaking; he feeds, heals, delivers, clothes us unweariedly; goodness and mercy follow us all the days of our lives, Psal. xxiii. 6; he regards us from our youth, and forsakes us not when we are grey-headed, Psal. lxxi. 17, 18. Most perfect are his works of special providence. Redemption is a perfect work; Christ held out in his sufferings till all was finished: though the Jews offered to believe in him if he would come down from the cross, yet would he not leave the work of man's redemption inconsummated. He finished the work which was given him to do; he saves to the utmost, delivers out of the hands of all enemies; nor does he leave these half destroyed, they are thrown into the bottom of the sea; he has

<small>Christus perseveravit pro te, ergo tu pro illo perseveres. Bern. de Temp. 56.</small>

not only touched, taken up, but quite taken away the sin of the world. Nor will he leave the work in the soul imperfect; he is "the author and finisher of our faith." His whole work shall be done upon Mount Zion; he will carry on his work of grace till it be perfected in glory, where the spirits of just men shall be made perfect, and the saints come unto a perfect man. (3.) Spiritual witherings and decayings are opposite to the word of God. 1. The word commands spiritual progressiveness: "Be thou faithful unto death," Rev. ii. 10. "Let us not be weary in well-doing," Gal. vi. 9. "Look to yourselves, that we lose not those things which we have wrought," 2 John 8. "Let us go on unto perfection," Heb. vi. 1. "Perfecting holiness in the fear of God," 2 Cor. vii. 1. "Take heed lest there be in any of you an evil heart of unbelief, in departing from the living God," Heb. iii. 12. 2. The word threatens spiritual decays: "If we sin wilfully after we have received the knowledge of the truth, there remaineth no more sacrifice for sins, but a certain fearful looking for of vengeance and fiery indignation, which shall devour the adversaries. It is a fearful thing to fall into the hands of the living God," Heb. x. 26, 27, 31. "I have somewhat against thee, because thou hast left thy first love," Rev. ii. 4. "If any man draw back, my soul shall have no pleasure in him," Heb. x. 38. 3. The word encourages proceeding in holiness: "I will give thee a crown of life," Rev. ii. 10. "Yet a little while, and he that shall come will come, and will not tarry," Heb. x. 37. "Behold, I come quickly; and my reward is with me," Rev. xxii. 12. "He that endureth to the end shall be saved." Nor need it seem strange that the proceeding of a godly man in holiness for a few years is rewarded with eternity; for as the sin of the wicked is punished eternally, because they, being obstinate and inflexible, would sin eternally should they always live; so the sincere desire and endeavour of the godly to proceed in holiness is crowned eternally, because, should they always live, they would always and progressively be holy. 4. Spiritual witherings and decays are opposite to the honour and worship of God. None can honour God who divides his service between him and other things. He accounts himself not served at all, unless always served. Who will think that employment vast and large, which a man takes up and lays down at his pleasure? What proportion bears slight and short obedience to the majesty of Him who is the best and the greatest? How can that work be deemed by any beholder sweet and delightful, of which men are as soon weary as of some grievous burden? Who will account that service profitable and advantageous, or its wages to eternity any other than a notion, when they who have entered into it think an hour long enough to continue in it? or will any think that God gives strength to his servants to perform it, who give it over before they have well begun? or that he delights in that holiness which his seeming friends take such frequent liberty to forsake at their pleasure? Prov. xvii. 17.

(2.) The sinfulness of witherings and decays appears in respect of ourselves. 1. Whatever professions have been made, it is certain there never was sincerity. Unstedfastness is a sure note of unsoundness; he never was, who ever ceases to be, a friend; for a friend loveth at all times. He who leaves Christ never loved him. They set not their heart aright, and their spirit was not stedfast with God, Psal. lxxviii. 8. 2. Spiritual withering renders all former profession unprofitable and in vain. He who continues not in, had as good never have entered into, the ways of God; nothing is held done as long as aught thereof remains to be done; we shall be judged according to what we are, not what we have been; Judas, not according to his apostleship wherein he lived, but according to his treachery and despair wherein he died, Matt. xxvii. 3—5: our beginning in the Spirit, followed with ending in the flesh, advantages not, Gal. iii. 3, 4; that is only well which ends well; it is not the contention, but the conquest which crowns; they win the prize, not who set out first, but continue last. 3. Spiritual withering makes our former profession and progress therein to injure us. It had not only been as well, but better, never to have known the way of righteousness. He who licks up his vomit never casts it up again. The house re-entered by Satan is more delightfully and strongly possessed by the impure spirit; the water cooled after heating is now colder than ever; the seeming breach between sin and the soul, being made up again, is like a disjointed bone well set, the union is stronger than ever; and it is more easy once to go on than often to begin. And as there was nothing Satan so much endeavoured as thy leaving God, so nothing will he so much hinder as thy returning again to God; yea, and it may be by this time God is justly provoked to leave that person to Satan, who would needs leave God for Satan. To conclude, none will be so inexcusable before God as they who leave the ways of holiness; for if those ways were bad, why did they enter into them? if good, why did they not continue in them?

(3.) The sinfulness of spiritual withering appears in respect of others. 1. They who remain strong and stable do not yet remain joyful, but are much distressed by the decays of any; though they fall not with them, yet they are cast down for them; yea, they should sin if they should not be sad; and how great a sin is it, to make it necessary for them to mourn, whom to rejoice is thy duty! "Now we live," saith Paul, "if ye stand fast in the Lord," 1 Thess. iii. 8. Their apostacy then would have been his death. 2. The weak are much endangered to be carried away with others for company; seldom doth any leave God singly: the worst, yea, the weakest, shall have too many followers. Although these seducers were carried away by reason of their emptiness, yet all that Jude could do, all the diligence he could use, was little enough to keep the Christians from being carried away with them. It is easier for a weak seducer to carry souls away, than for a strong Christian to keep them back. 3. The wicked are confirmed in the sin into which the decayed Christian is fallen, and also much deride and reproach that way of truth and holiness which the unstedfast have forsaken; they are confirmed in their sin, because their own way has now the addition of a proselyte, and the commendation of an enemy: now numbers are a great encouragement and a strong argument to a sinner in any wickedness, and the commendation of an enemy is equivalent to a universal good report; sinners will deride likewise and blaspheme the way of truth, as if either Christians had formerly embraced it for by-ends, or else as if it had not worth and excellency in it to deserve a stedfast persevering in it; and the dispraising of holiness by its seeming friends will appear to its enemies to be equivalent to a universal ill report.

Obs. 3. It is the duty of Christians to endeavour after spiritual fruitfulness. The apostle mentions unfruitfulness likewise as the sin and woe of these corrupt trees, seducers. This duty of bearing and bringing forth much fruit is frequently noted in Scripture: "Bring forth fruit meet for repentance;" Matt. iii. 8; Luke iii. 8. "Now he that ministereth seed to the sower," &c., "increase the fruits of your

Οὐδεὶς ἐραστὴς ὅστις οὐκ ἀεὶ φιλεῖ. Arist. Rhet. l. 2. c. 11.

righteousness," 2 Cor. ix. 10. "Being filled with the fruits of righteousness, which are by Jesus Christ," &c., Phil. i. 11. "The wisdom from above is full of good fruits," James iii. 17. "Every branch in me that beareth fruit he purgeth, that it may bring forth more fruit," John xv. 2. "He that abideth in me, and I in him, bringeth forth much fruit," ver. 5. "I have chosen you, that ye should bring forth fruit," ver. 16. "Being fruitful in every good work," Col. i. 10. As touching the nature and condition of these fruits,

(1.) They must be fruits of a right kind, Phil. i. 27; Eph. v. 3, 4; 1 Cor. xii. 31; good and spiritual fruits, of the same nature with the good seed that has been sown in us: when wheat is sown, tares must not come up; nor cockle, when barley is cast into the ground. Our fruit must be such as becomes the gospel, not fruits of the flesh. Not fruits merely of gifts, parts, abilities of utterance, knowledge, nor only of civil righteousness, just dealing toward men, freedom from scandals; not fruits only of external profession of religion, in prayer, hearing, &c.; but such as are suitable and proper to a supernatural root and principle, fruits worthy of amendment of life, Matt. iii.; love "out of a pure heart," 1 Tim. i. 5; spiritual fruits, fruits brought forth to a spiritual end; they must give a sweet and delightful relish, though possibly they are not very bulky. Our ends must be raised up to aim at God, and to sanctify him in all our duties. Our obedience must proceed more out of thankfulness, and less out of constraint of conscience; such fruits they must be as are reckoned, Gal. v. 22, 23, "Love, joy, peace, long-suffering, faith," &c. Thy fruit must be of a singularly excellent nature. A tree of righteousness, a branch of the true vine, must not bring forth grapes and thistles. If fornication, uncleanness, covetousness, &c. must not be once named among us, as becometh saints, then not be brought forth and owned. Muddy water is not a suitable stream to a crystal fountain. Brambles and briers are more fit for a wild common than a garden knot. Of the sinful actions committed by a saint, the wicked will say to God, as Jacob's sons did to their father of Joseph's coat, "See whether this be thy son's coat or no."

(2.) They must be fruits in point of production, apparency, and bringing forth. Fruits are not in, but upon the tree. Our goodness must not only appear, but yet it must appear: if it exist, it must and will be seen. Men must see our good works, that God may be glorified, Phil. i. 11. If they see them not, it must not be because we will not show them, but because they will not or cannot see them. The fountain which is full must also overflow. The hand must be filled as well as the heart with the fruits of righteousness. It is not having good in us, but doing good by us, for which we are called good. Our profiting in holiness must appear to all men, 1 Tim. iv. 15. We must shine as lights in the midst of a crooked and perverse generation. Our fruits must feed many.

(3.) They must be fruits suitable to the helps and furtherances bestowed upon us for producing them. If the soil be very fat, the watering very frequent, the cost and care very great, we expect the fruit should be very abundant. Indifferent hearts and lives are not good enough where God has bestowed excellent means. He is not a fruitful Christian who has but an ordinary growth under rich opportunities. Our returning must be proportionable to our receiving. They who enjoy much from God, and yet are no better than those who enjoy less, are therefore worse because they are not better. Whereas for the time, saith the apostle, you should have been teachers of others, &c., Heb. v. 12. "Unto whomsoever much is given, of him shall be much required," Luke xii. 48.

(4.) It must be fruitfulness in bringing forth all the fruits of righteousness. Fruits of the first and second table; of religion toward God, and of righteousness toward man. Fruits inward; good thoughts, desires, purposes, longings after God, good affections, holy joy, love, fear, sorrow. Fruits outward; good works, holy words: "Whatsoever things are honest, whatsoever things are true, whatsoever things are just, whatsoever things are pure, whatsoever things are lovely, whatsoever things are of good report," Phil. iv. 8. Observe the apostle's repetition of whatsoever; we must not pick and choose, and do whatsoever we please. Whatsoever the Lord commands we must do, Exod. ix. 8; xxiv. 3, 7; not examining what the service is which is commanded, but who the Master is who commands; growing up in Christ in all things; not preferring one thing before another; "being fruitful," as the apostle expresses it, "in every good work," Col. i. 10; having respect to all the commandments, Psal. cxix. 6; esteeming every precept "concerning all things to be right," ver. 128; not doing, with Herod, many things, but all things; thoroughly furnished to all good works: our feet must endure to walk in a stony as well as in a sandy path. As a man who is to plant an orchard will get some trees of every good fruit, so we must get every good fruit which we hear of, and set our hearts with it. The pulse of a gracious person beats evenly; and he is neither a maimed person to want any limb, nor a monster to have one limb so large that others want their due proportion.

(5.) They must be fruits, as of every good kind, so of every kind abundantly, not brought forth in a penurious, scanty measure. Imperfection must be our trouble as well as our pollution. The soil of a Christian's soul, like the land of Egypt in the seven plenteous years, must bring forth by handfuls. We must set no stints and limits to our Christian fruitfulness. We must know no enough, Phil. iii. 13. The degrees of a Christian's grace must be like numbers, the highest whereof being numbered, a higher than that may be named. We must look upon every grace like the faith of the Thessalonians, to have something lacking to it, 1 Thess. iii. 10. Perfection is our pattern, and proficiency is ever our duty. We are never gotten far enough till we are gotten home. He that thinks himself rich enough is nothing worth, and he that desires not to bear much fruit is no part of God's husbandry, John xv. 1, 2.

(6.) They must be fruits brought forth when the trees grow old. They must be borne constantly. Trees of righteousness bring forth most fruit in their old age; in this unlike other trees, who grow barren in their old age. They must ever be green and flourishing, Psal. xcii. 14. The bitter fruit of apostacy cannot be brought forth by a good tree. It had been better never to have been planted that we might bear fruit, and that we never had begun to bear fruit, than afterward to be plucked up for ceasing to bear fruit. The good ground bringeth forth fruit with patience; and glory and immortality is the portion only of those who are patient and continuing in well-doing.

(7.) They must be fruits in point of maturity; not only buds and blossoms, but brought forth to perfection. It is not enough for Christians only to have good motions and purposes, but their resolutions must also be brought to execution, and not perish like an abortive birth. Many make their purposes, as one saith, like our eves, and their performances like our holy-days: servants work hard upon the one, that they may play upon the other; so do they labour hard upon their purposes, but they are idle and play upon their performances. What a pity is it that many a fair blossom is nipped in the head!

(8.) They must be fruits in regard of seasonableness. We must bring forth fruit in due season, Psal. i. 3. Fruits are only acceptable in their season: pleasant fruits are brought forth in their months, Ezek. xlvii. 12. Words spoken, and works done, in season, are as apples of gold in pictures of silver. We must have our senses exercised to know fit seasons for all we do. Good duties must be done in a good and suitable time, and that adds much to the goodness of the action; we must order in this respect our conversation aright. If our corn should not ear till harvest were past, nor our trees bud till after midsummer, men would look but for poor store of fruit, and a slender crop. It is true, repentance, faith, and seeking reconciliation with God are continual acts, to be performed at all times, though even for these some times are more seasonable than others, as the time of health, strength, and youth; but hearing, reading, singing, solemn prayer, &c. may be unseasonably performed. Praying is not seasonably performed in the time of preaching, nor reading in the time of prayer. It is Satan's policy to mar duties, good for the matter, with an unseasonable manner of performing them. Seasonableness is the grace of our fruits.

(9.) Lastly, They must be fruits in respect of the propriety of them. They must be our own, not performed by a deputy or an attorney. The godly is compared to a tree that "brings forth his fruit," Psal. i. 3. It must not be borrowed: if our own lamps be without oil, we cannot borrow of our neighbours; the saints and angels have little enough for themselves. Papists in this respect build their confidence upon a sandy foundation. Another man's feeding or clothing himself cannot nourish or warm me; nor can another man's believing or working save me. The just must be saved by his own faith. People must not think to go to heaven by the goodness of their ministers, nor children by the holiness of their parents. Thy rejoicing, as the apostle speaks, must be in thyself, not another, Gal. vi. 4. If thy friend, thy pastor, thy parent, thy master be holy for himself and thee too, he shall go to heaven for himself and thee too.

To conclude this point with some directions how to become fruitful trees:

[1.] We must be removed from our natural root and stock, and set upon and ingrafted into a new one.

We must be transplanted from the first to the Second Adam. The tree must be good before the fruit can be so, Matt. xii. 33. "Men gather not grapes of thorns, nor figs of thistles," Matt. vii. 16. Till we are in Christ our best works are but corrupt fruits. According to our union with Christ, such is our communion with him and fruitfulness, John xv. Some are united to him only by the external tie of visible ordinances and profession; knit to him by that obligation made in baptism no otherwise than many grafts are that do not thrive or live in their stock, but only stand as bound about by a thread; and their communion with Christ is only external, without any spiritual sap or inward influence derived from him to them; and therefore their fruit is that which may grow in the wilderness of heathenism, which natural honesty and conscience bring forth. Our union to Christ must be real, supernatural. "Without me," saith he, "ye can do nothing:" we must abide in him, fetch all from him, depend upon him, John xv. 4—6. The fruits of righteousness are by Jesus Christ to the praise of God. We are to honour the Husbandman by making him our Lord, and by doing all for him; and the Root, by doing all in him and from him; we must be nothing in ourselves, either in regard of self-aims or self-abilities. From him is our fruit found. First a good tree, and then a fruit-bearing tree.

[2.] Shelter thy fruits from the blasting winds of pride. Walk humbly with thy God. The valleys men commonly build and plant in, and they are called the fruitful valleys. The lowly heart is the fruitful heart. God gives grace to the humble. Men look up to the hills, but they dwell in the valleys: "Though the Lord be high, yet hath he respect to the lowly," Psal. cxxxviii. 6. God and humility mutually delight in one another; God is always delighted in giving, humility in receiving; it being the poorest, and yet the richest grace. Should God pour grace upon a proud heart, it would be as the pouring of liquor upon the convex side of a vessel. "He hath filled the hungry with good things; and the rich he hath sent empty away," Luke i. 53.

[3.] Let no secret lust lie at the root of the tree. Grace is that flower at which sin and Satan always labour to be nibbling. The best plant may be spoiled with a worm at the root. Any one lust retained with love will blast the whole crop of thy graces. Beware of every root of bitterness. The Spirit of God is a tender, delicate thing; nor will it endure so harsh a companion as any one lust. If grace kill not sin, sin will kill grace. They can never be made friends. Pity to any one sin is cruelty to all thy graces; the sparing of the former is the spoiling of the latter. The growth of grace cannot consist with the love of poison. The least sin is terrible to the greatest saint.

[4.] Plant thyself by the rivers of water, Psal. i. 3; partake of those waters which flow from under the threshold of the sanctuary, Ezek. xlvii. 12. The inundation of the Nile made Egypt fruitful. Delight in a powerful ministry. It is as possible at the same time to grow in fruitfulness, and to decay in love to ordinances, as to increase the fire by taking away the fuel. "Apostles, pastors, teachers," &c. are given by Christ for our growth up to the fulness of the measure of the stature of Christ, Eph. iv. 13. As a Christian abates in appetite he will decay in strength.

[5.] Pray for the showers and dews of God's blessing. Thy planting and watering will not help without God give the increase. He who will have grace in plenty, will have prayer in fervency. Grace ever puts the soul upon begging for grace. The richest Christian has been oftenest begging for the alms of mercy, James i. 5. That wisdom which is fullest of good fruits must be begged from God, James iii. 17.

Obs. 4. The greatest flourishes and appearances of hypocrisy cannot reach the excellency of the least dram of sincerity. All a hypocrite can do amounts not to fruit. These seducers were "trees without fruit." If Solomon in all his glory was not arrayed like a poor lily of the field, much less is a hypocrite in all his glory beautified like the poorest real saint. The resplendent and beautiful body of the sun cannot in respect of life match the little ant upon the molehill. All the improvements of nature, let it be never so tilled, racked, manured, adorned, cannot reach the excellency of one dram of grace. A curious painter may go very far by his art in imitating of nature, but he can never reach by all his skill to the drawing or painting of life. It is easy to act a king upon the stage, it is not so easy to be a king on the throne. There is an emphasis in true sanctity which the most learned hypocrite cannot translate. The note of sincerity is too high for any but a saint to reach. Till the nature of the tree be changed, and of bad made good, the fruits are as none. How should this humble the proudest hypocrite! Could he bring to God all the gold and silver in Solomon's temple, it were, if brought by him, nothing, incomparably below one broken-hearted groan for sin, and fiducial breathing after Jesus Christ. All his truly good works may be summed up with a cipher; and though they glitter here, glow-worm like, in the dark night of this world, yet in the bright disquisition of the day of judgment they shall all vanish and disappear. Oh how great will the shame and disappointment of hypocrites be, who at that day shall see that all their days they have been doing nothing! To close this, what a comfort may this be to the poorest child of God, that God, in the midst of all his wants of these common blessings, has yet bestowed one upon him which is distinguishing! God bestows those blessings upon others which a saint, as such, needs not have, and that blessing upon him which the wicked, as such, cannot have. And how may a child of God improve this for comfort in the weakness, smallness, deficiencies, if they be his trouble, of his grace, considering it is fruit, true fruit; and it is more, though it be but one little basketful, nay, but one small cluster of grapes, than all the hypocrites in the world can show; and the least cluster as truly shows that is a vine which bears it, as the most plentiful increase that ever any vine brought forth!

Obs. 5. Incorrigibleness in sin is a dismal condition. These seducers were trees twice dead; the apostle despaired of their future living and becoming fruitful, and this was an estate that argued them extremely miserable. It is a woe to have a bad heart, but it is the depth of woe to have a heart that shall never be better. Sickness is an affliction, but sickness past recovery, a desperate sickness, is a desperate evil. How did it fetch tears from the eyes of Christ, that the things belonging to Jerusalem's peace were not only formerly unknown, but that now they were utterly hid from their eyes! "O Ephraim," (saith God,) "what shall I do unto thee? O Judah, what shall I do unto thee?" "If ye will not hear," saith Jeremiah to the incorrigible Jews, "my soul shall weep in secret places for your pride, and mine eye shall weep sore," &c., Jer. xiii. 17. "Rachel wept for her children, and would not be comforted," not because they were ill or sick, but were not. This incorrigibleness in sin, which frustrates and disappoints all the means of grace, provokes God to a total and angry removal of them; and makes him say, I will take no more pains with this desperate sinner; "He that is filthy, let him be filthy still," Rev. xxii. 11. It is that which, as the prophet speaks, wearies God. "Why should ye be stricken any more? ye will revolt more and more," Isa. i. 5. "I will not punish your daughters when they commit whoredom," Hos. iv. 14. "Ephraim is joined to idols; let him alone," ver. 17. When a tree is utterly dead, when it is pertinaciously barren, the hedge and wall shall be taken away and broken down; if it will be fruitless, it shall be fenceless; it shall neither be pruned nor digged, the clouds shall be forbidden to rain, Isa. v. 6. When the Physician of souls sees men rend in pieces his prescripts, and pull off his plasters, and throw away those wholesome potions which he administers to them, he gives them over, and suffers them to perish in their sins. Punish them he will, chasten them he will not. Cut them off he will, cure them he will not, Jer. vi. 29. When, instead of being refined in the fire, the metal will after all the hottest fires, and the constant blowing of the bellows, continue inseparable from its dross; when the bellows are burnt in the fire, and "the founder melteth in vain; reprobate silver shall men call them, because the Lord hath rejected them," Jer. vi. 29, 30. What is it but hell upon earth, for sinners to go to hell without control, to be given up to their heart's lusts, to treasure up wrath against the day of wrath; and, in a word, to be as bad as they will? O woeful recompence of spiritual pertinacy! The earth which, under all the drinking in of rain, "beareth thorns and briers, is rejected, and is nigh unto cursing," Heb. vi. 8. This double death, and irrecoverableness in sin, is a kind of foretaste of the second death. As perseverance in holiness crowns, so pertinacy in sin condemns; he who is obstinate in sin unto the end shall undoubtedly receive the curse of eternal death. How sore a judgment is it, so to be past feeling, that nothing cooler than hell-fire, and lighter than the loins of an infinite God, can make us sensible, though too late! O let us beware of the modest beginnings of sin, which certainly make way for immodest proceedings therein; every commission of sin is a strong engagement to a following act of wickedness; he who begins to go down to the chambers of death, knows not where he shall stop. In short, let no help to holiness leave thee as bad, for if so, it will leave thee worse, than it found thee, and present unreformedness will make way for incorrigibleness under the means.

Obs. 6. It is our greatest wisdom, and ought to be our chiefest care, to be preserved from apostacy. Take heed of being twice dead, i. e. of adding a death by apostacy to the death by original corruption. To this end, let us,

(1.) Be sure to have the truth of spiritual life in us; not only the external appearances of life, the leaves of religion, the form of godliness, and a name to live: he that would not die twice, must be sure he truly lives once; hypocrisy will end in apostacy; where the truth is not truly loved, it will be truly left. A tree that is unsound at the root, will soon cease from its faint puttings forth: the hollow heart will not hold out; the outward form without the inward power of godliness continues not in times of temptation. Labour for a faith of real reception, and please not thyself with that of mere illumination; the bellows of persecution which blow the sparks of sincerity into a flame, blow the blaze of hypocrisy into nothing.

(2.) Forecast the worst that can befall thee, and the best that can be laid before thee, to take thee off from the love and ways of holiness; reckon upon opposition in every way of God: he who meets not with the hatred of a man, may justly suspect his love to the truth; and he who expects not that hatred, will hardly continue his love to truth. When thou enterest upon religion, think not that thou goest to sea upon pleasure, but employment; not for recreation, but traffic; lest instead of holding out to thy intended port, thou presently makest to the next shore, upon the rising of the least storm. Though Christ requires thee not actually as yet to forsake all for him, yet he will have thee habitually prepared to do so, Luke xiv. 28—30, 33. Sever all worldly comforts from Christ in thy thoughts, and try how thou canst love him by and for himself, for his own beauty, without his clothes and external ornaments.

(3.) Take heed of the smallest decay, or a beginning to remit of thy holiness. And to this end, 1. Tremble at those sins which are seemingly but small; whatever has the nature of sin must be the object of hatred; the least enemy of the soul must not be despised. Though some sins may seem small comparatively, yet there is no one but must be accounted great considered in itself; the least sin herein resembling the earth, which though it be but a point to the heavens, yet is a vast and immeasurable body of itself. There is nothing little which offends a great God, or hurts an immortal soul. Poison and death are lodged in the least sin; and as unfaithfulness to God is discovered in a smaller as well as a greater sin, as towards men in a trifling as well as a weighty thing; so commonly it proceeds from showing itself in sins accounted slight, to manifest itself in courses notoriously and heinously sinful: the decay of a tree first appears in its boughs and twigs, but by little and little it goes on further, into the larger arms, and from them to the main body; and decay of grace is first seen in smaller matters, slight omissions. 2. And therefore, secondly, oppose sin in its bud and beginnings, in its first motions, overtures, solicitations: the greatest deluge begins with a drop; every sin defiling the conscience, makes a man the more careless of it. He who dares not wade to the ankles is in no danger of having the water reach as high as his neck. Sinners increase to more ungodliness; when they once descend, they know not where to stop: the beginnings of sin are modest, the progress adventurous, the conclusion may be impudent, in open apostacy. A drop of water may quench that spark which, if neglected till it grow to a flame, may violently destroy a whole town: the greatest crocodile at first laid in a little egg. Yea, thirdly, be afraid of the occasions of sin: the sparks in a flint let alone are quiet; but beat it with a steel, they come out and kindle a great fire: let not occasions of sin beat upon thy heart. It is easier to pass by the snare than to wind oneself out of it; if thou wouldst not like, long for, eat, and impart the forbidden fruit, gaze not on it, Gen. vi. 2; Psal. cxix. 37; Job xxxi. 1: a Christian's charity is not to be, and his prudence not to behold, a provocation to sin. God will preserve us in our ways, not in our wanderings. 4. Never look upon thyself as perfect, or thy progress in holiness as sufficient; he who thinks he has enough will soon come to have nothing; that we have will be gone, unless we strive to get more: look not backward in thy Christian race to see how many thou hast outstripped, but look forward on those who have gotten ground of thee: consider not so much how far thou hast gone, and how many come short of thee; as how far thou art to go, and how far thou comest short of commanded perfection: our greatest perfection in this life is to contend after perfection; we must never cease growing till we are grown into heaven. Christianity knows no enough: he who has the least grace has enough to be thankful; he who has the most has not enough to be either proud or idle. He will be stark naught who labours not to be as good as the best. In rowing up a river that runs with a strong stream, if we rest our oars, we fall down the stream; while we neglect to gain, we spend on the stock; he who hid his talent lost it. 5. Presume not upon thine own strength and power to stand; thou bearest not the root, but it bears thee; God's power only is our support, by it we are kept through faith to salvation: they who call not upon God go aside from God, Psal. xiv. 3, 4. He who first sets us up must also shore and keep us up; he who has brought us to himself must also hold us, that we depart not from himself: we are poor weak reeds, but tied to the strong pillar of God's power we shall stand: he who relies upon himself has a reed for his upholder: we cannot put too much confidence in God, or too little in ourselves. Peter's over-venturousness tripped up his heels, Matt. xxvi. 33. Let us not be like sick men, who, when they have had a good day or two, think themselves presently well again, and so putting off their warmer clothes, put on thinner garments, and adventure into the fresh air, whereupon follow irrecoverable relapses. It is the fear of God in the heart which keeps us from departing from him: let us fear always if we would fall never. "Be not high-minded, but fear." "Lean not," saith Solomon, "to thine own understanding," Prov. iii. 5: he who is his own teacher hath a fool to his master.

Obs. 7. God at length discovers unsound, empty, and decaying Christians to be what they are. These fruitless, dead trees are at length "plucked up by the roots;" their inside is turned outward. They who, going among the drove of professors, are but like sheep, shall be detected either here or hereafter to be but goats. Thus Cain, at the first a sacrificer, yet being a hypocrite, was given up to be a murderer, and was cast out of the sight of the Lord, out of his father's family, and from the ordinances. "Doeg, detained before the Lord" (1 Sam. xxi. 7) about religious offices, afterward discovers his unsoundness of heart by his cruelty; and more afterwards did God lay him open, when at his destruction it was seen and said, that "This is the man that made not God his strength," &c., Psal. lii. 7. The like may be said of Judas's, of whom Doeg was a type, discovery by his treachery; and of Saul's also by that horrid act of murdering the priests, and going to the witch, God also taking away his Spirit from him: they who are not of us will at length be suffered to go out from us. God leads those who secretly turn aside to crooked ways, with the workers of iniquity; though they did not seem to be workers of iniquity, yet God discovers them to be such by leading them forth with them. There are none who so much dishonour Christ as they who profess to be rooted in him, and yet are unfruitful and dead Christians. Christ is a fruitful soil, full of strength; and for any appearing to be in him to be barren and decay, is a great disparagement to him; every one will be ready to blame him for all their defects: therefore, that they may dishonour him no more, they are plucked up from that soil to which they only seemed to belong, for they were there only by a visible profession, not by a real rooting, as a lifeless stake is put into the ground; and in the civil law, till a tree has taken root it does not belong to the soil on which it is planted; and then it appears that they never were rooted in Christ. Please not (then) yourselves with a mere outward empty profession of godliness, with your standing among the trees of Christ in his orchard, merely in being accounted trees of righteousness, or only with the having a name to live. These things will be so far from hindering, that they will further your eradication. A dead, barren oak a man will haply suffer to stand in his wood, but not a dead vine in his vineyard. It was not a wild tree of the wood, which none ever expected should bear fruit, that Christ cursed, but an empty fig-tree, whose nature promised fruit. Root yourselves as much downward in inward holiness as you spread upward in outward profession, otherwise God will at length make your hypocrisy known, and will not suffer you always to abuse his own patience, the good opinions of beholders, and the place of your own standing; and the longer he lets you stand to deceive others, the greater shall your shame be when you shall be discovered.

This for the third resemblance, whereby the apostle describes the sin and wickedness of these seducers; "Trees without fruit, whose fruit withereth," &c.

Verse 13.

Raging waves of the sea, foaming out their own shame; wandering stars, to whom is reserved the blackness of darkness for ever.

The impiety and misery of these seducers are further described,

IV. As " raging waves of the sea, foaming out their own shame."

Two things are here to be explained.

1. What they are said to be, " Raging waves of the sea."

2. What they are said to get by being so, " Shame ;" they foamed out their own shame; like the raging waves, which, after their greatest unquietness, break themselves into foam.

1. What they are said to be, " Raging waves of the sea," κύματα ἄγρια θαλάσσης.

The word ἄγρια, here translated raging, signifies untamed, wild waves, roaring like the wild beasts of the wood. Hence the Vulgate renders this place *fluctus feri maris*; Erasmus, *undæ efferæ maris*; and Beza, *undæ maris efferatæ*; interpretations that betoken fierceness, wildness, turbulence. The same expression is in Wisd. xiv. 1; a man intending to pass through ἄγρια κύματα, fierce, troublesome, boisterous waves. One poet calls the waves of the seas *fluctus truces*, cruel, terrible; and another calls the waters of the sea *latrantes undas*, the barking waves; as if they made a noise like a barking dog when they were stirred and raised: and we frequently speak of angry, roaring, working, boisterous, rough, troublesome seas, and read in Scriptures of violent waves, Acts xxvii. 41. " The sea and waves roaring," Luke xxi. 25. " The ship tossed with waves," Matt. xiv. 24. The roaring of waves, Jer. li. 55; xxxi. 35; v. 22; Isa. li. 15. " The tumult of the people," and the noise of the seas and waves, are put together, Psal. lxv. 7. And therefore our apostle, in calling these seducers "raging waves," does not so much intend their instability, variableness, and fluctuation in mind and doctrine, their motion by every wind, and unstableness in the truth, though waters are unstable even to a proverb; nor only the pride and swelling arrogancy of these seducers, though the waves are called " proud waves," they oft lifting up themselves so high as if they would kiss the clouds, and making as if by their fall they would overspread the earth; but in calling them " raging waves," he rather intends, as I said, their troublesomeness and unquietness; and that in three respects.

(1.) Unquiet in respect of themselves. Their consciences were unquiet, tossed and troubled, without any inward tranquillity and calmness in the apprehension of reconciliation with God. Thus, saith the prophet, " The wicked are like the troubled sea, when it cannot rest, whose waters cast up mire and dirt. There is no peace, saith my God, to the wicked," Isa. lvii. 20, 21; xlviii. 22. Thus Eliphaz speaks, " The wicked travaileth with pain all his days," Job xv. 20. And to the same purpose Zophar, " Surely he shall not feel quietness in his belly," Job xx. 20. Inward peace belongs only to the faithful. It is only reported of them, " Great peace have they which love thy law," Psal. cxix. 165. It is only promised to them, " He will speak peace to his people," Psal. lxxxv. 8. God " will reveal to them abundance of peace." It is only requested for them, even that peace which passeth understanding to keep their hearts, 1 Cor. i. 3; Col. i. 2; 2 Thess. i. 2; peace from God being never desired for men to live in a state of war against God. Only the faithful have taken the right course to obtain it, Rom. v. 1, 9, 10. They alone are delivered from God's wrath, and have an interest in Christ who is our peace, Eph. ii. 14, and the Prince of peace; and have that Spirit which works it in us, and of whom true peace is a fruit and effect, Gal. v. 22. The wicked have not known the way of peace, Isa. lix. 8. They may have it in the brow, not in the breast; in *cortice*, not in *corde*; in the looks, not in the conscience; benumbed their consciences may be, pacified they cannot be. The guilt of sin is an unseen scourge, a hidden sore. He who has thorns run into the soles of his feet, wheresoever he goes, treads upon thorns: wicked men carry their furnace, their rack, their woe, their prison about them, wheresoever they go; nor can they any more lay these off than they can lay off themselves.

(2.) The apostle may compare these seducers to waves, as they are unquiet, troubled, and moved in regard of God, against and under whose will they were impatient, fretful, and unsubmissive. They did not quietly content themselves with their conditions. They were like chaff which flies in the face of him who fans it; there were within them waves of unquietness and impatience, raised by the winds of their pride. They were murmurers and complainers, both against God and man. Of this unquietness the apostle speaks afterwards, ver. 16.

(3.) They were as the troublesome and raging waves of the sea in respect of others; and this I conceive Jude principally intends in this place. The sea neither rests itself, nor suffers any thing to rest which is upon it; it tosses the ships, and tumbles the passengers therein from one side to another, who " reel to and fro like a drunken man;" and in its rage and fury often swallows up and devours both ship and men. The lives of those who are upon the sea hang by a thread, they themselves being neither reckoned among the dead, nor among the living. And thus these seducers were so restless and turbulent, that they found no rest but in their motions. Like those of whom Solomon speaks, who " sleep not except they have done mischief; and their sleep is taken away, unless they cause some to fall," Prov. iv. 16. And troublesome they were,

[1.] To the bodily and outward welfare of others; their names they tossed up and down by slanders and reproaches; they uttered many hard speeches against the faithful: their tongue, set on fire of hell, did set on fire the whole course of nature. What bitter and uncharitable censures have such fomented in all times against those who did not join and hold with them! They are wont to lower, browbeat, disdainfully frown, and look sourly upon them, as Cain upon Abel, with a discontented and fallen countenance. And what bitter enemies in all ages heretics, especially seducers, have been to the lives and safety of the godly and orthodox, has been before in part declared, and of old manifested by the Donatists and Arians, and more lately by the papists and Anabaptists, who all by their boisterous violence and cruelties showed themselves raging waves of the sea. They were troublesome enemies to all public order; they were fierce, heady, high-minded, traitors, inflaming and enraging men's spirits against all government and rule in church and state, putting all places into confusion and combustion by strifes, seditions, schisms; they were not afraid to " speak evil of dignities :" They set their mouth against the heavens, and their tongue walketh through the earth," Psal. lxxiii. 9.

Merito hæretici fluctibus maris similes esse dicuntur quod nunquam quieti sint, nusquam consistant, nova semper moliantur, jurgia misceant, seditionem excitent, schismata pariant, omnia denique perturbent ac pervertant. Justinian. Uti fluctus feri navim, ita ipsi turbulenti et seditiosi ecclesiam concutiunt. Lap.

[2.] These raging waves troubled and disquieted the spiritual welfare and peace of those Christians into whose societies they had crept, whom they tossed to and fro by the violent urging of their errors, and caused to fluctuate and waver in their judgments, overturning their faith, swallowing them up, and drowning them in perdition, by their erroneous and impious doctrines. Through the tossing and fury of these waves many souls suffered shipwreck, and lost the spiritual and precious merchandise of faith and holiness. With these waves of false teachers, and their doctrines, were the Galatians disquieted, when the apostle saith, "There be some" οἱ ταράσσοντες, "that trouble you," Gal. i. 7, or who muddy and stir you like water; and, "I would they were even cut off which trouble you," chap. v. 12.

Fluctus feri, sunt perversi doctores qui et in semetipsis inquieti semper, tumidi et amari sunt, et pacem ecclesiæ, firmitatemque semper impugnare non cessant.—Beda.

Thus we have opened the first branch of this resemblance.

2. What these "raging waves of the sea" are said to get and bring upon themselves by all their swelling and raging, and that was nothing but shame and disgrace; "Foaming out their own shame," ἐπαφρίζοντα τὰς ἑαυτῶν αἰσχύνας.

Vulg. Bez. Despumantes. Nonnulli, dispumantes. Despumare proprie valet spumam auferre. Dispumare, spumam ejicere. Quandoque confundi videntur. Syriace, qui in mare spumationis suæ indicant ignominiam suam. Arabice, sicut fluctus maris commoti, ebulliunt in confusionibus, seu delictis suis. Spumea semifero sub pectore murmurat unda. Virg.

The apostle saith not shame, but shames, αἰσχύνας, to note how great that shame and disgrace was which they discovered. And he saith, ἐπαφρίζοντα, foaming out their shames; that is, that by all their forementioned raging and troublesomeness they brought forth shame to themselves, as the raging waves of the sea bring forth foam.

Confusiones.—Vulg. Dedecora.—Bez.

And most aptly and elegantly, in the prosecution of the metaphor of "raging waves," our apostle says, that by their raging and swelling they brought forth disgrace and shame to themselves, as the raging waves of the sea bring forth foam. In these three respects did these raging waves, of whom the apostle speaks, bring forth shame to themselves, as the waves of the sea bring forth foam.

Instar tumentium undarum, quanto altius se superbientes attollunt, tanto amplius confusi quasi in spumas dissolvuntur et pereunt.—Bed.

(1.) Because that after all their troubling and disquieting the church by their erroneous, turbulent, and soul-destroying opinions and practices, both were found to have as much vanity, lightness, and emptiness as the foam of the sea: though in their swelling and proud elevation of themselves, and unquiet urging of their doctrines, they seemed like the huge waves, which threaten to touch and wash the very clouds, to be raised far above others in knowledge and spirituality, and especially in enjoying that liberty which they pretended went along with their practices and opinions, and so to have climbed, as it were, into the third heavens; yet soon did all their glorious appearances, as a highly raised billow of the sea, falling either upon a rock or the shore, end in mere froth and foam, emptiness and vanity. And indeed what are all the doctrines and opinions, opposed or not warranted by Scripture, whereby any pretend to benefit themselves and others, but gay and gilded nothings at the best? what have they in them but "a form of knowledge," Rom. ii. 20; "a show of wisdom," Col. ii. 23; "vain babbling; science falsely so called," 1 Tim. vi. 20; "strifes of words," ver. 4; "vain deceit," Col. ii. 8; froth and foam; "swelling words of vanity?" They bring no real relief and solid comfort to the soul. They are not bread, but chaff; not milk, but wind, to one who has holy hunger. And their emptiness a humble and serious Christian commonly perceives as soon as their errors are first broached and vented; and it will not be long ere the silly seducer and seduced shall know it also, either by being changed to a love of the truth, or by being punished for the love of error. Now what a shame was it for these seducers, after all their appearing importance with some rarely featured and beautiful truths, to swell with nothing but a tympany of pride and vanity; to seem to travail with a mountain, and to bring forth a mouse; to appear to be the only illuminated, accomplished doctors, accounting others but babes, pretending to be richly laden and fraught with the treasures of understanding, peace, liberty, ability, of all which they seemed to have the monopoly; and when all comes to all, to discover nothing but beggary, vanity, and disappointment of expectation, mere froth and foam!

(2.) These raging waves, the seducers, brought forth shame to themselves, as the raging waves of the sea bring forth foam, in respect of that impiety, corruption, filthiness, and uncleanness which they discovered by their swelling rage. What doth the sea after all its boiling and turbulence cast up, but mire and dirt, an unclean scum, a filthy froth? The more thick and muddy the waters are, the more scum and foam do they by their ebullitions and agitations send forth. How aptly did this agree to these impure seducers! Did not all their swelling, proud, and unquiet contentions end in profaneness and libertinism, as well as emptiness and vanity? Did they not turn the grace of our God into lasciviousness? Did not they who were lifted up to heaven in shows of spirituality and piety, afterward fall as low as hell into all carnal and unclean practices, by luxury, gluttony, and uncleanness? When they spake great swelling words of vanity, was it not to allure, through the lusts of the flesh, through much wantonness, those that were clean escaped from them who live in error? When they seemed to be looking up to the heavens by high speculations, and thereby would needs appropriate to themselves the name of Gnostics, or the knowing men, like that unwary star-gazer, they tumbled into the ditch of all filthiness and prodigious uncleanness. By their violent and turbulent venting of and contending for their opinions, whereby they tossed and shipwrecked poor souls, what did they bring forth, but looseness and profaneness, the casting off, reviling, and slandering of magistracy and all restraint, sedition, tumults, rapine, the liberty of being as bad as they would without control, the blaspheming of God? and, in short, while they promised liberty to others, they themselves were the servants of corruption. And was not the folly of these men of corrupt minds, and reprobate concerning the faith, made manifest to all men? 2 Tim. iii. 8, 9; and was there any shame in the world comparable to this, for men not only to appear altogether empty of what good they seemed to have and love, but wholly filled with all that evil which they seemed not to have, yea, to loathe? for this, the greatest, folly to be made known to all men, and for all their deluded followers to see that they who pretended to be healers of others, should be the most sick of any; and that they who were esteemed highest in holiness, should be found lowest in wickedness? Nothing is there of which a man should be so much ashamed as of sinning, and of no sinning so much as of sinning after an appearing height of and contention for holiness.

Non vacat probabilitate, per participium ἐπαφρίζοντα insinuatam effrænem venerem, cujus deam latine dictam Venerem, Græci Gentiles appellaverunt Ἀφροδίτην, a spuma quæ dicitur ἀφρός, quod e maris spuma orta videtur, vel quod sit ἀφροσύνης θεα, stultitiæ dea.—Lor. in loc. In medio quondam concreta profundo spuma sui, gratumque manet mihi nomen ab illa. Ovid. 4. Met.

(3.) These seducers brought forth shame to themselves, as the raging waves of the sea bring forth foam, in respect of the destruction and overthrow both of themselves and their errors. The waves of the sea cast forth their foam by being broken and dashed in pieces: they seemed indeed, when they were lifted up to heaven in their height and rage, to threaten the breaking or devouring of the rocks o. shore whenever they should fall; but when they fall, they only break themselves, the rock or shore still continuing unbroken and unhurt, and so they come to foam. And how evidently do seducers bring forth their shame, even as the dashed waves their foam, by their own and their errors' destructions! Errors have ever broken by beating upon the rock of truth, which hath in all ages stood firm against the rage of erroneous seducers. False doctrines, like the waves of the sea, may sometimes seem to cover the truth, but never can they conquer it, no more than the stubble can overcome the flame, the cloud the sun, the wave the rock. Truth has ever got by losing, and prevailed by being seemingly overcome; error has ever lost by gaining, and been overcome by seeming to conquer. By the advantages of time and Scripture discovery magnified errors come to be abhorred; and by heresies, as they who are approved are made manifest, so truth itself comes to be both approved and manifested. And as for heresiarchs and seducers, they have been broken in pieces by divisions, by disgrace and ignominy, by despair, though armed, ever to conquer naked truth; by external judgments upon their bodies, or else by the everlasting overthrow of their souls, they bringing upon themselves swift destruction: and what greater shame can possibly be brought forth, than that which comes by their own overthrow and destruction; and that after, nay by, their own elevation!

Sicut fluctus licet tumentes, litus et saxa verberantes ab iis repulsi resiliunt, abeuntque in spumas et evanescunt, sic et impetus tastds, ac furores haereticorum verberantes ecclesiam, in selpsos dissiliunt et evanescunt. Lap. in loc.

Obs. 1. There is no peace to the wicked when they are at the highest. The highest waves are yet unquiet: notwithstanding a sinner's outward swelling and greatness, he, like a limb of the body pained, though swelled, has a conscience inwardly vexatious. He is like a man who hath broken bones under a beautiful suit of apparel, disjointed fingers under a golden glove; like a book of direful tragedies bound up with a gilded fair cover; or, as somebody once said, like Newgate, having a comely outside structure, but within nothing but chains, dungeons, and blackness. There is no peace to the proudest, richest, and most honourable sinner. Till the inward distemper of the heart be removed, and that troubleheart, sin, be expelled, outward advancement can no more help him, than scratching can cure a boil while the blood is corrupt and infected, and no inward means used to cleanse it. Besides, true peace comes from enjoying communion with God, and from the apprehension of the removal of true woes and wretchedness: what true peace can appearing comforts bring to that man who remains under real wretchedness? Outward highness is but seeming and fictitious, spiritual miseries are truly and really such. He who cannot see that he is delivered from wrath to come, cannot be pacified with any enjoyments that are present: he is all his life long subject to bondage, Heb. ii. 15; and but like a rich or noble prisoner, who, though he is plentifully fed, respectably attended, and civilly treated by his keeper, is yet in an hourly expectation of condemnation. A child of God is more quiet upon the rack, than a sinner is upon a bed of down. His motto may well be, *Mediis tranquillus in undis.* Though he is in troubles, yet troubles are not in him. So long as the wind gets not into the bowels of the earth, there is no earthquake, though the wind bluster never so boisterously about and without the earth. If the terrors of God's wrath and the guilt of sin be kept out of the conscience, outward afflictions upon the body cannot cause any true trouble. We call it a fair day if there be a clear sunshine, and a fair sky over head, though it be dirty under foot; and if all be well upward, if God shine upon us with the light of his countenance, our condition is comfortable, though it be afflicted and uncomfortable in earthly respects. A saint has music in the house when there are storms without it, and when it rains upon the tiles. In a word, the godly have quiet rest in their motion; but the wicked have unquiet motion in their rest. How little are wicked men to be envied in their triumphs! How much better is it to have peace with God in trials, than to be his enemies in triumph!

Obs. 2. The erroneous are oft as disquieting and troublesome where they live as the waves of the sea; like the "raging waves of the sea." I have before largely spoken of their raging in point of bloodiness and cruelty, but they which are not gone so far as open persecution, are yet commonly men very turbulent and unquiet. They trouble and disquiet people's consciences, tossing them with the winds of their doctrines, not suffering them to hold any truth certainly, but with hesitation and doubting, casting in many scruples into their minds; with their doubtful disputations racking both the Scriptures and their hearers, by distracting their thoughts and apprehensions with what may be said for and against the truth, never studying to ground and stablish them in the knowledge thereof; leaving their disciples hereby like a cloud tossed with contrary winds, and a ball bandied between two rackets. Their only work indeed is to unsettle, and first to make people believe nothing, and to unbelieve, or at least to waver in their belief of what is true, that so they may be brought to believe that which is false: they who are drunken with error will have the spiritual staggers; they are as pendulous and uncertain as a meteor; they have no centre for their unsettled apprehensions. Schisms rend the coat, heresy disquiets and cuts the heart. Nor do seducers only disquiet and trouble others by unsettling them from the truth, but also by hurrying and driving people from one error to another. Sectaries rest not in one, but oft travel through all opinions. One error is a bridge to another. Errors are like circles in a pond, one begets another, a lesser makes way for a greater, a lower is but a step or stair to help to a higher; like a whirlpool, which first sucks in one part, and then the other, and never desists until it draws in the whole body. Seducers grow worse and worse, 2 Tim. iii. 13, and still increase to more ungodliness, 2 Tim. ii. 16. Heresy is a flood ever swelling, and a gangrene ever spreading. The Galatians were soon removed to another gospel. Nor are the erroneous less troublesome to the outward temporal peace of persons; witness the divisions and factions which they have made in families, between nearest relations, in congregations, cities, states. Heretics are commonly seditious and tumultuary. Novatus was, as Cyprian calls him, a firebrand to kindle sedition; an enemy to peace, turning the world upside down. What raging, outrageous waves were the Donatists, Circumcellions! Augustine in his Epistles tells us frequently of their rapines, robberies. How near sundry states, in these latter times, have been to subversion by the Anabaptists, they who write their histories have related at large. Nor will this unquietness of the erroneous seem strange, if we consider by

Fax et ignis ad conflanda seditionis incendia, hostis quietis, tranquillitatis adversarius, pacis inimicus. Cypr. 49. ad Cornel. August. Epist. 50. ad Bonif. Ep. 68. ad Januar.

whose blowing these waves are raised. It is the breath of that Æolus of hell which stirs them up; he will toss and trouble, though he cannot swallow up the ship of the church. All heretics are Satan's emissaries. He is the father of lies and liars, and a lying spirit in the mouth of every false prophet; and needs must they rage and run whom he stirs up. Nor is any thing so impatient of restraint as error. No heretics could ever patiently endure to be opposed: whenever either the winds of civil or ecclesiastical power, of sword or word, have blown against the tide of heresies, presently they grow rugged and boisterous. These seducers spake evil of dignities. Covetousness and pride, which oftenest put men upon error, are (both) impetuous lusts, and impatient of resistance. The thirst after gold and glory has troubled all the world. Seducers run greedily after their own gain, and compass sea and land to make proselytes. The papists had never raged against Luther if he had not struck at the pope's crown, and the monks' gluttony. And lastly, the truth is, when the heretical rage, it is much out of cowardice; for though they look highly and scornfully, yet they are so conscious of the craziness of their cause, that they cannot but be angry with every adversary. A sickly man cannot endure the sharp air, nor a sickly opinion the sharpness of opposition. They who are orthodox, and contend for truth, should hence be cautious: let them take heed of learning frowardness of the froward. God wants not our passions to promote his truth. Let the fury of the blind promote pity in those who have eyes; and let us break the rage of the waves only by being rocks of constancy, resolution, and zealous opposition. In short, let all those magistrates who will be favourers of the erroneous, consider whom they nourish, and withal whether it be not the greatest imprudence to cherish their destroyers, and to destroy their preservers; and whether they never heard of some who in opposition to church government, have helped up those that in opposition to civil government have pulled them down.

Obs. 3. It is the lot of the church to be amongst raging waves, to be troubled and disquieted in the world. The faithful on this side heaven are annoyed with the unquiet carriage of the wicked. The waterfloods oft are ready to overflow them, Psal. lxix. 15; they are in "the floods of great waters," Psal. xxxii. 6. "The floods of ungodly men," saith David, "made me afraid," Psal. xviii. 4. The people of God are oft accounted the troublers, but they are indeed the troubled of Israel. There is no resting-place for the feet of these doves in this deluge of sin and sorrow here below; they are tossed up and down in their names, estates, bodies, souls, by their enemies, as by raging waves. There is no more likelihood that they should be at rest upon earth, than there is that a man should be quiet upon the sea: nor is it indeed fit that it should be otherwise. The winds of trouble and unquietness blow them profit, and working waves work them much benefit. Hereby they are made to long for their haven, for that rest which remains for the people of God. If the world were a place of rest, they would be too ready here to set up their rest, and the thoughts of heaven would be troublesome, and they would be ready to say and hope that they should never be removed, and it is good to be here. The world is too sweet to them now it is so bitter; they suck at its breasts heartily even when the Lord rubs them over with wormwood. Oh what would they do were the world altogether sweet? If they love so much to smell to it when it is full of thorns, what would they do were it altogether roses? The more Noah's flood increased, the higher was the ark raised; and the troubles of the world raise the thoughts and desires of the faithful the nearer to heaven. The fruitful overflowings of Nile would hinder them from looking up to heaven for rain and refreshment. Tossings in the world make the people of God to be in the world rather patiently than delightfully. Again, by the tossings of the world they are put upon that holy exercise of prayer. He that would learn to pray, saith the proverb, must go to sea. Raging waves make the people of God call and cry for help. The disciples called to Christ when they were tossed; even the heathen mariners in a storm called every man upon his god, Jonah i. 5. The word θυέλλα, storm, is derived from two words, θύω λιαν, which signify much sacrificing. How earnestly did David and Hezekiah pray when they were upon the waves! Music, we say, sounds best upon the waters, and so do the prayers of the saints upon the waters of worldly troubles. "When he slew them, then they sought him," Psal. lxxviii. 34. "In their affliction," saith God, "they will seek me early." God oftentimes defers to deliver his people from trouble though they pray, that so the praying which he so much loves may still be continued; as we use to deal with some musicians, whom we will not presently reward for their music because we desire more of it. Again, were it not for these raging waves, the saints' depending upon and submissiveness to God could not be so manifested. Every one will trust him in a calm; it is only true faith that can rest upon him in a restless condition, and see a haven through all the waves. Nor does God teach his people patience but by being passive: "Tribulation," saith Paul, "worketh patience," Rom. v. 3. Trouble is *esca patientiæ* food, without which patience would starve. Some say the saints never can learn their lesson of patience but in the school of trouble. And further, the raging of the waves makes the people of God to magnify their Pilot and Preserver for his power, wisdom, and love. His power, which keeps the church, like another Mesopotamia, in the midst of the sea, and preserves it from being overturned, though not from being tossed; and which bounds those proud waves, so that they shall not overflow the church, even when the sea of the wicked world is so much in power and policy about it. His power likewise is seen, in that in the floods of great waters they shall not come near to the godly; not to his soul, to destroy its grace, and oft not to disturb its peace; it hereby appearing, that even when "the floods lift up their voice," yet "the Lord on high is mightier than the noise of many waters," Psal. xciii. 3, 4. To conclude, how plainly do the wisdom and love of God discover themselves toward the faithful, when they are tossed by the waves! his wisdom, in making the very rage of these waves to praise him; and instead of breaking his church, only to cleanse it; and instead of drowning it, to carry it to its haven, where it shall never be tossed more, and so skilfully to make it sail with every wind! His love, in that he will not refuse to bear his people company when they go through the waters, and to be their companion, yea, pilot in a storm, and then to give them a great calm within; and in a word, to assure them that they shall never be cast away with the wicked, though they may be cast among them. Let us not censure the faithful in their most tossed estate. There is not a drop of wrath in a sea of a saint's sufferings. Could you see how free his mind is, and his end shall be, from storms and tossings, you would rather envy than censure him: the waves which Satan raises show that he has a treasure, which that enemy would fain have cast away; but yet should he so far prevail, it is a treasure which will swim to shore with him. To conclude, let the faithful (of all people) most prepare for storms and waves: as it is best for them to be among raging waves, so it is too much for them, both to have a haven in their passage, and in the end of their passage too. As long as the people of God are sailing to that port the devil will toss them; and this he will do, though, nay because, he cannot destroy them. Let them be sure that by faith they get Christ into the ship, or rather into their souls, that by obedience they undertake their voyage for him, that their cause be good, and that by repentance they cast out every Jonah, and then let them fear no waves.

Obs. 4. The church has most trouble from those within her. She has sometimes, saith Bernard, had peace from heathens, never, <small>Pax a paganis, nunquam a filiis.</small> or but very rarely, from her own children. No adversaries were such raging waves as these, who were domestical. "Of yourselves," saith Paul, "shall men arise, speaking perverse things, to draw away disciples after them. Grievous wolves shall enter in among you, not sparing the flock," Acts xx. 29, 30. These seducers were not heathens without, but professors who had crept into the church. No evils are so great as those which come to the church from within. The intestine divisions, ruptures, heresies, schisms, have cost the church more lamentations than ever did her persecution from without. The heathen emperors never were so vexatious to her as Arians, Donatists, Anabaptists, papists. Outward enemies scratch the face, they within stab the heart, of the church. From the former she suffered, by the latter she both sinned and suffered; by the former she was under persecution from men, by the latter under provocation against God; by the former she was but solicited to tell where her great strength lay, by the latter she cut off her locks, threw away her own weapons, and betrayed her strength; by her suffering from without the enemies laboured to beat her off from continuing Christian, by her scandal within she beats them off from becoming Christians. Wonder not then that Satan has always used this homebred engine of evil against the church; namely, the ungodly carriage of those within her, and the stirring up troubles in her own house. He knows that there is no sword to this, and that they will never adventure their lives for God and one another in war, who will neither love God nor one another in peace. Oh how should Christians labour to disappoint and countermine this most destructive policy of Satan! Christians, if we must die, let us die like men, by a unanimous holy contention against the common enemy; not like fools, by giving him our sword, and destroying one another by heresies, schisms, profaneness in our own body.

Obs. 5. Sin is a person's greatest shame; that which should most make him ashamed and confounded in himself, and that which shall make him a spectacle of shame, disgrace, and infamy to others. "O my God," said Ezra, "I am ashamed, and blush to lift up my face to thee; for our iniquities are increased," &c., chap. ix. 6: there is the shame that sin should make in us. "Thou hast consulted shame to thy house by cutting off many people, and hast sinned against thy soul," Hab. ii. 10. "Let them be brought to shame," Psal. xl. 14. So Nahum iii. 5, "I will show," &c. "the kingdoms thy shame:" there is the shame that sin brings upon us. In the former respect sin should be shame; in the latter it shall be shame. It is sin only which deprives a man of true glory and excellency, and is the degradation of his nature. Men account that their shame, which to do or suffer is much below their port and rank. Oh how much goes that man below himself, who was created God's favourite and son, having his love fixed and image stamped upon him, the viceroy of the creation, a consort with angels; whose nature is taken into the union of the person of the Son of God, whose purchase was no less than the blood of God, whose soul is a little heaven for the great God to dwell in, whose body is the temple of the Holy Ghost, whose habitation shall be the empyrean heaven, a city, a kingdom purer, more glorious than a thousand suns, nay, in comparison whereof a thousand suns are but sackcloth; how much, I say, goes this excellent creature below himself, in being a thoroughfare, threshold, footstool, vassal to unclean spirits! yea, in having his heaven-born soul a very sink or common receptacle for that which is infinitely baser than all the offscouring and filth upon earth, or than any thing which has a being! How much lower is this descending, than for a king to embrace dunghills, or for Nebuchadnezzar to be a companion for beasts! Well might the apostle say, that of this condition the Romans were now ashamed, Rom. vi. 21. Indeed there is nothing but sin which truly disgraces a man; nothing but sin which disgraces a man in God's eye, whose estimate is the true standard of honour; nothing but sin makes us unfit for that habitation of glory; nothing shameful, unless sinning, but befell the Lord of glory; nothing but sin which will make us inglorious at the last day, when Christ shall appear with ten thousands of glorious saints and angels.

Oh how much are they mistaken who account sin their glory, who are ashamed of their glory, holiness, and glory in their shame, their sin! Are there not many who cannot blush in doing that at the hearing of which it is our duty to blush? Eph. v. 12. "They were not ashamed, neither could they blush," Jer. viii. 12; they have sinned away shame instead of being ashamed of sin, and will not now suffer nature to draw her veil of blushing before their abominations. When the colours and ensigns of a battle are lost, we then give up the battle for lost. Some have aptly called blushing the colour of virtue displayed by nature in the countenance. When Satan has taken away our colours, and custom of sin has banished even sense of sin, and shame for sin, our case seems to be desperate. Other evils which sin brings are curable, the anguish of conscience, the wrath of God, the breach of charity; but the shame of sin can, nay must, never be got out: the more holy we are now, the more should we be ashamed of our former sin. Oh that we could contemplate the shame of sin more in its departure, and less its beauty in its coming, and labour to look upon our old ways with new eyes, opened and enlightened by the Spirit of sanctification! and then it will be our greatest wonder that we should heretofore openly do that which we are now ashamed to think of.

To conclude this, how blessed are they whose sins are covered, whose transgressions are forgiven, Psal. xxxii. 1, who have bought and put on that white raiment whereby the shame of their nakedness cannot appear! If ever the sins of the godly are manifested, as I conceive they shall be, at the day of judgment, they shall be so far from bringing shame and confusion to them, that they shall be glorious trophies of God's mercy, Christ's merit, the strength of faith, and the truth of repentance.

Obs. 6. The shame of seducers is at length laid open and discovered. The great endeavour of these was to be magnified, or rather omnified; to have all others debased and nullified; to have themselves accounted the only men for knowledge, piety, privileges, and their ways the only ways of peace and liberty; but at length they lost and disgraced themselves, foamed out and discovered their own shame. (1.) Sometimes their shame is laid open, and foamed forth by the discovery of the emptiness and mere foam of their opinions, which are manifested to have had nothing of truth or solidity in them. At length they fall upon the shore, or dash upon the rock of the Scripture; and then instead of drowning the shore, or breaking the rock, they end in a little froth and emptiness, and in the breaking of themselves alone. Heresies are not permanent; the word of the Lord only endures for ever, it being a lasting fountain never to be dried up: but that which is against the Lord and his truth is but a land flood; though for the present it may swell and grow, yet it shall fall and sink, and in time vanish quite away. Heresies which have for a time borne all before them, as that of Arianism, which Augustine in grief and admiration tells us had invaded all the world, come by the advantages of time and Scripture discovery to be contemned and neglected. Error, like the painted beauty of some harlot, seems amiable when it walks in the dim twilight, where the orthodox preaching of the word shines not; but bring it to Scripture light, which it mainly shuns, and the more we look upon it, the more we shall suspect, and at length abhor it: the sun of Scripture scatters the fogs and mists of error: "Ye do err," saith Christ, "not knowing the Scriptures." How glorious have those adulterated beauties of the whore of Babylon, of image worship, transubstantiation, merit, &c., appeared in this nation of old, when the candle of Scripture was hid under a bushel! but afterward, it being set upon a candlestick, and giving light to all the house, how clearly did they all appear to be fictitious! and the hatred wherewith they are hated, I trust, by some is, as it was said of Amnon's to Tamar, greater than that love wherewith they were loved. (2.) Sometimes the shame of seducers is laid open and foamed forth by their looseness and profaneness of life; errors in doctrine producing commonly looseness in conversation. Thus the apostle speaks of some who should proceed no further, for their folly should be made manifest to all men, who should increase to more ungodliness, and grow worse and worse: hereby our Lord bids us discover them, "By their fruits ye shall know them." The vine of truth never produced the thistles and thorns of profaneness and looseness. A man of error is oft left to be a man of sin. Thus these seducers disgraced themselves by foaming out their uncleanness, cruelty, rebellion. Who will ever look upon these deformed issues to have truth, beautiful truth, for their mother? Well may he be suspected, who every step stumbles into profaneness, to have either no eyes or bad ones: thus papists, Anabaptists, Seekers, have been discovered by their taking pleasure in unrighteousness never to have believed the truth. (3.) Lastly, the Lord oft discovers their shame by their own destruction and disgraceful end, and by the judgments which he brings upon them. Arius's bowels gushed out, Nestorius's tongue was consumed with worms, and rotted out of his head, Cerinthus was killed by the fall of a house, Montanus hanged himself, Manes had his skin torn from his flesh: examples of this kind might fill a volume. How many seducers has God made pillars of salt by their deaths, who were unsavoury salt during their lifetime! how many of these stakes has God set up in the church, as in a pond, to keep men from adventuring into gulfs and whirlpools of error! Sometimes the hand of justice has found them out; witness the deaths of many Jesuits, of Baal's priests, of Anabaptists, and of other blasphemous heretics. And how oft have they been infamous for their strange deaths, who laboured to live *cæde scripturarum*, by the death and downfal of the Scripture! Oh then how much are they mistaken, who expect to get honour by being patrons of erroneous opinions!

While the pure lights of the church have burnt sweetly, and shined bright to after-ages, living when they were dead, the other have rotted in their names, faded in their honour, withered in their graces, and, in a word, even died while they lived; and what is there left of all these false pretended lights to posterity, but the smoke of an unsavoury snuff?

Obs. 7. The enemies of God cause their own shame and confusion; "foaming out their own shame." They are said to consult shame to their own house, Hab. ii. 10, i. e. their wisest consultations shall be turned into shame against them, or they shall be as surely ashamed, as if they had consulted or taken counsel to bring shame upon themselves. Though shame be not the end of the worker, yet shall it be the end of every work of ungodliness: wicked men twist their own halter, and by sin curiously weave their own confusion: shame is the natural production of every man's own sin. The wicked shall be "snared in the work of his own hands," Psal. ix. 16, and held "with the cords of his sins," Prov. v. 22. Be thy own friend, and none can be thy foe; disgrace not thyself, and then all the world cannot do it. It is not any thing cast upon us from without which is truly a shame, but something which grows out of a man's self; [Basil. de Ira. Οὐ τὸ πένεσθαι ἐπονείδιστον, ἀλλὰ τὸ μὴ φέρειν εὐγενῶς τὴν πενίαν. Pag. mihi 440.]

it is not poverty, reproach, pains, &c. that dishonour us, but impatience, revenge, unreformedness under all these. Every wicked man's dishonour is self-created. A sinner reaps no crop but that of which he himself was the sower; it is common equity that he who sows should reap; God will render to every one according to his own works. As grace is glory in the bud, and glory nothing but grace blown out; so sin is seminally and radically eternal shame and ignominy, and that shame is nothing but sin extended and displayed. So good is God, that he would not suffer sin unless thereby he were able to make it appear shameful; so much is God in love with his own glory, that he would never endure any to oppose his, unless thereby he intended to overthrow theirs; God never gave any of his enemies line, but to strangle themselves: we read of no enemies of God but they shamed themselves; Pharaoh, Ahithophel, Haman, Sisera, Sennacherib, Julian, &c. How should this comfort his people in the midst of all the height and glory of his enemies! Though they cannot pull them down, yet they shall lay their own glory in the dust; and how can God want weapons to beat his enemies, who can beat them with their own?

Obs. 8. Men by rage and fury lay open and discover their shame. When these seducers came to be raging waves, fierce and impetuous in their way, they soon disgraced themselves, and foamed out their own shame. A weak spirit is by nothing so much manifested as by wrath and passion: commonly men think that anger is an effect of magnanimity, whereas indeed it proceeds from weakness. An underling to passion has a base, low-built disposition, to which children and women, therefore called the weaker sex, are more subject than men. The Latins express all passion, anger especially, by the word *impotentia*, impotency and weakness; and hence Solomon, "He that hath no rule over his own spirit is like a city that is broken down, and without walls," Prov. xxv. 28: what so weak and beggarly, and so much at the cruel courtesy of every invader, as a city without all defence? Such a one is he whose raging passions sway him without control; he who scorns to be a servant to man, is a slave to lust, a base, sensual, brutish lust. The strong man (according to Scripture censure) is he who "is slow to anger;" nay, (saith Solomon,) [Non fortior judicandus est qui leonem, quam qui violentam in]

"He is better than the mighty; and he that ruleth his spirit than he that taketh a city," Prov. xvi. 32. Had a man conquered the world without him, and not his lust within him, he were but in a splendid, glittering servitude: well might he with Alexander sit down and weep, but not because there is no other world to conquer, but because there is still another, or rather because there are so many, and every one so much stronger than a world; I mean, unmortified passions. David in sparing Saul, and overcoming himself, was stronger than David when he overcame Goliath; for killing Goliath he was but promised to be Saul's son-in-law, but by subduing his own passion Saul deservedly conjectures that David should be his successor; "And now I know well," saith Saul, "that thou shalt surely be king," &c. Saul seeing in David a power to govern his own affections, foresaw that David was fit to rule a whole kingdom; but how unfit was Saul to be king of Israel, who was not a king over, but a slave to his own passion! A swine in an emperor's robe is most uncomely; and so is he who is a ruler over men without him, and a vassal to beasts within him. Men account it the greatest disgrace to be looked upon and called fools; but the Spirit of God makes wrath and passion the fool's coat or badge. Frequently do we read of a fool's wrath: "A fool's wrath is presently known," Prov. xii. 16. So, Prov. xxvii. 3, a fool's wrath is mentioned for its heaviness. And, "He that is hasty of spirit exalteth folly." And "anger resteth in the bosom of fools," saith Solomon, Eccl. vii. 9; it is loved, cherished, delighted in, as a thing laid in a man's bosom, and it resteth there, it departeth not. A wise man useth anger as physic in its proper time, but a fool uses it as his constant diet. It is an inmate to a fool; it is but a passenger through the heart of a wise man, it does not lodge in it all night, Eph. iv. 26. A man's discretion is to defer his anger, "and his glory to pass over a transgression," Prov. xix. 11; and James calls it the meekness of wisdom, chap. iii. 13. A governor of his passion is by some called *angelus in carne*, yea, *deus terrestris*. No lamb was ever so meek as was he who was Wisdom itself. "He that is slow to wrath is of great understanding," Prov. xiv. 29. Nor does the shame of these slaves to passion only appear in their name and estimate for folly, but in the shameful effects of this rage, where it masters any. "A stone is heavy," saith Solomon, "and the sand is weighty; but a fool's wrath is heavier than them both," Prov. xxvii. 3; a fool having no wisdom to moderate his passion, or to keep it, as a wise man does, from falling with its full weight. "Let a bear robbed of her whelps meet a man, rather than a fool in his folly." This cruellest of beasts shows not so much rage as a man in his fury. How oft has rage whetted tongue, teeth, swords, prepared snares, poisons, fires, &c., for destruction! How little does it distinguish betwixt friends and foes, sweeping away parents, children, brethren with its torrent! It regards neither venerable old age, nor the tenderness of age or sex, nor favours received, nor virtue and piety. It is a short madness, and an interregnum and eclipse of reason, forgetting even the ruin and destruction of the very party in whom it sways, making him neither to feel nor fear multilations, wounds, deaths. It makes a man to put off himself, changing him into a monster; and, as if he were to put on a mask, as Basil expresses it, it represents him another from himself, with eyes flaming, mouth foaming, teeth grinding, colour distempered, &c. Christians, as you love true honour, beware of being enslaved to passion, especially this of wrath and troublesomeness to others; stop its entrance; take heed, as Augustine excellently observes, when just anger knocks at the door, that the unjust crowd not in with it; from a twig it will grow to a beam: his advice is, rather than it should do so, to shut the door upon that anger which is just. In the midst of all thy injuries labour for a meek and a quiet spirit. In sinful contentions, he who is the conqueror is the slave: let not thy adversary be thy teacher, nor be thou his looking-glass to show him his shape in thyself; let him behold in thee a mind above, and deaf to, and impenetrable by reproaches; let not judgment be trodden under foot. If thine adversary deserve pity, why dost thou rage against him? if punishment, who dost thou imitate him? To conclude this, as Basil observes in his excellent discourse concerning anger, Never think thyself worthy of estimation from others, or others unworthy of estimation from thee; study the due ordering of thy irascible part; let it be at the command of grace, and then it will be helpful to thee against sin. Oh how happy were we if all our anger and indignation were set upon sin! we can never hate sin enough, unless we mix indignation with our hatred. Use thine anger like the dog, to spare those of the family, or the flock, I mean men; and set it upon the thief, the wolf, thine own lusts. Let not that which was given thee to be helpful to thee, be by thee made hurtful to thee; let the sword of anger spare Isaac, and sacrifice the ram; be angry, but sin not. Anger should not be destroyed, but sanctified. Be angry with the tempter, the devil, who stirs up thy brother to wrong thee; and be not like the furious dog, who bites the stone thrown, and meddles not with the hand that threw it. The man is to be pitied; Satan threw this stone at thee, he instigated thy brother's passion. In short, as the unicorn's horn upon the forehead of that fierce creature is most hurtful and destructive, but in the apothecary's shop most useful and salubrious; so passion, which men by nature abuse to the hurt of themselves and others, should by grace be made helpful and beneficial to both.

Obs. 9. It is the inward corruption of the heart which sends forth the foam of shameful actions. These seducers, like the sea, had that foam and filth first within them, which afterward they foamed out and sent forth. There could never be an unclean foam sent forth, unless there were first filthiness in the sea. All the unholiness and irregularity of practice comes from the depravity of the heart. Evil things are brought forth from the "evil treasure of the heart; out of the heart" (saith Christ) "come evil thoughts, murders, adulteries;" the heart is the womb of all sinful and impure issues: an unholy root sends forth bitter and sinful fruits. All the prodigious abominations which are made visible in the conversation proceed from an unsanctified disposition. Who sees not, then, at what door to lay all the deformed issues of men's practices? How foolishly are men displeased with themselves for their outward transgressions in their lives, while they tamely and quietly endure an unchanged and unrenewed heart! Why should any be displeased with that tree for bearing fruit, whose roots they will continue to manure and water? How vain and preposterous are those endeavours of reformation which are without inward renovation! If the tree continue bitter and corrupt, all the influences of heaven cannot make the fruit good. If we would have a holy life, we must labour for a changed heart. A Christian's reformation begins at the wrong end, when it begins at his fingers' ends.

As the heart first lives naturally, so spiritually. The foundation of most men's mortification is too shallow, it is not hearty and inward enough; and hence it is that their religion, in these days, is like our buildings, more slight and less durable than of old. It is foolish to think of drying up the streams when we nourish the fountain. David began at the right end when he desired the Lord to create in him a clean heart, Psal. li. 10: till the heart be healed we only skin the sore, we root not out the core of the corrupt matter; and hence the cure is only cloaked. Christians, would you heal the unwholesome water of your lives, you must first cast salt into the spring: get thy sea first made pure within at the bottom, and then thy foam, thy mire and dirt, will not be cast up; purge thy stomach, if thou wouldst not have an unsavoury breath; remove the inward impurity, and then thou wilt be rid of impure outward steams; lay thy mine under the foundation. "Cleanse your hands, ye sinners," saith James; but then the way prescribed is, "purify your hearts, ye double-minded," James iv. 8. New professions, expressions, sewed to an old disposition, will but make the rent the greater. And remember that,

Obs. 10. The unrenewed heart, if stirred and moved, soon discovers its foam and filthiness. These seducers, like the sea, put forth their unclean mire and dirt when disquieted and enraged. The waters which are dirtiest at the bottom appear fair and clear in a calm and serene day; but when the storms and winds arise, they then show what is in them: till the heart be cleansed, any occasion or temptation will draw forth its filthiness. If our lusts be not dead, but only sleeping, every jog will soon stir them up. London streets, inclinable of themselves to be dirty, are, we say, by a small shower made foul. A wicked man is but a chained lion or a tamed devil at the best. If he appear holy at any time, it is not because he is a sea without mire, but without storms; when his tide of nature is opposed by the winds, either of reprehension or chastisement, he will show himself but dirty water. We read not that the Ephesians foamed out their shame till they apprehended their Diana worship struck at, Acts xix. 28; nor that the Jews foamed out theirs, till Stephen had touched them for their hypocrisy, Acts vii. 54; nor that they railed and called Christ Samaritan, and one that had a devil, till he convinced them of their sin, and his own innocence, John viii. 48; nor did the Sodomites discover their shameful uncleanness so much till Lot reproved them: oh with how gentle a gale was their sea of sin troubled! Never did the secret sickness or wickedness of Ephraim so much show itself, nor were the evil humours so much provoked and stirred, until God went about to heal them; nor did the rage of Pharaoh's heart against God swell so prodigiously till God's judgment lay upon him. We see then how best to try the truth and strength of grace. O Christian, what art thou when stirred? dost thou not foam out dirt in a storm? art thou good when thou art pleased, calm when the tide of thy nature and the wind of word or providence go together? Truly this is no great matter; but observe thyself when occasions of sin meet thee, when winds cross thee, when reproofs and corrections would stop thee, and blow in thy very teeth: will thy heart, like the dunghill, stink when thou meetest with the sunshine of an allurement; or with the sea, foam when thou meetest with the wind of opposition? Canst thou then be calm with David, and say, "Let the righteous smite me?" and with Job, bless the Lord? and with the church say, "I will bear the indignation of the Lord, for I have sinned against him?" and with John Brown, that holy martyr, "Lord, I will bow, and thou shalt beat?" Canst thou kiss the rod, lay thy hand upon thy murmuring mouth, and desire that God would rather give thee submission to than deliverance from the stroke? Canst thou under severities heartily beg of the Lord that he would have his will of thee, by pulling down thy proud stomach before he throws away his smartest rod? And when the blasts of the word resist thy dearest corruption, and oppose thee in thy sweetest ways of sin; when the faithful minister levels his darts, and sets the point of the drawn sword of the Spirit most directly against thy bosom lust; canst thou then, I say, instead of rebelling, yield thyself a humble prisoner to Jesus Christ, fall down at his feet, and say, Lord, I submit, "what wilt thou have me to do?" blessed be thy strictest commands and threatenings against my sin, and blessed be the mouth of thy servant which uttered them? This is a happy sign that God has begun to cleanse thy heart from that filth which one unrenewed would have put forth upon these occasions.

Obs. 11. The turbulent and unquiet temper of a wicked man makes him differ much from a saint. The godly are endued with that wisdom from above which is peaceable; they offer no wrongs, they return no revenge; their peace from God inclines their heart to peaceableness toward men: a quiet conscience never produced an unquiet conversation. The peace of God makes those who have offered wrong to others willing to make satisfaction; and those who have suffered wrong from others, ready to afford remission. If the great God, who is offended, speaks peace to man, should not poor man, when an offender, offer peace much more to man? If God be pacified toward man upon his free grace, should not man be pacified to man, it being a commanded duty? The more God quiets us, the less shall we sinfully disquiet others. It is the portion of saints to find trouble in the world, not their property to cause trouble in the world. The reason why God's people are accounted unpeaceable in the world, is because they disquiet men's lusts; their will is for peace, but it is necessity which makes them contend. The peace of God rules in their hearts, Col. iii. 15; and when the unquiet affections of anger, hatred, revenge arise in them, like the judge or umpire of public wrestlings, this peace of God does $\beta\rho\alpha\beta\epsilon\dot{\nu}\epsilon\iota\nu$, rule by appeasing strifes and ending controversies. In short, the people of God are doves, sheep, not birds and beasts of prey: Christ gave the lamb, they will not have the lion or the tiger, for their cognizance. The unpeaceableness of godly men is because they have no more godliness. As the sons of God have a precept, so have they a property, to be harmless, Phil. ii. 15.

The last resemblance whereby the apostle describes the sin and misery of these seducers, is that of,

V. "Wandering stars, to whom is reserved the blackness of darkness for ever."

Two parts are here to be explained.
1. Their title, "Wandering stars."
2. Their estate, "To whom is reserved," &c.

In the first, their title, two things are to be opened.
(1.) What the apostle here terms these seducers.
(2.) Why he so terms them.
(1.) What he here terms them, viz. 1. "Stars;" and those, 2. "Wandering stars."

[1.] "Stars," $\dot{\alpha}\sigma\tau\dot{\epsilon}\rho\epsilon\varsigma$. Not to inquire whether the word $\dot{\alpha}\sigma\tau\dot{\eta}\rho$ be derived from the Hebrew שא signifying fire, because stars appear fiery, by poets called fires and flames; or $\dot{\alpha}\pi\dot{o}$ $\tau\tilde{\eta}\varsigma$ $\dot{\alpha}\sigma\tau\rho\alpha\pi\tilde{\eta}\varsigma$, because of its coruscation and shining, or from the word $\ddot{\alpha}\sigma\tau\alpha\tau\sigma\varsigma$, because a star is never standing still, but always in motion; nor to discourse of the magni- *ἀστήρ secundum aliquos derivatur ab שא quod astra πυρινὰ putent esse, id est, ignea, unde et ignes et flammae pro stellis, &c, sidus, quia sidat insidat, eodemque loco stet, Varro vocatum vult. Alii de-*

tude, numbers, motions, influences of the stars. The nature of a star properly so called, is the same with that of the heaven wherein it is placed; the Scripture mentions no difference between their nature; and the parts of simple bodies, as the heavens, are of the same nature with the whole. Besides, if the stars were not of the same nature with the heavens, they should be of an elementary nature, and so their motion would be direct and straight; whereas it is ever circular. And yet a star is not so transparent, subtile, and thin a body as is the other part of the heaven, for if so, it could not shine, reflect, and cast forth more light than the orb or heaven wherein it shines. A thin and diaphanous body, as the air, may receive, but not reflect light. It has therefore more thickness and condensation than the other parts of the heaven, that so it may reflect and cast forth those beams which are cast upon it by the sun; and in respect of that compactness and thickness wherein the star exceeds the other part of heaven, the orb or heaven in which the star shines is not unfitly compared to mere and pure water, but the star to water congealed or turned into ice, or, as some make the comparison, the heaven wherein the star is placed is like a broad and plain plank, or cloven board, but the star like the knot or knurle in the board.

ducunt a σὺν et εἴδω, scribendo cum y, sydus : q. sit signum in quo simul stellæ conspiciantur. Lorin. in loc.

[2.] "Wandering stars," ἀστέρες πλανῆται. There are two sorts of wandering stars. 1. Such as are commonly and properly called the seven planets, which are termed planets or wandering stars, not because they wander more than other stars, or are rovingly and uncertainly carried hither and thither, for they have a most constant and regular motion, which they duly fulfil in their set and definite times; but they are called wandering, or planets, because they proceed in their orb by various and different motions, keep not the same distance nor situation among themselves, nor one place under the firmament; nor are always of one distance from any of the fixed stars, but move sometimes more swiftly, sometimes more slowly; and are sometimes higher, sometimes lower; sometimes appearing with more light, sometimes with less, yea, sometimes not appearing at all, according to their particular motions.

Cicero planetas dictos existimat, per antiphrasim : q. minime errantes.

The other sort of wandering stars are but appearingly such, and improperly called such, and they are termed ἀστέρες διᾴττοντες, or, according to Aristotle, ἀστέρες διαθέοντες, such as dart, leap, and run hither and thither, and wander into several parts of the heavens, and oft fall down upon the earth; they being only hot and dry exhalations gathered together in a round heap, and yet not compacted thoroughly, elevated unto the highest part of the lower region, and there only kindled by antiperistasis; and seeking to ascend higher, by the sudden cold of the middle region are beaten back, and so appear as though stars should slide and leap from place to place. I conceive that Christ speaks of these stars Matt. xxiv. 29, where he saith, "The stars shall fall from heaven." Thus Aug. l. 2. de Civ. Dei, cap. 24. vid. Lud. Viv. Comment.

Ovid 2. Metaph. De cœlo lapsa sereno quæ si non cecidit, possit cecidisse videri, sæpe etiam stellas, vento impendente, videbis precipites cœlo labi. Virg. 1 Georg. Decidua sidera, Plin.

And that our apostle speaks of these stars, as it is the opinion of Junius, Perkins, Diodate, and also of sundry among the papists, as Cajetan, Lapide, Lorinus, it seems very probable, considering that though the seven planets have various and different motions in their orbs, yet their motions are so regular and constant, that they are certainly known even before they have fulfilled them, and also give clear direction to man concerning times and seasons, and the parts of the heavens and earth; and therefore it seems not probable that the apostle would call these seducers "wandering stars," or, as the Syriac, *seductrices*, or, as the Arabic, *caliginosas*, by comparing them to the seven planets. And besides, as the punishments contained in the former metaphors of trees, clouds, waves, are the continuations of the three foresaid resemblances; so the punishment which the apostle subjoins, "blackness of darkness," seems a continuation of the metaphor of "wandering stars," and is such as agrees not to the seven planets, but to these meteors or transitory impressions or exhalations, which, though for a time they flame and blaze brightly, yet quickly go out and end in smoke and black darkness.

(2.) Why doth our apostle here call these seducers "stars," and "wandering stars?"

[1.] By giving them this title of stars, I conceive our apostle intends either, 1. To show their duty, which was, as Christians, especially as teachers of others, to shine like stars before others, both by their doctrine and life, and by both to be holily influential upon them; or, 2. Rather, the apostle by calling them stars, would insinuate what they desired to be esteemed and accounted among the people, namely, the eminent and glorious lights of the church, such as were fixed in heaven in respect of their meditations and affections, such as directed others in the way to heaven, afforded spiritual heat and life and quickening to them; whereas, indeed, they were but false lights, wandering stars, such as led, or rather misled, people into the ways of error and destruction. And both these reasons of the apostle's calling these seducers stars, are made more than probable by that frequently used and elegant comparison of Scripture, wherein the ministers of the church are set forth by stars, Dan. viii. 10. "They who turn many to righteousness shall shine as the stars," Dan. xii. 3. "The seven stars are the angels of the seven churches," Rev. i. 20; ii. 1, 28; xii. 4. And most fitly may the ministers of the church be compared to stars,

1. For their nature : a star is of the same nature with the heavens, celestial, not elementary, Job xxv. 5. Ministers should be pure, blameless, inoffensive, 1 Tim. iv. 12; 2 Cor. vi. 6; they should teach *facienda et faciendo, voce et vita*, by lip and life, tongue and hand; their profession is holy; they are compared to angels, called holy angels; the prophets were called holy prophets : in their heart they should experimentally find their work of holiness, and in their conversations express it. It is the nature of a star to be receptive of light, and that from the sun. Ministers should abound in the light of knowledge. They are called lights; their lips should preserve knowledge, they should be apt to teach : and as the stars' beams are borrowed from the sun, the calling, gifts, abilities of the minister are from Christ; he has set them in his church, he is with them, without him they can do nothing; he gives them work, strength, success, wages, 1 Cor. iii. 5—7; Eph. iv. 11.

2. Stars in respect of their situation and position; they are high placed above the earth; and thus ministers should be stars advanced above others, both in respect of their calling, which of all others is the most excellent and honourable, and of their gifts of wisdom, &c., and also of that high regard and reverent esteem, double honour, which the faithful should bestow upon them. As they have the highest place in the church, so, walking worthy of their place, they should have the highest place in the hearts of believers; but especially they should be high and heavenly in their aims, affections, conversations.

They should carry themselves as the prophets and ministers of the Most High; they should not undertake their high and glorious function for low and base ends, for honour, wealth, ease, but for the advancing of Christ, the bringing of souls to heaven. Their affections must not be set upon these things which are below; money and possessions should lie at their feet, not their heart; an earthly-minded minister resembles a clod, not a star. Their conversation should be in heaven. A star would give no light if it were not in heaven. Instruction is made profitable to the people by the heavenly carriage of the minister. Stars are of a round, spherical figure; and an orb touches the earth not as a plane, but only *in puncto*. A little earth should seem enough to a minister, 1 Tim. vi. 8. And as the greatest stars, in regard of their distance from the earth, appear but small; so those ministers, who in gifts and graces are most eminent, are yet, in the opinions of men, small, vile, contemptible, the offscouring of the world, and basely esteemed, 1 Cor. iv. 9, 13: this is their lot, but withal it should be their care to be little in their own esteem, though never so highly advanced above others, considering that as God's free love gave them their place and glory, so their own pride may quickly take away both from them, Matt. xx. 26, 27.

3. Stars in respect of the different degrees of their glory. "One star differs," saith the apostle, "from another star in glory. There is one glory of the sun, another of the moon," 1 Cor. xv. 41. In Christ Jesus is the fulness of light and knowledge, and to his ministers he variously and differently dispenses his gifts: "There are differences of administrations, diversities of gifts, diversities of operations, though the same Spirit, Lord, God. To one is given by the Spirit the word of wisdom, to another the word of knowledge," &c., "the self-same Spirit dividing to every man severally as he will," 1 Cor. xii. 4—11. Ministers have gifts differing according to the grace that is given them. There are several notes in music, yet all make up one harmony; and there are sundry and different qualifications in ministers, yet all tending to the church's use and benefit. And therefore,

4. Stars in respect of their usefulness and benefit to the church. Stars are not made to be useful to themselves, but others. Ministers must not seek their own, but others' good. Stars give direction, light, influences, &c. It is a great help to mariners when they can see a star in a dark night. When Paul and they that sailed with him could see "neither sun nor star" for their direction, they were without all hope of coming safe to land, Acts xxvii. 20. Many poor souls are cast away for want of ministers to direct to Christ: they should be like that star which showed the wise men where to find Christ; and as they did, so people should rejoice with exceeding joy when they see such a star. Ministers, as stars, should give light to and be the light of the world, both in respect of doctrine and conversation. A minister must not hide his gifts, and put his candle under a bushel; nor should others extinguish these lights, either by withdrawing the oil of maintenance, or blowing them out with the wind of persecution. These stars must shine though dogs bark, though men shut their eyes, and in a night of persecution; yea, then most brightly. Their light should shine that God may be glorified. They must "be examples in word, conversation, charity," &c., 1 Tim. iv. 12; in all things showing themselves patterns of good works, "ensamples to the flock," that others may follow them, Tit. ii. 7; 1 Pet. v. 3; 1 Cor. iv. 16; xi. 1. In short, ministers, as stars, must be common goods, useful by their influences of warmth and moisture to refresh and to make fruitful the weary, the barren hearts of their hearers, to beget and increase grace in them; and although they see not a desired success of their labours, yet they must not refrain their influences, nor be discouraged with the earth's unfruitfulness.

God speaks of the Pleiades and Orion, which are a company of stars in the heavenly orb: "Canst thou bind the sweet influences of the Pleiades, or loose the bands of Orion?" Job xxxviii. 31. When the Pleiades arise, it is spring; they open the earth, they make herbs and flowers grow, the trees to sprout, and the plants to wax green. Orion produceth cold; the winter comes when that shows itself. Good ministers, as the Pleiades, quicken the heart, warm and make it fruitful in holiness. Bad ministers, like the stars of Orion, cool and deaden people's hearts to all goodness.

5. Stars in respect of their swift and constant motion. They must be stars for motion as well as for promotion. It is true, their motion should only be in their orb and sphere; they should not so visit others' diocesses as to neglect their own, nor be busybodies in other men's matters, nor entangle themselves in the affairs of this life, nor follow other vocations, lest they teach those of other vocations to fall into theirs; they must not leap out of their own element, nor forsake the employments of prayer, study, preaching, &c. In worldly affairs they should be as fish out of the water; but yet in their own orb let them move. Loitering is unsuitable to a harvestman: they must be workmen that need not be ashamed: it is better to be worn with using than rusting. Paul's glory was not that he lorded it, but that he laboured more than they all. They must never think their labour is ended till their life is ended; they must look upon their motion and work as circular, it must ever return; and the end of one service is to be the beginning of another. Their lives must be a succession of labours, praying, studying, preaching, conversing; yea, if God will, conflicting must be added, like the waves of the sea, overtaking one another. The wages will countervail for all.

6. Stars in respect of their duration and continuance. They are set in a firmament. All the powers of hell shall never utterly remove ministers. Till we all meet in the unity of the faith we shall have pastors and teachers. The ordinances of the stars are such as shall not depart from before God, Jer. xxxi. 36; they are established for ever. God has made a covenant with the day and night not to be broken, Jer. xxxiii. 25. Till the end of the world there shall be stars in the heaven, ministers in the church; Christ will be with them, and therefore they must needs be to the end of the world: could they have been pulled down, that work had long ago been done. When Satan the dragon did his utmost, he left two parts of three behind; and that third part which he swept down were not fixed in their orb, not faithful to their trust, but "wandering stars;" but they who are in the right hand of Christ shall never be plucked away: Christ will have his number always; and they who will go about to pull the stars out of his right hand, shall feel the strength of his right hand: the destroying of the ministry out of the church is but a vain attempt. And yet, though these stars shall shine to the end of the world, they shall shine no longer. When the night of sin and ignorance is at an end, when the Sun of righteousness shall arise, and the Lord Jesus himself shall come, there will be no more use of these stars. When we come to drink out of the fountain, we shall no more need the bottle. "Prophecies shall fail, tongues shall cease, knowledge shall vanish away. When that which is perfect is come, then that which is in part shall be done away," 1 Cor. xiii. 8, 10. Christ shall

both succeed and exceed them. All the stars in the firmament cannot make a day; nor can all the teachers in the world convey that light which Christ will afford in heaven. Oh how gloriously will our Sun shine, when all the once-glorious stars shall be swallowed up in his glory!

[2.] The apostle calls these seducers not simply stars, but "wandering stars." And why wandering stars? understanding such as are sliding, gliding, shooting, falling stars?

1. In regard of the matter of these stars. They were but earthly exhalations, when they seemed to shine in all their glory; they were not of that pure, celestial nature with those stars which they resembled; they had earthly, or, as Austin speaks of the rich glutton, they had *animas triticeas*, wheaten hearts; they sought themselves; their belly was their god; they minded earthly things. Earth and slime was their food and fuel: and when the earthly exhalation of profit, pleasure, and honour was spent, these stars went out. They were not like stars that shined to benefit the earth, but merely to be fed, and by being fed by the earth. They were slimy, sensual, unclean creatures, when they were most shining; servants of corruption. They taught false doctrines for filthy lucre's sake, and steered their course by the compass of profit; so that though the world, had they been true stars, should have been guided by them, they were guided by the world.

2. In respect of their outside shows and hypocrisy. Though they were but slimy matter, yet they had a bright and shining appearance; they transformed themselves into angels of light. They had a glorious outside, and an inglorious inside; like those false teachers among the Galatians, they did only εὐπροσωπῆσαι, make a fair show outwardly. A wandering star has nothing of a star but the show; and these nothing of ministers but only the title: they were confutations of their professions, being without knowledge, vain janglers; their science was falsely so called; though they might term themselves Gnostics, and pretend to be the only knowing men in the church, they left the Scripture, and only regarded fables. They were stars without influences; they neither furthered the holiness nor the peace of their hearers; their doctrines tended to carnal liberty and uncleanness; and soon their mistaken admirers found that peace and true liberty could never be obtained in such ways.

3. In respect of their instability. A wandering star keeps no certain course; the most skilful astrologer knows not which way it will move. They who leave the truth know not where they shall stop: the heart is only established with grace. A soul without holiness is a ship without ballast; it holds every thing, and truly holds to nothing. These seducers, like a skipping, dancing star, wavered, doubted, were sceptics in religion, not settled in the truths thereof, halting between several opinions; not placed upon a firm foundation, nor partaking of the full assurance of understanding; neither firm to the truth, nor to their own opinions; forgetting what they have been, not understanding what they are, and not knowing what they shall be.

4. In respect of seducing and misleading others. A wandering star is an unsafe guide. The word πλανῆται, here translated wandering, comes from a word which signifies to err or wander, as also to seduce, mislead, or make another to err; and is a word borrowed from travellers who are wandering in a wrong way. The Syriac read this place *stellæ seductrices*. The unwary mariner, who sails by a wandering star, may as well dash upon a rock or quicksand as hit upon his haven. The traveller who follows a wandering star must at best wander, and is in danger of falling into a river or quagmire. The blind lead the blind, and both fall into the ditch. The deceived seducer is also deceiving. Many follow these false, these fool's fires, though into pernicious ways. Seducers have most disciples; and though the leader shall be deepest in damnation, yet the follower will be as comfortless in falling with him, and as inexcusable in following him.

5. Lastly, Wandering stars in respect of their extinction, and being put out. These wandering stars continue not. Seducers may flash, and blaze, and flourish for a while, but they are not permanent. The true star shall stand as long as the firmament; it may be eclipsed, and there may be an interposition of clouds to hinder its appearing; but never shall there be a destruction of its light. How frequently have we seen the erroneous with their errors, like blazing meteors, go out in smoke, when the sweetly influential stars, the faithful ministers of the word, have still increased in their pure lustre!

Seducers, like transitory meteors and impressions, end in the smoke of shame and dishonour here, when their errors are discovered; and hereafter, when for their errors they are punished: whereas he who is a real, fixed, influential star, continues to shine both in the brightness of the truth which he holds forth, and in the glory of that recompence which he shall enjoy. In respect of the former, the brightness of truth, even dead, he lives; the truth which he preached lives for ever. Heaven and earth shall pass away, but not one jot of his heavenly doctrine. "Do the prophets," saith God by Zechariah, "live for ever? but my words and my statutes, which I commanded my servants the prophets, did they not take hold of your fathers?" Zech. i. 5, 6: the truth lives, though the man dies. The ministers may be bound, but "the word of God," saith Paul, "is not bound," its influence cannot be restrained. Heresy has often died with the heretic, but truth survives the preacher. In respect of the latter, the true stars, faithful ministers, shall shine as the stars in the firmament, with the light of glory, who have conveyed to so many the light of grace; whereas, should the wandering star not be extinguished, and end here in the darkness of ignominy and discovery of his black error, yet his end hereafter shall be the blackness of darkness in hell. This for opening the first particular, their title, "Wandering stars."

2. Their estate, "To whom is reserved the blackness of darkness for ever."

Three things here are briefly to be opened.

(1.) The horrible and dismal punishment itself; "blackness of darkness."

(2.) Its certainty and unavoidableness; it is "reserved" for them.

(3.) Its durableness and continuance; it is "for ever."

(1.) Their dismal misery is set out by "blackness of darkness."

As darkness is properly taken for the negation, defect, and privation of light; and according to the notation of the word, for such a want of light as hinders a man from walking; like that Egyptian darkness, by which people were constrained to sit still, and not to rise out of their place for three days: so the addition of this word ζόφος, blackness, notes a further increase of this darkness, such as is spoken concerning that in Egypt, that may be felt; and thereby the same thing is imported with that of "utter darkness," Matt. viii. 12; xxv. 30, i. e. such as is outmost and farthest removed from the region of light; for this phrase "blackness of darkness" intends as much as most black, thick darkness; it being a kind of Hebraical phrase, like unto that Matt. xxvi. 64, "the right hand of power," that is, a most powerful right hand. So a body of death, Rom. vii. 24, is put for a mortal body; and holiness of truth, Eph. iv. 24, for true holiness.

Caligo tenebrarum. Bez. Perfectio tenebrarum. Arab.

This thick, black, gross darkness is not to be understood properly for that negation or privation of light by reason of the absence of the sun, &c.; but metaphorically, for great calamities and miseries. And in Scripture there is a threefold misery set forth by darkness.

[1.] External misery: "When I looked for good, then evil came unto me: and when I waited for light, there came darkness," Job xxx. 26. So Isa. v. 30, "If one look unto the land, behold darkness and sorrow." So Isa. viii. 22, "They shall look unto the earth; and behold trouble and darkness." "Get thee into darkness, O daughter of the Chaldeans," &c., Isa. xlvii. 5; Amos v. 20.

[2.] Internal, comprehending, 1. Darkness and blindness of mind, the want of the saving knowledge of God and his ways: "To give light to them that sit in darkness and in the shadow of death," &c., Luke i. 79. "The light shineth in darkness," &c., John i. 5. "Ye were sometimes darkness, but now are ye light in the Lord," &c., Eph. v. 8; 1 Pet. ii. 9; 1 Thess. v. 4; John iii. 19. 2. Spiritual desertion, or the withdrawing of the light of God's countenance; and thus Heman complains that God had laid him in darkness, Psal. lxxxviii. 6. And, "Who is there among you that walketh in darkness, and hath no light?" Isa. l. 10.

[3.] Eternal darkness; the miserable condition of the damned in hell, by reason of their separation from God, called "utter darkness," Matt. xxii. 13; viii. 12, because farthest distanced from the light of God's pleased countenance; and this estate of misery is fitly compared to darkness, both in respect of the cause and the effect of darkness. 1. The (though only deficient) cause of darkness is the withdrawing of the light; so the separation from the favourable presence of God is the greatest misery of the damned, Matt. vii. 23; xxv. 46: the hell of hell, is to be without God's loving and gracious presence in hell. 2. The effect of darkness is horror, and affrightment, and trouble. There is no joy but in God's presence, in that there is fulness of joy, Psal. xvi.; but without it only weeping and wailing, blackness of darkness, thick darkness, *puræ tenebræ*, not the least glimpse and crevice of light and mixture of joy. And most fitly is this punishment of blackness of darkness threatened against these seducers, who transformed themselves into angels of light, and yet held not forth the light of the truth, but loved darkness more than light, and led others into the darkness of sin and error; and how just was it that they should suffer by thick, true, perfect darkness, who deluded the world with seeming and appearing light!

Æternis tenebris damnari decet qui, sese transfigurantes in angelos lucis, veram lucem non prædicarunt, sed suasmet magis tenebras et caligines dilexerunt, et in meras errorum tenebras alios præcipitaverunt. Lorin. in loc. Recte in tenebras tormentorum mittentur æternas, qui in ecclesiam Dei, sub nomine lucis, tenebras inducebant errorum. Beda.

(2.) The certainty and unavoidableness of this punishment. Jude saith this "blackness of darkness" is "reserved" for them, πετήρηται. The word properly imports the solicitous keeping and reserving a thing, lest it be lost or taken away by others; a keeping with watch and ward, most accurately and vigilantly, as a prisoner is kept. Hence in Acts iv. 3; v. 18, τήρησις is used to signify a prison. In this place, therefore, there is implied God's present forbearance to punish these seducers with the blackness of darkness, it being reserved and kept for them, not actually as yet inflicted upon them; but principally is intended the certainty and unavoidableness of this punishment, and the impossibility of the pertinacious sinner's escaping it. Nor is it any wonder that this state should be thus certainly reserved for them; the firm and irreversible decree, saith Lorinus, of God to punish them for ever, or that ordaining them of old to condemnation, mentioned ver. 4, is here denoted; so that as in God's decree heaven " is an inheritance reserved" for the faithful, this misery is reserved for the wicked. Needs must this punishment be reserved for incorrigible sinners, if we consider the truth, justice, power, omniscience of God. His truth, it being impossible for him to lie, and who is as true in his threatenings against the obstinate, as in his promises to the returning sinner. His justice, whereby he will not suffer sin always to go unpunished, and "will render to every one according to his deeds," Rom. ii. 6. His power, so great that none can deliver the wicked out of his hand; yea, so great, as that they can neither be able to keep out nor break out of prison. His omniscience, whereby none can escape or hide himself from his eye. In short, this blackness of darkness must certainly be reserved, if we consider the foolish diligence even of sinners themselves, daily hoarding up their own damnation, and "treasuring up wrath against the day of wrath," Rom. ii. 5; like some precious treasure, which they keep so carefully, as if they were afraid that any should bereave them of it.

Denotat firmum et ratum Divinæ justitiæ decretum de supplicio æterno. Lorin. in loc.

Κληρονομία τετηρημένη. 1 Pet. i. 4.

(3.) The duration and continuance of this their misery; the apostle saith it was "for ever." Misery indeed, and yet equity. Eternity it is that shall make their fire hot, their chains heavy, their darkness black and thick. How long does a dark night seem in this world! but how dark will a not merely long, but eternal, night seem in the next world! How hideous is that woe whereby the wicked shall ever strive to part with that which they shall never lose, and crave that which they shall never procure! If it be so great a misery for a starving prisoner to be kept without bread but for a day or two in a prison, and to see through his grate passengers laden with that plenty of provisions which he must not so much as touch, oh what a woe will it be for the damned ever to see the faithful feasting themselves in the fruition of God's presence, and to know that they shall eternally starve, and yet not die, in the want of the least drop, the smallest crumb of that full banquet of happiness, which the saints ever enjoy in God's presence!

Obs. 1. The world, without the word, lies in a condition of darkness. Ministers of the word are the stars, the light of the world; take them away, and every place is full of darkness. The people to whom Christ preached sat before in darkness, in the region and shadow of death, Matt. iv. 16. The Ephesians sometimes were darkness. Before the gospel is savingly delivered, we are under the power of darkness; and darkness is that term from which we are called when we are brought out of our natural estate. And in three respects is the world without the gospel in darkness.

(1.) In respect of ignorance. 1. It knows not God. The Gentiles are said to be such as knew not God. The word only discovers him savingly, because it only makes known God in Christ. The wisest of the heathens, till this light came, could not know him: "The world by wisdom knew not God;" they worshipped the unknown God. 2. It knows not the will and ways of God; and this follows from the former, for he who knows not what another is, cannot know what he loves. The will of God is only laid down in the word of God. There is no service pleases him but that which himself prescribes: The knowledge of the heathen only serves to render them inexcusable for not doing what they knew, not able sufficiently to understand all they had to do.

(2.) The world is in darkness in respect of wickedness and unrighteousness. A man in the dark sits still, and forbears to walk as he does who is in the light. Wicked men are unprofitable, slothful servants, inactive in the ways of God, not those by whom God gains. They are like the branches of the vine, in building good for nothing, Ezek. xv. 4. He who is in the dark, wanders, stumbles, or falls at every step he takes. Every wicked action is a falling into a slough, and down a precipice, a deviating from the way of God's commandments; and therefore sin is in Scripture called a work of darkness. Yea, they who are in the dark are not ashamed of the filthiest garments which they wear, or of the uncomeliest actions they perform; and they who are without the light of the word, in a night of sin and ignorance, blush not in the doing of those things which he who is spiritually enlightened is ashamed to hear, behold, or think of. "What profit," saith the apostle, "had ye in those things whereof ye are now ashamed?"

(3.) The world is in darkness in respect of fear, horror, and misery. Men in the dark tremble at the stirring of every twig. "There were they," saith David, "in great fear," Psal. xiv. 5. And it is called their fear: "Fear not," saith the prophet, "their fear," Isa. viii. 12. It is only the light of God's countenance which scatters the clouds of fear. Till fury be taken out of God, fear can never be removed out of men; but through the fear of death they are all their lifetime subject to bondage, Heb. ii. 15; when any misery befalls them, they tremble, as did the elders of Bethlehem at Samuel's coming, not knowing whether it comes peaceably or no; nor is it any wonder that the darkness of fear should here seize upon those who expect utter darkness hereafter in the everlasting separation from the light of God's countenance, wherein there is fulness of joy, and pleasures for evermore. We see then the true cause that the world has ever so much hated the word, which discovers its deeds of darkness. "I have given them thy word," saith Christ, "and the world hath hated them," John xvii. 14; and he who was the Word incarnate was also hated by the world, because he testified that the deeds thereof were evil. Hatred is the genius of the gospel, (saith Luther,) the shadow which ever attended upon the gospel's sunshine. Though saints are blameless and harmless, the sons of God without rebuke, Phil. ii. 15; yet if they will shine as lights in the midst of a crooked and perverse nation, they must look for opposition: but how irrational and groundless is this hatred of the world! for though the word manifests its deeds of darkness, yet withal it discovers its destruction in eternal darkness; and were the light thereof beheld and loved, it would prevent it, and lead by the light of grace to that of glory.

Obs. 2. Great is the difference between the light which shines here, and that which we shall behold hereafter. In the night of this world we have stars to give us light, we have "a light which shines in a dark place," 2 Pet. i. 19; but when the Sun shall arise, all these stars shall be put out. Prophets, evangelists, pastors, teachers, are given but till we all meet "in the unity of the faith, and of the knowledge of the Son of God," Eph. iv. 13, and then prophecies and tongues shall cease, knowledge shall vanish away; "when that which is perfect is come, that which is in part shall be done away;" when we shall behold the light of the Sun, we shall no more want star-light or candle-light; the immediate vision of God shall abolish these: the people of God shall be above ordinances and ministry, when they shall be above sin and error. In heaven all our difficulties and knots shall be untied; though here we are doubtful of many truths, yet in heaven we shall truly have cause to say, Now, Lord, thou speakest plainly, and not in parables. He who died in his childhood, in heaven knows more than the wisest Solomon ever did upon earth; and that little light or spark of joy which here the saints had, shall in heaven be blown into a flame; their bud of joy shall there be a full-blown flower: here light is sown, Psal. xcvii. 11; but there shall be a harvest, a fulness of joy. O. blessed estate!

Obs. 3. People should labour to walk and work by the light of the ministry. "Yet a little while," saith Christ, "is the light with you. Walk while ye have the light," John xii. 35. "Let us walk soberly," saith the apostle, "as in the day," Rom. xiii. 13. The light of the gospel must put Christians upon a twofold manner of walking and working; speedily, and accurately.

(1.) Speedily. Our light is not lasting, our candle may soon be put out; the most brightly shining minister shall ere long be put under the bushel of the grave, if he be not before blown out by the blast of Satan's rage, and the world's persecution: "Your fathers, where are they? and the prophets, do they live for ever?" Zech. i. 5. The light of life is but very short, but the light of the seasons of grace are far shorter. A book which is not our own, but only lent us to read, and that but for a day or two, we make much haste to read over. In the grave there is no more preaching, no more hearing of sermons; the living, the living, they only praise God, and preach to men: short seasons require speedy services. Oh what a shame is it that we should have torn so many books, worn out so many ministers, and yet have learned no more lessons! Which of us can promise to ourselves that our light shall shine half as long as we have formerly abused it, and wantonned in the shining of it? Oh what would damned spirits give for one glimpse of ministerial light again! would they not, think we, might they have such a favour, ply their work faster than ever they formerly did, or now we do? We have scribbled out much paper to no purpose, we are almost come to the end thereof, and had we not then need husband our time, and write the closer?

(2.) Let us walk and work accurately in the shining of ministerial light; decently, precisely. Though our light be but star-light in comparison of what it shall be in heaven, yet it is sun-light compared with that which shined in the time of the old law, and since the days of popery; we are now neither darkened with Jewish shadows nor popish fogs; we live under the clearest dispensation of the covenant of grace; we therefore live worse than did they in those times, because we live not better. How many kings and prophets would have thought themselves happy to have seen one of the days of the Son of man which we enjoy! Our great salvation neglected, will be damnation great and heightened. What a shame is it for us, that many have done their Master's work better by dim moon-light, than we do by clear sun-light! How shameful is it for us in the light of the gospel, to show ourselves in the filth and sordid rags of sin and profaneness! Cast off the works of darkness in a land of light.

Obs. 4. It is a high degree of impiety for any, especially for those who pretend to be instructers of souls, to mislead and seduce others from the right way. The sin of these seducers was to be false lights, and wandering and misguiding meteors, who pretended to be eminent and true teachers of souls, and to be both influential and directing stars. Severely do we find Christ denouncing woes against the scribes and Pharisees; and with much holy acrimony does he reprove them for being blind and misguiding guides, calling them several times fools, and blind, Matt. xxiii. 16, 17, 19. And ver. 26 he names the Pharisee, "Thou blind Pharisee." And, "Whosoever shall break one of the least of these commandments, and shall teach men so, he shall be called the least in the kingdom of heaven;" that is, shall be contemned, and not counted worthy to be so much as a member of the church of God in the new testament. The apostle Paul sharply expresses himself against seducing teachers, calling them the ministers of Satan, 2 Cor. xi. 15, "false apostles, deceitful workers," ver. 13, "grievous wolves, dogs," Acts xx. 29; Phil. iii. 2, &c. How sad a complaint is that of the prophet! "They which lead thee cause thee to err," Isa. iii. 12. And, "The leaders of this people cause them to err; and they that are led of them are destroyed," Isa. ix. 16. "And I have seen folly in the prophets of Samaria; they have caused my people Israel to err," Jer. xxiii. 13. No sins are so eminently and inexcusably sinful, as those committed against men's callings and professions. What wickedness greater than for a judge to be unjust, for a physician to be a murderer, for a seer to be blind, for a guide to misguide? It is not so heinously sinful for any, as for a teacher of souls, to be a deceiver of souls. Who shall show a soul the way to heaven, if a minister, like Elijah, who pretending to lead the blind Syrians to Dothan, guided them to Samaria, where they were in the midst of their enemies, shall lead them the way to hell? Who should save life, if they who should break the bread of life, give poison instead of bread? or if they whose lips should feed many, only infect and poison many? And further, what seduction is so destructive as soul seduction? Is the misery of leading men's bodies into ditches and quagmires by a fool's fire, comparable to the woe of being led into the pit of perdition, and the ditch of hell and damnation, by an erroneous minister? He that is misguided into hell can never be drawn out again: here it is true, *vestigia nulla retrorsum*, no coming back. The cheating a man of his money, though it be a loss, is a recoverable one; but he that is deceived of his soul, cheated out of his God, what has he more to lose, or what possibility has he ever to repair his damage? There is no folly so great as to be enticed out of life eternal, nor any deceit so cruel as to cheat the soul: nothing can be light wherewith the soul is hurt. Oh how deeply then is God provoked, when he delivers up a people to the misguidings of seducers! It is better ten thousand times to have a tyrannical prince over our bodies, than to have a treacherous pastor over our souls; and yet how do people groan and sigh under the former, and how slightly do they regard the latter! Surely, if for the sins of a people their magistrates are oppressive, for their sins it is that their ministers are erroneous. How just is it with God, that they who will not be disciples to truth, should be proselytes to error! that when none will follow the seeing guide, many should follow the pernicious ways of the blind guide! The true deserving cause of people's seduction is, as the prophet speaks, "The people love to have it so." "The prophets prophesy falsely, and the people love to have it so," Jer. v. 31. They will not endure sound doctrine; they will not suffer a Micaiah to instruct them, and therefore God sends them a Zedekiah to seduce them. They who received not the love of the truth had strong delusions sent them from God, and upon them the deceivableness of unrighteousness took hold, 2 Thess. ii. 10, 11. "The prophet is a fool," saith Hosea, "the spiritual man is mad, for the multitude of thine iniquity, and the great hatred," chap. ix. 7. The instructers of Israel were foolish, blind, and erroneous, because the iniquity of the people in rebelling against the light of truth had stirred up God thus to show his great hatred against them. God never sends darkness among a people till they shut their eyes against the light. If we will imprison truth, God may justly set seducers loose. O labour then to follow true, if you would not be misled by false, lights; and to be directed by fixed, if you would not be seduced by wandering, stars. To conclude this needful point, then, with caution both to ministers and people: to the former, I offer my humble thoughts in this hearty request, that they would consider, the best of them have sins enough of their own to answer for, without contracting more by misleading others. As inexcusable it is for ministers to lead people in a wrong way, as for people to follow ministers in a right way. If then we would not mislead any in this night of darkness and sin, let us be sure to be fixed stars ourselves; let us neither be planets nor meteors, let us be fixed to our Scripture principles, deliberately choosing what we should love, but then stedfastly loving what we have chosen. They who are to lift up their voice as a trumpet must not give an uncertain sound. A minister must be fixed in the Scripture orb, not having a particular motion of his own orb. If the stars and sea-marks change their places, and remove to and fro, the passengers who look for constant direction are in danger of being carried and cast upon quicksands and rocks. In all the reproaches a minister meets with for turning and moving, let his evident adhering to the word manifest that it is not the shore, but only the boatman, that moves: the times will at length come up to a minister if he be stedfast; however, let him take this for an invincible ground of encouragement, he shall be blessed in directing those who will not be directed by him. Whosoever doth and teacheth men to observe the commandments, saith Christ, shall be blessed, though he cannot prevail with men to observe them, Matt. v. 19. Christ propounds not the conversion of people as a property of a faithful minister, but the doing and teaching the will of God. To people, I present the needfulness of taking heed that they be not misled; to beware of wandering stars, false prophets, seducers. It is possible to follow a misleading guide with a good intention, but not with good success. It may be equally hurtful to receive the word of God as the word of man, and to receive the word of man as the word of God. Hearers must take nothing upon trust; they must love men for their doctrines, but not embrace doctrines for men; they must try the spirits, examine all by the word, and suffer no opinion to travel, unless it can show the Scripture pass, and pronounce its Shibboleth. The Scripture, like a sword of Paradise, should keep errors from entering into our hearts. We should not be like children, to gape at and to swallow whatever any person puts to our mouths. In understanding we should be men; and every opinion which cannot endure the beams of Scripture sun is to be thrown down as spurious. Build your faith upon no eminence of man; ever be more forward to examine than to admire what you hear; "call none Master but Christ:" the error of the master is always the temptation, oft the destruction, of the scholar.

Obs. 5. Great is God's forbearance towards sinners. Blackness of darkness is reserved for them, not presently inflicted upon them. Frequently does the Scripture proclaim God's long-suffering, and his being slow to anger. The apostle mentions his "forbearance and long-suffering," Rom. ii. 4. "He endured with much long-suffering the vessels of wrath fitted to destruction," Rom. ix. 22. He gave the old world a hundred and twenty years' space of repentance. He endured the manners of the Israelites "forty years in the wilderness," Acts xiii. 18. Four hundred years he spared the Canaanites, Gen. xv. 16. And sundry ways may this greatness of God's long-suffering be amplified. (1.) He forbears punishing sinners, though he see their sin, and is most sensible thereof: he sees all the circumstances of sin, the most secret and retired wickednesses in the heart, all are naked, ransacked, anatomized before him. Men forbear to punish men because they know not the secret machinations of mischief which are against them; but God, though he beholds all, yet he spares long. (2.) He does not only behold sin where it is, but loathes it wherever he beholds it; though he sees it every where with an eye of observation, yet no where with an eye of approbation. Sin is opposite to his very nature. Man may love sin, and yet be still a man; but if God should love sin, he should cease to be God; he is under sin as a cart pressed with sheaves, Amos ii. 13. All the hatred that man bears to all the things in the world which are either hateful or hurtful to him, is not comparable to God's detestation of the least sin. (3.) He is able to punish sin wherever he either looks upon it or loathes it. As the most secret sinner is within the reach of his eye, so the strongest sinner is within the reach of his arm; he is as able to throw a sinner into hell as to tell him of hell; he in all his forbearances loses not his power, but exercises his patience; he can, but will not punish. (4.) He does not only forbear punishment, but seeks to prevent it. He waits that he may be gracious. He is not willing that any should perish. He strikes more gently for a while, that he may not strike eternally; and he stays and warns so long, that he may not strike at all. (5.) He not only suffers sinners long, but all the while he puts forth mercy towards them, upholds their beings, feeds, heals, helps them. Sinners all the while they live spend upon the stock of mercy: God is at much loss and great charges in continuing those mercies which they wanton away unprofitably. (6.) He forbears to punish, without expecting any benefit to himself by it. If his long-suffering bring us to repentance, the good redounds to us; it is then, as the apostle speaks, salvation. He loses nothing if we are lost; he has no addition to his own happiness if we are happy. (7.) He is patient and long-suffering to sinners, who is much, nay, infinitely our superior, and more excellent than we are. Here a King, the King of kings, waits for beggars; our Lord and Master stands without at the door and knocks: O infinite condescension! How widely does God's carriage towards man differ from man's towards man! We, poor worms, have short thoughts: man will presently, upon every affront or neglect, be ready to call fire from heaven. It is well for poor sinning man he has to do with a long-suffering God; his fellow creature could not, would not be so patient. God truly shows himself a God, as well by sparing as by punishing: "I am God, and not man; and therefore," saith he, "the seed of Jacob are not destroyed." We further may gather that it is no sign that men are innocent because they are not punished. It follows not, because they are great, that therefore they are good; this follows only, God is good. Nor does God's forbearance prove a sinner pardoned, it only speaks him for a time, though the Lord knows for how short a time, reprieved. Justice is not dead, but sleepeth. God is sometimes said to hold his peace, never to be dumb; though he be long-suffering, yet he is not ever-suffering. God's patience shows not that God will always spare us, but that we should now repent. It is not a pillow for the presumptuous, but a cordial for the penitent. God will require interest hereafter for all his forbearance. Judgment delayed will be increased, unless prevented. Justice comes surely, though slowly, to the impenitent: the blackness of darkness is reserved for them who are unprofitable under light. If patience make thee not blush, power shall make thee bleed. O thou, though forborne sinner, labour for faith in threatenings; take heed of self-love, and shunning the thoughts of that severity, the feeling whereof thou canst not shun. Study the end of God's forbearance, and the vanity of all earthly refuges and reliefs against punishment reserved for an incorrigible sinner.

Obs. 6. Things earthly should teach us things heavenly. It is our duty to make a spiritual improvement of earthly objects. The apostle makes use of clouds, trees, stars, waves, to spiritual purposes. The world is a great school to teach us the knowledge of God. Though we have a superior doctrine, yet we must not neglect this. The prophets, apostles, and Christ, often used this kind of instruction by similitudes taken from the creatures; every one of which is a ladder made of many steps to raise up to God; a pair of spectacles, whereby we may read God the more clearly and plainly. Our meditation should be like a limbec, into which flowers being put, sweet water drops from it; and out of every earthly object put into our meditations, some heavenly considerations should be drawn and drop. All the creatures in general we should improve to the learning of God's nature, and our duty.

(1.) Of his nature. The invisible things of God are discovered by the creatures, Rom. i. 20. His power, in making them of nothing, and upholding them, as he made them, with his word. His eternity, for he that made them must needs be before them. His wisdom is manifest in the beauty, variety, and distinction, order and subordination of one to another, the exquisite cunning in the frame of the smallest creature. Indeed Augustine saith he more doubted whether he had a soul Soliloq. l. 31. in his body, (the effects whereof were evident,) than whether there were a God in the world. His bounty and goodness, in the endowments bestowed upon every one in its kind, his large provision for them all.

(2.) We should likewise improve all the creatures in general to the learning of our own duty. As, 1. To depend upon him for all necessaries, as they do for provisions, "their eyes waiting upon him," Psal. civ. 29: we must knock at his door, and go to his fountain, cast our care upon him. "In him we live, and move, and have our being," Acts xvii. 28. "Of him, through him, and to him, are all things," Rom. xi. 36: he is the great Householder of the world. Jezreel cries to the corn, wine, and oil, these cry and call to the earth, this calls to the heavens, but these call to God, upon whom they all depend; and shall not we do so? 2. All creatures teach us to love him and serve him, they being love-tokens, God loving us better than them; and all being instruments of punishment if we fail in our duty. They all serve the Lord by a perpetual law. The winds and the seas obey him; "fire, snow, hail," &c., Psal. cxlviii. 8. All the creatures, even frogs, grasshoppers, lice, are his soldiers. He is Commander-in-chief; they are all at his beck. In obedience to him they will run from themselves, and cease to be themselves; the sun will stand still, go back, the sea will be a solid wall, the fire will not burn, iron will swim, 2 Kings vi. 6. And they serve us all so constantly day and night; they serve us with their sweetest and choicest gifts; the sun with influence of heat and light, trees with delightful fruit, and beasts with fleece and life, to their own wasting and destruction. Oh how should we serve him even to the loss of the best things we have; and how should the constant standing of the creatures in that station wherein God at the first set them, make us ashamed of our apostacy from God, and rebellion against God! 3. All the creatures in general teach us earnestly to expect a better condition than that which we now enjoy. "The earnest expectation of the creature" (saith Paul) "waiteth for the manifestation of the sons of God," Rom. viii. 19. If there be something in the creatures (groaning and travailing in pain until now, tired out by man's sin, and made subject to vanity) like an earnest expectation of and waiting for this manifestation, should not man, who is the sinner, and has made the creature subject to vanity, who has also reason, and who shall partake of more happiness by that manifestation, much more desire and look for it? Shall man, of all creatures, rest in and be contented with a state of vanity? The very unreasonable, yea, insensible creatures, will teach us to soar to a more heavenly pitch of spirit.

And as all the creatures in general may (thus) be improved spiritually, so may every particular creature severally, whether in heaven or on the earth. For heavenly creatures, the psalmist tells us, "The heavens declare the glory of God, and the firmament showeth his handywork," Psal. xix. 1. "When I consider thy heavens, the work of thy fingers, the moon and the stars, which thou hast ordained; what is man?" &c., Psal. viii. 3. The pure and excellent matter of the heavens speaks the greater purity and excellency of the Workman. How pure also our hearts should be, which are his lesser heaven; and how pure they should be who expect to live in those heavens, into which no impure thing must enter! How hateful also sin is to God, who for man's sin will one day set this beautiful house on fire! The height of the heavens shows the infinite height, and honour, and majesty of him whose standing house is above all the visible heavens, whose palace, seat, and pavilion is in heaven above. The circular, round figure of the heavens teacheth us the infiniteness and perfection of the Maker. The firmness and stability of the heavens declares God's truth and unchangeableness, whose word is their pillar; the safety likewise of that place to lay up our treasures in: their swift motion and revolution in twenty-four hours instructs us of the readiness and swiftness which we should express in duty. The light of heaven, of so unknown a nature, shows us the incomprehensible nature of God. The diffusiveness and comfortableness of light speaks what comfort is in the light of his face, which, as light, though imparted to thousands, yet is not impaired or made less for the good of others. The purity of light contracting no filthiness, though looking into it, teaches us his holiness, who though he sees sin every where, yet loves it no where, and is ever in an irreconcilable opposition against all the works of darkness. The oneness, brightness, purity, greatness, influences, eclipses of the sun, teach us the Sun of righteousness, the Lord Christ, is the only Saviour, most swift to help, the brightness of his Father's glory, holy, powerful, infinitely useful and beneficial, the director, enlivener, cherisher of his church; and all this, though once eclipsed and clouded with a natural body and sufferings. The moon, her borrowing of light from the sun, her changes, spots, inferiority, governing of the night, disappearing at the rising of the sun, speaks the dependency of the church upon Christ, her many changes and various conditions in this life, her defects and deformities, subordination to Christ, as also the uncertainty and variableness of every worldly condition, the smallness and lowness of all earthly enjoyments, their spottedness with many cares, fears, wants, their usefulness only while we are in the night of this world, their disappearing and vanishing when the Sun of righteousness shall come in glory. The stars, in respect of the constancy, continuance of their courses in their orbs, communicativeness of light, differing one from another, their glittering and influences, declare the stability of God's promises to his church, which can never be broken, Jer. xxxi. 35, 36; our duty to continue in our own sphere, to afford our help and light to them who stand in need; the different degrees likewise of grace and glory hereafter, the clearest shining of grace in the night of affliction. Of the clouds we have spoken before. The air also, by its invisibleness, ubiquity, preservation of our life, should remind us that God is, though he is not seen; that he is every where, within me, without me, included in, excluded from no place; the Preserver also of our lives, in whom we live, move, and have our being. The winds, by their thinness, piercing, powerful motions, freedom, inconstancy, teach us, as God's invisibility, his irresistible power in his works of nature and grace, the free motion of the Spirit, and the secret working thereof in the heart, John iii. 7, 8; so the vanity and levity of man, and all human things, the inability of any creature to withstand God, the misery of those who are not built upon Christ as their rock and foundation, the unsettledness of the erroneous, tossed with every wind of doctrine. Of the earth likewise, with the creatures there, as well as the heavens, should we make a spiritual improvement. "Speak to the earth," saith Job, "and it shall teach thee," chap. xii. 8. "How excellent," saith David, "is thy name in all the earth!" The earth, by its hanging on nothing, its stability, plenty, lowness, the labouring about it, and its receiving of seed, instructs us of the infinite power and strength of God, the ability of his word to sustain the burdens of the soul, the riches of his throne, whose footstool is so decked; God's goodness to sinful man, in spreading and furnishing for him such a table; his care for his people, in so clothing the grass of the field, and providing for the very beasts; the unsuitableness of pride to man, the earth being his mother, whence he came and whither he goes; it teaches us also wisdom, to get our hearts above these drossy, earthly objects, and to have our conversation in heaven; the pains also which we ought to take to dig deep for wisdom, which is more precious than gold, and to receive the seed of the word in a prepared soil, a good and honest heart. The trees upon the earth, in respect of their variety of sorts, growth, shelter, fruitfulness, decay, teach us that difference which is among men: some are wild, trees of the wood, and of the field, without the church; others are planted in the garden and orchard of the church: some have neither the fruits of holiness nor the leaves of profession; others have leaves who are without fruit; others, trees of righteousness, have both: some are as the taller cedars, some as the lower shrubs, some are rich and noble, some poor and contemptible in the world; but when both are turned to ashes, then both alike: the ashes of a beggar are as good as those of a king. Some men fall by old age, and want of natural moisture, others are before their time cut down in their green years with the axe of death. There is no spiritual growth or continuance, unless we draw life from Christ our root: the more pruning, watering, and heavenly influences God bestows upon us, the more fruitful should we be; the more laden with fruit, the more we should bow ourselves down in humility and communicativeness. The very grass tells us we are withering creatures, and that the flourishing condition of the wicked is much more withering. The corn dying and fructifying teaches us the resurrection. "Ask now the beasts," saith Job, "and they shall teach thee," Job xii. 7. They all teach us the greatness of his possessions and riches, whose are the beasts upon a thousand hills: also the thankful knowing and owning of God; "The ox knoweth his owner, and the ass his master's crib." The lion teaches us the strength of Christ, and the cruelty of Satan. In the horse and mule we see our untaught and refractory nature; in the sheep our disposition to wander, and our duty to hear and follow our Shepherd, and our helplessness without him; also his meekness and patience, who, as a sheep before the shearers, was dumb, and opened not his mouth. In the lamb likewise observe him who was brought as a lamb to the slaughter; who was a Lamb for innocency and gentleness, a sacrificed Lamb for spotlessness and satisfaction. The dog and swine will remind us of the uncleanness of sinners, and especially of the odiousness of apostasy, which is a turning to the vomit, and to the wallowing in the mire. The serpent teaches us wisdom to preserve ourselves. The very ant, providence and diligence to lay up for the future. The despicable worm represents the lowness of him for our sin, who was a worm, and no man, Psal. xxii. 6. The taking of beasts in a snare should put us in mind of the snare of sin. Ask likewise, saith Job, of "the fowls of the air, and they shall tell thee," Job xii. 7. These may support faith, and scatter our distracting cares; they being fed, though they neither sow nor reap. Their observing also of their several seasons, the stork in the heavens knowing her appointed times, and the turtle, crane, and swallow observing the times of their coming, teach us to know the judgment of the Lord, and the day of our visitation. What a lively pattern of meekness and simplicity is the dove! The early chirping and singing of the birds in the morning, may teach man his duty to praise God as soon as he awakes in the morning; as a godly man once said to a bishop who was sleeping in bed too long in the morning, *Surrexerunt passeres, et stertunt pontifices.* How much greater is the care of Christ in protecting his servants, than that of a hen toward her chickens, in gathering them under her wings! "Speak to the fishes of the sea," saith Job; these have a speech, though they are mute. The sea itself, by its rage, fury, and foaming, shows us the inconstancy and troublesomeness of the world, the unquietness of wicked men, the power of him who who stills it and keeps it within its bounds. By its fulness, notwithstanding the running of so many floods and rivers out of it, it directs us to him who is an inexhaustible fountain of good, having never a whit the less for all he gives. The running of the rivers into the sea, whence they come, shows that as all is from him in bounty, so all must be returned to him by duty. The fish themselves will teach us the misery of want of government, when men are as the fishes of the sea, that have no ruler over them, but the greater devours the less, Hab. i. 14. Their sporting and skipping speaks the disposition of sinners, who sport in sin as their element before they are caught, Prov. x. 23; Tit. iii. 3; and the power of the gospel, whereby they are taken, Luke v. 10; Matt. iv. 19. The fewness of those which are caught in comparison of those which are left shows the small number of those who are taken with that net compared with those who are left. In catching fish with a net or hook unawares, we are taught the folly of men taken with the baits of sin, who think not of their time, but are taken as fish in an evil net. In short, the whole creation is a scripture of God, a book; and the heaven, the earth, the waters are three great leaves: the creatures contained in these are so many lines, by all which we may read a divinity lecture. Though the creature is not able to lead us into a saving knowledge of the mysteries of Christ, yet it gives us such advantages to know God as will leave us inexcusable in our ignorance. How should this doctrine humble us, who by our apostasy are become the scholars of the creatures! Christians, who have both reason and grace, may learn from those who have not so much as sense and life. Adam's knowledge of God led him to the knowledge of the creatures, but now man by the creature learns the knowledge of God; like Balaam's ass, the creatures now teach their master; man is now sent to their school, put back like an idle truant to the lowest form. How happy were man, could he learn of the very ass, which (as Bernard observes) will bear any load because he is an ass; but if we offer to thrust him down some steep hill, or drive him into the fire, he holds back, and shuns it; whereas a blockish sinner has no fear of that which brings eternal damnation! But, of all others, how justly reprovable are they who, instead of furthering their salvation, hasten their destruction by the creatures, in abusing them to excess, riot, and gluttony! *Oneramus asinum, et non cupit quia asinus est, at si in ignem impellere, si in foveam præcipitare velis, cavet quantum potest, quia vitam amat, et mortem timet. Bern.*

To conclude this point, for urging us to make a holy use of created objects, let us consider that there is a double use of every creature, natural and spiritual. If we content ourselves with the natural use without the spiritual, we do not take one half the comfort in the creature which God gave it for; and indeed, what do we more than the brute beast, which has a carnal and natural use of the creature as well as we? These seducers, for knowing things only naturally, are compared to brute beasts: let us not therefore, as children, look only upon pictures in our books, and gaze upon the gilded leaves and cover; but let us look to our lesson which we should learn therein. And let us know we never use the creatures as their lords, unless we see our Lord in them: a carnal man profits his body, a spiritual man his soul also, by them. Every creature may be a preacher to him in whom the Spirit first inwardly preaches. A man may be cast into such a condition, as whereby he may be hindered from good actions; but what, unless a bad heart, can hinder him from good meditation? And as it is with bees, though they gather honey from a flower, they leave it as fragrant and fresh as they found it; so we gathering spiritual thoughts from our worldly enjoyments and employments, instead of hurting and hindering them, we benefit and enrich ourselves, and advance them.

Verse 14, 15.

And Enoch also, the seventh from Adam, prophesied of these, saying, Behold, the Lord cometh with ten thousand of his saints, to execute judgment upon all, and to convince all that are ungodly among them of all their ungodly deeds which they have ungodly committed, and of all their hard speeches which ungodly sinners have spoken against him.

These two verses contain the third branch of the description of the lost estate of these seducers in respect of their sin and misery, which in these words are further set forth by the ancient and infallible prophecy of Enoch; and that prophecy is, 1. Declared and propounded here in these two verses. 2. Applied to these seducers in the following verse.

In the declaration and propounding thereof, I consider,

I. The preface prefixed by Jude before it.
II. The prophecy itself.

I. The preface, in these words, "Enoch, the seventh from Adam, prophesied of these." Wherein two particulars are considerable:

1. The excellent person here mentioned, "Enoch;" described from his descent and pedigree, "the seventh from Adam."

2. His honourable performance, he "prophesied of these."

In the prophecy itself of the last judgment, I find,

(1.) A note of incitement, to cause a regard to the following description of the judgment, in the word "behold."

(2.) That description of the judgment, to the regard of which we are incited; which description of the judgment has two parts:

[1.] The coming of the Judge to judgment.
[2.] The carriage of the Judge in judgment.
[1.] In his coming to judgment I observe,
1. His title, "The Lord."
2. His approach, "cometh."
3. His attendants, "with ten thousands of saints."
[2.] His carriage in judgment is observable,
1. Toward the wicked; wherein I consider,
(1.) The manner of his judging, which is to be by way of conviction; "to convince."
(2.) The parties to be judged, "all the ungodly:" which parties are considerable,
[1.] In their nature; so they are " ungodly."
[2.] In their numbers and extent; so they are said to be "all the ungodly."
(3.) The causes of the judgment, which are two:
[1.] Their works; considered, 1. In their general nature, said to be "ungodly." 2. In the particular manner how they were committed, "which they have ungodly," or ungodlily, "committed."
[2.] Their words; where is to be noted,
1. What kind of speeches they uttered, "hard speeches."
2. By whom they were uttered, "ungodly sinners."
3. Against whom, "against him."

In the application of this prophecy, (ver. 16,) Jude shows that these seducers were the ungodly which hereafter are to be judged; and this their ungodliness Jude there discovers by several signs:
1. Their discontentedness. 2. The following their lusts. 3. Their boasting. 4. Their admiration of men's persons.

I begin with the preface, and in that, 1. The person here mentioned, "Enoch, the seventh from Adam."

Three things here I shall inquire into by way of explication.

(1.) In what respect Enoch may be said to be "the seventh from Adam."

(2.) Why the Spirit of God in Scripture exactly sets down the genealogies and successions of the patriarchs, whereby it is known that Enoch was "the seventh from Adam."

(3.) Why Jude, choosing to allege the prophecy of Enoch, calls him "the seventh from Adam."

(1.) Enoch was the seventh person from Adam, so that both Adam and himself must be computed to be two of that number. [1.] Enoch was not so the seventh from, as to be the seventh after, or the seventh that came of Adam. The like expression is used Matt. 1. 17, "all the generations from Abraham to David are fourteen generations;" into which Abraham and David themselves must be taken to make them up fourteen. And thus the Scripture frequently reckons Enoch the seventh, as Luke iii. 37, 38; 1 Chron. i. 1—3; Gen. v. 3, 6, 9, 12, 15, 18. [2.] Enoch was not so the seventh person from Adam, as that there were no more than seven persons begotten from the time of Adam to Enoch; for all those six patriarchs mentioned before Enoch, are said to "beget sons and daughters," and of those sons and daughters there came likewise a great number; but Enoch is called "the seventh from Adam," because he was exactly the seventh in that particular direct line from Adam to him.

(2.) Why the Spirit of God so exactly mentions the succession of the patriarchs of old. [1.] To discover his care to keep and uphold his church, by showing where it was, in what families it continued, and how it was by his goodness preserved and propagated in all, even the worst and most corrupt ages of the world. The posterity of Cain was to be totally destroyed by the flood, and God swept them away with the besom of destruction; to what end, therefore, should they be so fully recorded? but the seed of Seth was to be preserved both in the deluge of waters, and of all succeeding calamities; and therefore their descents and successions are punctually recorded.

[2.] God hereby shows the great delight which he took in speaking of his church and children, and their concerns, above all other people in the world. The sacred history mentions the posterity of Cain but occasionally, and by the way, as the relation thereof had a necessary connexion with the history of the church, and as making it more clear and complete; and therefore the Scripture relates not either the successions or actions of those without the church in a constant course or series of history, nor doth it use that exactness and industry in treating of them, which it uses in setting down the affairs of the church. Hence it is (as Rivet well notes) that those things which seem to be of less moment and weight are so diligently described in Scripture story; as Jacob's flocks, his pilled rods of poplar and hazel, the conceiving of the flocks before them, and bringing forth cattle ring-straked, speckled, and spotted, &c., whenas the holy story passes over in neglective silence the beginnings and progress of the great empires and dominations of the world, as of the Assyrians, Egyptians, Grecians, &c., subjects, in appearance, more worthy of mentioning; the Lord herein, saith the forementioned author, being like a master of a family, who does not with so much care and delight regard his grounds and fields abroad, as he does his family and children with their carriage and concerns at home in his house, where he diligently and delightfully observes all the speeches, gestures, actions of his little ones, and whatever befalls them. *Vid. Riv. exercit. pag. 630, 631. in 30. Gen.* *Riv. in Gen. pag. 632.*

[3.] God, by this exact delivering the successions and genealogies of the patriarchs, would show the excellency and antiquity of the Scriptures, above all other historical writings in the world, which are not able to afford us a certain chronology concerning the times of the patriarchs before the flood.

[4.] Especially by recording the successions of the patriarchs, the Lord discovers who they were of whom the true Messiah came according to the flesh; and this he doth both for the honour of Christ as man, whose pedigree, that it might be perfect, was to be preserved and distinctly drawn as far as from Adam, as also for the confirmation of our faith touching his incarnation *Causa cur Lucas ascenderit ad*

*Adamum usque,
1. Ut doceret beneficia Messiæ, non saltem pertinere ad Abrahamum et eos qui illum secuti, sed ad patres Abrahamo anteriores, imo ad ipsum Adamum. 2. Ut vindicaret Messiæ gratiam, non saltem se extendere ad gentem Judaicam, et filios Abrahami, sed et ad multos Adami filios extra Abrahami posteritatem, qui benedictionis ejus debeant esse participes, Japheto adducto in tabernacula Semi.
Spanhem. Dub. Evang. 19. p. 91.*

the Scripture mentioning the order and names of all his progenitors, even from Adam; and thereby suffering us not to doubt of the truth of his human nature, unless we will imagine that all the names and successions of his progenitors mentioned from the beginning of the world to his birth, were fabulous and fictitious, and so make the continued line from Adam to Christ to be a continued lie, which to imagine were not more blasphemous and antiscriptural, than ridiculous and unreasonable. And the Scripture, by telling us that Christ came of those ancient patriarchs, would teach us that the benefits of the Messiah were extended to those who lived far, yea, farthest before him, to the patriarchs before the flood, and even to Adam himself, who by his sin gave occasion for a Saviour to visit poor man with mercy; and, as some note, by setting down the progenitors of Christ, who lived before the flood, and so long before Abraham, the Scripture would teach that the grace of Christ extended itself not only to the Jews and the seed of Abraham, but also to many of the sons of Adam who were not of the posterity of Abraham, but were to be made partakers of the blessing by Christ, when Japhet should be brought to dwell in the tabernacles of Shem.

(3.) Why Jude here terms Enoch "the seventh from Adam." Sundry reasons may be assigned. As,

[1.] To distinguish this Enoch from another of that name, who was the third from Adam, and of the posterity, yea, the immediate son of cursed Cain, mentioned Gen. iv. 17.

[2.] To show how holy and zealous Enoch was in sinful times. In a most dissolute and profane age, he prophesies of and foretells the destruction of sinners. Though he perhaps did them but little good by his prophecy, yet they did him as little hurt by their profaneness. This taper was not extinguished by the damps of a sinful generation; this star shined brightly in a black night: "Enoch the seventh," as afterward Noah the tenth, from Adam "walked with God" in a corrupt age, and did not only preserve his own holiness, but prophesy against others' unholiness.

[3.] He calls "Enoch the seventh from Adam," to gain the more credit and esteem to that prophecy which he is about to mention, and the more to convince these seducers of the truth thereof; in regard both, 1. Of the great antiquity, and, 2. The eminent piety of him who uttered this prophecy.

1. By the antiquity of a prophet who was "the seventh from Adam," the apostle wisely insinuates not only that even from the beginning of the world holy men have prophesied of the end thereof, but that even then the miserable end of the wicked was foretold; and that they who were most remote from these seducers, and who therefore were most impartial, and could not be biassed by affection to any sides or parties, prophesied of their overthrow.

2. By the eminent and renowned piety of this Enoch, the seventh from Adam, who walked so closely with God, and so pleased God that he accounted him too good to live long upon earth, and would not stay for his company in heaven till he had finished the ordinary time of living, but took him to himself before he had lived to half the years either of his father or his son; I say, by this admirable holiness of Enoch, Jude might stop the mouths of these seducers, and render them either unable to resist the evidence of this prophecy, or inexcusable in not submitting to it.

This eminent holiness of Enoch, is in Scripture expressed in these words, "He walked with God;" words few in number, but great in weight; and which, upon this apt occasion, I shall briefly explain.

By this walking with God, more generally is intended his giving up himself to the worship and service of God, in leading a holy life, rather than a peculiar ministration in discharging the office of the priesthood; this walking with God being the same with his walking in the way of God's commandments, and his ordering the whole course and frame of his conversation according to the will and commandment of God: and this metaphor of walking with God, is taken from two friends unanimously and willingly going the same course and path together as companions. More particularly this his walking with God,

(1.) Intends a setting of God before his eyes, and a living always as in his sight, and as being present with him, and thereby his humble reverencing of and fearing to offend God, and a studying to please him, and to approve himself to him; ("Walk before me, and be thou perfect," Gen. xvii. 1;) God's presence with us being as certain and undoubted as is his with whom we after a sensible manner and openly converse.

(2.) This walking with God intends a friendly and familiar acquaintance and conversing with God; for can two walk together unless they be agreed? God did not pass by Enoch as a stranger, nor use him as a page, only to go after him; but as a friend and companion he walked with God. These words, "he walked with God," the Sept. read εὐηρέστησε τῷ Θεῷ, "he pleased God." Whence the author of the Epistle to the Hebrews speaking of Enoch says, μεμαρτύρηται εὐηρεστηκέναι τῷ Θεῷ, "he had this testimony, that he pleased God," chap. xi. 5: so Abraham is called "the friend of God," and Christ calls his disciples his "friends." And his humble familiarity and acquaintance with God consisted, 1. In his apprehension of a propriety and interest in God. Without this he would have stood far from God, as a foe, a fire, not walked with God as a friend. Another's God cannot comfort us: a soul's solace stands in this pronoun, my, my Lord, my God. When Enoch foresaw that God was coming to execute judgment upon all the wicked, he then knew that God was his God and friend. 2. Enoch's familiar acquaintance with God, consisted in a friendly and mutual speaking and discoursing between God and him; this was no silent walking, no dumb show. God spake to him by exciting his graces, and putting into him holy motions, and telling his soul that he was his salvation, by directing him in his doubts; he spake to God by daily meditation, ready acceptance of his grace, by pouring forth all his cares by prayer into the bosom of his heavenly Father, by promising obedience, praying continually; see Psal. xxvii. 8; cxix. 164; taking his counsel in his doubts, Psal. cxix. 24. 3. This humble and holy acquaintance appeared in Enoch's exercising his fiduciary relying and reposing himself upon God, without anxiety and solicitousness, for providing for him in all his necessities: he cast all his care upon God, as a faithful Friend who cared for him; he wholly committed himself and all his affairs to his God; he did not wound himself with heart-cutting cares; he was not like the lion that roars after his prey, but like the sheep that depends upon the care of the shepherd: "The Lord is my shepherd, I shall not want." 4. Enoch's humble and sweet acquaintance with God, stood in his enjoying all his comforts in God, and God in them; he so much esteemed communion with God, that he accounted nothing sweet, but what he had with his love and smile; he was not a slave to sense, delighting himself only in the good things themselves which he enjoyed; he accounted every condition sweet or bitter, as far as God communicated himself in it, or withdrew himself from it: so that he was neither unduly lifted up in his enjoyments, nor dejected in his losses; the God of his delight being ever and evenly the same: nothing was delightful to Enoch by itself, but only God, other things only as they came with God; as, though water is only sweet when something sweet is put into it, yet honey and sugar are sweet alone by themselves.

(3.) This walking with God denotes spiritual motion; there cannot be walking without moving. Enoch neither stood by God, nor sat with God, but walked with God; the commandments of God were the way wherein he walked and moved, and every act of obedience was a several step taken in that way; in all his motions he observed some duty enjoined, and eschewed some sin forbidden, so that he praised God with the language of his conversation. He could not have walked unless he had been as practical as he was speculative and professing: only works speak, words are silent before God and man. Nor did he only practise this walking with God when he was exercised in the duties of God's immediate worship, but also when employed in the works of his particular place and calling. In performing the former, he was, as it were, in heaven; in the doing the latter, heaven was in him: the necessary employments of his calling took him not off from conversing with God, they did not make him at all renounce this. Paul, when he was making tents, did not cast off conversing with God; neither does piety make us idle in our places, nor does moderate diligence in our callings make us impious and profane; and indeed we cannot walk with God unless we serve him both in our general and particular callings.

To conclude this discourse of Enoch's walking with God, with a touch of the manner how he performed it; 1. He walked with God solely, he admitted no intruders into, or disturbers of his heavenly converse with his God; the world followed him as a servant, walked not with him as a companion: this God cannot endure: he rather used the world than enjoyed it; or rather, used it as if he used it not. God cannot bear the company of mammon; the love of God and the world cannot stand together. 2. He walked with God evenly, and in a direct course; he halted not, like the Israelites, 1 Kings xviii. 21, between two; he made straight paths for his feet; he gave allowance to no wanderings nor false ways: they who will walk in by-paths, walk not with God, but alone; and therefore Enoch walked in a straight path to heaven, and turned not aside to crooked ways, not treading in the way of any known sin. 3. He walked cheerfully, not unwillingly, or constrainedly, or sadly, his walking being with him who is the God of all comfort; and indeed God takes no pleasure in that man's company who accounts not walking with him a pleasure. Enoch was not by fear, or force, or restraint detained before the Lord, but he delighted himself in him, looking upon holy duties as his privileges as well as his tasks: nor indeed can any walk cheerfully, but when with God; his company makes the valley of the shadow of death to be a pleasant way, a bitter condition sweet, and a sweet condition sweeter. 4. He walked constantly, unweariedly with God, from strength to strength, till he appeared before him in the heavenly Zion. Enoch's goodness was not by fits and starts, like that of some hypocrites; he did not take a step or two, but walked with God. This his walking with God lasted as long as his continuing in the world; he did not set out well only in the beginning, but held out well also till the end of his race.

Obs. 1. The faithful must be holy in unholy times. Enoch in a corrupt age walked with God, and kept close to him when most left him. Saints must show that they are not of the world, when they are in it; they must not be conformed to the world, nor run with the world " to the same excess of riot," 1 Pet. iv. 4. As their righteousness must exceed the righteousness of hypocrites, so must it condemn the unrighteousness of the profane; the rest of their time they should not live to the lusts of men, but to the will of God; they are forbidden to follow a multitude to do evil, to go " in the way of evil men," Prov. iv. 14, to have " fellowship with the unfruitful works of darkness," Eph. v. 11. Elijah was zealous for God when he scarce could discern any to join with him. As Noah was saved by God when the earth was overwhelmed with an inundation of water, so did he walk with God when it was overspread with an inundation of wickedness. When David was looked upon as a monster, Isaiah and the faithful as wonders, yet they retained their integrity, Psal. lxxi. 7; Isa. viii. 18; Jer. xx. 7: when the wicked have almost made void the law, even then, nay therefore, must the godly love God's commandments, and esteem all his " precepts concerning all things to be right," Psal. cxix. 126—128. God is a Friend, a Father; and as this Friend loves us in the day of adversity, so should he be beloved in the day when his honour suffers. May not God say to those who temporize with his enemies for fear, or hope, Is this your kindness to your Friend? Is there any time wherein God hath left or forsaken us, and should there be any wherein we are weary of walking with God? Is God our Father, and can we endure with a tame patience to see him dishonoured? It is reported of a son, who though before dumb, yet seeing enemies about to kill his father, presently cried out, Kill not my father. The sons of God must glorify their Father, and shine as lights in a crooked and perverse nation, Phil. ii. 15. Nor can the truth, much less the strength of grace, or the power of godliness, ever be manifested, unless it appears in times of opposition: there is no power seen, where there are no difficulties contended with. Wherein doth the life of grace differ from death in sin, if Christians are carried down the unholy stream of their times? Grace will ever conflict with that sin, either in the soul or the world, which it is not able to conquer; it will condemn it, though it cannot execute it. And what more unreasonable, lastly, than for us to mete to God with one measure, and to expect that he should mete to us with another? How can we expect that he should love us in that day wherein he will leave the most, if we will not walk with him in this day when most forsake him? Study then, O saints, to give the name of God reparations for all the disgrace which wicked men cast upon it. Discover the true nobleness of your Christian spirit, and of minds spiritually generous, by gathering vigour and growing invincible, from the very oppositions of the wicked, and the impieties of your times.

Obs. 2. It is a singular and blessed privilege to walk with God. It was the great happiness and ennoblement of Enoch, this seventh from Adam. The happiness of walking with God appears in these particulars. (1.) It is a person's greatest honour. It is honourable to follow, much more to walk with a king; how great is the dignity then of walking with the King of kings! It is God's lowest condescension to walk with us, and our highest advancement to walk with him. The company of sin debases, and the walking with God dignifies a man. God with man, is the greatest with the least. Enoch was one of the greatest on earth, he was royally descended the seventh from Adam in the blessed line; he had six such tutors and teachers, viz. the six first patriarchs, to make him learned, as never man had; but that which is testified of him as his honour, was this his walking with God. Oh unconceivable dignity, conferred upon poor impure dust and ashes, to walk with him who is attended with ten thousand times ten thousand glorious saints and angels for his followers! (2.) In this walking with God is greatest delight and solace: solitariness is uncomfortable, company sweet, but none so delightful as God's company: he who has not God to bear him company is alone, though he has all the comforts of the world to accompany him. Of all the creatures, there was not found a fit companion for Adam, nor can any creature fitly suit the soul with its society. Good company is the life of our lives, the sweetness of our abodes on earth; but God's company is the truly good company; there is no melody in any concert to which this delight is not added. A man is said to be alone, though he have many beasts with him, if he be without the company of man; and a Christian is alone notwithstanding all the world is with him, if God be absent. "Whom," saith the psalmist, "have I in heaven but thee? and there is none upon earth that I desire besides thee," Psal. lxxiii. 25. A sinner is the truly solitary, sad person. Oh how sweetly contentful is his life, who when all his outward comforts leave him, can say as did Christ when his disciples left him alone, "Yet I am not alone, because the Father is with me," John xvi. 32. (3.) In walking with God there is true safety; what need that man fear who lies in the bosom, or walks by the side of such a Father, though he walks in the vale of the shadow of death? Who dares offer that man any injury that walks with a king? no evil is so insolent as to arrest us, when the King of kings graciously accompanies us. "Fear not, Abraham," saith God, "I am thy shield," Gen. xv. 1. If God be with us, who shall be against us? if he will help, what shall hurt us? his society is our true safety. So long as God was with Samson, the Philistines could not conquer him; but when the "Lord was departed from him," Judg. xvi. 20, he soon becomes a prey to his enemies. God's presence is a saint's life-guard; till God leave him, dangers are but trifles; he ever keeps those who walk with him, either from the presence of every misery, or from the hurt and misery of the misery. Lastly, In this walking with God is the greatest gain and profit to be found: what good thing can he deny us, who denies us not himself? God is not only a shield, but an exceeding great reward. How can he want who is with and has Him that is all things? God mine, and all mine. He will fulfil the desire of them that fear him: no good thing shall be wanting to them, Psal. xxiii. 1; nor will God deny them any blessing, which does not oppose their blessedness; nor any good, which hinders not from enjoying the chiefest good; and if he thinks it meet to keep away these externals, he will supply their absence with himself. "The Almighty will be thy defence, and thou shalt have plenty of silver," Job xxii. 25.

Quid timet homo in sinu Dei positus?

Obs. 3. Even of the longest-lived patriarchs there was a succession, not a constant continuation. Adam the first, Seth the second, Enos the third, &c., Enoch the seventh. One generation goeth, another cometh, Eccl. i. 4. The coming of new generations shows the going and passing away of the old; the latter crowds the former out of the world; one goeth away to make room for another. The longest-lived of these ancient patriarchs had in the world but his time and turn, which at length ended. It has been observed by some, that none of them lived, no, not Methuselah, a thousand years; and some say the reason thereof was, because God would by their dying before the end of a thousand years make good his threatening, "In the day thou eatest thereof thou shalt die;" it being said that a thousand years with God are but as one day: but in this there seems to be more wit than weight. A more solid reason of their dying within the foresaid term, seems to be because thereby God would show that the longest life of any of the sons of men, in respect of God himself, is but very short, and not able to reach to that space, which in respect of God's eternity is not a day: for which cause Cicero compares the longest life of man to that of that beast brought forth by the river Hippanis, which lives not above one day, and dying when the sun sets, dies then decrepit. Compare, saith he, our longest age with eternity, and we shall be found, after a sort, in the same age with that beast. It is added to the relation of the long lives of every one of the ancient patriarchs, "and he died." The repetition whereof seems not to be without great reason, which was not only to show the brittleness and frailty of man's continuance, even as nothing in comparison of eternity; but principally to show the immovable certainty of that threatening of death against the disobedience of our first parents, notwithstanding the vain and deceitful promise of the devil; as also manifest that the holiest men, whose death was the wages of sin, were in this life without that perfect holiness, required to the seeing of God; and therefore that they were to be cleansed by death, that with their body of flesh they laying off the corruption of their nature, might arise pure and spotless to immortality. The consideration whereof should put the strongest, and those who are most likely to live, upon a constant and serious meditation of death; and warn them not to expect immortality in this life, but daily to wait for their certain and appointed change. That blessed saint, now with God, Mr. Richard Rogers,* (who was another Enoch in his age, a man whose walking with God appeared by that incomparable directory of a Christian life, his book called the Seven Treatises, woven out of Scripture and his own experimental practice,) said in his lifetime that he should be sorry if every day were not to him as his last day. Every morning we arise let us say, Art thou my last day, or do I look for another? Let us live as if we were always dying, and yet as such as are ever to live. In short, the successions and conclusions of generations should put us upon holiness of life, for the preserving a sweet and precious remembrance of ourselves in that generation which follows, and especially that we may by our holy example transmit holiness to posterity; that we, with Enoch, walking with God, the church of God and a seed of saints may be continued as much as in us lies in our line. And truly, as otherwise we shall die while we live in the world, so hereby we shall live when we are taken out of the world, and be like civet, which when it is taken out of the box leaves a sweet savour behind it.

Confer longissimain nostram ætatem, cum æternitate, in ea propemodum ætate, qua illæ bestiolæ, reperiemur. Cic. l. 1. Tusc. quæst.

Obs. 4. All issue from Adam. As Enoch was, so all others were and are from Adam; from him all descend by natural propagation. He was the root, all others but branches; he the fountain, all others but streams. All were hewn out of this rock: an observation which puts us upon sundry useful considerations. It teaches us humility. As we were from Adam, so he was from the dust of the earth, and that dust from nothing. Our father was Adam, our grandfather dust, our great-grandfather nothing. They

* Sometime of Wethersfield in Essex, my dear and deceased grandfather.

who are proud that they can derive their pedigree so far as Adam, may be humble if they would go a little further. Remember whence thou art, and consider whither thou shalt go: nothing so unsuitable as pride for a clod of the earth. A man can never have too low thoughts of himself, but in the bowing down his nature to accompany with sin. He who would not endure pride in the angels of heaven, will not endure it in dust and ashes; and such even great Abraham calls himself; a fitter style, than most illustrious, high and mighty, invincible, &c. When thou art mounting up in proud and self-admiring thoughts, remember thou art from Adam, earthen Adam. Agathocles, a potter's son, when he came to be king, humbled himself with setting earthen vessels on his cupboard. If dust be sprinkled upon the wings of bees, their noises, hummings, risings, will (they say) quickly cease: when thou beginnest to grow proud, sprinkle thy thoughts with this remembrance, I am but dust. Further, we may hence gather the wonderful power of God's blessing, that of one so many millions should come; from one root such multitudes of branches. God can bless one into millions, and blast millions again into one, into nothing: God's powerful benediction multiplied Adam's numerous offspring. He whom God blesses shall be blessed; he whom God curses shall be cursed. We see the way to thrive in any kind; the blessing of God maketh rich, and without it thy own industrious endeavours will not help thee: he cursed the fig-tree, and it withered up at the roots. More particularly, we see from whom to beg the increase of posterity. It is from God that Jacob expected and desired, in his blessing, that Ephraim and Manasseh should grow into a multitude, Gen. xlviii. 16. See also Ruth iv. 11, 12. Hence also we may observe the goodness of God in continuing the blessing of increase to Adam, even after his fall; that sinful Adam should be the father of such a posterity: God might have said, Here is enough of one man, and too much; I will suffer no more to be of the kind. We destroy poisonous and hurtful creatures that they may not breed. But mark further, that merciful power of God to cause a holy offspring, a sanctified seed, though not such as coming of, yet to come of a sinful, fallen parent; that God should make white paper of dunghill rags; that any of Adam's unsanctified nature should partake of the Divine nature; in a word, that Enochs should be from Adam. Truly there was more mercy discovered in the changing one Enoch, than there would have been justice put forth in condemning a whole world. In a word, how should this our derivation from the first, put us upon labouring to get into the Second Adam; he who is but a man, a son of Adam, is a miserable man, a child of wrath. How careful should we be to get off from the old, dead, poisonous root and stock, and to be branches ingrafted into and growing upon the living, life-giving stock, the Lord Christ! In Adam, saith the apostle, all die, and in Christ all are made alive. "As we have borne the image of the earthy," so should we be restless till we bear that of "the heavenly," 1 Cor. xv. 49.

Obs. 5. It is our duty prudently to take our best advantages for truth's advancement. Thus Jude alleges here the prophecy of such a person as might in likelihood most draw respect and credit.

2. The honourable performance of Enoch, and that was his prophesying; he "prophesied of these."

Three things may be inquired into by way of explication.

1. What our apostle intends in this place by prophesying.

2. How Jude came by, or whence he received, the prophecy of Enoch.

3. Why he alleges and instances this particular prophecy.

1. What the apostle intends by prophesying. The word prophesy is in Scripture taken five several ways.

(1.) Sometimes it signifies no more than to be present at the public ministry, and to partake of the doctrine thereof. Thus I understand it in that place, "Every woman that prayeth or prophesieth with her head uncovered dishonoureth her head," 1 Cor. xi. 5; for otherwise women were not allowed to speak in the church. _{See Diodate's Annotations on 1 Cor. xi. 5.}

(2.) Prophecy is taken for the written word, 2 Pet. i. 20.

(3.) Elsewhere to prophesy signifies to expound, interpret, and apply the Scriptures to the edification of the church. "Despise not prophesyings," 1 Thess. v. 20; and, "He that prophesieth speaketh unto men to edification, and exhortation, and comfort," 1 Cor. xiv. 3.

(4.) Sometimes it signifies to know and to be able to declare things either past or present, which a man either by nature or industry is not able to know; and so it signifies to divine: thus it is taken Matt. xxvi. 68; Mark xiv. 65, &c., where they who had blinded Christ bid him, by way of derision, prophesy who it was that smote him: to this purpose said the Pharisee, Luke vii. 39, "This man, if he were a prophet, would have known," &c.

(5.) Strictly and properly to prophesy, is to foreshow or foretell things to come, or that afterward shall be fulfilled. Thus it is taken Acts xxi. 9, "Philip had four daughters, virgins, which did prophesy." Thus Ezek. xxi. 2, compared with ver. 7. So Ezek. xxix. 2; xxx. 2; xxxiv. 2; xxxviii. 2. And thus it must necessarily be taken in this place. "Enoch prophesied of these" by way of prediction, or he foretold their punishment.

2. Whence Jude received this prophecy or prediction of Enoch. To this some say that Jude took this prophecy out of an ancient book, written of old by this "Enoch the seventh from Adam." True it is, that in ancient times there were some writings dispersed abroad in the church, under the name of Enoch, and called by the name of Enoch's book; and of these Origen makes mention in his last homily on Numbers. And Tertullian, in his third chapter, *de habitu muliebri*, affirms that the book of Enoch was preserved by Noah in the ark and brought forth after the flood; and he attributes the opinion of its want of authority to the malice of the Jews, who, saith he, because some eminent testimonies concerning Christ may be produced out of it, endeavoured to suppress it. Augustine also mentions books bearing Enoch's name. That, then, there were such books called by the name of Enoch, it is not denied; but that Enoch was indeed the author of them, and that Jude made use of them, none can either probably or soberly suppose. The books, saith Augustine, which under the name of Enoch are produced are to be suspected for false, and none of his, because the Jews never accounted them canonical, nor kept them in the temple as such; and they abound with fables. Among the rest, that fond and erroneous conceit, so contrary both to Scripture and reason, that the angels in their assumed bodies went in unto the daughters of men, and so begat those giants mentioned Gen. vi. 4. Though this fabulous error, being entitled to so holy and ancient an author as Enoch, was embraced by Justin Martyr, Cyprian, Clemens Alexandrinus, and some _{Non sunt scripta in canone qui servabatur in templo. Cur autem hoc nisi quia suspectæ fidei, &c. Illa quæ sub Enochi nomine proferuntur, continent fabulas. Recte a prudentibus judicantur non ipsius esse credenda. Aug. l. 15. de Civ. Dei, c. 23.}

others. Besides, had there been any such true book or prophecy of Enoch in writing, no doubt but it would have been very famous and highly set by among the Jews, both for the antiquity and holiness of the author, as also for the preciousness of the matter, of which some mention would have been made by the holy prophets, or by Philo and Josephus, who were curious preservers and writers of Jewish antiquities, who yet never discovered to us that rare treasure. And that Moses was the first of all the holy writers, I think is the constant judgment of all learned divines, protestant and popish; nor does Christ acknowledge any holy writer to be more ancient than Moses; for, Luke xxiv. 27, it is said, that "beginning at Moses, he expounded unto them in all the Scriptures the things concerning himself." Now if Enoch had written a book, probable it is that Christ would have begun at him, he being so long before Moses, to have explained the prophecies of his humility and glory; the latter whereof this prophecy of Enoch, here mentioned by Jude, so clearly discovers. It is therefore the opinion of some learned men, that if there were in Jude's time any writing which went under Enoch's name, it was written by some Jews, who mixed some things good and true, which peradventure they received by tradition concerning the prophecies of Enoch, with other things false and fabulous; which book of theirs might be more and more in the progress of time corrupted, and was deservedly rejected as apocryphal. Possibly out of this book Jude might take this passage. The penmen of Holy Scripture have, not seldom, taken several passages which tended to edification out of profane authors, and thereby sanctified them to the use of the church, Acts xvii. 28; 1 Cor. xv. 33; Tit. i. 12; and yet, as Rivet well notes, since Jude saith that Enoch prophesied, it was necessary that Jude should have a peculiar revelation from the Holy Ghost, to assure him that the prophecy, recited by an apocryphal author, did indeed come from Enoch; for otherwise, should he only rely upon the authority of an apocryphal book, the prophecy related by Jude would no more be canonical than it was as set down by the apocryphal writer.

Libros Enochi plane suppositio esse ut mihi persuadeam, facit quod in ecclesia Dei ante Babylonicam captivitatem in nullis prophetarum libris fit mentio tam rari thesauri, quem non credibile est, si in rerum natura fuisset, Mosem latuisse, qui etiam scriptorum Enochi meminisset in hac historia si tunc extitissent. Rivet. in Exerc. in Gen. xlix.

Others, protestants and papists, assert, that after the death of the apostles, some impostors, taking occasion by Jude's alleging the prophecy of Enoch, published and set forth a book under the name of Enoch, that so by its bearing the name of one so pious and ancient, it might find the better acceptance. Of this opinion is the learned Gomarus, who withal gives a parallel instance of the feigning of an epistle, under Paul's name, to be written to the Laodiceans, by occasion of that passage of Col. iv. 16; so that according to this opinion some took occasion to write this fictitious book of Enoch by reading Jude's Epistle; not that Jude ever saw any book under Enoch's name extant, or took his prophecy out of it. Many learned men therefore very probably conceive that our apostle received this prophecy from common and undoubted tradition, transmitted from the patriarchs, and so handed from generation to generation, till such time as it seemed good to the Holy Ghost, by the apostle Jude, to make it a part of Scripture. And thus the apostle mentions the withstanding of Moses by Jannes and Jambres; Jacob's worshipping upon the top of his staff; Moses's saying that the sight upon the mount was so terrible, that "I exceedingly fear and quake." Thus it is said that Joseph's feet were hurt with fetters, and that he was laid in irons. All which passages, being no where mentioned in their proper stories, were received by tradition from generation to generation; the Spirit of God nevertheless sanctifying them, and giving them the stamp of Divine authority, to be most certain and infallible, by putting the penmen of holy writ to insert them into the Scripture. And by this which has been said, we answer, those who argue against this Epistle being canonical, from Jude's alleging, as they conceive, an apocryphal author, or his bringing in a tradition no where recorded in Scripture, the citing of these by our apostle, if he did cite them out of any author, being so far from making him apocryphal, that he makes them, so far as he uses them, canonical; as also, we hereby answer the papists, who because the apostles have sometimes transferred some things from human writings and tradition into Holy Scripture, take the boldness to do the like, and to join traditions with the Holy Scripture; not considering that they want that Spirit of discerning which the apostles had, who, by making use of traditions, gave them Divine authority. They were immediately influenced by the Holy Ghost in all their writings; but we are not endowed with the same measure of the Spirit, and therefore neither are able nor ought to imitate them herein.

Capta occasione ex prophetia Henochi commemorata a Juda, libros quasi antiquitus scriptos publicarunt. Perer. in Gen. Nieremberg de Orig. fac. scrip. pa. mihi 51.

3. The third thing to be explained is, why the apostle alleged and instanced this particular prophecy of Enoch.

The reasons why Jude made choice of this prophecy may be reduced to these two heads;

(1.) The first taken from the prophet.

(2.) The second from the prophecy itself.

And the consideration of the prophet Enoch induced Jude to use the prophecy, because the prophet was, 1. Eminent for his antiquity; he was the seventh from Adam: this seems to put great respect upon the prophecy; as if Jude had said, The sins of these seducers, which had judgment threatened against them almost from the very beginning of the world, so many thousands of years before they were committed, must needs be heinous and odious now when these sinners are acting them; and those sins which God has so anciently threatened, will at length be most severely punished. 2. This prophet was famous both for his piety and privileges; he was not only eminent for his piety in walking with God, which was his own benefit, and for his public usefulness, in warning and instructing that corrupt age in which he lived, keeping up the name of God in the world, opposing the profaneness of his times; but also for that glorious and unheard-of privilege of being taken to God, who thereby proclaimed him to be fit for no company but his own, and one for whom no place was good enough but heaven; a child, though sent abroad into the world as the rest, yet whom his Father so tenderly loved, that he would not suffer him to stay half so long from home as his other children; one who had done much work in a little time, and who having made a proficiency in that heavenly art of holiness above all his fellows, had that high degree of heavenly glory conferred upon him long before the ordinary time.

(2.) In respect of the suitableness of the prophecy itself to Jude's present occasion. And, 1. It was most suitable in respect of its certainty; it was a prophecy. Enoch prophesied, he spake from God, not uttering his own inventions, but God's inspirations; the foretelling of things to come being a Divine prerogative, and such which without revelation from God the creature cannot attain. And the Scripture assures us that it was God who "spake by the mouth of his holy prophets, which have been since the world began," Luke i. 70. How suitable was it to produce a prophecy sure to be fulfilled, coming from God by the mouth of a holy prophet, against these fearless, scornful sinners, who mocked at the last judgment! 2. Of its severity; what prophecy more fit for the secure scorners than a prophecy of judgment, the last, universal, unavoidable, unsupportable, eternal judgment? They might possibly slight the particular examples of God's judgments upon the angels, the Sodomites, the Israelites; but the arrow of the general judgment, prophesied of by Enoch against all the ungodly, would not perhaps be so easily shaken out of their sides. If any denunciation could affect them, surely it would be that which was prophetical; and if any prophetical denunciation, that of the last judgment. If the last judgment has made heathens tremble when but discoursed of before them, how should it dismay those who profess to know God when threatened against them! How bold in sin are they who will not fear the judgment! How can he who believes judgment to be dreadful, but dread to do that which shall be punished in that judgment? Even the devils at the sight of their Judge trembled to think of their judgment, Matt. viii. 29.

Obs. 1. The greatest honour to departed saints is to embrace their holy instructions. Enoch's person was not to be worshipped, but his prophecy to be believed. Saints are to be honoured by following their doctrines, by imitation of their practices, not by religious adoration. It is easy to commend their memories by our words, and to reverence their relics; but the art of Christianity appears in praising them with the language of our conversations, 1 Cor. xi. 1. The bark of a tree may be carried upon a man's shoulder without any pain or difficulty, but it requires strength and labour to carry away the body of the tree: the outside or shell of superstitious, popish adorations men easily perform; the heart and life of religion, which is that of the heart and life, men cannot away with. The Pharisees, who painted the sepulchres of the deceased prophets, opposed their piety, as also those holy ones in their times who were influenced by the same spirit of holiness which showed itself in those prophets of old. The Jews who boasted that they had Abraham for their father, did not the works of their father Abraham, but of their father the devil. Many are like Samson, that took honey out of the dead lion, praise dead ancient saints to be sweet and holy men; who, were they alive, would roar upon them for their lusts, would oppose and hate them: the right way (then) to reverence the godly who are departed this life, is to be led by that Spirit whereby they were led while they lived. [Honorandi propter imitationem, non adorandi propter religionem. Aug. de Ver. Rel. cap. 55.]

Obs. 2. Threatenings denounced by Divine warrant should deter us from sin. If Enoch's prophecy, which was of Divine authority, foretell judgments, they must not be slighted. As Divine promises should uphold and comfort us in our lowest and weakest estate; so should Divine threatenings make us tremble, and affright us from sin, in our greatest strength and highness. The Ninevites, by fearing evils foretold by Jonah against them, prevented the feeling of them. Josiah holily feared, and his "heart was tender," and he humbled himself when he heard what the Lord spake against Jerusalem, 2 Kings xxii. 19. When "Micah the Morashite prophesied in the days of Hezekiah king of Judah, saying, Zion shall be ploughed like a field," &c., Hezekiah feared, "and besought the Lord," Jer. xxvi. 18, 19. A judgment denounced by God cannot be kept off by power: there is no might or strength against the Lord. The hand of the Lord is not weakened, nor is his arm shortened, when he deals with his most potent adversaries. As God can create deliverances when he intends to show mercy, so can he create judgments when he purposes to punish. The truth of a threatening will break through the greatest improbabilities of its approaching. Though the Chaldeans were all as wounded men, if he threaten to punish by them, they shall be victorious against the unrepenting Jews, Jer. xxxvii. 10. There is no way of flying from God but by flying to him: the way to get out of the reach of judgments threatened, is to repent at the threatening of them: nothing but our repenting sincerely can make God repent mercifully. Oh how foolish a madness is it by politic endeavours to imagine a prevention of judgments divinely threatened, or by persecuting the prophet to think to overthrow the prophecy! "The prophets, do they live for ever?" yet "my words and my statutes, which I commanded my servants the prophets, did they not take hold of your fathers?" Zech. i. 5, 6. Paul suffered trouble "even unto bonds; but the word of God" (saith he) "is not bound," 2 Tim. ii. 9.

Obs. 3. Sinners should look upon the threatenings denounced against others for sin as belonging to them without repentance. The wicked against whom Enoch immediately prophesied were such as lived ungodlily in his time; and yet the apostle saith that he prophesied against these seducers: the reason is, because these lived in the same sins with those wicked ones of old. As the promises made to the godly who lived in former times belong to those who imitate them in succeeding ages, so the threatenings denounced against former sinners are denounced also against those who follow them in sin; and that by the constant analogy and proportion of justice, unless these repent, they shall likewise perish, Luke xiii. 3. Strong is the inference of the apostle, "If God spared not the natural branches, take heed lest he also spare not thee," Rom. xi. 21. Threatenings denounced against and inflicted upon those who lived in former times, manifest God's equal dislike of those who shall live in the same sins in succeeding ages; showing thereby that he is prepared, if they will also sin, to do what he has done against those who lived before them. Though God's forbearance towards some shows that sometimes he can spare sinners, yet his punishing others shows that he never loves sin. In all ages God is the same, he abhors sin in all the ages of the world; nor will he go out of his way to gratify men's lusts: changing is not God's property, but the sinner's duty. "If he turn not, he will whet his sword," Psal. vii. 12.

Obs. 4. Doctrines of greatest antiquity are only to be embraced as they consent with the testimonies which come from the infallible Spirit of God, Psal. cxix. 100. Enoch, though the seventh from Adam, and so very ancient, yet only is to be believed in what he said, as speaking by prophecy, and receiving what he delivered from Divine revelation. Whatever doctrines proceed not from or agree not to this, are, notwithstanding all pretences of antiquity, to be rejected as spurious. The papists who have no patronage from Scripture, have but a rotten support for their opinions which pretend to greatest antiquity. Custom without truth is but the antiquity of error. The most proudly swelling allegations of the ancients are but like a swollen leg, which though it be large, is yet but weak, and unable to bear up the body: the authority of religion must not be measured by time. We reverence the ancient fathers, and hold it our duty to rise up before the hoary head and to honour the person of [Mihi pro archivis est Jesus Christus. Ignat.] [Mos diabolicus est, ut per antiquitatis traducem commendetur fallacia. Aug. qu. 114. Nov. et Vet. Test.] [Cypr. Ep. 74.] [Religionis auctoritas non est tempore metienda. Arnob. contr. Gent. l. 2. Non veritas antiquitatis, sed an-]

tiquitas veritatis ecclesiæ authoritatem confert. Riv. contr. Q. 7. p. 224. the aged; but still with reservation of the respect we owe to their Father and ours, that "Ancient of days, the hair of whose head is like the pure wool," Dan. vii. 9. In opposition to him we must "call no man father," Matt. xxiii. 9. Nor yet is this said as if papists were able to produce better proof out of the testimony of the ancients for their errors than we can do for the truth; but to give the word of God its due, which is that rock upon which alone we build our faith. The truth is, papists have removed the ancient land-mark which the fathers set, that so they may invade another's possession; their traditions are new boundaries; their doctrines of merits, image worship, equivocation, transubstantiation, denial of priests' marriage, power of the pope, are new and upstart, not only to the Scripture, but even to the writings of the ancients.

So much for the preface.

II. The prophecy itself of the last judgment. And in that, first the note of incitement, to cause regard to the following description of the judgment, in the word "behold."

The word behold is in Scripture used principally these two ways.

1. As a note of manifestation of the truth, reality, certainty of a thing to be observed or believed. Thus it is used Matt. xxviii. 20, "Behold, I am with you to the end of the world." "Behold, I have given every herb bearing seed," Gen. i. 29. "Behold, I am with thee, and will keep thee," Gen. xxviii. 15. "Behold, the devil shall cast some of you into prison," Rev. ii. 10. "Behold, there come two woes more," Rev. ix. 12. "Behold, the hour is at hand; and the Son of man is betrayed," &c., Matt. xxvi. 45. "Behold, happy is the man whom the Lord correcteth," Job v. 17. "Behold, the eye of the Lord is upon them that fear him," Psal. xxxiii. 18; Rev. iii. 8, 9, 11, 20; Psal. xxxvii. 36; Zech. ix. 9; Matt. xxviii. 20; Gal. v. 2.

2. As a note of admiration, or to stir up attention for the great and stupendous wonderfulness of something that falls out. Thus it is taken 2 Kings vi. 17, "Behold, the mountain was full of horses and chariots of fire." "Behold, the veil of the temple was rent in twain," Matt. xxvii. 51. And, "Behold, there was a great earthquake," Matt. xxviii. 2. "Behold, a virgin shall conceive," Isa. vii. 14. "Behold, I show you a mystery," &c., 1 Cor. xv. 51; Luke xiii. 16; Acts i. 10; vii. 56; xii. 7; Gen. xxix. 6. The word behold in this place may, suitably to the subject in hand, the coming of Christ to judgment, be considered as denoting both these.

(1.) The certainty and truth thereof, it being a thing as sure as if it were before our eyes, and already accomplished, like that minatory prediction of the prophet concerning the house of Jeroboam, 1 Kings xiv. 14, "But what? even now;" a thing that ought to sink into the hearts of hearers, and that which they cannot too firmly and fixedly believe. The infallible predictions of Scripture which must be fulfilled, the judgments of God already executed upon some sinners, the fears of natural conscience, God's justice, which will render to every one according to his works; and lastly, the fitness that the body shall have its due retribution as well as the soul, all prove the certainty of the last judgment, Acts i. 11; Matt. xxiv. 30; 2 Thess. i. 7—12; Acts xvii. 32; xxiv. 25; Gen. xviii. 25; 1 Thess. i. 10; 2 Cor. v. 10; Rev. xx. 12.

(2.) The word behold may be considered as a note of admiration, denoting a most wonderful and strange thing, like that behold Hab. i. 5, "Behold, and wonder marvellously, for I will work a work in your days which ye will not believe, though it be told you." And this coming of Christ is wonderful and strange, 1. In respect of the wicked, to whom it is unexpected, they thereby being unprepared for it; it comes as a snare upon them, in a day wherein they look not for it, in an hour wherein they are not aware, Luke xii. 46, "as a thief in the night. When they shall say, Peace and safety; then sudden destruction cometh upon them, as travail upon a woman with child; and they shall not escape," 1 Thess. v. 2, 3. 2. It is wonderful in respect of the astonishing glory of the coming of Christ to judgment, together with the judgment itself, of which I have largely spoken before.

Obs. 1. Our thoughts only of those things which are truly great and glorious should be high and admiring. "Behold," saith Enoch, as noting the astonishing wonderfulness of the last judgment. This truly great thing should be looked upon as such. It is the folly of most men to look upon small things as great, and upon great things as small; human judgments affright and amaze them, the last judgment they slight and neglect. These want that rectified judgment of the apostle, who calls the day of judgment the appearing of the great God; and so preached of the judgment to come, that he made Felix tremble; whereas he tells us how little he estimated man's judgment, 1 Cor. iv. 3. Thus likewise our Saviour directs his disciples to contemn that which is small and contemptible, Fear not him that kills the body; and to dread that which is truly great and formidable, Fear him who can destroy both body and soul in hell, Matt. x. 28. When the disciples beheld with wonder, and showed to Christ the beautiful buildings of the temple, he, with a holy contempt of those outside beauties, tells them there shall not be one stone of all those stately structures left upon another that shall not be thrown down; and when Satan showed and offered him all the kingdoms of the world with their glory, he showed his contempt of the prospect and promotion, with a "Get thee behind me, Satan;" but when he observed the faith of the centurion, he wonders, and expresses his admiration to the people, Luke vii. 9.

Obs. 2. Great is our natural backwardness to mind and believe the coming of Christ to judgment. Enoch prefixes a note of incitement to his prophecy. The wicked take occasion to be secure, and to cast off the thought of Christ's coming, from the procrastination and delaying thereof. Men scoff at the promise of the coming of Christ, because (say they) " since the fathers fell asleep, all things continue as they were from the beginning of the creation," 2 Pet. iii. 4. That servant who said that his Lord delayed his coming, Luke xii. 45, instead of minding and preparing for it, beat his fellow servants, and also did eat, and drink, and was drunken. Hence it is that men say, Peace and safety, even when sudden destruction is coming upon them, 1 Thess. v. 3. Men are naturally led by sense; what they see not, feel not, they believe not. As Noah's flood was a type of the last judgment, so the disposition of men when that deluge approached resembled that which shall be in sinners at the coming of Christ. As in the days before the flood there was eating, drinking, marrying, &c., "so shall also the coming of the Son of man be," Matt. xxiv. 38, 39. And so great, likewise, is naturally every sinner's self-love, that they love to shun the thoughts of every thing which they love not; they are ready to say to themselves, as did Peter to Christ, "Be it far from thee; this shall not be unto thee;" they put far from them the last day, because they look upon it as the evil day, nay, the worst day; they love the world, and their hearts grow to it, and therefore it is death to them to think of an unsettlement. Their Sodom they so much delight in, that, like Lot's wife, they cannot endure to think of a shower of fire; herein resembling some, who are therefore unwilling to make their wills, because they cannot away with the thoughts of death. To rectify this distemper, as we should labour to find this great day a good day, and the great Lord our good Lord, and to be such that even out of this devouring lion we may take honey; so, consider that,

Obs. 3. The last judgment is to be looked upon as a matter of greatest certainty; not as a fiction, but as a most real and undoubted thing. We should look upon it to be as certain as if it were already with us. It is the policy of Satan, to make us diffident of that of which we should be confident, and confident of that of which we should be diffident. He presents his own lies as certainties, and God's truths as lies, or at the best as conjectural uncertainties; but our faith must take into its vast comprehension God's whole revealed will, part whereof is this of the last judgment. The last and dreadful judgment will never affright us from sin, if we look upon it in the devil's dress of uncertainty; for then we shall but sport with it, and make it our play-fellow instead of our monitor. Let us therefore labour to make it by prayer and meditation to sink into our hearts, and to believe it, though never so distant from or opposite to sense; taking heed lest the deferring thereof, and the present impunity of sinners, destroy or damp our belief of Christ's coming to judgment; considering that if every offender should now be openly punished, men would think that nothing would be reserved to the last judgment; as on the contrary, if no offender should be plagued, men would believe that there were no Providence. And let us beware lest we make that concealment of the last judgment to be an occasion of sin, which God intends should be an incentive to repentance.

Si nunc omne peccatum manifesta plecteretur poe.a, nihil ultimo judicio reservari crederetur: rursus, si nullum peccatum nunc puniret aperte divinitas, nulla esse divina providentia putaretur. Aug. de Civ. Dei, cap. 8.

This briefly for the note of incitement, "Behold."

2. The description of the judgment, and in that, first, the coming of the Judge to judgment; "The Lord cometh with ten thousand of his saints."

And here, 1. The title, 2. Approach, 3. Attendance of the Judge, are all worthy of consideration by way of explication.

(1.) Of the title, "Lord," I have spoken very largely before, and of the greatness of this Lord, the Judge, as he is God and man. The reasons also why he shall even as man judge the world I have mentioned, and how he excludes not Father and Holy Ghost. It will not be needful here again to repeat the fitness of Christ for judicature, in respect of his advancement after his humiliation, the necessity that the judicial proceeding should be visible, the great horror and amazement of his enemies, the comfort of the saints, the excellent qualifications of this Judge in regard of his righteousness, omniscience, strength, and fortitude, &c., Rev. vi. 16; 1 John ii. 28; Rev. v. 9; xix. 11; 1 Cor. iv. 5; Acts i. 11; x. 42; xvii. 13.

unc manifeste veniet judicaturus juste, qui occulte venerat judicandus injuste. Aug.

(2.) The approach of the Judge, "the Lord cometh," ἦλθε; in which word Jude uses the time past for the time to come, after the manner of the prophets, who are wont to speak of those things which are to come as if they were already past; and this he does for two reasons: First, to note the certainty of Christ's coming to judgment, it being as sure as if it were already. Secondly, to show the nearness thereof, Christ's coming is at hand: "The time is short" saith Paul, 1 Cor. vii. 29, its sails almost wound up. The Judge stands at the door. "He that shall come will come, and will not tarry." If he were coming in Enoch's time, if in the first, what is he then in the last times, as these are frequently called! Come, Lord Jesus, come quickly. "Behold, I come quickly," Rev. iii. 11. The bride's prayer and the Bridegroom's promise are both for speedy coming. "Behold, he cometh with clouds," Rev. i. 7; not, shall come; he is as good as come already. Christ cometh to us either in Spirit or in person.

[1.] In Spirit he cometh, 1. In the ministry, to win and persuade us to come to him: thus he went and preached in Noah's time to the spirits now in prison, 1 Pet. iii. 19. 2. In some special manifestation of his presence in mercy or judgment: the former, when he meets us with comfort, strength, and increase of grace, John xiv. 18, 23; the latter, in testification of displeasure, Rev. ii. 16; John xvi. 8.

[2.] In person he comes two ways. 1. *In carnem.* 2. *In carne.* 1. Into flesh, in humility in his incarnation, to be judged. 2. In flesh, in glory at the last day, to judge all flesh.

Where consider whence, whither, and when he cometh.

(1.) Whence he cometh. From heaven. "The Lord himself shall descend from heaven," 1 Thess. iv. 16; he shall come in the clouds of heaven: to heaven he ascended, and from heaven will he descend. "This Jesus, which is taken from you into heaven, shall so come in like manner as ye have seen him go into heaven," Acts i. 11. And it is necessary that Christ should come from heaven to judge, because it is not meet that the wicked should come thither, to him, though to be judged; for into that holy place can no unclean thing enter.

(2.) Whither cometh he? Some think that the judgment-seat shall be upon the earth, that the sentence may be given where the faults have been committed, and that in some place near Jerusalem, where the Judge was formerly unjustly condemned; and particularly some think it shall be in the valley of Jehoshaphat, though that place, Joel iii. 12, contains but an allegorical or typical prophecy. The apostle seems to intimate that the place of judgment shall be in the air, 1 Thess. iv. 17, where he mentions our being caught up to meet the Lord in the air, it being probable that the judgment shall be in that place where we shall meet the Judge, in the clouds of the air; and the Scripture saith he shall come in the clouds of heaven. Then the devils shall be conquered and sentenced in the very place wherein they have ruled all this while as princes. But over what place it seems to me a rashness to determine.

(3.) When shall he come? In the end of the world; but the particular age, day, or year is not known to man or angel, Mark xiii. 32: this secret the Spirit revealed not to nor taught the apostles, who yet were led by him into all necessary truths; and Christ must come as a thief in the night, and as in the days of Noah, when men knew nothing. And we are commanded to watch, and to be ever prepared, because we know not the hour. The childish curiosity of sundry in their computation of a set year, wherein the day of judgment shall be, rather deserves our caution than confutation.

3. The third thing to be opened in this coming of the Judge is his attendants, "ten thousand of his saints." The words in the original are ἐν μυριάσιν ἁγίαις αὐτοῦ, word for word, with his holy ten thousands, or myriads.

Four things may here offer themselves to be explained.

1. Their numbers; "ten thousand."

2. Their quality; they are holy ones, "ten thousand of his saints."

3. Their relation; they are his, his holy ten thousands.

4. Their action or employment; they are to come with the Lord.

(1.) Their numbers. The word μυριάς, in the Greek, properly signifies ten thousand. Thus, Acts xix. 19, where the apostle mentions μυριάδας πέντε, five myriads, it is rendered "fifty thousand." And Rev. ix. 16, δύο μυριάδες μυριάδων, two myriads of myriads, we translate "twenty thousand times ten thousand;" Vulg. *et* Erasm. *vicies millies dena millia*. Μυριάδες μυριάδων, Rev. v. 11. And Dan. vii. 10, μύριαι μυριάδες, according to the Septuagint, we render "ten thousand times ten thousand:" so Deut. xxxiii. 2; Psal. iii. 6; Dan. xi. 12; Luke xii. 1; Acts xxi. 20. And in those places where the word ten thousand is used (as here in Jude) without the addition of a word of another number, it imports an uncertain and very vast number, or an innumerable multitude; there being a certain number put for an uncertain, Heb. xii. 22.

(2.) Their quality or property, noted in this word holy, or "saints."

These here called holy, or saints, say some, are the angels, who in Scripture are oft said to be such with whom Christ comes at the last day, and also called holy; and not seldom is their coming with Christ and their holiness, as here, put together. Thus, Luke ix. 26, Christ is said to come in the "glory of the holy angels;" and, "The Son of man shall come, and all the holy angels with him," &c., Matt. xxv. 31. Sometimes they are called mighty angels: "The Lord Jesus shall be revealed from heaven with his mighty angels," 2 Thess. i. 7. And when God delivered the law upon Mount Sinai, it is said, "he came with ten thousands of his saints," Deut. xxxiii. 2; where by saints may be understood angels, who attended God in delivering the law; in which respect it is said that Israel "received the law by the disposition of angels," Acts vii. 53; and the law is said to be "the word spoken by angels," Heb. ii. 2. But others more rightly conceive, that by these holy myriads or ten thousands in this place, we are likewise to understand holy men as well as the holy angels; even the saints "shall appear with him in glory," Col. iii. 4. And more plainly, 1 Thess. iii. 13, "the coming of our Lord Jesus Christ" is foretold to be "with all his saints." And, "The righteous shall shine forth as the sun in the kingdom of their Father," Matt. xiii. 43. And these saints or righteous ones who are to attend upon Christ, shall be not only those who before were with Christ in heaven, but even those who shall be taken up in the clouds to meet Christ, and thereby shall be made a part of his attendants, 1 Thess. iv. 17. So that these myriads, this innumerable company, shall be made up of all the glorious angels and saints; it shall be a general assembly; all the servants shall wait upon their Master the Lord Jesus. We shall, saith the apostle, all meet, Eph. iv. 13; there shall not one be wanting: and if Christ bestows new liveries upon all his saints, they shall all, when adorned with them, yield their attendance to him in them.

But in what respect does the apostle call them "saints," or holy? Persons are holy in two respects. 1. In respect of destination, separation, or being set apart to holy services and employments. Thus the first-born were holy, Exod. xiii. 2, 12. Thus the prophets and apostles are oft called holy: Jeremiah was sanctified from the womb, Jer. i. 5. In this respect these holy angels and men may be called holy, as being set apart to the peculiar work and glorious employment of praising and glorifying of God for ever. 2. Persons may be holy in respect of true inherent holiness abiding in them. Thus likewise these angels and saints here mentioned may be called holy. For the angels, they were from their very creation perfectly holy, and afterward by the grace of confirmation made constant in holiness. As for holy men, though they were formerly made holy of not holy, privatively, that is, having lost their holiness, had holiness bestowed upon them by regeneration; and though they were made holy of less holy, by having increase and additions of holiness bestowed upon them in this life; yet at this great day they are with the angels perfectly holy likewise, the spirits of just men made perfect: in this life they were *perficientes*, perfecting; then shall they be *perfecti*, having as much holiness as they can hold, as much as God or themselves will desire, being without any mixtures of unholiness in them, all tears being wiped from their eyes, and all sins from their souls, and they presented faultless before that presence of glory, "not having spot, or wrinkle, or any such thing," but being "holy and without blemish," Eph. v. 27.

(3.) Their relation; they are called his, his holy ten thousands; and his they are in three respects. 1. In respect of creation; he made them all, whether saints or angels; as they are creatures, they are the works of his hands. 2. As they are saints, they are his also. Angels are his by being confirmed in their sanctity; holy men are his, because he was the deserving cause of their holiness, the pattern or exemplary cause of it; and lastly, by his Spirit, the efficient cause of their holiness, he is made sanctification to us, 1 Cor. i. 30; he sanctifies and cleanseth his church "with the washing of water by the word," Eph. v. 26. 3. They are his in point of service and attendance; for being sanctified, they wait upon him, and serve him in all holy employments here in the kingdom of grace, and hereafter shall they attend upon and come with him as his servants in his kingdom of glory.

(4.) Their employment; these "ten thousand of his saints" shall come with the Lord Jesus.

[1.] For his own glory; he will come in the glory of his holy angels; and he will likewise "come to be glorified in his saints, and admired in all them that believe in that day," 2 Thess. i. 10. How glorious these holy myriads or ten thousands shall make Christ at the day of judgment, both in regard of their excellencies and numbers! How will the beauty and multitudes of these subjects set forth the glory of the King of glory, who shall have myriads of servants, every one shining like myriads of suns, and every subject being indeed a king!

The first time he came as a servant to sinners, but the second time he shall come as the Lord of saints and angels. Then his forerunner was John Baptist, now he shall "descend with the voice of the archangel," 1 Thess. iv. 16; then he was attended with twelve poor contemptible men, but now with many millions of glorious angels: and the angels, more particularly, shall by their attendance make Christ's coming glorious in regard of their service and ministry; for they shall perform the work of the great day, in gathering together the elect, severing the tares from the wheat, they are called reapers, running at every command of Christ. And this work they shall do, 1. Powerfully; they are the angels of his power; they are principalities and powers, and excel in power; and at that day Christ's power shall be added to their own. 2. They shall do the work of Christ willingly; behold their readiness; the servants said, Shall we gather up the tares? Matt. xiii. 28. They who desire commission beforehand, will be ready enough when they have it. 3. They shall perform

x

it justly, holily, faithfully; they shall mingle no corrupt passions with their executions, nor corruptly respect any persons. "The seven angels are clothed in pure and white linen," Rev. xv. 6. 4. Diligently and perfectly, in a most strict and exact manner: though angels compared with God are imperfect, yet in comparison of God's law they have perfection, and no spot of sin cleaves to them; nor else could they continue in their glorious state, if they should not be answerable to God's law in the purity of their nature, and perfection of their work.

[2.] Christ will come with these ten thousands for the glory of his saints, and confusion of the wicked. Here saints have glorified him, but then he will glorify them; they who have here lien among the pots, shall shine with rays of majesty. What glory comparable to that of appearing with Christ in glory, of being privileged with the dignity of judging and condemning wicked men, yea angels? 1 Cor. vi. 3; and that not only, 1. By having the practices of these saints compared with those of the lost. Nor, 2. Only by their consenting to and approving of the sentence which Christ shall pass upon the wicked. But also, 3. In regard of that *dignitas assessoria*, that dignity whereby they shall be advanced to an honourable assessorship with the Lord Christ, in sitting, as it were, with him upon the throne of judicature. As likewise, 4. They in that judgment appearing with Christ, manifest victors over all their enemies, by trampling upon all the pride, malice, and weakness of devils and wicked men, and openly and holily insulting over them as vile, vanquished, and contemptible enemies.

Obs. 1. Our greatest wisdom and truest interest is to make Jesus Christ our friend against the last day. "The Lord cometh." He now is the Lord, but then he will openly declare himself to be so. How happy will they be who then put their trust in him, who have chosen and taken him to be their Lord! 2 Cor. v. 9. The service of Christ will then appear to be the only safety and dignity. The wicked who here take no care to make him their Lord, will, at that day, call him their Lord, Matt. vii. 22, and be sure to find and feel him their Lord. How unable will the enemies of Christ at the last day be to oppose him, the Lord that cometh from heaven! In regard of his very situation he will be above them, and have the advantage of them. Against earthly power they might make their party good: the ministers of Christ they opposed; but this mighty Lord, who shall come armed with an infinite power and dominion over all creatures, which shall be acknowledged by them all; (the angels shall observe and attend it; the heavens, earth, and elements shall be dissolved by it; the dead bodies of men shall be raised up out of the graves and out of the sea by it;) I say, this mighty Lord will easily and unavoidably crush them. A careful servant, that expects his master's return, will labour to have the work set him finished. If the bridegroom be coming, let the bride deck herself, like Rebekah, espying Isaac afar off, Gen. xxiv. 65. As Joshua exhorted Israel, chap. iii. 5, "Sanctify yourselves; for to-morrow the Lord will do wonders among you;" he means, in leading them to Canaan: so our Joshua commands us to be sanctified, because in the last day the Lord will do wonders in leading us to the heavenly Canaan. Let us separate from sin: a malefactor cannot stand before the judge, nor shall the wicked stand in judgment. Our care should be that we may be found of him in peace; and no peace can any one have with Christ who is not at war with sin. And how much better and easier is it to bear the yoke of service here in doing his will, than that of severity hereafter in undergoing his wrath!

Obs. 2. The saints have a strong ground for moderation in every condition. "The Lord cometh," and they shall come with him. The Lord's coming is the apostle's argument to urge moderation, Phil. iv. 5; Acts iii. 19; Eph. iv. 30; Luke xxi. 28. How patient and full of forbearance should they be in sustaining all their crosses and injuries! Contentedly should they here be accounted the refuse and offscouring of the world. Their Lord is coming, and they shall come with him in glory; though men here make them their footstool, yet Christ has allotted for every one of them a throne. In this world they are not accounted worthy of the society of men, but then they shall be in the company of angels, yea, Christ himself. Now Christ seems for a while to leave his family, every piece of household stuff appears to be misplaced, or all (as it were) to lie in a huddle or heap together, the most beautiful vessels to lie among the pots; but then the vessels of honour shall be set up in their places, and the vessels of dishonour thrown into theirs, Rom. viii. 23; 2 Tim. iv. 8; James v. 6—8; 1 Cor. iv. 5. It is not fit that our glory should appear so long as Christ's glory is hid. In the winter all the sap, and life, and fruit is hid in the root, and then the tree appears not what it is; but the summer coming, all that was within appears: so in this our winter, though we are the sons of God, yet it appears not what we shall be, but when Christ shall appear, we shall be like him, 1 John iii. 2.

Obs. 3. How cheerfully may saints think of the last judgment! This Lord is their Brother, their Saviour and Head, he it is who is coming: no wonder if "the bride say, Come," Rev. xxii. 17; and that the saints are called such as love his appearance, 2 Tim. iv. 8. A loving wife longs for the return of her husband from a far country. At that judgment-day the Judge will condemn none but malefactors; they who here are justified, shall then be declared to be so. It is true, Christ the Judge is here called a Lord; but yet he is so the saints' Lord, that he is also their Husband. How great is the difference betwixt a guilty malefactor's calling the judge my lord, and a loyal wife giving her husband that title! Who is he that condemns, if the Judge accept, acquit us? he it is that shall judge us who also died for our sins. The Father hath delivered all judgment to him, who himself was delivered for our sins, and "sent into the world, not to condemn the world, but that the world through him should be saved." How shall he who was sent into the world to save believers condemn them? How shall he who comes to condemn others for injuring them hurt them himself? How shall he who the first time came to be put to death for them, sentence them to die when he comes the second time? How should he throw them away, who was made their Head to gather them together? As therefore believers of the Old Testament longed to see the first coming of Christ, when he came in the form of a servant; so should believers of the New Testament desire the second coming of Christ in glory, when he shall come as a Lord: "The Lord cometh." The nearer the day of jubilee came, the more the joy of prisoners and debtors was increased; the nearer the day of our redemption approacheth, the more should we lift up our heads.

Obs. 4. Christ will be attended only by holy ones at the last day. Holy myriads. None shall meet with him in peace but they who first meet with him in purity. He will profess to the workers of iniquity at the last day that he knows them not. How unsuitable to the dignity of Christ will it be to be attended by those who have no better raiment than the filthy rags of sin! If Achish, an earthly king, had no need of madmen, what need will the King of glory have of unholy men? If he commands us here to have no fellowship with the works of darkness, will he himself in that day of light and glory show any love to them? How shall Christ at that day acquit those openly from the guilt of sin, who are not before parted from the filth of sin? Men here in this world are oft ashamed of holiness, but at the last day it will be the best ornament, the best defence; without it no man shall see God. How shall Christ present unclean ones without spot before the presence of his glory? They who will be ashamed of Christ here for his holiness, shall deservedly hereafter find Christ ashamed of them for their uncleanness.

Obs. 5. How great is the patience and long-suffering of the Lord Jesus Christ; who is contented so long to be hid, and not to show himself in glory to the end of the world, suffering, meanwhile, his glory to be veiled, yea, trampled on by the wicked! The heavens are now as a curtain between our eyes and his glory; he is out of sight, and, by most, out of mind; his patience is despised, and the promise of his coming derided; yea, his very saints do not so much believe, love, admire him as they should, in regard of their sins, and his hiding his face. He forbears to show forth his glory and power in judgment, not constrainedly, but voluntarily; not because he cannot punish, but because he would have sinners repent. And all this time of his forbearance he sees all the impieties committed against him, and indignities offered to him and his; yea, his hatred of all the sins which he beholds, is infinitely more keen and intense than that of all the saints and angels in the world. How unworthily and disgracefully was this Lord of glory used, when he veiled and hid his glory here upon earth! And yet, I say, with what patience and long-suffering does he forbear to manifest his majesty and greatness to the view of the world! We poor worms think a short time long and tedious, ere our enemies fall, and we rise; but Christ suffers very long. How patiently should we endure to have our glory obscured, and injuries unrevenged, since our Lord, our Master, the Judge himself, is the greatest sufferer, and yet voluntarily unrevenged!

Obs. 6. When angels and saints are in their greatest glory, obsequiousness and serviceableness to Christ becomes them. All the saints and angels of heaven shall worship and advance Christ, when they appear in their highest dignity; of him they will not be ashamed when they are in their best clothes, their robes of most shining glory; when they lay off all their infirmities, they throw off no love to Christ: as saints are made glorious in their bodies, so are those bodies joined to spirits made perfect in holiness, and that holiness will show itself in duty and obedience. How unlike to ten thousands of saints are they who think they are too good to honour Christ, when they are in outward glory and dignity! When they are in their rags, low and afflicted, they will then stoop to do something for Christ; but when in their best apparel, set up, advanced to any pitch of worldly eminence, they then think they shall spoil their clothes and disgrace their dignity by attending upon Christ. Do saints and angels wait upon him in their glory, and shall worms upon the dunghill think it much to serve him? Did he our Lord empty himself of glory to save, yea, serve us, and shall not we his servants serve him when filled with glory?

Thus far of the first part of the description of the judgment, viz. the coming of the Judge.

2. The carriage of the Judge in judgment, ver. 15; and in that, 1. His carriage toward all. 2. Particularly toward the wicked.

(1.) **Toward all, in these words, " to execute judgment upon all."**

For this first. Two things here require explication.

[1.] What the apostle here intends by execution of judgment. How judgment is here to be taken, and wherein the execution of judgment at the last day doth consist, I have spoken at large before.

[2.] How it is said that Jesus Christ shall execute judgment upon all, or concerning the universality of this judgment, I have likewise spoken before. Only as to this text, it is to be considered that the word κατὰ, here fitly translated upon, though sometimes it signifies *adversus*, against, cannot here be so rendered, because Jude speaks of the whole company of those who are to be judged, whom he distinguishes into good and bad in the next words, to convince all that are ungodly among them; and some, namely, the godly, shall not have judgment executed against them, although there shall be a judgment concerning and upon them, in respect of a happy sentencing. This word, then, κατὰ, I take to be equivalent to περὶ, in that sense in which it is used in 1 Cor. xv. 15, " We have testified" (κατὰ τοῦ Θεοῦ) of or concerning God, " that he raised up Christ," &c.

(2.) The carriage of the Judge toward the wicked.

[1.] The manner of his judging them is considerable; which is to be by way of conviction, "to convince," &c.

The word ἐξελέγχειν, here translated to convince, imports more than here is expressed, and indeed more than can be expressed in any one English word: the simple word ἐλέγχειν, the signification whereof by its composition is here increased and enlarged, is a word belonging to courts of judicature, and signifies two things, to prove, and to reprove.

1. To prove against one, or to accuse or convince one of a crime so clearly, evidently, and unanswerably, by arguments, reasons, or testimony, that nothing can be objected, alleged, or pretended against the proof by him who is accused, but he is thereby compelled to acknowledge the truth of the accusation. And answerably to this signification the word ἐλέγχειν is used John viii. 9, " They which heard it," ἐλεγχόμενοι, " being convicted by their own conscience, went out," &c. So ver. 46, " Which of you" ἐλέγχει, " convinceth me of sin." " He is convinced," ἐλέγχεται, &c.; " the secrets of his heart are made manifest," &c., 1 Cor. xiv. 24, 25.

2. To reprove, or reprehend, or correct; and that verbally and by word, as Luke iii. 19, " Herod the tetrarch" ἐλεγχόμενος, " being reproved by him (John) for Herodias," &c. So Eph. v. 11, " Have no fellowship with the unfruitful works of darkness, but rather" ἐλέγχετε, " reprove them." So Tit. ii. 15, ἔλεγχε, " rebuke with all authority," &c. And really or by deed, as Heb. xii. 5; Rev. iii. 19, where rebuking is expounded by chastening. The word ἐξελέγχειν here used by Jude, may aptly import either of these significations, and by its composition makes either the more full and significant. For the first, at the last day Christ shall bring to the remembrance of sinners those things which they have done, so set their sins in order before them, and so evidently convince, irradiate, and dilate their consciences, that then they shall bring in such full and impartial evidence against them as shall silence them, and stop their mouths; they shall have nothing to object, but shall be compelled to acknowledge what they have done, and do thereby deserve. And this inward conviction of conscience they shall no more be able to shake off than to shake off themselves and their very being; they shall see this lightning, though they should labour to shut their eyes: the witness, the guilty, the judge, the tormenter, and scourge are all one. Sinners shall have a self-conviction, an internal conviction. They shall in that day take part with Christ against themselves, who have here taken part with their lusts

against Christ. This is that opening of the books, mentioned Rev. xx. 12. Wicked men's consciences shall in the last day be opened, though here they are sealed books. In this life they were bribed, and gave in partial and imperfect evidence; but then they shall bring in the truth, the whole truth, and nothing but the truth. That writing which heretofore was almost imperceptible, shall, being held to the fire of Divine vengeance, be made legible. And then, 2. As Christ shall convince them evidently, so shall he reprove them severely, vex them in his sore displeasure; the Lamb will then be turned Lion; he whose bowels heretofore made a noise, shall now thunder in his indignation. This reproof shall be both verbal and real.

(1.) Verbal, and by word of mouth. That part of the judgment which stands in disquisition or examination, according to the most, shall be transacted, not by voice, but in silence, in every one's conscience, as the books which shall be opened at the last day are not material, but those of the consciences, Rom. ii. 15, 16; Rev. xx. 12. That part which stands in denouncing sentence, at least in respect of the general sentence, which shall be pronounced either for the elect or against the reprobate, shall be despatched (I conceive) by pronouncing a verbal sentence. Thus most of the schoolmen think, encouraged thereto by Augustine, who saith, Christ shall come openly hereafter with a voice, who, coming the first time in obscurity, was silent before the judge; and they doubt not but that He who shall openly be seen in a visible shape, shall openly be heard by an audible voice. Now how dreadful will that definitive sentence of loss and pain be, " Depart from me into everlasting fire!" words brimful of woe, and wherein is summed up the whole wretchedness of the lost. All the happiness of the creature has but one neck, and that cut in sunder by the one blow of a sentence of departure from God.

<small>Christus in voce evidens apparebit, qui priùs, cum venisset occultus, ante judicem siluit. Aug. l. 20. de Civ. Dei, cap. 24. Qui omnibus se conspiciendum exhibebit in gloria majestatis, etiam omnibus audiendum se præbebit in voce judicis. Estius in Sent. 4. dist. 47. sec. 1.</small>

(2.) Real. The sentence shall be executed. The sentence shall not be a thunderclap without a thunderbolt, nor a report without a bullet; but this word shall be operative, efficacious, a working word, a fiery stream, proceeding from the throne of the Judge, and sweeping the condemned into hell, 2 Thess. i. 9.

Obs. 1. It is the greatest folly to shelter our sin with hopes of secrecy. As all things are open and naked before the eyes of our Judge now, so will he make them apparent before our own eyes hereafter. God is not mocked. " Can any man hide himself in secret places that I should not see him?" Jer. xxiii. 24. Though sinners now think that God is such a one as themselves, yet will God hereafter reprove them, and set their sins in order before them, Psal. l. 21. Every sinner is fully and clearly manifest before God, yea, naked, unquartered, and exposed before his eyes, as when a man anatomize a body, whereby he curiously finds out every little vein or muscle, though they are never so close and hidden. The ungodly shall be convinced of the most concealed wickednesses, and their mouth shall be shut as soon as ever God's book is opened. We may delude men, we cannot deceive God: they cannot convince unless men be witnesses against thee; God will convince thee by making thine own conscience witness for him against thee. Yea, of those sins which are unknown to thee, shalt thou be convinced by Him who knows all things. We should be, then, so far from sheltering those sins which we know, that we ought to be humbled for such as we know not.

Thus of the first particular, in the carriage of the Judge toward the wicked, viz. the manner of his judging them, namely, by way of conviction.

2. The parties to be judged follow in the next place, who are here said for their quality to be "ungodly," and for their number, all the ungodly. Of this before at large.

3. The causes of and matters about which they shall be judged are next considerable, and they are twofold.

The first, their ungodly deeds; "their ungodly deeds which they have ungodly committed."

Not to enlarge upon this first particular here considerable, viz. the general nature of their deeds, here said to be ungodly, as being sufficiently known by the former consideration of the parties who were called ungodly. By which it is manifest that ungodly deeds are primarily and properly such as are committed immediately against God himself, and so against the first table, in the profane opposing of God's worship and honour, in which respect ungodliness is distinguished from unrighteousness, which properly breaks the commandments of the second table. And yet secondarily, and in a more large consideration, ungodliness here comprehends any sin committed either against God or man, and so against any commandment of the law; for even that sin which is directly against man, has in it a defect and a withdrawing of some duty due to God. If it be inquired why the apostle only here saith ungodly, and not unrighteous deeds also, it is answered, for three reasons.

[1.] Because ungodliness and unrighteousness are inseparable. Wherever ungodliness is, there will be no conscience made of unrighteousness: as the two tables were given, so are they broken and embraced both together; and he who breaks one makes no conscience of breaking the other, the authority of the Giver being the same.

[2.] Because ungodliness is the cause of unrighteousness. He who has a profane, godless heart, will not stick at any act of injustice. It is the fear of God which is to depart from evil. As holiness puts a man upon righteousness, so profaneness upon unrighteousness. Pharaoh knew not God, and therefore he oppressed Israel.

[3.] Because these seducers flattered themselves with pretences of eminent godliness and holiness, though they took a liberty to live in many vices and unclean extravagancies. The apostle several times in this Epistle brands them with the name of ungodly ones, and threatens judgment for their ungodliness.

Secondly, The manner after which they were committed, and that was ungodlily, "which they have ungodly committed."

The words "ungodly committed" are contained in one word, ἠσέβησαν; if it may be rendered by any one Latin word, it must be *impiarunt;* nor can it be in any one English word properly expressed, but must be rendered either to do or perform or live ungodlily. The same word is expressed but in one place besides this in all the New Testament, and that place is 2 Pet. ii. 6, where it is rendered living ungodly. In the opening hereof, I shall only show what it is to commit an evil work ungodlily.

1. More generally, it notes the proceeding of these ungodly deeds from an ungodly, unsanctified principle, an unholy, unrepentant heart, a mind devoted and addicted to ungodliness. This is not the fruit which grows upon a good tree, nor the spot of God's people, who, though sometimes they do that which is ungodly, withdraw that duty which is due to God, and commit that evil which is against the will of God; yet, as the psalmist speaks, they do not wickedly, as these did, depart from God, Psal. xviii. 21. The wicked are they who " do wickedly against the

covenant," Dan. xi. 32. And of the wicked, it is said that they " shall do wickedly," Dan. xii. 10.

But, 2. That which this doing ungodlily more particularly intends, is the performing of wickedness after a wicked and ungodly manner, and that principally these four several ways.

(1.) By purposing and intending of sin. The wicked is not overtaken with a sudden fit of temptation, but resolves on sin long before; he makes provision for his lust; he is like a man who lays himself to sleep, draws the curtains, puts out the candle, and he intends, and in a sort overtakes his sleep in sin; " he setteth himself in a way that is not good," Psal. xxxvi. 4.

(2.) Ungodly deeds are performed after an ungodly manner by devising and contriving ungodliness: the wicked devise mischief, Prov. vi. 14. " He that deviseth to do evil shall be called a mischievous person." The "heart that deviseth wicked imaginations" is one of the seven things which the Lord hates, Prov. vi. 16, 18. Against those "who devise iniquity, and work evil upon their beds," is a woe denounced, Micah ii. 1. The wicked are workers of iniquity, Matt. vii. 23; they are curious, cunning artificers in and contrivers of sin; ungodliness is their art, trade, and mystery; they are wise to do evil, and men in malice, though children in understanding; they are skilful practitioners in sin.

(3.) By delighting and taking pleasure in the committing of sin. Wicked men are willingly obedient to it; they yield themselves to execute its commands, and they universally resign the whole consent of the will to the obedience of it. Sin is as pleasant to sinners as bread and wine: " They eat the bread of wickedness, and drink the cup of violence," Prov. iv. 17. They " rejoice to do evil, and delight in the frowardness of the wicked," Prov. ii. 14. Wickedness is sweet in their mouths, and they hide it under their tongues, Job xx. 12. As it is not doing good, but delighting in doing it, that makes it done well; so neither is it simply doing evil, but doing it delightfully, that makes it done ungodlily: " It is as sport to a fool to do mischief," Prov. x. 23.

(4.) By continuing and persisting in sin. Wicked men grow worse and worse, their ways increase to more ungodliness, they run on in them without repentance; none say, "What have I done?" It is weakly done to fall, but it is wickedly done to lie still; it is bad to stand in the way of sinners, much worse to sit in the seat of the scornful.

Obs. 1. The godly sin not as do the wicked. The sinful actions of the godly proceed not from a heart altogether void of a sanctified principle; there is in them the seed of God, the Divine nature, a renewed part, from which their wicked works never issue. In committing the most ungodly of their actions, they themselves are not altogether ungodly; and they are overtaken unawares with sin; they sin of infirmity and weakness; with the purpose of their hearts they cleave unto the Lord, Acts xi. 23, though by sin they are diverted from their holy resolutions, and turned out of the way; they overtake not sin, but are overtaken by it; like a good marksman, they aim and level right at the mark, though Satan and their own unregenerate part sometimes jogging them, as it were, by the elbow, make them in their performances swerve and deviate from the same. Nor do the godly go about sin with the witty wickedness and skilfulness of the ungodly; they are brought up to another trade, being children in malice, and men in understanding; they are under the captivity of sin, which though it may haply have a victory, and exercise tyranny over them as a usurper, does not exercise a reign over them as a king; they are taken sometimes in a temptation by that which the apostle calls νόμον αἰχμαλωτίζοντα, Rom. vii. 23, a captivating law, which as by the point of the spear, or edge of the sword, forcibly overcomes them, but it does not bring their whole will to a complete consent and subjection to it; they do what they hate, Rom. vii. 15. There is ever something in them which hates sin, which though it does not always succeed to prevent sin, yet it always supplies with repentance after the commission of sin; and though some kind of consent went before to conceive sin, yet it shall not follow after to allow it being committed. Of these things more before, concerning walking in the way of Cain.

<small>In discordia carnis et spiritus non facile obtinetur tam perfecta victoria, ut etiam quæ sunt adimpenda, non illigent, et quæ sunt interficienda, non vulnerent. Leo de Jejun. sep. mens. ser.</small>

Obs. 2. The wicked sin not of infirmity. They do not fall into but follow sin; they are not pulled into sin against their will or unawares, but they wallow in it; they are not surprised by sin, but they sell themselves to it; not sinning fraillly, but ungodlily; they are not, after purpose to walk in the ways of God's commandments, withdrawn unawares out of the way, but they please themselves in wandering; and, like the beggar, they are never out of their way, or truly displease themselves for being so, when they are most so. Let no wicked man then flatter himself by pretending such a sin is his infirmity: sins of weakness are not committed wickedly, nor is there wanting so much strength in any saint as to strive against them, and to arise up from them.

Obs. 3. The manner of committing sin is that which shall condemn. As the manner of doing good is that which commends a good action, so the manner of committing evil is that which makes it most deformed in God's sight. There is no sin shall condemn which is not committed wickedly; that which is sincerely opposed and repented of shall never destroy: when the virgin cried out, she was not to die. Instead of destroying us for it, we shall be delivered from it. Hence it is that sundry sins of the wicked (mentioned in Scripture) were more severely punished than those committed by the godly, though, as to the nature of the sin itself, the latter seemed much more heinous. A child of God sins not, so neither shall he smart, as the sinner.

This briefly for the first sort of causes or matters about which the wicked shall be judged, " their ungodly deeds which they have ungodly committed."

2. " Their hard speeches spoken against him."

The words " hard speeches " are comprised in this one word σκληρὰ, hard, which must nevertheless be restrained to speeches, in respect of the word which follows, namely, spoken. This word σκληρὰ, hard, according to the force of its own signification, imports that hardness which comes from the dryness of a thing, and which thereby is unpleasing, harsh, rugged, and so hurtful to the touch; and works or words may be said to be hard, when they are grievous, harsh, unpleasing, churlish, rough: thus it is said that the Egyptians made the lives of the Israelites bitter, according to the Septuagint, ἐν τοῖς ἔργοις τοῖς σκληροῖς, " with hard bondage," Exod. i. 14. " His," God's, " hand is " σκληρὰ, " sore upon us, and upon Dagon our god," 1 Sam. v. 7. So it is said of Nabal, 1 Sam. xxv. 3, that he was σκληρὸς καὶ πονηρὸς, " churlish and evil," &c. 1 Kings xii. 4 is mentioned the σκληρὰ δουλεία, " grievous service " of Solomon. " The king

<small>Nonnulli codices post σκληρῶν addunt λόγων. Lorin. Sed verba per verbum loquendi satis intelligunctur. Id. Vis Græcæ vocis σκληροῦ, duritiem importat ex ariditate, quam ariditatem spiritualiter habent hi quorum cor durum est, et quorum animæ dici possunt sine aqua, quia humore gratiæ destituuntur. Lorin. in loc. In Sept. Υἱοὶ Σαρουίας σκληρότεροί μου εἰσὶν, 2 Sam. iii. 39. Ὁ πολεμὸς σκληρός, 2 Sam. ii. 17. Vid. et Isa. xxvii. 8; xlviii. 4; Cant. viii. 6.</small>

answered the people" σκληρά, "roughly," 1 Kings xii. 13; or, as here in Jude, "hard speeches." "Joseph spake" σκληρά, "roughly," Gen. xlii. 7. "I knew that thou art" σκληρὸς, "an hard man," Matt. xxv. 24.

By these hard speeches therefore Jude intends, though not such as were afflictive, hurtful to Christ; for as our good words cannot benefit him, so neither can our bad ones harm him; yet such as among men are accounted harsh, grievous, and offensive; such as were spoken in opposition, contempt, obstinacy, stubbornness against him. And thus two ways they spake hard speeches against Christ.

1. Directly; when they spake falsely, blasphemously, and irreverently, against his person, natures, or offices.

2. Indirectly they spake against him, in speaking against his word, and the persons whom he would have them reverence.

(1.) In speaking against his word, they deride and mock at its promises, which they allowed to be encouragements to them to live as they list. The gospel of grace they turn into lasciviousness, and profess that it gives them liberty to cast off all obedience; and therefore all the precepts, they say, are antiquated, and of no other use now than to show from what they are delivered. The purity and holiness required therein they deride as needless niceness, as the fetching of a wearisome compass, and the going the farthest way about in the journey and course of Christianity. The threatenings of the word they securely scoff at, as if they were but empty sounds, reports without bullets, thunder-claps without bolts; they scorn to be stopped in their carnal and sensual prosecutions, as they of old did by the foretelling of a flood, by the denunciation of a day of judgment; scoffingly inquiring, "Where is the promise of his coming?" 2 Pet. iii. 4. They look upon examples of judgment as fables, or nothing at all concerning them: the examples of Divine patience they boldly turn into presumption, with Lamech, "If Cain shall be avenged sevenfold, truly Lamech seventy and sevenfold," Gen. iv. 24.

(2.) They speak against him in speaking against the persons of others. Their governors and superiors they reproach, and speak evil of dignities. Though they allowed not the magistrate to use the sword against them, yet they abused that which was sharper than a sword against him. Against private Christians they spake,

[1.] Boastingly and proudly. And thus, Psal. xxxi. 18, David's enemies spake hard things, proudly; and Psal. xciv. 4, they "speak hard things, and boast themselves," namely, by threatening such things which were grievous to be borne, insufferable and insupportable; they herein resembling the waves of the sea, which in their proud swelling seem to threaten the swallowing up of ships and shore.

[2.] They speak hard things against Christians by slandering and defaming them, casting undue aspersions upon them, 1 Pet. iv. 4. Because these could not find, they made and minted many accusations against them; and that both by uttering those things against them which were false and evil, as also by uttering true things after a false and sinful manner, as by blazing of secret infirmities, amplifying offences beyond their due proportion, lessening and depraving the good which was in or done by them, perverting and destroying the sense and meaning of their words.

[3.] They speak hard things against Christians by censuring and judging them; they uncharitably passed sentence against their persons and practices, declaring the former to be hypocrites because they would not be profane, and to have no more than, because they had so much as the appearance of holiness; they judged harshly of their future state, and of those actions which to these censurers were unknown, for they spake evil of what they knew not; they ever judged the worst.

[4.] They speak hard things by mocking and deriding the godly: the holy strictness and preciseness of the saints occasioned their scorn. These libertines derided them, as if they had made an idol of conscience, because they durst not run with them to the same excess of riot. They turned the glory of holy men into shame; for that which made the godly more than men, they abused them as children. As, in likelihood, those sturdy giants in Enoch's time scoffed both at his purity and predictions; so did these sensual monsters mock at the Christians, both for their being such manner of persons, and also for the motive of their being so, the promise of the coming of Christ to judgment. Luke xxiii. 11, ἐμπαίξας.

Obs. 1. The excellency of any way or persons exempts them not from hard words. Even Christ himself had hard words uttered against him; Christ endured, and therefore he had the contradiction of sinners. Where wicked men cannot find, they will make a cause to speak against Christ, and rather than they will have none at all, this shall be it, that they can find none. The good word of the ungodly is no commendation to the commended. What evil have I done, said one to a wicked man, that thou shouldst speak well of me? A man is much known by those who accompany and commend him. The commendation of sinners, since Christ had their contradiction, should rather make thee suspect than soothe thyself. If thou wilt be like Christ in being holy, thou must be like him in being disgraced. Expect not to have the good word of sinners, nor be troubled for wanting it. In short, let us not think the worse of Christ or his ways because they meet with the unkind word of the world; rather let us be so experimentally acquainted with the worth and goodness of both, that we may be able to confute the hard words of the wicked; to say, We have found Christ good, when others shall give him hard words; nay, that we may be the more incited to speak for Christ, the more ungodly men speak against him. To conclude, let us be harsh to our lusts, and to our sinful natures, and be sensible of the harshness and hurtfulness of sin, and then we shall both account Christ good, and speak good, not hard words of him.

Obs. 2. A wicked tongue is rugged, harsh, grating. It speaks hard things. It is not made of bone, nor is there a bone in it, as some observe, but yet it utters words that are harder than bones, yea, sharper than swords. It has made incurable gashes in the name. The poison latent in and vented by the tongue is deadly. The mockings of the tongue are called cruel. Many men have adventured to lose their lives rather than they would endure the rugged and unpleasing expressions of the tongue. Reproaches are like the living coals of juniper, which burn hottest, and some say they may be kept a whole year, Psal. cxx. 4. The tongue, like fire, though it be a good servant, is a bad master. The unicorn's horn is very salubrious and beneficial when the apothecary uses it in his shop, but very hurtful when upon the head of that fierce and wild creature. Hence we should be warned to take heed of having a tongue hurtful to others, as also to labour to shield ourselves with innocence and patience against this cruelly cutting instrument, and to find that the ruggedness and harshness of others' tongues may be only as a file or wisp, to take away the rust and filth of our corruption; remembering that even the best saints oft want the rubber of a sinner's tongue to make them clean, and that they may make as good a use of the reproaching tongue of an enemy, as of the reproving or comforting tongue of a friend; and that hereby the swords of the tongue shall let out the corruption of their sores, and do them good against the will of their enemies.

Obs. 3. For our words we are responsible before the tribunal of Christ. Words pass away in respect of the sound, not in respect of the guilt and effect; even of idle words men shall give account, Matt. xii. 36, ἀργα, workless words, which benefit not, and administer no grace to the hearer; how much more then for hurtful words! If a man may sin by silence, how much more by hurtful speaking! The sins of the tongue much dishonour God. Of all creatures, man alone had the glory of speech bestowed upon him; and indeed to what end should an irrational creature be furnished with language? his tongue was to proclaim his reason, and that by setting forth the glory of his Maker. Man was made to glorify God, and the tongue is that instrument whereby he should principally do it. To offend God then by the tongue, is to fight against him with his own weapon, and to turn his own artillery upon himself. Further, the sinful tongue, of all other parts, does most injury to others, not only by vexing and afflicting them with calumnies, reproaches, disgraces, but also infecting them, and scattering its poison to tempt and draw to sin and error. How great should our care be to throw the salt of grace into the streams of our words, to labour that our speech should be always gracious, and, as the apostle speaks, seasoned with salt! Col. iv. 6; and that both by cleansing the fountain, the heart, as also by setting a watch before the door of our lips, and by giving entrance to no expressions but such as can bring a pass from the Scripture; adding to that double guard, the teeth and lips, with which nature has hedged in the tongue, a third, namely, the fear of God, which is the best keeper both of heart and tongue; always remembering, that though words seem to vanish and to die as soon as we have spoken, yet that our words have not done with us when we have done with them, but that even of our seemingly perished expressions, and forgotten, if sinful, words, shall we at the last day be convinced. The arrows of our words, shot so high that they seem to be lost and out of sight, will afterward fall upon the heads of those who shot them up.

Obs. 4. Christ accounts the words spoken against his people as uttered against himself. These troublesome, rugged-tongued sectaries handled the names of others rudely; but at the last day Christ will convince them of these hard speeches; their foolish tongues shall recoil upon themselves, and rebound, like an arrow shot against a brazen wall, from the reviled innocents to the nocent revilers. Jesus Christ will give his saints more than treble damages, nay, fourfold restitution, for all the reproaches which they have sustained; sinners shall restore the stolen reputations of saints, and that with interest. It is a righteous thing with God to render tribulation to all who even this way trouble his people. Christ well knows that all the hard speeches against his servants were uttered for his sake; because they did not run with the wicked to the same excess of riot, they were therefore followed by them with excessive reproaches. David said it was for his sake that Saul killed the priests of the Lord; he could not come at David, and therefore he destroyed his friends. The wicked cannot reach the person, and therefore they tear the picture; but Christ will hereafter suffer none to be losers by him that have been losers for him: the revilings uttered against saints will at the last appear to have been spoken against the truly great ones, the favourites of the King of glory: "Were ye not afraid," saith God to Aaron and Miriam, "to speak against my servant Moses?" He speaks to them as slandering a great person.

Verse 16.

These are murmurers, complainers, walking after their own lusts; and their mouth speaketh great swelling words, having men's persons in admiration because of advantage.

In this verse our apostle excellently applies the forementioned prophecy of the last judgment unto these seducers, showing by sundry apt and pregnant proofs that these seducers were guilty of that ungodliness for which the wicked at the last day were to be judged. And they discover their ungodliness these four ways.

1. By being "murmurers, complainers."
2. By following "their lusts."
3. By boasting; speaking "great swelling words."
4. By their admiration of "men's persons."

1. They discover their ungodliness by showing themselves "murmurers, complainers."

I shall herein show who are here meant by "murmurers, complainers;" and then why Jude expresses himself against them, or what is the greatness or heinousness of this their sin, in being "murmurers, complainers."

(1.) Who are here meant by "murmurers, complainers."

The first word, γογγυσται, "murmurers," imports an expressing of discontentedness against another in our words; and that not aloud, with a high voice, but with a voice somewhat low, muttering, and grumbling. The word γογγύζω comes, say some, from γρυζω, *grunnio*, to grunt as fat swine; and so imports secretly to speak against others, saith Gerard, with hatred and impatience. Thus they who received but a penny for their work, thinking themselves wronged, ἐγόγγυζον, "murmured against the good man of the house," Matt. xx. 11. And the scribes and Pharisees ἐγόγγυζον, murmured against Christ and his disciples for eating with publicans and sinners. And "the Jews murmured," ἐγόγγυζον, "at him, because he said, I am the bread of life," John vi. 41. So ver. 43, 61, of the same chapter. So 1 Cor. x. 10, "Neither murmur ye," μηδὲ γογγύζετε, "as some of them also murmured," ἐγόγγυσαν, "and were destroyed of the destroyer." Though sometimes, as Beza notes, the word is taken for any close, secret whispering of a matter without offence and indignation, as John vii. 12, 32, yet most frequently and properly it is used in the former signification. This murmuring may be either against men, or against God himself; the word here used by Jude, by its own force, signifies not one more than another. Against man have men frequently murmured, as the Israelites against Moses and Aaron; nor is any thing more usual, than for people to murmur, especially against their governors, out of envy, impatience, or discontent; a sin questionless which these seducers were deeply guilty of, who despised dominions, and spake evil of dignities: and yet because the apostle had accused them for that sin before, ver. 8, and also threatened destruction against them for it, ver. 11; because also the next word, complainers, wherein the apostle shows the cause of their murmuring, notes a complaining of

Suum more grunnire. Murmure, lenis aquæ strepitus denotatur, et a Græco verbo μορμύρειν descendere videtur.

Submissa voce mussitare. Bez.

that lot, portion, and condition set out by God for us; I rather conceive that this murmuring here, with which Jude charges these seducers, was their muttering of impatient, discontented expressions against God himself, with whom they were angry and displeased; a distemper which, allowed, is an evident sign of an ungracious, ungodly heart, the thing which also Jude here intends to prove, and contrary to that quiet and silent submissiveness of the godly, who, with David, are dumb, and open not their mouth, because the Lord doth it, Psal. xxxix. 9, who will be pleased with God, and with whatever he does, when he is most angry with them, who will justify him when he seems to condemn them. A sin likewise is this murmuring against God, of which the ungodly Israelites are frequently accused; as Deut. i. 27; Exod. xv. 24; and for which they were severely punished. Concerning those who by murmuring showed themselves displeased with God, the apostle tells us that God was not well pleased with them, for they were overthrown in the wilderness: their displeasure was wicked and sinful, but yet weak and impotent; God's was holy and righteous, and withal potent and irresistible. Man has no ability with his anger; he may hate God, but he cannot hurt him; nay, instead thereof, he only hurts himself; every arrow which he shoots up to God falling down upon his own head.

The other expression whereby Jude sets forth their sin is μεμψίμοιροι, translated complainers, which does not, as indeed I think no one word can, fully express the force of the word used by the apostle, which signifies complainers, blamers, or accusers of that part, portion, or allotment which was set out for them in the world; the word being made up of two, the one μέμψις, which signifies blaming or complaining; the other μοῖρα, a lot, portion, or division. The apostle then by this word μεμψίμοιροι, complainers of their lot and portion, explains the former, γογγυσταί, murmurers; by it showing what it was at which these people murmured, namely, that their condition in the world was not so rich, great, and honourable as was that of some others; they murmured, as if God had unequally distributed their estate and portion; because they had not as much as others, they thought they had not enough, nay, nothing. Haply they were displeased that they were not the governors of the world, that any were above them; and indeed this was the true reason why they spake evil of dignities, and opposed magistrates, not because they hated ruling, but because they themselves were not the rulers. And this further clearing of their sin by the apostle further proves them ungodly, the apostle's scope; for in complaining of their lot and portion, what did they, but accuse God either of want of righteousness or wisdom in his distributions and dispensations, as if either he had defrauded them of their due, or not understood fitly to proportion their estates? And what can be more contrary to godliness, which, as the apostle speaks, is joined with contentment or self-sufficiency, 1 Tim. vi. 6, than discontentedly never to be sufficed with what God has laid out for us? what more unlike that holy disposition of saints, whereby they say with David, "The Lord is the portion of mine inheritance: the lines are fallen unto me in pleasant places; yea, I have a goodly heritage?" Psal. xvi. 5, 6. Discontentedness with our times and estates is that which the Holy Ghost deservedly chargeth with sinful folly. Say not thou, What is the cause that the former days were better than these? for thou dost not inquire wisely concerning this, Eccl. vii. 10; that is, Do not, by considering of the goodness of former times, complain discontentedly of God's providence in ordering thee to live in those which he has allotted for thee.

(2.) Why Jude expresses himself against their murmuring and complaining, or what is the heinousness considerable in this their sin. I answer, our apostle by charging them herewith, as I said, intends to prove them ungodly men, and such bold sinners as uttered hard speeches against God. Now how much ungodliness lays open itself by this sin of murmuring discontentedness against God's administrations, appears, by considering what those sins are whereof this sin is made up and consists, and wherewith it is ever accompanied.

[1.] In this is contained that great sin of unbelief and distrustfulness. He who complains of his portion, does not believe that God is his portion, and will supply him accordingly. He who believes that God is his portion, needs not complain of his portion; no, he that can say with David, "The Lord is the portion of mine inheritance," will undoubtedly add, "the lines are fallen unto me in pleasant places; I have a goodly heritage," Psal. xvi. 5, 6. That God who is self-sufficient is all-sufficient; sufficient for the soul, fills every corner thereof. The bee in the hive puts not forth its sting, nor doth the soul, when centred upon God, disquiet us. So that this murmuring discontentedness clearly argues that the soul departs from the living God, and looks not upon him as a God able and willing to relieve it in its exigences; a sin, doubtless, very heinous, and such as much dishonours God's all-sufficiency, and that which God oft punished in Israel, and which was the companion, or rather the cause, of all their murmurings against him; as appears Psal. lxxviii. 19, 20, "Can God furnish a table in the wilderness? He smote the rock," but "can he give bread also? can he provide flesh for his people?"

[2.] This sin discovers, as a fruit of the former, the going out of the heart after some other portion besides God, nay, more than God; which because it cannot obtain in so large a measure as it desires, like a child that cries because it is pinched in a strait coat much too little for it, a man becomes unquiet and complaining. Now how great an impiety is it to lament and complain more for the want of trifles, than for the want of that great soul-satisfying good, namely, that God who has all in him that may do or make us good! like a foolish mother, who, having many lovely children, will not look upon them, but only regards and delights herself with dolls, or puppets made of rags. How deservedly great is that complaint of God, "They have forsaken me the fountain of living waters, and have hewed them out cisterns, broken cisterns, that can hold no water!" How inexcusable a wickedness was it for the king of Israel, instead of seeking God, to go to Baal-zebub the god of Ekron for the recovery of his health! What greater disloyalty, than for a soul, like Potiphar's wife, to wrangle and rage because it cannot obtain its servant, the creature, to satisfy its unclean desires, and to despise the chaste and truly comfortable embracements of its Lord, to whom it is married, and tied by dearest and strictest bonds!

[3.] This murmuring discontentedness discovers the great sin of unthankfulness for what portion we enjoy. A murmurer cannot be thankful; nor can he who is thankful for what he has murmur for what he is without; but he wonders that God should give him any thing, not frets because God does not give him every thing: he saith, (with Jacob,) "I am less than the least of all thy mercies;" and does not mutter against God for not bestowing upon him greater. This distemper of discontent, contrarily, causes men to think so much of what they want, that they quite forget what they already have received. Thus the Israelites discontentedly murmured for what they had not, and unthankfully forgat what they had. Discontentedness makes heavy mercies to sink to the bottom, and to be forgotten, and light wants and troubles to swim on the top; and it makes men so fretful in that a few are above them, that they are utterly unthankful for their being above so many. God loses a friend in the discontented person for but doing with his own as he pleases.

[4.] In this is manifested the sin of a proud conceit of our own worth and deservings, a sinful self-justification when God's dispensations are severe and afflictive. He who complains of God's dealing, secretly applauds his own deservings; he who murmurs against God's hand, shows that he is not angry with his own heart; he always saith, See, what have I lost! how many comforts I want! but he never saith, What have I done? how many corruptions has my heart, which make me unfit to enjoy a fuller portion in the world! All the fault is laid upon God, nothing upon himself, as if his sin never threw one mite into the treasury of his sufferings; he counts God a hard master, and himself a good servant; and if it be a great sin in the courts of men to acquit the wicked, and to condemn the innocent, how inexcusable a wickedness is it to condemn God and acquit ourselves! A discontented complainer saith not with David, "I and my father's house have sinned: these sheep, what have they done?" nor with the humble soul, "The Lord is righteous; and I will bear the indignation of the Lord, because I have sinned against him;" but flies in the face of God, instead of falling down at his feet. In one word, this discontent is a shield for sin, and is a sword against God.

[5.] This sin unduly and sacrilegiously usurps God's own seat and throne: what does he who complains of God's administrations, but in effect profess that he would be in the room of God, to order the world after his own mind; and that he has more wisdom, care, justice, and therefore fitness, to dispose of men, and to allot them their portions, than God himself? Interpretatively, he says, like Absalom, There is none that takes care to order men's affairs: oh that I were king of the world! then should things be better ordered than now they are. And he saith to God, as that master of the feast to his self-advancing guest, Come down, sit lower, and give way to thy betters to sit above thee. Whereas, alas, should such silly Phaetons as we but govern the world, as they fable he did the chariot of the sun, for one day, we should set all things on fire; nay, should we be left to cut out our own portions, and be our own carvers, how soon should we cut our own fingers! And how can He whose will is the rule of rectitude do any thing unrighteously? Man does a thing because it is just, but therefore is a thing just because God does it: "Far be it from God," saith Elihu, "that he should do wickedness; and from the Almighty, that he should commit iniquity," Job xxxiv. 10: who can be more careful than He who is more tender over his, than a mother is over her sucking child? who so wise as the only wise God, whose eyes run to and fro throughout the whole earth; nay, who indeed is all eye to behold all the concernments of the sons of men?

[6.] Lastly, This sin of discontentedness with our own private allotments takes men off from minding the more public and weighty concernments of God's church; making them disregard and forget it in all her sufferings and hazards. What more than this sin causes men to mind their own, and not the things of Jesus Christ, and to lose the thoughts thereof in a crowd of discontented cares for themselves? It is impossible for him that is overmuch in mourning for himself to be mindful of or mournful for Zion. Now what an unworthy distemper is this, for men to live as if God had made them only to mind their own private conditions in the world, to regard only the painting of their own cabins, though the ship be sinking; and so as it may be well with themselves, to be careless how it fares with the whole church of Christ! We should rejoice that God would set up a building of glory to himself, though upon our ruins; and that Christ rises, though we fall; that his kingdom comes, though ours goes; that he may be seen and honoured, though we stand in a crowd and be hidden.

Obs. 1. God has divided, set out for every one his portion here in the world. These seducers, in complaining of their part and allotment, show that God appoints to every one his *demensum* or proportion that he thinks fittest for them. God is the great Householder of the world, and Master of that great family; and as it was the custom of ancient times to divide and give to every one his portion of meat and drink, and his set allowance of either, whence we read, Psal. xi. 6, of the portion of the wicked's cup; so God deals out to every one what estate he thinks meetest. To some he gives a Benjamin's portion in the world, five times so much as to others; he is the sovereign disposer of us and of all our concerns, and he best knows what is best for us; and to his people he ever gives them that allotment which best suits with their obtaining the true good, himself, and ever affords them, if not what they would, yet what they want. Oh how should this consideration work us to a humble contentedness with all our allotments, and make us bring our hearts to our condition, if we cannot bring our condition to our hearts! In a word, when we see that the condition of others is higher than ours, let us consider that it is better to wear a fit garment than one much too big, though golden.

Obs. 2. No estate of outward fulness can quiet the heart, and still its complaints. These seducers feasted sumptuously, fed themselves to the full, and fared high; and yet, for all that, they murmured and complained. The rich man in the gospel, in the midst of all his abundance, cries out, "What shall I do?" Luke xii. 17. Neither the life, nor the comfort of the life, consists in the abundance of the things which we enjoy. None complain so much as they who have the greatest plenty. Though Nabal had in his house the feast of a king, yet soon after his heart died in him, and he became like a stone, 1 Sam. xxv. 37. Nabal's heart was like the kidney of a beast, which though enclosed in fat, is itself lean. Solomon in his glory reads a lecture of the creature's vanity. Ahab and Haman were as discontented in heart, as great in estate. Vast is the disproportion between the soul and all worldly objects, for they being but momentary and vanishing, dead and inefficacious, earthy and drossy, are unsuitable to the soul's excellency and exigences. It is not the work of worldly abundance to take away covetousness, but of grace in the heart: the lesson of contentment must be learned in a higher school than outward plenty.

Obs. 3. They who deserve worst complain and murmur most, and are most ready to think that they are most hardly dealt with. None are so unthankful as the unworthy. Israelites murmur. Absalom is discontented. Haman cries out, "What doth all this avail me?" &c. Whereas Jacob tells God that he was not worthy of the least of all the mercies and truth which God had showed him, Gen. xxxii. 10. Job praised and submitted to God when he took from him as well as when he gave to him. None see their unworthiness so little as they who are fullest of unworthiness; and till a man see himself deserving nothing, he will ever complain of God when he abridges him of any thing. Besides, the wicked mortify no lusts, and therefore they are angry when their lusts are not fulfilled; but especially they look not upon God as their portion in Christ: and who can be content or praise God that has no spiritual blessings to bless him for? How readily then, instead of being angry with God's dispensations, should we chide our own corruptions, and oft blush, that so many saints have been so patient under mountains, and that such sinners as we should so complain under feathers!

Obs. 4. It is our duty to take heed of this sinful distemper of murmuring against and complaining of God's dealing with us. To this end, in the most unpleasing dispensation of providence, (1.) Study more what thou deservest, than consider what thou sustainest. Whatever thy condition be, thou hast deserved that it should have been worse. The fire is not answerable to thy fuel. Wonder more at what good thou hast, than at what thou wantest; and at the evil thou art without, than at that which thou undergoest. The godly say, "He hath not dealt with us after our sins, nor rewarded us after our iniquities." It is his mercy that we are not consumed. Our God hath punished us less than our iniquities. (2.) Mourn more for thy incorrigibleness under, than the unpleasantness of any providence; that thou hast been so long in the fire, and lost no more of thy dross; that folly is still so bound up in thy heart, notwithstanding all thy rods of correction, and that thou art that foolish child which stays so long in the place of breaking forth of children, Hos. xiii. 13. (3.) Labour more to make thy shoulder strong than to get thy burden taken off, and rather to be fit to endure cross providences than to have them ended. To this end, [1.] Look more upon providence as concluding than as at present, Prov. xxiii. 18; in the end thou shalt say the wilderness was the best way to Canaan, and that God dealt better by thee than thou couldst have done by thyself. Wait the winding up of providence, prejudge not God's proceedings; he oft turns water into wine. God's farthest way about will prove better than thy shorter cut. [2.] Clear up thy interest in Christ, and so possess thyself of true riches. If God be thy portion, thou wilt never complain it is small or smart. [3.] Labour to kill lust, which is the sting of every trouble, making a sweet condition bitter, and a bitter condition more bitter. Rather mend thy house than complain of the rain getting into it. Get affections weaned from the world. Count the greatest worldly gain small, and then thou wilt never think the greatest loss great. Love every thing, besides Christ, as about to leave and loathe it. [4.] Endeavour after submissiveness of heart. Say rather, Oh that I had patience under than riddance from my trouble! Study for an annihilated will, or rather to have thy will losing itself in God's. [5.] Compare thy lot with theirs who have less than thou hast, and yet deserve more than thou dost. If thy drink be small, others drink water; if thine be water, others drink gall; if thine be gall, others drink blood; if thine be blood, others drink damnation. [6.] Consider more whence every providence is than what it is: it is bitter in the stream, but sweet in the fountain. Observe the hand of a sovereign Lord, a wise Governor, a merciful Father, a righteous Judge. In precepts, consider not what is commanded, but who commands. In providence, not what is the correction, but who is the Corrector: the former will make thee obedient in doing; the latter, in suffering.

(4.) Remember, if thou hast a murmuring tongue, God has a hearing ear. God hears thee when thou mutterest most secretly, most inwardly. He who hears the groans of his own Spirit, hears the grumblings of thine. "The Lord," saith Moses, "heareth your murmurings," Exod. xvi. 7—9. If his ear be open, let thy mouth be stopped; be afraid thy God should hear thee. Murmuring is a great provocation.

(5.) Meditate of the folly and vanity of this sin of discontented murmuring against God. 1. Consider it cannot benefit and relieve us, Eccl. vii. 10. I may say of sinful complaining as Christ of sinful care, Which of you by complaining can add one cubit to his stature? Never did any find ease or obtain their desire by contending with God. An impatient murmurer is like a man sick of a burning fever, who tumbles and tosses from one side of the bed to the other for coolness, but till his distemper be removed he gets no ease. God must have his will; there is no escaping from him but by submitting to him. It is a vain thing for a man in a boat, by pulling with a cable at the rock, to think to draw the rock to him. 2. It is a distemper which disquiets him most in whom it is. The impatient murmurer is his own martyr, his afflictions are self-created. He would take it very ill to have another do half so much against him, as he does against his own soul. All his trouble is from his own pride, through which comes all contention with God and man. It is fulness of the stomach which makes a man sea-sick, and the proud heart which causes all the vexation in a troublesome estate. The arrow of murmuring shot up against God, falls down upon the head of him who shot it. The wild bull in the net, instead of breaking it, does by struggling the more hamper himself. 3. This sin of discontentedness deprives a man of all that spiritual benefit which he may reap by the troublesomeness of his worldly allotments. Were not men peevish and unsubmissive, they might take honey out of the carcass of every lion-like and tearing trouble. They might learn those lessons of heavenly-mindedness, meekness, faith, mortification, which would countervail for every cross. The silent and submissive acceptance of a severe dispensation turns every stone thrown at us into a precious stone, and produces the peaceable fruit of righteousness; whereas murmuring discontentedness makes us spend that time in beating ourselves, and wrangling with God, which we might profitably improve in labouring for a sanctified use of every dispensation.

This for the first proof that these seducers were those ungodly ones who shall be judged at the last day, viz. because they were "murmurers, complainers."

2. "Walking after their own lusts."

Two things are here to be opened. 1. Their guides who led them; "their own lusts." 2. Their following these guides; they walked after them.

(1.) Their guides are set down, 1. By way of specification; it is said they were "lusts." 2. By their relation, or their appropriation to these seducers; and so they are said to be "their own."

1. They are specified and denominated "lusts." Two things here are considerable. 1. What is meant by lusts. 2. Wherein their hurtfulness stands. [1.] The word ἐπιθυμία, lust, is indifferently used concerning lust, good or bad, denoting by its proper force only an ardent, earnest desire. And therefore there are lusts not only lawful and indifferent, being the motions of the concupiscible power, desiring such objects as tend to the preservation of nature, as meat, drink, rest, &c., Luke xvi. 21; but also holy and spiritual; in which respect the Spirit is said to lust against the flesh, Gal. v. 17, in regard of that new and holy inclination of the regenerate, whereby they endeavour to put off the old man, and to put on the

new. That which in insensible things is ὄρεξις, in the sensible and rational is ἐπιθυμία. But here, as elsewhere very frequently, the word ἐπιθυμία intends carnal, sinful, and corrupt lust. And this is twofold.

[1.] Original; that inordinate disposedness, that inbred and primitive pravity of nature, standing in an aversion from all good, and propension to all evil; the root not only of all wicked desires in the will, but also of all the evil thoughts in the understanding; and it is called lust, because it principally discovers itself by sinful lustings, and by them manifests its vigour and strength. And of this speaks the apostle James, chap. i. 15, " When lust hath conceived," &c.

[2.] Actual, is every sinful rising or inordinate motion against the law of God, every evil desire springing from the root of original concupiscence. And of these speaks the apostle, Eph. ii. 3, " We had our conversation in times past in the lusts of our flesh," &c.; and also Eph. iv. 22, " That ye put off concerning the former conversation the old man, which is corrupt according to the deceitful lusts." " Let not sin reign in your mortal body, that ye should obey it in the lusts thereof," Rom. vi. 12. Our natural corruption is the root which sends forth these lusts as its branches, and upon them grow those bitter fruits mentioned Gal. v. 19, 20, " Adultery, fornication, uncleanness, lasciviousness, idolatry, witchcraft, heresies," &c. Now these lusts are of two sorts. 1. The vicious inclinations of our minds, or of the upper or rational soul. We must not restrain lusts to the sensitive or lower part of the soul only, which they call the unreasonable, exempting the mind and reason from these blemishes; these lusts of the flesh into which the radical pollution of nature has diffused itself belonging to the understanding and reason also, as well as to the other inferior faculties; the very wisdom of the flesh being, as the apostle speaks, enmity against God, and such as cannot be subject to his law and will, Rom. viii. 7; for from hence is all impiety, idolatry, superstition, heresy, rejection of the truth; and indeed all those sins which directly are committed against the first table; and the apostle expressly mentions the wills of the mind, Eph. ii. 3, whereby he understands that superior part called διανοητική, intellective and discursive; and the apostle, speaking of those who drew others to the superstitious worship of angels, discovers that flesh is found in their very mind or understanding, in these words, " vainly puffed up by his fleshly mind," ὑπὸ τοῦ νόος τῆς σαρκὸς αὑτοῦ, Col. ii. 18. 2. The lower and more brutish appetites in the sensitive part of the soul, the motions to uncleanness, drunkenness, gluttony, the lusts called " of the flesh," 1 John. ii. 16, the vehement motions of the soul after sensual delights and carnal pleasures, which oft degenerate into beastly excess. These are called the θελήματα σαρκὸς, the wills of the flesh, Eph. ii. 3; joined also with pleasures, "serving divers lusts and pleasures," Tit. iii. 3; and called "worldly lusts," Tit. ii. 12; Rom. xiii. 14; 1 Pet. i. 14; ii. 11.

The original contagion of man's nature having poisoned and corrupted all the cogitations of the mind and conceptions of the heart, from them diffuses itself through the affections and inferior appetites, stirs up innumerable inordinate passions, to the breach of the second table of the law. And from the corruption of this inferior part the whole depravation of nature is, I conceive, called flesh; it drawing the unregenerate from things above and heavenly, to such as are below and earthly; from spiritual to corporal objects; from the Creator to the creature; and after a sort transforms a man into a beast. And these carnal desires, sensual lusts, are the guides which our apostle saith these seducers followed, as is evident from what he had expressed against them in the fourth verse, " turning the grace of God into lasciviousness ;" and ver. 8, " filthy dreamers defile the flesh ;" and ver. 10, " what they know naturally, as brute beasts, in those things they corrupt themselves ;" and ver. 12, " feeding themselves without fear," &c. And from these ungodly lusts, as he after calls them, the apostle may well prove them ungodly men.

[2.] The sinfulness of these sensual lusts appears in respect, 1. Of their objects, when such things are desired and craved as are forbidden, whether persons or things. 2. Of their measure, when things lawful are desired unlawfully because excessively; the desires after food, apparel, sleep, recreations, or any other sensual delights, being boundless, and concupiscence unlimited; when in eating men so gluttonize that their souls in their bodies are like a candle in a greasy lantern; when we grasp the world till we make our sinews crack. Oh how unsuitable is it for men to grow cold in prayer and hearing, and to sweat in the world; to account a little grace enough, and enough wealth a little! 3. Of their end, when things are desired not for the glory of God, but for our own pleasure, greatness, and benefit; not for the advancing of God, but ourselves; when we seek great things for ourselves, not for fitting us to duty, but for our carnal interest : all the good things we crave should be scaffolds to erect a building of honour to God, not to erect a structure of glory to ourselves. It is the part of an epicure, not of a Christian, to make his enjoyments centre in himself, and to sing with that sensualist in the midst of abundance, " Soul, thou hast much goods," &c., " take thine ease, eat, drink, and be merry." 4. Of their effects; and so they are sinful in being, 1. Entangling and encumbering; like long garments, which being let down about the heels, hinder from walking, and trip up in the race; and therefore the apostle commands us to gird up the loins of our minds. Hence by some they are not unfitly called the bird-lime of our spiritual wings; and by others compared to a string tied to a bird's leg, with which, flying unto the trees, she is hampered in the boughs. Inordinate lusts stop the Christian's progress heavenward; they hinder him in prayer, meditation, hearing, practising; they "choke the word," Mark iv. 19; and from the lusting of the flesh against the Spirit, the apostle saith, " Ye cannot do the things that ye would," Gal. v. 17 : women are led into error with divers lusts, 2 Tim. iii. 6. <small>Viscus spiritualium pennarum.</small>

(2.) These lusts are deceitful; so they are called expressly by the apostle, ἐπιθυμίαι τῆς ἀπάτης, cupiditates deceptionis, Eph. iv. 22, and that in several respects. 1. They are not what they seem to be. All the pleasures which are found in them are but false and appearing, not true, and real, and proper. But secondly, and especially, they are termed lusts of deception or error, because they do not what they promise; they are deluding and disappointing of that expectation which they raise up in any one. They promise honour, pleasure, riches, &c., but they perform nothing less, and make a man more miserable after all his endeavouring to satisfy them, than he was before; by their embraces they strangle. They who sow to the flesh, of the flesh reap corruption : lusts end in death, and therefore in disappointment. Like a chimney-piece, they are fair without, black within. They promise a Rachel, they give a Leah. They give not what, but contrary to what, they promise. What was Achan's wedge of gold, but an instrument to rive his body and soul asunder ? and what did his Babylonish garment clothe him with, but confusion ?

Hence they who will be rich are said to fall into many foolish lusts; that is, such as make them fools who fall into them, 1 Tim. vi. 9. Solomon speaks of a lustful fool, who went "as an ox to the slaughter, or as a fool to the correction of the stocks."

(3.) These lusts are defiling; they are unclean lusts, corrupt and corrupting. The old man is said to be "corrupt according to deceitful lusts," Eph. iv. 22. Christ tells us that the lusts which are within defile a man, Matt. xv. 18. They corrupt and defile the very body, as I have shown before, much more the soul, making it an unclean cage of unclean birds; they defile all we are, yea, all we do, prayers, hearings, sacraments. We lift up impure hands if in wrath.

(4.) Disquieting lusts; they are called noisome or hurtful, βλαβερας ἐπιθυμίας, damosas cupiditates, 1 Tim. vi. 9. Every man set upon lust troubles his own flesh. How many more are made martyrs to their lusts than to God himself! Oh the diseases, losses, torments, disgraces that uncleanness, drunkenness, ambition, wrath, covetousness, &c., have brought upon their vassals, who indeed are no other than very hackneys, whipped and driven through thick and thin in obedience to their lusts! But most of all do they fight against the soul, 1 Pet. ii. 11; by reason of their contrariety they tear and pull it several ways. They disquiet the conscience. The very worst and foulest days of a saint are better than the days of a sinner's sunshine. How many racks and silent scourges do sinners carry in their bosoms for satisfying their lusts! In a word, they drown the soul in perdition, and produce an eternity of pain for a moment of pleasure. To all this I might add the unquietness of men's lusts to others who live near them: "From whence," saith James, "come wars and fightings among you? come they not hence, even of your lusts?" chap. iv. 1.

This for the first particular, the denomination of these guides which these seducers followed; they were "lusts."

2. The relation of these lusts to these seducers is mentioned; the apostle calls them "their own;" and so they were in several regards, 2 Tim. iv. 3; James iv. 1, 3; 2 Pet. iii. 3; Jude 18.

(1.) In respect of propagation and derivation. Lust is the legacy left by our progenitors. It is a natural, inbred, hereditary propensity to sin, from which all those unholy motions and inordinate inclinations proceed, after which these seducers walked. Men are carried to the service of lust by the tide of nature as well as by the wind of temptation. Lusts are more truly ours than any thing left us by our parents.

(2.) In respect of seat and habitation. Lusts are our own because they are in us, in our hearts; they lie liegers for Satan in the soul, and there they are his proxies, spokesmen, and advocates. And therefore Christ saith, "Out of the heart proceed murders, adulteries, fornications, thefts," &c., Matt. xv. 19. Men lodge not strangers, but their own: "My children are with me in bed," Luke xi. 7. Lusts are our own, then, because we harbour them, lodge them, bed them, give them house-room, heart-room.

(3.) Their own in point of provision. Men provide for their own children and charge; and much more do they for their own lusts. The apostle speaks of making "provision for the flesh, to fulfil the lusts thereof," Rom. xiii. 14. The high fare, the impure dalliances, unclean objects of these seducers, were all provisions for their lusts. The work of the covetous, glutton, proud, &c., is to project for and provide fuel for lusts, like the poor Israelites, who painfully gathered stubble to please their task-masters.

(4.) Their own in point of protection and defence: as men provide for, so likewise protect their own. These seducers would not endure the wind to blow upon their lusts; hence it was that they spake evil of dignities appointed to curb their lusts. Hence they were raging waves, and gave the faithful hard words. Sometimes sinners protect their lusts with denial, with excuses, allegations of Scripture, appearances of sanctity; and if none of these will do, with fire and sword, open rage and opposition; yea, with tears and lamentations, as those women who wept for Tammuz, as if some gainful good were taken from them; as Micah cried for his gods; and as the harlot's bowels yearned over her own child.

(5.) Lastly, Their own in point of peculiarity of delight and dearness. Some lusts are peculiarly a man's own: such as to which he is given by constitution; so some men are addicted to gluttony, drunkenness, some to uncleanness, some to covetousness, others to ambition, &c. By interest; calling, the time, age, or place wherein he lives. David kept himself, as he saith, from his own iniquity, Psal. xviii. 23; that is, as I conceive by the subject of that psalm, from murdering Saul, a sin to which his interest tempted him. The reason why some men follow not some lusts, is because some are not so peculiarly their own; but stop them in the prosecution of their own, and then they show themselves.

Thus of the first branch of explication, the guides.

2. The following of these guides; "walking after," &c.

Πορευόμενοι, "walking;" a usual metaphor in Scripture to set forth the course of a man's life, whether good or bad. Zacharias and Elisabeth "were righteous," πορευόμενοι, "walking in all the commandments," &c., Luke i. 6. False teachers the apostle calls πορευομένους, those who "walk after the flesh," 2 Pet. ii. 10. So 2 Pet. iii. 3; 1 Pet. iv. 3.

And most fitly is this their following their lusts called a walking, in respect, 1. Of their motion, labour, and unquietness in the prosecution of them. A man who walks, sits not still, but is laborious and restless. None are such true drudges as they who serve their lusts, as Paul speaks, Tit. iii. 3. 2. It is called walking in respect of skilfulness. They who walk in a path are versed in it, and skilled in it, know every step of it: wicked men are wise to do evil, they are curious and witty workers of iniquity, Matt. vii. 23. 3. Walking, because of progressiveness. He who walks stands not at a stay, but goes on from step to step: the wicked grow worse and worse, they daily add something to their stature in sin; they add sin to sin; they never think they have done enough for lust; they are daily throwing some more mites into the treasuries of God's wrath and their own wickedness. 4. Walking, because they are going and tending to some term or place. The wages of sin, and the end of every lust, is death; though hell be not the end of the worker, yet is it of the work: every lust is hell in the bud, and it has fire and brimstone in the substance of it; damnation is its centre. 5. Walking, in point of a voluntary obsequiousness. Wicked men obey their lusts, willingly walk after the commands and dictates thereof. Saints are dragged, sinners walk after lust; they are not driven; they seek after their own heart, and their own eyes, after which they go a whoring, Numb. xv. 39. They are taken captives of the devil at his will, 2 Tim. ii. 26, ἐζωγρημένοι; taken alive by his baits without any resistance. Whatever lust, the devil's spokesman, dictates, they obey.

Obs. 1. All the visible abominations and notorious extravagancies in the world come from within. Lust is the womb of all the drunkenness, gluttony, adultery, murders: these things come from within, the heart; from the lusts that war in our members come wars and fightings. These seducers fell into all profaneness and licentiousness by following their lusts. A lustful heart makes a lewd life; that is the Trojan horse, from whence issue all hurtful practices. We see then the folly of only external mortification: what is the whipping of the flesh, lying in the ashes, voluntary poverty, outward abstinences, without inward mortification, but the plucking off the leaves without the withering of the root? The lusts must be destroyed inwardly, before ever practices can be with success amended outwardly. Christ so cursed the fig-tree that it withered at the root; that was the way for fruit never to grow on it more.

Obs. 2. In reformation it is not enough to forsake the evils we have no desires after, but we must leave our lusts, yea, our own lusts, those evils to which we are most inclined. Some men will say they are no sectaries, why, heresy is not their lust; others say they are not drunkards, when drunkenness is not their lust; the prodigal pleases himself that he is no covetous griper, &c.: but this is a token of sincerity, to forsake our own evil ways; and like those who, fighting with an enemy, mar every good piece of ground, to strike at those sins, which by custom, constitution, interest we are most addicted to.

Obs. 3. The course of a wicked man in sin is very earnest and impetuous. It is with a sinful lusting and an eager desire. Of this at large before, in Balaam's running greedily.

Obs. 4. It is the duty of faithful instructers, with holy Jude here, to tell men of their own lusts, to strike at those sins to which they see them most inclined. Thus did the prophets, who lifted up their voice like a trumpet, and told Judah of their transgressions. Thus did Christ, who reproved not only idolatry, but pharisaism and hypocrisy, the sins of his time. Otherwise ministers do but like unfaithful soldiers, who in war discharge not against the enemy, but shoot up into the air: though striking at men's lusts makes ministers hateful, yet it speaks them faithful.

Obs. 5. Miserable is the condition of the poor misled followers of seducing teachers. The seducer follows his lust, and the follower is led by the seducer; here it is true, the blind leads the blind. In all solicitations to follow others, we should consider whether they are led by Christ or by lust. Be followers of others only as they are led by Christ. You set your watches not by the clock, but by the sun; do so with your hearts.

Obs. 6. Great may be the comfort to God's people in case of inward, if hateful temptations. When motions come into the godly, and they do not lust after, but dislike them, nor entertain them with spiritual dalliance, they may be assured that those evils shall not be charged upon them. Before a temptation can be a sin, it must have somewhat of lusting in it. Christ was tempted as we are, and yet he sinned not, because he rejected his temptations. How great a comfort may it be, when Christ is thy love, and lust thy load!

Obs. 7. Though wicked men have their own several peculiar lusts, yet they all agree together against Christ. Pilate and Herod consent in this third. Envy moved the high priests against Christ, covetousness stirred up Judas, popularity Pilate, but all these lusts concentred in opposing Christ. Pharisees and Sadducees unite their forces against him, though they were mortal enemies between themselves. A fever and a lethargy are contrary to one another, yet both are against health; and therefore let not people please themselves in opposing some kind of sins, let them ask themselves whether there be not that within them that is enmity to Christ. And what a strong argument may this be to the godly, who have their lesser differences, to unite for Christ against sin!

Obs. 8. Every man's woe and wickedness arise from himself, his own lusts. The root of all is in ourselves. Every man forges his own confusion, and coins his own calamity. None is hurt purely from another. A man, as Augustine saith, is an Eve to himself. We must not altogether blame suggestions and temptations without. The devil tempted David to number the people, and to look at Bathsheba while bathing; but after both he confesses that he had sinned. It may in this case be said, *Nolenti non fit injuria;* None can hurt him that will not hurt himself. "Every man is tempted when he is drawn away of his own lust." Poison would never hurt unless taken in. The strongest enemy cannot hurt us, nor the falsest delude us, if we will be true to ourselves. Were there not a complying principle, outward objects of sin would draw out nothing but detestations; as in Christ, in whom, because Satan found nothing, he could do nothing against him. And it is the duty of the godly to make use of ungodly examples, not for imitation, but greater abhorrence. Saints, like fire in cold weather, should be hotter and holier for living in times of greatest coldness and profaneness. The best men have oft lived in worst places; as Lot, Elijah, Obadiah, &c., and shined as lights in the midst of a crooked nation; and redeemed the time, although, nay because, the days were evil. It is not outward power and opportunity to sin, but inward poison that makes us sin; and therefore in all our humiliations we should more angrily smite upon our own thighs, than upon any outward occasional furtherances to sin.

Obs. 9. The servitude and slavery of a man that follows his lust is very miserable. "Serving divers lusts," Tit. iii. 3. Oh how true a drudge is he that is a lackey to his lusts, and who has lusts for his leaders and commanders! (1.) A servant is hindered from doing any thing but what his master pleases. A servant to his lusts is in the bond of iniquity; hindered not only from doing, but even from willing to do any thing but what pleases his lusts; he is alienated from the life of God, cannot hear, pray, meditate holily: sometimes he is *in arcta custodia,* in close custody, not so much as able to go about the very outward works of holiness; at least he is *in libera custodia;* he cannot do them any further than his lusts allow, never spiritually; he is Satan's captive. The Romans cut off the thumbs of their slaves, that so they might be able to handle the oar, but not the sword; so the devil hinders his slaves from holy services, but leaves them in a posture of activity for sin. Satan gives some of his slaves longer line than he gives to others, but he ever keeps them in his power. (2.) A servant is servilely employed: the Gibeonites were "hewers of wood, and drawers of water." A sinner is put upon basest and hardest works; like the Israelites in Egypt, who had their shoulders under burdens, and were put upon base and dirty drudgeries. Issachar couched under his burden like an ass. A wicked man takes pains to go to hell; his employments are most painful and vile: the working days of a saint are better than the holidays of a sinner. Christ's yoke is easy, and his burden light. (3.) A servant is beaten, breast-beaten, back-beaten. Oh the wounds of conscience that sinners get in the service of their lusts! there is no peace to them; they carry furnaces in their breasts, silent scourges; not to speak of the wounds upon their bodies, health, names, estates. (4.) A servant is rewarded; but what are the sinner's wages? Summed up they are in that one word, (how comprehensive!) death. The very work of a saint is abundant wages; the very wages of a sinner his greatest woe. After sinners have drudged for lusts all the days of their lives, Satan lodges them in flaming sheets at night. He who has now been their tempter will then be their tormenter. And yet how unlike is a servant to lusts to a servant unto men!

[1.] The work of a man's servant is at length at an end; a sinner's work is never done: *peccator nunquam feriatur,* sinners have no holidays; they drudge without intermission: on the sabbath they sin, in prayer, hearing, sacraments, in eating, drinking, recreations; on earth, in hell.

[2.] A man's servant is weary of his servitude, groans like the Israelites under his bondage, and desires delivery. A slave to lust loves to be so still; he is a bored slave that will not be free, but accounts every one his enemy that would deliver him; he thinks his servitude his liberty, his prison his palace.

[3.] Among men, one master has many servants, but spiritually one servant has many masters; "serving," saith the apostle, "divers lusts and pleasures," Tit. iii. 3; yea, these masters are contrary, some haling this way, others another. Covetousness hales one way, prodigality and pride another; ambition drags one way, uncleanness another. A sinner by these lusts is drawn as by wild horses.

<small>Quot habet dominos qui unum non habet!</small>

[4.] Among men, the master is better and more honourable than the servant; but a servant to lusts serves masters that are infinitely below and baser than himself; a man never goes below himself but when he serves them. Every lust is Satan's offspring: how unworthy is that servitude when a heaven-born soul has such a master! Only sin disennobles intellectual nature, making men sinners, and angels devils. Concerning the means of opposing and overcoming lusts I have treated before.

3. *Their boasting.* The third proof which our apostle brings to show that these seducers were ungodly men, and to be judged at the last day, is set down in the words, wherein he taxes them of their proud, arrogant boasting, "their mouth speaketh great swelling words." These words, "great swelling words," are in the Greek expressed in this one word, ὑπέρογκα, which signifies not only big, bulky, bunching out, or swelling, but all these to a very great measure, or, as some, beyond measure; the composition increasing the signification, and importing that these seducers spake words of a vastly rising, swelling, mountainous bigness. Thus Plutarch useth the word ὑπέρογκος, when he saith that λέξις ὑπέρογκος, turgid or swelling speech, is very unfit to be used about civil affairs. And a very apt and true accusation is this brought against these false teachers by Jude; it having been the constant course of heretics to speak very high and swelling words, of arrogant boasting. Jerom applies this expression of swelling words to Jovinian, whom, saith he, the apostle describes speaking with swollen cheeks, and puffed-up expressions.

<small>Vulg. superba. Bez. tumida. Tigur. vehementer fastuosa. Alii, prætumida, supra modum turgida, immensa. Projicit ampullas et sesquipedalia verba. Horat.</small>

<small>Ἡ μὲν λέξις ὑπέρογκος ἀπολίτευτός ἐστι. De Educ. lib.</small>

<small>Descripsit sermo apostolicus Jovinianum loquentem buccis tumentibus et inflata verba trutinantem. Hier. l. 1. Contr. Jovin.</small>

Two things may here be opened. 1. What the apostle meant by "great swelling words." 2. Wherein stands the sinfulness of using them.

1. For the first. In two respects might their words be called swelling: 1. In respect of the things that they spake. 2. Of their manner of speaking them.

1. In respect of the things they spake; and that, (1.) Of God; and so they might speak great swelling words against him either when they blasphemed him in their murmuring and complaining of his providences, or otherwise in uttering blasphemous expressions against his glorious and Divine excellencies. We read of those who "set their mouth against the heavens," Psal. lxxiii. 9; and of the beast it is said, that "there was given him a mouth speaking great things and blasphemies," Rev. xiii. 5. Antichrist "exalteth himself above all that is called God," 2 Thess. ii. 4. Pope Nicholas blasphemously decreed that the pope was not subject to the secular power, because God could not be judged by man. The pope calls himself a god on earth; to him, he saith, is given all power in heaven and in earth; he takes away the sins of the world; he is the lion of the tribe of Judah, the saviour of the world, &c.

<small>Oraculis vocis mundi moderaris habemus, Et merito in terris crederis esse Deus. Omnia quæ Dei, quæ Christi sunt, sibi usurpat; tollit peccata mundi, dominans a mari ad mare. Leo de tribu Judæ, mundi salvator, &c. Illi acclamatur, Tu es omnia, et super omnia: tibi data est omnis potestas in cœlo et in terra. Vid. Paræum. in Apoc. 13. v. 3.</small>

(2.) They might speak great swelling words in respect of others. 1. Magistrates, of whom they spake evil, and whom they despised, and from subjection to whom they openly professed that they were exempted. 2. Their words in respect likewise of common persons might be swelling; as, 1. By threatening curses against them who would not embrace their errors: threatening words are swelling words. Thus Goliath, Rabshakeh, Jezebel, Benhadad uttered their swelling threats. 2. By great and swelling defamations, making their throats open sepulchres to bury the names of those who opposed them; they being valiant in calumniation, but weak in confutation; they spake evil of what they knew not. 3. By promising great and admirable privileges of peace, pleasure, liberty to those who would embrace their errors. Thus we read, 2 Pet. ii. 18, while they spake "great swelling words of vanity, they allure through the lusts of the flesh," i. e. by promising pleasure; and ver. 19, "they promise them liberty;" like mountebanks, they proclaimed the virtue of their salves, the better to put them off. Thus the false prophet Zedekiah, making him horns of iron, promised that with those the king should push the Syrians till he had destroyed them. Thus the devil, that great seducer, promised to Christ all the kingdoms of the world and their glory, if he would fall down and worship him, Matt. iv. 9.

(3.) Their words were swelling in regard of themselves and those of their own party, whom they cried up with full mouths for their knowledge and piety: hence they arrogated to themselves the title of Gnostics, or knowing men, and perfect ones; they commended themselves, as if they alone had the monopoly of wisdom, and had only insight into deep and profound mysteries; as if all others in comparison of them were poor, short-sighted people, and as far short of them for quick-sightedness as the owl is short of the eagle. Thus Tertullian describes them, when he saith, They all swell, they all promise wisdom, they are perfect catechumens before they are taught: how malapert are the very women, who are so bold as to teach, contend, &c.! Irenæus likewise, describing the pride of the Gnostics, saith, they call themselves perfect, as if none were able to equalize them for the greatness of their knowledge; as if Peter, or Paul, or any of the apostles, were inferior to them for knowledge; the greatness whereof they make as if they had drunk up and devoured; boasting of such a height as if they were above all virtue. Pride, saith Jerom, is the mother of their iniquity,

<small>Omnes tument, omnes scientiam pollicentur, ante sunt perfecti catechumeni, quam edocti. Ipsæ mulieres hæreticæ quam procaces? quæ audeant docere, contendere, exorcismis agere, curationes repromittere, forsan et tingere. Tert. de Præscrip. c. 41. Perfectos seipsos vocant, &c. Iren l. 1. c. 9. Matrem habent iniquitatis suæ superbiam, dum semper se scire altiora jactitant. Hier. in Hos. v. Ὑπὲρ τὸν ἀποστόλων φρονοῦντες,</small>

while they boast of their knowledge in the highest mysteries. They think higher of themselves, saith Clemens Alexandrinus, than ever did the apostle.

φυσιούμενοι καί φρυαττόμενοι. 1. Pædag. c. 6.

Arius, that pestilent heretic, as Athanasius reports, proudly boasted that he had received his doctrine from the elect of God, men that knew God, and had received the anointing of the Spirit. But concerning the high boastings of heretics I have spoken before.

2. They might be said to speak swelling words, in respect of the manner of speaking those things which they uttered; and that both in respect, 1. Of their voice; and, 2. Style.

(1.) In respect of their voice; it might be with that height and loudness which savoured of a proud boisterousness. Peter, 2 Epist. ii. 18, mentioning their speaking " great swelling words," uses the word φθεγγόμενοι, which properly signifies their lifting up their voices, and making a great noise, a bellowing or roaring like beasts; as if these seducers placed their victory in the loud contention of their voices. Thus the idolatrous Ephesians lifted up their voices to the height, when they cried out with so much rage, " Great is Diana of the Ephesians," Acts xix. 28, 34.

Indicatur hæreticos resonare, vociferari, mugire, sonum sine fructu emittere, in clamore vocisque contentione victoriæ summam constituere. Lorin. in 2 Pet. ii. 18.

(2.) In respect of their style or phrase wherein they uttered what they spake. It has been the course of seducers to speak bubbles of words, sublime strains, strong lines, big and new expressions, that they, being not understood, may be admired: what they want in the weight of matter, they make up in the persuasiveness of wooing words. Their novel doctrines were clothed with new and formerly unheardof expressions. They laid aside the form of wholesome words, 2 Tim. i. 13, consented not to it; but being proud, they doted about strifes of words, 1 Tim. vi. 3, 4: their speeches in this respect are aptly by the apostle twice called " vain babblings," κενοφωνίας, mere empty cracks of words, windy expressions, without any substance; or, as Chrysostom, καινοφωνίας, new-coined expressions. Thus Paul, Rom. xvi. 18, tells us of some that διὰ τῆς χρηστολογίας καὶ εὐλογίας, " by good words and fair speeches," by a winning, meretricious wording of what they delivered, " deceived the hearts of the simple;" and Peter, 2 Epist. ii. 3, πλαστοῖς λόγοις, " with feigned words they make merchandise of you." They resembled merchants, who commend their wares to sale by using false words fitted to that purpose. Seducers' doctrines, like some empty boxes in the apothecaries' shops, or some sorry book that the stationer has a mind to put off, shall have goodly titles affixed to them. And commonly, especially at the first broaching of an error, seducers are wont to shadow and cloud what they utter in obscure and doubtful expressions, and to swathe their heresy while it is yet in its infancy in the clothing of obscurity.

2. The sinfulness of using these great swelling words is considerable,

(1.) In the hypocrisy of it. Seducers put beautiful colours upon that which within is blackness and rottenness, gay titles upon empty books and boxes; they speak lies in hypocrisy. Oh how contrary is this both to a God of truth, and the truth of God! they deal with their persons and opinions as some popes have done, who, in naming themselves, have such names of holiness imposed upon them, as are most contrary to their ungodly natures and dispositions.

(2.) In the seducing others, who by hearing the high promises, and viewing the holy appearances of godliness affixed to opinions and persons, are led away to their own destruction after them both. Words are too oft esteemed according to the estimate of the speaker. Tertullian observes that sundry were edified into error by the example and high reputation of those that had fallen into error: though we should judge of persons by their faith, yet commonly we do judge of faith by persons. Having the gifts and persons of men in admiration has drawn many to follow their pernicious ways. Men of renown, like Korah's accomplices, perish not alone; and yet is there any who hath not sins enough of his own to answer for, unless he become likewise a misleader of others, and so contract their sins upon himself likewise?

Tert.de Præscrip. contr. Hær. c. 3.

(3.) In the destructiveness of this arrogant boasting to him who uses it. How impossible is it that ever he should blush at those errors and impieties whereof he boasts! They who will speak highly of their own follies are furthest from amendment, and, by consequence, furthest from mercy. The boasting Pharisee was further from mercy than the blushing publican, Luke xviii. 12, 14. Recovery cannot be obtained but in a way of confession. A proud boaster obstructs to himself the way of his own happiness; others may, he must, miscarry. And how hard is it for one who has spoken highly of his own person or opinion, ever to veil his proud and sinful gallantry by a humble and holy retractation!

Obs. 1. None are so ready to commend themselves as they who are least commendable. They who are lowest in worth are commonly highest in boasting: they who are emptiest of grace swell most with pride. Wicked men advance, saints debase themselves. Goliath, Rabshakeh, Benhadad, Jezebel, Nebuchadnezzar, Sennacherib, &c. were all egregious boasters. And among other titles which the apostle gives those wicked men, he calls them " boasters," 2 Tim. iii. 2. But mark the language of saints: Abraham calls himself dust and ashes. Jacob speaks himself not worthy of the least of all God's mercies. David saith, and that as a type of Christ, that he was " a worm, and no man." Agur, that he was " more brutish than any man, and had not the understanding of man." When Paul had said that he " laboured more than they all," he corrects himself by adding, " not I, but the grace of God with me," 1 Cor. xv 10. Though Luke writes that Matthew made Christ a great feast, yet Matthew himself saith Christ did eat with him, Luke v. 29; Matt. ix. 10, 11. As humility makes way for more grace, so grace ever makes way for more humility. They who have most grace ever most see their own want of grace: that which a man boasts of when he is in his natural estate, he blushes at when God opens his eyes; he is now, saith the apostle, ashamed of it, Rom. vi. 21. Paul, a Pharisee, accounted himself blameless and perfect; Paul, a Christian, reckoned himself the chief of sinners, and the least of saints. Of some we say, when they are single, they want nothing but a wife; but when they are married, they want every thing else. They who are without grace say they want little or nothing; they who have grace see they want every thing. They are poor people who cry in London streets what they have; the richest merchant holds his peace, and proclaims not his wealth to the world. Besides, a wicked man makes himself his end, and improves all his endowments to self-advancement; and therefore the more wicked, the more he sets up himself by boasting of what he has. Moses was a beautiful child, and his parents hid him; they who have most beauty most hide it: a child of God, like Moses, when God appeared in the bush, hides his face and pulls off his shoes; covers what is comely, and confesses what is deformed and uncomely. Pride, then, is both a sign and a cause of want of grace: a saint ever sees he has enough to be thankful, and thinks he never has enough to be proud.

Obs. 2. Self-advancement is a sin and folly to be shunned. Let another praise thee, and not thyself; a stranger, and not thine own lips. They who strove in the Olympic games, when victors, never put the crown upon their own heads, but that honour was done them by another. It is our duty to do things worthy of praise, our sin and folly to praise ourselves for doing them. Our works should praise us, not our words. It is said of Greg. Nazianzen, that he was high in his performances, but low in his opinion. It is our duty to carry ourselves so, as our very enemies may be forced to speak well of us; and some have noted that the word נכרי stranger, Let a stranger praise, &c., Prov. xxvii. 2, sometimes signifies an enemy in Scripture; but we ourselves are of all men the unfittest for that employment: praise is comely in thy enemy's mouth, not comely in thy friend's, uncomely in thine own. The performances which, another reporting them, appear glorious, being related by thyself, lose all their lustre; because they who praise their own good deeds are thought not therefore to report them because they did them, but therefore to have done them that afterward they might report them. A man in commending does not, yea, undoes what he is doing. "Thou bearest record of thyself," said the Pharisees; "thy record is not true." When Paul mentioned his own necessary praise, he saith he "speaks foolishly," 2 Cor. xi. 16, 17, 21, and that he was "become a fool in glorying," 2 Cor. xii. 11, though he were compelled thereto. A man should not therefore do any good that he may have a good report, but therefore, and only therefore, desire a good report that he may be in the greater capacity of doing good. If a man commend himself, he should do it modestly and constrainedly, for the advantage of the gospel. Paul speaks his commendation as belonging to a third person, "I knew a man," &c., 2 Cor. xii. 2; and ver. 11, "Ye have compelled me," &c. But ordinarily we should neither praise nor dispraise ourselves; even the latter of these being the giving of others an occasion to praise us, and oft a putting of praise, as one saith aptly, to usury, that we may receive it with the greater advantage. To conclude, if it be a sin to praise ourselves when we have done good, how great an impiety is it to glory in evil! the former discovers the corruption of a man, the latter of a devil. Lastly, though it be a sin for a man to commend himself, yet it is our duty to praise the good we see in and done by others, that God may be honoured, who was the Author of all good, and men encouraged; the doer to proceed, the beholder to imitate him.

Obs. 3. Great swelling words should not seduce us from the truth. We should not regard the words, but the weight of every teacher; nor who speaks, but what is spoken: "The kingdom of God is not in word, but in power," 1 Cor. iv. 20. We must not dislike truth because the bearer's words are low and contemptible, nor embrace error because the words of him who brings it are lofty and swelling. A Christian should be a man in understanding, not like a little child, ready to swallow whatever the nurse puts to the mouth. We should ever be more forward to examine by Scripture, with the noble Bereans, the truth of what is taught us, than to be bewitched, like the foolish Galatians, with the words of any teacher; suspect the cause that needs them, and the men that use them: as a rotten house, so a rotten cause, needs most props. Truth, like a beautiful face, needs no painting. Though he were one that speaks big, nay, with the tongue of an angel, nay, were an angel; yet if he preached another gospel, we should hold him accursed. Christians should labour for knowledge to discern between great words and good words, or rather between good words and good matter.

This for the third proof that these seducers were those ungodly men who should be judged at the last day, viz. because they spake "great swelling words."

4. Their admiration of men's persons; "having men's persons in admiration because of advantage."

In which words our apostle, 1. Describes what they did; they had "men's persons in admiration." 2. Discovers why they did it; for "advantage."

1. What they did; "having men's persons in admiration."

That we may understand the sin wherewith these seducers are here charged in admiring persons, we must first open these two expressions.

1. Persons, and admiring, or having them in admiration.

2. Show what admiring of persons is here by the apostle condemned, and why.

1. The word persons in the original is πρόσωπα: now though πρόσωπον signifies the face, and properly answers to a Hebrew word of the same signification, yet in Scripture it is taken several ways. Not to speak of the divers acceptations of the word in Scripture when attributed to God, as being too remote from our present purpose; when it is used concerning the creature, (1.) It is given to things without life; as Matt. xvi. 3; Luke xii. 56, "Ye can discern the face of the sky;" that is, the outward show or appearance. Luke xxi. 35; Acts xvii. 20, we read of the "face of the earth;" in which places it is taken for the superficies or outside. (2.) Most frequently to man; and so, 1. Properly, it signifies his face and countenance. Thus Matt. vi. 16, "They disfigure their faces;" and ver. 17, "Wash thy face." So Matt. xxvi. 67, "Then did they spit in his face." 2. His person; as 2 Cor. i. 11, "The gift bestowed upon us by the means of many persons," ἐκ πολλῶν προσώπων. 3. His bodily presence, 1 Thess. ii. 17, "We being taken from you" προσώπῳ, "in presence." 4. A man as accomplished with his gifts, excellencies, or endowments, real or appearing; which are outwardly beheld, or looked upon to belong to him; for which he is oft unduly respected, either in regard of his own body, mind, or outward condition; and thus it is taken Matt. xxii. 16; Mark xii. 14, where the Herodians tell Christ that he regarded not πρόσωπον, "the person of men;" and Acts x. 34, "God is no respecter of persons." So Rom. ii. 11. And thus I take it in this place, where Jude accuses these servile seducers for their excessive sinful flattering of men in eminence, advanced in respect of their outward state of wealth, honour, &c., for their own private gain and advantage.

The other expression is admiring, or, as we render it, having in admiration, θαυμάζοντες. It signifies two things. (1.) To wonder at a thing in respect of its strangeness, unusualness, at which men look very earnestly and intently. Thus it is taken Matt. viii. 27, where it is said that Christ rebuking the winds and the sea, the men marvelled, ἐθαύμασαν. So Matt. xxi. 20, when the fig-tree withered, it is said the disciples marvelled; when Christ had with such admirable wisdom answered the insnaring question of the Herodians, it is said they marvelled, Matt. xxii. 22; xxvii. 14; Luke i. 21, 63; iv. 22; xi. 38.

(2.) It signifies highly to honour, fear, or reverence the person or thing which we look upon as strange;

and thus some take it Matt. viii. 10, when Christ heard of the centurion's faith, it is said, ἐθαύμασε, "he marvelled;" that is, say some, he respected and honoured his faith. *Vid. Ravanel in Tit. admiratio.* Thus it is taken in this place of Jude. These seducers honoured highly, advanced, and praised the endowments and qualifications of great men for advantage; and probable it is, that the apostle expresses their honouring of men's persons by admiring them, because the Septuagint so translates those places where honour and respect to persons is mentioned. When Naaman the Syrian is said to be honourable, the Septuagint render the phrase τεθαυμασμένος προσώπω, admired in his person. So Deut. x. 17, "The Lord regardeth not persons." 2 Chron. xix. 7.

2. What admiring of persons is to be condemned as unlawful. Certainly all kind of admiring persons is not unlawful before God, nor disallowed by the apostle. Honour to the persons of others may lawfully be given, even for those gifts and endowments wherewith God has furnished them, whether outward or inward: for the outward glory and majesty which God gave Nebuchadnezzar, "all people trembled and feared before him," Dan. v. 19. And God commands honour to parents natural and political; and the elders who rule well are to be counted worthy of double honour. And some are deservedly preferred before others for their age, calling, gifts, graces, relation to us. But several ways admiring of persons is unlawful. I shall reduce them all to these two heads; as this admiration of man more particularly concerns, 1. God. 2. Man. (1.) The admired. (2.) The admirer. (3.) Others.

1. As it may concern God. And thus we admire men sinfully,

(1.) When we so admire man as that we honour him without eyeing God's command. The lowest service must be done in obedience to the highest Master: our earthly parent must be honoured and admired because our heavenly Father enjoins it. An earthly master must not be honoured and served with an eye only to his command, but out of conscience of duty to God's command. Herein must we resemble that noble Roman, who, disdaining to bow before a foreign prince, when he came into his presence, let fall his ring, which he stooping to take up, and thereupon the prince insulting, the Roman utters these words, *Non tibi, sed annulo*; I bow not to thee, but to take up my ring. Or as that Frederic Barbarossa, who kneeling down before the pope to receive his crown, said, *Non tibi, sed Petro*; Not to thee, but to Peter. The apostle makes the application when he enjoins servants to "be obedient unto masters as unto Christ; not as men-pleasers, but as the servants of Christ," Eph. vi. 5, 6; and "not as men-pleasers, but," &c., "fearing God," Col. iii. 22.

(2.) When we so admire men as to honour and serve them in those things which they command against God. Our earthly lord must be obeyed, but our heavenly Lord must be preferred. When these two come in competition, we are disobedient unless we be disobedient. Against my heavenly Father's will I neither owe burial to my dead, nor obedience to my living father. Whether it be right to obey God or man, saith the apostle, "judge ye," Acts iv. 19. "Ephraim is oppressed and broken in judgment, because he willingly walked after the commandment," Hos. v. 11.

(3.) When we so admire men for any excellency as not to give the glory thereof to God. The sweetness of the stream must not make us forget the fountain. Men must be honoured as instruments, not adored as deities. It was cursed, and it proved costly flattery which was given to Herod, when the people shouted, "It is the voice of a god, and not of a man: because he gave not God the glory," he was smitten, "and eaten of worms," Acts xii. 22, 23. That must not be offered to any which the best never durst take, namely, the praise of having or doing any thing of themselves. How fearful have holy men been in their highest performances, lest any of God's glory should cleave to their fingers! When Peter had wrought that great miracle of healing the cripple, and the people greatly wondered, fearing the sinful admiring of his person, he takes all honour from himself, and casts it upon Christ: "Ye men of Israel," saith he, "why look ye so earnestly on us, as though by our own power or holiness we had made this man to walk? The God of Abraham," &c., "hath glorified his Son Jesus," &c., Acts iii. "Barnabas and Paul rent their clothes" when the people were about to sacrifice to them, Acts xiv. 14. "I laboured," saith Paul, "more abundantly than they all; yet not I, but the grace of God which was with me," 1 Cor. xv. 10. "Our sufficiency is of God," 2 Cor. iii. 5. "Who is Paul, or who is Apollos, but ministers by whom ye believed? I have planted, Apollos watered; but God gave the increase. So then neither is he that planteth any thing," &c., 1 Cor. iii. 5—7: the Corinthians' faith was not to "stand in the wisdom of men, but in the power of God," 1 Cor. ii. 5. People are commonly in extremes, either they deify men, or nullify them; either they make them dwarfs or giants: but for people so to admire any men as to ascribe their conversion or edification to them; as if men were not only God's instruments and Christ's servants, but Gods and Christs themselves; and as if their grace were from the abilities of the teacher, and not from the power of Christ; is a very plainly sinful admiring of men's persons, even to an unchairing of Christ, and a lifting up of man into his seat; to a depriving the Shepherd and Bishop of our souls, and a substituting another in his room. In a word, it is all one, as to thank the axe for building the house, and to attribute nothing to the carpenter. Nor indeed is it any other than idolatry.

(4.) When we so admire and honour men as to put that trust and confidence in them which we owe only to God. "Thou," saith Job, "art my confidence," Job xxxi. 24. "He is the confidence of all the ends of the earth," Psal. lxv. 5. "Put your trust in the Lord," Psal. iv. 5. "Trust in him at all times," Psal. lxii. 8; so Psal. xxxvii. 5. But men, though never so full of love, skill, strength, must not have our trust. "Put not confidence in a guide," Micah vii. 5. "It is better to trust in the Lord than to put confidence in princes," Psal. cxviii. 9. "Every man at his best state is altogether vanity," Psal. xxxix. 5. "Cease from man, whose breath is in his nostrils; for wherein is he to be accounted of?" Isa. ii. 22. Man is to be used as a wand in our hand, not leaned upon as our staff or support; in subordination to, not instead of God; only as one that can help us, if God will help him; as one that of himself cannot move, or undertake, much less accomplish any good for us. Oh how oft has God snapped in sunder all these rotten crutches in England! and how many lectures of vanity has he read upon men in greatest admiration!

(5.) When we so admire men as to fear their power more than God's. Men are sinfully admired, both when they, being for us, appear to us so great as that God need not help us; and when they, being against us, appear so great as that God cannot help us. Man is idolized both by looking upon him as one that can work without God, and much more by looking upon him as able to work against God. How sinfully did the Israelites admire the persons of the giants in

Canaan, in respect of their strength and stature! How sinfully did David admire Saul, when against God's promise he said he should perish by his hand! Thus the Israelites sinfully admired the Egyptians, when upon the sight of them, notwithstanding the word and works of God, they tell Moses in their march that he took them "away to die in the wilderness," Exod. xiv. 11. "Who art thou, that thou shouldst be afraid of a man that shall die?" &c., "and forgettest the Lord thy Maker?" Isa. li. 12, 13. The fearing of man is the forgetting of God.

(6.) When we admire men's goodness, or what of God we see in men, their persons, loving the message for the messenger, the liquor for the vessel, holy instruction for the sake of him who gives it; and so hearing the word of God as the word of man: this is to prefer a man of God before God in a man, or rather man before God; and, contrary to what Tertullian speaks, not to judge of persons by faith, but of faith by persons.

2. Admiration of persons is sinful as it concerns man. (1.) As it concerns the admired; and so admiration of persons is sinful,

[1.] When we admire such persons as are not able to bear their own admiration. A proud man having done any thing commendably, is not fit to be commended. Some weak brains will be turned with a small quantity of wine; others more strong will endure more. Herod was intoxicated with applause, when the people cried him up for a god; but Paul and Barnabas rend their clothes, and are ready to sacrifice themselves, when the people meditate a sacrificing to them. A weak stomach cannot concoct fat morsels; he is a man of strong grace who can hear his own commendations without hurt. Nothing more discovers a man than praising him. "As the fining pot for silver, and the furnace for gold; so is a man to his praise," Prov. xxvii. 21.

[2.] When we so admire persons as thereby to make a prey of them, or to overthrow either their bodies or souls. Thus the Herodians admired and honoured Christ, telling him that he was true, and taught the way of God in truth, and regarded "not the person of man," Matt. xxii. 16; but all this was but to entangle and destroy him, by bringing him on to answer a captious question. Thus afterward Christ was betrayed with a kiss; and not seldom have we known that men have lain in ambush behind the thickets of commendation and admiration, and so unsuspectedly fallen upon the unwary and credulous hearer. Jael gives her nail soon after her milk; and poison is oftenest drunk in gold. Thus after the death of Jehoiada, the princes of Judah came and made obeisance to king Joash, whereby they prevailed with him to leave the house of the Lord, and to serve groves and idols, 2 Chron. xxiv. 17, 18; and thus, as ecclesiastical history tells us, Simon Magus cried up Nero above the clouds, and accounted and called him a god, to make him the greater enemy to the Christians. Thus Tertullus admired the person of Felix, that thereby he might stir him up against Paul, Acts xxiv. 2, 3.

[3.] When we so admire persons as to cover, hide, and excuse their sin because of their greatness; a sin the greater, because greatness ought to be so far from being a cloak for, that it is an aggravation of sin, and makes it the more heinous. A wicked person in Scripture phrase is but a vile person, and by so much the more vile, by how much the more he corrupts and abuses any eminent gifts and endowments which God has bestowed upon him. The word speaks as basely of rich wicked ones, as they think contemptibly of God's people. That wicked king was very low in the eyes of the holy prophet, who said, "Were it not that I regard the person of Jehoshaphat king of Judah, I would not look toward thee, nor see thee," 2 Kings iii. 14. Unsanctified greatness is most likely to be pernicious, and therefore should be most reprehended.

(2.) Admiration of persons is sinful as it concerns the admirer; and so,

[1.] When we so admire persons as thereby only to advance and advantage ourselves; and that, 1. Either in profit and gain; or, 2. In honour or reputation. 1. In profit: and thus these seducers here admired great ones, and honoured their greatness for their own advantage, servilely cringing and crouching to them for filthy lucre; they gave them great titles, and flattered them in sin, and assented to them in every thing, that they might fill their purses; and, as Peter speaks, through covetousness, did they with feigned words make merchandise of people, hereby showing that they neither served Christ, nor indeed those whom they flattered, but their own bellies; at once laying off both the Christians and the man. 2. In honour and reputation: and for this end sometimes the persons of great men are admired, as Mr. Fox tells us that the bloody tiger, Stephen Gardiner, was wont to admire the person of Henry VIII., speaking of him to others with greatest honour, and calling him his gracious lord and master, only to be looked upon as his favourite, though he knew that the king never loved him. But for honour hypocrites commonly admire the persons of good men; admire their persons, I say, though they imitate not their practices. Thus Saul desired the presence of Samuel, to be honoured before the people. Thus the scribes and Pharisees admired the dead prophets, only to be accounted, as they were, holy.

[2.] When we so admire persons as withal to imitate their sins and imperfections. Thus these seducers were so admired, as that many followed their damnable errors, putting no difference between their faces and the warts, their speaking and stammering. The falls and folly of the admired are commonly the snares of the admirers; and the error of the master oft the temptation of the scholar. It is very hard to admire the person of another, and not to imitate his imperfections.

(3.) Admiration of persons is sinful as it concerns and hurts others; and so,

[1.] When for some commendable actions or endowments we so admire a person, who is in most things very discommendable, and a known wicked person, that thereby we give occasion to the hearer, who is, though wicked, yet not so wicked as he, to judge his own condition very good, and to bless and flatter himself in his sin, as thinking that he deserves commendation as well as or better than the other. This I have ever thought to be one stratagem whereby the hands of the wicked have been strengthened in sin; and a stumbling-block which some either weakly or wickedly have laid before others. Thus I have oft heard, even with grief, when in funeral sermons a profane drunkard, a swearer, an adulterer, or one perhaps at the most but civilly honest, for some few good deeds has been cried up and even sainted by the preacher, that the most wicked persons have been ready to saint themselves, and to say, If such a one were commendable, and praised by our minister for a good man, I thank God it is much better with me, I never was guilty of half his extravagancies, and I see I may be a good man, yea, and commended when I am dead, notwithstanding my failings, though I be not so pure as some are. Oh how unsuitable is it, that by funeral sermons men should be made more unfit for death! to paint those in the pulpit who are punished in hell! and that a minister should be strewing that dead body with flowers, whose soul is bathing in flames! For my part, though I should not deny due commendation, even at a funeral, to some eminently exemplary saint, or publicly useful instrument; yet mostly, I think, his speech concerning the deceased may suffice, who said, If he were good, he did not desire; if bad, he did not deserve, praise.

[2.] When we so admire the persons of some instructers, as to neglect and despise others who haply deserve better than they: the sin of the Corinthians, when the apostle tells them of their glorying in men, 1 Cor. iii. 21; some teachers being so gloried in peculiarly, as if they were only worth hearing, and none else to be regarded. Some accounted Paul the only teacher, some delighted only in Apollos, some magnified Peter as the alone worthy man; thus they thought of men above what was meet, and they were puffed up for one against another. They gloried in some, disdaining all others as not to be named with them, though teachers of the same truth, because they had a high conceit of their learning, wit, eloquence, holiness, or the like qualifications. A great sin doubtless, and, I fear, the common sin of this city. How unthankful for the bounty of Christ do men make themselves hereby, who gave all the ministers of the gospel to be theirs for their good! "All things," saith the apostle, "are yours, whether Paul, or Apollos, or Cephas," 1 Cor. iii. 21, 22. It is unthankfulness to a bountiful prince, when he bestows many lordships on his favourite, if he should regard one of them only, and despise all the rest. Yea, how injuriously is the Spirit of Christ hereby reproached! for the despising those who are of small gifts is a reproaching of the Spirit of God, as if he were defective in his gifts; whereas their variety sets forth the fulness and freeness of God's Spirit, who divideth "to every man severally as he will," and "worketh all these," 1 Cor. xii. 11. Besides, this sin is oft the main cause of schisms in the church. It makes people divide themselves under different teachers whom they admire, and it causes teachers to take away those who affect them, from other teachers whom they affect not so much. Now this sin of schism, in itself very great, is made much greater by being occasioned by those very gifts of men which God bestowed upon them to this end, that there might "be no schism in the body, but that the members should have the same care one for another," 1 Cor. xii. 25. Nor is there any sin which more exposes the Christian religion to so much contempt and obloquy than this kind of admiring of persons; for hereby several companies of Christians are made like the several schools of philosophers, some of which followed Plato, some Aristotle, some Epicurus; and the doctrines of faith are but accounted as the proper opinions of several teachers; and all zeal for them is conceived to arise not from a certain knowledge of heavenly truth, but from peculiar humour and strength of fancy. And how great a stumbling-block must this needs be to those who are without, how will it hinder them from embracing the truth, and lay it open to derision! Yet further, the sinfulness of this sort of man-admiration appears, because hereby both the despised person is so grieved and discouraged, that he is enfeebled and disabled in his work; and also he who is admired is not only puffed up with pride, and thereby induced to adulterate the word, invent and broach errors, that still he may be advanced above all others by going in a different way from them; but also put upon the pleasing of men by sinful flatteries, instead of profiting them by faithful reprehensions. To conclude this consideration, nothing begets so great an aptness in men to receive errors as this sinful admiration; nor has any seed of heresies and superstitions proved so fruitful as this. Affection commonly makes men take down falsehood, and error is easily received from them whom we much admire; and God often leaves admired teachers to err for trial of the people, and the punishing of their vanity in making God's truth to stand at the devotion of the teacher for its acceptance, and trampling upon the holy and, perhaps, learned labours of those who are more seeing and faithful than the admired.

[3.] When we so admire men's persons as to give all respect to men in outward greatness, though perhaps wicked, despising the poor saints because poor: this James reproves, "My brethren, have not the faith of our Lord Jesus Christ in respect of persons," James ii. 1: when wickedness in robes is magnified, and holiness in rags contemned. Oh how unworthy is it that the gold ring and costly apparel should be preferred before the robe of Christ's righteousness and the jewel of grace! that godliness and good examples should be rejected for their want of a gold ring! that he who shall have a throne in heaven must here be a footstool upon earth!

[4.] When elections and offices are passed and bestowed partially, for friendship, favour, money, kindred; a sin by much aggravated when men have taken oaths to a corporation to the contrary; and it is oft a great temptation to the party who enters by money to sell justice dear.

[5.] When we so admire the person of one as to do injustice in judgment, whether civil or ecclesiastical; which is when our affection so blinds our judgment by some outward respect or appearance, that we will not determine righteously, the cause being overbalanced with such foreign considerations as have no affinity with it. Thus men are in judicature sometimes swayed with foolish pity, sometimes with cowardly fear: both these the Lord forbids. "Thou shalt not respect the person of the poor, nor honour the person of the mighty," Lev. xix. 15. This sin would make God a patron of iniquity, the sentence being pronounced from God, Deut. i. 17.

Obs. 1. The condition of men in greatest outward eminence and dignity is oft very miserable. None have so many flatterers, and therefore none so few friends, as they: flatterers, as worms, breed in the best fruit. When a poor illiterate man is admonished for sin, a rich, a learned man is admired in, nay, haply for sin. As the bodies, so the souls of kings and great men, have oftenest poison given them. Hushai humoured Absalom, Ziba flattered David, the people admired Herod; Jezebel soothed Ahab out of sadness into sin; Ahab had four hundred false prophets who flattered him into wickedness, and but one faithful Micaiah to tell him the truth. The common sound in the ears of princes is, *Quod libet, licet,* Your will is a law; as if they could not be carried fast enough into sin by the tide of their own nature, unless driven also by the wind of the flatterer's breath. The running water has no certain colour of its own, but is coloured like the soil which is under it; so flatterers fit themselves to every humour. Aristippus, for flattering Dionysius, was called the court-spaniel, *canis aulicus.* Flatterers are crows that hover about the carcass of greatness, friends in prosperity only, summer friends; like lookers upon a dial, they only regard men when the sun of prosperity shines upon them.

None are so little to be envied by others, or so much to be careful of themselves, as they who are in dignity; they should much more delight in words that are bitter and wholesome, than in such as are sweet and destructive. It was a holy and wise resolution of David, "He that walketh in a perfect way, he shall serve me; he that worketh deceit shall not dwell with me," Psal. ci. 6, 7. And Psal. cxli. 5, "Let the righteous smite me; it shall be a kindness," &c. "Faithful are the words of a friend; but the kisses of an enemy are deceitful," Prov. xxvii. 6. "A flattering mouth worketh ruin," Prov. xxvi. 28; xxviii. 23.

Obs. 2. How just is God in staining the pride of worldly glory! The persons of great ones are oft admired and adored as gods, and therefore God makes them often lower than men. God oft even smites godly men when they are over-admired. That late renowned Gustavus of Sweden feared as truly as humbly, when he said he thought that God would take him off, because men too much admired him. When we unduly set men up, God deservedly pulls them down. How many golden calves, how much sinfully-adored greatness, has God ground to powder of late years in England! We are angry that it is done, but why are we so well pleased with that sin which did it?

Obs. 3. How sinful is it to admire our own persons! If it may be ungodly to admire others in their outward excellencies, how much more then ourselves, who are conscious of so many inward defilements and deformities!

Obs. 4. It is a sin to receive, much more to seek for, admiration from others. If it be a sin to offer it, it must be a sin to receive it. The receiver of vainglory is as a thief in God's account, though others bring it to him: "Ye receive honour one of another." If men admire us sinfully against our wills, it is not our sin; if we close with the temptation, we become partners in their wickedness. We cannot be too worthy of having praise, nor too wary in hearing it. All our commendations should fall upon us as sparks upon wet tinder; humility should damp all our praises.

It is as unsafe for a proud person to have praises fly about him, as for a disarmed man to stand among flying bullets. A gracious heart can only digest both his sufferings and elevations, so as neither to be impatient under the former, nor to be proud under the latter; they alone set every crown of commendation upon the head of Jesus Christ. How vain and sinful is it to hunt after our own bane, and God's dishonour, popular applause!

Obs. 5. The proudest spirits are oft the basest. These arrogant seducers, who spake great swelling words, unworthily cringed and basely crouched in the admiring of persons for their own advantage. None now are so proud in their highness, nor so base in their lowness, as they: see an evident example in Benhadad, who though at first he proudly demanded of Ahab his silver and gold, wives and children, and the plunder of all his houses, and boasted that the dust of Samaria should not suffice for handfuls for his army; yet being overcome, he sends his servants to Ahab with sackcloth on their loins, and ropes about their necks, with a petition for the life of his servant Benhadad, 1 Kings xx. 5, 6, 10, 31, 32. The late bishops who tyrannized over their poor brethren, were yet the most servile flatterers, even to the servants of the king, for their own advantage. Oh how different is this temper from that true and heavenly nobleness of saints; who, with Elihu, cannot "accept any man's person," and "know not to give flattering titles!" Job xxxii. 21, 22; who in their own cause, though high, they bow as low as the reed; yet in the cause of God, when they are lowest, they are as stout and strong as the oak, yea, as hard as the adamant! There is a silent glory, and a secret generosity, that discovers itself in the poorest saint. A rich, honourable sinner is a beggar in robes; a poor, disgraced, imprisoned saint is a king in rags. Paul at the bar discovers more true nobleness and magnanimity than Felix upon the bench. The former reproved sin, and speaks of judgment with courage; the latter hears him with a servile trembling: the scribes and Pharisees taught with servile flattery, Christ with authority, and not as they.

[Marginal note: See Mr. Pryn in the Life of the late Archbishop of Canterbury.]

Obs. 6. It is our duty to preserve ourselves from this note of ungodliness, and practice of ungodly ones, admiring of persons. To this end,

(1.) Get an untainted, renewed judgment: a carnal eye sees nothing glorious but carnal, outside objects. Moses had a rectified judgment, a sanctified estimate; he prized the reproach of Christ above the treasures of Egypt, Heb. xi. 26. A skilful eye discerns the excellency of a picture curiously drawn, though it be not adorned with gold; yea, though it be set in a rotten frame; and contemns the gaudery of that workmanship which is only rich, and has nothing of art. A rich sinner is but a vile person in a saint's eye, an honourable leper. The four monarchies in Scripture emblems are but four beasts, violent, base, sensual. Ahab is not worth looking upon by a holy Elijah; as beholders are, so will things be accounted; the world loves its own; a child is taken with a doll more than with the conveyance of a great estate.

(2.) Study the nature of a person's true glory; this, grace I mean, is spiritual, hidden, not sensible and outward. The best of a man, and that which is truly admirable, is within: "The King's daughter is all glorious within," Psal. xlv. 13. Grace is veiled; the man of the heart is a hidden man, 1 Pet. iii. 4. That which is most to be desired of a man is that which cannot be seen, his goodness. We admire the lesser because we see not the greater beauties: the worst of a man is that which the eye sees. He who admires only the wealth and outward grandeur of a person, neglecting his grace, is as ridiculous as he who reverences a prince's robes, and despises his person.

(3.) Study the vanity of all common endowments and accomplishments wherewith the most gaudy sinner is adorned; consider they are but beauties in fancy and appearance, outside glitterings, at the best but well-acted vanities. There is not one of them but God puts upon his enemies; with them he oft gilds potsherds; they are paint which is put upon the worst faces, and waterings upon the rottenest stuffs, such as alter not the nature of him who has them, who is still but a swine under all his robes, an ass though crowned, or though carrying the rites of Isis. All the honour, parts, domination, riches in the world, amount not to the excellency of the least dram of true grace; they are not objects noble enough for a Christian's admiration. I remember when I was a child, that I heard a godly gentlewoman relate, that that holy man of God, old Mr. Culverwell, heartily chid her for saying that she wondered how such a formerly poor man, of whom they were speaking, came to be so exceeding rich: Oh! saith he, are these toys fit for such a one as thou art to wonder at? Besides, there is no robe of worldly excellency but must be laid off. The greatest potentate must stand naked of them at the day of judgment; nay, before; their honour descends not with them to the grave; when they crowd into that narrow hole, all their gaudy ornaments will be swept off. The dust of an emperor is no sweeter than that of a beggar.

(4.) Study God's dispensations; in them we shall see that he is no respecter of persons; he has commonly set the greatest respect upon those things and persons which are of least account in the world. He hath chosen the base things of the world, poor fishermen for disciples, nay, great sinners. The things of God were hidden from the wise and prudent, and revealed to babes. God chose not the eagle or lion, but dove and lamb, for sacrifice; "the poor of this world rich in faith," James ii. 5. "He accepteth not the persons of princes, nor regardeth the rich more than the poor," Job xxxiv. 19.

(5.) Study thine own profession, which is that thou art a saint, not a sensualist; that thou art a servant of Christ, not of men; that thou expectest to admire God for ever in glory, not worms upon a dunghill; that thou art called out of the world, and crucified to it, and that they who are spiritual and heavenly are thy brethren, thy companions, thy fellow members. Oh how heinous an evil is it for Christians to despise Christians, the heroes of heaven, and to admire the wicked, Satan's slaves! Oh what a dishonour is it to Christ, and a confutation of thy Christianity, when thou who art acquainted with higher glories, admirest grovelling worms! In short, remember thy Master never admired any thing but grace, regarding that in a poor woman, when he despised all the glory of the world.

(6.) Banish self-interest and carnal designs out of all the respects thou givest to others: the aiming at honour or riches will pervert thy estimate, and make thee admire those that can most advantage thee. This will make a great saint basely to fall down before unsanctified greatness. Luther could not admire the pope, because he admired neither money nor preferment. Covetous designs will make thee, with these seducers, to honour those where there is most gain, not most grace. Mortification is the best remedy against sinful admiration.

2. The motive of their admiring of others, or why they did it, viz. for advantage, besides what I have spoken in this last branch, I refer the reader to p. 230, &c., 235, concerning the "running," &c. "for reward."

Verse 17, 18, 19.

But, beloved, remember ye the words which were spoken before of the apostles of our Lord Jesus Christ; how that they told you there should be mockers in the last time, who should walk after their own ungodly lusts. These be they who separate themselves, sensual, having not the Spirit.

The body and substance of this Divine Epistle, continued from the preface in the first two verses, to the conclusion in the last two verses, contains an exhortation to the Christians "earnestly to contend for the faith;" in the managing whereof,

1. The apostle sets down the reasons of his sending them this exhortation.
2. The exhortation itself; both contained in ver. 3.
3. Several arguments to move the Christians to embrace that exhortation, from the 3rd to the 17th verse.
4. And fourthly, sundry directions to guide and teach the Christians how to observe that exhortation, from the 17th to the 24th verse.

Of the three former we have largely, by God's assistance, spoken; now we come to speak of the fourth and last, the directions: and these directions are of two sorts.

First, Such as concern, 1. Christians themselves; and, 2. Others.

I. The former, in relation to "themselves," are principally five.

1. The improving and recollecting of "the words of the apostles," who foretold the carriage of these seducers, contained in these three, the 17th, 18th, and 19th verses.
2. Edification on their holy faith, ver. 20.
3. Supplication in the Holy Ghost, ver. 20.
4. Conservation of themselves in the love of God, ver. 21.
5. Expectation of the coming of Christ, ver. 21.

II. Such directions as concern their carriage toward others are laid down ver. 22, 23.

The first is the improving of the testimony of the apostles. In which testimony I note five particulars.

1. To whom it is commended; to his "beloved."
2. How it was to be improved; by remembering it.
3. From whom it proceeded; "the apostles of our Lord Jesus Christ."
4. Wherein it consisted; in a prediction that there should be mockers, walking after their ungodly lusts.
5. To whom it is applied, viz. to these seducers; "These be they who separate themselves," ver. 19.

1. Concerning the first, the persons to whom this testimony is commended, such as he calls "beloved," I have at large spoken before, p. 52, 53.

2. As also concerning the second, viz. their recalling it to remembrance, p. 107, 108. We proceed,

3. To the third, from whom this testimony proceeded, viz. "the apostles of our Lord Jesus Christ."

In explication hereof I might enlarge on the nature of the apostolical function, and in showing what Jude means by this term "apostles," and wherein stands the difference between them and ordinary ministers of Christ; as namely, in respect of immediate calling, their authentic authority in writing and speaking, their work and office to plant churches, to work miracles, to give the Holy Ghost by imposition of hands, and to use the apostolical rod against obstinate offenders. But to pass by these, as not concerning our purpose, and as being spoken to by others;

Two things in relation to this testimony here alleged by Jude may be touched by way of explication.

1. What apostles these were of whom Jude speaks, and where this testimony is to be found.
2. Why Jude makes use of that testimony which came from them, and tells us that it did come from them.

1. Who these apostles were that gave this prediction which Jude here alleges, and where they gave it. Although possibly sundry of the apostles might by word of mouth testify what Jude here mentions, yet I doubt not but he principally relates to their writings. And in them they frequently foretell and forewarn of these seducers. Matthew tells us from Christ's mouth, that "many false prophets shall rise, and deceive many," chap. xxiv. 11. John tells the Christians that there are many antichrists, whereby they knew that it was the last time, 1 Epist. ii. 18. Possibly Jude might intend these proofs among others; but I conceive, with Œcumenius, that he principally aims at that which Paul and Peter before him had foretold concerning these seducers. Paul warned of these seducers in sundry of his Epistles. Peter particularly in his Second. Paul especially foretells of them, 1 Tim. iv. 1, "The Spirit speaketh expressly, that in the latter times some shall depart from the faith, giving heed to seducing spirits," &c. And 2 Tim. iii. 1—4, "This know, that in the last days perilous times shall come;" (and the description of those who shall make the times so perilous exactly agrees to these seducers, as I have shown throughout this Epistle of Jude;) "for men shall be lovers of their own selves, covetous, boasters, proud, blasphemers," &c., "incontinent, fierce, despisers of those that are good, traitors, heady, highminded, lovers of pleasures more than lovers of God."

Sermo videtur esse tum de verbis scriptis, tum de prædicatis. Lor. in 2 Pet. iii. 2.

And 2 Tim. iv. 3, "The time will come when they will not endure sound doctrine; but after their own lusts shall they heap to themselves teachers." Plainly likewise Paul foretells the coming of seducers: "I know this, that after my departure shall grievous wolves enter in among you, not sparing the flock: also of your own selves shall men arise, speaking perverse things, to draw away disciples after them," Acts xx. 29, 30. But especially Jude seems to intend the remembering of that prediction concerning seducers which Peter gives us, "There shall come in the last days scoffers, walking after their own lusts," 2 Epist. iii. 3. And our apostle, in exhorting the Christians to remember the words of the apostles, wherein they foretold the coming of these mockers, seems to some to imitate Peter, who in the forementioned place, ver. 2, exhorted the Christians to remember the command of the apostles, (namely, to avoid the doctrines of seducers,) "knowing that there shall come in the last days mockers," &c.

2. Why Jude makes use of their testimony, and tells us that it came from them. It was not without weighty reason that Jude makes use of the apostles' testimony, and mentions the coming thereof from the apostles, and that in respect of those apostles, Jude himself, and these Christians.

(1.) In respect of those apostles: by mentioning their foretelling of these mockers, Jude shows the great care which those faithful servants of Christ had of the church's welfare, their desires being that the church should get good by them, and live holily and peaceably when they had done living; and that they might by their writings live even when they were dead, to be serviceable to the church of Christ.

(2.) In respect of Jude himself: he mentions the words of the apostles, to show his humility in acknowledging the grace and gifts of God bestowed upon others, and the sweet accord and agreement between them and him in the doctrines which he delivered to them in this Epistle concerning these seducers, that hereby he might gain the more credit to himself and present service, there being a joint concurrence between him and the other apostles: as to this end he had before told the Christians that James was his brother in respect of parentage, so here he tells them that he and the other apostles were brethren in respect of judgment and opinion. All the apostles were stars enlightened by the same sun; they drew the waters of life out of the same fountain, plucked the fruits of wholesome doctrines off from the same tree; and by producing the testimony of so many others who witnessed the same thing with him, he more clearly evidenced that he had spoken nothing but the truth against these seducers, whom he had so sharply reproved.

(3.) In respect of the Christians to whom he wrote: he mentions the apostles, [1.] To show how zealous they ought to be against these seducers and their doctrines, because the apostles, who were so holy and unerring, had given the Christians warning of them, and with such vehemency spoken against them, as if they were desirous to leave hatred of error as their legacy to their spiritual children. [2.] To preserve these Christians against discouragements, by seeing such ungodly, soul-subverting seducers rage and prevail in the church; it being no other than what was foretold by those who could not be deceived, John xvi. 4; and therefore they were not to look upon it as if some strange thing had happened to them. [3.] To direct the Christians to the right means to discover, and so to avoid, all those seducers and seductions wherewith the church of God was then infested. The words of the apostles being observed, these characters of seducers which they had delivered might be so plainly seen to agree to these who had crept into the church, that the one being known, the other could not be hid; and they being seen, surely ought to be shunned.

Obs. 1. Great should be the care of the ministers of Christ to warn the church of approaching evils, especially of seducers. The apostles of Christ foretold the coming of these seducers among the Christians: Paul "warned every one night and day with tears," Acts xx. 31. They are watchmen, and it is their duty to give warning of every enemy. They should be unfaithful to your souls, if they should be friends to your adversaries. Their loving and faithful freeness herein creates them many enemies; but they can much more easily endure the wrath of man here for discharging, than the wrath of God hereafter for neglecting their duty. It is better that the lusts of seducers should curse them awhile, than the souls of their people to all eternity. Ministers must defend as well as feed their flock, and keep away poison as well as give them meat; drive away the wolf as well as provide pasture. Cursed be that patience which can see the wolf, and yet say nothing. If the heresies of seducers be damnable, the silence of ministers must needs be so too.

Obs. 2. It is our duty to acknowledge and commend the gifts and graces of God bestowed upon others with respect. Jude honourably mentions these apostles, both for the dignity of their function, and also for the faithfulness of their discharge thereof, by forewarning the Christians. The prudent commending of the gifts and graces of another is the praising of the Giver, and the encouragement of the receiver. The good we see in any one is not to be damped, but cherished; nor should the eminence of our own make us despise another's endowments. Peter, though he had oft heard Christ himself preach, and had long been conversant with Christ upon earth; though at pentecost the Spirit was poured upon him; yet he thought it no derogation from his worth to make an honourable mention of Paul, to read his Epistles, and to allege the authority of his writings, 2 Pet. iii. 15. Peter does not say, Why is not my word as credible as Paul's? but without any self-respect he appeals to Paul, honours Paul, and fetches in Paul for the warrant of his writings. Oh how unworthy is it either to deny or diminish the worth of others! How unsuitable is it to the spirit of Christianity, when mere shame compels a man to speak something in commendation of another, to come with a but in the conclusion of our commendation; But in such or such a thing he is faulty and defective! This kind of commendation is like an unskilful farrier's shoeing a horse, who never shoes but he pricks him.

Obs. 3. The consent between the penmen of Scripture is sweet and harmonious; they were all breathed upon by the same Spirit, and breathed forth the same truth and holiness. Jude and the rest of the apostles agree unanimously against these seducers. Moses and all the prophets accord with the apostles in their testimony of Christ, Luke xxiv. 27. Peter and Paul agree harmoniously, 2 Pet. iii. 15. All holy writers teach one and the same faith. They were several men, but not of several minds. The consideration whereof affords us a notable argument to prove the Divine authority of Scripture, all the penmen whereof, though of several conditions, living in several ages, places, and countries, yet teach the same truth, and confirm one another's doctrine. 2. It teaches in the exposition of Scripture to endeavour to make them all agree. When other writers oppose the Scripture, we should kill the Egyptian, and save the Israelite; but when the holy writers seem, for they never more than seem, to jar one with another, we should study to make them agree, because they are brethren. But, 3. and especially, The consideration hereof should put all Christians upon agreeing in believing and embracing the truth: if the writers agreed, the readers should do so too; but chiefly the preachers of the word should take heed of difference among themselves in interpreting the Scripture. Concord among teachers is as necessary as is the help of the left hand needful to the right. When the children fall out in interpreting their father's testament, the lawyer only gains; and when ministers are at variance among themselves, heretics only rejoice, and get advantage to extol and promote error. In a word, as the apostle holily exhorts, we should "walk by the same rule, and mind the same thing," Phil. iii. 16; and "speak the same thing;" labouring that there may be no division among us, but that we "be perfectly joined together in the same mind and in the same judgment," 1 Cor. i. 10. All contention among ministers should be, who shall be foremost in giving of honour, and gaining of souls.

Manus dextra non tantopere indiget ministerio sinistrae, quam necessaria est ecclesiae doctoribus concordia. Gerhard, 2 Pet. iii. 15.

Obs. 4. Scripture is the best preservative against seduction. The apostle directs the Christians to make use of the words of the apostles to that end. The Scripture is the best armoury to afford weapons against seducers. It is only the sword of the Spirit, the word of God, that slays error. Jesus Christ made use of it when he conflicted with that arch-seducer the devil, Matt. iv. The reason why people are children tossed about with every wind of seduction, is, because they are children in Scripture knowledge. They are children which commonly are stolen in the streets, not grown men. "Ye err," saith Christ to the Sadducees, "not knowing the Scripture." The Scripture is the light which shines in a dark place; an antidote against all heretical poison; a touchstone to try counterfeit opinions; that sun, the lustre whereof, if any doctrines cannot endure, they are to be thrown down as spurious. And this discovers the true reason of Satan's rage against the word in all ages: never did any thief love the light, nor any seducer delight in the word. Heretics fly the Scripture as the owl the sun: when that arises, they fly to their holes; when that sets, they fly abroad and lift up their voice. It is Satan's constant design that there may not be a sword found in Israel. Our care should be to arraign every error at the bar of Scripture, and to try whether it can speak the Scripture shibboleth, whether it has given them letters of commendation or no, or a pass to travel up and down the church or no. If to Scripture they appeal, to Scripture let them go; and let us, with those noble Bereans, with pure, humble, praying, unprejudiced hearts, "search the Scriptures whether those things are so."

Obs. 5. They who are forewarned should be forearmed. It is a shame for them who have oft heard and known the doctrines of the apostles to be surprised by seducers. Jude expects that these Christians who knew what the apostles had delivered, should strenuously oppose all seduction. To stumble in the light is inexcusable. To see a young beginner seduced is not so strange, but for an old disciple, a grey-headed gospeller, to be misled into error, how shameful is it! and yet how many such childish old ones as these are doth England, London, afford! who justly, because they are ever learning, and never coming to the knowledge of the truth, but remain unprofitable hearers of truth, are left by God to be easily followers of error.

4. The fourth particular which I considered in Jude's producing of the testimony of the apostles, was, wherein this testimony consisted, or the testimony itself, laid down in the 18th verse in these words, that "there should be mockers in the last time, who should walk after their own ungodly lusts." In which words these seducers are described, 1. From the time wherein they appeared. 2. From their qualities or conditions wherewith they appeared; according to which the apostle saith they were, 1. Mockers. 2. Such as walked after their lusts.

1. The time when they appeared; their appearance was in "the last time."

Two things here briefly require explication.
1. What "the last time" is.
2. Why these seducers showed themselves "in the last time."

1. What "the last time" is. By the phrase ἔσχατος χρόνος, "the last time," the Scripture means sometimes a continuation or length of time, sometimes an end of time. When by the last time it means a continuation of time, it intends a space, which, in respect of that compass of time of which it is the last part, may fitly be called the last time. Thus the life of man being made up of several ages, the last space thereof, old age, may be called its last time. Thus within the compass of a year, there being four seasons, the last season, winter, may be called the last time of a year. Or sometimes by the last time is meant *terminus temporis*, the very end or expiring of time; as the moment wherein a man dies is his last time, or the last day of December is the end or last time of the year.

"Ἔσχατος παρὰ τὸ σχεῖν, in quo necesse est ut consistamus. Ultimum dicitur, ultra quod pergere non licet.

1. Ultimum tempus. 2. Ultimum temporis.

Now thus "the last time" is the end of the world, and it is ever expressed in the singular number, and usually called "the last day," as four times John vi., and once in John xi. And thus in 1 Pet. i. 5 the last time is used, where the apostle mentions that "salvation ready to be revealed in the last time."

"The last time" in this place must needs be taken in the former sense, viz. for a space which is the last age of the world, or the last part of its time; and thus those places are ever to be taken where we read of the last times, or days, in the plural number; as 1 Pet. i. 20, it is said that Christ was manifested in the "last times," which times have continued many hundreds of years. So Heb. i. 2, "God hath in these last days spoken by his Son." So 2 Tim. iii. 1, "In the last days perilous times shall come." And Acts ii. 17, "In the last days, I will pour out of my Spirit." So 2 Pet. iii. 3. And thus it is taken in this place. Nor does the Holy Ghost intend these last times by a word of the singular number in any place, as I remember, save only in this place of Jude. Now by these last times in general, are meant all those times from the revelation of Christ to the end of the world, in which space the kingdom of Christ was founded and advanced in the world; which times, because, saith the learned Mead, they are under the last monarchy, viz. the Roman, are called the last times. Hence it is said, 1 Pet. i. 20, "Christ was manifested in these last times;" and Gal. iv. 4, "When the fulness of time was come, God sent forth his Son," &c. Others think that these times after the coming of Christ to the end of the world are called the last times on account of those which went before, wherein the state of the church was oft changed, and the covenant frequently renewed; but now by the death of Christ the covenant of grace being so established, that it is never again to be renewed or changed; but the condition of the church is to be in a fixed state to the end of the world, and no other to succeed it; these are called the last times.

Vid. Mead in his learned discourse of the Apostacy of the Last Times.

2. Why these profane seducers arose in these last times.

(1.) The last times are times of presumption and security, and therefore of dissoluteness and impiety. In former times judgments were threatened, the dissolution and destruction of all things foretold; but because the execution hereof is not beheld, therefore they who live in these times are encouraged to sin. Because sentence against their evil works is not speedily executed, therefore are their hearts set to do evil. This security Christ foretells should be in the last of the last days, namely, at his coming to judgment: "As in the days before the flood they were eating and drinking, marrying and giving in marriage," &c.; "so shall also the coming of the Son of man be," &c. And this continuance of all things as they were from the beginning occasioned these seducers to scoff at the promise of his coming, 2 Pet. iii. 4. The nearer they came to feeling, the further they were from fearing of punishment.

(2.) They who live in the last days are more skilful practitioners in sin, wittily wicked, understand more how to contrive sin and work iniquity, by the improved experiences of their own and former times. Thus, as it is in every other art, so likewise in that of sinning, by length of time, custom, and experience, it is improved to a greater degree of fineness and exactness. The sinners of the last times are men, they of former times were but children, in wickedness. That old serpent, the older he grows, the more of the serpent he has, and so it is with the seed of the serpent.

(3.) In the last times the kingdom of Jesus Christ is to be more enlarged and advanced, and therefore the malice of Satan is the more increased. As Christ rises in glory, so will Satan and sinners more swell with rage and envy. It is said, that those people who live in places where the sun is hottest and most scorching, every morning curse the rising sun; and thus in times where the gospel reaches men with its holy heat and light, they curse and malign it. Hatred is the genius of the gospel; and as wicked men the more raged at Christ the older he grew; so the more his gospel spreads, the more Satan despites it.

(4.) Lastly, In the last times the devil's time grows short, and therefore his wrath grows great. Satan labours to supply the shortness of his time with the sharpness of his assaults. Besiegers make their last onset upon town or castle the most resolute and terrible of all others. Satan now sets upon souls by seduction the more furiously, because when these times are at an end he shall never be suffered to do so any more; like a malicious tenant, who, perceiving that his term is almost expired, does what he can to ruin the house; or like a bloody tyrant, who, suspecting the loss of his usurped sovereignty, makes havoc among his subjects.

Obs. 1. The wicked are worst in the best times. In the last days, wherein the light of the gospel, the knowledge of Christ, and the means of grace are most abundant, the wicked are most wicked. In the land of uprightness they live unholily. As the means of grace can make no man good of themselves; so, by reason of our oppositeness to holiness, they occasion us to be far worse. A Judas in the fellowship of Christ—a Doeg detained before the Lord—an unreformed person under the means of reformation, is most pertinaciously such. The means of grace without the grace of the means, only draws forth our rage against them. Let not men therefore please themselves because either the times or places wherein they live are holy, unless these find themselves bettered by them. The higher we are lifted up, the sorer will be our fall: we cannot sin at so cheap a rate in these last times as formerly. Sins in the last times find out the lowest places in hell. Let this likewise be an apology for the gospel. Lay not the sins of gospel times to the gospel's charge, since men are not wicked because the gospel is so much preached, but because it is no more than preached, not lived and practised also.

Obs. 2. The dispensation of the covenant of grace is now unalterable. In former times it has appeared under several dresses and forms; but now in the last times we must look for no renovation or change thereof. The present administration of the covenant goes next to the end of the world, and shall be closed up of the last day.

Obs. 3. God is abundant in the discovery and dispensing his grace even in times wherein men profanely abuse it: the gospel is in the last times most liberally afforded, though most ungratefully neglected and abused.

Obs. 4. Of all times, the last require most care in our carriage. They who live in them enjoy the helps and advantages of the former. Jesus Christ is most clearly discovered. We should do our work better by sun-light, than others have by twilight, else it will be our inexcusable shame. We should imitate God: as his last works, his works in the last times, are his best; so should ours be, the best of our lives should be in the bottom of time: nay, herein our very adversary should teach us; if his rage against God increases because his time of doing hurt is short, should not our zeal increase because the time of our doing good is short? Besides, in the last times we have greatest temptations, most examples of sin: when the times are worst, we should be best; and if we cannot make the times good, they should not make us bad. In dirty ways we should tuck up our garments, we should keep ourselves from this untoward generation, and "shine as lights in a crooked and perverse nation," and give God's glory reparations for all it suffers from the wicked.

Obs. 5. The people of God should bear and forbear.

(1.) Bear their crosses: these are the last times, the end of time is approaching, and with time all their troubles shall end. "Be patient," saith James, "for the coming of the Lord draweth nigh," and "the Judge standeth at the door." And Heb. x. 37, "Yet a little while, and he that shall come will come, and will not tarry." And 1 Pet. i. 6, "Now for a season ye are in heaviness." The elect, which cry day and night to him, shall be avenged speedily, Luke xviii. 7, 8. And, "Our light affliction is but for a moment," 2 Cor. iv. 17. We count a moment a thousand years, but in Scripture computation a thousand years are but a moment. Nothing should be great to him to whom is known the greatness of eternity. He who keeps a city for his prince, though it be straitly besieged, will hold out, if relief be approaching. Our relief, redemption from all troubles, draws nigh: oh how great a shame and vexation will it afterward be to deliver up ourselves by impatience to apostacy, since our relief is within the sight of the besieged, we being in the last times! 1 Cor. vii. 29—31.

(2.) Forbear, use comforts moderately: "Let your moderation be known: the Lord is at hand," Phil. iv. 5. A tenant being in the last year of his house, builds not, plants not. He is a madman who sets up a stately fabric upon that ground which is troubled with earthquakes, and sure shortly to sink. "Lay up treasures in heaven;" labour for "everlasting habitations," "a city that hath foundations." Because "the time is short," they that marry should be as if they married not, &c., "they that buy, as if they possessed not," &c.; "for the fashion of this world passeth away." "Love not the world," 1 John ii. 15; it "passeth away," ver. 17. Use perishing comforts with perishing affections; love them as always about to leave them.

Thus of the first part, in the testimony itself, viz. the time when these seducers were to appear; "the last time."

2. Their qualities, which are here said to be two. First, mocking. Secondly, walking after their lusts. The first is set forth in this word "mockers."

Two things I shall here briefly show by way of explication.

1. What we are to understand by "mockers."
2. How great the sin is, to be "mockers."

1. What we are to understand by "mockers." The word ἐμπαῖκται properly signifies such who deride and mock at others, as if they were but foolish and silly children; or such who scorn or scoff at any thing, as if it were but foolish and childish. And to this signification of the word agree those expressions whereby mocking is shown; as sometimes by, (1.) Scornful and contemptuous speeches: thus Joseph's brethren called him the "dreamer;" Elijah was called "bald-head;" Christ "the King of the Jews," &c. (2.) Deriding and scornful gestures, as fleering with the nose, making of mouths, nodding of the head, Psal. xxii. 7, making a wide mouth, putting out of the tongue, Isa. lvii. 4, and shooting out the lip, Prov. xvi. 30; Psal. xxii. 7; putting out of the finger, Isa. lviii. 9; clapping of the hands, Lam. ii. 15. (3.) Scornful and abusive dealings: thus Christ was crowned with thorns, clad in purple, a reed was put into his hand, he was spit upon, &c.

From ἐμπαίζω, ἐμπαίζειν est proprie, instar pueri aliquem tractare, ludificare, et irridere. Gerh. Harm. de Passione, pag. mihi 106.

Gal. vi. 7, Μυκτηρίζομαι. Μυκτήρ nasum significat. Naso suspendit adunco. Horat. Serm. 1.

But that we may understand what the apostle here means by mockers, we must consider this malicious and contemptuous derision or mocking in his objects, against which it is committed. It is expressed either against man, or God himself.

(1.) Against man; and that for several causes. As,

[1.] For his country. So some interpret that passage, Ezek. xxxvi. 6, where God tells the Israelites that they "have borne the shame of the heathen;" and that they should not "bear the reproach of the people any more," ver. 15. It seems that the heathen objected to the Jews the frequent sterilities and famines of their land, or the destructions and captivities which for their sins they had endured. Julian the apostate called Christ, by way of contempt, the Galilean; and, to some, it seems a contemptuous proverb, "Can there any good thing come out of Nazareth?" John i. 46.

[2.] For his poverty and meanness. Christ in and for his sufferings was mocked, Matt. xx. 19; xxvii. 29, 31. Thus Tobiah mocked the poor Jews when building, saying, "If a fox go up, he shall even break down their stone wall," Neh. iv. 3. And thus Solomon tells us, that he "who mocketh the poor reproacheth his Maker," Prov. xvii. 5. The contempts of this nature reflect upon God himself, who, when "the rich and poor meet together, is the maker of them both," Prov. xxii. 2.

[3.] For his deformity, or any infirmity of body. And so they mocked Elisha, when they said, "Go up, thou bald-head," 2 Kings ii. 23. Thus men are mocked for their low stature, their black and unbeautiful complexion, their weakness, &c.

[4.] For his religion or godliness. The godly suffered "cruel mockings," Heb. xi. 36. Thus Michal mocked David for dancing before the ark, 2 Sam. vi. 20. Thus Festus tells Paul that too much learning had made him mad, Acts xxvi. 24. This sort of mocking was that which the Babylonians expressed against the Jews in their captivity: Let us hear your Hebrew songs, Psal. cxxxvii. 3. Such, some conceive, was Ishmael's mocking of Isaac, Gen. xxi. 9. And this was that derision expressed against those who had received the gifts of the Holy Ghost, profane scoffers saying that they were drunk with new wine, Acts ii. 13. David was "the song of the drunkards," Psal. lxix. 12. "I and the children whom the Lord hath given me are for signs and wonders," Isa. viii. 18.

[5.] For his office and employment. And thus they asked Jehu wherefore that mad fellow, meaning the prophet, came to him, 2 Kings ix. 11.

(2.) Mocking (with highest impiety) is expressed against God himself; and that sometimes as in respect of his works of judgment, so oftenest of his word; as either commanding, reprehending, or threatening. Thus when Christ had preached against covetousness, the Pharisees, who were covetous, derided him. Thus when the Lord called the secure scorners "to weeping and mourning, to baldness and girding with sackcloth; there was joy and gladness, slaying of oxen and killing of sheep, eating flesh and drinking wine," &c., Isa. xxii. 12, 13. When Hezekiah's posts went with letters to stir up Israel to celebrate the passover at Jerusalem, they were mocked, 2 Chron. xxx. 10. Sad is the complaint of Jeremiah, chap. xx. 7, 8, "I am in derision daily, every one mocketh me," &c., "the word of the Lord is made a reproach unto me, and a derision, daily." And in 2 Chron. xxxvi. 16, "They mocked the messengers of the Lord, and despised his words," &c. When Paul discoursed "of the resurrection, some mocked," Acts xvii. 32; and of this mocking at God's word our apostle accuses these seducers, I conceive, in this place. I doubt not but they mocked at dominions and dignities, at the holiness and godly strictness of these Christians, as at a needless and vain severity; but here Jude seems to run parallel with Peter, who tells us that the mockers of the last times showed themselves such, by deriding at the promise of Christ's coming, asking, "Where is the promise of his coming? for since the fathers fell asleep all things continue as they were," &c., 2 Pet. iii. 4. These sensual atheists then turning the grace of God into wantonness, and giving over themselves to following their lusts, securely derided and scoffed at any directions to holiness, or denunciations of judgments, which opposed them in their ungodly courses, as vain and contemptible fables.

2. The great sinfulness of mocking.

(1.) It is a sin of unspeakable profaneness, very heinous in respect of the glorious excellency of that God whom we mock. It is a great offence to mock man, a weak worm, a king, our parents; but to mock the great God is a surpassing wickedness. What does the profane mocker, but, according to the meaning of his name, carry himself toward God as if all his power, justice, threatenings, commands, ordinances were childish toys?

(2.) In respect of that gross unbelief which is in it. Men are therefore mockers because they are unbelievers; threatenings, commands, promises, are therefore derided because they are distrusted. "Where is the promise," said these mockers, "of his coming?" 2 Pet. iii. 4; all which the God of truth saith is accounted but a notion, a fable.

(3.) It argues the greatest contempt of God's long-suffering and forbearance. That goodness of God which should lead to repentance, is to scorners a pillow of security; and what greater disingenuousness, than to make God a sufferer because he makes not us to suffer, and to strike him because he strikes not us, to fight against him with his own weapons!

(4.) It makes all the means of grace ineffectual. Scorners will not be bettered: Rebuke a scorner, and he will hate thee, Prov. ix. 7, 8. The strength of this sin makes all the helps of holiness to be but weak; they all slide off as water from an oiled post. A scorner is (as it were) a brazen wall, which beats back all the arrows of reprehension. Mocking argues obdurateness in sin; it extinguishes light natural, and opposes light spiritual. The admonishing of a scorner is the holding of a looking-glass before a blind man, who indeed by his breath may blemish the glass, but cannot behold himself.

(5.) It notes progressiveness in sin, and arriving even at the top of impiety: the beginnings of sin are modest. It is bad to sin, as at the first sinners do, though with blushing and concealment; but afterward by continuing in sin, not only to grow insensible of it, to proclaim it, to maintain it, but to scorn all reproofs and threatenings against it; this shows a sinner is higher by the head and shoulders in sin than other men, and one who is gone so far in ungodliness that he seldom turns. The LXX. express the Hebrew word which signifies a scorner by the word ἀκόλαστος, Prov. xx. 1, which signifies incorrigible, that which cannot be tamed, because there is no hope of a scorner. Commonly mockers are either idolatrous or profane. The little children who mocked Elisha, and called him bald-head, came out of that idolatrous city where Jeroboam had set up his calf; and idolatrous Jeroboam and his courtiers were great scorners, Hos. vii. 5; probably they scoffed at those who would not yield to that idolatrous worship that Jeroboam had set up. Oft also profaneness and sensuality causes mocking. When the king was sick with wine, "he stretched out his hand with scorners," Hos. vii. 5. When wicked men are most pampered, they scoff most at piety. Religion makes them sport at their feasts; "mockers in feasts," Psal. xxxv. 16.

(6.) Scorners are the greatest instruments of Satan; the main promoters of his cause, and advancers of his kingdom. The Hebrew word scorners, according to the LXX. is expressed by the word λοιμῶν, Psal. i. 1, which signifieth plagues, in the chair of plagues, because scorners are plagues to the place where they live, and infect many. Scorners are they who sit in the chair, and are the doctors of impiety, and the *antesignani* and ringleaders of all mischief. They are the spokesmen and proctors of Satan. Nor do any bring such instruments of cruelty to wound religion and religious ones as do scoffers. Mocking is called a persecution, Gal. iv. 29; and mockings are called "cruel mockings," Heb. xi. 36. By no devices does Satan so much dishearten men from religion, and afflict for religion, as by this. By no means has he more instructed those who would be bad, and discouraged others from being good.

Obs. 1. Great is the patience and forbearance of God. None but a God would spare those impudent and bitter scoffers, which he is so able to punish. Men are under nothing so impatient as under scoffs and derisions. How full of vexation are they, when either they have not wit enough to return scoff for scoff, or strength enough to return stripes and blows for scoffs! But God is as full of patience to endure scoffers, as of power to confound them. Surely, God as truly shows himself a God by sparing as by punishing these his enemies.

Obs. 2. How just will the confusion of scorners be! Nothing is more suitable and deserved than for the impudent in sin to be dashed out of countenance, to be beaten with their own weapon. The Lord "scorneth the scorners," Prov. iii. 34. He will mock at the calamities of those when they come, who mocked at God before they came, Prov. i. 26. None was a more bitter scoffer at the godly than that cruel Doctor Story, who, when the meek and lamb-like martyr, blessed Mr. Denly, Fox, Martyrolog. was singing a psalm at the stake, wounded his face by throwing a faggot at it, adding this bitter and profane scoff, That he had spoiled a good old song: but never was mocker so handsomely mocked, for in Queen Elizabeth's times, he being beyond sea, authorized to go on ship-board to search out the heretical books, (as they called them,) which he hoped to find in the ship of an English merchant, and going down into lower parts thereof to ransack it for that purpose, the hatches were presently clapped down upon him, the sails hoisted up, he brought into England, and deservedly for treason executed at Tyburn.

Obs. 3. It is our duty patiently to carry ourselves under mockings. It has been the lot of the saints in all ages to meet with them: "Thou makest us a by-word among the heathen," Psal. xliv. 14. "We are become a reproach and derision to them that are round about us," Psal. lxxix. 4. And, "I became a reproach," saith David, "to them: when they looked upon me, they shaked their heads," Psal. cix. 25. Tertullian tells us that the Christians in his time were mocked for ignorance. The heathens painted the God of the Christians with an ass's head, and a book in his hand, to signify that though they pretended learning, yet they were silly and unlearned people. Such who kept the sabbath were said to have a disease upon them, on account of which they were fain to rest once in the week. Athanasius was called Sathanasius, for being an adversary to the Arians. Cyprian was abused by the name of Coprian, one that gathers up dung. But why speak I of the mockings which befell Christians; they were the portion of Christ himself. Our Head was crowned with these thorns; they spit in his face, gave him a reed for a sceptre, bowed before him; though he was despised, yet he endured the shame, Heb. xii. 2. If mocking were the diet drink of Christ, should not we patiently taste now and then a drop thereof? yea, none can bear so much contempt as God doth daily. Besides, by impatience under scoffs we hurt ourselves more than scoffers can. If we would not vex and disturb our own souls by impatience, our enemies could not hurt us by reproaches; and, indeed, this self-disquieting is the only way to gratify our enemies, whose alone aim by mocking is to trouble and disturb us. And by fretfulness and rage we are liable to discover as much evil as our enemies can discover by all their scoffs; and though we are unjustly reproached, yet we may discover so much folly and passion as to be a just cause of reproach. We live among reproachers and scoffers, and without patience we shall never have comfortable lives, but the comfort and quiet of our lives will ever lie at the mercy of others. The greatest evil of reproach is from him that receives it. As it is with meat, so it is with mockings. It is not the goodness and sweetness of meat in itself that makes it good and sweet to me, but it is to me as my stomach and body are affected; and scoffs and reproaches are not evils as they come from him that casts them upon us, but the greatest part of the evil of reproaches comes from the affection of the receiver. Further, remember there is more honour in bearing scoffs patiently, than there is disgrace in having them cast upon us wrongfully. Every fool can cast a reproach, but only the wise man can bear it well. Chrysostom tells us that the reproacher is below a man, but the patient under reproach is equal to an angel. Consider, likewise, that God takes the care of our names as well as of our souls. When David's enemies spake mischievous things against him, he tells us, Psal. xxxviii. 12, 13, that he heard not; but, ver. 15, he saith that God hears. The less we hear, the more God will hear. They who mock here, shall be mocked hereafter; and they who are here mocked, shall then be honoured. And how countervailing a mercy is it to be delivered from eternal reproach! Meditate also how much contempt and mocking many justly suffer for their sins. Many care not how much shame they endure in the service of a base lust. Who are so basely looked upon as the drunkards, covetous? and yet they go on, and bless themselves, notwithstanding their reproach. What cause have we then to go on in the ways of God, though all the world mock us! Consider also what honour God has put upon thee for the present. He has, if thou art godly, brought thee to the honourable estate of sonship, and put his glory upon thy soul, and honoured thee by that near relation thou hast to Christ. How base was Haman's spirit, who being so honoured by the king, was so vexed because Mordecai would not bow to him! And truly it is a sinful baseness in saints, that when God has raised them to such glory as to be members of and co-heirs with his Son, and provided for them the glory of heaven; yet for all this, when they have but a mock from men, to be so discouraged and cast down, as if all the honour that God had put upon them were nothing. Think likewise how much religion has been scoffed at for your sake; and is it so great a matter for you to be mocked for religion? Chrysostom saith, that when for us our Lord is blasphemed, it is worse than if we perished. Consider also the goodness of God in keeping in those many secret wickednesses of thy heart from appearing, which, had they been suffered by God to break forth, would have been matter enough of scorn and reproach, whereas now the enemies are fain to watch and pry for some occasion, and yet can hardly find any. Remember also that there is more danger in being honoured than contemned by men. Luther said his greatest fear was the praise of men, and that reproach was his joy, and that he would not have the glory and fame of Erasmus. Lastly, The bearing of scoffs patiently is a great help to our progress in godliness. As they who have overcome the evil of shame in a way of sin grow hardened in sin; so they who regard no reproach cast upon them for holiness will steadily proceed therein. And that we may bear the most cruel mockings patiently, (1.) Labour to get good by them. If thou seest another so vigilant to find thee out to reproach thee, how vigilant shouldst thou be over thyself to find out what is in thee to humble thee! Herein, as David speaks, be "wiser than thine enemies," Psal. cxix. 98; and the less credit thou hast in the world, labour for the more in heaven. (2.) Persuade thy soul of the reality of the honour that is in the ways of God: consider thy honour here is real, true, and hereafter it shall be visible to all. (3.) Pity your reproachers; be troubled for their sin instead of thine own disgrace. (4.) Spread thy condition before the Lord when thou art mocked, Psal. cix. 4: prayer was David's best medicine against mocks, Psal. lvii. 2, 3. (5.) Labour for holy magnanimity and greatness of spirit. Great men think themselves above reproaches; exercise thy soul with the great things of eternity. It is a weak-spirited man who cannot endure contempt. St. John's spirit was so holily high, that he calls all the malicious words of Diotrephes but trifling, φλυαρῶν, 3 John 10. (6.) Return not scoff for scoff; for hereby, as you will harden scoffers in their sin, who will think they do not worse than you, and show that you think there is a greater evil in suffering than sinning; so you are put to base shifts, as if you thought that you had no other remedy for an ill name but an ill tongue; and you deprive yourselves of relief from God: and ever remember that he who is willingly overcome in the fight of scoffing is ever the better man. (7.) Keep conscience quiet; let not thy heart reproach thee, Job xxvii. 6. Winds move not the earth unless they get within it: be careful of what you do, and then you need not care what men say.

Obs. 4. It is our duty to shun the sin of scoffing, especially at the people, word, and ways of God. To this end,

(1.) See the beauty and excellency of them. Men deride that which they account base and contemptible. Let not worldly bravery dazzle your eyes. Study the glory of holiness, the comeliness and rationality of every way of God. Learning and religion meet with no other mockers but the ignorant.

(2.) Consider Satan's end in stirring up mockers against the ways and people of God: the devil knows there is no such likely way to darken religion, and to damp the hearts of people from embracing it, as by these; and therefore it is observable, that Julian, one of the subtlest enemies that ever the cause of God had, would not oppose religion by open persecution, but sought all means to cast contempt upon it by jeers and scoffs, and hereby he drew off multitudes from it.

(3.) Labour for faith in threatenings: faith fears a threatened evil as much as sense mourns under an inflicted evil: faith takes into its vast comprehension the threatenings of judgments as well as the promises of mercies; and causes holy fear in respect of the former, as it quells unholy fear in respect of the latter.

(4.) Study the end of God's forbearance. It is not that thou shouldst mock at God, but repent of sin. Scoffers turn the motive to repentance into an encouragement of rebellion. God is not long-suffering, that the wicked should be securely sinning. How unavoidable is his destruction who is ruined by the means of recovery! 2 Chron. xxv. 16; xxxvi. 16.

(5.) Study the vanity of all earthly refuges. Judgment will throw them all down; the overflowing scourge will break down these weak banks, nor will any fancied defences appear any other than paper towers when wrath approaches. "Can thy heart endure, or thy hands be strong," saith God, "in the day when I shall deal with thee?" Ezek. xxii. 24. It is not so easy to resist judgments when they come, as it is to scoff at them before they come. Scoffers, when vengeance meets them, will be found to be but like cowardly soldiers, who though they vaunt, and boast, and swagger before the enemy comes, will run away as soon as they see him come.

Obs. 5. It is our duty to take heed that mockers at our holiness hinder us not in the ways of holiness. Though the clouds darken the light of the sun, yet the sun ceases not its course. Was there ever such a fool as to be scoffed out of his inheritance? and yet it is a greater folly to be scoffed out of holiness: this will make us a reproach before God, angels, and saints, yea, and before our very enemies, who will, when they have got their will of us, the more vilify and contemn us; whereas, if we persist in holiness, they inwardly admire us. They who sought by scoffing to hinder Nehemiah's work, would have mocked him much more, had they caused him to give over He that will not suffer scoffers for God's name, shall deservedly suffer it for his own sin.

The second property of these seducers was their walking "after their own ungodly lusts," of which I have spoken largely before, ver. 16.

The fifth and last particular in this first direction, viz. the remembering the words of the apostles, is the application of their testimony to these seducers, ver. 19, in these words, " These are they who separate themselves, sensual, having not the Spirit." In which words the apostle shows that these who separate themselves from the church were scorners, and that these who were sensual and void of the Spirit followed their ungodly lusts. Or in the words Jude expresses, 1. The sin of these seducers in separating themselves. 2. The cause thereof, which was, (1.) Their being sensual; and, (2.) Their not having the Spirit. For the first, their separation.

Two things are here to be opened.

1. What the apostle intends by separating themselves.

2. Wherein the sinfulness thereof consists.

<small>Segregantes, separantes, disterminantes, exterminantes.</small> 1. What the apostle intends by separating themselves. The words are ἀποδιορίζοντες ἑαυτούς. The word ἀποδιορίζοντες, several ways rendered by several interpreters, may signify the unbounding of a thing, and the removing it from those bounds and limits wherein it was set and placed; for the words ὁρίζω and διορίζω signify to terminate or circumscribe a thing within limits and bounds, and <small>Thus the preposition ἀπό is frequently taken in Scripture.</small> the preposition ἀπό added to it may import the taking away or exempting a thing from those bounds and limits wherein it was contained; and this interpretation of making themselves boundless, as being a generation of libertines that would be kept within no bounds or compass of restraint by Scripture, magistrates, church discipline, &c., agrees both with the word ἀποδιορίζοντες, and also the whole series of the Epistle and context, in which the apostle immediately before saith they walked after their own lusts, and immediately after saith they were sensual, given over to sensual pleasures. These seducers were sons of Belial, without a yoke, like yokeless heifers. Scope and liberty were their study. They would needs make the way to heaven, as he who went over a narrow bridge with spectacles before his eyes desired to make the bridge, seem broader than it was. This interpretation I dare not reject, I desire to present it to the learned; but though upon my maturest thoughts I much incline to it, yet seeing the stream of interpreters going another way, I shall not refuse the second, according to which the word ἀποδιορίζοντες imports the parting and separating of one thing from another by bounds and limits put between them, and the putting of bounds and limits for distinction and separation between several things, a resemblance taken from fields or countries which are distinguished and parted from each other by certain boundaries and landmarks set up to that end; and thus it is commonly taken by interpreters in this place, wherein these seducers may be said to separate themselves, divide or bound themselves from others, either first, doctrinally: or secondly, practically.

(1.) Doctrinally, by false and heretical doctrines, whereby they divided themselves from the true and faithful, who were guided by the truth of the Scripture, and walked according to the rule of the word; hence these seducers were deceiving and deceived, and brought in damnable heresies, and many followed their pernicious ways, 2 Pet. ii. 2; and they spake perverse things to draw away disciples after them. And thus they separated themselves from the church,

[1.] By holding that the grace of God gave men liberty to live as they pleased, and by maintaining unchristian libertinism, because Christ had purchased Christian liberty for us; whereas the word teaches the contrary, namely because the grace of God hath appeared, therefore that we should deny ungodliness and worldly lust, Tit. ii. 11, 12.

[2.] By teaching that among the people of God there ought to be no civil magistrate, no superiority, nor any to restrain and hinder people from going on in what ways they pleased; whereas the word commands every soul to be subject.

[3.] By denying the day of judgment, at which they scoffed as at a vain scarecrow, because it was deferred; whereas the faithful were to account the long-suffering of the Lord salvation, 2 Pet. iii. 15, to labour to be made meet for the approach of Christ, and to look for the mercy of the Lord to eternal life.

(2.) Practically, they might separate themselves as by bounds and limits.

[1.] By profaneness, and living in a different way from the saints, namely, in all looseness and uncleanness; for as the faithful separate and difference themselves from the wicked by their holy and heavenly conversation, so the wicked divide themselves from the faithful by profaneness, and falling from the profession of godliness into all manner of looseness and irregularity; and thus the ungodly make such bounds between themselves and saints as saints dare not break over, ungodliness being too high a wall for a godly man to scale, or rather too deep a moat for him to swim over and wade through.

[2.] By schismaticalness, and making of separation from and divisions in the church. Because they proudly despised the doctrines or persons of the Christians as contemptible and unworthy, or because they would not endure the holy severity of the church's discipline, they, <small>Discessionem faciunt ab ecclesia quia disciplinæ jugum ferre nequeunt. Calv. in loc.</small> saith Calvin, departed from it. They might make rents and divisions in the church by schismatical withdrawing themselves from fellowship and communion with it. Their heresies were perverse and damnable opinions, their schism was a perverse separation from church communion; the former was in doctrinals, the latter in practicals. The former was opposite to faith, this latter to charity. By faith all the members are united to the Head, by charity <small>Schismaticos facit non diversa fides, sed communionis disrupta societas. Aug. Contr. Faust. l. 20. c. 3.</small> one to another; and as the breaking of the former is heresy, so their breaking of the latter was schism. And this schism stands in dissolving the spiritual band of love and union among Christians, and appears in withdrawing from the performance of those duties which are both the signs of and helps to Christian unity; as prayer, hearing, receiving of sacraments, &c. For because the dissolving of Christian union chiefly appears in the undue separation from church communion, therefore this rending is rightly called schism. It is usually said to be twofold, negative and positive. The first, the negative, is <small>Camero de schismate.</small> when there is only *simplex secessio*, when there is only a bare secession, a peaceable and quiet withdrawing from communion with a church without making head against that church from which they depart. 2. The other, the positive, is when persons so withdrawing consociate and draw themselves into a distinct and opposite body, setting up a church against a church, or, as divines express it, from Augustine, an altar against an altar; and this it is which in a peculiar manner, and by way of eminency, is called by the name of schism, and becomes sinful either in respect of the groundlessness, or the manner thereof. 1. The groundlessness, when there is no casting of persons out of the church by an unjust censure of excommunication, no departure by unsufferable persecution, no heresy nor idolatry in the church maintained, no necessity, if communion be held with a church, of communicating in its sins and corruptions. 2. The manner of separation makes it unlawful, when it is made without due endeavour and waiting for reformation of the church from which the departure is; and such a rash departure is against charity, which suffers both much and long, 1 Cor. xiii. 4, all tolerable things. It is not presently distasted; when the most just occasion is given, it first uses all possible means of remedy. The surgeon reserves dismembering as the last remedy. It looks upon a sudden breaking off from communion with a church, which is a dismembering, not as surgery, but butchery; not as medicinal, but cruel.

2. The sinfulness of this separation. Not to speak of the sinfulness of separation by heresies and profaneness, having shown it at large before, but briefly to manifest the sinfulness of schismatical separation. I shall not spend time to compare it with heresy, though some have said that schism is the greater sin of the two. Augustine tells the Donatists, that schism was a greater sin than that of the Traditores, who in time of persecution, through fear, delivered up their Bibles to the persecutors to be burnt; a sin at which the Donatists took so much offence, that it was the ground of their separation. But to pass by these things: by these three considerations especially the sinfulness of schism shows itself.

Sunt qui peccatum schismatis adæquent peccato heresis; sunt qui illud adhuc præ isto exaggerent. Musc. loc. Com. de Schism. Aug. Cont. Donat. lib. 2. cap. 6.

In respect of Christ, the parties separating, and those from whom they separate.

1. In respect of Christ. (1.) It is a horrible indignity offered to his body, dividing Christ, as the apostle speaks, 1 Cor. i. 13, and makes him appear as the head of two bodies: how monstrous and dishonourable is the very conceit hereof!

(2.) It is rebellion against his command, his great command of love. The grace of love is by some called the queen of graces; and it is greater than faith in respect of its object, not God only, but man; its duration, which is eternal; its manner of working, not in a way of receiving Christ, as faith, but of giving out the soul to him; and the command of love is the greatest command in respect of its comprehensiveness, taking in all the commandments, the end of them all being love, and it being the fulfilling of them all, Eph. iv. 3; Phil. ii. 2; John xiii. 34.

(3.) It is opposite to one great end of Christ's greatest undertaking, his death, which was that his saints should be one, John xvii. 21—23.

(4.) It tends to frustrate his prayer for unity among saints, John xvii., and endeavours that Christ may not be heard by his Father.

(5.) It opposes his example: "By this shall all men," saith he, "know that ye are my disciples, if ye love one another." Love is the livery and cognizance which Christ gives to every Christian. If there be no fellowship among Christians, there is no following of Christ. "Let this mind be in you which was in Christ Jesus," Phil. ii. 5.

(6.) It is injurious to his service and worship. How can men pray, if in wrath and division? How can Christians fight with heaven, and prevail, when they are in so many divided troops? What worthiness can be in those communicants who celebrate a feast of love with hearts full of rancour and malice?

2. In respect of the parties separating. For,

(1.) It causes a decay of all grace. By divisions among ourselves we endeavour to divide ourselves from Him, in and from whom is all our fulness. All wickedness follows contention. Upon the stock of schism commonly heresy is grafted. There is no schism, saith Jerom, but ordinarily it invents and produces some heresy, that the separation may seem the more justifiable. The Novatians and Donatists from schism fell to heresies: our own times sadly comment upon this truth, equally arising to both. The farther lines are distanced one from another, the greater is their distance from the centre; and the more divided Christians are among themselves, the more they divide themselves from Christ. Branches divided from the tree receive no sap from the root. The soul gives life to members which are joined together, not plucked asunder.

Nullum schisma non sibi aliquam confingit hæresim, ut recte ab ecclesia recessisse videatur. Hierom. in Tit.

(2.) Schism is the greatest disgrace to the schismatics. A schismatic is a name much disowned, because very dishonourable. All posterity loads the name of sinful separatists with disgrace and abhorrence. He spake truly, who said, The sin and misery of schism cannot be blotted out with the blood of martyrdom. He cannot honourably give his life for Christ who makes divisions in his church, for which Christ gave his life.

3. In respect of the church from which this separation is made; for, (1.) It is injurious to the honour of the church, whose greatest glory is union, Cant. vi. 9. How can a body be rent and torn without impairing its beauty? Besides, how disgraceful an imputation is cast upon any church, when we profess it unworthy for any to abide in it, that Christ will not, and therefore that we cannot, have communion with it!

(2.) It is injurious to the peace and quietness of the church. Schismatics more oppose the peace of the church than do heathens. If the natural body be divided and torn, pain and smart must needs follow. The tearing and rending of the mystical body goes to the heart of all sensible members. They often cause the feverish distempers of hatred, wrath, seditions, envyings, murders. Schism in the church puts the members out of joint, and disjointed bones are painful. "All my bones," saith David, "are out of joint." Church divisions cause sad thoughts of heart: true members are sensible of these schisms, though artificial ones feel nothing. None rejoice but our enemies. Oh impiety! to make Satan music, and to make mourning for the saints!

(3.) It is opposite to the edification of the church. Division of tongues hindered the building of Babel, and doubtless division in hearts, tongues, hands, heads, must needs hinder the building of Jerusalem: while parties are contending, churches and commonwealths suffer. In troublous times the walls and temple of Jerusalem went but slowly on. Though Jesus Christ, the Head, be the only fountain of spiritual life, yet the usual way of Christ's strengthening and perfecting it is the fellowship of the body, that by what every joint supplies the whole may be increased: when church members are put out of joint, they are made unserviceable, and unfit to perform their several offices. They who were wont to join in prayer, sacraments, fasting, and were ready to all mutual offices of love, are now fallen off from all.

(4.) It is opposite to the future estate of the church in glory. In heaven the faithful shall be of one mind. We shall all meet, saith the apostle, "in the unity of the faith," Eph. iv. 13, when we are come to our manly age. Wrangling is the work of childhood and folly, and a great piece of the folly of our childhood. Luther and Calvin are of one mind in heaven, though their disciples wrangle here on earth.

Obs. 1. Naturally men love to be boundless; they will not be kept within any spiritual compass, nor endure to be held in any bounds. This, according to one signification of the word ἀποδιορίζοντες, the apostle Jude aims at in this place. Wicked men are sons of Belial; they cannot endure the yoke of Christ, though it be sweet and easy. They break his bonds asunder, and cast away his cords from them, Psal. ii. 3. Men love to have liberty to damn their own souls. They backslide like "a backsliding heifer," Hos. iv. 16. Though men account it no unwelcome straitening to them to have a fence between them and their bodily enemies, yet they cannot endure those limits and bounds of God's law or corrections which stop them from sin; their fear of hurt makes them love preservation, their love of pleasure makes them desirous of sinful liberty. How good a sign of a gracious heart is it, rather to desire to be in Christ's enclosure than in Satan's champaign! to account Christ's service our liberty, and Satan's liberty our bondage! How just also is God in suffering sinners to take their course and swing in the ways of sin and destruction! They who will not be kept within God's compass, are deservedly left to Satan's disposal. They who are backsliding heifers, who will not endure the yoke, are justly threatened to be suffered to be as a lamb in a large place, without a keeper or preserver. They shall have their fill of liberty; but their liberty is like that of the deer, which, though it were gotten out of the park-pale, yet it was at the cruel courtesy of the hounds. On the contrary, God is very gracious in stopping up his church's way, though with a "thorny hedge," Hos. ii. 6. O happy thorns, that stop us in our ways to hell! Such thorns are better than roses. The setting up of the thorny hedge is a promise, a branch of the covenant.

Obs. 2. Our separation from Rome cannot be charged with schism.

This will evidently appear, if we consider either the ground or the manner of our separation.

(1.) For the ground and cause thereof. Our separation from Rome was not for some slight and tolerable errors, but damnable heresies and gross idolatries. The heresies fundamental, and idolatries such as those who hold communion with her cannot but partake of. In respect of both which the church of Rome was first apostatized before ever we separated; nor was there any separation from it as it had any thing of Christ, or as it was Christian, but as it was Roman and popish. The apostacy of the Roman church, which was the ground of our separation, appeared sundry ways. [1.] In that she thrust the Lord Jesus, the great and only Teacher of the church, out of the chair, and in it placed the pope as the infallible doctor of the church, to whom she ties her belief, and subjects her faith, though he always may, and oft does, rise up against Christ himself. [2.] The Scriptures, the alone rule of faith, the Romanists slight and impiously despise, and make them an insufficient rule of faith, by joining their over-fond and false traditions to it, by preferring a vicious and barbarous interpretation before the sacred originals, by making the Holy Scriptures to have neither life, nor soul, nor voice, till the interpretation of the church, or rather of the pope, be added. [3.] They have depraved the great and main article of faith concerning the justification of a sinner, the nature of which, though the Scripture makes to stand in the remission of sins, and the application of Christ's righteousness by faith, yet they ascribe it partly to Christ's, and partly to our own merits and righteousness, in which respect that of the apostle suits with them, "Christ is become of no effect to you who are justified by the law." [4.] Though the worshipping of the immortal and invisible God under any visible image or representation, or the likeness of a mortal creature, is frequently and expressly forbidden in Scripture; yet they set forth and teach the worshipping of the Father under the image of an old man, the Son under the image of a lamb, and the Holy Ghost of a dove. *Ecclesiæ Romanæ usus admittit hasce trinitatis imagines, eæque pinguntur non* And Cajetan confesses that they draw these images of the Trinity, not only to show, but to adore and worship them. *solum ut ostendantur, sed ut adorentur. In 3. Aq. 9. 29. Art. 3.* To these I might add their maiming, or rather marring, the sacrament of the Lord's supper, their denying the cup to the laity, their ascribing of remission and expiation of sin to the sacrifice of the mass, their seven sacraments, their praying to saints, and ascribing to the Virgin Mary the bestowing grace and glory, pardon of sin, *Psalt. Rom.* &c.; their dispensations with the most hideous and hellish abominations, as murders, incest, sodomy, &c., for money.

(2.) For the second, the manner of our separation. It was not uncharitable, rash, heady, and unadvised, nor before all means were used for the cure and reformation of the Romanists, by the discovery of their errors, that possibly could be devised; notwithstanding all which, though some have been enforced to an acknowledgment of them, they still obstinately persist in them. Our famous godly and learned reformers would have healed Babylon, but she is not healed; many skilful physicians have had her in hand, but like the woman in the gospel, she grew so much the worse. By prayer, preaching, writing, yea, by sealing their doctrine with their blood, have sundry eminent instruments of Christ endeavoured to reclaim the popish from their errors; but instead of being reclaimed, they anathematized them with the most dreadful curses; excommunicated, yea, murdered and destroyed multitudes of those who endeavoured their reducement, not permitting any to trade, buy, or sell, to have either religious or civil communion with them, except they received the beast's mark in their hands and foreheads. All which considered, we might safely forsake her, nay, could not safely do otherwise. Since, instead of our healing Babylon, we could not be preserved from her destroying us, we deservedly departed from her, and every one went into his own country; and unless we had so done, we could not have obeyed the clear precept of the word, Jer. li. 9. "Come out of her, my people," &c. Rev. xviii. 4. Timothy is commanded to withdraw himself from perverse and unsound teachers, 1 Tim. vi. 3, 5. Though Paul went into the synagogue, disputing and persuading the things concerning the kingdom of God; yet "when divers were hardened and believed not, but spake evil of that way, he departed from them, and separated the disciples," Acts xix. 9. And expressly is communion with idolaters forbidden, 1 Cor. x. 14. And 2 Cor. vi. 14—17, "What fellowship hath righteousness with unrighteousness? what communion hath light with darkness? what concord hath Christ with Belial? what agreement hath the temple of God with idols? Come out from among them, and be ye separate." And Hos. iv. 15, "Though thou, Israel, play the harlot, yet let not Judah offend; and come ye not unto Gilgal, neither go ye up to Beth-aven." Though in name that place was Beth-el, the house of God; yet because Jeroboam's calf was set up there, it was indeed Beth-aven, the house of vanity. If Rome be a Beth-aven for idolatry and corrupting of God's worship, our departure from it may be safely acknowledged and justified. In vain therefore do the Romanists, Stapleton, Sanders, and others, brand our separation from them with the odious imputation of Donatism and schism; it being evident out of Augustine, that the Donatists never objected any thing against, nor could blame any thing in, the church from which they separated, either for faith or worship; whereas we have unanswerably proved the pseudo-catholic Roman church to be notoriously guilty both of heresy *Nic. Sanderus de Visib. Monar. Eccles. præfat. ad lect. Staplet. demonstrat. Princ. fid. l. 4. c. 10.*

and idolatry; and our adversaries themselves grant, in whatever church either of those depravations are found, communion with it is to be broken off. I shall conclude this discourse with that passage out of Musculus concerning schism. There is a double schism, the one bad, the other good; the bad is that whereby a good union, the good that whereby a bad union, is broken asunder. If ours be a schism, it is of the latter sort.

Schisma aliud malum, aliud bonum. Malum quo bona, bonum quo mala, scinditur unitas. Musc. de Schism.

Obs. 3. The voluntary and unnecessary dividing and separation from a true church is schismatical. When we put bounds and partitions between it and ourselves, we sin, say some, as did these seducers here taxed by Jude. If the church be not heretical or idolatrous, or do not by excommunication, persecution, &c. thrust us out of its communion; if it be such a one as Christ the Head has communion with; we the members ought not by separation to rend and divide the body. To separate from congregations where the word of truth and gospel of salvation are held forth in an ordinary way, as the proclamations of princes are held forth upon pillars to which they are affixed; where the light of the truth is set up as upon a candlestick to guide passengers to heaven, 1 Tim. iii. 15; to separate from them to whom belong the covenants, and where the sacraments, the seals of the covenant, are for substance rightly dispensed; where Christ walketh in the midst of his golden candlesticks, Rev. i. 13, and discovers his presence in his ordinances, whereby they are made effectual to the conversion and edification of souls in an ordinary way; where the members are saints by a professed subjection to Christ and his gospel, and probably have promised this explicitly and openly; where there are many who in the judgment of charity may be conceived to have the work of grace really wrought in their hearts, by walking in some measure answerable to their profession; I say, to separate from these, as those with whom church communion is not to be held and maintained, is unwarrantable and schismatical. Pretences for separation, I am not ignorant, are alleged; frequently and most plausibly that of mixed communion, and of admitting into church fellowship the vile with the precious, and those who are chaff, and therefore ought not to lodge with the wheat. I answer, (1.) Not to insist upon what some have urged, viz. that this has been the stone at which most schismatics have stumbled, and the pretence which they have of old alleged, as having ever had a *spiritum excommunicatorium*, a spirit rather putting them upon dividing from those who they say are unholy, than putting them upon any godly endeavours of making themselves holy, as is evident in the examples of the Audæans, Novatians, Donatists, Anabaptists, Brownists, &c. (2.) Let them consider whether the want of the exact purging and reforming of these abuses proceed not rather from some unhappy obstructions and political restrictions, whether or no caused by those who make this objection, God knows, in the exercise of discipline, than from the allowance or neglect of the church itself. Nay, (3.) Let them consider whether when they separate for sinful mixtures, the church be not at that very time purging out those sinful mixtures; and is that a time to make a separation from a church by departing from it, when the servants of Christ are making a separation in that church by reforming it? But, (4.) Let it be seriously weighed, that some sinful mixtures are not a sufficient cause of separation from a church. Has not God his church even where corruption of manners has crept into it, if purity of doctrine be maintained? and is separation from that church lawful, from which God does not separate? Did the apostle, because of the sinful mixtures in the church of Corinth, direct the faithful to separate? Must not he who will forbear communion with a church till it be altogether freed from mixtures, tarry till the day of judgment? till when we have no promise that Christ will gather out of his church whatsoever doth offend. (5.) Let them consider whether God has made private Christians stewards in his house, to determine whether those with whom they communicate are fit members of the church or not; or rather, whether it is not their duty, when they discover tares in the church, instead of separating from it, to labour that they may be found good corn, that so when God shall come to gather his corn into his garner, they may not be thrown out? Church officers are ministerially trusted with the ordering of the church, and for the opening and shutting of the doors of the church's communion by the keys of doctrine and discipline; and herein, if they shall either be hindered or negligent, private Christians shall not be entangled in the guilt of their sin, if they be humbled, and use all lawful means for remedy, though they do communicate. (6.) Let them search whether there is any scripture warrant to break off communion with the church in the ordinances, when there is no defect in the ordinances themselves, only upon this ground, because some are admitted to them who, because of their personal miscarriages, ought to be debarred. The Jews of old, though they separated when the worship itself was corrupted, 2 Chron. xi. 14, 16, yet not because wicked men were suffered to be in outward communion with them, Jer. vii. 9, 10. Nor do the precepts or patterns of the Christian churches for casting out offenders give any liberty to separation, in case of failing to cast them out; and though permitting scandalous persons is blamed, yet not communicating with them. The command not to eat with a brother who is a fornicator or covetous, &c., 1 Cor. v. 11; Rev. ii. 14, 15, 20, 24, concerns not religious, but civil communion, by a voluntary, familiar, intimate conversation, either in being invited or in inviting, as is clear by these two arguments. 1. That eating which is here forbidden with a brother is allowed to be with a heathen; but it is the civil eating which is only allowed to be with a heathen; therefore it is the civil eating which is forbidden to be with a brother. 2. The eating here forbidden is for the punishment of the guilty, not for a punishment to the innocent; but if religious eating at the sacrament were forbidden, the greatest punishment would fall upon the innocent, the godly. Now though such civil eating was to be forborne, yet it follows not at all, much less much more, that religious eating is forbidden, 1. Because civil eating is arbitrary and unnecessary; not so religious, which is enjoined, and a commanded duty. 2. There is danger of being infected by the wicked in civil, familiar, and arbitrary eatings; not so in joining with them in a holy and commanded service and ordinance. 3. Civil eating is done out of love either to the party inviting or invited, but religious is done out of love to Jesus Christ, were it not for whom we would neither eat at sacrament with wicked men, nor at all.

To conclude this: Separation from churches from which Christ does not separate is schismatical. Now it is clear in the Scripture that Christ owns churches where faith is found for the substance, and their worship gospel worship, though there are many defects and sinful mixtures among them. And what I have said concerning the schism of separation because of the sinful mixtures of those who are wicked in practice, is as true concerning separation from them who are erroneous in judgment, if the errors of those from whom the separation is made are not fundamental, and hinder communion with Christ the Head. And much more clear, if clearer can be, is the schismaticalness of those who separate from and renounce all communion with those churches which are not of their own manner of constitution, and modelled according to the platform of their own particular church order. To refrain fellowship and communion with such churches who profess Christ their Lord, whose faith is sound, whose worship is gospel worship, whose lives are holy, because they come not into that particular way of church order which we have pitched upon, is a schismatical rending of the church of Christ to pieces. Of this the church of Rome are most guilty, who most plainly ἀποδιορίζειν ἑαυτούς, and circumscribe and bound the church of Christ within the limits and boundaries of the Roman jurisdiction, even so that they cast off all churches in the world, yea, and cut them off from all hope of salvation, who subject not themselves to their way. Herein likewise those separatists among ourselves are heinously faulty, who censure and condemn all other churches, though their faith, worship, and conversation be never so Scriptural, merely because they are not gathered into church order according to their own patterns. In Scripture, churches are commended and dignified according as their fundamental faith was sound, and their lives holy; not according to the regularity of their first manner of gathering. And notwithstanding the most exact regularity of their first gathering, when churches have once apostatized from faith and manners, Christ has withdrawn communion from them, and most severely censured them. And this making of the first gathering of people into church fellowship to be the rule to direct us with whom we may hold communion, will make us refuse some churches upon whom are seen the Scripture characters of true churches, and join with others only upon a human testimony, because men only tell us they were orderly gathered.

Obs. 4. It should be our care to shun separation. To this end,

(1.) Labour to be progressive in the work of mortification: the less carnal we are, the less contention and dividing will be among us. "Are ye not carnal?" saith the apostle; and he proves it from their divisions. Separation is usually, but very absurdly, accounted a sign of a high-grown Christian. We wrangle because we are children, and are men in malice because children in holiness: wars among ourselves proceed from the "lusts that war in our members," James iv. 1.

(2.) Admire no man's person. The excessive regarding of some, makes us despise others in respect of them. When one man seems a giant, another will seem a dwarf in comparison of him. This caused the Corinthian schism. Take heed of man worship as well as image worship; let not idolatry be changed, but abolished. Of this largely before, upon "Having men's persons in admiration."

(3.) Labour for experimental benefit by the ordinances. Men separate to those churches which they account better, because they never found those where they were before to them good. Call not ministers good, as the young man in the gospel did Christ, complimentally only; for if so, you will soon call them bad. Find the setting up of Christ in your hearts by the ministry, and then you will not dare to account it antichristian. If, with Jacob, we could say of our Beth-els, God is here; we would set up pillars, nay, be such, for our constancy in abiding in them.

(4.) Neither give nor receive scandals; give them not to occasion others to separate, nor receive them to occasion thine own separation; watch exactly, construe doubtful matters charitably. Look not upon blemishes with multiplying glasses, or old men's spectacles. Hide them, though not imitate them. Sport not yourselves with others' nakedness. Turn separation *from* into lamentation *for* the scandalous.

(5.) Be not much taken with novelties. New lights have set this church on fire; for the most part, they are taken out of the dark lanterns of old heretics. They are false and fools' fires to lead men into the precipice of separation. Love truth in an old dress; let not antiquity be a prejudice against, nor novelty an inducement to the entertainment of truth.

(6.) Give not way to lesser differences. A little division will soon rise up to greater: small wedges make way for bigger. Our hearts are like tinder, a little spark will inflame them. Be jealous of your hearts when contentions begin, stifle them in the cradle. Paul and Barnabas separated about a small matter, the taking of an associate, Acts xv. 36—40.

(7.) Beware of pride, the mother of contention and separation. Love not the pre-eminence; rather be fit for than desirous of rule; despise not the meanest; say not, I have no need of thee. All schisms and heresies are mostly grafted upon the stock of pride. The first rent that was ever made in God's family was by the pride of angels, ver. 14, and that pride was nothing else but the desire of independence.

(8.) Avoid self-seeking: he who seeks his own things and profit will not mind the good and peace of the church. O take heed lest thy secular interest draw thee to a new communion, and thou colour over thy departure with religion and conscience.

Thus we have spoken of the first, viz. what these seducers did; "separate themselves."

2. The cause of their separation, or what they were, in these words; "sensual, having not the Spirit." Wherein,

1. Their estate is propounded; they were "sensual."

2. Explained; "having not the Spirit."

But, 1. In what respect were they "sensual," and "having not the Spirit."

2. Why does the apostle here represent them to be such.

1. In what respect were they "sensual."

The word ψυχικοί, here translated sensual, comes from ψυχή, *anima*, the soul; so that ψυχικὸς signifies primarily one who has a soul. And in Scripture the word is used three ways. (1.) Sometimes it is joined with the word body, in opposition to a glorified body; and then the body is called a natural body, that is, such a body as is informed, governed, moved by the soul; or is subject to animal affections and operations, as generation, nutrition, augmentation, &c.; or such a body as is sustained and upheld by the actions of the soul, as it receives from it life and vegetation; that is, by the action of the vegetative power, the chief whereof is nutrition, which cannot be without nourishment; so that this natural body wants the constant help of nourishment for its preservation, in which respect it is distinguished from a glorified body. (2.) This word ψυχικὸς is in Scripture opposed to regenerate, and so imports one who has in him nothing excellent but a rational soul, who is governed only by the natural light of reason, who has in him only natural abilities and perfections. And when it is thus taken, our learned translators translate ψυχικὸς by the word natural, 1 Cor. ii. 14, intending one who is guided by natural reason, he being there opposed to πνευματικὸς, the spiritual man, who is endued with and guided by a Divine and supernatural illumination. (3.) It is taken for one who, <small>Vid. Aquin. Cajet. Estium, Pareum. in 1 Cor. xv. 44. Piscat. Bez.</small>

being guided by no better light than that of his own natural reason, or rather who, being altogether addicted to the service of that part which is called ψυχή, the soul, 1 Thess. v. 23, whereby is meant the sensitive and inferior part of the soul, the sensual appetite, common to man with the beasts, as distinct from πνεῦμα, the spirit, or intellectual and rational part, follows the dictates of that his sensual appetite, and the inclinations of his sensitive soul, and his only bent and intent is upon satisfaction by worldly delights; his study and care is for the sensitive and vegetative part, and for those things which belong to the animal and present life: and hence it is that some learned men, and amongst others Lorinus, conceive that ψυχικοί, sensual, comes from ψυχή, as ψυχή is (in Scripture) used to denote life, and the functions of life common to us with beasts. Thus Christ saith, "Take no thought for your life," τῇ ψυχῇ, "what ye shall eat, or what ye shall drink," &c. "Is not the life," ἡ ψυχή, "more than meat," &c.? Matt. vi. 25. And in this notion of sensuality Tertullian, after he began to favour Montanism, took the word ψυχικοί, when he fastened that odious name of *physici* upon the orthodox, because they refused to condemn second marriages. And in this place likewise, with submission to more mature judgments, I conceive that ψυχικοί is intended to denote their brutish and unruly sensuality. Thus the Arabic interpreter, and Œcumenius, with sundry others, likewise understand it. Thus likewise our learned translators thought, who interpreted the word sensual, as conceiving that Jude intended that they altogether served their sensitive and vegetative soul, and (as beasts) followed their senses, and lived in the lusts of the flesh, not according to the Spirit, prosecuting those carnal objects with all industry which tend to preserve their present life, and choosing rather to leave the church, than to abridge themselves of any bodily pleasures. And the apostle by this word seems to me to make their brutish sensuality and propensities to be the cause of their separation; as if he said, They will not live under the strict discipline where they must be curbed and restrained from following their lusts; no, these sensualists will be alone by themselves in companies, where they may have their fill of all sensual pleasures, and where they may gratify their genius to the utmost. And this exposition of ψυχικοί most aptly agrees also to that first interpretation of ἀποδιορίζοντες, viz. such who will be boundless, and kept within no limits or compass, but like a company of beasts shut up in a field, who seeing better pasture in that on the other side of the hedge, and desirous also of more scope, break the fence, and leap over the bars, that they may both run and raven. The more I think of ἀποδιορίζοντες, the more I incline to think the apostle intends thereby to represent them boundless, extravagant libertines.

The apostle represents them "having not the Spirit."

The word spirit, not to speak of the many acceptations of the word, when attributed to the creatures, to angels, the soul, &c., when attributed to God, is taken either, (1.) Οὐσιωδῶς, essentially, and so God is called a Spirit, a spiritual essence, John iv. 24; and the Divine nature of Christ is set forth by the word Spirit, 1 Tim. iii. 16; 1 Pet. iii. 18; Heb. ix. 14. Or, (2.) Ὑποστατικῶς, personally, in which respect it notes the Third Person in the blessed Trinity: and thus it is taken, either, 1. Properly, for the Third Person, Matt. xxviii. 19; John i. 32; xiv. 26; Eph. i. 13; 1 Thess. i. 6, &c.; or, 2. Improperly and metonymically, for the effects and gifts of the Holy Spirit, ordinary or extraordinary; in which respect some are said to be anointed with the Spirit, to have the Spirit on and in them, to be filled with the Spirit, Luke ii. 25; iv. 18; Acts ii. 17, 18; Tit. iii. 6; Acts viii. 15, 16; x. 44; Luke i. 41; Acts iv. 8, 31; vi. 3, 5; vii. 55; xiii. 9, 52; 1 Cor. i. 4; 2 Cor. vi. 6; Gal. iii. 2; v. 17; and in this respect these seducers are said not to have the Spirit, viz. the saving, working, gifts, graces of the Spirit, to teach, act, and rule them, to sanctify and purify them, &c., which they wanting, it was no wonder that they were sensual and given over to the sinful prosecution of all carnal delights and pleasures: not having the Spirit, they could not walk in the Spirit, Gal. v. 16, 17; not having the Spirit to lust in them against the flesh, they must needs be carried away with the lusts of the flesh, as acting them without contradiction, Rom. viii. 1, 9.

2. Why does the apostle so represent them. The apostle seems to add this their sensuality and want of the Spirit to their separating themselves, not only to show that sensuality was the cause of their separation, and the want of the Spirit the cause of both; but as if he intended directly to thwart and cross them in their pretences of having a high and extraordinary measure of spiritualness above others, by their dividing themselves from others, who, as these seducers might pretend, were in so low a form of Christianity, and had so little spiritualness, that they were not worthy to keep them company; whereas Jude tells these Christians that these seducers were so far from being more spiritual than others, that they were mere sensualists, and had nothing in them of the Spirit at all. For by their boundless separation and sensuality, they showed that, (1.) They had not the Spirit of wisdom, discerning, and illumination, to discover to them the beauty of that holiness and truth which were in the ways of the saints which they hated and forsook, and to guide and lead them to that happiness which they should look after for themselves. The Spirit is a Spirit of truth, John xiv. 17; xv. 26, of knowledge, of judgment, Isa. xi. 2; xxvi. 8. The Spirit guides into all truth, and is a voice which saith, "This is the way;" whereas these seducers were led by a fool's fire into the bogs and precipices of delusion and damnation by a lying spirit, a spirit of error, 1 John iv. 6.

(2.) They had not the Spirit of renovation to change their natures, of sanctification and holiness to mortify their lusts. The Spirit of God is a holy Spirit, Rom. i. 4; a Spirit of grace, Zech. xii. 10. "Through the Spirit we mortify the deeds of the flesh," Rom. viii. 13; whereas these impure monsters wallowed in all manner of sensuality and uncleanness, and showed that they were acted by an unclean, impure spirit; that they walked not after the Spirit, but the flesh.

(3.) They had not the Spirit of meekness, love, peace: these are the fruits of the Spirit, Gal. v. 22, 23. The Spirit makes us enjoy peace in ourselves, and study peace with others; whereas these incendiaries made rents and schisms in the church of Christ; by their divisions they showed themselves carnal.

(4.) They had not the Spirit of liberty and activity in the ways of God, 2 Cor. iii. 17; they were without any quickening of the Spirit; they were not able to do any good work, nor enlivened in any way of holiness; but slaves and prisoners, even in *arcta custodia*, to Satan and their own lusts; the servants of corruption, though they boasted of liberty.

Obs. 1. Commonly sensuality lies at the bottom of sinful separation and making of sects. "Separate themselves, sensual" &c. It is oft seen that they who divide themselves from the faithful, either in opinion or practice, aim at looseness and libertinism. Such were the Nicolaitans and the disciples of Jezebel, Rev. ii. 6, 20, who seduced the people of God to commit fornication. Heretics are seldom without their harlots; Simon Magus had his Helena, Montanus his Maximilla, Donatus his Lucilia, Priscillian his Galla, Pope Sergius his Marozia, Gregory the Seventh his Matildis, Alexander the Sixth his Lucretia, Leo the Tenth his Magdalena, Paul the Third his Constantia. Rome, which condemns all the churches in the world, sets an easy rate upon all the impure practices of luxury, natural and unnatural. The Anabaptists allow plurality of wives; and some of them have said that none of their sect can commit adultery with another's wife, according to the etymology of *adulterium*, for all their sect, say they, are so knit the one to the other, that they are all one body. John of Leyden had thirteen wives, and gave a liberty to every one to marry as many as they pleased.

Ad alterum.

Obs. 2. It is possible for those who are sensual and without the Spirit to boast of spiritualness.

Obs. 3. Sanctity and sensuality cannot agree together. If a man be sensual, he has not the Spirit; if he have the Spirit, he will not be sensual. Sowing to the Spirit, and to the flesh, are opposed, Gal. vi. 8. The opposition also is remarkable, " Be not drunk with wine," &c., " but be filled with the Spirit," Eph. v. 18: when sense is gratified, the Spirit is opposed. Mark the like opposition also Rom. viii. 13, " If ye live after the flesh, ye shall die: but if ye through the Spirit do mortify the deeds of the body, ye shall live." " But put ye on the Lord Jesus, and make no provision for the flesh, to fulfil the lusts thereof," Rom. xiii. 14. And, " The flesh lusteth against the Spirit, and the Spirit against the flesh," Gal. v. 17: these have contrary originals; the one is from earth, the other from heaven. The motions of sensual lusts and the Spirit are contrary, one downward, another upward; a man cannot look those contrary ways at once. Lust, like the woman's disease in the gospel, bows us down to the earth; the Spirit moves to the things above. Like two balances, if one go up, the other goes down; they put upon contrary practices, Gal. v. 17. " Walk in the Spirit, and ye shall not fulfil the lust of the flesh," ver. 16. They both endeavour to take up, and each to engross and monopolize, the whole man, soul and body; they will neither endure to have their dominion over man parted. They can admit of no accommodation; whatever means or helps advance the one, suppress and expel the other. The fuel of lust (worldly excess) extinguishes the Spirit; the preservatives of the Spirit, prayer, word, fasting, meditation, are the poisons of lusts. Oh the madness then of those who think to serve these contrary masters! Matt. vi. 24. If one be loved, the other must be forsaken. The allowance of any inordinate lust is inconsistent with the Spirit. How great should our care be to take the Spirit's part against the flesh! (1.) By a thorough, hearty, inward work of mortification, and the plucking up of lust by the roots, not only by snibbing the blade. (2.) By a holy and watchful moderation in worldly enjoyments, behind which Satan, like the Philistines, ever lies in ambush when the lust, like Delilah, is tempting. (3.) By diverting thy joys and pleasure upon heavenly objects; and, (4.) By labouring for a sanctified improvement of all the stoppages in the way of lust, and God's breaking down thy bridges in thy march.

Obs. 4. They who want the Spirit are easily brought over to sensuality. They had not the Spirit, and no wonder if sensual. Natural light is not enough to overcome natural lusts. He who is but a mere man may soon become a prey to sensuality. *Væ soli*, woe to him who has not this Spirit to renew him, nay, constantly to reside in him, and to actuate him! Even saints themselves, when the Spirit withdraws and leaves them to themselves, how sensual have they proved! David, Lot, Samson are proofs. Let thy great care be then to keep the Spirit from departing. It was David's prayer, "Take not thy Holy Spirit from me," Psal. li. 11. Take heed of giving way to sins of pleasure, or to sins of deliberation, or to repeated sins, or to sins against conscience, or to the sin of pride and presumption of thine own strength. Delight not in sinful company. Beware of worldlymindedness. Follow the dictates of the Spirit, and listen to its first motions. Fruitfully improve the ordinances wherein the Spirit delights to breathe.

VERSE 20.

But ye, beloved, building up yourselves on your most holy faith, praying in the Holy Ghost.

THE second direction to teach the Christians how to observe the former exhortation to contend for the truth, and to oppose seducers, is building up themselves on their most holy faith; yet so as this and the next direction are set down as dispositions and means to keep themselves in the love of God, mentioned in the next verse. In this the apostle shows, and we ought to explain, three things.

1. The builders, or the parties directed; " **Beloved.**" Of these I have before treated.

2. Their foundation; their " most holy faith."

3. Their building thereon, in these words; " building up yourselves on," &c.

2. The foundation; their " most holy faith."

In this I might inquire, (1.) What is meant by " faith." (2.) How it is called " your faith." (3.) How it is called " most holy."

(1.) What is meant by " faith." By faith I understand the doctrine of faith; for enlargement upon which, and reasons why the word is called faith, I refer the reader to what I have spoken, p. 62, 63.

(2.) This faith is called " your faith;" and the doctrine of faith was theirs, [1.] Because of ministration. It was delivered to the saints, and by God given to them, and to others for their sakes.

[2.] Because they received it, were moulded into it. It was so delivered to them, that they (as the apostle speaks) were delivered into it; as it was ministered to them so it was accepted by them. It was not scorned, rejected; but received, embraced, yea, contended for by them. It was effectually theirs as well as ministerially.

[3.] Theirs it was in regard of the fruit and benefit of it. It was theirs for the salvation of their souls, 1 Pet. i. 9. It was to them a savour of life, not a sentence of condemnation.

(3.) It is called " most holy faith."

[1.] To put a difference between those unholy and fabulous dreams of these seducers, the most impure inventions of the Gnostics, Jewish fables, &c.

Vid. Lorin. in loc.

[2.] Considered in itself; and that,

First, In its supreme author and efficient cause, the Holy Ghost. It was θεόπνευστος, by Divine inspiration, 2 Tim. iii. 16.

Secondly, In the instruments of conveying it, who were " holy men of God," who "spake as they were moved by the Holy Ghost," 2 Pet. i. 21.

Quænam Pauli Epistola non melle dulcior, non lacte candidior. Hierom.

Thirdly, In the matter of it, which is altogether holy: "Every word of God is pure." The threatenings holy, denounced against sin; the precepts holy, and such as put us only upon holiness; the comforts and promises holy, parts of a holy covenant, and such as only comfort in the practice of holiness, and encourage to holiness, and are made to holy ones.

Fourthly, In the effects of it. It works and exciteth holiness in nature, heart, life. It is that which being believingly looked into, makes the beholders holy like itself; as the rods of Jacob which, laid before the sheep, made them bring forth young ones of the same colour with those rods.

3. Their building on this foundation is contained in these words, "building up yourselves." Two things are in this branch comprehended: How we are to understand this building up, and this building up of themselves.

(1.) How we are to understand this building up. Ἐποικοδομοῦντες imports three things. 1. A fitting and a joining the building to the foundation. 2. A skilful disposing of the materials and parts of the building. 3. A progressiveness and proceeding therein, even to perfection: and all these are aptly applicable to that spiritual purpose of our apostle in this place; for by this expression he intends to put them upon labouring for confirmation and stability in their Christian course, by sitting fast to the word, the foundation of faith; and as a building which is firmly fixed and immovably set upon its foundation, stedfastly to abide in and rest upon the truth of the word, that all the winds, and waves, and oppositions of seducers may not be able to unsettle and remove them. And this it is which the apostle, Col. ii. 7, intends by the very same expression, ἐποικοδομούμενοι, "built up;" in which he exhorts the Christians to stability in Christ and his truth, by being joined to him as the building is to the foundation. And hence it is that Christ commended the wisdom of that man who "built his house upon a rock," Matt. vii. 24, and blamed the folly of him who "built his house upon the sand," ver. 26. He that heareth my words, saith he, "and doeth them, I will liken him unto a wise man, that built his house upon a rock." The firm and unfeigned belief of the doctrine of faith is as the resting and depending upon the rock or foundation. It is true, faith sets us upon Christ as a foundation personal or mediatory, upon whom alone we depend for life and salvation; but faith sets us upon the word as the foundation Scriptural or manifestative, or that for the truth of which, and of its discoveries, we believe in and depend upon Christ. And hence it is, that as Christ is in Scripture called a foundation, Eph. ii. 20, "the chief corner-stone," a stone for a foundation, and besides whom no other foundation can be laid, 1 Cor. iii. 11; so is the word adorned with the same title, Eph. ii. 20, where by "the foundation of the apostles and prophets," we are to understand their doctrines; and the way to build upon Christ, is by building upon his word as our foundation; for Christ is not a foundation of happiness every way that man frames in his own heart, but only as God offers him in the word of the gospel; and Christ makes it all one to build and believe on his word as on himself. "He that rejecteth me, and receiveth not my words," John xii. 48. And, "If ye abide in me, and my words abide in you," John xv. 7. As we rest upon a man by trusting to his word, so we build upon Christ by building on his word; and the word being rooted in our hearts, unites us to Christ.

[2.] The apostle, by this phrase of "building up," puts the Christians upon a right ordering of the materials and parts of the building; for in the building the materials are not only to be laid, but skilfully to be laid upon the foundation; and this comprehends two things. 1. The providing of good materials. 2. The placing of them fitly.

For the first. In buildings, sundry profitable and useful materials are provided, as brass, iron, stone, timber, lime, lead, glass, &c.; and in this spiritual building there must be parcels of all graces, faith, hope, love, knowledge, &c. Faith must be those brazen gates to let in Christ into the soul, and to shut out Satan; watchfulness and courage must be as the stone wall to oppose the approaches of our enemies; patience, the dormers bearing the weight of the house, and every burden that may be laid upon it; love, the cement to bind and knit all together; knowledge, as the windows to lighten the house; hope, as the glass or casements to look out and wait for things believed.

2. These must be fitly placed; and that, 1. So as that all the parcels may be set upon the foundation; all must lean upon Jesus Christ as manifested in Scripture, Phil. iv. 13. Grace of itself is but a creature, and defectible; he can only continue life and vigour to it: without Christ the greatest and highest graces will but be *pondera ad ruinam*, and could neither be set up nor kept up: grace will prove but deceitful, unless it stands upon the strength of Christ the foundation. 2. All the parts must be disposed and contrived for the best advantage of, and so as they may be most useful to, the dweller. Every grace must be for God, as it is from him. Who builds a house, and does not expect to be accommodated and benefited by it? 3. There must be a due proportion between part and part, and such a laying out of the one, that there may not be too great an abridgement or hindering of the beauty and largeness of the other. Christians must have all the parts of holiness and parcels of grace. There must not be so much allotted for one room that nothing is left for another: a Christian must not be all for knowledge, and nothing for love; all for zeal, and nothing for humility; all for humility, nothing for courage. A Christian must neither be maimed nor monstrous. 4. All the parts must be built according to the line and rule of the word. The tabernacle was according to the pattern in the mount, Exod. xxv. 40. A Christian must walk and build by rule, entertain every grace, and perform every duty which is enjoined, and because it is enjoined; he must not live according to example, but rule.

[3.] By this expression of "building up," the apostle puts these Christians upon progressiveness and perfection in the work of Christianity; he not only enjoins every Christian to be busy in building, but by this word ἐποικοδομοῦντες, he denotes a building up till the work be finished, an increasing in building, even to its consummation. This also is intimated by the note of opposition, δε, but, in the connexion, to those who fall off; whereby he would teach the Christians not to give over the work till they be builded up a perfected building for Christ. Hence it is that Peter, though not in the same words, yet to the same effect, directs the Christians to "grow in grace," 2 Pet. iii. 18; and to add grace to grace, "Add to your faith virtue; and to virtue knowledge," &c., 2 Pet. i. 5; and Eph. iv. 15, to a growing up into Christ in all things. It is true, building is a slow and leisurely work, a work of time; but yet it must be a progressive and proceeding work; it is done by little and little, but yet many littles will bring forth much, and make a beautiful building at length. What more dishonourable than for a man to begin, and not to be able to finish? Luke xiv. 30. The disgrace hereof Christ mentions in the gospel. No change so unworthy and dishonourable as to begin in the Spirit, and end in the flesh. And not to go forward in Christianity is to go backward; and they who build not up, pull down. There is no standing still in this work: the want of a roof impairs the walls; the leaving of the building imperfect and unfinished, by not adding what is wanting, tends to the ruin of that which is already set up: "We lose those things which we have wrought," 2 John 8. And this pains and progressiveness in this work is about a building which is not temporal, and in time to fall down, but spiritual and eternal.

2. How are we to understand the building up themselves. It may be demanded, 1. What is meant by themselves, ἑαυτούς. 2. How they may be said to be able to build up themselves.

1. For the first. The word themselves, added to building up, may import a building up of one another, ἑαυτοὺς pro ἀλλήλους, and intend a mutual duty to be put forth and exercised between Christian and Christian; and thus the apostle uses the word ἑαυτούς, Col. iii. 16, where he exhorts them to admonish ἑαυτούς, one another; and Eph. iv. 32, to forgive one another: and this mutual and fraternal helping of one another forward in our Christian progress is elsewhere frequently commanded in Scripture; "exhorting one another," Heb. xi. 25, and "edify one another," 1 Thess. v. 11. Christians by their counsels, comforts, exhortations, examples, should advance one another's spiritual welfare; but though this be a truth, and here not excluded, yet this hinders not but that primarily the apostle intends that every one should promote his own particular holiness, and progress in the faith of the gospel.

2. For the second. It may be doubted how we can build up ourselves. Is edification man's work? Are we not God's workmanship? *Answ.* I grant spiritual houses cannot build themselves more than any other. Our houses are not naturally houses of God, but made so to our hands. Unless the Lord build the house all labour is vain. And the apostle points at the Builder, when in the next words he bids these Christians pray in the Holy Ghost. But he here writes to the regenerate, who have the Spirit, by whom and whose grace they have spiritual liberty afforded to them; and being drawn, they run; and being acted upon, they are active. Inward and habitual grace was the sole work of the Spirit infusing: that which is practical is the work of the regenerate person flowing from infused grace.

Non libertate gratiam, sed gratia libertatem. Aug.

2. Though we are God's workmanship and building, yet he builds by means; and by such precepts as these he exhorts us to submit ourselves to the means, to yield ourselves to be hewn, squared, and laid in the building.

For observations drawn, 1. From the title, "Beloved;" as also, 2. From the apostle's expressing the doctrine of faith by the term faith; see p. 52, 53, 63.

From the pleasant and significant metaphor of building, I observe, that,

Obs. 1. The faithful are the house of God. By this resemblance the church is not seldom set forth. "Moses was faithful in all his house," Heb. iii. 2. "How to behave thyself in the house of God," 1 Tim. iii. 15. "In a great house there are vessels," &c., 2 Tim. ii. 20. "Whose house we are, if we hold fast," &c., Heb. iii. 6. "The time is come that judgment must begin at the house of God," &c., 1 Pet. iv. 17. "Ye are God's building," 1 Cor. iii. 9. "Ye also, as lively stones, are built up a spiritual house," 1 Pet. ii. 5. And this resemblance of a house aptly belongs to the faithful, either in respect of Christ, themselves, or God.

(1.) Christ is the foundation of this house; he was a "corner-stone," Isa. xxviii. 16, on which both the Jews and Gentiles meet; he is called a stone for a foundation, Eph. ii. 20. Christ is a foundation, [1.] In point of sustentation; upon him the faithful build their hope and expectations; upon him all their grace and holiness is built; he is "a living stone," 1 Pet. ii. 4, that sends life and influence into all the stones of the building set upon him; upon him all their comforts are built; all their rejoicing is in him. Take away Christ, and all their joy falls to the ground; upon him are built all their duties, both in respect of power to perform them, and in respect of acceptance from God when they are performed. [2.] Christ is a foundation in respect of union. Between the building and this foundation, this is the ground of sustentation: this union, set out sometimes by a matrimonial union, sometimes by a union between head and members, sometimes by that between root and branches, &c., is, on the part of Christ, by his Spirit laying hold on us, and infusing spiritual life into us, and affording to us all supplies of grace, Rom. viii. 9; 1 Cor. xii. 8. On our part, by faith, putting and setting us into him, as also receiving and drawing grace from him, Phil. i. 19. [3.] Christ is a foundation in point of hiddenness: the building is seen, the foundation is hidden; he is a hid treasure. 1. His person is not yet seen. "When he shall appear," 1 John iii. 2. "Whom having not seen," &c., 1 Pet. i. 8. 2. His benefits and graces are hidden. Our life is a hidden life, hidden not only to the wicked, but even oft to the godly themselves, who behold not their own happiness either of grace or glory. This life is the obscurity of their adoption; his face is frequently hidden from them, and the tokens of his presence removed.

And for the excellency of this foundation, [1.] He is the sole foundation. No other foundation can be laid, 1 Cor. iii. 11. No other appointed by God, Acts iv. 12. No other ever embraced by saints. No other ever revealed by the word. No other needed beside. No other willing or able to bear the weight of the building. No other was fit to have the honour of our affiance and dependence.

[2.] He is a strong foundation; so strong that he bears up every stone, every saint of all sizes that ever was or shall be laid upon him, and all their weights and pressures; he bears them up always, so that they shall never fall. They who are built upon this Rock are safe, Matt. vii. 25; "as Mount Zion, which cannot be moved." The word shall fall, but not a saint, because Christ falls not. The gates of hell, the floods of temptation, shall never totally prevail: a child of God shall never sin away all his holiness; he may sin, not perish, not sin to death. Grace may be abated, not abolished; shaken in, not out of the soul. Of all given to Christ he hath lost none; his sheep never perish, John x. 29.

(2.) The church is a house in respect of believers, who are the stones of which this house is built up; and these stones are naturally, 1. Rugged and unpolished, till they are hewn, smoothed, and made fit for the building, Hos. vi. 5. The word of God takes away their natural asperity, and makes them fit for the building, and submissive to God's disposal, and fit for his purpose. 2. These stones are of several sizes, some greater, some lesser. Christians are of divers degrees, some more eminent, some more obscure; some of stronger, others of weaker graces. 3. The stones which are different in their size are yet cemented and united one to another. As there is a union of faith betwixt the building and the foundation, so there is a union of love between the parts of the building. And hence the whole body is said to be "fitly joined together and compacted," Eph. iv. 16. The greatest stone in the building cannot say to the least, it hath no need thereof. The Foundation disdains not the least pebble, no more should the strongest stone in the building.

(3.) The church is a house in respect of God.

[1.] He dwells in this house. He has two houses: that above, of glory; this below, of grace; and he who dwells every where by his essence, dwells in his church by the presence of his grace. God takes more delight in his church than in all the world. He rests in this house.

[2.] He furnishes his house with all necessaries, yea, ornaments, his ordinances, graces, &c.

[3.] He protects his house: he that destroyeth the temple of God, him will God destroy. His enemies shall answer for dilapidations, for every breach they have made.

[4.] He repairs his house; and when his enemies have broken it, he restores it, and makes up its breaches; it shall never utterly be destroyed.

[5.] He purges and cleanses his house; disorders and abuses are too ready to creep into it; it oft wants reformation. Judgment begins at the house of God. "You have I known of all the families of the earth, therefore I will punish you," Amos iii. 2. Man regards not much what lies in his field, but he is curious that nothing offensive be laid in his house. Judgments begin at the sanctuary. Sins in the church are most heinous. Christians are so much worse than others, by how much they should be better. The meditation of this resemblance should therefore put us upon trial and strengthening of our union to Christ our foundation, upon dependency on and trusting to him. It serves also to strengthen the love, nearness, and dearness of believers, living stones; to make us dedicate ourselves to the Lord, as his house and temple; to offer up the daily sacrifice of prayer and praise to him; to tell Satan and lust, whenever they sue for a room in our house, that every room is taken up for God, that his enemy must not be let in. We are the temple of God; O let us not make ourselves a temple of idols by covetousness, or a taphouse by drunkenness, or a sty by any swinish lusts. To conclude this, labour for the costly furniture of holiness for thy house; use the perfume of prayer, the washing of godly sorrow; give the Lord costly entertainment. Repair all thy breaches by repentance. Run not too long to ruin. Patiently bear the Lord's visitation, and the means he uses to mend and cleanse thee. And lastly, depend upon him for care and protection in all dangers.

Obs. 2. The word of God is the foundation of a Christian. "Build yourselves on your faith." It is a foundation to bear a saint out in all his duties, comforts, belief of truths. (1.) All our duties, services must be built upon the word. That which will not stand with the word must be no part of the building: the word must be the foundation of practice; he that walks by this rule, peace shall be upon him, Gal. vi. 16. It is not the showing of any warrant of man that will bear thee harmless at the day of judgment. (2.) The word is the foundation of a Christian's comfort; no promises but Scripture promises but may deceive. No other promises can bear the weight of an afflicted soul: "Unless thy law had been my delight, I should have perished in my affliction," Psal. cxix. 92. "Thy statutes were my songs in the house of my pilgrimage," Psal. cxix. 54. (3.) But especially the word is the foundation of a Christian's belief of truths asserted; we can only securely assent to the assertions of the word. That which I read not I believe not. A written word is the only food of faith; the formal object of faith is the truth manifested in Scripture; every truth has an *esse credibilis*, because it was delivered in the written word, and spoken by God. Faith is carried to its object under the notion of infallibility, which can never be without Divine revelation; all human testimony being fallible, though not false; and hence it is that the revelation of God in his word is only propounded by God as a foundation of faith, Deut. xvii. 18. These things "are written, that ye might believe," John xx. 31. "We have a more sure word of prophecy; whereunto ye do well to take heed," 2 Pet. i. 19. So 1 John v. 13, "These things have I written to you that believe on the name of the Son of God." "To the law and to the testimony," Isa. viii. 20. "Search the Scriptures; for in them ye think ye have eternal life," John v. 39. And this word of God has only been embraced by the faithful in all ages as the foundation of their faith. Whenever they would prove any thing to be believed, they have gone to the written word for a foundation of belief. Thus the noble Bereans, who "searched the Scriptures daily, whether those things were so," Acts xvii. 11. Thus Paul grounded what he wrote upon Scripture, Acts xiii. 33; 1 Cor. ii. 9; xv. 54; Rom. xiv. 11; and professed that he "believed all things written in the law and the prophets," Acts xxiv. 14; and that he said "no other things than those which the prophets and Moses did say should come," Acts xxvi. 22. So that the doctrine of faith revealed in the Scripture must be the foundation to bear us up and out in all duties to be performed, comforts to be entertained, and truths to be embraced. And hence, as we may see the misery of those who have no foundation at all, holding their religion only for form, fashion, example, or fear of superiors, which sandy bottoms will never keep them up from sin, nor bear them out in sufferings, especially death and judgment; so we should labour to improve the doctrine of faith as our foundation in all the forementioned respects:

Baron. contr. Turnbullum.

[1.] By having a deep sense and feeling of our misery; so that not finding in ourselves whereon to found ourselves, we may be driven to look after the foundation discovered in the Scripture, which is only Jesus Christ.

[2.] By faith, whereby we give a supernatural assent to the word, and spiritually discern its truth; whereby, likewise, we apply the word to ourselves, and are knit to it as a foundation, as mingling it with faith. Although the doctrine of faith is a foundation in itself, yet it is not so to us, unless we believe it, and apply it to ourselves by the gift of faith.

[3.] By labouring that the word may take so deep a root in the heart, that it may descend into the affections, and there be embraced until it has wrought an experience of its own delightful sweetness.

[4.] By several needful considerations. 1. By considering that it never failed any that ever depended upon it, having in all practices, distresses, debates upheld them. The public faith of heaven was never broken; the promises, commands, and assertions of the word have borne saints out in all difficulties. 2. By considering that every other foundation will fail; whether fancied by ourselves, or suggested by others, it is but a lying vanity. 3. By studying the nature of him whose word it is, who is the Rock of ages, in whom is no shadow of change, for whom it is impossible to lie to us, or deny himself.

Sundry observations which might have been made concerning stedfastness and proceeding in Christianity, and the usefulness of a constant progress therein to keep us from seduction, proving that the best way for Christians not to be losers of what they have is to be labourers for what they want, I shall not mention, as having largely insisted thereupon before, p. 50, 51, 266, 267, 273, &c., 277, 278.

Thus of the second direction whereby the apostle teaches the Christians to embrace the foregoing exhortation of contending for the faith, viz. edification on the faith. The third follows, viz. "praying in the Holy Ghost," whereby he instructs them withal how to build prosperously, viz. by taking in God's help; and how to keep themselves in the love of God, which is the direction next ensuing.

Two things are here to be opened.
1. What he commands, prayer.
2. The manner of performing it, "in the Holy Ghost."

1. What he commands, prayer; "praying."

I shall not here handle the duty of prayer in a common-place way, by insisting either upon the sundry sorts of prayer, petition for good things, deprecation to remove evil things, intercession for others, imprecation against others, thanksgiving for ourselves or others; or upon the circumstances of prayers for time, place, measure. Only as to the former, I shall note, that when this word prayer is set alone, as it is here in Jude, it comprises all the kinds under it; when it is joined with thanksgiving alone, it comprises all kinds belonging to request; when it is joined with deprecation or intercession, it is restrained to a desire of good things for ourselves. But as to the present occasion, I shall only show what prayer is in regard of its general nature.

Προσευχή.
Δέησις.
Ἔντευξις.
Εὐχαριστία.

The word in the original here used, προσευχόμενοι, praying, imports an earnest wishing or craving of such things which are according to our desire, because by prayer we open our hearts' desire to God. There are sundry rhetorical, brief, commendatory descriptions used by learned men to set forth prayer; as, the key of heaven and of all God's cabinets, the conduit of mercy, faith flaming, Jacob's ladder, an invisible and invincible weapon, a victory over the Omnipotent, the consumption of cares, a box of ointment broke upon the head of Christ, the perfume of heaven, the mount of transfiguration, the soul's messenger, Satan's scourge, the ascending of the mind to God, ἀνάβασις τοῦ νοῦ πρὸς Θεόν. To wave these, though sweet and pious expressions, prayer is more fitly called, according to the nature and import of the word προσευχή, a right opening of the desire of the heart to God; or, as the apostle, Phil. iv. 6, a making known our desires to him; or, as some, a religious speech directed to God after a due sort, concerning things appertaining to his glory and our good.

Ὁμιλία τῆς ψυχῆς πρὸς Θεόν.
Damasc. de Orthod. Fid. l. 3. c. 24.

(1.) First, the will is filled in prayer with desires, and then these desires flame forth, blaze upward, and are opened to God. Formally, prayer is an act of the will, and has its conception in the heart; and,

(2.) Then its birth is the expression of our desires, however uttered. And these desires are expressed sundry ways, either by an inward or an outward word, there being a twofold speech; the first ὁ ἔξω λόγος, and προφορικὸς, a speech uttered with the voice; the second ὁ ἔσω λόγος, and ἐνδιαθετὸς, a speech conceived in the mind: prayer is not the outward voice only or chiefly, but the inward of the soul. Sighs are articulate. Moses is said to cry to God, when we read not of his uttering any words, Exod. xiv. 15; and "Hannah spake in her heart, but her voice was not heard," 1 Sam. i. 13; her prayer was *oratio mentalis*, an inward mental prayer: and this is the strongest voice of all, and by it we speak loudest in the ears of God. Hence prayer is called the lifting of the heart to God, Psal. xxv. 1, and the pouring forth of the soul before the Lord, Psal. lxii. 8; 1 Sam. i. 15; Psal. cxlii. 2; 2 Tim. ii. 22; Psal. cxix. 7. As for that prayer which is only the outward speech of the mouth, without the inward of the heart, it is rather lip-labour than prayer. Desires are usually made known by outward means, words, signs: words most exactly set forth the intent of the heart; yet signs also, as lifting up the hands or eyes, stretching abroad the arms, bowing the knees, both express and excite inward affection. But by inward means, as sighs and groans, God discerns a man's desires as well as by words and signs, he understanding the motions of the heart as well as of the tongue. And hence it is that God knowing the secrets of the heart, and understanding our thoughts afar off, prayer is not made to make known our desires to God, as if otherwise God would be ignorant of them, but to testify man's obedience to that order which God has set down, God appointing prayer in this way a means to obtain needful blessings; and that very wisely, as,
1. That by making known our wants to God we may not only know, but acknowledge God to be the author and fountain of all blessings, and so upon the receiving thereof ascribe the praise to God. 2. That it may appear we understand our own desires, and have sense of the thing we want. 3. That others may mutually join with us in prayer. 4. That our affections may be the more enlarged; for as desires help us to words, so words inflame our desires. 5. To prevent distraction and interruption in our thoughts.

(3.) Prayer is made to God only. It is a principal point of Divine service. 1. God only is religiously to be worshipped and served, Matt. iv. 10. 2. God only knows whether we pray or no, i. e. from the heart. 3. God only is every where present to hear the suits of all, Jer. xxiii. 23, 24. 4. God only is almighty, and able to grant whatsoever we ask.

(4.) In prayer, as the desires must be made known to God, so after a due manner; but of that in the next part, "in the Holy Ghost."

2. The manner of performing this duty is "in the Holy Ghost," ἐν Πνεύματι Ἁγίῳ.

In Scripture sometimes mention is made of praying in the spirit of man, as 1 Cor. xiv. 15, "I will pray" τῷ πνεύματι, "with the spirit," or in the spirit, i. e. (say some,) my understanding and my heart or soul, so as I may both understand, and also be affected with what I pray. And Eph. vi. 18, the apostle enjoins praying in the Spirit, which may be understood either of God's Spirit or man's; but in this place particular and express mention is made of the Holy Spirit, or the Spirit of God, in which we are to pray; whereby is meant by the assistance, motion, inspiration, strength, help, and guiding of the Spirit; for this sense agrees with the preposition ἐν, here translated in, which is in Scripture oft of the same signification with διὰ, by, as Matt. v. 34—36, "Swear neither" ἐν τῷ οὐρανῷ, "by heaven, nor" ἐν τῇ γῇ, "by the earth, nor" ἐν τῇ κεφαλῇ, "by thy head;" and in 2 Cor. vi. 6, 7, it is eight times thus taken; and it is most suitable to other places of Scripture, where the Spirit of God is mentioned with prayer, as Zech. xii. 13, where is promised the spirit of supplication, that is, the Spirit, as giving, bestowing, and working the gift and grace of prayer; as in 2 Cor. iv. 13, we read of "the spirit of faith," i. e. the Spirit working faith; and Rom. viii. 15, we read of "the Spirit," ἐν ᾧ, by which "we cry, Abba, Father." James v. 16, we find mentioned δέησις ἐνεργουμένη, which properly signifieth a prayer wrought in us, and excited, and so imports the efficacy and influence of the Holy Ghost in enabling us to pray. And the apostle, Rom. viii. 26, most fully expresses this truth. 1. Affirmatively, "The Spirit helpeth our infirmities," and "maketh intercession for us." 2. Negatively, saying, We know not what to pray. Whence it is clear, not that the Spirit of God truly and properly prays for us, as our High Priest and Mediator, or as one of us for another, for then would there be more than one Mediator, 1 Tim. ii. 5, and God would request to God, the Holy Ghost being God, but not man also, as was Christ; but that the Spirit of God stirs us up to pray, quickens and puts life into our dead and dull spirits, yea, and infuses into us such desires, sighs, and groans, and suggests to us such words, as are acceptable to God, which for their truth and sincerity, for their vehemence and ardency, for their power and efficacy, are unutterable; they pierce through the heavens, and enter to the throne of grace, and there make a loud cry in the ears of God. More particularly, from these expressions of both these apostles, Paul and Jude, we may consider wherein this assistance of the Holy Ghost, or this praying by the Holy Ghost, stands and consists; and that is, 1. In respect of the matter; 2. Of the manner, of our prayer.

Attributing the office of Mediator to the Holy Ghost was one of the heresies of Arius.

(1.) In respect of the matter of our prayer. We pray in the Holy Ghost, as he instructs and teaches us to ask such things as are κατὰ Θεὸν, according to the will of God, lawful and good things, Rom. viii. 27; 1 John v. 14. The Spirit of God stirs us not up to desire what his word forbids us to desire. We know not what is good for ourselves, and God has oft heard us by denying us. Though when we ask bread our father gives us not a stone; yet when we ask a stone God has oft given us bread. The thing asked, if by the Spirit, is warrantable: the Spirit puts us upon asking, especially, spiritual blessings, as our lusts put us upon craving things which are their fuel. The Spirit of wisdom desires not its own poison.

(2.) We pray in the Holy Ghost in respect of the manner of our praying. And that,

[1.] As it enables us to pray sincerely and heartily. God's Spirit is a Spirit of truth. And whenever we pray in his Spirit, we pray likewise in our own, and his stirs up ours to pray. The prayer of a saint goes not out of feigned lips. The Spirit lifts up the hand and the heart together, Psal. xxv. 1; lxxxvi. 4; Lam. iii. 41.

[2.] As it enables us to pray with fervency. The motions of the Spirit, as they are regular in regard of the object, so vehement in regard of the manner. Its groans are such as "cannot be uttered," Rom. viii. 26. The symbols of the Spirit were fiery tongues, and "a rushing mighty wind," Acts ii. 2, 3. As a bullet flies no farther than the force of the powder carries it, so prayer goes no farther than the fervour of the Spirit drives it. Prayer is called a knocking, a seeking, and figured by wrestling, Gen. xxxii. 24—26; Hos. xii. 4; nay, called a wrestling, Rom. xv. 30. The importunity required in prayer is called ἀναίδεια, impudence, Luke xi. 8: sluggish prayers are no spiritual prayers. The device of shooting a letter at the end of a dart, used as I have sometimes heard in sieges, is a fit emblem of a soul sending its epistle to heaven. As the Spirit wrought vehemently in those holy men who were θεοφόρητοι, and φερόμενοι ὑπὸ Πνεύματος, moved by the Holy Ghost to speak the word of God to men, so it works fervently in those who are to speak in prayer to God. David mentions the setting forth of his prayer as incense, and incense burnt before it ascended: there must be fired affections, before our prayers will go up. The tribes, Acts xxvi. 7, are said to serve God ἐν ἐκτενείᾳ, which signifies a stretching forth themselves with all their might.

Προσεύχειν cognationem habet cum verbo προσέχειν, quod significat attendere, animumque advertere. Oratio attenta fundi debet.

[3.] As it enables us to pray in faith. The Spirit is called the Spirit of faith, 2 Cor. iv. 13, and the Spirit of Christ; as it is sent from him, so it sends us to him. The Spirit so intercedes in us on earth for the operation and framing of our prayers, that it sends us to Him who intercedes for us in heaven for the acceptance of our prayers: "Through Christ we have access by one Spirit unto the Father," Eph. ii. 18. And hence the Spirit enables us to pray "in faith, nothing wavering," James i. 6, in confidence that through the faith of him our prayers shall be successful, in such a way as our gracious Father in Christ sees best for us. This is called the "full assurance of faith," Heb. x. 22, and a praying "without doubting," 1 Tim. ii. 8; faith applying the promise, "Whatsoever ye shall ask the Father in my name, he will give it you," John xiv. 13; xvi. 23.

[4.] As it enables us to pray in holiness, with pure hearts and hands. He is a Spirit of holiness; his office is to make us holy, and wherever he witnesses he washes. If he be a Spirit of faith to strengthen our confidence in Christ, he is a Spirit of holiness to cause our conformity to Christ; hence the Spirit of grace is mentioned with the Spirit of supplication. As the Spirit makes us come boldly before the throne of grace; so he makes us come purely before it too, as being a throne of glory. "If I regard iniquity in my heart," saith David, "the Lord will not hear me," Psal. lxvi. 18. "I will wash my hands in innocency: so will I compass thine altar." This legal washing is evangelically improved. "Lifting up holy hands," 1 Tim. ii. 8; Heb. x. 22.

[5.] Lastly, as it enables us to pray in love. The Spirit of love, for so he is called 2 Tim. i. 7, never in prayer witnesses God's love to us, unless he draws ours to him, nay, for his sake to others. He never makes us lift up hands without doubting, unless also without wrath, 1 Tim. ii. 8; and when he makes us at peace with ourselves, he makes us peaceable with others, Matt. v. 24.

Obs. 1. Without the Spirit there is no praying. They who are totally destitute of the Spirit, in their natural condition, can no more pray in faith than a dead man can crave help of another. They may have the gift of prayer, but not, in that state, the grace of prayer: "We are not sufficient of ourselves to think any thing as of ourselves." The wicked call not upon God. There is no natural man but is spiritually deaf and dumb. All natural men are in this respect ἄλογα ζῶα, brute and mute. If a man have not the Spirit of grace, he must needs be destitute of the Spirit of supplication. He is a mere stranger to those prayer graces, faith, fervency, holiness, love, &c. He derides at prayer, I mean prayer by the Spirit. The wicked howl upon their beds, not pray in the Spirit; they may say a prayer, not pray a prayer, as it is said of Elijah, who prayed in prayer, ἐν προσευχῇ προσηύξατο, James v. 17; they do but make a loud noise like a wind instrument. They are but like Balaam, into whose mouth God put a word, without any heat of love or zeal in his soul. But why speak I of natural men, when without the acting of the Spirit in our regenerate state all our abilities to pray are presently gone? as a wheel which is turned about with a hand, if the hand be taken away, the wheel will soon stand still. It is necessary that to the first grace following grace be added: man, after he is regenerate, still needs the present, effectual, continual work of the Spirit. Preventing grace is not effectual, unless helped with a supply of second grace. It is true even of the regenerate, "Without me ye can do nothing:" God gives first the will, and then the deed, and continuance of doing that which is truly good. Grace must be every way grace, else it will be no grace at all. He that hath begun a good work in us must also perfect it, Phil. i. 6. Oh how heavily do even saints draw and drive, when they have sinned away the Spirit of prayer! When saints have yielded to sin, they are like a bird whose wings are besmeared with birdlime, they cannot fly up to heaven. How lamely and miserably, I have sometimes thought, did David pray upon his murder and adultery! The fire which consumed the burnt-offering came out from the Lord, Lev. ix. 24.

Obs. 2. How excellent and honourable a work is that of prayer! The whole Trinity has a work in this holy exercise: the Holy Ghost frames our requests; the Son offers them up to his Father, Rev. viii. 3, with his incense the prayers of the saints are offered, he prays them, as it were, over again; and the Father accepts these prayers thus framed and offered up.

Obs. 3. As without the Spirit there is no prayer, so without prayer a man evidently shows himself to have nothing of the Spirit. Wherever the Spirit is, there will be praying in the Spirit: if the Spirit live in us, it will breathe in us. God never yet had, nor ever will have, a dumb child. They who are the Lord's will name him, 2 Tim. ii. 19. They who are saints "call upon Christ," 1 Cor. i. 2. Breathing is a true property of life. As soon as ever Paul was converted he prayed, Acts ix. 11.

Obs. 4. Needs must the prayers of the saints be acceptable. They are by the Holy Ghost, his very groans, and by him our spirits are made to groan. Prayer prevails not only over creatures, but even over the very Creator himself. One faithful man's prayer is more forcible than a whole army, Exod. xvii. 11. There is a shadow of omnipotency in prayer. It was said of Luther, he could do what he would. Needs must that petition be granted which the framer receives. The Lord cannot more be out of love with prayer, than with his own will. Prayer is but a kind of counterpane or reflection of God's own pleasure.

Obs. 5. How good is God to his poor saints! He not only grants their prayers, but makes their prayers. God not only provides a gift, but a hand also to take it with; not a feast only, but a stomach; both grace for the desire, and the very grace of desire. Oh how sweet also are the conditions of the covenant of grace! God bids us pray, and helps us to pray; commands us duty, and enables to perform it; gives work, wages, and strength.

Obs. 6. It is our greatest wisdom to get and keep the Spirit. If either we never had it, or lose it, we cannot pray.

(1.) It is obtained in the ministry of the gospel. The Spirit is peculiar to the gospel, and not belonging to the law, if considered alone by itself as a distinct covenant; for so it genders only to bondage. "Received ye the Spirit by the works of the law, or by the hearing of faith?" q. d. Ye received the Spirit by hearing the gospel. The gospel is called "the ministration of the Spirit," 2 Cor. iii. 8.

(2.) It is kept by following his motions and suggestions. Make much of his presence; the Spirit is a delicate thing; grieve him not by negligence in using his gifts, Eph. iv. 30, pride, eagerness after the world, sensuality, ungodly company, premeditated, repeated sins. If the Spirit be gone, thy best friend is gone. It was David's prayer, "Take not thy Holy Spirit from me." Without the Spirit, thou art like lockless Samson, as another man; poor, weak Samson, when the Lord was departed! thou art like a ship wind-bound. No stirring without the Spirit's gales. Lord, what were my life if I could not pray! it would even be my burden; and how can I pray without thy Spirit? As a man cannot preach without external mission, so not pray without internal motion.

Obs. 7. How happy are saints in all straits! they have the Spirit to help them to pray. There is nothing but sin can drive or keep away the Spirit; sufferings, prisons, banishments, cannot. And hast thou the Spirit, it is better, like Jonah, to be praying in a whale's belly, than without the Spirit to be devout in a gilded chapel. Suppose thy friends cannot, will not visit thee, the Spirit is a guest that cannot be excluded. Like Joseph, he delights to manifest himself to his when all are gone out. Holy Mr. Dod was wont to say, Never despair of him who can but pray. Suppose men cut out thy tongue, or stop thy mouth, they cannot hinder thee from praying in the Spirit, because they cannot prevent the Spirit from praying in thee.

VERSE 21.

Keep yourselves in the love of God, looking for the mercy of our Lord Jesus Christ unto eternal life.

THE fourth direction whereby the apostle guides them to observe his exhortation to contend for the faith against seducers and seduction, is contained in these words, "Keep yourselves in the love of God." A very apt and suitable course for the aforesaid end and purpose; for he that will be a friend to God, can never be in love with error, which draws the soul away from God and his truth.

Two particulars are here in this direction contained.

1. That thing about which the Christians were to be employed, or the object, "the love of God."

2. How they were to be employed about it, viz. by keeping themselves therein: there is the act.

So that by way of explication two things may be inquired after.

1. What the apostle intends by "the love of God."

2. What by keeping themselves therein.

1. By the love of God, I here understand not that love whereby God loves man, but that whereby man loves God, rests in him, and cleaves to him as the most absolute good; of this both in respect of its several kinds and properties, as also in several observations, I have spoken, p. 36, 40, 43, &c. To avoid tediousness and repetition, I shall refer to that place.

2. For the second, by keeping themselves in this love, I understand perseverance in loving God, or a preserving of the love of God in their hearts, from all those things whereby they might be enticed to let it go and part with it; and this preservation or keeping stands in using those means which God has ordained to preserve in us our love towards him; which is done by sundry considerations and practices.

1. The considerations which preserve our love.

(1.) God's loveliness and soul-ravishing perfections, and his blessed suitableness to our soul's exigences; when we know him to be a full good, as having all the scattered excellencies of all the world, and all the persons and things therein, in himself, and infinitely more; a filling good, and able to satisfy our desires to the brim; may well make us persevere in love to him.

(2.) By considering that he loves us, loved us first, and perseveres and rests in his love, Zeph. iii. 17. The more we walk in this sun, the hotter we shall be; nay, were our hearts as cold as stones, the sunshine of his love upon us should heat us with love toward him again.

(3.) That every one of us keeps up a love to something: the poorest of us has a love, and if not for God, for that which is infinitely below him, yea, which is unworthy of us.

(4.) That we have nothing besides love to give him.

(5.) That he accepts of it instead of all other things, seeks it, bespeaks it, Deut. x. 15.

(6.) That we always profess we love him, and have chosen him, Josh. xxiv. 22.

(7.) That it is a greater dishonour to him to cease to love him, than never to have begun to love him at all.

(8.) That the keeping of ourselves in his love is the true keeping of love to ourselves, Deut. v. 19. We are the gainers by loving him; we forsaking his love and our own mercy at once.

2. The practices which preserve our love. As,

(1.) By keeping ourselves in a constant hatred of all sin. As love to sin grows, love to God will decay. These are as two buckets; as the one comes up, the other goes down.

(2.) By keeping ourselves in the delight of God's friends and favourers, who will ever be speaking well of him, and by taking heed of those misrepresentations that sinners make of him and his ways.

(3.) By keeping ourselves in delight of the ordinances, wherein his glory and beauty are displayed, and communion with himself is enjoyed, and our love is increased by these in exercising it.

(4.) By endeavouring for a holy remissness in loving other things; when we love the world as always about to leave and loathe it. A soul weaned from these breasts will only feed upon communion with and the enjoyments of God. "If any man love the world, the love of the Father is not in him," 1 John ii. 15. No outward object should be further beloved than as it is either a pledge of God's love to us, or an incitement of ours to him; in short, nothing should be loved much but only He whom we cannot love too much.

(5.) Lastly, by keeping up and increasing of brotherly love among ourselves; for though the love of God is the cause which makes us love our brethren, yet the love of our brethren is not only a sign, but an excellent preservative of our loving God. In every saint we may see God's image, he is God's best picture; now though the love of a man makes us love his picture, yet the often delightful looking upon his picture continues and inflames our love toward him. The fire of love to God will be extinguished in a heart cold and frozen to the saints; our love to God and the godly grow and decay together. The sun on the dial moves, though not so swiftly, yet according to the proportion of its motion in the heavens; and so though our love to God be more swift and intense than that to the saints, yet this is proportioned to that: without love to a brother we can have no assurance of God's love to us, nor any continuance of our love to God. He who has not the love of a brother toward saints, cannot have the love of a son toward God.

Obs. 1. We are very ready to decay and grow remiss in our love to God. "Keep yourselves," saith Jude. The word τηρήσατε, keep, notes such a keeping as that wherewith we keep a prisoner; our gadding hearts should be kept with all diligence. It is hard to get, and not easy to keep up our spiritual fervour. The love of most grows cold: water grows cold of itself, but it gets heat from the fire; we grow remiss of ourselves, fervent from the Spirit. When we go from prayer, sacraments, hearing, though our hearts have been warmed, yet upon our going into our worldly employments we are ready soon to fall into a spiritual chilness, as those whose heat having come outward, going into the sharp air, are very ready to catch cold. A tender person had need to take heed of leaving off any clothes; and our hearts, upon leaving off of duty, are subject to abate in the heat of their affections. God complains of those who had "lost their first love," Rev. ii. 4. Our hearts are like green wood, wherein fire cannot be kept without continual blowing: grace of itself is defectible, and without constant supplies of the Spirit, it would soon come to nothing. It is only kept by the power of God. Parents will not trust their little children to have their money in their own keeping. How had we need beg of God to keep this jewel of love for us, and to preserve it from being stolen from us!

Obs. 2. The best things should be most carefully kept. Spirituals are only worth the keeping, and indeed only can be kept. Men cannot always either keep the world, or their love to it. Judas threw away his thirty pieces, and his love to them, at the same time. There will come a time when we shall say we have no pleasure in these things, Eccl. xii. 1. It is good sometimes in a way of duty to part with these things; for to be sure we shall part with them in a way of necessity. How poor is that man who has no better treasure than that which is at the courtesy of the thief and moth! Oh how great is their folly who will keep every thing but that which deserves their care; to lay up trash under lock and key, and to lay their gold and jewels abroad in the streets! If thou canst keep thy God, thy love, be not troubled, though thou partest with thy gold.

Obs. 3. How great, how full a good is God! Even when we have him, and have had him never so long, he has enough within him to draw forth fresh and fresh loves toward him. The more we love him, the more we should love him. The glorious saints in heaven sing a new song, because it is a song of love. It is new to them, and sweet, though they have been singing it so many thousands of years. We soon grow weary of our worldly toys after we have had them awhile. As they are withering objects, so our delight in them is a withering delight; they are fulsome, rather than delightful and filling. It is true profane Esau said, "I have enough;" and a saint saith, I have enough; but with as much difference are both these enoughs, as when one man saith, I have enough by taking a little fulsome physic, and a thirsty man saith, I have enough by drinking a sufficient draught of thirst-satisfying water. Before worldly enjoyments are had, they seem beautiful; but when they are once obtained, they soon clog the soul. Here is the excellency of spirituals, they sweetly fill and satisfy, and yet at the same time we ever desire and hunger for more.

Obs. 4. The preserving of our love to God is an excellent preservative against sectaries and false teachers. He who loves God will fear to break the unity and peace of the church; also he will ἀληθεύειν ἐν ἀγάπῃ, follow "the truth in love," Eph. iv. 15. Error comes from men's affection; a cold, corrupt, and vapouring stomach makes an aching head. A corrupt, cold heart, which wants the heat of love to God, makes an erroneous head. And besides, God has bound himself to keep them from error and folly who love him. If a man love and keep the commands and will of God, he shall know his will. God never leaves them that will not leave him first. A man will not forsake a friend, a lover. Sweet and suitable is that expression, Psal. xci. 14, "Because he hath set his love upon me, therefore will I deliver him;" and Psal. cxlv. 20, "The Lord preserveth all them that love him." "Be merciful unto me," saith David, "as thou usest to do unto those that love thy name," Psal. cxix. 132. Though heresies and false teachers come, yet these, as Paul speaks, 1 Cor. xi. 19, shall but make those which are approved to be manifest. They shall discover true love to God, not destroy it. And fidelity will be the more apparent, like that of loyal subjects in times of sedition, in the treachery of others. To conclude, this love is a breastplate, as the apostle calls it, 1 Thess. v. 8, to repel all the darts of error. Oh then what need have we to go abroad with this breastplate in these times wherein these deadly arrows fly so thick! And consider here the true cause that so many are wounded with them. Christians want their breastplate; their hearts are not kept, nor their love preserved for God.

The last direction which our apostle prescribes is contained in these words, "looking for the mercy of our Lord Jesus Christ unto eternal life." An excellent and suitable direction! The expectation of a reward in heaven countervails and sweetens all their labour and faithfulness in opposing the enemies of truth upon earth; and withal keeps up their love to God, who commands their resisting of error and seduction.

Two things are here principally contained. 1. A duty; "looking for the mercy of our Lord Jesus Christ:" where he sets down, 1. What was to be regarded; "the mercy of Christ." 2. How it was to be regarded; by "looking for" it. 2. An inducement encouraging to the performance of that duty; "eternal life."

In the first branch two things are to be explained. 1. What the apostle means by "mercy," and "the mercy of Christ."

2. What by "looking for" it.

1. What is meant by "mercy," τὸ ἔλεος. I have discoursed on those words, "Mercy to you," p. 26, 27. To avoid needless repetition, I only say, that mercy as attributed to man is such a sympathy or compassion of heart as inclines us to relieve the miserable.

But as attributed to God and Christ in glory, as here, it notes either, 1. A gracious disposition or inclination to help and succour us in our distresses. As for sympathy and compassion, they are not, as learned Zanchius observes, essential to mercy in itself, but accidental to it, in regard of our present state. 2. The effects and expressions of mercy, or the actual helping of us out of our distresses; and so God is said to have mercy on us, and show mercy to us.

De Na. Dei, l. 4. c. 4. q. 1.

Now these effects of mercy are either common or special. Common, such as are afforded to all men and creatures, Psal. cxlvii. 9; Luke vi. 36, &c. Special, bestowed upon the elect, who are the vessels of mercy, and who only have the inward effects of mercy, in preventing and following grace; the outward, in justifying and glorifying mercy bestowed upon them. And thus mercy is principally to be taken in this place, and that peculiarly for those gracious expressions and discoveries of mercy which shall be shown toward the faithful in acquitting and delivering them at Christ's second coming, or coming to judgment. And this is called mercy in Scripture, 2 Tim. i. 18, where the apostle, speaking of Onesiphorus, prays "that he may find mercy of the Lord in that day." And deservedly it is so called; for,

(1.) It comes from the purpose and intention of free favour and good will. "This is the Father's will which hath sent me, that I should lose nothing," &c., John vi. 39. "Fear not, little flock; it is your Father's good pleasure to give you the kingdom," Luke xii. 32. The means and the end, the bestowing of grace and glory, are both referred to the Father's pleasure. Election to this state was from free grace; and in that respect the elect are called vessels of mercy.

(2.) In it there are the greatest effects and discoveries of mercy. A removal of all sin, sorrow, tears, temptations; outward, inward, eternal evils; woes from ourselves, other men, devils, God himself. A confluence of all good, of perfect grace in the soul, glory on the body and soul; by it we enter into the vision and fruition of the chiefest good. A supply of all exigences. A fulness of joy, rivers, nay, a fountain of pleasures. In one word, in this respect, it is not so much a mercy, one mercy, as a bundle of mercies, and the perfection and consummation of them all. It is called by the apostle τὸ ἔλεος, "the mercy," that mercy, by way of excellency. God here had much mercy in his heart, but his hands will be full of mercy at the coming of Christ.

(3.) It is mercy because it is bestowed upon the miserable. Indeed the saints are vessels of mercy, and, in comparison of the reprobate, happy in this life; but yet in comparison of the glorified they are miserable, and that in respect of the remainders of sin in the soul, the frequent eclipses of God's lightsome and loving countenance, temptations from devils, and opposition and persecution from a cruel and unkind world; they are here in a valley of tears, surrounded with shame, sicknesses, pains, losses, deaths. Their eyes run down with rivers of tears; they are men of sorrow, yea, sorrow is not only their condition, but their duty; but sorrow and sighing shall flee away, and all tears shall be wiped from their eyes, when this mercy comes.

(4.) It is mercy because bestowed upon those who could not merit and deserve it. "Eternal life is the gift of God," Rom. vi. 23. It could never be deserved by doing nor suffering, Rom. viii. 17; Gal. iv. 7; Rom. xi. 35; 1 Cor. iv. 7; Phil. ii. 13. The best men are unprofitable servants. All our good is either *ipse, aut ab ipso*, either God, or from God; all we do is due debt, all we receive is from free grace. Our very "sufferings are not worthy of the glory that shall be revealed in us," Rom. viii. 18. We are not purchasers, but heirs of this happiness. Our works, as they are good, are not ours, but God's mere gifts; as they are ours they are impure and imperfect. Besides, none can give any thing to God equivalent to what he has already received, therefore he cannot deserve that which he has not received. I am less, saith Jacob, than the least of thy mercies, Gen. xxxii. 10. What shall I render for them, saith David, Psal. cxvi. 12. There is no proportion between a finite work and an infinite reward, a reward no less than the infinite rewarder himself. It is the alone free grace of this God whereby we come to partake of his glory.

Οὐ κατὰ ὀφείλημα τῶν ἔργων, ἀλλὰ κατὰ χάριν τοῦ μεγαλοδώρου Θεοῦ. Basil in Psal. xiv.

2. But why is it "the mercy of our Lord Jesus Christ?"

(1.) It is his *ratione meriti;* he has purchased it by his merit. The obedience of Christ was not only satisfactory, but meritorious, by reason of the infiniteness of the person, there being an infinitely greater excess and proportion of virtue in his obedience than of malignity in our disobedience; by virtue of which merit a purchase is made of this mercy, as well as a removal made of our misery. Christ's merit at his first procures mercy at his second coming.

(2.) It is his *respectu præparationis;* he has prepared us for it by sending his Spirit into us to make us meet to partake of this mercy. He has bestowed upon us the earnest of our inheritance, and the first-fruits of the Spirit, given us a part in the first resurrection. The heaven without us is from his merit, the heaven within us from his Spirit.

(3.) It is his *respectu donationis*, of giving and exhibiting it at his coming. It is he who shall be the Judge to acquit the saints, that shall pronounce the blessed sentence, "Come, ye blessed," &c., that shall give his faithful soldiers "a crown of righteousness at that day," 2 Tim. iv. 7, 8, that shall "present us faultless before the presence of glory," Jude 24.

Secondly, We are to consider what is "looking for" this mercy. Προσδεχόμενοι denotes properly an earnest receiving of it, or taking it to us as some welcome guest or stranger whom we take in; a disposition commended in and commanded to the saints, Tit. ii. 13, προσδεχόμενοι, "looking for that blessed hope;" and Christ commands his to be like men προσδεχομένοις, that look for their lord, Luke xii. 36. And this comprehends several particulars under it; as,

(1.) Meditation of this mercy. I may think of that which I do not look for, but I cannot look for that of which I do not think. The wife that looks for the return of her welcome husband, spends her thoughts upon him; By this time, thinks she, he is come to such a place, to-night he lodges in such a house. The thoughts of saints run upon this mercy of Christ. The reason why they are called strangers here, is because they dwell so much in their thoughts of another condition, Heb. xi. 13; Psal. xxxix. 12; 1 Pet. i. 17; ii. 11. Every saint is made to look upwards. Beneficial and great things are much thought on. The covetous man thinks of his treasure, the labourer of his hire, the prisoner of his enlargement, the heir of his possession. And great things are greatly observed, and serious matters seriously regarded. Trivial toys and enjoyments cannot hinder a saint from the thoughts of this great mercy; yea, all other things are but so many steps to raise his meditation to it. Wicked men are bowed downward in their contemplation as in their condition. Saints are low in the latter, high in the former. They are as unlike as a piece of dirt and a ball. Cast dirt upon the earth, it lies still; cast a ball on it, and it rebounds upward.

(2.) Belief of this mercy. The looking for this mercy imports a groundedness of expectation. A saint looks for nothing without the foundation of a promise. Faith certainly lays hold on that certain word; and hence hope has such a certainty as never makes us ashamed. There is a full assurance of hope, called therefore the sure and stedfast anchor of the soul, Heb. vi. 11, 19. This expectation is not overcome by human sense and reason, but climbs above them. Faith gives a reality to things not seen, Heb. xi. 1. This looking is for that which is clean contrary to sense. It is a hope above hope; they who have it see the mercy of Christ's coming even through a cloud of sin and misery, and look at things within the veil, Heb. vi. 19.

(3.) Ardent desires after this mercy. This looking for it implies the welcomeness and acceptableness of it; and it is a looking for mercy. Saints are both said to be lookers for and lovers of it, 2 Tim. iv. 8; they are sick of love to it. "The bride saith, Come," Rev. xxii. 17. Come, Lord Jesus, come quickly, shuts up the Scripture, and sums up the church's wishes. There is a grief for his absence, and a groaning desire after his presence: "We groan within ourselves, waiting," &c., Rom. viii. 23. As no worldly difficulty can disappoint, so no worldly enjoyment can bribe the soul's desires. A saint, with Abraham, stands at his tent door, or, with Sisera's mother, looks out of the window, and saith, "Why is his chariot so long in coming?" It hasteth. We cannot thus look for Christ unless we love him: the devils and the wicked have a fearful, the faithful a longing, looking for Christ, 2 Thess. iii. 5; 2 Pet. iii. 12.

(4.) It imports patience of expectation. The faithful will stay God's leisure for his dole of mercy, as beggars at a door that continue there till there be leisure to serve them. They make not haste, Isa. xxviii. 16, though they dwell in an unkind world, and among them that hate peace. Though they are wounded with crosses, yet they say, with Augustine, Lord, here burn, wound, cut, the mercy of Christ makes amends for all. Though they are environed with a body of death, and had infinitely rather, if God pleased, change a necessity of sinning for a necessity of obeying; yet they contentedly think God's time is the best for removing, though the worst of evils. "Through faith and patience they inherit the promises," Heb. vi. 12. This looking for the Spirit of Christ is called ὑπομονή, patience itself, 2 Thess. iii. 5. Mercy must not be bestowed, nay, it will be no mercy, if patience be not tried. Certainty countervails all delays.

(5.) This looking contains in it a joyful expectation of that great good for which we look. Though the deferring makes the heart sad and sick; yet the expecting thereof makes the heart glad and cheerful. We rejoice under the hope of the glory of God, Rom. v. 2. In whom believing, we "rejoice with joy unspeakable and full of glory," 1 Pet. i. 8. If Abraham, looking for the day of Christ's humility two thousand years before, rejoiced; must not believers needs rejoice in looking for the day of his and their own glory approaching so near, it being now, as it were, the last minute of the last hour before the day of our marriage, redemption, coronation?

(6.) It denotes prudent vigilance. What we look for, we watch for; when we look either for friend or foe, we keep ourselves waking. Hence Luke makes this looking and watching all one, chap. xi. 36, 37. They who look for an enemy will watch to prevent his coming, as Christ speaks of the thief. They who look for a friend will watch to welcome and entertain him. All who look for mercy, labour to be found in peace, 2 Pet. iii. 14; they look up as watchmen upon their tower, they keep their loins girt, and they are in the posture of servants expecting their Lord; they are afraid of surfeits and sleeping by worldly pleasures. They who reach after this mercy must let worldly trifles fall out of their hand. The better the mercy to be enjoyed is, the fitter we should be to receive. A prepared mercy suits not with an unprepared heart. Every day to a saint should be as his last. And of every one he should say, Art thou the last, or look I for another? Am I now in a meet posture to receive the mercy of Christ?

To shut up this: It is not strange that Jude enjoins these saints to look for this mercy of Christ, considering the suitableness of this exhortation to the persons exhorted, who, 1. Are saints, such as have the Spirit, which saith, Come, whose motions are upward, who are begotten again to this lively hope, who, as they are men, look upward with their faces; so, as they are saints and new men, look upward with their spirits, and wait for Christ from heaven, 1 Thess. i. 10, and love his appearance, 2 Tim. iv. 8; such as are like the young ones of the fowls of heaven, who though they may be hatched under a hen's wing, yet, being grown, they presently fly abroad. The saints are born, and for a time live, in the world, yet they soon show that they are not of this world, who, 2. Also were so opposed and tempted by seducers, that, (1.) Looking for the crown of life was little enough to make them constant to the death. (2.) Considering for whom they were to look, their Master, their Husband, Head, their Saviour, the Lord Jesus Christ. (3.) Considering for what they looked, mercy, to be bestowed at a time when they should want it most, even at Christ's coming, when nothing else will help. Lastly, considering the great beneficialness of this mercy, it was such a mercy whereby they should be possessed of eternal life; which is the second branch to be opened.

2. The inducement encouraging to the duty of

looking for the mercy of Christ. It was a mercy whereby they should be brought to eternal life. Of this, though we shall enjoy it so much, yet can we speak but little. Under two words, eternal life, the Scripture frequently sets forth the state of the saints of heaven; which for its blessedness is called life, and for its durableness eternal.

(1.) Life. There is a threefold life. Natural, consisting in the conjunction of the body and soul. Spiritual, which is eternal life begun, in respect of grace, here. Eternal life, in respect of glory hereafter, whereby is understood all the happiness to be enjoyed in heaven. As under the word death, the greatest of evils, are comprehended all the miseries inflicted for sin in this and the next state; so in that of life, of all things the most precious and the most prized, are contained all the blessings to be enjoyed here and hereafter: but because our happiness cannot be perfect and consummate till we come to heaven, that condition is principally and frequently called life; which life stands in our immediate communion with God in a unitive vision, of in seeing and enjoying him, Matt. v. 8; 1 John iii. 2; Psal. xvi. 11, &c. Heaven is a low thing without God, saith Augustine. Whatever is less than himself is less than our desires. In him is contained infinitely more than either we want, or all other things in the world have: his presence shall be our life, and, as it were, enliven all things else, which without him, as here they are, so there would be dead things. In the immediate, full, and perfect, not in respect of the object, but subject, uninterrupted, reflexive, unmixed, enjoyment of this God stands life.

(2.) Life in respect of its duration is called eternal; as never to be interrupted and intermitted, so without any end or amission; and indeed this it is which makes all the enjoyments of heaven to be truly such, and as the faggot-band whereby all the particular parcels of happiness are bound and tied together, and without which they would be all scattered and lost. Frequently is the life of glory said to be eternal, John iii. 15; viii. 51; xi. 25, &c., 'pleasures for evermore," "a treasure in the heaven that faileth not," Luke xii. 33, an "eternal weight of glory," 2 Cor. iv. 17, a treasure beyond the reach of thief and moth, &c. God the fountain and treasury of life can never be exhausted. The saints can never be willing to part with this God. Enemies shall never be able to separate them. A complete happiness, to be truly and also necessarily happy.

Obs. 1. The looking for the mercy of Christ quickens us in our course of Christianity. The apostle directs them to contend for the faith by "looking for the mercy of our Lord Jesus," &c.

(1.) It purges the heart from sin. Whosoever hath this hope purifieth himself, 1 John iii. 3. He who looketh for Christ looks to be like him, and therefore conforms himself to Christ in purity. He who looks for great revenues within a few years will not cut off his hopes, but rather remove impediments. We may say of sinners, as of some men who are adventurous in the world, They have nothing to lose. The looking for mercy, and the living in sin, cannot stand together. The love of sin is the confutation of our hopes.

(2.) The looking for this mercy damps our affections to the things of the world. He who beholds the glorious sunshine of Christ's appearance hath his eyes so dazzled, that he can behold no beauty in any thing besides. He is like Jacob, who when he was to go to rich Egypt and a dear Joseph, was not to regard his stuff. Earthly objects, which to earthly minds seem glorious, to a believer have no glory, by "reason of the glory that excelleth," 2 Cor. iii. 10.

Though Jezebel paints her face, he throws her down, and treads her under foot.

(3.) It makes us conscientious in holy duties. Paul charges Timothy to keep the command without spot by an argument drawn from Christ's appearance; and upon this ground, of looking for a reward from the chief Shepherd, Peter warns the elders to feed the flock. As we cannot conceive what manner of mercy, for it is glory which we look for; so neither can we express what manner of persons we should be, or what manner of performances ours should be for holiness, 1 Cor. xv. 58. "What manner of persons," saith the apostle," ought we to be?" 2 Pet. iii. 11.

(4.) It engages to patience under every difficulty and distress. "Behold, I come quickly: hold that fast which thou hast," Rev. iii. 11. Thus 1 John ii. 28, "Little children, abide in him, that when he shall appear we may have confidence," &c. He who beholds a kingdom appointed for him, will abide with Christ in his temptations. The drawing nigh of the Lord's coming is the apostle's ground of patience, James v. 8; 2 Thess. i. 6, 7. John Huss and Jerom of Prague appealed from the unjust sentences of men, to the righteous judgment of Christ. This day's misery is not worthy of that day's mercy, Rom. viii. 18; 2 Cor. iv. 17. No more comparable with it than is the uncovering of the head a trouble comparable to the honour of receiving a crown. Saul held his peace, though he were despised, because he was king, 1 Sam. x. 27. How easily should our sea of honey swallow up our drop of vinegar! Though godliness brings sufferings, yet it affords encouragements; like Egypt, which though it were full of poisonous creatures, yet full of antidotes. The reason why we are cast away in tempests, is for want of this anchor of hope of the mercy of Christ. Let then, O Christians, the looking for this mercy engage you to duty. Remember such mercy to be received deserves better services to be performed. As God's mercy and faithfulness are put together, so let not his mercy and our faithfulness be severed, Psal. xxxvi. 5. Brethren, if any shame could befall the saints at the day of judgment, it would be for this, that they who have done so little on earth for God, should receive so much in heaven from God.

Obs. 2. It is mercy, not merit, that must stand us in stead at the last day.

Obs. 3. How much are they mistaken who expect mercy, and yet have no interest in Christ! It is the "mercy of Christ." Christless persons are merciless persons; merciless because they show no mercy, and merciless because they receive no mercy: true saving mercy is derived from God through Christ. He "hath blessed us with all spiritual blessings in Christ." God in himself is a full fountain, but in his Son he only is an overflowing fountain, of mercy. He who is in Christ a God of mercy, is in himself a God of wrath. It was a saying of Luther, Let me have nothing to do with an absolute God. We are only accepted in the Son of his love. It is his blood which only quenches the fire of his Father's wrath. As soon mayst thou extract water out of a consuming fire, as a drop of mercy out of an unreconciled majesty. Say not then, poor ignorant sinner, He that made me will save me, God is a merciful God. What mercy for him who despises mercy by refusing Christ? Think not with a fawning presumption to say, God is my God. I tell thee he is only so thy God, as that he is also thy Judge.

Obs. 4. They who have Christ for theirs cannot be under wrath. Their portion is mercy. In all conditions they meet with mercy. It is mercy when it is misery; let their straits, poverty, disgraces, death, judgment come, it is all mercy. The day of judgment shall be to them a day of mercy; nay, therefore a day of mercy because a day of judgment, for God shall be most just in showing them that mercy which by Christ is so dearly purchased. So that even as they may appeal from the justice of God to his mercy, so may they, in a sort, expect mercy from his justice. How willingly then may saints submit to every Divine, though smart, dispensation! God may be severe, never unmerciful toward them. There is not a drop of wrath in a sea of their sufferings. If God scourge them, it is in mercy. Oh how great is the difference between an executioner's axe and a father's rod!

Obs. 5. It is our wisdom to be made fit to look for the mercy of Christ. See p. 152.

Obs. 6. It is our duty to be quickened in looking for this mercy of our Lord Jesus Christ. Its certainty, greatness, speediness, are all motives; of which see p. 150, 151.

VERSE 22, 23.

And of some have compassion, making a difference: and others save with fear, pulling them out of the fire; hating even the garment spotted by the flesh.

WE have handled the first sort of directions guiding these Christians how to contend for the faith, viz. such as chiefly concern themselves.

The directions of the second sort, viz. such as concern their carriage towards others, are contained in these two verses, wherein the Christians are directed to use a different deportment and carriage toward the different delinquents which were among the seduced for their recovery.

The first kind of deportment and carriage is that of Christian lenity and gentleness towards some, in ver. 22.

The second is that of holy austerity and severity toward others, ver. 23.

Their carriage of Christian gentleness toward some is enjoined, 1. More generally, by setting down the thing to be done, viz. their showing of compassion. 2. More particularly, how they should extend their compassion, in way of making a difference between offenders.

Two things are here briefly to be explained.
1. What Jude intends by having "compassion of some."
2. What by "making a difference."

Vulg. ἐλέγχετε, arguite.
1. "Have compassion," ἐλεεῖτε. By compassion here we must not only understand inward sympathy, no, nor yet only inclination to help the miserable, but principally the expressing of both by outward real tokens and effects of mercy; and here more particularly these expressions were to be put forth toward such of the seduced followers of these ungodly seducers, of whose recovery the saints had most hope.

Not that the apostle exhorts the Christians by a preposterous patience, either, 1. To wink at and dissemble their sins and errors, and silently to forbear the discovering of them to the offenders. Silence in a reprover was by Luther called an irremissible sin, and the greatest hatred to the offender; and if sin be bold, reprehension must not be bashful. Or, 2. Much less to soothe and flatter sinners in their errors and impieties; a wickedness which is in Scripture frequently charged upon and reproved in false prophets; and the contrary duty of faithful and upright reprehension is both commanded and encouraged. "Lift up thy voice; show my people their transgressions, and the house of Jacob their sin," Isa. lviii. 1; Ezek. iii. 17. And, "He that rebuketh a man afterwards shall find more favour than he that flattereth with the tongue," Prov. xxviii. 23.

But by this showing of compassion toward some offenders, he intends an endeavour, in convincing of and reproving for sin, to reduce them from their falls and follies in a mild, gentle, meek manner, and a mixing or seasoning all the means used for their reduction and repentance with Christian gentleness and sweetness, so that the offender may not be swallowed up of grief and despair. The same counsel is given by Paul, Gal. vi. 1, namely, of restoring a fallen brother "in the spirit of meekness;" and 2 Tim. ii. 25, of "instructing those who oppose themselves in meekness." In the former place Paul bids them καταρτίζειν, "restore such an one," &c., the word signifying to set a joint or bone that is broken, to show the care and skill of him who undertakes the employment of a reprover. Sinful severity is too ready to creep into and corrupt the duty of reprehension. Commonly men are either too remiss if they endeavour gentleness, or too austere if they labour for faithfulness. But it must be with a reprover as with a surgeon, who binds not up the wound either *duriter* or *segniter*, either too slack or too hard. This Christian gentleness shows itself towards the offender in restoring him several ways. (1.) By propounding a reproof in our own person, and declaring how great a sin it would have been for ourselves to have done thus or thus. So Paul, 1 Cor. iv. 6, "These things," saith he, "I have in a figure transferred to myself and to Apollos for your sakes," that by this wise way he might reprove them and their teachers in making sects and factions. (2.) By conveying the sharpest reproofs in sweet and gentle words, and accompanying them with courteous carriage. The pill of a reprehension is to be gilded and sugared over with gentleness: soft words do best with strong arguments. The iron of Naphtali's foot was dipped in oil. (3.) By conveying the reproof in a parable, as Nathan did in convincing David of his sin; who hereby was made his own judge, and spared the prophet the unpleasing pains of a large application. (4.) By persuading the reprehended of our love to their persons, and convincing them that it is not the person who has sinned, but the sin of the person, which we strike at. A man will take any thing from one that loves him. A surgeon we will not strike, though he cut us deep, whereas we will not endure half those wounds from a murderer without returning stroke for stroke. (5.) By mixing hopes of pardon with the severest reprehensions and denunciations. When God had humbled Adam, he concludes with the promise of the Seed of the woman. Thus Joseph dealt with his brethren when he had humbled them. Thus Nathan with David. The needle of the law is but to make way for the thread of the gospel, and the most legal reprehension must be uttered with an evangelical purpose and intention.

2. This compassion must be exercised by putting a difference, διακρινόμενοι. The word having several readings and significations, is differently rendered by interpreters. The Vulgate reading the place ἐλέγχετε διακρινομένους, interprets it *arguite judicatos*, reprove them as being judged, without hope of recovery, making the apostle speak of the openly and incorrigibly wicked, and so Beza saith he found it in three Greek copies. But this is overthrown by comparing this with the next exhortation, "and others save with fear;" the opposition is destroyed by this exposition. Others reading, also, ἐλέγχετε for ἐλεεῖτε, though they hold to διακρινόμενοι, yet interpret it ar-

guite judicati, reprove some while ye are judged; that is, faithfully admonish them, though they condemn and censure you; but since the word διακρινόμενοι may signify discerning or putting a difference, and this signification is most suitable to the apostle's scope, which is wisely to direct them to discern between offender and offender; and since the word διακρινόμενοι is of a middle signification, and may be as well taken actively as passively; I therefore doubt not but it is most aptly rendered by Beza *habito delectu,* putting a difference; that is, between those who are more gently, and those who are more severely to be dealt with, by reason of their several demerits and dispositions.

More particularly, this putting of a difference between some and others is considerable in respect of the parties offending, and in the way of their offending.

1. In respect of the parties offending. (1.) Difference is to be put between magistrates in public authority, and private persons. In reproving the former more prudence and caution is required; their authority being to be honoured, when their faults are reprehended. (2.) Difference is to be put between those of more soft, tender, and humble dispositions, and those who are more rugged and pertinacious. A Venice glass is not to be rubbed so hard as an iron or brass vessel. A word will do more with some than a blow will do with another. A gentle admonition will be more prevalent with one, than a dreadful commination will be with another. The reed will be more easily bowed than the sturdy oak. "The fitches are not threshed with a threshing instrument, neither is the cart wheel turned about upon the cummin; but the fitches are beaten out with a staff, and the cummin with a rod," Isa. xxviii. 27. (3.) Difference is to be put between those of nearer relation to us and others. Snakes or foxes I will destroy in my own and my neighbour's garden, but with more hatred and indignation in my own than in his. Sinners in mine own family, my own servants, children, relations, I should oppose and reprove for sin with more zeal than another's. By how much an enemy is nearer to me, by so much the more sharp is the conflict with him.

2. In the way of their offending. (1.) Some offend either in judgment or practice, of ignorance, blind zeal, as the Jews who had zeal for God, but not according to knowledge, Rom. x. 2. Paul persecuted the church of God ignorantly. Others of malice and obstinacy, who know they offend, and yet persist. Between these a great difference is to be put, Tit. iii. 10; Phil. iii. 15. Some of simple ignorance, who have not the means of knowledge; others of wilful and affected ignorance, who are willingly ignorant, and refuse the means of knowledge. (2.) Some offend secretly, and so the scandal is the smaller; the offence being known but to few, haply but to one: others sin publicly, and the sun is a blushing beholder of their enormities, and they are observed by all. If the offence be private, first admonish the party between thee and him; if he hear thee not, tell the church. If he offend publicly, he must, for preventing the like in others, be openly reproved, 1 Tim. v. 20. The plaster must be as broad as the sore. (3.) Some sin of infirmity, overborne by the violence of sudden passion; others of premeditated, contrived forecast. The latter is to be more humbled. The one fell by a slip and trip, as it were; the other lay down, yea, made his bed as easy as he could before. (4.) Some have fallen but once, it is the first fault, the first time they were overtaken; others live in and practise sin as their trade, their element. Gentle physic will serve for a begun distemper, a chronic disease is cured more hardly and harshly. (5.) Some are leaders and captains in wickedness, perhaps heresiarchs, and masters and authors of heresy, the contrivers and commanders of impiety; others are poor misled, seduced souls, like Absalom's followers. Now the heads of treason and conspiracies are most severely punished: "Mark them which cause divisions," Rom. xvi. 17. (6.) Lastly, Some offend in matters of highest and most vast importance; haply their error is fundamental, as papists in justification by works, idol worship, &c.; possibly their practice has been bloody, their offence adultery, incest, &c.: others offend in matters not of so high a nature, as haply in an error disciplinary; or if in doctrine, not overturning the foundation, but building of hay and stubble upon it. All sins want an equal price and merit for satisfaction, but not an equal severity in our reprehension.

Obs. 1. Those duties which seem most opposite must be reconciled in our practice; holy mourning and rejoicing, love and hatred, holy anger and meekness, zeal and compassion. Job was holily both patient and impatient; patient under his crosses, impatient against the sinful counsel of his wife. Moses was the meekest man, and yet eminent for zeal: when he was with God, he prayed for the people; when with the people, he pleaded even with the sword for God. Holy duties never interfere among themselves. In vain do men pretend the distance of the commands, as if they could not be brought together. Holiness never destroys holiness. There is a connexion between every duty. The faithful prefer not one duty before another, but are uniform in observing the commands. Causam populi apud Deum precibus; causam Dei apud populum gladiis allegavit. Greg.

Obs. 2. Compassion is most suitable to a Christian. They have obtained mercy; they are elect of God, and put on bowels of mercy, Col. iii. 12. They are peculiarly commanded to be merciful from the pattern of God's mercy, Luke vi. 36; to sympathize with others in their afflictions, 1 Pet. iii. 8. Christ and all the saints are herein our copy, Jer. ix. 1; Matt. ix. 36; Luke xix. 41; 2 Cor. xi. 9. Grace dries not up, but diverts the stream of our affections. Holy men have ever been most tender-hearted. Insensibleness of others' miseries is neither suitable to us as men or Christians. According to the former we are the same with others, according to the latter grace has made the difference. If Christians be hard-hearted, who should be soft and tender?

Obs. 3. The souls of people are true objects of mercy. No misery is so great as that of souls: they who are spiritually miserable cannot pity themselves; though their words speak not, yet their woes do. We weep over a body from which the soul is departed, and shall we not do so much more over a soul from which God is departed? What in this world is so noble, excellent, precious as the soul? We pity not so much a base-born beggar in his distresses, but when we behold some high-born prince brought to beggary, how do our bowels yearn! The soul is heaven-born, noble in regard of its original and endowments. O weep to think that hell should have such excellent furniture as precious souls; that these who are, or rather were once so high, should fall so low. I wonder not at Paul's industry, entreaties, wooings, solicitations, in doing good to souls, Acts xx.; his advice to Timothy to be instant in season and out of season, to exhort, &c., 2 Tim. iv. 2. Paul was an excellent orator, and all his oratory was to woo and win upon souls, and to persuade men to be saved. Never did malefactor so plead for his own life, as did Paul plead with men to accept of life. Though the more he loved, the less he was beloved; though the more he sued to people, the more he suffered from them; yet he patiently suffered all this for the elect's sake. He labours abundantly. He becomes all things to all men, that he might by all means save some, 1 Cor. ix. 22; 2 Cor. x. 1. He besieges souls with beseechings throughout all his Epistles, Eph. iv. 1—3; Rom. xii. 1; 2 Thess. ii. 1. It is impossible to be too importunate with souls; even boldness here is holy. Courtesy must veil to Christianity.

Obs. 4. Compassion is not to be denied to the fallen, as if there were no hope of their restitution and salvation. Paul commands that they should be restored who are overtaken with a sin, Gal. vi. 1. As the best of saints have sometimes fallen, so they have also been raised, and afterwards better than ever before. He who doth but stumble, gets ground by his stumbling. Jonah, Peter, and David stumbled, yea, fell foully, but they were raised, and received, and afterward were more holy and watchful than ever before. And although Christ saith that, Whosoever shall deny me before men shall be denied before my Father, &c., yet this is meant of a total and final denial, Heb. vi. 4—6; and although a wilful, malicious, universal renouncing of the known truth admits of no sacrifice for sin, yet the gospel excludes none from pardon that can be humbled and sincerely sorrowful for their falls. Greatly therefore did the Novatians err, in teaching that sins committed after conversion are unpardonable. Christian meekness must both wholly restrain unjust, and temper even just anger; our zeal must not transgress its due limits. We live not among the perfect, but such as are subject to many slips; and we have frequent want of God's meekness and gentleness towards us in our daily falls and follies. Considering what we both have been, and may again be, we should pity the fallen. If two travellers fall into a deep ditch, the one being helped out, must not deny help to the other.

Obs. 5. Wisdom is requisite in every one that would recover a fallen brother. There must be a wise discerning between offender and offender. The setting of a soul in joint is a point of skill and dexterity. It is not for every horseleech to meddle with this art. Every unskilful workman is not to tamper with men's souls. The apostle puts those that are spiritual (Gal. vi. 1; 1 Cor. xiv. 37) upon this employment, such as had received a greater portion of the graces of the Spirit, and were stronger than others. He who speaks a word to the weary must have the tongue of the spiritually learned, Phil. iii. 13. The wisest course must be chosen for recovering the fallen. The physician administers not the same medicine to every patient, but he varies his prescriptions according to the nature of the disease, or the constitution of the diseased. Oh that Christians would employ their wisdoms for God! We see how wise men are to damn and undo their souls, and how witty seducers are to mislead others into sin and error; why should not Christians then study the heavenly art of saving and delivering the souls of others?

Obs. 6. The gifts of God are not bestowed upon us for ourselves alone, but for the good of others. Every private Christian, in some sort, should be a public good. The possession of our gifts belongs to us, but the use of them to others also. No Christian is a treasurer, but a steward of God's gifts. The more spiritual any man is, the more he is bound to restore others. The hotter the sun shines upon the wall, the more it warms the passenger. The more mercy has relieved thee, the greater obligation lies upon thee to relieve others. As any man hath received the gift, so let him minister unto others, 1 Pet. iv. 10. It is not having good in us, but the doing of good by us, that makes us called good.

The apostle directs these Christians how to carry themselves towards others, more obstinate and pertinacious sinners, namely, with holy severity, in these words, "And others save with fear, pulling them out of the fire; hating even the garment spotted by the flesh."

The words consist of two parts.
1. A duty enjoined; to save others with fear.
2. The manner of performing it:
(1.) Vehemently and earnestly, "pulling them out of the fire."
(2.) Vigilantly and warily, "hating even the garment spotted," &c.

1. For the first, the duty; "others save with fear." What intends the apostle by these "others;" what by saving; and what by saving them "with fear?"

(1.) By "others," he means those who were to be looked upon as unlike those of whom he had spoken in the foregoing part, that were to be dealt with in a way of Christian compassion. This is clear by the adversative expression δὲ, and, or rather, but. So that as those of whom they were to have compassion were of the more hopeful and corrigible sort, who had haply fallen out of ignorance, infirmity, or blind zeal; so these others were such as were more obstinate and stubborn in their sin and errors, and who did more knowingly and maliciously offend; and by this indefinite expression, "others," he intends those more hateful sinners of any rank or degree whatsoever, high or low, rich or poor, there being no sinful respect of persons to be had in this terrifying them from their accursed impieties.

(2.) He directs to save these others; that is, to deliver them from that sin into which they had fallen, and destruction into which they were falling. Saving is in Scripture attributed to God, to Christ, to men.

[1.] To God, who is the supreme author of our safety and deliverance, by whose proper power we are made safe from evils, either in respect of common salvation or preservation afforded to all men, or of peculiar salvation bestowed upon those who believe; according to that of 1 Tim. iv. 10, "He is the Saviour of all men, especially those who believe."

[2.] To Christ, who is called a Saviour, Luke ii. 11; Matt. i. 21, the only Saviour, Acts iv. 12, a strong, sufficient Saviour, a horn of salvation, able to the utmost to save; and that both by delivering by his merit and Spirit from the condemning and destroying, as also from the reigning and defiling, power of all our spiritual enemies.

[3.] To men, who are frequently in Scripture said to save, and to be saviours. " Saviours shall come up on Mount Zion," Obad. 21. "How knowest thou, O man, whether thou shalt save thy wife?" 1 Cor. vii. 16. "Thou shalt save thyself, and them that hear thee," &c., 1 Tim. iv. 16; James v. 20. Not as if men were the authors of our salvation, but instruments and subordinate helps and means appointed by God to serve his providence in saving themselves or others, whether from bodily or spiritual enemies. Words proper to the Supreme Cause being thus in Scripture attributed to the instrument, who, though he be by God appointed to use the severest means towards any, yet all is to be done in order to their salvation and recovery, 1 Cor. v. 5; 2 Tim. ii. 25, 26. The most sharp and cutting reproofs are to be used that the reproved "may be sound in the faith," Tit. i. 13.

(3.) He directs to the saving of these others with fear, ἐν φόβῳ. The apostle means by terrifying them, or making them afraid of continuing in their sin, lest they fall into destruction of soul and body. So that hereby the apostle intends the using Christian severity towards these others, as by showing compassion he directed them to use Christian lenity and gentleness towards the former. For though Jude intends not that these to whom he wrote should put forth or exercise ways of terror in a civil or earthly respect, by corporal punishments, in which respect the magistrate is called a terror to evil works, Rom. xiii. 3; yet spiritually, and by using spiritual means, and for the saving of the spirit, he directs them to terrify these offenders: and this may be done two ways, either charitatively, or by authoritative means. [1.] Charitatively, or in a way of Christian charity; and thus one Christian is bound to terrify another from sin, and not to suffer him without reproof and denunciation of God's judgments to go on in any way of wickedness. And this, though severity, is a token of love, and the refraining from it interpreted by the Spirit of God to be hatred. "Thou shalt not hate thy brother," Lev. xix. 17. [2.] Authoritatively, or by those whom God has put into office for this end, among others, to reduce offenders, and save them by fear. And this authoritative affrighting from sin is either doctrinal or disciplinary.

The doctrinal is put forth three ways.

(1.) By information, and clear discovering of the nature of sin in itself, and showing the difference between good and evil, and the hatefulness of sin both in its nature and effects. For want of this knowledge many a soul has perished.

(2.) By application and conviction, and bringing home the sin to the conscience of the offender. Thus Nathan, "Thou," saith he to David, "art the man." Thus Peter to those converts, "Him," meaning Christ, "ye have taken, and by wicked hands have crucified and slain." Thus also Stephen, "Ye do always resist the Holy Ghost," Acts vii. 51. Thus God bids the prophet to tell the people of "their transgression," Isa. lviii. 1. Ministers must not be like fencers, who so strike every where, that indeed they strike no where; but the two-edged sword of the word they must sheath in the bowels of sinners, and lay the deformed brat of sin at the right door; and so must we preach, that in our ministry the Spirit may convince of sin, John xvi. 8.

(3.) By commination and denouncing of punishments for sin, that so by hearing them men may not feel them. Offenders must be warned of the wrath to come: Knowing the terror of the Lord, we warn men. Thus frequently the prophets denounced judgments against sinners.

There is a disciplinary affrighting from sin; consisting, (1.) In solemn and particular admonition of a party offending, with a declaration of judgment against him in case of obstinacy. A sinner is first to hear this from the church. (2.) Suspension from the Lord's supper, and denying the pledges of grace to the wicked as unworthy of them. How should the child be ashamed who is debarred from sitting at his Father's table with the rest of his brethren! How can he think himself fit to partake of benefits signified in the sacrament, to sit down in the kingdom of glory, who is duly excluded from participating of the signs thereof in the kingdom of grace? (3.) Excommunication, whereby obstinate sinners are cast out of the church, and delivered up to Satan, and accounted as heathens, and reckoned among the number of Satan's servants, who rules in the world, and therefore to have him hereafter pay them their wages, 1 Cor. v. 5; Matt. xviii. 17; 1 Tim. i. 20.

Obs. 1. We must be careful to save others as well as ourselves. No man should be willing to be saved alone. A Christian should not be a Cain; he is in a sort his brother's keeper. Nor are the ministers solely the watchers over or saviours of their people. None of us are neither born the first nor second time for ourselves. In many cases every sheep is to be a shepherd. Hence those exhortations of provoking one another, Heb. x. 24. Looking diligently lest any of you fail of the grace of God, Heb. xii. 15. "Exhorting one another." Salvation is large enough for ourselves and others. If God's eye be good, ours should not be evil. The doing good to others' souls is encouraged, James v. 20; and rewarded, Dan. xii. 3. It is the nature of grace to propagate itself. The Spirit appeared in the likeness of fiery tongues, and both fire and tongues are very communicative; the one of itself and heat, the other of sound and voice. Our relations of brethren, fellow members, &c., call for this expression of love; yea, the contrary practice of sinners, who damn and defile one another's souls, may put us upon this duty. How great then is their sin who destroy the souls of others by error and seduction, and ungodly example, &c., who watch over others for evil, and, to make proselytes for hell, are factors for Satan, and agents for that prince of darkness! If their own sin and damnation will be so heavy a burden, what will other men's sins and damnations also be to them in hell! Oh what a holy covetousness should be in every saint to propagate holiness and leaven others with grace in the world! O pray, Lord, let hell never be the fuller for me or mine, but heaven for both! In respect of the privilege of saving souls, it is by some said that saints on earth excel the very glorified in heaven.

Obs. 2. Necessity should be the mother of severity. Others, i. e. they who will be by no other means reclaimed, upon whom compassion will not work, must be saved by fear. First gentle means must be used, severe afterwards. Severity, though good, is but accidentally good, not in itself, but only because of man's stubbornness: medicines were only brought in and kept up by sickness. The bee gives its honey naturally, its sting only when provoked. We should run to compassion, but be driven to rigour. If the birds will be driven away, it is needless to shoot them: our will must bring forth peace; necessity, war. Paul was much more willing to come to the Corinthians with the spirit of meekness, than with the rod of severity. Even when we are most deeply engaged in rigour, let all see that in afflicting others we more afflict ourselves.

Obs. 3. Severity is to be regulated not by outward respects, but by the merit of the offence. Others, that is, they who are more obdurate, not who are further from us in relation, or poorer, &c., should be affrighted. Though the nature of the offence should make us put a difference in our rigours, yet other considerations foreign to the cause should not. Some are fiery hot in terrifying the poorer sort, whereas the rich are like the mount that might not be touched; an ungodly base respecting of persons!

Obs. 4. Even a man may be a saviour of souls. See the proofs in the explication. Paul speaks of labouring by all means to gain some; and we read of those who catch men, and win souls; and Christ mentions the gaining of thy brother. How great an honour doth God cast upon weak worms! If the Supreme Cause be pleased to attribute salvation to men because of ministry, should not men attribute salvation to God in regard of efficacy? How careful should we be to honour that God who so dignifies dust and ashes! Lay that crown at his feet which he sets on thy head. How industrious should this likewise make us in doing good to others! The Lord reckons it as our own. Though he guided thy hand every letter, yet he saith thou hast written the fair copy, whereas indeed only the blots and blurs were thine. Though thou didst but lay on the plaster, yet he attributes the cure to thee, who couldst never put virtue into the salve. To conclude this, how fearful should any be of despising the ministry of man! Though salvation sometimes be attributed to ourselves, that we may not be negligent, and properly to God, that we may not idolize man; yet it is often ascribed to others, that we may not contemn their help.

Obs. 5. Severity should be exercised to this end, to save. The scope of using the sharpest rebukes by spiritual physicians should be cure. Merciful intentions must be lodged under severest performances. The end of excommunication must be the saving of the spirit. The most cutting reproofs must be given to others "that they may be sound in the faith," Tit. i. 13. Even the most dreadful censures of the church are not mortal, but medicinable. In the body of the church, members are wounded and cut, that themselves and the whole body may be saved. And herein ecclesiastical censures excel civil punishments; the latter being to preserve the public peace, and for warning to others; the former being principally to save the offender's soul. How sharply did Peter reprove Simon Magus, when he said, "Thy money perish with thee," and "thou art in the gall of bitterness!" and yet he adds, "Repent and pray," &c. We must not reprove men to disgrace their persons, but to shame their sins; and neither insulting over men's falls, nor despairing of their risings. And therefore let not people fume and rage against the constrained rigour of the faithful, especially ministers; for it is not butchery, but surgery. As reprehension faithfully ministered shows the strength of zeal; so meekly received, the sincerity of grace. A godly heart would not one threatening less to be in the Bible. It is a bloodless martyrdom humbly to embrace the strokes of a reprover. To conclude, how ridiculously profane are the papists, whose loudest thunderings out of excommunication are against the holiest persons! But Christ's Spirit is not in their counsels, nor will he refuse graciously to meet thee unjustly ejected, as he did the blind man sinfully cast out by the Jews.

Obs. 6. Severity to sin is mercy to the soul. This affrighting made way for saving. Holy severity is a wholesome thing. The nipping frosts of winter, though not so pleasant as summer sunshine, yet are as needful for the earth, they killing the worms and vermin. Jacob is said to bless his sons, and yet he sharply censured three, Gen. xlix. 28. The smitings of the righteous are desirable to a saint. They are precious ointment. They slay sin, and save the soul. How wild a madness is it then to be angry with them, who by telling thee truth love thy peace! None but fools oppose faithful reprovers; and who are such, that if the truth be told them, will not be pleased, and if they be pleased, the truth is not told them. Such a disposition as this is an evident token that God has a purpose to destroy them, 2 Chron. xxv. 16. How much is this cruelty to their own souls to be pitied by every reprover! They oppose reproofs and their own happiness both at once. Let them read their dismal doom, "He, that being often reproved hardeneth his neck, shall suddenly be destroyed, and that without remedy," Prov. xxix. 1. Let those whom God has appointed to be reprovers, take heed lest like drones they lose their stings. If sinners be not saved, it should be their trouble; if they be neither reproved nor saved, it is their sin also. O let not the sinner's frenzy drive any minister into a palsy.

Obs. 7. Wicked men are oft fearless in sin, though on hell's brink. These sinners were to be made to fear, but otherwise they were fearless, they were without fear or shame, bold, presumptuous sinners. The sweetness of sin so bewitches, that the bitterness of sin does not affright. Sinners look upon wrath through the wrong end of the prospective glass, so that it seems remote. They put on Satan's spectacles, which greatens mercy, and lessens wrath, to the eyes of sinners; they are faithless, therefore fearless.

Obs. 8. Bold presumption makes way for fear. These libertines, who fed themselves without fear, and feared no judgment, but mocked at the promise of Christ's coming, if ever they came to salvation, went by the way of fear. Oh that you would think of this in your bold adventurings upon sin! your audacious undertakings must all be undone, and picked out stitch by stitch. That which was thy glory, thy rejoicing, thy valour, will afterward be thy shame, thy sorrow, thy fear. And truly it is happy if the Lord make it so before it be too late. Holy fear is no sign of unmanly cowardice.

This for the first part, the duty; "others save with fear." The second follows, the manner of performing it; and first for the vehemency and holy earnestness thereof, "pulling them out of the fire." This has two branches. 1. A sinner's woe. 2. A saint's work. The first is, to be in the fire. The second is, to pull them out of the fire.

1. Let me explain a sinner's woe, being in the fire.
2. A saint's work, pulling out of the fire.

1. A sinner's woe. Not to enlarge upon the several metaphorical acceptations of the word fire in Scripture, it is sometimes used to set forth,

(1.) Sin. All sin: "Wickedness burneth as the fire," Isa. ix. 18. More particularly the burning lust of uncleanness: "They burned in lust one toward another," Rom. i. 27. And, "It is better to marry than to burn," 1 Cor. vii. 9. Thus with this fire Sodom burnt, before it burnt with fire from heaven; and this agrees to these impure wretches compared to Sodomites, ver. 6, for sin and punishment; and this fire of lust has gluttony for its fuel.

(2.) Misery and trouble. And these are compared to fire, 1. As probatory and refining. Thus Isa. xxxi. 9, "Fire in Zion, and furnace in Jerusalem." So 1 Pet. iv. 12, "Fiery trial which is to try you." Or, 2. As it is painful and tormenting, in which respect hell-torments may be compared to fire. Or, 3. As it is violent and irresistible. 4. As it is diffusive and spreading. 5. As it smutches and takes away beauty. 6. As it is dangerously destructive and consuming: hence the wrath of God is compared unto fire, "Fire is kindled in my anger, which shall burn upon you." So Ezek. xxii. 31; and Heb. xii. 29, "Our God is a consuming fire." Hence the people returned from Babylon is said to be "a brand plucked out of the fire," Zech. iii. 2, to which place Jude probably alludes; and this I take to be the meaning of the Holy Ghost in this place, where he speaks of these seducers as being in the fire, to set forth their dangerously miserable estate, and destructive courses. These sinners, without recovery by Christians, were certainly to be destroyed and consumed here and hereafter. They corrupted themselves, ver. 10; and they who sow to the flesh reap corruption, Gal. vi. 8. And the consumption and destructiveness of this fire is worse than that of natural fire, [1.] Because a sinner lying under wrath is consumed spiritually. His precious soul is destroyed; and this is worse than if his house, his money, his child, his body were consumed in fire. The fire which destroys the soul consumes not the dross, but the gold. [2.] In this fire a sinner is destroyed insensibly; he feels no pain, fears no hurt. Men shun material fire, but they run into this fire. Fools make a sport of sin and wrath; sin is their element, they are displeased with any who would pluck them out of it. Like the horse, they will not stir, though they be in never so much danger by the approaching flames. [3.] He is destroyed pitilessly; there are few that rescue and pluck him out of the fire. Every one will quench the fire which burns the house, few labour to quench the fire which burns the soul. There are few faithful reprovers. Who warns his neighbour of God's wrath? most are afraid to black or burn their fingers. Most men pour oil rather than water to these flames. [4.] He is destroyed everlastingly. Natural fire consumes so as it ends and eats up that which it burns; this fire is ever destroying, never destroys. Without the blood of Christ it is unquenchable: a sinner shall ever burn in it, but never be burnt up in it. That which makes other fire so dreadful, namely, to make an end of things, would make this fire merciful.

2. A saint's work; the plucking out of this fire, ἁρπάζοντες. The word properly signifies the soldiers' violent rushing or seizing upon a town or castle for plunder or prey. "The kingdom of heaven suffereth violence, and the violent" ἁρπάζουσι, "take it by force." And more particularly,

This plucking sinners out of their misery as out of fire, imports,

(1.) Speediness. When a thing is in the fire it endures no delays. Sin, like poison, admits of no dalliance. The abiding in spiritual fire but a little longer may make the recovery impossible; no deliberation so dangerous. It is needless here to call a council. While we are lingering and doubting, the fire is devouring. Satan, like a subtle enemy, never desires to treat but for his own advantage.

(2.) It imports solicitousness and care, a holy fear of the future event, the ruin of that which is to be plucked out of the fire. Paul was afraid of the Galatians, Gal. iv. 19. Holy love is solicitous, does its best, but fears the worst. Titus had an earnest care for the good of the Corinthians, 2 Cor. viii. 16; and their burning calamity caused in Paul burning care. "Who is offended," saith he, "and I burn not?"

(3.) Pity and commiseration. The more violence and speed is used in plucking a good thing out of the fire, the more tender pity is expressed. If pity should be showed to thy neighbour's beast, or to his house, much more to his own body, but most of all to his soul. It is reported of Æneas, that his pity made him take his father upon his shoulder, and carry him out of the flames of Troy. It is storied, Gen. xix. 16, that while Lot, his wife, and daughters lingered in Sodom, upon which fire was falling, the Lord being merciful to him, the angels brought him forth, and set him without the city. This mercy in this spiritual plucking out is here imported.

(4.) Esteem and appreciation. Men pluck that with eagerness out of the fire which they value and set by. A piece of potsherd they neglect, but a costly garment, some rare book, or much more a dear child, oh how earnestly are they snatched out of the flames! The estimate which ought to be had of souls is much greater. Heaven-born, beautifully-endowed, eternal souls are so precious that Christ shed his blood for them, and Satan only delights in shedding theirs.

(5.) Hazard and endangering of him who plucks the party out of the fire. They who will take a thing out of the fire commonly burn their own fingers. The most zealous adventurers for souls have seldom escaped the scorching rage and fury of the wicked. Truth begets hatred both in others, and oft in him whom we labour to save. Satan will not let go his hold willingly. All the militia of hell is raised against the faithful saving of souls. All the holy prophets, apostles, ministers, more or less, must feel the scorching of the fire, if they will be plucking out of souls. The saviours of souls must be sufferers for souls, and herein resemble the great Saviour, who for souls was the greatest sufferer.

(6.) Diligence and earnest industry. This is principally here intended according to the signification of the word ἁρπάζοντες. They who pluck a precious thing out of the fire, do it with putting forth all their vigour and pains. They who will save souls, must apply heart and head to this employment. Faithful ministers are ever laborious. They are peculiarly called labourers. They labour in the word and doctrine. "As much as in me is, I am ready to preach the gospel," Rom. i. 15. This work he made his business, and he gave himself to it. In comparison of this his diligence for other things was but negligence. For three years together he warned every one with tears, Acts xx. 31. He was willing to "spend and be spent," 2 Cor. xii. 15. He was fervent in spirit in this serving of the Lord. In plucking a precious thing out of the fire, the finger is not held up, but violently is the thing laid hold upon and drawn forth with our hand.

Obs. 1. The hell of a sinner is begun in this life; he is even here in the fire; hell-fire is but his greater sensibleness of that fire of wrath wherein he even now is. As heaven, so hell, is now in this world *in semine*. In hell the damnation of the wicked is but displayed; here it is, though wrapped up as the flag about the staff. Sinners in this life are treasuring up of wrath. Put sin into its best dress, it is but gilded damnation. The fire of God's wrath is kindled on this side hell, and it burns inward, only in hell it blazes out. The incorrigible are condemned already. They are even here the children of perdition, and there is nothing between them and the fire of hell but a thin wall of flesh. And therefore,

Obs. 2. How madly merry is every sinner! Fond creature, to bribe and soothe thy burning soul with toys and rattles! How unseasonable and unsuitable is thy mirth, when thou art burning thy soul; and yet, as the idolaters of old, when they sacrificed their children to idols, makest music and singing! This doth every secure sinner. Oh how much better is it here to mourn and shed the tears of godly sorrow, especially to get the blood of Jesus Christ to quench the flames before they blaze out in hell, where they will be unquenchable.

Obs. 3. The devil has his martyrs; nay, the most are burnt for irreligion. Wicked men here burn themselves, not as saints, to escape, but, in regard of the end of the work, to embrace eternal burnings. It should be a shame to consider how mad sinners are upon and patient in the flames of wrath and sin, and how impatient saints are in those flames out of which all the heat and hurt is taken. *Per quot pericula itur ad majus periculum!*

Obs. 4. Even they who are in the fire may be pulled out. There is a peradventure mentioned of God's giving repentance even to opposers, 2 Tim. ii. 25. "Such," saith the apostle, "were some of you," 1 Cor. vi. 11, ταῦτα, such trash, such rubbish. Manasseh, Magdalene, and Paul, the greatest of sinners, and those Christians hateful and hating one another, serving divers lusts, and children of wrath, found mercy, Eph. ii. 3; Tit. iii. 3. God sometimes turns people in their race of sin when they are gotten almost to their goal, hell-gates, and receives prodigals who smell of the hogs' trough, and recovers brands which are singed, yea, almost consumed. The freeness of his grace, the riches of mercy, the depth of his wisdom, the greatness of his power, are all hereby magnified: we must not despair of the most seemingly desperate. We may censure the actions, not determine the ends, though of great sinners. To conclude, the greater the misery and the more scorching the fire is out of which any of us have been plucked, the stronger is the engagement upon us to save others, and to serve our Saviour.

Obs. 5. The faithful are very useful and beneficial to the world. It is a misery when any thing dear to us falls into the fire; but this is by much the greater when there is no man near to pluck it out of the fire. They who save our goods from the flames are commended for helpful people; but they who save souls from the wrath of God and the fire of hell, are much more necessary. The people of God are falsely accounted the troublers and incendiaries of the world, whereas their work is to recover out of the fire, not to cause and increase the fire. There are none so miserable as they who may be suffered to lie in sin as long as they please, without controllers or recoverers, who may be as bad as they please, without check or reprehension.

Obs. 6. The greatest diligence in the recovery of souls is very excusable. The most earnest plucking of our treasure or child out of the fire wants not an apology. The best things require most labour about them. Trifles, fancies, riches, honours, deserve not our diligence. No persuasions should be so vehement, no pains so great, as those we take for souls. We may easily be too importunate and painful when we labour for our bodies, but it is impossible to be so when we labour to benefit ours or others' souls. It is a holy impudence to be bold in urging any to pity their better part. It is a sinful bashfulness to be so courteous to forget Christianity. We can never warn men too much of their spiritual danger. It is very good manners in Christianity to stay and knock again, though we have knocked more than thrice at the door of a sinner's conscience. Either here or hereafter his conscience will commend us, though now his lusts are angry with us. How willing therefore should eople be to take holy importunity for their souls' good in good part! If importunity overcame an unrighteous judge to do good to another, how much more should it prevail with us for our good! Let not ministers complain that they spread out their hands to a gainsaying people.

Cum periculo ignis temporalis eripiendus est peccator ex igne æterno.

2. In this manner of recovering these offenders the apostle enjoins, in the second place, that it should be done with vigilancy and wariness; in these words, "hating even the garment spotted by the flesh." And this he adds to the former, to warn the Christians that in their conversing with these offenders, when they laboured to recover them, they should take heed of getting any hurt from them, having to deal with them as physicians, not as companions.

Two things are here briefly to be explained.

1. The thing to be hated, "the garment spotted," &c.
2. How and why it was to be hated.

1. "The garment spotted with the flesh." Many impertinent and over-curious expositions by popish writers are given us of this place: some understand this "garment spotted by the flesh" properly, as if Jude intended that the filthy uncleanness and obscenities of these impure sinners did not only defile their manners and actions, but even their very clothes and garments, by reason of their nearness to their defiled flesh; and even these, say they, Jude bids these Christians to shun or not touch, to show their hatred of carnal uncleanness. But Justinian seems rightly to conceive that this is an exposition of more lightness than to savour of apostolic gravity. Others by this garment understand that natural unholiness which Paul calls the old man with his deeds, and commands the Christians to put off as an old filthy garment, Col. iii. 9.

But this is not agreeable to the scope of the apostle, which is not to direct the Christians what to put off and hate in themselves, but to shun and hate that which might be conveyed from others to themselves. The best exposition is that given by learned Calvin, and some others, who say, that by this "garment spotted by the flesh, the apostle intends that which seems to have any affinity or nearness to the vices of these sinners which were among them. And this is very much confirmed, 1. By the word καὶ, here translated even, which, as Calvin notes, *ad amplificationem valet,* has the force of amplification, and imports as if the apostle had said in a full speech, hating not only the flesh itself, but even the garment spotted or infected by the flesh; and also, 2. By that apt allusion which in these metaphorical expressions, Jude makes to that commanded rite of the ceremonial law, whereby the Israelites were ceremonially unclean, not only by touching the flesh of one who had a running issue, or the matter itself that issued forth, but even by touching the seat, bed, saddle, garments of such a person, Lev. xv. 4—6, &c.; so that this direction of "hating the garment spotted by the flesh," imports as much as if Jude had said, Know, O Christian, though I have exhorted you to have compassion of the persons of these sinners, and to labour with them that they might be plucked out of their miserable state, yet I would have you warily to take heed to yourselves, lest while you are about curing them they infect you, and lest that while you lend them your hand to draw them out of the pit, they, being stronger than you, pull you in to them. Nay, so far must you be from allowing and liking their gross and ungodly practices, that you must abstain from whatever has any neighbourhood or nearness to their sins. For not only would I have you kept from touching the infecting and defiling flesh, the sin itself; but I exhort you to hate even the very clothes, or that which sits any thing near to it, or borders upon it, or has affinity to it. And this direction principally comprehends two particulars.

(1.) That they should hate all incentives, occasions, inducements, or inlets to sin, and that both in respect of themselves and others. 1. In respect of themselves. It is safest keeping far from the brink of the river. He who has fallen, and yet will walk in slippery places, shows that yet he has not been bruised enough. Thus Eve's looking on the apple, when it drew on her appetite, her parely with the serpent, should have been avoided. 2. In respect of others. Paul was very careful to avoid occasions of making others sin, though things which he avoided were neither sinful in themselves, nor to him. Paul's eating of flesh was lawful in itself, and lawful to him, and yet rather than he would offend his weak brother, he would never do it while the world stands, 1 Cor. viii. 13; Rom. xiv. 21. Paul was sometimes here travailing in birth with his little children, Gal. iv. 19; and was like a careful mother, who forbears many meats for fear of doing her child hurt. Thus Paul refused to circumcise Titus, fearing the confirmation of the Jews in their error, Gal. ii. 3.

(2.) That they should avoid that which carries a show of evil, and is liable to misconstruction. Thus Paul refused using his liberty in taking a lawful maintenance for his labours, lest a sinister interpretation of covetousness and mercenary affection should have been put upon it by his adversaries. Though here it must be noted, that in all necessary duties we must yield absolute obedience to God, though to the world it appear never so evil. Christ preached himself the bread of life, though the Jews were offended, John vi. Daniel will pray three times a day, though it cost him his life. John will preach against Herodias, though all the court be offended. For though evil must not be done that good may come of it, yet good must be done, though evil may come of it. Thus in doctrine we must abstain from such speeches which, though they may have a right interpretation, yet carry a show of evil. To say we are saved by works may have a true interpretation, but it is better to abstain from it, because it has an appearance of popish merit. To call evangelical ministers priests may be truly expounded, but it were better to avoid the expression, because of the show of popish sacrifice and priesthood. The words of heretics are to be avoided. And if we will keep the faith of the Scriptures, we must keep the words of the Scriptures. Those things which are *male colorata*, though not *in se mala*, which have an ill colour, though not an ill nature, must be shunned.

Cæsar said of his wife, that she ought to be without suspicion of fault, as well as without fault. Valentinian having a drop of the water sprinkled upon his garment which was cast about by the priests in their heathenish services, cut out that piece of cloth upon which that drop fell from the rest of the garment. The ancient Christians would not set up lights and bays at their doors, though for this they were persecuted as enemies to the emperor, because the temple and the doors of idolaters were wont to be thus garnished. Tertul. lib. de Idol. These primitive Christians would not endure that any Christian should look toward Jerusalem praying, because they would avoid show of Judaism. Augustine thought it in his time unlawful to fast on the sabbath day, because the Manichees did so. God appointed his own ceremonies, that a wall of partition might be put between the Israelites and heathens; in which respect his people are forbid to eat swine's flesh, the ordinary food of the Gentiles, to make their heads bald, to shave their beards, to cut their flesh. And Aquinas thinks, that because the heathens set their temples eastward, therefore God's was set westward, *ad arcendam idololatriam*, saith he. Aquin. 1 a. 20. 3. q. Not only apparent sins, but sins in appearance, are to be avoided by Christians. Even accompanying with sinners is suspicious, as well as acting their impieties is heinous, Eph. v. 7. Tell me, said a good man once, where thou hast been, and I will tell thee what thou hast done. A man sins as well by not reproving a swearer as by swearing. He that does not preserve the law does not observe it. This, say some, was one reason why David refused to take the thrashing-floor, oxen, &c., as a gift, but would buy them, because he would avoid the show of covetousness.

For the second, why this "garment spotted," &c. was to be hated, i. e. inwardly loathed, outwardly shunned.

In respect of God, of themselves, and of others.

1. God. (1.) It is his command; he would have his to adorn the gospel, to shine as lights, to abstain from all appearance of evil, and be holy in repute as well as in reality. (2.) His honour is hereby advanced. The further we keep from defiling ourselves, the more we keep from dishonouring him. It is the glory of the gospel, when men cannot lay any thing like an evil to our charge, and when they cannot speak reproachfully and truly at the same time. (3.) His example is hereby imitated. He hates all that is evil and like evil. The conformity of our affections with the Lord is very acceptable. How highly is the church of Ephesus commended for hating the doctrine "of the Nicolaitanes, which," saith the Lord, "I also hate." There is in God no shadow of change, and therefore nothing like sin; he is of purer eyes than to behold sin, or to look upon iniquity.

2. Themselves. (1.) It is a true note of sincerity to shun evil in its very likeness. He who hates a person loves not his very picture. This is a main difference between a sound Christian and a hypocrite. A wicked man will abstain from evil in extremes, but commonly he cares not for petty and appearing evils. Hence, tell him of such and such a sin, his reply usually is, Give me some plain, manifest scriptures against it; scriptures which oppose his sin by consequence and proportion will not serve the turn. It must only be a plain, bare-faced evil that he will forsake. A hypocrite loves the appearance of good more than goodness itself; the godly hates the very appearance of evil as well as the evil itself. (2.) It is his wisdom to avoid the appearance of evil. He who will never give way to so much as an appearing, shall not be overthrown with a real evil. He who will not touch will not taste, much less swallow down a sin. And he who cares not to avoid the appearance of evil, by little and little comes to esteem the evil and the appearance both alike: the beginnings of sin are modest, and yet make way to immodest proceedings. (3.) He takes the wisest course to preserve his good name. He who abstains from appearing evils, provides for his conscience and reputation at once, and stops the mouths of accusers abroad, as well as of the accuser in his own bosom.

3. Others, the weak and the wicked. (1.) They who shun the very resemblance of sin, make those who are any thing inclinable to follow them more exact and precise in their walking. Commonly, if a leader will adventure upon an appearing, a follower will be imboldened thereby to commit a real evil; for though when we behold men strict in holiness, we are too ready to hope that we may be allowed to come a little short of them, yet when we see any take liberty to do that which inclines to evil, we are prone to imagine that we may go a little beyond them. They who write copies must write a fair hand; trifles in a leader are blasphemies. As reports lose nothing in the telling, so sin loses nothing in the imitating. Commonly the scholar outgoes the master. (2.) They who allow themselves in appearing evils harden wicked men, who ever make the faults of such seem bigger and more than they are, and for fifty write down a hundred; and ever make use of the appearing evils of saints as shields and apologies to bear them out in their greatest enormities.

Obs. 1. Sin and sinners are spotting and defiling, they stain what they touch. The allusion here is to a running issue defiling the thing it touches.

Obs. 2. The people of God in this world are subject to defilements. Jude, in exhorting the Christians to carry themselves compassionately towards sinners, directs them likewise to carry themselves warily, lest they get hurt from them. It is as hard to be in the world, and not to be polluted by it, as to be among infectious persons, and not to be infected. The best of saints have a principle in them which will make them catch infection. The great industry of worldly persons is to pollute the godly. The power of religion is principally seen in keeping a man unspotted of the world, James i. 27. The people of God had need gird up their loins, and carry themselves watchfully in every place and condition: spots are easily seen in white garments, and defilements on those who have more than ordinary purity. The men of the world are spotting, defiling creatures. They are such vessels of dishonour which a man cannot touch without pollution. A vessel of honour must "purge himself from these," 2 Tim. ii. 21. And how great cause have saints to long for that place, where they shall be freed from places of and temptations to sin! In infectious times we use to covet the country, and to desire an open and fresh air. It is for scullions to be among the pots, and for worldly men to love to live in the world.

Obs. 3. Reprehension of sin must be accompanied with sincere hatred to sin. It was not enough for these Christians to make offenders afraid, unless they also hated that thing from which they terrified them. That man will be but an ineffectual reprover, and seldom works upon the heart, who speaks only from the lip. The best oratory is that which proceeds from experience: "Knowing," saith Paul, "the terror of the Lord, we persuade men." He who does but act the reprover, seldom benefits the reproved. But should such a notional teacher of others do them good, what benefit comes to himself? surely he would be like an unskilful servant, who opens the gate for his master, but lets it fall to again, so that he himself is hindered from following.

Obs. 4. Appearances of good are to be loved and respected. If any thing like to sin is to be loathed, then the very shews and pictures of holiness are to be regarded. Christ looked upon the young man in the gospel, and loved him. The outward humiliation of Ahab went not without its reward. His appearing repentance had an appearing recompence. And God, saith Calvin, would show how much he loved the truth of grace by rewarding the shadow thereof. We love the picture for the person's sake. Much more we should love and cherish the least spark or drachm of true grace; the very smoking flax, and bruised reed. It is murder to kill a little infant of a span long as well as a full-grown man.

Obs. 5. A Christian's honour is exactness in his conduct. He must walk accurately, not only abstaining from gross, but even from the finest-spun sins, the very show and appearance thereof. Every earthly artist is so much regarded as he can show exactness in his profession. In false religions exactness is highly set by; how great a sin and shame then is it that exactness in the most honourable art should only be reproached! The enemies of preciseness most oppose Christianity; nay, they who are ashamed of holy strictness, are ashamed of the greatest glory.

Obs. 6. Great is the safety of the ways of God. They preserve from coming near the confines of sin and destruction. The farther from sin, the more distant from danger. He who keeps himself far from sin, needs not fear though troubles come never so near. "The beloved of the Lord shall dwell in safety by him," Deut. xxxiii. 12; though they are not taken out of the world, yet they are kept from the evil, and so as that the evil one toucheth them not, John xvii. 15.

Obs. 7. Religion provides for our fame as well as for our conscience. It keeps us from any appearance of a spot or suspicion of a sin. Sin martyrs the name, but holiness puts us upon those things only which are of good report; our names are only scratched by the briers of sin. In keeping our purity we cannot part with our reputation, unless it be among those whose praise is our reproach, and whose reproach is our praise.

VERSE 24, 25.

Now unto him that is able to keep you from falling, and to present you faultless before the presence of his glory with exceeding joy, to the only wise God our Saviour, be glory and majesty, dominion and power, both now and ever. Amen.

WE have finished, by God's assistance, the two first parts of this Divine Epistle, viz.

The title, contained in the two first verses; and,

The body and substance of the Epistle, contained from the 3rd verse to the 23rd.

The third part, the conclusion, laid down in ver. 24, 25, remains to be handled; though I shall rather briefly touch than handle these two verses; both because my scope when I began this Epistle was to insist upon the body and substance thereof; and because I have already at large spoken of the main part of the 24th verse, viz. Christ preserving us from falling; and also because the substance of the 25th verse is handled by those who comment upon the Lord's prayer, and both largely and learnedly by Doctor Gouge in his Exposition of that prayer.

These two verses shut up this whole Epistle with a sacred and solemn doxology, and the celebration of God's name by praise and thanksgiving. And three parts are herein principally considerable.

I. The person to whom praise is given, the Lord Christ, set forth three ways.

1. By his power to keep these Christians from falling, and to present them faultless before, &c.

2. By his wisdom; "the only wise God."

3. By his goodness; "our Saviour."

II. What the praise is that is given him, viz. the praise of "glory, majesty, dominion, power," all amplified by their duration, "now and ever."

III. The manner how this praise is given him, intended in this word, "Amen."

I. The person to whom praise is given is so described by our apostle, as that the faith of these Christians may be the more confirmed in praying for and expecting those things to which Jude in this Epistle had exhorted them.

1. He is set forth by his power, (1.) To preserve them from falling. Of this power of Christ to preserve from falling into sin and misery I have at large spoken, p. 17, 18, on these words, "preserved in Jesus Christ."

(2.) He is set forth by his power to present them "faultless before the presence of his glory with exceeding joy." In which words are contained a description of the glorious state of the church in heaven. This state is generally propounded, and particularly exemplified.

1. In the general proposition the saints are said to be presented "before the presence of his glory."

2. The particular exemplification thereof is,

(1.) Privative, by removing of all deformity, noted in the word "faultless."

(2.) Positive, by partaking of fulness of joy, noted in this expression, "with exceeding joy."

1. The saints are to be presented. The word present, στῆσαι, imports, 1. To place or set, as Matt. iv. 5; xviii. 2; to dispose of a thing to a station. And, 2. To place it in a way of firmness and stability, to establish it, Rom. iii. 31; Matt. xii. 26. The same thing is intended both here and Eph. v. 27, where the apostle speaks of Christ's presenting to himself a glorious church; in which place the word παραστήσῃ, present, is taken from the custom of solemnizing a marriage. First the spouse was wooed, and then set before or presented to her husband, that he might take her for his

wife to be with him. Thus Eve was presented by God to Adam, that he might take her for his wife, Gen. ii. 22, and Esther was presented to Ahasuerus; to which custom Paul elegantly alludes 2 Cor. xi. 2, " I have espoused you to one husband, that I may" παραστῆσαι, " present you as a chaste virgin to Christ." And this presentation is said to be before the presence of his glory, κατενώπιον τῆς δόξης αὐτοῦ. By this glory is meant the beaming forth, discovery, manifestation of the excellency of Christ before the saints; that of which Christ speaks, John xvii. 24, " Father, I will that they also whom thou hast given me be with me where I am, that they may behold my glory." By which glory I understand not only that glory of soul and body which he has in common with the saints, subjectively abiding and inherent in him; but also that which is bestowed upon the human nature by the personal union, and its exaltation to the right hand of God, above all saints and angels. Before the presence of this his glory shall the saints be placed. Κατενώπιον, before it, *coram, in conspectu,* in the full view of it, in a clear and open vision, right against it. The sunshine of Christ's glory shall be full upon them, and they look full upon it; yea, so as to be made partakers of it in their measure: this sun looking upon them will make them shine also, Matt. xiii. 43. The spouse of Christ shall shine with his beams, and be advanced to his dignity, so far as she is capable of it; she shall eat and drink with him at his table in his kingdom, Luke xxii. 30; and it is said she shall be presented "a glorious church," Eph. v. 27.

Thus we see this glorious estate is generally propounded. But,

2. It is particularly exemplified; and that,

(1.) Negatively; and so it is said he will present the saints without spot, ἀμώμους, irreprehensible, unblamable, such as in whom the greatest carper, or strictest and most curious beholder, shall not be able to behold any thing amiss, no defect of what should be, or excess of what should not be. The church shall not have "spot, or wrinkle, or any such thing," no stain or scar, no freckle or deformity; nothing of stain or contagion received from others, no wrinkle, no defect of spiritual moisture, nothing which may make her seem uncomely in Christ's eye: not only great and heinous sins, which are great botches and boils, but every least speck and wrinkle, shall be taken away. Now sin is subdued, but then it shall be rooted out. Here saints are freed from the power of it, but then from the presence of it also. He who will wipe away all tears from the eyes of his church, will undoubtedly take away all matter of mourning from her soul. Heaven would not be heaven to a saint, could any spot continue in heaven. But when sin is gone, sorrow must needs fly away: if the fountain be dried up, the streams must needs follow. Sin brought in tears, and tears shall go away with sin. Because saints shall be presented faultless, therefore with exceeding joy. For,

(2.) This glory is exemplified positively, "with exceeding joy," ἀγαλλιάσει: the word imports an exceeding joy, with an outward leaping, dancing, or some such cheerful motion of body, an exultation which is expressed in the gesture. Unspeakable is the joy in the hoping for this glory, 1 Pet. i. 8; how great will the joy be of having it! A bunch of grapes greatly delights, what then will all the crop of Canaan! It is called not only fulness of joy, but joy itself, Matt. xxv. 21, 23: and needs must it be so; for what is joy but the quieting and resting of the soul in its object, the filling it to the brim with what it desired? Joy is the stilling of all our longings, a cessation of all our cravings. Joy to desire is what rest is in respect of motion. When motion ends, then comes rest. When desire is filled, then comes joy. Now what crevice or corner of the soul is there which shall not be satisfied in heaven by the immediate and perfect fruition of that chief good, God himself, who is the heaven of heaven, and who shall fill the soul, as those waterpots of Galilee were filled, up to the very brims? There shall be no empty spaces left in the soul untaken up. He who has fulness enough to fill himself, a vast ocean, must needs have enough to fill the soul, comparatively a small vessel. He who is self-sufficient, all-sufficient, must needs be soul-sufficient.

Thus the person is described in respect of his power.

2. He is set forth by his wisdom, in these words, "The only wise God."

(1.) He is called " God ;" of which largely before, p. 101, 102.

(2.) He is called "wise." He oft in Scripture has the name wisdom itself, Prov. viii. 22—24, &c. Christ is called the wisdom of God. This his wisdom, as here attributed to God, is twofold. 1. His wisdom of science, or theoretical wisdom, whereby he is omniscient, and with one immutable, eternal act of understanding perfectly sees and perceives, observes and knows, all things. 2. His wisdom of working, whereby he does all things, both in respect of creation and providence, with infinite wisdom, Job xii. 13. According to the former he is said to be "a God of knowledge," 1 Sam. ii. 3. There is no " creature that is not manifest in his sight: all things are naked and opened unto his eyes," Heb. iv. 13. " Known unto God are all his works," Acts xv. 18. He seeth under the whole heaven. According to the latter he is said to make all his works in wisdom, Psal. civ. 24. By wisdom he "made the heavens," Psal. cxxxvi. 5. "By wisdom hath he founded the earth, and established the world," Prov. iii. 19; Jer. x. 12; Isa. xl. 28; Psal. xcii. 6.

(3.) He is said to be " only wise." Not to exclude the wisdom of the Father and Holy Ghost, but the wisdom of all the creatures; as God the Father is called the only true God, not to exclude the Son and Holy Ghost : and though the creatures have wisdom, yet is not theirs comparable to Christ's, nor deserves the name of wisdom. 1. For his wisdom of science, which is universal, perfect, complete. [1.] He knows himself and all things, John xxi. 17; 1 John iii. 20. " Known to God are his works," Acts xv. 18. " His understanding is infinite," Psal. cxlvii. 5. Whereas the greatest part of what man knows is the least part of what he doth not know. [2.] He knows " things to come," Isa. xli. 23. Men and devils cannot foretell future contingents, but either by God's discovery, or conjecturally. His prescience has so many witnesses as he has made prophets. [3.] He knows all things possible, though they never shall actually be; his knowledge is as large as his power, and his power is such as that he can do more than he ever will do. An artificer may frame that house in his head which he never will set up with his hand. " God calleth those things which be not as though they were," Rom. iv. 17. [4.] He knows all things clearly, particularly, distinctly. All things are anatomized, ripped up before him, Heb. iv. 13. His knowledge is not, as ours, general or confused. We are said to know a man, though we know not a hundred things in a man. [5.] He knows the least things; every circumstance of every action. His knowledge extends itself to every hair of the head, Matt. x. 30, every sparrow that lights on the ground. [6.] He knows things with one simple view; not as man, by sense, opinion,

Præscientia Dei tot habet testes quot facit prophetas. Tert.

relation, reasoning, and discoursing, and drawing conclusions from propositions, and gathering knowledge of that which is less known by that which is more known. He is not for knowledge beholden, as we are, to the images and representations of things, which first are printed on our fancy, and thence offered to our understanding. He goes not out of himself to the objects for knowledge. He knew them before they were. [7.] He knows the most secret things, even the very thoughts of the heart; he knows them when they are, he knows them before they are; as what we do think, so what we will think; he puts thoughts into us, he publishes, punishes, reproves thoughts, Jer. xi. 20; xvii. 10; 1 Kings viii. 39; Psal. cxxxix. 2; xciv. 11; Ezek. xiv. 3; 1 Cor. iv. 5; Matt. ix. 4. [8.] He knows permanently, nothing slips out. He forgets nothing; his knowledge can neither be diminished nor increased.

And, 2. For the wisdom of his working. [1.] He only is originally wise; the wisdom of the wisest is from him. Bezaleel's wisdom was bestowed by him; he teaches men wisdom. All wisdom, either speculative or practical, is from Christ; every candle received light from his. The very husbandman's discretion is from God, Isa. xxviii. 26. [2.] He only is exactly, perfectly, thoroughly wise; all his works, for number, measure, and weight, are done to the height of wisdom, not one of the creatures could have been made in greater wisdom. The fairest copy that was ever written by the sons of men had some blots and scratches in it. The wisest men sometimes slip, and sleep like the wise virgins. [3.] He only is irresistibly wise, there is no wisdom against him, Prov. xxi. 30; none can go beyond him. He destroys the wisdom of the wise, and bringeth "to nothing the understanding of the prudent," 1 Cor. i. 19.

3. The person praised is set forth from his goodness and compassion in saving. Concerning the meaning of the word "Saviour," as also from what Christ saves, and how excellent a salvation his is, see p. 56, 57.

II. The main part of this doxology is the praise itself which is here given to Christ, viz. the praise of "glory, majesty, dominion, power," all set forth by the duration, "now and ever."

1. "Glory." By it I understand that infinite and incomprehensible excellency by which Christ excels all, and for which he is to be honoured above all. The glory of a thing is that excellency thereof which causes it to be in high esteem, and procures fame and renown unto it. The glory of his essence is the Godhead itself. When Moses desired God to show him his glory, God answered, "Thou canst not see my face; for there shall no man see me, and live," Exod. xxxiii. 20; so that God's glory is his face, and his face is himself. This glory is the fountain of all glory and excellence in the creature. All the creatures shine in any excellency with beams borrowed from God's glory, as the stars shine with the light they receive from the sun. And its brightness obscures all other glory. The glorious angels have wings to cover their faces; otherwise the brightness of God's glory would dazzle them. The glory of God is without measure, infinite, above comprehension, a light to which none can approach, 1 Tim. vi. 16. When God darted a faint ray of this glory upon Moses's face, they were afraid to come nigh him. How much more may any creature be afraid to come to God by reason of the incomprehensible shining of his glorious face! When the sun shines, the stars are not seen. When God's glory shines, no other is seen.

2. "Majesty," μεγαλωσύνη, majesty or magnificence. By this we are to understand that admirable highness and greatness, amplitude, splendour, dignity of Christ, as God, which appears principally in his works, thereby making himself wonderful, Psal. cxi. 3. The works of the Lord are great, and called wonderful. The royal majesty of Solomon, Ahasuerus, Nebuchadnezzar, in their apparel, buildings, feastings, and attendance, were but sordid and contemptible in comparison of God's majesty shown forth in the truth, wisdom, justice, goodness, power of his works. In respect of these the psalmist saith, he is "clothed with honour and majesty." *quadam et splendida propositione agitatio atque administratio. Cic. de Juvent.*

3. "Dominion," κράτος, properly signifying strength, Luke i. 51; sometimes power, and by consequent dominion. I here understand by κράτος, the strength and ability of Christ, whereby he can do whatsoever he will. This strength and might extends itself to every thing that by power may be done. "Is any thing too hard for the Lord?" Gen. xviii. 14. "With God nothing shall be impossible," Luke i. 37. "With God all things are possible," Mark x. 27. He is God Almighty, παντοκράτωρ. All things are within the compass of his power but such as import impotency and imperfection, as matters of iniquity, contradiction, passion, infirmity. All the power of the creature is derived from and subordinate to this, Psal. cxv. 3; cxlvii. 5; Eph. iii. 20, 21.

4. "Power," ἐξουσία. The word signifies authority and power. It properly imports a liberty to do as one list. By it in this place Jude, I conceive, intends that supreme sovereignty and authority which Christ has over all things, in governing and commanding them. He is an absolute Lord. *Ab ἔξεστι, non est jus proprie, sed efficacia, talis quæ quod vult, æquum aut iniquum, facile effectum dat. Grot. in John xix. 10.*

2. All these are amplified from their duration, "now and ever," καὶ νῦν καὶ εἰς πάντας τοὺς αἰῶνας. "Now," that is, in this life, and in all the ages of the world. The original word, αἰὼν, properly signifies that which is for ever; and because an age is the usual and longest distinction of time, this same word is put for age. And when there is no end of that which is spoken of, the plural number ages, or all ages, is used to set out the everlastingness of it. And this eternity properly taken is proper to God. For though other things are said sometimes to be for ever, and may have sempiternity or everlastingness, which looks forward to that which is to come; yet they have not eternity, which looks backward and forward, and cannot, as here the properties of God, be said to be without beginning and end. Besides, the very continuance of every creature is alterable and dependent, Acts xvii. 28; Rom. xi. 36. All the glory, majesty, power, dominion of the creature is as the flower of the field, fading; indeed every thing in this world, like flowers, the sweeter they are, the shorter lived they are, and the sooner withering; the more beautiful, as they say of glass, the more brittle.

III. Lastly, In this Divine doxology is considerable after what manner, or with what affection, this praise is given: this is set down in the word "Amen;" which imports a confirmation of all that was said before, as is clear from 1 Kings i. 36. The Greek translators turn it γένοιτο, be it done. And the root from whence the word cometh signifies as much; but it was held fit by the primitive church, for the greater dignity of the word, saith Augustine, not to translate it. Some have noted that it cannot be translated without losing much of its weight; for when it is added to a speech, it is, 1. A note of assent; and therefore it was not used only by the Jews at prayer, but at the *Amen signaculum orationis Dominicæ. Hier. in Matt. vi. Non est interpretatum, non ut esset negatum, sed ne vilesceret nudatum. Aug. Tract. in John 41. Judæi non solum ad omnes preces, sed ad omnes conciones et expositiones allego-*

Magnificentia, est rerum magnarum et excelsarum cum animi ampla

sermons and expositions delivered by the rabbins, to testify that the people assented and agreed to all that they taught. Hence Amen may not unfitly be called, as it were, a kind of audible subscription. Thus the apostle directs the Christians to speak in a known tongue, that the unlearned, understanding what he hears, may give his assent to it by saying Amen, 1 Cor. xiv. 16. 2. It imports earnest desire. Hence Jeremiah said Amen to the false prophecy of Hananiah, concerning the return of the captives to their land, to show how earnestly he desired that it might be so, Jer. xxviii. 6. 3. Stedfast faith, or a trusting that the thing to which we say Amen shall so be as was spoken, either when petitioned by us, or promised by God. And hence it is that Christ having made a promise of his second coming, the church saith Amen, Rev. xxii. 20.

ricas, dicere debent Amen, ut per hoc significent, quod credant id omne quod rabbini loquuntur. Buxtorf. de Synagog. Judaic. c. 1. p. 64.

Having thus briefly explained this concluding doxology, I might draw from its several parts very many large and fruitful observations. But because I have noted many of them in the forenamed places, where I have met with the same subjects contained in these verses, as also because I only intended to touch upon this doxology, I shall conclude with these general notes.

Obs. 1. Praising God is a work very suitable to saints.

Obs. 2. After all exhortations for obtaining any good, God must be acknowledged the Author of that good.

Obs. 3. It is our duty to praise God for future blessings, for what we have in hope as well as for what we have in hand.

Obs. 4. Spiritual blessings principally deserve our praises.

Obs. 5. In our addresses to God we should have such apprehensions and use such expressions concerning him as may most strengthen our faith.

Obs. 6. Our speeches concerning Christ must be with highest honour and reverence.

Obs. 7. Praise should conclude that work which prayer began.

Obs. 8. The concluding thanksgivings which are affixed to writings are only to be given to God, Rom. xvi. 27; 2 Tim. iv. 18; Heb. xiii. 21. I have ever with the deepest abhorrence of soul looked upon the endings of many popish books, especially of those made by Jesuits, who share their concluding praises between God and saints. Thus Tannerus concludes his first tome of School Divinity, Pineda his Comment on Ecclesiastes, with returns of praise to God and the Virgin. Sanctius ends his on the Kings and Chronicles with ascribing the glory to God, the Virgin Mary, Ignatius, and Francis Xavier; all which, saith he blasphemously, I have called upon as my patrons and defenders in performing this work. Thus Baronius ends the first tome of his Annals with ascribing the praise thereof to God the Father, Son, and Holy Ghost, and, to use his own words, to the most holy Virgin Mary, the mother of God, and our reconciler. But Cornelius a Lapide exceeds all in blasphemy and idolatry, who divides all the praises between St. Paul and the Virgin Mary at the end of his Comment on Paul's Epistles. He tells Paul, that by his strength and intercession he had performed that work, and he desires him to grant that the Holy Ghost may make his writings beneficial to others; yet he tells the Virgin Mary that he owes himself and all his works to her, and that she has made his dull mind and hand as the pen of a ready writer.

Clausulæ doxologicæ Deo propriæ. Estius in 2 Pet.

Quos mihi ad hoc opus patronos et tutelares advocavi, pag. 1659.

Virgini Dei genetrici Mariæ et divini numinis conciliatrici. Baron. ad fin. Tom. 1. Annal.

Tua ope et intercessione da, ut quod hic exterius scripsi, interius Spiritus Sanctus suggerat. Cornel. a Lapide in Heb. xiii. ad fin.

Cui me, meaque omnia debeo, utpote quæ me in hoc opere direxit, juvit, instruxit, efficitque, ut tarda, et impolita mens et manus mea fierent calamus scribæ velociter scribentis. Id. ibid.

For myself, all good that I can do, or in this or any other service have done, I humbly desire may be returned only to the honour and praise of my most dear and blessed Lord and Saviour Jesus Christ, whose grace was the principle of all that is rightly done in this performance, whose Spirit was my guide in doing it, whose word was my rule, whose glory was my end, whose merit can alone procure acceptance for me and all my services, and the everlasting enjoyment of whose presence is my soul's desire and longing. Amen.

THE END.

GENERAL INDEX.

A

	PAGE
ABILITIES, proportioned to services required	128
Accuse, the meaning of the word	204
Adam, greater happiness by the Second than the first	21
all issue from	209
Admiration should only be of things truly great	303
of men's persons, what, and why condemned	321
from others sinfully received	324
of men, helps against	324
Affections, corrupt, darken the judgment	213
Affliction, the lot of God's Israel	113
Ages, a proneness to sin in all	169
Agreement in sinning among the wicked	159, 183
Alliance in faith the nearest	4
Ambition knows no bounds	242
Amen, what it comprehends	359
Angels, the word, their nature and office	125, 126
their attendance shows God's glory	127
much above man	128
their first estate, what	129
their own habitation, what	130
the cause of their fall discussed	133
their first sin	134, 135
their defection final and total	135
how reserved to judgment	144
about what they contend	196
the bad overpowered by the good	199
Antiquity, how far to be followed	302
Apostacy, the imitation of the devil	136
preservations against it	277
Apostates, they are the worst who have seemed the best	137
Apostles, which of them intended by Jude	325
why Jude makes use of the testimony of the	326
Appearances of evil to be loathed and shunned	356
of good ought to be loved	357
Appetite, sensual, deceitful	217
Archangel, whether only one	191
wherein his superiority	191
Authority, God opposes the opposers of lawful	244

B

	PAGE
Balaam, his country, parentage, and office	228, 229
his error, what	229
Beginnings in holiness, engagements on us to go on	57
Behold, the word, how used in Scripture	303
Best gifts of God most freely given to saints	49, 59
Blessings, spiritual, satisfactory	59

	PAGE
Boasting, of seducers, and their own vain-glorious appearance	265
the work of the wicked	318
must not seduce us from the truth	320
helps against	320
Body abused by sin and uncleanness	171
Bondage of Israelites in Egypt, how cruel	110
Bounds, men naturally love not to be held within any	353
Building up ourselves in the faith, what is implied by	339
how this is done by ourselves	340
Burial, decent, to be afforded to the deceased	200

C

	PAGE
Cain, who he was, his birth, name	220
his ways	221
his course, why called a way	221
went in the way of	222
Called ones should carry themselves suitably to their calling	26
Caller, God is the	23
Calling required for undertaking Divine employments	3
Care to be taken of those who are below us	129
Cause, the worst has commonly the most abettors	119
Censure not to be passed upon every one accused	195
Certainty of the misery of the wicked	290
Chains, what Jude understands by	137
of devils, how and why everlasting	138
Chance, there is none in regard of God	85
Change of a sanctified person very great	13
Chastisements on church differ from punishing of sinner	156
Christ, how the cause of our preservation	19
liable to all dangers out of	20
have recourse in all dangers to	21
no peace without	34
how Lord and only Lord	98—100
power of	100
true God	101
infinite wisdom, justice, love, &c. shown in the incarnation of	102
the only Saviour	102
his members dignified and blessed	103
denied, how many ways	103
the denial of, how sinful	104
denying, how to keep from	105
his high advancement	127
Christianity does not destroy, but strengthens, the powers that be	177

	PAGE
Church, we should not be offended at the wicked in the	77
Satan attempts in sundry ways to injure the most hurt by subtlety	77
most hurt by subtlety	78
wonder not that seducers are in the	85
shall not be utterly destroyed	115
most opposed by Satan when God begins to keep it	115
what given to it not to be alienated from it	253
trouble its portion	282
her greatest trouble within herself	283
unnecessary separation from it sinful	335
preservatives against unnecessary separation from the	336
Clouds, their nature, use	257
why seducers are called	257
wherein they resemble ministers	261
without water, wherein they resemble seducers	265
Commands of God easy in the end, though hard at first	117
Commendation of themselves by the least commendable	319
Company of the wicked, the lot of the good	253
Compassion toward others' souls after sinning	351
Condemnation, taken several ways	79
to which the seducers were appointed, what	79
woe of seducers, why called	80
of wicked begun in this life	80
of wicked, how to be shunned	81
Conflicts, directions for spiritual	70—73
Consent between the inspired penmen harmonious	326
Contention for best things the greatest	72
Contentions, our cause should be good in all	200
Contentment our duty	29
in our wants, by having God for us	92
Conviction at the last day, what	307
Core, pedigree, employment, posterity of	237, 238
his gainsaying, and its sin	239
destruction of	241
Corruption, attendant on natural knowledge	214
Courtesy, Christianity no enemy to	53
Covetousness, an incentive to all sin	235
Cowardice, none in not daring to sin	207
Curse on the creatures for man's sin	150

D

	PAGE
Darkness, why used to depict the misery of the wicked	141
different kinds of it	289
the world lies in	290
Dead servants of Christ most honoured by the wicked	203
how seducers are said to be twice	270
Death, the sorts of—spiritual	270
Decays in grace repugnant to a Christian's welfare	49
Defilement, the best in this world subject to	356
Defiling by sins of unchastity	171
Deformity of sinners	249
Deliverance of Israel out of Egypt, how great	109—113
of church not hindered by difficulties	116
not given until welcome	116
Deliverances abused make way for judgments	119
Denial of Christ	104
Despair, how to be armed against temptations to	85
to be shunned even by the worst	161
Destruction, total, never befalls Israel	115
Devil, cannot hurt us unless he get us within his chain	139
rages because his time is short	146
the name considered	191
in what respects an accuser	192
a hurtful spirit	194
a harsh master	195
dispute between Michael and the	197
Devils, not reformed by torments	139
can do nothing without God's permission	139

	PAGE
Difference, how to make between sinners a	350
Dignity, to be in duty the greatest	193
Diligence, about greatest matters should be shown the greatest	54
greatest in service of Christ	100
Doctrine of faith, how unalterable	68
precious	69
Doctrines suitable to the condition of the people to be preached	60
derogatory to Christ's honour to be shunned	101
Dominion, meaning of the word	172
what kind attributed to magistrates	173, 174
how despised	175
sinful to despise	176
how attributed to God	176
Dreamers, why seducers are called	185
Duration of the misery of the wicked	290

E

	PAGE
Eagerness of sinners in sin	233
suspicious when excessive	236
Earthly greatness vain at the last day	151
heavenly things to be learnt from things	293
Egyptians' cruelty to Israel	110—112
Enemies of the faithful, many	18, 57
of Christ cannot escape	100
of church, cruel to it	114
fulfil God's will in their very attempts to frustrate it	116
of God easily overcome by God	209
of God cause their own shame	284
Enoch, how the seventh from Adam	297
why Jude so calls him	297
his prophecy, whence received	300
why referred to by Jude	301
Envy, stirred up in the wicked by God's goodness	113
the evil and folly of	225
its mark is excellency	243
Exactness in carriage the honour of a Christian	357
Example, we easily follow even the worst	160
what Jude means by the word δειγμα	167
how the Sodomites were an	167
Examples of great ones in sin often followed	160
of caution, why the Lord gives them	168
how to derive benefit from them	170
Exhortation, how to be used by ministers	61
a help to be embraced	62
Expectations, the most hopeful, disappointed by sin	120
in earthly blessings often disappoint us	223

F

	PAGE
Faith, diversely taken	62
why the word of God is called	63
how contended for by Christians	70
why called "holy"	338
how built up in	339
Faithfulness of God in fulfilling his promises	116
Fame preserved by religion	357
Fear, the grounds of	206
of God, the bridle of sin	207
saving others with	251
Feasting, not always unlawful	254
we are too prone to cast away holy fear in	256
Feasts of charity	246
Feeding, how by the seducers	248
how without fear	249
Fewness of saints no derogation from the word	66
Filthiness of sin and sinners	250
Fire, wherewith the Sodomites were consumed, what, and how	163
the wrath of God more dreadful than	353
six things denoted by the plucking out of the	354
Flattery, great men made miserable by	323
Foaming out their own shame by seducers	284

GENERAL INDEX.

	PAGE
Forbearance of punishment no sign of total immunity	85
of God towards sinners great	293
Fornication of Sodom as understood by Jude	157
Freeness of God greatest in giving the best blessings	59
of the gospel	89, 90
ought to be in our services	90
Fruit, how persons are said to be without	269
Fruitfulness, in grace honours God	47
pleases God	47
makes us beneficial to others	48
our duty and dignity	48
promotes our comfort here and hereafter	48
the means to	276
Fruits, what sorts the wicked may bear	268
how those of the wicked are withering	269
some borne by the worst trees	273
Fury, men's shame discovered by their rage and	284

G

Gainsaying of Core, what meant by it	239
its sinfulness	240
Garments spotted by the flesh	355
Gentleness to be used in exhortation	62
Gifts and graces of others to be commended	326
not bestowed on us for our own benefit alone	351
Glory, our graces being derived from God should be devoted to his	15
of God to be maintained	19
saints most offended at opposition to God's	209
God just in staining the world's	324
Gluttony the sinfulness of	255, 256
God, what is meant by a propriety in	90
why called by Jude our God	90, 91
advantages of a propriety in	92
not sufficient to have a common propriety in	92
how to obtain this propriety in	92
they should manifest it who have a propriety in	92
his goodness occasions wantonness	95
gracious to abusers of grace	96
Christ proved to be	99, 100
greatly to be feared	129
gracious in greatest severity	169
the same in all ages	169
his greatness and dominion	193
Goodness of cause exempts it not from opposition	72
Gospel, we ought to praise God much for the	25
covet to be interested in the benefits of the	90
contempt of it a heinous sin	166
Grace, in us an ornament to our kindred	7
converting, excels restraining	12
repair to God when in want	16
to be maintained	16
what is meant by the multiplication of	46
though ours be multiplied, we must not despise the helps to	49
a saint allows not himself in any deficiency of	50
multiplied from God	50
in this life incomplete	50
for every child God has enough of	51
where begun, more shall be bestowed	51
given by God suitably to all the exigences of the saints	51
what it signifies	89
understood in several ways	89
why the doctrine of the gospel is called	89
neglected, leaves no escape	90
how turned into lasciviousness	93
the sinfulness of turning it into lasciviousness	95
its doctrine to be taught warily	96
not to be abused	97

H

Hard speeches, what sorts of	309
often uttered against the best deserving	310
Hatred of others for increasing in grace, impious	49
of sin must accompany reprehension of sin	357
Heart, not bettered by best of outward administrations	95
if unholy, sucks poison out of the best things	96
sinful actions spring from inward corruption of the	285, 316
unrenewed, when stirred, discovers its filth	286
not quieted with outward fulness	313
Heaven, the dangers of this life should commend to us	57
but one way to	59
its joys despised by sinners because joined with holiness	132
the habitation of the glorified	132
Hinderance of others from increasing in grace sinful	48
Holiness cannot be hid	13
of a sanctified person not purely negative	13
great love of God to	15
the excellency of	15, 131
much opposed by its enemies	18
and truth only can plead antiquity	131
opposition universal between sin and	199
Holy ones only to attend Christ at the last day	306
House of God, why saints are called the	340
Human helps to be used for the advancement of truth	7
Humility, our graces administer matter of	15
the ordaining of the wicked to condemnation should incite the best to	85
the more eminent we are, the greater should be our	193
Hypocrisy sinful in its shows	265
Hypocrites unstedfast	20
at last discovered	278

I

Ignorance, the sorts of	211
the cause of opposing the ways of God	212
Ignorant, sinful for them to speak evil of what they know not	211
persons most ready to speak	211
must forbear to speak evil	212
Illumination should be accompanied with purity of affection	206
Importunity to be used for the good of souls	62
Imprecations to be avoided	219
Incarnation, man's nature dignified by Christ's	102
Incorrigibleness in sin a dismal state	277
Innocence is no shelter from opposition	242
Insensibility of sinner great	183
Instructors of others sin greatly in seducing	292
must strike at the sins to which we are most inclined	317
Instruments, the meetest used by Satan	74
of public good often ill requited	243
Irrational, every sinner is	132
Israelites, great deliverance and destruction of the	109, &c.
God's mercy and severity great to the	120

J

James, how the brother of the Lord	6
held in high esteem by the church	6
holiness in life and death of	6
Jude, signification of the name	1
author of this epistle	1
parentage of	1

GENERAL INDEX.

Jude, distinguished from Judas Iscariot by sundry names 1, 2
    how and why he styles himself the servant of Christ 3
    why called the brother of James . . 6, 7
Judge at the last day, Christ, and why . 147—149
Judgment, God merciful in . . . 120
    of the last day, what . . . 143
    if rash, sinful 145
    happiness of those who shall be able to stand in the 146
Judgment-day, in it the greatest enemies of God weak 146
    why called a day, and how . . 146
    in what sense great . . . 147
    to be regarded as most certain . . 150
    to be longed for . . . 152
    labour to make this great day prove a good day to us . . . 152
    happiness of saints in respect of the . 152
    may be cheerfully thought of by the saints 152
    our backwardness to think of the . 303
Judgments, not kept off by worldly strength . 156
    spiritual, the sorest . . . 186

K

Knowing naturally, what it means . . 214
    like brute beasts, why . . 214
Knowledge, of the Christians mentioned by Jude . 108
    very commendable in Christians . . 108
    of Scripture, needful for all . . 109
    a strong engagement to practice . . 109
    of truth unchangeable . . . 109
    a great sin to speak evil against . . 213
    spiritual, opposed, causes the loss of the reasonable 216
Known evils to be spoken against . . 213

L

Lasciviousness, as meant by Jude . . 93
Last times, in which the seducers appeared . 327
    require most care and watchfulness . 328
    therefore the people of God should bear and forbear 328
Law, difference between the gospel and the . 90
Laziness to be avoided in our heavenly course . 237
Leaders in sin, their impiety . . 234, 241
Liberty, most cruel are the pleaders for . 228
    in sin, a token of God's anger . . 237
    in forsaking God's service no . 140
Life, new, of a sanctified person, wherein it consists . 10
Light, that here and hereafter greatly different . 291
    of the word, labour to walk by the . 291
Longest lived, there was a succession even of the . 299
Looking for future happiness, wherein it consists . 347
    quickens to present duty 348
Lord, in what respects Christ is called . . 98
    how Christ is only . . . 99
    supper of the, a love-feast . . 250
    comes, how 304
Lords, worldly, must govern warily and conscientiously 100
Love, of God, ever expressive . . 16
    several kinds of . . . 35
    to God, its properties . . 36—38, &c.
    to man, its properties . . 42, 43
    to God, from God . . . 43
    the best thing we can render to God is . 44
    ill-placed, if set on the creature . . 44
    to be set on God . . . 44
    if set on God, will be also given to man . 45
    God shows his goodness by enjoining mutual . 46
    of God, not to be measured by outward events . 225
    toward God, how preserved . . 345
    of God, proneness to decay in . . 345

Love of God an excellent preservative against error . 345
Lust, men made to err through love of . . 171
    loves not to be bridled . . . 178
    is never satisfied . . . 233

M

Magistracy strengthened by Christianity . . 177
Magistrates, how they defend the faith . 70, 71
    suffered to be burdensome to a people, a sign of God's wrath . . 176
    God is seen in causing men's subjection to 176
    their power to be improved for God . 176
    most opposed by the ungodly . . 177
    why called dignities . . . 178
    spoken ill of in several ways . . 179
    the sin of speaking evil of . . 179
    should beware of blemishing their dignity 180
    God is highly provoked when he pours contempt upon . . . 181
    to preserve their authority by becoming means is lawful for . . 182
    not to be flattered . . . 182
Majesty, how attributed to God . . 359
Man, by sin made a hurtful creature . . 74
    God's care great of the safety of . 166
    full of disorder by sin . . . 216
    merely such, steady in no relation . 242
Manner of committing sin is that which shall condemn 309
Martyrs, the devil has his . . . 354
Men, why seducers are called . . 74
    rest not content in being merely . 74
    beware of those who are merely natural . 74
    to them God more gracious than to angels . 141
Mercy, the several kinds of . . . 27
    of God distinguished according to the several requirements of his people . . 27, 28
    properties of God's . . . 28, 29
    impiety and folly of those who abuse God's . 29
    imitate God in showing . . 30
    in judgment God remembers . . 120
    different significations of the word . 346
    of Christ, why it is so called . . 346
Mercies, we should labour for the best and choicest . 30
    before God wounds persons by judgments, he labours to win them by . 119
    an unholy heart not benefited by even miraculous 119
Michael, signification of the name . . 190
    his person, office, and place . 190, 191
Ministers, should be of untainted reputation . 7
    the beauty of agreement among . 7
    the dignity and duty of . . 25
    ought to promote and pray for the peace of others 35
    the holiness of the people is the crown of the 48
    their duty to love their people . . 52
    their labour should proceed from love . 53
    the people should study to be fit for the love of their . . . 53
    their love must be ardent . . 53
    love to their persons causes love to their doctrines 53
    why they should labour to be beloved . 53
    the utmost they can do is to use diligence . 54
    diligence the commendation of . 54, 262
    if diligent, not to be neglected . . 55
    their desire should be to benefit as many as possible 55
    great is the dignity of their office . 65
    must contend for the faith in a twofold manner 71
    not to be discouraged by the forgetfulness of the people . . . 108
    must not contrive but recall doctrines . 108

GENERAL INDEX.

Ministers, ought to commend their people's proficiency 109
 must be full clouds . . . 262
 are upheld by God's power . . 263
 must not in this world look for a quiet condition 263
 why compared to stars . . 287
Ministry, not to be entered on by the uncalled . 243
Mockers, what we are to understand by . 329
 their confusion just . . . 330
Mocking, the great sinfulness of . . 329
 be patient under 330
Moderation not always commendable . . 73
Mortification, nature of true . . 8, &c.
 outside, or mere superstitious . 13
Moses, reason of the contention about the body of . 197
Murmuring, what is meant by . . 311
 great folly and sinfulness of . 312
 most frequent among the least deserving 313
 remedies against . . . 314

N

Names, commend us not to God . . . 2
 the best made odious by the wicked . 2
 baptismal, should admonish of duty . 2
 we should do nothing to which we are not willing to put our . . . 3
Nature, all sinful practices arise from the depravation of 131
 of man, very depraved . . 160
Necessity, diversely taken in Scripture . . 59
Needful, benefitting of souls an employment the most 60
New doctrines to be avoided . . . 68
 lights, meaning of the phrase . 68
Now and ever, meaning of the phrase . . 359
Number of sinners, when greatest, are unable to withstand God 119

O

Obedience to men, to be such only as Christ allows . 100
Occasions of evil to be shunned . . . 355
Offenders, can be made by God their own afflicters . 140
 open examples should be made of open . 168
Omniscience of God 145
Once, the word, how used . . . 66
 how faith delivered . . . 66
Order, comeliness of 194
Ordinances of Christ to be highly esteemed . 103
Ordination to condemnation . . . 79
 this of old . . . 81
 of God opposed by corrupt nature . 161
Own, how lusts are said to be their . . 316

P

Pains-taking of sinners in sin . . . 161
Parents, ought to be thankful for their children . 223
 though bad, may have good children . 241
Parts, excellent, often given to the worst . 234
Patience of God toward sinners . . . 165
 helped by having a God to befriend us . 210
Patriarchs, their succession mentioned for sundry reasons 296
Peace, several kinds of . . . 31
 of conscience, its excellency . . 33
 to be found in the ways of holiness only . 34
 means to preserve . . . 35
 belongs not to the wicked . . 281
People should be fit objects for the love of their pastor 53
 must not neglect their own souls, nor their minister 55
Perfections, the highest created, defectible . 136
Performances of Cains please not God . . 224

Permission of God, the devil can do nothing without the 139
Perseverance, opposers of it confuted . . 19
Persuading of others to serve Christ best done by becoming his servants ourselves . . 5
Plenty, the greatest earthly, given to the greatest sinners 155
 of places occasions impiety of inhabitants . 155
Plucked up by the roots . . . 272
Portion of every one set out by God . . 313
Power, of God to preserve the word . . 68
 in turning the will . . . 236
 how attributed to God . . 359
 of Satan limited . . . 208
Prayer, a help to love God . . . 46
 nature of 342
 made to God only . . . 342
 in the Holy Ghost . . . 342
 cannot be performed without the Spirit . 343
Presence of God, the greatest wisdom to obtain it in glory . . . 142
 a comfort against all distresses . 143
Present you before the presence of his glory . 357
Preservation of the godly, threefold . . 16
 in holiness perpetual . . 18
Presumption ends in despair . . . 228
Pretexts, specious, cast on foul courses . . 96
Prevention of sin in others from our own sufferings for sin 169
Pride, how unbeseeming . . . 29
 first sin of the angels . . 134
 very incident to a high estate . 136
Profession, if mere, will end in ungodliness . 88
 contradicted by practice amounts to a denial of Christ . . . 105
Progressiveness in sin usual . . . 161
Propagation of sin to ours . . . 223
Prophecy of Enoch, whence Jude received the . 300
Prophesying, meaning of the word . . 300
Proportion, there is often between sin and punishment a 116
Proudest spirits the basest . . . 324
Providence of God for man's peace . . 176

Q

Quickening, the best Christians want . . 62

R

Railing, import of the word . . . 204
 accusation, the sin of . . 205
 the means to avoid . . . 206
Rain, resemblance between the word and . 258
Reason, sensual objects not to be contended with by the mere light of . . . 216
Rebuking of Satan, what it imports . . 207
 why Michael desires to be engaged in . . . 208
 causes him to desist from mischief 208
Remembrance, what 107
 why needful . . . 107
Repeated truths not to be slighted . . 107
Reprobation, a double act in . . . 82
 absolute . . . 82
 immutable . . . 83
 exceptions against the doctrine prevented . . . 83, 84
 of others not to be judged of . 85
 we ought to be most thankful if exempted from . . . 85
Restraint differs from reformation . . 139
Revenge unsuitable to a saint . . . 209
Reward, error of Balaams and seducers for . 229
Righteousness of God in punishing sinners . 165
Rome, fitly called spiritual Sodom . . 160
 our separation from it justified . 334

S

	PAGE
Safety, sinners without	20, 57
in the ways of God	357
Saints, in this life we must be	12
esteemed of God	13
causelessly complained of as troublers	14
safe	18, 57, 129
in two respects	65
to whom the faith was delivered	65
keepers of the word	66
the world indebted to the	66
the cause of Satan's rage against the	66
wherein consists the strength of	70
their straits often great	114
difference between the sleep of the wicked in sin and that of	187
Salvation, different acceptations of the word	56
the state of the faithful called	57
of the faithful begun here	57
Scripture appointed for	57
in what sense called common	58, 59
because common, to be the more laboured for	59
Sanctification, different meanings of the word	8
the parts of	8—10
changes not our substance, but only our disorder	12
admits of no agreement with sin	13
puts no limits to grace	13
how God is the author of	14
in what respect attributed to God the Father	14
Satan, our great adversary	69
fights where he cannot prevail	72
labours most to spoil the best things	72
uses the meetest instruments	74, 233
contends with the strongest	200
molests the most advanced	200
aims in all contentions to draw us to sin	201
can adduce fair reasons for the foulest practices	202
delights in opposing God's honour	202
attempts to make the holiest the greatest occasions of sin	203
Saved, none should be willing to be so alone	59
Schism, the nature of	332
the sinfulness of	333
Secrecy, no shelter for sin	308
Seducers, danger from	60
a necessary part of the ministry to oppose	60
slighted by the apostle	74
infamous	75
numerous	75
vigilancy required against	75
the subtlety of	76, 77
Christian often mistaken in	78
modest in the beginning of sin	78
their shame at length laid open	283
compared to wandering stars	287
Self-advancement, a sin and folly to be shunned	320
Self-soothing, and flattery dangerous	187
helps against	188
Sensual, wherein seducers were	336
Sensuality, the cause of sinful separation	337
opposes sanctity	338
Separating themselves, what the apostle means by this	332
Separation from God, misery of	141, &c.
Servant of Christ, in three respects	3
Servants of Christ, there should be unity among the	100
of God, the worst are often compelled both to entertain and express a high opinion of the	203
Severity, not be regulated by outward respects	352
necessity should be the mother of	352
to sin is mercy to the soul	353
to be exercised with a view of saving	353
Shame, when sinful	49

	PAGE
Sin, how fearful we should be of	21
heinousness of	30
loves not to be seen in its own colours	78
the greatest evil in the world	92
of angels	134
nothing so truly vile and base as	136
a course and trade in, makes us resemble Satan	139
the pleasures not comparable to the pains of	140
boldness in it, madness	151
sleeping in, threefold	184
helps against sleeping in	188
a person's greatest shame	283
Sincerity, inconsistent with unstedfastness	19
best test of	236
Sinners, most irrational	132
gross is the delusion of	142
how foolish are	145
compared to sleepers	184
it is a high commendation to shun sin, when necessitated to converse with	206
eagerness in sin	233
know not where they shall stop	237
deformity of	249
Sinning of the godly and wicked different	228
Slanderers are Satan's first-born	196
Slanders, to be expected by saints	195
how to prevent	196
Sleep of saints differs from that of the wicked in sin	187
in sin, helps against	188
Sleepers compared to sinners	184
Sleeping	184
Snares attend the best enjoyments	95
Sodom and Gomorrha	153
the cities about	154
why rather named by Jude than the other cities	154
why mentioned rather than the inhabitants	154
Spots, what, and why the seducers are so called	246
Straits of saints are often great	114

T

Teachers of others, first to be taught themselves	59
Ten thousands, signification of the word	305
the saints are called in three respects his holy	305
Thanksgivings attached to writings should be ascribed only to God	360
Thirst after the word, of what kind	264
Threatenings, Divine, should terrify from sin	302
against some should warn others	302
Times, we should be best in the worst	73
heinous are the sins of these latter	169
we must act holily in the worst	298
the wicked worst in the best	328
Titles, flattering, not to be given	100
Toleration, impurity not prevented by	161
Tongue, sinful extravagancy of an unmortified	180
fears not to lash dignities	180
if wicked, is rugged, harsh, and grating	310

U

Unbelief, why Israel was most punished for	121
soon discovered by difficulties	122
allowed, keeps up other sins	122
our great proneness to	123
not excused by the greatest dangers	123
remedies against	124
Unbelievers, meaning of the word in Scripture	120
greatest enemies to themselves	123
Uncleanness, the different kinds of	158
the odiousness of	159
helps against	162
followed peculiarly with vengeance	164
body abused by	171
Ungodliness, wherein it consists	87

		PAGE
Ungodly, meaning of the term	. .	86
though reputed godly, men may be	.	88
tremble to be	. . .	89
deeds, how ungodlily committed	.	309
their sinning different from that of the saints	. . . .	309
sin not from infirmity	. .	309
Unholiness unsuitable to those to whom the faith is delivered	. . . . .	66
Unity to be pursued by saints	. .	59
Unpeaceableness not caused by godliness	.	35
saints differ from the wicked in	.	286
Unstable, the, are empty	. . .	266
Unstableness, threefold	. . .	259
causes of	. . .	260
Unstedfastness, preservatives against	.	266

V

		PAGE
Variety of places ordered by God's wisdom for habitation	. . . . . .	154
Vengeance, different meanings of the word	.	163
Vocation, several sorts of	. . .	21
effectual, sixfold	. . .	22
not for own worthiness	. .	23
consists not of mere moral persuasion		24
not to be defeated by the liberty of the will	. . . . .	24

W

		PAGE
Walking with God, wherein it consists	.	297
privilege of	. .	298
after lust, wherein it consists		316
War of a Christian, laborious, dangerous	.	73
Warned, should be forearmed	. .	327
Warning often betters not sinners	. .	155
given by God before he strikes	.	219
of seducers, must be given by ministers		326
Waves, raging, why seducers are called	.	279
Way, there is to heaven but one	. .	59
of Cain	. . . .	222
Weakness in ourselves for spiritual conflicts	.	73

		PAGE
Wisdom, of the wicked often comes too late	.	117
to have Christ our friend the greatest	.	306
needful in a repairer	. .	351
of God, what, and how excellent	.	358
Withering in holiness unsuitable to a Christian	.	273
Woe, meaning of the word	. . .	218
the end of wickedness	. .	218
of every one from himself	. .	317
Woes, spiritual, the worst	. . .	218
to be denounced against the wicked by ministers	. . . . .	219
Word, the, most worthy of our assent	.	63
their condition miserable who want	.	63
they are stable who rest upon	.	63
how said to be delivered	. .	63
the necessity of its being delivered	.	64
God the author of	. . .	64
be thankful for	. . .	64
the sin of obtruding on others a faith not contained in	. . . .	64
the sin of parting with	. .	65
to be delivered to, not kept from, others		66
the sin of those who pretend they can live without	. . . .	68
perfect	. . .	68
God's blessing to be expected on	.	68
of God pure	. . .	168
of God, a Christian's foundation	.	341
Words, responsible to Christ for our	.	311
spoken against saints, accounted by Christ as spoken against himself	.	311
swelling	. . . .	318
sin of great and swelling	. .	319
Worldly increase, not worth contending for	.	48
enjoyments, not to value ourselves by	.	92
Wrath of God, very dreadful	. .	166
changes the use of the creatures	.	166
Writing, excellency in four respects of	.	55
sin of those who abuse	. .	56
to be used for others' salvation	.	58
Written word, our readiness to swerve from the goodness of God in bestowing the	.	56
impiety of those who slight the	.	56
its necessity as a rule	. .	60

SOLID GROUND PURITAN CLASSICS

In addition to *An Exposition Upon the Epistle of Jude* by William Jenkyn, we are delighted to offer several other PURITAN CLASSICS to the people of God in the beginning of the twenty-first century.

HEAVEN UPON EARTH: *Jesus, The Best Friend in the Worst Times*
James Janeway

Written after the Black Plague of 1665 and the Great Fire of London of 1666, James Janeway appeals to his reader to recognize in Jesus Christ the Best Friend in the Worst of Times. Be prepared for a spiritual feast fit for the children of a great King. Dr. Joel Beeke states, *"This book is an invaluable handbook on how to grow in intimacy with God through His Son."*

A COMMENTARY ON THE EPISTLE TO THE HEBREWS
Exegetical and Expository
William Gouge

"We greatly prize Gouge. Upon any topic which he touches he gives outlines which may supply sermons for months." -C.H. Spurgeon

"We are so grateful to Solid Ground Christian Books for reprinting Gouge's magnum opus, *A Commentary on the Epistle to the Hebrews*... It is a golden exposition of the fullness of Christ." - Dr. Joel Beeke

A SHORT EXPLANATION OF THE EPISTLE TO THE HEBREWS
David Dickson

"We need say no more than get it, and you will find abundance of suggestions for profitable trains of thought. Dickson is a writer after our own heart. For preachers he is a great ally. There is nothing brilliant or profound; but everything is clear and well arranged, and the unction runs down like the oil from Aaron's head." - C.H. Spurgeon

THE REDEEMER'S TEARS WEPT OVER LOST SOULS
John Howe

Here is a fine biblical exposition of Luke 19:41,42 (Jesus weeping over Jerusalem), with appropriate application that is as suitable today as when Howe wrote it. The first part portrays the Savior as He looked down upon Jerusalem—a stirring scene filled with divine pathos. Then follows a series of explanations and admonitions, all breathing a compassionate anxiety to win the lost for Christ.

In addition to these titles, we are hoping to do *Of Domestical Duties* by Gouge, *A Body of Divinity* by James Ussher, and *The Works of Thomas Manton*. Keep your eyes and ears open to note our progress on these projects and more.

Burning Issues Series

Solid Ground Christian Books has developed a reputation for "uncovering buried treasure" from the past and bringing them back to a new generation. We thank God for the world-wide ministry He has opened to us over the past five years.

We are pleased to announce that we have launched a new series of books called BURNING ISSUES. These are not reprints of old books but new books from contemporary Reformed authors. What do we mean by BURNING ISSUES?

We intend by this term the following three things:

First, BURNING ISSUES is a series of books that will address the "Burning Issues" of the 21st Century Church and World. It is our sincere desire to have these books speak to our day from the unchangeable wisdom of Holy Scripture. SGCB is convinced that the Word of God is not only inspired, infallible and inerrant, but also SUFFICIENT to address every "burning issue" of our day, and RELEVANT to the needs of the 21st century and on into eternity.

Second, BURNING ISSUES is a series of books written by men who will write from a "Burning Heart." Our books will not be written by men who are writing because they simply want to get something "off their chest", but men who will echo the words of the Psalmist who said in Psalm 39:2,3: "I was mute with silence, I held my peace even from good; And my sorrow was stirred up. My heart was hot within me; While I was musing, the fire burned. Then I spoke with my tongue."

Third, BURNING ISSUES is a series of books written with the distinct goal that it will produce "Burning Hearts" in those who read each one. We will not be satisfied simply to publish these books and send them forth, but will earnestly pray that all who pick up and read our books will experience what was descried by the Emmaus Road disciples in Luke 24:32 "Did not our heart burn within us while He talked with us on the road, and while He opened the Scriptures to us?"

Thus far we have the following titles available or on the way:

YEARNING TO BREATHE FREE? *Thoughts on Immigration, Islam and Freedom* by David Dykstra

This provocative book was recently featured in WORLD Magazine (October 28, 2006).

PULPIT CRIMES: *The Criminal Mishandling of God's Word* by James R. White

This thought-provoking book is the perfect gift to give to the local pastor who has been compromising the pulpit against his own conscience. Vital for the pulpit and the pew!

TWO MEN FROM MALTA: *A Passionate and Rational Appeal to Roman Catholics* by Joe Serge and Joel Nederhood

A newspaperman from Canada and a pastor with a worldwide radio and television ministry team to present the truth of God's Word to thoughtful Roman Catholics who want the truth.

COMMON FAITH & COMMON CULTURE: *How Christianity Defeats Paganism* by Joe Bianchi

Wayne Mack says of this book, "I commend this book to you and encourage you to buy it and then read it through at least twice and share it with others."

Call us at 205-443-0311
E-mail us at sgcb@charter.net
Visit our web site at http://solid-ground-books.com

www.ingramcontent.com/pod-product-compliance
Lightning Source LLC
Chambersburg PA
CBHW081420160426
42814CB00039B/200